Table A-2 Present Value of an Annuity of $1 per Period for n Periods:

$$PVIFA_{k,n} = \sum_{t=1}^{n} \frac{1}{(1+k)^t} = \frac{1 - \dfrac{1}{(1+k)^n}}{k} = \frac{1}{k} - \frac{1}{k(1+k)^n}$$

Number of Periods	1%	2%	3%	4%	5%	6%	7%	8%	9%	10%	12%	14%	15%	16%	18%	20%	24%	28%	32%
1	0.9901	0.9804	0.9709	0.9615	0.9524	0.9434	0.9346	0.9259	0.9174	0.9091	0.8929	0.8772	0.8696	0.8621	0.8475	0.8333	0.8065	0.7813	0.7576
2	1.9704	1.9416	1.9135	1.8861	1.8594	1.8334	1.8080	1.7833	1.7591	1.7355	1.6901	1.6467	1.6257	1.6052	1.5656	1.5278	1.4568	1.3916	1.3315
3	2.9410	2.8839	2.8286	2.7751	2.7232	2.6730	2.6243	2.5771	2.5313	2.4869	2.4018	2.3216	2.2832	2.2459	2.1743	2.1065	1.9813	1.8684	1.7663
4	3.9020	3.8077	3.7171	3.6299	3.5460	3.4651	3.3872	3.3121	3.2397	3.1699	3.0373	2.9137	2.8550	2.7982	2.6901	2.5887	2.4043	2.2410	2.0957
5	4.8534	4.7135	4.5797	4.4518	4.3295	4.2124	4.1002	3.9927	3.8897	3.7908	3.6048	3.4331	3.3522	3.2743	3.1272	2.9906	2.7454	2.5320	2.3452
6	5.7955	5.6014	5.4172	5.2421	5.0757	4.9173	4.7665	4.6229	4.4859	4.3553	4.1114	3.8887	3.7845	3.6847	3.4976	3.3255	3.0205	2.7594	2.5342
7	6.7282	6.4720	6.2303	6.0021	5.7864	5.5824	5.3893	5.2064	5.0330	4.8684	4.5638	4.2883	4.1604	4.0386	3.8115	3.6046	3.2423	2.9370	2.6775
8	7.6517	7.3255	7.0197	6.7327	6.4632	6.2098	5.9713	5.7466	5.5348	5.3349	4.9676	4.6389	4.4873	4.3436	4.0776	3.8372	3.4212	3.0758	2.7860
9	8.5660	8.1622	7.7861	7.4353	7.1078	6.8017	6.5152	6.2469	5.9952	5.7590	5.3282	4.9464	4.7716	4.6065	4.3030	4.0310	3.5655	3.1842	2.8681
10	9.4713	8.9826	8.5302	8.1109	7.7217	7.3601	7.0236	6.7101	6.4177	6.1446	5.6502	5.2161	5.0188	4.8332	4.4941	4.1925	3.6819	3.2689	2.9304
11	10.3676	9.7868	9.2526	8.7605	8.3064	7.8869	7.4987	7.1390	6.8052	6.4951	5.9377	5.4527	5.2337	5.0286	4.6560	4.3271	3.7757	3.3351	2.9776
12	11.2551	10.5753	9.9540	9.3851	8.8633	8.3838	7.9427	7.5361	7.1607	6.8137	6.1944	5.6603	5.4206	5.1971	4.7932	4.4392	3.8514	3.3868	3.0133
13	12.1337	11.3484	10.6350	9.9856	9.3936	8.8527	8.3577	7.9038	7.4869	7.1034	6.4235	5.8424	5.5831	5.3423	4.9095	4.5327	3.9124	3.4272	3.0404
14	13.0037	12.1062	11.2961	10.5631	9.8986	9.2950	8.7455	8.2442	7.7862	7.3667	6.6282	6.0021	5.7245	5.4675	5.0081	4.6106	3.9616	3.4587	3.0609
15	13.8651	12.8493	11.9379	11.1184	10.3797	9.7122	9.1079	8.5595	8.0607	7.6061	6.8109	6.1422	5.8474	5.5755	5.0916	4.6755	4.0013	3.4834	3.0764
16	14.7179	13.5777	12.5611	11.6523	10.8378	10.1059	9.4466	8.8514	8.3126	7.8237	6.9740	6.2651	5.9542	5.6685	5.1624	4.7296	4.0333	3.5026	3.0882
17	15.5623	14.2919	13.1661	12.1657	11.2741	10.4773	9.7632	9.1216	8.5436	8.0216	7.1196	6.3729	6.0472	5.7487	5.2223	4.7746	4.0591	3.5177	3.0971
18	16.3983	14.9920	13.7535	12.6593	11.6896	10.8276	10.0591	9.3719	8.7556	8.2014	7.2497	6.4674	6.1280	5.8178	5.2732	4.8122	4.0799	3.5294	3.1039
19	17.2260	15.6785	14.3238	13.1339	12.0853	11.1581	10.3356	9.6036	8.9501	8.3649	7.3658	6.5504	6.1982	5.8775	5.3162	4.8435	4.0967	3.5386	3.1090
20	18.0456	16.3514	14.8775	13.5903	12.4622	11.4699	10.5940	9.8181	9.1285	8.5136	7.4694	6.6231	6.2593	5.9288	5.3527	4.8696	4.1103	3.5458	3.1129
21	18.8570	17.0112	15.4150	14.0292	12.8212	11.7641	10.8355	10.0168	9.2922	8.6487	7.5620	6.6870	6.3125	5.9731	5.3837	4.8913	4.1212	3.5514	3.1158
22	19.6604	17.6580	15.5969	14.4511	13.1630	12.0416	11.0612	10.2007	9.4424	8.7715	7.6446	6.7429	6.3587	6.0113	5.4099	4.9094	4.1300	3.5558	3.1180
23	20.4558	18.2922	16.4436	14.8568	13.4886	12.3034	11.2722	10.3711	9.5802	8.8832	7.7184	6.7921	6.3988	6.0442	5.4321	4.9245	4.1371	3.5592	3.1197
24	21.2434	18.9139	16.9355	15.2470	13.7986	12.5504	11.4693	10.5288	9.7066	8.9847	7.7843	6.8351	6.4338	6.0726	5.4509	4.9371	4.1428	3.5619	3.1210
25	22.0232	19.5235	17.4131	15.6221	14.0939	12.7834	11.6536	10.6748	9.8226	9.0770	7.8431	6.8729	6.4641	6.0971	5.4669	4.9476	4.1474	3.5640	3.1220
26	22.7952	20.1210	17.8768	15.9828	14.3752	13.0032	11.8258	10.8100	9.9290	9.1609	7.8957	6.9061	6.4906	6.1182	5.4804	4.9563	4.1511	3.5656	3.1227
27	23.5596	20.7069	18.3270	16.3296	14.6430	13.2105	11.9867	10.9352	10.0266	9.2372	7.9426	6.9352	6.5135	6.1364	5.4919	4.9636	4.1542	3.5669	3.1233
28	24.3164	21.2813	18.7641	16.6631	14.8981	13.4062	12.1371	11.0511	10.1161	9.3066	7.9844	6.9607	6.5335	6.1520	5.5016	4.9697	4.1566	3.5679	3.1237
29	25.0658	21.8444	19.1885	16.9837	15.1411	13.5907	12.2777	11.1584	10.1983	9.3696	8.0218	6.9830	6.5509	6.1656	5.5098	4.9747	4.1585	3.5687	3.1240
30	25.8077	22.3965	19.6004	17.2920	15.3725	13.7648	12.4090	11.2578	10.2737	9.4269	8.0552	7.0027	6.5660	6.1772	5.5168	4.9789	4.1601	3.5693	3.1242
35	29.4086	24.9986	21.4872	18.6646	16.3742	14.4982	12.9477	11.6546	10.5668	9.6442	8.1755	7.0700	6.6166	6.2153	5.5386	4.9915	4.1644	3.5708	3.1248
40	32.8347	27.3555	23.1148	19.7928	17.1591	15.0463	13.3317	11.9246	10.7574	9.7791	8.2438	7.1050	6.6418	6.2335	5.5482	4.9966	4.1659	3.5712	3.1250
45	36.0945	29.4902	24.5187	20.7200	17.7741	15.4558	13.6055	12.1084	10.8812	9.8628	8.2825	7.1232	6.6543	6.2421	5.5523	4.9986	4.1664	3.5714	3.1250
50	39.1961	31.4236	25.7298	21.4822	18.2559	15.7619	13.8007	12.2335	10.9617	9.9148	8.3045	7.1327	6.6605	6.2463	5.5541	4.9995	4.1666	3.5714	3.1250
55	42.1472	33.1748	26.7744	22.1086	18.6335	15.9905	13.9399	12.3186	11.0140	9.9471	8.3170	7.1376	6.6636	6.2482	5.5549	4.9998	4.1666	3.5714	3.1250

Financial
Management
and Policy

Ninth Edition

James C. Van Horne
Stanford University

Financial Management and Policy

Prentice Hall, Englewood Cliffs, New Jersey 07632

Library of Congress Cataloging-in-Publication Data

Van Horne, James C.
    Financial management and policy / James C. Van Horne. -- 9th ed.
        p.   cm.
    Includes bibliographical references and index.
    ISBN 0-13-322074-5
    1. Corporations--Finance.   I. Title.
    HG4011.V34   1992
    658.15--dc20   91-15089
                                                                        CIP

Acquisition editor: Whitney Blake
Production coordinator: Patrick Reynolds
Production editor: Nancy Savio-Marcello
Copy editor: Marie Lines
Interior and cover design: Jerry Votta
Cover photograph: The Image Bank™
Prepress buyer: Trudy Pisciotti
Manufacturing buyer: Robert Anderson

©1992, 1989, 1986, 1983, 1980, 1977, 1974, 1971, 1968 by Prentice-Hall, Inc.
a Simon & Schuster Company
Englewood Cliffs, New Jersey 07632

Printed in the United States of America
10   9   8   7   6   5   4   3   2   1

ISBN 0-13-322074-5

Prentice-Hall International (UK) Limited, *London*
Prentice-Hall of Australia Pty. Limited, *Sydney*
Prentice-Hall Canada Inc., *Toronto*
Prentice-Hall Hispanoamericana, S.A., *Mexico*
Prentice-Hall of India Private Limited, *New Delhi*
Prentice-Hall of Japan, Inc., *Tokyo*
Prentice-Hall of Southeast Asia Pte. Ltd., *Singapore*
Editora Prentice-Hall do Brasil, Ltda., *Rio de Janeiro*

To Mimi, Drew, Stuart, and Stephen

CONTENTS

3

MARKET RISK AND RETURNS   51

4

MULTI VARIABLE AND FACTOR VALUATION   87

5

VALUATION FROM A RELATIVE STANDPOINT   105

PART 2
INVESTMENT IN ASSETS AND REQUIRED RETURNS

Through the Looking Glass: Competitive
Advantage, Deluxe Style   133

6

PRINCIPLES OF CAPITAL INVESTMENT   134

7

RISK AND MANAGERIAL OPTIONS IN CAPITAL BUDGETING   169

8

CREATING VALUE THROUGH CAPITAL INVESTMENTS 204

9

REQUIRED RETURNS FOR COMPANIES, DIVISIONS, AND ACQUISITIONS 234

PART 3

FINANCING AND DIVIDEND POLICIES

10

THEORY OF CAPITAL STRUCTURE 268

11

MAKING CAPITAL STRUCTURE DECISIONS   305

12

DIVIDEND-PAYOUT RATIO AND VALUATION   326

13

OTHER ASPECTS OF DIVIDEND POLICY   351

PART 4

MANAGEMENT OF LIQUIDITY AND CURRENT ASSETS

Through the Looking Glass:
Levi Strauss Goes Back to Basics   373

14

WORKING CAPITAL MANAGEMENT AND EFFICIENT MARKET CONSIDERATIONS   374

15

MANAGEMENT OF CASH AND MARKETABLE SECURITIES   388

16

MANAGEMENT OF ACCOUNTS RECEIVABLE AND INVENTORIES   419

PART 5
SHORT- AND INTERMEDIATE-TERM FINANCING

17

UNSECURED SHORT-TERM FINANCING   458

18
SECURED LOANS AND TERM FINANCING   480

19
LEASE FINANCING   503

PART 6
LONG-TERM FINANCING

20
CHANGING FINANCIAL MARKETS   526

21

ISSUING SECURITIES   544

22

FIXED-INCOME FINANCING AND PENSION LIABILITY   566

23

OPTION FINANCING: WARRANTS, CONVERTIBLES, AND EXCHANGEABLES   603

PART 7
EXPANSION AND RESTRUCTURING

24

MERGERS AND THE MARKET FOR CORPORATE CONTROL   630

25

CORPORATE RESTRUCTURING   666

26

INTERNATIONAL FINANCIAL MANAGEMENT   685

PART 8
TOOLS OF FINANCIAL ANALYSIS AND CONTROL

27

FINANCIAL RATIO ANALYSIS   724

28

FINANCIAL PLANNING   762

APPENDIX A: REMEDIES FOR A FAILING COMPANY   797

APPENDIX B: PRESENT-VALUE TABLES AND NORMAL PROBABILITY DISTRIBUTION TABLE   804

INDEX   815

PREFACE

Financial theory and practice continue to change rapidly. Hence, this edition is another major revision. Not only have substantial advances been made in valuation and in the theory of finance, but the environment has changed dramatically since the last edition. Finance has taken an even greater strategic focus as managers cope with how to create value within a corporate setting. Proper utilization of resources, balancing various stakeholder claims, information effects and financial signaling, the globalization of finance, regulatory and tax law changes, and a host of other considerations now permeate the landscape of financial decision making.

In this edition, I have tried to capture many of the things that have happened as well as to better express previous ideas, thereby enhancing the learning experience. The purpose of *Financial Management and Policy* remains one of providing three things. First, by developing an understanding of the rapidly evolving and exciting theory of finance, it enables readers to evaluate how close the firm's investment, financing, and dividend decisions come to an objective of maximizing shareholder wealth. Second, it familiarizes readers with the ways in which analytical techniques are applied to a variety of financial issues. Third, it supplies the institutional material necessary for a solid understanding of the environment in which financial decisions are made.

The book has been thoroughly reviewed and updated throughout in materials and problems. More substantive changes include the following.

A new, extensive section appears in Chapter 2 on bond returns and valuation. With respect to stock valuation, there is a new section on retained earnings and dividend growth.

Chapter 3 has been substantially rewritten to include a new treatment of security portfolio risk, efficient sets, and global diversification effects. A new treatment of market risk premiums also appears.

Chapter 4 is new, and it examines the extended capital asset pricing model, factor models, and arbitrage pricing theory (APT). This rich chapter is a natural outgrowth of the two previous chapters on valuation.

In Chapter 5, there is a new section on debt options and their valuation. In addition, some of sections on stock option valuation have been rewritten to make them clearer.

The information necessary to analyze an acquisition has been brought into Chapter 6.

Managerial options are an entirely new thrust in Chapter 7. Here the options to expand, to abandon, to postpone, and to downsize are explored.

Chapter 8 has been substantially revised to focus on value creation in a corporate setting. The use of APT factor models to determine required returns is taken up. There is a new section on the adjusted present-value (APV) method and its use versus the weighted average cost of capital (WACC). In Chapter 9, there is also an expanded treatment of the WACC.

In Chapter 10, on capital structure theory, there are revised and improved treatments of tax effects and of bankruptcy costs. In the follow-up chapter on the use of debt, coverage ratio analysis has been improved, and there is a new appendix on bankruptcy costs.

Share repurchase valuation has been redone in Chapter 13 with a new formulation of the proper repurchase price.

There is expanded discussion of marketable securities in Chapter 15, and new material on practical aspects of managing receivables appears in Chapter 16. A new section on expert systems applications to credit is in Chapter 17.

Chapter 20 includes such changes as extended coverage of inflation and interest rates, a new section on nominal contracting effects, and a new treatment of financial innovation.

Improvements in Chapter 21 involve rights versus public security offerings, and information effects.

Significant changes occur in Chapter 22: a new treatment of sinking funds, of the call feature and its valuation, and of recent developments in private placements. There is a new, rather extensive appendix on hedging fixed-income instruments, including futures markets, debts options, and interest-rate swaps.

In Chapter 23, convertible and exchangeable securities are analyzed according to arbitrage efficiency when the various features are decomposed.

Chapter 24, on acquisitions and the market for corporate control, has been substantially rewritten to reflect changing theory, practice, and the legal environment.

The subsequent chapter on corporate restructuring has also been substantially revised to reflect the changed environment for leveraged buyouts. Moreover, there is a new section on leveraged recapitalizations.

Because finance is becoming increasingly globalized, Chapter 26, on international finance, has been completely rewritten. There is an entirely new consideration of the types of exchange-rate risk exposure. Exposure management, starting with the determination of natural hedges and then examining cash management and intercompany accounts, financing hedges, and finally currency hedges, is new. The last includes currency forward contracts, futures contracts, currency options, and currency swaps. Finally, there is a new treatment of the macro factors that govern exchange-rate behavior.

In Chapter 27, the cash-flow-to-capitalization analysis has been redone, and the materials on predicting financial distress have been revised. Finally, in Chapter 28, there is a new section on accounting statements of cash flows.

The order of the chapters reflects my preferences for teaching the course, but the instructor may approach them in whatever order seems appropriate. The tools of financial analysis and planning appear at the end of the book because many students have encountered them in courses in accounting. For those readers, Part 8 can serve as a review. If the class does not have this background, the professor may wish to take up the material at an early juncture. Extensive selected references at the end of the chapters give the reader direct access to literature on which the chapter is partly based. The appendixes at the end of some chapters invite the reader to go into certain topics in greater depth, but the book's continuity is maintained if this material is not covered.

ANCILLARY MATERIALS

A number of materials are available to supplement the book. For the professor, there is a comprehensive *Instructor's Manual*, which contains suggestions for organizing the course and solutions to all the problems that appear at the ends of the chapters. Also available are transparency masters of most of the figures in the text. Finally, there is a test item file of extensive questions and problems, both in hard copy in the form of a book and on computer-disk. These materials can be obtained from Prentice Hall.

Also available is *Financial Management Computer Applications*, written by Stuart B. Van Horne and myself. This booklet and disks may be used with Lotus 1-2-3 or with Macintosh Excel. They contain programs that are useful in connection with analytical and valuation issues found in this book. A number of self-correction exercises are found in the supplement. In addition, certain chapter-end problems in this book have been designated where the computer programs are useful. All the problems can be solved by hand; the use of the computer simply makes it easier. Concerning the book itself, several self-correction problems appear at the end of each chapter. These are in addition to the regular problems.

The finance area is constantly undergoing change. It is both stimulating and rather awesome. I hope that *Financial Management and Policy* imparts some of this excitement and contributes to a better understanding of corporate finance. You, the reader, are the final judge and I welcome your suggestions.

James C. Van Horne   *Palo Alto, California*

Financial
Management
and Policy

PART 1

FOUNDATIONS
OF FINANCE

Merck Is America's Most-Admired Corporation

Each year *Fortune* magazine polls thousands of businesspeople and asks them to rate companies according to eight key attributes. These attributes are: quality of products or services; innovativeness; ability to attract, develop, and keep talented people; financial soundness; community and environmental responsibility; quality of management; use of corporate assets; and long-term investment value. In 1990, Merck, a pharmaceutical company, was tops for the fourth year in a row. In the first four attributes, it was ranked number 1. In the remaining four, it was ranked number 2 or number 3. Merck is driven to drug innovation and to creating competitive advantage for itself in the markets it serves. The financial numbers emanating from this philosophy are impressive—a steady and consistent growth in sales and earnings, and climbing share price.

As Dr. P. Roy Vagelos, the company's chairman, explains, "It's understanding that the most important thing you can contribute as a human being is improving the lives of millions of people. We do that every year, introducing drugs and vaccines that will change the course of diseases or prevent diseases. Pharmaceuticals is a very fragmented market, and a company that can put everything together for a series of years should be able to gather up a much larger and more significant share of the market."

Not surprisingly, Merck stockholders have fared very well over the years, and many of them are institutional investors. The company consistently creates value. Shareholders realize an annual return of some 30 percent, among the highest for American stocks.

1

GOALS AND FUNCTIONS OF FINANCE

The financial manager plays a dynamic role in a modern company's development. With growing influence that now extends far beyond records, reports, the firm's cash position, paying bills, and obtaining funds, the financial manager is concerned with (1) investing funds in assets and (2) determining the best mix of financing and dividends in relation to a company's overall valuation.

Investment of funds in assets determines the size of the firm, its profits from operations, its business risk, and its liquidity. Obtaining the best mix of financing and dividends determines the firm's financial charges and its financial risk; it also impacts its valuation. All of this demands a broad outlook and an alert creativity that will influence almost all facets of the enterprise.

EVOLUTION OF FINANCE

Long considered a part of economics, corporation finance emerged as a separate field of study in the early 1900s. At first, it dealt with only the instruments, institutions, and procedural aspects of capital markets. Accounting data and financial records were not the kind we use today, nor were there regulations making it necessary to disclose financial data. But interest in promotion, consolidations, and mergers was mounting. The formation of U.S. Steel Corporation in 1900 started a trend of combinations that involved issuance of huge blocks of fixed-income and equity securities.

As the century moved into the 1920s, technological innovation and new industries created a need for more funds, prompting the study of finance to emphasize liquidity and financing of the firm. Attention turned to external financing rather than internal management. Arthur Stone Dewing's *Financial Policy of Corporations* (1920), one of the scholarly texts of the period, drew together existing thought, promulgated new ideas, and patterned the teaching of finance for many years. Widespread interest in securities, particularly common stock, became intense toward the end of the decade, making the investment banker a particularly significant figure to study in corporate finance of the period.

The depression of the 1930s necessarily focused the study of finance on

2

defensive aspects of survival, preservation of liquidity, bankruptcy, liquidation, and reorganization. The principal concern in external financing was how a lender could create self-protection. Conservatism, naturally, dominated, with considerable emphasis on a company's maintaining a sound financial structure. The large number of abuses with debt, particularly debts connected with public utility holding companies, were uncovered when many companies collapsed. These failures, together with fraudulent maltreatment of numerous investors, brought cries for regulation. It came quickly, accompanied by increased governmental controls on business. Regulation also increased the amount of financial data disclosed by companies, and that disclosure had another by-product. Financial analysis became more encompassing as the analyst could compare the financial condition and performance of various companies.

Finance, during the 1940s through the early 1950s, took the traditional approach that had evolved during the 1920s and 1930s. It analyzed the firm from the viewpoint of an outsider such as a lender or investor, but it did not emphasize decision making within the firm. Although the study of external financing was still largely descriptive, students did learn more about analyzing cash flows of the firm, and more was being said about planning and control of these flows from within.

In the middle 1950s, capital budgeting and allied considerations moved to the forefront.[1] Supported by concurrent emphasis on present value, they became a catalyst for sweeping changes to come. New methods and techniques for selecting capital investment projects led to a framework for efficient allocation of capital within the firm. The financial manager now dealt with the total funds committed to assets and the allocation of capital to individual assets on the basis of an appropriate and objective acceptance criterion.

Then came the computer. From the 1950s on, complex information systems began to provide the financial manager with data from which to make sound decisions. Powerful analytical tools could be applied to financial problems. Operations research and decision theory techniques found widespread use, making possible more disciplined and fruitful financial analysis. The electronic age has profoundly affected the means by which companies bank, pay their bills, collect monies owed them, transfer cash, determine financing and hedging strategies, manage currency-risk exposure, and so forth.

GROWTH OF MODERN FINANCE

These developments brought the financial manager to grips with the way in which investors and creditors valued the firm and how a particular decision affected their respective valuations. Valuation models were developed for use in financial decision making. Interestingly enough, many of the dividend valuation models developed during the 1950s for the valuation of the firm were offshoots of the classic 1938 work of John Burr Williams.[2] Unfortunately, the impact of this work was not felt in finance for nearly 20 years. With the concern for valuation in the 1950s, however, came a critical evalua-

---

[1] In the early 1950s, Friederich and Vera Lutz expounded a comprehensive theory of the firm in their famous book *The Theory of Investment of the Firm* (Princeton, NJ: Princeton University Press, 1951). Much of the work on capital budgeting owes its origin to Joel Dean's renowned book *Capital Budgeting* (New York: Columbia University Press, 1951). These works served as building blocks for subsequent theoretical and managerial development in finance.

[2] *The Theory of Investment Value* (Amsterdam: North-Holland, 1964).

tion of the capital structure and the dividend policy of the firm in relation to its valuation as a whole. The path-breaking articles by Modigliani and Miller in 1958 and 1961 on these topics set the stage for extended theoretical inquiry, which continues today.[3] Never before had academic and practitioner thinking been so jarred as when these authors argued that with efficient financial markets and no imperfections, the debt and dividend policies of a firm really did not matter from the standpoint of valuation. Much of the subsequent work on these topics has tried to identify market imperfections that would give rise to a valuation effect.

Development of portfolio theory and its eventual application to financial management was a major event in the 1960s. First exposited by Markowitz in 1952, the theory was later extended and considerably refined by Sharpe, Lintner, Fama, and a number of others.[4] Basically, this theory tells us that the risk of an individual asset should not be judged on the basis of possible deviations from its expected return but rather in relation to its marginal contribution to the overall risk of a portfolio of assets. Depending on the degree of correlation of that asset with other assets in the portfolio, the asset will be more or less risky. Concurrent with this development was considerable theoretical and empirical work on the functioning of financial markets. The simple notion that the firm's debt and equity instruments are traded in markets that may be more or less efficient, depending on the circumstances, was not fully understood until much of the work on portfolio theory and efficient markets had been done.

Further refinement of Sharpe's capital asset pricing model for valuing financial assets brought with it the application of these ideas to financial management in the 1970s. The model suggested that some of the risk of the firm was not relevant to investors in the firm's stock, as this risk could be diversified away in the portfolios of stocks they held. It also brought an increased focus on market imperfections when one judged the firm's selection of assets, financing, and dividends. Recently, the capital asset pricing model has undergone challenge, particularly from an empirical standpoint. The arbitrage pricing theory, an alternative, less restricted approach, has created a good deal of interest due at least in part to valuation depending on multiple factors.[5] The idea here is that arbitrage embracing several risk dimensions brings about market equilibrium. Subject to recent empirical testing, this theory is undergoing refinement and holds promise for corporate finance. In the ensuing chapters, we will devote considerable attention to the implications of these notions for financial management.

In a landmark contribution in the 1970s, Black and Scholes developed the option pricing model for the relative valuation of financial claims.[6] The existence of an options market makes it possible for an investor to establish a riskless hedged position by buying shares and, at the same time, writing op-

---

[3] Franco Modigliani and Merton H. Miller, "The Cost of Capital, Corporation Finance and the Theory of Investment," *American Economic Review*, 48 (June 1958), 261–97; and "Dividend Policy, Growth, and the Valuation of Shares," *Journal of Business*, 34 (October 1961), 411–33.

[4] See Harry M. Markowitz, *Portfolio Selection: Efficient Diversification of Investments* (New York: John Wiley, 1959); William F. Sharpe, "Capital Asset Prices: A Theory of Market Equilibrium under Conditions of Risk," *Journal of Finance*, 19 (September 1964), 425–42; John Lintner, "Security Prices, Risk and Maximal Gains from Diversification," *Journal of Finance*, 20 (December 1965), 587–616; and Eugene F. Fama and Merton H. Miller, *The Theory of Finance* (New York: Holt, 1972).

[5] See Stephen A. Ross, "The Arbitrage Theory of Capital Asset Pricing," *Journal of Economic Theory*, 13 (December 1976), 341–60.

[6] Fischer Black and Myron Scholes, "The Pricing of Options and Corporate Liabilities," *Journal of Political Economy*, 81 (May–June 1973), 637–54.

tions on the stock. In efficient financial markets, the return on such a position should be the risk-free rate. If this holds, precise formulas for valuing various types of options are possible. With this basic notion, a number of scholars have valued convertible securities and warrants and have treated as options such things as the capital structure of the firm, the desire by lenders for restrictions on the borrower, and the call feature on corporate bonds. The application of the option pricing model to corporate finance is expanding and has been a rich lode of intellectual inquiry in recent years.

In the 1980s, we witnessed a number of intellectual advances in the valuation of the firm in an uncertain world. Increased attention was paid to the effect of market imperfections on value. The role of personal taxes in conjunction with corporate taxes was a particularly fruitful area. Information economics gave us certain insights into the market behavior of financial instruments. The notion of an imcomplete market, where investors' desires for particular types of securities are not filled, places the corporation in the role of marketing special types of financial claims. More precision is being added to financial theory, and we can expect this trend to continue.

Differences in the information known by management, investors in the company's securities, and other stakeholders, such as customers, suppliers, and employees, has been a particularly fruitful area of inquiry in recent years.[7] Various financial decisions—issuing securities, dividend policy, investment in assets, acquisitions, and other forms of corporate restructuring—are studied as to their signaling effect. In particular, asymmetric information between management and investors may result in a change in valuation occurring when one or more of the above actions are taken by a company. As management will want to signal information to enhance share price, this leads to predictable behavior. We explore financial signaling throughout this book.

In the 1990s, finance has played an ever more vital strategic role within the corporation. The chief financial officer (CFO) has emerged as a team player in creating value. To determine whether value is being created, one must know what suppliers of capital require the company to earn. That becomes the underlying opportunity cost against which product, investment, and operating decisions must be judged. Otherwise free cash flow should be returned to shareholders for employment, by them, in other investment opportunities. If this does not occur, the market for corporate control comes into play, and the company becomes a takeover candidate. The CFO must juxtapose this delicate balance and bring it to bear in a company's overall decision-making process. Another reality of the 1990s is the globalization of finance. As the financial markets of the world become increasingly integrated, the financial manager must search for "best price" across national boundaries, often with currency and other hedges.

External factors are increasingly impacting the financial manager. A number of things have happened. Beginning in 1980 and accelerating rapidly, we have had deregulation of the financial services industry in the United States. Competition among suppliers of capital and among providers of financial services is extremely keen. We are also mindful of the fact that the

---

[7] Numerous scholars have studied this issue. Among others, one might wish to read Stewart C. Myers and Nicholas S. Majluf, "Corporate Financing and Investment Decisions When Firms Have Information That Investors Do Not Have," *Journal of Financial Economics,* 13 (June 1984), 187–222; Merton H. Miller and Kevin Rock, "Dividend Policy and Asymmetric Information," *Journal of Finance,* 40 (September 1985) 1031–51; Paul Asquith and David W. Mullins, Jr., "Signaling with Dividends, Stock Repurchases, and Equity Issues," *Financial Management,* 15 (Autumn 1986), 27–44; and Bradford Cornell and Alan C. Shapiro, "Corporate Stakeholders and Corporate Finance," *Financial Management,* 16 (Spring 1987), 5–14.

last dozen years have been characterized by considerable volatility in inflation, in interest rates, and in currency exchange rates. Major tax law changes affecting financial instruments are occurring with increased regularity. Economic uncertainty worldwide, periodic energy cost shocks, foreign loan problems, domestic loan problems arising from the highly levered transactions era of the 1980s, some speculative excesses, and ethical concerns over certain financial dealings—all have been part of the financial landscape in recent years. The confluence of these events has resulted in continual change in the external environment in which a company operates. The financial manager simply must adapt if his or her company is to be well served.

The evolution of finance has greatly impacted the role and importance of financial management. Finance has changed from primarily a descriptive study to one that encompasses rigorous analysis and normative theory; from a field that was concerned primarily with the procurement of funds to one that includes the management of assets, the allocation of capital, and the valuation of the firm in the overall market; and from a field that emphasized external analysis of the firm to one that stresses decision making within the firm. Finance today is best characterized as ever changing, with new ideas and techniques. The role of the financial manager is considerably different from what it was 20 years ago and from what it will no doubt be in another 20 years. Academics and financial managers must grow to accept the changing environment and master its challenge. In this regard, they must thoroughly understand the underlying objective of the firm.

OBJECTIVE OF THE FIRM

In this book, we assume that the objective of the firm is to create value for its shareholders. Value is represented by the market price of the company's common stock, which, in turn, is a reflection of the firm's investment, financing, and dividend decisions. The idea is to acquire assets whose expected return exceeds their cost, to finance with those instruments where there is particular advantage, tax or otherwise, and to undertake a meaningful dividend policy for stockholders.

PROFIT MAXIMIZATION VERSUS VALUE CREATION

Frequently, maximization of profits is regarded as the proper objective of the firm, but it is not as inclusive a goal as that of maximizing shareholder wealth. For one thing, total profits are not as important as earnings per share. A firm could always raise total profits by issuing stock and using the proceeds to invest in Treasury bills. Even maximization of earnings per share, however, is not a fully appropriate objective, partly because it does not specify the timing or duration of expected returns. Is the investment project that will produce a $100,000 return 5 years from now more valuable than the project that will produce annual returns of $15,000 in each of the next 5 years? An answer to this question depends on the time value of money. Few stockholders would think favorably of a project that promised its first return in 100 years, no matter how large this return. We must take into account the time pattern of returns in our analysis.

Another shortcoming of the objective of maximizing earnings per share is that it does not consider the risk or uncertainty of the prospective earnings stream. Some investment projects are far more risky than others. As a result, the prospective stream of earnings per share would be more uncertain if these projects were undertaken. In addition, a company will be more or less risky depending on the amount of debt in relation to equity in its capital structure. This financial risk is another uncertainty in the minds of investors when they judge the firm in the marketplace. Finally, an earnings per share objective does not take into account any dividend the company might pay.

For the reasons given, an objective of maximizing earnings per share may not be the same as maximizing market price per share. The market price of a firm's stock represents the value that market participants place on the firm.

MANAGEMENT VERSUS STOCKHOLDERS

The objectives of management may differ from those of the firm's stockholders. In a large corporation, the stock may be so widely held that stockholders cannot even make known their objectives, much less control or influence management. Often ownership and control are separate, a situation that allows management to act in its own best interests rather than those of the stockholders.

We may think of management as agents of the owners. Stockholders, hoping that the agents will act in the stockholders' best interests, delegate decision-making authority to them. Jensen and Meckling were the first to develop a comprehensive theory of the firm under agency arrangements.[8] They show that the principals, in our case the stockholders, can assure themselves that the agent (management) will make optimal decisions only if appropriate incentives are given and only if the agent is monitored. Incentives include stock options, bonuses, and perquisites, and they are directly related to how close management decisions come to the interests of stockholders. Monitoring can be done by bonding the agent, systematically reviewing management perquisites, auditing financial statements, and explicitly limiting management decisions. These monitoring activities necessarily involve costs, an inevitable result of the separation of ownership and control of a corporation. The less the ownership percentage of the managers, the less the likelihood that they will behave in a manner consistent with maximizing shareholder wealth and the greater the need for outside stockholders to monitor their activities.

A NORMATIVE GOAL

Because the principle of maximization of shareholder wealth provides a rational guide for running a business and for the efficient allocation of resources in society, we use it as our assumed objective in considering how financial decisions *should* be made. The purpose of capital markets is to allocate savings efficiently in an economy, from ultimate savers to ultimate users of funds who invest in real assets. If savings are to be channeled to the most

[8] Michael C. Jensen and William H. Meckling, "Theory of the Firm: Managerial Behavior, Agency Costs and Ownership Structure," *Journal of Financial Economics*, 3 (October 1976), 305–60.

promising investment opportunities, a rational economic criterion must govern their flow. By and large, the allocation of savings in an economy occurs on the basis of expected return and risk. The market value of a company's stock, embodying both of these factors, therefore reflects the market's trade-off between risk and return. If decisions are made in keeping with the likely effect on the market value of its stock, a firm will attract capital only when its investment opportunities justify the use of that capital in the overall economy. Any other objective is likely to result in the suboptimal allocation of funds and therefore lead to less than optimal capital formation and growth in the economy.

This is not to say that management should ignore social responsibility, such as protecting consumers, paying fair wages, maintaining fair hiring practices and safe working conditions, supporting education, and becoming actively involved in environmental issues like clean air and water. Many people feel that a company has no choice but to act in socially responsible ways; they argue that shareholder wealth and, perhaps, the corporation's very existence depend on its being socially responsible. Because criteria for social responsibility are not clearly defined, however, it is difficult to formulate a consistent objective. When society, acting through Congress and other representative bodies, establishes the rules governing the trade-off between social goals and economic efficiency, the task for the corporation is clearer. The company can be viewed as producing both private and social goods, and the maximization of shareholder wealth remains a viable corporate objective.

DEVELOPMENT OF THE BOOK

The functions of finance involve three major decisions the firm must make: the investment decision, the financing decision, and the dividend decision. Each must be considered in relation to the objective of the firm; an optimal combination of the three will maximize the value of the firm to its shareholders. Because the decisions are interrelated, we must consider their joint impact on the market price of the firm's stock, so we shall briefly examine each of them and their place in the subsequent chapters of this book.

INVESTMENT DECISION

The investment decision is the most important of the three decisions when it comes to the creation of value. Capital investment is the allocation of capital to investment proposals whose benefits are to be realized in the future. Because the future benefits are not known with certainty, investment proposals necessarily involve risk. Consequently, they should be evaluated in relation to their expected return and risk, for these are the factors that affect the firm's valuation in the marketplace. Included also under the investment decision is the decision to reallocate capital when an asset no longer economically justifies the capital committed to it. The investment decision, then, determines the total amount of assets held by the firm, the composition of these assets, and the business-risk complexion of the firm as perceived by suppliers of capital. The theoretical portion of this decision is taken up in Part 2. Using an appropriate acceptance criterion, or required rate of return, is fundamental to the investment decision. Because of the paramount and integrative importance of this issue, we shall pay considerable attention to determining the appropriate required rate of return for an investment project, for a division of a company, for the company as a whole, and for a prospective acquisition.

In addition to selecting new investments, a firm must manage existing assets efficiently. Financial managers have varying degrees of operating responsibility for existing assets; they are more concerned with the management of current assets than with fixed assets. In Part 4, we shall explore ways in which to manage current assets efficiently in order to maximize profitability relative to the amount of funds tied up in an asset. Determining a proper level of liquidity is very much a part of this management, and its determination should be in keeping with the firm's overall valuation. Although financial managers have little or no operating responsibility for fixed assets and inventories, they are instrumental in allocating capital to these assets by virtue of their involvement in capital investment.

In Parts 2 and 7, we consider mergers and acquisitions from the standpoint of an investment decision. These external investment opportunities can be evaluated in the same general manner as an investment proposal that is generated internally. The market for corporate control is ever present in this regard, and this topic is taken up in Part 7. Growth in a company can be internal, external, or both, domestic, and international; therefore, Part 7 also considers growth through international operations. With the globalization of finance in recent years, this book has placed substantial emphasis on international aspects of financial decision making.

FINANCING DECISION

In the second major decision of the firm, the financing decision, the financial manager is concerned with determining the best financing mix or capital structure. If a company can change its total valuation by varying its capital structure, an optimal financing mix would exist, in which market price per share could be maximized. In Chapters 10 and 11 of Part 3, we take up the financing decision in relation to the overall valuation of the firm. Our concern is with exploring the implications of variation in capital structure on the valuation of the firm. In Parts 5 and 6, we examine the various methods by which a firm obtains short-, intermediate-, and long-term financing. The emphasis is on not only certain valuation underpinnings but also the managerial aspects of financing, as we analyze the features, concepts, and problems associated with alternative methods.

Part 6 also investigates the interface of the firm with the capital markets and the ever-changing environment in which financing decisions are made. In Part 7, corporate restructuring is explored. While aspects of corporate restructuring fall across all three of the major decisions of the firm, this topic invariably involves financing.

DIVIDEND DECISION

The third important decision of the firm is its dividend policy, which is examined in Chapters 12 and 13 of Part 3. The dividend decision includes the percentage of earnings paid to stockholders in cash dividends, the stability of absolute dividends about a trend, stock dividends and splits, and the repurchase of stock. The dividend-payout ratio determines the amount of earnings retained in the firm and must be evaluated in the light of the objective of maximizing shareholder wealth. The value, if any, of a dividend to investors must be balanced against the opportunity cost of the retained earnings lost as a means of equity financing. Thus, we see that the dividend decision should be analyzed in relation to the financing decision.

FINANCIAL MANAGEMENT

Financial management involves the solution of the three major decisions. Together, they determine the value of a company to its shareholders. Assuming that our objective is to maximize this value, the firm should strive for an optimal combination of the three interrelated decisions, solved jointly. The decision to invest in a new capital project, for example, necessitates financing the investment. The financing decision, in turn, influences, and is influenced by, the dividend decision, for retained earnings used in internal financing represent dividends forgone by stockholders. With a proper conceptual framework, joint decisions that tend to be optimal can be reached. The main thing is that the financial manager relate each decision to its effect on the valuation of the firm.

Because valuation concepts are basic to understanding financial management, these concepts are investigated in depth in Chapters 2 through 5. Thus, the first five chapters serve as the foundation for the subsequent development of the book. They introduce key concepts: the time value of money, market efficiency, risk-return trade-offs, valuation in a market portfolio context, and the valuation of relative financial claims using option pricing theory. These concepts will be applied in the remainder of the book.

In an endeavor to make optimal decisions, the financial manager makes use of certain analytical tools in the analysis, planning, and control activities of the firm. Financial analysis is a necessary condition, or prerequisite, for making sound financial decisions; we examine the tools of analysis in Part 8. One of the important roles of a CFO is to provide accurate information on financial performance. This material appears at the end of the book in order to set it apart from the book's sequence of development. Depending on the reader's background, it can be taken up early or used for reference purposes throughout.

QUESTIONS

1. In what direction has the field of finance evolved in recent years?
2. Why should a company concentrate primarily on wealth maximization instead of profit maximization?
3. "A basic rationale for the objective of maximizing the wealth position of the stockholder as a primary business goal is that such an objective may reflect the most efficient use of society's economic resources and thus lead to a maximization of society's economic wealth." Briefly evaluate this observation.
4. Beta-Max Corporation is considering two investment proposals. One involves the development of 10 discount record stores in Chicago. Each store is expected to provide an annual after-tax profit of $35,000 for 8 years, after which the lease will expire and the store will terminate. The other proposal involves a classical record of the month club. Here, the company will devote much effort to teaching

the public to appreciate classical music. Management estimates that after-tax profits will be zero for 2 years, after which they will grow by $40,000 a year through year 10 and remain level thereafter. The life of the second project is 15 years. On the basis of this information, which project do you prefer? Why?

5. What are the major functions of the financial manager? What do these functions have in common?

6. Interest rates are said to embrace the real rate of interest for a given maturity plus a premium for inflation. What effect does continually fluctuating inflation have on corporate financing? on corporate planning overall?

7. Should the managers of a company own sizable amounts of stock in the company? What are the pros and cons?

8. In recent years, there have been a number of environmental, pollution, hiring, and other regulations imposed on businesses. In view of these changes, is maximization of shareholder wealth still a realistic objective?

9. As an investor, do you believe that some managers are paid too much? Do not their rewards come at your expense?

10. How does the notion of risk and reward govern the behavior of financial managers?

SELECTED REFERENCES

CORNELL, BRADFORD, and ALAN C. SHAPIRO, "Corporate Stakeholders and Corporate Finance," *Financial Management*, 16 (Spring 1987), 5–14.

DESCHAMPS, BENOIT, and DILEEP MEHTA, *Chief Financial Officer: Strategy Formulation and Implementation*. New York: John Wiley, 1988.

DONALDSON, GORDON, "Financial Goals: Management vs. Stockholders," *Harvard Business Review*, 41 (May–June 1963), 116–29.

FAMA, EUGENE F., "Agency Problems and the Theory of the Firm," *Journal of Political Economy*, 88 (April 1980), 288–307.

FINDLEY, M. CHAPMAN, III, and G. A. WHITMORE, "Beyond Shareholder Wealth Maximization," *Financial Management*, 3 (Winter 1974), 25–35.

FRUHAN, WILLIAM E., JR., *Financial Strategy*. Homewood, IL: Richard D. Irwin, 1979.

JENSEN, MICHAEL C., and WILLIAM H. MECKLING, "Theory of the Firm: Managerial Behavior, Agency Costs and Ownership Structure," *Journal of Financial Economics*, 3 (October 1976), 305–60.

RAPPAPORT, ALFRED, *Creating Shareholder Value*. New York: Free Press, 1986.

ROLL, RICHARD, and STEPHEN A. ROSS, "The Arbitrage Pricing Theory Approach to Strategic Portfolio Planning," *Financial Analysts Journal*, 40 (May–June 1984), 14–26.

SEITZ, NEIL, "Shareholder Goals, Firm Goals and Firm Financing Decisions," *Financial Management*, 11 (Autumn 1982), 20–26.

TREYNOR, JACK L., "The Financial Objective in the Widely Held Corporation," *Financial Analysts Journal*, 37 (March/April 1981), 68–71.

WILLIAMSON, OLIVER E., "Corporate Finance and Corporate Governance," *Journal of Finance*, 43 (July 1988), 567–92.

2

CONCEPTS IN VALUATION

To make itself as valuable as possible to shareholders, a firm must choose the best combination of decisions on investment, financing, and dividends. If any of these decisions are part of your job, you will have a hand in shaping your company's *return-risk character* and your firm's value in the eyes of suppliers of capital. *Risk* can be defined as the possibility that the actual return will deviate from that which was expected. Expectations are continually revised on the basis of new information about the investment, financing, and dividend decisions of the firm. In other words, on the basis of information about these three decisions, investors formulate expectations as to the return and risk involved in holding a common stock.

Common stocks are going to be important to us in this chapter and the next two, as we study the valuation of financial market instruments. These are groundwork chapters on which we shall later base our analyses of decisions on investment, financing, and dividends. We shall consider the expected return from a security and the risk of holding it. Assuming that investors are reasonably well diversified in their security holdings, we can ultimately value a firm; but first we must consider the time value of money and how to calculate the terminal value, the present value, and the internal rate of return from an investment. These considerations involve principles that we shall use repeatedly throughout the book in valuing stocks, bonds, and other securities.

THE TIME VALUE OF MONEY

Now we look at one of the most important principles in all of finance, the relationship between $1 in the future and $1 today. For most of us, $1 in the future is less valuable. Moreover, $1 two years from now is less valuable than $1 one year from now. We will pay more for an investment that promises returns over years 1 to 5 than we will pay for an investment that promises identical returns for years 6 through 10. This relationship is known as the *time value of money*, and it permeates almost every nook and cranny of finance. Let us see what is involved.

COMPOUND INTEREST AND TERMINAL VALUES

The notion of compound interest is central to understanding the mathematics of finance. The term itself merely implies that interest paid on a loan or an investment is added to the principal. As a result, interest is earned on interest. This concept can be used to solve a class of problems illustrated in the following examples. To begin with, consider a person who has $100 in a savings account. If the interest rate is 8 percent compounded annually, how much will the $100 be worth at the end of a year? Setting up the problem, we solve for the terminal value (or future value as it is also known) of the account at the end of the year (TV_1)

$$TV_1 = \$100(1 + .08) = \$108$$

For a deposit of 2 years, the $100 initial deposit will become $108 at the end of the first year at 8 percent interest. Going to the end of the second year, $108 becomes $116.64, as $8 in interest is earned on the initial $100, and $0.64 is earned on the $8 interest paid at the end of the first year. In other words, interest is earned on previously earned interest, hence the name *compound interest*. The terminal value at the end of the second year is $100 times 1.08 squared, or 1.1664. Thus

$$TV_2 = \$100(1.08)^2 = \$116.64$$

At the end of 3 years, the depositor would have

$$TV_3 = \$100(1 + .08)^3 = \$125.97$$

Looked at in a different way, $100 grows to $108 at the end of the first year if the interest rate is 8 percent, and when we multiply this amount by 1.08 we obtain $116.64 at the end of the second year. Multiplying $116.64 by 1.08 we obtain $125.97 at the end of the third year.

Similarly, at the end of n years, the terminal value of a deposit is

$$TV_n = X_0(1 + r)^n \qquad (2\text{-}1)$$

where X_0 = amount of savings at the beginning
  r = interest rate

A calculator makes the equation very simple to use.

Table 2-1, showing the terminal values for our example problem at the end of years 1 through 10, illustrates the concept of interest being earned on interest. Equation (2-1) is our fundamental formula for calculating terminal values. Obviously, the greater the interest rate r and the greater the number of periods n, the greater the terminal value.

Although our concern has been with interest rates, the concept involved applies to compound growth of any sort. Suppose the earnings of a firm are $100,000, but we expect them to grow at a 10 percent compound rate. At the end of years 1 through 5 they will be as follows:

YEAR	GROWTH FACTOR	EXPECTED EARNINGS
1	(1.10)	$110,000
2	$(1.10)^2$	121,000
3	$(1.10)^3$	133,100
4	$(1.10)^4$	146,410
5	$(1.10)^5$	161,051

TABLE 2-1
**Illustration of compound interest with $100 initial deposit
and 8 percent interest**

PERIOD	BEGINNING VALUE	INTEREST EARNED DURING PERIOD (8 PERCENT OF BEGINNING VALUE)	TERMINAL VALUE
1	$100.00	$ 8.00	$108.00
2	108.00	8.64	116.64
3	116.64	9.33	125.97
4	125.97	10.08	136.05
5	136.05	10.88	146.93
6	146.93	11.76	158.69
7	158.69	12.69	171.38
8	171.38	13.71	185.09
9	185.09	14.81	199.90
10	199.90	15.99	215.89

Similarly, we can determine the level at the end of so many years for other problems involving compound growth. The principle is particularly important when we consider certain valuation models for common stock, as we shall do later in this chapter.

Tables of Terminal Values.   Using Eq. (2-1), we can derive tables of terminal values (also known as future values). Table 2-2 is an example showing interest rates of 1 to 15 percent. In the 8 percent column, note that the terminal values shown for $1 invested at this compound rate correspond to our calculations for $100 in Table 2-1. Notice, too, that in rows tabulating 2 or more

TABLE 2-2
Terminal value of $1 at the end of _n_ years

YEAR	1%	2%	3%	4%	5%	6%
1	1.0100	1.0200	1.0300	1.0400	1.0500	1.0600
2	1.0201	1.0404	1.0609	1.0816	1.1025	1.1236
3	1.0303	1.0612	1.0927	1.1249	1.1576	1.1910
4	1.0406	1.0824	1.1255	1.1699	1.2155	1.2625
5	1.0510	1.1041	1.1593	1.2167	1.2763	1.3382
6	1.0615	1.1262	1.1941	1.2653	1.3401	1.4185
7	1.0721	1.1487	1.2299	1.3159	1.4071	1.5036
8	1.0829	1.1717	1.2668	1.3686	1.4775	1.5938
9	1.0937	1.1951	1.3048	1.4233	1.5513	1.6895
10	1.1046	1.2190	1.3439	1.4802	1.6289	1.7908
11	1.1157	1.2434	1.3842	1.5395	1.7103	1.8983
12	1.1268	1.2682	1.4258	1.6010	1.7959	2.0122
13	1.1381	1.2936	1.4685	1.6651	1.8856	2.1329
14	1.1495	1.3195	1.5126	1.7317	1.9799	2.2609
15	1.1610	1.3459	1.5580	1.8009	2.0789	2.3966
20	1.2202	1.4859	1.8061	2.1911	2.6533	3.2071
25	1.2824	1.6406	2.0938	2.6658	3.3864	4.2919
50	1.6446	2.6916	4.3839	7.1067	11.4674	18.4201
100	2.7048	7.2446	19.2186	50.5049	131.5010	339.3014

years, the proportional increase in terminal value becomes greater as the interest rate rises. This heightened growth is impressive when we look a century ahead. A dollar deposited today will be worth only $2.70 if the interest rate is 1 percent, but it will fatten to $1,174,313 if the interest rate is 15 percent. Behold (or let your heirs behold) the wonders of compound interest.

COMPOUNDING MORE THAN ONCE A YEAR

Up to now, we have assumed that interest is paid annually. Although this assumption is easiest to work with, we consider now the relationship between terminal value and interest rates for different periods of compounding. To begin, suppose interest is paid semiannually and $100 is deposited in a savings account at 8 percent. This means that for the first 6 months the return is one-half of 8 percent, or 4 percent. Thus, the terminal value at the end of 6 months will be

$$TV_{1/2} = \$100\left(1 + \frac{.08}{2}\right) = \$104.00$$

and at the end of a year it will be

$$TV_1 = \$100\left(1 + \frac{.08}{2}\right)^2 = \$108.16$$

This amount compares with $108.00 if interest were paid only once a year. The $0.16 difference is attributable to the fact that during the second 6 months, interest is earned on the $4.00 in interest paid at the end of the first 6

TABLE 2-2
(cont.)

7%	8%	9%	10%	12%	15%
1.0700	1.0800	1.0900	1.1000	1.1200	1.1500
1.1449	1.1664	1.1881	1.2100	1.2544	1.3225
1.2250	1.2597	1.2950	1.3310	1.4049	1.5209
1.3108	1.3605	1.4116	1.4641	1.5735	1.790
1.4026	1.4693	1.5386	1.6105	1.7623	2.0114
1.0577	1.5869	1.6771	1.7716	1.9738	2.331
1.6058	1.7138	1.8280	1.9487	2.2107	2.600
1.7182	1.8509	1.9926	2.1436	2.4760	3.090
1.8385	1.9990	2.1719	2.3579	2.7731	3.5179
1.9672	2.1589	2.3674	2.5937	3.1058	4.056
2.1049	2.3316	2.5804	2.8531	3.4785	4.624
2.2522	2.5182	2.8127	3.1384	3.8960	5.3503
2.4098	2.7196	3.0658	3.4523	4.3635	6.128
2.5785	2.9372	3.3417	3.7975	4.8871	7.0757
2.7590	3.1722	3.6425	4.1772	5.4736	8.171
3.8697	4.6610	5.6044	6.7275	9.6463	16.3665
5.4274	6.8485	8.6231	10.8347	17.0001	32.9190
29.4570	46.9016	74.3575	117.3907	289.0022	1.083.6574
867.7149	2,199.7569	5,529.0304	13,780.5890	83,522.2657	1,174,313.4510

months. The more times during a year that interest is paid, the greater the terminal value at the end of a given year.

The general formula for solving for the terminal value at the end of year n where interest is paid m times a year is

$$TV_n = X_0 \left(1 + \frac{r}{m}\right)^{mn} \qquad (2\text{-}2)$$

To illustrate, suppose that in our previous example interest were paid quarterly and that we wished again to know the terminal value at the end of one year. It would be

$$TV_1 = \$100 \left(1 + \frac{.08}{4}\right)^4 = \$108.24$$

which, of course, is higher than it would have been with semiannual or annual compounding.

The terminal value at the end of 3 years for the example with quarterly interest payments is

$$TV_3 = \$100 \left(1 + \frac{.08}{4}\right)^{12} = \$126.82$$

compared to a terminal value with semiannual compounding of

$$TV_3 = \$100 \left(1 + \frac{.08}{2}\right)^6 = \$126.53$$

and with annual compounding of

$$TV_3 = \$100 \left(1 + \frac{.08}{1}\right)^3 = \$125.97$$

The greater the number of years, the greater the difference in terminal values arrived at by two different methods of compounding.

As m approaches infinity, the term $(1 + r/m)^{mn}$ approaches e^{rn}, where e is approximately 2.71828 and is defined as

$$e = \lim_{m \to \infty} \left(1 + \frac{1}{m}\right)^m \qquad (2\text{-}3)$$

with ∞ being the sign for infinity. To see that e approaches 2.71828 as m increases, simply increase m in the above expression from, say, 5 to 10 to 100 and solve for e. The terminal value at the end of n years of an initial deposit of X_0 where interest is compounded continuously at a rate of r is

$$TV_n = X_0 e^{rn} \qquad (2\text{-}4)$$

For our example problem, the terminal value at the end of 3 years would be

$$TV_3 = \$100(2.71828)^{(.08)(3)} = \$127.12$$

This compares to terminal values with annual, semiannual, quarterly, and monthly compounding of $125.97, $126.53, $126.82, and $127.02, respectively. Thus, continuous compounding results in the maximum possible terminal value at the end of n periods for a given rate of interest. As m is increased in Eq. (2-2), the terminal value increases at a decreasing rate until ultimately it approaches the terminal value achieved with continuous compounding.

PRESENT VALUES

Not all of us live by the credit card alone; some like to save now and buy later. For a $700 purchase 1 year from now, how much will you have to put aside in a bank paying 8 percent on 1-year deposits? If we let A_1 represent the amount of money you wish to have 1 year from now, PV the amount saved, and k the annual interest rate, we have

$$A_1 = PV(1 + k) \qquad (2\text{-}5)$$

For our example problem, this becomes

$$\$700 = PV(1.08)$$

Solving for PV, we obtain

$$PV = \frac{\$700}{1.08} = \$648.15$$

Deposit $648.15 today and take home $700 one year hence. Stated another way, $648.15 is the *present value* of $700 to be received at the end of 1 year when the interest rate involved is 8 percent.

BEYOND ONE PERIOD

The present value of a sum to be received 2 years from now is

$$PV = \frac{A_2}{(1 + k)^2} \qquad (2\text{-}6)$$

which, for our example problem, would be

$$PV = \frac{\$700}{(1.08)^2} = \frac{\$700}{1.1664} = \$600.14$$

Thus, $700 two years from now has a lower present value than $700 one year from now. That is the whole idea of the time value of money.

In solving present-value problems, it is useful to express the interest factor separately from the amount to be received in the future. For example, our problem can be expressed as

$$PV = \$700\left[\frac{1}{(1.08)^2}\right] = \$600.14$$

In this way, we are able to isolate the interest factor, and this isolation facilitates present-value calculations. In such calculations, the interest rate is known as the *discount rate*, and henceforth we will refer to it as such.

So far we have considered present-value calculations for amounts of money to be received only 1 and 2 years in the future; however, the principles are the same for amounts to be received further in the future. The present value of $1 to be received at the end of n years is

$$PV = \frac{1}{(1 + k)^n} \qquad (2\text{-}7)$$

The present value of $1 to be received 5 years from now, when the discount rate is 10 percent, is

$$\$1\left[\frac{1}{(1.10)^5}\right] = \$.62092$$

The dollar we shall get 5 years from now is worth approximately 62 cents today if the discount rate is 10 percent.

Fortunately, present-value tables relieve us of having to make these calculations every time we have a problem to solve. Table A at the end of the book shows present values of $1, known as discount factors, for discount rates from 1 percent to 40 percent and for periods 1 through 25 in the future. We see in the table that for a 10 percent discount rate, the discount factor for 5 years in the future is .62092, just as we calculated. For 1 year, 2 years, and 3 years in the future, we see that the discount factors are .90909, .82645, and .75131, respectively. These discount factors are merely the result of the following calculations: $1/(1.10)$, $1/(1.10)^2$, and $1(1.10)^3$.

If we had an uneven series of cash flows—$1 one year hence, $3 two years hence, and $2 three years from now—the present value of this series, using a 10 percent discount rate, would be

PV of $1 to be received at end of 1 year	$1(.90909) =	.90909
PV of $3 to be received at end of 2 years	$3(.82645) =	2.47935
PV of $2 to be received at end of 3 years	$2(.75131) =	1.50262
	Present value of series	$4.89106

With a present-value table, we are able to calculate the present value for any series of future cash flows in this manner.

PRESENT VALUE OF AN ANNUITY

The procedure can be simplified for a series of even cash flows. A series of this sort is known as an *annuity*. Suppose $1 is to be received at the end of each of the next 3 years. The calculation of the present value of this stream, using a 10 percent discount rate, is

PV of $1 to be received in 1 year	=	.90909
PV of $1 to be received in 2 years	=	.82645
PV of $1 to be received in 3 years	=	.75131
Present value of series		$2.48685

With an even series of future cash flows, it is unnecessary to go through these calculations. The discount factor, 2.48685, can be applied directly. Simply multiply $1 by 2.48685 to obtain $2.48685.

Present-value tables for even series of cash flows allow us to look up the appropriate compound discount factor (see Table B at the end of the book). We note that the discount factor for an even series of cash flows for 3 years, using a 10 percent discount rate, is 2.4868, as we calculated. Thus, for an even series of cash flows, we simply multiply the appropriate discount factor times the cash flow. If the discount rate is 8 percent and a $5 cash flow is to be received at the end of each year during the next 4 years, we multiply

$$\$5(3.3121) = \$16.56$$

Using the present-value Tables A and B at the end of the book, we are able to calculate the present value of various future streams of cash flows.

If we trace across any of the rows in Tables A and B, we see that the higher the discount rate, the lower the discount factor. It is not a linear relationship, because the discount factor decreases less and less as the discount rate increases. Therefore, the present value of an amount of money to be received in the future decreases at a decreasing rate as the discount rate increases. The relationship is illustrated in Fig. 2-1. At a zero rate of discount, the present value of $1 to be received in the future is $1. In other words, there is no time value of money. As the discount rate increases, however, the present value declines but at a decreasing rate. As the discount rate approaches infinity, the present value of the future $1 approaches zero.

With most calculators, it is possible to solve for present and terminal values, either directly or indirectly. The more sophisticated calculators have built-in functions, so one can solve directly; otherwise, one must make calculations for each cash flow and store them in memory. In addition to calculators, computer-based spreadsheet programs have present- and terminal-value functions built in that allow solution of the numbers inputted. There still are occasions when it is easier to use the tables, however, and that is the reason for our attention to them.

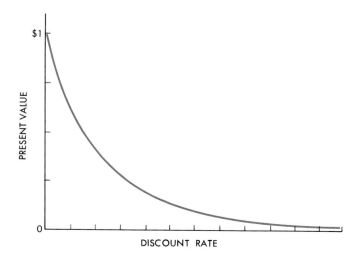

FIGURE 2-1

Relationship between present value and the discount rate

AMORTIZING A LOAN

An important use of present-value concepts is in determining the payments required under an installment type of loan. Installment payments are prevalent in mortgage loans, auto loans, consumer loans, and certain business loans. The distinguishing feature is that the loan is repaid in equal periodic payments that embody both interest and principal. These payments can be made monthly, quarterly, semiannually, or annually.

To illustrate with the simplest case of annual payments, suppose you borrow $22,000 at 12 percent to be repaid over the next 6 years. Equal installment payments are required at the end of each year, and these payments must be sufficient in amount to repay the $22,000 together with providing the lender a 12 percent return. To determine the amount of payment, we set up the problem as follows:

$$\$22,000 = \sum_{t=1}^{6} \frac{x}{(1.12)^t} \tag{2-8}$$

Looking in Table B at the end of the book, we find that the discount factor for a 6-year annuity with a 12 percent discount rate is 4.1114. Solving for x in Eq. (2-8), we have

$$\$22,000 = 4.1114x$$

$$x = \frac{\$22,000}{4.1114} = \$5,351$$

Thus, annual payments of $5,351 will completely amortize a $22,000 loan in 6 years. Each payment consists partly of interest and partly of principal repayment. The amortization schedule is shown in Table 2-3. We see that annual interest is determined by multiplying the principal amount outstanding at the beginning of the year by 12 percent. The amount of principal payment is simply the total installment payment minus the interest payment. Notice that the proportion of the installment payment composed of interest declines over time, whereas the proportion composed of principal increases. At the end of 6 years, a total of $22,000 in principal payments will have been

TABLE 2-3
Amortization schedule for illustrated loan

END OF YEAR	(1) INSTALLMENT PAYMENT	(2) PRINCIPAL AMOUNT OWING AT YEAR END	(3) ANNUAL INTEREST $(2)_{t-1} \times .12$	(4) PRINCIPAL PAYMENT $(1) - (3)$
0	—	$22,000	—	—
1	$ 5,351	19,289	$ 2,640	$ 2,711
2	5,351	16,253	2,315	3,036
3	5,351	12,853	1,951	3,400
4	5,351	9,044	1,542	3,809
5	5,531	4,778	1,085	4,266
6	5,531	0	573	4,778
	$32,106		$10,106	$22,000

made and the loan will be completely amortized. Later in the book, we will derive amortization schedules for loans of this type. The breakdown between interest and principal is important because only the former is deductible as an expense for tax purposes.

PRESENT VALUE WHEN INTEREST IS COMPOUNDED MORE THAN ONCE A YEAR

When interest is compounded more than once a year, the formula for calculating present values must be revised along the same lines as for the calculation of terminal value. Instead of dividing the future cash flow by $(1 + k)^n$ as we do when annual compounding is involved, the present value is determined by

$$PV = \frac{A_n}{\left(1 + \dfrac{k}{m}\right)^{mn}} \qquad (2\text{-}9)$$

where, as before, A_n is the cash flow at the end of year n, m is the number of times a year interest is compounded, and k is the discount rate. The present value of $100 to be received at the end of year 3, the discount rate being 10 percent compounded quarterly, is

$$PV = \frac{\$100}{\left(1 + \dfrac{.10}{4}\right)^{(4)(3)}} = \$74.36$$

The present value of $100 at the end of 1 year with a discount rate of 100 percent compounded monthly is

$$PV = \frac{\$100}{\left(1 + \dfrac{1}{12}\right)^{12}} = \$38.27$$

When interest is compounded continuously, the present value of a cash flow at the end of the year n is

$$PV = \frac{A_n}{e^{rn}} \qquad (2\text{-}10)$$

where e is approximately 2.71828. The present value of $100 to be received at the end of 3 years with a discount rate of 10 percent compounded continuously is

$$PV = \frac{\$100}{2.71828^{(.10)(3)}} = \$74.08$$

On the other hand, if the discount rate is compounded only annually, we have

$$PV = \frac{\$100}{(1.10)^3} = \$75.13$$

Thus, the fewer times a year the discount rate is compounded, the greater the present value. This relationship is just the opposite of that for terminal values. To illustrate the relationship between present value and the number of times a year the discount rate is compounded, consider again our example involving $100 to be received at the end of 3 years with a discount rate of 10 percent. The following present values result from various compounding intervals.[1]

COMPOUNDING	PRESENT VALUE
Annually	$75.13
Semiannually	74.62
Quarterly	74.36
Monthly	74.17
Continuously	74.08

We see that the present value decreases but at a decreasing rate as the compounding interval shortens, the limit being continuous compounding.

INTERNAL RATE OF RETURN OR YIELD

The internal rate of return or yield for an investment is the discount rate that equates the present value of the expected cash outflows with the present value of the expected inflows. Mathematically, it is represented by that rate, r, such that

$$\sum_{t=0}^{n} \left[\frac{A_t}{(1 + r)^t} \right] = 0 \qquad (2\text{-}11)$$

where A_t is the cash flow for period t, whether it be a net cash outflow or inflow, n is the last period in which a cash flow is expected, and Σ denotes the sum of discounted cash flows at the end of periods 0 through n. If the initial cash outlay or cost occurs at time 0, Eq. (2-11) can be expressed as

$$A_0 = \frac{A_1}{(1 + r)} + \frac{A_2}{(1 + r)^2} + \cdots + \frac{A_n}{(1 + r)^n} \qquad (2\text{-}12)$$

Thus, r is the rate that discounts the stream of future cash flows (A_1 through A_n) to equal the initial outlay at time 0—A_0. We implicitly assume that the cash inflows received from the investment are reinvested to realize the same rate of return as r. More will be said about this assumption in Chapter 6, but keep it in mind.

To illustrate the use of Eq. (2-12), suppose we have an investment opportunity that calls for a cash outlay at time 0 of $18,000 and is expected to provide cash inflows of $5,600 at the end of each of the next 5 years. The problem can be expressed as

[1] For semiannual compounding, m is 2 in Eq. (2-9) and mn is 6. With monthly compounding, m is 12 and mn is 36.

$$\$18{,}000 = \frac{\$5{,}600}{(1 + r)} + \frac{\$5{,}600}{(1 + r)^2} + \frac{\$5{,}600}{(1 + r)^3} + \frac{\$5{,}600}{(1 + r)^4} + \frac{\$5{,}600}{(1 + r)^5} \qquad (2\text{-}13)$$

Solving for the internal rate of return, r, involves an iterative procedure using present values. Fortunately, computer programs and sophisticated calculators can do this for us. If you are curious about a manual method, however, consider again our example. The cash-flow stream is represented by an even series of cash flows of $5,600, to be received at the end of each of the next 5 years. We want to determine the discount factor that, when multiplied by $5,600, equals the cash outlay of $18,000 at time 0. Suppose we start with 3 discount rates—14 percent, 16 percent, and 18 percent—and calculate the present value of the cash-flow stream. Using the different discount factors shown in Table B at the end of the book, we find

DISCOUNT RATE	DISCOUNT FACTOR	CASH FLOW EACH YEAR	PRESENT VALUE OF STREAM
18%	3.1272	$5,600	$17,512.32
16	3.2743	5,600	18,336.08
14	3.4331	5,600	19,225.36

When we compare the present value of the stream with the initial outlay of $18,000, we see that the internal rate of return necessary to discount the stream to $18,000 falls between 16 and 18 percent, being closer to 16 than to 18 percent. To approximate the actual rate, we interpolate between 16 and 17 percent as follows:

	DISCOUNT RATE	PRESENT VALUE
	16%	$18,336.08
	17	17,916.08
Difference	1%	$ 420.00
$\dfrac{336.08}{420.00} = .80$	$16\% + .80\% = 16.8\%$	

Thus, the internal rate of return necessary to equate the present value of the cash inflows with the present value of the outflows is approximately 16.8 percent. Interpolation gives only an approximation of the exact percent; the relationship between the two discount rates is not linear with respect to present value.

When, as above, the cash-flow stream is an even series and the initial outlay occurs at time 0, there really is no need for trial and error. We simply divide the initial outlay by the cash flow and search for the nearest discount factor. Using our example, we divide $18,000 by $5,600, obtaining 3.214. The nearest discount factor on the 5-year row in Table B at the end of the book is 3.2743, and this figure corresponds to a discount rate of 16 percent. Inasmuch as 3.214 is less than 3.2743, we know that the actual rate lies between 16 and 17 percent and we interpolate accordingly. When the cash-flow stream is an uneven series, the task is more difficult, and here we must resort to trial and error. With practice, however, a person can come surprisingly close in selecting discount rates from which to start.

Actually, a present-value table is nothing more than a bond-yield table that takes account of compound interest. In Chapter 6, we will compare the present-value and internal-rate-of-return methods for determining investment worth and go deeper into the subject. With what we have learned so far, we are able to proceed with our examination of the valuation of financial instruments.

BOND RETURNS

The first instrument to consider is a bond. It calls for a stated amount of money to be paid to the investor either at a single future date, maturity, or at a series of future dates, including final maturity. The first situation is a pure discount bond, or zero coupon bond as it is known, whereas the second corresponds to a coupon bond. In what follows, we present the rudiments of bond valuation. A detailed exposition is found in a supplementary text.[2]

PURE DISCOUNT
(ZERO COUPON) BONDS

A pure discount bond is one where the issuer promises to make a single payment at a specified future date. This single payment is the same as the *face value* of the instrument, usually expressed as $100.[3] The present value of a zero coupon bond is

$$P = \frac{\$100}{\left(1 + \dfrac{r}{2}\right)^{2n}} \qquad (2\text{-}14)$$

where P is the present market price of the bond, $100 is its face value, r is the yield to maturity, and n is the maturity. The yield is simply the internal rate of return discussed earlier. The normal pricing convention is to use semiannual compounding as shown, as opposed to annual compounding.

Suppose Betatron Corporation issued a zero coupon bond with a face value of $100 and a maturity of 10 years and that the yield to maturity is 12 percent. This implies a market price of

$$P = \frac{\$100}{(1.06)^{20}} = \$31.18$$

The investor puts up $31.18 today for the promise to receive $100 in ten years. The return of 12 percent compounded semiannually is embraced in the discount from face value—$31.18 versus $100 ten years hence.

If the price were $35 and we wished to solve for the yield, we would set up the problem as follows:

---

[2] James C. Van Horne, *Financial Market Rates and Flows*, 3d ed. (Englewood Cliffs, NJ: Prentice Hall, 1990).

[3] The actual face value of virtually all bonds is $1,000 per bond. However, the pricing convention is in terms of $100.

$$\$35 = \frac{\$100}{\left(1 + \dfrac{r}{2}\right)^{20}}$$

We then solve for the rate of discount that equates $35 today with $100 twenty periods hence. This is done in the same manner as illustrated for internal-rate-of-return calculations. When we do so, we find this rate to be 5.39 percent. Doubling this percent to put things on an annual basis, the yield to maturity is 10.78 percent. The lesser discount from face value, $35 versus $31.18 in our earlier example, results in a lower yield.

COUPON BONDS

Most bonds are not of a pure discount variety, but rather pay a semiannual interest payment along with a final principal payment of $100 at maturity. To determine the return here, we solve the following equation for r, the yield to maturity:

$$P = \frac{C/2}{\left(1 + \dfrac{r}{2}\right)} + \frac{C/2}{\left(1 + \dfrac{r}{2}\right)^{2}} + \cdots + \frac{C/2}{\left(1 + \dfrac{r}{2}\right)^{2n}} + \frac{\$100}{\left(1 + \dfrac{r}{2}\right)^{2n}} \qquad (2\text{-}15)$$

where P is the present market price of the bond, C is the annual coupon payment, and n is the number of years to maturity.

To illustrate, if the 10 percent coupon bonds of UB Corporation have 12 years to maturity and the current market price is $96 per bond, Eq. (2-15) becomes

$$\$96 = \frac{\$5}{\left(1 + \dfrac{r}{2}\right)} + \frac{\$5}{\left(1 + \dfrac{r}{2}\right)^{2}} + \cdots + \frac{\$5}{\left(1 + \dfrac{r}{2}\right)^{24}} + \frac{\$100}{\left(1 + \dfrac{r}{2}\right)^{24}}$$

When we solve for r, we find the yield to maturity of the bond to be 10.60 percent.

Given any three of the following four factors—coupon rate, final maturity, market price, and yield to maturity—we are able to solve for the fourth. Fortunately, elaborate bond value tables are available, so we need not go through the calculations. These tables are constructed in exactly the same manner as present-value tables. The only difference is that they take account of the coupon rate and of the fact that the face value of the bond will be paid at the final maturity date.

Were the market price $105, so that the bond traded at a premium instead of at a discount, the yield-to-maturity—substituting $105 for $96 in the equation—would be 9.30 percent. On the basis of these calculations, several observations are in order:

1. When a bond's market price is less than its face value of $100 so that it sells at a discount, the yield-to-maturity exceeds the coupon rate.
2. When a bond sells at a premium, its yield-to-maturity is less than the coupon rate.
3. When the market price equals the face value, the yield-to-maturity equals the coupon rate.

The yield-to-maturity, as calculated above, may differ from the holding-period yield if the security is sold prior to maturity. The holding-period yield is the rate of discount that equates the present value of interest payments, plus the present value of terminal value at the end of the holding period, with the price paid for the bond. For example, suppose the above bond were bought for $105, but interest rates subsequently increased. Two years later the bond has a market price of $94, at which time it is sold. The holding-period return is

$$\$105 = \frac{\$5}{\left(1 + \dfrac{r}{2}\right)} + \frac{\$5}{\left(1 + \dfrac{r}{2}\right)^2} + \frac{\$5}{\left(1 + \dfrac{r}{2}\right)^3} + \frac{\$5}{\left(1 + \dfrac{r}{2}\right)^4} + \frac{\$94}{\left(1 + \dfrac{r}{2}\right)^4}$$

Here r is found to be 2.23 percent. While the bond originally had a yield-to-maturity of 9.30 percent, the subsequent rise in interest rates resulted in its being sold at a loss. Although the coupon payments more than offset the loss, the holding-period yield was quite low.

PERPETUITIES

It is conceivable that we might be confronted with an investment opportunity that, for all practical purposes, is a perpetuity. With a perpetuity, a fixed cash inflow is expected at equal intervals forever. The British consol, a bond with no maturity date, carries the obligation of the British government to pay a fixed coupon perpetually. If the investment required an initial cash outflow at time 0 of A_0 and were expected to pay A^* at the end of each year forever, its yield is the discount rate, r, that equates the present value of all future cash inflows with the present value of the initial cash outflow

$$A_0 = \frac{A^*}{(1 + r)} + \frac{A^*}{(1 + r)^2} + \cdots + \frac{A^*}{(1 + r)^n} \tag{2-16}$$

In the case of a bond, A_0 is the market price of the bond and A^* the fixed annual interest payment. When we multiply both sides of Eq. (2-16) by $(1 + r)$, we obtain

$$A_0(1 + r) = A^* + \frac{A^*}{(1 + r)} + \frac{A^*}{(1 + r)^2} + \cdots + \frac{A^*}{(1 + r)^{n-1}} \tag{2-17}$$

Subtracting Eq. (2-16) from Eq. (2-17), we get

$$A_0(1 + r) - A_0 = A^* - \frac{A^*}{(1 + r)^n} \tag{2-18}$$

As n approaches infinity, $A^*/(1 + r)^n$ approaches 0. Thus

$$A_0 r = A^* \tag{2-19}$$

and

$$r = \frac{A^*}{A_0} \tag{2-20}$$

Here r is the yield on a perpetual investment costing A_0 at time 0 and paying A^* at the end of each year forever. Suppose that for \$100 we could buy a security that was expected to pay \$12 a year forever. The yield of the security would be

$$r = \frac{\$12}{\$100} = 12\%$$

Another example of a perpetuity is a preferred stock. Here a company promises to pay a stated dividend forever. (See Chapter 22 for the features of preferred stock.) If Zeebok Shoes Inc. had a 9 percent, \$50 face value preferred stock outstanding and the appropriate yield in today's market were 10 percent, its value per share would be

$$A_0 = \frac{\$4.50}{.10} = \$45$$

This is known as capitalizing the \$4.50 dividend at a 10 percent rate.

DURATION OF DEBT INSTRUMENT

Instead of maturity, bond investors and portfolio managers frequently use the duration of the instrument as a measure of the average time to the various coupon and principal payments. More formally, duration is

$$D = \sum_{t=1}^{n} \frac{C_t \times t}{(1 + r)^t} \Big/ P \qquad (2\text{-}21)$$

where C_t = interest and/or principal payment at time t
　t = length of time to that payment
　n = length of time to final maturity
　r = yield to maturity
　P = value or market price of the bond

Suppose a 9 percent bond with 4 years to maturity paid interest annually. Its yield to maturity is 10 percent and its market value is \$96.83 per bond. The duration of the instrument is

$$D = \frac{\dfrac{\$9 \times 1}{1.10} + \dfrac{\$9 \times 2}{(1.10)^2} + \dfrac{\$9 \times 3}{(1.10)^3} + \dfrac{\$109 \times 4}{(1.10)^4}}{\$96.83}$$

$$= 3.52 \text{ years}$$

This represents the weighted average time to the interest and principal payments. Notice in the formula that the higher the coupon rate, the less the duration, all other things the same. This is merely to say that more of the total return is received early on as opposed to what would be the case with a low coupon bond. For a zero coupon, there is but one payment at maturity, and the duration of the bond equals its maturity. For coupon bonds, duration is less than maturity.[4]

One of the reasons that duration is widely used in the investment community is that the volatility of a bond's price is related to it. Under certain idealized circumstances (which we will not probe), the percentage change in price is proportional to duration times the percentage change in 1 plus the yield.

$$\frac{\Delta P}{P} = -D\frac{\Delta r}{(1 + r)} \qquad (2\text{-}22)$$

Suppose in our example interest rates increased from 10 percent to 11.1 percent. This corresponds to a 1 percent increase in $1 + r$, as 1.10 goes to 1.111. Using Eq. (2-22), the predicted change in price would be

$$-3.52\frac{.011}{(1.10)} = -.0352$$

In other words, the price of the bond would be expected to decline by 3.52 percent.

The longer the duration of a debt instrument, the greater its volatility with respect to changes in market interest rates. In addition to bond analysis, the financial manager may find the duration measure useful in lease analysis and in capital budgeting.

THE RETURN FROM A STOCK INVESTMENT

The common stockholders of a corporation are its residual owners; their claim to income and assets comes after creditors and preferred stockholders have been paid in full. As a result, a stockholder's return on investment is less certain than the return to a lender or to a preferred stockholder. On the other hand, the return to a common stockholder is not bounded on the upside as are returns to the others.

SOME FEATURES OF COMMON STOCK

The corporate charter of a company specifies the number of *authorized* shares of common stock, the maximum that the company can issue without amending its charter. Although amending the charter is not a difficult procedure, it does require the approval of existing stockholders, which takes time. For this reason, a company usually likes to have a certain number of shares that are authorized but unissued. When authorized shares of common stock are sold, they become *issued* stock. *Outstanding* stock is the number of shares issued and actually held by the public; the corporation can buy back part of its issued stock and hold it as *Treasury* stock.

A share of common stock can be authorized either with or without par

---

[4] Duration tends to increase at a decreasing rate with maturity, but there can be peculiarities in the case of discount bonds of long maturity. For a detailed analysis of duration and maturity, see Van Horne, *Financial Market Rates and Flows.*

value. The par value of a stock is merely a stated figure in the corporate charter and is of little economic significance. A company should not issue stock at a price less than par value, because stockholders who bought stock for less than par would be liable to creditors for the difference between the below par price they paid and the par value. Consequently, the par values of most stocks are set at fairly low figures relative to their market values. Suppose a company sold 10,000 shares of new common stock at $45 a share and the par value of the stock was $5 per share. The equity portion of the balance sheet would be

Common stock ($5 par value)	$ 50,000
Additional paid-in capital	400,000
Shareholders' equity	$450,000

The *book value* of a share of stock is the shareholders' equity of a corporation less the par value of preferred stock outstanding divided by the number of shares outstanding. Suppose in the case above the company is now 1 year old and has generated $80,000 in after-tax profit but pays no dividend. Shareholders' equity is now $450,000 + $80,000 = $530,000, and book value per share is $530,000/10,000 = $53.

Although one might expect the book value of a share of stock to correspond to the liquidating value (per share) of the company, frequently it does not. Often assets are sold for less than their book values, particularly when liquidating costs are involved. In some cases certain assets—notably land and mineral rights—have book values that are modest in relation to their market values. For the company involved, liquidating value may be higher than book value. Thus, book value may not correspond to liquidating value and, as we shall see, it often does not correspond to market value. What, then, determines market value?

RETURN ON INVESTMENT

When people buy common stock, they give up current consumption in the hope of attaining increased future consumption. They expect to collect dividends and eventually sell the stock at a profit. But this is only one part of a lifetime of consumption, and wealth has to be allocated accordingly. A colleague of mine once remarked that he'd like to use his money in such a way that it would be completely spent when he died. If the person could know how long he was going to live, he could apportion his wealth so that it would give him maximum satisfaction from present and future consumption. He would know the exact returns available from investment and the timing of these returns, as well as future income from noninvestment sources. Investment would be merely a means of balancing present against future comsumption.

Not knowing what lies ahead, investors are unable to plan lifetime consumption patterns with certainty. Because the returns from investment and the timing of those returns are uncertain, they compensate for the lack of certainty by requiring an expected return sufficiently high to offset it. But what constitutes the return on a common stock? For a 1-year holding period, the benefits associated with ownership include the cash dividends paid during

the year together with an appreciation in market price, or capital gain, realized at the end of the year. More formally, the one-period return is

$$r = \frac{\text{Dividends} + (\text{Ending price} - \text{Beginning price})}{\text{Beginning price}} \tag{2-23}$$

where the term in parentheses in the numerator is the capital gain or loss during the holding period.

Suppose you were to purchase a share of stock of a corporation for $50.
The company is expected to pay a $2 dividend at the end of the year, and its
market price after the payment of the dividend is expected to be $55 a share.
Thus, your expected return would be

$$r = \frac{\$2.00 + (\$55.00 - \$50.00)}{\$50.00} = .14$$

where r is the expected return. Another way to solve for r is

$$\$50.00 = \frac{\$2.00}{(1 + r)} + \frac{\$55.00}{(1 + r)}$$

When we solve for the rate of discount that equates the present value of the
dividend and terminal value at the end of 1 year with the purchase price of
the stock at time 0, we find it to be 14 percent. You expect a 14 percent return
on your investment.

Now suppose that instead of holding the security 1 year, you intend to
hold it 2 years and sell it at the end of that time. Moreover, you expect the
company to pay a $2.70 dividend at the end of year 2 and the market price of
the stock to be $60 after the dividend is paid. Your expected return can be
found by solving the following equation for r:

$$\$50.00 = \frac{\$2.00}{(1 + r)} + \frac{\$2.70}{(1 + r)^2} + \frac{\$60.00}{(1 + r)^2}$$

When we solve for r by the method described earlier, we find it to be 14 percent also. For general purposes, the formula can be expressed as

$$P_0 = \sum_{t=1}^{2} \frac{D_t}{(1 + r)^t} + \frac{P_2}{(1 + r)^2} \tag{2-24}$$

where P_0 is the market price at time 0, D_t is the expected dividend at the end
of period t, Σ sigma denotes the sum of discounted dividends at the end of periods 1 and 2, and P_2 is the expected terminal value at the end of period 2.

If your holding period were 10 years, the expected rate of return would
be determined by solving the following equation for r:

$$P_0 = \sum_{t=1}^{10} \frac{D_t}{(1 + r)^t} + \frac{P_{10}}{(1 + r)^{10}} \tag{2-25}$$

But if a perpetual trust fund had bought the stock, and the trustee expected to
hold it forever, the expected return would consist entirely of cash dividends
and perhaps a liquidating dividend. Thus, the expected rate of return would

be determined by solving the following equation for r:

$$P_0 = \sum_{t=1}^{\infty} \frac{D_t}{(1 + r)^t}$$

(2-26)

where ∞ is the sign for infinity.[5] What we are saying here is that the formula takes account of all possible future dividends that might be paid.

ARE DIVIDENDS THE FOUNDATION?

It is clear that the intended holding periods of different investors will vary greatly. Some will hold a stock for only a few days; others might expect to hold it forever. Investors with holding periods shorter than infinity expect to be able to sell the stock at a price higher than they paid for it. This assumes, of course, that at that time there will be investors willing to buy it. As buyers, they will, in turn, judge the stock on expectations of future dividends and future terminal value beyond that point. That terminal value, however, will depend on other investors at that time being willing to buy the stock. The price they are willing to pay will depend on their expectations of dividends and terminal value. And so the process goes through successive investors. Note that the total cash return to all successive investors in a stock is the sum of distributions by the company, whether they be regular cash dividends, liquidating dividends, or share repurchases. (See Chapter 13 for a discussion of share repurchase as part of an overall dividend decision.) Thus, cash distributions are all that stockholders as a whole receive from their investment; they are all the company pays out. Consequently, the foundation for the valuation of common stock must be dividends. These are construed broadly to mean any cash distribution to shareholders, including share repurchases.

The logical question to be raised is, why do the stocks of companies that pay no dividends have positive, often quite high, values? The answer is that investors expect to be able to sell the stock in the future at a price higher than they paid for it. Instead of dividend income plus terminal value, they rely only on the terminal value. In turn, terminal value will depend on the expectations of the marketplace at the end of the horizon period. The ultimate expectation is that the firm eventually will pay dividends, broadly defined, and that future investors will receive a cash return on their investment. In the interim, however, investors are content with the expectation that they will be able to sell the stock at a subsequent time because there will be a market for it. In the meantime, the company is reinvesting earnings and, it is hoped, enhancing its future earning power and ultimate dividends.

DIVIDEND DISCOUNT MODELS

We saw in Eq. (2-26) that the return on investment is the rate of discount that equates the present value of the stream of expected future dividends with the current market price of the stock. Dividend discount models are designed to

[5] For longer holding periods, portfolio theorists usually work with continuously compounded rates of return. The assumption is that the portfolio's return follows a lognormal distribution. While the expression of returns on a continuously compounded basis is preferred, it is difficult for the reader to follow in a basic finance course. For ease of understanding, we work with returns based on discrete time periods. If you are interested in continuously compounded returns, see the last section of Chapter 5, where they are employed in connection with option valuation.

compute this implied stock return under specific assumptions as to the expected growth pattern of future dividends. Merrill Lynch, First Boston, and a number of other investment banks routinely publish such calculations for a large number of stocks, based on their particular model and security analysts' estimates of future earnings and dividend-payout ratios. In what follows we examine such models, beginning with the simplest one.

PERPETUAL GROWTH MODEL

If dividends of a company are expected to grow at a constant rate, the calculation of the implied return is an easy matter. If this constant rate is g, Eq. (2-26) becomes

$$P_0 = \frac{D_0(1 + g)}{(1 + r)} + \frac{D_0(1 + g)^2}{(1 + r)^2} + \cdots + \frac{D_0(1 + g)^\infty}{(1 + r)^\infty} \qquad (2\text{-}27)$$

where D_0 is the dividend per share at time 0. Thus, the dividend expected in period n is equal to the most recent dividend times the compound growth factor $(1 + g)^n$.

Assuming r is greater than g, Eq. (2-27) can be expressed as[6]

$$P_0 = \frac{D_1}{r - g} \qquad (2\text{-}28)$$

where D_1 is the dividend per share at time 1. Rearranging, the expected return becomes

$$r = \frac{D_1}{P_0} + g \qquad (2\text{-}29)$$

The critical assumption in this valuation model is that dividends per share are expected to grow perpetually at a compound rate of g. For some companies, this assumption may be a fair approximation of reality. To illustrate the use of Eq. (2-29), suppose A & G Company's dividend per share at $t = 1$ was expected to be $3, to grow at a 7 percent rate forever, and the current market price was $50 a share. The expected return would be

---

[6] If we multiply both sides of Eq. (2-27) by $(1 + r)/(1 + g)$ and subtract Eq. (2-27) from the product, we obtain

$$\frac{P_0(1 + r)}{(1 + g)} - P_0 = D_0 - \frac{D_0(1 + g)^\infty}{(1 + r)^\infty}$$

Because r is greater than g, the second term on the right side will be zero. Consequently,

$$P_0\left[\frac{(1 + r)}{(1 + g)} - 1\right] = D_0$$

$$P_0\left[\frac{(1 + r) - (1 + g)}{1 + g}\right] = D_0$$

$$P_0(r - g) = D_0(1 + g)$$

$$P_0 = \frac{D_1}{r - g}$$

If r is less than g, it is easy to determine that the market price of the stock would be infinite. See David Durand, "Growth Stocks and the Petersburg Paradox," *Journal of Finance*, 12 (September 1957), 348–63.

$$r = \frac{\$3}{\$50} + .07 = 13\%$$

and this return would be expected in every future period. For companies in the mature stage of their life cycle, the perpetual growth assumption is not unreasonable.

Conversion to a Price/Earnings Ratio. With the perpetual growth model, we can easily go from dividend valuation, Eq. (2-28), to price/earnings ratio valuation. Suppose a company retained a constant portion of its earnings each year, call it b. The dividend-payout ratio (dividends per share divided by earnings per share) also would be constant:

$$1 - b = \frac{D_1}{E_1} \qquad (2\text{-}30)$$

where E_1 is earnings per share in period 1. Equation (2-28) can be expressed as

$$P_0 = \frac{(1 - b)E_1}{r - g} \qquad (2\text{-}31)$$

Rearranging, this becomes

$$\frac{P_0}{E_1} = \frac{(1 - b)}{r - g} \qquad (2\text{-}32)$$

where P_0/E_1 is the price/earnings ratio based on expected earnings in period 1. In our earlier example, suppose A & G Company had a retention rate of 40 percent. Therefore

$$\frac{P_0}{E_1} = \frac{(1 - .40)}{.13 - .07} = 10 \text{ times}$$

With a $50 share price, expected earnings in period 1 would be $5 per share.

Retained Earnings and Dividend Growth. Without external financing, the source of dividend growth is the retention of earnings and the return on this retention, namely the return on equity (ROE). By retaining earnings, a company is able to invest the funds and, as a result, would be expected to earn more than it did the year before. In turn, a higher dividend would be expected to be paid. If there were no retention and all earnings were paid out as dividends, there would be no net investment. In our idealized world, we implicitly assume that an amount equal to depreciation is invested to maintain the earnings of the company (no growth). Net investment is investment over and above depreciation, and it is possible only with retention.

If expected ROE is constant over time, growth in dividends, g, can be expressed as

$$g = b \times \text{ROE} \qquad (2\text{-}33)$$

where b is a constant retention rate. As before, the fraction, $1 - b$, is the dividend-payout ratio.

To illustrate, suppose Gonzalez Freight Company earned $5.00 per share last year. Its retention rate is 60 percent, so it paid out $5.00(1 − .60) = $2.00 in dividends per share. The historical ROE of the company is 15 percent. If things do not change, this implies that earnings per share for this period, E_1, will be

$$E_1 = \$5.00 + \$5.00(.60).15 = \$5.45$$

and that dividends per share, D_1, will be

$$D_1 = \$5.45(1 - .60) = \$2.18$$

Thus, the dividend is increased from $2.00 to $2.18 per share on the basis of the additional earnings made possible by retaining a portion of last year's earnings. The growth rate in dividends per share is

$$g = \$2.18/\$2.00 = 9\%$$

which, of course, is the same as that determined through Eq. (2-33):

$$g = .60 \times 15\% = 9\%$$

In subsequent years, dividends per share also would be expected to grow by 9 percent.

Is such growth realistic? It depends on the opportunities available for investment and their likely return. For most companies, a perpetual growth model is inappropriate. Typically, both the rate of return on equity and the retention rate change over time. The import of the above, however, is that the retention of earnings permits growth of future earnings and dividends. It is not the only source of growth; external financing and increased returns on equity through better capital investment opportunities also are sources. In Chapters 8 and 9, we discuss how to create value through capital investments. For now, we merely need to be mindful that retention is an important source of growth.

GROWTH PHASES

When the pattern of expected growth is such that a perpetual growth model is not appropriate, modifications of Eq. (2-27) can be used. A number of valuation models are based on the premise that the growth rate will taper off eventually. For example, the transition might be from a present above-normal growth rate to one that is considered normal. If dividends per share were expected to grow at a 14 percent compound rate for 10 years and then grow at a 7 percent rate, Eq. (2-27) would become

$$P_0 = \sum_{t=1}^{10} \frac{D_0(1.14)^t}{(1 + r)^t} + \sum_{t=11}^{\infty} \frac{D_{10}(1.07)^{t-10}}{(1 + r)^t} \tag{2-34}$$

Note that the growth in dividends in the second phase uses the expected dividend in period 10 as its foundation. Therefore, the growth-term exponent is $t - 10$, which means that in period 11 it is 1, in period 12 it is 2, and so forth. The transition from an above-normal to a normal rate of growth could be specified as more gradual than the rate just given. For example, we might expect dividends to grow at a 14 percent rate for 5 years, followed by an 11 percent rate for the next 5 years, and a 7 percent growth rate thereafter. The more growth segments that are added, the more closely the growth in dividends will approach a curvilinear function. But even Microsoft cannot grow at an above-normal rate forever. Typically, companies grow at a very high rate initially, after which their growth opportunities slow down to a rate that is normal for companies in general.

Share price, then, is the summation of the present values of expected future dividends in each of the growth phases:

$$P_0 = PV(\text{phase 1}) + PV(\text{phase 2}) + \cdots + PV(\text{phase n}) \qquad (2\text{-}35)$$

In this three-phase example, suppose the present dividend is $2 per share and the present market price is $40. Therefore

$$\$40 = \sum_{t=1}^{5} \frac{\$2(1.14)^t}{(1 + r)^t} + \sum_{t=6}^{10} \frac{D_5(1.11)^{t-5}}{(1 + r)^t} + \sum_{t=11}^{\infty} \frac{D_{10}(1.07)^{t-10}}{(1 + r)^t} \qquad (2\text{-}36)$$

In a multiphase growth situation such as this, solving for the rate of return that equates the stream of expected future dividends with the current market price is arduous. If you have a lot of problems to solve, it is worthwhile to program the computer with an algorithm to solve for r. In the absence of such, one must resort to trial and error similar to that illustrated for the internal rate of return. The difficulty, of course, is in knowing where to begin. With a three-phase situation, we might start by employing the middle growth rate in a perpetual growth model to approximate the actual r. With an initial growth of 14 percent, the expected dividend at the end of year 1 is $2(1.14) = $2.28. Using 11 percent as our perpetual growth rate, r = ($2.28/$40) + .11 = 16.7%. If we then employ 16 percent as a starting discount rate, the present value of the right-hand side of Eq. (2-36) is as shown in Table 2-4.

TABLE 2-4
Present value of multiphased growth problem—16 percent

TIME	DIVIDEND	PRESENT VALUE OF DIVIDEND (16%)	PRESENT VALUE OF YEAR 10 MARKET PRICE (16%)
1	$2.28	$ 1.97	
2	2.60	1.93	
3	2.96	1.90	
4	3.38	1.87	
5	3.85	1.83	
6	4.27	1.75	
7	4.74	1.68	
8	5.27	1.61	
9	5.84	1.54	
10	6.49	1.47	
		$17.55	

$$P_{10} = \frac{\$6.49(1.07)}{.16 - .07} = \$77.16 \qquad \$17.49$$

Total present value (dividends + ending price) = $17.55 + $17.49 = $35.04

For the last growth phase, the perpetual growth model can be used to derive expected share price at the end of year 10, based on constantly growing dividends thereafter. The resulting market price of $77.16 shown in the table is then discounted at 16 percent to its present value at time 0. When this amount is added to the total present value of dividends, we obtain an overall present value of $35.04. As this amount is less than the share price of $40, we must try a lower discount rate. Repeating the calculations for 15 percent, we obtain the results shown in Table 2-5. As $39.81 is almost $40, we know that r is slightly less than 15 percent. Therefore, the expected rate of return that equates the stream of expected future dividends with the market price is approximately 15 percent.[7]

For any stream of expected future dividends, we can solve for the rate of discount that equates the present value of this stream with the current share price. While this is tedious when there is multiphased growth, the calculations can be streamlined. If enough computations are involved, it is worthwhile to program a computer algorithm. The rate of discount for which we solve is, by definition, the expected return on investment in the stock. However, we must be mindful that the accuracy of this estimate depends on the precision with which we are able to forecast expected future dividends.[8]

An Approximation Model for Three-Phase Growth. Russell J. Fuller and Chi-Cheng Hsia have derived an approximation formula for determining the required rate of return when the dividend discount model involves three phases of growth.[9] They call their formula the H model, where the required return is expressed as

$$r = (D_0/P_0)[(1 + g_3) + H(g_1 - g_3)] + g_3 \qquad (2\text{-}37)$$

where D_0 = present dividend per share
P_0 = present market price per share
g_3 = long-run growth rate in final phase
$H = (A + B)/2$, where A is the number of years in phase 1, and B is the end of phase 2
g_1 = growth rate in phase 1

For our previous example, this formula is expressed as

$$r = (\$2/\$40)[1.07 + 7.5(.14 - .07)] + .07 = 14.975\%$$

This percentage is very close to that solved for above. The H model is particularly useful when the first two growth phases are relatively short in number of years, the first growth rate does not exceed r, and the growth rate for the second phase is about half way between the growth rates for the first and last phases. The further a situation is from these conditions, the poorer the ap-

[7] The precise discount rate is 14.96 percent, but to avoid further tediousness, we do not interpolate for it.
[8] For an analysis of the effect of quarterly dividends and compounding, ex-dividend day effects, and other refinements of the dividend discount model, see Jeremy L. Siegel, "The Application of the DCF Methodology for Determining the Cost of Equity Capital," *Financial Management,* 14 (Spring 1985), 46–53.
[9] Russell J. Fuller and Chi-Cheng Hsia, "A Simplified Common Stock Valuation Model," *Financial Analysts Journal,* 40 (September–October 1984), 40–56.

TABLE 2-5
Present value of multiphased growth problem—15 percent

TIME	DIVIDEND	PRESENT VALUE OF DIVIDEND (15%)	PRESENT VALUE OF YEAR 10 MARKET PRICE (15%)
1	$2.28	$ 1.98	
2	2.60	1.97	
3	2.96	1.95	
4	3.38	1.93	
5	3.85	1.91	
6	4.27	1.85	
7	4.74	1.78	
8	5.27	1.72	
9	5.84	1.66	
10	6.49	1.60	
		$18.35	

$$P_{10} = \frac{\$6.49(1.07)}{.15 - .07} = \$86.80 \qquad \$21.46$$

Total present value (dividends + ending price) = $18.35 + $21.46 = $39.81

proximation. However, for many situations involving three-phase growth, the H model provides a quick and reasonably accurate approximation of the discount rate.

Solving for the Present Value. In another situation, suppose a company were expected to pay no dividends for 2 years and then begin to pay dividends. In year 3, the dividend is expected to be $1 per share. In year 4, it is expected to be $1.50, $2.20 in year 5, and $3.00 in year 6. After this period of "supernormal" growth, dividends are expected to grow at a constant 10 percent compound annual rate. Suppose the appropriate required rate of return were 18 percent and we wished to determine the present value of the dividend stream. Setting up the problem in a manner similar to Table 2-4, we have

TIME	DIVIDEND	PRESENT VALUE AT 18%
1	0	0
2	0	0
3	$1.00	$0.61
4	1.50	0.77
5	2.20	0.96
6	3.00	1.11
Terminal value	41.25*	15.28
Total present value		$18.73

$$*p_6 = \frac{\$3(1.10)}{.18 - .10} = \$41.25$$

Thus, the present value of the dividend stream is $18.73.

PRICE/EARNINGS HORIZON VALUE

For both of the growth-phase examples, a perpetual dividend growth assumption was invoked to obtain a terminal value at the end of some horizon—10 or 6 years. This terminal value also can be determined by assuming a price/earnings ratio at the horizon and multiplying earnings per share by it. To illustrate, we disaggregate dividends into earnings per share and the dividend-payout ratio. Suppose earnings per share for a company were expected to grow at a 25 percent rate the first 4 years, 15 percent the next 4, and 8 percent thereafter. Moreover, the dividend-payout ratio is expected to increase with the transition from the initial growth phase to the eventual mature phase of the company.

As a result, we might have the following for the three phases:

PHASE	EPS GROWTH	DIVIDEND-PAYOUT RATIO
1–4 years	25%	20%
5–8 years	15%	26%, 32%, 38%, 44%
Year 9 and beyond	8%	50%

Suppose the price/earnings ratio at the end of year 8 were expected to be 10 times. Suppose further that this ratio is based on expected earnings per share in year 9. If present earnings per share (at time 0) are $3.00, the expected cash flows to the investor are as shown in Table 2-6. In the table, we see that the terminal value at the end of year 8 is determined by multiplying expected earnings per share in year 9 by the price/earnings ratio of 10 to obtain $138.30.

To determine the implied expected return to the investor, we solve for the rate of discount that equates the cash-flow stream shown in the last column with the market price per share at time 0. If this price were $52, the implied return would be 15.59 percent when we solve for the internal rate of return. If we knew the required rate of return and wished to determine the

TABLE 2-6
Expected Dividend and Terminal Value Cash Flows for Example

TIME	EARNINGS PER SHARE	DIVIDEND PAYOUT	DIVIDEND PER SHARE	CASH FLOW TO INVESTOR
1	$3.75	.20	$0.75	$0.75
2	4.69	.20	0.94	0.94
3	5.86	.20	1.17	1.17
4	7.32	.20	1.46	1.46
5	8.42	.26	2.19	2.19
6	9.69	.32	3.10	3.10
7	11.14	.38	4.23	4.23
8	12.81	.44	5.64	5.64

Year 9 EPS = $12.81(1.08) = $13.83
P_8 = $13.83 × 10 PE = $138.30

8 Terminal value				138.30

present value of the cash-flow stream, we would simply present value each of the cash flows in the table and sum them. If the required return were 17 percent, the present value would be $47.45 per share. With these examples, we illustrate the mechanics by which dividend discount models may be used to determine either the expected return or the present value for a stock.

MEASURING RISK—
THE STANDARD DEVIATION

So far we have worked with only the expected return from holding a security. In a world of uncertainty, this return may not be realized. Risk can be thought of as the possibility that the actual return from holding a security will deviate from the expected return. The greater the magnitude of deviation and the greater the probability of its occurrence, the greater is said to be the risk of the security. Figure 2-2 shows the probability distributions of possible returns for two securities.

Because the actual return of security B has a greater likelihood of deviating from its expected return than that of security A, we say that it has greater risk. Although the investor is principally concerned with downside risk, or the possibility of a negative return, for ease of use our measure of risk takes into account all divergence of the actual return from that which was expected.

To illustrate this measure, suppose an investor believed that the possible 1-year returns from investing in a particular common stock were those shown in Table 2-7. This probability distribution can be summarized in terms of two parameters: the *expected* return and the *standard deviation*. The expected return is[10]

---

[10] The average shown is an arithmetic mean that is appropriate as a measure of central tendency of a probability distribution. If we were concerned with the rate of wealth accumulation over time that arose from a security investment, however, the measure would not be appropriate. Here the average return is a multiplicative function of the returns realized each year. A geometric average annual return should be used, and it is

$$\overline{R} = \sqrt[m]{(1 + R_1)(1 + R_2)(1 + R_3) \cdots (1 + R_m)} - 1$$

where m is the total number of years involved, $\sqrt[m]{}$ is the m-root sign, and R_t is the return on investment in year t. This measure gives us the average compound rate of growth of wealth from beginning to end, time 0 to time m.

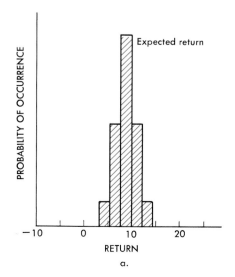

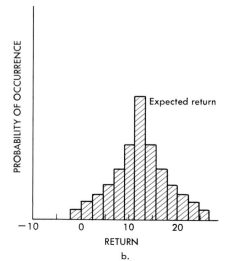

FIGURE 2-2

Illustration of risk

TABLE 2-7
Probability distribution of possible returns for a 1-year holding period

Probability of occurrence	.05	.10	.20	.30	.20	.10	.05
Possible return	−.10	−.02	.04	.09	.14	.20	.28

$$\overline{R} = \sum_{i=1}^{n} R_i P_i \tag{2-38}$$

where R_i is the return for the ith possibility, P_i is the probability of concurrence of that return, and n is the total number of possibilities. The standard deviation is

$$\sigma = \sqrt{\sum_{i=1}^{n} (R_i - \overline{R})^2 P_i} \tag{2-39}$$

where $\sqrt{}$ represents the square root. It also can be expressed as $[\ ]^{1/2}$. The square of the standard deviation, σ^2, is known as the variance of the distribution.

To illustrate these measures, consider again the distribution of possible returns shown in Table 2-7. The expected return is

$$\overline{R} = -.10(.05) - .02(.10) + .04(.20) + .09(.30) + .14(.20)$$
$$+ .20(.10) + .28(.05)$$
$$= 9\%$$

The standard deviation is

$$\sigma = [(-.10 - .09)^2.05 + (-.02 - .09)^2.10 + (.04 - .09)^2.20$$
$$+ (.09 - .09)^2.30 + (.14 - .09)^2.20 + (.20 - .09)^2.10$$
$$+ (.28 - .09)^2.05]^{1/2}$$
$$= [.00703]^{1/2}$$
$$= 8.38\%$$

USE OF STANDARD DEVIATION INFORMATION

When we deal with *discrete* probability distributions, we do not have to calculate the standard deviation in order to determine the probability of specific outcomes. To determine the probability of the actual return in our example being less than zero, we look at Table 2-7 and see that the probability is 15 percent. When we deal with *continuous* distributions, the procedure is slightly more complex.

For the normal bell-shaped probability distribution, .68 of the distribution falls within one standard deviation of the expected value, .95 falls within two standard deviations, and over .99 within three standard deviations. By expressing differences from the expected value in terms of standard deviations, we are able to determine the probability that the actual return will be greater or less than such and such an amount.

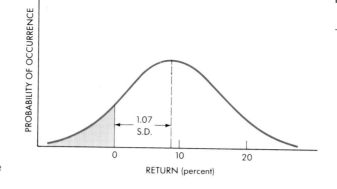

FIGURE 2-3
Probability distribution of
possible returns for example

Suppose our distribution had been a *normal* distribution with an expected return equal to 9 percent and a standard deviation of 8.38 percent and we wished to determine in this case, also, the probability that the actual return would be less than zero. Standardizing the deviation from the expected value, we have 9%/8.38% = 1.07 standard deviations. Turning to the normal probability distribution Table C at the end of the book, we find that there is approximately a 14 percent probability that the actual return will be more than 1.07 standard deviations from the mean of the distribution. Therefore, there is a 14 percent likelihood that the actual return on investment will be zero or less. The probability distribution is illustrated in Fig. 2-3. The shaded area represents 1.07 standard deviations to the left of the mean, and as indicated, this area represents 14 percent of the total distribution.

Thus, the dispersion, or wideness, of the probability distribution of possible returns reflects the degree of the investor's uncertainty. A distribution with a small standard deviation relative to its expected value indicates little dispersion and a high degree of confidence in the outcome. A distribution with a large standard deviation relative to its expected value indicates a high degree of uncertainty about the possible return on investment. In the immediate discussion, we assume that probability distributions can be summarized in terms of two parameters: the expected value and the standard deviation.

MEAN-VARIANCE UTILITY

For a risk-averse investor, utility increases at a decreasing rate with successive increments in wealth.[11] Therefore, the greater the variance, or standard deviation, of the probability distribution of possible returns for an investment, the less the expected utility of that investment and the less desirable it becomes.

By way of illustration, suppose an investor's utility of wealth function can be expressed by the following equation,[12]

$$U = 2X - .05X^2$$

[11] The utility approach considered in this section has its origin in the classic work of John von Neumann and Oskar Morgenstern, *Theory of Games and Economic Behavior*, rev. ed. (Princeton, NJ: Princeton University Press, 1955). For an excellent discussion of the axioms as they pertain to investments, see Eugene F. Fama and Merton H. Miller, *The Theory of Finance* (New York:Holt, 1972), pp. 192–96; and J. Hirshleifer, *Investment, Interest, and Capital* (Englewood Cliffs, NJ: Prentice Hall, 1970), Chap. 8.

[12] Eventually the quadratic equation shown will result in decreases in utility for subsequent increases in wealth. As is customary, we ignore this segment and define the relevant range as that where the first derivative is positive.

where U is the number of utiles and X is the increments of wealth in units of $1,000. Two investments are being considered: Investment 1 has a 50 percent probability of providing a $10,000 increment in wealth and a 50 percent probability of a $20,000 increment, while investment 2 has a 50 percent probability of providing a $12,000 increment in wealth and a 50 percent probability of providing an $18,000 increment. We note that both investments have the same expected monetary value, $15,000, but that investment 1 has a higher variance. The expected utilities of the two investments are

$$U_1 = [2(10) - .05(10)^2].5 + [2(20) - .05(20)^2].5 = 17.5$$
$$U_2 = [2(12) - .05(12)^2].5 + [2(18) - .05(18)^2].5 = 18.3$$

Thus, investment 1, which has the greater variance of possible outcomes, has a lower expected utility. For the risk averter, the certainty equivalent of a risky investment is always less than its expected monetary value. In our investment 1 example, the increment in wealth associated with 17.5 utiles is $12,929.[13] This certainty equivalent is less than the investment's expected monetary value of $15,000. The difference of $2,071 might be thought of as the risk premium. It is the amount the investor is willing to give up to remove the gamble involved in the investment. These illustrations show why the variance of a distribution is an appropriate measure of risk.

In the chapter that follows, we assume that investors select stocks according to the principle of maximizing expected utility. Expected utility is determined on the basis of the probability distribution of possible returns from an investment. We also assume that investors can summarize their beliefs about the probability distribution of possible returns from an investment or portfolio of investments in terms of two parameters of the distribution.[14] These parameters are the expected value and the standard deviation, both illustrated earlier. In the next chapter, we follow up on these ideas by showing how the utility preferences of investors can be applied to the selection of portfolios of securities.

SUMMARY

Investment, financing, and dividend decisions have significant impact on the firm's valuation. A key concept underlying valuation is the time value of money. In considering this topic, the determination of both terminal values and present values was illustrated. Both formulas may be modified for compounding more than once a year. Using present-value techniques, we are able to isolate differences in the timing of cash flows for various investments. Also

---

[13] Setting up the problem for the quadratic equation, we have $-.05X^2 + 2X - 17.5 = 0$. The quadratic equation is

$$X = \frac{-b \pm \sqrt{b^2 - 4ac}}{2a}$$

$$= \frac{-2 \pm \sqrt{(2)^2 - 4(-.05)(-17.5)}}{2(-.05)} = 12.929, 27.071$$

As the second root applies to decreases in utility, we ignore it.

[14] For an analysis of the conditions under which this is possible, see David P. Baron, "On the Utility Theoretic Foundation of Mean-Variance Analysis," *Journal of Finance*, 32 (December 1977), 1683–98.

using these techniques, we showed how to amortize a loan and how to compute the internal rate of return on an investment. Frequent use of present values and internal rates of return will occur in subsequent chapters.

Bonds can be either pure discount ones, where only one payment is made at maturity, or coupon bonds, where interest payments are made semi-annually through maturity, at which time the bond's face value is paid as well. Yield to maturity is the rate of discount that equates the present value of promised future payments to investors with the current market price of the bond. Formulas were presented for solving for market price, given the yield, or for yield, given the market price. In addition, the valuation of perpetuities was addressed, one example of which is preferred stock. The duration of a bond is a measure of its average life on a present-value basis, where both the times to interest payments and the time to the final principal payment are considered.

In purchasing a common stock, the investor gives up present consumption with the expectation of increasing future consumption. The expected return is the rate of discount that equates the present market value of the stock with the present value of the stream of expected future dividends. Because cash dividends are all that investors as a whole receive from their investment, these dividends are the foundation for valuation. A dividend valuation model is consistent with the fact that many investors expect to sell their stock in the future and realize a capital gain. Given the basic valuation model, we saw how it could be modified to solve for different expectations of future growth, be they for perpetual growth or for phased growth. With respect to the latter, a terminal value is determined at some horizon, by assuming either a perpetual growth dividend situation or a price/earnings ratio multiple.

In addition to the expected return on investment, we are concerned with risk. For our purposes, *risk* is defined as the deviation of the actual return from that which was expected. To measure the wideness of the distribution of possible returns, the standard deviation is computed. By relating the standard deviation to a specific difference from the expected return, we are able to determine the probability of occurrence of that outcome. Investors attempt to maximize their expected utility, which is a function of expected return and standard deviation. In the subsequent chapter, we show how these concepts are applied to the selection of a portfolio of securities and the implications of such selection for the required rate of return and valuation of the individual firm.

SELF-CORRECTION PROBLEMS

1. The following cash-flow streams need to be analyzed:

CASH-FLOW STREAM	YEAR END				
	1	2	3	4	5
1	$100	$200	$200	$300	$300
2	600	—	—	—	—
3	—	—	—	—	1,200
4	200	—	500	—	300

a. Calculate the terminal value of each stream at the end of year 5 with an interest rate of 10 percent.

b. Compute the present value of each stream if the discount rate is 14 percent.

c. Compute the internal rate of return of each stream if the initial investment at time 0 were $600.

2. Sanchez Hydraulics Company has outstanding a 14 percent coupon bond with three years to maturity. Interest payments are made semiannually. Assume a face value of $100.

a. If the market price of the bond is $104, what is the yield to maturity? If it were $97, what would be the yield? If it were $100?

b. If the bond's yield were 12 percent, what would be its price? If it were 15 percent? If 14 percent?

c. Instead of a coupon bond, suppose it were a zero coupon, pure discount instrument. If the yield were 14 percent, what would be the market price? (Assume semiannual compounding.)

3. Delphi Products Corporation currently pays a dividend of $2 per share and this dividend is expected to grow at a 15 percent annual rate for 3 years, then at a 10 percent rate for the next 3 years, after which it is expected to grow at a 5 percent rate forever.

a. What value would you place on the stock if an 18 percent rate of return were required?

b. Would your valuation change if you expected to hold the stock only 3 years?

4. For Delphi Products Corporation in Problem 3, suppose the company were expected to have a price/earnings ratio of 8 times at the end of year 6. Moreover, earnings per share in year 7 are expected to be $7.50. If the present market price per share is $35, what is the expected return on investment? (Assume that terminal value at the end of year 6 is based on year 7 earnings.)

5. Fox River Associates is analyzing a new line of business and estimates the possible returns on investment as

Probability	.1	.2	.4	.2	.1
Possible return	−10%	5%	20%	35%	50%

a. What are the expected value of return and standard deviation?

b. Assume that the parameters in part a pertain to a normal probability distribution. What is the probability the return will be zero or less? less than 10 percent? more than 40 percent? (Assume a normal distribution.)

PROBLEMS

1. The following are exercises in terminal values:

a. At the end of 3 years, how much is an initial deposit of $100 worth, assuming an annual interest rate of (1) 10 percent? (2) 100 percent? (3) 0 percent?

b. At the end of 3 years, how much is an initial deposit of $100 worth, assuming a quarterly compounded interest rate of (1) 10 percent? (2) 100 percent?

c. Why does your answer to part b differ from that to part a?

d. At the end of 10 years, how much is an initial deposit of $100 worth, assuming an interest rate of 10 percent compounded (1) annually? (2) semiannually? (3) quarterly? (4) continuously?

2. The following are exercises in present values:

a. $100 at the end of 3 years is worth how much today, assuming a discount rate of (1) 10 percent? (2) 100 percent? (3) 0 percent?

b. What is the aggregate present value of $500 received at the end of each of the next 3 years, assuming a discount rate of (1) 4 percent? (2) 25 percent?

c. $100 is received at the end of 1 year, $500 at the end of 2 years, and $1,000 at the end of 3 years. What is the aggregate present value of these receipts, assuming a discount rate of (1) 4 percent? (2) 25 percent?

d. $1,000 is to be received at the end of 1 year, $500 at the end of 2 years, and $100 at the end of 3 years. What is the aggregate present value of these receipts, assuming a discount rate of (1) 4 percent? (2) 25 percent?

e. Compare your solutions in part c with those in part d and explain the reason for the differences.

3. The following are exercises on internal rates of return (IRRs):

a. An investment of $1,000 today will return $2,000 at the end of 10 years. What is its IRR?

b. An investment of $1,000 today will return $500 at the end of each of the next 3 years. What is its IRR?

c. An investment of $1,000 today will return $1,000 at the end of 1 year, $500 at the end of 2 years, and $100 at the end of 3 years. What is its IRR?

d. An investment of $1,000 will return $60 per year forever. What is its IRR?

4. Graph the present value of $1 per year for 5, 10, 15, 20, and 25 years at 0, 10, 20, 30, and 40 percent rates of discount. Explain the difference in the slopes of the curves.

5. Selyn Cohen is 65 years old and recently retired. He wishes to provide retirement income for himself and is considering an annuity contract with Monument Life Insurance Company. Such a contract pays him an equal amount each year he lives. For this cash-flow stream, he must put up so much money at the beginning. According to actuarial tables, his life expectancy is 15 years, and that is the duration on which the insurance company bases its calculations regardless of how long Cohen actually lives.

a. If Monument Life uses an interest rate of 5 percent in its calculations, what must Cohen pay at the outset for an annuity providing him $10,000 per year? (Assume annual payments are at the end of each of the 15 years.)

b. What would be the purchase price if the interest rate were 10 percent?

c. If Cohen had $30,000 to put into an annuity, how much would he receive each year if the insurance company used a 5 percent interest rate in its calculations? a 10 percent rate?

6. On a contract, you have a choice of receiving $25,000 six years from now or $50,000 twelve years hence. What is the implied discount rate that equates these two amounts?

7. You borrow $10,000 at 14 percent for 4 years. The loan is repayable in four equal installments at year ends.

a. What is the annual payment that will completely amortize the loan over 4 years? (You may wish to round to the nearest dollar.)

b. Of each payment, what is the amount of interest? the amount of principal?

8. Establish loan amortization schedules for the following loans to the nearest cent. (See Table 2-3 for an example.) This problem should only be done with the computer program in the supplement.

a. A 36-month loan of $8,000 with equal installment payments at the end of each month. The interest rate is 1 percent per month.

b. A 25-year mortgage loan of $184,000 with equal installment payments at the end of each year. The interest rate is 10 percent per annum.

9. Barquez Mines, Inc., is considering investing in Chile. It makes a bid to the government to participate in the development of a mine, the profits of which will be realized at the end of 5 years. The mine is expected to produce $5 million in cash to Barquez at that time. Other than the bid at the outset, no other cash flows will occur, as the government will reimburse the company for all costs. If Barquez requires a return of 20 percent, what is the maximum bid it should make for the participation right if interest is compounded (a) annually? (b) semiannually? (c) quarterly? (d) continuously?

10. Booker Brown, Inc., has a 10 percent bond outstanding with 7 years remaining to

maturity. Interest payments are semiannual, and the instrument's face value is $100.

a. If the yield to maturity is 11.6 percent, what is the bond's market price? If 9.2 percent?

b. If the market price were $110, what would be the yield to maturity? if $94?

11. Kerby Manufacturing Corporation sells a zero coupon bond for $38 with 8 years to maturity. At maturity the company will pay the bond's holder $100. What is the bond's yield to maturity if a semiannual convention to valuation is employed?

12. Caroline Islands Resorts has 1,750,000 shares of authorized common stock having a $1 par value. Over the years it has issued 1,532,000 shares, but presently 63,000 are held as Treasury stock. The paid-in capital of the company is presently $5,314,000.

a. How many shares are now outstanding?

b. If the company were able to sell stock at $19 per share, what would be the maximum amount it could raise under its existing authorization, including Treasury shares?

c. What would be its common stock and paid-in capital accounts after the financing?

13. The stock of the Health Corporation is currently selling for $20 and is expected to pay a $1 dividend at the end of the year. What will be the rate of return to investors who buy the stock now and sell it for $23 after collecting the dividend?

14. North Great Timber Company will pay a dividend of $1.50 next year. After this, earnings and dividends are expected to grow at an 8 percent annual rate indefinitely. Investors now require a rate of return of 12 percent. The company is considering several business strategies and wishes to determine the effect of these strategies on the market price per share of its stock.

a. Continuing the present strategy will result in the expected growth rate and required rate of return shown.

b. Expanding timber holdings and sales will increase the expected dividend growth rate to 10 percent but will increase the risk of the company. As a result, the rate of return required by investors will increase to 15 percent.

c. Integrating into retail stores will increase the dividend growth rate to 9 percent and increase the required rate of return to 13 percent.

From the standpoint of market price per share, which strategy is best?

15. Zachery Zorro Company presently pays a dividend of $1.60 per share and the market price per share is $30. The company expects to increase the dividend at a 20 percent annual rate the first 4 years, at a 13 percent rate the next 4 years, and then grow the dividend at a 7 percent rate thereafter. This phased-growth pattern is in keeping with the expected life cycle of earnings. What is the stock's expected return on investment?

16. Northern California Fruit Company's latest earnings are $2.00 per share. Earnings per share are expected to grow at a 20 percent compound annual rate for 4 years, at a 12 percent annual rate for the next 4 years, at 6 percent thereafter. The dividend-payout ratio is expected to be 25 percent the first 4 years, 40 percent the next 4 years, and 50 percent thereafter. At the end of year 8, the price/earnings ratio for the company is expected to be 8.5 times, where year 9 expected earnings per share are used in the denominator.

a. If the required rate of return is 14 percent, what is the present market price per share?

b. If the present market price per share is $30, what is the stock's expected return?

17. Wally Whittier is considering investing in a security that has the following distribution of possible returns:

Probability	.10	.20	.30	.30	.10
Return	−.10	.00	.10	.20	.30

a. What is the expected value of return and standard deviation associated with the investment?

b. Is there much downside risk? How can you tell?

18. Shirley Batavia is analyzing an investment in a shopping center. The expected return on investment is 20 percent. The probability distribution of possible returns is a normal bell-shaped distribution with a standard deviation of 15 percent.

a. What are the chances that the investment will result in a negative return?

b. What is the probability that the return will be greater than 10 percent? than 20 percent? than 30 percent? than 40 percent? than 50 percent?

SOLUTIONS TO
SELF-CORRECTION PROBLEMS

1. a. Terminal value of each cash flow and total future value of the stream:

CASH-FLOW STREAM	YEAR					TOTAL TERMINAL VALUE
	1	2	3	4	5	
1	$146.41	$266.20	$242	$330	$300	$1,284.61
2	878.46	—	—	—	—	878.46
3	—	—	—	—	1,200	1,200.00
4	292.82	—	605	—	300	1,197.82

b. Present value of each cash flow and total present value of stream:

CASH-FLOW STREAM	YEAR					TOTAL PRESENT VALUE
	1	2	3	4	5	
1	$87.72	$153.89	$134.99	$177.62	$155.81	$710.03
2	526.31	—	—	—	—	526.31
3	—	—	—	—	623.24	623.24
4	175.44	—	337.49	—	155.81	668.74
Discount factor	.87719	.76947	.67497	.59208	.51937	

c. Internal rates of return: 1 = 20.20%; 2 = 0% (a $600 outlay followed by a $600 receipt results in a zero IRR); 3 = 14.87%; and 4 = 18.34%. To illustrate cash-flow stream 4 by trial and error.

YEAR	CASH FLOW	18% DISCOUNT FACTOR	18% PRESENT VALUE	19% DISCOUNT FACTOR	19% PRESENT VALUE
0	−$600	1.00000	−$600.00	1.00000	−$600.00
1	200	.84746	169.49	.84034	168.07
3	500	.60863	304.32	.59342	296.71
5	300	.43711	131.13	.41905	125.72
Total			$ 4.94		−$ 9.50

$$IRR = .18 + \frac{\$4.94}{\$4.94 + \$9.50} = 18.34\%$$

2. a. (1) Setting up the problem in keeping with Eq. (2-15) and solving for r, the yield to maturity is found to be 12.36%. The yield is less than the coupon rate when the bond trades at a price premium above its face value.

(2) The yield here is 15.72%. Yield is more than the coupon rate for a bond trading at a discount.

(3) Whenever the market price equals the face value, yield equals the coupon rate, 14% in this case.

b. (1) Setting up this problem again in keeping with Eq. (2-15) and solving for price, we find it to be $104.92.

(2) In this case, price is found to be $97.65.

(3) Price equals the face value of $100 when yield equals the coupon rate.

c. $P = \$100/(1.07)^6 = \$66.63$

3. a.

END OF	DIVIDEND	PRESENT VALUE OF DIVIDENDS 18%
Year 1	$2.00(1.15) = $2.30	× .84746 = $ 1.95
Year 2	2.00(1.15)² = 2.64	× .71818 = 1.90
Year 3	2.00(1.15)³ = 3.04	× .60863 = 1.85
Year 4	3.04(1.10) = 3.35	× .51579 = 1.73
Year 5	3.04(1.10)² = 3.68	× .43711 = 1.61
Year 6	3.04(1.10)³ = 4.05	× .37043 = 1.50
		Total = $10.54

Year 7 dividend = $4.05(1.05) = $4.25

Market value at end of year 6 = $\dfrac{4.25}{.18 - .05}$ = $32.69

Present value of expected dividend to be received at end of years 1, 2, and 3 = $1.95 + $1.90 + $1.85 = $5.70.

b. Present value of market value at end of year 3 = $1.73 + $1.61 + $1.50 + $12.11 = $16.95.

Present value of expected dividend to be received at end of years 1, 2, and 3 = $1.95 + $1.90 + $1.85 = $5.70.

Total value = $16.95 + $5.70 = $22.65. Thus, the value is the same for an investor with a 3-year time horizon.

4. Terminal value at the end of year 6 equals $7.50 EPS × 8 P/E ratio = $60.00. The expected cash flows to the investor are (in dollars).

			YEAR			
0	1	2	3	4	5	6
−35.00	2.30	2.64	3.04	3.35	3.68	64.05

Solving for the rate of discount that equates the present values of the cash inflows with the cash outflow of $35 at time 0, we find it to be 16.50 percent.

5. a. By visual inspection of a symmetrical distribution, the expected value of return is seen to be 20 percent. (This can be easily confirmed mathematically.) The standard deviation is

$$SD = [(-.10 - .20)^2 .1 + (.05 - .20)^2 .2 + (.20 - .20)^2 .4$$
$$+ (.35 - .20)^2 .2 + (.50 - .20)^2 .1]^{1/2}$$

$$= 16.43\%$$

b. For a zero or less return, standardizing the deviation from the expected value of return one obtains $(0 - 20\%)/16.43\% = -1.217$ standard deviations. Turning to Table C at the back of the book, 1.217 falls between standard deviations of 1.20 and 1.25. These standard deviations correspond to areas under the curve of .1151 and .1056, respectively. Interpolating

$$.1151 - (.1151 - .1056)\left(\frac{1.217 - 1.20}{1.25 - 1.20}\right) = .1118$$

This means there is approximately an 11.18 percent probability the actual return will be zero or less.

For a 10 percent or less return, standardizing the deviation we obtain $(10\% - 20\%)/16.43\% = -.609$ standard deviations. Referring to Table C at the back of the book and going through the same computations as above, we obtain

$$.2743 - (.2743 - .2578)\left(\frac{.609 - .60}{.65 - .60}\right) = .2713$$

Here there is approximately a 27.13 percent probability the actual return will be 10 percent or less.

For a 40 percent or more return, standardizing we obtain $(40\% - 20\%)/16.43\% = 1.217$ standard deviations. This is the same as in our first instance involving a zero return or less, except that it is to the right as opposed to the left of the mean. Therefore, the probability of a 40 percent or more return is approximately 11.18 percent.

SELECTED REFERENCES

BAUMAN, W. SCOTT, "Investment Returns and Present Values," *Financial Analysts Journal*, 25 (November–December 1969), 107–18.

BRIGHAM, EUGENE F., and JAMES L. PAPPAS, "Duration of Growth, Changes in Growth Rates, and Corporate Share Prices," *Financial Analysts Journal*, 22 (May–June 1966), 157–62.

CISSELL, ROBERT, HELEN CISSELL, and DAVID C. FLASPOHLER, *Mathematics of Finance*, 8th ed. Boston: Houghton Mifflin, 1990.

FAMA, EUGENE F., "Components of Investment Performance," *Journal of Finance*, 27 (June 1972), 551–67.

——, and MERTON H. MILLER, *The Theory of Finance*. New York: Holt, 1972.

FULLER, RUSSELL J., and CHI-CHENG HSIA, "A Simplified Common Stock Valuation Model," *Financial Analysts Journal*, 40 (September–October 1984), 49–56.

HAUGEN, ROBERT A., *Modern Investment Theory*, 2d ed. Englewood Cliffs, NJ: Prentice Hall, 1990.

HICKMAN, KENT, and GLENN H. PETRY, "A Comparison of Stock Price Predictions Using Court Accepted Formulas, Dividend Discount, and P/E Models," *Financial Management*, 19 (Summer 1990), 76–87.

MALKIEL, BURTON G., "Equity Yields, Growth, and the Structure of Share Prices," *American Economic Review*, 53 (December 1963), 467–94.

MODIGLIANI, FRANCO, and GERALD A. POGUE, "An Introduction to Risk and Return," *Financial Analysts Journal*, 30 (March–April 1974), 68–80, and (May–June 1974), 69–86.

SHARPE, WILLIAM F., and GORDON J. ALEXANDER, *Investments*, 4th ed. Englewood Cliffs, NJ: Prentice Hall, 1990.

SIEGEL, JEREMY J., "The Application of the DCF Methodology for Determining the Cost of Equity Capital," *Financial Management*, 14 (Spring 1985), 46–53.

TIMME, STEPHEN G., and PETER C. EISEMANN, "On the Use of Consensus Forecasts of Growth in the Constant Growth Model: The Case of Electric Utilities," *Financial Management*, 18 (Winter 1989), 23–35.

VAN HORNE, JAMES C., *Financial Market Rates and Flows*, 3d ed. Englewood Cliffs, NJ: Prentice Hall, 1990.

———, and WILLIAM F. GLASSMIRE, JR., "The Impact of Unanticipated Changes in Inflation on the Value of Common Stocks," *Journal of Finance*, 27 (December 1972), 1081–92.

3

MARKET RISK
AND RETURNS

Prospective investors are consumers, shopping. They are influenced by advertising, by the company's image, and, predominantly, by price. Investors usually do not fill their shopping bags with only one investment opportunity, and they try to be sophisticated shoppers when they select a portfolio of securities. Like consumer researchers, let us follow them around to see how they make their choices, how the individual firm is valued in the market, and how market equilibrium is achieved.

EFFICIENT FINANCIAL MARKETS

Market efficiency, an underlying idea in this chapter, means that the market price of a security represents the market's consensus estimate of the value of that security. If the market is efficient, it uses all information available to it in setting a price. Investors who choose to hold a security are doing so because their information leads them to think that the security is worth at least its current market price. Those who do not purchase the stock interpret their information as a lower appraisal.

An efficient financial market exists when security prices reflect all available public information about the economy, about financial markets, and about the specific company involved. The implication is that market prices of individual securities adjust very rapidly to new information. As a result, security prices are said to fluctuate randomly about their "intrinsic" values. New information can result in a change in the "intrinsic" value of a security, but subsequent security price movements will follow what is known as a *random walk* (changes in price will not follow any pattern).[1] Contrary to often quoted passages of Shakespeare and Santayana, history—at least in the stock market—is not repetitious or helpful. This simply means that one cannot use past security prices to predict future prices in such a way as to profit on average. Moreover, close attention to news releases will be for naught. Alas, by the time you are able to take action, security price adjustments will already have occurred, according to the efficient market notion.

Expressed more formally, market efficiency means that the unanticipated portion of the return earned on a security is unpredictable and, over a

[1] For a formalized presentation of this condition, see Eugene F. Fama, "Efficient Capital Markets: A Review of Theory and Empirical Work," *Journal of Finance,* 25 (May 1970) 384–87.

sufficient number of observations, it does not differ systematically from zero. The unanticipated portion is simply the actual return less that which was expected based on some fundamental analysis (e.g., its "intrinsic" value). Put differently, it is the surprise element. Using the definitions of Fama, weak-form market efficiency means that the unanticipated return is not correlated with previous unanticipated returns.[2] Semistrong-form market efficiency means it is not correlated with any publicly available information. Finally, with strong-form market efficiency, the unanticipated return is not correlated with any information, be it publicly available or insider.

On balance, the evidence indicates that the market for stocks, particularly those listed on the New York Stock Exchange, is reasonably efficient. Security prices appear to be a good reflection of available information, and market prices adjust quickly to new information. Market participants seem to be ready to seize on any recurring price pattern; and in doing so, they drive price changes about a security's "intrinsic" value to a random walk. About the only way one can consistently profit is to have insider information, that is, information about a company known to officers and directors but not to the public. If security prices impound all available public information, they tell us a good deal about the future. In efficient markets, one can hope to do no better.

James H. Lorie, Peter Dodd, and Mary T. Hamilton,[3] as well as a number of others, point out that the efficient market theory presents a curious paradox: The hypothesis that stock markets are efficient will be true only if a sufficiently large number of investors disbelieve its efficiency and behave accordingly. In other words, the theory requires that there be a sufficiently large number of market participants who, in their attempts to earn profits, promptly receive and analyze all the information that is publicly available concerning companies whose securities they follow. Should this considerable effort devoted to data accumulation and evaluation cease, financial markets would become markedly less efficient. In this book, we assume that financial markets are reasonably efficient in the information sense described. However, we do not rule out market imperfections that, on occasion, can affect security pricing.

ARBITRAGE EFFICIENCY

Another definition of market efficiency has to do with arbitrage. *Arbitrage* simply means finding two things that are essentially the same and buying the cheaper and selling, or selling short, the more expensive. Suppose there exist two risk-free bonds: Bond 1 is priced at $1,000 and pays $100 at the end of year 1 and $1,100 at the end of year 2; Bond 2 costs $800 and pays $1,000 at the end of year 2. Presently you own 8 of Bond 1. If you continue to hold them, you will receive $800 at the end of year 1. If a risk-free party were to pay you 10 percent for the use of these funds from the end of year 1 to the end of year 2, the $800 would grow to $880. The total amount of funds you would have at the end of year 2 would be $880 plus (8 × $1,100), or $9,680. For Bond 2, $8,000 invested today would grow to $10,000 at the end of year 2. Clearly, you should sell your holdings in Bond 1 for $8,000 and invest in Bond 2.

[2] Ibid.
[3] *The Stock Market*, 2d ed. (Homewood, IL: Richard D. Irwin, 1985).

As others recognize this arbitrage opportunity, they will do the same. Selling Bond 1, of course, exerts downward pressure on its price, while buying Bond 2 brings upward pressure on its price. Arbitrage actions will continue until the two bonds provide the same funds at the end of year 2. The simple, but powerful, notion here is that security prices adjust as market participants search for arbitrage profits. When such opportunities have been exhausted, security prices are said to be in equilibrium. In this context a definition of market efficiency is the absence of arbitrage opportunities, their having been eliminated by arbitragers.

SECURITY PORTFOLIOS

In the last chapter, we measured the expected return and risk for a single security. For a portfolio of two or more securities, things are different. The expected return, r_p, is straightforward:

$$r_p = \sum_{j=1}^{m} r_j A_j \qquad (3\text{-}1)$$

where r_j is the expected return on security j, A_j is the proportion of total funds invested in security j, and m is the total number of securities in the portfolio. The Greek sigma denotes the summation from security 1 through security m. Equation (3-1) merely says that *the expected return for a portfolio is a weighted average of expected returns for securities making up that portfolio.*

PORTFOLIO RISK

The risk of a portfolio is not a simple weighted average of the standard deviations of the individual securities. Portfolio risk depends not only on the riskiness of the securities constituting the portfolio but also on the relationship among those securities.

By selecting securities that have little relationship with each other, an investor is able to reduce relative risk. *Diversification*, combining securities in a way that will reduce relative risk, is illustrated in Fig. 3-1. Here the returns over time for security A are cyclical in that they move with the economy in general. Returns for security B, however, are mildly countercyclical. Equal amounts invested in both securities will reduce the dispersion of the return on total investment.

In another example involving less than countercyclical behavior, two securities have one-period returns under three possible states of nature:

STATE	PROBABILITY OF STATE OCCURRING	RETURN ON SECURITY A	RETURN ON SECURITY B
Boom	.25	28%	10%
Normal	.50	15	13
Recession	.25	−2	10

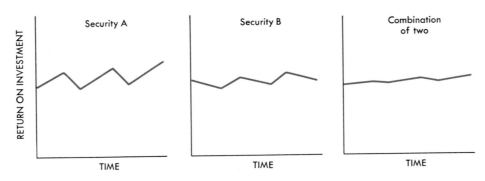

FIGURE 3-1
Effect of diversification

The expected return and standard deviation of the probability distribution of possible returns for the two securities are[4]

	SECURITY A	SECURITY B
Expected return	14.0%	11.5%
Standard deviation	10.7	1.5

If equal amounts of money are invested in the two securities, the expected return of the portfolio is 14.0%(.5) + 11.5%(.5) = 12.75%. The weighted average of the individual standard deviations is simply 10.7%(.5) + 1.5%(.5) = 6.1 percent.

However, this is not the standard deviation of the overall portfolio. The returns for a portfolio consisting of equal investments in both securities are

STATE	PROBABILITY OF STATE OCCURRING	RETURN ON PORTFOLIO
Boom	.25	19%
Normal	.50	14
Recession	.25	4

where the return on the portfolio is simply the weighted average of the returns on the individual securities. The expected return for the portfolio is 19%(.25) + 14%(.50) + 4%(.25) = 12.75%, the same as before. However, the standard deviation of the portfolio is

$$[(.19 - .1275)^2 .25 + (.14 - .1275)^2 .50 + (.04 - .1275)^2 .25]^{1/2} = 5.4\%$$

where the exponent of $\frac{1}{2}$ for the outside brackets means the square root. We

[4] The expected return and standard deviation are determined by using Eq. (2-38) and Eq. (2-39) in Chapter 2.

see that the portfolio standard deviation is less than the weighted average of the individual standard deviations, 6.1 percent. The reason why the weighted average of the standard deviations fails to yield the correct standard deviation of the portfolio is that it ignores the relationship, or covariance, between the returns of the two securities.

COVARIANCE OF RETURNS

It is clear that one cannot in general calculate the standard deviation of a portfolio's returns simply by taking the weighted average of the standard deviations for the individual securities. Instead, the standard deviation of a probability distribution of possible portfolio returns is

$$\sigma_p = \sqrt{\sum_{j=1}^{m} \sum_{k=1}^{m} A_j A_k \sigma_{jk}} \tag{3-2}$$

where m is the total number of securities in the portfolio; A_j is the proportion of the total funds invested in security j; A_k is the proportion invested in security k; and σ_{jk} is the covariance between possible returns for securities j and k. (The covariance term will be illustrated shortly.)

The two Σs mean that we consider the covariances for all possible pairwise combinations of securities in the portfolio. For example, suppose m were four. The matrix of covariances for possible pairwise combinations would be

$$
\begin{matrix}
\sigma_{1,1} & \sigma_{1,2} & \sigma_{1,3} & \sigma_{1,4} \\
\sigma_{2,1} & \sigma_{2,2} & \sigma_{2,3} & \sigma_{2,4} \\
\sigma_{3,1} & \sigma_{3,2} & \sigma_{3,3} & \sigma_{3,4} \\
\sigma_{4,1} & \sigma_{4,2} & \sigma_{4,3} & \sigma_{4,4}
\end{matrix}
$$

The combination in the upper left-hand corner is $1, 1$, which means that $j = k$ and that our concern is with the variance of security 1. That is, $\sigma_1 \sigma_1 = \sigma_1^2$ in Eq. (3-2), or the standard deviation squared. As we trace down the diagonal, there are four situations in all where $j = k$, and we would be concerned with the variances in all four. The second combination in row 1 is $\sigma_{1,2}$, which signifies the covariance between possible returns for securities 1 and 2. Note, however, that the first combination in row 2 is $\sigma_{2,1}$, which signifies the covariance between securities 2 and 1. In other words, we count the covariance between securities 1 and 2 twice. Similarly, we count the covariances between all other combinations not on the diagonal twice. The double summation signs in Eq. (3-2) simply mean that we sum all variances and covariances in the matrix of possible pairwise combinations. In our matrix, it is 16, represented by 4 variances and 6 covariances counted twice.

The covariance of the possible returns of two securities is a measure of the extent to which they are expected to vary together rather than independently of each other. More formally, the covariance term in Eq. (3-2) is

$$\sigma_{jk} = r_{jk} \sigma_j \sigma_k \tag{3-3}$$

where r_{jk} is the expected correlation between possible returns for securities j and k, σ_j is the standard deviation for security j, and σ_k is the standard deviation for security k. The standard deviations of the probability distributions of possible returns for securities j and k are determined by the methods taken up in the preceding chapter. When $j = k$ in Eq. (3-3), the correlation coefficient is 1.0, and $\sigma_j \sigma_k$ becomes σ_j^2. That is, we are concerned only with the own variance of securities along the diagonal of the matrix.

The formula in Eq. (3-2) makes a very fundamental point. The standard deviation for a portfolio depends not only on the variances of the individual securities but on the covariances between various pairs. As the number of securities in a portfolio increases, the covariance terms become more important relative to the variance terms. This can be seen by examining the matrix. In a two-security portfolio, there are two own variance terms along the diagonal, $\sigma_{1,1}$ and $\sigma_{2,2}$, and two covariance terms, $\sigma_{1,2}$ and $\sigma_{2,1}$. For a four-security portfolio, there are 4 own variance terms and 12 covariance terms. For a large portfolio then, total variance depends primarily on the covariances among securities. For example, with a 30-security portfolio, there are 30 own variance terms in the matrix and 870 covariance terms. As a portfolio expands further to include all securities, only covariance is important.

The value of a correlation coefficient always lies in the range from -1 to $+1$. A correlation coefficient of 1.00 indicates that an increase in the return for one security is always associated with a proportional increase in the return for the other security, and similarly for decreases. A correlation coefficient of -1.00 indicates that an increase in the return for one security is always associated with a proportional decrease in the return for the other security, and vice versa. A zero coefficient indicates an absence of correlation, so that the returns of each security vary independently of the other. However, most stock returns tend to move together, so the correlation coefficient between two stocks is positive.

ILLUSTRATION OF CALCULATIONS

To illustrate the determination of the parameters of a two-security portfolio, suppose Simplicity Foods Inc.'s stock has an expected return of 12 percent and a standard deviation of 11 percent, while that of Fast Eddys Electronics Company has an expected return of 18 percent and a standard deviation of 19 percent. The expected correlation between the two security returns is .20. By investing equal portions in each of the two stocks, the expected return for the portfolio is

$$R_p = 12\%(.50) + 18\%(.50) = 15\%$$

This, of course, is simply a weighted average.

If we calculate a weighted average of the standard deviations, we find it to be 15 percent. In fact, this would be the portfolio standard deviation if the correlation coefficient were 1.0. However, Eq. (3-2) tells us the standard deviation is lower when the correlation coefficient is less than 1.0. For a correlation coefficient of .20, the standard deviation is

$$\sigma_p = [(.5)^2 (1.00)(.11)^2 + (2)(.5)(.5)(.20)(.11)(.19) + (.5)^2 (1.00)(.19)^2]^{\frac{1}{2}}$$

$$= 11.89\%$$

From Eq. (3-2), we know that the covariance between the two stocks must be counted twice. Therefore, we multiply the covariance by two. When

$j = 1$ and $k = 1$ for stock 1, the proportion invested (.5) must be squared, as must the standard deviation (.11). The correlation coefficient, of course, is 1.00. The same thing applies to stock 2 when $j = 2$ and $k = 2$. The important principle to grasp is that as long as the correlation coefficient between two securities is less than 1.00, the standard deviation of the portfolio will be less than the weighted average of the two individual standard deviations.

A TWO-SECURITY EFFICIENT SET

We see this is the case when equal investments are made in Simplicity Foods and Fast Eddys Electronics. The standard deviation is 11.89 percent versus 15.00 percent if the correlation coefficient is 1.0. The difference is due to the diversification effect. For other combinations of our two securities, we have the following, again using Eq. (3-1) and (3-2) to make the calculations:

PORT-FOLIO	PROPORTION SIMPLICITY	PROPORTION FAST EDDYS	PORTFOLIO RETURN	PORTFOLIO STANDARD DEVIATION
#1	1.0	0	12.0%	11.00%
#2	.8	.2	13.2	10.26
#3	.6	.4	14.4	11.02
#4	.4	.6	15.6	13.01
#5	.2	.8	16.8	15.79
#6	0	1.0	18.0	19.00

To visualize things graphically, Figure 3-2 describes the relationship between expected return and risk when the proportions invested in each security are varied. The dots correspond to the six portfolios described above. The curve that connects them is known as the *opportunity set*, and it depicts the risk-return trade-off. Several features in the figure are important.

First, the diversification effect is seen by comparing the curved line with the straight dashed line, which connects an all Simplicity Foods investment (portfolio #1) with an all Fast Eddys Electronics investment (portfolio #6). The straight line would describe the opportunity set if perfect positive corre-

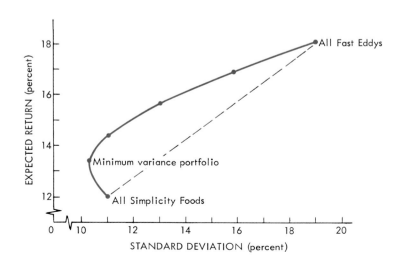

FIGURE 3-2

Opportunity set for investment in a two-security portfolio

lation prevailed—i.e., if the correlation coefficient were 1.0. With a correlation coefficient of only .20, a considerable diversification effect is evidenced by the distance between the two lines.

Second, it is possible to reduce the standard deviation from what occurs with a 100 percent investment in Simplicity Foods by investing in the riskier security, Fast Eddys Electronics. This counterintuitive result is due to the diversification effect. Unexpected returns from one security often are offset by opposite movements in returns for the other security. On average, the two-security returns move in the same direction, but with a correlation coefficient of only .20 there are offsets. By investing a moderate amount in Fast Eddys Electronics, one can lower the standard deviation. Therefore, the opportunity set curve is backward bending for awhile.

Third, the portfolio depicted farthest to the left is known as the *minimum variance portfolio*. It is the one with the lowest standard deviation that comes about by varying the mix of securities held. In our case, the minimum variance portfolio consists of 80 percent in Simplicity Foods and 20 percent in Fast Eddys Electronics. Using Eq. (3-2), one finds that a 19 percent investment in Fast Eddys Electronics or a 21 percent investment results in a slightly higher standard deviation. The minimum variance portfolio is 80–20. It should be noted that backward bending does not necessarily occur with diversification. It depends on the correlation coefficient, as we will illustrate in the next section.

Fourth, no one would want to own a portfolio with a lower expected return than that provided by the minimum variance portfolio. Therefore, the backward-bending portion of the opportunity set curve is infeasible. The *efficient set* is the portion of the curve going from the minimum variance portfolio, #2, to the one with the maximum expected return, #6, consisting of all Fast Eddys Electronics stock.

Fifth, it is only possible to be on the opportunity set line, not above or below it. With only two securities, altering the proportions held affects only one's position on the line.

DIFFERENT CORRELATIONS

With higher correlation between returns, the diversification effect is lower. Figure 3-3 depicts the opportunity set curve for our example when the correlation coefficient is .60, in addition to .20 and 1.00. As seen, the distance from the straight line, representing perfect positive correlation, is lessened. Also, there is no backward bend to the curve. Any investment in Fast Eddys Electronics results in a higher standard deviation than occurs with a 100 percent investment in the safer stock, Simplicity Foods. Therefore, the minimum variance portfolio consists of all funds being invested in Simplicity Foods. The efficient set now is represented by the entire opportunity set line. As seen in the figure, the lower the correlation coefficient between security returns, the more bowed the opportunity set curve and the greater the diversification effect.

The example suggests that by diversifying one's holdings to include securities with less than perfect positive correlation among themselves, the investor is able to reduce the standard deviation of the probability distribution of possible returns relative to the expected return. In other words, risk is lowered relative to expected return.

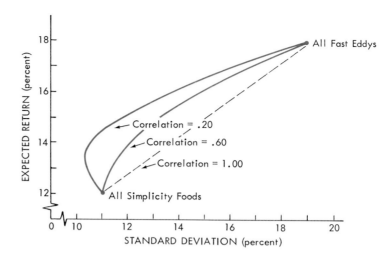

FIGURE 3-3

Opportunity sets for two-security portfolios with different correlation coefficients

MULTIPLE SECURITY PORTFOLIO ANALYSIS AND SELECTION

The same principles hold when we go to portfolios containing more than two securities. An example of the opportunity set here is shown in Figure 3-4. This set is based on the subjective probability beliefs of an individual investor. It reflects all possible portfolios of securities as envisioned by the investor, every point in the shaded area representing a portfolio that is attainable. Note that this opportunity set is different from that for a two-security portfolio, as illustrated in Figure 3-2. In that figure, we saw that all possible combinations of the two securities fell on a single line. In Figure 3-4, they fall within a rather large area. As the number of securities available for investment increases, the number of pairwise and multiple combinations increases geometrically.

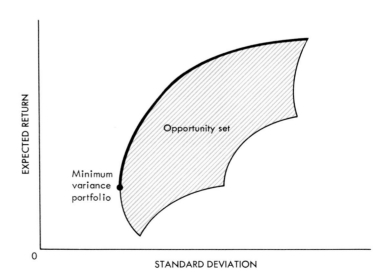

FIGURE 3-4

Hypothetical opportunity set

As before, the minimum variance portfolio is the one farthest to the left, possessing the lowest standard deviation. Notice in the figure that the outward edge of the opportunity set is backward bending for awhile. This occurs for the same reason that it did for our two-security portfolio example—the diversification effect of offsetting returns. The efficient set, or efficient frontier as it also is called, is described by the dark line at the top of the opportunity set. It goes from the minimum variance portfolio to the portfolio with the highest expected return.

According to the Markowitz mean-variance maxim, an investor should seek a portfolio of securities that lies on the efficient set.[5] A portfolio is not efficient if there is another portfolio with a higher expected return and a lower standard deviation, a higher expected return and the same standard deviation, or the same expected return but a lower standard deviation. If your portfolio is not efficient, you can increase the expected return without increasing the risk, decrease the risk without decreasing the expected return, or obtain some combination of increased expected return and decreased risk by switching to a portfolio on the efficient frontier. As can be seen, the efficient set is determined on the basis of dominance. Portfolios of securities tend to dominate individual securities because of the reduction in risk obtainable through diversification. As discussed before, this reduction is evident when one explores the implications of Eqs. (3-2) and (3-3).

UTILITY FUNCTIONS AND INVESTOR CHOICE

The best mix of expected return and standard deviation for a security portfolio depends on the investor's utility function. If you are a risk-averse investor who associates risk with divergence from expected value of return, your utility function might be depicted graphically as in Fig. 3-5. The expected return is plotted on the vertical axis, while the standard deviation is along the horizontal. The curves are known as *indifference curves*; the investor is indifferent between any combination of expected return and standard deviation on a particular curve. In other words, a curve is defined by those combinations of expected return and standard deviation that result in a fixed level of expected utility.[6]

The greater the slope of the indifference curves, the more averse the investor is to risk. As we move to the left in Fig. 3-5, each successive curve represents a higher level of expected utility. It is important to note that the exact shape of the indifference curves will not be the same for different investors. While the curves for all risk-averse investors will be upward-sloping, a variety of shapes are possible, depending on the risk preferences of the individual. As an investor, you want to hold that portfolio of securities that places you on the highest indifference curve.

In addition to portfolios of risky securities along the efficient set in Fig-

---

[5] Harry M. Markowitz, *Portfolio Selection: Efficient Diversification of Investments* (New York: John Wiley, 1959), Chaps. 7 and 8.

[6] For further discussion and proof that indifference curves for a risk-averse investor are concave, see Eugene F. Fama and Merton H. Miller, *The Theory of Finance* (New York: Holt, 1972), pp. 226–28.

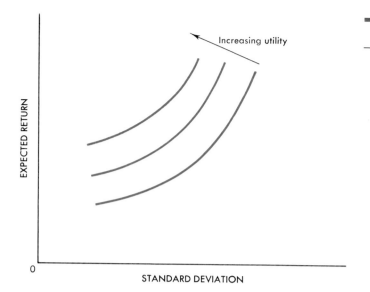

FIGURE 3-5

Hypothetical
indifference curves

ure 3-4, you will usually be able to invest in a risk-free security that yields a certain future return. This security might be a Treasury security that is held to maturity. Although the expected return may be low, relative to other securities, there is complete certainty of return. Suppose for now that you can not only lend at the risk-free rate but borrow at it as well. (We relax this assumption later on.) To determine the optimal portfolio under these conditions, we first draw a line from the risk-free rate, R_f, on the *expected return* axis through its point of tangency with the opportunity set of portfolio returns, as illustrated in Fig. 3-6. This line then becomes the new efficient frontier. Note that only one portfolio of risky securities—namely, *m*—would be considered; it

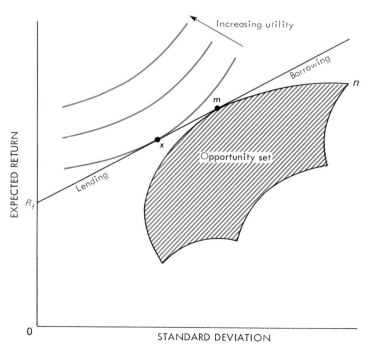

FIGURE 3-6

Selection of optimal portfolio when risk-free asset exists

now dominates all others, including those on the efficient frontier of the opportunity set.

Any point on the straight line tells us the proportion of the risky portfolio, m, and the proportion of loans or borrowings at the risk-free rate. To the left of point m, you would hold both the risk-free security and portfolio m. To the right, you would hold only portfolio m and would borrow funds, in addition to your initial investment funds, in order to invest further in it. The farther to the right in the figure, the greater borrowings will be. The overall expected return = (w) (expected return on risky portfolio) + (1 − w) (risk-free rate), where w is the proportion of total wealth invested in portfolio m, and 1 − w is the proportion invested in the risk-free asset. If lending were involved, w would be less than 1.0; if borrowing occurred, it would be greater than 1.0. The overall standard deviation is simply w times the standard deviation of the risky portfolio. No account is taken of the risk-free asset because its standard deviation is zero.

The optimal investment policy is determined by the point of tangency between the straight line in Fig. 3-6 and the highest indifference curve.[7] As shown in the figure, this point is portfolio x, and it consists of lending at the risk-free rate and investing in the risky security portfolio, m. If borrowing were prohibited, the efficient set would no longer be a straight line throughout but would consist of line $R_f mn$. The optimal portfolio would be determined in the same manner as before, namely, the tangency of the efficient set with the highest indifference curve.

If market participants have homogeneous expectations, in market equilibrium point m represents a portfolio of all securities available in the market, weighted by their respective total market values. By definition, this weighted average portfolio is the *market portfolio*. The straight line in the figure describes the trade-off between expected return and risk for various holdings of the risk-free security and the market portfolio. Thus, two things are involved: the price of time and the price of risk. The former is depicted by the intercept of the line on the vertical axis. The risk-free rate, then, can be thought of as the reward for waiting. The slope of the line represents the market price of risk. It tells us the amount of additional expected return that is required for an increment in standard deviation.

SEPARATION THEOREM

The attitude of individual investors toward bearing risk affects only the amount that is loaned or borrowed. It does not affect the optimal portfolio of risky assets. Turning to Fig. 3-6, we would select portfolio m of risky assets no matter what the nature of our indifference curves. The reason is that when a risk-free security exists, and borrowing and lending are possible at that rate, the market portfolio dominates all others. As long as they can freely borrow and lend at the risk-free rate, two investors with very different preferences will both choose portfolio m.

Thus, the individual's utility preferences are independent of or separate from the optimal portfolio of risky assets. This condition is known as the *sep-*

---

[7] For a more sophisticated and mathematical discussion of the point of tangency, see Fama and Miller, *Theory of Finance*, pp. 223–26 and 243–50. For ease of understanding, we have purposely kept the presentation graphical.

aration theorem.[8] Put another way, it states that the determination of an optimal portfolio of risky assets is independent of the individual's risk preferences. Such a determination depends only on the expected returns and standard deviations for the various possible portfolios of risky assets. In essence, the individual's approach to investing is two phased: First determine an optimal portfolio of risky assets; then determine the most desirable combination of the risk-free security and this portfolio. Only the second phase depends on utility preferences. The separation theorem is very important in finance. As we will see, it allows the management of a corporation to make decisions without reference to the attitudes toward risk of individual owners. Rather, security price information can be used to determine required returns, and decisions will be so guided.

GLOBAL DIVERSIFICATION

By investing across world financial markets, one can achieve greater diversification than by investing in a single country. As we discuss in Chapter 26, the economic cycles of different countries are not completely synchronized. A weak economy in one country may be offset by a strong economy in another. Moreover, exchange-rate risk and other risks discussed in that chapter add to the diversification effect. During the last two decades, non-U.S. stocks have provided both a higher return and a higher standard deviation on average than have U.S. stocks.

The situation is illustrated in Fig. 3-7. Here the opportunity set of risky securities for the United States is shown by the lightly shaded area. The global

---

[8] This theorem was originally stated by J. Tobin, "Liquidity Preference as Behavior towards Risk," *Review of Economic Studies*, 25 (February 1958), 65–86.

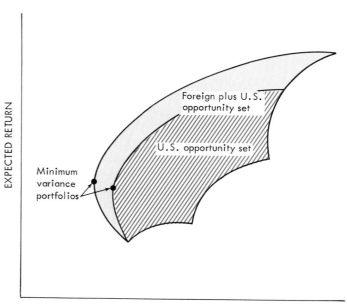

FIGURE 3-7
The effect of global diversification

opportunity set is superimposed on this, and the increment is shown by the dark shaded area. We see that the outer edge of the global opportunity set is backward bending in the lower left-hand portion of the figure. While on average foreign stocks have a higher standard deviation than U.S. stocks, the diversification effect more offsets this for moderate increments of foreign stocks into one's portfolio. As a result of greater backward bending, the global minimum variance portfolio has less risk than the domestic minimum variance portfolio. At the other end of the efficient set, the increased number of possible portfolio combinations, some of which have higher expected returns and risk, results in an extension up and to the right. Finally, higher foreign returns result in a higher efficient set than occurs with only U.S. stocks. One caveat. Just because foreign stock returns have been higher than U.S. stock returns in the past does not mean that this will occur in the future.

CAPITAL ASSET PRICING MODEL

Based on these considerations of behavior by the risk-averse investor, there is implied an equilibrium relationship between risk and expected return for each security. In market equilibrium, a security will be expected to provide a return commensurate with its *unavoidable* risk. This is simply the risk that cannot be avoided by diversification. The greater the unavoidable risk of a security, the greater the return that investors will expect from the security. The relationship between expected return and unavoidable risk, and the valuation of securities that follows, is the essence of the capital asset pricing model (CAPM). This model was developed by William F. Sharpe (1990 Nobel prize winner in economics) and John Lintner in the 1960s, and it has had important implications for finance ever since.[9] While other models also attempt to capture market behavior, the capital asset pricing model is simple in concept and has real-world applicability.

As with any model, there are assumptions to be made. First, we assume that capital markets are highly efficient where investors are well informed, transaction costs are zero, there are negligible restrictions on investment and no taxes, and no investor is large enough to affect the market price of the stock. We assume also that investors are in general agreement about the likely performance and risk of individual securities and that their expectations are based on a common holding period, say, 1 year. Under these conditions, all investors will perceive the opportunity set of risky securities in the same way and will draw their efficient frontiers in the same place.

There are two types of investment opportunities with which we will be concerned. The first is a risk-free security whose return over the holding period is known with certainty. Frequently, the rate on a Treasury security is used as surrogate for the risk-free rate. The second investment opportunity with which we are concerned is the market portfolio of common stocks. It is represented by all available stocks, weighted according to their market values outstanding. As the market portfolio is a somewhat unwieldy thing with

[9] See William F. Sharpe, "Capital Asset Prices: A Theory of Market Equilibrium under Conditions of Risk," *Journal of Finance* 19 (September 1964), 425–42; John Lintner, "The Valuation of Risk Assets and the Selection of Risky Investments in Stock Portfolios and Capital Budgets," *Review of Economics and Statistics*, 47 (February 1965), 13–37; and Eugene F. Fama, "Risk, Return, and Equilibrium—Some Clarifying Comments," *Journal of Finance*, 23 (March 1968), 29–40.

which to work, most people use a surrogate such as Standard & Poor's 500-Stock Index. Broader indexes include the New York Stock Exchange's Index of all stocks listed on that exchange and the Wilshire 5000 Index, which covers 5,000 stocks and includes exchanges other than the NYSE as well as the over-the-counter market.

THE CHARACTERISTIC LINE

Now we are in a position to compare the expected return for an individual stock with the expected return for the market portfolio. In our comparison, it is useful to deal with returns in excess of the risk-free rate. The *excess return* is simply the expected return less the risk-free return. If the expected relationship is based on past experience, excess returns would be calculated from historical data. Suppose we felt that monthly returns over the last 5 years were a good proxy for the future. For each of the last 60 months we then would compute excess returns for the particular stock involved and for the market portfolio, as represented by Standard & Poor's 500-Stock Index. The monthly return for both is the ending price minus the beginning price plus any dividend that was paid, all over the beginning price. From these returns, the monthly risk-free rate is subtracted to obtain excess returns.

Instead of using historical returns, one might obtain future return estimates from security analysts who follow the stock. Here the focus is on the stock's likely future return *conditional* on a specific market return. For example, if the market return for next period is x percent, what is likely to be the stock's return? By posing the question in this way for various market returns, conditional estimates are obtained for a range of possible stock returns. An added refinement might be to ask for some measure of the analyst's uncertainty about the conditional estimates. This might be accomplished simply by requesting a pessimistic estimate, a most likely estimate, and an optimistic estimate, again conditional on a given market return. Thus, there are two ways to go about determining the relationship between excess returns for a stock and excess returns for the market portfolio. We can use historical data, under the assumption that the relationship will continue into the future, or we can go to security analysts to obtain future estimates. As the second approach usually is restricted to investment organizations with a number of security analysts, we will illustrate the relationship using the historical approach.

Having calculated historical excess returns for the stock and for the market portfolio, we plot them. Figure 3-8 compares expected excess returns for a stock with those for the market portfolio. The dots represent the monthly plots of the excess returns, 60 in all. The colored line fitted to the dots describes the historical relationship between excess returns for the stock and excess returns for the market portfolio. This line is known as the *characteristic line*, and it is used as a proxy for the expected relationship between the two sets of excess returns.

A SECURITY'S ALPHA

The graph reveals that the greater the expected excess return for the market, the greater the expected excess return for the stock. Three measures are important. The first is known as the *alpha*, and it is simply the intercept of the characteristic line on the vertical axis. If the excess return for the market

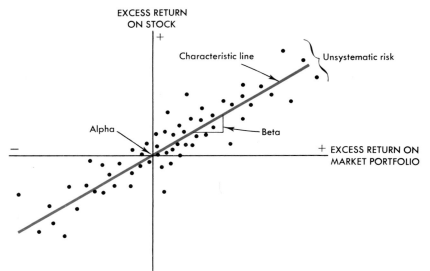

EXCESS RETURN
ON STOCK

Characteristic line

Unsystematic risk

Alpha

Beta

+ EXCESS RETURN ON
MARKET PORTFOLIO

FIGURE 3-8
Relationship between
excess returns for stock and
excess returns for market
portfolio

portfolio were expected to be zero, the alpha would be the expected excess return for the stock. In theory, the alpha for an individual stock should be zero.

If it were less than zero, as a rational investor you would avoid the stock because you could do better with some combination of risk-free asset and the market portfolio (minus the stock). If enough people avoid it, of course, the price will decline and the expected return will increase. How long will this go on? In theory, until the alpha rises to zero. One can visualize the equilibration process by supposing the characteristic line in Fig 3-8 were below, but parallel to, the line shown. As the security declines in price, its expected return rises and the characteristic line shifts upward to where eventually it passes through the origin. If the alpha were positive, the opposite equilibrium process would occur; people would rush to buy the security, and this would cause the price to rise and expected return to decline.[10] We assume, then, that the alpha for a particular stock is zero.

THE SYSTEMATIC RISK AS MEASURED BY BETA

The second measure with which we are concerned, and most important for our purposes, is the *beta*. The beta is simply the slope of the characteristic line. It depicts the sensitivity of the security's excess return to that of the market portfolio. If the slope is one, it means that excess returns for the stock vary proportionally with excess returns for the market portfolio. In other words, the stock has the same unavoidable or systematic risk as the market as a whole. A slope steeper than one means that the stock's excess return varies more than proportionally with the excess return of the market portfolio. Put

[10] The alpha for the market portfolio is simply a weighted average of the alphas for the individual stocks making up the portfolio. In efficient markets, rational investors seize upon any deviation from zero of the alpha of an individual stock. As the alphas of individual stocks will be driven to zero, the weighted average of alphas of stocks comprising the market portfolio also must be zero. It should be pointed out that some empirical tests have shown positive alphas for low beta stocks and negative alphas for high beta stocks. Various reasons have been advanced for this occurrence.

another way, it has more systematic risk than the market as a whole. This type of stock is often called an "aggressive" investment. A slope less than one, as is the case in Fig. 3-8, means that the stock has less unavoidable or systematic risk than does the market as a whole. This type of stock is often called a "defensive" investment.

The greater the slope of the characteristic line for a stock, as depicted by its beta, the greater its systematic risk. This means that for both upward and downward movements in market excess returns, movements in excess returns for the individual stock are greater or less, depending on its beta. If the beta for a particular stock were 1.70 and the market excess return for a specific month were −2.00 percent, this would imply an expected excess return for the stock of −3.40 percent. Thus, the beta represents the systematic risk of a stock due to underlying movements in security prices. This risk cannot be diversified away by investing in more stocks because it depends on things such as changes in the economy and in the political atmosphere, which affect all stocks. In summary, the beta of a stock represents its contribution to the risk of a highly diversified portfolio of stocks.

Empirical work on the stability of historical beta information over time suggests that past betas are useful in predicting future betas; however, the ability to predict seems to vary with the size of the portfolio. The larger the number of securities in a portfolio, the greater the stability of the beta for that portfolio over time. Even for the individual stock, however, past beta information has been found to have reasonable predictive value. In addition to portfolio size, betas tend to show greater stability as longer time intervals are studied.

A number of organizations regularly compute and publish betas for actively traded stocks. The better-known services include Merrill Lynch and Value Line. The typical analysis involves either monthly or weekly returns on the stock and on the market index for 3 to 5 years in the past. For example, Merrill Lynch uses monthly returns for 5 years in the past, whereas Value Line uses weekly returns, again for 5 years in the past. The interval employed seems to make a difference. Weekly calculated betas tend to be less than monthly calculated betas for high beta levels, but higher for low levels of beta.[11] Thus, one must be mindful of the return interval used in the calculations, for calculated betas of high-risk and of low-risk securities change differently as the interval is increased.

Because beta information is readily available from various services, one is saved the task of computing it. An example of betas for a sample of companies using weekly returns is shown in Table 3-1. The betas of most stocks range from .7 to 1.4, though some are lower and some are higher. If the past systematic risk of a stock seems likely to prevail in the future, the historical beta can be used as a proxy for the expected beta coefficient.

Adjusting Historical Betas.   There appears to be a tendency for the measured betas of individual securities to revert eventually toward the beta of the market portfolio, 1.0, or toward the beta of the industry of which the company

---

[11] Frank K. Reilly and David J. Wright, "A Comparison of Published Betas," *Journal of Portfolio Management*, 14 (Spring 1988), 64–69; and Puneet Handa, S. P. Kothari, and Charles Wasley, "The Relation between the Return Interval and Betas," *Journal of Financial Economics*, 23 (June 1989), 79–100. The reasoning of the latter is that a security's return covariance with the market return and market's return variance may not change proportionately as the return interval is increased.

TABLE 3-1
Betas for selected companies, August 1990

STOCK	BETA
Atlantic Richfield	.85
American Building Maintenance	.75
Birmingham Steel	1.10
Clorox	.90
Delta Airlines	1.05
Dow Chemical	1.20
Exxon	.85
Fuji Photo (ADR)	.80
General Electric	1.10
Hewlett-Packard	1.20
Illinois Power	.60
Illinois Tool Works	1.40
Kellogg	1.00
Motorola	1.40
New York Times	1.00
Paine Webber Group	1.60
Procter & Gamble	.95
Salomon Inc.	1.50
Sears Roebuck	1.15
Texas Utilities	.75
Waste Management	1.10
Wells Fargo & Co.	1.00

is a part. This tendency may be due to economic factors affecting the operations and financing of the firm and perhaps to statistical factors. To adjust for this tendency, Merrill Lynch, Value Line, and certain others calculate an *adjusted beta*. To illustrate, suppose the reversion process were toward the market beta of 1.0. If the measured beta were 1.5 and a .70 weight were attached to it and .30 to the market beta, the adjusted beta would be 1.5(.70) + 1.0(.30) = 1.35. The same could be done if the reversion process were toward an industry average beta of, say, 1.2. As one is concerned with the beta of a security in the future, it may be appropriate to adjust the measured beta if the reversion process just described is clear and consistent.

Another approach to adjusting betas involves a type of Bayesian analysis. The historical beta is calculated, as we have done, but it then is adjusted to give a better estimate of the beta that will prevail in the near future. To make the adjustment, such things as the debt ratio, the size of the stock (total market value of all the company's shares), industry classification, dividend yield, and even the stock's price/earnings ratio are brought into play.[12] This "other" information is subjected to regression analysis or to other statistical techniques to produce a weighting of the importance of the factor involved. On the basis of the weightings, the historical beta is adjusted. To be sure, a stock's historical beta still has a positive and usually substantial effect on explaining returns, but estimates sometimes are improved with the addition of some of the factors mentioned earlier. Adjusting historical betas is difficult business, because the process is seldom clear and consistent.

[12] For a general discussion of these issues, see Barr Rosenberg, "The Capital Asset Pricing Model and the Market Model," *Journal of Portfolio Management*, 7 (Winter 1981), 5–16.

The last of the three measures with which we are concerned is the unsystematic, or avoidable, risk of a security. Unsystematic risk derives from the variability of the stock's excess return *not* associated with movements in the excess return of the market as a whole. This risk is described by the dispersion of the estimates involved in predicting a stock's characteristic line. In Fig. 3-8, the unsystematic risk is represented by the relative distance of the dots from the solid line. The greater the dispersion, the greater the unsystematic risk of a stock. By diversification of stocks in our portfolio, however, we can reduce unsystematic risk.

Thus, the total risk involved in holding a stock comprises two parts:

$$\begin{array}{ccc} \text{Total risk} = & \text{Systematic risk} & + & \text{Unsystematic risk} \\ & \text{(nondiversifiable} & & \text{(diversifiable} \\ & \text{or unavoidable)} & & \text{or avoidable)} \end{array} \qquad (3\text{-}4)$$

The first part is due to the overall market risk—changes in the nation's economy, tax reform by the Congress, a change in the world energy situation—risks that affect securities overall and, consequently, cannot be diversified away. In other words, even the investor who holds a well-diversified portfolio will be exposed to this type of risk. The second risk component, however, is unique to a particular company, being independent of economic, political, and other factors that affect securities in a systematic manner. A wildcat strike may affect only one company; a new competitor may begin to produce essentially the same product; a technological breakthrough can make an existing product obsolete. However, by diversification this kind of risk can be reduced and even eliminated if diversification is efficient. Therefore, not all of the risk involved in holding a stock is relevant; part of it can be diversified away.

Unsystematic risk is reduced at a decreasing rate toward zero as more randomly selected securities are added to the portfolio. Various studies suggest that 15 to 20 stocks selected randomly are sufficient to eliminate most of the unsystematic risk of a portfolio. Thus, a substantial reduction in unsystematic risk can be achieved with a relatively moderate amount of diversification. Conceptually, diversification can be viewed in the manner portrayed in Fig. 3-9. As the number of randomly selected securities held in the portfolio is increased, the total risk of the portfolio is reduced in keeping with the reduction of unsystematic risk. Such a reduction is at a decreasing rate, however. Efficient diversification reduces the total risk of the portfolio to the point where only systematic risk remains.

For the typical stock, unsystematic risk accounts for around 75 percent of the total risk or variance of the stock. Expressed differently, systematic risk explains only about 25 percent of the total variability of an individual stock. The proportion of total risk explained by movements of the market is represented by the R-square statistic for the regression of excess returns for a stock against excess returns for the market portfolio. (R-square measures the proportion of the total variance of the dependent variable that is explained by the independent variable; it is simply the correlation coefficient squared.) The proportion of total risk unique to the stock is one minus R-square.

The proportion of systematic to total risk depends on the particular stock. The excess-return relationship depicted in Fig. 3-8 is an example of relatively little unsystematic risk; the observations are tightly clustered around the characteristic line. Contrast this with a more typical situation, such as that

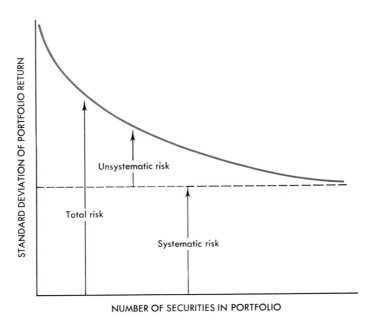

FIGURE 3-9

Total, unsystematic, and systematic risk

shown in panel a of Fig. 3-10. Here the observations are scattered rather widely around the characteristic line, indicating a good deal of unsystematic risk. However, this variability can be reduced through diversification. Suppose you diversify by investing in 10 stocks whose weighted average beta is the same as the slope of the characteristic line in panel a. The result might be that shown in panel b. We see that with reasonable diversification, the scatter of excess-return observations about the characteristic line is reduced considerably. It is not eliminated because it would take more stocks to do that. However, the scatter is much less than it is for the individual security, and this is the essence of diversification.

The capital asset pricing model assumes that all risk other than systematic risk has been diversified away. Stated differently, if capital markets are efficient and investors at the margin are well diversified, the important risk of a stock is its unavoidable or systematic risk. The risk of a well-diversified

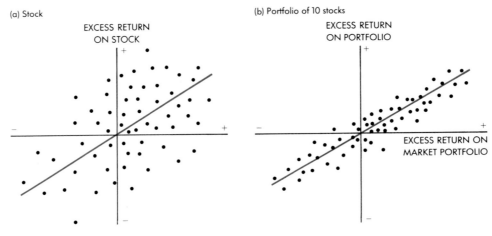

FIGURE 3-10

Relationships between excess returns

portfolio is a value-weighted average of the systematic risks (betas) of the stocks comprising that portfolio. Unsystematic, or diversifiable, risk plays no role.

EXPECTED RETURN FOR INDIVIDUAL SECURITY

For the individual security, then, the relevant risk is not the standard deviation of the security itself (total risk), but the marginal effect the security has on the standard deviation of an efficiently diversified portfolio (systematic risk). As a result, a security's expected return should be related to its degree of systematic risk, not to its degree of total risk. Systematic risk is the thing that matters to an investor holding a well-diversified portfolio. If we assume that unsystematic risk is diversified away, the expected rate of return for stock j is

$$\overline{R}_j = R_f + (\overline{R}_m - R_f)\beta_j \tag{3-5}$$

where again R_f is the risk-free rate, $\overline{R}_m$ is the expected overall return for the market portfolio, and β_j is the beta coefficient for security j as defined earlier. The greater the beta of a security, the greater the risk and the greater the expected return required. By the same token, the lower the beta, the lower the risk, the more valuable it becomes, and the lower the expected return required.

Put another way, the expected rate of return for a stock is equal to the return required by the market for a riskless investment plus a risk premium. In turn, the risk premium is a function of (1) the expected market return less the risk-free rate, which represents the risk premium required for the typical stock in the market; and (2) the beta coefficient. Suppose the expected return on Treasury securities is 10 percent, the expected return on the market portfolio is 15 percent, and the beta of Pro-Fli Corporation is 1.3. The beta indicates that Pro-Fli has more systematic risk than the typical stock. Given this information and using Eq. (3-5), we find that the expected return for Pro-Fli's stock would be

$$\overline{R}_j = .10 + (.15 - .10)1.3 = 16.5\%$$

What this tells us is that, on average, the market expects Pro-Fli to show a 16.5 percent annual return. Because Pro-Fli has more systematic risk than the typical stock in the marketplace, its expected return is higher. Suppose now that we are interested in a defensive stock, First Safety Inc., whose beta coefficient is only .7. Its expected return is

$$\overline{R}_j = .10 + (.15 - .10)0.7 = 13.5\%$$

Because this stock has less systematic risk than the typical stock in the market, its expected return is less. Therefore, different stocks will have different expected returns, depending on their betas.

The beta of a portfolio is simply a weighted average of the betas of the securities comprising the portfolio. If a portfolio consisted of .60 of Pro-Fli Corporation and .40 of First Safety Inc., the beta of the portfolio would be

$$\beta_p = .60(1.3) + .40(0.7) = 1.06$$

If the risk-free rate and expected market return were the same as above, the portfolio's expected return would be

$$\overline{R}_p = .10 + (.15 - .10)1.06 = 15.3\%$$

This is the same as the weighted average of the two expected returns previously calculated.

EXPECTED RETURN EXPRESSED DIFFERENTLY

Equation (3-5) can be expressed in a different way.[13] If we go back to our discussion of the calculation of covariance, we know that the beta of a security is a measure of the responsiveness of its excess returns to those of the market portfolio. Mathematically, this responsiveness is nothing more than the covariance between possible returns for security j and the market portfolio divided by the variance of the probability distribution of possible returns for the market portfolio. Therefore, the beta of security j can be expressed as

$$\beta_j = (r_{jm}\sigma_j\sigma_m)/\sigma_m^2 \qquad (3\text{-}6)$$

where $(r_{jm}\sigma_j\sigma_m)$ is the covariance of returns for security j with those of the market. In turn, it embodies r_{jm}, the expected correlation between possible returns for security j and the market portfolio; σ_j, the standard deviation of the probability distribution of possible returns for security j; and σ_m, the standard deviation of the probability distribution of possible returns for the market portfolio. Finally, σ_m^2 is the variance of the market portfolio.

Substituting Eq. (3-6) into Eq. (3-5), we obtain

$$\overline{R}_j = R_f + \frac{\overline{R}_m - R_f}{\sigma_m^2}(r_{jm}\sigma_j\sigma_m) \qquad (3\text{-}7)$$

In Eq. (3-7) it is possible to cancel by σ_m in the last term, leading to the equation

$$\overline{R}_j = R_f + \frac{\overline{R}_m - R_f}{\sigma_m}(r_{jm}\sigma_j) \qquad (3\text{-}8)$$

This equation may be interpreted in the following way: The expected return of security j consists of the risk-free rate and a risk premium represented by the remaining term on the right-hand side. This risk premium term can be analyzed further: σ_j represents the total risk of security j, but of this total risk, only a fraction measured by r_{jm} is systematic. In other words, the diversified investor can avoid a fraction $(1 - r_{jm})$ of the risk represented by σ_j. The fraction $(\overline{R}_m - R_f)/\sigma_m$ represents the market relationship between systematic risk and the risk premium required by the market. It can be thought of as the market price of systematic risk and is equal to the slope of the line in Fig. 3-6. The risk premium, or return in excess of the risk-free rate, is equal to the product of the systematic risk $(r_{jm}\sigma_j)$ and the market price of that risk, $(\overline{R}_m - R_f)/\sigma_m$.

---

[13] This section can be passed over without loss of continuity by those not interested in a mathematical representation of expected return.

The systematic risk of security j, measured in absolute terms, is (r_{jm}, σ_j). Alternatively, we may choose to measure the systematic risk in relative terms by relating it to the risk of the market portfolio, σ_m. If we divide $(r_{jm}\sigma_j)$ by the measure of market risk, σ_m, we obtain the beta of security j:

$$\beta_j = (r_{jm}\sigma_j)/\sigma_m \qquad (3\text{-}9)$$

We can therefore use β_j as a measure of the relative systematic risk of security j.

THE SECURITY MARKET LINE

In market equilibrium, the relationship between an individual security's expected rate of return and its systematic risk, as measured by beta, will be linear. The relationship is known as the *security market line,* and it is illustrated in Fig. 3-11. Under the assumptions of the capital asset pricing model, all securities lie along this line. The figure shows that the expected return on a risky security is a combination of the risk-free rate plus a premium for risk. This risk premium is necessary to induce risk-averse investors to buy a risky security. We see that the expected return for the market portfolio is $\bar{R}_m$, consisting of the risk-free rate, R_f, plus the risk premium, $\bar{R}_m - R_f$. Inasmuch as the unsystematic risk of a security can be eliminated by the well-diversified investor, investors overall are not compensated for bearing such risk according to the capital asset pricing model. The investor in only a single security will be exposed to both systematic and unsystematic risk but will be rewarded for only the systematic risk that is borne.

In fact, it is possible for a security with a great deal of total risk to have actually lower systematic risk than a security with only a moderate amount of total risk. Take the case of a new mining company endeavoring to discover gold and silver in the Rocky Mountains. While the total risk of the company is considerable, the finding of gold and silver deposits is almost a chance event. As a result, the security's return bears little relation to the market overall. In a well-diversified portfolio, its unsystematic risk is unimportant. Only its systematic risk matters, and this by definition is low, say, a beta of .4. On the other hand, the return from a stock of a large manufacturing company such as

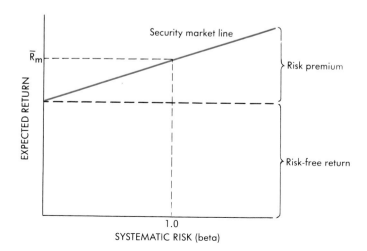

FIGURE 3-11
The security market line

General Electric or a large retailer such as Sears is closely tied to the overall economy. Such stocks have only moderate unsystematic risk, so that their total risk may be less than that of the new mining company. Their systematic risk, however, is approximately that of the market as a whole, say, a beta of 1.0.

As an individual security, the mining company may be considerably more risky than General Electric or Sears, but as part of a well-diversified portfolio, it is much less risky. Consequently, its expected or required return in the market will be less. This counterintuitive example points to the importance of differentiating systematic risk from total risk. Although there is a tendency for stocks with large systematic risk to have large unsystematic risk as well, there can be exceptions to this generalization.

Under- and Overvaluations. Thus, in market equilibrium the capital asset pricing model implies an expected return-risk relationship for all individual securities (the security market line.) If an individual security has an expected return-risk combination that places it above the security market line, it will be undervalued in the market. That is, it provides an expected return in excess of that required by the market for the systematic risk involved: $\overline{R}_j > R_f + (\overline{R}_m - R_f)\beta_j$. As a result, the security will be attractive to investors. According to the theory, the increased demand will cause the price to rise. How far? Until the expected return declines sufficiently for the security to lie on the security market line and, thereby, for $\overline{R}_j = R_f + (\overline{R}_m - R_f)\beta_j$. An overvalued security is characterized by an expected return-risk combination that places it below the security market line. This security is unattractive, and investors holding it will sell it and those not holding it will avoid it. The price will fall and expected return rise until there is consistency with the security market line and with equilibrium pricing.[14]

Market Risk Premium. The expected market risk premium, $\overline{R}_m - R_f$, has ranged from 3 to 7 percent in recent years. This is not the range of risk premiums actually realized, but the range of expected risk premiums for investing in the market portfolio of stocks as opposed to a risk-free asset. For the 1926–1988 period, stock returns exceeded the return on Treasury bills by 8.4 percent using the arithmetic mean.[15] Put differently, the investor was rewarded with an excess return above Treasury bills of 8.4 percent on average for the 63-year time frame. For the geometric average of annual returns, the excess return, again above Treasury bills, was 6.2 percent. For cumulative wealth changes over long sweeps of time, the geometric average is the appropriate measure, whereas the arithmetic average best expresses the excess return for a single year.

Is the historical excess return of common stocks over Treasury bills a good estimate of the future market risk premium? If current expectations of risk mirror this historical happening, it would be. If the current risk-free rate were 7 percent, the expected market return for one year would be

$$\overline{R}_m = 7\% + 8.4\% = 15.4\%$$

---

[14] For caveats concerning the use of deviations from the security market line as measures of superior performance, see Philip H. Dybvig and Stephen A. Ross, "Differential Information and Performance Measurement Using a Security Market Line," *Journal of Finance*, 40 (June 1985), 383–99.

[15] *Stocks, Bonds, Bills and Inflation 1990 Yearbook* (Chicago: Ibbotson Associates, 1990).

By knowing the risk-free rate, we could always determine the expected return on the market portfolio simply by adding on 8.4 percent. Although simple in application and advocated by a number of financial economists, there are problems.

For one thing, the average risk-free rate for the 63 years was only 3.6 percent, much lower than recently. For another, there is controversy as to whether a short-, intermediate-, or long-term security should be used. Third, it is not clear whether the arithmetic or the geometric average is best. It makes a difference—8.4 percent versus 6.2 percent. For the one-year expected return, the arithmetic average is more appropriate. However, if our concern is with a long-lived capital investment project, the geometric average may be better. Apart from these issues is the question of whether expectations were realized. If common stocks provided higher returns than expected over the period studied, the excess return over Treasury bills would be a biased and high estimate of the true market risk premium. As indicated at the outset, *ex ante* or beforehand estimates of the market risk premium have ranged from 3 to 7 percent in recent years. Just because actual excess returns have been greater does not mean that previous expectations were wrong. Finally, the market risk premium is likely to change over time with changing risk aversion in society. In turn, this is a function of economic and interest-rate cycles.

Thus, there is disagreement as to what is the appropriate market risk premium. My preference is an ex ante, beforehand estimate by investment analysts and economists, as opposed to the historical excess return. This allows for a change in the risk premium over time. The issue will be addressed further in Chapters 8 and 9, when we consider required rates of return for capital investments by corporations. For now, bear in mind the controversy on which reasonable people differ.

IMPLICATIONS FOR THE VALUATION OF THE FIRM

We have been exploring some of the foundations of valuation in a market context. Our exploration has not been complete, but we are getting a background for a deeper look into the valuation implications of decisions by the individual firm. As we have seen, value depends not only on the security or firm itself but also on other securities available for investment. By analyzing decisions in relation to their likely effect on expected return and systematic risk, we are able to judge their effect on valuation. According to the presentation so far, unsystematic risk or risk unique to the firm is not important because it can be diversified away. More will be said about this shortly.

In keeping with the capital asset pricing model and the separation theorem, we are able to make certain generalizations about the valuation of a firm, without having to determine directly the risk preferences of investors. If management wishes to act in the best interests of the owners, it will attempt to maximize the market value of the stock. Recall from Chapter 2 that the market value per share can be expressed as the present value of the stream of expected future dividends:

$$P_0 = \sum_{t=1}^{\infty} \frac{D_t}{(1 + k)^t} \tag{3-10}$$

where P_0 is the market price per share at time 0, D_t is the expected dividend at the end of period *t*, and *k* is the required rate of return. The CAPM approach allows us to determine the appropriate discount rate to employ in discounting expected dividends to their present value. That rate will be the risk-free rate plus a premium sufficient to compensate for the systematic risk associated with the expected dividend stream. The greater the systematic risk, of course, the greater the risk premium and the return required and the lower the value of the stock, all other things being the same. Thus, we are pointed toward determining required rates of return for individual securities.

Seemingly, all decisions of the firm should be judged in a market context, using the CAPM. Recall, however, that the model presented has a number of simplifying assumptions, some of them untenable in the real world. To the extent that they do not hold, unique or unsystematic risk may become a factor affecting valuation. Indeed, a good portion of our discussion in Parts 2 and 3 is devoted to exploring market imperfections that make unique risk a factor of importance.

Nonetheless, the CAPM serves as a useful framework for evaluating financial decisions. The basic tenets of the model hold even when assumptions are relaxed to reflect real-world conditions. Given that investors tend to be risk averse, a positive trade-off exists between risk and expected return for efficient portfolios. Moreover, expected returns for individual securities should bear a positive relationship to their marginal contributions of risk to the market portfolio (i.e., systematic risk).

CERTAIN ISSUES WITH THE CAPM

To put across important concepts, we have presented the capital asset pricing model (CAPM) without a number of issues surrounding its usefulness. To better understand the model, we explore certain problem areas in this section. Further extensions are taken up in the next chapter.

ZERO BETA VERSION OF THE CAPM

One of the assumptions of the CAPM is that the investor can both borrow and lend at the risk-free rate. Obviously, the investor can lend at this rate. If the borrowing rate is higher, however, an imperfection is introduced, and the line in Fig. 3-6 depicting the trade-off between expected return and standard deviation is no longer linear throughout. In Fig. 3-12, it is straight for the segment originating from the risk-free lending rate on the vertical axis to portfolio *L* on the efficient frontier. Because the borrowing rate is higher, however, another tangency point on the efficient frontier, *B*, is introduced. The relevant portion of this line is from point *B* to the right; it represents borrowing to invest in portfolio *B*. The segment of the line between *L* and *B* is curved and is simply a portion of the efficient frontier of the opportunity set of risky securities. As is evident from the figure, the greater the spread between the borrowing and the lending rates, the greater the curved segment.

If the market portfolio lies between points *L* and *B*, it is possible to use a *zero beta portfolio* in place of the risk-free asset in the capital asset pricing model.[16] Drawing a dashed line tangent to the efficient frontier at market port-

[16] Fischer Black, "Capital Market Equilibrium with Restricted Borrowing," *Journal of Business*, 45 (July 1972), 444–54. See also Richard Roll, "Orthogonal Portfolios," *Journal of Financial and Quantitative Analysis*, 15 (December 1980), 1005–11.

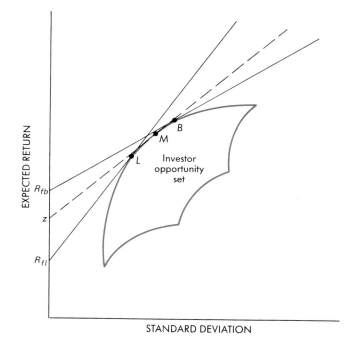

FIGURE 3-12
**Effect of differing
borrowing and lending
rates**

folio *M*, we see that it intercepts the vertical axis between the borrowing rate, R_{fb}, and the lending rate, R_{fl}. The intercept z represents the return on a zero beta portfolio. This simply means a portfolio with no covariability with the market portfolio, which may be created by short selling.[17] Depending on their utility preferences, investors will hold some combination of the zero-beta portfolio and the market portfolio, *m*. The same general picture emerges as if investors could both borrow and lend at the risk-free rate, except the dashed line in the figure has a different slope. The expected return for the individual security, *j*, becomes

$$\overline{R}_j = z + (\overline{R}_m - z)\beta_j \qquad (3\text{-}11)$$

where z is the expected return associated with a zero beta asset, and the other symbols are the same as before.

It is important to note that the z intercept in Fig. 3-12 is inferred from return information on stocks; we cannot look up the zero-beta return in a newspaper, as we can the return on Treasury securities. However, one can estimate the zero beta security market line and from that the zero beta return.

The procedure frequently employed is to estimate future dividends for a large sample of companies, which is representative of the market portfolio. Solving for the discount rate that equates the present value of the dividend stream with the market price of the stock, one obtains the expected return for each of the companies in the sample. These expected returns, together with their respective betas, are then plotted on a scatter diagram. A line is fitted to

---

[17] In a short sale, the investor borrows securities and sells them in the market. Eventually the securities must be replaced, and this is done by purchasing them in the market. Often a short sale is in anticipation of a decline in price so that the securities borrowed can be replaced at a price lower than that for which they were sold. However, the motivation can be simply to create a hedge.

the observations. This line represents the zero beta security market line, some-times also known as the "empirical" SML.

The intercept of the zero-beta SML on the vertical axis is the estimated zero-beta return. As this intercept typically exceeds the risk-free lending rate, the zero-beta security market line is flatter than the security market line based on the risk-free rate (Fig. 3-11). However, all securities presumably will lie along the zero-beta security market line, and essentially the same risk-return conclusions are possible whether we use a zero-beta portfolio or the risk-free lending rate in the capital asset pricing model.

HETEROGENEOUS EXPECTATIONS, TRANSACTION AND INFORMATION COSTS

Relaxation of another major assumption, homogeneous expectations, complicates the problem in a different way. With heterogeneous expectations, a complex blending of expectations, wealth, and utility preferences of indi-vidual investors emerges in the equilibrating process. This complex equili-brating process has been examined by the author elsewhere and will not be presented here.[18] The principal implication is that precise generalizations are not possible. With only moderate heterogeneity in expectations, however, the basic tenets of the capital asset pricing model still hold, and rough estimates of the expected return-risk trade-offs for portfolios and individual securities are possible. Still, the lack of precise description must be recognized.[19]

Transaction costs also affect market equilibrium. The greater these costs, the less investors will undertake transactions to make their portfolios truly efficient. Rather than portfolios being on the efficient set, some may be on one side or the other because transaction costs more than offset the advantages of being right on the line. In other words, there may be bands on either side of the efficient set within which portfolios would lie. The greater the transaction costs, the wider the bands might be. Similarly, when securities are not infinitely divisible, as is the case in the real world, investors are able to achieve an efficient portfolio only up to the nearest share of stock or the nearest bond. Recall that another assumption of perfect capital markets is that all information about a firm is instantaneously available, free, to all investors. To the extent that there are delays and costs, there will be differing expecta-tions among investors for these reasons alone. The effect here is the same as that for heterogeneous expectations. In general, the greater the imperfections, the more important the unique, or unsystematic, risk of the firm. Remember that the CAPM assumes that this risk can be diversified away. If it cannot, cer-tain implications of the model do not entirely hold.

FAULTY USE OF MARKET INDEX

There are problems in the use of any index as a proxy for the overall market portfolio. The "true" market portfolio consists of all assets—stocks, bonds, real estate, and human capital. Richard Roll has analyzed the problem

[18] James C. Van Horne, *Financial Market Rates and Flows*, 3d ed. (Englewood Cliffs, NJ: Prentice Hall, 1990), Chap. 3.
[19] Another assumption is that the probability distributions of possible returns on all portfolios are normal. As long as the distributions are nearly symmetric, however, this condition is met in a practical sense.

of using the wrong security market line and has categorized errors that can occur.[20] Roll does not suggest that the capital asset pricing model is somehow void of meaning, but that tests of it are suspect and must be evaluated with caution. Unless the true market portfolio is known and employed, tests of the CAPM are likely to result in faulty measurement of security performance. As the proxy market index is only a subset of the true market portfolio, it is unlikely to capture the basis of the underlying market equilibration process. Therefore, the measurement of security performance for various investment strategies will be ambiguous. In addition to Roll's criticism, it is bothersome that a stock's beta shows considerable variation depending on whether the New York Stock Exchange Index, the Standard & Poor's 500-Stock Index, Wilshire's 5,000 Stock Index, or some other index is employed.

SOME FINAL OBSERVATIONS

The CAPM is intuitively appealing in that expected return logically follows from the risk a security adds to an overall portfolio. Although faulty, empirical testing is in general agreement with the risk-return trade-off hypothesized. Because of its simplicity, the CAPM is widely used, both in the securities industry and in corporate finance. It gives straightforward implications for market equilibration and for required rates of return on risky assets.

However, the model is not without its challenges, as we have touched on in this section.[21] Extensions of the CAPM and alternative models are being actively developed. These models, where multiple variables and factors are employed, hold much promise. In the next chapter, we examine them. Whether they gain the wide acceptance of the CAPM remains to be seen.

SUMMARY

Capital markets are said to be efficient when security prices fully reflect all available information. In such a market, security prices adjust very rapidly to new information. Another definition of market efficiency is the lack of security arbitrage opportunities, their having been eliminated by arbitragers.

The risk of a portfolio depends not only on the standard deviations of the individual securities comprising the portfolio but also on the correlation of possible returns. For a two-security portfolio, an opportunity set line describes the risk-return trade-off for various combinations. The diversification effect sometimes causes the opportunity set line to bend backward, with the minimum variance portfolio having a lower standard deviation than that of the least-risky security. The efficient set is the portion of the opportunity set

[20] "A Critique of the Asset Pricing Theory Tests," *Journal of Financial Economics,* 4 (March 1977), 129–76; and "Performance Evaluation and Benchmark Errors," *Journal of Portfolio Management,* 6 (Summer 1980), 5–12.

[21] An additional challenge to the traditional capital asset pricing model is a consumption-based CAPM, where markets equilibrate in terms of people's desires for real consumption and investment (inflation adjusted). See Douglas T. Breeden, "An Intertemporal Asset Pricing Model with Stochastic Consumption and Investment Opportunities," *Journal of Financial Economics,* 7 (September 1979), 265–96; and Douglas T. Breeden, Michael R. Gibbons, and Robert H. Litzenberger, "Empirical Tests of the Consumption-Oriented CAPM," *Journal of Finance,* 44 (June 1989), 231–62.

line going from the minimum variance portfolio to the one with the highest expected return.

By diversifying our holdings to include securities that are not perfectly correlated with each other, we can reduce risk relative to expected return. We wish to maximize utility as depicted by our indifference curves in relation to the opportunity set of risky securities available. With the existence of a risk-free security, the focus becomes a line from the risk-free rate to the point of tangency with the opportunity set. This point is the market portfolio, given our assumptions. The most desirable combination of risk-free security and market portfolio is determined by the point of tangency of investors' indifference curves with the capital market line. This two-phased approach to investing constitutes the separation theorem.

The capital asset pricing model allows us to draw certain implications about the expected return of a specific security. The key assumptions in the model are that perfect capital markets exist and that investors have homogeneous expectations. In this context, the relevant risk of a security is its undiversifiable risk. This risk is described by the slope of the characteristic line, where security returns in excess of the risk-free rate are related to excess returns for the market portfolio. Known also as beta, it is used as a measure of the systematic risk of a security. The total risk of a security can be divided into systematic and unsystematic components. Systematic risk is risk that cannot be diversified away, for it affects all securities in the market. Unsystematic risk is unique to the particular security and can be eliminated with efficient diversfication.

The market equilibrium relationship between systematic risk (beta) and expected return is known as the security market line. With this approach, we are able to estimate required rates of return for individual securities. The original CAPM can be modified to include consideration of the zero-beta version of the model. A number of problems plague empirical testing of the CAPM, and imperfections also detract from its usefulness. However, the model is widely used and has stood the test of time. In the next chapter, we explore alternative valuation models. In yet other parts of the book, we draw implications of the CAPM and of other models for financial decisions.

SELF-CORRECTION PROBLEMS

1. You are able to both borrow and lend at the risk-free rate of 9 percent. The market portfolio of securities has an expected return of 15 percent and a standard deviation of 21 percent. Determine the expected return and standard deviations of the following portfolios:

   a. All wealth is invested in the risk-free asset.

   b. One-third is invested in the risk-free asset and two-thirds in the market portfolio.

   c. All wealth is invested in the market portfolio. Furthermore, you borrow an additional one-third of your wealth to invest in the market portfolio.

2. Zwing-Zook Enterprises has a beta of 1.45. The risk-free rate is 10 percent and the expected return on the market portfolio is 16 percent. The company presently pays a dividend of $2 a share and investors expect it to experience a growth in dividends of 10 percent per annum for many years to come.

   a. What is the stock's required rate of return according to the CAPM?

b. What is the stock's present market price per share, assuming this required return?

3. The common stocks of Blatz Company and Stratz, Inc., have expected returns of 15 percent and 20 percent, respectively, while the standard deviations are 20 percent and 40 percent. The expected correlation coefficient between the two stocks is .36. What is the expected value of return and standard deviation of a portfolio consisting of 40 percent Blatz and 60 percent Stratz? of one with 40 percent Stratz and 60 percent Blatz?

PROBLEMS

1. Rosita Ramirez invests the following sums of money in common stocks having expected returns as follows:

SECURITY	AMOUNT INVESTED	EXPECTED RETURN
Morck Drug	$6,000	14%
Kota Chemical	11,000	16
Fazio Electronics	9,000	17
Northern California Utility	7,000	13
Grizzle Restaurants	5,000	20
Pharlap Oil	13,000	15
Excell Corporation	9,000	18

a. What is the expected return (percentage) on her portfolio?

b. What would be her expected return if she quadrupled her investment in Grizzle Restaurants while leaving everything else the same?

2. Securities D, E, and F have the following characteristics with respect to expected return, standard deviation, and correlation between them:

			CORRELATION COEFFICIENTS		
	R	σ	D-E	D-F	E-F
Company D	.08	.02	.4	.6	
Company E	.15	.16	.4		.8
Company F	.12	.08		.6	.8

What is the expected return and standard deviation of a portfolio composed of equal investments in each?

3. Dot Thermal Controls Company's common stock has an expected return of 20 percent and a standard deviation of 22 percent. Sierra Nevada Electric Company's stock has an expected return of 12 percent and a standard deviation of 11 percent. The correlation coefficient between returns for the two stocks is .30.

a. What portfolio expected returns and standard deviations arise from investing varying proportions of your funds in these two stocks? Vary your proportions in increments of .10, going from 1.00 in Sierra Nevada Electric and 0 in Dot Thermal Controls to .90 and .10, to .80 and .20, and so forth.

b. Approximately what is the minimum variance portfolio? What is the efficient set?

c. If the correlation coefficient were .70, what would happen to the diversification effect and to the minimum variance portfolio?

4. The following portfolios are available in the market:

PORTFOLIO	A	B	C	D	E
Expected return	.15	.07	.13	.17	.11
Standard deviation	.11	.02	.08	.15	.05

a. Assume that you can invest in only one of these portfolios; that is, it is not possible to mix portfolios. Plot the risk-return trade-off. Which portfolio do you prefer?

b. Assume now that you are able to borrow and lend at a risk-free rate of 6 percent. Which portfolio is preferred? Would you borrow or lend at the risk-free rate to achieve a desired position? What is the effect of borrowing and lending on the expected return and on the standard deviation?

5. Suppose the market portfolio had an expected return of 20 percent and a standard deviation of 15 percent. The risk-free rate is 10 percent, and all the assumptions of the capital asset pricing model hold. What is the expected return and standard deviation if you invest your wealth (1) entirely in the risk-free asset? (2) one-half in the risk-free asset and one-half in the market portfolio? (3) all in the market portfolio? (4) all in the market portfolio and borrow half again as much for additional investment in the market portfolio?

6. On the basis of an analysis of past returns and of inflationary expectations, Marta Gomez feels that the expected return on stocks in general is 14 percent. The risk-free rate on Treasury securities is now 8 percent. Gomez is particularly interested in the return prospects for Kessler Electronics Corporation. Based on monthly data for the past 5 years, she has fitted a characteristic line to the responsiveness of excess returns of the stock to excess returns of Standard & Poor's 500-Stock Index and has found the slope of the line to be 1.67. If financial markets are believed to be efficient, what return can she expect from investing in Kessler?

7. For the past 2 years, Natchez Steamboat Company and Standard & Poor's 500-Stock Index have had the following excess monthly returns:

	NATCHEZ STEAMBOAT	STANDARD & POOR'S 500-STOCK INDEX
January 19—1	−4%	−2%
February	−5	−6
March	2	−1
April	1	3
May	7	5
June	−1	2
July	−1	−3
August	8	4
September	3	1
October	−10	−5
November	2	1
December	4	4
January 19—2	3	2
February	−3	−4

	NATCHEZ STEAMBOAT	STANDARD & POOR'S 500-STOCK INDEX
March	1	1
April	5	3
May	8	7
June	0	−1
July	−1	−2
August	−7	−4
September	2	3
October	−2	1
November	−5	−5
December	−3	−1

a. Plot these observations on graph paper and fit a characteristic line to them by eye.

b. What is the approximate beta for Natchez Steamboat Company?

c. Does the stock present much unsystematic risk? How can you tell?

8. Jane Leslie Richardson, manager of stock investments for the Delta Pension Fund, detects a tendency in the betas of certain stocks to regress toward the average beta of the industry of which they are a part. She is considering weighting factors of .60, .70, and .80 for the measured betas. The following information is available:

	MEASURED BETA	INDUSTRY BETA
Red Rocker Homes	1.40	1.80
Zaleski Electronics	1.50	1.10
Fairgold Foods	1.00	.90
Pottsburg Water Distilling	.80	1.10

For each of the three weighting factors, what is the adjusted beta for these stocks?

9. In the context of the capital asset pricing model, what is the expected return of security j if it has the following characteristics and if the following information holds for the market portfolio?

Standard deviation, security j	.20
Standard deviation, market portfolio	.15
Expected return, market portfolio	.13
Correlation between possible returns for security j and the market portfolio	.80
Risk-free rate	.07

a. What would happen to the required return if the standard deviation of security j were higher?

b. What would happen if the correlation coefficient were less?

c. What is the functional relationship between the required return for a security and market risk?

10. At present, suppose the risk-free rate is 10 percent and the expected return on the market portfolio is 15 percent. The expected returns for four stocks are listed together with their expected betas.

STOCK	EXPECTED RETURN	EXPECTED BETA
1. Stillman Zinc Corporation	17.0%	1.3
2. Union Paint Company	14.5	.8
3. National Automobile Company	15.5	1.1
4. Parker Electronics, Inc.	18.0	1.7

a. On the basis of these expectations, which stocks are overvalued? Which are undervalued?

b. If the risk-free rate were to rise to 12 percent and the expected return on the market portfolio rose to 16 percent, which stocks would be overvalued? Which would be undervalued? (Assume the expected returns and the betas stay the same.)

11. Corliss Services, Inc., provides maintenance services to commercial buildings. Presently, the beta on its stock is 1.08. The risk-free rate is now 10 percent; the expected return for the market portfolio is 15 percent. Corliss is expected to pay a $2 per share dividend at the end of the year and to grow in nominal terms at a rate of 11 percent per annum for many years to come. Based on the capital asset pricing model and other assumptions you might make, what is the market price per share of the stock?

12. The following stocks are available for investment:

	BETA
Zeebock Enterprises	1.40
Topaz Jewels Inc.	.80
Yum Yum Soups Company	.60
Fitzgerald Securities Company	1.80
Ya Hoo Fisheries	1.05
Square Deal Services	.90

If you invest 20 percent of your funds in each of the first four securities, and 10 percent in each of the last two, what is the beta of your portfolio? If the risk-free rate is 8 percent and the expected return on the market portfolio 14 percent, what will be the portfolio's expected return?

13. The market portfolio has an expected return of 15 percent and a standard deviation of 20 percent. The standard deviation of Bartez Pharmaceutical Company's stock is 25 percent and its correlation coefficient with the market portfolio is .50.

a. What is the beta of Bartez's stock? (*Hint:* Review the section on the expected return for the individual security.)

b. What would happen to the beta if Bartez's standard deviation were 40 percent? if the correlation coefficient were .60?

c. Of the total variance of the stock in the original example, what portion is accounted for by systematic risk? by unsystematic risk? (The correlation coefficient squared is R-squared.) What in general would happen to the total variance of a portfolio if a portion of the Bartez stock were sold and the proceeds were invested in unrelated stocks having the same beta?

14. What are the critical assumptions in the capital asset pricing model? What are the implications of relaxing these assumptions?

1. The expected return is $(w)R_m + (1 - w)R_f$ and the standard deviation is $(w)\sigma_m$, where w is the proportion of total wealth invested in the risky market portfolio of securities, m, and R_f is the risk-free rate.

   a. $R_p = (0).15 + (1.0).09 = 9\%$

      $\sigma_p = (0).21 = 0\%$

   b. $R_p = (\frac{2}{3}).15 + (\frac{1}{3}).09 = 13\%$

      $\sigma_p = (\frac{2}{3}).21 = 14\%$

   c. $R_p = (\frac{4}{3}).15 - (\frac{1}{3}).09 = 17\%$

      $\sigma_p = (\frac{4}{3}).21 = 28\%$

   Both expected return and standard deviation increase linearly with increases in the proportion of wealth invested in the risky market portfolio of securities.

2. a. $R_{zz} = 10\% + (16\% - 10\%)1.45 = 18.70\%$

   b. If we use the perpetual dividend growth model, we would have

   $$P_0 = \frac{D_1}{R_{zz} - g} = \frac{\$2(1.10)}{.187 - .10} = \$25.29$$

3. a. $R_p = .4(15\%) + .6(20\%) = 18\%$

      $\sigma_p = [(.4)^2(1.0)(.2)^2 + 2(.4)(.6)(.36)(.2)(.4) + (.6)^2(1.0)(.4)^2]^{\frac{1}{2}}$

      $= [.0778]^{\frac{1}{2}} = 27.9\%$

   For the standard deviation, the middle term denotes the covariance $(.36)(.2)(.4)$ times the weights of .4 and .6, all of which is counted twice—hence the 2 in front. For the first and last terms, the correlation coefficients for these own variance terms are 1.0.

   b. $R_p = .6(15\%) + .4(20\%) = 17\%$

      $\sigma_p = [(.6)^2(1.0)(.2)^2 + 2(.6)(.4)(.36)(.2)(.4) + (.4)^2(1.0)(.4)^2]^{\frac{1}{2}}$

      $= [.0538]^{\frac{1}{2}} = 23.2\%$

   The lesser proportional investment in the riskier asset, Stratz, results in a lower expected return as well as a lower standard deviation.

SELECTED REFERENCES

BLACK, FISCHER,"Capital Market Equilibrium with Restricted Borrowing," *Journal of Business*, 45 (July 1972), 444–54.

BLUME, MARSHALL E., "Betas and Their Regression Tendencies," *Journal of Finance*, 30 (June 1975), 785–96.

BREEDEN, DOUGLAS T., MICHAEL R. GIBBONS, and ROBERT H. LITZENBERGER, "Empirical Tests of the Consumption-Oriented CAPM," *Journal of Finance*, 44 (June 1989), 231–62.

CONNOR, GREGORY, "A Unified Beta Pricing Theory," *Journal of Economic Theory*, 34 (December 1984), 13–31.

CUTLER, DAVID M., JAMES M. POTERBA, and LAWRENCE H. SUMMERS, "What Moves Stock Prices?" *Journal of Portfolio Management*, 15 (Spring 1989), 4–12.

EVANS, JACK, and STEPHEN H. ARCHER, "Diversification and the Reduction of Dispersion: An Empirical Analysis," *Journal of Finance*, 23 (December 1968), 761–67.

FAMA, EUGENE F., "Efficient Capital Markets: A Review of Theory and Empirical Work," *Journal of Finance*, 25 (May 1970), 383–417.

———, "Components of Investment Performance," *Journal of Finance*, 27 (June 1972), 551–67.

———, and MERTON H. MILLER, *The Theory of Finance*, New York: Holt, 1972.

HARRINGTON, DIANA R., *Modern Portfolio Theory, the Capital Asset Pricing Model and Arbitrage Pricing Theory: A User's Guide*, 2d ed. Englewood Cliffs, NJ: Prentice Hall, 1987.

HAUGEN, ROBERT A., *Modern Investment Theory*, 2d ed. Englewood Cliffs, NJ: Prentice Hall, 1990.

LINTNER, JOHN, "Security Prices, Risk and Maximal Gains from Diversification," *Journal of Finance*, 20 (December 1965), 587–616.

LORIE, JAMES H., PETER DODD, and MARY T. HAMILTON, *The Stock Market*, 2d ed. Homewood, IL: Richard D. Irwin, 1985.

MARKOWITZ, HARRY M., *Portfolio Selection: Efficient Diversification of Investments*. New York: John Wiley, 1959.

MODIGLIANI, FRANCO, and GERALD A. POGUE, "An Introduction to Risk and Return," *Financial Analysts Journal*, 30 (March–April 1974), 68–80, and (May–June), 68–86.

MULLINS, DAVID W., JR., "Does the Capital Asset Pricing Model Work?" *Harvard Business Review*, 60 (January–February 1982), 105–14.

REILLY, FRANK K., *Investment Analysis and Portfolio Management*, 3d ed. Hinsdale, IL: Dryden, 1989.

———, and DAVID J. WRIGHT, "A Comparison of Published Betas," *Journal of Portfolio Management*, 14 (Spring 1988), 64–69.

ROLL, RICHARD, "A Critique of the Asset Pricing Theory Tests. Part I: On Past and Potential Testability of the Theory," *Journal of Financial Economics*, 4 (March 1977), 129–76.

———, "Performance Evaluation and Benchmark Errors," *Journal of Portfolio Management*, 6 (Summer 1980), 5–12.

ROSENBERG, BARR, "The Capital Asset Pricing Model and the Market Model," *Journal of Portfolio Management*, 7 (Winter 1981), 5–16.

ROSS, STEPHEN A., "Information and Volatility: The No-Arbitrage Martingale Approach to Timing and Resolution Irrelevancy," *Journal of Finance*, 44 (March 1989), 1–18.

SHARPE, WILLIAM F., "A Simplified Model for Portfolio Analysis," *Management Science*, 10 (January 1963), 277–93.

———, "Capital Asset Prices: A Theory of Market Equilibrium under Conditions of Risk," *Journal of Finance*, 19 (September 1964), 425–42.

———, and GORDON J. ALEXANDER, *Investments*, 4th ed. Englewood Cliffs, NJ: Prentice Hall, 1990.

SHLEIFER, ANDREI, and LAWRENCE H. SUMMERS, "Crowds and Prices: Towards a Theory of Inefficient Markets," working paper, Center for Research in Security Prices, University of Chicago (1990).

TOBIN, JAMES, "Liquidity Preference as Behavior towards Risk," *Review of Economic Studies*, 25 (February 1958), 65–86.

VAN HORNE, JAMES C., *Financial Market Rates and Flows*, 3d ed. Englewood Cliffs, NJ: Prentice Hall, 1990, Chap. 3.

4

MULTI VARIABLE AND FACTOR VALUATION

In the last chapter, prospective investors were seen to be consumers, shopping. The product attribute of importance was the relationship of a security's return with that of the overall market. Other attributes, however, may influence the perceived risk of a security to our shopper and, hence, its price in the marketplace. The purpose of this chapter is to explore things additional to beta that may provide a better explanation of the risk-return trade-off for securities. We begin with extensions to the capital asset pricing model (CAPM) and then move on to factor models in general. Finally, we consider the arbitrage pricing theory (APT), which involves multiple factors, as an alternative model to the CAPM.

EXTENDED CAPM

The capital asset pricing model is a single factor model where expected return is related to beta. As we know from the previous chapter, beta is the reaction coefficient of a security's return to that of the overall market, as typified by some broad index such as Standard & Poor's 500-Stock Index. To repeat what was in Chapter 3, a security's expected return, R_j, is

$$\overline{R}_j = R_f + (\overline{R}_m - R_f)\beta_j \qquad (4\text{-}1)$$

where R_f is the risk-free rate, $\overline{R}_m$ is the expected return on the market portfolio, and β_j is the security's beta. By adding additional variables to this equation, one hopes to obtain not only higher explanatory power but insight into other influences on security returns. In turn, these influences affect financial decision making, the thrust of this book. In what follows, we present various extensions to the CAPM.

ALLOWANCE FOR A TAX EFFECT

The return that an investor realizes from holding a stock is composed of two parts: (1) dividends, if any, received during the holding period and (2) the capital gain or loss that occurs when the stock is sold. If all investors paid ei-

87

ther no taxes or the same taxes on dividends and capital gains, the CAPM generalizations made about an individual stock would be unaffected by whether the company paid high or low dividends. In many countries, capital gains are taxed at a more favorable rate than dividends. Under the 1986 Tax Act in the United States, dividend income and capital gains were taxed at the same rate at the federal level. However, capital gains income is not recognized until the stock is sold. If held until death, the capital gain is largely unrecognized. Therefore, there are present-value advantages to capital gains versus dividend income. With the passage of the 1990 Tax Act, a small differential in tax in favor of capital gains reemerged for the maximum tax-bracketed individual—28 percent versus 31 percent.

Suppose we expect Alpha Company to have a 12 percent dividend yield for the year (dividends divided by initial value) and a 3 percent capital gain on initial value, while Baker Company is expected to have a 2 percent dividend yield and a 12-1/2 percent capital gain. The expected before-tax return of Alpha Company, 15 percent, is higher than that of Baker Company, 14-1/2 percent. If an investor is in a 30 percent tax bracket, but the "effective economic" tax on capital gains is 24 percent, the after-tax returns are as follows:

	ALPHA COMPANY			BAKER COMPANY		
	Before Taxes	Tax Effect	After Taxes	Before Taxes	Tax Effect	After Taxes
Dividend yield	12%	(1 − .30)	8.40%	2.0%	(1 − .30)	1.40%
Capital gain	3	(1 − .24)	2.28	12.5	(1 − .24)	9.50
Expected return	15%		10.68%	14.5%		10.90%

We see that despite the lower expected return before taxes, the expected after-tax return is higher for Baker Company, owing to a greater portion of the return being realized in capital gains. On the other hand, a tax-exempt investor, such as a pension fund, would prefer Alpha Company, with its higher before-tax expected return, all other things being the same.

Whether there is a systematic preference in the market as a whole for capital gains over dividends is a subject that must await a more detailed exploration in Chapter 12. In this chapter, we wish to explore only the implications for the capital asset pricing model if such a preference is assumed. Most significant is that holding risk constant, high dividend stocks may have to provide higher expected returns before taxes than will low dividend stocks, in order to offset the tax effect.

If this is so, and again we emphasize the unsettled nature of the argument, the expected before-tax return on security j would be a function of both the stock's beta and its dividend yield:

$$\bar{R}_j = R_f + b\beta_j + t(d_j - R_f) \qquad (4\text{-}2)$$

where R_f = risk-free rate
  β_j = the security's beta
  b = a coefficient indicating the relative importance of beta
  d_j = dividend yield on security j
  t = a coefficient indicating the relative importance of the tax effect

This equation tells us that the greater the dividend yield, d_j, the greater the expected before-tax return that investors require. If t were .1 and the dividend yield were to rise by 1.0 percent, the expected return would have to increase by .1 percent to make the stock attractive to investors. Put another way, the market trade-off would be $1.00 of dividends for $.90 of capital gains.

If there is a systematic bias in the market in favor of capital gains, the expected return on a stock would depend on both its beta and its dividend yield. Instead of the two-dimensional (expected return-beta) security market line in Fig. 3-11 in Chapter 3, we need a three-dimensional surface of the sort shown in Fig. 4-1. In this approach, devised by William F. Shape, we see that expected return is on the vertical axis, whereas beta and dividend yield are on the other axes. Looking at expected return and dividend yield, we see that the higher the dividend yield, the higher the expected return. Similarly, the higher the beta, the higher the expected return. Instead of a security market line, we have a security market surface, depicting the three-dimensional relationship among expected return, beta, and dividend yield. Whether the use of such a trade-off surface is appropriate and practical depends on the fundamental existence of a tax effect and its proper measurement, a topic we consider in depth in Chapter 12.

THE PRESENCE OF INFLATION

In our presentation of valuation principles, we implicitly assumed that market equilibration occurred in nominal terms; however, we know that investors are concerned with inflation, and they factor this into account when making an investment decision. The realized real return for a security can be expressed as

$$R_j^r = R_j - \rho \tag{4-3}$$

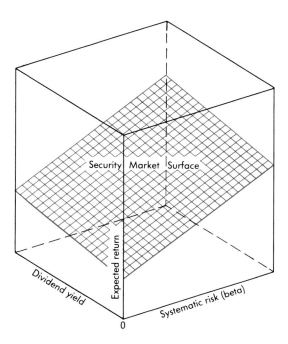

FIGURE 4-1
Three-dimensional security market
surface illustrating a tax effect

where R_j^r = the return for security j in real terms
R_j = the return for security j in nominal terms
ρ = inflation during the period

If inflation is highly predictable, investors simply will add an inflation premium onto the real return they require, and markets will equilibrate in the manner described earlier in the chapter. As long as inflation is predictable, it is not a source of uncertainty. Therefore, the risk of a security can be described by its systematic and unsystematic risk, regardless of whether these risks are measured in real or nominal terms. (See Chapter 20 for a discussion of inflation's impact on interest rates.)[1]

When inflation is uncertain, however, things are different. By uncertainty, we mean that the market does not anticipate changes that occur in the rate of inflation. Whether uncertain inflation is good or bad for a stock depends on the covariance of this uncertainty with that of the stock. If the return on a stock increases with unanticipated increases in inflation, this desirable property reduces the systematic risk of the stock in real terms and provides a hedge. Contrarily, if the stock's return goes down when unanticipated inflation occurs, this is undesirable because it increases the systematic risk of the stock in real terms.

We would expect that the greater the covariance of the return of a stock with unanticipated changes in inflation, the lower the expected nominal return the market will require. If this is so, one could express the expected nominal return of a stock as a positive function of its beta and a negative function of its covariance with unanticipated inflation. We might have

$$\overline{R}_j = R_f + b\beta_j - i\frac{\text{(inflation covariance)}}{\sigma_i^2} \tag{4-4}$$

where i is a coefficient indicating the relative importance of a security's covariance with inflation, σ_i^2 is the variance of inflation, and the other variables are the same as defined for Eq. (4-2). In effect, the last variable is a beta for the sensitivity of security returns to changes in inflation. By dividing by inflation's variance, things are expressed on a relative as opposed to an absolute basis.

Similar to the dividend-yield case, we could construct a three-dimensional security market surface. This surface would have nominal security returns increasing with beta and decreasing with relative inflation covariance. In other words, covariance with inflation may be a desirable property and lower the return that investors require. Many stocks have negative covariances; their returns tend to decline with unanticipated increases in inflation, and vice versa. This may be an undesirable characteristic and such a security may require a higher return, all other things the same. While all of this is simple enough in concept, it is difficult to predict the sensitivity of an individual stock (or even stocks overall) to unanticipated changes in inflation. Efforts to do so often result in no additional predictive ability for the model.

---

[1] See James C. Van Horne, *Financial Market Rates and Flows*, 3d ed. (Englewood Cliffs, NJ: Prentice Hall, 1990).

LIQUIDITY AND SIZE EFFECTS

Extensions other than dividend and inflation effects have been made to the CAPM. Other variables include liquidity, size, price/earnings ratio, seasion, and industry.[2] *Liquidity* is the ability to sell a security quickly and without significant price concession. Presumably, investors prefer high to low liquidity and, if this is true, would have a three-dimensional security market surface, similar to Fig. 4-1, but where the degree of illiquidity replaces the dividend yield on one of the axes.

Closely related to liquidity is *size*, as measured by the relative market capitalization of a company. From time to time, a "small stock effect" appears, where small capitalization stocks provide a higher return than large capitalization stocks, holding other things constant. Presumably, small stocks provide less utility to the investor and require a higher return. Often the size variable is treated as the decile in which the company's market capitalization falls relative to the market capitalizations of other companies.

PRICE/EARNINGS RATIO EFFECT

A price/earnings ratio effect has been observed. Holding constant beta, observed returns tend to be higher for low P/E ratio stocks and lower for high P/E ratio stocks. Expressed differently, low P/E ratio stocks earn excess returns above what the CAPM would predict, and high P/E ratio stocks earn less than what the CAPM would predict. This is a form of mean reversion, and it adds explanatory power to the CAPM. With only this variable added, the model becomes

$$\bar{R}_j = R_f + b\beta_j - p(P/E_j - P/E_m) \tag{4-5}$$

where p is a coefficient reflecting the relative importance of a security's price/earnings ratio, P/E_j is the price/earnings ratio of that security, and P/E_m is the weighted average price/earnings ratio for the market portfolio. We should point out that this is but one of a number of ways to express the variable.

As with the other additional variables, we can construct a three-dimensional security market surface with the price/earnings ratio along one of the axes. This is shown in Figure 4-2, and we see that expected return increases with beta and decreases with the P/E ratio. The addition of this variable has been found to be important in tempering return estimates derived from the CAPM. Expressed differently, beta does not capture all the risk associated with holding a stock, and additional explanatory power may come from including the price/earnings ratio.

---

[2] For a discussion of various extensions to the CAPM, see Donald B. Keim, "The CAPM and Equity Return Regularities," *Financial Analysts Journal*, 42 (May–June 1986), 19–34; Yakov Amihud and Haim Mendelson, "Liquidity and Stock Returns," *Financial Analysts Journal*, 42 (May–June 1986), 43–48; Rolf W. Banz, "The Relationship between Return and Market Value of Common Stocks," *Journal of Financial Economics*, 9 (March 1981), 3–18; S. Basu, "The Relationship between Earnings Yield, Market Value and Return for NYSE Common Stocks: Further Evidence," *Journal of Financial Economics*, 12 (June 1983), 129–56; Laxmi Chand Bhandari, "Debt/Equity Ratio and Expected Common Stock Returns: Empirical Evidence," *Journal of Finance*, 43 (June 1988), 507–28; and William F. Sharpe and Gordon J. Alexander, *Investments*, 4th ed. (Englewood Cliffs, NJ: Prentice Hall, 1990) Chap. 8.

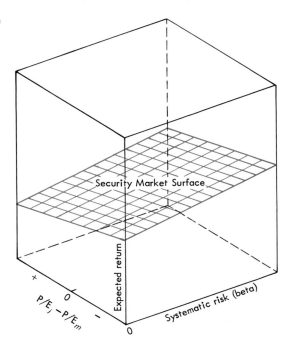

FIGURE 4-2
Three-dimensional security market
surface illustrating a
price/earnings ratio effect

SEASONAL AND INDUSTRY EFFECTS

Seasonal effects have to do with the month and/or the day of the week in which a security trade takes place. Different returns on investment may occur depending on these factors. The "January effect," for example, refers to a pattern of excess returns that on a number of occasions occurs during that month. Even more of an anomaly is that these gains tend to be concentrated in the first five trading days of the month and in the stocks of small companies.

Others have tried to isolate *industry* effects by using dummy variables to depict whether or not a security falls into a particular industry, such as energy. As variables additional to beta are used to approximate the expected return from a security, we have what is known as the *extended capital asset pricing model.*

FINAL OBSERVATIONS
ON THE EXTENDED CAPM

Of the variables used to extend the CAPM, size and the price/earnings ratio have been found to be the most consistent and significant in their effect. The dividend-yield effect is the most controversial, as we shall see in Chapter 12. For multiple variables,

$$\overline{R}_j = R_f + b\beta_j + c(\text{variable \#2}) + d(\text{variable \#3})$$
$$+ e(\text{variable \#4}) + \cdots + m(\text{variable \#n}) \tag{4-6}$$

where, again, b, c, d, e, and m are coefficients reflecting the relative importance of the variable involved. When variables other than beta are added, a better data fit generally is obtained. These variables have been found to successfully explain some of a security's total return not explained by beta.

The extensions to the CAPM taken up in this section do not negate the model's underlying importance. They simply permit more precise measurement of the required return for a particular stock, as well as provide a richer, more realistic description of the market equilibrium process. However, beta still remains the dominant determinant of security returns. The extensions discussed embellish the model, supplementing but not supplanting beta. Devotees still cry, long live beta!

FACTOR MODELS IN GENERAL

Perhaps the most important challenge to the CAPM is the arbitrage pricing theory (APT). As this theory involves a factor model approach, we first consider such models in general. Like the extended CAPM, factor models suggest that expected returns are affected by a number of risks. Such models assume that security returns are generated by a set of underlying factors, often economic. The extended CAPM may include economic variables. However, the key variable is beta, which is not necessarily the case with factor models of the sort we consider now. The difference is subtle, but important.

TWO-FACTOR MODEL

To illustrate a two-factor model, suppose the actual return on a security, R_j, can be explained by the following:

$$R_j = a + b_{1j}F_1 + b_{2j}F_2 + e_j \qquad (4\text{-}7)$$

where a is the return when all factors have zero values, F_n is the value (uncertain) of factor n, b_{nj} is the reaction coefficient depicting the change in the security's return to a one-unit change in the factor, and e_j is the error term. The error term is security specific, or unsystematic.

As with our discussion in the last chapter, unsystematic risk can be diversified away by holding a broad portfolio of securities as opposed to only one. With a portfolio, security specific risk is not a thing of value. The error terms of individual securities are unrelated to each other; i.e., their correlation coefficients are zero. Under these circumstances, only the factor risks are important. They represent unavoidable risk, whereas unsystematic risk can be avoided by diversification.

For the factors, it is the unanticipated or "surprise" element that matters. For example, an announcement of a change in commodity price levels is comprised of two parts: the expected and the unanticipated. If inflation is a factor affecting expected returns, the expected component already is embraced in security prices. It is the unanticipated that causes equilibrium conditions to be upset and for security prices to change. Thus,

$$\text{Announcement of} \atop \text{change in factor} = \text{Expected} \atop \text{component} = \text{Unanticipated} \atop \text{component} \qquad (4\text{-}8)$$

To repeat, the second component is the surprise element and the thing that moves security prices, which, in turn, allows us to study the process. The expected component already is discounted in the sense that a security's price reflects it. Put another way, it is the unanticipated that constitutes risk, not the expected. Therefore, the factors in Eq. (4-7) relate to unanticipated changes.

The expected return on a security, in contrast to the actual return in Eq. (4-7), is

$$(E)\overline{R}_j = \lambda_0 + \lambda_1 b_{1j} + \lambda_2 b_{2j} \tag{4-9}$$

The λ_0 parameter corresponds to the return on a risk-free asset. The other λ parameters represent risk premiums for the types of risk associated with particular factors. For example, λ_1 is the expected excess return (above the risk-free rate) when $b_{1j} = 1$ and $b_{2j} = 0$.[3] The parameters can be positive or negative. A positive λ reflects risk aversion by the market to the factor involved. A negative parameter indicates value being associated with the factor, in the sense of a lesser return being required.

Suppose Torquay Resorts Limited's stock is related to two factors where the reaction coefficients, b_{1j} and b_{2j}, are 1.4 and 0.8, respectively. If the risk-free rate is 8 percent, and λ_1 is 6 percent and λ_2 is -2 percent, the stock's expected return is

$$(E)\overline{R}_j = .08 + .06(1.4) - .02(0.8) = 14.8\%$$

The first factor reflects risk aversion and must be compensated for with a higher expected return, while the second is a thing of value to investors and lowers the return they expect. Thus, the λ's represent market prices associated with factor risks.

Figure 4-3 illustrates a two-factor model where the lambdas are both pos-

[3] Nai-fu Chen, "Some Empirical Tests of the Theory of Arbitrage Pricing," *Journal of Finance*, 38 (December 1983), 1194.

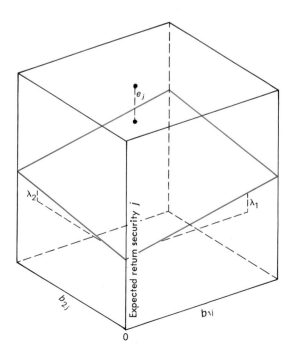

FIGURE 4-3

Three-dimensional illustration of a two-factor model

itive. The reaction coefficients for the two factors are shown along two axes, while expected return is along the vertical axis. The market price, λ_{1j}, is the angle of the security market surface to the b_{1j} line, while λ_{2j} is the angle of the surface to the b_{2j} line. The error term, e_j, is illustrated by the distance off the surface. This is a random occurrence, by definition. If persistent, we would expect it to be eliminated by arbitrage, to be illustrated shortly.

Now you might ask, How does this differ from the three-dimensional figures used to illustrate the extended CAPM? Both involve two-factor models, but with Figs. 4-1 and 4-2, one of the factors was beta. The CAPM does not assume an underlying structure to security returns, whereas factor models often do.

MORE THAN TWO FACTORS

The same principles hold when we go to more than two factors. Here the expected return is

$$(E)\overline{R}_j = \lambda_0 + \lambda_1 b_{1j} + \lambda_2 b_{2j} + \cdots + \lambda_n b_{nj} \tag{4-10}$$

where the number of factors is n. Again, each λ represents a market price of risk. For example, λ_1 represents the expected return in excess of the risk-free rate when the reaction coefficient for the first factor, b_{1j}, is 1.0, and the b's for all other factors are zero. Each factor is an undiversifiable, or unavoidable, risk. The greater a security's reaction coefficient with respect to a factor, the more the risk and the higher the required return. Thus, Eq. (4-10) tells us that a security's expected return is the risk-free rate, λ_0, plus risk premiums for each of the n factors. Factor models are based on the idea that security prices move together or apart in reaction to common forces as well as to by chance. The objective is to isolate the noise, or chance, element in order to get at the common forces.

One way to do so is with a statistical technique called factor analysis. Here actual returns on securities are analyzed as to their covariances to see if any common factors can explain them. The factors that emerge are examined to see if they correspond to economic or behavioral variables that may or may not be suggested by theory. Another approach is to specify various factors on the basis of theory and then proceed to test them. This leads us to the much acclaimed arbitrage pricing theory.

ARBITRAGE PRICING THEORY

Like the CAPM, arbitrage pricing theory (APT) is an equilibrium model as to how security prices are determined. Originally developed by Stephen A. Ross, this theory is based on the idea that in competitive financial markets arbitrage will ensure that riskless assets provide the same expected return.[4] Arbitrage simply means finding two things that are essentially the same and buying the cheaper and selling, or selling short, the more expensive. The model is based

---

[4] Stephen A. Ross, "The Arbitrage Theory of Capital Asset Pricing," *Journal of Economic Theory*, 13 (December 1976), pp. 341–60.

on the simple notion that security prices adjust as investors form portfolios in search of arbitrage profits. When such profit opportunities have been exhausted, security prices are said to be in equilibrium. In this context, a definition of market efficiency is the absence of arbitrage opportunities, their having been eliminated by arbitragers.

The APT suggests that the market equilibration process is driven by individuals eliminating arbitrage profits across these multiple factors. The model does not tell us what the factors are or why they are economically or behaviorally relevant. It merely states that there is a relationship between security returns and a limited number of factors. That is, security returns move together because of some common attributes. One of the factors might be the market return, as in the CAPM, but this need not be the case.

THE ARBITRAGE PROCESS

According to the APT, two securities with the same reaction coefficients, the b's in Eq. (4-10), should provide the same expected return. What happens if this is not the case? Investors rush in to buy the security with the higher expected return and sell, or sell short, the security with the lower expected return.

Suppose returns required in the market by investors are a function of two factors according to the following equation, where the risk-free rate is 7 percent:

$$(E)\overline{R}_j = .07 + .04(b_{1j}) - .01(b_{2j})$$

Quigley Manufacturing Company and Zolotny Basic Products Corporation both have the same reaction coefficients to the factors, such that $b_{1j} = 1.3$ and $b_{2j} = 0.9$. Therefore, the required return for both securities is

$$(E)\overline{R}_j = .07 + .04(1.3) - .01(0.9) = 11.3\%$$

However, Quigley's stock is depressed, so its expected return is 12.8 percent, while Zolotny's share price is relatively high; its expected return is only 10.6 percent. A clever arbitrager should buy Quigley and sell or sell short Zolotny. If she has things right and the only risks of importance are captured by factors 1 and 2, the two securities have the same overall risk. Yet because of mispricing, one security provides a higher expected return than its risk would dictate, while the other provides a lower return. This is a money game, and our clever arbitrager will want to exploit the opportunity as long as possible.

As arbitragers recognize the mispricing and engage in the transactions suggested, price adjustments will occur. The price of Quigley stock will rise, and its expected return will fall, while the price of Zolotny stock will fall, and its expected return will rise. This will continue until both securities have an expected return of 11.3 percent.

According to the APT, rational market participants will exhaust all opportunities for arbitrage profits. Market equilibrium will occur when expected returns for all securities bear a linear relationship to the various reaction coefficients, the b's. Thus, the foundation for equilibrium pricing is arbitrage. The APT implies that market participants act in a manner consistent with general agreement as to what are the relevant risk factors that move security prices. Whether this assumption is a reasonable approximation of reality is a subject of much controversy.

ROLL-ROSS AND THEIR FIVE FACTORS

Richard Roll and Stephen A. Ross believe the truth lies in five specific factors.[5] They suggest that different securities have different sensitivities to these systematic factors and that the major sources of security portfolio risk are captured in them. The five factors are (1) changes in expected inflation, (2) unanticipated changes in inflation, (3) unanticipated changes in industrial production, (4) unanticipated changes in the yield differential between low- and high-grade bonds (the default-risk premium), and (5) unanticipated changes in the yield differential between long-term and short-term bonds (the term structure of interest rates). The first three factors affect primarily the cash flow of the company and, hence, its dividends and growth in dividends. The last two affect the market capitalization, or discount, rate.

Substituting into Eq. (4-10), the Roll-Ross model may be expressed as

$$
\begin{aligned}
(E)\overline{R}_j = \lambda_0 &+ \lambda_1(b_{1j}E\Delta \text{ inflation}) + \lambda_{2j}(b_2 U\Delta \text{ inflation}) \\
&+ \lambda_{3j}(b_3 U\Delta \text{ industrial production}) \\
&+ \lambda_{4j}(b_4 U\Delta \text{ bond risk premium}) \\
&+ \lambda_{5j}(b_5 U\Delta \text{ long minus short rate})
\end{aligned}
\tag{4-11}
$$

where $E\Delta$ is an expected change, $U\Delta$ represents an unanticipated change, and the other symbols are the same as before. According to this equation, the expected return on a security, $(E)\overline{R}_j$, exceeds the risk-free rate by the sum of the products of the market prices of risk, the λ's, and the sensitivity coefficients, the b's. The sensitivity coefficients simply tell us the average response of the security's return to an unanticipated change in a factor, holding other factors constant.

According to this model, investors are characterized as having risk preferences along five dimensions. Each investor would formulate a portfolio of securities depending on his or her desired risk exposure to each of the factors. Different investors will have different risk attitudes. For example, some may want little inflation risk but be willing to tolerate considerable productivity risk and default risk. Roll-Ross argue that the CAPM beta is too restricted a measure of risk. Several stocks may have the same beta but vastly different factor risks. If investors in fact are concerned with these factor risks, the CAPM beta would not be a good indicator of the expected return for a stock.

What would be? According to the Roll-Ross version of the arbitrage pricing theory, or similar versions, knowing the λ's (the market prices of various risks, expressed in terms of premiums above the risk-free rate) and the b's (the response coefficients for specific security returns to changes in factors) in Eq. (4-11) would be sufficient. In an empirical study for the 1958–84 period,

[5] "An Empirical Investigation of the Arbitrage Pricing Theory," *Journal of Finance*, 35 (December 1980), 1073–1103; "The Arbitrage Pricing Theory Approach to Strategic Portfolio Planning," *Financial Analysts Journal*, 40 (May–June 1984); and Nai-Fu Chen, Richard Roll, and Stephen A. Ross, "Economic Forces and the Stock Market," *Journal of Business*, 59 (July 1986), 383–403.

Chen, Roll, and Ross estimate the following parameters for *monthly* returns:[6]

$$(E)\bar{R}_j = .00412 - .00013(b_1 E\Delta \text{ inflation}) - .00063(b_2 U\Delta \text{ inflation})$$
$$+ .01359(b_3 U\Delta \text{ industrial production})$$
$$+ .00721 (b_4 U\Delta \text{ bond risk premium}) \qquad (4\text{-}12)$$
$$- .00521 (b_5 U\Delta \text{ long minus short rate})$$

Suppose the *b*'s for CRR Corporation are: $b_1 = 1.8$, $b_2 = 2.4$, $b_3 = 0.9$, $b_4 = 0.5$, and $b_5 = 1.1$. Under these conditions, the expected return for the stock is

$$(E)\bar{R}_{crr} = .00412 - .00013(1.8) - .00063(2.4) + .01359(0.9)$$
$$+ .00721(0.5) - .00521(1.1)$$
$$= 1.25\%$$

Remember that this expected return, 1.25 percent, is a monthly as opposed to annual return. Roll-Ross estimates for individual stocks are available to security analysts who subscribe to their service and to financial managers through ALCAR, a financial consulting firm.

OTHER EMPIRICAL TESTING

If the parameters for this or some other model could be estimated with reliability and we were confident that we had specified the risk factors of importance, it would be an easy matter to determine the expected return for a security. As illustrated for the Roll-Ross model, we would simply multiply the λ's by the *b*'s and sum them. This weighted product would represent the total risk premium for security *j*, to which we would add the risk-free rate to obtain the expected return.

But life is not so simple. There is not agreement as to the risk factors of importance. For example, Michael A. Berry, Edwin Burmeister, and Marjorie B. McElroy use the unanticipated inflation, bond risk premium, and long- minus short-term interest-rate factors previously described, but they also employ unanticipated changes in the expected growth rate of profits, and residual market risk.[7] The latter is that part of the S&P 500-stock return that is not explained by the other four factors. They claim this captures any missing factors. What we have, of course, is an extended CAPM. Others have specified different factors or have used factor analysis, previously described, to determine them. As the articles cited below reflect, empirical tests of the APT are inconclusive.[8] Disagreement abounds, both as to the factors to employ and as to parameter estimate consistency from test to test and over time.

---

[6] Nai-Fu Chen, Richard Roll, and Stephen A. Ross, "Economic Forces and the Stock Market," 383–403.

[7] Michael A. Berry, Edwin Burmeister, and Marjorie B. McElroy, "Sorting Out Risks Using Known APT Factors," *Financial Analysts Journal*, 44 (March–April 1988), 29–42.

[8] In addition to the articles already cited, see Jay Shanken, "The Arbitrage Pricing Theory: Is It Testable?" *Journal of Finance*, 37 (December 1982), 1129–40; Marc R. Reinganum, "The Arbitrage Pricing Theory: Some Empirical Results," *Journal of Finance*, 36 (May 1981), 312–22; D. Chinhyung Cho, Edwin J. Elton, and Martin J. Gruber, "On the Robustness of the Roll and Ross Arbitrage Pricing Theory," *Journal of Financial and Quantitative Analysis*, 19 (March 1984), 1–10; Phoebus J. Dhrymes, Irwin Friend, and N. Bulent Gultekin, "A Critical Reexamination of the Empirical Evidence on the Arbitrage Pricing Theory," *Journal of Finance*, 39 (June 1984), 323–46;

It can never be conclusively demonstrated that the APT is superior to the CAPM, or vice versa. Both models involve expectations of risks and of returns. Such expectations are not directly observable but must be estimated, and these estimates are subject to wide error. As more testing of the APT occurs, perhaps the areas of disagreement will diminish. The APT shows much promise, and a number of people have gravitated toward the Roll-Ross model.

IMPLICATIONS OF THE APT FOR THIS BOOK

Because multiple risks are considered, the arbitrage pricing theory is intuitively appealing. We know that different stocks may be affected differently by different risks. A retailing company may have more exposure to unanticipated inflation than does a basic foods company. A machine tool company may be dramatically affected by what happens to industrial production, whereas a utility may be little affected. By relating security returns to underlying risk factors, we can better understand the economic forces that affect share price. In Chapters 8 and 9, which deal with required rates of return, we probe further into the use of multifactor valuation models.

For a number of stocks, a multifactor model gives a better estimate of the required return on equity than does the one-factor CAPM. For other stocks, such as the broadly based American Home Products Corporation, the CAPM has high explanatory power and additional factors contribute little. For this reason, some of the more "practical" uses of the APT begin with a CAPM estimate, and then add other risk factors to get more explanatory power. This, of course, is a variant of the extended CAPM.

In the chapters that follow, we look primarily to the CAPM as a means for describing the equilibrium behavior of security prices. This is due to its wide acceptance. Where appropriate, we will describe the implications that arise when an APT approach is used. Whether the APT should replace the CAPM is a subject of much debate. Some of it is warranted, but some is not because the two models are compatible. Although the APT may become the principal theory of asset pricing, with the CAPM as a subset of it, this is not the case as yet.

SUMMARY

The capital asset pricing model may be extended to include variables other than beta. Whether expected return is comprised of dividends or capital gains may make a difference in valuation. If there is a systematic bias in favor of

Dorothy H. Bower, Richard S. Bower, and Dennis E. Logue, "Arbitrage Pricing Theory and Utility Stock Returns," *Journal of Finance*, 39 (September 1984), 1041–54; Philip H. Dybvig and Stephen A. Ross, "Yes, the APT Is Testable," *Journal of Finance*, 40 (September 1985), 1173–88; Charles Trzcinka, "On the Number of Factors in the Arbitrage Pricing Model," *Journal of Finance*, 41 (June 1986), 346–68; Bruce N. Lehmann and David M. Modest, "The Empirical Foundations of the Arbitrage Pricing Theory," *Journal of Financial Economics*, 21 (September 1988), 213–54; and Gregory Connor and Robert A. Korayczyk, "Risk and Return in an Equilibrium APT: Application of a New Test Methodology," *Journal of Financial Economics*, 21 (September 1986), 383–403.

capital gains, the required return on a high-dividend-paying stock will be greater than that on a low-paying one. To the extent investors are concerned with inflation, they may value the security whose returns covary with unanticipated changes in inflation and, accordingly, require a lower return, all other things the same. Liquidity and market capitalization size of a company may be desirable characteristics and require a lower return.

A price/earnings ratio effect may occur where observed returns are higher for low P/E ratio stocks than beta alone would predict, and vice versa. Expressed differently, the expected return on a high P/E ratio stock would be less than that on a low P/E ratio stock, holding beta constant. Finally, seasonal and industry effects may have an influence on expected security returns. Of the variables used to extend the CAPM, size and P/E ratio effects are the most consistent in their impact. Multiple variables added to beta increase the explanatory power of the model.

Like the extended CAPM, factor models relate expected returns to multiple risks. The idea is to capture unavoidable risk in the factors employed. Here risk relates to unanticipated changes in the factors. The lambda parameters reflect the market prices of risk for the various factors. One benefit of a factor model is that it allows analysis of the way different risks affect a particular security. The factors employed may arise from a statistical technique called factor analysis or from specification on the basis of theory.

The arbitrage pricing theory (APT) is an equilibrium model based on individuals arbitraging across multiple factors. By eliminating arbitrage opportunities, arbitragers make the market efficient. Roll and Ross have specified five factors that they think capture unavoidable risk, and their model has enjoyed good usage. Still there is not agreement as to the factors that are important, nor has empirical testing produced parameter stability and consistency over time. The APT has not displaced the CAPM in use, but it holds considerable promise for corporate finance.

SELF-CORRECTION PROBLEMS

1. Rubinstein Robotics Corporation has a beta of 1.25. The risk-free rate is 8 percent and the expected return on the market portfolio is 15 percent. Share price is $32, earnings per share $2.56, and dividends per share $1.28.
   a. What is the expected return using the CAPM without extension?
   b. If dividends increase the required return on stocks with the result that the t coefficient in Eq. (4-2) is .10 while the b coefficient is .075, what is the stock's expected return if we assume the equation holds?
   c. The price/earnings ratio for the market portfolio is 11, the p coefficient in Eq. (4-5) is −.006, and the b coefficient is .075. What is the stock's expected return if that equation holds?

2. The return on Hendershott Hinge Company's stock is related to factors 1 and 2 as follows:

$$(E)\overline{R}_j = \lambda_0 + .6\lambda_1 + 1.3\,\lambda_2$$

   where .6 and 1.3 are sensitivity, or reaction, coefficients associated with each of the factors as defined in the chapter. If the risk-free rate is 7 percent, the λ_1 risk premium is 6 percent, and λ_2 is 3 percent, what is Hendershott's expected return?

3. Suppose a three-factor APT model holds and the risk-free rate is 6 percent. There are two stocks in which you have a particular interest: Montana Leather Com-

pany and Bozeman Enterprises. The market-price lambdas and reaction coefficients for the two stocks are as follows:

FACTOR	λ	b_{ml}	b_{be}
1	.09	.5	.7
2	−.03	.4	.8
3	.04	1.2	.2

If you were to invest equally in the two securities, what would be the expected return on your portfolio? If you were to invest one-third in Montana Leather Company and two-thirds in Bozeman Enterprises?

PROBLEMS

1. Perez Paint Company pays a dividend of $3 per share and share price is $40. Presently the risk-free rate is 5 percent and the expected return on the market portfolio is 12 percent. The company's beta is .80. The b coefficient in Eq. (4-2) is .07 and the d coefficient is .10.

   a. What is the expected return for the company's stock if the equation holds?

   b. What would happen if the b coefficient were .08 and the d coefficient were .25? Under what circumstances would this occur?

2. Norway Fiord Boat Company has a beta of 1.40. The risk-free rate is presently 8 percent, and the inflation extension to the CAPM, Eq. (4-4), holds. The b coefficient in the equation is .075, and the i coefficient is .03. The inflation covariance/variance ratio for the company is .25. What is the stock's expected return? In words, what would happen if negative instead of positive covariance occurred?

3. Suppose the expected return for a stock were a function of beta and size according to following formula:

$$\bar{R}_j = R_f + .08\beta_j - .002(\text{size decile})$$

   where size is the decile in which security j falls with respect to total market capitalization, 10 being the largest. The risk-free rate is presently 9 percent.

   a. Tobias Tire Company has a beta of 1.10 and is in the second decile with respect to market capitalization size. What is its expected return?

   b. Cooper Chemical Company has a beta of 1.12 and is in the ninth decile with respect to size. What is the expected return of this company's stock? Why does it differ from that of Tobias Tire Company?

4. Fullerton-Bristol, Inc., has a beta of .90, a market price per share of $27.20, and earnings per share of $3.40. The risk-free rate is 6 percent, the price/earnings ratio for the market portfolio is 12 times, and Fullerton-Bristol is in the sixth decile with respect to market capitalization (10 is the largest). Suppose the expected return for a security is expressed as

$$\bar{R}_j = R_f + .08(\beta_j) - .001(\text{P/E}_j - \text{P/E}_m) - .002(\text{size})$$

   where P/E_m is the price/earnings ratio of the market portfolio and size is the decile of market capitalization. What is the stock's expected return?

5. Leeny Kelly Company's stock is related to the following factors with respect to actual return:

$$R_j = a + .8(F_1) + 1.2(F_2) + .3(F_3) + e_j$$

a. Suppose that the a term for the stock is 14 percent and that for the period the unanticipated change in factor 1 is 5 percent, factor 2 minus 2 percent, and factor 3 minus 10 percent. If the error term is zero, what would be the stock's actual return for the period?

b. Now suppose that we wish to solve for the expected return. If the risk-free rate is 8 percent, $\lambda_1 = 4$ percent, $\lambda_2 = 2$ percent, and $\lambda_3 = 6$ percent, what is the stock's expected return?

6. Security returns are generated by factors according to the following formula:

$$R_j = R_f + b_{1j} F_1 + b_{2j} f_2 + b_{3j} f_3 + e_j$$

Assume $R_f = 5$ percent, $F_1 = 6$ percent, $F_2 = 7$ percent, and $F_3 = 8$ percent. Assume also the following for two securities, X and Y:

$b_{1x} = .10$	$b_{1y} = .80$
$b_{2x} = 1.20$	$b_{2y} = .20$
$b_{3x} = .90$	$b_{3y} = .40$

What actual return would you forecast for the two securities?

7. Based on their present share prices and expected future dividends, Bosco Enterprises, Target Markets, Inc., and Selby Glass Company have expected returns of 16 percent, 14 percent, and 20 percent, respectively. The risk-free rate presently is 7 percent. Required returns on investment are determined according to the following factor model:

$$(E)\bar{R}_j = \lambda_0 + .12(b_{1j}) + .04(b_{2j})$$

The reaction coefficients for the companies are as follows:

	b_{1j}	b_{2j}
Bosco	.80	.20
Target	.10	1.10
Selby	1.20	.40

a. Which securities are overpriced in the sense of the required return being more than the expected return? underpriced?

b. As an arbitrager, what would you do? How long would you do it for?

8. The expected return for Sawyer Coding Company's stock is described by the Roll-Ross model. Sawyer's reactions coefficients are as follows: $b_1 = 1.4$, $b_2 = 2.0$, $b_3 = 0.7$, $b_4 = 1.2$, and $b_5 = 0.8$. Using the lambda estimates of Chen, Roll, and Ross, what is the expected monthly return for this security?

9. How does the arbitrage pricing theory (APT) differ from the capital asset pricing model (CAPM)? What are the similarities of the two models?

SOLUTIONS
TO SELF-CORRECTION
PROBLEMS

1. a. $R_{rrc} = .08 + 1.25(.15 - .08) = 16.75\%$
   b. The dividend yield for Rubinstein Robotics Corporation is $1.28/$32 = 4.00\%.

   $$R_{rrc} = .08 + .075(1.25) + .1(.04 - .08) = 16.98\%$$

The equation implies that dividend income is not as attractive as capital gains. Therefore, a higher return is required for the high-dividend-paying stock. In this case, dividend yield is less than the risk-free rate, so the effect is negative.

The price/earnings ratio of the stock is $32/$2.56 = 12.5 times.

$$R_{rrc} = .08 + .075(1.25) - .006(12.5 - 11.0) = 16.48\%$$

A higher than average price/earnings ratio implies an expectation of a lower expected return than the CAPM without extension would predict.

2. The expected return for Hendershott Hinge stock using a factor model is

$$(E)\overline{R}_j = .07 + (.6).06 + (1.3).03 = 14.5\%$$

3.

$$(E)\overline{R}_{ml} = .06 + .09(.5) - .03(.4) + .04(1.2) = 14.1\%$$

$$(E)\overline{R}_{be} = .06 + .09(.7) - .03(.8) + .04(.2) = 10.7\%$$

Portfolio expected return where the two investments are equally weighted:

$$(E)\overline{R}_p = .5(14.1\%) + .5(10.7\%) = 12.4\%$$

Portfolio expected return with one-third invested in Montana Leather Company and two-thirds in Bozeman Enterprises:

$$(E)\overline{R}_p = .333(14.1\%) + .667(10.7\%) = 11.83\%$$

The return may be higher or lower because we cannot reduce unsystematic risk to zero with so small a portfolio.

CHAPTER 4
Multi Variable and
Factor Valuation

SELECTED REFERENCES

Berry, Michael A., Edwin Burmeister, and Marjorie B. McElroy, "Sorting Out Risks Using Known APT Factors," *Financial Analysts Journal*, 44 (March–April 1988), 29–42.

Bower, Dorothy H., Richard S. Bower, and Dennis E. Logue, "Arbitrage Pricing Theory and Utility Stock Returns," *Journal of Finance*, 39 (September 1984), 1041–54.

Chen, Nai-Fu, "Some Empirical Tests of the Theory of Arbitrage Pricing," *Journal of Finance*, 38 (December 1983), 1194.

———, Richard Roll, and Stephen A. Ross, "Economic Forces and the Stock Market," *Journal of Business*, 59 (July 1986), 383–403.

Cho, D. Chinhyung, Cheol S. Eun, and Lemma W. Senbet, "International Arbitrage Pricing Theory: An Empirical Investigation," *Journal of Finance*, 41 (June 1986), 313–29.

Connor, Gregory, and Robert A. Korajczyk, "Risk and Return in an Equilibrium APT: Application of a New Test Methodology," *Journal of Financial Economics*, 21 (September 1988), 255–90.

———, "An Intertemporal Equilibrium Beta Pricing Model," *Review of Financial Studies*, 2, No. 3 (1989), 373–92.

Dybvig, Philip H., and Stephen A. Ross, "Yes, the APT Is Testable," *Journal of Finance*, 40 (September 1985), 1173–88.

Friend, Irwin, Yoram Landskroner, and Etienne Losq, "The Demand for Risky Assets under Uncertain Inflation," *Journal of Finance*, 31 (December 1976), 1287–98.

Haugen, Robert A., *Modern Investment Theory*, 2d ed. Englewood Cliffs, NJ: Prentice Hall, 1990, Chaps. 8 and 9.

Keim, Donald B., "The CAPM and Equity Return Regularities," *Financial Analysts Journal*, 42 (May–June 1986), 19–34.

Lehmann, Bruce N., and David M. Modest, "The Empirical Foundations of the Arbitrage Pricing Theory," *Journal of Financial Economics*, 21 (September 1988), 213–54.

Litzenberger, Robert H., and Krishna Ramaswamy, "The Effect of Personal Taxes and Dividends on Capital Asset Prices," *Journal of Financial Economics*, 7 (June 1979), 163–95.

Reinganum, Marc R., "The Arbitrage Pricing Theory: Some Empirical Results," *Journal of Finance*, 36 (May 1981), 313–22.

ROLL, RICHARD, and STEPHEN A. ROSS, "An Empirical Investigation of the Arbitrage Pricing Theory," *Journal of Finance*, 35 (December 1980), 1073–1103.

——, "The Arbitrage Pricing Theory Approach to Strategic Portfolio Planning," *Financial Analysts Journal*, 40 (May–June 1984), 14–26.

ROSS, STEPHEN A., "The Arbitrage Theory of Capital Asset Pricing," *Journal of Economic Theory*, 13 (December 1976), 341–60.

SHARPE, WILLIAM F., and GORDON J. ALEXANDER, *Investments*, 4th ed. Englewood Cliffs, NJ: Prentice Hall, 1990, Chaps. 8 and 9.

TRZCINKA, CHARLES, "On the Number of Factors in the Arbitrage Pricing Model," *Journal of Finance*, 41 (June 1986), 347–68.

WEI, K. C. JOHN, "An Asset-Pricing Theory Unifying the CAPM and APT," *Journal of Finance*, 43 (September 1988), 881–92.

5

VALUATION FROM A RELATIVE STANDPOINT

So far, our valuation of a firm's stock has been based on its expected stream of dividends and on its risk to investors with diversified portfolios. That valuation was specific—absolute. Now we are going to make relative evaluations of options, contracts that give the holder the right but not the obligation to buy or sell a designated security at a specific price.

Amid the variety of option contracts, the most prevalent is the *call option*, which gives the holder the right to buy a security at a specified *exercise price*. We might have a call option to buy one share of ABC Corporation's common stock at $10 through December 21 of the current year. Thus, the option has an exercise price of $10 through December 21, which is the expiration date. In contrast, a *put option* gives the holder the right to sell a share of stock at a specified price up to the expiration date; it is the mirror image of a call option. More complex options may involve combinations of the call and put options. With so many options being traded, active option markets developed. The Chicago Board Options Exchange was the first of these, and it is the largest.

We are restricting our discussion to call options because other options are not relevant to our needs in later chapters. A basic understanding of option valuation involves concepts that may be applied to financial theory and the valuation of certain financial instruments. The number of those applications has grown in recent years and now includes the valuation of convertible bonds, warrants, callable bonds, the equity and debt values of the firm, rights offerings, executive stock options, loan guarantees, standby agreements, and insurance contracts. These growing applications make option valuation highly pertinent to financial management.

EXPIRATION DATE VALUE OF AN OPTION

A *European option* can be exercised only at its expiration date; an *American option* can be exercised at any time up to and including the expiration date. We shall begin by assuming that we have a European option on a stock that does not pay dividends. Later, we relax both assumptions.

The value of the call option at its expiration date is simply

$$V_o = \max (V_s - E, 0)$$

where V_s is the market price of one share of stock, E is the exercise price of the option, and max means the maximum value of $V_s - E$ or zero, whichever is greater. To illustrate the formula, suppose one share of Selby Corporation's stock is $25 at the expiration date, and the exercise price of a call option is $15. Therefore, the value of the option is $25 − $15 = $10. Note that the value of the option is determined solely by the value of the stock less the exercise price; however, the option cannot have a negative value. When the value of the stock is below the exercise price, the value of the option is zero. If the stock value in the example above were $12, the value of the option would not be $12 − $15 = −$3, but rather, it would be zero.

In Fig. 5-1, the value of the stock is on the horizontal axis, and the value of the option at the expiration date is on the vertical axis. When the value of the stock exceeds the exercise price, the option has a positive value and increases in a linear one-to-one manner with increases in the value of the stock. When the value of the stock equals or is less than the exercise price, the option has a value of zero.

To determine whether an investor holding an option gains or loses, we must take account of the price, or premium, paid for the option. If we disregard, for the moment, the time value of money and transactions costs, the investor's gain or loss is simply the value of the option at the expiration date less the price paid for it. To break even, the value of the stock must exceed the exercise price by an amount equal to the premium paid for the option. This is illustrated in the top panel in Fig. 5-2. Here we see that the investor suffers a loss until the stock rises in price to the point where it equals the exercise price of the option plus the premium. After that, as the stock rises in price, the holder of the option gains.

For the writer, or seller, of the option, the opposite picture emerges. In the lower panel of the figure, the writer receives the premium and realizes a gain as long as the value of the stock at the expiration date is less than the exercise price plus the premium. If it is more, the seller loses, and losses deepen with increases in the value of the stock. In options, then, the expiration date gain or loss to the investor and to the writer of the option are mirror images of

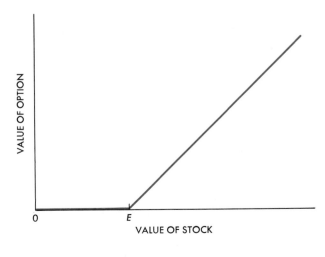

FIGURE 5-1

Value of option at expiration

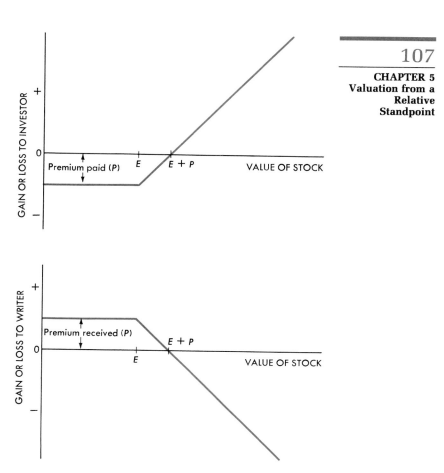

FIGURE 5-2
Gain or loss of option to
the investor and to the
writer of the option

each other. It is a zero-sum game where one can gain only at the expense of
the other.

VALUATION WITH
ONE PERIOD TO EXPIRATION:
A GENERAL CONSIDERATION

Consider now the option with one period to expiration. Again we assume a
European option, which can be exercised only at the expiration date. While
we do not know the value of the stock at the expiration date, we assume that
we are able to formulate probabilistic beliefs about its value one period hence.

Figure 5-1 illustrates the theoretical relationship between the now, beginning of period price of a share of common stock and the price of an option
to buy that stock. The 45° line represents the theoretical value of the option. It
is simply the current stock price less the exercise price of the option. When
the price of the stock is less than the exercise price of the option, the option
has a zero theoretical value; when more, it has a theoretical value on the line.

As long as there is some time to expiration, it is possible for the market
value of an option to be greater than its theoretical value. The reason for this
is the very nature of the contract: It is an option that affords the holder
flexibility with respect to the purchase of stock. Suppose the current market

price of ABC Corporation's stock is $10, which is equal to the exercise price. Theoretically, the option has no value; however, if there is some probability that the price of the stock will exceed $10 before expiration, the option has a positive value, inasmuch as it *may* permit the holder to exercise it advantageously. Suppose further that the option has 30 days to expiration and that there is a .3 probability that the stock will have a market price of $5 per share at the end of 30 days, .4 that it will be $10, and .3 that it will be $15. The expected value of the option at the end of 30 days is thus

$$0(.3) + 0(.4) + (\$15 - \$10)(.3) = \$1.50$$

It is therefore possible for an option to have a positive value even if it is on stock valued less than or equal to the exercise price. Because the option cannot go below zero in value, even when the stock price less the exercise price is negative, the option is frequently worth more than its theoretical value. How much more depends in part on the time to expiration. Figure 5-3 illustrates the general relationship between stock prices and option prices for various terms to expiration.[1]

BOUNDARIES FOR OPTION VALUATION

The highest value the option can take is the value of the stock, represented by the 45° line X. This value can be reached, presumably, only if the option has a very long time to expiration, perhaps forever, and if the option is not expected to be exercised until far into the future. Under these circumstances, the present value of the exercise price to be paid in the future approaches zero. As a result, the value of the option approaches the value of the associated stock. The lowest value the option can take, of course, is its theoretical value, represented in the figure by zero up to the exercise price and by line Y for values of the stock greater than the exercise price. One might think

[1] Perhaps the first to draw attention to this type of presentation was Paul A. Samuelson, "A Rational Theory of Warrant Pricing," *Industrial Management Review*, 6 (Spring 1965), 103–32.

FIGURE 5-3

Relation between stock price and option price for various expiration dates

of the theoretical value line as representing the values of an option with only a moment to expiration. Thus, lines X and Y constitute the boundaries for the value of the option in relation to the value of the associated stock.

For most options, however, the relationship lies between these two boundaries. In general, it can be described by a convex relationship in which the value of the option commands the greatest premium over its theoretical value at the exercise price, and the premium declines with increases in the value of the stock beyond that point. If the stock price is less than the exercise price in the figure, the option is said to be trading "out of the money." The farther to the left, the deeper the option is out of the money, and the less likelihood it will have value at the expiration date. If the current stock price exceeds the exercise price, the option is said to be trading "in the money," whereas if it equals the exercise price, the option is trading "at the money."

TIME TO EXPIRATION AND INTEREST RATE

In general, the longer the expiration date, the greater the value of the option relative to its theoretical value. One reason for this is that there is more time in which the option may have value. Moreover, the greater the time to expiration, the lower the present value of the exercise price to be paid in the future; and this, too, enhances the value of the option, all other things staying the same. As the expiration date of an option approaches, however, the relationship between the option value and the stock value becomes more convex. In Fig. 5-3, line 1 represents an option with a shorter time to expiration than that for line 2; and line 2, an option with a shorter time to expiration than that for line 3.

Another feature of option valuation is the time value of money. When you acquire a stock by means of an option, you make an initial down payment in the price you pay for the option. Your "final" payment is not due until you exercise the option some time in the future. This delay (to the time you pay the exercise price) is more valuable the higher interest rates are in the market. Thus, an option will be more valuable the longer the time to expiration and the higher the interest rate.

VOLATILITY OF THE STOCK

Usually the most important factor in the valuation of options is the price volatility of the associated security. More specifically, the greater the possibility of extreme outcomes, the greater the value of the option to the holder, all other things the same. The greater the volatility, the higher the market line curve in Figure 5-3. If a stock is not likely to change much in price, an option on it is worth little, and the curve will be very near the lower boundary, Y. With volatility, the option will be valuable. We may, at the beginning of a period, be considering options on the two stocks shown in Table 5-1. The expected value of stock price at the end of the period is the same for both stocks:

TABLE 5-1
Probability distributions of two stocks at the end of the period

Probability of occurrence	.10	.25	.30	.25	.10
Price of stock A	$30	$36	$40	$44	$50
Price of stock B	$20	$30	$40	$50	$60

$40. For stock B, however, there is a much larger dispersion of possible outcomes. Suppose the exercise prices of options to purchase stock A and stock B at the end of the period are the same, $38. Thus, the two stocks have the same expected values at the end of the period, and the options have the same exercise price.

The expected value of the option for stock A at the end of the period, however, is

$$\text{Option } A = 0(.10) + 0(.25) + (\$40 - \$38)(.30) + (\$44 - \$38)(.25)$$
$$+(\$50 - \$38)(.10)$$
$$= \$3.30$$

whereas that for stock B is

$$\text{Option } B = 0(.10) + 0(.25) + (\$40 - \$38)(.30) + (\$50 - \$38)(.25)$$
$$+(\$60 - \$38)(.10)$$
$$= \$5.80$$

Thus, the greater dispersion of possible outcomes for stock B leads to a greater expected value of option price on the expiration date. In turn, this is due to the fact that the value of an option cannot be less than zero. As a result, the greater the dispersion, the greater the magnitude of favorable outcomes as measured by the stock price minus the exercise price. Increases in the volatility of the stock therefore increase the magnitude of favorable outcomes for the option buyer and, hence, increase the value of the option.

This is illustrated in Figure 5-4, where two stocks with different end-of-period share price distributions are shown. The exercise price, E, is the same, so the lower boundary for expiration-date option values is also the same. This is shown by the dark "hockey stick" line at the bottom of the figure. The probability distribution of end-of-period share price is wider for stock B than it is for stock A, reflecting greater volatility. As stock B provides a greater chance for a big payoff, its option is worth more.

We shall see later in the chapter that the value of an option does not depend on the expected value of the stock price. Suppose there are two stocks

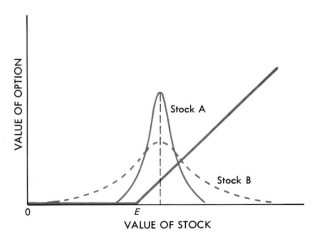

FIGURE 5-4
**Volatility and option values
for two stocks**

with equal volatility and option features, but one stock has a greater expected future value than the other. Despite the higher expected return on this stock, the option values for the two are the same. It is the variance, or volatility, of the stock price that is important. This statement is a fundamental proposition of option valuation, and it will permeate our application of this concept to various problems in financial management. Our example has been kept purposely simple in looking at the value of the option at the end of the period. The determination of value at the beginning of the period involves the present value of outcomes at the end of the period and is more complicated. We shall explore this determination in the sections that follow; however, the fundamental importance of the volatility of security price in the valuation of options continues to hold as in our example.

To summarize where we are up to now, the value, or price, of a call option will change as follows when the variables listed below increase:

INCREASE IN VARIABLE	OPTION VALUE CHANGE
Stock volatility	Increase
Time to expiration	Increase
Interest rate	Increase
Exercise price	Decrease
Current stock price	Increase

Keeping these relationships in mind will help us as we probe deeper into option valuation.

THE USE OF A HEDGED POSITION AND MARKET EQUILIBRIUM

Having two related financial assets—a stock and the option on that stock—we can set up a risk-free hedged position. In this way, price movements in one of the financial assets will be offset by opposite price movements in the other. Consider again a European option, 6 months to expiration, on a stock that pays no dividend. Moreover, assume that there are no transaction costs involved in buying and selling stock or in buying or writing options. In addition to the return on the option and the return on the stock, the opportunity cost of funds is important when it comes to establishing a hedged position. We assume this cost is the risk-free rate, denoted by r, perhaps the rate of return on Treasury bills.

AN ILLUSTRATION OF HEDGING

Consider now a time-branching process where at the end of the 6-month period there are two possible values for the common stock. One value is higher than the current value of the stock, and it is denoted by uV_s. The other is a lower value, denoted by dV_s. Because V_s represents the current value of the stock, u represents one plus the percentage increase in value of the stock from the beginning of the period to the end, and d represents one minus the percentage decrease in the value of the stock.[2] Associated with the upward movement of the stock is a probability of q, and with the downward movement, a probability of $1 - q$.

Figure 5-5 gives some numbers and probabilities to these symbols. There is a two-thirds probability that the stock will increase in value by 20 percent and a one-third probability that it will decline in value by 10 percent. The expected value of stock price at the end of the period is $55, which, on the basis of a $50 investment, represents a return of 10 percent. Assume now that the risk-free rate, r, is 5 percent for the 6-month period and that the exercise price of the option is $50. With this information, we see in the lower right-hand column of the figure that the value of the option at the end of the period is either $10 or 0, depending on whether the stock rises or falls in value.

In this situation, a hedged position can be established by buying the stock (holding it long) and by writing options. In our example, the idea is to establish a riskless hedged position. The appropriate hedge ratio of stock to options (also called the option delta) can be determined by

$$\text{Hedge ratio} = \frac{uV_o - dV_o}{uV_s - dV_s} = \frac{\$10 - 0}{\$60 - \$45} = \frac{2}{3}$$

where uV_o is the end-of-period value of the option when the stock price, uV_s,

[2] In order that pure arbitrage opportunities not exist, u must exceed and d must be less than one plus the risk-free rate. This example is based in part on John Cox, "A Discrete Time, Discrete State Option Pricing Model" (unpublished teaching note, Graduate School of Business, Stanford University).

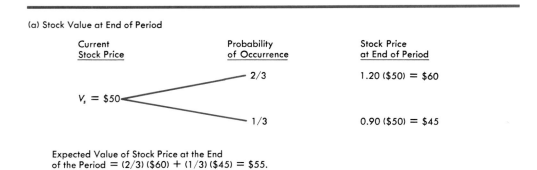

(a) Stock Value at End of Period

Current Stock Price	Probability of Occurrence	Stock Price at End of Period
$V_s = \$50$	2/3	1.20 ($50) = $60
	1/3	0.90 ($50) = $45

Expected Value of Stock Price at the End of the Period = (2/3) ($60) + (1/3) ($45) = $55.

(b) Option Value at End of Period

Stock Price at End of Period	Probability of Occurrence	Option Value at End of Period
$60	2/3	Max. ($60 − $50, 0) = $10
$45	1/3	Max. ($45 − $50, 0) = 0

Expected Value of Option Value at End of the Period = (2/3) ($10) + (1/3)(0) = $6.667

FIGURE 5-5
Hedged position example

is $60 at the end of the period, and dV_o is the value of the option when the stock price, dV_s, is $45 at the end of the period. This hedge ratio means that the person who wishes to hedge should purchase two shares of stock (the long position) and write three options (the short position).

By undertaking such transactions, the end-of-period values for the two future states will be[3]

STOCK PRICE AT END OF PERIOD	VALUE OF LONG POSITION IN STOCK	VALUE OF SHORT POSITION IN OPTION	VALUE OF COMBINED HEDGED POSITION
$60	2($60) = $120	−3($10) = −$30	$90
45	2($45) = $ 90	−3(0) = 0	90

We see that when the stock price at the end of the period is $60, the value of two shares of stock is $120. However, we must subtract from this value the negative value of our short position in options of $30 to get the overall value of our hedged position. When the stock price is $45, two shares are worth $90, and in this case there is no loss on the short position. Therefore, the overall position is perfectly hedged in the sense of providing the same value at the end of the period, regardless of the stock price outcome.

DETERMINING THE VALUE OF THE OPTION

The return on this hedged position depends on the value of the option, or the premium, at the beginning of the period. Since the hedged position is riskless, in efficient financial markets we would expect the return on this position to equal the risk-free rate, or 5 percent per 6-month period. We know that the ending value of the hedged position is $90 and that the investment in the two shares of stock at the beginning of the period is $100. The overall investment in the hedged position at the beginning of the period is $100 less the price received on the three options that are written. In other words, the short position results in a cash inflow, whereas the long position results in a cash outflow. Our concern is with the net position.

The value of the option at the beginning of the period, which must prevail if the overall return is to be 5 percent per 6-month period, can be determined by solving the following equation for V_{oB}:

$$[\$100 - 3(V_{oB})]1.05 = \$90$$

$$3.15V_{oB} = \$105 - 90$$

$$V_{oB} = \frac{\$15}{3.15}$$

$$V_{oB} = \$4.762$$

Thus, the overall investment in the hedged position at the beginning of the

---

[3] Again we have assumed the absence of transaction costs.

period is $100 − 3($4.762) = $85.714. The return on this hedged position is ($90 − $85.714)/$85.714 = 5 percent, or the risk-free rate. In other words, the return on the hedged position is the same as that which could be realized by investing $85.714 in a risk-free asset. As both investments are risk free, they should promise the same rate of return.

In summary, the option should be priced so that when it is combined with the stock in a hedged position, the return on the position equals the risk-free rate. To the extent that excess returns are available on a fully hedged position, people will have an incentive to take such positions. The impact of their transactions on relative prices will drive out any excess returns that might be earned. As a result, prices will adjust until the return on the hedged position is the risk-free rate and the option is neither overpriced nor underpriced. In the Appendix to this chapter, we show market equilibration across call options, shares of stock, and put options, employing what is known as the put-call parity theorem. This should give the interested reader a better understanding of how arbitrage works to bring about market equilibrium.

So far, we have worked with simple examples to provide a basic understanding of option pricing. A number of restrictive assumptions were imposed, and the derivation of the option's value was relevant for only the example presented. In the next section, we consider a more exacting option valuation framework.

THE BLACK-SCHOLES OPTION MODEL

In a seminal paper, Fischer Black and Myron Scholes developed a precise model for determining the equilibrium value of an option.[4] They then went on to observe that the option pricing concepts can be used to value other contingent claims. In particular, the model provides rich insight into the valuation of debt relative to equity. This application and others are taken up later in the book, after we have the foundations provided in this chapter. The Black-Scholes model has been extended and refined in major ways, and new applications are unfolding. The model has both theoretical importance for valuing contingent claims and practical importance for identifying overvalued and undervalued options in the market.

THE MODEL IN GENERAL

A number of assumptions are in order before we can discuss the model:

1. Only European options are considered, that is, options that can be exercised only at expiration.
2. There are no transaction costs. Options and stocks are infinitely divisible, and information is available to all without cost.
3. No imperfections exist in writing an option or selling a stock short.
4. The short-term interest rate is known and constant throughout the duration of the option contract. Market participants can both borrow and lend at this rate.
5. The stock pays no dividend.

[4] "The Pricing of Options and Corporate Liabilities," *Journal of Political Economy*, 81 (May–June 1973), 637–54.

6. Stock prices behave in a manner consistent with a random walk in continuous time.
7. The probability distribution of stock returns over an instant of time is normal.
8. The variance of the return is constant over the life of the option contract and is known to market participants.

Given these assumptions, we can determine the equilibrium value of an option. Should the actual price of the option differ from that given by the model, we could establish a riskless hedged position and earn a return in excess of the short-term interest rate in the manner illustrated in the previous section. As arbitragers entered the scene, the excess return would eventually be driven out and the price of the option would equal that value given by the model.

To illustrate a hedged position, suppose the appropriate relationship between the option and the stock of XYZ Corporation were that shown in Fig. 5-6. Suppose further that the current market price of the stock were $20 and the price of the option $7. At $20 a share, the slope of the line in Fig. 5-6 is one-half. A hedged position could be undertaken by buying a share of stock for $20 and writing two options at $7 each. The "net money" invested in this position is $20 − 2($7) = $6.

This combination of holding one share of stock long and two options short leaves us essentially hedged with respect to risk. If the stock drops slightly in value, the value of the short position goes up by approximately an equal amount. We say *approximately* because with changes in the price of the common and with changes in time, the ideal hedge ratio changes. With a stock price increase, for example, the slope of the line in Fig. 5-6 increases. Therefore, fewer options would need to be written. If the stock price declines, the slope decreases and more options must be written to maintain a hedge. As a general rule, the higher the stock price relative to the exercise price, the less risky the option and the fewer options that must be used in a hedge. In addition to stock price changes, the actual value line in Figure 5-6 will shift downward as time goes on and the expiration date approaches. Thus, one's position must be continually adjusted for changes in the stock price and for changes in time if a riskless hedged position is to be maintained.

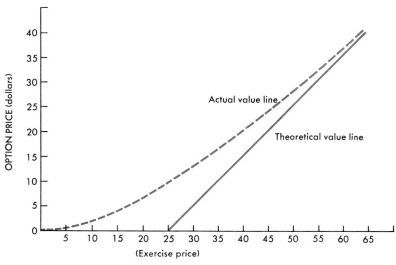

FIGURE 5-6

Relation between the option price and the stock price for XYZ Corporation

In this context, the equilibrium value of an option, V_o, that entitles the holder to buy one share of stock is shown by Black and Scholes to be

$$V_o = V_s N(d_1) - \frac{E}{e^{rt}} N(d_2) \qquad (5\text{-}1)$$

where V_s = the current price of the stock
$\qquad E$ = the exercise price of the option
$\qquad e$ = 2.71828, the base of natural logarithms
$\qquad r$ = the short-term annual interest rate continuously compounded
$\qquad t$ = the length of time in years to the expiration of the option
$\qquad N(d)$ = The value of the cumulative normal density function

$$d_1 = \frac{\ln (V_s/E) + [r + \frac{1}{2}(\sigma^2)]t}{\sigma \sqrt{t}}$$

$$d_2 = \frac{\ln (V_s/E) + [r - \frac{1}{2}(\sigma^2)]t}{\sigma \sqrt{t}}$$

$\ln$ = the natural logarithm
σ = the standard deviation of the annual rate of return on the stock continuously compounded

The important implication of this formula is that the value of the option is a function of the short-term interest rate, of the time to expiration, and of the variance rate of return on the stock, but it is not a function of the expected return on the stock. The value of the option in Eq. (5-1) increases with the increase of either or all of the terms: for duration to expiration of the option, t, for the variance rate, σ^2, and for the short-term interest rate, r. The reasons for these relationships were discussed earlier in the chapter. Of the three factors affecting the value of the option, however, the short-term interest rate generally has the least impact. With increases in t, r, and σ^2 in Eq. (5-1), the value of the option approaches the value of a share of stock as a limit.[5]

Given the valuation equation for options, Black and Scholes derive the ratio of shares of stock to options necessary to maintain a fully hedged position. It is shown to be $N(d_1)$, which was defined earlier. Thus, the Black-Scholes model permits the quantification of the various factors that affect the value of an option.[6]

---

[5] Black and Scholes, "Pricing of Options and Corporate Liabilities," p. 644.

[6] The option pricing model can be integrated with the capital asset pricing model. From Chapter 3, we know that the expected excess return for a stock is $R_s - R_f = \beta_s(R_m - R_f)$, where R_s is the expected return on the stock, R_f is the risk-free rate, R_m is the expected return on the market portfolio, and β_s is the beta of the stock. If we assume that the short-term interest rate in the option pricing model is the same as R_f, the expected excess return for an option on the stock can be expressed as

$$R_o - R_f = \left(\frac{V_s}{V_o} \frac{\partial V_o}{\partial V_s} \right)(R_s - R_f)$$

where R_o is the expected return on the option, V_s is the value of the stock, and V_o is the value of the option. Combining these two equations, we have

$$R_o - R_f = \left(\frac{V_s}{V_o} \frac{\partial V_o}{\partial V_s} \right)\beta_s(R_m - R_f)$$

Therefore, the beta of the option is

$$\left(\frac{V_s}{V_o} \frac{\partial V_o}{\partial V_s} \right)\beta_s$$

As the stock price changes, so does the beta of the option.

SOLVING THE FORMULA

In solving the formula, we know four of the five variables: the current stock price, the time of expiration of the option, the exercise price, and the short-term interest rate. The key unknown, then, is the standard deviation of the stock price. Black and Scholes assume that the stock's continuously compounded rate of return is normally distributed with constant variance.[7] The usual approach to the problem is to use the recent past volatility of the stock as a proxy for its volatility during the life of the option. We might use weekly observations of stock prices over the last year and derive the annualized standard deviation of the natural logarithm of price relatives.[8] There are other ways to estimate volatility, but we will not get into them as they are beyond the scope of this chapter. The reader interested in more detail is referred elsewhere.[9]

To illustrate the use of the Black-Scholes option pricing formula, suppose that on the basis of an analysis of past volatility we found the standard deviation of the stock's continuously compounded return to be .40. By referring to a financial newspaper, we are able to look up the other four terms necessary to solve the option pricing formula. Suppose we find the following:

Stock price, V_s = $30

Exercise price option, E = $28

Short-term annual rate of interest
   continuously compounded, r = .10

Time to expiration, t = .50 (one-half year)

Solving first for d_1 and d_2 we obtain

$$d_1 = \frac{\ln (30/28) + [.10 + 1/2(.40)^2].50}{.40\sqrt{.50}} = \frac{.158993}{.282843} = .562$$

$$d_2 = \frac{\ln (30/28) + [.10 - 1/2(.40)^2].50}{.40\sqrt{.50}} = \frac{.078993}{.282843} = .279$$

The expression $\ln (30/28)$ can be solved either by using a calculator having such a function or by looking it up in a natural log table. In our example, $\ln (30/28) = .068993$.

In Eq. (5-1), $N(d_1)$ and $N(d_2)$ are the probabilities that a random variable with a standardized normal distribution will take on values less than d_1 and less than d_2. With the bell-shaped normal distribution, slightly over two-thirds of the distribution falls within one standard deviation on either side of the mean, 95 percent within two standard deviations, and 99.7 percent within

[7] Although this assumption is open to question, solving the problem without a stationarity assumption is exceedingly complex. The valuation formula is very sensitive to the standard deviation employed as an estimate of the volatility of the stock.

[8] A *price relative* is simply the stock price this week divided by the stock price last week. If the stock price this week is $33 and the price last week was $31.50, the price relative is $33/31.50 = 1.04762. The natural logarithm of this number is .04652, and it can be found in a natural log table or on a calculator equipped with this function. Given a listing of 52 price relatives and their natural logarithms, we can easily derive the standard deviation (52 weeks to the year). To annualize this weekly standard deviation, it must be multiplied by the square root of 52.

[9] See Mark Rubinstein and John C. Cox, *Option Markets* (Englewood Cliffs, NJ: Prentice Hall, 1985), Chap. 6; and John Hull, *Options, Futures, and Other Derivative Securities* (Englewood Cliffs, NJ: Prentice Hall, 1989), Chaps. 3–5.

three standard deviations. In Table C at the end of the book, an abbreviated table for the normal distribution tells us the area of the distribution that is so many standard deviations to the left or to the right of the mean. A d_1 of .562 lies between the standard deviations of .55 and .60 shown in the table, corresponding to .2912 and .2743 areas of the distribution respectively. Interpolating, we come up with

$$.2912 - \left(\frac{.12}{.50}\right)(.2912 - .2743) = .287$$

This represents the area of a normal distribution that is .562 or more standard deviations greater than the mean. To determine the area of the normal distribution that is less than .562 standard deviations, we merely subtract .287 from one.[10] Therefore

$$N(d_1) = N(.562) = 1 - .287 = .713$$

For the d_2 of .279, we see in Table C that it lies between the standard deviations of .25 and .30. Interpolating here, we obtain

$$.4013 - \left(\frac{.29}{.50}\right)(.4013 - .3821) = .390$$

Therefore

$$N(d_2) = N(.279) = 1 - .390 = .610$$

Given $N(d_1)$ and $N(d_2)$ together with the information on the stock price, the exercise price, the interest rate, and the length of time to expiration of the option, we are able to compute the equilibrium value of the option using Eq. (5-1). For our example problem,[11]

$$V_o = \$30(.713) - \frac{\$28}{e^{(.10)(.50)}}(.610) = \$5.14$$

Thus, the Black-Scholes option pricing model suggests that an option to buy one share of stock having the characteristics specified is worth $5.14. Rather than solve for this value by hand, computer programs are available that will do it for you with dispatch. One such program can be found in Chapter 12 of the supplement *Financial Management Computer Applications* by James C. Van Horne and Stuart B. Van Horne.

The value of $N(d_1)$ tells us the appropriate hedge ratio to employ. In our example, the ratio is .713. This means that a movement in the stock price will be accompanied by a .713 movement in the option price. To hedge, the individual should purchase .713 shares of stock for each option that is written.

---

[10] If the value of d_1 were negative, we would be concerned with the area of the distribution that was to the left of the standard deviation. As a result, we would not subtract it from one. It is only with positive values that we subtract the area of the normal distribution from one.

[11] In the equation, $e = .271828$, as stated earlier. Many calculators have this function, which allows for easy solution of the problem. Without this help, we must resort to a table of natural logarithms.

With these proportions, price movements of the two financial assets will be offsetting. The equation above also tells us that if the actual market price is more or less than $5.14, it is over- or undervalued. However, caution is necessary in interpreting the results because our estimate of the stock's future volatility is based on its past volatility. This may or may not be an accurate proxy for the future. As the formula is quite sensitive to the standard deviation employed, caution is necessary in judging whether an option is over- or undervalued. In Table 5-2, Black-Scholes option values are shown for other assumptions concerning the standard deviation, stock price, exercise price, interest rate, and the time to expiration.

SOME REFINEMENTS

As previously mentioned, the hedge ratio of stocks and options must be adjusted as prices and volatility change. In theory, continuous adjustment is necessary to maintain a risk-free hedge. Such continuous changes do not occur in practice. There are delays in execution and there are transaction costs.

TABLE 5-2
Option prices from Black-Scholes equation for various parameter values
(price of underlying stock = $40)

STANDARD DEVIATION	EXERCISE PRICE	$r = 5\%$		
		$t = 1$ Month	$t = 4$ Months	$t = 7$ Months
.20	35	5.15	5.77	6.42
.20	40	1.00	2.18	3.02
.20	45	.02	.51	1.11
.30	35	5.22	6.26	7.19
.30	40	1.46	3.08	4.20
.30	45	0.16	1.26	2.24
.40	35	5.39	6.90	8.11
.40	40	1.92	3.99	5.38
.40	45	.42	2.11	3.44

$r = 10\%$			$r = 15\%$		
$t = 1$ Month	$t = 4$ Months	$t = 7$ Months	$t = 1$ Month	$t = 4$ Months	$t = 7$ Months
5.30	6.29	7.26	5.44	6.81	8.11
1.09	2.54	3.67	1.19	2.94	4.38
.03	.65	1.47	.03	.82	1.91
5.36	6.72	7.92	5.50	7.18	8.66
1.55	3.42	4.79	1.64	3.78	5.42
.18	1.45	2.66	.20	1.67	3.12
5.52	7.31	8.76	5.65	7.73	9.42
2.00	4.31	5.94	2.09	4.65	6.52
.45	2.33	3.87	.48	2.57	4.34

These factors must be weighted against the benefits. Most people who use the Black-Scholes model, or a similar one, adjust the hedge ratio every so often, perhaps once or twice a week. When prices are changing rapidly, more frequent adjustment is necessary than in a stable market period. In practice, one cannot obtain a perfect hedge, only approximate it.

With the Black-Scholes formula, we can estimate the volatility of a stock if we know the other variables. Assuming equilibration between the stock and options markets, the estimated variability of the stock can be backed out of the formula. In other words, if we know the market price of the stock, the market price of the option, the expiration and exercise price of the option, and the short-term interest rate, we can solve the formula for the standard deviation of return for the stock. In practice, much attention is paid to the variance assumption involved in the associated asset. In valuing an option or a contract with option features, often it will be prefaced by saying "value is based on a 23 percent standard deviation assumption," or something to this effect.

The Black-Scholes formula, extensions of it, and other formulas of the same general sort are widely used on Wall Street.[12] In recent years, the avenues for shifting risk have expanded enormously—options markets on stocks and fixed-income securities, futures markets on financial assets and commodities, and currency markets. With combinations of securities held outright, securities sold short, options contracts, futures contracts, and currency contracts, it is possible to derive myriad "synthetic" securities. With precision, the investment or financial manager can lay off the desired degree of risk. This can be done either directly or through an investment bank or other adviser. The development of options markets is an integral part of the risk-shifting movement described and the evolution of complex options strategies.

AMERICAN OPTIONS

In the preceding section, we assumed a European option on a stock paying no dividends and then proceeded to value it in a hypothetical example of the stock's volatility, its price, the exercise price of the option, the length of time to expiration, and the short-term interest rate. We now need to determine the effect on the value of an option when we drop the assumptions of a European option and no dividends.

An American option can be exercised by the holder any time up to the expiration date. Because the American option provides all the rights of a European option plus the ability to exercise it before the expiration date, its value must be at least that of an identical European option. In certain cases, it will be worth more; however, it has been demonstrated that an American option on a non-dividend-paying stock should not be exercised before the expiration date.[13] The holder gives up the option value as well as the time value of money in paying the exercise price early. Without early exercise, the American and European options will be priced the same if they are alike in all other

---

[12] For an excellent discussion of the assumptions inherent in the Black-Scholes model and various extensions to more realistic assumptions, see Fischer Black, "How to Use the Holes in Black-Scholes," *Journal of Applied Corporate Finance*, 1 (Winter 1989), 67–73.

[13] Robert C. Merton, "Rational Theory of Option Pricing," *Bell Journal of Economics*, 4 (Spring 1973), 142–45. With a non-dividend-paying stock, the value of a perpetual option will equal the value of the underlying stock.

respects. Only for options on dividend-paying stocks is the distinction between the European and the American option important. To this issue we
now turn.

THE EFFECT OF DIVIDENDS

A cash dividend on a common stock tends to lower the value of the option on that stock. The higher the dividend, the lower the option's value, all
other things staying the same. In essence, a cash dividend represents the partial liquidation of a company to which the stockholders, but not the option
holders, are entitled. With a complete liquidating dividend, the price of the
stock will go to zero, as will the price of the option. When a stock goes ex-
dividend,[14] the market price of the stock will drop by an amount somewhat
less than that of the dividend, depending on the tax effect.[15] The greater the
present value of cash dividends likely to be paid prior to the expiration of the
option, the lower its value, all other things staying the same. This relationship
is illustrated in Fig. 5-7. The curved lines represent actual option values for
different levels of dividend. The greater the dividend, as represented by a
higher number, the lower the value of the option relative to its theoretical
value, all other things staying the same.

A cash dividend may affect the timing in exercising an American option,
since there is an obvious advantage in buying the stock in time to receive the
dividend. The disadvantage in early exercise of the option is the opportunity
cost of the interest that would have been earned on the exercise price. Dividend and interest become a trade-off in choosing the optimal time to exercise
the option. One way to adjust for the presence of dividends in the Black-
Scholes option pricing model is to treat all expected future dividends up to
the expiration date as though they had been paid. The present value of these
dividends is subtracted from the current price of the stock. The option pricing

---

[14] In declaring a dividend, the board of directors specifies an ex-dividend date. At that date, the
stock trades ex-dividend in that investors who purchase it are not entitled to the declared dividend.

[15] See Chapter 12 for a discussion of the ex-dividend behavior of common stocks in relation to
taxes.

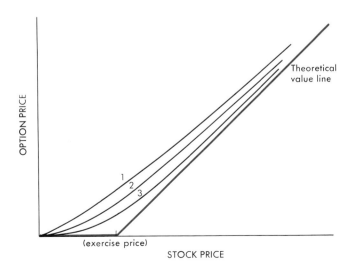

FIGURE 5-7

**Relation between stock
price and option price
for different levels of
dividend**

formula then is based on this adjusted price, as opposed to the actual price of the stock. This, of course, sidesteps the possibility of early exercise, which remains a problem.

Richard Roll, followed by Robert Geske and modified slightly by Robert E. Whaley, develops a formal model to deal with call options on stocks with known dividends.[16] Essentially, the model is a modification of the Black-Scholes model that incorporates the dividend, the time to the ex-dividend date, and the decline in stock price on this date as a proportion of the dividend. Empirical tests of the model show a lower prediction error for dividend-paying stocks, particularly where the dividend is large, than occurs with the Black-Scholes model adjusted by deducting the present value of dividend payment from the stock price.[17] However, there still is a tendency for the model to overestimate values of options written on high-variance stocks and underpredict values of options written on low-variance stocks as well as overestimate values for "in the money" options and underestimate values for "out of money" options.[18]

While the presence of cash dividends complicates the picture, the basic tenets of the Black-Scholes option pricing model continue to hold. For many options, the expiration date is relatively near, and the quarterly dividends likely to be paid on the stock before the option's expiration are not material. In situations of this sort, it may not be worthwhile to make a dividend adjustment, particularly if the next ex-dividend date is some time away. For applications of the model later in this book, no dividend adjustments will be made because our focus will be on the conceptual insights provided by the model.

DEBT AND OTHER OPTIONS

In addition to stock options, there are options on other securities. Rather than an option on a specific stock, one might prefer an *index option*. Here an option is written on a broad portfolio of stocks, such as Standard & Poor's 500-Stock Index or the New York Stock Exchange Index. The option written pertains to the level of stock prices in general. Another option is a *foreign currency option*. Here an option is written on the number of units of a foreign currency that a U.S. dollar will buy. It could be British pounds or German deutschemarks. This type of option is discussed in Chapter 26 when we take up international financial management. Finally, there are interest-rate options.

[16] Richard Roll, "An Analytic Formula for Unprotected American Call Options on Stocks with Known Dividends," *Journal of Financial Economics*, 5 (November 1977), 251–58; Robert Geske, "A Note on an Analytical Valuation Formula for Unprotected American Call Options on Stocks with Known Dividends," *Journal of Financial Economics*, 7 (December 1979), 375–80; and Robert E. Whaley, "On the Valuation of American Call Options on Stocks with Known Dividends," *Journal of Financial Economics*, 9 (June 1981), 207–11. See also Robert Geske and Kuldeep Shastri, "Valuation by Approximation: A Comparison of Alternative Option Valuation Techniques," *Journal of Financial and Quantitative Analysis*, 20 (March 1985), 45–71; and Robert E. Whaley, "On Valuing American Futures Options," *Financial Analysts Journal*, 42 (May–June 1986), 49–59.

[17] See William E. Sterk, "Comparative Performance of the Black-Scholes and Roll-Geske-Whaley Option Pricing Models," *Journal of Financial and Quantitative Analysis*, 18 (September 1983), 345–54. Also see Whaley, "On the Valuation of American Call Options," and Whaley, "Valuation of American Call Options on Dividend-Paying Stocks: Empirical Tests," *Journal of Financial Economics*, 10 (March 1982), 29–58.

[18] N. Bulent Gultekin, Richard J. Rogalski, and Seha Tinic, "Option Pricing Model Estimates: Some Empirical Results," *Financial Management*, 11 (Spring 1982), 58–69.

INTEREST-RATE OPTIONS

There are options on specific debt instruments as well as futures options on such instruments as Eurodollars, Treasury bills, Treasury notes, and Treasury bonds. A *futures contract* is a standardized agreement that calls for the delivery of a security, such as a Treasury bill, at some specified future date. If interest rates rise and security prices fall, the buyer of the contract loses and the writer of the contract gains, and vice versa. As futures prices tend to move in concert with prices on actual debt instruments, futures options are really a bet on interest-rate movements. If interest rates rise and security prices fall, the call option holder loses, whereas the put option holder gains, and vice versa. With a debt option, the potential loss is limited to the premium paid, just as with a stock option.

USE OF DEBT OPTIONS

Options are particularly suited to hedging risk in one direction. Consider a fixed-rate loan commitment by a financial institution. If interest rates rise, a high proportion of the commitments will be taken down, necessitating the financial institution to make loans at below market rates of interest. By purchasing a put option, however, the financial institution offsets the value loss that occurs with higher interest rates. If interest rates decline, customers will renegotiate their loans at lower rates and let their commitments expire.

Thus, the risk to the financial institution is one-sided—rising interest rates. Effectively, the financial institution has written a put option to its customers. To hedge, it may purchase a put option in the market.

So far we have discussed only put options. However, one can buy call options or write either type of option. The various configurations of price movements are shown in Fig. 5-8. The colored lines represent expiration date

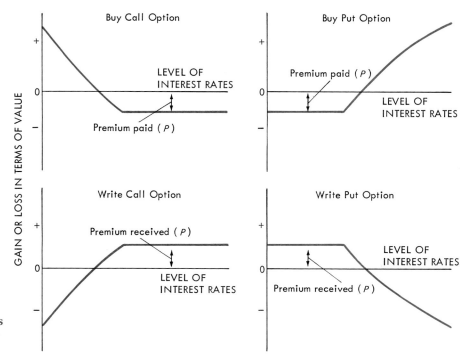

FIGURE 5-8

Profit or loss in options position with a change in interest rates values of the options as interest rates change. Note that with interest rates on the horizontal axis, the lines are opposite to what would be the case if prices were used. Also, the lines are curvilinear, reflecting the relationship between value changes and interest rates. Thus, debt options can be used in a number of ways to hedge risk or to place bets on the direction and/or volatility of interest rates.

VALUATION OF DEBT OPTIONS

Option pricing models in the spirit of Black-Scholes may be used to value debt options (substituting futures prices and variances for stock prices and variances in the formula). As with any option, the key is the volatility of returns for the associated asset. In this case, volatility has to do with the variability of interest rates. However, there are some important differences between debt options and stock options. As a result, various scholars have fashioned valuation models that recognize the unique aspects associated with debt options. As these models are examined in a companion book, we will not do so here.[19] Most alter the Black-Scholes model in minor to moderate ways, but the principles of option valuation examined in this chapter continue to hold.

SUMMARY

A call option gives the holder the right to buy a share of stock at a specified price, the exercise price. A European option can be exercised only at the expiration date, whereas an American option can be exercised any time up to and including the expiration date. The value of the option at the expiration date is the value of the stock minus the exercise price, or it may be zero. It cannot be a negative value. The most important factor affecting the value of the option is the price volatility of the stock; the greater the volatility, the more valuable the option, all other things staying the same. In addition, the longer the time to the expiration date and the higher the interest rate, the greater the value of the option, all other things the same.

With a stock and an option on the stock, it is possible to establish a riskless hedged position by buying the stock and by writing options or selling them short. The hedge ratio determines the portion of stock held long in relation to the options in the short position. (A riskless hedge could be established also by buying options and selling the stock short.) With a discrete time example, we showed how the value of the hedged position was the same regardless of the stock price outcome. In efficient financial markets, the rate of return on a perfectly hedged position would be the risk-free rate. If this is the case, it is possible to determine the appropriate value of the option at the beginning of the period.

The Black-Scholes option pricing model provides an exact formula for determining the value of an option based on the volatility of the stock, the

---

[19] James C. Van Horne, *Financial Market Rates and Flows*, 3d ed. (Englewood Cliffs, NJ: Prentice Hall, 1990), pp. 219–24.

price of the stock, the exercise price of the option, the time to expiration of the option, and the short-term interest rate. With an example, we showed how this formula could be used, and we discussed some of the problems. The model is based on the notion that investors are able to maintain reasonably hedged positions over time and that arbitrage will drive the return on such positions to the risk-free rate. As a result, the option price will bear a precise relationship to the stock price. The Black-Scholes model provides considerable insight into the valuation of contingent claims, and certain refinements of it were examined.

In comparing American and European options, we found that an American option on a stock that pays a dividend may have less value than a European option on a stock that does not pay a dividend. Finally, debt options permit a wide variety of hedging against interest-rate movements or speculating on such movements. One-directional hedging through debt options might be used to cap the interest-rate cost of a loan, for example.

APPENDIX
Put-Call Parity

In the equilibration process driven by arbitrage, there is a relationship between put, call, and stock prices. To illustrate, assume European type put and call options where both have the same exercise price, $30, and the same expiration date. Suppose our strategy is to sell one put option and to buy one call option. If we ignore for now the premiums earned and paid, the expiration date values of the two options are as shown in Fig. 5-9. We see that the expiration date value of our put-call strategy is the stock price less the exercise price

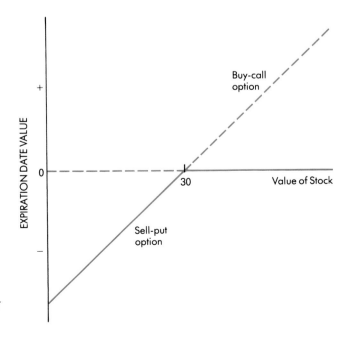

FIGURE 5-9

Expiration date values of put and call options

of $30, described by the diagonal line throughout. Now suppose we buy the stock and borrow the exercise price of the options with a loan maturing at the expiration date. The expiration date value of our position, ignoring interest, is also the stock price minus $30. Thus, the two strategies produce the same result.

In market equilibrium with zero arbitrage opportunity, there will be a precise relationship between the market values of the put and the call options and the stock. We have established that the payoff from a strategy of buying a call and selling a put is the same as that from buying the stock and borrowing the exercise price. Taking account of the time value of money, the relationship can be expressed as

$$V_c - V_p = V_s - PV(E) \tag{5A-1}$$

where V_c = value of call option
V_p = value of put option
V_s = value of share of stock
$PV(E)$ = present value of the exercise price, where the time interval is the time to expiration of the options.

Rearranging Eq. (5A-1), we obtain

$$-V_s + PV(E) + V_c - V_p = 0 \tag{5A-2}$$

which is the put-call parity theorem. This basic expression can be rearranged further to solve for any one of the four values, given the other three. For the value of the call, it is

$$V_c = V_s + V_p - PV(E) \tag{5A-3}$$

For the value of the put, it is

$$V_p = -V_s + V_c + PV(E) \tag{5A-4}$$

and for the value of the stock

$$V_s = V_c - V_p + PV(E) \tag{5A-5}$$

Suppose a put option had a value of $3, both options had an exercise price of $30 and 6 months to expiration, the interest rate was 4 percent for 6 months, and share price was $35. If there were no opportunities for arbitrage, the value of the call option would be

$$V_c = \$35 + \$3 - \$28.80 = \$9.20$$

If the call option value were other than this, there would be opportunity for arbitrage.

Thus, the put-call parity theorem may be used to determine whether the stock and the options are priced correctly. Zero arbitrage opportunity means that there is market equilibrium in the prices of all three securities, as was the case in the chapter discussion for the call option and the stock.

1. Loco Baking Company's common stock has a present market price per share of $28. A 6-month call option has been written on the stock with an exercise price of $30. Presently the option has a market value of $3. At the end of 6 months, you estimate the market price of the stock to be $24 per share with a probability of .1, $28 with a probability of .2, $32 with a probability of .4, $37 with a probability of .2, and $43 with a probability of .1.

   a. What is the expected value of share price 6 months hence? What is the expiration value of the option if that expected value of share price should prevail?

   b. What is the expected value of option price at expiration, assuming that the option is held to this time? Why does it differ from the option value determined in part a?

   c. Presently, what is the theoretical value of the option? Why does it have a positive value?

2. Prudencio Jiminez Company's share price is now $60. Six months hence, it will be either $75 with probability .70 or $50 with probability .30. A call option exists on the stock that can be exercised only at the end of 6 months at an exercise price of $65.

   a. If you wished to establish a perfectly hedged position, what would you do on the basis of the facts just presented?

   b. Under each of the two possibilities, what will be the value of your hedged position?

   c. What is the expected value of option price at the end of the period?

3. A call option enables the holder to acquire one share of stock at $45 a share for each option held. The option has 6 months until its expiration. The market price of the stock is currently $40 a share, and the expected standard deviation of its continuously compounded return over the near future is .30. The short-term annual interest rate is 10 percent.

   a. On the basis of this information, what is the proper value of the option using the Black-Scholes option pricing model? (The calculations can be made with a reasonably sophisticated calculator or with an ordinary calculator and various tables.)

   b. What is the appropriate hedge ratio and how does it work?

PROBLEMS

1. Given the following data, determine the value of the call options at their expiration dates.

OPTION	MARKET PRICE PER SHARE AT THE EXPIRATION DATE	EXERCISE PRICE OF THE OPTION
A	$10	$12
B	25	21
C	48	52
D	7	5

2. The X-Gamma Company and the X-Theta Company have actively traded options on their stocks with the same exercise price, $30. The current market prices of the two stocks are the same, $27 per share; yet the current market price of the X-Gamma option is $2.25, while that of the X-Theta option is $3.90. How can this difference in option prices occur?

3. Julia Malone is considering writing a 30-day option on Video Sonics Corporation, which is currently trading at $60 per share. The exercise price will also be $60 per share, and the premium received on the option will be $3.75. At what common stock prices will she make money, at what price will she begin to lose money, and at what prices will she lose $5 and $10 on each option that is written?

4. The stocks of Carson Can Company and Tahoe Forest Products Company are expected to have the following probability distributions with respect to market price per share 6 months hence.

PROBABILITY OF OCCURRENCE	CARSON CAN	TAHOE FOREST PRODUCTS
.15	$34	$22
.20	38	28
.30	40	36
.20	42	44
.15	46	50

Options exist for each of these stocks, and both have an exercise price of $38 and an expiration date 6 months from now.

a. What is the expected value of market price per share 6 months hence for the two companies?

b. What is the expected value of option price for the two options at expiration, assuming the options are held to this time?

c. Reconcile your answers to parts a and b.

5. Shinto Carbon Steel Company's stock price at the beginning of a 6-month period is $40 per share. At the end of the period, there is a 50 percent chance that the stock will increase in value to $50 and a 50 percent chance that it will fall in value to $38 per share. An option on the stock can be exercised only at the end of the period and at an exercise price of $41. The risk-free rate is now 5 percent per period.

a. How would you establish a perfectly hedged position, using the stock and the option?

b. Show how the value of your position will be the same regardless of the stock price outcome.

6. In Problem 5, what will be the market price of the option at the beginning of the period if financial markets are efficient and rational? What would happen if the actual market price of the option were in excess of the price you compute? What would happen if it were less?

7. Zilcon Laboratories, Inc., is a new high-technology company whose common stock sells for $23 per share. A call option exists on this stock with 3 months to expiration. It has an exercise price of $18 and sells for $5.30. You have made a careful study of the stock's volatility and conclude that a standard deviation of .50 is appropriate for the next 3 months. Currently the annual rate on short-term Treasury bills is 6 percent.

a. Using the Black-Scholes option pricing model, is the option overvalued, undervalued, or priced just right? (These calculations are possible with a reasonably sophisticated calculator or with a plain calculator and various tables.)

b. If you believe in these numbers, what should you do?

8. For Zilcon Laboratories, Inc., in Problem 7, determine the value of the option with the following changes, holding all else constant, and explain why the change in the value of the option occurs.

  a. The length of time to expiration is 1 year instead of 3 months.
  b. The short-term interest rate is 8 percent instead of 6 percent.
  c. The standard deviation is .10 instead of .50.

9. A 6-month call option on the stock of Costello Equipment Company permits the holder to acquire one share at $30. Presently share price is $25, and the expected standard deviation of its continuously compounded return is .20. The short-term annual interest rate is 8 percent.

  a. What is the value of the option according to the Black-Scholes formula?

  b. What would be the value if the current share price were $30? $35? How do these premiums over lower boundary theoretical values compare with that when share price is $25? Why the differences?

  c. Suppose now that the original conditions hold, but we do not know the standard deviation. If the option price is $2, what is the implied standard deviation? (*Note:* This question should be undertaken only if you have a computer program at your disposal. In this regard, see the supplement, Van Horne/Van Horne, *Financial Management Computer Applications,* Chapter 12. Do not do by hand.)

Appendix Problem

1. A put and a call option each have an expiration date 6 months hence and an exercise price of $10. The interest rate for the 6-month period is 3 percent.

  a. If the put has a market price of $2 and stock is worth $9 per share, what is the value of the call?

  b. If the put has a market price of $1 and the call $4, what is the value of the stock per share?

  c. If the call has a market value of $5 and market price of the stock is $12 per share, what is the value of the put?

SOLUTIONS TO SELF-CORRECTION PROBLEMS

1. a. *EV* of share price = $24(.1) + $28(.2) + $32(.4) + $37(.2) + $43(.1) = $32.50

Option value = $32.50 − $30.00 = $2.50

  b. *EV* of option price = 0(.1) + 0(.2) + ($32 − $30)(.4) + ($37 − $30)(.2) + ($43 − $30)(.1) = $3.50

At values of share price less than $30, the option has zero value, as opposed to a negative value. This boundary on the downside results in a higher expected value of option price than in part a, where the implicit assumption is a negative option price when share price is either $24 or $28.

  c. Theoretical value of option = max ($28 − $30, 0) = 0

The option has a positive value because the probability distribution of possible share prices 6 months hence is relatively wide. If the market's assessment corresponds to yours, that would explain the positive option price.

2. a. Hedge ratio = $\dfrac{uV_o - dV_o}{uV_s - dV_s} = \dfrac{\$10 - 0}{\$75 - \$50} = .4$

This hedge ratio means that you should purchase two shares of stock in a long position for every five options you write (your short position). By so doing, you will have established a perfectly hedged position.

b. This hedged position may be illustrated by determining the value of your position under each of the two possibilities:

STOCK PRICE	VALUE OF LONG POSITION IN STOCK	VALUE OF SHORT POSITION IN OPTION	VALUE OF COMBINED HEDGED POSITION
$75	2($75) = $150	−5($10) = −$50	$100
50	2($50) = $100	−5($0) = 0	100

Thus, the value of the hedged position is the same regardless of the stock outcome.

c. EV of option price = ($75 − $65)(.70) + 0(.30) = $7

3. a.
$$d_1 = \frac{\ln (40/45) + [.10 + 1/2(.30)^2].50}{.30\sqrt{.50}} = -.213$$

$$d_2 = \frac{\ln (40/45) + [.10 - \frac{1}{2}(.30)^2].50}{.30\sqrt{.50}} = -.426$$

$N(d_1) = N(-.213) = .416$
$N(d_2) = N(-.426) = .335$

$$V_o = \$40(.416) - \frac{\$45}{e^{(.10)(.50)}}(.335) = \$2.30$$

Since d_1 and d_2 are negative, we do not subtract them from one as we do when they are positive.

b. The appropriate hedge ratio is $N(d_1) = .416$. This means that for every option written or sold short, the individual should buy .416 share of common stock.

SELECTED REFERENCES

BLACK, FISCHER, "Fact and Fantasy in the Use of Options," *Financial Analysts Journal*, 31 (July–August 1975), 36–72.

———, "How to Use the Holes in Black-Scholes," *Journal of Applied Corporate Finance*, 1 (Winter 1989), 67–73.

———, and MYRON SCHOLES, "The Pricing of Options and Corporate Liabilities," *Journal of Political Economy*, 81 (May–June 1973), 637–54.

BRENNAN, MICHAEL J., and EDUARDO S. SCHWARTZ, "Finite Difference Methods and Jump Processes Arising in the Pricing of Contingent Claims: A Synthesis," *Journal of Financial and Quantitative Analysis*, 13 (September 1978), 461–74.

COX, JOHN C., and STEPHEN A. ROSS, "The Valuation of Options for Alternative Stochastic Processes," *Journal of Financial Economics*, 3 (January–March 1976), 145–79.

———, and MARK RUBINSTEIN, "Option Pricing: A Simplified Approach," *Journal of Financial Economics*, 7 (September 1979), 229–63.

GALAI, DAN, "Empirical Tests of Boundary Conditions for CBOE Options," *Journal of Financial Economics*, 6 (June–September 1978), 187–212.

GESKE, ROBERT, "A Note on an Analytical Valuation Formula for Unprotected American Call Options on Stocks with Known Dividends," *Journal of Financial Economics*, 7 (December 1979), 375–80.

———, and RICHARD ROLL, "On Valuing American Call Options with the Black-Scholes European Formula," *Journal of Finance*, 39 (June 1984), 443–55.

GULTEKIN, N. BULENT, RICHARD J. ROGALSKI, and SEHA TINIC, "Option Pricing Model Estimates: Some Empirical Results," *Financial Management*, 11 (Spring 1982), 58–69.

HAUGEN, ROBERT A., *Modern Investment Theory*, 2d ed. Englewood Cliffs, NJ: Prentice Hall, 1990, Chaps. 17 and 18.

HULL, JOHN, *Options, Futures and Other Derivative Securities*. Englewood Cliffs, NJ: Prentice Hall, 1989.

JARROW, ROBERT A., and ANDREW RUDD, *Option Pricing*. Homewood, IL: Richard D. Irwin, 1983.

MACBETH, JAMES D., and LARRY J. MERVILLE, "An Empirical Examination of the Black-Scholes Call Option Pricing Model," *Journal of Finance*, 34 (December 1979), 1173–86.

MASON, SCOTT P., and ROBERT C. MERTON, "The Role of Contingent Claims Analysis in Corporate Finance," *Recent Advances in Corporate Finance*, Edward I. Altman and Marti G. Subrahmanyam, eds. Homewood, IL: Richard D. Irwin, 1985.

MERTON, ROBERT C., "A Rational Theory of Option Pricing." *Bell Journal of Economics*, 4 (Spring 1973), 141–82.

ROLL, RICHARD, "An Analytic Valuation Formula for Unprotected American Call Options with Known Dividends," *Journal of Financial Economics*, 5 (November 1977), 251–58.

RUBINSTEIN, MARK, and JOHN C. COX, *Options Markets*. Englewood Cliffs, NJ: Prentice Hall, 1985.

SHARPE, WILLIAM F., and GORDON J. ALEXANDER, *Investments*, 4th ed. Englewood Cliffs, NJ: Prentice Hall, 1990, Chap. 18.

STERK WILLIAM E., "Comparative Performance of the Black-Scholes and Roll-Geske-Whaley Option Pricing Models," *Journal of Financial and Quantitative Analysis*, 18 (September 1983), 345–54.

VAN HORNE, JAMES C., *Financial Market Rates and Flows*, 3d ed. Englewood Cliffs, NJ: Prentice Hall, 1990. Chaps. 7, 9, 10.

WHALEY, ROBERT E., "On the Valuation of American Call Options on Stocks with Known Dividends," *Journal of Financial Economics*, 9 (June 1981), 207–11.

———, "Valuation of American Call Options on Dividend-Paying Stocks: Empirical Tests," *Journal of Financial Economics*, 10 (March 1982), 29–58.

———, "On Valuing American Futures Options," *Financial Analysts Journal*, 42 (May–June 1986), 49–59.

PART 2

INVESTMENT IN ASSETS AND REQUIRED RETURNS

Competitive Advantage, Deluxe Style

Deluxe Corporation has been described as being on the trailing edge of technology.[*] In a computer age moving toward a checkless society, it is likened to a buggy-whip company. Deluxe has stuck steadfastly to what it knows best—printing checks and deposit tickets used by banks and their depositors and producing other business forms used in financial transactions. Surely this is a sick company in a sick industry. Or is it?

The company consistently shows returns on equity investment (ROE) of 25 to 30 percent, among the highest in American industry. It is careful to acquire assets and other companies that fit into its overall strategy of competitive advantage within the financial transactions industry. Technology improvement, cost advantage over competitors, and marketing advantage are its hallmarks. Although the company has expanded into electronic services, the bulk of its profits comes from old-fashioned "block and tackling," that is, prompt, dependable service—filling most orders within two days—and high-quality products. This formula has consistently provided stockholder returns in excess of what the financial markets require. Not every company needs to be in high tech to build value for its owners.

[*] Alan C. Shapiro, "Corporate Strategy and the Capital Budgeting Decision," *Financial Management Collection*, 1 (Winter 1986), 2.

6

PRINCIPLES OF CAPITAL INVESTMENT

When a business firm makes a capital investment, it incurs a current cash outlay for benefits to be realized in the future. We know that we must judge a proposed investment by its expected return. How close will it come to the return required by investors? The answer to that question relates the effect of an investment decision on the price of the stock. Although our objective in the subsequent four chapters is to come to grips with this issue, first we must take up certain fundamental concepts, and that is the purpose of this chapter.

To simplify the presentation of these basics, we assume for now that the required rate of return on investment projects is given and is the same for all projects. This assumption necessitates our holding constant the financing and dividend decisions of the firm. Moreover, it implies that the selection of any investment project or combination of projects does not alter the business-risk complexion of the firm as perceived by suppliers of capital.

It is important to stress that in the next chapters we shall relax these assumptions. By that time, we shall understand the rudiments of capital budgeting.

THE ADMINISTRATIVE FRAMEWORK

Successful administration of capital investments by a company involves

1. Generation of investment proposals
2. Estimation of cash flows for the proposals
3. Evaluation of cash flows
4. Selection of projects based on an acceptance criterion
5. Continual reevaluation of investment projects after their acceptance

The first four are examined in this chapter, although the fourth is analyzed in much greater depth in Chapters 8 and 9. The fifth is taken up in Chapter 7 when we consider the question of divestiture.

Depending on the firm involved, investment proposals can emanate from various sources. For purposes of analysis, projects may be classified into one of five categories:

1. New products or expansion of existing products
2. Replacement of equipment or buildings
3. Research and development
4. Exploration
5. Others

The fifth category comprises miscellaneous items such as the expenditure of funds to comply with certain health standards or the acquisition of a pollution-control device. For a new product, the proposal usually originates in the marketing department. On the other hand, a proposal to replace a piece of equipment with a more-sophisticated model usually emanates from the production area of the firm. In each case, efficient administrative procedures are needed for channeling investment requests.

Most firms screen proposals at multiple levels of authority. For a proposal originating in the production area, the hierarchy of authority might run from (1) section chiefs to (2) plant managers to (3) the vice-president for operations to (4) a capital expenditures committee under the financial manager to (5) the president to (6) the board of directors. How high a proposal must go before it is finally approved usually depends on its size. The greater the capital outlay, the greater the number of screens usually required. Plant managers may be able to approve moderate-sized projects on their own, but only higher levels of authority approve larger ones. Because the administrative procedures for screening investment proposals vary greatly from firm to firm, it is not possible to generalize. The best procedure will depend on the circumstances.

The level and type of capital expenditure appear to be important to investors, as they convey information about the expected future growth of earnings. John J. McConnell and Chris J. Muscarella test this notion with respect to the level of expenditures of a company. They find that an increase in capital expenditure intentions, relative to prior expectations, results in increased stock returns around the time of the announcement, and vice versa for an unexpected decrease.[1]

ESTIMATING CASH FLOWS

One of the most important tasks in capital budgeting is estimating future cash flows for a project. The final results we obtain are really only as good as the accuracy of our estimates. Since cash, not income, is central to all decisions of the firm, we express whatever benefits we expect from a project in terms of cash flows rather than income. The firm invests cash now in the hope of receiving cash returns in a greater amount in the future. Only cash receipts can be reinvested in the firm or paid to stockholders in the form of dividends. In capital budgeting, good guys may get credit, but effective managers get cash. In setting up the cash flows for analysis, a computer spreadsheet program is invaluable. It allows one to change assumptions and quickly produce a new cash-flow stream. In the supplement, *Financial Management Computer Applications*, a program format for this purpose is presented.

---

[1] "Corporate Capital Expenditure Decisions and the Market Value of the Firm," *Journal of Financial Economics*, 14 (September 1985), 399–422.

For each investment proposal, we need to provide information on expected future cash flows on an after-tax basis. In addition, the information must be provided on an *incremental* basis, so that we analyze only the difference between the cash flows of the firm with and without the project. For example, if a firm contemplates a new product that is likely to compete with existing products, it is not appropriate to express cash flows in terms of the estimated sales of the new product. We must take into account some probable "cannibalization" of existing products, and we must make our cash-flow estimates on the basis of incremental sales. The key is to analyze the situation with and without the new investment. Only *incremental* cash flows matter.

In this regard, sunk costs must be ignored. One is concerned with incremental costs and benefits; the recovery of past costs is irrelevant. They are bygones and should not enter into the decision process. Also, we must be mindful that certain costs do not necessarily involve a dollar outlay. If we have allocated plant space to a project and this space can be used for something else, its opportunity cost must be included in the project's evaluation. If a presently unused building can be sold for $300,000, that amount should be treated as a cash outlay at the outset of the project. Thus, in deriving cash flows we must consider appropriate opportunity costs.

To illustrate the information needed for a capital budgeting decision, consider the following situation. Dilly Duck Apparel Company is considering the introduction of a new clothes line. To launch the product line, the company will need to spend $150,000 for special equipment and the initial advertising campaign. The marketing department envisions the product life to be 6 years and expects incremental sales revenue to be

YEAR 1	YEAR 2	YEAR 3	YEAR 4	YEAR 5	YEAR 6
$60,000	$120,000	$160,000	$180,000	$110,000	$50,000

Cash outflows include labor and maintenance costs, material costs, and various other expenses associated with the product. As with sales, these costs must be estimated on an incremental basis. In addition to these outflows, the company will need to pay higher taxes if the new product generates higher profits, and this incremental outlay must be included. Cash outflows *should not* include interest costs on debt employed to finance the project. Such costs are embodied in the required rate of return to be discussed in Chapters 8 and 9. To deduct interest charges from net cash flows would result in double counting.

Suppose that on the basis of these considerations, Dilly Duck Apparel estimates total incremental cash outflows to be

YEAR 1	YEAR 2	YEAR 3	YEAR 4	YEAR 5	YEAR 6
$40,000	$70,000	$100,000	$100,000	$70,000	$40,000

Because depreciation is a noncash expense, it is not included in these outflows. The expected net cash flows from the project are

	INITIAL COST	YEAR 1	YEAR 2	YEAR 3	YEAR 4	YEAR 5	YEAR 6
Cash inflows		$60,000	$120,000	$160,000	$180,000	$110,000	$50,000
Cash outflows	$150,000	40,000	70,000	100,000	100,000	70,000	40,000
Net cash flows	−$150,000	$20,000	$ 50,000	$ 60,000	$ 80,000	$ 40,000	$10,000

Thus, for an initial cash outflow of $150,000 the company expects to generate net cash flows of $20,000, $50,000, $60,000, $80,000, $40,000, and $10,000 over the next 6 years. These cash flows represent the relevant information we need in order to judge the attractiveness of the project. The development of cash-flow data of this sort is facilitated greatly by the use of a spreadsheet program.

Patterns of Cash Flows.   The net cash flows for this example are plotted in the top panel of Fig. 6-1. We notice that the initial cash outlay, or invest-

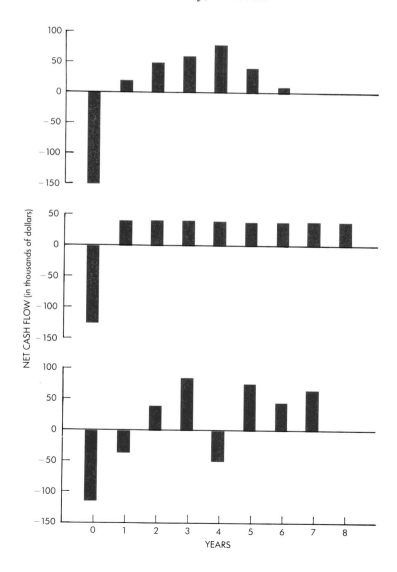

FIGURE 6-1
Patterns of cash flows

ment, is followed by positive and increasing net cash flows through year 4, after which they drop off as the project becomes older. Many other patterns are possible, both with respect to the life of the project and to the annual cash flows. In the middle panel, the initial cash outlay is followed by a stream of eight equal net cash inflows. From Chapter 2, we recognize this pattern to be an *annuity*. In the bottom panel, two distinct investment phases are shown. The first is at time 0 and continues into year 1 where there are heavy advertising and promotion expenses. In year 4, additional investment is needed to upgrade production capability and to promote the product some more. These outlays more than offset operating cash inflows, so there is a net cash outflow for the year. In the next two years, the project generates net cash inflows. Finally, the project terminates at the end of year 7. At that time, a salvage value is realized that results in a higher net cash inflow than in year 6. These examples illustrate that the patterns of expected net cash flows can vary considerably over time, depending on the project.

REPLACEMENT DECISIONS AND DEPRECIATION

To go to a somewhat more complicated replacement decision example involving taxes, suppose we are considering the purchase of a new machine to replace an old one, and we need to obtain cash-flow information in order to evaluate the attractiveness of this project. The purchase price of the new machine is $18,500, and it will require an additional $1,500 to install, bringing the total cost to $20,000. We can sell the old machine for its depreciated book value of $2,000. The initial net cash outflow for the investment project, therefore, is $18,000. The new machine should cut labor and maintenance costs and effect other cash savings totaling $7,100 a year before taxes for each of the next 5 years, after which it will probably not provide any savings, nor will it have a salvage value. These savings represent the net savings to the firm if it replaces the old machine with the new. In other words, we are concerned with the difference between the cash flows resulting from the two alternatives: continuing with the old machine or replacing it with a new one.

Because a machine of this sort has a useful life in excess of 1 year, we cannot charge its cost against income for tax purposes but must depreciate it. We then deduct depreciation from income in order to compute taxable income. Under the tax laws when this edition was written, capital assets fall into defined cost recovery classes depending on their nature. These classes of property have periods, or depreciable lives, of 3, 5, 7, 10, 15, 20, $27\frac{1}{2}$, and $31\frac{1}{2}$ years. A general description of the classes follows shortly. For now, suppose the machine we are considering falls into the 5-year property class for cost recovery (depreciation) purposes. Later in the chapter, we consider the exact depreciation that may be deducted under existing tax law. For simplicity of illustration, we assume straight-line depreciation.

As a result, the annual depreciation charge is 20 percent of the total depreciable cost of $20,000, or $4,000 a year. Assume additionally that the corporate income tax rate is 40 percent. Moreover, assume that the old machine has a remaining depreciable life of 5 years, that there is no expected salvage value at the end of this time, and that the machine also is subject to straight-line depreciation. Thus, the annual depreciation charge on the old machine is 20 percent of its depreciated book value of $2,000, or $400 a year. Because we are interested in the incremental impact of the project, we must subtract depreciation charges on the old machine from depreciation charges on the new one to obtain the incremental depreciation charges associated with the project. Given the information cited, we now are able to calculate the expected net cash flow (after taxes) resulting from the acceptance of the project.

	BOOK ACCOUNT	CASH-FLOW ACCOUNT
Annual cash savings	$7,100	$7,100
Depreciation on new machine	4,000	
Less: Depreciation on old machine	400	
Additional depreciation charge	$3,600	
Additional income before taxes	3,500	
Income tax (40%)	1,400	1,400
Additional income after taxes	$2,100	
Annual net cash flow		$5,700

In figuring the net cash flow, we simply deduct the additional cash outlay for federal income taxes from the annual cash savings. The expected annual net cash inflow for this replacement proposal is $5,700 for each of the next 5 years; this figure compares with additional income after taxes of $2,100 a year. The cash-flow and net profit figures differ by the amount of additional depreciation. As our concern is not with income as such, but with cash flows, we are interested in the right-hand column. For an initial cash outlay of $18,000, then, we are able to replace an old machine with a new one that is expected to result in net cash savings of $5,700 a year over the next 5 years. As in the previous example, the relevant cash-flow information for capital budgeting purposes is expressed on an incremental, after-tax basis.

METHODS FOR EVALUATION

Once we have collected the necessary information, we are able to evaluate the attractiveness of the various investment proposals under consideration. Because our purpose in this chapter is to examine the basic concepts of capital budgeting, we assume that the risk or quality of all investment proposals under consideration does not differ from the risk of existing investment projects of the firm and that the acceptance of any proposal or group of investment proposals does not change the relative business risk of the firm. The investment decision will be either to accept or to reject the proposal. In this section, we evaluate four methods of capital budgeting:

1. Average rate of return
2. Payback
3. Internal rate of return
4. Net present value

The first two are approximate methods for assessing the economic worth of a project. For simplicity, we assume throughout that the expected cash flows are realized at the end of each year.

AVERAGE RATE OF RETURN

This accounting measure represents the ratio of the average annual profits after taxes to the investment in the project. In the previous example of the new machine, the average annual book earnings for the 5-year period are $2,100, and the initial investment in the project is $18,000. Therefore

$$\text{Average rate of return} = \frac{\$2,100}{\$18,000} = 11.67\% \tag{6-1}$$

If income were variable over the 5 years, an average would be calculated and employed in the numerator. Once the average rate of return for a proposal has been calculated, it may be compared with a required rate of return to determine if a particular proposal should be accepted or rejected.

The principal virtue of the average rate of return is its simplicity; it makes use of readily available accounting information. Once the average rate of return for a proposal has been calculated, it may be compared with a required, or cutoff, rate of return to determine if a particular proposal should be accepted or rejected. The principal shortcomings of the method are that it is based on accounting income rather than on cash flows and that it fails to take account of the timing of cash inflows and outflows. The time value of money is ignored: benefits in the last year are valued the same as benefits in the first year.

Suppose we have three investment proposals, each costing $9,000 and each having an economic and depreciable life of 3 years. Assume that these proposals are expected to provide the following book profits and cash flows over the next 3 years.

	PROJECT A		PROJECT B		PROJECT C	
PERIOD	Book Profit	Net Cash Flow	Book Profit	Net Cash Flow	Book Profit	Net Cash Flow
1	$3,000	$6,000	$2,000	$5,000	$1,000	$4,000
2	2,000	5,000	2,000	5,000	2,000	5,000
3	1,000	4,000	2,000	5,000	3,000	6,000

Each proposal will have the same average rate of return: $2,000/$9,000, or 22.22 percent; however, few, if any, firms would regard the three projects as equally favorable. Most would prefer project A, which provides a larger portion of total cash benefits in the first year. For this reason, the average rate of return leaves much to be desired as a method for project selection.

PAYBACK

The payback period of an investment project tells us the number of years required to recover our initial cash investment. It is the ratio of the initial fixed investment over the annual cash inflows for the recovery period. For our example

$$\text{Payback period} = \frac{\$18,000}{\$5,700} = 3.16 \text{ years} \qquad (6\text{-}2)$$

If the annual cash inflows are not equal, the job of calculation is somewhat more difficult. Suppose annual cash inflows are $4,000 in the first year, $6,000 in the second and third years, and $4,000 in the fourth and fifth years. In the first 3 years, $16,000 of the original investment will be recovered, followed by $4,000 in the fourth year. With an initial cash investment of $18,000, the payback period is 3 years + ($2,000/$4,000), or $3\frac{1}{2}$ years.

If the payback period calculated is less than some maximum acceptable payback period, the proposal is accepted; if not, it is rejected. If the required payback period were 4 years, the project in our example would be accepted. The major shortcoming of the payback method is that it fails to consider cash flows after the payback period; consequently, it cannot be regarded as a measure of profitability. Two proposals costing $10,000 each would have the same payback period if they both had annual net cash inflows of $5,000 in the first 2 years; but one project might be expected to provide no cash flows after 2 years, whereas the other might be expected to provide cash flows of $5,000 in each of the next 3 years. Thus, the payback method can be deceptive as a yardstick of profitability. In addition to this shortcoming, the method does not take account of the magnitude or timing of cash flows during the payback period. It considers only the recovery period as a whole.

The payback method continues in use, nevertheless, frequently as a supplement to other, more sophisticated methods. It does afford management limited insight into the risk and liquidity of a project. The shorter the payback period, supposedly, the less risky the project and the greater its liquidity. The company that is cash poor may find the method to be very useful in gauging the early recovery of funds invested. There is some merit to its use in this regard, but the method does not take into account the dispersion of possible outcomes—only the magnitude and timing of the expected value of these outcomes relative to the original investment. Therefore, it cannot be considered an adequate indicator of risk. When the payback method is used, it is more appropriately treated as a constraint to be satisfied than as a profitability measure to be maximized.

INTERNAL RATE OF RETURN

Because of the various shortcomings in the average rate of return and payback methods, it generally is felt that *discounted cash-flow methods* provide a more objective basis for evaluating and selecting investment projects. These methods take account of both the magnitude and the timing of expected cash flows in each period of a project's life. The two discounted cash-flow methods are the internal-rate-of-return and the present-value methods described in Chapter 2. Recall that the internal rate of return for an investment proposal is the discount rate that equates the present value of the expected cash outflows with the present value of the expected inflows. It is represented by that rate, r, such that

$$\sum_{t=0}^{n} \left[\frac{A_t}{(1 + r)^t} \right] = 0 \qquad (6\text{-}3)$$

where A_t is the cash flow for period t, whether it be a net cash outflow or inflow, and n is the last period in which a cash flow is expected. If the initial cash outlay or cost occurs at time 0, Eq. (6-3) can be expressed as

$$A_0 = \frac{A_1}{(1 + r)} + \frac{A_2}{(1 + r)^2} + \cdots + \frac{A_n}{(1 + r)^n} \tag{6-4}$$

Thus, r is the rate that discounts the stream of future cash flows—A_1 through A_n—to equal the initial outlay at time 0, A_0. For our example, the problem can be expressed as

$$\$18,000 = \frac{\$5,700}{(1 + r)} + \frac{\$5,700}{(1 + r)^2} + \frac{\$5,700}{(1 + r)^3} + \frac{\$5,700}{(1 + r)^4} + \frac{\$5,700}{(1 + r)^5} \tag{6-5}$$

Solving for r by means of a computer, a programmed calculator, or the manual method described in Chapter 2, we find the internal rate of return for the project to be 17.57 percent.

Acceptance Criterion. The acceptance criterion generally employed with the internal-rate-of-return method is to compare the internal rate of return with a required rate of return, known also as the cutoff, or hurdle, rate. If the internal rate of return exceeds the required rate, the project is accepted; if not, it is rejected. If the required rate of return is 12 percent and this criterion is used, the investment proposal being considered will be accepted. Accepting a project with an internal rate of return in excess of the required rate of return should result in an increase in the market price of the stock, because the firm accepts a project with a return greater than that required to maintain the present market price per share. Chapters 8 and 9 will say much more about relating the investment decision to the objective of the firm. We assume for now that the required rate of return is given.

Recognize, however, that capacity expanding investment projects may differ from cost-reduction projects and, hence, require a different return. Edward M. Miller reasons that capital expanding projects are highly related to the level of economic activity, producing sizable cash flows when the economy is prosperous.[2] Drawing on concepts presented in Chapter 3, the systematic risk of the project would be high. Replacement projects, on the other hand, are cost reducing and would likely produce benefits across more states of the economy. As a result, they would possess lower systematic risk and require a lower return to satisfy investors.

NET PRESENT VALUE

Like the internal-rate-of-return method, the present-value method is a discounted cash-flow approach to capital budgeting. With the present-value method, all cash flows are discounted to present value, using the required rate of return. The net present value of an investment proposal is

---

[2] Edward M. Miller, "On the Systematic Risk of Expansion Investment," *Quarterly Review of Economics and Business,* 28 (Autumn 1988), 67–77.

$$NPV = \sum_{t=0}^{n} \frac{A_t}{(1 + k)^t} \qquad (6\text{-}6)$$

where k is the required rate of return. If the sum of these discounted cash flows is zero or more, the proposal is accepted; if not, it is rejected. Another way to express the acceptance criterion is to say that the project will be accepted if the present value of cash inflows exceeds the present value of cash outflows. The rationale behind the acceptance criterion is the same as that behind the internal-rate-of-return method. If the required rate of return is the return investors expect the firm to earn on the investment proposal, and the firm accepts a proposal with a net present value greater than zero, the market price of the stock should rise. Again, the firm is taking on a project with a return greater than that necessary to leave the market price of the stock unchanged.

If we assume a required rate of return of 12 percent after taxes, the net present value of our example problem is

$$
\begin{aligned}
NPV &= -\$18,\!000 + \frac{\$5,\!700}{(1.12)} + \frac{\$5,\!700}{(1.12)^2} + \frac{\$5,\!700}{(1.12)^3} + \frac{\$5,\!700}{(1.12)^4} + \frac{\$5,\!700}{(1.12)^5} \\
&= -\$18,\!000 + \$20,\!547 \\
&= \$2,\!547
\end{aligned}
\qquad (6\text{-}7)
$$

Again, one can solve the problem by computer, by calculator, or by reference to the appropriate present-value table at the end of the book. Using Table B because an annuity is involved, we find the appropriate discount factor 3.6048 and multiply $5,700 by it to obtain $20,547. Subtracting the initial outlay of $18,000, we obtain $2,547. Inasmuch as the net present value of this proposal is greater than 0, the proposal should be accepted, using the present-value method.

With the internal-rate-of-return method, we are given the cash flows, and we solve for the rate of discount that equates the present value of the cash inflows with the present value of the outflows. We then compare the internal rate of return with the required rate of return to determine whether the proposal should be accepted. With the present-value method, we are given the cash flows and the required rate of return, and we solve for the net present value. The acceptability of the proposal depends on whether the net present value is zero or more.

MUTUAL EXCLUSION AND DEPENDENCY

In evaluating a group of investment proposals, we must determine whether the proposals are independent of each other. A proposal is *mutually exclusive* if the acceptance of it precludes the acceptance of one or more other proposals. For example, if the firm is considering investment in one of two temperature-control systems, acceptance of one system will rule out acceptance of the other. Two mutually exclusive proposals cannot both be accepted.

A *contingent* or *dependent* proposal depends on the acceptance of one or more other proposals. The addition of a large machine may necessitate construction of a new wing to house it. Contingent proposals must be part of our thinking when we consider the original, dependent proposal. Recognizing the dependency, we can make investment decisions accordingly.

PROFITABILITY INDEX

The profitability index, or benefit-cost ratio, of a project is the present value of future net cash flows over the initial cash outlay. It can be expressed as

$$PI = \frac{\sum_{t=1}^{n} \frac{A_t}{(1 + k)^t}}{A_0} \qquad (6\text{-}8)$$

For our example

$$PI = \frac{\$20,547}{\$18,000} = 1.14 \qquad (6\text{-}9)$$

As long as the profitability index is 1.00 or greater, the investment proposal is acceptable. In calculating the profitability index, we compute the net rather than the aggregate index. The aggregate index is simply the present value of cash inflows over the present value of cash outflows. We use the net index to differentiate the initial cash outlay from subsequent cash outlays. The initial outlay is discretionary because the firm can either commit funds to the project or employ them elsewhere. Subsequent cash outflows are not discretionary in this sense; they are embodied in the system. The aggregate index does not differentiate between the cash outlay the firm has to put up initially and subsequent cash outlays.[3] For this reason, the net profitability index is a more rational measure of profitability than is the aggregate index.

For any given project, the net-present-value method and the profitability index give the same accept-reject signals. If we must choose between mutually exclusive projects, the net-present-value measure is preferred because it expresses in absolute terms the expected economic contribution of the project. In contrast, the profitability index expresses only the relative profitability.

NPV VERSUS IRR

In general, the net-present-value and internal-rate-of-return methods lead to the same acceptance or rejection decision. In Fig. 6-2, we illustrate graphically the two methods applied to a typical investment project. The figure shows the curvilinear relationship between the net present value of a project and the discount rate employed. When the discount rate is 0, net present value is simply the total cash inflows less the total cash outflows of the project. Assuming that total inflows exceed total outflows and that outflows are followed by inflows, the typical project will have the highest net present value when the discount

[3] See Bernhard Schwab and Peter Lusztig, "A Comparative Analysis of the Net Present Value and the Benefit-Cost Ratio as Measures of the Economic Desirability of Investments," *Journal of Finance*, 24 (June 1969), 507–11.

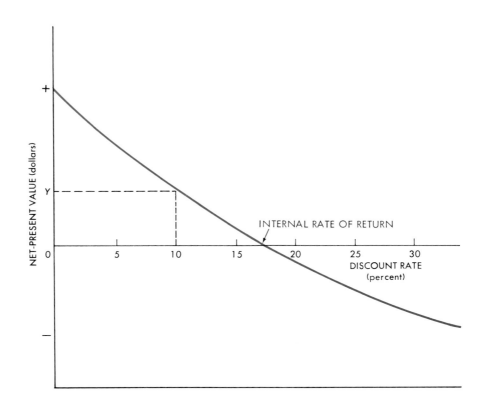

FIGURE 6-2
Relation between
discount rate and net
present value

rate is 0. As the discount rate increases, the present value of future cash inflows decreases relative to the present value of outflows. As a result, NPV declines. The crossing of the NPV line with the 0 line establishes the internal
rate of return for the project.[4]

If the required rate of return is less than the internal rate of return, we
would accept the project, using either method. Suppose that the required rate
were 10 percent. As seen in Fig. 6-2, the net present value of the project then
would be Y. Inasmuch as Y is greater than 0, we would accept the project, using the present-value method. Similarly, we would accept the project using
the internal rate of return method because the internal rate of return exceeds
the required rate. For required rates greater than the internal rate of return, we
would reject the project under either method. Thus, we see that the internal
rate of return and present-value methods give us identical answers with respect to the acceptance or rejection of an investment project.

COMPOUNDING RATE DIFFERENCES

We must, however, identify important differences between the methods.
When two investment proposals are mutually exclusive, so that we can select
only one, the two methods may give contradictory results. To illustrate the nature of the problem, suppose a firm had two mutually exclusive investment
proposals that were expected to generate the following cash flows.

[4] We must recognize the possibility of multiple internal rates of return. See the Appendix at the
end of this chapter.

	CASH FLOWS				
YEAR	0	1	2	3	4
Proposal A	−$23,616	$10,000	$10,000	$10,000	$10,000
Proposal B	−23,616	0	5,000	10,000	32,675

Internal rates of return for proposals A and B are 25 percent and 22 percent, respectively. If the required rate of return is 10 percent, however, and we use this figure as our discount rate, the net present values of proposals A and B are $8,083 and $10,347, respectively. Thus, proposal A is preferred if we use the internal-rate-of-return method, whereas proposal B is preferred if we use the present-value method. If we can choose but one of these proposals, we obviously have a conflict.

The conflict between these two methods is due to differences in the implicit compounding of interest. The IRR method implies that funds are compounded at the internal rate of return. For proposal A, the assumption is that $23,616 invested at 25 percent will compound in a way that will release $10,000 at the end of each of the next 4 years. The present-value method implies compounding at the required rate of return used as the discount rate. For proposal A, the assumption is that the $8,083 present value plus the $23,616 initial outflow, or $31,699, invested at 10 percent will compound in such a way that it will release $10,000 at the end of each of the next 4 years. Only if the required rate of return were 16.65 percent would the net present value of the two proposals be the same, $4,006. Below 16.65 percent, proposal B has a higher NPV; above, proposal A has the higher NPV.

SCALE OF INVESTMENT

In addition to the problem of different implicit compounding rates, a problem arises if the initial cash outlays are different for two mutually exclusive investment proposals. Because the results of the internal-rate-of-return method are expressed as a percentage, the scale of investment is ignored. Without allowance for this factor, a 50 percent return on a $100 investment would always be preferred to a 25 percent return on a $500 investment. In contrast, the results of the present-value method are expressed in absolute terms. If the investment proposals were each for 1 year, we would have the following, assuming a required rate of return of 10 percent:

	CASH FLOWS			
	Year 0	Year 1	IRR	NPV (10%)
Proposal X	−$100	$150	50%	$36.36
Proposal Y	−500	625	25	68.18

With respect to absolute returns, the second proposal is superior, despite the fact that its internal rate of return is less. The reason is that the scale of investment is greater, which affords a greater net present value.

MULTIPLE RATES OF RETURN

A final problem with the internal-rate-of-return method is that multiple IRRs are possible. A necessary, but not sufficient, condition for this occurrence is that the cash-flow stream changes sign more than once. All of our examples depicted situations where a cash outflow was followed by one or more cash inflows. In other words, there was but one change in sign, which ensured a unique internal rate of return. However, some projects involve multiple changes in sign. At the end of the project, there may be a requirement to restore the environment. This often happens in the extractive industry where the land must be reclaimed at the end of the project. With a chemical plant, there are sizable dismantling costs. Whatever the cause, these costs result in a cash outflow at the end of the project and, hence, in more than one change in sign in the cash-flow series.

Whether these changes in sign cause more than one IRR depends also on the magnitudes of the cash flows. As the relationship is complicated and requires illustration, we address the problem in detail in the Appendix at the end of the chapter. While most projects have but one change in sign in the cash-flow stream, some have more. When this occurs, the financial manager must be alert to the possibility of multiple internal rates of return. As shown in the Appendix, no one internal rate of return makes sense economically when there are multiple IRRs, and an alternative method of analysis must be used.

With multiple IRR situations, calculators and computer programs often are fooled and produce only one IRR. Perhaps the best way to determine if a problem exists is to calculate the net present value of a project at various discount rates. If the discount rate were increased from zero in 25 percent increments up to, say, 1,000 percent, the NPV could be plotted on a graph similar to that shown in Fig. 6-2. If the NPV line connecting the dots crosses the zero NPV line more than once, you have a multiple IRR problem.

SUMMARY OF THE SHORTCOMINGS OF THE IRR METHOD

We have seen that the present-value method always provides correct rankings of mutually exclusive investment projects, whereas the internal-rate-of-return method sometimes does not. With the IRR method, the implied reinvestment rate will differ, depending on the cash-flow stream for each investment proposal under consideration. For proposals with a high internal rate of return, a high reinvestment rate is assumed; for proposals with a low internal rate of return, a low reinvestment rate is assumed. Only rarely will the internal rate of return calculated represent the relevant rate for reinvestment of intermediate cash flows. With the present-value method, however, the implied reinvestment rate—namely, the required rate of return—is the same for each proposal. In essence, this reinvestment rate represents the minimum return on opportunities available to the firm.

In addition, the net-present-value method takes account of differences in the scale of investment. If our objective is truly value maximization, the only theoretically correct opportunity cost of funds is the required rate of return. It is consistently applied with the net-present-value method, thereby avoiding the reinvestment rate and scale of investment problems. Finally, the possibility of multiple rates of return hurts the case for the IRR method.

With all of these criticisms, why is it used at all? The reason is that many managers find the IRR easier to visualize and interpret than they do the NPV measure. One does not have to specify a required rate of return in the calculations. To the extent that the required rate of return is but a rough estimate, the internal-rate-of-return method may permit a more satisfying comparison of projects for the typical manager. Put another way, they feel comfortable with a return measure as opposed to an absolute NPV figure. As long as the company is not confronted with many mutually exclusive projects or with unusual projects having multiple sign changes in the cash-flow stream, the IRR method may be used with reasonable confidence. When such is not the case, the shortcomings noted must be borne in mind. Either modifications in the IRR method or a switch to the NPV method needs to occur.

DEPRECIATION AND OTHER REFINEMENTS IN CASH-FLOW INFORMATION

In our machine replacement example, we assumed straight-line depreciation, the depreciable life of the asset equaling its economic life, no salvage value, and no working capital requirement. Our purpose was to keep the example simple so that we could analyze the methods for evaluating expected profitability. We shall now digress for a while in order to examine the effect of these real-world considerations on the magnitude and timing of cash flows.

METHOD OF DEPRECIATION

In our earlier example, we assumed straight-line depreciation when computing cash flows. However, a more advantageous method of depreciation is available for tax purposes. Under the 1986 Tax Reform Act, there are eight property classes for cost recovery (depreciation) purposes. The property category in which an asset falls determines its depreciable life for tax purposes.

3-Year Class. Includes property with a midpoint life of 4 years or less. The midpoint life of various types of assets is determined by the Treasury Department under the asset depreciation range (ADR) system.

5-Year Class. Includes property with an ADR midpoint life of 4 to 10 years. Included in this class are most machinery, automobiles, light trucks, most technological and semiconductor equipment, switching equipment, small power production facilities, and research and experimental equipment.

7-Year Class. Includes property with an ADR midpoint of 10 to 16 years and railroad track and single-purpose agriculture structures.

10-Year Class. Includes property with an ADR midpoint life of 16 to 20 years.

15-Year Class. Includes property with a midpoint of 20 to 25 years and telephone distribution plants.

20-Year Class. Includes property with an ADR midpoint of 25 years or more, other than real property described below.

$27\frac{1}{2}$-*Year Class.* Includes residential rental property.

$31\frac{1}{2}$-*Year Class.* Other real estate.

For the 3-year, 5-year, 7-year, and 10-year property classes, the method of depreciation is the 200 percent declining-balance method. This method switches to straight line in the year that provides the quickest write-off. Moreover, a half-year convention is used in the first year and in the year following the last year. For the 15-year and 20-year property classes, 150 percent declining-balance depreciation is used with subsequent switching to straight line. Finally, for the $27\frac{1}{2}$-year and $31\frac{1}{2}$-year classes, straight-line depreciation is used throughout.

To illustrate for the 5-year property class, assume an asset costing $10,000 is acquired at the start of the year. The formula for the declining-balance method is $m(1/n)$, where m is the multiplier and n is the number of years in the property class. For our example, $2(1/5) = 40$ percent. However, in the first year a one-half-year convention is employed, so first-year depreciation is 20 percent, or $2,000. At the end of the third year, it is favorable to switch to straight-line depreciation. Thus, the depreciation schedule is

YEAR	DEPRECIATION	DEPRECIATION CHARGE	BALANCE
0			$10,000
1	.2 of $10,000	$2,000	8,000
2	.4 of $8,000	3,200	4,800
3	.4 of $4,800	1,920	2,880
4	$2,880/2.5 years	1,152	1,728
5	$2,880/2.5 years	1,152	576
6	$2,880 × .20	576	0

At the beginning of the fourth year, the balance remaining is divided by the remaining life to get straight-line depreciation. The remaining life is $2\frac{1}{2}$ years, owing to the half-year convention in the sixth year. Finally, in the sixth year, the remaining balance is $576, or one-fifth of the balance at the end of the third year.

Instead of making such calculations, the Treasury publishes depreciation percentages of original cost for each property class. For the first four property categories, they are

RECOVERY YEAR	3-YEAR	5-YEAR	7-YEAR	10-YEAR
1	33.33%	20.00%	14.29%	10.00%
2	44.45	32.00	24.49	18.00
3	14.81	19.20	17.49	14.40
4	7.41	11.52	12.49	11.52
5		11.52	8.93	9.22
6		5.76	8.93	7.37
7			8.92	6.55
8			4.46	6.55
9				6.56
10				6.55
11				3.28

These percentages correspond to the principles taken up in our previous calculations, and they should be used for determining depreciation.

SETTING UP THE CASH FLOWS

In most cases, the capital recovery (depreciation) period is shorter than the economic life of the asset. To illustrate how we might go about using depreciation tables and setting up the cash flows for analysis, suppose a company were considering an asset costing $100,000 that fell in the 5-year property class. The asset was expected to produce annual before-tax cash savings of $32,000 in each of the first 2 years, $27,000 in each of the next 2 years, $22,000 in both the fifth and the sixth years, and $20,000 in the seventh and last year. Assume further a 40 percent tax rate (federal and state) and no salvage value. Setting up the cash flows is facilitated greatly with a spreadsheet program like Lotus 1-2-3. The annual net cash flows are as follows:

	0	1	2	3	4	5	6	7
1. Cost	(100,000)							
2. Annual savings		32,000	32,000	27,000	27,000	22,000	22,000	20,000
3. Depreciation		20,000	32,000	19,200	11,520	11,520	5,760	
4. Income		12,000	0	7,800	15,480	10,480	16,240	20,000
5. Taxes (40%)		4,800	0	3,120	6,192	4,192	6,496	8,000
6. Net cash flow (1) + (2) − (5)	(100,000)	27,200	32,000	23,880	20,808	17,808	15,504	12,000

We see that the tax shield occurs only in the first 6 years, after which the full cash savings are subject to taxation. As a result, the cash flow is lower. This shift in timing over what would occur with straight-line depreciation has a favorable present-value effect. To determine the net present value of the project, we discount the cash flows shown in row 6 by the required rate of return and sum them. If the required rate of return were 12 percent, the net present value would be $3,405 and the internal rate of return 13.25 percent, both measures indicating acceptance of the project. Cash flows for other projects can be set up similarly.

SALVAGE VALUE AND TAXES

The cash-flow pattern will change toward the better if the asset is expected to have salvage, or scrap, value at the end of the project. As the asset will be fully depreciated at that time, the salvage value realized is subject to taxation at the ordinary income tax rate. Suppose the asset were sold for $10,000 at the end of year 7. With a 40 percent tax rate, the company will realize cash proceeds of $6,000 at the end of the last year. This amount then would be added to the net cash inflow previously determined to give the total cash flow in the last year.

If the asset is sold before it is fully depreciated, the tax treatment is different. In general, if an asset is sold for more than its depreciated book value but for less than its cost, the firm pays taxes at the full corporate rate. If the asset is sold for more than its cost, this excess is subject to the capital-gains tax treatment, which sometimes is more favorable. As such calculations are complicated, the reader is referred to the tax code and/or to a tax attorney when faced with the tax treatment of a sale of an asset.

WORKING CAPITAL REQUIREMENT

In addition to the investment in a fixed asset, it is sometimes necessary to carry additional cash, receivables, or inventories. This investment in working capital is treated as a cash outflow at the time it occurs. For example, if $15,000 in working capital is required in connection with our example, there would be an additional cash outflow of $15,000 at time 0, bringing the total outflow to $115,000. At the end of the project's life, the working capital investment presumably is returned. Therefore, there would be a $15,000 cash inflow at the end of year 7. As a result, the cash inflow in that year would be $27,000 instead of $12,000.

This switching of cash flows obviously is adverse from a present-value standpoint: $15,000 is given up at time 0 and is not gotten back until 7 years later. Again using 12 percent as the required rate of return, the net present value of row 6 of our previous example, rearranged as suggested, is −$4,810. The IRR is now 10.57 percent. These figures compare with $3,405 and 13.25 percent determined before. Thus, an initial working capital investment of $15,000 causes the project to be unacceptable, whereas before it was acceptable. While total cash flows are not affected, their timing is affected.

WHAT HAPPENS WHEN CAPITAL IS RATIONED?

Capital rationing occurs any time there is a budget ceiling, or constraint, on the amount of funds that can be invested during a specific period of time, such as a year. Such constraints are prevalent in a number of firms, particularly in those that have a policy of financing all capital expenditures internally. Another example of capital rationing occurs when a division of a large company is allowed to make capital expenditures only up to a specified budget ceiling, over which the division usually has no control. With a capital rationing constraint, the firm attempts to select the combination of investment proposals that will provide the greatest profitability.

Your firm may have the following investment opportunities, ranked in descending order of profitability indexes (the ratio of the present value of future net cash flows over the initial cash outlay):

PROPOSAL	4	7	2	3	6	5	1
Profitability index	1.25	1.19	1.16	1.14	1.09	1.05	0.97
Initial outlay	$400,000	$100,000	$175,000	$125,000	$200,000	$100,000	$150,000

If the budget ceiling for initial outlays during the present period is $1 million, and the proposals are independent of each other, you would select proposals in descending order of profitability until the budget was exhausted. With capital rationing, you would accept the first five proposals, totaling $1 million in initial outlays. In other words, you do not necessarily invest in all proposals that increase the net present value of the firm; you invest in an acceptable proposal only if the budget constraint allows such an investment. You will not invest in proposal 5, even though the profitability index in excess of 1.00 would suggest its acceptance. The critical aspect of the capital rationing constraint illustrated is that capital expenditures during a period are strictly limited by the budget ceiling, regardless of the number of attractive investment opportunities.

Under capital rationing, the objective is to select the combination of investment proposals that provides the highest net present value, subject to the budget constraint for the period. If this constraint is strictly enforced, it may be better to accept several smaller, less profitable proposals that allow full utilization of the budget than to accept one large proposal that results in part of the budget's being unused. Admittedly, a fixed one-period constraint is highly artificial. Companies engaging in capital rationing seldom will set a budget so rigidly that it does not provide for some flexibility. In addition, the cost of certain investment projects may be spread over several years. Finally, a one-period analysis does not take account of intermediate cash flows generated by a project. Some projects provide relatively high net cash flows in the early years; these cash flows serve to reduce the budget constraints in the early years because they may be used to finance other investment projects. For the reasons discussed, when capital is rationed, management should consider more than one period in the allocation of limited capital to investment projects.

A budget ceiling carries its cost, too, when it bars us from taking advantage of an opportunity that provides a return in excess of that required. In our first example, the opportunity forgone by the $1 million budget ceiling is proposal 5, which has a profitability index of 1.05. Though all cash flows are discounted at the required rate of return, we do not necessarily accept proposals that provide positive net present values. We see which proposals we can accept before we exhaust the budget. In so doing, we may reject projects that provide positive net present values, as was shown with proposal 5.

Capital rationing usually results in an investment policy that is less than optimal. In some periods, the firm accepts projects down to its required rate of return; in others, it rejects projects that would provide returns substantially in excess of the required rate. If the required rate of return corresponds to the project's cost of capital, and the firm actually can raise capital at that approximate cost, should it not invest in all projects yielding more than the required rate of return? If it rations capital and does not invest in all projects yielding more than the required rate, is it not forgoing opportunities that would enhance the market price of its stock?

In the final analysis, the firm should accept all proposals yielding more than their required rates of return. By so doing, it will increase the market price per share, because it is taking on projects that will provide a return higher than necessary to maintain the present market price per share. Certainly, there are circumstances that complicate the use of this rule. In general, however, this policy should tend to maximize the market price of the stock over the long run.

In general, an inflationary economy distorts capital budgeting decisions. For one thing, depreciation charges are based on original rather than replacement costs. As income grows with inflation, an increasing portion is taxed, with the result that real cash flows do not keep up with inflation. Consider an investment proposal costing $24,000 under the assumption that no inflation is expected, that depreciation is straight line over 4 years, and that the tax rate is 40 percent. The following cash flows are expected to occur.

YEAR	CASH SAVINGS	DEPRECIATION	TAXES	CASH FLOW AFTER TAXES
1	$10,000	$6,000	$1,600	$8,400
2	10,000	6,000	1,600	8,400
3	10,000	6,000	1,600	8,400
4	10,000	6,000	1,600	8,400

Depreciation is deducted from cash savings to obtain taxable income, on which taxes of 40 percent are based. Without inflation, depreciation charges represent the "cost" of replacing the investment as it wears out. Because nominal income on which taxes are paid represents real income, the last column represents real cash flows after taxes. The internal rate of return that equates the present value of the cash inflows with the cost of the project is 14.96 percent.

Consider now a situation in which inflation is at a rate of 7 percent per annum and cash savings are expected to grow at this overall rate of inflation. The after-tax cash flows become

YEAR	CASH SAVINGS	DEPRECIATION	TAXES	CASH FLOW AFTER TAXES
1	$10,700	$6,000	$1,880	$ 8,820
2	11,449	6,000	2,180	9,269
3	12,250	6,000	2,500	9,750
4	13,108	6,000	2,843	10,265

Although these cash flows are larger than before, they must be deflated by the inflation rate if one is concerned with the real as opposed to the nominal rate of return. Therefore, the last column becomes

	YEAR			
	1	2	3	4
Real after-tax cash flow	$8,243	$8,096	$7,959	$7,831

153

As we see, the real after-tax cash flows are less than before and decline over time. The reason is that depreciation charges do not change in keeping with inflation, so that an increasing portion of the tax savings is subject to taxation. As taxes increase at a rate faster than inflation, real after-tax cash flows must decline. The internal rate of return based on real after-tax cash flows is 12.91 percent, compared with 14.96 percent without inflation.

The presence of inflation therefore results in lower real rates of return and less incentive for companies to undertake capital investments. The cash-flow situation is improved with accelerated depreciation, but the same unfavorable comparisons hold. There simply is a disincentive for companies to undertake capital expenditures, so they typically invest less, seek investments with faster paybacks (shorter economic lives), and become less capital intensive during periods of inflation.[5]

THE BIAS IN CASH-FLOW ESTIMATES

In estimating cash flows, it is important that the individual company take anticipated inflation into account. Often there is a tendency to assume that price levels will remain unchanged throughout the life of the project. Frequently, this assumption is imposed unknowingly; future cash flows simply are estimated on the basis of existing prices. A bias arises in the selection process, however, in that the required rate of return for the project is usually based on current capital costs, which in turn embody a premium for anticipated inflation.[6]

Assume a situation in which the hurdle rate for a project is its required rate of return as perceived by investors and creditors. (The ways by which it is measured are taken up in Chapter 8.) There is general agreement that security prices are influenced by inflation. As we will discover in Chapter 8, the relationship is far from simple and it is not stable over time. Rather than get into these arguments now, we simply assume that capital costs embody in them some kind of premium for inflation.

The key factor is that if the acceptance criterion, namely, the required rate of return, includes a premium for anticipated inflation, then the estimated cash flows also must reflect inflation. Such cash flows are affected in several ways. Inflows may rise if they come from products sold at higher prices; outflows may increase with higher wages and materials costs. But future inflation does not affect depreciation charges on existing assets. Once the asset is acquired, these charges are known with certainty. The effect of anticipated inflation on cash inflows and cash outflows will vary with the nature of the project. In some cases, cash inflows, through price increases, will rise faster than cash outflows; in other cases, the opposite will hold. No matter what the relationship, it is important that it be embodied in the cash-flow estimates. Otherwise, a bias of the type described before arises.

INFLATION BIAS

To illustrate inflation bias, let us consider a project that cost $100,000 at time 0 and was expected to provide cash-flow benefits over the next 5 years. Assume straight-line depreciation of $20,000 a year and a corporate tax rate

---

[5] For an analysis of these points, see Charles R. Nelson, "Inflation and Capital Budgeting," *Journal of Finance,* 31 (June 1976), 923–31.

[6] This section is based on James C. Van Horne, "A Note on Biases in Capital Budgeting Introduced by Inflation," *Journal of Financial and Quantitative Analysis,* 6 (January 1971), 653–58.

(federal and state) of 40 percent. Cash flows were estimated on the basis of price levels at time 0, future inflation ignored, and these estimates were

	PERIOD				
	1	2	3	4	5
Expected cash inflow, I_t	$30,000	$40,000	$50,000	$50,000	$30,000
Expected cash outflow, O_t	10,000	10,000	10,000	10,000	10,000
	$20,000	$30,000	$40,000	$40,000	$20,000
Times (1 − tax rate)	.60	.60	.60	.60	.60
	$12,000	$18,000	$24,000	$24,000	$12,000
Depreciation times tax rate	8,000	8,000	8,000	8,000	8,000
Net cash flow	$20,000	$26,000	$32,000	$32,000	$20,000

The calculation of net cash flows in this manner results in exactly the same answer as when we determined net income after depreciation, taxes on this net income, and then subtracted taxes from annual savings to obtain the net cash flow. (The portrayal above is consistent with Eq. (6-10) presented below.) If the project's required rate of return were 13 percent, the net present value of the project would be −$9,280. The negative figure would doom the project to rejection.

Results are biased, however, in the sense that the discount rate embodies an element attributable to anticipated future inflation, whereas the cash-flow estimates do not. Suppose that the existing rate of inflation, as measured by changes in the price-level index, were 10 percent and that this rate was expected to prevail over the next 5 years. If cash inflows and cash outflows were both expected to increase at this rate, the net present value of the project would be

$$NPV = \sum_{t=1}^{5} \frac{[I_t(1.10)^t - O_t(1.10)^t][1 - .40] + 20,000[.40]}{(1.13)^t} - 100,000$$

$$= \$11,056 \tag{6-10}$$

where I_t is the cash inflow in year t, O_t is the cash outflow in year t, and $20,000 is the annual depreciation in year t, which is multiplied by the tax rate to give the tax shield cash savings. Because the net present value is positive, the project would be acceptable now, whereas before it was not. To reject it under the previous method of estimating cash flows would result in an opportunity loss to stockholders, for the project provides a return somewhat in excess of that required by investors.

The example illustrates the importance of taking anticipated inflation into account explicitly when estimating future cash flows. Too often there is a tendency not to consider its effect in these estimates. Because anticipated inflation is embodied in the required rate of return, not to take account of it in the cash-flow estimates will result in a biased appraisal of the project and, in turn, the possibility of a less than optimal allocation of capital.

It is essential, then, to compare apples with apples or oranges with oranges. If a nominal required return is used, which usually is the case, then nominal cash flows should be employed and these cash flows should take account of expected future inflation. If a real required rate of return is used, then the cash-flow estimates should not be adjusted for inflation. Consistency is critical, as illustrated in our example. More exact inflation adjustment procedures for capital investment are described elsewhere, but consistency in assumptions is the important lesson to be learned.[7] In Chapter 20, we shall consider further the impact of inflation on the cost of financing.

INFORMATION TO ANALYZE AN ACQUISITION

Investment proposals under consideration are not necessarily generated internally. A proposal can consist of the acquisition of a company or a portion thereof. The topic of acquisitions is treated in Chapter 24; in the present chapter and in Chapter 9, we consider the capital budgeting aspects of the problem. In principle, the prospective acquisition is much the same as any investment proposal; there is an initial outlay of cash or stock, followed by expected future benefits. The major difference is that, with an acquisition, the initial cost may not be established; indeed, it frequently is subject to bargaining. The framework for analyzing the expected return involved with an acquisition is similar to that discussed earlier. The critical thing is the accurate measurement of incremental cash flows, a topic to which we now turn.

MEASURING FREE CASH FLOWS

To consider an acquisition in a capital budgeting framework, expected future cash flows must be expressed on a basis consistent with those for investment proposals generated internally. In evaluating the prospective acquisition, the buying company should first estimate the future cash income that the acquisition is expected to add. Because we are interested in the marginal impact of the acquisition, these estimates should embody any expected economies, known as *synergism*, that are involved in the merger. (In Chapter 24, we explore synergy in greater detail.)

In an acquisition, there are the usual problems in estimating future cash flows. The process may be somewhat easier than for a capital budgeting proposal, however, because the company being acquired is a going concern. The acquiring company buys more than assets; it buys experience, an organization, and proven performance. The estimates of sales and costs are based on past results; consequently, they are likely to be more accurate than the estimates for a new investment proposal.

We are interested in what is known as *free cash flows*. These are the cash flows that remain after we subtract from expected revenues expected costs and the capital expenditures necessary to sustain, and hopefully improve, the cash flows.

In making the various estimates, it is important to isolate from consideration the capital structure that results from the merger. The reason is that once the merger is consummated, the buying company can modify the capital structure that results from the merger. Therefore, prospective incremental cash income from the acquisition should be estimated before interest charges.

---

[7] See Van Horne, "A Note on Biases in Capital Budgeting Introduced by Inflation"; and Alfred Rappaport and Robert A. Taggart, Jr., "Evaluation of Capital Expenditure Proposals under Inflation," *Financial Management*, 11 (Spring 1982), 5–13.

In other words, we attempt to measure the expected incremental earning power of the acquisition, apart from considerations of financing.

Expected incremental cash income should be adjusted for taxes. As was the case earlier, we deduct expected depreciation charges from cash income and compute the amount of taxes to be paid on the residual. By subtracting expected taxes from expected incremental cash income, we obtain cash income after taxes for each future period. From this expected cash income after taxes, we must subtract any new investments the acquiring firm believes it will have to make in order to generate the expected stream of earnings. The residual represents the expected cash flow for the period. It is important that we take account of these investments; otherwise, incremental cash-flow estimates will be biased upward.

Expected future earnings after taxes are frequently—and erroneously—treated as cash flows of a firm being considered for acquisition. The problem is that an earnings estimate for a future period usually is predicated on reinvesting a portion of earnings from previous periods.[8] To use expected earnings in evaluating an acquisition results in double counting, as does the use of expected future earnings per share in a dividend valuation model. In summation, the appropriate measure of incremental cash flow is expected earnings after taxes plus depreciation in each future period, less any investment required in that period.

PREPARING THE CASH FLOWS FOR ANALYSIS

To illustrate the information needed, suppose the incremental cash flows shown in Table 6-1 were expected from an acquisition. In the case of an acquisition investment, the life of the project is indefinite. In many cases, analysts assume some horizon such as 20 years, beyond which incremental cash flows are not estimated. While the present-value effect of these distant cash flows usually is not material, we choose to show cash flows into perpetuity, denoted by ∞, so that the valuation of a merger is consistent with the valuation of a common stock. In addition to expected free cash flows, the acquiring firm may wish to specify other possible cash-flow series. This can be done

---

[8] It is also assumed that funds generated through depreciation allowances are reinvested to maintain the company's existing level of earnings.

TABLE 6-1
Illustration of incremental cash flows from an acquisition

	AVERAGE FOR YEARS (IN THOUSANDS)				
	1–5	6–10	11–15	16–20	21–∞
Expected cash income from acquisition before taxes	$1,500	$2,000	$2,500	$3,000	$3,200
Taxes	−500	−700	−1,000	−1,200	−1,300
Expected cash income after taxes	$1,000	$1,300	$1,500	$1,800	$1,900
Investment required	−800	−900	−800	−700	−600
Net cash flow	$ 200	$ 400	$ 700	$1,100	$1,300

with a probability tree of possible free cash flows, a method taken up in Chapter 7.

The free cash flows for our example are shown at the bottom of the table, and these are the basis on which value is judged. If such cash flows were discounted at an appropriate required return (to be taken up in Chapter 9), we would obtain the expected present value of the acquisition. If the cash price to be paid is known, it should be subtracted from the expected present value to obtain the expected *net* present value. With this information, one is able to evaluate the acquisition in the same manner as described earlier. In most cases, however, the price to be paid is not set and must be negotiated.

NONCASH PAYMENTS AND LIABILITY ASSUMPTION

Now what if the acquisition were for other than cash? In many cases, the buyer assumes the liabilities of the company it acquires. Moreover, payment to the acquired company's stockholders may involve common stock, preferred stock, debt, cash, or some combination. Does not this complicate the matter? It does, but we must keep our eye on the overriding valuation principle. That is the value of the incremental free cash flows. The present-value figure obtained in the cash-flow format illustrated represents the maximum "cash-equivalent" price to be paid. If securities other than cash are used in the acquisition, they should be converted to their cash-equivalent market values. If the acquiring firm assumes the liabilities of the acquired company, these too should be converted to their market values. Thus, the present value of incremental free cash flows sets an upper limit on the market value of all securities, including cash, used in payment, together with the market value of any liabilities assumed in the acquisition. In this way, we are able to separate the investment worth of an acquisition from the way it is financed.

In Chapter 9, we shall investigate the question of whether an acquisition should be evaluated in isolation or as one of many companies whose stocks are publicly traded. Our concern in this chapter has been with the information needed for the various types of evaluation possible. We leave to later the valuation principles inherent in this problem.

SUMMARY

Capital budgeting involves the outlay of current funds in anticipation of future cash-flow benefits. Collection of cash-flow information is essential for the evaluation of investment proposals. The key is to measure incremental cash flows with and without the investment proposal being analyzed. Depreciation under the accelerated cost recovery system has a significant effect on the pattern of cash flows and, hence, on present value. Also affecting the pattern of cash flows is the presence of salvage value and a working capital requirement.

Capital budgeting methods, including the average rate of return and payback methods, were examined under the assumption that the acceptance of any investment proposal does not change the business-risk complexion of the firm as perceived by suppliers of capital. The two discounted cash-flow methods—internal rate of return and net present value—are the only appropriate means by which to judge the economic contribution of an investment proposal. The important distinctions between the internal-rate-of-return method and the present-value method involve the implied compounding rate, the scale of investment, and the possibility of multiple internal rates of return. Depending on the situation, contrary answers can be given with respect to the acceptance of mutually exclusive investment proposals. On theoretical grounds, a case can be made for the superiority of the present-value method, though in practice the IRR is popular.

Capital rationing is likely to result in investment decisions that are less than optimal. Inflation creates a disincentive for capital investment because depreciation charges do not reflect replacement costs, and a firm's taxes grow at a faster rate than inflation. In estimating cash flows, one should take account of anticipated inflation. Otherwise a bias arises in using an inflation-adjusted required return and non-inflation-adjusted cash flows, and there is a tendency to reject some projects that should be accepted.

In general, we can evaluate an acquisition in much the same manner and with much the same kind of information that we use for evaluating an investment proposal generated internally. Free cash flows, after capital expenditures, are estimated taking account of likely synergies. The present value of these cash flows sets an upper limit on the market value of all securities, including cash, to be paid together with the market value of any liabilities assumed.

APPENDIX
Multiple Internal Rates of Return

In a well-known article, Lorie and Savage pointed out that certain streams of cash flows may have more than one internal rate of return.[9] To illustrate the problem, suppose we had the following stream of cash flows corresponding to the "pump" proposal of Lorie and Savage.

YEAR	0	1	2
Cash flow	−$1,600	$10,000	−$10,000

In this example, a new, more effective pump is substituted for an existing pump. On an incremental basis, there is an initial outlay followed by net cash inflows resulting from the increased efficiency of the new pump. If the quantity of oil, for example, is fixed, the new pump will exhaust this supply quicker than the old pump would. Beyond this point of exhaustion, the new

[9] See James H. Lorie and Leonard J. Savage, "Three Problems in Rationing Capital," *Journal of Business*, 28 (October 1955), 229–39.

pump alternative would result in an incremental outflow, because the old pump would still be productive.

When we solve for the internal rate of return for the above cash-flow stream, we find that it is not one rate but two: 25 percent and 400 percent. This unusual situation is illustrated in Fig. 6-3, where the discount rate is plotted along the horizontal axis and net present value along the vertical axis. At a 0 rate of discount, the net present value of the project is simply the sum of all the cash flows. It is −$1,600 because total cash outflows exceed total cash inflows. As the discount rate increases, the present value of the second-year outflow diminishes with respect to the first-year inflow and the present value of the proposal becomes positive when the discount rate exceeds 25 percent. As the discount rate increases beyond 100 percent, the present value of all future cash flows (years 1 and 2) diminishes relative to the initial out-flow of −$1,600. At 400 percent, the present value of all cash flows again be-comes 0.

This type of proposal differs from the usual case, shown in Fig. 6-2, in which net present value is a decreasing function of the discount rate, and in which there is but one internal rate of return that equates the present value of all inflows with the present value of all outflows. An investment proposal may have any number of internal rates of return, depending on the cash-flow pattern. Consider the following series of cash flows:

YEAR	0	1	2	3
Cash flow	−$1,000	$6,000	−$11,000	$6,000

In this example, discount rates of 0, 100, and 200 percent result in the net present value of all cash flows equaling 0.

The number of internal rates of return is limited to the number of rever-sals of sign in the cash-flow stream. In the example, we have three reversals and three internal rates of return. Although a multiple reversal in signs is a necessary condition for multiple internal rates of return, it is not sufficient for

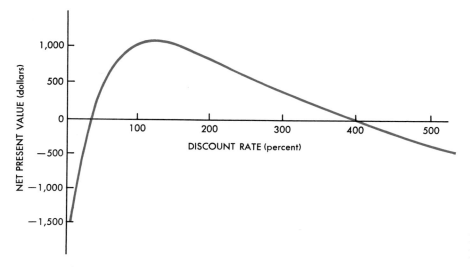

FIGURE 6-3
Dual rates of return

such an occurrence. The occurrence of multiple internal rates of return also depends on the magnitude of cash flows. For the following series of cash flows, there is but one internal rate of return (32.5 percent), despite two reversals of sign.

YEAR	0	1	2
Cash flow	−$1,000	$1,400	−$100

We note that the equation for solving for the internal rate of return, Eq. (6-3), is an nth degree polynomial, having n years in which cash flows occur. Therefore, the formula has n roots. For conventional investment proposals, only one of the roots is positive and $n - 1$ roots are negative or imaginary. As a result, the proposal is said to have a *unique* internal rate of return. In other words, the net-present-value line in Fig. 6-2 crosses the zero line only once. With a nonconventional investment proposal, such as those illustrated, more than one of the roots are real numbers, and the present-value line crosses the zero line more than once. For dual rates of return, for example, two of the roots are positive numbers.

When confronted with a proposal having multiple rates of return, how does one decide which is the correct rate? In our dual-rate example, is the correct rate 25 percent or 400 percent? Actually, neither rate is correct, because neither is a measure of investment worth. In essence, the firm has "borrowed" $10,000 from the project at the end of year 1 and will pay it back at the end of year 2. The relevant question is, What is it worth to the firm now to have the use of $10,000 for 1 year beginning at the end of year 1? This question, in turn, depends on the investment opportunities available to the firm for that period of time. If the firm could earn $2,000 on the use of these funds and realize these earnings at the end of the period, the value of this opportunity would be $2,000, to be received at the end of year 2. This amount would then be compared with the initial outlay of $1,600 to determine whether the project is worthwhile. Similarly, other proposals can be evaluated in this manner to determine whether they are worthwhile.

In general, holding risk constant, a company wishes to lend at as high a rate as possible and to borrow at as low a rate as possible. In the case of a project having multiple changes in signs, both lending and borrowing are involved. The best way to tackle the problem is to separate cash flows into their lending and borrowing components and then to use the net-present-value approach. In this way, the appropriate minimum required rate of return can be used on the lending side and the appropriate borrowing rate on that side.

SELF-CORRECTION PROBLEMS

1. Briarcliff Stove Company is considering a new product line to supplement its range line. It is anticipated that the new product line will involve cash investments of $700,000 at time 0 and $1.0 million in year 1. After-tax cash inflows of $250,000 are expected in year 2, $300,000 in year 3, $350,000 in year 4, and $400,000 each year thereafter through year 10. While the product line might be

viable after year 10, the company prefers to be conservative and end all calculations at that time.

  a. If the required rate of return is 15 percent, what is the net present value of the project? Is it acceptable?

  b. What is its internal rate of return?

  c. What would be the case if the required rate of return were 10 percent?

  d. What is the project's payback period?

2. Carbide Chemical Company is considering the replacement of two old machines with a new, more efficient machine. The old machines could be sold for $70,000 in the secondary market. Their depreciated book value is $120,000 with a remaining useful and depreciable life of 8 years. Straight-line depreciation is used on these machines. The new machine can be purchased and installed for $480,000. It has a useful life of 8 years, at the end of which a salvage value of $40,000 is expected. The machine falls into the 5-year property class for accelerated cost recovery (depreciation) purposes. Due to its greater efficiency, the new machine is expected to result in incremental annual savings of $120,000. The company's corporate tax rate is 34 percent, and if a loss occurs in any year on the project it is assumed that the company will receive a tax credit of 34 percent of such loss.

  a. What are the incremental cash inflows over the 8 years and what is the incremental cash outflow at time 0?

  b. What is the project's net present value if the required rate of return is 14 percent?

3. The Platte River Perfect Cooker Company is evaluating three investment situations: (1) produce a new line of aluminum skillets, (2) expand its existing cooker line to include several new sizes, and (3) develop a new higher-quality line of cookers. If only the project in question is undertaken, the expected present values and the amounts of investment required are

PROJECT	INVESTMENT REQUIRED	PRESENT VALUE OF FUTURE CASH FLOWS
1	$200,000	$290,000
2	115,000	185,000
3	270,000	400,000

If projects 1 and 2 are jointly undertaken, there will be no economies; the investments required and present values will simply be the sum of the parts. With projects 1 and 3, economies are possible in investment because one of the machines acquired can be used in both production processes. The total investment required for projects 1 and 3 combined is $440,000. If projects 2 and 3 are undertaken, there are economies to be achieved in marketing and producing the products but not in investment. The expected present value of future cash flows for projects 2 and 3 is $620,000. If all three projects are undertaken simultaneously, the economies noted will still hold. However, a $125,000 extension on the plant will be necesary, as space is not available for all three projects. Which project or projects should be chosen?

4. Insell Corporation is considering the acquisition of Fourier-Fox, Inc., which is in a related line of business. Fourier-Fox presently has a cash flow of $2 million per year. With a merger, synergism would be expected to result in a growth rate of this cash flow of 15 percent per year for 10 years, at the end of which level cash flows would be expected. To sustain the cash-flow stream, Insell will need to invest $1 million annually. For purposes of analysis and to be conservative, Insell limits its calculations of cash flows to 25 years.

  a. What expected annual cash flows would Insell realize from this acquisition?

  b. If its required rate of return is 18 percent, what is the maximum price Insell should pay?

PROBLEMS

1. Lobears, Inc., is considering two investment proposals, labeled Project A and Project B, with the characteristics shown in the accompanying table.

	PROJECT A			PROJECT B		
PERIOD	Cost	Profit after Taxes	Net Cash Flow	Cost	Profit after Taxes	Net Cash Flow
0	$9,000	—	—	$12,000	—	—
1		$1,000	$5,000		$1,000	$5,000
2		1,000	4,000		1,000	5,000
3		1,000	3,000		4,000	8,000

For each project, compute its average rate of return, its payback period, and its net present value, using a discount rate of 15 percent.

2. What criticisms may be offered against the average rate of return method as a capital budgeting technique? What criticisms may be offered against the payback method?

3. Zaire Electronics can make either of two investments at time 0. Assuming a required rate of return of 14 percent, determine for each project: (a) the payback period; (b) the net present value; (c) the profitability index; and (d) the internal rate of return. Assume the accelerated cost recovery system for depreciaton and that the asset falls in the 5-year property class and the corporate tax rate is 34 percent.

PROJECT	COST	1	2	3	4	5	6	7
A	$28,000	$8,000	$8,000	$8,000	$8,000	$8,000	$8,000	$8,000
B	20,000	5,000	5,000	6,000	6,000	7,000	7,000	7,000

4. Two mutually exclusive projects have projected cash flows as follows:

PERIOD	0	1	2	3	4
A	−$10,000	$5,000	$5,000	$5,000	$5,000
B	− 10,000	0	0	0	30,000

a. Determine the internal rate of return for each project.

b. Assuming a required rate of return of 10 percent, determine the net present value for each project.

c. Which project would you select? What assumptions are inherent in your decision?

5. The city of San Jose needs a number of new concrete-mixer trucks. It has received several bids and has closely evaluated the performance characteristics of the various trucks. Each Patterbilt truck costs $74,000, but it is "top-of-the-line" equipment. The truck has a life of 8 years, assuming that the engine is rebuilt in

 163

the fifth year. Maintenance costs of $2,000 a year are expected in the first 4 years, followed by total maintenance and rebuilding costs of $13,000 in the fifth year. During the last 3 years, maintenance costs are expected to be $4,000 a year. At the end of 8 years, the truck will have an estimated scrap value of $9,000.

A bid from Bulldog Trucks, Inc., is for $59,000 a truck; however, maintenance costs for this truck will be higher. In the first year, they are expected to be $3,000, and this amount is expected to increase by $1,500 a year through the eighth year. In year 4, the engine will need to be rebuilt, and this will cost the company $15,000 in addition to maintenance costs in that year. At the end of 8 years, the Bulldog truck will have an estimated scrap value of $5,000.

The last bidder, Best Tractor and Trailer Company, has agreed to sell San Jose trucks at $44,000 each. Maintenance costs in the first 4 years are expected to be $4,000 the first year and to increase by $1,000 a year. For San Jose's purposes, the truck has a life of only 4 years. At that time it can be traded in for a new Best truck, which is expected to cost $52,000. The likely trade-in value of the old truck is $15,000. During years 5 through 8, the second truck is expected to have maintenance costs of $5,000 in year 5, and these are expected to increase by $1,000 each year. At the end of 8 years, the second truck is expected to have a resale or salvage value of $18,000.

a. If the city of San Jose's cost of funds is 8 percent, which bid should it accept? Ignore any tax consideration, as the city pays no taxes.

b. If its opportunity cost were 15 percent, would your answer change?

6. Thoma Pharmaceutical Company may buy DNA testing equipment costing $60,000. This equipment is expected to reduce clinical staff labor costs by $20,000 annually. The equipment has a useful life of 5 years, but falls in the 3-year property class for cost recovery (depreciation) purposes. No salvage value is expected at the end. The corporate tax rate for Thoma is 38 percent, and its required rate of return is 15 percent. (If profits after taxes on the project are negative in any year, the firm will receive a tax credit of 38 percent of the loss in that year.) On the basis of this information, what is the net present value of the project? Is it acceptable?

7. In Problem 6, suppose 6 percent inflation in labor cost savings is expected over the last 4 years, so that savings in the first year are $20,000, savings in the second year are $21,200, and so forth.

a. If the required rate of return is still 15 percent, what is the net present value of the project? Is it acceptable?

b. If the working capital requirement of $10,000 were required in addition to the cost of the equipment and this additional investment were needed over the life of the project, what would be the effect on net present value? (All other things are the same as in part a.)

8. The Lake Tahoe Ski Resort is studying a half-dozen capital improvement projects. It has allocated $1 million for capital budgeting purposes. The following proposals and associated profitability indexes have been determined. The projects themselves are independent of one another.

PROJECT	AMOUNT	PROFITABILITY INDEX
1. Extend ski lift 3	$500,000	1.21
2. Build a new sports shop	150,000	.95
3. Extend ski lift 4	350,000	1.20
4. Build a new restaurant	450,000	1.18
5. Add to housing complex	200,000	1.20
6. Build an indoor skating rink	400,000	1.05

With strict capital rationing, which of these investments should be undertaken?

b. Is this an optimal strategy?

9. Rioka Corporation can invest in a project that costs $100,000 and has a useful life of 5 years. The expected cash flows from the project are

		YEAR		
1	2	3	4	5
$20,000	$40,000	$40,000	$30,000	$20,000

The company's tax rate is 50 percent, and its cost of capital based on present conditions in the financial markets is 12 percent. The company uses straight-line depreciation and will depreciate the project over 5 years.

a. Compute the net present value of the project without the consideration of inflation.

b. If inflation of 7 percent per annum is expected over the life of the project and cash flows are adjusted upward, what is the project's net present value?

10. The R.Z. Frank Company may acquire Aziz Car Leasing Company. Frank estimates that Aziz will provide incremental net income after taxes of $2 million in the first year, $3 million the second, $4 million the third, $5 million in each of the years 4 through 6, and $6 million annually thereafter. Owing to the need to replenish the fleet, heavier than usual investments are required in the first 2 years. Capital investments and depreciation charges are expected to be

YEAR	1	2	3	4	5	6	7 on
Capital investment (in millions)	$5	$5	$4	$4	$4	$4	$4
Depreciation (in millions)	$3	$4	$4	$4	$4	$4	$4

The overall required rate of return is 15 percent. Compute the present value of the acquisition based on these expectations. If you had a range of possible outcomes, how would you obtain the information necessary to analyze the acquisition?

11. An investment has an outlay of $800 today, an inflow of $5,000 at the end of 1 year, and an outflow of $5,000 at the end of 2 years. What is its internal rate of return? If the initial outlay were $1,250, what would be its IRR? (*Hint:* This case is an exception rather than the rule.)

12. An investment has an inflow of $200 today, an outflow of $300 at the end of 1 year, and an inflow of $400 at the end of 2 years. What is its internal rate of return? (*Hint:* Try calculating NPVs for a wide range of required returns.)

SOLUTIONS TO
SELF-CORRECTION PROBLEMS

1. a.

YEAR	CASH FLOW	DISCOUNT FACTOR (15%)	PRESENT VALUE
0	$ (700,000)	1.00000	$(700,000)
1	(1,000,000)	.86957	(869,570)
2	250,000	.75614	189,035
3	300,000	.65752	197,256
4	350,000	.57175	200,113
5-10	400,000	2.1638 *	865,520
	Net present value		= $(117,646)

* 5.0188 for 10 years − 2.8550 for 4 years

As the net present value is negative, the project is unacceptable.

b. IRR = 13.21%

If the trial-and-error method were used, we would have the following:

YEAR	CASH FLOW	14% DISCOUNT FACTOR	14% PRESENT VALUE	13% DISCOUNT FACTOR	13% PRESENT VALUE
0	$(700,000)	1.0000	$(700,000)	1.0000	$(700,000)
1	(1,000,000)	.87719	(877,190)	.88496	(884,960)
2	250,000	.76947	192,368	.78315	195,788
3	300,000	.67497	202,491	.69305	207,915
4	350,000	.59208	207,228	.61332	214,662
5-10	400,000	2.3024	920,960	2.4517	980,680
	Net present value		$(54,143)		$ 14,085

Interpolating gives us

$$13\% + \frac{\$14,085}{\$54,143 + \$14,085} = 13.21\%$$

As the IRR is less than the required rate of return, the project would not be acceptable.

c. The project would be acceptable.

d. Payback period = 6 years

$$-\$700,000 - \$1,000,000 + \$250,000 + \$300,000 + \$350,000$$

$$+ \$400,000 + \$400,000 = 0$$

2. a. Incremental cash inflows:

166

	1	2	3	4	5	6	7	8
1. Savings	$120,000	$120,000	$120,000	$120,000	$120,000	$120,000	$120,000	$120,000
2. Depreciation, new	96,000	153,600	92,160	55,296	55,296	27,648		
3. Depreciation, old	15,000	15,000	15,000	15,000	15,000	15,000	15,000	15,000
4. Incremental depreciation	81,000	138,600	77,160	40,296	40,296	12,648	(15,000)	(15,000)
5. Profit before tax (1) − (4)	39,000	(18,600)	42,840	79,704	79,704	107,352	135,000	135,000
6. Taxes (34%)	13,260	(6,324)	14,566	27,099	27,099	36,500	45,900	45,900
7. Operating cash flow (1) − (6)	106,740	126,324	105,434	92,901	92,901	83,500	74,100	74,100
8. Salvage value × (1 − .34)								26,400
9. Net cash flow	$106,740	$126,324	$105,434	$ 92,901	$ 92,901	$ 83,500	$ 74,100	$100,500

Incremental cash outflow:

Cost − Sale of old machines − Tax savings on book loss

$480,000 − $70,000 − .34($120,000 − $70,000) = $393,000

b. Net present value of $393,000 outflow and net cash inflows on line 9 above at 14 percent = $75,139
The project is acceptable.

3.

PROJECT	INVESTMENT REQUIRED	PRESENT VALUE OF FUTURE CASH FLOWS	NET PRESENT VALUE
1	$200,000	$290,000	$ 90,000
2	115,000	185,000	70,000
3	270,000	400,000	130,000
1, 2	315,000	475,000	160,000
1, 3	440,000	690,000	250,000
2, 3	385,000	620,000	235,000
1, 2, 3	680,000	910,000	230,000

Projects 1 and 3 should be chosen, as they provide the highest net present value.

4. a.

YEAR	CASH FLOW	INVESTMENT	CASH FLOW	PRESENT VALUE OF NET CASH FLOW (18%)
1	$2,230,000	$1,000,000	$1,130,000	$ 957,630
2	2,645,000	"	1,645,000	1,181,406
3	3,041,750	"	2,041,750	1,242,670
4	3,498,013	"	2,498,013	1,288,450
5	4,022,714	"	3,022,714	1,321,259
6	4,626,122	"	3,626,122	1,343,224
7	5,320,040	"	4,320,040	1,356,147
8	6,118,046	"	5,118,046	1,361,605
9	7,035,753	"	6,035,753	1,360,821
10–25	8,091,116	"	7,091,116	8,253,350
b. Total present value				$19,666,562

The maximum price that is justified is approximately $19\frac{2}{3}$ million. It should be noted that these calculations use present-value tables. For cash flows going from years 10 to 25, we subtract the discount factor for 9 years of annuity payments, 4.3030, in Appendix B at the end of the book from that for 25 years, 5.4669. The difference, $5.4669 - 4.3030 = 1.1639$ is the discount factor for cash flows for an annuity starting in year 10 and going through year 25. If a present-value function of a calculator is used, a slightly different total may be given due to rounding in the present-value tables.

SELECTED REFERENCES

BACON, PETER W., "The Evaluation of Mutually Exclusive Investments," *Financial Management*, 6 (Summer 1977), 55–58.

BRENNER, MENACHEM, and ITZHAK VENEZIA, "The Effects of Inflation and Taxes on Growth Investments and Replacement Policies," *Journal of Finance*, 38 (December 1983), 1519–28.

HERBST, ANTHONY, "The Unique, Real Internal Rate of Return: Caveat Emptor!" *Journal of Financial and Quantitative Analysis*, 13 (June 1978), 363–70.

JENSEN, MICHAEL C., "The Takeover Controversy: Analysis and Evidence," *Midland Corporate Finance Journal*, 4 (Summer 1986), 6–32.

KEANE, SIMON M., "The Internal Rate of Return and the Reinvestment Fallacy," *Journal of Accounting and Business Studies*, 15 (June 1979), 48–55.

LEVY, HAIM, and MARSHALL SARNAT, *Capital Investment & Financial Decisions*, 4th ed. Englewood Cliffs, NJ: Prentice Hall, 1990.

LOGUE, DENNIS E., and T. CRAIG TAPLEY, "Performance Monitoring and the Timing of Cash Flows," *Financial Management*, 14 (Autumn 1985), 34–39.

LORIE, JAMES H., and LEONARD J. SAVAGE, "Three Problems in Rationing Capital," *Journal of Business*, 28 (October 1955), 227–39.

McCONNELL, JOHN J., and CHRIS J. MUSCARELLA, "Corporate Capital Expenditure Decisions and the Market Value of the Firm," *Journal of Financial Economics*, 14 (September 1985), 399–422.

MILLER, EDWARD M., "On the Systematic Risk of Expansion Investment," *Quarterly Review of Economics and Business*, 28 (Autumn 1988), 67–77.

MYERS, STEWART C., "Notes on an Expert System for Capital Budgeting," *Financial Management*, 17 (Autumn 1988), 23–31.

PINCHES, GEORGE E., "Myopia, Capital Budgeting and Decision Making," *Financial Management*, 11 (Autumn 1982), 6–19.

RAPPAPORT, ALFRED, and ROBERT A. TAGGART, JR. "Evaluation of Capital Expenditure Proposals under Inflation," *Financial Management*, 11 (Spring 1982), 5–13.

SCHWAB, BERNHARD, and PETER LUSZTIG, "A Comparative Analysis of the Net Present Value and the Benefit-Cost Ratios as Measures of the Economic Desirability of Investments," *Journal of Finance*, 24 (June 1969), 507–16.

SEITZ, NEIL E., *Capital Budgeting and Long-Term Financing Decision*, Hinsdale, IL: Dryden, 1990.

VAN HORNE, JAMES C., "A Note on Biases in Capital Budgeting Introduced by Inflation," *Journal of Financial and Quantitative Analysis*, 6 (March 1971), 653–58.

———, "Capital Budgeting under Conditions of Uncertainty as to Project Life," *Engineering Economist*, 17 (Spring 1972), 189–99.

———, "The Variation of Project Life as a Means for Adjusting for Risk," *Engineering Economist*, 21 (Spring 1976), 151–58.

WEINGARTNER, H. MARTIN, *Mathematical Programming and the Analysis of Capital Budgeting Problems*. Copyright © H. Martin Weingartner, 1963.

———, "Some New Views on the Payback Period and Capital Budgeting Decisions," *Management Science*, 15 (August 1969), 594–607.

———, "Capital Rationing: n Authors in Search of a Plot," *Journal of Finance*, 32 (December 1977), 1403–31.

7

RISK AND MANAGERIAL OPTIONS IN CAPITAL BUDGETING

Up to now we have worked with expected cash flows when assessing the worth of an investment project. In so doing, we ignored a fact of life. Expectations may not be realized. There is risk associated with the cash-flow estimates as, alas, there is risk associated with most elements of our lives. In the eyes of investors and creditors, a company's business-risk complexion may change as a result of the investments it chooses. The valuation impact of uncertain investments is going to occupy us for three chapters, beginning with this one, in which we take up the information necessary to make intelligent evaluations.

In addition to risk, investment projects sometimes embody in them options for subsequent management decisions. Once a project is accepted, management may have flexibility to make changes that will affect subsequent future cash flows and/or the project's life. We call this ability a *managerial* option, in order to distinguish it from a *financial* option, presented in Chapter 5. However, the same valuation principles are at work. Thus, this chapter deals with how risk and managerial options may alter the treatment of capital budgeting taken up in the last chapter.

QUANTIFYING RISK AND ITS APPRAISAL

From Chapter 2, recall that *risk* was defined as the variability of possible outcomes from that which was expected. Put another way, it is the surprise element in the actual return, the other element being the expected outcome. As in Chapter 2, we will use the standard deviation as a measure of risk. This measure gives us information about the tightness of the probability distribution of possible outcomes. If investors and creditors are risk averse—and all available evidence suggests that they are—it behooves management to incorporate the risk of an investment proposal into its analysis of the proposal's worth. Otherwise, capital budgeting decisions are unlikely to be in accord with an objective of maximizing share price.

169

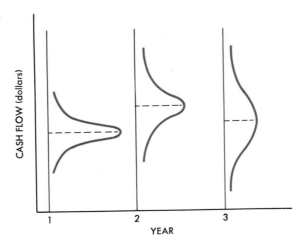

FIGURE 7-1

Illustration of changing risk over time

We begin by considering a single project in which the cash flows are independent from period to period. Our concern is with measuring the overall riskiness of an investment proposal when the probability distributions of cash-flow outcomes for different periods are not necessarily the same. Figure 7-1 illustrates this idea; both the expected value of cash flow and the dispersion of the probability distributions change over time. Once we have presented the basic method of analysis under the assumption of independent probability distributions, we shall move on to consider varying degrees of correlation of cash flows over time.

ASSUMPTION OF INDEPENDENCE

With independence of cash flows over time, the outcome in period t does not depend on what happened in period $t - 1$. Stated differently, there is no causative relationship between cash flows from period to period. The mean of the probability distribution of possible net present values for a proposal is

$$NPV = \sum_{t=0}^{n} \frac{\overline{A_t}}{(1 + R_f)^t} \tag{7-1}$$

where $\overline{A_t}$ is the expected net cash flow in period t, R_f is the risk-free rate, and n is the number of periods over which cash flows are expected.

The risk-free rate is used at this time as the discount rate because we attempt to isolate the time value of money. To include a premium for risk in the discount rate would result in double counting with respect to our analysis. The required rate of return for a project embodies a premium for risk. If this rate is used as the discount rate, we would be adjusting for risk in the discounting process itself. (The greater the discount rate, the greater the risk adjustment, assuming a constant risk-free rate.) We then would use the probability distribution of net present values to judge the risk of the proposal. However, the probability distribution is obtained using a risk-adjusted discount rate. In essence, we would adjust for risk a second time in our analysis of the dispersion of the probability distribution of possible net present values.

Because of the problems inherent in double counting for risk, we take account only of the time value of money in the discounting process.[1]

Given the assumption of serial independence of cash flows for various future periods, the standard deviation of the probability distribution of net present values is

$$\sigma = \sqrt{\sum_{t=0}^{n} \frac{\sigma_t^2}{(1 + R_f)^{2t}}} \qquad (7\text{-}2)$$

where σ_t is the standard deviation of the probability distribution of possible net cash flows in period t. To illustrate the calculations involved with Eq. (7-1) and Eq. (7-2), suppose we had an investment proposal costing $10,000 at time 0 and expected to generate net cash flows during the first three periods with the probabilities shown in Table 7-1. The means of net cash flows for periods 1, 2, and 3, are $5,000 $4,000, and $4,000, respectively. The standard deviation of possible cash flows for period t, σ_t, is computed by

$$\sigma_t = \sqrt{\sum_{x=1}^{5} (A_{xt} - \overline{A}_t)^2 \, P_x t} \qquad (7\text{-}3)$$

where A_{xt} is the xth possible net cash flow, $\overline{A}_t$ is the mean net cash flow for period t, and P_{xt} is the probability of occurrence of A_{xt}.

In the example, the standard deviation of possible net cash flows for period 1 is

$$\sigma_1 = [.10(3,000 - 5,000)^2 + .25(4,000 - 5,000)^2 + .30(5,000 - 5,000)^2$$
$$+ .25(6,000 - 5,000)^2 + .10(7,000 - 5,000)^2]^{1/2}$$
$$= \$1,140$$

Because the probability distributions for periods 2 and 3 have the same dispersion about their expected values as that for period 1, σ_2 and σ_3 are $1,140 also. Given this information, we are able to calculate the net present value for

---

[1] This is not to say that to accept or reject a proposal we should discount at the risk-free rate the mean cash flows. Indeed, in Chapter 8, we show that the appropriate discount rate is the required rate of return, which embodies a premium for the project's risk. For discounting the dispersion of the distribution, however, we use the risk-free rate for the foregoing reasons.

TABLE 7-1
Expected cash flows for example problem

PERIOD 1		PERIOD 2		PERIOD 3	
Probability	Net Cash Flow	Probability	Net Cash Flow	Probability	Net Cash Flow
.10	$3,000	.10	$2,000	.10	$2,000
.25	4,000	.25	3,000	.25	3,000
.30	5,000	.30	4,000	.30	4,000
.25	6,000	.25	5,000	.25	5,000
.10	7,000	.10	6,000	.10	6,000

171

CHAPTER 7
Risk and
Managerial
Options in Capital
Budgeting

the proposal as well as the standard deviation. If we assume a risk-free rate of 8 percent, the net present value for the proposal is

$$NPV = -10,000 + \frac{5,000}{(1.08)} + \frac{4,000}{(1.08)^2} + \frac{4,000}{(1.08)^3} = \$1,234$$

Using Eq. (7-2), under the assumption of mutual independence of cash flows over time, the standard deviation is

$$\sigma = \sqrt{\frac{1,140^2}{(1.08)^2} + \frac{1,140^2}{(1.08)^4} + \frac{1,140^2}{(1.08)^6}} = \$1,700$$

STANDARDIZING THE DISPERSION

The expected value and the standard deviation of the probability distribution of possible net present values give us a considerable amount of information by which to evaluate the risk of the investment proposal. If the probability distribution is approximately normal (bell-shaped), we are able to calculate the probability of a proposal's providing a net present value of less or more than a specified amount. The probability is found by determining the area under the curve to the left or to the right of a particular point of interest.

To go to our previous illustration, suppose we wish to determine the probability that the net present value will be zero or less. To determine this probability, we first calculate the difference between zero and the net present value for the project. In our example, this difference is −$1,234. We then standardize this difference by dividing it by the standard deviation of the probability distribution of possible net present values. The formula is

$$S = \frac{X - NPV}{\sigma} \tag{7-4}$$

where X is the outcome in which we are interested, NPV is the mean of the probability distribution, and σ is the standard deviation. In our case

$$S = \frac{0 - 1,234}{1,700} = -.726$$

This figure tells us that a net present value of zero lies .726 standard deviations to the left of the mean of the probability distribution of possible net present values.

To determine the probability that the net present value of the project will be zero or less, we consult the normal probability distribution table (Table C) at the end of this book. (More detailed tables are found in most statistics texts.) With respect to the problem at hand, we find with interpolation that there is a .23 probability that an observation will be less than −.726 standard deviation from the mean of that distribution. Thus, there is a .23 probability that the net present value of the proposal will be zero or less. Put another way, there is a .23 probability that the internal rate of return of the project will be less than the risk-free rate. If we assume a continuous distribution, the probability density function of our example problem can be shown as in Fig. 7-2.

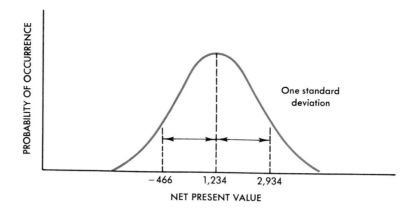

FIGURE 7-2
Probability density function, example problem

The mean of the probability distribution of possible net present values is $1,234. One standard deviation on either side of the mean gives us net present values of −$466 and $2,934. With a normal distribution, .683 of the distribution or area under the curve falls within one standard deviation on either side of the mean.[2] Thus, we know that there is approximately a two-thirds probability that the net present value of the proposal examined will be between −$466 and $2,934. We know also that there is a .23 probability that the net present value will be less than zero and a .77 probability that it will be greater than zero. By expressing differences from the mean in terms of standard deviations, we are able to determine the probability that the net present value for an investment proposal will be greater or less than a particular amount.

Knowledge of these probabilities is fundamental for a realistic assessment of risk. Suppose the firm is considering another mutually exclusive investment project, proposal Y. The probability density function for this proposal is shown in Fig. 7-3, as is that for our example problem, proposal X. We see that the mean net present value for proposal Y, $2,260, is higher than that for proposal X, $1,234, but there is also greater dispersion of the probability distribution. If risk is directly related to dispersion, proposal Y has both a higher expected profitability and a greater risk than does proposal X.

[2] Approximately .954 of a normal distribution falls within two standard deviations on either side of the mean and .997 within three standard deviations.

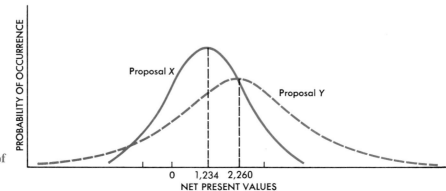

FIGURE 7-3
Probability distribution of net present values for proposals X and Y

INFORMATION GENERATED

The approach just outlined can be adapted to internal rates of return. What is involved is expression of the distribution in terms of possible internal rates of return as opposed to net present values. By varying the discount rate, R_f, in Eq. (7-2), we obtain standard deviations for different discount rates. For each standard deviation, the probability that net present value will be zero or less can be computed. These probabilities then are plotted with the discount rate along the horizontal axis in ascending order and with the corresponding probabilities on the vertical axis. A probability distribution of possible internal rates of return emerges from which the mean and standard deviation can be computed. Using the standard deviation together with the mean of possible internal rates of return, one is able to perform the same type of analysis as before.

In the examples, we have assumed normal probability distributions. Although this property is desirable for purposes of calculation, it is not a necessary condition for the use of the foregoing approach. Even when the distribution is not normal, we usually are able to make reasonably strong probability statements by using Tchebycheff's inequality. This approach is based on the fact that regardless of the form of the distribution, there is a close relationship between the magnitude of deviations from the mean of the distribution and probability.[3] Again, we are interested in the area under the curve, or probability density function, that is to the left or right of a particular net present value or internal rate of return. By computing this area, we are able to determine the probability that the index will be greater or less than a particular amount and judge the risk of the project accordingly.

Biases in Obtaining Information. Before closing this section, we must point out that the main difficulty associated with risky investments lies in obtaining cash-flow estimates from people, not in the mathematical manipulation of the data obtained. People being what they are, biases invariably creep into the process. Sometimes the incentive compensation of managers is linked to the return on assets relative to some standard. If this standard is based on the expected return for investment projects, managers are likely to bias their estimates downward. In this way they are more likely to be able to exceed the standard. To ensure unbiased cash-flow forecasts, it is essential that the compensation of those doing the forecasting is divorced from subsequent performance.

Bias may arise because of the nature of the selection process. An individual may make unbiased cash-flow estimates for projects arising in that person's area of responsibility. For some projects, these estimates will prove to be too high, whereas for others they will be too low. However, on average, the estimates are unbiased in the sense that over- and underestimates cancel out. But not all projects are accepted. The forecasts are given to a higher level of management, which, in turn, makes the accept-reject decision. Acceptance, of course, depends on a project's likely return relative to its risk. In this regard, there may be a tendency to select projects where costs are underestimated and revenues overestimated.[4] Even though a person's overall estimates are unbi-

---

[3] For an extensive discussion and application of this technique, see Stephen L. Buzby, "Extending the Applicability of Probabilistic Management and Control Models," *Accounting Review*, 49 (January 1974), 42–49.

[4] Keith C. Brown, "A Note on the Apparent Bias of Net Revenue Estimates for Capital Investment Projects," *Journal of Finance*, 29 (September 1974), 1215–16, first pointed out this bias.

ased, this tendency will result in those selected being biased. If this happens, actual returns on accepted investment projects will be lower on average than their projected returns. Decision tree approaches have been advanced for adjusting for this type of bias.[5]

175

CHAPTER 7
Risk and
Managerial
Options in Capital
Budgeting

In the adjustment for biases, one problem faced in any organization is overadjustment. Sam makes a forecast that he regards as unbiased and sends it up through the chain of command for final project approval. Linda believes Sam to be consistently biased and adjusts the forecast before sending it forward. Pete does not trust Linda's adjusted forecast, so he makes an adjustment to correct for the perceived bias. And so the process goes until the information finally reviewed by top management bears little resemblance to that originally provided by Sam. Also, there is the problem of accountability. Because capital investment projects involve returns over many years, it is difficult to go back to the person who made the forecast with the actual results. That person often has been transferred or has left the company. While the best approach to correcting biases may be to present a forecaster with the actual results for a number of projects and to compare these results with the forecasts, this often is not possible for long-lived projects.

In addition to the biases described, others also are possible. Although the focus of this chapter is on the quantitative organization of data, we must be mindful of the fact that the accuracy of the final results depends heavily on behavioral considerations. Every effort must be made to provide an environment conducive to the unbiased forecasting of project cash flows.

DEPENDENCE OF CASH FLOWS OVER TIME

In the preceding section, we assumed serial independence of cash flows from one future period to another. For most investment proposals, however, the cash flow in one future period depends in part on the cash flows in previous periods. If an investment proposal turns bad in the early years, the probability is high that cash flows in later years also will be lower than originally expected. To assume that an extremely unfavorable or favorable outcome in the early life of an investment proposal will not affect the later outcome is unrealistic in most investment situations. The consequence of cash flows being correlated over time is that the standard deviation of the probability distribution of possible net present values or possible internal rates of return is larger than it would be if we assumed independence. The greater the degree of correlation, the greater the dispersion of the probability distribution. The mean net present value, however, is the same, regardless of the degree of correlation over time. In this section, we explore varying degrees of dependence of cash flows over time.

Perfect Correlation. Cash flows are perfectly correlated over time if they deviate in exactly the same relative manner—if actual cash flows for all periods show the same relative deviation from the means of their respective probability distributions of expected cash flows. In other words, the cash flow in period t depends entirely on what happened in previous periods. If the ac-

---

[5] See Edward M. Miller, "Uncertainty Induced Bias in Capital Budgeting," *Financial Management*, 7 (Autumn 1978), 12–18; Keith C. Brown, "The Rate of Return of Selected Investment Projects," *Journal of Finance*, 33 (September 1978), 1250–53; and Seymour Smidt, "A Bayesian Analysis of Project Selection and of Post Audit Evaluations," *Journal of Finance*, 34 (June 1979), 675–88.

tual cash flow in period t is X standard deviations to the right of the mean of the probability distribution of possible cash flows for that period, actual cash flows in all other periods will be X standard deviations to the right of the means of their respective probability distributions. Stated differently, the cash flow in any period is a linear function of the cash flows in all other periods. The formula for the standard deviation of a perfectly correlated stream of cash flows over time is

$$\sigma = \sum_{t=0}^{n} \frac{\sigma_t}{(1 + R_f)^t} \qquad (7\text{-}5)$$

To illustrate its use, consider the same example as before. The standard deviation for the proposal, using Eq. (7-5), is

$$\sigma = \frac{1{,}140}{(1.08)} + \frac{1{,}140}{(1.08)^2} + \frac{1{,}140}{(1.08)^3} = \$2{,}938$$

This compares with a standard deviation of \$1,700 when we used Eq. (7-2) under the assumption of serial independence over time. Thus, the standard deviation for a perfectly correlated stream of cash flows is significantly greater than the standard deviation for the same stream under the assumption of mutual independence. The standard deviation for a less than perfectly correlated stream of cash flows will be somewhere between these two values.[6] The probabilistic analysis of a project with a perfectly correlated stream of cash flows over time is the same as that illustrated previously for a project with an uncorrelated stream.

Moderate Correlation. Where the cash flows of the firm are neither approximately independent nor perfectly correlated over time, the classification of the cash-flow stream as one or the other is not appropriate. One method for dealing with the problem of moderate correlation is with a series of conditional probability distributions. Suppose the investment in a project costing \$10,000 at time 0 is expected to generate net cash flows in periods 1, 2, and 3 with the probabilities in Table 7-2. The table shows 27 possible cash-flow series. The last column depicts the joint probability of occurrence of a particular cash-flow series. For series 1, the joint probability of a −\$6,000 cash flow in period 1 being followed by cash flows of −\$2,000 and \$5,000 in periods 2 and 3, respectively, is .25 × .30 × .25 = .01875. Similarly, joint probabilities for the other cash-flow series can be determined in this manner.

The use of conditional probability distributions enables us to take account of the correlation of cash flows over time. In the above example, the cash flow in period 3 depends on what happened in periods 1 and 2; however, the correlation of cash flows over time is not perfect. With a given cash flow in period 1, the cash flow in period 2 can vary within a range. Similarly, the cash flow in period 3 can vary within a range, depending on the outcomes in periods 1 and 2.

---

[6] Frederick S. Hillier, "The Derivation of Probabilistic Information for the Evaluation of Risky Investments," *Management Science*, 9 (April 1963), 443–57, combines the assumptions of mutual independence and perfect correlation of cash flows in developing a model to deal with mixed situations. Essentially, the overall cash flows of the firm are separated and classified as either independent or perfectly correlated over time. A formula is derived for calculating the standard deviation.

TABLE 7-2
Illustration of conditional probability distribution approach

PERIOD 1		PERIOD 2		PERIOD 3			JOINT
Initial Probability $P(1)$	Net Cash Flow	Conditional Probability $P(2\mid 1)$	Net Cash Flow	Conditional Probability $P(3\mid 2,1)$	Net Cash Flow	CASH-FLOW SERIES	PROBABILITY $P(1,2,3)$
				.25	5,000	1	.01875
		.30	−$ 2,000	.50	7,000	2	.03750
				.25	9,000	3	.01875
				.25	7,000	4	.02500
.25	−$6,000	.40	1,000	.50	9,000	5	.05000
				.25	11,000	6	.02500
				.25	9,000	7	.01875
		.30	4,000	.50	11,000	8	.03750
				.25	13,000	9	.01875
				.30	10,000	10	.03750
		.25	3,000	.40	12,000	11	.05000
				.30	14,000	12	.03750
				.30	12,000	13	.07500
.50	− 4,000	.50	6,000	.40	14,000	14	.10000
				.30	16,000	15	.07500
				.30	14,000	16	.03750
		.25	9,000	.40	16,000	17	.05000
				.30	18,000	18	.03750
				.25	15,000	19	.01875
		.30	8,000	.50	17,000	20	.03750
				.25	19,000	21	.01875
				.25	17,000	22	.02500
.25	− 2,000	.40	11,000	.50	19,000	23	.05000
				.25	21,000	24	.02500
				.25	19,000	25	.01875
		.30	14,000	.50	21,000	26	.03750
				.25	23,000	27	.01875

The calculation of the mean net present value using this approach is the same as in Eq. (7-1). The standard deviation may be determined mathematically for the simple case by

$$\sigma = \sqrt{\sum_{x=1}^{l} (NPV_x - \overline{NPV})^2 P_x} \qquad (7\text{-}6)$$

where NPV_x is the net present value for series x of net cash flows, covering all periods, $\overline{NPV}$ is the mean net present value of the proposal, and P_x is the probability of occurrence of that series. For the example, there are 27 possible series of cash flows, so that $l = 27$. The first series is represented by a net cash flow of −$10,000 at time 0, −$6,000 at time 1, −$2,000 at time 2, and $5,000 at time 3. The probability of occurrence of that series is .01875.

Unfortunately, for complex situations the mathematical calculation of the standard deviation is unfeasible. For these situations, we can *approximate* the standard deviation by means of simulation. With this method, we use random sampling to select cash-flow series for evaluation and calculate the net present value or internal rate of return for each selected series. When a random sample of sufficient size has been built up in this way, the mean and standard deviation of the probability distribution are estimated from the sample; this information is then analyzed in much the same manner as before.

We have seen that our assumption as to the degree of correlation of cash flows over time is an important one. If cash flows are highly correlated over time, the risk of a project will be considerably greater than if they are mutually independent, all other things being the same. Although independence often is assumed for ease of calculation, this assumption greatly underestimates project risk if in fact the cash flows are highly correlated over time. Thus, it is important to give careful consideration to the likely degree of dependence of cash flows over time. Otherwise, the assessment of risk may well be distorted. Of the approaches for dealing with the problem, the use of conditional probabilities is the most accurate, although the most difficult to implement. Other approaches to moderately correlated cash flows could be illustrated, but the discussion in this section as well as in the next is sufficient to give a flavor of how to go about it.[7]

A SIMULATION APPROACH

In considering risky investments, we can use simulation to approximate the expected return and dispersion about the expected return for an investment proposal. By *simulation,* we mean testing the results of an investment decision before it actually occurs. The testing itself is based on a model coupled with probabilistic information. A simulation model proposed by Hertz considers the following factors in deriving a project's earnings stream:

MARKET ANALYSIS

1. Market size
2. Selling price
3. Market growth rate
4. Share of market (which results in physical sales volume)

INVESTMENT COST ANALYSIS

5. Investment required
6. Residual value of investment

OPERATING AND FIXED COSTS

7. Operating costs
8. Fixed costs
9. Useful life of facilities[8]

---

[7] Carmelo Giacotto, "A Simplified Approach to Risk Analysis in Capital Budgeting with Serially Correlated Cash Flows," *Engineering Economist,* 29 (Summer 1984), 273–86, uses a Markov model to estimate the expected return and risk involved in less than perfectly correlated cash flows over time. In his model, cash flows are assumed to follow a growth path with a random disturbance term. The model may be used when uncertainty increases with futurity and is another example of an approach to correlated cash flows over time.

[8] David B. Hertz, "Risk Analysis in Capital Investment," *Harvard Business Review,* 42 (January–February 1964), 95–106; and Hertz, "Investment Policies That Pay Off," *Harvard Business Review,* 46 (January–February 1968), 96–108.

Probability distributions are assigned to each of these factors, based on management's assessment of the probable outcomes.

Once the probability distributions are determined, the next step is to determine the average rate of return that will result from a random combination of the nine factors listed. To illustrate the simulation process, assume that the market-size factor had the following probability distribution:

179

CHAPTER 7
Risk and
Managerial
Options in Capital
Budgeting

Market size (in thousand units)	450	500	550	600	650	700	750
Probability	.05	.10	.20	.30	.20	.10	.05

Now suppose that we have a roulette wheel with 100 numbers, on which numbers 1 to 5 represent a market size of 450,000 units; 6 to 15 represent a market size of 500,000; 16 to 35, a market size of 550,000 units, and so on through 100. As in roulette, we spin the wheel, and the ball falls in one of the 100 slots: number 26. For this trial, then, we simulate a market size of 550,000 units. Fortunately, we do not need a roulette wheel to undertake a simulation; the same type of operation can be carried out on a computer in a much more efficient manner.

Simulation trials are undertaken for each of the other eight factors. The first four factors (market analysis) give us the annual sales per year; factors 7 and 8 give us the operating costs and fixed costs per year. Together, these six factors enable us to calculate the annual earnings per year. When trial values for these six factors are combined with trial values for the required investment, the useful life, and the residual value of the project, we have sufficient information to calculate the return on investment for that trial run. Thus, the computer simulates trial values for each of the nine factors and then calculates the return on investment based on the values simulated. The process is repeated a number of times. Each time we obtain a combination of values for the nine factors and the return on investment for that combination. When the trial is repeated often enough, the rate of return obtained can be plotted in a frequency distribution.

From this frequency distribution, we are able to evaluate the expected return and the dispersion about this expected return, or risk, in the same manner as before; in other words, we can determine the probability that an investment will provide a return greater or less than a certain amount. By comparing the probability distribution of rates of return for one proposal with the probability distribution of rates of return for another, management is able to evaluate the respective merits of different risky investments. Hertz's simulation method has been used extensively and applied to a wide variety of investment projects.

Two points should be made about the simulation method illustrated. Although the simulation model computes the average rate of return on investment, the method could easily be modified to calculate the internal rate of return, the net present value, or the profitability index. In addition, although Hertz allows for dependency among the nine factors, the model presented treats the factors as though they were independent. To the extent that dependency exists among factors, it must be taken into account in determining the probability distributions. For example, there is likely to be significant correlation between the market size and the selling price. These interrelationships add considerable complexity to the estimating procedure. Notwithstanding the added complexity of estimating and specifying the relationships among factors, it must be done if the model is to provide realistic results.

TOTAL RISK FOR MULTIPLE INVESTMENTS

We have been measuring risk for a single investment project. When multiple investment projects are involved, the measurement may differ from that for a single project, owing to the properties of diversification.[9] Diversification of securities was discussed in Chapter 3, and this concept applies also to capital assets; however, it is noteworthy that investment in capital assets differs from investment in securities. For one thing, capital assets typically are not divisible, whereas securities are. Moreover, it usually is much more costly, and sometimes impossible, to divest oneself of a capital asset, whereas selling a marketable security is relatively easy. Finally, there is the problem of mutual exclusion and contingency that does not occur with securities. All of these factors make diversification with respect to capital assets more "lumpy" than diversification with securities. Whether diversification of capital assets is a thing of value for the firm is a subject of considerable controversy, one that will be analyzed in the next two chapters. Our purpose here is only to show how to measure risk for combinations of risky investments, not to ponder whether such measurement is worthwhile. That comes later.

As was true earlier, the two pieces of information we seek are the mean and standard deviation of the probability distribution of possible net present values for the combination of projects being analyzed. The mean usually is simply a weighted average for the projects making up the combination. From Chapter 3, we know that the total variance, or risk, of a combination of risky investments depends to a large extent on the degree of correlation between the investments. The standard deviation of the probability distribution of possible net present values for a portfolio of capital investments can be expressed as

$$\sigma = \sqrt{\sum_{j=1}^{m} \sum_{k=1}^{m} r_{jk}\sigma_j\sigma_k} \tag{7-7}$$

where m is the total number of assets in the portfolio, r_{jk} is the expected correlation between the net present values for investments j and k, σ_j is the standard deviation for investment j, and σ_k the standard deviation for investment k.

Equation (7-7) indicates that the standard deviation, or risk, of a portfolio of projects depends on (1) the degree of correlation between various projects and (2) the standard deviation of possible net present values for each project. We note that the higher the degree of positive correlation, the greater the standard deviation of the portfolio of projects, all other things remaining constant. Moreover, the greater the standard deviations of the individual projects, the greater the standard deviation of the portfolio, if the correlation is positive. The standard deviations of the individual investment projects, necessary for the calculation of Eq. (7-7), are obtained through the methods presented earlier in the chapter.

[9] The development of this section assumes that the reader has studied portfolio selection in Chapter 3.

CORRELATION BETWEEN PROJECTS

181

CHAPTER 7
Risk and
Managerial
Options in Capital
Budgeting

As was the case with a portfolio of securities discussed in Chapter 3, the correlation between expected net present values of two projects may be positive, negative, or zero, depending on the nature of the association. A correlation coefficient of 1.00 indicates that the net present values of two investment proposals vary directly in the same proportional manner; a correlation coefficient of −1.00 indicates that they vary inversely in the same proportional manner; and a zero correlation coefficient usually indicates that they are independent.

For most pairs of investment projects, the correlation coefficient lies between 0 and 1.00. The lack of negatively correlated projects is due to most investments being correlated positively with the economy. Still it is possible to find projects having low or moderate degrees of correlation. Management might have reason to expect only slight correlation between an investment project involving an industrial product and one involving a new consumer product. It might, however, expect high positive correlation between investments in a milling machine and a turret lathe if both machines are to be used in the production of industrial lift trucks. Projects in the same general line of business tend to be highly correlated with each other, while projects in essentially unrelated lines of business tend to have low degrees of correlation.

If you are trying to obtain a realistic standard deviation from Eq. (7-7), you must carefully estimate correlation coefficients. Perhaps your investment project will be similar to an earlier one, and your historical data will help you to compute correlation coefficients. If not, you may have to rely on an assessment of the future. It is not unreasonable to expect management to make fairly accurate estimates of the correlation between investment projects. When the actual correlation differs from the expected, the situation can be a learning process, and estimates on other projects can be revised.

To illustrate calculations with Eq. (7-7), suppose a firm has a single existing investment project, 1, and it is considering an additional project, 2. The projects have the following expected net present values, standard deviations, and correlation coefficients:

	EXPECTED NET PRESENT VALUE	STANDARD DEVIATION	CORRELATION COEFFICIENT
Project 1	$12,000	$14,000	1.00
Project 2	8,000	6,000	1.00
Projects 1 and 2			.40

The expected net present value of the combination of projects is simply the sum of the two separate net present values:

$$NPV = \$12,000 + \$8,000 = \$20,000$$

The standard deviation for the combination, using Eq. (7-7), is

$$\sigma = \sqrt{r_{11}\sigma_1^2 + 2r_{12}\sigma_1\sigma_2 + r_{22}\sigma_2^2}$$

$$= \sqrt{(1.00)(14,000)^2 + (2)(.40)(14,000)(6,000) + (1.00)(6,000)^2}$$

$$= \$17,297$$

Thus, the expected net present value of the firm increases from $12,000 to $20,000, and the standard deviation of possible net present values from $14,000 to $17,297 with the acceptance of project 2.

As can be imagined, if the number of projects is large the calculations become cumbersome. Chi-Cheng Hsia and Russell J. Fuller develop a simplified model for approximating the total variance of discounted cash flows for multiple projects.[10] If the stochastic process governing cash-flow behavior is first-order autoregressive, the model provides reasonable approximations with far fewer calculations than occur with Eq. (7-7).

FEASIBLE COMBINATIONS AND DOMINANCE

With the foregoing procedures, you can determine the mean and the standard deviation of the probability distribution of possible net present values for a combination of investments. A combination includes all existing investment projects and one or more proposals under consideration. We assume that a firm has existing investment projects generating expected future cash flows and that disinvestment with respect to these projects is not possible. Existing projects comprise a subset that is included in all combinations. Proposals under consideration are assumed to represent all future proposals on the investment horizon.

The next step involves analyzing feasible combinations of existing projects and proposals under consideration according to their net present values, and standard deviations, to see which combinations dominate. In Fig. 7-4, a scatter diagram, the expected value of net present value is along the horizontal axis; the standard deviation is on the vertical axis. Each dot represents a feasible combination of proposals under consideration and existing investment projects for the firm.

Collectively, the dots represent the total set of feasible combinations of investment opportunities available to the firm. This set corresponds to the opportunity set of security portfolios discussed in Chapter 3, the major difference being that combinations of investment projects are not as divisible as

---

[10] Chi-Cheng Hsia and Russell J. Fuller, "A Simplified Model for Measuring Total Risk of Discounted Cash Flows," working paper, Portland State University and Washington State University (1988).

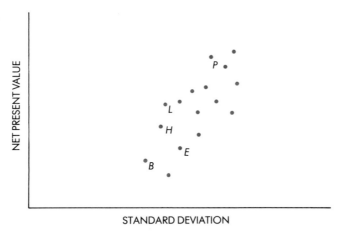

FIGURE 7-4
Opportunity and project portfolio

portfolios of securities. Certain dots in Fig. 7-4 dominate others in the sense that they represent a higher net present value and the same standard deviation, a lower standard deviation and the same net present value, or both a higher net present value and a lower standard deviation. The dots that dominate others are those that are farthest to the left, and they correspond to the efficient frontier for an opportunity set of security portfolios.

If E represents the existing portfolio of investment projects, it is dominated by combination P with respect to net present value, by combination B with respect to standard deviation, and by combinations H and L with respect to both net present value and standard deviation. Other dots dominate E, but these are not on the frontier. With the type of information in Fig. 7-4, most combinations of investment proposals can be eliminated simply because they are dominated by other combinations. In Chapter 9, we take up the evaluation of this information and the acceptance criterion. Our purpose in this chapter is only to present the measurement of portfolio risk.

We observe that the combination of projects ultimately chosen determines the new investment proposal or proposals that will be accepted. An exception occurs only when the portfolio selected is composed of existing projects. In this situation, no investment proposals under consideration would be accepted. In our case, the portfolio of existing projects is represented by dot E in Fig. 7-4. Therefore, the selection of any of the four outlying portfolios would imply the acceptance of one or more new investment proposals. Those investment proposals under consideration but not in the portfolio finally selected would be rejected, of course. The incremental net present value and standard deviation can be determined by measuring on the horizontal and vertical axes the distance from dot E to the dot representing the combination finally selected. Instead of working with net present values, the framework described can be expressed in terms of internal rates of return. The reader should easily be able to visualize this change, for the principles are the same.

MANAGERIAL OPTIONS

For the capital budgeting projects so far considered, cash flows were assumed out to some horizon and then discounted to present value. Investment projects are not necessarily set in concrete once they are accepted. Managers can, and often do, make changes that affect subsequent cash flows and/or the life of the project. Slavish devotion to discounted cash-flow methods (DCF) often ignores future managerial flexibility. That is, the flexibility to alter old decisions when conditions change.

VALUATION IN GENERAL

The presence of managerial options enhances the worth of an investment project. Its worth can be viewed as the net present value of the project, calculated in the usual way, together with the value of the option(s).

$$\text{Project worth} = \text{NPV} + \text{Option value} \qquad (7\text{-}8)$$

The greater the number of options and the greater the uncertainty surrounding their use, the greater the second term in the equation and the greater the project's worth.

183

CHAPTER 7
Risk and
Managerial
Options in Capital
Budgeting

The types of managerial options available include

1. The option to vary output. An important option is to expand production if conditions turn favorable and to contract production if conditions turn bad.
2. The option to abandon. If a project has abandonment value, this effectively represents a put option to the project's owner.
3. The option to postpone. For some projects there is the option to wait, thereby obtaining new information.

Sometimes these options are treated informally as qualitative factors when judging the worth of a project. It may be no more than "if such and such occurs, we will have the opportunity to do this." Managerial options are more difficult to value than are financial options; the option formulas taken up in Chapter 5 often do not work. Rather, resort must be made to decision trees, simulations, and ad hoc approaches.

THE OPTION TO EXPAND

For a manufacturing plant, management often has the option to make a follow-on investment. Gummy Glue Company is evaluating a new, revolutionary glue. It can build a plant that is capable of producing 25,000 cans a month. That level of production is not economical, either from a manufacturing or from a marketing standpoint. As a result, the project's new present value is expected to be −$3 million. According to classical DCF analysis, the project should be rejected.

However, the new glue could be a winner. If it takes off, Gummy Glue Company could then invest in a new plant, say 2 years hence, which would triple output and be highly efficient. However, the opportunity for this level of demand is not available unless an initial investment is made. (Without the initial investment, the company would not have first-mover advantage.)

There is a 50-50 chance the market will take off. If it does, the net present value of the new investment at the end of year 2 will be $15 million. When discounted at the required rate of return, the NPV at time 0 is $11 million. If the market does not take off, the company will not invest further and incremental NPV at the end of year 2, by definition, is zero. The situation is depicted in Figure 7-5.

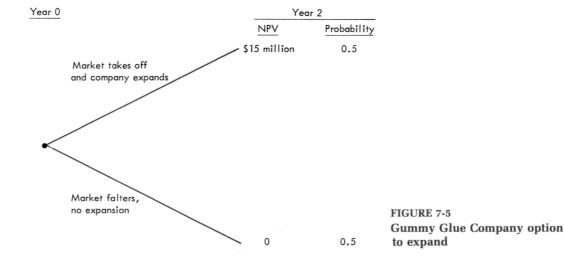

Year 0	Year 2	
	NPV	Probability
Market takes off and company expands	$15 million	0.5
Market falters, no expansion	0	0.5

FIGURE 7-5
Gummy Glue Company option
to expand

The mean of the distribution of possible NPVs associated with the option is 0.5($11 million) + 0.5(0) = $5.5 million. Using Eq. (7-8),

$$\text{Project worth} = -\$3 \text{ million} + \$5.5 \text{ million}$$

$$= \$2.5 \text{ million}$$

185

CHAPTER 7
Risk and
Managerial
Options in Capital
Budgeting

Even though the initial project has a negative NPV, the option to expand more than offsets it. Because it embraces a valuable option, the project should be accepted. For sequential decisions of this sort, a decision tree allows analysis of the subsequent chance events.[11]

INITIAL REGIONAL VERSUS NATIONAL DISTRIBUTION

A variation of this theme involves new product distribution. Major Munch Cereal Company is considering the introduction of a new cereal, honey-coated oat flakes. Initially, it must decide whether to distribute the product in the Midwest or nationally. Regional distribution will require an expenditure of $1 million for a new plant and for the initial marketing effort. Depending upon demand during the first two years, the company then would decide whether or not to expand to national distribution. If it goes from regional to national distribution, it will need to spend an additional $3 million for expansion of the existing plant and to make an additional marketing effort. Of course, Major Munch can distribute nationally from the very outset. If it does, it will cost $3 million to construct a plant and to launch the marketing of the product. We see that there are economies associated with distributing nationally at the outset. For one thing, building a large plant is less expensive than building a small one and having to enlarge it later. Moreover, there are economies in marketing.

Thus, the $1 million initial investment buys Major Munch Cereal Company an option to be exercised at the end of two years either to distribute nationally or to continue regional distribution. The nature of the option is illustrated graphically by the decision tree shown in Fig. 7-6. The squares represent decision points. The first decision is whether to distribute regionally or nationally. The circles represent chance event nodes. If the company decides to distribute nationally at the outset, there is 0.4 probability that demand will prove to be high, 0.4 that demand will turn out to be medium, and 0.2 that it will be low. On the other hand, if the company distributes regionally, there is 0.5 probability that demand will be high, 0.3 probability that it will be medium, and 0.2 probability that it will be low. At the end of year 2, the company must decide whether to continue to distribute regionally, in which case demand will continue to be high, low, or medium, or whether it should distribute nationally, in which case the national demand is shown by the subsequent chance event in the figure.

The expected net present values for the various branches are shown in Table 7-3. This information is derived from the expected cash-flow streams for each branch using the risk-free rate as the discount rate. If Major Munch switches from regional to national distribution at the end of year 2, there is a cash expenditure of $3 million, and this represents a negative cash flow at

[11] For a simplified analytical approach to sequential decision problems, see Clarence C. I. Kwan and Yufei Yuan, "Optimal Sequential Selection in Capital Budgeting: A Shortcut," *Financial Management*, 17 (Spring 1988), 54–59.

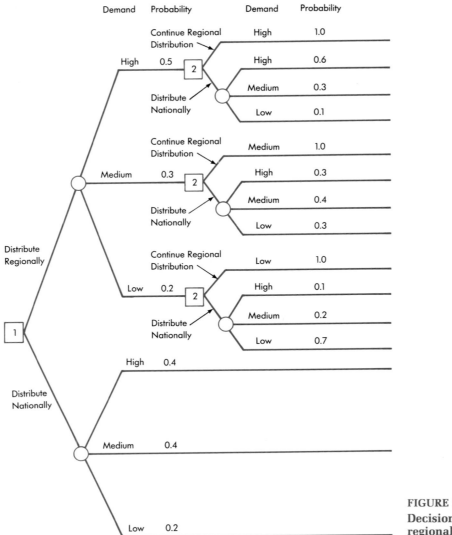

FIGURE 7-6
Decision tree; national versus regional distribution

that time. This outflow is in addition to the cash outflow of $1 million at time 0 for the regional plant. We need now to incorporate these net present values into our decision tree. In Fig. 7-7, they are shown at the branch tips, indicating the expected net present values associated with the sequence of decisions and chance events comprising the branch.

Optimal Set of Decisions. You may determine the optimal sequence of decisions by "rolling back" the tree from the right-hand side. In other words, first appraise the most distant decisions; namely, the choice of whether or not to switch from regional to national distribution. To do so, determine the mean net present value for national distribution, given that demand for the regional distribution proves to be high, medium, or low. The mean net present value is simply the net present values at the branch tips times the probabilities of occurrence. For high regional demand, the net present value for subsequent national distribution is

186

187

CHAPTER 7
Risk and
Managerial
Options in Capital
Budgeting

TABLE 7-3
Expected net present values for various branches of decision tree (000 omitted)

	NET PRESENT VALUE
Regional distribution throughout:	
High demand	$ 947.4
Medium demand	136.2
Low demand	− 637.1
Regional distribution followed by national distribution:	
High regional–high national demand	4,096.9
High regional–medium national demand	1,573.1
High regional–low national demand	− 704.1
Medium regional–high national demand	3,377.4
Medium regional–medium national demand	932.6
Medium regional–low national demand	− 1,426.8
Low regional–high national demand	2,411.2
Low regional–medium national demand	51.9
Low regional–low national demand	− 2,307.5
National distribution throughout:	
High demand	3,830.5
Medium demand	851.6
Low demand	− 1,927.3

$$NPV = 0.6(4,096.9) + 0.3(1,573.1) + 0.1(-704.1)$$
$$= \$2,859.6 \tag{7-9}$$

This amount appears at the chance event node for national distribution, given high regional demand.

In a similar fashion, the means of net present value for national distribution, given medium and low regional demands, are computed and shown at the appropriate chance event nodes. We note in Fig. 7-7 that the net present value for national distribution, given low regional demand, is −$1,363,800. This figure compares with an expected net present value of −$637,100 if the company continues with regional distribution. Thus, if regional demand is low, the company should not distribute nationally but should continue to distribute regionally. On the other hand, if regional demand turns out to be either high or medium, Major Munch should go to national distribution, for the net present value is higher than it is if the firm continues with regional distribution. By backward induction, then, you are able to determine the optimal decision at the most distant decision point.

The next step is to determine the optimal decision at the first decision point; that is, to decide whether to distribute nationally or regionally at the outset. The mean net present value for regional distribution, given optimal decisions at decision point 2, is

$$NPV = 0.5(2,859.6) + 0.3(958.2) + 0.2(-637.1) = \$1,589.8 \tag{7-10}$$

Note that if regional demand is high or medium, we use the net present value associated with subsequent national distribution. If regional demand is low, we use the net present value associated with continuing regional distribution. The net present value for initial national distribution is

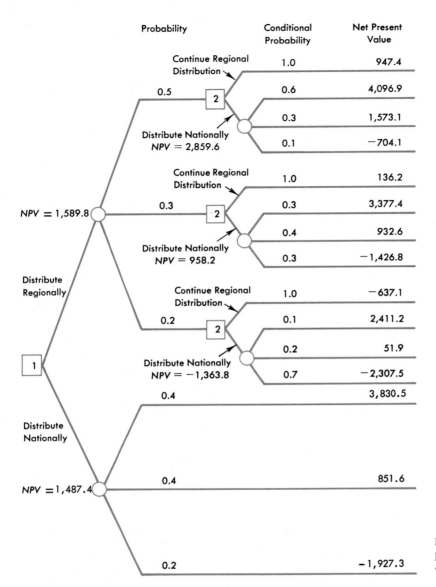

Probability	Conditional Probability	Net Present Value

Continue Regional Distribution — 1.0 — 947.4

0.5 — 2

Distribute Nationally NPV = 2,859.6

0.6 — 4,096.9
0.3 — 1,573.1
0.1 — −704.1

NPV = 1,589.8

Continue Regional Distribution — 1.0 — 136.2

0.3 — 2

Distribute Nationally NPV = 958.2

0.3 — 3,377.4
0.4 — 932.6
0.3 — −1,426.8

Distribute Regionally

Continue Regional Distribution — 1.0 — −637.1

0.2 — 2

Distribute Nationally NPV = −1,363.8

0.1 — 2,411.2
0.2 — 51.9
0.7 — −2,307.5

0.4 — 3,830.5

1

Distribute Nationally

0.4 — 851.6

NPV = 1,487.4

0.2 — −1,927.3

FIGURE 7-7
Decision tree; net present values of branches

$$NPV = 0.4(3,830.5) + 0.4(851.6) + 0.2(-1,927.3)$$

$$= \$1,487.4$$

(7-11)

Thus, the mean net present value for initial regional distribution exceeds that for initial national distribution. This occurs despite the fact that it is more economical to build the plant and initiate the marketing effort all at once. However, initial regional distribution gives the company the option to expand only if demand proves strong. The mean of the distribution of NPVs is $102,400 higher, after recovery of the $1 million "cost" of the managerial option to expand.

THE OPTION TO ABANDON

189

CHAPTER 7
Risk and
Managerial
Options in Capital
Budgeting

A second option is that to abandon a project after it is undertaken. This may consist of selling the asset, where a company realizes cash upon its disposal. However, an asset does not have to be sold to realize abandonment value. It simply may be employed in another area of the enterprise. In either case, an abandonment value can be estimated. Effectively, the ability to abandon a project represents a put option for the company.

The economic rationale for abandonment is the same as that for capital budgeting. Funds should be removed from a project, or disinvested, whenever the project does not economically justify their use. In general, an investment project should be abandoned when (1) its abandonment value exceeds the present value of the project's subsequent future cash flows, and (2) it is better to abandon then than in the future. With the ability to abandon, the worth of an investment project may be enhanced.

$$\text{Project worth} = \begin{array}{c} \text{NPV without} \\ \text{abandonment} \\ \text{option} \end{array} + \begin{array}{c} \text{Value of} \\ \text{abandonment} \\ \text{option} \end{array} \qquad (7\text{-}12)$$

The recognition of later abandonment may have a significant effect upon project selection.

The abandonment rule posed can be expressed more formally as[12]

1. Compute the present value of the sum of cash flows expected to be generated from the project and the expected abandonment value at the end of the holding period. If there were n years remaining in the life of the project, we would have the following formula:

$$PV_{\tau \cdot a} = \sum_{t=\tau+1}^{a} \frac{A_t}{(1 + k)^{(t-\tau)}} + \frac{AV_a}{(1 + k)^{(a-\tau)}} \qquad (7\text{-}13)$$

where $PV_{\tau \cdot a}$ = present value at time τ of expected future net cash flows through period a, plus the present value of the expected abandonment value at the end of period a
$\quad a$ = period in which the project is abandoned
$\quad A_t$ = expected net cash flow of the project in period t
$\quad k$ = required rate of return
$\quad AV_a$ = expected abandonment value at the end of period a

2. For $a = n$, compute $PV_{\tau \cdot a}$. If $PV_{\tau \cdot n}$ is greater than the current abandonment value, AV_τ, we continue to hold the project and evaluate it at time $\tau + 1$, based on our expectations at that time.

3. If $PV_{\tau \cdot n}$ is less than or equal to AV_τ, we compute $PV_{\tau \cdot a}$ for $a = n - 1$. If $PV_{\tau \cdot n-1}$ is greater than AV_τ, we continue to hold the project as in (2) above. If $PV_{\tau \cdot n-1} \le AV_\tau$, we compute $PV_{\tau \cdot a}$ for $a = n - 2$ and compare it with AV_τ. This

---

[12] See Alexander A. Robichek and James C. Van Horne, "Abandonment Value and Capital Budgeting," *Journal of Finance*, 22 (December 1967), 557–89; Edward A. Dyl and Hugh W. Long, "Comment," *Journal of Finance*, 24 (March 1969), 88–95; and Robichek and Van Horne, "Reply," ibid., 96–97.

procedure is continued until either a decision to hold the project is reached or $a = \tau + 1$.

4. If $PV_{\tau \cdot a} \leq AV_\tau$ for all $\tau + 1 \leq a \leq n$, then we would abandon the project at time τ.

In other words, these steps would have us abandon a project only if the present value of possible future benefits is less than the current abandonment value and if it appears better to abandon now than in the future. When the above rules suggest that a project should be given up, we would make less than optimum use of capital if we continued.

AN ABANDONMENT ILLUSTRATION

Wonka Tractor Company is considering a new plant to produce the Wonka III lawn tractor. This tractor will be produced for only one or two years, as the Wonka IV, now on the drawing boards, will replace it. The proposal costs $3 million, and the cash flows and their probabilities of occurrence are shown as a series of conditional probabilities in Table 7-4. For simplicity of illustration, we assume that after the second year, the proposal is not expected to provide any cash flow or residual value. We also assume an expected abandonment value of $1.5 million at the end of the first period. There are nine possible series of cash flows over the two-year period, the first series representing a cash flow of $1.0 million in period 1, followed by a cash flow of 0 in period 2. The joint probability of each series of cash flows is shown in the last column of the table; for the first series, it is 0.25 × 0.25 = 0.0625.

If we assume a required rate of return of 10 percent and use this rate as our discount factor, we are able to determine the expected net present value of the proposal without abandonment by (1) computing the net present value for each cash-flow series; (2) obtaining the expected net present value for each series by multiplying the computed net present value by the probability of occurrence of that series; and (3) adding the expected net present values of all

TABLE 7-4
Conditional probability distribution series for abandonment example

PERIOD 1		PERIOD 2		
Cash Flow (000 omitted)	Initial Probability $P(1)$	Cash Flow (000 omitted)	Conditional Probability $P(2|1)$	JOINT PROBABILITY $P(1,2)$
$1,000	0.25	$ 0	0.25	0.0625
		1,000	0.50	0.1250
		2,000	0.25	0.0625
2,000	0.50	1,000	0.25	0.1250
		2,000	0.50	0.2500
		3,000	0.25	0.1250
3,000	0.25	2,000	0.25	0.0625
		3,000	0.50	0.1250
		3,500	0.25	0.0625
Abandonment value $1,500		$0		

sequences. Carrying out these computations, we find the mean net present value to be $445,246.

When we allow for the possibility of abandonment, however, the results change dramatically. Following the decision rules specified earlier, Wonka Tractor would divest itself of the project if its abandonment value at the end of period 1 exceeds the expected cash flows for the subsequent period, discounted at 10 percent. Because cash flows are expected for only two periods, the possibility of abandoning the project beyond period 1 does not exist. Consequently, a number of the computational steps involved in the abandonment decision rules discussed are not applicable in this case. Referring again to Table 7-4, we find that we should abandon the project at the end of the first period if the cash flow in that period turns out to be $1 million. The reason is that the mean present value of possible cash flows in period 2, discounted to period 1, $909,091, is less than the abandonment value at the end of the period, $1.5 million. If the cash flow in period 1 turns out to be either $2 million or $3 million, however, abandonment would not be worthwhile because the mean present value of period 2 cash flows discounted to period 1 exceeds $1.5 million.

When we allow for abandonment, the expected cash flows shown in Table 7-4 must be revised; these revisions are shown in Table 7-5. Recalculating the mean net present value for the proposal, based upon the information, we find it to be $579,544. A significant improvement occurs because a portion of the downside is eliminated if the project is abandoned when events turn unfavorable.[13]

The option to abandon is more valuable the greater the volatility of cash flows for a project. The abandonment option, like other managerial options, lets the good times roll while mitigating the effect of bad outcomes by exercise of the option. To the extent the option has value, it may change a reject signal for a project to an accept signal.

191

CHAPTER 7
Risk and
Managerial
Options in Capital
Budgeting

[13] In studying plant closings, David W. Blackwell, W. Wayne Marr, and Michael F. Spivey, "The Impact of Plant Closings on the Wealth of Shareholders," working paper, Tulane University (1988), find that share price shows a small, but statistically significant, decline around the time of the announcement. They interpret this finding as consistent with the expectation of lower future cash flows. Similar results were found by George P. Tsetsekos and Michael J. Gambola, "Stock Price Reaction to Plant Closing Announcements: Financial Performance and Reasons for Closings," working paper, Drexel University (March 1990).

TABLE 7-5
Conditional probability distribution series for revised case

PERIOD 1		PERIOD 2		
Cash Flow (000 omitted)	Initial Probability $P(1)$	Cash Flow (000 omitted)	Conditional Probability $P(2\|1)$	JOINT PROBABILITY $P(1,2)$
$2,500	0.25	$ 0		0.2500
2,000	0.50	1,000	0.25	0.1250
		2,000	0.50	0.2500
		3,000	0.25	0.1250
3,000	0.25	2,000	0.25	0.0625
		3,000	0.50	0.1250
		3,500	0.25	0.0625

In addition to evaluating new investment proposals, the procedure outlined above can be used for continually evaluating existing investment projects, deciding whether it is better to continue with the project or to abandon it and employ the funds elsewhere. Even though the project is profitable, it may make sense to abandon it if the abandonment value is sufficiently high. In other words, the optimal time to abandon is the point where the combination of expected future cash flows and future abandonment value has the highest present value. Through the continual assessment of projects, a company is able to weed out those that no longer are economically viable.

THE OPTION TO POSTPONE

For some investment projects, there is the option to wait. That is, the project does not have to be undertaken immediately. By waiting, you obtain new information on the market, on prices, on costs, and perhaps on other things. However, you give up the interim cash flows and, possibly, "first mover" advantage in the marketplace.

A mining operation, where the site is owned, involves a decision to begin extraction now or to wait. Here the new information has largely to do with the price of the metal.[14] The cost of exercising the option is the extraction cost. With commodities, such as metals, the value of the option depends importantly on the volatility of commodity price. In other words, the mine is an option on the commodity contained therein. With an operating mine, there is the option to shut it down if price goes too low. This does not mean abandonment, as the mine continues to be owned and can be reopened. Michael J. Brennan and Eduardo S. Schwartz derive optimal points at which to open or shut a gold mine, depending on the price of gold.[15] They treat the problem as a complex option.

Most business decision situations do not hinge on the price of a commodity. As a result, they do not lend themselves to formulation in the option pricing context presented in Chapter 5. Still the principles are similar, though improvisation is necessary. Consider a new product decision where management has the option to launch now or to defer. If the product is launched now, the company will realize cash flows earlier than if it waits. This is like having an option on a dividend-paying stock. Exercise now and you get the near future dividends, but you give up the option. If you wait, you may be able to exercise to more advantage. The greater the volatility of possible outcomes, of course, the greater the value of the option.

If the option value for a new product is large, management may wish to defer product launch even though the project has a positive net present value if undertaken now. However, one must make sure the option remains open. Much can change in the new product area, and you lose first mover advantage. However, American Home Products Corporation, one of the most profitable companies in America, consistently has followed a strategy of waiting for

---

[14] If the mine is not owned, the price to buy reserves will go up or down with the price of the metal. As a result, there is no option.

[15] Michael J. Brennan and Eduardo S. Schwartz, "A New Approach to Evaluating Natural Resource Investments," *Midland Corporate Finance Journal*, 3 (Spring 1985), 37–47. Additionally, see Robert L. McDonald and Daniel R. Siegel, "Investment and the Valuation of Firms When There Is an Option to Shut Down," *International Economic Review*, 26 (June 1985), 331–49; Robert L. McDonald and Daniel R. Siegel, "The Value of Waiting to Invest," *Quarterly Journal of Economics*, 101 (November 1986), 707–27; and Avinash Dixit, "Entry and Exit Decisions under Uncertainty," *Journal of Political Economy*, 97 (June 1989), 620–38.

a product market to develop before launching a "me too" product or a product extension. Through advertising and marketing clout, the company quickly gains market share and a profitable position.

193

CHAPTER 7
Risk and
Managerial
Options in Capital
Budgeting

OBSERVATIONS ON MANAGERIAL OPTIONS

The managerial options discussed—expansion, abandonment, and postponement—have a common thread. Because they limit the downside, the greater the variance or uncertainty associated with the future, the more valuable these options. As our preceding discussion reflects, there are differences between financial options and managerial options. Option pricing theory tells us an exact relationship between the value of an option and the price of the associated asset, based on the idea that a riskless hedged position should provide a return no more than or less than the risk-free rate. Market equilibration depends on highly efficient, arbitrage-driven financial markets. Because product markets are not nearly so efficient, managerial options are different.

You cannot use risk neutrality to factor out implied variances, as you can with financial options. The exercise price of a managerial option can change over time. Moreover, volatility is difficult to measure, as you seldom have past market value changes on which to base an estimate. The opportunity cost to waiting to exercise a managerial option is not nearly as precise as giving up dividends on a dividend-paying stock. These and other differences cause a managerial option to be much more difficult to value than a financial option.

Still, the overall option pricing framework can be applied to managerial options, despite the difficulty in measurement. Recognition of management flexibility can alter an initial decision to accept or reject a project. A reject decision using classical DCF analysis can be reversed if the option value is high enough. An accept decision can be turned into a postponement decision if the option value more than offsets the early cash flows. While a DCF approach to determining net present value is an appropriate starting place, in many cases it needs to be modified for managerial options.

SUMMARY

Because investment proposals entail differing degrees of business risk, we must analyze not only their expected profitability but also the possible deviations from that expectation. Risk is expressed in terms of the dispersion of the probability distribution of possible net present values or possible internal rates of return and is measured by the standard deviation.

By measuring the standard deviation under a variety of assumptions and using it in relation to the expected value of the distribution, we try to determine the probability that certain events will occur. Risk can be measured under the assumption of serial independence of cash flows over time or when cash flows from one period to the next are dependent over time. For dealing with situations of moderate correlation of cash flows over time, probability trees are useful. Simulation techniques often can be applied to the problem of how to analyze risky investments. Although the portfolio approach has merit only under certain circumstances, it is one way to measure the marginal risk of a project in relation to others that exist or are being considered.

Managerial options often are important in capital budgeting. This term simply means flexibility of management to alter a previous decision. An investment project's worth can be viewed as its net present value, calculated using classical discounted cash-flow analysis, together with the value of the option. The greater the uncertainty surrounding the use of the option, the greater its value. Managerial options include the option to expand, the option to abandon, and the option to postpone. Consideration of these various options can cause a reject decision on a capital budgeting project to turn into an accept decision and an accept decision to turn into a decision to postpone. In analyzing managerial options, decision trees often are used to come to grips with the sequential nature of the problem.

In the next two chapters, we consider the evaluation of investments when we have information about risk and expected return developed in this chapter. We shall investigate the acceptance or rejection of risky investments in relation to the objective of maximizing share price. Our discussion will involve us in the valuation of the firm and in the considerable theoretical controversy that surrounds the question of risky investments and acquisitions. Again, we point out that Chapters 7 through 9 must be treated as a package.

SELF-CORRECTION PROBLEMS

1. Gomez Drug Products Company could invest in a new drug project with an estimated life of 3 years. If demand for the new drug in the first period is favorable, it is almost certain that it will be favorable in periods 2 and 3. By the same token, if demand is low in the first period, it will be low in the two subsequent periods as well. Owing to this likely demand relationship, an assumption of perfect correlation of cash flows over time is appropriate. The cost of the project is $1 million, and possible cash flows for the three periods are

PERIOD 1		PERIOD 2		PERIOD 3	
Prob.	Cash Flow	Prob.	Cash Flow	Prob.	Cash Flow
.10	$ 0	.15	$ 100,000	.15	$ 0
.20	200,000	.20	400,000	.20	150,000
.40	400,000	.30	700,000	.30	300,000
.20	600,000	.20	1,000,000	.20	450,000
.10	800,000	.15	1,300,000	.15	600,000

Assuming that the risk-free rate is 8 percent and that it is used as the discount rate, calculate the expected value and standard deviation of the probability distribution of possible net present values. Assuming a normal distribution, what is the probability of the project providing a net present value of zero or less, of $300,000 or more, of $1,000,000 or more? Is the standard deviation calculated larger or smaller than it would be under an assumption of independence of cash flows over time?

2. Zello Creamery Company would like a new product line—puddings. The ex-

pected value and standard deviation of the probability distribution of possible net present values for the product line are $12,000 and $9,000, respectively. The company's existing lines are ice cream, cottage cheese, and yogurt. The expected values of net present value and standard deviation for these product lines are

195

CHAPTER 7
Risk and
Managerial
Options in Capital
Budgeting

	NET PRESENT VALUE	σ
Ice cream	$16,000	$8,000
Cottage cheese	20,000	7,000
Yogurt	10,000	4,000

The correlation coefficients between products are

	ICE CREAM	COTTAGE CHEESE	YOGURT	PUDDING
Ice cream	1.00			
Cottage cheese	.90	1.00		
Yogurt	.80	.84	1.00	
Pudding	.40	.20	.30	1.00

a. Compute the expected value and the standard deviation of the probability distribution of possible net present values for a combination consisting of existing products.

b. Compute the expected value and standard deviation for a combination consisting of existing products plus pudding. Compare your results in parts a and b. What can you say about the pudding line?

3. Feldstein Drug Company is considering a new drug, which would be sold over the counter without a prescription. To develop the drug and to market it on a regional basis will cost $12 million over the next 2 years, $6 million in each year. Expected cash inflows associated with the project for years 3 through 8 are $1 million, $2 million, $4 million, $4 million, $3 million, and $1 million, respectively.

If the project is successful, at the end of year 5 the company will have the option to invest an additional $10 million to secure a national market. The probability of success is .60; if not successful, the company will not invest the $10 million and there will be no incremental expected cash flows. If successful, however, cash flows are expected to be $6 million higher in each of the years 6 through 10 than would otherwise be the case with a probability of .50, and $4 million higher with a probability of .50. The company's required rate of return for the project is 14 percent.

a. What is the net present value of the initial project? Is it acceptable?

b. What is the worth of the project if we take account of the option to expand? Is the project acceptable?

PROBLEMS

1. The probability distribution of possible net present values for project X has an expected value of $20,000 and a standard deviation of $10,000. Assuming a normal distribution, calculate the probability that the net present value will be zero or less; that it will be greater than $30,000; and that it will be less than $5,000.

2. The Dewitt Corporation has determined the following discrete probability distributions for net cash flows generated by a contemplated project:

PERIOD 1		PERIOD 2		PERIOD 3	
Prob.	Cash Flow	Prob.	Cash Flow	Prob.	Cash Flow
.10	$1,000	.20	$1,000	.30	$1,000
.20	2,000	.30	2,000	.40	2,000
.30	3,000	.40	3,000	.20	3,000
.40	4,000	.10	4,000	.10	4,000

a. Assume that probability distributions of cash flows for future periods are independent. Also, assume that the after-tax risk-free rate is 7 percent. If the proposal will require an initial outlay of $5,000, determine the mean net present value.

b. Determine the standard deviation about the mean.

c. If the total distribution is approximately normal and assumed continuous, what is the probability of the net present value being zero or less?

d. What is the probability that the net present value will be greater than zero?

e. What is the probability that the profitability index will be 1.00 or less?

f. What is the probability that the profitability index will be greater than 2.00?

3. Ponape Lumber Company is evaluating a new saw with a life of 2 years. The saw costs $3,000, and future after-tax cash flows depend on demand for the company's products. The probability tree of possible future cash flows associated with the new saw is

YEAR 1		YEAR 2		
Initial Probability	Cash Flow	Conditional Probability	Cash Flow	BRANCH
.4	$1,500	.3	$1,000	1
		.4	1,500	2
		.3	2,000	3
.6	$2,500	.4	$2,000	4
		.4	2,500	5
		.2	3,000	6

a. What are the joint probabilities of occurrence of the various branches?

b. If the risk-free rate is 10 percent, what are the mean and standard deviation of the probability distribution of possible net present values?

c. Assuming a normal distribution, what is the probability the actual net present value will be less than zero?

4. Xonics Graphics is evaluating a new technology for its reproduction equipment. The technology will have a 3-year life and cost $1,000. Its impact on cash flows is subject to risk. Management estimates that there is a 50:50 chance that the technology will either save the company $1,000 in the first year or save it nothing at all. If nothing at all, savings in the last 2 years would be zero. Even worse, in the second year an additional outlay of $300 may be required to convert back to the original process, for the new technology may result in less efficiency. Man-

agement attaches a 40 percent probability to this occurrence, given the fact that the new technology "bombs out" in the first year. If the technology proves itself, second-year cash flows may be either $1,800, $1,400, or $1,000, with probabilities of .20, .60, and .20, respectively. In the third year, cash inflows are expected to be $200 greater or $200 less than the cash flow in period 2, with an equal chance of occurrence. (Again, these cash flows depend on the cash flow in period 1 being $1,000.) All the cash flows are after taxes.

197

CHAPTER 7
Risk and
Managerial
Options in Capital
Budgeting

a. Set up a probability tree to depict the foregoing cash-flow possibilities.

b. Calculate a net present value for each three-year possibility, using a risk-free rate of 5 percent.

c. What is the risk of the project?

5. The Hume Corporation is faced with several possible investment projects. For each, the total cash outflow required will occur in the initial period. The cash outflows, expected net present values, and standard deviations are as follows. (All projects have been discounted at a risk-free rate of 8 percent, and it is assumed that the distributions of their possible net present values are normal.)

PROJECT	COST	NET PRESENT VALUE	σ
A	$100,000	$10,000	$20,000
B	50,000	10,000	30,000
C	200,000	25,000	10,000
D	10,000	5,000	10,000
E	500,000	75,000	75,000

a. Determine the coefficient of variation for each of these projects. (Use cost plus net present value in the denominator of the coefficient.)

b. Ignoring size, do you find some projects clearly dominated by others?

c. May size be ignored?

d. What is the probability that each of the projects will have a net present value greater than 0?

e. What decision rule would you suggest for adoption of projects within this context? Which (if any) of the foregoing projects would be adopted under your rule?

6. The Bertz Company uses a simulation approach to judge investment projects. Three factors are employed: market demand, in units; price per unit minus cost per unit; and investment required at time 0. These factors are felt to be independent of one another. In analyzing a new consumer product, Bertz estimates the following probability distributions:

ANNUAL DEMAND		PRICE MINUS COST PER UNIT		INVESTMENT REQUIRED	
Prob.	Units	Prob.	Dollars	Prob.	Dollars
.05	10,000	.10	$3.00	.30	$1,800,000
.10	20,000	.20	4.50	.40	2,000,000
.20	30,000	.40	6.00	.30	2,300,000
.30	45,000	.20	7.00		
.20	60,000	.10	8.00		
.10	75,000				
.05	90,000				

a. Using a random number table or some other random process, simulate 20 or more trials for these three factors and compute the return on investment for each trial. (*Note:* Return = profit/investment.)

b. Approximately what is the most likely return? How risky is the project?

7. The Windrop Company will invest in two of three possible proposals, the cash flows of which are normally distributed. The expected net present value (discounted at the risk-free rate) and the standard deviation for each proposal are given as follows:

	1	2	3
Expected net present value	$10,000	$8,000	$6,000
Standard deviation	4,000	3,000	4,000

Assuming the following correlation coefficients for each possible combination, which two proposals dominate?

Proposals	1	2	3	1 and 2	1 and 3	2 and 3
Correlation coefficients	1.00	1.00	1.00	.60	.40	.70

8. The Plaza Corporation is confronted with several combinations of risky investments.

OLD PORTFOLIOS	NET PRESENT VALUE	σ
A	$100,000	$200,000
B	20,000	80,000
C	75,000	100,000
D	60,000	150,000
E	50,000	20,000
F	40,000	60,000

NEW PORTFOLIOS	NET PRESENT VALUE	σ
G	$120,000	$170,000
H	90,000	70,000
I	50,000	100,000
J	75,000	30,000

a. Plot the portfolios.

b. Which portfolios dominate?

9. The Ferret Pet Company is considering a new location. If it constructs an office and 100 cages, the cost will be $100,000 and the project is likely to produce net cash flows of $17,000 per year for 15 years, after which the leasehold on the land expires and there will be no residual value. The company's required return is 18

percent. If the location proves favorable, Ferret Pet will be able to expand by another 100 cages at the end of 4 years. The cost per cage would be $200. With the new cages, incremental net cash flows of $17,000 per year for years 5 through 15 would be expected. The company believes there is a 50-50 chance that the location will prove to be a favorable one.

a. Is the initial project acceptable?

b. What is the value of the option? the worth of the project with the option? Is it acceptable?

10. The Kazin Corporation is introducing a new product, which it can distribute initially either in the state of Georgia or in the entire Southeast. If it distributes in Georgia alone, plant and marketing will cost $5 million, and Kazin can reevaluate the project at the end of three years to decide whether to go regional. To go regional at the end of the three years would cost another $10 million. To distribute regionally from the outset would cost $12 million. The risk-free rate is 4 percent. In either case, the product will have a life of six years, after which the plant will be worthless. Given the following data, what policy should Kazin adopt?

199

CHAPTER 7
Risk and
Managerial
Options in Capital
Budgeting

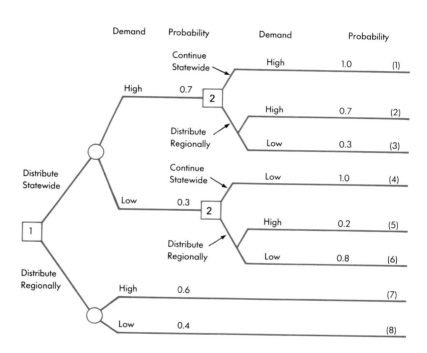

Decision tree; national versus regional distribution

Expected cash flows (in thousands)

				YEARS			
BRANCH	0	1	2	3	4	5	6
1	− $ 5,000	$1,000	$ 3,000	$ 5,000	$ 7,000	$ 4,000	$2,000
2	− 5,000	1,000	3,000	− 7,000	10,000	20,000	8,000
3	− 5,000	1,000	3,000	− 7,000	8,000	6,000	4,000
4	− 5,000	200	400	1,000	2,000	1,000	200
5	− 5,000	200	400	− 11,000	8,000	15,000	5,000
6	− 5,000	200	400	− 11,000	3,000	4,000	4,000
7	− 12,000	3,000	10,000	15,000	20,000	12,000	5,000
8	− 12,000	1,000	2,000	3,000	4,000	3,000	1,000

11. ABC Corporation is ordering a special-purpose piece of machinery costing $9,000 with a life of 2 years, after which there is no expected salvage value. The possible incremental net cash flows are

	YEAR 1		YEAR 2	
Cash Flow	Probability	Cash Flow	Conditional Probability
$6,000	.3	$2,000	.3
		3,000	.5
		4,000	.2
7,000	.4	4,000	.3
		5,000	.4
		6,000	.3
8,000	.3	6,000	.2
		7,000	.5
		8,000	.3

The company's required rate of return for this investment is 8 percent.

a. Calculate the mean of the probability distribution of possible net present values.

b. Suppose now that the possibility of abandonment exists and that the abandonment value of the project at the end of year 1 is $4,500. Calculate the new mean NPV, assuming the company abandons the project if it is worthwhile to do so. Compare your calculations with those in part a. What are the implications?

SOLUTIONS TO
SELF-CORRECTION PROBLEMS

1. The expected values of the distributions of cash flows for the three periods are $400,000, $700,000, and $300,000.

The standard deviations of the cash flows for the three periods are

$$\sigma_1 = [.1(0 - 400,000)^2 + .2(200,000 - 400,000)^2$$
$$+ .2(600,000 - 400,000)^2 + .1(800,000 - 400,000)^2]^{1/2}$$
$$= [48,000,000,000]^{1/2} = \$219,089$$

$$\sigma_2 = [.15(100,000 - 700,000)^2 + .2(400,000 - 700,000)^2$$
$$+ .2(1,000,000 - 700,000)^2 + .15(1,300,000 - 700,000)^2]^{1/2}$$
$$= [144,000,000,000]^{1/2} = \$379,474$$

$$\sigma_3 = [.15(0 - 300,000)^2 + .2(150,000 - 300,000)^2$$
$$+ .2(450,000 - 300,000)^2 + .15(600,000 - 300,000)^2]^{1/2}$$
$$= [36,000,000,000]^{1/2} = \$189,737$$

The standard deviation of the probability distribution of possible net present values under the assumption of perfect correlation of cash flows over time is

201

CHAPTER 7
Risk and
Managerial
Options in Capital
Budgeting

$$\sigma = \frac{\$219{,}089}{(1.08)} + \frac{\$379{,}474}{(1.08)^2} + \frac{\$189{,}737}{(1.08)^3} = \$678{,}818$$

The mean net present value of the project is

$$NPV = -\$1{,}000{,}000 + \frac{\$400{,}000}{(1.08)} + \frac{\$700{,}000}{(1.08)^2} + \frac{\$300{,}000}{(1.08)^3} = \$208{,}659$$

The standardized differences for zero, $300,000, and $1 million are:
For zero or less

$$S = \frac{0 - 208{,}659}{678{,}818} = .307$$

For $300,000 or more

$$S = \frac{300{,}000 - 208{,}659}{678{,}818} = .135$$

For $1,000,000 or more

$$S = \frac{1{,}000{,}000 - 208{,}659}{678{,}818} = 1.166$$

From Table C at the end of the book, these standardized differences correspond to probabilities of approximately .38, .45, and .12, respectively. The standard deviation calculated under this assumption is much larger than it would be under an assumption of independence of cash flows over time.

2. a. Net present value = $16,000 + $20,000 + $10,000 = $46,000
Standard deviation = $[(8{,}000)^2 + (2)(.9)(8{,}000)(7{,}000)$
$+ (2)(.8)(8{,}000)(4{,}000) + (7{,}000)^2$
$+ (2)(.84)(7{,}000)(4{,}000) + (4{,}000)^2]^{1/2}$
$= [328{,}040{,}000]^{1/2} = \$18{,}112$

  b. Net present value = $46,000 + $12,000 = $58,000
Standard deviation = $[328{,}040{,}000 + (9{,}000)^2$
$+ (2)(.4)(9{,}000)(8{,}000) + (2)(.2)(9{,}000)(7{,}000)$
$+ (2)(.3)(9{,}000)(4{,}000)]^{1/2} = [513{,}440{,}000]^{1/2}$
$= \$22{,}659$

The coefficient of variation of existing projects (σ/NPV) = 18,112/46,000 = .39. The coefficient of variation for existing projects plus puddings = 22,659/58,000 = .39. While the pudding line has a higher coefficient of variation (9,000/12,000 = .75) than existing products, indicating a higher degree of risk, the correlation of this product line with existing lines is sufficiently low as to bring the coefficient of variation for all products including puddings in line with that for only existing products.

3.

	CASH FLOWS (IN MILLIONS)		
TIME	Initial Project	Scenario #1 Prob. = .3	Scenario #2 Prob. = .3
1	− $6		
2	− 6		
3	1		
4	2		
5	4	− $10	− $10
6	4	6	4
7	3	6	4
8	1	6	4
9		6	4
10		6	4
NPV (14%)	− $2.57	$5.51	$1.94

a. At time 0, the initial project has an NPV of −$2.57 million and it would be rejected.

b. Option value = 0.3($5.51) + 0.3($1.94) + 0.4(0)

= $2.23 million

Worth of project = −$2.57 + $2.23 = −$.34 million

While the option value raises the worth of the project substantially, it does not entirely offset the initial project's negative NPV. Therefore, we still would reject the project.

SELECTED REFERENCES

AGGARWAL, RAJ, and LUC A. SOENEN, "Project Exit Value as a Measure of Flexibility and Risk Exposure," *Engineering Economist,* 35 (Fall 1989), 39–54.

BEY, ROGER P., "Capital Budgeting Decisions When Cash Flows and Project Lives are Stochastic and Dependent," *Journal of Financial Research,* 6 (Fall 1983), 175–87.

———, and J. CLAYTON SINGLETON, "Autocorrelated Cash Flows and the Selection of a Portfolio of Capital Assets," *Decision Sciences,* 8 (October 1978), 640–57.

BRENNAN, MICHAEL J., "Latent Assets," *Journal of Finance,* 45 (July 1990), 709–30.

———, and EDUARDO S. SCHWARTZ, "A New Approach to Evaluating Natural Resource Investments," *Midland Corporate Finance Journal,* 3 (Spring 1985), 37–47.

BUTLER, J. S., and BARRY SCHACHTER, "Estimation Risk and Risk Adjusted Discount Rates," *Financial Management,* 18 (Winter 1989), 13–22.

DIXIT, AVINASH, "Entry and Exit Decisions under Uncertainty," *Journal of Political Economy,* 97 (June 1989), 620–38.

GIACCOTTO, CARMELO, "A Simplified Approach to Risk Analysis in Capital Budgeting with Serially Correlated Cash Flows," *Engineering Economist,* 29 (Summer 1984), 273–86.

HERTZ, DAVID B., "Risk Analysis in Capital Investment," *Harvard Business Review,* 42 (January–February 1964), 95–106.

HESPOS, RICHARD F., and PAUL A. STRASSMANN, "Stochastic Decision Trees for the Analysis of Investment Decisions," *Management Science,* 11 (August 1965), 244–59.

HILLIER, FREDERICK S., "The Derivation of Probabilistic Information for the Evaluation of Risky Investments," *Management Science,* 9 (April 1963), 443–57.

HSIA, CI-CHENG, and RUSSELL J. FULLER, "A Simplified Model for Measuring Total Risk of Discounted Cash Flows," working paper, Portland State University and Washington State University (1988).

JOY, O. MAURICE, "Abandonment Values and Abandonment Decisions: A Clarification," *Journal of Finance,* 31 (December 1976), 1225–28.

KWAN, CLARENCE C. Y., and YUFEI YEAN, "Optimal Sequential Selection in Capital Budgeting: A Shortcut," *Financial Management,* 17 (Spring 1988), 54–59.

LEVY, HAIM, and MARSHALL SARNAT, "The Portfolio Analysis of Multiperiod Capital Investment under Conditions of Risk," *Engineering Economist,* 16 (Fall 1970), 1–19.

MCDONALD, ROBERT L., and DANIEL R. SIEGEL, "Investment and the Valuation of Firms When There Is an Option to Shut Down," *International Economic Review,* 26 (June 1985), 331–49.

———, "The Value of Waiting to Invest," *Quarterly Journal of Economics,* 101 (November 1986), 707–27.

MAGEE, J. F., "How to Use Decision Trees in Capital Investment," *Harvard Business Review,* 42 (September–October 1964), 79–96.

MILLER, EDWARD M., "Uncertainty Induced Bias in Capital Budgeting," *Financial Management,* 7 (Autumn 1978), 12–18.

ROBICHEK, ALEXANDER A., and JAMES C. VAN HORNE, "Abandonment Value and Capital Budgeting," *Journal of Finance,* 22 (December 1967), 557–89; EDWARD A. DYL and HUGH W. LONG, "Comment," *Journal of Finance,* 24 (March 1969), 88–95; and ROBICHEK and VAN HORNE, "Reply," ibid., 96–97.

Sɪᴄᴋ, Gᴏʀᴅᴏɴ A., "A Certainty-Equivalent Approach to Capital Budgeting," *Financial Management*, 15 (Winter 1986), 23–32.

Sᴛᴀᴛᴍᴀɴ, Mᴇɪʀ, and Jᴀᴍᴇs F. Sᴇᴘᴇ, "Project Termination Announcements and the Market Value of the Firm," *Financial Management*, 18 (Winter 1989), 74–81.

Tʀɪɢᴇᴏʀɢɪs, Lᴇɴᴏs, and Sᴄᴏᴛᴛ P. Mᴀsᴏɴ, "Valuing Managerial Flexibility," *Midland Corporate Finance Journal*, 5 (Spring 1987), 14–21.

Vᴀɴ Hᴏʀɴᴇ, Jᴀᴍᴇs C., "Capital-Budgeting Decisions Involving Combinations of Risky Investments," *Management Science*, 13 (October 1966), 84–92.

———, "The Analysis of Uncertainty Resolution in Capital Budgeting for New Products," *Management Science*, 15 (April 1969), 376–86.

———, "Capital Budgeting under Conditions of Uncertainty as to Project Life," *Engineering Economist*, 17 (Spring 1972), 189–99.

———, "The Variation of Project Life as a Means for Adjusting for Risk," *Engineering Economist*, 21 (Spring 1976), 151–58.

203

CHAPTER 7
Risk and
Managerial
Options in Capital
Budgeting

8

CREATING VALUE THROUGH CAPITAL INVESTMENTS

Our eyes are still on the stockholders, and the maximization of their value. By investing monies in products and projects, a company creates value if the expected return exceeds the return required by the financial markets for the risk involved. In previous chapters, we measured the risk of individual and combined investments. But knowing how risky is not enough; we must know how costly the risk is—that is, its market price. The idea is a simple one; we try to determine the opportunity cost of a capital investment by relating it to a financial market investment with the same risk.

FOUNDATIONS OF VALUE CREATION

In general, corporations that are situated in attractive industries and/or attain a sustainable competitive advantage within an industry are able to earn excess returns and create value. These are the things that give rise to positive net-present-value projects, ones that provide expected returns in excess of what the financial markets require.

INDUSTRY ATTRACTIVENESS

At a recent annual meeting of Berkshire Hathaway, the renowned investor Warren Buffett said, "it is better to be an average management in a wonderful business than a marvelous management in a lousy business." In this regard, he suggested that television networks were not a wonderful business, although they were when there were only three. "When you get right down to it, networks are in the business of selling eyeballs. There will continue to be erosion as the eyeballs have more choices" (cable, etc.).

Favorable industry characteristics include the growth phase of a product cycle, barriers to entry, and other protective devices such as patents, temporary monopoly power, and/or oligopoly pricing where nearly all competitors are profitable. Industry attractiveness has to do with the relative position of an industry in the spectrum of return-generating possibilities.

COMPETITIVE ADVANTAGE

Competitive advantage involves the relative position of a company within an industry. The company could be multidivisional, in which case competitive advantage needs to be judged industry by industry. The avenues to competitive advantage are several: cost advantage, marketing and price advantage, and superior organizational capability (corporate culture).[1] Competitive advantage is eroded with competition. Relative cost or marketing superiority, for example, is conspicuous and will be attacked. As before, the mark of a successful company is one that continually identifies and exploits opportunities for excess returns. Only with a sequence of short-run advantages can any overall competitive advantage be sustained.

Thus, industry attractiveness and competitive advantage are principal sources of value creation. The more favorable these are, the more likely the company is to have expected returns in excess of what the financial markets require for the risk involved.

THE VALUATION UNDERPINNINGS

As we know, most investors are concerned with unavoidable risk, the risk that cannot be avoided by diversification of the stocks, bonds, and other financial assets they hold. The required rate of return on investment is the return on a risk-free asset plus the market price of risk to the investor due to one or more factors. The required return can be expressed in terms of a factor model using multiple risk components to characterize unavoidable risk (Chapter 4), in terms of the single-factor capital asset pricing model (CAPM) where the factor is the return on the market portfolio (Chapter 3), or the CAPM extended to include additional variables (Chapter 4). As these models were previously discussed, we do not dwell on them here.

Whatever the valuation model, for a given degree of risk the financial markets expect a company to earn a minimum required return commensurate with the risk involved. Suppose the security market line of the CAPM were the appropriate equilibrium trade-off between risk and required return. This is shown graphically in Fig. 8-1. The greater the systematic risk, the greater the return the financial markets require of an investment opportunity. All projects with expected internal rates of return lying on or above the line should be accepted, for they provide excess returns. Acceptable projects are depicted by x's. All projects lying below the line, shown by zeros, would be rejected. The acceptance of projects lying above the line should result in an increase in share price. With a higher risk-adjusted return than the market requires, investors will bid up the price of the stock.

The goal of the firm in this context is to search for investment opportunities lying above the line. Since external financial markets offer security portfolios that lie along the security market line, it makes little sense for the firm to invest in internally generated investment proposals unless they lie above the line. If product markets were perfect, one could not expect to find such opportunities. Investment opportunities would lie along or below the line, and the firm could expect to earn no more than the required rate of return. Thus, the

---

[1] For an extensive discussion of this concept and much more, see Michael E. Porter, *Competitive Advantage* (New York: Free Press, 1985).

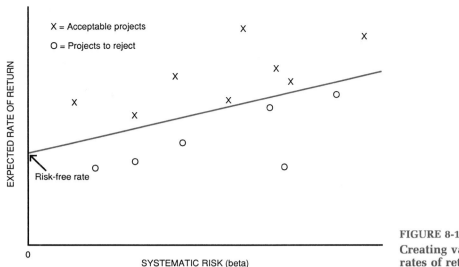

FIGURE 8-1
Creating value through required rates of return

combination of perfect product markets along with perfect capital markets would rule out the ability of firms to earn excess returns for their stockholders. Put another way, firms could expect to earn no more on a project than the return the market requires on the basis of the systematic risk involved.

If product markets are less than perfect, however, it is possible to find projects with expected returns above the security market line. The portion of the return over and above the opportunity rate required by capital suppliers is known as an economic rent. While competition among firms tends to drive economic rents to zero (expected returns toward the security market line), sufficient lags may allow excess returns to be earned temporarily. The mark of a successful company is one that continually identifies and exploits opportunities for excess returns. Only with a sequence of short-run advantages can any overall competitive advantage be sustained.[2]

We note that the important thing is to earn excess returns, as measured by the distance above the security market line, regardless of the risk spectrum in which the opportunity arises. That is, the opportunity may be in a safe, mature business or in a riskier, growth-oriented business. There is nothing magical about growth per se; the key is to exploit opportunities wherever they arise. It is not the greatest return nor the greatest growth that matters, but the greatest return relative to the standard imposed by the financial markets. In this way, value is created.

Separation of Required Return and the Firm. Another implication is that the required rate of return for the project does not depend on the company undertaking the investment. Given the project's systematic risk, the market requires a single return. Therefore, the required rate of return on the project is the same for any firm that might invest in it. Stated differently, the systematic risk of a project is the same for all firms; therefore, the project's required return is the same. This is not to say that the project is equally valuable to all firms. Some firms will derive greater incremental cash flows from it than will

[2] For a discussion of such advantages, together with examples, see Alan C. Shapiro, "Corporate Strategy and the Capital Budgeting Decision," *Financial Management Collections*, 1 (Winter 1986), 1–14.

others. Because of differences in expertise, management efficiency, synergism, and so forth, the expected return can vary among firms. Consequently, the project will be more valuable to some firms than to others, but the acceptance standard will be the same for all firms considering the project.

Diversification Is Not of Value. Because the market models (CAPM, extended CAPM, APT) assume that investors, in their portfolios of stocks, diversify away all risk other than systematic risk, diversification by the firm in its portfolio of capital assets is not a thing of value. In other words, the model implies that the firm is unable to do something for investors—namely, diversify—that they cannot do for themselves. Now one could argue that while investors are able to diversify across companies whose stocks are publicly traded, they cannot diversify across capital assets held by these companies. In other words, they purchase shares in the income stream of the company as a whole, not in the income streams of the individual assets of the company.

Investors do not need to acquire direct claims on capital assets, however, in order to accomplish such diversification. As long as there is information available about the actual returns on individual assets, investors can effectively diversify across capital assets of individual companies. In essence, an investor can replicate the return stream of the individual capital asset held by a firm.[3] Suppose a firm holds three productive assets, A, B, and C, and complete information exists about the actual ex post returns on these assets. To "invest" in asset A but not in assets B and C, the investor could buy x percent of the stock of the company. He then would sell claims against himself based on promises to pay x percent of the future income streams associated with assets B and C. That is, in a particular year, if asset B were to provide a $100 return and asset C a $200 return, he would pay $100x and $200x to the holders of the claims. In this way, the investor effectively replicates the income stream of a single capital asset of a firm, that of asset A in our example.

It is in this sense that investors are able to diversify effectively across capital assets of individual firms. Another way to visualize the matter is to think of A, B, and C as divisions of a company. If a group of large investors wanted to acquire A but not B and C, they could buy the whole company and sell off divisions B and C. This *value additive* principle states that the value of the whole is equal to the sum of the separate asset parts. As a result of this principle, the firm is said not to be able to do something for investors through diversification of capital assets that they cannot do for themselves. Investment projects should, therefore, be evaluated on the basis of only their systematic risk, not on the basis of their total risk nor the incremental risk they contribute to the firm as a whole. More about this later.

MEASURING REQUIRED MARKET-BASED RETURNS

Having discussed value creation in general, we want to focus on how to go about establishing the return the financial markets require. We assume initially that the project is financed entirely by equity, that the firm considering

---

[3] See Lawrence D. Schall, "Asset Valuation, Firm Investment, and Firm Diversification," *Journal of Business*, 45 (January 1972), 13–21, for amplification on this point as well as proof of the irrelevancy of diversification decisions by the firm.

the project is all equity financed, and that all financial market information pertains to unlevered situations. Later we modify the approach for leverage, but our understanding of the basics is made easier if we first ignore this consideration.

Under these circumstances, the required rate of return for a project can be expressed as a function of its beta, in a CAPM context, or of its factor risks, in an APT factor model context. (See Chapters 3 and 4.) Note that the required return derived is market based, using tradable securities. The return on investment for capital projects, however, usually is expressed in terms of the internal rate of return. This measure is based on the time-magnitude relationship between cash inflows and the initial cash outflow. It does not take account of the changes in market value of the project from period to period. Thus, there is a problem of incompatibility between the return measure for a security and that for a capital project.

SURROGATE MARKET INFORMATION

One way to come to grips with the problem is to try to express the profitability of an investment project in terms of its cash flow during the period and its change in value from the beginning of the period to the end. In this way, the two return measures would be compatible. The one-period return for an investment project would be

$$R_t = \frac{V_t + A_t - V_{t-1}}{V_{t-1}} \tag{8-1}$$

where V_t = the market value of the project at the end of period t
A_t = net cash flow received at the end of period t

The difficulty, of course, is in estimating the value of the project at the end of a period. One approach is to use externally determined market values for the asset. A secondary market of sorts may exist, as it does for machine tools, where prices are established for used machines of various ages. Other assets have similar markets where prices can be determined. Even though the market values involved are those in the product markets as opposed to those in financial markets, market value changes are still employed in the approach. Later in this section, we shall derive the required rate of return using this method, but first let us take up other surrogates.

PROXY COMPANIES

In many cases, a project is similar to a company whose stock is publicly traded, so in a CAPM context we can use that company's beta in deriving the required rate of return. For large projects, such as new products, one frequently can identify publicly traded stocks of companies engaged entirely or almost entirely in the same type of operation.

Suppose a steel company is considering the formation of a real estate subsidiary. We can determine the betas for a number of real estate companies with publicly traded stocks and use them to derive the required rate of return for the project. Note that the relevant required rate of return is not for the steel company but for other real estate firms. Stated differently, the market views the steel company's venture in the same way it views other firms engaged solely in real estate. By concentrating on companies in the same line as the business the firm desires to enter, we can find surrogates that approximate the systematic risk of the project. Exact duplication of the project's risk is unlikely, but reasonable approximations are possible.

One should endeavor to identify companies of a similar nature to the project in question. The search for similars usually is industry based. Sometimes one will turn to the SIC (Standard Industrial Classification) code to determine an initial sample. When a project falls in a single industry classification, the job is relatively easy. From the sample of proxy companies, their betas are arrayed. If outliers are felt not to be comparable with the project in question, they might be culled. Rather than compute an arithmetic average of the sample betas, I find it better to use a modal or median value. The idea is to come up with a beta that broadly portrays the business risk of the investment project. One can only hope to approximate, given the data problems.

To illustrate, say that 1.6 is the median beta for a sample of real estate companies whose stocks are publicly traded and whose basic businesses are similar to the venture contemplated by the steel company. We can use this beta as a surrogate for the beta of the project. If we expect the average return on the market portfolio of stocks to be 15 percent and the risk-free rate to be 10 percent, the required rate of return for the project will be $R_k = .10 + (.15 - .10)1.6 = 18\%$. Therefore, 18 percent is used as the required rate of return for the project. If the real estate venture can be expected to provide an internal rate of return in excess of, or equal to, this rate, the project will be accepted. If not, it will be rejected.

For publicly held stocks, we do not have to calculate the betas ourselves. We can—and should for projects of this sort—obtain it from a number of services, including Merrill Lynch, First Boston, and the Value Line Investment Survey. Historical beta information is computed on the basis of weekly or monthly data for 3 to 5 years in the past. Whether the historical beta should be adjusted on the basis of additional information will depend on the considerations taken up in Chapter 4.

APT FACTOR MODEL APPROACH

For use of factor models, computations are more involved. If you are confident in the factor risks specified and in the consistency of parameter estimates, we learned in Chapter 4 that it is straightforward to solve for the required rate of return for a proxy company. You do the following: (1) take the firm's reaction coefficients to the various factor risks; (2) multiply them by their respective lambdas, the market prices of the factor risks; (3) sum the products; and (4) to this sum add the risk-free rate.

Suppose the risk factors of importance were unexpected changes in inflation, unexpected changes in overall economic output, and unexpected changes in default risk premiums between low- and high-grade bonds. Some proxy companies will have greater sensitivity to inflation than they do to the other factors. Other companies are more sensitive to default risk, and so forth. All of this was discussed in Chapter 4. The import is that APT factor models allow determination of the underlying sensitivities of an asset to broad economic and financial factors. These factors represent unavoidable (systematic) risk for the asset.

Instead of risk being captured by the proxy company's beta, it is a function of the responsiveness coefficients for each of the factors of importance. If these coefficients were readily available, as are betas for stocks, if the lambda risk premiums (market prices of risk) were known, and if we were confident that the factors specified were the appropriate ones, there would be no problem. As discussed in Chapter 4, however, there is not agreement as to what factors are important. Moreover, empirical inconsistencies appear in the measurement of the responsiveness coefficients.

The APT factor model approach is going through refinement and has found considerable application in security analysis. It has potential for corporate finance, but as yet it has not been widely used, in contrast to the CAPM. In the remainder of this chapter and in the next, applications will involve the CAPM. However, many of the principles and insights obtained apply to APT factor models. The reader should bear this in mind when approaching the issues to be discussed.

USE OF ACCOUNTING BETAS

Another approach to calibrating risk is to develop betas for a company, or part thereof, based on accounting data. Here an accounting measure of return for a company or project, such as the return on assets, is related to an economywide index of returns, such as the average return on assets for nonfinancial corporations. Regressing the former on the latter, a beta or regression coefficient is determined that is said to depict the systematic risk of returns for the company or division. The procedure for determining and evaluating accounting betas is analogous to that used for market betas previously illustrated. The appeal of this approach is that it does not require data on market returns for the project. Such data often are difficult, if not impossible, to obtain. In contrast, data on accounting returns are readily available.

Recognizing the advantages of data availability, we question only whether accounting betas are good surrogates for market betas. While various empirical studies show a significant statistical association between accounting and market betas for companies, the explanatory power is only moderate. For the individual company, the ability to predict market betas on the basis of accounting betas is too low to make the approach anything but a crude approximation; therefore, we concentrate on developing market return information.[4]

ILLUSTRATION OF DERIVATION
OF REQUIRED RATE OF RETURN

In this section, we illustrate the derivation of the required rate of return for a project when the beta surrogate of a publicly traded company is not available. The example has been simplified to work with annual as opposed to monthly or weekly data.

---

[4] For development of the accounting market beta issue as well as empirical tests in this regard, see William Beaver, Paul Kettler, and Myron Scholes, "The Association between Market-Determined and Accounting-Determined Risk Measures," *Accounting Review*, 45 (October 1970), 654–82; William Beaver and James Manegold, "The Association between Market-Determined and Accounting-Determined Measures of Systematic Risk: Some Further Evidence," *Journal of Financial and Quantitative Analysis*, 10 (June 1975) 231–84; Ned C. Hill and Bernell K. Stone, "Accounting Betas, Systematic Operating Risk, and Financial Leverage," *Journal of Financial and Quantitative Analysis*, 15 (September 1980), 595–637; and Pieter T. Elgers and Dennis Murray, "The Impact of Choice of Market Index on the Empirical Evaluation of Accounting Risk Measures," *Accounting Review*, 57 (April 1982), 358–75.

TABLE 8-1
History of machine used by Albar Dairy Products Company

211

CHAPTER 8
Creating Value
through Capital
Investments

YEAR END	(1) PURCHASE PRICE	(2) EXTERNAL MARKET VALUE	(3) ACTUAL NET CASH FLOW (AFTER TAX)	(4) ANNUAL RETURN $\dfrac{(2)_t + (3)_t - (2)_{t-1}}{(2)_{t-1}}$
Start	$110,000	$110,000		
1		$100,000	$20,000	.091
2		84,000	27,000	.110
3		64,000	22,000	.024
4		53,000	26,000	.234
5		40,000	20,000	.132
6		33,000	18,000	.275
7		24,000	13,000	.121
8		19,000	12,000	.292
9		13,000	8,000	.105
10	Salvage value	9,000	5,000	.077

Suppose Albar Dairy Products Company is looking at a multiple-purpose machine costing $110,000 for use in production of cottage cheese. The company has had similar machines in the past and feels that it is appropriate to use past behavior as a proxy for the future. The history of a comparable machine is shown in Table 8-1. In this table, the external market price of the asset is an estimate of the price prevailing in the market for used machines. This value is set by the forces of supply and demand. The return computed in column (4) is simply the external value at the end of the year less the beginning value plus the net cash flow that occurred, all over the beginning value.

Now that the project cash flows are expressed in terms of market-based annual returns, we are able to compute the beta. Our procedure is to determine the slope of the least squares linear regression line, where the excess return of the project is regressed against the excess return of the market index.[5] For purposes of illustration, this slope, or regression coefficient, is computed by hand. Thankfully, computer routines exist to compute the relevant statistics associated with a regression analysis. Still, it is instructive to go through the calculations, and that is one of the purposes of this illustration.

Suppose Standard & Poor's 500-Stock Index returns for each of the past 10 years are those shown in column (1) of Table 8-2. The risk-free rate, shown in column (2), might simply be the yield available on one-year Treasury securities. In column (3) of the table, the excess return for the market index is determined simply by subtracting the risk-free rate from the market return. In the next column, this excess return is squared and the sum appears at the bottom. The return on the project (shown in the last column of Table 8-1) is reported in column (5) of Table 8-2. In column (6), the excess return on the project is determined. In the last column, the cross product is calculated by multiplying the excess return for the market by the excess return for the project. At the bottom of the columns, the sums of the numbers of the columns are determined, and in the next row, the average is computed for the five return columns. The average is simply the total divided by the number of years, which is 10.

[5] The least squares method fits a regression line to the observations so that the sum of the squares of the deviations from that line is as small as possible. The method is described in most statistics texts.

TABLE 8-2
Computation of excess returns for market index and project and cross product

YEAR	(1) MARKET RETURN R_{mt}	(2) RISK-FREE RATE	(3) EXCESS MARKET RETURN (M) (1) − (2)	(4) EXCESS MARKET RETURN SQUARED $(M)^2$ $(3)^2$	(5) PROJECT RETURN R_{kt}	(6) EXCESS RETURN PROJECT (K) (5) − (2)	(7) CROSS PRODUCT EXCESS RETURNS (MK) (3) × (6)
1	.11	.05	.06	.0036	.091	.041	.0025
2	.17	.07	.10	.0100	.110	.040	.0040
3	(.02)	.06	(.08)	.0064	.024	(.036)	.0029
4	.25	.08	.17	.0289	.234	.154	.0262
5	.18	.06	.12	.0144	.132	.072	.0086
6	.28	.07	.21	.0441	.275	.205	.0431
7	(.08)	.07	(.15)	.0225	.121	.051	(.0077)
8	.27	.09	.18	.0324	.292	.202	.0364
9	.14	.07	.07	.0049	.105	.035	.0025
10	.00	.08	(.08)	.0064	.077	(.003)	.0002
Total	1.30	.70	.60	.1736	1.461	.761	.1187
Average return	.13	.07	.06		.146	.076	

The beta, or slope of the regression line, is determined by the following formula:

$$\text{Beta} = \frac{\Sigma MK - n\overline{MK}}{\Sigma M^2 - n\overline{M}^2} \qquad (8\text{-}2)$$

where ΣMK is the sum of the cross products, n is the number of years, $\overline{M}$ is the average excess market return, $\overline{K}$ is the average excess project return, and ΣM^2 is the sum of the squares of excess market returns. For our example in Table 8-2, the beta is

$$\text{Beta} = \frac{.1187 - (10)(.06)(.076)}{.1736 - (10)(.06)^2} = \frac{.0731}{.1376} = .53 \qquad (8\text{-}3)$$

Again we stress that computer routines can easily solve for the slope of a linear regression line, which is the beta as defined. A beta of .53 suggests that the project has only moderate systematic risk. Recall from Chapter 3 that any beta less than 1.00 is said to characterize a defensive investment. Given the beta, we have the most important piece of information necessary to calculate the project's required rate of return.

Two additional pieces of information are necessary, however, before we can make such a computation: the expected risk-free rate and the market rate of return. As with the beta, one is interested in likely *future* outcomes. Suppose, for purposes only of illustrating the immediate example, one felt that the arithmetic means of the risk-free rates and market returns that prevailed over the 10-year period in our example were reasonable proxies for the future. (We will discuss how these estimates should be made shortly.) From Table 8-2, these averages are 7 percent and 13 percent, respectively. With this additional information, we now are able to estimate the required rate of return for the project. Using Eq. (8-2), it is

$$R_k = R_f + (\bar{R}_m - R_f)\beta_k = .07 + (.13 - .07).53 + .102 \qquad (8\text{-}4)$$

where R_f and $\bar{R}_m$ are the arithmetic means of risk-free rates and actual S&P 500-stock index returns, respectively. Thus, the required rate of return for the project is 10.2 percent. The reason the required return is less than the average return for the market index, 13 percent, is that the project has a relatively low covariance with the market index.

The critical assumption is that past experience is a good proxy for the future; that is, the association between project returns and market returns is likely to be the same in the future as it has been in the past. In addition, future returns on a riskless investment and on the market portfolio must be expected to be approximately the same as their returns in the past. If these assumptions hold, R_k can be used as an approximation of the project's required rate of return. Expected net cash flows for the new, but similar, project would be discounted at this rate. If the net present value were positive, the project would be accepted; if not, it would be rejected. To illustrate the acceptance criterion, suppose the expected net cash flows for the project under consideration were

TIME	0	1	2	3	4	5	6	7	8	9	10
Expected net cash flow after tax (in thousands)	$(110)	$42	$38	$32	$27	$23	$18	$15	$12	$10	$8

When we discount this cash-flow stream at the proposed required rate of return of 10.2 percent, we find the net present value to be $46,144. Because this figure is positive, the proposal should be accepted according to the method employed.

The procedure is crude in that we use the past beta as a proxy for the future; nevertheless, all required-rate-of-return calculations are similarly plagued. The real problem is when the project being evaluated is unlike past projects with which the firm or outside specialists have had experience. Here estimates of the responsiveness of project returns to market returns must be estimated subjectively, and they are vulnerable to considerable error.

If the project is relatively self-contained, such as a new division, it should be compared with another firm or subsidiary of a firm. If the firm or subsidiary has publicly traded stock, it is an easy matter to use such returns to compute the beta and the required rate of return for the project. As suggested earlier in our example of a steel company investing in a real estate venture, this proxy is likely to be accurate. Whenever possible, then, comparisons of a project with publicly held (proxy) companies should be used. In practice, this has proved feasible, as a number of companies have identified publicly traded companies that correspond in general to internal investment projects.

RISK-FREE RATE AND MARKET RETURN

In addition to beta, it is important that the numbers used for the market return and the risk-free rate be the best estimates of the future possible. The past probably will not be a good proxy. Changing inflation and interest rates make arithmetic averages of the past, of the sort undertaken in Table 8-2, unlikely predictors of future returns. Rather than use ex post returns, ex ante returns should be employed.

The risk-free rate is controversial, not as to the security that should be used but the maturity. Most agree that the proper instrument is a Treasury security. But the proper maturity is another matter. As the CAPM is a one-period model, some contend a short-term rate, such as that for 3-month Treasury bills, is in order. Others argue that because capital investment projects are long-lived, a long-term Treasury bond rate should be used. Still others, myself included, feel more comfortable with an intermediate-term rate, such as that on 1- or 2-year Treasury notes. This is a middle position in a rather murky area. With an upward-sloping yield curve (the relationship between yield and maturity), the longer the maturity the higher the risk-free rate, but also the less the variability of interest rates.

For the expected return on the market portfolio of stocks, as usually depicted by Standard & Poor's 500-Stock Index or the New York Stock Exchange Index, one can use consensus estimates of security analysts, economists, and others who regularly predict such returns. Goldman Sachs, Merrill Lynch, and other investment banks make these predictions, often on a monthly basis. These estimated annual returns are for the immediate future.

The *expected* return on the market portfolio has exceeded the risk-free rate by anywhere from 3 to 7 percent in recent years. Expressed differently, the ex ante market risk premium has ranged from 3 to 7 percent. This is not the range of risk premiums actually realized over some holding period, but the range of expected risk premiums. This 3 to 7 percent spread represents the expected risk premium for investing in the market portfolio of stocks as opposed to a risk-free asset. Another approach to estimating the future market return is simply to add a risk premium to the risk-free rate. If the present return on an appropriate Treasury security is 9 percent and a risk premium of 5 percent is appropriate, the expected return on the market portfolio is 14 percent. This figure can then be used as the market return, and the risk-free rate will be 9 percent.

MODIFICATION FOR LEVERAGE

So far we have assumed all equity financing and that the beta employed pertains to an unlevered situation. It is appropriate now to modify the approach for leverage. The beta, and hence the required return of a project, is a function of both business risk and the degree of leverage. If the tenets of the capital asset pricing model hold, the relationship shown in Fig. 8-2 will prevail. As a company increases its degree of debt financing, the project's beta and required return increase in the linear manner shown. With respect to leverage, it is important that the beta used for the project corresponds with the way the firm intends to finance.

If a proxy company is used to determine the project's beta, and it has significant leverage while we do not, the use of its beta will bias things toward a higher required return on equity than is justified. This occurrence can be seen in the figure, where we assume the proxy company has leverage of x. As a result, its required return is r_x. Now if we employ no leverage, our true required return for the project is r_0. By using the proxy company's beta, however, we end up with a much higher required return. The difference between

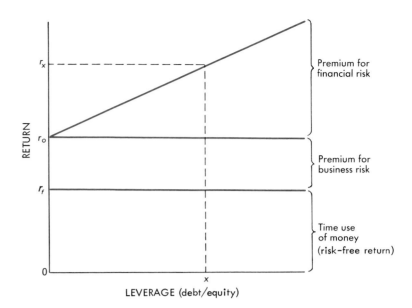

FIGURE 8-2
Relationship between the required
return on equity and leverage

r_x and r_o is due solely to differences in leverage. In essence, the firm unnecessarily penalizes itself in the return it requires. As can easily be visualized, the opposite occurs if the proxy company uses no leverage and we are levered.

ADJUSTING THE BETA FOR LEVERAGE

When the leverage of the proxy company differs significantly from the leverage the firm wishes to employ, it may be desirable to adjust the beta of the proxy company. The procedure presented below takes as given the assumptions of the capital asset pricing model. In the end, we shall qualify the results for the considerations to be taken up in Chapter 10, where the question of capital structure is examined in depth.

With corporate income taxes, interest payments are deductible for tax purposes. Under these circumstances, Hamada, as well as others, has demonstrated that the required rate of return for a stock is[6]

$$R_j = R_f + \left(\frac{\overline{R}_m - R_f}{\sigma_m^2}\right)(r_{ju,m}\sigma_{ju}\sigma_m)\left[1 + \frac{D}{S}(1 - T_c)\right] \qquad (8\text{-}5)$$

where R_f = risk-free rate

R_m = the expected return on the market portfolio

σ_m = standard deviation of the probability distribution of possible market returns

σ_{ju} = standard deviation of the probability distribution of possible returns for security j *in the absence of leverage*

$r_{ju,m}$ = correlation coefficient between returns for security j *in the absence of leverage* and the market portfolio

D/S = the debt-to-equity ratio in market value terms

T_c = corporate tax rate

[6] Robert S. Hamada, "Portfolio Analysis, Market Equilibrium and Corporation Finance," *Journal of Finance,* 24 (March 1969), 19–30.

The important thing to note is that the covariance between returns, which is the second bracketed term in the equation, is as if the company had an all-equity capital structure.

Equation (8-5) can be expressed in terms of the more familiar beta:

$$R_j = R_f + (R_m - R_f)\beta_{ju}\left[1 + \frac{D}{S}(1 - T_c)\right] \tag{8-6}$$

where β_{ju} is the beta measuring the responsiveness of the excess return for the security *in the absence of leverage* to the excess return for the market portfolio. Thus, the overall required rate of return is composed of the risk-free rate, R_f, plus a premium for business risk, $(R_m - R_f)\beta_{ju}$, and a premium for financial risk:

$$(R_m - R_f)\beta_{ju}\left[\frac{D}{S}(1 - T_c)\right]$$

The measured, or observed, beta for the stock, β_j, embodies both risks and is simply

$$\beta_j = \beta_{ju}\left[1 + \frac{D}{S}(1 - T_c)\right] \tag{8-7}$$

Rearranging, the beta for the stock *in the absence of leverage* is

$$\beta_{ju} = \frac{\beta_j}{\left[1 + \frac{D}{S}(1 - T_c)\right]} \tag{8-8}$$

An Example. Given these expressions, we are able to derive the beta *in the absence of leverage* for a particular stock. Suppose the measured beta, β_j, for security *j* were 1.4; the debt-to-equity ratio, *D/S*, were .70; and the tax rate were 40 percent (federal and state). Therefore, the beta *in the absence of leverage* would be

$$\beta_{ju} = \frac{1.4}{[1 + .7(.6)]} = .99$$

If we now wished to determine the beta for a different amount of leverage, we would use Eq. (8-7). Suppose we were interested in using security *j* as a proxy for the systematic risk of our project. However, we employ a debt-to-equity ratio of .3 as opposed to the .7 for security *j*. Therefore, the adjusted beta would be

$$\text{Adjusted } \beta_j = .99[1 + .3(.6)] = 1.17$$

This beta contrasts with .99 for security *j in the absence of leverage* and with 1.40 for security *j* with a debt-to-equity ratio of .7.

Important Caveats. In summary, we are able to derive an adjusted beta for a security under the assumption of a different proportion of debt than what occurs. We first estimate the beta for the stock *in the absence of leverage* and then adjust this figure for the proportion of leverage we wish to employ. The final result is an approximation of the beta that would prevail if the external company were to employ the desired proportion of debt. Again, it should be emphasized that the beta adjustment procedure is crude.

It assumes that capital markets are perfect except for the presence of corporate taxes. Indeed, the only adjustment, and a linear one at that, is for corporate taxes. To the extent that future debt levels and the tax shield are uncertain, James A. Miles and John R. Ezzell demonstrate that leverage contributes less to value than the adjustment formula implies.[7] As a result, the unlevered beta is less than that determined by the Hamada beta adjustment formula, Eq. (8-8). Put another way, the required return on equity is overestimated with this formula.

On the other hand, when the debt issued is risky, the true unlevered beta will be somewhat higher than the formula suggests.[8] The point is that different imperfections affect the beta adjustment differently. Rather than get into these now, in Chapter 10 we look at imperfections in an overall assessment of the impact of capital structure on valuation. Until then, keep in mind the caveats, particularly when large beta adjustments are involved.

WEIGHTED AVERAGE REQUIRED RETURN

The final step is to use the adjusted beta to determine the cost of equity capital for the project and then to go on to determine a weighted average required return. The best way to describe these steps is by extending our previous illustration. Suppose the risk-free rate is 8 percent, the cost of debt funds to our company is 10 percent, and the expected return on the market portfolio is 13 percent. The after-tax cost of debt funds is

$$R_{debt} = .10(1 - \text{tax rate})$$

$$= .10(1 - .4) = .06$$

The cost of equity, using the capital asset pricing model approach, is

$$R_{equity} = R_f + (\bar{R}_m - R_f)\text{adjusted } \beta_j$$

$$= .08 + (.13 - .08)1.17 = .1385$$

Both of these costs are expressed on an after-tax basis.

WEIGHTED COST

Once we have individual costs for debt and equity funds, we must blend them. The weighted average cost of capital (WACC) is expressed as follows:

$$\text{WACC} = \begin{pmatrix} \text{Proportion} \\ \text{of debt} \end{pmatrix} \begin{pmatrix} \text{Debt} \\ \text{cost} \end{pmatrix} + \begin{pmatrix} \text{Proportion} \\ \text{of equity} \end{pmatrix} \begin{pmatrix} \text{Equity} \\ \text{cost} \end{pmatrix} \quad (8\text{-}9)$$

[7] "Reformulating Tax Shield Valuation: A Note," *Journal of Finance*, 40 (December 1985), 1485–92.

[8] See Thomas E. Conine, Jr., "Corporate Debt and Corporate Taxes: An Extension," *Journal of Finance*, 35 (September 1980).

Returning to our example, a debt-to-equity ratio of .3 means that we employ 3 parts of debt for every 10 parts of equity. Therefore, the proportion of debt is $3/(3 + 10)$ and the proportion of equity is $10/(3 + 10)$. With these weights and the costs of funds previously calculated, the weighted average required return for the project is

$$R_{project} = .06\left(\frac{3}{13}\right) + .1385\left(\frac{10}{13}\right) = .1204$$

Thus, the required return on the project is approximately 12 percent when we adjust the beta for differences in leverage and then use the adjusted beta and the leverage we wish to employ to determine a weighted average required return. This required return would be used as the acceptance criterion for the project, according to the capital asset pricing model method.

QUALIFICATIONS

Again we point out that the beta adjustment procedure assumes perfect capital markets with the exception of the presence of corporate taxes. When in Chapter 10 we examine the issue of leverage in depth, we shall find that personal taxes lessen the overall corporate tax advantage associated with debt. As a result, the adjustment would be somewhat less. The presence of bankruptcy costs and other imperfections further complicates the picture. These topics must await Chapter 10, when we can evaluate them as an integrated whole. The adjustment procedure described provides an approximate beta when the proportion of debt is varied, but we must recognize it as an approximation.

Multiperiod Problem. We must remember also that the CAPM is single period in time frame. On the other hand, capital budgeting projects to which the required return is applied are typically multiperiod. Although it usually is safe to go from one to the other, additional care must be exercised in some situations. When the asset's systematic risk, as depicted by its beta, is roughly constant over the project's life, there are few problems. If the beta of a project changes significantly over time, however, we must allow for this change. Some projects are riskier initially, then become safer as uncertainty is resolved with time; other projects become riskier with time. When an asset's beta changes significantly over time, it may be appropriate to use different betas and, consequently, different discount rates for different future periods.

In an alternative approach, the certainty equivalent technique would adjust the cash flows for systematic risk by relating them to returns for the market portfolio. Expressed differently, cash-flow betas instead of return betas are derived and then are used to reduce the expected cash flows for systematic risk. These and other adjustment techniques are possible, but beyond the scope of this chapter. The reader interested in the problem should refer to the articles listed in the footnote.[9] Despite the multiperiod problem, for ease of

[9] See Richard Roll and Marcus C. Bogue, "Capital Budgeting of Risky Projects with Imperfect Markets for Physical Capital," *Journal of Finance*, 29 (May 1974), 606–12; Michael J. Brennan, "An Approach to the Valuation of Uncertain Income Streams," *Journal of Finance*, 28 (June 1973), 661–74; Stewart C. Myers and Stuart M. Turnbull, "Capital Budgeting and the Capital Asset Pricing Model: Good News and the Bad News," *Journal of Finance*, 32 (May 1977), 321–32; Eugene F. Fama, "Risk-Adjusted Discount Rates and Capital Budgeting under Uncertainty," *Journal of Financial Economics*, 5 (1977), 3–24; and Gordon A. Sick, "Multiperiod Risky Project Valuation: A Mean-Covariance Certainty-Equivalent Approach," in *Advances in Financial Planning and Forecasting*, ed. C. F. Lee (Greenwich, CT: JAI Press, 1987).

exposition we assume that a project's beta is roughly constant over time. As a result of this and other assumptions, we assume a constant risk-adjusted discount rate through future time.

ADJUSTED PRESENT VALUE

An alternative to the weighted average cost of capital (WACC) is the adjusted present-value method (APV), first proposed by Stewart C. Myers.[10] With an APV approach, project cash flows are broken down into two components: unlevered operating cash flows; and those associated with financing the project. These components then are valued so that

$$APV = \frac{\text{Unlevered}}{\text{value}} + \frac{\text{Value of}}{\text{financing}} \qquad (8\text{-}10)$$

The disaggregation of cash flows is undertaken so that different discount rates may be used. As operating cash flows are more risky, they are discounted at a higher rate.

More formally, the adjusted present value is

$$APV = \sum_{t=0}^{n} \frac{OC_t}{(1 + k_u)^t} + \sum_{t=0}^{n} \frac{\text{Int.}_t(T_c)}{(1 + k_i)^t} - F \qquad (8\text{-}11)$$

where OC_t is the after-tax operating cash flow in period t, k_u is the required rate of return in the absence of leverage (all-equity financing), Int._t is the interest payment on debt in period t, T_c is the corporate tax rate, k_i is the cost of debt financing, and F is the after-tax flotation cost associated with financing (debt, equity, or both). The first component on the right-hand side of the equation represents the net present value of operating cash flows discounted at the unlevered cost of equity capital. The second component is the present value of the interest tax shield on any debt employed to finance the project. The discount rate is the corporate cost of borrowing, the idea being that the realization of the tax shield bears a risk comparable to that embraced in the cost of debt funds. Finally, any flotation costs are subtracted from the sum of the first two components.

AN ILLUSTRATION

Gruber-Elton Paper Company is considering a new production machine costing $2 million that is expected to produce after-tax cash savings of $400,000 per year for 8 years. The required rate of return on unlevered equity is 13 percent. If this was all there was, the net present value of the project would be (in thousands):

$$NPV = -\$2,000 + \sum_{t=1}^{8} \frac{\$400}{(1.13)^t} = -\$80$$

Under these circumstances, the project would be rejected. Ned Gruber and

[10] Stewart C. Myers, "Interactions of Corporate Financing and Investment Decisions—Implications for Capital Budgeting," *Journal of Finance*, 29 (March 1974), 1–25.

Martin Elton, the founders of the company, are heartbroken, as they really wanted the machine.

But all is not lost! After all, it is the policy of the company to finance capital investment projects with 50 percent debt, as that is the target debt-to-total capitalization of the company. Gruber-Elton Paper Company is able to borrow $1 million at 10 percent interest to finance the new machine in part. (The balance will come from equity funds.) The principal amount of the loan will be repaid in equal year-end installments of $125,000 through the end of year 8. If the company's tax rate (federal and state) is 40 percent, we can compute the interest tax shield and its present value, and they are shown in Table 8-3. We see in column (4) that the present value of the interest tax shield is $132 (in thousands).

The adjusted present value of the project is now (in thousands)

$$APV = -\$80 + \$132 = \$52$$

Gruber and Elton are happy because the project is now acceptable and they can bask in the glory of a shiny new, softly purring machine.

But what about flotation costs? These are the costs of lawyers, investment bankers, printers, and other fees involved in issuing securities. They pertain to both new debt and equity, with those for the latter usually being higher. Suppose in our example the company incurs after-tax flotation costs of $40,000. These reduce the company's cash flows so the adjusted present value becomes

$$APV = -\$80 + \$132 - \$40 = \$12$$

The project is still acceptable, but it provides less benefit than in the absence of flotation costs.

WACC VS. APV

We have presented two methods for determining the value of a project, the weighted average cost of capital and the adjusted present-value method.

TABLE 8-3
Present value of interest tax shield for Gruber-Elton Paper Company (in thousands)

YEAR	(1) DEBT AT BEGINNING OF YEAR	(2) INTEREST (1) × 10%	(3) TAX SHIELD (2) × 40%	(4) PRESENT VALUE AT 10% DISCOUNT RATE
1	$1,000	$100	$40	$36
2	875	88	35	29
3	750	75	30	23
4	625	62	25	17
5	500	50	20	12
6	375	38	15	8
7	250	25	10	5
8	125	12	5	2
Total				$132

The APV method is a general theoretical rule that embraces the WACC method as a subcase. In his article, Myers shows certain biases involved in the WACC method, and there have been a number of challenges and counter-challenges.[11]

Whenever a capital investment occurs, there is an interaction of investment and financing. As a general rule, as long as the firm maintains a relatively constant debt ratio over time and it invests in projects like those it already owns, the WACC method gives an accurate portrayal of the project's worth. This is merely to say that financial risk and business risk are relatively invariant over time. If a company should depart radically from previous financing patterns and/or invest in an entirely new line of business (like widgets when it is a seed company), then the APV approach provides a more accurate answer theoretically.

The advantage of the WACC method is that it is easy to understand and widely used. The APV method is pleasing to many academics, but is not widely used in business. The APV method is not without its difficulties. Implied is that there are no imperfections other than corporate taxes and flotation costs. In other words, the interest tax shield and flotation costs are all that matters when it comes to financing. We explore other imperfections in Chapter 10, when we evaluate capital structure decisions from a broader perspective. For now recognize the differences in approach, but also the fact that for most situations the two approaches give identical accept/reject decisions. More will be said about the WACC method in the next chapter.

TOTAL RISK ANALYSIS

So far in this chapter our focus has been on the return required for so much systematic, or unavoidable, risk. We know from Chapter 3, however, that the total risks of an investment is the sum of both systematic and unsystematic risks. The latter is the risk that can be diversified away. If some of the assumptions of the capital asset pricing model or APT factor models do not hold, the effect of a project on the total risk of the firm may be important.

Leaving aside for the moment whether or not these assumptions hold, we want to explore the evaluation of risky investments if they do not hold. That is, we assume that the *only* thing that is important is the risk and return of the individual firm and that projects are evaluated with respect to their marginal impact on these two factors. In the subsequent section, we examine the critical assumptions of the capital asset pricing model and APT factor models and attempt to reconcile them with the total variability approach presented in this section. Our attention now, however, is directed to the evaluation of risky investments solely in relation to their impact on the total risk and return of the firm.

---

[11] See James Miles and John R. Ezzell, "The Weighted Average Cost of Capital, Perfect Capital Markets and Project Life: A Clarification," *Journal of Financial and Quantitative Analysis*, 15 (September 1980), 719–30; Donald R. Chambers, Robert S. Harris, and John J. Pringle, "Treatment of Financing Mix in Analyzing Investment Opportunities," *Financial Management*, 11 (Summer 1982), 24–41; and Robert A. Taggart, Jr., "Consistent Valuation and Cost of Capital Expressions with Corporate and Personal Taxes," working paper, National Bureau of Economic Research (August 1989).

EVALUATION OF COMBINATIONS
OF RISKY INVESTMENTS

From Chapter 7, we know that the marginal risk of an individual proposal to the firm as a whole depends on its correlation with existing projects
as well as its correlation with proposals under consideration that might be
accepted. The appropriate information is the standard deviation and expected
value of the probability distribution of possible net present values for all feasible combinations of existing projects and investment proposals under consideration. Now we must select the most desirable combination. Later in the
chapter, we shall ask the fundamental question, Should a portfolio approach
be used at all? We assume now that management is interested only in the
marginal impact of an investment proposal on the risk complexion of the firm
as a whole.

The selection of the most desirable combination of investments will
depend upon management's utility preferences with respect to net present
value and variance, or standard deviation. If management is averse to risk and
associates risk with the variance of net present value, its utility function may
be similar to that shown in Fig. 8-3. As discussed in Chapter 3, the curves in
the figure are indifference curves; management is indifferent to any combination of expected value of net present value and standard deviation on a particular curve. Thus, a specific curve portrays the trade-off between the two
parameters for a particular company. The indifference curves in Fig. 8-3
suggest that management's utility function is risk averse, indicating decreasing marginal rates of substitution between standard deviation and net present
value. As the dispersion of possible net present values of the firm increases, it
takes increasing amounts of net present value for management to accept additional increments of risk.

As we move to the left and up in Fig. 8-3, each successive curve represents a higher level of utility. Thus, management would choose the combination of investments that lies on the highest indifference curve, the one farthest
to the left, because this curve represents the greatest utility. This combination
is determined by the intersection of a dot, point L, with the highest indifference curve. Point L represents the portfolio of existing projects and proposals

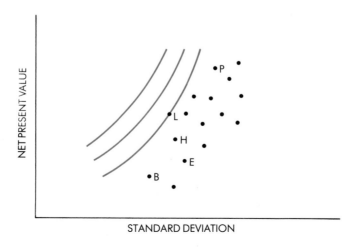

FIGURE 8-3

Selection of the best
portfolio

offering the most desirable combination of expected value of net present value and risk. But remember that this presentation is mainly conceptual. It assumes that a utility function for management can be graphed, when in fact, a group utility function can be derived only under very restricted conditions.[12]

PROJECT COMBINATION DOMINANCE

The framework for evaluating combinations of risky investments just developed is useful nevertheless, even if management's utility function is not defined. With the information shown by the dots in Fig. 8-3, management can eliminate most combinations, simply because they are dominated by other combinations. Unless management is quite averse to risk, it probably would consider only four portfolios of risky investments: *B*, *H*, *L*, and *P*. From these, management would choose the one that appeared to offer the best combination of expected return and risk.

This selection determines which new investment proposals to accept, but if the portfolio contained only existing projects, no investment proposals would be accepted. If the portfolio of existing projects were represented by portfolio *E* in Fig. 8-3, however, the selection of any of the four portfolios would imply the acceptance of one or more new investment proposals. Proposals not in the portfolio finally selected would be rejected, of course.

In summary, management is able to determine which investment proposals under consideration offer the best marginal contribution of net present value and standard deviation to the firm as a whole. In determining the standard deviation for a portfolio, management considers the correlation between an investment proposal and existing or other proposed investments. This evaluation implies that the total risk of the firm is what is important; therefore, investment decisions should be made in light of their marginal impact on total risk. The evaluation is firm-risk oriented in the sense that management does not consider explicitly the impact of the project on investors' portfolios, only on the portfolio of assets of the firm.

RECONCILIATION OF THE TWO APPROACHES

We have taken two paths toward evaluating risky investments. On one we evaluated a project in relation to its systematic risk; on the other we analyzed the incremental impact of the project on the business-risk complexion of the firm as a whole. Which was the right way?

Let us go back to one foundation of the two market models—CAPM and APT factor. We know that the risk or total variability of asset returns is comprised of unavoidable, or systematic, risk as well as asset specific risk. The market models assume that efficient investors can diversify away asset specific, or unsystematic, risk. Consequently, this residual risk does not affect value. If the assumptions of the market models do not entirely hold under real-world conditions, unsystematic risk may affect the value of the firm. In

---

[12] See Robert Wilson, "The Theory of Syndicates," *Econometrica*, 36 (January 1968), 119–32.

this case, the impact of a project on the firm's total variability of returns would be of some importance.

CRITICAL ASSUMPTIONS

A crucial assumption in the market models is that the cost of insolvency or bankruptcy is zero. If a firm fails, assets presumably can be sold for their economic value. No legal or selling costs are incurred. After creditors have been paid, the residual proceeds are distributed to stockholders. As long as assets can be sold at their economic value in a frictionless world, investors can effectively diversify their risk. Under real-world conditions, however, assets often have to be sold in bankruptcy at distress prices. Moreover, there are selling costs, legal fees, and other out-of-pocket costs. Finally, and probably most important, there are a number of delays and inefficiencies involved in the process of going through a bankruptcy. Impending bankruptcy repels suppliers, who fear that the company may not be able to pay them. Employees leave in anticipation of doom. Sales drop off as customers worry about the reliability of the product and service. These developments make operations inefficient, to say the least.

A cumbersome legal process delays creditor takeover, during which asset values deteriorate. All of this becomes a "drain on the system" to suppliers of capital, and it works either directly or indirectly to the detriment of stockholders, the residual owners of the firm. The idea is that there are a number of stakeholders in the company—debt holders and common stockholders to be sure, but also customers, employees, governments, and people in communities where facilities are located. When total risk increases, the cost of doing business rises. In turn, this weakens the company's chances for survival. If there were no costs to bankruptcy and the firm could go through a costless reorganization or liquidation, stockholders might not care as long as the firm were committed to doing those things that it did best. However, with significant bankruptcy costs, stockholders will be affected and may view diversification of assets in a different light.

The probability of a firm's becoming insolvent depends on its *total* risk, not just on its *systematic* risk; therefore, a case can be made for choosing projects in light of their effect on both the systematic and the total (systematic plus residual) risk of the firm. Put another way, when insolvency or bankruptcy costs are significant, investors may well be served by the firm's paying attention to the total risk of the firm, not just to its systematic risk. Risky capital budgeting proposals can alter the total risk of the firm apart from their effect on its systematic risk. To the extent that residual risk is a factor of at least some importance, total risk should be evaluated.

Other market imperfections also make asset specific or residual risk important. For example, the market models (CAPM and APT factor) assume that investors can lend and borrow at the same rate, that there are no transaction costs, and that information is available without cost to all market participants. In the real world, the borrowing rate typically exceeds the lending rate, there are transaction costs, and investors incur costs in obtaining information. All of these factors limit the effectiveness with which investors are able to diversify away asset-specific, or residual, risk. As a result, residual risk becomes a factor of at least some importance in valuation. Although these imperfections probably are not as important as the cost of insolvency or bankruptcy for the capital investment decision, nonetheless they contribute to the importance of residual risk.

A DUAL APPROACH

Where does this leave us? It suggests that we should consider the impact of a project on both the systematic risk and the total risk of the firm. If both the market model approach and the total variability approach for evaluating a project give clear accept or reject signals, we should act upon them. The obvious problem is when one approach gives an accept signal and the other a reject signal. When this occurs, management needs to assess which approach is more applicable. If the common stock of the company involved is publicly held, if the possibility of insolvency is remote, and if the firm can realistically express expected project returns in terms of changes in market-based capitalized values, a strong case can be made for the signal given by a market model.

If the stock is traded in a market with high transaction and information costs, if the possibility of insolvency or bankruptcy is significant, and if the expression of project returns in terms of market-based returns is crude, greater reliance should be placed on the total variability approach. Even here, however, a portion of the residual risk can be diversified away. Even when there are problems in expressing project returns on a basis consistent with a market model, one should not ignore the implications of the approach.

Obviously, the methods proposed are not operationally perfect. Still, they represent a means for judging risky investments. In the years to come, we can expect the state of the art to be improved. It is clear that the impact of a project on risk is important and must be considered if the firm is to make investment decisions that maximize shareholder wealth. It also is clear that management must consider the effect of a project not only on the risk complexion of the firm but on the systematic risk to investors. The idea that the market for common stocks is relatively efficient forces a firm in this direction if its objective is truly one of maximizing shareholder wealth.

SUMMARY

Value is created through capital investments by exploiting opportunities for excess returns, those providing returns in excess of what the financial markets require for the risk involved. The avenues to value creation are industry attractiveness and competitive advantage; these are the things that give rise to positive net-present-value projects. The successful company continually identifies and exploits such opportunities, giving it a sequence of short-run advantages.

In evaluating risky investments, a market model (CAPM or APT factor) relates the acceptance of a project to the systematic risk of investors. Projects are evaluated in a market context, and the required rate of return is computed for each project. The approach was illustrated with an example.

A problem of incompatibility between the usual measures of return for stocks and for capital investment projects can be reduced by expressing project returns in terms of changes in capitalized value. Still better, a publicly traded proxy company can be used in the calculation of beta for the project under review. When the firm finances partially with debt or when a proxy company uses more or less leverage, it may be necessary to modify the CAPM approach. An adjustment formula for beta was illustrated, as was the calculation of a weighted average required return for a project.

In addition to the weighted average cost of capital (WACC), the adjusted present value (APV) method was considered. In the latter approach, project-operating cash flows are discounted at the unlevered cost of equity, interest tax shields at the cost of borrowing, and flotation costs are subtracted from the sum of the present values. The idea is that there are two components to a project: its unlevered value and the net value of financing. The differences between the APV and WACC methods were explored, and it was determined that imperfections other than corporate taxes cloud the issue.

Instead of using a market model, one can evaluate projects with respect to their incremental impact on the total return and risk of the firm. Here one is concerned with various combinations of existing investment projects and investment proposals under consideration. In a portfolio framework, the trade-off between risk and expected net present value for different combinations of investments can be analyzed. Management then can choose the best combination of risk and return for the firm as a whole. In an attempt to reconcile the two approaches under real-world conditions, we saw that the market models depend on several assumptions, like the absence of bankruptcy costs. When we allow for the cost of bankruptcy as well as for other market imperfections, asset-specific or residual risk becomes a factor of importance. In such cases, a dual system for evaluating risky investments can be used where both a market model and the total variability approaches are employed.

SELF-CORRECTION PROBLEMS

1. Determine the required return on equity for the following project situations, using the capital asset pricing model.

SITUATION	EXPECTED RETURN MARKET PORTFOLIO	RISK-FREE RATE	BETA
1	15%	10%	1.00
2	18	14	.70
3	15	8	1.20
4	17	11	.80
5	16	10	1.90

What generalizations can you make?

2. Esto Perpetua Corporation is considering investing in a new product line, computer printers. The company presently has a debt-to-equity ratio of .60 in market-value terms and would use that ratio in financing the new product line. This line will cost the company $4 million at the outset and is expected to produce the following after-tax net cash flows:

YEAR	1	2	3	4	5	6	7
Cash flow (in thousands)	$500	$1,000	$1,400	$1,700	$1,800	$1,300	$600

Esto Perpetua has identified a publicly traded company that is in the same printer business it wishes to enter. This proxy company has a beta of 1.25. The risk-free rate is 10 percent, and the expected return on the market portfolio is 16 percent. Esto Perpetua has a corporate tax rate of 40 percent, and its cost of debt funds is 13 percent.

a. Assuming that the proxy company had approximately the same debt ratio and tax rate as Esto Perpetua, what is the project's required rate of return using the CAPM approach? What is the net present value of the project?

b. If both companies employed no debt, but everything else was the same, how would your solutions to part (a) change?

c. Suppose the proxy company had a debt-to-equity ratio of .20 instead of .60, but everything else was the same. Adjust the beta for leverage and determine a new required return assuming that Esto Perpetua still wishes to finance with a .60 ratio of debt to equity. What is the project's net present value now?

d. Suppose the debt incurred in financing the project remained outstanding throughout the seven years. If there were no flotation costs, what would be the project's adjusted present value (APV) under the conditions of a?

3. You are evaluating two separate projects as to their effect on the total risk and return of your corporation. The projects are expected to result in the following:

	NET PRESENT VALUE OF COMPANY (IN THOUSANDS)	STANDARD DEVIATION (IN THOUSANDS)
Existing projects only	$6,000	$3,000
Plus project 1	7,500	4,500
Plus project 2	8,200	5,000
Plus projects 1 and 2	9,700	6,100

a. Would you invest in one or both projects?

b. What would you do if a capital asset pricing model approach to the problem suggested a different decision?

PROBLEMS

1. Acosta Sugar Company has estimated that the overall return for Standard & Poor's 500-Stock Index will be 15 percent over the next 10 years. The company also feels that the interest rate on Treasury bills will average 10 percent over this interval. The company is thinking of expanding into a new product line: almonds. It has had no experience in this line but has been able to obtain information on various companies involved in producing and processing nuts. Although no company examined produces only almonds, Acosta's management feels that the beta for such a company would be 1.10 once the almond operation was ongo-

ing. There is some uncertainty about the beta that will actually prevail. Management has attached the following probabilities to possible outcomes:

Probability	.2	.3	.2	.2	.1
Beta	1.00	1.10	1.20	1.30	1.40

    a.   What is the required rate of return for the project using the mode beta of 1.10?

    b.   What is the range of required rates of return?

    c.   What is the expected value of required rate of return?

2.   The North Bend Bait Company is contemplating an investment to get it into the production and sale of spinning rods and reels. Heretofore, it has produced only artificial baits. The financial manager of the company, Bruno Litzenberger, feels that the only way to analyze the merit of the project is with a capital asset pricing model approach. Fortunately, Super Splash Spinning Corporation, a publicly held company, produces only spinning fishing equipment. Litzenberger feels it appropriate to use this company as a benchmark for measuring risk. Neither North Bend Bait nor Super Splash employs any leverage.

    The actual returns to investors in Super Splash over the last 10 years were those shown in the following table. Also shown are 1-year returns for Standard & Poor's 500-Stock Index and the risk-free rate.

	ANNUAL RETURNS		
YEAR END	Super Splash	Market Index	RISK-FREE RATE
19-0	.14	.11	.05
19-1	.21	.17	.07
19-2	(.06)	(.02)	.06
19-3	.30	.25	.08
19-4	.24	.18	.06
19-5	.34	.28	.07
19-6	(.12)	(.08)	.07
19-7	.32	.27	.09
19-8	.19	.14	.07
19-9	(.10)	.00	.08
Average return	.146	.13	.07

Litzenberger believes that the average annual return for the market index and the average annual return for the risk-free rate over the 10-year period are reasonable proxies for the returns likely to prevail in the future.

    a.   Compute the beta for Super Splash Spinning Corporation.

    b.   What is the required return for the project? What assumptions are critical?

3.   The spinning rod and reel project in Problem 2 costs $575,000 and is expected to provide the following incremental net cash flows.

YEAR	1	2	3	4	5	6	7	8	9	10
Net cash flow (in thousands)	$50	$100	$125	$125	$150	$150	$150	$125	$100	$75

229

**CHAPTER 8
Creating Value
through Capital
Investments**

No cash flows are predicted beyond 10 years, as North Bend Bait Company has found that the product life for profitable operations is about 10 years. Should the company undertake the spinning equipment project?

4. Rich Diggings Gold Mining Company, which employs no leverage, is considering the purchase of a new dredge. During the last 10 years, it has used an old dredge that is about worn out. A viable secondary market exists for dredges. With proper conversion, they can be used for purposes other than gold mining. The external market values, as well as the actual incremental cash flows generated as a result of having the old dredge, were as follows:

	PURCHASE PRICE	EXTERNAL MARKET VALUE	ACTUAL NET CASH FLOW
Start	$400,000	$400,000	$ —
19-1	—	360,000	108,000
19-2	—	300,000	61,600
19-3	—	250,000	65,000
19-4	—	220,000	85,000
19-5	—	180,000	75,200
19-6	—	150,000	69,600
19-7	—	120,000	33,000
19-8	—	80,000	72,400
19-9	—	50,000	22,800
19-0	—	40,000	18,000

a. Compute the annual returns, using external market values as the base.

b. If the information on annual returns for the market index and for the risk-free rate is the same as that shown in Problem 2, compute the required return for the project, assuming that past relationships are a reasonable proxy for the future.

c. Suppose the new dredge costs $575,000 and the expected cash flows are exactly the same as in Problem 3 for the spinning equipment project. Should the new dredge be purchased? If your answer differs from that in Problem 3, explain the reason why.

5. In Problem 4, suppose Rich Diggings Gold Mining Company were to finance the project with 40 percent debt at an interest rate of 9 percent and 60 percent equity. The company has a tax rate of 35 percent. If nothing else changes, what is the weighted average required rate of return for the project? Will the project be more or less attractive?

6. Willie Sutton Bank Vault company has a debt-to-equity ratio (market value) of .75. Its present cost of debt funds is 15 percent, and it has a marginal tax rate of 40 percent. Willie Sutton Bank Vault is eyeing the automated bank teller business, a field that involves electronics and is considerably different from its own, so the company is looking for a benchmark or proxy company. The Peerless Machine Company, whose stock is publicly traded, produces only automated teller equipment. Peerless has a debt-to-equity ratio of .25, a beta of 1.15, and an effective tax rate of .40.

a. If Willie Sutton Bank Vault Company wishes to enter the automated bank teller business, what systematic risk (beta) is involved if it intends to employ the same amount of leverage in the new venture as it presently employs?

b. If the risk-free rate presently is 13 percent and the expected return on the market portfolio is 17 percent, what return should the company require for the project if it uses a capital-asset pricing model approach?

7. Grove Plowing, Inc., is considering investing in a new snow plow truck costing $30,000. The truck is likely to provide a cash return after taxes of $10,000 per year for 6 years. The unlevered cost of equity capital of the company is 16 percent. The company intends to finance the project with 60 percent debt, which will bear an interest rate of 12 percent. The loan will be repaid in equal annual principal payments at the end of each of the 6 years. Flotation costs on financing amount to $1,000, and the company is in a 30 percent tax bracket.

a. What is the adjusted present value (APV) of the project? Is the project acceptable?

b. What would happen if expected after-tax cash flows were $8,000 per year instead of $10,000?

8. The Empire Mining Company's existing portfolio of assets has an expected value of net present value of $30 million and a standard deviation of $20 million. The company is considering four new explorations. The 16 possible portfolios have the following characteristics:

POSSIBLE PORTFOLIO	EXPECTED NET PRESENT VALUE (IN MILLIONS)	STANDARD DEVIATION (IN MILLIONS)
1. Existing assets (EA) only	$30	$20
2. EA plus 1	33	23
3. EA plus 2	32	21
4. EA plus 3	35	24
5. EA plus 4	34	25
6. EA plus 1 and 2	35	23
7. EA plus 1 and 3	38	25
8. EA plus 1 and 4	37	26
9. EA plus 2 and 3	37	24
10. EA plus 2 and 4	36	25
11. EA plus 3 and 4	39	28
12. EA plus 1, 2, and 3	40	26
13. EA plus 1, 2, and 4	39	27
14. EA plus 1, 3, and 4	42	30
15. EA plus 2, 3, and 4	41	28
16. EA plus 1, 2, 3, and 4	44	31

a. Plot these various portfolio possibilities on graph paper.

b. With a firm-risk approach to evaluating risky investments, which portfolio do you prefer?

9. Two mutually exclusive investment proposals are under consideration. The following information is relevant:

	MEAN NET PRESENT VALUE	STANDARD DEVIATION
Proposal A	$10,000	$ 5,000
Proposal B	12,000	10,000

What is the probability that the actual net present value will be zero or less? Which proposal would you accept?

1.

SITUATION	EQUATION	REQUIRED RETURN
1	10% + (15% − 10%)1.00	15.0%
2	14% + (18% − 14%).70	16.8
3	8% + (15% − 8%)1.20	16.4
4	11% + (17% − 11%).80	15.8
5	10% + (16% − 10%)1.90	21.4

The greater the risk-free rate, the greater the expected return on the market portfolio and the greater the beta, the greater will be the required return on equity, all other things being the same. In addition, the greater the market risk premium $(\bar{R}_m - R_f)$, the greater the required return, all other things being the same.

2. **a.** Cost of equity = 10% + (16% − 10%)1.25 = 17.5% (using the proxy company's beta).

$$\text{Cost of debt} = 13\%\,(1 - .4) = 7.8\%$$

$$\text{Weighted average required return} = 7.8\%\left(\frac{.60}{1.60}\right) + 17.5\%\left(\frac{1.00}{1.60}\right)$$

$$= 13.86\%$$

$$NPV = -\$4,000 + \frac{\$500}{(1.1386)} + \frac{\$1,000}{(1.1386)^2} + \cdots + \frac{\$600}{(1.1386)^7}$$

$$= \$950,000 \text{ (to the nearest \$1,000)}$$

indicating that the project is acceptable.

b. Required rate of return on project = 17.5%

$$NPV = -\$4,000 + \frac{\$500}{(1.175)} + \frac{\$1,000}{(1.175)^2} + \cdots + \frac{\$600}{(1.175)^7}$$

$$= \$396,000$$

Still acceptable, but less profitable with the higher discount rate.

c. Using Eq. (8-7)

$$\beta_{\text{unlevered}} = \frac{1.25}{[1 + (.20)(1 - .4)]} = 1.116$$

$$\text{Adjusted } \beta = 1.116[1 + (.60)(1 - .4)] = 1.52$$

Thus, the adjusted beta is higher than before, owing to the proxy company having less leverage than Esto Perpetua.

$$\text{Cost of equity} = 10\% + (16\% - 10\%)1.52 = 19.12\%$$

$$\text{Weighted average required return} = 7.8\%\left(\frac{.60}{1.60}\right) + 19.12\%\left(\frac{1.00}{1.60}\right)$$

$$= 14.87\%$$

231

$$NPV = -\$4,000 + \frac{\$500}{(1.1487)} + \frac{\$1,000}{(1.1487)^2} + \cdots + \frac{\$600}{(1.1487)^7}$$

$$= \$813,000 \text{ (to the nearest \$1,000)}$$

d. (1) The unlevered beta is

$$\beta_{unlevered} = \frac{1.25}{[1 + (.60)(1 - .40)]} = .919$$

The cost of unlevered equity funds = 10% + (16% − 10%) .919 = 15.51%. The net present value of the operating cash flows is

$$NPV(O) = -\$4,000 + \frac{\$500}{(1.1551)} + \cdots + \frac{\$600}{(1.1551)^7}$$

$$= \$687,000 \text{ (to the nearest \$1,000)}$$

(2) With a debt-to-equity ratio of .60, the company employs 6 parts of debt for every 10 parts of equity.
Debt financing = $4 million (6/16) = $1.5 million
Tax shield per year = $1.5 million × 13% interest × 40% tax rate = $78,000
Present value of $78,000 per year for 7 years discounted at 13% = $345,000 (to the nearest $1,000)
(3) APV = $687,000 + $345,000 = $1,032,000 (to the nearest $1,000)
The project is acceptable using the adjusted present value method.

3. a. The coefficients of variation (standard deviation/NPV) for the alternatives are

Existing projects	.50
Plus project 1	.60
Plus project 2	.61
Plus projects 1 and 2	.63

The coefficient of variation increases with either or both investments. A reasonably risk-averse decision maker will prefer the existing projects to any combination of new project additions to existing projects. If this is the case, both new projects will be rejected. The actual decision will depend on your risk preferences. Presumably, these preferences will be influenced by the presence of bankruptcy costs.
b. If the CAPM approach gives an opposite decision, the key to deciding would be the importance of market imperfections. As indicated earlier, if a company's stock is traded in imperfect markets, if the possibility of insolvency is substantive, and if bankruptcy costs are significant, more reliance should be placed on a total variability approach because it recognizes residual plus systematic risk. If things point in the opposite direction, more reliance should be placed on the CAPM results.

SELECTED REFERENCES

ANG, JAMES S., and WILBUR G. LEWELLEN, "Risk Adjustment in Capital Investment Project Evaluations," *Financial Management*, 11 (Summer 1982), 5–14.
BEAVER, WILLIAM, PAUL KETTLER, and MYRON SCHOLES, "The Association between Market-Determined and Accounting-Determined Risk Measures," *Accounting Review*, 45 (October 1970), 654–82.
BEAVER, WILLIAM, and JAMES MANEGOLD, "The Association between Market-Determined

and Accounting-Determined Measures of Systematic Risk: Some Further Evidence," *Journal of Financial and Quantitative Analysis*, 10 (June 1975), 231–59.

BEN-SHAHAR, HAIM, and FRANK M. WERNER, "Multiperiod Capital Budgeting under Uncertainty: A Suggested Application," *Journal of Financial and Quantitative Analysis*, 12 (December 1977), 859–78.

CHAMBERS, DONALD R., ROBERT S. HARRIS, and JOHN J. PRINGLE, "Treatment of Financing Mix in Analyzing Investment Opportunities," *Financial Management*, 11 (Summer 1982), 24–41.

HAMADA, ROBERT S., "Portfolio Analysis, Market Equilibrium and Corporation Finance," *Journal of Finance*, 24 (March 1969), 13–31.

LESSARD, DONALD R., and RICHARD S. BOWER, "An Operational Approach to Risk Screening," *Journal of Finance*, 28 (May 1973), 321–38.

MANDELKER, GERSHON, and S. GHON RHEE, "The Impact of the Degrees of Operating and Financial Leverage on Systematic Risk of Common Stock," *Journal of Financial and Quantitative Analysis*, 19 (March 1984), 45–58.

MILES, JAMES A., and JOHN R. EZZELL, "Reformulating Tax Shield Valuation: A Note," *Journal of Finance*, 40 (December 1985), 1485–92.

MYERS, STEWART C., "Procedures for Capital Budgeting under Uncertainty," *Industrial Management Review*, 9 (Spring 1986), 1–15.

———, "Interactions of Corporate Financing and Investment Decisions—Implications for Capital Budgeting," *Journal of Finance*, 29 (March 1974), 1–25.

———, and STUART M. TURNBULL, "Capital Budgeting and the Capital Asset Pricing Model: Good News and Bad News," *Journal of Finance*, 32 (May 1977), 321–32.

ROLL, RICHARD, and MARCUS C. BOGUE, "Capital Budgeting of Risky Projects with Imperfect Markets for Physical Capital," *Journal of Finance*, 29 (May 1974), 606–12.

ROSENBERG, BARR, and ANDREW RUDD, "The Corporate Use of Beta," *Issues in Corporate Finance*. New York: Stern, Stewart, Putnam & Macklis, 1983, 42–52.

SCHALL, LAWRENCE D., "Asset Valuation, Firm Investment, and Firm Diversification," *Journal of Finance*, 45 (January 1972), 11–28.

SHAPIRO, ALAN C., "Corporate Strategy and the Capital Budgeting Decision," *Financial Management Collections*, 1 (Winter 1986), 1–14.

SICK, GORDON A., "A Certainty Equivalent Approach to Capital Budgeting," *Financial Management*, 15 (Winter 1986), 23–32.

TAGGART, ROBERT A., JR., "Consistent Valuation and Cost of Capital Expressions with Corporate and Personal Taxes," working paper, National Bureau of Economic Research (August 1989).

TURNBULL, STUART M., "Market Value and Systematic Risk," *Journal of Finance*, 32 (September 1977), 1125–42.

VAN HORNE, JAMES C., "Capital-Budgeting Decisions Involving Combinations of Risky Investments," *Management Science*, 13 (October 1966), 84–92.

———, "The Analysis of Uncertainty Resolution in Capital Budgeting for New Products," *Management Science*, 15 (April 1969), 376–86.

9

REQUIRED RETURNS FOR COMPANIES, DIVISIONS, AND ACQUISITIONS

Extending our evaluation of risky investments to the company as a whole, to its divisions and prospective acquisitions, we focus on determining the required rate of return for each. For a company or subunit, there is an aggregation of assets. As we shall see, the use of an aggregate required rate of return is appropriate only when those assets are homogeneous with respect to risk and investment proposals under consideration are of the same character. If investment projects widely vary in risk, an aggregate required rate of return is not appropriate as an acceptance criterion.

The advantage to using an aggregate required rate is its simplicity. Once we have computed it, we can evaluate projects by using a single rate that does not change unless underlying conditions change. We avoid the problems involved in computing individual required rates of return for each investment proposal, as in the preceding chapter. If an aggregate required rate of return is used, however, projects must correspond to the foregoing conditions.

This chapter will parallel Chapter 8 to some extent. First, we consider the required rate of return under the assumptions of a market model and then move on to consider other means for measuring it. The degree to which the former approach needs modification depends on the strength of one's convictions regarding the assumptions inherent in the model. We begin with the cost of capital of a company and then consider the required rate of return for a division. As in the previous chapter, the idea is to identify opportunities that provide expected returns in excess of what the financial markets require, either for the company or for the division. In turn, the availability of such opportunities depends on industry attractiveness and competitive advantage within an industry. Finally, we consider the evaluation of a potential acquisition and the appropriate acceptance criterion for that decision. As with Chapter 8, this chapter draws on the valuation foundations laid out in Chapters 2 through 4.

The overall cost of capital or required return of a firm is composed of the costs of the various components of financing. The cost of equity capital is the most difficult to measure and will occupy most of our attention. We also consider the costs of debt and preferred stock. To the extent that the historical cost of a source of funds closely parallels the present cost, historical costs may give us some insight, but we are concerned with the *marginal cost* of a specific source of financing. Only if the past is a good surrogate for the future are historical costs of use to us. After covering the various individual costs, we will show how they can be combined into an overall cost of capital for the company.

COST OF EQUITY CAPITAL
IN A MARKET CONTEXT

In theory, *cost of equity capital* can be defined as the minimum rate of return that a company must earn on the equity-financed portion of its investments in order to leave unchanged the market price of its stock. From the preceding chapter and Chapter 3, we know that the capital asset pricing model implies that the required return on a stock is

$$R_j = R_f + (\overline{R}_m - R_f)\beta_j \qquad (9\text{-}1)$$

where R_f is the risk-free rate, $\overline{R}_m$ is the expected return on the market portfolio, and β_j is the measure of the responsiveness of the excess return for the security to the excess return for the market portfolio.

In Chapter 8, we listed several services that provide beta information for stocks. Suppose that from such a service we find the beta of K-Bob Toy Company to be 1.58, and that the expected risk-free rate is 8 percent while the expected market return is 13 percent. According to the CAPM, the company's required return on equity is

$$R_{\text{K-Bob}} = .08 + (.13 - .08)1.58 = 15.90\%$$

With this approach, we hope to approximate the cost of equity capital for the company. The critical assumption is that the past relationship between a security's return and the market return will hold in the future. In addition, it is important that the market return and the risk-free rate represent expected future returns. When past returns seem not to be good proxies for the future, it is better to estimate these returns directly. As taken up in Chapter 8, there is controversy concerning the maturity to employ for the risk-free security. As also mentioned in that chapter, the ex ante, or beforehand, market risk premium (expected market return less the risk-free rate) has been between 3 and 7 percent.

Once the required rate of return for security j has been determined, it is used as the cost of equity capital. In essence, it is the rate that investors expect the firm to earn on its equity after corporate taxes are paid. However, it is not the after-tax return to investors; rather, it is their pretax return. Put another way, R_j represents the before-tax return to investors that the firm must earn after it has paid taxes at the corporate level.

APT FACTOR MODEL ESTIMATES

As we know from Chapters 4 and 8, multifactor models can be used to obtain estimates of a company's required return on equity. Instead of systematic, or unavoidable, risk being captured by a company's beta, it is a function of multiple economic and financial factors. A stock's responsiveness coefficients to each of these factors are multiplied by the market prices of the factor risks, the lambdas. These products are summed, and to this sum the risk-free rate is added to obtain an estimate of the stock's required return.

Although a good deal of work has been done on factor model applications to security analysis, as yet such models have not been widely used in corporate finance. There is not agreement as to the risk factors of importance, nor are the reaction coefficients and lambda risk premiums readily available. Still, such models have considerable potential for determining required rates of return and undoubtedly will become more important in this regard. (See Chapter 4.)

UNSYSTEMATIC RISK AND OTHER QUALIFICATIONS

With either the CAPM or an APT factor model, unsystematic risk is assumed to be diversified away. As long as financial markets are highly efficient and without imperfections, the required return on equity would be determined by a company's systematic, or unavoidable, risk(s). When these assumptions are relaxed to take account of real-world conditions, the unsystematic, security-specific risk of a stock may take on a degree of importance. We know that the total risk of a security is composed of its systematic risk(s) as well as its unsystematic risk. The assumption of the market models is that only the former is important.

Chapter 8, however, showed that the costs of bankruptcy work to the detriment of stockholders. In essence, these costs represent external drains on the system. As they cannot be diversified away by investors, the total risk of the firm becomes a factor of concern. Stated differently, the probability of a firm going bankrupt depends on the total variability of its cash flows. If there were no costs associated with a creditor takeover, investors would concern themselves only with the systematic risk of a security. As long as the assets of the bankrupt firm could be sold or traded at their economic values, no penalty would be involved. The fact that an individual firm might go bankrupt would be embraced in the overall systematic risk that investors were willing to tolerate in their portfolios.

With bankruptcy costs, however, there is a penalty to the investor. The greater the cost of bankruptcy and the greater the probability of its occurrence, the more concerned the investor will be with the total risk of the firm. Holding systematic risk constant, the greater the unsystematic risk of a company, the greater the expected bankruptcy costs to be incurred. As a result, investors will demand a higher required return for the company than that dictated by its systematic risk alone. Therefore, the required rate of return given by a market model needs to be adjusted upward if this factor is to be taken into account. Stipulating the exact adjustment is difficult in practice, though in theory it can be rigorously specified.[1] We know that the greater the probability of bankruptcy, the greater the upward adjustment that is necessary. Depending on the situation, often a rough estimate of the expected cost of bankruptcy is possible and can be used to adjust upward the required rate of return.

237

CHAPTER 9
Required Returns
for Companies,
Divisions, and
Acquisitions

In addition to bankruptcy costs, other relaxations in the assumptions of a market model, as so far developed and applied, will cause an upward revision in the required rate of return. As taken up in Chapters 3 and 4, a number of imperfections bear upon the equilibrium pricing of a security. The greater the imperfections and the greater the measurement problems, the greater the adjustment (usually upward) in the required return on equity generated by a market model.

DIVIDEND DISCOUNT MODEL APPROACH

In measuring the cost of equity capital, we are concerned with approximating the rate of return required by investors. A market model approach, with appropriate adjustments, is one means by which we can do this. Another way we might approach the problem of determining the required rate of return is to estimate the stream of expected future dividends per share, as perceived by investors at the margin, and then solve for the rate of discount that equates this stream with the current market price of the stock.

Briefly recalling Chapter 2, we can view the value of a share of stock to investors as the present value of the expected future stream of income paid to them. Because dividends are all that stockholders as a whole receive from their investment, this stream of income is the cash dividends paid in future periods and, perhaps, a final liquidating dividend. At time 0, the value of a share of stock is

$$P_0 = \frac{D_1}{(1 + k_e)} + \frac{D_2}{(1 + k_e)^2} + \cdots + \frac{D_\infty}{(1 + k_e)^\infty}$$

$$P_0 = \sum_{t=1}^{\infty} \frac{D_t}{(1 + k_e)^t}$$

(9-2)

where P_0 is the value of a share of stock at time 0; D_t is the dividend per share expected to be paid in period t; and k_e is the appropriate rate of discount.

We suggested in Chapter 2 that investors formulate subjective probability distributions of dividends per share expected to be paid in various future periods. For the individual investor, the D_t in Eq. (9-2) are the expected values, or means, of these probability distributions. For the market as a whole, the D_t represent the expected values for investors at the margin, and k_e is the market discount factor appropriate for the risk involved. The *cost of equity capital* is defined as the market rate of discount, k_e, that equates the present value of all expected future dividends per share with the current market price of the stock. This cost is found by solving Eq. (9-2) for k_e.

---

[1] For a state-preference approach to the measurement of bankruptcy costs, see James C. Van Horne, "Optimal Initiation of Bankruptcy Proceedings by Debt Holders," *Journal of Finance,* 31 (June 1976), 897–910.

Growth Situations. If dividends per share are expected to grow at a constant rate, g, and k_e is greater than g, we discovered in Chapter 2 that

$$P_0 = \frac{D_1}{k_e - g} \tag{9-3}$$

where D_1 is the dividend per share expected to be paid at the end of period 1. Thus, the cost of equity capital would be

$$k_e = \frac{D_1}{P_0} + g \tag{9-4}$$

The critical assumption, of course, is that dividends per share are expected to grow at a compound rate of g forever. In certain situations, this assumption may be a fair approximation of investor expectations. If ABC Company's expected dividend per share at the end of period 1 is $2, the current market price is $40, and earnings and dividends per share are expected to grow about 10 percent per annum, the company's cost of equity capital is

$$k_e = \frac{\$2}{\$40} + .10 = 15\%$$

For k_e to be realistic, expectations in the marketplace must be such that dividends per share are believed to grow in fact at a rate of g. The important factor, then, is measuring the growth in dividends per share as perceived by investors at the margin.

When the expected growth in dividends per share is other than perpetual, a modification of Eq. (9-2) can be used. As Chapter 2 pointed out, a number of valuation models assume that the growth rate will eventually taper off. Frequently, the transition is from an above-normal growth rate to one that is considered normal. If dividends were expected to grow at a 15 percent compound rate for 5 years, at a 10 percent rate for the next 5 years, and then grow at a 5 percent rate, we would have

$$P_0 = \sum_{t=1}^{5} \frac{D_0(1.15)^t}{(1 + k_e)^t} + \sum_{t=6}^{10} \frac{D_5(1.10)^{t-5}}{(1 + k_e)^t} + \sum_{t=11}^{\infty} \frac{D_{10}(1.05)^{t-10}}{(1 + k_e)^t} \tag{9-5}$$

We see that the current dividend, D_0, is the base on which the expected growth in future dividends is built. By solving for k_e, we obtain the cost of equity capital as defined. One would use the method illustrated in Chapter 2 to solve for k_e. For example, if the current dividend, D_0, were $2 a share and market price per share, P_0, were $70, k_e in Eq. (9-5) would be 10.42 percent. For other patterns of expected future growth, the equation can be easily modified to deal with the situation.

The more growth segments we specify, of course, the more the growth pattern will approximate a curvilinear relationship. From Chapter 2, we learned how to determine the terminal value at the beginning of the last growth segment. This terminal value can be based on expected future dividends, as in Eq. (9-5), in which case the perpetual dividend growth model is used, or on earnings per share multiplied by an assumed price/earnings ratio.

For all growth situations, the important thing is to solve for the k_e that equates the current market price of the stock with the expected future dividends perceived by investors at the margin. Because the expected growth in dividends is not directly observable, we must estimate it. Herein lies the major difficulty involved in estimating the cost of equity capital. For reasonably stable patterns of past growth, one might project this trend into the future. However, we must temper the projection to take account of current market sentiment. Insight into such sentiment can come from investment advisers who have made analyses of the industry and company and from articles about the company in financial newspapers and magazines.

239

CHAPTER 9
Required Returns
for Companies,
Divisions, and
Acquisitions

Implications of Approach.   If measurement were exact and certain assumptions held, the discount rate determined by this method would be the same as the required rate of return determined by a market model approach. When assumptions underlying a market model do not seem appropriate, the second approach serves as a useful benchmark for adjusting the required rate of return. By now it should be apparent that measuring the cost of equity capital of a company is an inexact science. We can only hope to approximate it as carefully as possible.

The methods suggested enable us to make such an approximation more or less accurately, depending on the situation. For a large company whose stock is actively traded on the New York Stock Exchange and whose systematic risk is close to that of the market as a whole, we can usually estimate more confidently than we can for a moderate-sized company whose stock is inactively traded in the over-the-counter market and whose systematic risk is very large. We must live with the inexactness involved in the measurement process and try to do as good a job as possible. Now let us turn to measuring the costs of other types of financing, which pose far fewer problems than the cost of equity capital, as the brevity of their treatment will attest.

COST OF DEBT

To derive the explicit cost of debt, we solve for the discount rate, k, that equates the net proceeds of the debt issue with the present value of interest plus principal payments. Then we adjust the explicit cost obtained for the tax effect. If we denote the after-tax cost of debt by k_i, it can be approximated by

$$k_i = k(1 - t) \qquad (9\text{-}6)$$

where k is the internal rate of return or yield and t is the marginal tax rate. Because interest charges are tax deductible, the after-tax cost of debt is substantially less than the before-tax cost. If a company were able to sell a new issue of 20-year bonds with a 12 percent coupon rate and realize net proceeds (after underwriting expenses) of $1,000 for each $1,000 face value bond, k would be 12 percent. If the income tax rate were 40 percent

$$k_i = 12.00(1 - .40) = 7.20\%$$

We note that the 7.20 percent after-tax cost in our example represents the marginal, or incremental, cost of additional debt. It does not represent the cost of debt already employed.

If a firm has the policy of maintaining a given proportion of debt in its capital structure, debt is never really paid. Individual debt instruments are paid, of course, but they are replaced by new debt. Thus, debt can be regarded as a permanent part of the financing mix. Under these circumstances, the appropriate formula for calculating the explicit cost of debt is the formula for a perpetuity:

$$k_i = \frac{C_t}{I_0}(1 - t) \qquad (9\text{-}7)$$

where C_t = fixed interest cost in all periods and I_0 = proceeds of the issue.

Uncertainty of Tax Shield. It is important to point out that the adjustment of the cost of debt for taxes holds only if the company has now, and will have in the future, a marginal tax rate of t. An unprofitable company that pays no taxes would have a cost of debt equal to the before-tax cost, k. Therefore, if interest payments on debt are to be entirely and immediately deductible for tax purposes, reported earnings must be zero or positive. If not, the loss may be carried back 3 years and applied to taxes previously paid.[2] If reported earnings are sufficient in those years, the firm receives a tax refund, and the cash-flow effect is nearly the same as that which occurs if operations in the current year are profitable. If reported earnings in the prior 3 years do not offset the current year loss, however, the residual is carried forward to be applied to reported profits during the subsequent 15 years. In this case, part or all of the interest tax subsidy is postponed. In addition to the uncertainty regarding reported income, there is uncertainty regarding the corporate tax rate itself. Congress may change it, as we all know.

Since interest payments may not be tax deductible, their full burden could fall upon a firm's cash flow. Consequently, it may be inappropriate to treat the cost of debt as the interest rate times one minus the tax rate. Assuming there are time states during the life of the instrument in which the tax shield is not entirely applicable, this computation understates the cost of debt financing. The greater the number of time states in which the tax shield cannot be used, the more important it becomes to consider this factor in cost of debt analyses. In general, the greater the business risk of a firm and the closer it approaches marginal profitability, the more important it becomes to allow for the possibility of losing the tax shield advantage associated with the employment of debt funds.

COST OF PREFERRED STOCK

The cost of preferred stock is a function of its stated dividend. As we discuss in Chapter 22, this dividend is not a contractual obligation of the firm but is payable at the discretion of the board of directors. Consequently, unlike debt, it does not create a risk of legal bankruptcy. To holders of common stock however, preferred stock is a security interest that takes priority over theirs. Most corporations that issue preferred stock intend to pay the stated dividend.[3] As preferred stock has no maturity date, its cost may be represented as

$$k_p = \frac{D}{I_0} \qquad (9\text{-}8)$$

[2] The loss must be first applied to the earliest preceding year and, if not entirely consumed, to the next earliest year, then to the preceding year.

[3] The consequences of not paying the dividend are examined in Chapter 22.

where D is the stated annual dividend and I_0 represents the proceeds of the preferred stock issue. If a company were to sell an 11 percent preferred stock issue ($50 par value) and realize net proceeds of $48.37 a share, the cost of the preferred stock would be $5.50/$48.37 = 11.37%. Note that this cost is not adjusted for taxes, because the preferred stock dividend is paid after taxes. Thus, the explicit cost of preferred stock usually is greater than that for debt.

However, the preferred stock has a desirable feature to the corporate investor. The tax law provides that 70 percent of the dividends received by one corporation from another is exempt from taxation. This attraction on the demand side usually results in yields on preferred stocks being slightly below those on bonds of the same company. It is only after taxes that debt financing becomes more attractive.

241

CHAPTER 9
Required Returns
for Companies,
Divisions, and
Acquisitions

OTHER TYPES OF FINANCING

Although equity, debt, and preferred stock are the major sources, other types of financing include leasing, convertible securities, warrants, and other options. Because determining the costs of these types of financing involves some special and rather complex valuation issues, we postpone their treatment until Chapters 19 and 23. Also, we ignore payables, accruals, and deferred taxes, not because they are unimportant sources of financing, but because they have no explicit interest cost. For our purposes in this chapter, knowing the costs of equity, debt, and preferred stock financing is sufficient for illustrating the overall cost of capital of a firm. When costs are later determined for other types of financing, they can be inserted in the weighting scheme about to be discussed.

WEIGHTED AVERAGE COST OF CAPITAL

Once we have computed costs of individual components of the capital structure, we may weight them according to some standard and calculate a weighted average cost of capital. As an illustration of the *mechanics* of the calculations, suppose a firm had the following capital structure at the latest statement date, where the amounts shown represent market values.

	AMOUNT	PROPORTION
Debt	$30 million	30%
Preferred stock	10 million	10
Common-stock equity	60 million	60
	$100 million	100%

Common stock equity includes both common stock issues and retained earnings. In calculating proportions, it is important that we use market-value as opposed to book-value weights. Because we are trying to maximize the value of the firm to its shareholders, only market-value weights are consistent with our objective. Market values are used in the calculation of the costs of the various components of financing, so market-value weights should be used in determining the weighted average cost of capital.

To continue with our illustration, suppose the firm computed the following after-tax costs for the component methods of financing.

	COST
Debt	7.20%
Preferred stock	11.37
Common-stock equity	15.00

Therefore, the weighted average cost of capital for this example problem is

	(1) PROPORTION	(2) COST	(3) WEIGHTED COST (1) × (2)
Debt	30%	7.20%	2.16%
Preferred stock	10	11.37	1.14
Common-stock equity	60	15.00	9.00
			12.30%

Thus, with the assumptions of this example, 12.3 percent represents the weighted average cost of the component methods of financing where each component is weighted according to market-value proportions.

SOME LIMITATIONS

With the calculation of a weighted average cost of capital, the critical question is whether the figure represents the firm's "true" cost of capital. The answer to this question depends on how accurately we have measured the individual marginal costs, on the weighting system, and on certain other assumptions. Assume for now that we are able to measure accurately the marginal costs of the individual sources of financing; let us examine the importance of the weighting system.

Marginal Weights. The critical assumption in any weighting system is that the firm will in fact raise capital in the proportions specified. Because the firm raises capital *marginally* to make a *marginal* investment in new projects, we need to work with the marginal cost of capital to the firm as a whole. This rate depends on the package of funds employed to finance investment projects. In other words, our concern is with new or incremental capital, not with capital raised in the past. In order for the weighted average cost of capital to represent a marginal cost, the weights employed must be marginal; that is, the weights must correspond to the proportions of financing inputs the firm intends to employ. If they do not, capital is raised on a marginal basis in proportions other than those used to calculate this cost.

As a result, the "true" weighted average cost of capital will differ from that calculated and used for capital investment decisions. An obvious bias results. If the "true" cost is greater than that which is measured, certain investment projects will be accepted that will leave investors worse off than before. On the other hand, if the "true" cost is less than the measured cost, projects will be rejected that could increase shareholder wealth. Therefore, the 12.3 percent weighted average cost of capital computed in our example is realistic only if the firm intends to finance in the future in the same proportions as its existing capital structure.

Raising capital is "lumpy," and strict proportions cannot be maintained. For example, a firm would have difficulty financing each project with 30 percent debt, 10 percent preferred stock, and 60 percent equity. In practice, it may finance with debt in one instance and with preferred stock or equity in another. Over time, most firms are able to finance in roughly a proportional manner. It is in this sense that we try to measure the marginal cost of capital for the package of financing employed. In other words, weighted average cost of capital calculations should ignore temporary deviations from a target capital structure, even though these deviations detract from the theoretical correctness of the weighted average cost method.

Change in Capital Structure. A problem occurs whenever the firm wishes to change its capital structure. The costs of the component methods of financing usually are based on the existing capital structure, and these costs may differ from those that rule once the firm has achieved its desired capital structure. Because the firm cannot measure directly its costs at the desired capital structure, these costs must be estimated. During the period of transition from the present capital structure to one that is desired, the firm usually will rely on one type of financing until the desired capital structure is achieved. Although there may be some discrepancy, it is best to use the estimated weighted average cost of capital based on the financing mix to be employed once the firm reaches its target capital structure.

Flotation Costs. Flotation costs involved in the sale of common stock, preferred stock, or a debt instrument affect the profitability of a firm's investments. In many cases, the new issue must be priced below the market price of existing financing; in addition, there are out-of-pocket flotation costs. Owing to flotation costs, the amount of funds the firm receives is less than the price at which the issue is sold. The presence of flotation costs in financing requires that an adjustment be made in the evaluation of investment proposals.

That adjustment is made by adding flotation costs of financing to the project's initial cash outlay. Suppose an investment proposal costs $100,000, and to finance the project the company must raise $60,000 externally. Both debt and common stock are involved, and after-tax flotation costs come to $4,000. Therefore, $4,000 should be added to $100,000, bringing the total initial outlay to $104,000. In this way, the proposal is properly "penalized" for the flotation costs associated with its financing. The expected future cash flows associated with the project are discounted at the weighted average cost of capital. If the project were expected to provide annual cash inflows of $12,000 forever and the weighted average cost of capital were 10 percent, the project's net present value would be

$$NPV = \frac{\$12,000}{.10} - \$104,000 = \$16,000$$

243

CHAPTER 9
Required Returns
for Companies,
Divisions, and
Acquisitions

This amount contrasts with a net present value of $20,000 if no adjustment is made for flotation costs.

Thus, the adjustment for flotation costs is made in the project's cash flows and not in the cost of capital. A second approach calls for an upward adjustment in the discount rate when flotation costs are present. Under this procedure, each component cost of capital would be recalculated by finding the discount rate that equates the present value of cash flows to suppliers of capital with the net proceeds of the security issue. The resulting component costs then would be weighted and combined to produce an overall "adapted" cost of capital for the firm. NPVs calculated using this method generally will be higher than those calculated when we adjust the initial outlay for flotation costs. It has been shown that adjusting the cost of capital for flotation costs results in a biased estimate of "true" value.[4] We agree with the arguments and favor the adjustment of initial outlay method.

CONCEPTUAL CHALLENGES

As taken up in Chapter 8, the adjusted present-value method (APV) is an alternative to discounting project cash flows by the weighted average cost of capital (WACC). In cases where business and financial risk change significantly as a result of joint investment/financing decisions, it can be demonstrated that the APV method provides a more accurate estimate of the value of a project.[5] As the two methods were compared in the previous chapter, we do not repeat that discussion here. While the APV method is pleasing to a number of academics, practitioners generally favor the WACC. Changing business risk can be dealt with by focusing on the business unit or on the project as opposed to the company as a whole. In what follows we will employ the WACC, but the reader should be mindful of the problems raised in the last chapter.

RATIONALE FOR WEIGHTED AVERAGE COST

The rationale behind the use of a weighted average cost of capital is that by financing in the proportions specified and accepting projects yielding more than the weighted average required return, the firm is able to increase the market price of its stock. This increase occurs because the investment projects accepted are expected to return more on their equity-financed portions than the cost of equity capital, k_e. Once these expectations are apparent to the marketplace, the market price of the stock should rise, all other things remaining the same. The firm has accepted projects that are expected to provide a return greater than that required by investors at the margin, based on the risk involved.

[4] For a defense of the procedure, see Simon E. Keane, "The Investment Discount Rate—In Defence of the Market Rate on Interest," *Accounting and Business Research* (Summer 1976), 234; and John R. Ezzell and R. Burr Porter, "Flotation Costs and the Weighted Average Cost of Capital," *Journal of Financial and Quantitative Analysis*, 11 (September 1976), 403–13. For additional refinements, see F. K. Wright, "New-Issue Costs and Capital Budgeting," *Journal of Business Finance and Accounting*, 14 (Summer 1987).

[5] See Stewart C. Myers, "Interactions of Corporate Financing and Investment Decisions—Implications for Capital Budgeting," *Journal of Finance*, 29 (March 1974), 1–25; and James Miles and John R. Ezzell, "The Weighted Average Cost of Capital, Perfect Markets, and Project Life: A Clarification," *Journal of Financial and Quantitative Analysis*, 5 (September 1980), 719–30.

Using Eq. (9-2) as our valuation model and holding constant the dividend policy of the firm, we see that the acceptance of the projects raises expected future dividends per share, D_t, in the numerator of the equation. If the equity-financed portion of the new investment projects consists of a common stock offering, market price per share will rise with an upward shift in expectations of future dividends per share. Embodied in these expectations is the dilution that necessarily will occur with the common stock offering. In other words, the rise in expected future earnings must be sufficient to raise expected future *dividends per share*, not just expected future dividends.

If the equity-financed portion of the new investment project consists of retained earnings, no dilution will occur. Here the rise in expected future dividends per share must be sufficient so that when the incremental increases are discounted by the market discount rate, k_e, their present value exceeds the equity capital employed in the projects. One can visualize the process as the firm's employing investors' capital at time 0 to invest in a project whose cash-flow benefits are expected to give rise to higher future dividends. For the project to be worthwhile, the present value of the incremental dividends must equal or exceed the equity capital employed in it. If the present value exceeds the equity capital employed in the project, the market price of the stock P_0 will rise. If the present value is just equal to the amount of equity capital employed, P_0 will remain unchanged.[6]

A Pool of Financing. The weighted average cost of capital approach implies that investment projects are financed out of a pool of funds, as opposed to being individually financed out of debt, preferred stock, common stock, or what have you. To see this concept in the context of the capital asset pricing model, refer to Fig. 9-1. Here we have the familiar security market line with the required returns on debt, preferred stock, and common stock for a particular company. The cost of capital of the company is a weighted average of the required rates of return of the various components. If projects are accepted with a systematic risk of X and an expected return of k_0, the expected return will be just sufficient to compensate the various security holders at their required rates of return: k_i, k_p, and k_e. As a result, the investment will leave share price unchanged. If the expected return from the project is higher than k_0, with systematic risk the same, then this return will be more than sufficient to compensate debt holders, preferred stockholders, and common stockholders. The maximum claims of debt holders and preferred stockholders being fixed, most of the benefit will accrue to the common stockholders. In other words, their expected return will be in excess of that required, k_e. As a result,

---

[6] As an aside, market price per share will rise over time if the firm invests in projects whose return on the equity-financed portion just equals the cost of equity capital. This situation is known as expansion. In essence, dividends per share would rise over time because of the increase in earnings occasioned by the reinvestment of retained earnings. As a result, the present value of expected future dividends also would rise over time. For example, if a perpetual growth model were applicable

$$P_0 = \frac{D_1}{k_e - g}$$

If expectations and the market rate of discount remained unchanged, the market price at time 1 would be

$$P_1 = \frac{D_2}{k_e - g}$$

Because D_2 is greater than D_1, P_1 will be greater than P_0. Similarly, it can be shown that $P_t > P_{t-1}$ for all t under our assumptions.

245

CHAPTER 9
Required Returns
for Companies,
Divisions, and
Acquisitions

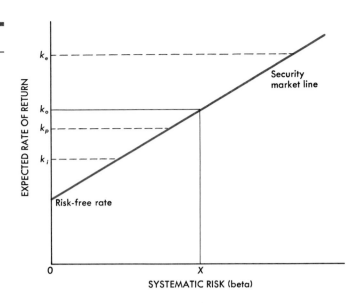

FIGURE 9-1
Required rates of return for debt (k_i), preferred stock (k_p), common stock equity (k_e), and the overall cost of capital (k_o) for an individual company

share price will increase as investors bid up the price of the stock until equilibrium is restored.

QUALIFICATIONS

The use of a weighted average cost of capital figure must be qualified for the points raised earlier. It assumes that the investment proposals being considered do not differ in systematic risk from that of the firm as a whole and that the unsystematic risk of the proposals does not provide any diversification benefits to the firm, if indeed unsystematic risk is a factor of importance. Only under these circumstances is the cost of capital figure obtained appropriate as an acceptance criterion. These assumptions are extremely binding. They imply that the projects of a firm are completely homogeneous with respect to risk and that only projects of exactly the same risk will be considered.

In practice, of course, the issue is one of degree. If the conditions are approximately met, the company's weighted average cost of capital may be used as the acceptance criterion. If a firm produced only one product and all proposals considered were in conjunction with the marketing and production of that product, the use of the firm's overall cost of capital as the acceptance criterion might be appropriate. (Even here, however, there may be significant enough differences in risk among investment proposals to warrant separate consideration.) For a multiproduct firm with investment proposals of varying risk, the use of an overall required rate of return is inappropriate. Here the required rate of return for the specific proposal should be used, as determined with the methods proposed in the preceding chapter. The key, then, is the homogeneity with respect to risk of existing investment projects and proposals under consideration.

THE UNDERINVESTMENT PROBLEM

When a company finances with debt, there may be an incentive problem concerning capital investments. We have argued that a positive net-present-value project should be accepted, but this may not always happen. Suppose the project works more to the benefit of debt holders than to that of stockholders. An example might be a project that lowers the relative risk of the firm because of diversification properties. This may enhance debt holder wealth, but only at the expense of stockholders. The decline in stockholder value via the risk dimension may more than offset any favorable cash-flow characteristics. As a result, the project will be rejected by management, in behalf of stockholders, even though it has a positive NPV to security holders overall.[7]

247

CHAPTER 9
Required Returns
for Companies,
Divisions, and
Acquisitions

An analogy is that of a levered farmer who decides not to buy crop insurance. Whereas a farmer without debt might purchase such insurance, the levered farmer may well reason that lenders will benefit much more in the event of a payoff.

The underinvestment proposition can be put in an option pricing model framework. Stockholders can be thought of as having an option to buy back the company from debt holders (the option writer) if its total value exceeds the face value of the debt. As with any option, its value increases as the variability of the associated asset, in this case the value of the overall firm, increases and declines when variability decreases. A possible remedy is for investors to own both stocks and bonds in the company. If the incentives of debt holders and stockholders can somehow be brought together by this means or by contracting between the two parties, the underinvestment problem disappears. In a practical world where this does not occur, the problem can arise.

DIVISIONAL REQUIRED RETURNS

So far we have considered the required return for the company overall, under the assumption that existing and proposed investment projects are homogeneous with respect to risk. Where the use of a companywide cost of capital is inappropriate as an acceptance criterion, the use of a divisional cost of capital may be valid. By *division*, we mean some subunit of a company that carries on a set of activities that can be differentiated from the other activities of the firm. Usually these activities are differentiated along product or service lines as well as along management lines. Henceforth, we will refer to these subunits as divisions, whether they be called subsidiaries, divisions, business units, or whatever.

Each division employs in it assets that must be financed. The question is, What is an appropriate acceptance criterion? Again the key is homogeneity. If the products or services involved are homogeneous with respect to risk, and new investment proposals are of the same sort, a case can be made for a divisional cost of capital as the acceptance criterion. It represents the transfer price of capital from the company to the division. Stated differently, it is the rate of return the company expects the division to earn on its capital investments. The question is, What is the proper rate of return for a division, assuming the activities of that division are homogeneous with respect to risk?

---

[7] For an analysis of the underinvestment problem, see Stewart C. Myers, "Determinants of Corporate Borrowing," *Journal of Financial Economics*, 5 (November 1977), 147–75. In a later paper, Myers, "Signaling and Accounting Information," working paper, National Bureau of Economic Research (December 1989), suggests that accounting alleviates the underinvestment problem by differentiating expenditures affecting income from capital expenditures.

USING PROXY COMPANIES

The concepts taken up in the preceding chapter and earlier in this one can be applied here. Having gone through the mechanics of measurement several times before, we know how to make the necessary calculations, so we may concentrate on implications.

As with individual investment projects and the company as a whole, we can use the capital asset pricing model to determine a required rate of return on equity for a division. We would try to identify "pure-play" companies with publicly traded stocks that were engaged solely in the same line of business as the division. This would involve a careful comparison of the products and services involved. For an electrical products division, one would concentrate on companies engaged solely in the manufacture and sale of electrical products. Sometimes the matching can only be approximate. The important thing is to try to find publicly traded companies that have nearly the same degree of systematic risk as the division.

Once we carefully identify a sample of proxy companies according to procedures described in Chapter 8, we determine their betas.[8] Rather than compute an arithmetic average of the sample betas, I prefer to use a modal or median value as the measure of central tendency. With this representative proxy beta, we then calculate the required return on equity for the division according to the procedures illustrated earlier. In other words, the summary beta information for companies whose stock is publicly traded is substituted for that of the division.[9] (If the arbitrage pricing theory method is used, its application would be as described in Chapter 8.)

When it is difficult to identify companies that closely parallel a division, one can resort to the methods taken up in the last chapter, where we measured the beta for a project based on the market value of the specific asset. The much preferred and more accurate way, however, is to find a company whose stock is publicly traded. Typically, this is much easier for a division than it is for an individual investment project. There usually are companies that carry on activities similar to those of the division. The principal exception would be an industry composed entirely of multidivision companies. Even here, it may be possible to glean information on systematic risk, provided that the multidivision companies are not the same in what they do. Suppose Katz Enterprises, a multidivision company, has a division similar in business to your division, but it also has two other divisions. You know Katz's overall beta. If

[8] For illustrations of this approach with actual companies, see James C. Van Horne, "An Application of the Capital Asset Pricing Model to Divisional Required Returns," *Financial Management*, 9 (Spring 1980), 14–19; and Diana R. Harrington, "Stock Prices, Beta and Strategic Planning," *Harvard Business Review*, 61 (May–June 1983), 157–64. For a different approach to determining divisional required returns by an actual company, see Benton E. Gup and Samuel W. Norwood III, "Divisional Cost of Capital: A Practical Approach," *Financial Management*, 11 (Spring 1982), 20–24; and Robert S. Harris, Thomas J. O'Brien, and Doug Wakeman, "Divisional Cost-of-Capital Estimation for Multi-Division Firms," *Financial Management*, 18 (Summer 1989), 74–84. Finally, for an excellent overall discussion of the application of the CAPM to divisional required returns, see Barr Rosenberg and Andrew Rudd, "The Corporate Use of Beta," *Issues in Corporate Finance* (New York: Stern, Stewart, Putnam & Macklis, 1983), pp. 42–52.

[9] Russell J. Fuller and Halbert S. Kerr, "Estimating the Divisional Cost of Capital: An Analysis of the Pure-Play Technique," *Journal of Finance*, 36 (December 1981), 997–1009, collected proxy company betas for the various divisions of some 60 multidivision firms. The authors found that an appropriately weighted average of the betas of the proxy firms closely approximated the beta of the multidivision firm. Although an adjustment for leverage was made, the results here did not provide as good an estimate of the multidivision firm beta as did the unadjusted betas.

proxy companies (pure plays) are available for its two other divisions, you can obtain betas for them. These betas then are weighted by the values of the divisions. Given the overall beta of Katz Enterprises, you can solve for the beta of the division in question. This is due to the fact that betas are additive. The derived estimate will be crude, but it may be better than estimates based on things other than stock valuation. If there is more than one unknown, we might solve a system of simultaneous equations across multiple companies for beta. While feasible in concept, such efforts bog down in measurement problems.

PROPORTION AND COST OF DEBT FUNDS

The amount of nonequity financing assigned to a division is an important consideration. For the foregoing procedure to hold, it should approximate the same relative amount as that used by the proxy company. In other words, the proportion of nonequity financing allocated to a division cannot be significantly out of line with that of the external company being used. Otherwise, one will not get a reasonable proxy for the systematic risk of the division. Where the proportions are not nearly the same, the proxy company's beta should be adjusted before it is used as the cost of equity capital for the division. The procedure for adjusting the beta for leverage was described and illustrated in Chapter 8.[10] Using this procedure, we can approximate the beta for the proxy company, if it were to have the same relative proportion of nonequity financing as that contemplated for the division. (The caveats mentioned in Chapter 8 concerning the use of the beta releverage formula hold here.) The cost of equity capital for the division then can be determined in the same manner as before.

For the cost of debt for a division, many use the company's overall borrowing cost. Even here adjustments can and should be made if a division has significantly more or less risk than the company as a whole. The notion that equity costs differ according to a division's systematic risk applies to debt costs as well. Both types of costs are determined in the capital markets according to a risk-return trade-off. The greater the risk, the greater the interest rate that will be required. While a case can be made for differentiating debt costs among divisions according to their systematic risks, few companies do it. For one thing, there are mechanical difficulties in computing the beta, for the market index must include debt instruments. It is possible to make adjustments in interest rates based on the relative debt capacities of the various divisions of a company. However, the division itself is not ultimately responsible for its debt. The company as a whole is responsible. Because of diversification of cash flows among divisions, the probability of payment for the whole may be greater than the sum of the parts. For these reasons, few companies have tried to apply a market model to divisional debt costs as they have to equity costs. Still, it may be appropriate to vary debt costs for divisions depending on their risk, even though the adjustment is partly subjective.

---

[10] For a refinement of this formula for risky debt, personal taxes, and bankruptcy costs, see Joseph Yagil, "Divisional Beta Estimation under the Old and New Tax Laws," *Financial Management*, 16 (Winter 1987), 16–21.

249

CHAPTER 9
Required Returns
for Companies,
Divisions, and
Acquisitions

DETERMINING A DIVISION'S OVERALL REQUIRED RETURN

If the company allocated the same proportion of nonequity funds to each of its divisions, the next step is straightforward. Given the cost of equity capital previously determined and costs of nonequity financing, we derive a weighted average required rate of return for the division. The weighting process and the calculation of the weighted average required rate of return are the same as in the previous section. What we end up with is a required rate of return for investment proposals undertaken by that division. This is the return required by investors for projects having the same relative systematic risk as the division.

When different divisions are allocated significantly different proportions of nonequity funds, determining the overall required return for a division is more complicated. If one division is allocated a much higher proportion of debt, it will have a lower overall required return on paper. But is it truly lower? Should one division be allowed to significantly lower its required return simply by taking on more leverage? Is this fair to other divisions? Apart from the incentive issue, what are the problems to the company as a whole?

High leverage for one division may cause the cost of debt funds for the overall company to rise. This marginal increase should not be allocated across divisions, but rather it should be pinpointed to the division responsible. Second, the high leverage incurred by the division may increase the uncertainty of the tax shield associated with debt for the company as a whole. As discussed earlier in this chapter, if the firm's earnings should decline so that the tax deductibility of interest payments is postponed or lost, the cost of debt funds to the company overall rises dramatically. Finally, high leverage for one division increases the volatility of returns to stockholders of the company, together with the possibility of insolvency and bankruptcy costs being incurred. In turn, this will cause them to increase the required return on equity to compensate for the increased risk. (The way this comes about is taken up in Chapter 10.)

For these reasons, the "true" cost of debt for the high leverage division may be considerably greater than originally imagined. If this is the case, some type of premium should be added to the division's required return in order to reflect more accurately the true cost of capital for the division. The difficulty is in deciding on what premium is appropriate; and adjustments usually are partly subjective. Still, it is possible to get a reasonable handle on incremental interest costs and, perhaps, some crude approximation of the probability that the tax shield may be postponed or lost.

AN ALTERNATIVE APPROACH

In the weighted average cost of capital approach described, costs of equity capital are derived from proxy companies, while costs of debt and the weighting of capital costs are decisions of the company itself. An alternative approach is to determine the overall cost of capital, comprised of both debt and equity funds, of proxy companies. This approach takes as given the costs of debt and equity funds, together with the weights employed. The median weighted average cost of capital of the sample companies (or some other measure of central tendency) then is used as the required rate of return for the division.

Thus, both external capital costs and financing weights are applied to the division. The problem, of course, is when a division uses a significantly different proportion of nonequity funds than the proxy companies. When this occurs, adjustments need to made. However, they need to be made in the previous approach. Both approaches have shortcomings, so the use of one or the other depends on the situation.

251

CHAPTER 9
Required Returns
for Companies,
Divisions, and
Acquisitions

IMPLICATIONS FOR PROJECT SELECTION

With one of the two methods described, an overall divisional required return is estimated. We then allocate or transfer capital throughout the firm on a risk-adjusted return basis. The higher the systematic risk of a division, the higher the required rate of return. This approach provides a consistent framework for allocating capital among divisions with greatly different risks. Too often in a multidivision firm, a single cutoff rate is used for project selection. An edict comes from above stating that "no project shall be undertaken unless it provides a return of 15 percent!" The problem is that certain "safe" projects with little systematic risk are rejected because they do not provide a return above the company's stated goal. Yet some of these projects may provide expected returns greater than the "true" cost of capital for the division. In contrast, divisions characterized by large systematic risk may accept projects with expected returns higher than the companywide norm but lower than they should earn, considering the systematic risk involved.

Figure 9-2 illustrates this problem. The horizontal dashed line is the company's overall cost of capital, and the bars represent the required returns for the various divisions of the company, based on their systematic risk. The x's and o's represent investment projects of the type described. The expected returns of the x's are below the company's overall cost of capital but above the division's required return. The o's have expected returns above the company's cost of capital but below the division's required return. The rejection of the x projects and acceptance of the o's is suboptimal. The x's provide expected returns in excess of the returns required by the market for the systematic risk involved; the o's provide expected returns lower than those required. The

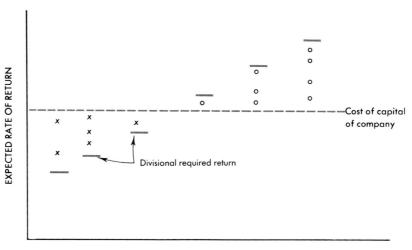

FIGURE 9-2

Comparison of companywide cost of capital and divisional required returns.

problem may seem obvious, but this very thing happens either directly or indirectly in many a multidivision company.

The incentives in such a company are such that divisions with low systematic risk often are too conservative in project generation and selection, while divisions with large systematic risk are too aggressive. Too often a company puts money in those divisions providing the greatest growth opportunities and rations capital to other divisions, so that they will accept only projects consistent with the overall growth objectives. Frequently, the high-growth divisions have a license to do almost anything they want, as long as the expected returns on the projects selected are above the company's overall required return. When some of the projects selected provide too low an expected return for the systematic risk involved, the company may become riskier without commensurate increases in expected return.

The incentive scheme is skewed in the direction of growth and the acceptance of risky projects. "Safe" divisions may be starved for capital, even though they are able to generate investment proposals that are expected to provide returns in excess of those required for the systematic risk involved. The problem is a mistaken belief that growth in itself is the panacea for all problems. The value of a firm rests on two foundations: expected return and risk. Growth in the former is good, but growth in the latter is bad. Whether the overall result is good or bad depends on the combined effect of these two factors.

What is needed is a system for allocating capital to divisions on a risk-adjusted return basis. The approach presented provides such a means. As long as investment proposals emanating from the division are homogeneous with respect to systematic risk, the approach will result in consistent investment decisions being made among the divisions of a company. When investment proposals are not homogeneous, management should evaluate them on a proposal-by-proposal basis, using the methods taken up in the preceding chapter.

UNSYSTEMATIC RISK CONSIDERATIONS

In our discussion of the required rate of return for a division, we considered only the systematic risk of that division and implied that the market evaluates the parts of a company, in our case its divisions, separately according to their systematic risk. (The reasoning behind this assumption was taken up in the preceding chapter, so we will not repeat it here.) As in all of our previous discussions, the question becomes, What happens if unsystematic risk is important? As we know, the greater the imperfections in the capital markets, generally the greater the importance of unsystematic risk—not the unsystematic risk of the division, but the unsystematic or firm specific risk of the company as a whole. Take the imperfection of bankruptcy costs. A particular division might experience difficulties and go into bankruptcy on its own, but the company as a whole would not, because of the offsetting performance of other divisions that are not experiencing such adversities. It is only if the firm as a whole goes bankrupt that bankruptcy costs are incurred.

Following the methods outlined in the preceding chapter, we can determine the impact of a division on the total risk of the firm (that is, its systematic and unsystematic risk). In that chapter, a dual approach for evaluating risky investments was presented. Recall that this approach consisted of evaluating investment proposals according to a market model and then according to their incremental impact on the total risk of the firm. Accept or reject decisions are reached for both approaches. Where these decisions are the same, there is no problem. When conflicting decisions are reached, however, the final decision depends on the perceived importance of imperfections in the capital markets. On the basis of their importance, one approach would seem preferable and lead to a decision.

253

CHAPTER 9
Required Returns
for Companies,
Divisions, and
Acquisitions

The same dual approach can be applied to the evaluation of the divisions of a company. Such an approach results in using a market model to determine the "underlying" required rate of return for the division commensurate with the systematic risk involved. When we analyze the impact of the various divisions on the total risk of the firm, we can also consider the diversification properties of those divisions. This consideration is important only if imperfections in the capital markets make the unsystematic risk of a firm a significant factor to investors. Thus, we are able to take account of unsystematic risk in the same manner as we did for individual investment projects.

EVALUATION OF ACQUISITIONS

We saw in Chapter 7 that we can analyze an acquisition according to its expected return and risk in the same manner as we analyze any capital investment. The relevant expected future cash flows are *free cash flows,* those left over after making all investments necessary to produce the expected cash-flow stream. In what should by now be a familiar procedure, we examine the issue under the assumptions of a market model and then under conditions in which unsystematic risk might be a factor of at least some importance.

Acquisitions are treated in two parts. In this chapter, we cover valuation issues surrounding an investment in assets, following up on concepts already developed. In Chapter 24, we delve into mergers and takeovers more globally, including empirical evidence on valuation.

MARKET MODEL IMPLICATIONS

Given the assumptions of a market model (CAPM or APT factor), it is clear that investors are able to achieve the same diversification as the firm can achieve for them. This point is particularly apparent in the acquisition of a company whose stock is publicly held. In fact, the investor has an advantage in being able to diversify by buying only a few shares of stock, whereas the acquisition for the buying company is much more "lumpy." Thus, the acquiring firm is unable to do something for investors that they are not able to do for themselves at least as efficiently. Therefore, pure diversification by the firm through acquisitions is not a thing of value.[11] The whole will simply equal the sum of the parts.

This is not to say that an acquisition will not enhance the value of the firm to its shareholders. Indeed, economies may be involved that benefit the acquiring firm and its stockholders. The prospect of synergism may make a

---

[11] For further discussion and demonstration of this point, see Corry Azzi, "Conglomerate Mergers, Default Risk, and Homemade Mutual Funds," *American Economic Review,* 68 (March 1978), 161–72; and Haim Levy and Marshall Sarnat, "Diversification, Portfolio Analysis, and the Uneasy Case for Conglomerate Mergers," *Journal of Finance,* 25 (September 1970), 795–802.

prospective acquisition more attractive to one company than to another, but diversification itself would not be beneficial. Conglomerate mergers for the sole purpose of diversification would be suspect; they would not enhance shareholder wealth. If an acquisition is to be worthwhile, there must be the prospect of synergism. In other words, the acquiring company must be able to effect operating economies, distribution economies, or other things of this sort if the acquisition is to be a thing of value.

Purchase Price and Required Return. It is an easy matter to measure the required rate of return for the acquisition of a company whose stock is publicly traded. Direct market information is available, so one is able to calculate the required rate of return on equity using the procedures illustrated earlier. No proxy company is necessary. If the acquisition involves taking on the selling company's debt, this debt must be taken into account. The purchase price we use in evaluating a prospective acquisition is the market value of its debt plus the amount paid to the stockholders of the selling company. Suppose Magna Corporation is considering acquiring Carta Company by paying the stockholders of Carta $3 million. Magna will assume Carta's debts, which have a market value of $2 million. For purposes of calculation, the purchase price of this acquisition is $5 million.

Against this purchase price, one must balance the expected incremental after-tax cash flows arising from the acquisition. The appropriate discount rate is a weighted average required return for the selling company. The cost of equity is computed directly from market information, as discussed earlier. The cost of debt is the current yield in the marketplace for the selling company's debt, multiplied by one minus the tax rate. For our example, Carta Company employs two parts of debt for every three parts of equity, so these weights would be used in determining a weighted average required return. The expected after-tax cash flows from the acquisition then are discounted at the weighted average required return. If the present value of these cash flows exceeds the purchase price, the acquisition is worthwhile; if not, it should be rejected. All of this follows from our earlier study of the rules of project acceptability.

Importance of Operating Efficiencies. The important thing to remember is that under the assumptions of a market model, the present value of cash flows will exceed the purchase price only if there are operating economies and/or improved management. Stated differently, in the absence of cash-flow improvements such that $2 + 2 = 5$, called synergy, the expected return arising from the acquisition will be no more than the required return. This suggests that the analysis of a prospective acquisition should focus on the likelihood of economies. For the acquiring company, this usually means doing those things that it does well. Acquiring a company in an unrelated line of business in which management has no expertise is unlikely to produce economies. Too many companies have done that, mistakenly believing that it is the only way to achieve growth. When inefficiencies develop, the acquiring company earns an incremental return less than that required by the market for the systematic risk involved. As a result, the market price of the stock drops below the price it would have sold for if the acquisition had not been made.

If the stock of the prospective acquisition is priced efficiently in the market, the acquiring company will pay at least what the company is worth as an independent entity. If a premium is paid—and it usually must be paid—then the acquiring company pays more than the acquisition is worth as an independent operation. This premium, however, can be offset by economies, so that the acquisition provides an incremental expected return equal to or greater than that required by the market, given the systematic risk involved. In evaluating an acquisition, one should concentrate on the prospect of operating economies. We will discover in Chapter 24 that other considerations come into play—information effects, tax reasons, wealth transfers, and personal agendas. However, the bedrock of value creation is operating economies.

255

CHAPTER 9
Required Returns
for Companies,
Divisions, and
Acquisitions

A DIVERSIFICATION EFFECT?

If unsystematic risk is felt to be important or if management is concerned only with the impact of an acquisition on the expected risk and return of the firm as a whole, the evaluation process needs to be altered. One can evaluate an acquisition from the standpoint of the "portfolio" effect on the firm. This was illustrated for investment proposals in Chapter 8, and the procedures are the same for an acquisition. To reiterate briefly in this context, recall our Chapter 7 discussion of how to derive the probability distribution of possible incremental present values arising from an acquisition. If the price to be paid has been established, it should be subtracted from the expected present value to obtain the expected net present value. The next step is to estimate the correlation coefficients for the relationship between the net present value for the prospective acquisition and the net present values for existing projects and investment proposals under consideration.

The acquisition then becomes one more investment proposal in a portfolio of projects to be considered. The methods of analysis and selection are the same as those employed in the preceding chapter. Management chooses the best combination of expected net present value and risk. If the portfolio of projects represented by this combination includes the prospective acquisition, the firm should acquire the company involved. In this way, an acquisition is evaluated in the same manner as any internally generated investment proposal. A decision is made with attention to the marginal impact of the acquisition on the total risk of the firm.

Whether a market model approach is altered depends on the importance of the diversification effect. In turn, its importance depends on imperfections in the capital market. If significant imperfections exist, such as bankruptcy costs, a case can be made for the importance of diversification properties of an investment.[12] As with individual assets or divisions, the acquisition then would be evaluated according to the systematic risk involved as well as according to its incremental impact on the total risk of the firm.

Debt Holders versus Equity Holders. Even in the absence of bankruptcy costs, Wilbur G. Lewellen argues that mergers result in "financial synergism," beneficial to investors.[13] By merging, he contends, the debt capacity of the

[12] For an analysis of the conditions under which an acquisition benefits stockholders, see Robert C. Higgins and Lawrence D. Schall, "Corporate Bankruptcy and Conglomerate Merger," *Journal of Finance*, 30 (March 1975), 106–11; and James H. Scott, Jr., "On the Theory of Conglomerate Mergers," *Journal of Finance*, 32 (September 1977), 1235–50.

[13] "A Pure Financial Rationale for the Conglomerate Merger," *Journal of Finance*, 26 (May 1971), 521–37. For further amplification, see Li Way Lee, "Co-insurance and Conglomerate Merger," *Journal of Finance*, 32 (December 1977), 1527–37.

combined entity will be greater than the sum of the individual debt capacities of the two companies involved. If, in a world of taxes, debt funds are "cheaper" than equity funds, borrowing more will increase the value of the equity. The reason debt capacity supposedly increases is that the variance about the mean of two streams of cash flows often can be reduced by combining them. By reducing the dispersion of the probability distribution of possible cash flows relative to the mean of the distribution, the probability that principal and interest payments on the debt will not be met is reduced.

As a result, lenders are willing to lend more to the combined entity than to the two companies separately. (The reduction in relative dispersion of cash flows affords them a greater degree of protection.) One might be tempted to argue that a lender can achieve this diversification on his or her own. Although it is true that lenders can diversify loans, they are unable to reduce the probability that independent companies will default because their cash flows cannot be merged. Only through an actual merger are these cash flows fused and *relative* dispersion reduced. For reasons of "financial synergism," then, Lewellen argues that mergers, and particularly conglomerate mergers, enhance shareholder wealth.

A number of authors reach a different conclusion when they come at the issue from a different valuation perspective.[14] They agree that a merger between two firms reduces the bankruptcy risk to creditors by providing a form of coinsurance in the sense that the premerger cash flows of the two firms are fused. They argue, however, that under perfect capital market assumptions, this fusion benefits only the debt holders. The market price of the debt instruments rises, and because the total value of the company remains the same under the assumptions of perfect capital markets, equity values fall. In other words, there is a wealth transfer from equity holders to debt holders. Thus, diversification does not change the total value of the firm, although there can be a redistribution of value between equity holders and debt holders.

Diversification in the Presence of Market Imperfections. When we allow for such things as bankruptcy costs and taxes, it may be possible to increase the value of the firm through merging, apart from any synergistic effects. By diversifying through a merger, the probability of bankruptcy can be reduced. As a result, there will be a reduction in the expected costs of bankruptcy, assuming these costs are positive and significant. As we demonstrated earlier, this reduction will increase the value of the firm, all other things staying the same. In a world of corporate income taxes and the deductibility of interest, a merger may reduce expected total future tax payments if there are future states in which one company would go bankrupt while the other would not. In this situation, a merger may permit the losses of the one firm to be applied against the profits of the other. As a result, the future taxes paid may be less for the merged company than they are for the two firms separately. This occurrence would result in the merged company's having a greater value than the sum of the parts, all other things the same.

Both of these factors (bankruptcy costs and taxes) are defined as market imperfections. While we would not imagine these imperfections to have a

[14] See Higgins and Schall, "Corporate Bankruptcy and Conglomerate Merger"; Dan Galai and Ronald W. Masulis, "The Option Pricing Model and the Risk Factor of Stock," *Journal of Financial Economics*, 3 (January–March 1976), 66–69; E. Han Kim and John J. McConnell, "Corporate Merger and the Co-insurance of Corporate Debt," *Journal of Finance*, 32 (May 1977), 349–63; and Paul Asquith and E. Han Kim, "The Impact of Merger Bids on the Participating Firms' Security Holders," *Journal of Finance*, 37 (December 1982), 1209–28.

large impact on the value of the acquiring firm, they nonetheless may be important enough to make the diversification effect of a merger a significant factor. In most cases, however, the really important thing to evaluate in a prospective acquisition is the prospect for operating economies. This focus is particularly appropriate if a premium in stock value must be offered to acquire the company. In the final analysis, the value of acquisitions to equity holders and debt holders is an empirical question, and the evidence is reviewed in Chapter 24.

257

**CHAPTER 9
Required Returns
for Companies,
Divisions, and
Acquisitions**

SUMMARY

The use of the cost of capital for a company or division as an acceptance criterion is predicated on its activities being homogeneous with respect to risk and on investment proposals under consideration being of the same sort. A company has available to it an assortment of financing methods, each with a cost. By far the most difficult to measure is the cost of equity capital. One way to measure it is with a market approach. With this approach, we are able to determine the return investors require the company to earn on equity, given the systematic risk involved. To the extent that imperfections exist in the capital markets and they are felt to be important, this rate of return may have to be adjusted upward to reflect the significance of unsystematic risk. Another way to measure the cost of equity capital is to solve for the rate of discount that equates the stream of expected future dividends, as perceived by investors at the margin, with the current market price of the stock.

Once the costs of the individual methods of financing are determined, a weighted average cost of capital for the firm can be computed. The market-value weights employed should correspond to the proportions with which the firm intends to finance. Once computed, the weighted average cost becomes the basis for accepting or rejecting investment projects. The rationale for its use was explored in detail, as was its shortcomings. Again, a key condition is the homogeneity of existing investment projects and investment proposals under consideration. When this condition does not hold, the overall company's cost of capital should not be used as an acceptance criterion.

Often the condition is met for divisions of a company but is not met for the company as a whole. Again using a market model approach, one can determine the required return on equity for the division. The important thing is to identify publicly traded companies whose lines of business and systematic risk closely parallel the division's. These companies then are proxies for developing beta information, which may be adjusted for leverage. Once we determine a representative cost of equity capital for the division, we combine it with other costs in a weighted average required return for the division. Certain problems arising from the differential utilization of nonequity financing among divisions were explored, and an alternative method of using proxy companies' overall costs of capital was investigated. We then discussed the implications of the proxy company approach to divisional project selection and concluded that the approach has considerable merit for allocating capital among the divisions of a company on a risk-adjusted return basis. We then extended our discussion to allow for unsystematic risk being a factor of importance and analyzed it along the lines proposed in the preceding chapter.

In the final section, we took up the evaluation of acquisitions. If most of the assumptions of a market model hold, it is clear that investors are able to achieve the same diversification on their own as the acquiring company is able to do for them. Therefore, diversification by the firm in acquisitions would not be a thing of value. This argues that a company should focus its analysis on the likelihood of operating economies when studying prospective acquisitions. Only operating economies will result in incremental value being gained. We then examined the conditions under which the diversification effect in mergers might be a factor of importance and how equity holders and debt holders expropriate wealth from each other.

SELF-CORRECTION PROBLEMS

1. Over the last 6 years, the following excess returns (above the risk-free rate) were experienced on the market index and on the stock of Kay Wyman Stores, Inc.:

YEAR	1	2	3	4	5	6
Excess-return market	.08	(.02)	.14	.18	(.06)	.04
Excess-return Wyman	.12	(.07)	.26	.28	(.12)	.07

Using the capital asset pricing model approach illustrated in the last chapter, on the basis of these limited data determine the company's cost of equity capital if the risk-free rate is 8 percent and the expected return on the market portfolio 14 percent. Compare the cost of equity capital derived with that derived for Problem 3 (Rayfil Manufacturing Company) if you do that problem.

2. Silicon Wafer Company presently pays a dividend of $1. This dividend is expected to grow at a 20 percent rate for 5 years and at 10 percent per annum thereafter. The present market price per share is $20. Using a dividend discount model approach to estimating capital costs, what is the company's expected, or required, return on equity?

3. Novus Nyet Company has two divisions: Health Foods and Specialty Metals. Each of these divisions employs debt equal to 30 percent of its total requirements, with equity capital used for the balance. The current borrowing rate is 14 percent and the company's tax rate is 40 percent. Novus Nyet wishes to establish a minimum return standard for each division based on the risk of that division. This standard then would serve as the transfer price of capital to the division.

    The company has thought about using the capital asset pricing model in this regard. It has identified two samples of companies, with the following mode-value characteristics:

	BETA	DEBT/TOTAL CAPITALIZATION RATIO	TAX RATE
Health Foods	.90	.50	.40
Specialty Metals	1.25	.30	.40

The risk-free rate presently is 12 percent and the expected return on the market portfolio 17 percent. Using the CAPM approach, what required returns on investment would you recommend for these two divisions?

4. The Williams Warbler Company is contemplating acquiring the Acme Brass Company. Incremental cash flows arising from the acquisition are expected to be the following:

259

CHAPTER 9
Required Returns
for Companies,
Divisions, and
Acquisitions

	AVERAGE OF YEARS (IN THOUSANDS)		
	1–5	6–10	11–∞
Cash flow after taxes	$100	$150	$200
Investment required	50	60	70
Net cash flow	$ 50	$ 90	$130

Acme has an all-equity capital structure. Its beta is .80, based on the past 60 months of data relating its excess return to that of the market. The risk-free rate is 9 percent, and the expected return on the market portfolio is 14 percent.

a. What is the maximum price that Williams Warbler Company might pay for Acme?

b. On what assumptions does a price that high depend?

PROBLEMS

1. On March 10, International Copy Machines (ICOM), one of the "favorites" of the stock market, was priced at $300 per share. This price was based on an expected annual growth rate of at least 20 percent for quite some time in the future. In July, economic indicators turned down, and investors revised downward to 15 percent their estimate for growth of ICOM. What should happen to the price of the stock? Assume the following:

   a. A perpetual-growth valuation model is a reasonable representation of the way the market values ICOM.

   b. The firm does not change its dividend, the risk complexion of its assets, nor its degree of financial leverage.

   c. The dividend next year will be $3 per share.

2. Zosnick Poultry Corporation has launched an expansion program that, in 6 years, should result in the saturation of the Bay Area marketing region of California. As a result, the company is predicting a growth in earnings of 12 percent for 3 years, 6 percent for years 4 through 6, then constant earnings for the foreseeable future. The company expects to increase its dividend per share, now $2, in keeping with this growth pattern. Currently, the market price of the stock is $25 per share. Estimate the company's cost of equity capital.

3. During the last 6 years, excess returns above the risk-free rate were the following for the market index and for the common stock of Rayfil Manufacturing Company:

YEAR	1	2	3	4	5	6
Excess-return market	.08	(.02)	.14	.18	(.06)	.04
Excess-return Rayfil	.02	.06	.22	.17	(.02)	(.03)

Over this same period, the risk-free rate averaged 8 percent. On the basis of these limited observations and using the past as a proxy for the future, compute the cost of equity capital of the firm in the context of the capital asset pricing model. (Use the method illustrated in the last chapter.)

4. Assuming that a firm has a tax rate of 30 percent, compute the after-tax cost of the following:

a. A bond, sold at par, with a 10.40 percent coupon

b. A preferred stock, sold at $100 with a 10 percent coupon and a call price of $110, if the company plans to call the issue in 5 years (use an approximation method)

c. A common stock selling at $16 and paying a $2 dividend, which is expected to be continued indefinitely

d. The same common stock if dividends are expected to grow at the rate of 5 percent per year and the expected dividend in year 1 is $2

5. The Kalog Precision Tool Company was recently formed to manufacture a new product. The company has the following capital structure in market value terms:

13% debentures of 2005	$ 6,000,000
12% preferred stock	2,000,000
Common stock (320,000 shares)	8,000,000
	$16,000,000

The common stock sells for $25 a share, and the company has a marginal tax rate of 40 percent. A study of publicly held companies in this line of business suggests that the required return on equity is about 17 percent for a company of this sort. (A capital asset pricing model approach was used to determine the required rate of return.)

a. Compute the firm's present weighted average cost of capital.

b. Is the figure computed an appropriate acceptance criterion for evaluating investment proposals?

6. The Tumble Down D Ranch in Montana is considering investing in a new mechanized barn, which will cost $600,000. The new barn is expected to save $90,000 in annual labor costs indefinitely (for practical purposes of computation, forever). The ranch, which is incorporated and has a public market for its stock, has a weighted average cost of capital of 14.5 percent. For this project, Howard Kelsey, the president, intends to use $200,000 in retained earnings and to finance the balance half with debt and half with a new issue of common stock.

After-tax flotation costs on the debt issue amount to 2 percent of the total debt raised, whereas flotation costs on the new common stock issue come to 15 percent of the issue. What is the net present value of the project after allowance for flotation costs? Should the ranch invest in the new barn?

7. Ponza International, Inc., has three divisions. One is engaged in leisure wear, one in graphics, and one in household paint. The company has identified proxy com-

panies in these lines of business whose stocks are publicly traded. Neither Ponza International nor the proxy companies employ debt in their capital structures. On the basis of analyzing these stocks in relation to the market index, Ponza has estimated that the systematic risks of its three divisions are as follows:

261

CHAPTER 9
Required Returns
for Companies,
Divisions, and
Acquisitions

	LEISURE	GRAPHICS	PAINT
Beta	1.16	1.64	.70

The expected return on the market index is 13 percent in the foreseeable future, and the risk-free rate is currently 7 percent. The divisions are evaluating a number of projects, which have the following expected returns:

PROJECT	DIVISION	EXPECTED RETURN
1	Graphics	18%
2	Paint	12
3	Paint	10
4	Leisure	26
5	Leisure	13
6	Graphics	21
7	Paint	14
8	Graphics	16

a. Which projects should be accepted and which rejected?

b. What are the assumptions involved in your acceptance criterion?

8. a. In your answer to Problem 7a, what would happen if Ponza International had a debt-to-total-capitalization ratio of 40 percent and intended to finance each of the projects with 40 percent debt, at a 6 percent after-tax interest cost, and 60 percent equity? (Assume that everything else was the same, with the exception that the proxy companies now have debt ratios corresponding to that of Ponza.)

b. In words, what would happen to your answer to Problem 7a if market imperfections made unsystematic risk a factor of importance?

9. Cougar Pipe Company is considering the cash acquisition of Red Wilson Rod, Inc., for $750,000. The acquisition is expected to result in incremental cash flows of $125,000 in the first year, and this amount is expected to grow at a 6 percent compound rate. In the absence of the acquisition, Cougar expects net cash flows of $600,000 this coming year (after capital expenditures), and these are expected to grow at a 6 percent compound rate forever. At present, investors and creditors require a 14 percent overall rate of return for Cougar Pipe Company. Red Wilson Rod is much more risky, and the acquisition of it will raise the company's overall required return to 15 percent.

a. Should Cougar Pipe Company acquire Red Wilson Rod, Inc.?

b. Would your answer be the same if the overall required rate of return stayed the same?

c. Would your answer be the same if the acquisition increased the surviving company's growth rate to 8 percent forever?

SOLUTIONS TO SELF-CORRECTION PROBLEMS

1.

YEAR	EXCESS MARKET RETURN (M)	EXCESS MARKET RETURN SQUARED (M)²	KAY WYMAN EXCESS RETURN (J)	CROSS-PRODUCT EXCESS RETURNS (MJ) (1) × (2)
1	.08	.0064	.12	.0096
2	(.02)	.0004	(.07)	.0014
3	.14	.0196	.26	.0364
4	.18	.0324	.28	.0504
5	(.06)	.0036	(.12)	.0072
6	.04	.0016	.07	.0028
Total	.36	.0640	.54	.1078
Average return	.06		.09	

$$\text{Beta} = \frac{\Sigma\ MJ - n\overline{M}\overline{J}}{\Sigma\ M^2 - n\overline{M}^2} = \frac{.1078 - (6)(.06)(.09)}{.0640 - (6)(.06)^2} = \frac{.0754}{.0424} = 1.778$$

Cost of equity capital $= .08 + (.14 - .08)1.778 = .18668$

The cost of equity capital for Kay Wyman Stores is approximately 18.7 percent. It is higher than the cost of equity capital for Rayfil because of the much higher beta. This indicates a significantly greater degree of systematic undiversifiable risk.

2. Through trial and error, one ends up using 18 percent and 19 percent as discount rates.

END OF YEAR	DIVIDEND PER SHARE	PRESENT VALUE AT 18%	PRESENT VALUE AT 19%
1	$1.20	$1.02	$1.01
2	1.44	1.03	1.02
3	1.73	1.05	1.03
4	2.07	1.07	1.03
5	2.49	1.09	1.04
Present value, 1–5 years		$5.26	$5.13

Year 6 dividend $= \$2.49(1.10) = \$2.74$

Market prices at the end of year 5 using a perpetual growth dividend valuation model:

$$P_5 = \frac{\$2.74}{.18 - .10} = \$34.25; \quad P_5 = \frac{\$2.74}{.19 - .10} = \$30.44$$

Present value at time 0 for amounts received at end of year 5:

$$\$34.25 \text{ at } 18\% = \$14.97; \quad \$30.44 \text{ at } 19\% = \$12.76$$

	18%	19%

263

CHAPTER 9
Required Returns
for Companies,
Divisions, and
Acquisitions

	18%	19%
Present value of 1–5 years	$ 5.26	$ 5.13
Present value of 6–∞ years	14.97	12.76
Present value of all dividends	$20.23	$17.89

Therefore, the discount rate is closer to 18 percent than it is to 19 percent. Interpolating

$$k_e = 18\% + \frac{.23}{20.23 - 17.89} = 18.10\%$$

and this is the estimated return on equity that the market requires.

3. If the proxy companies are used in a CAPM approach, it is clear that different systematic risks are involved in the two divisions. The proxy companies in the health food business have more debt than Novus Nyet Company. In this case, the beta probably should be adjusted for leverage, using the technique presented in Chapter 8. The beta in the absence of leverage would be

$$\beta_u = \frac{.90}{\left[1 + \left(\dfrac{.50}{.50}\right)(1 - .4)\right]} = .5625$$

where (.50/.50) is the debt-to-equity ratio. The adjusted beta for the proportion of debt Novus Nyet employs in its division is

$$\text{Adjusted } \beta = .5625 \left[1 + \left(\frac{.30}{.70}\right)(1 - .4)\right] = .7071$$

or, with rounding, .71.

Given an adjusted proxy beta of .71 for health foods and a proxy beta of 1.25 for specialty metals, the required returns on equity become

	EQUATION	REQUIRED EQUITY RETURN
Health Foods	12% + (17% − 12%) .71	15.55%
Specialty Metals	12% + (17% − 12%)1.25	18.25

The after-tax cost of debt funds for both divisions is 14%(1 − .4) = 8.40%. The weighted average required return for each division becomes

	DEBT COST	WEIGHT	EQUITY COST	WEIGHT	WEIGHTED AVERAGE REQUIRED RETURN
Health Foods	8.40%	.3	15.55%	.7	13.41%
Specialty Metals	8.40	.3	18.15	.7	15.30

The figures in the last column would be used as minimum, or required, returns for the two divisions.

4. a. The estimated required rate of return for the acquisition is

$$R_{Acme} = R_f + (\bar{R}_m - R_f)\beta_{Acme}$$
$$= .09 + (.14 - .09).80 = .13$$

Using this rate to discount the net cash flows, we obtain

YEARS	NET CASH FLOW		PRESENT VALUE FACTOR	PRESENT VALUE
1–5	$ 50	×	3.5172	= $175,860
5–10	90	×	(5.4262 − 3.5172)	= 171,810
11–∞	130	×	[(1/.13) − 5.4262]	= 294,594
				$642,264

The maximum price that should be paid is $642,264.

b. To pay this price, the assumptions of the capital asset pricing model must hold. The company is being valued according only to its systematic risk. The effect of the acquisition on the total risk of Williams Warbler Company is assumed not to be a factor of importance to investors. Additionally, we assume that the measurement of beta is accurate and that the estimates of R_f and $\bar{R}_m$ are reasonable.

SELECTED REFERENCES

ARDITTI, FRED D., and HAIM LEVY, "The Weighted Average Cost of Capital as a Cutoff Rate: A Critical Analysis of the Classical Textbook Weighted Average," *Financial Management*, 6 (Fall 1977), 24–34.

ASQUITH, PAUL, and E. HAN KIM, "The Impact of Merger Bids on the Participating Firms' Security Holders," *Journal of Finance*, 37 (December 1982), 1209–28.

AZZI, CORRY, "Conglomerate Mergers, Default Risk and Homemade Mutual Funds," *American Economic Review*, 68 (March 1978), 161–72.

CHAMBERS, DONALD R., ROBERT S. HARRIS, and JOHN J. PRINGLE, "Treatment of Financing Mix in Analyzing Investment Opportunities," *Financial Management*, 11 (Summer 1982), 24–41.

CONINE, THOMAS E., JR., and MAURY TAMARKIN, "Division Cost of Capital Estimation: Adjusting for Leverage," *Financial Management*, 14 (Spring 1985), 54–58.

FULLER, RUSSELL J., and HALBERT S. KERR, "Estimating the Divisional Cost of Capital: An Analysis of the Pure-Play Technique," *Journal of Finance*, 36 (December 1981), 997–1009.

GUP, BENTON E., and SAMUEL W. NORWOOD III, "Divisional Cost of Capital: A Practical Approach," *Financial Management*, 11 (Spring 1982), 20–24.

HALEY, CHARLES W., and LAWRENCE D. SCHALL, "Problems with the Concept of the Cost of Capital," *Journal of Financial and Quantitative Analysis*, 13 (December 1978), 847–70.

HAMADA, ROBERT S., "Portfolio Analysis, Market Equilibrium and Corporation Finance," *Journal of Finance*, 24 (March 1969), 13–31.

HARRINGTON, DIANA R., "Stock Prices, Beta and Strategic Planning," *Harvard Business Review*, 61 (May–June 1983), 157–64.

HARRIS, ROBERT S., THOMAS J. O'BRIEN, and DOUG WAKEMAN, "Divisional Cost-of-Capital Estimation for Multi-Division Firms," *Financial Management*, 18 (Summer 1989), 74–84.

HARRIS, ROBERT S., and JOHN J. PRINGLE, "Risk-Adjusted Discount Rates—Extensions from the Average-Risk Case," *Journal of Financial Research*, 8 (Fall 1985), 237–44.

265

CHAPTER 9
Required Returns
for Companies,
Divisions, and
Acquisitions

HIGGINS, ROBERT C., and LAWRENCE D. SCHALL, "Corporate Bankruptcy and Conglomerate Merger," *Journal of Finance*, 30 (March 1975), 93–114.

KIM, E. HAN, and JOHN J. MCCONNELL, "Corporate Merger and the Co-insurance of Corporate Debt," *Journal of Finance*, 32 (May 1977), 349–63.

LEVY, HAIM, and MARSHALL SARNAT, "Diversification, Portfolio Analysis and the Uneasy Case for Conglomerate Mergers," *Journal of Finance*, 25 (September 1970), 795–802.

LEWELLEN, WILBUR G., "A Pure Financial Rationale for the Conglomerate Merger," *Journal of Finance*, 26 (May 1971), 521–37.

MILES, JAMES A., and JOHN R. EZZELL, "The Weighted Average Cost of Capital, Perfect Capital Markets, and Project Life: A Clarification," *Journal of Financial and Quantitative Analysis*, 15 (September 1980), 719–30.

MYERS, STEWART C., "Determinants of Corporate Borrowing," *Journal of Financial Economics*, 5 (November 1977), 147–75.

SCHALL, LAWRENCE D., "Asset Valuation, Firm Investment, and Firm Diversification," *Journal of Business*, 45 (January 1972), 11–28.

TAGGART, ROBERT A., JR., "Consistent Valuation and Cost of Capital Expressions with Corporate and Personal Taxes," working paper, National Bureau of Economic Research (August 1989).

VAN HORNE, JAMES C., "Optimal Initiation of Bankruptcy Proceedings by Debt Holders," *Journal of Finance*, 31 (June 1976), 897–910.

———, "An Application of the Capital Asset Pricing Model to Divisional Required Returns," *Financial Management*, 9 (Spring 1980), 14–19.

YAGIL, JOSEPH, "Divisional Beta Estimation under the Old and New Tax Laws," *Financial Management*, 16 (Winter 1987), 16–21.

See Chapter 24 for additional references on acquisitions.

PART 3

FINANCING AND DIVIDEND POLICIES

Growing Toys "R" Us Conservatively

Few companies have had the success of Toys "R" Us,[*] a large retailer of toys and children's clothing. By gauging consumer demand with a highly sophisticated information system, the company carefully manages its inventories. The result is that fewer funds are tied up and there is little obsolescence. Also feeding the bottom line is a corporate staff kept at a bare minimum. "We operate very lean and very efficient," says Michael Goldstein, chief financial officer of the company. This is despite having sales of over $6 billion.

Still, the company's aggressive growth must be funded. How do Goldstein and the company do it? Conservatively. The company's debt-to-capitalization ratio is only about 10 percent. Most financing is with internally generated funds. With its heady growth the company has chosen not to pay a dividend, even a token one. The result is that all profits are plowed back into the company to fuel growth. What debt financing that occurs sometimes is with commercial paper, at low cost. So far investors have enjoyed ever-appreciating share value. As the company matures, it will be interesting to see whether the no-dividend policy is changed.

[*] "Michael Goldstein of Toys 'R' Us: Going Beyond Financials," *Institutional Investor*, 24 (June 1990), 122.

10

THEORY OF CAPITAL STRUCTURE

In Part 2, we looked into allocating capital to investment proposals, when we had a given financing mix. In this chapter and the next, we are going to find out whether the way in which investment proposals are financed matters, and if it does matter, what the optimal capital structure is. If we finance with one mix of securities rather than another, is the market price of the stock affected? If the firm can affect the market price of its stock by its financing decision, it will want to undertake a financing policy that will maximize market price. For simplicity, we examine the question of capital structure in terms of the proportion of debt to equity; however, the principles taken up in this chapter can be easily expanded to include consideration of the specific type of security being issued.

First, we explore the theory with respect to the valuation of the firm. Our examination involves a partial equilibrium analysis that holds constant the investment and dividend decisions of the firm and tries to determine the effect of a change in financing mix on share price. In this regard, we focus on the arbitrage process as the means by which equilibrium is achieved. Upon completion of this presentation, we then show how the problem ties into a market model. This treatment will provide not only an easier understanding of the problem but also a richer insight. Following this, we relax the initial assumptions and study the impact of various capital-market imperfections on the way in which capital structure decisions affect the valuation of the firm, including incentives and financial signaling. In Chapter 11, we consider how a firm in practice can determine a capital structure suitable for its particular situation.

INTRODUCTION TO THE THEORY

Even a casual review of the literature brings one quickly to the key question of whether or not capital structure matters. Can the firm affect its total valuation and its required return by changing its financing mix? In this section, we are going to find out what happens to the total valuation of the firm and to its cost of capital when the ratio of debt to equity, or degree of leverage, is varied. We use a capital market equilibrium approach because it allows us to abstract from factors other than leverage that affect valuation.

ASSUMPTIONS AND DEFINITIONS

To present the analysis as simply as possible, we make the following assumptions:

1. There are no corporate or personal income taxes and no bankruptcy costs. (Later, we shall remove these assumptions.)
2. The ratio of debt to equity for a firm is changed by issuing debt to repurchase stock or issuing stock to pay off debt. In other words, a change in capital structure is effected immediately. In this regard, we assume no transaction costs.
3. The firm has a policy of paying 100 percent of its earnings in dividends. Thus, we abstract from the dividend decision.
4. The expected values of the subjective probability distributions of expected future operating earnings for each company are the same for all investors in the market.
5. The operating earnings of the firm are not expected to grow. The expected values of the probability distributions of expected operating earnings for all future periods are the same as present operating earnings.

Given these assumptions, we are concerned with the following three rates:

$$k_i = \frac{F}{B} = \frac{\text{Annual interest charges}}{\text{Market value of debt outstanding}} \qquad (10\text{-}1)$$

In this equation, k_i is the yield on the company's debt, assuming this debt to be perpetual.

$$k_e = \frac{E}{S} = \frac{\text{Earnings available to common stockholders}}{\text{Market value of stock outstanding}} \qquad (10\text{-}2)$$

The earnings/price ratio is the required rate of return for investors in a firm whose earnings are not expected to grow and whose dividend-payout ratio is 100 percent. With our restrictive assumptions, then, the earnings/price ratio represents the market rate of discount that equates the present value of the stream of expected future dividends with the current market price of the stock. It should not be used as a general rule to depict the required return on equity, for with expected growth it usually is a biased and low estimate (see Chapter 9 on measuring capital costs). We use it only because of its simplicity in illustrating the theory of capital structure. The final rate we consider is

$$k_o = \frac{O}{V} = \frac{\text{Net operating earnings}}{\text{Total market value of the firm}} \qquad (10\text{-}3)$$

where $V = B + S$. Here, k_o is an overall capitalization rate for the firm. It is defined as the weighted average cost of capital and may also be expressed as

$$k_o = k_i\left(\frac{B}{B+S}\right) + k_e\left(\frac{S}{B+S}\right) \qquad (10\text{-}4)$$

We want to know what happens to k_i, k_e, and k_o when the degree of leverage, as denoted by the ratio B/S, increases.

NET OPERATING INCOME APPROACH

One approach to the valuation of the earnings of a company is known as the net operating income approach. To illustrate it, assume that a firm has $1,000 in debt at 10 percent interest, that the expected value of annual net operating earnings is $1,000, and that the overall capitalization rate, k_o, is 15 percent. Given this information, we may calculate the value of the firm as

O	Net operating income	$1,000
k_o	Overall capitalization rate	.15
V	Total value of firm	$6,667
B	Market value of debt	1,000
S	Market value of stock	$5,667

The earnings available to common stockholders, E, is simply net operating income minus interest payments, or $1,000 − $100 = $900. The implied required return on equity is

$$k_e = \frac{E}{S} = \frac{\$900}{\$5,667} = 15.88\%$$

With this approach, net operating income is capitalized at an overall capitalization rate to obtain the total market value of the firm. The market value of the debt then is deducted from the total market value to obtain the market value of the stock. Note that with this approach the overall capitalization rate, k_o, as well as the cost of debt funds, k_i, stay the same regardless of the degree of leverage. The required return on equity, however, increases linearly with leverage.

To illustrate, suppose the firm increases the amount of debt from $1,000 to $3,000 and uses the proceeds of the debt issue to repurchase stock. The valuation of the firm then is

O	Net operating income	$1,000
k_o	Overall capitalization rate	.15
V	Total value of firm	$6,667
B	Market value of debt	3,000
S	Market value of stock	$3,667

The implied required return on equity is

$$k_e = \frac{E}{S} = \frac{\$700}{\$3,667} = 19.09\%$$

We see that the required equity return, k_e, rises with the degree of leverage. This approach implies that the total valuation of the firm is unaffected by its capital structure. Figure 10-1 shows the approach graphically. Not only is the total value of the firm unaffected, but so too is share price. To illustrate, assume in our example that the firm with $1,000 in debt has 100 shares of common stock outstanding. Thus, the market price per share is $56.67 ($5,667/100). The firm issues $2,000 in additional debt and, at the same time,

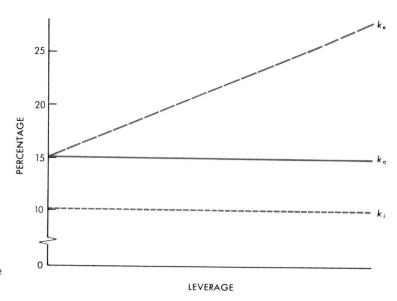

FIGURE 10-1
Capital costs: net operating income
approach

repurchases $2,000 of stock at $56.67 per share, or 35.29 shares in total if we permit fractional shares. It then has $100 - 35.29$ shares = 64.71 shares outstanding. We saw in the example that the total market value of the firm's stock after the change in capital structure is $3,667. Therefore, the market price per share is $3,667/64.71 = 56.67, the same as before the increase in leverage and recapitalization.

The critical assumption with this approach is that k_o is constant, regardless of the degree of leverage. The market capitalizes the value of the firm as a whole; as a result, the breakdown between debt and equity is unimportant. An increase in the use of supposedly "cheaper" debt funds is offset exactly by the increase in the required equity return, k_e. Thus, the weighted average of k_e and k_i remains unchanged for all degrees of leverage. As the firm increases its degree of leverage, it becomes increasingly more risky. Investors penalize the stock by raising the required equity return directly in keeping with the increase in the debt-to-equity ratio. As long as k_i remains constant, k_e is a constant linear function of the debt-to-equity ratio. Because the cost of capital of the firm, k_o, cannot be altered through leverage, the net operating income approach implies that there is no one optimal capital structure.

So far our discussion of the net operating income approach has been purely definitional; it lacks behavioral significance. Modigliani and Miller, in their famous 1958 article, offered behavioral support for the independence of the total valuation and the cost of capital of the firm from its capital structure.[1] Before taking up the implications of their position, however, we examine the traditional approach to valuation.

TRADITIONAL APPROACH

The traditional approach to valuation and leverage assumes that there is an optimal capital structure and that the firm can increase the total value of the firm through the judicious use of leverage. The approach suggests that the firm initially can lower its cost of capital and raise its total value through

[1] Franco Modigliani and Merton H. Miller, "The Cost of Capital, Corporation Finance and the Theory of Investment," *American Economic Review*, 48 (June 1958), 261–77.

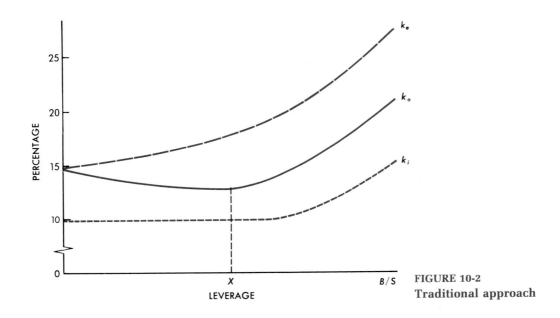

FIGURE 10-2

Traditional approach

leverage. Although investors raise the required rate of return on equity, the increase in k_e does not offset entirely the benefit of using "cheaper" debt funds. As more leverage occurs, investors increasingly penalize the firm's required equity return until eventually this effect more than offsets the use of "cheaper" debt funds.

In one variation of the traditional approach, shown in Fig. 10-2, k_e is assumed to rise at an increasing rate with leverage, whereas k_i is assumed to rise only after significant leverage has occurred. At first, the weighted average cost of capital declines with leverage because the rise in k_e does not offset entirely the use of cheaper debt funds. As a result, the weighted average cost of capital, k_o, declines with moderate use of leverage. After a point, however, the increase in k_e more than offsets the use of cheaper debt funds in the capital structure, and k_o begins to rise. The rise in k_o is supported further, once k_i begins to rise. The optimal capital structure is the point at which k_o bottoms out. In the figure, this optimal capital structure is point X. Thus, the traditional position implies that the cost of capital is not independent of the capital structure of the firm and that there is an optimal capital structure.

MODIGLIANI-MILLER POSITION

Modigliani and Miller (MM) in their original position advocate that the relationship between leverage and the cost of capital is explained by the net operating income approach. They make a formidable attack on the traditional position by offering behavioral justification for having the cost of capital, k_o, remain constant throughout all degrees of leverage. As their assumptions are important, it is necessary to spell them out.

1. Capital markets are perfect. Information is costless and readily available to all investors. There are no transactions costs, and all securities are infinitely divisible. Investors are assumed to be rational and to behave accordingly.

272

2. The average expected future operating earnings of a firm are represented by subjective random variables. It is assumed that the expected values of the probability distribution of all investors are the same. The MM illustration implies that the expected values of the probability distributions of expected operating earnings for all future periods are the same as present operating earnings.

3. Firms can be categorized into "equivalent return" classes. All firms within a class have the same degree of business risk. As we shall see later, this assumption is not essential for their proof.

4. The absence of corporate income taxes is assumed. MM remove this assumption later.

Simply put, the Modigliani-Miller position is based on the idea that no matter how you divide up the capital structure of a firm among debt, equity, and other claims, there is a conservation of investment value.[2] That is, because the total investment value of a corporation depends on its underlying profitability and risk, it is invariant with respect to relative changes in the firm's financial capitalization. Thus, the total pie does not change as it is divided into debt, equity, and other securities. The sum of the parts must equal the whole; so regardless of financing mix, the total value of the firm stays the same, according to MM. The idea is illustrated with the two pies in Fig. 10-3. Different mixes of debt and equity do not alter the size of the pie—total value stays the same.

The support for this position rests on the idea that investors are able to substitute personal for corporate leverage, thereby replicating any capital structure the firm might undertake. Because the firm is unable to do something for its stockholders (leverage) that they cannot do for themselves, capital structure changes are not a thing of value in the perfect capital market world that MM assume. Therefore, two firms alike in every respect except capital structure must have the same total value. If not, arbitrage will be possible, and its occurrence will cause the two firms to sell in the market at the same total value.

ARBITRAGE SUPPORT ILLUSTRATED

Consider two firms identical in every respect except that company A is not levered, while company B has $30,000 of 12 percent bonds outstanding. According to the traditional position, company B may have a higher total value and lower average cost of capital than company A. The valuation of the

[2] This idea was first espoused by John Burr Williams, *The Theory of Investment Value* (Amsterdam: North-Holland, 1938), pp. 72–73.

FIGURE 10-3
Illustration of capital
structure irrelevancy

FIRM VALUE   FIRM VALUE

two firms is assumed to be the following:

		COMPANY A	COMPANY B
O	Net operating income	$10,000	$10,000
F	Interest on debt		3,600
E	Earnings available to common stockholders	$10,000	$ 6,400
k_e	Required equity return	.15	.16
S	Market value of stock	$66,667	$40,000
B	Market value of debt		30,000
V	Total value of firm	$66,667	$70,000
k_o	Implied overall capitalization rate	15%	14.3%
B/S	Debt-to-equity ratio	0	75.0%

MM maintain that this situation cannot continue, for arbitrage will drive the total values of the two firms together. Company B cannot command a higher total value simply because it has a financing mix different from company A's. MM argue that by investing in company A, investors in company B are able to obtain the same dollar return with no increase in financial risk. Moreover, they are able to do so with a smaller investment outlay.[3] Because investors would be better off with the investment requiring the lesser outlay, they would sell their shares in company B and buy shares in company A. These arbitrage transactions would continue until company B's shares declined in price and company A's shares increased in price enough to make the total value of the two firms identical.

If you are a rational investor who owns 1 percent of the stock of company B, the levered firm, worth $400 (market value) you should

1. Sell the stock in company B for $400.
2. Borrow $300 at 12 percent interest. This personal debt is equal to 1 percent of the debt of company B, your previous proportional ownership of the company.
3. Buy 1 percent of the shares of company A, the unlevered firm, for $666.67.

Prior to this series of transactions, your expected return on investment in company B's stock was 16 percent on a $400 investment, or $64. Your expected return on investment in company A is 15 percent on a $666.67 investment, or $100. From this return you must deduct the interest charges on your personal borrowings, so your net dollar return is

Return on investment in company A	$100
Less: interest ($300 x .12)	36
Net return	$ 64

Your net dollar return, $64, is the same as it was for your investment in company B; however, your cash outlay of $366.67 ($666.67 less personal borrow-

---

[3] This arbitrage proof appears in Franco Modigliani and Merton H. Miller, "Reply to Heins and Sprenkle," *American Economic Review,* 59 (September 1969), 592–95.

ings of $300) is less than the $400 investment in company B, the levered firm. Because of the lower investment, you would prefer to invest in company A under the conditions described. In essence, you "lever" the stock of the unlevered firm by taking on personal debt.

The action of a number of investors undertaking similar arbitrage transactions will tend to drive up the price of company A shares, lower its k_e, drive down the price of company B, and increase its k_e. This arbitrage process will continue until there is no further opportunity for reducing one's investment outlay and achieving the same dollar return. At this equilibrium, the total value of the two firms must be the same. As a result, their average costs of capital, k_o, also must be the same. The principle involved is simply that investors are able to reconstitute their former positions by offsetting changes in corporate leverage with changes in personal leverage.

IRRELEVANCE IN A CAPM FRAMEWORK

It is important to realize that MM's proof of the proposition that leverage is irrelevant does not depend on the two firms' belonging to the same risk class. This assumption was invoked for easier illustration of the arbitrage process. However, equilibrium occurs across securities of different companies on the basis of expected return and risk. If the assumptions of the capital asset pricing model hold, as they would in perfect capital markets, the irrelevance of capital structure can be demonstrated using the CAPM.

Consider the expected return and systematic risk of a levered company. The firm's expected return is simply a weighted average of the expected returns for the debt and equity securities.

$$k_o = \left(\frac{B}{B + S}\right)k_i + \left(\frac{S}{B + S}\right)k_e \qquad (10\text{-}5)$$

where, as before, B is the market value of debt, S is the market value of stock, k_i is now the expected return on the firm's debt, and k_e is the expected return on its stock. Rearranging this equation and canceling out, we obtain[4]

$$k_e = k_o + \frac{B}{S}(k_o - k_i) \qquad (10\text{-}6)$$

Here we see that the expected return on the stock increases in proportion to increases in the debt-to-equity ratio.

As described by beta, the systematic risk of the overall firm is simply a weighted average of the betas of the individual securities of the firm.

$$\beta_{\text{firm}} = \left(\frac{B}{B + S}\right)\beta_{\text{debt}} + \left(\frac{S}{B + S}\right)\beta_{\text{stock}} \qquad (10\text{-}7)$$

Rearranging and canceling out as we did before, we obtain

---

[4] The rearrangement to obtain Eq. (10-6) is

$$k_e = \frac{k_o - \left(\dfrac{B}{B + S}\right)k_i}{\left(\dfrac{S}{B + S}\right)} = \left(\frac{B + S}{S}\right)k_o - \left(\frac{B}{S}\right)k_i = k_o + \frac{B}{S}(k_o - k_i)$$

$$\beta_{\text{stock}} = \beta_{\text{firm}} + \frac{B}{S}(\beta_{\text{firm}} - \beta_{\text{debt}}) \qquad (10\text{-}8)$$

Thus, an increase in the debt-to-equity ratio increases not only the expected return of a stock but also its beta. With perfect capital markets, both increase proportionally, so that they offset each other with respect to their effect on share price. The increase in return is just sufficient to offset the additional return required by investors for the increment in beta. Therefore, share price being invariant with respect to leverage can be shown in the context of the CAPM equilibrating process of risk and expected return.

TAXES AND CAPITAL STRUCTURE

The irrelevance of capital structure rests on an absence of market imperfections. No matter how one slices the corporate pie between debt and equity, there is a conservation of value, so that the sum of the parts is always the same. In other words, nothing is lost or gained in the slicing. To the extent that there are capital market imperfections, however, changes in the capital structure of a firm may affect the total size of the pie. That is to say, the firm's valuation and cost of capital may change with changes in its capital structure. One of the most important imperfections is the presence of taxes. In this regard, we examine the valuation impact of corporate taxes in the absence of personal taxes and then the combined effect of corporate and personal taxes.

CORPORATE TAXES

The advantage of debt in a world of corporate taxes is that interest payments are deductible as an expense. They elude taxation at the corporate level, whereas dividends or retained earnings associated with stock are not deductible by the corporation for tax purposes. Consequently, the total amount of payments available for both debt holders and stockholders is greater if debt is employed.

To illustrate, suppose the earnings before interest and taxes are $2,000 for companies X and Y, and they are alike in every respect except in leverage. Company Y has $5,000 in debt at 12 percent interest, whereas company X has no debt. If the tax rate (federal and state) is 40 percent for each company, we have

	COMPANY X	COMPANY Y
Earnings before interest and taxes	$2,000	$2,000
Interest, income to debt holders	0	600
Profit before taxes	2,000	1,400
Taxes	800	560
Income available to stockholders	$1,200	$ 840
Income to debt holders plus income to stockholders	$1,200	$1,440

Thus, total income to both debt holders and stockholders is larger for levered company Y than it is for unlevered company X. The reason is that debt holders receive interest payments without the deduction of taxes at the corporate level, whereas income to stockholders is after corporate taxes have been paid. In essence, the government pays a subsidy to the levered company for the use of debt. Total income to all investors increases by the interest payment times the tax rate. In our example, this amounts to $600 \times .40 = \$240$. This figure represents a tax shield that the government provides the levered company. If the debt employed by a company is permanent, the present value of the tax shield using the perpetuity formula is

$$\text{Present value of tax shield} = \frac{t_c rB}{r} = t_c B \qquad (10\text{-}9)$$

where t_c is the corporate tax rate, r is the interest rate on the debt, and B is the market value of the debt. For company Y in our example

$$\text{Present value of tax shield} = .40(\$5,000) = \$2,000.$$

What we are saying is that the tax shield is a thing of value and that the overall value of the company will be $2,000 more if debt is employed than if the company has no debt. This increased valuation occurs because the stream of income to all investors is $240 per year greater. The present value of $240 per year discounted at 12 percent is $240/.12 = $2,000. Implied is that the risk associated with the tax shield is that of the stream of interest payments, so the appropriate discount rate is the interest rate on the debt. Thus, the value of the firm is

$$\text{Value of firm} = \begin{array}{c}\text{Value if}\\\text{unlevered}\end{array} + \begin{array}{c}\text{Value of}\\\text{tax shield}\end{array}$$

For our example, suppose the required equity return for company X, which has no debt, is 16 percent. Therefore, the value of the firm if it were unlevered would be $1,200/.16 = $7,500. The value of the tax shield is $2,000, so the total value of company Y, the levered firm, is $9,500.

We see in Eq. (10-9) that the greater the amount of debt, the greater the tax shield and the greater value of the firm, all other things the same. Thus, the original MM proposition as subsequently adjusted for corporate taxes suggests that an optimal strategy is to take on a maximum amount of leverage.[5] Clearly, this is not consistent with the behavior of corporations, and alternative explanations must be sought.

UNCERTAINTY OF TAX SHIELD

As pointed out in the last chapter, the tax savings associated with the use of debt are not certain. If reported income is consistently low or negative, the tax shield on debt, as denoted by $t_c B$ in Eq. (10-9), is reduced or even eliminated. As a result, the near full or full cash-flow burden of interest payments would be felt by the firm. If the firm should go bankrupt and liquidate, the potential future tax savings associated with debt would stop altogether. We must recognize also that Congress can change the corporate tax rate. Finally, the greater the possibility of going out of business, the greater the proba-

---

[5] Franco Modigliani and Merton H. Miller, "Corporate Income Taxes and the Cost of Capital: A Correction," *American Economic Review*, 63 (June 1963), 433–42.

bility the tax shield will not be effectively utilized. All of these things make the tax shield associated with debt financing less than certain.

Another argument in this vein is by De Angelo and Masulis, and it has to do with tax shelter redundancy.[6] The notion here is that companies have ways other than interest on debt to shelter income—leasing, foreign tax shelters, investment in intangible assets, and the use of option and future contracts, to name a few. If earnings in a given year are sufficiently low, these other tax shields may entirely use up the earnings at hand. As a result, the tax liability would be zero, and the company would be unable to utilize interest payments as a tax deduction.

De Angelo and Masulis reason that as a company takes on more debt, it increases the probability that earnings in some years will not be sufficient to offset all the tax deductions. Some of them may be redundant, including the tax deductibility of interest. While this argument has merit, it is mitigated to some extent by the presence of tax loss carryback and carryforward provisions. In addition, the 1986 and 1990 Tax Acts reduce considerably the tax shelters available to the corporation, though the tax deductibility of interest remains intact. As a result of the "drying up" of some of these other alternatives, the tax redundancy argument is less compelling.

However, the uncertain nature of the interest tax shield, together with the possibility of at least some tax shelter redundancy, may cause firm value to rise less with leverage than the corporate tax advantage alone would suggest. This is illustrated in Figure 10-4, where the corporate tax effect is shown by the top line.[7] As leverage increases, the uncertainty associated with the interest tax shield comes into play. At first, the diminution in value is slight. As more leverage occurs, tax shield uncertainty causes value to increase at an ever-decreasing rate and perhaps eventually to turn down. Under these conditions, the value of the firm is

---

[6] Harry De Angelo and Ronald W. Masulis, "Optimal Capital Structure under Corporate and Personal Taxation," *Journal of Financial Economics*, 8 (March 1980), 3–29. See also James A. Miles and John R. Ezzell, "Reformulating Tax Shield Valuation: A Note," *Journal of Finance*, 40 (December 1985), 1485–92. Jeffrey K. Mackie-Mason, "Do Taxes Affect Corporate Financing Decisions?" working paper, National Bureau of Economic Research (June 1988), found empirically that the higher a company's nondebt tax shields, the less likely it was to issue debt at the margin.

[7] Mathematically, the value line with a corporate tax effect is slightly concave with respect to the debt-to-equity ratio. See A. Appleyard and N. Strong, "Textbook Inconsistencies in Graphing Valuation Equations: A Note," *Financial Review*, 20 (November 1985), 361–67; and Thomas E. Conine, Jr., and Maurry Tamarkin, "Textbook Inconsistencies in Graphing Valuation Equations: A Further Note," *Financial Review*, 23 (May 1988), 237–41.

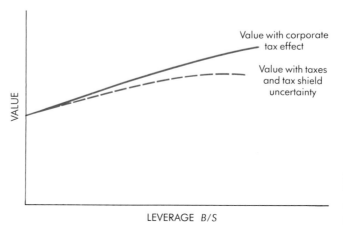

FIGURE 10-4
Value of firm with corporate taxes and tax shield uncertainty

$$\begin{array}{c} \text{Value of} \\ \text{firm} \end{array} = \begin{array}{c} \text{Value if} \\ \text{unlevered} \end{array} + \begin{array}{c} \text{Pure value of} \\ \text{corporate tax} \\ \text{shield} \end{array} - \begin{array}{c} \text{Value lost through} \\ \text{tax shield} \\ \text{uncertainty} \end{array}$$

The last two factors combined give the present value of the corporate tax shield. The greater the uncertainty associated with the shield, the less important it becomes.

CORPORATE PLUS PERSONAL TAXES

Apart from tax shield uncertainty, the presence of taxes on personal income may reduce or possibly eliminate the corporate tax advantage associated with debt. If returns on debt and on stock are taxed at the same personal tax rate, however, the corporate tax advantage remains. This can be seen by taking our earlier example and applying a 30 percent personal tax rate to the debt and stock returns:

	COMPANY X	COMPANY Y
Debt income	0	$600
Less: Personal taxes of 30%		− 180
Debt income after personal taxes	0	420
Income available to stockholders	$1,200	$840
Less: Personal taxes of 30%	− 360	− 252
Stockholders' income after personal taxes	$ 840	$588
Income to debt holders and stockholders after personal taxes	$840	$1,008

Although the total after-tax income to debt holders and stockholders is less than before, the tax advantage associated with debt remains.[8]

Looking at the matter as we did in our earlier discussion, we discover that the present value of the corporate tax shield would be the following when personal taxes are present:

$$\text{Present value of tax shield} = \left[1 - \frac{(1 - t_c)(1 - t_{ps})}{1 - t_{pd}} \right] B \qquad (10\text{-}10)$$

where t_c and B, as before, are the corporate tax rate and market value of the firm's debt; t_{ps} is the personal income tax applicable to common stock income; and t_{pd} is the personal tax rate applicable to debt income.[9] If the return on

[8] In the previous example, the total incomes to debt holders and stockholders were $1,200 and $1,440 for the unlevered and levered company examples, or a ratio of 1.2. In this example, the ratio is $1,008/$840 = 1.2 as well.

[9] To see why this is so, we know that the total income available to both stockholders and debt holders is

$$[(EBIT - rB)(1 - t_c)(1 - t_{ps})] + [rB(1 - t_{pd})]$$

where the after-tax income to stockholders is depicted by the first major bracketed term and that to debt holders by the second, and EBIT is earnings before interest and taxes. Rearranging, we obtain

$$EBIT(1 - t_c)(1 - t_{ps}) + rB(1 - t_{pd}) \left[1 - \frac{(1 - t_c)(1 - t_{ps})}{1 - t_{pd}} \right]$$

The first part of this equation is the income from an unlevered company after corporate and personal taxes have been paid. If an individual buys a bond for B, he or she receives, in the construct

debt is taxed at the same personal tax rate as that on stock, $t_{pd} = t_{ps}$. As a result, these two terms cancel out in Eq. (10-10), and the present value of the corporate tax shield becomes

$$\text{Present value of tax shield} = t_c B$$

which is the same as Eq. (10-9). Therefore, the corporate tax advantage of debt remains exactly the same if debt income and stock income are taxed at the same personal tax rate.

We know that stock income is composed both of dividends and capital gains, however. Dividend income by and large is taxed at the same personal tax rate as interest income. Capital gains often are taxed at a lower rate. Sometimes the differential is explicit in that the tax rate is less. Even when capital gains are taxed at the same rate as ordinary income, however, there is an advantage to the capital gain. For one thing, it is postponed until the security is sold. For those who give appreciated securities as gifts to charitable causes, the tax may be largely avoided, as it is if a person dies. For these reasons, the effective tax on capital gains in a present-value sense is less than that on interest and dividend incomes, even when the federal tax rate is the same. We will have more to say about current tax law shortly.

For now we assume that overall stock income (dividends and capital gains) is taxed at a lower personal tax rate than debt income (interest). In this situation, the corporate tax advantage associated with debt is reduced. To illustrate, we begin with an extreme assumption. All stock income is realized as capital gains and the tax rate on such gains is zero; therefore, t_{ps} is equal to zero. Assume, however, that the personal tax rate applicable to debt income, t_{pd}, is positive.

In this situation, a company will need to decide whether to finance with debt or with stock. If a dollar of operating earnings is paid out as interest to debt holders, the company pays no corporate tax on it because interest is deductible as an expense. Therefore, the income to the investor after personal taxes are paid is

$$\text{After-tax income for debt holders} = \$1(1 - t_{pd})$$

If the dollar of operating earnings is directed instead to stockholders, the company pays a tax on those earnings at the corporate tax rate. The residual would be income to stockholders; and because we assume that the personal tax rate on stock income is zero, it would go directly to them. Therefore

$$\text{After-tax income for stockholders} = \$1(1 - t_c)$$

If the company is concerned with only after-tax income to the investor, it would finance either with debt or with stock, depending on the relative values of t_{pd} and t_c. If the personal tax rate on debt income exceeds the corporate tax rate, the company would finance with stock, because the after-tax income to

---

of our previous examples, $rB(1 - t_{pd})$ annually forever. Therefore, the value of the last part of the second equation is

$$\left[1 - \frac{(1 - t_c)(1 - t_{ps})}{1 - t_{pd}}\right]B$$

which is Eq. (10-10).

the investor would be higher. If t_{pd} is less than t_c, however, it would finance with debt, because after-tax income to the investor would be greater here. If t_{pd} equals t_c, it would be a matter of indifference whether debt or stock were employed.

MERTON MILLER'S ARGUMENT

In a provocative presidential address to the American Finance Association, Merton Miller proposed that with both corporate and personal taxes, capital structure decisions by the firm were irrelevant.[10] That is, changes in capital structure have no effect on the firm's total valuation. This position is the same as Modigliani-Miller's original proposition in a world of no taxes, but it contrasts sharply with their 1959 corporate tax adjustment article, in which they found that debt had substantial advantage. Simply put, Miller's model suggests that in market equilibrium personal and corporate tax effects cancel out. He assumes that the personal tax rate on stock income, t_{ps}, is zero. Accordingly, his model implies that at the margin, the personal tax rate on debt income, t_{pd}, must equal the corporate tax rate, t_c. As illustrated in the previous section, when $t_{pd} = t_c$, changes in the proportion of debt in the capital structure do not change the total after-tax income to investors. As a result, capital structure decisions by the corporation would be irrelevant.

Investor Clienteles and Market Equilibrium.   Different investors, however, have different personal tax rates. Some investors, such as pension funds, are tax exempt; others, such as high-income individuals, are in high tax brackets. Holding risk constant, the tax-exempt investor would want to invest in debt; the high tax bracket investor would want to hold the company's stock. Miller's position is based on the idea that when the market is in disequilibrium, corporations alter their capital structures to take advantage of clienteles of investors in different tax brackets. If there is an abundance of tax-exempt investors, a company will increase the supply of its debt to appeal to this clientele. As companies increase the supply of debt, however, the tax-exempt clientele's ability to absorb more debt is exhausted, and further debt must be sold to higher tax bracket clienteles. Companies will stop issuing debt when the marginal personal tax rate of a clientele investing in the instrument equals the corporate tax rate. At this point, the market for debt and stock is said to be in equilibrium, and an individual company no longer can increase its total value by increasing or decreasing the amount of debt in its capital structure. In market equilibrium, then, corporations are said to be unable to increase their value by changing their degree of leverage. As a result, according to Miller, capital structure decisions for the individual firm would be irrelevant.

One can think of the equilibration process as corporations marketing their securities in much the same way as they market their products. They identify an unsatisfied demand and then design a product to fit this market niche. In the case of capital structure, the product is a financial instrument and the niche is an unsatisfied investor clientele. This clientele is unsatisfied simply because there are not enough securities available of the type necessary to satisfy its tax motivated investment desires. The market is incomplete, and corporations should seek to offer those securites in excess demand.

[10] Merton H. Miller, "Debt and Taxes," *Journal of Finance*, 32 (May 1977), 266–68.

Note that for all companies there is a total optimal capital structure that depends on the tax brackets of different clienteles of investors and the amounts of funds these clienteles have to invest. Corporations overall will want to issue enough debt to satisfy the total demand of investors in tax brackets less than the corporate tax rate. One implication is that if the corporate tax rate were to increase relative to the personal tax rate, the equilibrium would be upset, and the new equilibrium would call for higher total debt-to-equity ratios for companies overall. If the personal tax rate were increased relative to the corporate tax rate, the new equilibrium would involve lower debt-to-equity ratios for companies overall. If the two sets of tax rates go up or down proportionally, there will be no effect. Once the new equilibrium is achieved, however, Miller's position is that the individual firm cannot alter its capital structure to advantage.[11] Thus, the irrelevance argument applies only to market equilibrium, not to disequilibrium. In what follows, we assume that the individual firm is a price taker. In other words, it is unable to affect market equilibrium prices by its individual capital structure actions.

Some Counterarguments.   So far we have taken as given Miller's assumption that the personal tax rate on stock income is effectively zero. In support of this contention, Miller and Scholes argue in a subsequent article that through various tax shelters, individuals are able to postpone realizing a capital gain until they die, at which time capital gains are not taxed.[12] Also, Miller and Scholes suggest that wealthy individuals may use interest expenses on personal borrowings to offset dividend income, so that the effective tax rate on dividends is zero. We know from Treasury tax data, however, that most individuals pay taxes on dividends. Moreover, companies do pay dividends, so some of the return on stock is taxed at essentially the same rate as that for interest income. Furthermore, some capital gains are realized, and taxes are paid on these gains, so the assumption of a zero personal tax on stock income is suspect. The Miller proposition depends on some people's personal tax rate being higher than the corporate tax rate. However, the 1986 and 1990 Tax Acts lowered the top bracket for personal taxes to approximately 32 percent, while that for corporate taxes is 34 percent.

Also disturbing is the relationship between corporate debt and stock returns and returns available on tax-exempt municipal bonds. If the tax rate on stock income is zero, we would expect there to be an equilibration of returns between common stocks and tax-exempt bonds, because the tax rate on municipal debt income is zero. Typically, the yield on municipal debt is about 75 percent of that of corporate debt of the same quality rating,[13] implying a tax rate of 25 percent for the marginal investor. This implied rate is less than the top corporate tax rate, which should prevail on municipal securities if the market equilibrating process advanced by Miller holds. At a 25 percent im-

---

[11] An incomplete market is said to exist when the number and types of securities in the market do not correspond entirely to objects of choice by individuals with respect to time-state contingent claims. Put another way, in an incomplete market, distinct marketable securities do not correspond to every contingency in the world. Under these circumstances, it may be possible for a company to tailor a security issue to a particular class of investor to take advantage of the situation. As a result, capital structure changes could affect the valuation of the firm apart from any other consideration, but the effect here is not systematic as to direction. See J. Hirshleifer, *Investment, Interest and Capital* (Englewood Cliffs, NJ: Prentice Hall, 1970), pp. 264–75.

[12] "Dividends and Taxes," *Journal of Financial Economics*, 6 (December 1978), 333–64.

[13] See James C. Van Horne, *Financial Market Rates and Flows*, 3d ed. (Englewood Cliffs, NJ: Prentice Hall, 1990), Chap. 12.

plied tax rate on municipal debt, wealthy individuals presumably would not be attracted to investing in stocks but would invest in municipal bonds instead. On the supply side of the equation, we know that different corporations have different effective tax rates at the margin. This makes the market equilibration process two-sided and more likely that there will be a net tax effect associated with corporate leverage.

With the 1986 Tax Act, the top tax rate on personal income fell by more than the top corporate tax rate. If the distributions of marginal tax rates for individuals and corporations follow the same pattern, debt financing will be more attractive than before. Furthermore, the taxation of capital gains, upon realization, at nearly the same rate as that on ordinary income, raises the marginal personal tax rate on overall stock income relative to that on debt income. This, too, worked to increase the present value of the tax shield associated with leverage.

A RECAPITULATION

The Miller proposition is provocative and certainly has led us to a better understanding of how taxes affect capital structure. In addition to the arguments presented, theoretical arguments can be marshaled against the idea that the presence of personal taxes completely offsets the corporate tax effect.[14] Moreover, the 1986 and 1990 Tax Acts for all practical purposes make it impossible to achieve a Miller tax equilibrium. Still, there would appear to be some lessening of the corporate tax effect owing to personal taxes. Not a complete offset, as Miller suggests, but some offset nonetheless.

Perhaps this can best be visualized if we reconsider Eq. (10-10). We suggested earlier that if the personal tax rate on stock income, t_{ps}, equaled that on debt income, t_{pd}, the present value of the tax shield associated with leverage would be $t_c B$, which is the corporate tax rate times the market value of the debt. If t_{ps} is less than t_{pd}, the tax advantage associated with debt is less than $t_c B$. Suppose the marginal corporate tax rate is 34 percent, the marginal personal tax rate on debt income is 31 percent, and the market value of DSS Corporation's perpetual debt is $1 million. Now suppose the effective marginal personal tax rate on stock income is 28 percent. As a result, the present value of the tax shield is

$$\text{Present value of tax shield} = \left[1 - \frac{(1 - .34)(1 - .28)}{(1 - .31)} \right] \$1 \text{ million}$$

$$= \$311,304$$

If the effective personal tax rate on stock income is .20 instead of .28, we have

$$\text{Present value of tax shield} = \left[1 - \frac{(1 - .34)(1 - .20)}{(1 - .31)} \right] \$1 \text{ million}$$

$$= \$234,783$$

[14] Robert H. Litzenberger and James C. Van Horne, "Elimination of the Double Taxation of Dividends and Corporate Financial Policy," *Journal of Finance*, 33 (June 1978), footnote 10, demonstrate that Miller's position is inconsistent with market clearing and that a tax advantage of debt remains. Amir Barnea, Robert A. Haugen, and Lemma W. Senbet, "An Equilibrium Analysis of Debt Financing under Costly Tax Arbitrage and Agency Problems," *Journal of Finance*, 36 (June 1981), 569–81, demonstrate that with costs associated with tax avoidance and certain unresolved agency problems, the Miller proposition does not hold.

Thus, the corporate tax advantage associated with debt is less if the effective personal tax rate on debt income exceeds that on stock income. Moreover, the greater the personal tax on debt income relative to stock income, the lower the corporate tax shield.

We have seen that the tax advantage associated with leverage is reduced but not eliminated when we allow for the presence of personal taxes and different tax rates among market participants. Again, we assume that the individual firm does not affect the overall market equilibrium process, but rather is a price taker. Under these circumstances, an optimal leverage strategy would still call for the corporation to have a large proportion of debt. This is despite the fact that tax shield uncertainty may lessen the net tax effect with extreme leverage. As corporations overall are not highly levered, we must search for other factors affecting the valuation of the corporation when it alters the proportion of debt in its capital structure.

EFFECT OF BANKRUPTCY COSTS

Another important imperfection affecting capital structure decisions is the presence of bankruptcy costs. We know from earlier chapters that bankruptcy costs are more than legal and administrative expenses of bankruptcy; they involve inefficiencies in operating a company when it is about to go bankrupt as well as liquidation of assets at distress prices below their economic values.

If there is a possibility of bankruptcy, and if administrative and other costs associated with bankruptcy are significant, the levered firm may be less attractive to investors than the unlevered one. With perfect capital markets, zero bankruptcy costs are assumed. If the firm goes bankrupt, assets presumably can be sold at their economic values with no liquidating or legal costs involved. Proceeds from the sale are distributed according to the claim on assets described in the Appendix at the end of the book. If capital markets are less than perfect, however, there may be administrative costs, and assets may have to be liquidated at less than their economic values. These costs and the shortfall in liquidating value from economic value represent a drain in the system from the standpoint of debt holders and equity holders.

In the event of bankruptcy, security holders as a whole receive less than they would in the absence of bankruptcy costs. To the extent that the levered firm has a greater possibility of bankruptcy than the unlevered one has, the levered firm would be a less attractive investment, all other things the same. The possibility of bankruptcy usually is not a linear function of the debt-to-equity ratio, but it increases at an increasing rate beyond some threshold.[15] As a result, the expected cost of bankruptcy increases in this manner and would be expected to have a corresponding negative effect on the value of the firm and on its cost of capital.[16] Creditors bear the ex post cost of bankruptcy, but

---

[15] Using a state-preference approach in a world of taxes and bankruptcy penalties, Alan Kraus and Robert H. Litzenberger, "A State-Preference Model of Optimal Financial Leverage," *Journal of Finance*, 28 (September 1973), 911–22, show that with discrete states of nature, the relationship between the value of the firm and the amount of debt is jagged. Value is increased with leverage up to the point where a further debt increase causes a change from a state in which the firm would be solvent to one in which it would be insolvent. At that point the market value drops, owing to bankruptcy penalties. It increases with subsequent leverage (because of the tax advantage of debt) only to fall when another change in state occurs.

[16] See James C. Van Horne, "Optimal Initiation of Bankruptcy Proceedings by Debt Holders," *Journal of Finance*, 31 (June 1976), 897–910.

they will probably pass on the ex ante cost to stockholders in the form of higher interest rates. Hence, the stockholders would bear the burden of ex ante bankruptcy costs and the subsequent lower valuation of the firm. Because bankruptcy costs represent a "dead weight" loss, investors are unable to diversify away these costs even though the market equilibration process is assumed to be efficient.

Now it may be argued that if creditors and stockholders could get together informally, they could work out an agreement outside of the court. By so doing, bankruptcy costs could be avoided, with both parties sharing in the gain.[17] Even if such a work out were "costless," Ronald M. Giammarino shows that creditors often prefer costly arbitration.[18] The crux of his argument is that there is asymmetric information between the two parties, and enforcement of contracts is costly.

As a result, investors are likely to penalize the price of the stock as leverage increases. The nature of the penalty is illustrated for a no-tax world in Fig. 10-5. Here the required rate of return for investors, k_e, is broken into its component parts. There is the risk-free rate, R_f, plus a premium for business risk. This premium is depicted on the vertical axis by the difference between the required rate of return for an all-equity capital structure and the risk-free rate. As debt is added, the required rate of return rises and this increment repre-

[17] Robert A. Haugen and Lemma W. Senbet, "The Irrelevance of Bankruptcy Costs to the Theory of Optimal Capital Structure," *Journal of Finance*, 33 (June 1978), 383–94, argue that bankruptcy costs are not a factor of importance. They assume that rationality prevails on the part of customers, suppliers, employees, and creditors, so that when bankruptcy approaches, the company simply reorganizes by selling stock and repurchasing debt. They reason that all parties have an incentive to avoid the costs of a formal reorganization and will seek an informal reorganization instead where the costs are lower. The authors distinguish between a bankruptcy, where debt holders take over the company, and a liquidation. The latter is said to be a rational abandonment decision on the part of the firm (see Chap. 7) and is independent of the event of bankruptcy. The argument that bankruptcy costs are insignificant depends on complete rationality by all parties in a distress situation, no restrictions on arbitrage, and no imperfections when it comes to selling stock and repurchasing debt. Based on fragmentary evidence, bankruptcy costs appear to be positive and significant.

[18] Ronald M. Giammarino, "The Resolution of Financial Distress," *Review of Financial Studies*, 2, No. 1 (1989), 25–49. A similar conclusion is reached by David T. Brown, "Changing Incentive Conflicts in Reorganization: The Role of Bankruptcy Law," *Review of Financial Studies*, 2, No. 1 (1989), 109–23.

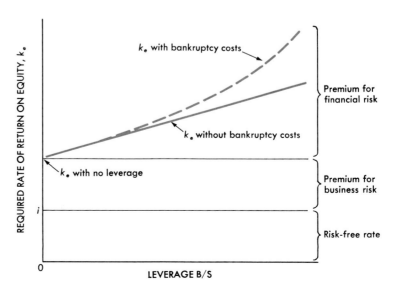

FIGURE 10-5

Required rate of return for equity capital when bankruptcy costs exist but there are no taxes

sents a financial risk premium. In the absence of bankruptcy costs, the required return would rise in a linear manner according to our earlier discussion of taxes, and this relationship is shown. However, with bankruptcy costs and an increasing probability of bankruptcy with leverage, the required rate of return would be expected to rise at an increasing rate beyond some point. At first there might be a negligible probability of bankruptcy, so there would be little or no penalty. As leverage increases, so does the penalty; for extreme leverage, the penalty becomes very substantial indeed.

However, the penalty may differ according to the type of company. Sheridan Titman suggests that companies that produce unique, specialized products impose a higher cost of insolvency on customers, employees, and suppliers than do companies producing less-unique products.[19] The idea is that such stakeholders develop specialized, or customized, skills and capital that are not easily transferable. As a result, the costs of bankruptcy will differ according to the type of firm. Titman finds that companies in unique lines of business tend to have lower debt ratios, a finding consistent with this idea.

TAXES AND BANKRUPTCY COSTS

Our earlier discussion of taxes and capital structure concluded that leverage is likely to result in a net tax advantage (the corporate tax effect offset by the personal tax effect). As the company increases its leverage, the present value of the tax shield will increase. In this restricted context, the total value of the firm is

$$\text{Value of firm} = \begin{array}{c}\text{Value as}\\\text{unlevered}\\\text{firm}\end{array} + \begin{array}{c}\text{Present value}\\\text{of net tax}\\\text{shield on debt}\end{array} \qquad (10\text{-}11)$$

If we allow for bankruptcy costs and if the probability of bankruptcy increases at an increasing rate with leverage, extreme leverage is likely to be penalized by investors. (As discussed earlier, bankruptcy costs represent a drain in the system to security holders.) In a world of both taxes and bankruptcy costs, it is likely that there would be an optimal capital structure. Whereas the net tax effect would have a positive influence on value, bankruptcy costs would exert a negative influence. The value of the firm would increase as leverage was first employed because of the tax advantage of debt. Gradually, however, the prospect of bankruptcy would become increasingly important. This, together with tax shield uncertainty, would cause the value of the firm to increase at a decreasing rate. As more and more leverage was undertaken, eventually the net tax effect would be offset, and the value of the firm would decline. We can express the above as

$$\text{Value of firm} = \begin{array}{c}\text{Value as}\\\text{unlevered}\\\text{firm}\end{array} + \begin{array}{c}\text{Present value}\\\text{of net tax}\\\text{shield on debt}\end{array} - \begin{array}{c}\text{Present value}\\\text{of bankruptcy}\\\text{costs}\end{array} \qquad (10\text{-}12)$$

The joint effect of taxes and bankruptcy costs is illustrated in Fig. 10-6.

---

[19] Sheridan Titman, "The Effect of Capital Structure on a Firm's Liquidation Decision," *Journal of Financial Economics*, 13 (March 1984), 137–51. For empirical evidence, see Sheridan Titman and Roberto Wessels, "The Determinants of Capital Structure Choice," *Journal of Finance*, 43 (March 1988), 1–19.

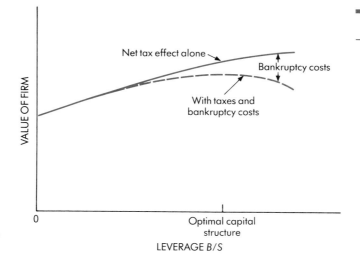

FIGURE 10-6
Value of firm with taxes
and bankruptcy costs

The net tax effect line is shown to taper off as more leverage is undertaken, in keeping with the mathematics and with tax shield uncertainty. However, bankruptcy costs are what cause value eventually to decline in the figure. The optimal capital structure by definition is the point at which the value of the firm is maximized. Thus, we have a trade-off between the tax effects associated with leverage and the nonlinear expected bankruptcy costs that come when leverage is pushed beyond a point. While taxes and bankruptcy costs are probably the most important imperfections when it comes to capital structure decisions, there are others that bear on the problem.

OTHER IMPERFECTIONS

Other capital market imperfections impede the equilibration of security prices according to their expected returns and risks. As a result, these imperfections may result in leverage having an effect on the value of the firm apart from taxes and bankruptcy costs. The imperfections must be not only material but also one-directional. We know that transaction costs restrict the arbitrage process described earlier, but the net effect of this imperfection is not predictable as to direction if, in fact, there is a net effect at all. In what follows, we examine certain additional imperfections that may have a predictable effect on the capital structure question.

CORPORATE AND HOMEMADE LEVERAGE NOT BEING PERFECT SUBSTITUTES

The perceived risks of personal leverage and corporate leverage may differ. Despite the implication in the MM analysis that personal and corporate leverage are perfect substitutes, there are various reasons for suspecting that this may not be the case. For one thing, if investors borrow personally and pledge their stock as collateral, they are subject to possible margin calls. Many investors view this possibility with alarm. Moreover, personal leverage involves a certain amount of inconvenience for investors, which they do not experience with corporate leverage. In addition, stockholders have limited liability with a stock investment, whereas their liability with personal loans is unlimited. Moreover, the cost of borrowing may be higher for the individual than for the corporation. For these reasons, personal leverage may not be a perfect substitute for corporate leverage in the minds of many investors.

Arbitrage need not occur in terms of the individual actually borrowing in the market, however. The same thing may be accomplished by changing one's holdings of bonds. Moreover, the arbitrage process is not confined to individuals. If opportunities for profit exist, financial intermediaries may enter the scene and replicate the financial claims of either the levered or the unlevered company and buy the stock of the other. The free entry of financial intermediaries without cost will ensure the efficient functioning of the arbitrage process, which in turn will result in the irrelevance of corporate leverage. Therefore, we are inclined to discount the importance of this argument.

INSTITUTIONAL RESTRICTIONS

Restrictions on investment behavior may retard the arbitrage process. Many institutional investors, such as pension funds and life insurance companies, are not allowed to engage in the "homemade" leverage that was described. Regulatory bodies often restrict stock and bond investments to a list of companies meeting certain quality standards, such as only a "safe" amount of leverage. If a company breaches that amount, it may be removed from the acceptable list, thereby precluding certain institutions from investing in it. This reduction in investor demand can have an adverse effect on the market value of the company's financial instruments.

Glenn argues that the combination of restrictions on the investment behavior of financial institutions, together with restrictions on short sales, results in there being an optimal capital structure for the firm.[20] By way of definition, a *short sale* is the borrowing of a security and selling it with the obligation to deliver the borrowed security back to the lender some time in the future. The short seller hopes to buy the security back at a lower price than the price at which it was sold, thereby realizing a profit from the two transactions. Restrictions on the investment behavior of institutions will result in those securities approved for investment selling at higher prices than otherwise would be the case. As long as there are impediments to short selling, unrestricted investors, through arbitrage, will not be able to eliminate the premiums in prices for securities that are approved investments for restricted institutional investors. Under these circumstances, an optimal capital structure exists, according to Glenn. For most firms, it would involve issuing the maximum amount of debt consistent with obtaining a preferential investment grade rating suitable for institutional investors.

If other imperfections and behavioral factors dilute the arbitrage argument of MM, the point at which the firm value line turns down with leverage in Fig. 10-6 would be sooner or later than that depicted. The greater the importance of the other imperfections we have discussed, the less effective the arbitrage process becomes, and the greater the case that can be made for an optimal capital structure.

[20] David W. Glenn, "Super Premium Security Prices and Optimal Corporate Financing Decisions," *Journal of Finance*, 31 (May 1976), 507–24.

Capital structure decisions lead to a number of incentive issues among equity holders, debt holders, management, and other stakeholders in the corporation. In this section we examine these issues, followed by the question of financial signaling. These considerations can, and often do, influence the choice of security used in financing, as well as whether to finance, and invest, at all. To begin, we look at debt versus equity in an option pricing model framework. This serves as a foundation for the subsequent discussion.

DEBT HOLDERS VERSUS EQUITY HOLDERS[21]

Using the concepts developed in Chapter 5, the equity of a firm can be viewed as a call option on the firm's total value, the value being the associated or underlying asset of the option. The writers of the option are the debt holders. For simplicity, assume that debt is represented by discount bonds that pay only at maturity.[22] We can then view stockholders as having sold the firm to the debt holders with an option to buy it back at a specified price. The option has an exercise price equal to the face value of debt, and its expiration date is the maturity of the debt.[23]

The value of the option at the expiration date, which by definition is the value of the stock, is

$$V_o = \max(V_f - D, 0) \qquad (10\text{-}13)$$

where V_f is the value of the firm at the expiration date, D is the face value of the debt which is the exercise price of the option, and max means the maximum value of $V_f - D$ or zero, whichever is greater. The value of the debt at the expiration date is simply

$$V_d = \min(V_f, D) \qquad (10\text{-}14)$$

where min means V_f or D, whichever is less. In other words, if V_f is greater than D, the debt holders are entitled only to the face value of the debt, and the stockholders exercise their option. If V_f is less than D, the debt holders as owners of the firm are entitled to its value. The stockholders receive nothing. Note that the value of their option at expiration cannot be negative, because they have limited liability.

These notions are illustrated in Fig. 10-7, where in the left panel the value of debt is shown and in the right panel the value of equity. The value of the firm at the expiration date of the debt is shown along the horizontal axis in both panels, with the face value of the debt again being represented by D. Depending on whether the value of the firm is above or below D, equity and

[21] Unless the reader has covered Chapter 5 this section should be passed over.
[22] The interest rate is embodied in the discount. If the bond had a face value of $1,000, a maturity of 1 year, and a discount of $120, the interest rate would be $120/$880 = 13.64%.
[23] See Fischer Black and Myron Scholes, "The Pricing of Options and Corporate Liabilities," *Journal of Political Economy*, 81 (May–June 1973), 649–51.

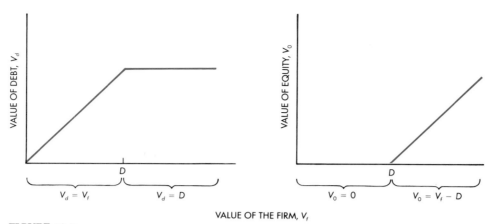

FIGURE 10-7
Value of debt and equity at the debt's expiration date

debt values will be those shown. We see, then, that the debt holder–stockholder relationship can be pictured in an option pricing framework.

EFFECT OF VARIANCE AND THE RISKINESS OF ASSETS

We know from Chapter 5 that the greater the variance or volatility in value of the underlying asset, the greater the value of the option, all other things the same. Therefore, it is in the interest of the option holders, in this case the stockholders, to increase the variance of the firm. With a given exercise price of D, an increase in the dispersion of the probability distribution of possible firm values increases the value of their option. Thus, by increasing the riskiness of the assets of the firm, stockholders can increase the value of their option. This works to the disadvantage of the debt holders because there will be a corresponding decrease in the market value of their investment.

To illustrate, we use the Black-Scholes option pricing model from Chapter 5. In this regard, the same assumptions are made as before.[24] Suppose that the total value of Belgrazia Tube Company is $4 million, and it has just issued debt with a face value of $3 million payable entirely at the end of 5 years. At present the standard deviation of the continuously compounded rate of return on the overall value of the company is .12. Also, the short-term, risk-free rate is 6 percent. Given this information, we first solve for d_1 and d_2 in the Black-Scholes option pricing formula.

$$d_1 = \frac{\ln (\$4/\$3) + [.06 + 1/2(.12)^2]5}{.12\sqrt{5}} = \frac{.623682}{.268328} = 2.32 \qquad (10\text{-}15)$$

In the equation, ln refers to the natural log and 5 to the length of time to the expiration of the option. For d_2, we have

$$d_2 = \frac{\ln (\$4/\$3) + [.06 - 1/2(.12)^2]5}{.12\sqrt{5}} = \frac{.551682}{.268328} = 2.06 \qquad (10\text{-}16)$$

[24] These include no transaction costs, no taxes, no financial market imperfections, no restrictions on short sales, no dividends on the stock, a known and constant short-term interest rate at which parties can both lend and borrow, and the value of the firm following a random walk in continuous time with a constant variance rate over time.

290

In Table C at the end of the book, the area of a normal distribution to the right of 2.30 standard deviations is .0107 and to the right of 2.35 standard deviations, .0094. Interpolating, we find that 2.32 standard deviations correspond to .0102. Therefore, the area of the distribution less than 2.32 standard deviations to the right of the mean is $1 - .0102 = .9898$. For the area 2.06 standard deviations to the right of the mean, we find by interpolating that this standard deviation corresponds to .0197. The area of the distribution less than 2.06 standard deviations is $1 - .0197 = .9803$. Therefore, $N(d_1) = .9898$, and $N(d_2) = .9803$. Solving for the option pricing formula, Eq. (5-2) in Chapter 5, we obtain

$$V_o = \$4 \text{ million } (.9898) - \frac{\$3 \text{ million}}{e^{(.06)(5)}}(.9803) = \$1,780,526 \qquad (10\text{-}17)$$

where $e = 2.71828$ and the exponent is the interest rate times the length of time to expiration. Thus, the value of the stock is \$1,780,526, and the value of the debt is $\$4,000,000 - \$1,780,526 = \$2,219,474$.

Suppose now that Belgrazia Tube Company dramatically increases the riskiness of its business so that the standard deviation of its continuously compounded rate becomes .36 in contrast to .12 before. Going through the same kind of calculations as before, the value of the stock is found to be \$2,084,431. This contrasts with \$1,780,526 before. The value of the debt is $\$4,000,000 - \$2,084,431 = \$1,915,569$, in contrast to \$2,219,474 before.

By increasing the riskiness of the company, stockholders are thus able to increase the value of their stock at the direct expense of the debt holders. The reason for this occurrence is that stockholders have an option on the total value of the firm. As with any option, increased variance of the underlying asset increases the option's value.

CHANGING THE PROPORTION OF DEBT

With the perfect market assumptions of the option pricing model, changing the proportion of debt in the capital structure will not affect the total value of the firm. In other words, the Modigliani-Miller irrelevance proposition holds. Such a change will affect the relative valuations of the debt and of the equity, however. We know that the option pricing formula can be used to determine the value of the common stock and that by deducting this value from the value of the total firm we can determine the value of the debt. By comparing values for different proportions of debt, we are able to determine the relationship between the proportion of debt and valuation.

To understand this, use our last example but assume that the face value of the debt is \$1 million instead of \$3 million. Putting these numbers into the Black-Scholes formula, the value of the stock is found to be \$3,266,681. The value of the debt is $\$4,000,000 - \$3,266,681 = \$733,319$. Recall from our previous example that with \$3 million in debt, these values were \$2,084,431 and \$1,915,569, respectively. The percentage increases for the debt are

			PERCENTAGE CHANGE
Face value of debt	\$1,000,000	\$3,000,000	200%
Value of debt	733,319	1,915,569	161

Thus, the increase in the face value of the debt is accompanied by a smaller percentage increase in the value of the debt, holding constant the total value of the firm. The reason is that the probability of default has increased, and with the greater default risk, the value of the debt (per dollar of face value) is reduced.

In the context of the option pricing model, issuing debt and retiring stock—thereby increasing the proportion of debt in the capital structure—will result in a decline in the price of the existing debt (per dollar of face value) and an increase in share price. If the face value of each bond were $1,000, there would be 1,000 bonds outstanding at $1 million in debt and 3,000 bonds outstanding at $3 million in debt. The value per bond at the lower level of debt is $733,319/1,000 = $733.32 per bond. At the higher level, it is $1,915,569/3,000 = $638.52. In essence, the stockholders have expropriated some of the wealth of the existing debt holders. The new debt holders are not hurt, because they lend money on the basis of the default risk associated with the new capital structure. In our example, they would lend $638.52 for each $1,000 face value bond. Only the old debt holders suffer. Similar to a change in the overall risk of the firm in our previous discussion, wealth transfers from the old debt holders to the stockholders.

PROTECTIVE COVENANTS

Debt holders can protect themselves against expropriation by imposing constraints on the company at the time the loan is made. Known as protective covenants, these covenants may be used to restrict the stockholders' ability to increase the asset riskiness of the company and/or its leverage. In Chapter 18, we describe protective covenants in detail and show how they may be used in an option pricing model context. The reputation of the borrower may affect the terms of the loan. New borrowers with short track records generally face more restrictions and monitoring than does a company with a longstanding, high credit rating.[25]

The Modigliani-Miller argument for the irrelevance of capital structure requires that security holders protect themselves against capital structure changes that work to erode their position. "Me-first" rules ensure that one party cannot gain at the expense of the other. Although stockholders usually gain and old debt holders usually lose, it is possible for the reverse to occur. With certain protective covenants, debt holders might obtain a claim on future retained earnings at the expense of stockholders. Therefore, stockholders also must assure themselves that their position is not eroded without compensation. To the extent that "me-first" rules are not effective, capital structure decisions may be relevant even in the absence of taxes and bankruptcy costs.

THE UNDERINVESTMENT PROBLEM
IN REVERSE

The incentive problem between equity holders and debt holders could lead to investment in negative net present value projects.[26] The underinvestment problem, the opposite, was described in Chapter 9. Recall that it was

[25] Douglas W. Diamond, "Reputation Acquisition in Debt Markets," *Journal of Political Economy*, 97, No. 4 (1989), 828–62.
[26] I am indebted to John McConnell for this insight.

that any capital investment that lowered the relative variance of debt holder returns increased the creditworthiness of their claim. The market value of the debt should rise, and this represents a wealth transfer from equity holders, all other things the same. This wealth transfer may cause the firm, in behalf of its stockholders, to forgo a positive NPV project simply because debt holders reap too much of the benefit relative to equity holders.

In the opposite direction, a company with substantial leverage may be able to extract a wealth transfer from debt holders to equity holders by making the company even riskier through its investment decisions. If the wealth transfer were large enough, share price might increase even with a negative NPV project. In other words, the financial risk associated with leverage accentuates underlying business risk. To the extent the firm undertakes negative NPV projects as leverage becomes extreme, the value line in Fig. 10-6 would turn down more sharply than shown.

AGENCY COSTS MORE BROADLY DEFINED

The expropriation of wealth and the "me-first" rules illustrate the need for debt holders to monitor the actions of equity holders. Monitoring requires the expenditure of resources, and the costs involved are one form of *agency costs*. As discussed in Chapter 1, Jensen and Meckling have expounded a sophisticated theory of agency costs.[27] Among other things, they show that regardless of who makes the monitoring expenditures, the cost is borne by stockholders. Debt holders, anticipating monitoring costs, charge higher interest. The higher the probable monitoring costs, the higher the interest rate, and the lower the value of the firm to its shareholders, all other things the same.

Complete protection would require the specification of extremely detailed protective covenants and extraordinary enforcement costs. Virtually every decision of the firm would need to be monitored. Not only would there be substantial legal and enforcement costs, but the firm would operate inefficiently. All of these agency costs go to reduce the overall value of the firm. As residual owners of the firm, stockholders have an incentive to see that such monitoring costs are minimized—up to a point. There is a trade-off. In the absence of any protective covenants, debt holders may charge very high interest rates, and these rates may cost stockholders more than the agency costs associated with reasonable protective covenants.

It is not that monitoring costs per se are bad for the owners of a company; it is that monitoring needs to be efficient. As more and more safeguards and enforcement procedures are imposed, debt holders' protection rises, but at a decreasing rate. Beyond a point, the reduction in interest rate is more than offset by escalating agency costs, which ultimately are borne by the stockholders. An optimal balance needs to be struck between monitoring costs and the interest rate charged on a debt instrument at the time it is sold. Some activities of the firm are relatively inexpensive to monitor; others are expensive. Dividend and financing decisions can be monitored with only moderate cost, whereas the production and investment decisions of the firm are much more costly to monitor. The relative costs of monitoring need to be taken into account in determining the protective covenants that should be used.

[27] Michael C. Jensen and William H. Meckling, "Theory of the Firm: Managerial Behavior, Agency Costs and Ownership Structure," *Journal of Financial Economics*, 3 (October 1976), 305–60. For a somewhat different approach, see Stewart C. Myers, "Determinants of Corporate Borrowing," *Journal of Financial Economics*, 5 (November 1977), 147–75.

In addition, the firm should endeavor to see that efficient monitoring occurs. To the extent that management together with an outside auditor or appraiser can produce information at a lower cost than the lender can, it should undertake the production of such information. (This assumes that the "quality" of the information is the same.) The important thing to realize is that ultimately the costs of monitoring are borne by the stockholders. It is always in their interest to see that monitoring is efficiently administered. Some things are inherently difficult to monitor. Control over investment in intangibles, such as R&D and advertising, for example, are difficult to capture in a debt contract. In order to control agency costs, equity holders may need to limit the amount of debt financing.

The presence of monitoring costs acts as a disincentive to the issuance of debt. If capital markets were perfect with the exception of these costs and we lived in a no-tax world, the firm would not want to issue any debt. In the real world of corporate income tax, the issuance of debt is attractive. Like bankruptcy costs, though, monitoring costs may limit the amount of debt that it is optimal for a firm to issue. It is likely that beyond a point the amount of monitoring required by debt holders increases with the amount of debt outstanding. When there is little or no debt, lenders may engage in only limited monitoring, whereas with a great deal of debt outstanding they may insist on extensive monitoring. In turn, this monitoring may involve considerable costs. As a result, Fig. 10-6, showing the relationship among taxes, bankruptcy costs, and firm value, would need to be modified. Monitoring costs would act as a further factor decreasing firm value for extreme leverage. The situation is illustrated in Fig. 10-8. The optimal capital structure occurs at point x, somewhat before that which occurs with taxes and bankruptcy costs alone, point y.

DEBT AND THE INCENTIVE
TO MANAGE EFFICIENTLY

Working in the other direction is the notion that high debt levels create incentives for management to be more efficient.[28] By taking on the cash-flow obligation to service debt, it is claimed that management's "feet are held close

[28] A number of people have made this argument, but it is articulated perhaps best in Michael C. Jensen, "The Takeover Controversy: Analysis and Evidence," *Midland Corporate Finance Journal*, 4 (Summer 1986), 12–21.

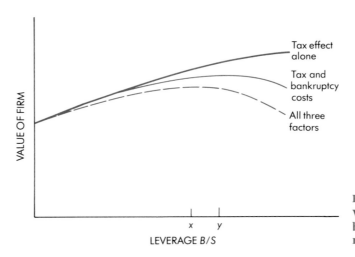

FIGURE 10-8

Value of firm with taxes, bankruptcy costs, and monitoring costs

to the fire." As a result, there is said to be an incentive not to squander funds in wasteful activities, whether it be an investment, a perquisite, a company plane, or whatever. The idea is that levered companies may be leaner because management cuts the fat. Contrarily, the company with little debt and significant free cash flow, after investing in all worthwhile projects, may have a tendency to squander funds. In the absence of other incentives, "running scared" to make debt payments may have a salutary effect on efficiency.

FINANCIAL SIGNALING

Closely related to monitoring costs and agency relationships is the notion of signaling. Because strict managerial contracts are difficult to enforce, managers may use capital structure changes to convey information about the profitability and risk of the firm. The implication is that insiders know something about the firm that outsiders do not. As a manager, your pay and benefits may depend on the firm's market value. That gives you an incentive to let investors know when the firm is undervalued. You could make an announcement, "Our firm is undervalued," but you are more sophisticated than that, and you know that investors would probably be as convinced as if you were boasting about your child. So you alter your firm's capital structure by issuing more debt. Increased leverage implies a higher probability of bankruptcy, and since you would be penalized contractually if bankruptcy occurred, investors conclude that you have good reason to believe that things really are better than the stock price reflects.[29] Your actions speak louder than words. Increased leverage is a positive sign.

ASYMMETRIC INFORMATION

More formally, a signaling effect assumes there is information asymmetry between management and stockholders. When financing an investment project management will want to issue the overvalued security, if it is acting in the interests of current stockholders. As Myers and Majluf suggest, it will issue stock if it believes the existing stock is overvalued and debt if it believes the stock is undervalued.[30] However, investors are not unmindful of this phenomenon, so debt issues are regarded as "good news" and stock issues as "bad news."

The greater the asymmetry in information between insiders (management) and outsiders (security holders), the greater the likely stock price reaction to a financing announcement. In general, empirical evidence is consistent with the asymmetry of information idea. Around the time of the announce-

---

[29] For an extended analysis of this effect, see Stephen A. Ross, "The Determination of Financial Structure: The Incentive Signaling Approach," *Bell Journal of Economics*, 8 (Spring 1977), 23–40; and Hayne E. Leland and David H. Pyle, "Informational Asymmetries, Financial Structure, and Financial Intermediation," *Journal of Finance*, 32 (May 1977), 371–88. See also Wayne L. Lee, Anjan V. Thakor, and Gautam Vora, "Screening, Market Signalling, and Capital Structure Theory," *Journal of Finance*, 38 (December 1983), 1507–18.

[30] Stewart C. Myers and Nicholas S. Majluf, "Corporate Financing and Investment Decisions When Firms Have Information That Investors Do Not Have," *Journal of Financial Economics*, 13 (June 1984), 187–222. For refinement along the lines of adverse selection, see Michael Brennan and Alan Kraus, "Efficient Financing under Asymmetric Information," *Journal of Finance*, 42 (December 1987), 1225–43.

ment, leverage-increasing transactions tend to result in positive excess returns to stockholders, whereas leverage-decreasing transactions result in the opposite. The evidence overall is consistent with a financial signaling effect accompanying the choice of security employed in the capital structure.

FROM WHERE DOES VALUE COMETH?

This is not to say that capital structure changes cause changes in valuation. Rather, it is the signal conveyed by the change that is significant. This signal pertains to the underlying profitability and risk of the firm, as that is what is important when it comes to valuation. Financial signaling is a topic of considerable interest in the writing on finance, but the various models are difficult to evaluate. Unless the managerial contract is very precise, the manager is tempted to give false signals. Moreover, there simply may be more effective and less costly ways to convey information than by altering the firm's capital structure. We shall have more to say about this phenomenon when we consider dividend policy in Chapter 12.

SUMMARY

A great deal of controversy has developed over whether the capital structure of a firm, as determined by its financing decision, affects its overall value. Traditionalists argue that the firm can lower its cost of capital and increase market value per share by the judicious use of leverage. Modigliani and Miller, on the other hand, argue that in the absence of taxes and other market imperfections, the total value of the firm and its cost of capital are independent of capital structure. This position is based on the notion that there is a conservation of investment value. No matter how you divide the pie between debt and equity claims, the total pie or investment value of the firm stays the same. Therefore, leverage is said to be irrelevant. We saw that behavioral support for the MM position was based upon the arbitrage process.

In a world of corporate income taxes, there is a substantial advantage to the use of debt; and we showed how the present value of the tax shield might be measured. This advantage is lessened with tax shield uncertainty, particularly if leverage is high. When we allow for personal income taxes and a higher personal tax rate on debt income than on stock income, we find the tax advantage of debt to be further reduced. Merton Miller argues that it is zero, and his argument, as well as certain refuting evidence, was examined. Bankruptcy costs work to the disadvantage of leverage, particularly extreme leverage. A combination of net tax effect with bankruptcy costs will result in an optimal capital structure. Other market imperfections—such as institutional restrictions on lender and stock investor behavior—impede the equilibration of security prices according to expected return and risk. As a result, leverage may affect the value of the firm.

One can analyze the capital structure problem in an option pricing model framework giving stockholders an option to buy back the firm at the maturity of the debt. As with any option, an increase in the variance of the associated asset—in this case, the value of the firm—will increase the value of the option. It is to the stockholders' advantage to increase variance, either by increasing the riskiness of the assets of the firm or by increasing the proportion of debt. Debt holders can protect themselves against this occurrence by imposing protective covenants. This protection involves monitoring costs, which are a form of agency costs. Stockholders, who ultimately bear the cost of monitoring, have an incentive to see that it is efficient. Beyond some threshold, monitoring costs are likely to increase at an increasing rate with leverage. Like bankruptcy costs, monitoring costs may limit the amount of debt in an optimal capital structure. In the context of agency costs, other incentive issues affecting capital structure decisions were analyzed.

Financial signaling occurs when capital structure changes convey information to security holders. It assumes an asymmetry in information between management and stockholders. Management behavior results in debt issues being regarded as "good news" by investors and stock issues as "bad news." Empirical evidence seems to be consistent with this notion. In the next chapter, we shall find out how a firm can choose an appropriate capital structure.

SELF-CORRECTION PROBLEMS

1. Abacus Calculation Company and Zoom Calculators, Inc., are identical except for capital structures. Abacus has 50 percent debt and 50 percent equity, while Zoom has 20 percent debt and 80 percent equity. (All percentages are in market-value terms.) The borrowing rate for both companies is 13 percent in a no-tax world, and capital markets are assumed to be perfect.

   a. If you own 2 percent of the stock of Abacus, what is your dollar return if the company has net operating income of $360,000 and the overall capitalization rate of the company, k_o, is 18 percent? What is the implied required rate of return on equity?

   b. Zoom has the same net operating income as Abacus. What is the implied required equity return of Zoom? Why does it differ from that of Abacus?

2. Massey-Moss Corporation has earnings before interest and taxes of $3 million and a 40 percent tax rate. It is able to borrow at an interest rate of 14 percent, whereas its required rate of return on equity in the absence of borrowing is 18 percent.

   a. In the absence of personal taxes, what is the value of the company in an MM world with no leverage? with $4 million in debt? with $7 million in debt?

   b. Personal as well as corporate taxes now exist. The marginal personal tax rate on common stock income is 25 percent and the marginal personal tax rate on debt income is 30 percent. Determine the value of the company using Eq. (10-10) for each of the three debt alternatives in part a. Why do your answers differ?

3. L'Etoile du Nord Resorts is considering various levels of debt. Presently, it has no debt and a total market value of $15 million. By undertaking leverage, it believes that it can achieve a net tax advantage (corporate and personal combined) equal to 20 percent of the amount of the debt. However, the company is concerned with bankruptcy and agency costs as well as lenders increasing their interest rate if it borrows too much. The company believes that it can borrow up to $5 million without incurring any of these costs. However, each additional $5 million increment in borrowing is expected to result in the three costs cited being incurred. Moreover, they are expected to increase at an increasing rate with leverage. The present-value cost is expected to be the following for various levels of debt:

Debt (in millions)	$5	$10	$15	$20	$25	$30
PV cost of bankruptcy, agency, and increased interest rate (in millions)	0	.6	1.2	2.0	3.2	5.0

Is there an optimal amount of debt for the company?

PROBLEMS

1. The Malock Company has net operating earnings of $10 million and $20 million of debt with a 7 percent interest charge. In all cases, assume no taxes.

   a. Using the net operating income approach and an overall capitalization rate of 11 percent, compute the total market value, the stock market value, and the implied required return on equity for the Malock Company prior to the sale of additional debt.

   b. Determine the answers to part a if the company were to sell the additional $10 million in debt.

2. The Kelly Company and the Green Company are identical in every respect except that the Kelly Company is not levered, while the Green Company has $2 million in 12 percent bonds outstanding. There are no taxes, and capital markets are assumed to be perfect. The valuation of the two firms is the following:

	KELLY	GREEN
Net operating income	$600,000	$600,000
Interest on debt	0	240,000
Earnings to common	$600,000	$360,000
Required equity rate	.15	.16
Market value of stock	$4,000,000	$2,250,000
Market value of debt	0	2,000,000
Total value of firm	$4,000,000	$4,250,000
Implied overall capitalization rate, k_o	15.00%	14.12%
Debt-to-equity ratio, B/S	0	0.89

   a. You own $22,500 worth of Green stock. Show the process and the amount by which you could reduce your outlay through the use of arbitrage.

   b. When will this arbitrage process cease?

3. The Blalock Corporation has a $1 million capital structure and will always maintain this book-value amount. Blalock currently earns $250,000 per year before taxes of 50 percent, has an all-equity capital structure of 100,000 shares, and pays all earnings in dividends. The company is considering issuing debt in order to retire stock. The cost of the debt and the price of the stock at various levels of debt are given in the accompanying table. It is assumed that the new capital structure would be reached all at once by purchasing stock at the current price. In other words, the table is a schedule at a point in time.

AMOUNT OF DEBT	AVERAGE COST OF DEBT	PRICE OF STOCK PER SHARE
—	—	$10.00
$100,000	10.0%	10.50
200,000	10.0	10.80
300,000	10.5	11.00
400,000	11.0	11.15
500,000	12.0	10.50
600,000	14.0	9.50

   a. By observation, what do you think is the optimal capital structure?

   b. Construct a graph in terms of k_e, k_i, and k_o based on the data given.

   c. Are your conclusions in part a confirmed?

4. Zapatta Cottonseed Oil Company has $1 million in earnings before interest and taxes. Currently it is all equity financed. It may issue $3 million in perpetual debt at 15 percent interest in order to repurchase stock, thereby recapitalizing the corporation. There are no personal taxes.

   a. If the corporate tax rate is 40 percent, what is the income to all security holders if the company remains all equity financed? if it is recapitalized?

   b. What is the present value of the debt tax shield?

   c. The required return on equity for the company's stock is 20 percent while it remains all equity financed. What is the value of the firm? What is the value if it is recapitalized?

5. Loveless Electrical Products Company has $4 million in debt outstanding. The corporate income tax rate is 35 percent. In an extensive study of investors, G. Rosenberg and Associates, an outside consulting firm, has estimated that the marginal personal tax rate on common stock income for investors overall is 25 percent. Dividends and capital gains are both included in this income. The firm also has estimated that the marginal personal tax rate on debt income is 30 percent.

   a. Determine the tax advantage to Loveless Electrical Products Company for the use of debt under the assumption of corporate income taxes but no personal income taxes. (Assume the debt is perpetual and that the tax shield will be the same throughout.)

   b. Determine the tax advantage with both corporate and personal income taxes. Why does your answer to part b differ from that to part a?

   c. What would be the tax advantage if the personal tax rate on common stock income were 30 percent? if it were 20 percent? (Assume that all else stays the same.)

6. Petroles Vintage Wine Company is presently family owned and has no debt. The Petroles family is considering going public by selling some of their stock in the company. Investment bankers tell them the total market value of the company is $10 million if no debt is employed. In addition to selling stock, the family wishes to consider issuing debt that, for computational purposes, would be perpetual. The debt then would be used to purchase stock, so the size of the company would stay the same. Based on various valuation studies, the net tax advantage of debt is estimated at 22 percent of the amount borrowed when both corporate and personal taxes are taken into account. The investment banker has estimated the following present values for bankruptcy costs associated with various levels of debt:

DEBT (IN MILLIONS)	PRESENT VALUE OF BANKRUPTCY COSTS
$1	0
2	$50,000
3	100,000

[continued]

DEBT (IN MILLIONS)	PRESENT VALUE OF BANKRUPTCY COSTS
4	200,000
5	400,000
6	700,000
7	1,100,000
8	1,600,000

Given this information, what amount of debt should the family choose?

7. Acme-Menderhall Corporation is trying to determine an appropriate capital structure. It knows that as its leverage increases, its cost of borrowing will eventually increase, as will the required rate of return on its common stock. The company has made the following estimates for various leverage ratios:

		REQUIRED RATE OF RETURN ON EQUITY	
DEBT/(DEBT + EQUITY)	INTEREST RATE ON BORROWINGS	Without Bankruptcy and Agency Costs	With Bankruptcy and Agency Costs
0	—	10 %	10 %
.10	8 %	$10\frac{1}{2}$	$10\frac{1}{2}$
.20	8	11	$11\frac{1}{4}$
.30	$8\frac{1}{2}$	$11\frac{1}{2}$	12
.40	9	$12\frac{1}{4}$	13
.50	10	$13\frac{1}{4}$	$14\frac{1}{2}$
.60	11	$14\frac{1}{2}$	$16\frac{1}{4}$
.70	$12\frac{1}{2}$	16	$18\frac{1}{2}$
.80	15	18	21

a. At a tax rate of 50 percent (federal and state), what is the weighted average cost of capital of the company at various leverage ratios in the absence of bankruptcy and agency costs? What is the optimal capital structure?

b. With bankruptcy and agency costs, what is the optimal capital structure?

8. Mohave Sand and Transit Company currently has an overall value of $8 million. The debt has a face value of $4 million and is represented by discount bonds that mature in 3 years. The standard deviation of the continuously compounded rate of return on overall value is 20 percent. The short-term risk-free rate is currently 6 percent.

a. Treating the stock as an option and using the Black-Scholes option model, Eq. (5-2) in Chapter 5, determine the value of the equity and the value of debt.

b. If the company were to increase the riskiness of its business so that the standard deviation became 50 percent, what would happen to the value of the stock and to the value of the debt?

c. Does one party gain at the expense of the other? If this is the case, how can the other party protect itself?

9. Suppose in Problem 8 that Mohave Sand and Transit Company decided to issue $2 million in additional debt (face value) with a 3-year maturity and repurchase $2 million in stock.

a. What is the effect on the value of the stock and on the value of the debt if the standard deviation is 50 percent?

b. Does the value of the debt increase proportionally with the increase in its face value? Why or why not?

10. Archer-Deloitte Company wishes to finance a $15 million expansion program and is trying to decide between debt and equity. Management believes the mar-

ket does not appreciate the company's profit potential and that the stock is undervalued. What security do you suppose it will use in financing, and what will be the market's reaction? What if management felt the stock were overvalued?

SOLUTIONS TO
SELF-CORRECTION PROBLEMS

1. a. (1)

Net operating income	$ 360,000
Overall capitalization rate	.18
Total value of firm	$2,000,000
Market value of debt (50%)	1,000,000
Market value of stock (50%)	1,000,000
Net operating income	$ 360,000
Interest on debt (13%)	130,000
Earnings to common	$ 230,000

2% of $230,000 = $4,600

(2) Implied required equity return = $230,000/$1,000,000 = 23%

b. (1)

Total value of firm	$2,000,000
Market value of debt (20%)	400,000
Market value of equity (80%)	1,600,000
Net operating income	$ 360,000
Interest on debt (13%)	52,000
Earnings to common	$ 308,000

Implied required equity return = $308,000/$1,600,000 = 19.25%

(2) It is lower because Zoom uses less debt in its capital structure. As the equity capitalization is a linear function of the debt-to-equity ratio when we use the net operating income approach, the decline in required equity return offsets exactly the disadvantage of not employing so much in the way of "cheaper" debt funds.

2. a. Value if unlevered (000 omitted):

EBIT	$3,000	
Profit before taxes	3,000	
Taxes	1,200	
Profit after taxes	$1,800	
÷ required equity return	.18	
Value if unlevered	$10,000	($10 million)

Value with $4 million in debt:

$$\text{Value} = \text{Value if unlevered} + \text{Value of tax shield}$$

$$\text{Value} = \$10,000 + .40(\$4,000) = \$11,600$$

Value with $7 million in debt:

$$\text{Value} = \$10,000 + .40(\$7,000) = \$12,800$$

Due to the tax subsidy, the firm is able to increase its value in a linear manner with more debt.

b. Value if unlevered (000 omitted): the same as before, namely, $10,000 (10 million). Value with $4 million in debt:

$$\text{Value} = \$10,000 + \left[1 - \frac{(1 - .40)(1 - .25)}{1 - .30} \right] \$4,000$$

$$= \$11,429$$

Value with $7 million in debt:

$$\text{Value} = \$10,000 + \left[1 - \frac{(1 - .40)(1 - .25)}{1 - .30} \right] \$7,000$$

$$= \$12,500$$

The presence of personal taxes reduces the tax advantage associated with corporate debt. As long as the personal tax on stock income is less than that on debt income, however, the net tax advantage to debt is positive. As a result, the value of the firm rises with more debt, but not as rapidly as if there were no personal taxes or if the personal tax rate on stock and debt income were the same.

3. (in millions)

(1) LEVEL OF DEBT	(2) FIRM VALUE UNLEVERED	(3) PV OF TAX SHIELD (1) × 0.20	(4) PV OF BANKRUPTCY, AGENCY, AND INCREASED INTEREST COSTS	VALUE OF FIRM (2) + (3) − (4)
0	$15	0	0	$15.0
$ 5	15	$1	0	16.0
10	15	2	$ .6	16.4
15	15	3	1.2	16.8
20	15	4	2.0	17.0
25	15	5	3.2	16.8
30	15	6	5.0	16.0

The market value of the firm is maximized with $20 million in debt.

SELECTED REFERENCES

BAXTER, NEVINS D., "Leverage, Risk of Ruin, and the Cost of Capital," *Journal of Finance*, 22 (September 1967), 395–404.

BERKOVITCH, ELAZAR, and E. HAN KIM, "Financial Contracting and Leverage Induced Over- and Under-Investment Incentives," *Journal of Finance*, 45 (July 1990), 765–94.

BLACK, FISCHER, and JOHN C. COX, "Valuing Corporate Securities: Some Effects on Bond Indenture Provisions," *Journal of Finance*, 31 (May 1976), 351–68.

BLACK, FISCHER, and MYRON SCHOLES, "The Pricing of Options and Corporate Liabilities," *Journal of Political Economy*, 81 (May–June 1973), 637–54.

BRENNAN, M. J., "Taxes, Market Valuation and Corporate Financial Policy," *National Tax Journal*, 23 (December 1970), 417–27.

CORNETT, MARCIA MILLON, and NICKOLAOS G. TRAVLOS, "Information Effects Associated with Debt-for-Equity and Equity-for-Debt Exchange Offers," *Journal of Finance*, 44 (June 1989), 451–68.

DE ANGELO, HARRY, and RONALD W. MASULIS, "Optimal Capital Structure under Corporate and Personal Taxation," *Journal of Financial Economics*, 8 (March 1980), 3–29.

DIAMOND, DOUGLAS W., "Reputation Acquisition in Debt Markets," *Journal of Political Economy*, 97, No. 4 (1989), 828–62.

GIAMMARINO, RONALD M., "The Resolution of Financial Distress," *Review of Financial Studies*, 2, No. 1 (1989), 25–49.

GLENN, DAVID W., "Super Premium Security Prices and Optimal Corporate Financing Decisions." *Journal of Finance*, 31 (May 1976), 507–24.

HAMADA, ROBERT S., "Portfolio Analysis, Market Equilibrium, and Corporation Finance," *Journal of Finance*, 24 (March 1969), 13–31.

HARRIS, MILTON, and ARTUR RAVIV, "Capital Structure and the Informational Role of Debt," *Journal of Finance*, 45 (June 1990), 321–49.

HAUGEN, ROBERT A., and LEMMA W. SENBET, "The Irrelevance of Bankruptcy Costs to the Theory of Optimal Capital Structure," *Journal of Finance*, 33 (June 1978), 383–94.

JENSEN, MICHAEL C., and WILLIAM E. MECKLING, "Theory of the Firm: Managerial Behavior, Agency Costs and Ownership Structure," *Journal of Financial Economics*, 3 (October 1976), 305–60.

KIM, E. HAN, "A Mean-Variance Theory of Optimal Structure and Corporate Debt Capacity," *Journal of Finance*, 33 (March 1978), 45–64.

————, JOHN J. McCONNELL, and IRWIN SILBERMAN, "Capital Structure Rearrangements and Me-First Rules in an Efficient Capital Market," *Journal of Finance*, 32 (June 1977), 789–810.

KRAUS, ALAN, and ROBERT H. LITZENBERGER, "A State-Preference Model of Optimal Financial Leverage," *Journal of Finance*, 28 (September 1973), 911–22.

LITZENBERGER, ROBERT H., "Some Observations on Capital Structure and the Impact of Recent Recapitalizations on Share Prices," *Journal of Financial and Quantitative Analysis*, 21 (March 1986), 47–58.

————, and JAMES C. VAN HORNE, "Elimination of the Double Taxation of Dividends and Corporate Financial Policy," *Journal of Finance*, 33 (June 1978), 737–49.

MACKIE-MASON, JEFFREY K., "Do Taxes Affect Corporate Financing Decisions?" working paper, National Bureau of Economic Research (June 1988).

————, "Do Firms Care Who Provides Their Financing?" working paper, National Bureau of Economic Research (July 1989).

MILES, JAMES A., and JOHN R. EZZELL, "Reformulating Tax Shield Valuation: A Note," *Journal of Finance*, 40 (December 1985), 1485–92.

MILLER, MERTON H., "Debt and Taxes," *Journal of Finance*, 32 (May 1977), 261–78.

————, "The Modigliani-Miller Propositions after Thirty Years," *Journal of Economic Perspectives*, 2 (Fall 1988), 99–120.

————, and MYRON S. SCHOLES, "Dividends and Taxes," *Journal of Financial Economics*, 6 (December 1978), 333–64.

MODIGLIANI, FRANCO, and M. H. MILLER, "The Cost of Capital, Corporation Finance and the Theory of Investment," *American Economic Review*, 48 (June 1958), 261–97.

————, "The Cost of Capital, Corporation Finance and the Theory of Investment: Reply," *American Economic Review*, 48 (September 1958), 665–69; "Taxes and the Cost of Capital: A Correction," ibid., 53 (June 1963), 433–43; "Reply," ibid., 55 (June 1965), 524–27; "Reply to Heins and Sprenkle," ibid., 59 (September 1969), 592–95.

MYERS, STEWART C., "Determinants of Corporate Borrowing," *Journal of Financial Economics*, 5 (November 1977), 147–75.

————, "Capital Structure Puzzle," *Journal of Finance*, 39 (July 1984), 575–92.

————, and NICHOLAS S. MAJLUF, "Corporate Financing and Investment Decisions When Firms Have Information That Investors Do Not Have," *Journal of Financial Economics*, 13 (June 1984), 187–222.

Ross, Stephen A., "The Determination of Financial Structure: The Incentive-Signalling Approach," *Bell Journal of Economics*, 8 (Spring 1977), 23–40.

Rubinstein, Mark E., "A Mean-Variance Synthesis of Corporate Financial Theory," *Journal of Finance*, 28 (March 1973), 167–82.

Smith, Clifford W., Jr., "Investment Banking and the Capital Acquisition Process," *Journal of Financial Economics*, 15 (January/February 1986), 3–29.

———, and Jerold B. Warner, "On Financial Contracting: An Analysis of Bond Covenants," *Journal of Financial Economics*, 7 (June 1979), 117–61.

Titman, Sheridan, "The Effect of Capital Structure on a Firm's Liquidation Decision," *Journal of Financial Economics*, 13 (March 1984), 137–51.

———, and Roberto Wessels, "The Determinants of Capital Structure Choice," *Journal of Finance*, 43 (March 1988), 1–19.

Van Horne, James C., "Optimal Initiation of Bankruptcy Proceedings by Debt Holders," *Journal of Finance*, 31 (June 1976), 897–910.

11

MAKING CAPITAL STRUCTURE DECISIONS

Now let us put ourselves in the role of financial manager seeking an appropriate capital structure for our firm. We may use various methods of analysis—none completely satisfactory in itself, but taken collectively, they give us enough information to make a rational decision. Like all financial managers, we shall not be able to identify the precise percentage of debt that will maximize share price, but we must try to determine an approximate proportion of debt to employ for that objective. In the last part of the chapter, we explore briefly the questions of timing and flexibility of a single security issue.

EBIT-EPS ANALYSIS

One widely used means of examining the effect of leverage is to analyze the relationship between earnings before interest and taxes (EBIT) and earnings per share (EPS). Essentially, the method involves the comparison of alternative methods of financing under various assumptions as to EBIT.

CALCULATION OF EARNINGS PER SHARE

To illustrate an EBIT-EPS analysis of leverage, suppose Cherokee Tire Company, with long-term capitalization of $10 million consisting entirely of common stock, wishes to raise another $5 million for expansion through one of three possible financing plans. The company may finance with (1) all common stock, (2) all debt at 12 percent interest, or (3) all preferred stock with an 11 percent dividend. Present annual earnings before interest and taxes are $2 million, the income tax rate is 40 percent, and 200,000 shares of stock are now outstanding. Common stock can be sold at $50 per share under financing option 1, which translates into 100,000 additional shares of stock.

To determine the EBIT break-even, or indifference, points between the various financing alternatives, we begin by calculating earnings per share for some hypothetical level of EBIT. Suppose we wished to know what earnings per share would be under the three financing plans if EBIT were $2.4 million. The calculations are shown in Table 11-1. We note that interest on debt is deducted before taxes, while preferred stock dividends are deducted after taxes. As a result, earnings available to common stockholders are higher under the

TABLE 11-1
Calculations of earnings per share under three financing alternatives

	COMMON	DEBT	PREFERRED
Earnings before interest and taxes (hypothetical)	$2,400,000	$2,400,000	$2,400,000
Interest	—	600,000	—
Earnings before taxes	$2,400,000	$1,800,000	$2,400,000
Income taxes	960,000	720,000	960,000
Earnings after taxes	$1,440,000	$1,080,000	$1,440,000
Preferred stock dividend	—	—	550,000
Earnings available to common stockholders	$1,440,000	$1,080,000	$ 890,000
Number of shares	300,000	200,000	200.000
Earnings per share	$4.80	$5.40	$4.45

debt alternative than they are under the preferred stock alternative, despite the fact that the interest rate on debt is higher than the preferred stock dividend rate.

BREAK-EVEN, OR INDIFFERENCE, ANALYSIS

Given the information in Table 11-1, we are able to construct a break-even, or indifference, chart. On the horizontal axis we plot earnings before interest and taxes and on the vertical axis, earnings per share. For each financing alternative, we must draw a straight line to reflect EPS for all possible levels of EBIT. To do so, we need two datum points for each alternative. The first is the EPS calculated for some hypothetical level of EBIT. For $2.4 million in EBIT, we see in Table 11-1 that earnings per share are $4.80, $5.40, and $4.45 for the common, debt, and preferred stock financing alternatives. We simply plot these earnings per share at the $2.4 million mark in EBIT. Technically it does not matter which hypothetical level of EBIT we choose for calculating EPS. On good graph paper, one level is as good as the next.

The second datum point is simply the EBIT necessary to cover all fixed financial costs for a particular financing plan, and it is plotted on the horizontal axis. For the debt alternative, we must have EBIT of $600,000 to cover interest charges; so $600,000 becomes the horizontal axis intercept. For the preferred stock alternative, we must divide total annual dividends by one minus the tax rate in order to obtain the EBIT necessary to cover these dividends. Thus, we need $916,667 in EBIT to cover $550,000 in preferred stock dividends, assuming a 40 percent tax rate. Again, preferred dividends are deducted after taxes, so it takes more in before-tax earnings to cover them than it does to cover interest. Given the horizontal axis intercepts and earnings per share for some hypothetical level of EBIT, we draw a straight line through the two sets of points. The break-even, or indifference, chart for Cherokee Tire Company is shown in Fig. 11-1.

We see from the figure that the earnings per share indifference point between the debt and common stock financing alternatives is $1.8 million in EBIT. If EBIT is below that point, the common stock alternative will provide

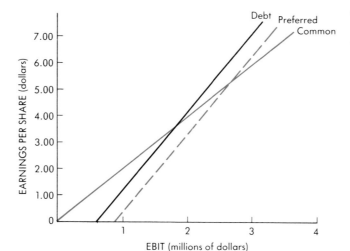

FIGURE 11-1
EBIT-EPS break-even, or
indifference, chart for
three financing
alternatives

higher earnings per share; above that point the debt alternative is best. The indifference point between the preferred stock and the common stock alternatives is $2.75 million in EBIT. Above that point, the preferred stock alternative is favored with respect to earnings per share; below it, the common stock alternative is best. Note that there is no indifference point between the debt and preferred stock alternatives. The debt alternative dominates for all levels of EBIT and by a constant amount of earnings per share; $0.95.

Indifference Point Mathematically. The indifference point between two methods of financing can be determined mathematically by

$$\frac{(EBIT^* - C_1)(1 - t)}{S_1} = \frac{(EBIT^* - C_2)(1 - t)}{S_2} \tag{11-1}$$

where $EBIT^*$ = the EBIT indifference point between the two methods of financing for which we solve

C_1, C_2 = annual interest expenses or preferred stock dividends on a before-tax basis for financing methods 1 and 2

t = corporate tax rate

S_1, S_2 = number of shares of common stock to be outstanding after financing for methods 1 and 2

Suppose we wished to determine the indifference point between the common stock and the debt-financing alternatives in our example. We would have

$$\frac{(EBIT^* - 0)(.6)}{300,000} = \frac{(EBIT^* - 600,000)(.6)}{200,000} \tag{11-2}$$

Rearranging, we obtain

$$.6(EBIT^*)(200,000) = .6(EBIT^*)(300,000) - .6(600,000)(300,000)$$

$$60,000 \; EBIT^* = 108,000,000,000$$

$$EBIT^* = \$1,800,000$$

The indifference point in EBIT, where earnings per share for the two methods of financing are the same, is $1.8 million. This amount can be verified graphically in Fig. 11-1. Thus, indifference points for financial leverage can be determined either graphically or mathematically.

USE OF EBIT-EPS INFORMATION

Constructing an EBIT-EPS chart shows the financial manager how alternative methods of financing have different impacts on earnings per share. We note that as long as the firm is able to earn more than 12 percent before taxes on its investment, debt financing will show an EPS advantage. We know from our earlier discussion, however, that the impact on expected return is only one side of the coin. The other side is the effect that financial leverage has on risk. An EBIT-EPS chart does not permit a precise analysis of risk. Nonetheless, certain generalizations are possible. For one thing, the financial manager should compare the indifference point between alternatives, like debt versus common stock financing, with the most likely level of EBIT. The higher the expected level of EBIT, assuming that it exceeds the indifference point, the stronger the case that can be made for debt financing, all other things the same.

In addition, the financial manager should assess the likelihood of future EBITs actually falling below the indifference point. If the probability is negligible, the use of the debt alternative would be supported. On the other hand, if EBIT is now only slightly above the indifference point and the probability of EBIT's falling below this point is high, we may conclude that the debt alternative is too risky. In summary, the greater the level of EBIT and the lower the probability of downside fluctuation, the stronger the case that can be made for the use of debt. To facilitate the evaluation of downside fluctuations, you may wish to superimpose the probability distribution of possible EBIT on an indifference chart, like the one shown in Fig. 11-1.

Financial leverage magnifies the underlying business risk of the firm when it comes to the variability of earnings per share. EBIT-EPS break-even analysis gives us insight into the return-risk trade off that governs valuation.[1] However, no one method of analysis of leverage is satisfactory by itself. When several methods of analysis are undertaken simultaneously, generalizations are possible.

CASH-FLOW ABILITY
TO SERVICE DEBT

When considering the appropriate capital structure, we should analyze also the cash-flow ability of the firm to service fixed charges. The greater the dollar amount of senior securities the firm issues and the shorter their maturity, the greater the fixed charges of the firm. These charges include principal and interest payments on debt, lease payments, and preferred stock dividends. Be-

---

[1] For an extension of break-even analysis that brings in valuation concepts, see Haim Levy and Robert Brooks, "Financial Break-Even Analysis and the Value of the Firm," *Financial Management*, 15 (Autumn 1986), 22–26.

fore assuming additional fixed charges, the firm should analyze its expected future cash flows, for fixed charges must be met with cash. The inability to meet these charges, with the exception of preferred stock dividends, may result in financial insolvency. The greater and more stable the expected future cash flows of the firm, the greater the debt capacity of the company.

COVERAGE RATIOS

Among the ways we can gain knowledge about the debt capacity of a firm is through the use of coverage ratios. In the computation of these ratios, one typically uses earnings before interest and taxes as a rough measure of the cash flow available to cover debt-servicing obligations. Perhaps the most widely used coverage ratio is times interest earned, which is simply

$$\text{Times interest earned} = \frac{\text{EBIT}}{\text{Interest on debt}} \qquad (11\text{-}3)$$

Suppose the most recent annual earnings before interest and taxes for a company were $6 million, and interest payments on all debt obligations were $1.5 million. Therefore, times interest earned would be four times. This tells us that EBIT can drop by as much as 75 percent and the firm still will be able to cover its interest payments out of earnings.

A coverage ratio of only one indicates that earnings are *just* sufficient to satisfy the interest burden. Although generalizations about what is an appropriate interest coverage ratio are difficult, one usually is concerned when the ratio gets much below 3 : 1. Circumstances differ, however. In a highly stable industry, a relatively low times interest earned ratio may be appropriate, whereas it is not appropriate in a highly cyclical industry.

Debt Service Coverage. Note that the times interest earned ratio tells us nothing about the ability of the firm to meet principal payments on its debt. The inability to meet a principal payment constitutes the same legal default as failure to meet an interest payment. Therefore, it is useful to compute the coverage ratio for the full debt-service burden. This ratio is

$$\text{Debt-service coverage} = \frac{\text{EBIT}}{\text{Interest} + \dfrac{\text{Principal payments}}{1 - \text{Tax rate}}} \qquad (11\text{-}4)$$

Here principal payments are adjusted upward for the tax effect. The reason is that EBIT represents earnings before taxes. Because principal payments are not deductible for tax purposes, they must be paid out of after-tax earnings. Therefore, we must adjust principal payments so that they are consistent with EBIT. If principal payments in our previous example were $1 million per annum and the tax rate were 40 percent, the debt-service coverage ratio would be

$$\text{Debt-service coverage} = \frac{\$4 \text{ million}}{\$1.5 \text{ million} + \dfrac{\$1 \text{ million}}{1 - .4}} = 1.26$$

A coverage ratio of 1.26 means that EBIT can fall by only 21 percent before earnings coverage is insufficient to service the debt.[2] Obviously the closer the ratio is to 1.0, the worse things are, all other things the same. Even with a coverage ratio of less than one, a company may still meet its obligations if it can renew some of its debt when it comes due.

The financial risk associated with leverage should be analyzed on the basis of the firm's ability to service total fixed charges. While lease financing is not debt per se, its impact on cash flows is exactly the same as the payment of interest and principal on a debt obligation. (See Chapter 19 for an analysis of lease financing.) Annual lease payments, therefore, should be added to the numerator and denominator of Eq. (11-4) to reflect properly the total cash-flow burden associated with financing.

As with the times interest earned ratio, there are no exact rules of thumb for what constitutes a good or bad debt-service ratio. It varies according to the business risk of the firm. This is illustrated in Fig. 11-2, which shows the probability distributions of EBIT for two hypothetical companies. The expected value of EBIT is the same for both companies, as is the debt-service burden as described by the denominator in Eq. (11-4). Therefore, the debt-service coverage ratios also are the same, $100/$60 = 1.67. Company A, however, has much more business risk. The probability that EBIT will fall below the debt-service burden is depicted by the shaded areas in the figure. We see that this probability is much greater for company A than it is for company B. While a debt-service coverage ratio of 1.67 may be appropriate for company B, it may not be appropriate for company A. Simply put, a company with stable cash flows is able to take on relatively more fixed charges. This explains why electric utility companies have low coverage ratios when compared with manufacturing companies.

As we discuss in Chapter 27, on financial ratios, two comparisons should be undertaken with a coverage ratio. First, it should be compared with past and expected future ratios of the same company. Called trend analysis, the comparison determines if there has been an improvement or a deterioration in coverage over time. The second comparison is with similar companies, perhaps in the same industry. The idea here is to try to isolate business risk as nearly as possible by comparing like companies. Sources of data and types of analysis possible are described in Chapter 28, so we do not dwell on them here.

[2] The percentage is determined by $1 - (1/1.26) = .21$.

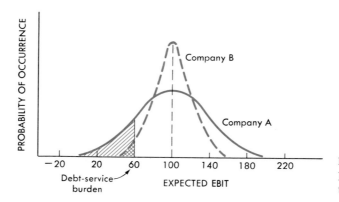

FIGURE 11-2

Possible EBIT in relation to debt-service burden

Ultimately, we want to make generalizations about the appropriate amount of debt (and leases) for a firm to have in its financing mix. It is clear that the ability of a going-concern firm to service debt over the long run is tied to earnings. Therefore, coverage ratios are an important tool of analysis. Like all ratios, they are subject to certain limitations and, consequently, cannot be used as a sole means for determining a firm's financing. The fact that EBIT falls below the debt-service burden does not spell immediate doom for the company. Often alternative sources of funds, including renewal of the loan, are available, and these sources must be considered.

Earnings before Interest, Taxes, and Depreciation. Instead of focusing on EBIT in the coverage ratio, some analysts add back depreciation. EBITD is earnings before interest, taxes, and depreciation, and it portrays the total operating cash flow of a company. To the extent that all such cash flow can be dedicated to debt service, EBITD is appropriate to use in the numerator of the coverage ratio. However, certain capital expenditures may be necessary to keep the business operating. To the extent that these expenditures approximate depreciation, EBITD is not a good measure of the cash available for debt service. Under these circumstances, it is better to use EBIT in the numerator of the coverage ratio.

PROBABILITY OF CASH INSOLVENCY

The vital question for the firm is not so much whether a coverage ratio will fall below one, but what the chances of insolvency are. The answer depends on whether all sources of payment—EBITD, cash, a new financing arrangement, or the sale of assets—are collectively deficient. A coverage ratio tells only part of the story. To address the broader question of cash insolvency, we must obtain information on the possible deviation of actual cash flows from those expected. As we discuss in Chapter 28, cash budgets can be prepared for a range of possible outcomes, with a probability attached to each. This information is extremely valuable to the financial manager in evaluating the ability of the firm to meet fixed obligations. Not only expected earnings are taken into account in determining this ability, but other factors as well: the purchase or sale of assets, the liquidity of the firm, dividends, seasonal patterns, and any other factors impacting on cash flows. Given the probabilities of particular cash-flow sequences, the financial manager is able to determine the amount of fixed charges and debt the company can undertake while still remaining within the insolvency limits tolerable to management.

Management may feel that a 5 percent probability of being out of cash is the maximum it can tolerate, and that this probability corresponds to a cash budget prepared under pessimistic assumptions. In this case, debt might be undertaken up to the point where the cash balance under the pessimistic cash budget is just sufficient to cover the fixed charges associated with the debt. In other words, debt would be increased to the point at which the additional cash drain would cause the probability of cash insolvency to equal the risk tolerance specified by management. It is not necessary that debt be increased to this point, of course. Note that the method of analysis simply provides a means for assessing the effect of increases in debt on the risk of cash insolvency. On the basis of this information, management would determine the most appropriate level of debt.

Donaldson has proposed a similar type of analysis.[3] He suggests that the ultimate concern of a company is whether cash balances during some future period will be involuntarily reduced below zero. Therefore, he advocates examining the cash flows of the company under the most adverse circumstances; that is, in his definition, under recession conditions. These conditions may or may not be the most adverse; however, in keeping with the spirit of his proposal, the firm should evaluate its cash flows under adverse circumstances. Donaldson defines the net cash balance in a recession as

$$CB_r = CB_0 + NCF_r \qquad (11\text{-}5)$$

where CB_0 = cash balance at start of recession
NCF_r = net cash flows during recession

Donaldson then calculates a probability distribution of expected net cash flows and analyzes the cash-flow behavior of a firm during a recession.[4] Combining the beginning cash balances, CB_0, with the probability distribution of recession cash flows, NCF_r, he prepares a probability distribution of cash balances in the recession—CB_r.

To ascertain its debt capacity, a firm first would calculate the fixed charges associated with additional increments of debt. For each addition, the firm then would determine the probability of being out of cash, based on the probability distribution of cash balances during the recession. As before, management could set tolerance limits on the probability of being out of cash. Suppose the firm were considering issuing $20 million in additional debt, and the annual fixed charges were $3 million. By subtracting $3 million from the expected cash balances shown for the probability distribution of CB_r, we obtain the probability of distribution of CB_r with the addition of $20 million in debt. If the probability of being out of cash with this increment of debt is negligible, Donaldson would contend that the company has unused debt capacity. Therefore, it would be possible to increase the amount of debt until the probability of being out of cash equaled the risk tolerance of management.

Inventory of Resources. Donaldson extends his analysis to calculate the probability of *cash inadequacy.* Our discussion before was in terms of *cash insolvency,* which is defined as lack of cash after all nonessential expenditures have been cut. Cash inadequacy is said to occur if the firm is out of cash after making certain desired expenditures such as dividends, R&D expenditures, and capital expenditures. Thus, cash insolvency is the extreme form of cash inadequacy. In all cases, the firm should take stock of the resources it has at its disposal to meet an unexpected cash drain. Typically, a number of alternatives are available, ranging from the use of surplus cash to the sale of fixed assets at distress prices.

The firm's resources can be categorized into uncommitted reserves, reduction of planned outflows, and liquidation of assets. These categories and their various subsets are shown in Table 11-2. The first category of resource

---

[3] Gordon Donaldson, *Corporate Debt Capacity* (Boston: Division of Research, Harvard Business School, 1961). See also Donaldson, "Strategy for Financial Emergencies," *Harvard Business Review, 47* (November–December 1969), 67–79.

[4] The determinants of net cash flows with which he works are sales collections, other cash receipts, payroll expenditures, raw materials expenditures, and nondiscretionary cash expenditures. By analyzing each of these determinants, he determines the range and probability of recession net cash flows.

TABLE 11-2
Inventory of resources to meet possible cash drains

RESOURCES	AVAILABLE FOR USE WITHIN		
	One Quarter	One Year	Three Years
Uncommitted reserves:			
Instant reserves			
Surplus cash	$		
Unused line of credit	$		
Negotiable reserves			
Additional bank loans			
Unsecured	$		
Secured	$		
Additional long-term debt		$	
Issue of new equity		$	
Reduction of planned outflows:			
Volume-related			
Change in production schedule	$		
Scale-related			
Marketing program		$	
R&D budget		$	
Administrative overhead		$	
Capital expenditures		$	
Value-related			
Dividend payments		$	
Liquidation of assets:			
Shutdown		$	
Sale of unit			$
	$	→$	
		$	→$
Total resources			$

represents contingency reserves held by the firm as insurance against adverse outcomes—not to be used if everything goes according to plan, but there in case things do not go that way. For the most part, these reserves can be tapped in a short period of time. The second category represents operating cuts and cuts in dividends. Cash is realized from these cuts only over time. Usually, changes in operations are at the expense of long-term profitability. In other words, future profitability is sacrificed in order to release cash to meet current obligations. The final category is the most draconian of all. By liquidating assets, management cuts into the very bone of the company.

Once an inventory of resources has been compiled, the adequacy of these resources should be judged in relation to potential cash drains. Embodied in this analysis should be the fixed charges associated with various levels of debt. Thus, the liquidity of the firm should be analyzed in relation to its debt capacity.

CASH-FLOW ANALYSIS
AND DEBT-TO-EQUITY RATIOS

The analysis of the cash-flow ability of the firm to service fixed charges is perhaps the best way to analyze financial risk, but there is some question as to whether the external market analyzes a company in this manner. Sophisticated lenders and institutional investors certainly analyze the amount of fixed charges and evaluate financial risk in keeping with the ability of the firm to service these charges, but individual investors may judge financial risk more by the book value proportions of debt to equity.

There may or may not be a reasonable correspondence between the ratio of debt to equity and the amount of fixed charges relative to the firm's cash-flow ability to service these charges. Some firms may have relatively high ratios of debt to equity but substantial cash-flow ability to service debt. Consequently, the analysis of debt-to-equity ratios alone can be deceiving, and an analysis of the magnitude and stability of cash flows relative to fixed charges is extremely important in determining the appropriate capital structure for the firm. To the extent that creditors and investors analyze a firm's cash-flow ability to service debt, and management's risk preferences correspond to those of investors, capital structure decisions made on this basis tend to maximize share price.

OTHER METHODS OF ANALYSIS

COMPARISON OF CAPITAL STRUCTURE RATIOS

Another method of analyzing the appropriate capital structure for a company is to evaluate the capital structure of other companies having similar business risk. Companies used in this comparison may be those in the same industry. If the firm is contemplating a capital structure significantly out of line with that of similar companies, it is conspicuous in the marketplace. This is not to say that the firm is wrong. Other companies in the industry may be too conservative in their use of debt. The optimal capital structure for all companies in the industry might call for a higher proportion of debt to equity than the industry average. As a result, the firm may well be able to justify more debt than the industry average. Because investment analysts and creditors tend to evaluate companies by industry, the firm should be prepared to justify its position if its capital structure is noticeably out of line in either direction. (See Chapter 27 for a discussion of the comparison of financial ratios with industry averages.)

SURVEY OF INVESTMENT ANALYSTS AND LENDERS

The firm may profit by talking with investment analysts, institutional investors, and investment houses to obtain their views on the appropriate amount of leverage. These analysts examine many companies and are in the business of recommending stocks. They therefore have an influence on the market, and their judgments with respect to how the market evaluates leverage may be worthwhile. Similarly, a firm may wish to interview lenders to see how much debt it can undertake before the cost of borrowing is likely to rise. Finally, the management of a company may develop a "feel" for what has happend to the market price of the stock when they have issued debt. As suggested in Chapter 9, to evaluate the impact of a financial decision on share price, the financial manager must think the way investors think.

SECURITY RATINGS

Whenever a company sells a debt or preferred stock issue to public investors, as opposed to private lenders such as banks, it must have the issue rated by one or more rating services. The principal rating agencies are Moody's Investors Service and Standard & Poor's. The issuer of a new corporate security contracts with the agency to evaluate and rate the issue as to quality as well as to update the rating throughout the life of the instrument. For this service, the issuer pays a fee. In addition, the rating agency charges subscribers to its rating publications. While the assignment of a rating for a new issue is current, changes in ratings of existing securities tend to lag the events that prompt the change.

Both agencies use much the same letter grading. The ratings used by Moody's and Standard & Poor's, as well as brief descriptions, are shown in Table 11-3. In their ratings, the agencies attempt to rank issues according to their probability of default. The first four grades are considered investment-quality issues, whereas other rated securities are considered speculative. The highest grade securities, whose risk of default is felt to be negligible, are rated triple A. For each rating category a modifier of 1, 2, or 3 is applied. For example, Aa-1 means that a security is in the higher end of the Aa rating category. Baa-3 indicates that a security is in the lower end of the Baa category. The ratings by the agencies are widely respected and are recognized by various government regulatory agencies as measures of default risk. In fact, many investors accept them without further investigation of the risk of default.

The rating agencies look at a number of things before assigning a grade: trends in ratios of liquidity, debt, profitability, and coverage; the firm's business risk, both historically and expected; present and likely future capital requirements; specific features associated with the instrument being issued; the relative proportion of debt; and, perhaps most important, the cash-flow ability

TABLE 11-3
Ratings by investment agencies

MOODY'S INVESTORS SERVICE		STANDARD & POOR'S	
Aaa	Best quality	AAA	Highest grade
Aa	High quality	AA	High grade
A	Upper medium grade	A	Higher medium grade
Baa	Medium grade	BBB	Medium grade
Ba	Possess speculative elements	BB	Speculative
B	Generally lack characteristics of desirable investment	B	Very speculative
Caa	Poor standing; may be in default	CCC-CC	Outright speculation
Ca	Highly speculative; often in default	C	Reserved for income bonds on which no interest is being paid
C	Lowest grade	DDD-D	In default, with rating indicating relative salvage value

Note: The top four categories indicate "investment grade quality" securities; the categories below the dashed line are reserved for securities below investment grade.

to service principal and interest payments. If a public security offering is contemplated, the financial manager must be mindful of ratings when determining how much leverage is appropriate. If taking on additional debt lowers your firm's security ratings from an investment- to a speculative-grade category (junk bonds)—thus making the security ineligible for investment by many institutional investors—you will want to factor this into account before making a decision.[5] It may well be that the advantages of debt outweigh the lower security rating. However, a significant lowering of a security rating usually is a manifestation of fundamental problems that may raise the implicit as well as the explicit cost of leverage. Therefore, you will want to consider the likely effect of a change in capital structure on your company's security rating.

COMBINATION OF METHODS

We have discovered a number of methods of analysis that can be brought to bear on the question: What is an appropriate degree of leverage for our company? These include EBIT-EPS analysis, cash-flow ability to service debt, the leverage ratio of our firm relative to others, survey of investment analysts and lenders, and an evaluation of the effect of a decision on our security rating. In addition to these factors, you will want to know the changing interest cost for various levels of debt. The maturity structure of the debt is important as well, but we take this up later in the book. We focus here only on the broad issue of the degree of leverage to employ. All the analyses should be guided by the conceptual framework presented in the previous chapter.

The implicit cost of leverage, that is, the effect on a stock's value in the marketplace, is not easy to determine. Nevertheless, by undertaking a variety of analyses, the financial manager should be able to determine, within some range, the appropriate capital structure. By necessity, the final decision has to be somewhat subjective, but it can be based upon the best information available. In this way, the firm is able to obtain the capital structure most appropriate for its situation—the one it hopes will maximize the market price of the stock, all other factors held constant.

TIMING AND FLEXIBILITY

Once a firm has determined an appropriate capital structure, it still has the problem of timing security issues. When external financing is required, a company often faces the question of how to time an issue appropriately and whether to use debt or common stock. Because financing is "lumpy," it is difficult for a firm to maintain strict proportions in its capital structure. Frequently, it must decide whether to finance now with a stock issue and later with a debt issue, or vice versa. Consequently, it is forced to evaluate the alternative methods of financing in light of general market conditions and expectations for the company itself.

If the future were certain, it would be an easy matter to determine today an optimal financing sequence for many years to come. The sequence would

---

[5] For a further discussion of security ratings and default risk, see James C. Van Horne, *Financial Market Rates and Flows*, 3d ed. (Englewood Cliffs, NJ: Prentice Hall, 1990), Chap. 8.

be timed to take advantage of known future changes in the stock market and in the market for fixed-income securities. Unfortunately, prices in financial markets, particularly in the equity market, are unstable. Instead of making decisions based on a sure thing, decisions must be based on management's best estimate of the future. In addition, there are the financial signaling and incentive issues taken up in the last chapter. Usually, the announcement of a debt issue has a favorable impact on share price, as we know from that discussion.

If a firm chooses this alternative, however, it may sacrifice a certain amount of flexibility. By *flexibility,* we simply mean that today's financing decision will keep open future financing options. Remember that a company cannot issue debt continually without building its equity base. It is neither desirable, given our discussion in the preceding chapter, nor possible, once default risk becomes too great. Therefore the equity base must be increased over time, and this is where flexibility becomes important. If a company undertakes a substantial debt issue and things take a turn for the worse, the firm may be forced to issue stock on unfavorable terms in the future. To preserve its flexibility in tapping the capital markets, it may be better for a firm to issue stock now so that it will have unused debt capacity for future needs. The preservation of unused debt capacity can be a consideration of consequence for the company whose funds requirements are sudden and unpredictable. It gives the company financial maneuverability by virtue of leaving the options open.

We must bear in mind that if the financial markets are efficient, all available information is reflected in the price of the security. Under these circumstances, the market price of the security is the market's best estimate of the value of that security. If management is no better than the average investor at forecasting future market prices, efforts by a company to time security offerings will be for naught. In other words, management will be wrong about as often as it is right. If timing is to be a thing of value, management's expectations must be more correct than those of the market. In Part 6, we examine specific methods of long-term financing, the timing of a specific security issue, and the flexibility afforded by the instrument.

SUMMARY

In choosing an appropriate capital structure, the financial manager should consider a number of factors. Considerable insight can be gained from an analysis of the cash-flow ability of the firm to service fixed charges associated with debt, preferred stock, and leasing. One way to determine this ability is through the analysis of coverage ratios. However, coverage ratios consider only the earnings of a company as a means to service debt. A more inclusive analysis involves the probability of cash insolvency and takes into account all resources available to service debt. Using this type of analysis, the financial manager is better able to estimate the debt capacity of the firm.

Another method for gaining insight into the question of the appropriate capital structure involves analyzing the relationship between earnings before interest and taxes and earnings per share for alternative methods of financing. When this analysis is expanded to consider the level of and likely fluctuations in EBIT, light is shed on the question of financial risk.

In addition, the financial manager can learn much from a comparison of capital structure ratios for similar companies, and through discussions with investment analysts, investment bankers, and other lenders. Security ratings on public issues of debt and preferred stock necessarily are of concern to the financial manager and are a part of any decision. Collectively, the methods of analysis taken up in this chapter should provide sufficient information on which to base a capital structure decision. Once an appropriate capital structure has been determined, the firm should finance investment proposals in roughly those proportions.

Finally, we examine the problem of timing a debt or equity issue. Where sequential financing is involved, the choice of debt or equity appreciably influences the future financial flexibility of the firm.

APPENDIX
Bankruptcy Costs

In both this chapter and the last, bankruptcy costs were seen to reduce the degree of leverage that might be considered optimal. The cost of bankruptcy can be thought of as being composed of two parts: (1) direct costs, represented by out-of-pocket fees that arise in the course of going through a bankruptcy; and (2) indirect costs, represented by the "shortfall" in value arising from delays and economic inefficiencies in operating a company when it is about to go bankrupt.

The first facet involves fees and other compensation to third parties: filing fees with the court, referee and trustee fees, attorney fees, appraiser fees, accountant fees, auctioneer and liquidator fees, reporting and transcribing fees, as well as others. These costs represent a direct cash drain from suppliers of capital. In Chapter 8, we saw that impending bankruptcy frightens suppliers, customers, and employees, with the result that operations usually become less efficient. This inefficiency also works to the detriment of suppliers of capital.

Unfortunately, the empirical evidence on bankruptcy costs is limited, owing in part to the difficulty involved in extracting information from the chaotic records available in the bankruptcy courts. Those studies that have been undertaken are rather far ranging in their estimates. For direct, out-of-pocket bankruptcy costs, the estimates range from 4 percent of value to over 20 percent, depending on the type of company analyzed and other sample characteristics.[6] Studies of indirect costs suggest that they are larger than direct costs. While the evidence is fragmentary, it seems clear that total bankruptcy costs are not trivial.

For a sample of bankrupt companies under reorganization, Julian R. Franks and Walter N. Torous find significant deviations from the rule of absolute priority.[7] As explained in Appendix A at the end of this book, absolute

---

[6] Jerold Warner, "Bankruptcy Costs: Some Evidence," *Journal of Finance*, 32 (May 1977), 337–47; James S. Ang, Jess H. Chua, and John J. McConnell, "The Administrative Costs of Corporate Bankruptcy: A Note," *Journal of Finance*, 37 (March 1982), 219–26; Michelle J. White, "Bankruptcy Costs and the New Bankruptcy Code," *Journal of Finance*, 38 (May 1983), 477–88; and Edward I. Altman, "A Further Empirical Investigaton of the Bankruptcy Cost Question," *Journal of Finance*, 39 (September 1984), 1067–89.

[7] Julian R. Franks and Walter N. Torous, "An Empirical Investigation of U.S. Firms in Reorganization," *Journal of Finance*, 44 (July 1989), 747–69.

priority calls for the claims of one class of claimants (say, the bondholders) to be settled in full before there is any distribution to a junior claimant (like the preferred stockholders). The authors suggest that stockholder-oriented management has bargaining power, because it controls the company during the reorganization proceedings. Sometimes creditors will give up part of their claim to expedite the process. Franks and Torous liken management's position to an option, which allows them to protract the reorganization proceedings and to incur costs, borne largely by creditors. Thus, there is a willing shifting of wealth away from creditors so that bankruptcy costs overall are reduced.

In summary, bankruptcy costs—both direct and indirect—are an impediment to capital flows and the efficient functioning of financial markets.

SELF-CORRECTION PROBLEMS

1. Dorsey Porridge Company presently has $3 million in debt outstanding bearing an interest rate of 12 percent. It wishes to finance a $4 million expansion program and is considering three alternatives: additional debt at 14 percent interest, preferred stock with a 12 percent dividend, and the sale of common stock at $16 per share. The company presently has 800,000 shares of common stock outstanding and is in a 40 percent tax bracket.

   a. If earnings before interest and taxes are presently $1.5 million, what would be earnings per share for the three alternatives, assuming no immediate increase in profitability?

   b. Develop a break-even, or indifference, chart for these alternatives. What are the approximate indifference points? To check one of these points, what is the indifference point mathematically between debt and common?

   c. Which alternative do you prefer? How much would EBIT need to increase before the next alternative would be best?

2. Torstein Torque and Gear Company has $7.4 million in long-term debt having the following schedule:

	AMOUNT (IN THOUSANDS)
15% serial bonds, payable $100,000 in principal annually	$2,400
13% first mortage bonds, payable $150,000 in principal annually	3,000
18% subordinated debentures, interest only until maturity in 10 years	2,000
	$7,400

Torstein's common stock has a book value of $8.3 million and a market value of $6.0 million. The corporate tax rate, federal and state, is 50 percent. Torstein is in a cyclical business: its expected EBIT is $2.0 million with a standard deviation of $1.5 million. The average debt-to-equity ratio of other companies in the industry is .47.

   a. Determine the times interest earned and the debt-service coverage of the company at the expected EBIT.

   b. What are the probabilities these two ratios will go below one-to-one?

   c. Does Torstein have too much debt?

3. Sowla Electronics currently has $2 million in cash and marketable securities, a $3 million bank line of credit of which $1.3 million is in use, pays a cash dividend on its stock of $1.2 million annually, plans capital expenditures of $4 million a year, and devotes $2 million a year to advertising and special promotions. In addition, it spends $2 million a year on research and development. The company's sales are highly correlated with swings in sales of integrated circuits. Currently, the firm is enjoying good times with annual after-tax profits and depreciation (cash flow) totaling $7 million. As it sells mainly to jobbers, finished goods inventories are minimal.

   a. If the integrated circuit cycle moves into a recession and cash flow drops by $5 million, what would you do? Do you have proper flexibility now for the unforeseen?

   b. What if a negative cash flow of $9 million per annum were experienced?

PROBLEMS

1. The Lemaster Company is a new firm that wishes to determine an appropriate capital structure. It can issue 16 percent debt or 15 percent preferred stock. Moreover, common can be sold at $20 per share. In all cases, total capitalization of the company will be $5 million, and it is expected to have a 30 percent tax rate. The possible capital structures are

PLAN	DEBT	PREFERRED	EQUITY
1	0%	0%	100%
2	30	0	70
3	50	0	50
4	50	20	30

   a. Construct an EBIT-EPS chart for the four plans.

   b. Determine the relevant indifference points.

   c. Using Eq. (11-1), verify the indifference points on your graph for the dominant plans.

   d. Which plan is best?

2. Gallatin Quarter Company makes saddles. During the preceding calendar year, it earned $200,000 after taxes. The company is in a 40 percent tax bracket, it had no debt outstanding at year end, and it has 100,000 shares of common stock outstanding. At the beginning of the current year, it finds that it needs to borrow $300,000 at an interest rate of 10 percent, in order to expand its operations.

   a. What are earnings per share before and after financing if EBIT stays the same?

   b. What are the absolute and percentage increases in earnings per share if EBIT increases by 50 percent?

3. Hi Grade Regulator Company currently has 100,000 shares of common stock outstanding with a market price of $60 per share. It also has $2 million in 6 percent bonds. The company is considering a $3 million expansion program that it can finance with (1) all common stock at $60 a share, (2) straight bonds at 8 percent interest, (3) preferred stock at 7 percent, or (4) half common stock at $60 per share and half 8 percent bonds.

   a. For a hypothetical EBIT level of $1 million after the expansion program, calculate the earnings per share for each of the alternative methods of financing. Assume a corporate tax rate of 50 percent.

b. Construct an EBIT-EPS chart. What are the indifference points between alternatives? What is your interpretation of them?

4. Hi Grade Regulator Company (see Problem 3) expects the EBIT level after the expansion program to be $1 million, with a two-thirds probability that it will be between $600,000 and $1,400,000.

    a. Which financing alternative do you prefer? Why?

    b. Suppose the expected EBIT level were $1.5 million and there were a two-thirds probability that it would be between $1.3 million and $1.7 million. Which financing alternative would you prefer? Why?

5. Fazio Pump Corporation presently has 1.1 million shares outstanding and $8 million in debt bearing an interest rate of 10 percent on average. It is considering a $5 million expansion program financed with either (1) common stock at $20 per share being realized, (2) debt at an interest rate of 11 percent, or (3) preferred stock with a 10 percent dividend rate. Earnings before interest and taxes (EBIT) after the new funds are raised are expected to be $6 million, and the company's tax rate is 35 percent.

    a. Determine likely earnings per share after financing for each of the three alternatives.

    b. What would happen if EBIT were $3 million? $4 million? $8 million?

    c. What would happen under the original conditions if the tax rate were 46 percent? if the interest rate on new debt were 8 percent and the preferred stock dividend rate were 7 percent? if the common could be sold for $40 per share?

6. The Power Corporation currently has 2 million shares outstanding at a price of $20 each and needs to raise an additional $5 million. These funds could be raised with stock or 10 percent debentures. Expected EBIT after the new funds are raised will be normally distributed with a mean of $4 million per year forever and a standard deviation of $2 million. Power Corporation has a 50 percent tax rate. What is the probability that the debt alternative is superior with respect to earnings per share?

7. Cornwell Real Estate Speculators, Inc., and the Northern California Electric Utility Company have the following EBITs and debt-servicing burdens:

	CORNWELL	NORTHERN CALIFORNIA
Expected EBIT	$5,000,000	$100,000,000
Annual interest	1,600,000	45,000,000
Annual principal payments on debt	2,000,000	35,000,000

The tax rate for Cornwell is 40 percent; for Northern California Electric Utility, 36 percent. Compute the times interest earned ratio and the debt-service coverage ratio for the two companies. With which company would you feel more comfortable if you were a lender? Why?

8. Gamma Tube Company plans to undertake a $7.5 million capital improvement program and is considering how much debt to use. It feels that it could obtain debt financing at the following interest rates (assume that this debt is perpetual):

Amounts	First $3 million	Next $2 million	Next $1.5 million	Next $1 million
Interest cost	10 percent	11 percent	12 percent	13 percent

The company has made projections of its net cash flows (exclusive of new financing) during a period of adversity such as a recession. In a recession, it expects a net cash flow of $3 million with a standard deviation of $2 million (as-

321

sume a normal distribution). Its beginning cash balance is $1 million. If the company is willing to tolerate only a 5 percent probability of running out of cash during a recession, what is the maximum proportion of the $7.5 million capital improvement program that can be financed with debt? (Ignore any tax considerations.)

SOLUTIONS TO SELF-CORRECTION PROBLEMS

1. a. (000 omitted):

	DEBT	PREFERRED STOCK	COMMON STOCK
EBIT	$1,500	$1,500	$1,500
Interest on existing debt	360	360	360
Interest on new debt	560	—	—
Profit before taxes	$ 580	$1,140	$1,140
Taxes	232	456	456
Profit after taxes	$ 348	$ 684	$ 684
Preferred stock dividend	—	480	—
Earnings available to common stockholders	$ 348	$ 204	$ 684
Number of shares	800	800	1,050
Earnings per share	$ .435	$ .255	$ .651

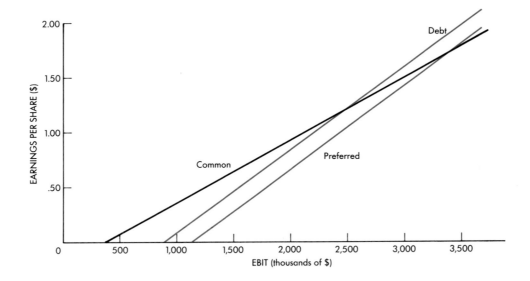

b. Approximate indifference points:
   Debt and common, $2.7 million in EBIT
   Preferred and common, $3.6 million in EBIT
   Debt dominates preferred by the same margin throughout. There is no indifference point.

Mathematically, the indifference point between debt and common (000 omitted) is

$$\frac{(EBIT^* - \$920)(1 - .4)}{800} = \frac{(EBIT^* - \$360)(1 - .4)}{1{,}050}$$

$$.6(EBIT^*)(1{,}050) - .6(\$920)(1{,}050) = .6(EBIT^*)(800) - .6(\$360)(800)$$

$$630(EBIT^*) - 480(EBIT^*) = \$579{,}600 - \$172{,}800$$

$$150(EBIT^*) = \$406{,}800$$

$$EBIT^* = \$2{,}712$$

Note that for the debt alternative, the total before-tax interest is $920, and this is the intercept on the horizontal axis. For the preferred stock alternative, we divide $480 by (1 − .4) to get $800. When this is added to $360 in interest on existing debt, the intercept becomes $1,160.

c. For the present EBIT level, common is clearly preferable. EBIT would need to increase by $2,712,000 − $1,500,000 = $1,212,000 before an indifference point with debt is reached. One would want to be comfortably above this indifference point before a strong case for debt should be made. The lower the probability that actual EBIT will fall below the indifference point, the stronger the case that can be made for debt, all other things staying the same.

2. a. Total annual interest (in thousands):

15% of $2.4 million	$ 360
13% of $3.0 million	390
18% of $2.0 million	360
	$1,110

Total annual principal payments = $100 + $150 = $250. EBIT necessary to service = $250/(1 − .5) = $500.
Times interest earned = $2,000/$1,110 = 1.80
Debt-service coverage = $2,000/$1,610 = 1.24

b. Deviation from mean before ratio is one-to-one:

$$\text{Times interest earned: } \$2{,}000 - \$1{,}110 = \$890$$

$$\text{Debt-service coverage: } \$2{,}000 - \$1{,}610 = \$390$$

Standardizing the deviation and using Table C at the back of the book:

	TIMES INTEREST EARNED	DEBT-SERVICE COVERAGE
Standardized deviation ratio	890/1,500	390/1,500
Standardized deviation	.593	.260
Probability of occurrence (Table C)	.28	.40

The probabilities that the two ratios will be less than one-to-one are approximately 28 percent and 40 percent. These probabilities assume the distribution of possible EBITs is normal.

c. There is a substantial probability, 40 percent, that the company will fail to cover its interest and principal payments. Its debt ratio of $7.4 million/$8.3 million = .89 is much higher than the industry norm of .47. Its book value of debt to market value of stock ratio is even higher. Although the information is limited, based on what we have, it would appear that Torstein has too much debt. However, other factors, such as liquidity, may mitigate against this conclusion.

3. a. There is not a precise solution to this problem; rather, it is a judgment call. In the problem are listed various possibilities for coming to grips with the cash-flow short fall. In addition, there may be others, such as the sale of plant and equipment. A cash flow of $7 million is $1.8 million more than capital expenditures and the dividend. If the cash flow were to fall by $5 million, this annual surplus would disappear. In addition, other things must give. One probably would use most of the cash and marketable securities, but not all. The bank line should be fully utilized, or nearly so. In a slack period, it may be possible to cut capital expenditures. Due to competition, the company probably should maintain advertising and promotion expenses at approximately the same level. Otherwise, sales may suffer even more. To build for the future, the company probably should not cut its R&D expenditures, although something could give here. The dividend may be reduced, but there will be an adverse informational effect. (See Chapters 12 and 13.) If the recession is expected to be short, many firms will try to maintain their dividend.

Based on this discussion, a possible proposal to offset the $5 million in reduced cash flow might be (000 omitted)

Elimination of previous annual surplus	$1,800
Decrease in cash and marketable securities	900
Additional borrowings under line of credit	1,700
Capital expenditure reduction	600
	$5,000

Again, there is no right or wrong solution. If $5 million is the maximum decline in cash flow and the industry recession is expected to be short in duration, the firm probably has adequate financial flexibility. Once in a recession, however, it should try to negotiate a larger line of credit so that it has some margin for error.

b. If the cash-flow shortfall is $9 million, the solution must be harsher. Capital expenditures will need to be cut further, and all other items will need to be cut. The dividend, if maintained at all, will be sharply reduced. Indeed, survival becomes the theme. If the bank line cannot be increased, a possible remedy might be (000 omitted)

Elimination of previous surplus	$1,800
Decrease in cash and marketable securities	1,000
Additional borrowings under line of credit	1,700
Capital expenditures reduction	2,000
Reduction in R&D expenditures	800
Reduction in advertising and promotions	800
Reduction of dividend	900
	$9,000

Obviously, the company has utilized a good deal of its resources to stem the cash-flow decline. Further cuts will be needed if the recession continues. Additional financing will need to be sought, as the firm is completely inflexible after one really bad year. Again, these are only examples of solutions.

DIAMOND, DOUGLAS W., "Reputation Acquisition in Debt Markets," *Journal of Political Economy*, 97, No. 4 (1989), 828–62.

DONALDSON, GORDON, *Corporate Debt Capacity*. Boston: Division of Research, Harvard Business School, 1961.

————, "Strategy for Financial Emergencies," *Harvard Business Review*, 47 (November–December 1969), 67–79.

LEVY, HAIM, and ROBERT BROOKS, "Financial Break-Even Analysis and the Value of the Firm," *Financial Management*, 15 (Autumn 1986), 22–26.

MYERS, STEWART C., "Capital Structure Puzzle," *Journal of Finance*, 39 (July 1984), 575–92.

PINEGAR, J. MICHAEL, and LISA WILBRICHT, "What Managers Think of Capital Structure Theory: A Survey," *Financial Management*, 18 (Winter 1989), 74–81.

PIPER, THOMAS R., and WOLF A. WEINHOLD, "How Much Debt Is Right for Your Company," *Harvard Business Review*, 60 (July–August 1982), 106–14.

12

DIVIDEND-PAYOUT RATIO AND VALUATION

The third major decision of the firm is its dividend policy, the percentage of earnings it pays in cash to its stockholders. Dividend payout, of course, reduces the amount of earnings retained in the firm and affects the total amount of internal financing. Consequently, it must be considered in relation to the overall financing decision. In this chapter, we evaluate dividend policy in light of our objective, namely, to maximize the value of the firm to its shareholders. Shareholder wealth includes not only the market price of the stock but also the current dividend. Again, we assume that business risk is held constant; that is, the acceptance of any investment proposal does not affect the business-risk complexion of the firm as perceived by suppliers of capital.

The dividend-payout ratio obviously depends on the way earnings are measured. For ease of exposition, we use accounting net earnings but assume that these earnings conform to true economic earnings. In practice, net earnings may not conform and may not be an appropriate measure of the ability of the firm to pay dividends. Certain writers argue that cash flow, the sum of earnings and depreciation, is a better measure of the capacity of a firm to pay dividends. Even better might be free cash flow, that remaining after all worthwhile investment opportunities have been financed. Still others suggest that changes in stock prices are the best approximation of permanent earnings changes.[1]

Like the other major decisions of the firm—the investment and the financing decisions—the dividend decision has both theoretical and managerial facets. This chapter—structured much the same as Chapter 10, on capital structure theory—begins with an investigation of dividend payout under perfect capital-market assumptions. Then follows a systematic analysis of the implications of various market imperfections and of financial signaling. Finally, the chapter itemizes what a company in practice should analyze in approaching a dividend decision. Chapter 13 will take us to other aspects of dividend

---

[1] See Terry A. Marsh and Robert C. Merton, "Dividend Behavior for the Aggregate Stock Market," *Journal of Business,* 60 (January 1987), 1–40, for this last approach as well as a summary of other approaches.

policy: dividend stability, stock dividends and stock splits, repurchase of stock, and procedural and legal considerations.

Before we can say whether dividend payout affects shareholder wealth, we must look at the firm's policy solely as a financing decision involving the retention of earnings. Each period the firm must decide whether to retain its earnings or to distribute part or all of them to shareholders as cash dividends. (We rule out share repurchase for now.) As long as there are investment projects with returns exceeding those that are required, it will use retained earnings, and the amount of senior securities the increase in equity base will support, to finance these projects. If the firm has retained earnings left over after financing all acceptable investment opportunities, these earnings then will be distributed to stockholders in the form of cash dividends. If not, there will be no dividends. If the number of acceptable investment opportunities involves a total dollar amount that exceeds the amount of retained earnings plus the senior securities these retained earnings will support, the firm will finance the excess with a combination of a new equity issue and senior securities.

When we treat dividend policy as strictly a financing decision, the payment of cash dividends is a passive residual. The amount of dividend payout will fluctuate from period to period in keeping with fluctuations in the amount of acceptable investment opportunities available to the firm. If these opportunities abound, the percentage of dividend payout is likely to be zero. On the other hand, if the firm is unable to find profitable investment opportunities, dividend payout will be 100 percent. For situations between these two extremes, the payout will be a fraction between zero and one.

The treatment of dividend policy as a passive residual determined solely by the availability of acceptable investment proposals implies that dividends are irrelevant; the investor is indifferent between dividends and retention by the firm. If investment opportunities promise a return greater than their required return, the investor is happy to have the company retain earnings. Contrarily, if the return is less than the required return, the investor prefers dividends. A residual theory of dividend policy does not necessarily mean that dividends need fluctuate from period to period in keeping with fluctuations in investment opportunities. A firm may smooth out actual payments by saving some funds in surplus years, in anticipation of deficit years. If forecasting is relatively accurate, the firm can establish its dividend payment at a level at which the cumulative distribution over time corresponds to cumulative residual funds over the same period. The fact that dividends do not correspond to residual funds period by period does not negate the residual theory of dividends.

The critical question is whether dividends are more than just a means of distributing unused funds. Should dividend policy be an active decision variable as opposed to a passive one? To answer these questions, we must examine more thoroughly the argument that dividends are irrelevant, so that changes in the payout ratio (holding investment opportunities constant) do not affect shareholder wealth.

IRRELEVANCE OF DIVIDENDS

Modigliani and Miller's 1961 article is the most comprehensive argument for the irrelevance of dividends.[2] They assert that, given the investment decision of the firm, the dividend-payout ratio is a mere detail. It does not affect the wealth of shareholders. MM argue that the value of the firm is determined by the earning power of the firm's assets or its investment policy and that the manner in which the earnings stream is split between dividends and retained earnings does not affect this value. The critical assumptions are

1. Perfect capital markets in which all investors are rational. Information available to all at no cost, instantaneous transactions without cost, infinitely divisible securities, and no investor large enough to affect the market price of a security.
2. An absence of flotation costs on securities issued by the firm.
3. A world of no taxes.
4. A given investment policy for the firm, not subject to change.
5. Perfect certainty by every investor as to future investments and profits of the firm. (MM drop this assumption later.)

DIVIDENDS VERSUS TERMINAL VALUE

The crux of MM's position is that the effect of dividend payments on shareholder wealth is offset exactly by other means of financing. Consider first selling additional stock in lieu of retaining earnings. When the firm has made its investment decision, it must decide whether to retain earnings or to pay dividends and sell new stock in the amount of these dividends in order to finance the investments. MM suggest that the sum of the discounted value per share after financing and dividends paid is equal to the market value per share before the payment of dividends. In other words, the stock's decline in market price because of external financing offsets exactly the payment of the dividend. Thus, the stockholder is said to be indifferent between dividends and the retention of earnings and subsequent capital gains.

The market price of a share of stock at the beginning of a period is defined as equal to the present value of the dividend paid at the end of the period plus the market price at the end of the period. Thus

$$P_0 = \frac{1}{1 + \rho}(D_1 + P_1) \qquad (12\text{-}1)$$

where P_0 = market price per share at time 0
ρ = capitalization rate for firm in that risk class (this rate is assumed to be constant throughout time)
D_1 = dividend per share at time 1
P_1 = market price per share at time 1

Assume that n is the number of shares of record at time 0 and that m is the number of new shares sold at time 1 at a price of P_1. Equation (12-1) then

[2] Merton H. Miller and Franco Modigliani, "Dividend Policy, Growth, and the Valuation of Shares," *Journal of Business*, 34 (October 1961), 411–33.

can be rewritten as

$$nP_0 = \frac{1}{(1 + \rho)}[nD_1 + (n + m)P_1 - mP_1] \qquad (12\text{-}2)$$

In words, the total value of all shares outstanding at time 0 is the present value of total dividends paid at time 1 on those shares plus the total value of all stock outstanding at time 1, less the total value of the new stock issued. The total amount of new stock issued is

$$mP_1 = I - (X - nD_1) \qquad (12\text{-}3)$$

where I = total new investments during period 1
X = total new profit of firm for the period

Equation (12-3) merely states that the total sources of funds must equal total uses. That is, net profit plus new stock sales must equal new investments plus dividends.

The total amount of financing by the sale of new stock is determined by the amount of investments in period 1 not financed by retained earnings. By substituting Eq. (12-3) into Eq. (12-2), MM find that the nD_1 term cancels out and

$$nP_0 = \frac{1}{(1 + \rho)}[(n + m)P_1 - I + X] \qquad (12\text{-}4)$$

Because D_1 does not appear directly in the expression and because X, I, $(n + m)P_1$, and ρ are assumed to be independent of D_1, MM conclude that the current value of the firm is independent of its current dividend decision. What is gained by stockholders in increased dividends is offset exactly by the decline in the terminal value of their stock. MM go on to show that nP_0 is unaffected not only by current dividend decisions but by future dividend decisions as well. Under the assumption of perfect certainty by all investors, the price of the stock at time 1, time 2, and time n is determined solely by Eq. (12-4). Thus, stockholders are indifferent between retention and the payment of dividends (and concurrent stock financing) in all future periods. As a result, shareholder wealth is unaffected by current and future dividend decisions; it depends entirely on the expected future earnings stream of the firm.

If both leverage and dividends are irrelevant, the firm would be indifferent to whether investment opportunities were financed with debt, retained earnings, or a common stock issue. One method of financing would be as satisfactory as the next. Now one might ask, How does this correspond to our earlier chapters when we said that dividends are the foundation for the valuation of common stocks? While it is true that the market value of a share of stock is the present value of all expected future dividends, the timing of the dividends can vary. The irrelevance position simply argues that the present value of future dividends remains unchanged even though dividend policy changes their timing. It does not argue that dividends, including liquidating dividends, are never paid, only that their postponement is a matter of indifference when it comes to market price per share.

IRRELEVANCE UNDER UNCERTAINTY

In a world of perfect capital markets and the absence of taxation, dividend payout would be a matter of irrelevance even with uncertainty. This argument involves the same reasoning as that for the irrelevance of capital structure and for the irrelevance of diversification of corporate asset decisions. Investors are able to replicate any dividend stream the corporation might pay. If dividends are less than desired, investors can sell portions of their stock to obtain the desired cash distribution. If dividends are more than desired, investors can use dividends to purchase additional shares in the company. Thus, investors are able to manufacture "homemade" dividends in the same way they devise "homemade" leverage in capital structure decisions.

For a corporate decision to be a thing of value, the company must be able to do something for stockholders that they cannot do for themselves. Because investors can manufacture "homemade" dividends, which are perfect substitutes for corporate dividends under the above assumptions, dividend policy is irrelevant. As a result, one dividend policy is as good as the next. The firm is unable to create value simply by altering the mix of dividends and retained earnings. As in capital structure theory, there is a conservation of value so that the sum of the parts is always the same. The total size of the pie is what is important, and it is unchanged in the slicing.

TAXES AND DIVIDENDS

The irrelevance of dividend argument assumes an absence of market imperfections. To the extent imperfections exist, they may support the contrary position, namely, that dividends are relevant. We shall examine various imperfections bearing on the issue, beginning with taxes. After we consider the theory, we will look at various empirical evidence bearing on the topic.

UNIMPORTANCE OF CORPORATE INCOME TAXES

Unlike the capital structure decision, corporate income taxes have no bearing on dividend relevance. Under present law, earnings of the firm are taxed at the corporate level, regardless of whether or not a dividend is paid. In other words, it is the profit after corporate taxes that is divided between dividends and retained earnings. Corporate income taxes could affect dividend relevance if tax laws were changed, as would occur under various methods to eliminate the double taxation of dividends.

TAXES ON THE INVESTOR

Taxes paid by the investor are another matter. To the extent that the personal tax rate on capital gains is less than that on dividend income, there may be an advantage to the retention of earnings. While the 1986 and 1990 Tax Acts brought these two rates close together, the capital gains tax is deferred until the actual sale of stock. Effectively, the stockholder is given a valuable timing option when the firm retains earnings as opposed to paying dividends. As brought out in Chapter 10, the capital gains tax may be avoided if appreciated securities are given as gifts to charitable causes or if the person dies. For these reasons, the effective (present value) tax on capital gains is less than that on dividend income.

As we described in Chapter 4, a differential tax on dividends and capital gains may result in a "yield tilt." That is, a dividend-paying stock will need to provide a higher expected before-tax return than will a non-dividend-paying stock of the same risk. This is said to be necessary to offset the tax effect on dividends. According to this notion, the greater the dividend yield of a stock, the higher its expected before-tax return, all other things being the same. Thus, security markets would equilibrate in terms of systematic risk, dividend yield, and, perhaps, other factors. Principal proponents of this position include Litzenberger and Ramiswamy.[3]

However, investors do not necessarily experience the same taxation on the two types of income. Institutional investors, such as retirement and pension funds, pay no tax on either dividends or capital gains. For corporate investors, intercompany dividends are taxed at a rate below that applicable to capital gains. For example, if Laurel Corporation owns 100 shares of Hardy Corporation, which pays $1 per share dividend, 70 percent of the dividend income is tax exempt. In other words, Laurel Corporation would pay taxes on $30 of dividend income at the corporate tax rate. The overall tax effect will be less than if Hardy Corporation had share appreciation of $100 and all of this were taxed at the capital gains rate. Accordingly, there may be a preference for current dividends on the part of corporate investors. Despite these exceptions, for many investors there exists a present-value differential in taxes between a dollar of dividend and a dollar of retained earnings.

INVESTOR CLIENTELE NEUTRALITY

With different tax situations, clienteles of investors may develop with distinct preferences for dividend- or non-dividend-paying stocks. Many corporate investors will prefer dividend-paying stocks, whereas wealthy individual investors may prefer stocks that pay no dividends. Tax-exempt investors will be indifferent, all other things the same. If dividend-paying stocks were priced in the marketplace to provide a higher return than non-dividend-paying stocks, however, they would not be indifferent. They would prefer dividend-paying stocks.

If various clienteles of investors have dividend preferences, corporations should adjust their dividend payout to take advantage of the situation. Expressed differently, corporations should tailor their dividend policies to the unfulfilled desires of investors and thereby take advantage of an incomplete market. (See Chapter 10 and its footnote 11 for a discussion of incomplete markets.) Suppose two-fifths of all investors prefer a zero dividend payout, one-fifth prefer a 25 percent payout, and the remaining two-fifths prefer a 50 percent payout. If most companies pay out 25 percent of their earnings in dividends, there will be excess demand for the shares of companies paying zero dividends and for the shares of companies whose dividend-payout ratio is 50

[3] Robert H. Litzenberger and Krishna Ramiswamy, "The Effect of Personal Taxes and Dividends on Capital Asset Prices," *Journal of Financial Economics*, 7 (June 1979), 163–95; Litzenberger and Ramiswamy, "Dividends, Short Selling Restrictions, Tax Induced Investor Clienteles and Market Equilibrium," *Journal of Finance*, 35 (May 1980), 469–82; and Litzenberger and Ramiswamy, "The Effects of Dividends on Common Stock Prices: Tax Effects or Information Effects?" *Journal of Finance*, 37 (May 1982), 429–44.

percent. Presumably, a number of companies will recognize this excess demand and adjust their payout ratios in order to increase share price. The action of these companies eventually will eliminate the excess demand.

In equilibrium, the dividend payouts of corporations will match the desires of investor groups. At this point, no company would be able to affect its share price by altering its dividend. As a result, even with taxes, dividend payout would be irrelevant. Black and Scholes are principal proponents of the neutral position, based on corporations adjusting the supply of dividends to take advantage of any mispricing of stocks in the marketplace.[4]

Another argument against clientele effects is that investors can use combinations of put and call options to isolate movements in stock price. By so doing, the investor effectively strips the dividend from the capital gains component of the stock. If investors are able to separate dividends from capital gains to suit their needs, the tax-induced clientele argument for particular stocks is weakened. Yet another argument on the demand side follows.

MILLER AND SCHOLES ARGUMENT

In a different attack, Miller and Scholes argue that it is possible for investors to avoid paying taxes on dividends.[5] With such avoidance, of course, any tax bias in favor of retention of earnings disappears. The Miller and Scholes "tax dodge" involves a stockholder borrowing a sufficient amount of funds to produce one dollar of interest expense for each dollar of dividend income. The amount borrowed is invested in a single-payment annuity or some other type of tax-deferred investment. The interest expense is offset against dividend income, so the investor pays no immediate tax. The capital gain on the investment of the borrowed funds is sheltered. If this gain is postponed until the time of death, no capital gains tax would be paid. Thus, the argument is one of investors transforming dividends into capital gains that are postponed.

Suppose you have invested $20,000 in Dolce Corporation common stock, and the stock has an 8 percent dividend yield. You receive $1,600 in dividends. In addition to dividend yield, the stock is expected to show annual price appreciation of 6 percent. Now you borrow $40,000 at 12 percent interest and invest the proceeds of the loan in additional Dolce Corporation stock. The interest on this loan is deductible for tax purposes. As a result, your tax position would be

	ORDINARY INCOME	EXPECTED PRICE APPRECIATION
Dividends received ($60,000 × .08)	$4,800	Gain ($60,000 × .06) $3,600
Less: Interest expense ($40,000 × .12)	4,800	
Net ordinary income	$ 0	

[4] Fischer Black and Myron Scholes, "The Effects of Dividend Yield and Dividend Policy on Common Stock Prices and Returns," *Journal of Financial Economics*, 1 (May 1974), 1–5. Rosita P. Chang and S. Ghon Rhee, "The Impact of Personal Taxes on Corporate Dividend Policy and Capital Structure Decisions," *Financial Management*, 19 (Summer 1990), 21–31, find a significant degree of correlation between financial leverage and dividend-payout ratio, which is consistent with the simultaneous occurrence of leverage and dividend tax clientele effects.

[5] Merton H. Miller and Myron S. Scholes, "Dividends and Taxes," *Journal of Financial Economics*, 6 (December 1978), 333–64.

Thus, the dividend income is neutralized by the interest expense. As long as the stock is not sold, the price appreciation will go unrealized for tax purposes. Consequently, no taxes will be paid. We see that dividend income is transformed into capital gains. Of course, borrowing funds increases the overall risk of your position. You cannot get something (incremental price appreciation of $2,400 above the $1,200 you otherwise would expect) for nothing. The added return is the result of increased risk. If you wish to bear no more risk than before, Miller and Scholes suggest that you use an insurance annuity. Instead of borrowing $40,000, borrow $13,333, again at 12 percent interest. Then take the $13,333 and invest it in a risk-free insurance annuity. Such an annuity implies that the insurance company invests the funds in a risk-free asset and agrees to repay, at some future date, the $13,333 plus compound interest at the risk-free rate. Thus, the risk-free asset offsets your borrowing, and you incur no increase in risk on your overall position. At the outset, your balance sheet includes the following items:

ASSETS		LIABILITIES	
Dolce Corporation stock	$20,000	Borrowings	$13,333
Single-time insurance annuity	13,333		
Your current tax return would be			
Dividends received			
($20,000 × .08)	$ 1,600		
Less: Interest expense			
($13,333 × .12)	1,600		
Net taxable income	$ 0		

Thus, you will pay no taxes on your dividend income. When the annuity is realized, you will have to pay tax, but this realization is off in the future, and presumably you will postpone it. Instead of an insurance annuity, you might increase your contribution to a pension fund. In both cases, the institutions involved are not taxed on their investment income, so they provide vehicles for the postponement of taxes. The idea is to borrow so that interest payments offset dividends received; as a result, no taxes are paid. The second step is to neutralize the risk of borrowing and to postpone the realization of capital gains.

Although the steps just outlined work to reduce the tax bias that favors retention over dividends, there is some question about how easy they are to accomplish. Often it is difficult to find insurance or other vehicles by which taxes can be conveniently postponed. Moreover, the specific tax provision that allows such a tax dodge is highly restrictive. For one thing, the 1986 Tax Reform Act restricts interest deductibility to home mortgages. This and other limitations cause many to regard the Miller-Scholes tax avoidance strategy as unworkable in practice.

TAX EFFECT: A QUICK SUMMATION

We are left with an unsettled situation in which the effect of taxes on dividends is not clear. Even if there is an effect, however, it has been lessened with the 1986 and 1990 Tax Acts. As a result of them, we might expect demand for higher-yielding stocks to increase. Before examining empirical evidence on the subject, we must look at other factors that may influence the payment of dividends.

INFLUENCE OF OTHER FACTORS ON DIVIDENDS

FLOTATION COSTS

The irrelevance of dividend payout is based on the idea that in accordance with the investment policy of the firm, funds paid out by the firm must be replaced by funds acquired through external financing. The introduction of flotation costs favors the retention of earnings in the firm. For each dollar paid out in dividends, the firm nets less than a dollar after flotation costs per dollar of external financing. Moreover, the smaller the size of the issue, the greater in general the flotation costs as a percentage of the total amount of funds raised. In addition, stock financing is "lumpy" in the sense that small issues are difficult to sell even with high flotation costs.

TRANSACTION COSTS AND DIVISIBILITY OF SECURITIES

Transaction costs involved in the sale of securities tend to restrict the arbitrage process in the same manner as that described for debt. Stockholders who desire current income must pay brokerage fees on the sale of portions of their stock if the dividend paid is not sufficient to satisfy their current desire for income. This fee varies inversely, per dollar of stock sold, with the size of the sale. For a small sale, the brokerage fee can be a rather significant percentage. Because of this fee, stockholders with consumption desires in excess of current dividends will prefer that the company pay additional dividends. Perfect capital markets also assume that securities are infinitely divisible. The fact that the smallest integer is one share may result in "lumpiness" with respect to selling shares for current income. This, too, acts as a deterrent to the sale of stock in lieu of dividends. On the other hand, stockholders not desiring dividends for current consumption purposes will need to reinvest their dividends. Here again, transaction costs and divisibility problems work to the disadvantage of the stockholder, although in the opposite direction. Thus, transactions costs and divisibility problems cut both ways, and one is not able to draw directional implications about dividends versus retained earnings.

INSTITUTIONAL RESTRICTIONS

Certain institutional investors are restricted in the types of common stock they can buy or in the portfolio percentages they can hold in these types. The prescribed list of eligible securities is determined in part by the duration over which dividends have been paid. If a company does not pay a dividend or has not paid dividends over a sufficiently long period of time, certain institutional investors are not permitted to invest in the stock.

Universities, on the other hand, sometimes have restrictions on the expenditure of capital gains from their endowment. Also, a number of trusts have a prohibition against the liquidation of principal. In the case of common stocks, the beneficiary is entitled to the dividend income, but not to the proceeds from the sale of stock. As a result of this stipulation, the trustee who manages the investments may feel constrained to pay particular attention to dividend yield and seek stocks paying reasonable dividends. Though the two influences described are small in aggregate, they work in the direction of a preference for dividends as opposed to retention and capital gains.

PREFERENCE FOR DIVIDENDS

Finally, we must allow for the possibility of a preference for dividends on the part of a sizable number of investors. The payment of dividends may resolve uncertainty in the minds of some. Also, such payments may be useful in diversification of investments in an uncertain world. If in fact investors can manufacture "homemade" dividends, such a preference is irrational. Nonetheless, sufficient statements from investors make it difficult to dismiss the argument. Perhaps, for either psychological or inconvenience reasons, investors are unwilling to manufacture "homemade" dividends.

Hersh M. Shefrin and Meir Statman reason that some investors are reluctant to sell shares because they will experience regret if the stock subsequently rises in price.[6] For them, dividends and the sale of stock for income are not perfect substitutes. A second argument the authors advance is that while many investors are willing to consume out of dividend income they are unwilling to "dip into capital" in order to do so. Again, dividends and the sale of stock are not perfect substitutes for these investors. For psychological reasons, then, certain investors prefer dividends. Whether they are numerous enough to make a difference is an empirical question, about to be addressed.

FINANCIAL SIGNALING

Cash dividends may be viewed as a signal to investors.[7] Presumably, firms with good news about their future profitability will want to tell investors. Rather than make a simple announcement, dividends may be increased to add conviction to the statement. When a firm has a target-payout ratio that is stable over time and it changes this ratio, investors may believe that management is announcing a change in the expected future profitability of the firm. The signal to investors is that management and the board of directors truly believe things are better than the stock price reflects. In this vein, Merton H. Miller and Kevin Rock suggest that investors draw inferences about the firm's internal operating cash flows from the dividend announcement.[8] The notion is based on asymmetric information. Management knows more about the true state of the company's earnings than do outside investors.

[6] Hersh M. Shefrin and Meir Statman, "Explaining Investor Preferences for Cash Dividends," *Journal of Financial Economics*, 13 (June 1984), 253–82.

[7] See Sudipto Bhattacharya, "Imperfect Information, Dividend Policy, and the 'Bird-in-the-Hand' Fallacy," *Bell Journal of Economics*, 10 (Spring 1979), 259–70.

[8] Merton H. Miller and Kevin Rock, "Dividend Policy under Asymmetric Information," *Journal of Finance*, 40 (September 1985), 1031–51. The authors also analyze management trying to fool the market by increasing dividends and the implications of such an expectation for stockholders and for the equilibrating mechanism.

Accordingly, the price of the stock may react to this change in dividends. To the extent dividends provide information on economic earnings not provided by reported accounting earnings and other information, share price will respond. Put another way, dividends speak louder than words under these circumstances. The rationale behind a dividend signaling effect is similar to a capital structure signaling effect described in Chapter 10. However, it generally is agreed that the effect is more important for dividends than it is for capital structure.

Two examples illustrate intent. In the late 1980s, Dow Chemical Company increased its dividend by 14 percent as a means, according to its chief financial officer, of signaling optimism for U.S. and foreign operations. In the mid-1980s, Nalco Chemical Company debated cutting its dividend in light of earnings pressure. Having increased dividends for 24 consecutive years, it was decided that a cut, no matter how justified, would signal undue pessimism.

EMPIRICAL TESTING AND IMPLICATIONS FOR PAYOUT

While we have seen that a number of factors may explain dividends' impact on valuation, many are difficult to test. Most empirical testing has concentrated on the tax effect and on financial signaling. This is not to say that such things as flotation costs, transactions costs, institutional restrictions, and preference for dividends have no effect; only that whatever effect they might have is swamped by the two effects discussed. Empirical testing has taken several forms.

EX-DIVIDEND DAY TESTS

One of the mainstays has involved the ex-dividend behavior of common stock prices. As we explain in Chapter 13, companies paying dividends establish an ex-dividend date. Investors buying the stock before that date are entitled to the dividend declared; purchases on or after the ex-dividend date are not entitled to the dividend. In a nontaxable world, the stock should drop in value by the amount of the dividend on the ex-dividend day. If you are a taxable investor, however, and buy the stock before the ex-dividend day, you will need to pay taxes on the dividend. In contrast, if you wait until the ex-dividend day to buy the stock, you will pay no taxes on the dividend, since there is no dividend, and any price movement presumably is subject only to the capital-gains tax. A number of authors reason that if there is a tax effect, owing to capital gains being taxed at a lower rate than dividend income, a stock should decline in price by less than the dividend on the ex-dividend day. Expressed differently, investors would value a dollar of dividends less than they would a dollar of capital gains.

An earlier study of the phenomenon was by Elton and Gruber.[9] In a sample of companies, they found that on average a stock declined by .78 of the dividend on the ex-dividend date. They interpret this result as consistent with a clientele effect where investors in high tax brackets show a preference for capital gains over dividends, and vice versa.

[9] Edwin J. Elton and Martin J. Gruber, "Marginal Stockholder Tax Rates and the Clientele Effect," *Review of Economics and Statistics*, 52 (February 1970), 68–74.

There have been a number of other studies of share price behavior on the ex-dividend day.[10] In general, the evidence is consistent with the foregoing, namely, that stock prices decline on the ex-dividend day but by less than the amount of the dividend. Many view these findings as consistent with a tax effect where dividends are taxed more heavily than are capital gains, and stock prices reflect this differential.

DIVIDEND-YIELD APPROACH

A second approach to the tax effect question is to study the relationship between dividend yields and stock returns, where other influences on returns are isolated. One of the earlier studies here was by Black and Scholes.[11] In testing a modification of the capital asset pricing model to measure the deviation of a stock's dividend yield from that of the market portfolio, they find the coefficient of the variable to be insignificant. Stocks with high payout ratios did not provide returns significantly different from those with low payout ratios. The authors interpret this finding as consistent with the idea that dividend policy does not matter. The differential tax explanation of dividend yield and stock returns has been challenged by others as well.[12]

As we know from Chapter 4, however, many authors have found a positive relationship between expected before-tax returns and dividend yields, holding other things constant. Perhaps the leading investigators here are Litzenberger and Ramiswamy, but there have been a number of others.[13] The findings of these scholars are said to be consistent with high-dividend stocks providing higher expected before-tax returns than low-dividend stocks to offset the tax effect. As a result, we would have the "yield tilt" illustrated in Chapter 4.

Nai-fu Chen, Bruce Grundy, and Robert F. Stambaugh also test for a yield tilt effect and find, as do others, that the dividend coefficient is significantly positive when the CAPM is employed.[14] However, when a de-

---

[10] Avner Kalay, "The Ex-Dividend Day Behavior of Stock Prices: A Re-examination of the Clientele Effect," *Journal of Finance*, 37 (September 1982), 1059–70; Kenneth M. Eades, Patrick J. Hess, and E. Han Kim, "On Interpreting Security Returns during the Ex-Dividend Period," *Journal of Financial Economics*, 13 (March 1984), 3–34; Patrick J. Hess, "The Ex-Dividend Day Behavior of Stock Returns: Further Evidence on Tax Effects," *Journal of Finance*, 37 (May 1982), 445–56; James M. Poterba and Lawrence H. Summers, "New Evidence That Taxes Affect the Valuation of Dividends," *Journal of Finance*, 39 (December 1984), 1397–1416; Costas P. Kaplanis, "Options, Taxes and Ex-Dividend Day Behavior," *Journal of Finance*, 41 (June 1986), 411–24; and Michael J. Barclay, "Dividends, Taxes and Common Stock Prices: The Ex-Dividend Day Behavior of Common Stock Prices before the Income Tax," *Journal of Financial Economics*, 19 (September, 1987), 31–44.

[11] Black and Scholes, "The Effects of Dividend Yield and Dividend Policy on Common Stock Prices and Returns."

[12] Miller and Scholes, "Dividends and Taxes"; and Marshall Blume, "Stock Returns and Dividend Yields: Some More Evidence," *Review of Economics and Statistics*, 62 (November 1980), 567–77.

[13] Litzenberger and Ramiswamy, "The Effect of Personal Taxes and Dividends on Capital Asset Prices," and "Dividends, Short Selling Restrictions, Tax Induced Investor Clienteles and Market Equilibrium." See also Sasson Bar-Yosef and Richard Kolodny, "Dividend Policy and Capital Market Theory," *Review of Economics and Statistics*, 58 (May 1976), 181–90; Alan J. Auerbach, "Stockholder Tax Rates and Firm Attributes," *Journal of Public Economics*, 21 (March 1983), 107–27; Roger Gordon and David Bradford, "Taxation and the Stock Market Valuation of Capital Gains and Dividends: Theory and Empirical Results," *Journal of Public Economics*, 14 (March 1980), 109–36; Poterba and Summers, "New Evidence That Taxes Affect the Valuation of Dividends"; and James S. Ang and David R. Peterson, "Return, Risk, and Yield: Evidence from Ex Ante Data," *Journal of Finance*, 40 (June 1985), 537–48.

[14] Nai-fu Chen, Bruce Grundy, and Robert F. Stambaugh, "Changing Risk Premiums, and Dividend Yield Effects," Merton Miller Conference in Honor of His 65th Birthday (August 1988).

fault-risk premium variable is added (junk bond rate minus Treasury bond rate) to the extended CAPM, the dividend coefficient is not significantly different from zero. They conclude that the dividend-yield measure is likely to be correlated with a number of economic phenomena. To detect a tax-induced penalty for dividends, if indeed there is one, is very difficult, according to the authors.

Thus, the question of taxes and dividend payout is in an unsettled state empirically. It may be that a tax effect, if any, is too sensitive to be picked up by the economic models. After the passage of the 1986 Tax Reform Act, dividend-payout ratios of American corporations increased somewhat. This behavior is consistent with a tax effect lessening as the differential taxation between dividends and capital gains narrows. However, it does not establish the presence of a tax effect prior to the 1986 Tax Act.

FINANCIAL SIGNALING STUDIES

Testing for a financial signaling effect has involved a different methodology. Typically, an event study is employed where daily share price changes, relative to the market, are analyzed around the announcement of a dividend change. A number of studies report findings consistent with a dividend announcement effect: increases in dividend leading to positive excess returns and decreases to negative excess returns.[15] The effect seems to be more pronounced for companies that previously overinvested free cash flow in projects with returns less than what the financial markets require.[16] After all, those cash flows belong to the stockholders and should not be invested in negative NPV projects.

In a study of firms initiating dividends for the first time or after a long hiatus, Asquith and Mullins discover significant excess returns.[17] They interpret this finding as supporting the view that dividends convey valuable information to investors over and above that available from other sources. As would be expected, companies that omit dividends because of poor present earnings and future prospects suffer a share price decline.[18]

---

[15] See, for example, Joseph Aharony and Itzhak Swary, "Quarterly Dividend and Earnings Announcements and Stockholders' Returns: An Empirical Analysis," *Journal of Finance,* 35 (March 1980), 1–12; Guy Charest, "Dividend Information, Stock Returns and Market Efficiency," *Journal of Financial Economics,* 6 (June–September 1978), 297–330; J. Randall Woolridge, "Dividend Changes and Security Prices," *Journal of Finance,* 38 (December 1983), 1607–15; Terry E. Dielman and Henry R. Oppenheimer, "An Examination of Investor Behavior during Periods of Large Dividend Changes," *Journal of Financial and Quantitative Analysis,* 19 (June 1984), 197–216; Kenneth M. Eades, Patrick H. Hess, and E. Han Kim, "Market Rationality and Dividend Announcements," *Journal of Financial Economics,* 14 (December 1985), 581–604; Aharon R. Ofer and Daniel R. Siegel, "Corporate Financial Policy, Information, and Market Expectations: An Empirical Investigation of Dividends," *Journal of Finance* (September 1987), 889–911; and Paul M. Healy and Krishna G. Palepu, "Earnings Information Conveyed by Dividend Initiations and Omissions," *Journal of Financial Economics,* 21 (September 1988), 149–75.

[16] Larry H. P. Lang and Robert H. Litzenberger, "Dividend Announcements: Cash Flow Signalling vs. Free Cash Flow Hypothesis," *Journal of Financial Economics,* 24 (September 1989), 181–91.

[17] Paul Asquith and David W. Mullins, Jr., "The Impact of Initiating Dividend Payments on Shareholders' Wealth," *Journal of Business,* 56 (January 1983), 77–96. See also Gordon R. Richardson and Stephan E. Sefcik, "A Test of Dividend Irrelevance Using Volume Reactions to a Change in Dividend Policy," *Journal of Financial Economics,* 17 (December 1986), 313–33; and Healy and Palepu, "Earnings Information Conveyed by Dividend Initiations and Omissions."

[18] Healy and Palepu, *op. cit.*

A SUMMING UP WITH IMPLICATIONS
FOR CORPORATE POLICY

339

CHAPTER 12
Dividend-Payout
Ratio and
Valuation

As reflected in the foregoing discussion, the empirical evidence is mixed as to there being a tax effect that requires a higher before-tax return the greater the dividend. While the majority of the evidence is consistent with a "yield tilt," a number of studies do not support a tax effect; they are consistent with neutrality. If there was a "yield tilt" effect before the 1986 Tax Act (altered slightly by the 1990 Tax Act), it surely was substantially reduced or eliminated with the act. In contrast to the results for a tax effect, most empirical studies suggest that dividends convey information and that there is a signaling effect. Where does this leave us with respect to directions for a corporation?

A company should endeavor to establish a dividend policy that will maximize shareholder wealth. Almost everyone agrees that if a company does not have sufficiently profitable investment opportunities, it should distribute any excess funds to its stockholders. As we have said before, these funds belong to them, not to management to squander on wasteful expenditures. The firm need not pay out the exact unused portion of earnings every period. Indeed, it may wish to stabilize the absolute amount of dividends paid from period to period. But over the longer run the total earnings retained, plus the senior securities the increasing equity base will support, will correspond to the amount of profitable investment opportunities. Dividend policy still would be a passive residual determined by the amount of investment opportunities.

For the firm to be justified in paying a dividend larger than that dictated by the amount left over after profitable investment opportunities, there must be a net preference for dividends in the market. It is very difficult to "net out" the arguments just discussed to arrive at the bottom line. Only institutional restrictions and some investors' preference for dividends argue for dividends. The other arguments suggest either a neutral effect or a bias favoring retention. There does appear to be some positive value associated with a modest dividend as opposed to none at all. This occurrence may be due to institutional restrictions and a signaling effect.

Beyond that, the picture is very cloudy, and some argue that even a modest dividend has no effect on valuation. Few academic scholars argue that dividends significantly in excess of what a passive policy would dictate will lead to share price improvement. With personal taxes and flotation costs, shareholders are money behind when a company issues stock to pay dividends. The arguments are for either a neutral effect or a negative effect owing to tax reasons. Before making a final observation, let us consider some practical things.

MANAGERIAL CONSIDERATIONS IN DETERMINING A DIVIDEND PAYOUT

So far we have discussed only the theoretical aspects of dividend policy. Yet, when a company establishes a dividend policy, it looks at a number of things. These considerations should be related back to the theory of dividend payout and the valuation of the firm. In what follows, we take up various factors that firms in practice can and should analyze when approaching a dividend decision.

FUNDS NEEDS OF THE FIRM

Perhaps the place to begin is with an assessment of the funds needs of the firm. In this regard, cash budgets and projected source and use of funds statements (topics taken up in Chapter 28) are of particular use. The key is to determine the likely cash flows and cash position of the company in the absence of a change in dividend. In addition to looking at expected outcomes, we should factor in business risk, so that we may obtain a range of possible cash-flow outcomes. The procedure is spelled out in Chapter 28, so we need not dwell on it here.

In keeping with our earlier discussion of the theory of dividend payout, the firm wishes to determine if anything is left over after servicing its funds needs, including profitable investment projects. In this regard, a company should look at its situation over a reasonable number of future years to iron out fluctuations. The likely ability of the firm to sustain a dividend should be analyzed relative to the probability distributions of possible future cash flows and cash positions. On the basis of this analysis, a company can determine its likely future residual funds.

Over the life cycle of a company, we would expect no dividends to be paid early on. As it matures and begins to generate excess cash, dividends are paid—a token dividend at first, but bigger ones as relatively fewer productive investment opportunities are found. In the late stages, "harvesting" may occur. Here a company self-liquidates by paying substantial dividends to its stockholders. Even for "nonharvest" situations, we would expect the mature company to pay sizable dividends.

LIQUIDITY

The liquidity of a company is a prime consideration in many dividend decisions. As dividends represent a cash outflow, the greater the cash position and overall liquidity of a company, the greater its ability to pay a dividend. A company that is growing and profitable may not be liquid, for its funds may go into fixed assets and permanent current assets. Because the management of such a company usually desires to maintain some liquidity cushion to give it flexibility and a protection against uncertainty, it may be reluctant to jeopardize this position in order to pay a large dividend. The liquidity of the company is strongly influenced by the firm's investment and financing decisions. The investment decision determines the rate of asset expansion and the firm's need for funds, and the financing decision determines the way in which this need will be financed.

ABILITY TO BORROW

A liquid position is not the only way to provide for flexibility and thereby protect against uncertainty. If a firm has the ability to borrow on comparatively short notice, it may be relatively flexible. This ability to borrow can be in the form of a line of credit or a revolving credit from a bank or simply the informal willingness of a financial institution to extend credit. In addition, flexibility can come from the ability of a company to go to the capital markets with a bond issue. The larger and more established a company, the better its access to capital markets. The greater the ability of the firm to borrow, the greater its flexibility and the greater its ability to pay a cash dividend. With ready access to debt funds, management should be less concerned with the effect that a cash dividend has on its liquidity.

ASSESSMENT OF ANY VALUATION INFORMATION

To the extent that there are insights into the effect of a dividend on valuation, they should be gathered. Most companies look at the dividend-payout ratios of other companies in the industry, particularly those having about the same growth. It may not matter that a company is out of line with similar companies, but it will be conspicuous; and usually a company will want to justify its position. Also, a company should judge the informational effect of a dividend. What do investors expect? Here security analysts and security reports are useful. The company should ask itself what information it is conveying with its present dividend and what it would convey with a possible change in dividend. As much of this was discussed in the previous section, we limit our remarks here.

CONTROL

If a company pays substantial dividends, it may need to raise capital at a later time through the sale of stock. Under such circumstances, the controlling interest of the company may be diluted if controlling stockholders do not or cannot subscribe for additional shares. These stockholders may prefer a low dividend payout and the financing of investment needs with retained earnings. Control can work two ways, however. When a company is being sought by another company or by individuals, a low dividend payout may work to the advantage of the "outsiders" seeking control. The outsiders may be able to convince stockholders that the company is not maximizing shareholder wealth and that they (the outsiders) can do a better job. Consequently, companies in danger of being acquired may establish a high dividend payout in order to please stockholders.

NATURE OF STOCKHOLDERS

When a firm is closely held, management usually knows the dividend desires of its stockholders and may act accordingly. If most stockholders are in high tax brackets and prefer capital gains to current income, the firm can establish a low dividend payout. The low payout, of course, would be predicated upon having profitable investment opportunities for the retained earnings. The corporation with a large number of stockholders can judge their desires for dividends only in a market context.

RESTRICTIONS IN BOND INDENTURE OR LOAN AGREEMENT

The protective covenants in a bond indenture or loan agreement often include a restriction on payment of dividends. The restriction is employed by the lenders to preserve the company's ability to service debt. Usually, it is expressed as a maximum percentage of cumulative earnings. When such a restriction is in force, it naturally influences the dividend policy of the firm. Sometimes the management of a company welcomes a dividend restriction imposed by lenders because it does not then have to justify to stockholders the retention of earnings. It need only point to the restriction.

SOME FINAL OBSERVATIONS

In determining a dividend payout, the typical company will analyze a number of factors already described. These factors largely dictate the boundaries within which a dividend can be paid. When a company pays a dividend in excess of its residual funds, it implies that management and the board of directors believe the payment has a favorable effect on shareholder wealth. The frustrating thing is that we have so little in the way of clear generalizations from the empirical evidence. The lack of firm footing for predicting the long-run effect of a specific dividend policy on valuation makes the dividend decision more difficult in many ways than either the investment or financing decisions.

Considerations taken up in the section above allow a company to determine with reasonable accuracy what would be an appropriate passive dividend strategy. An active dividend policy involves an act of faith, because it demands that a portion of the cumulative dividends ultimately be replaced with common stock financing. Such a strategy is undertaken in a foggy area, but one in which most academics have difficulty believing shareholder wealth will be enhanced. Notwithstanding, many companies profess a belief that dividend payout affects share price and behave in a manner consistent with dividends mattering.

If dividends are not an efficient means for transmitting excess funds to stockholders, we might ask, What is? One means is the repurchase of stock, a topic taken up in the next chapter. This alternative results in capital gains income as opposed to dividend income. Even if both incomes are taxed the same, capital gains can be postponed, which makes share repurchase a more tax-efficient way of distributing excess liquidity. What if the liquidity is not excess, but merely held as a store of value pending future investment opportunities? After all, a cash dividend or a share repurchase is an irreversible decision.

If a company seeks a passive investment, money market securities are tax disadvantaged. The company pays a tax at the corporate level, and stockholders pay personal taxes upon eventual distribution. A better passive investment might be a diversified portfolio of common stocks. The portfolio could be selected to match the systematic risk of the firm, though this is not necessary. Dividend income on the portfolio is 70 percent exempt from corporate taxation. While the remaining 30 percent is taxed at the corporate tax rate, the overall tax bite is not large. If a firm wishes to hold liquidity for future investment opportunities, the diversified portfolio of common stocks makes good sense theoretically and is low cost.

The critical question in dividend policy is whether dividends have an influence on the value of the firm, given its investment decision. If dividends are irrelevant, as Modigliani and Miller believe, the firm should retain earnings only in keeping with its investment opportunities. If there are not sufficient investment opportunities providing expected returns in excess of the required return, the unused funds should be paid out as dividends.

The key issue is whether dividends are more than just a means of distributing unused funds. If they do affect the value of the common stock, dividend policy becomes more than a passive variable determined solely by the investment opportunities available. The firm could affect shareholder wealth by varying its dividend-payout ratio. As a result, there would be an optimal dividend policy.

With perfect capital markets and an absence of taxes, stockholders can manufacture "homemade" dividends and make dividend payout irrelevant. With differential taxes on dividends and capital gains, there seemingly is a bias in favor of retention; however, different investors are affected differently. Some may be able to avoid taxes on dividends, and this tax dodge was investigated, as was the clientele theory, where corporations alter the supply of dividends in keeping with the tax situation of investor clienteles.

The market imperfection of flotation costs biases things in favor of retention because retention is less expensive than the common-stock financing used to replace the dividend. Quality restrictions on the investment behavior of financial institutions work in the direction of a preference for dividends. Finally, for psychological reasons, certain investors may prefer dividends to the retention of earnings and capital gains. Financial signaling implies that dividends may be used to convey information. That information, rather than the dividend itself, affects valuation.

Empirical testing of dividend policy has focused on whether there is a tax effect and whether dividends serve as signals in conveying information. The evidence is conflicting with respect to the former, ranging from a neutral effect to a negative effect. However, there seems to be agreement that dividends provide financial signals. In final analysis, we are unable to state whether the dividend payout of the firm should be more than a passive decision variable. Most academics think not. Admittedly, many companies behave as if dividend policy is relevant, but the case for it is not conclusive.

In the last section, we examined various managerial considerations when a company is faced with a dividend decision. These factors include the funds needs of the firm, liquidity, ability to borrow, assessment of any valuation information, control and the nature of stockholders, and restrictions in bond indentures or loan agreements. In the next chapter, we extend our analysis of the dividend payout and examine other aspects of dividend policy.

SELF-CORRECTION PROBLEMS

1. The Beta-Alpha Company expects with some degree of certainty to generate the following net income and to have the following capital expenditures during the next 5 years (in thousands):

YEAR	1	2	3	4	5
Net income	$2,000	$1,500	$2,500	$2,300	$1,800
Capital expenditures	1,000	1,500	2,000	1,500	2,000

The company currently has 1 million shares of common stock outstanding and pays dividends of $1 per share.

a. Determine dividends per share and external financing required in each year if dividend policy is treated as a residual decision.

b. Determine the amounts of external financing in each year that will be necessary if the present dividend per share is maintained.

c. Determine dividends per share and the amounts of external financing that will be necessary if a dividend-payout ratio of 50 percent is maintained.

d. Under which of the three dividend policies are aggregate dividends maximized? external financing minimized?

2. Do-Re-Me Corporation makes musical instruments and experiences only moderate growth. The company has just paid a dividend and is contemplating a dividend of $1.35 per share 1 year hence. The present market price per share is $15, and stock price appreciation of 5 percent per annum is expected.

a. If the required return on equity were 14 percent and we lived in a no-tax world, what would be the market price per share at the end of the year using the Miller-Modigliani model? What would be the price if no dividend were paid?

b. Jose Hernandez, a stockholder, is in a 30 percent tax bracket for ordinary income, but his effective tax rate for capital gains is 26 percent. If he were to hold the stock 1 year, what would be his expected after-tax return in dollars for each share held?

c. Explain in general how Hernandez might avoid taxes on his dividend income à la Miller and Scholes.

3. For each of the companies described below, would you expect it to have a medium/high or a low dividend-payout ratio? Explain why.

a. A company with a large proportion of inside ownership, all of whom are high-income individuals

b. A growth company with an abundance of good investment opportunities

c. A company experiencing ordinary growth that has high liquidity and much unused borrowing capacity

d. A dividend-paying company that experiences an unexpected drop in earnings from a trend

e. A company with volatile earnings and high business risk

PROBLEMS

1. Financial data on two companies are shown in the accompanying table. What differences reflected in these data give insight into dividend policy and valuation?

	CLEVELAND MACHINE TOOL COMPANY			FOX ELECTRONICS COMPANY		
	Earnings per Share	Dividends per Share	Range P/E Ratio	Earnings per Share	Dividends per Share	Range P/E Ratio
19x9	$3.02	$1.50	8-12	$1.18	$ .15	25-32
19x8	3.19	1.50	9-14	1.02	.10	25-35
19x7	3.10	1.25	13-18	.81	.10	30-40
19x6	2.90	1.25	10-17	.72	.10	30-40
19x5	1.06	1.25	13-17	.48	.05	35-45
19x4	2.03	1.25	14-18	.41	.05	40-50
19x3	2.87	1.25	15-23	.29	.05	45-55
19x2	2.13	1.25	11-16	.20	.04	40-50
19x1	1.32	1.00	8-13	.14	.00	30-45
19x0	2.21	1.00	10-15	.13	.00	30-40

2. Malkor Instruments Company treats dividends as a residual decision. It expects to generate $2 million in net earnings after taxes in the coming year. The company has an all-equity capital structure and its cost of equity capital is 15 percent. The company treats this cost as the opportunity cost of retained earnings. Because of flotation costs and underpricing, the cost of common stock financing is higher. It is 16 percent.

    a. How much in dividends (out of the $2 million in earnings) should be paid if the company has $1.5 million in projects whose expected return exceeds 15 percent?

    b. How much in dividends should be paid if it has $2 million in projects whose expected return exceeds 15 percent?

    c. How much in dividends should be paid if it has $3 million in projects whose expected return exceeds 16 percent? What else should be done?

3. The Mann Company belongs to a risk class for which the appropriate required equity return is 15 percent. It currently has outstanding 100,000 shares selling at $100 each. The firm is contemplating the declaration of a $5 dividend at the end of the current fiscal year, which just began. Answer the following questions based on the Modigliani and Miller model and the assumption of no taxes.

    a. What will be the price of the stock at the end of the year if a dividend is not declared? What will it be if one is?

    b. Assuming that the firm pays the dividend, has net income of $1 million, and makes new investments of $2 million during the period, how many new shares must be issued?

    c. Is the MM model realistic with respect to valuation? What factors might mar its validity?

4. The University of Northern California pays no taxes on the dividend income and capital gains received on its various endowment funds. Over the years, it has steadily bought the stock of IVM Corporation for its alumni fellowship fund. The alumni campaign is such that the bulk of alumni giving occurs in the months of June and December. Coincidentally, IVM pays a semiannual dividend in these months. In the past, the university has not paid attention to whether it bought the stock before or after the ex-dividend dates of June 10 and December 10. (Before the ex-dividend date, investors are entitled to the dividend; after, they are not.) The feeling has been that the stock will decline by the amount of the dividend on the ex-dividend date, so it really does not matter when the stock is purchased.

    Shirley McDonald, the finance officer of the university, has just completed a study showing that over the years IVM's stock price on average declined by only 90 percent of the dividend per share on the ex-dividend date. She attributes this occurrence to the fact that a number of investors are interested in capital gains.

As a result, these investors buy the stock after the ex-dividend date, and the impact of their purchases causes the stock to decline by less than the amount of the dividend. In view of this finding, should the university change the timing of its purchases of IVM stock? If so, how should it change?

5. Corinth Kazabek is in a 28 percent tax bracket for ordinary income, but her effective tax rate on capital gains is 24 percent. She has invested $15,000 in Insell Corporation. This stock has a 6 percent dividend yield and is expected to have price appreciation of 9 percent per annum.

   a. If she plans to sell the stock after 1 year, what will be Kazabek's expected after-tax dollar return?

   b. Kazabek is able to borrow on personal account at an interest rate of 12 percent. Her intention is to borrow and invest the proceeds of the loan in additional Insell stock. If she wishes to neutralize total dividend income with interest expense, how much will she borrow?

   c. Under part b, what will be her expected after-tax dollar return, assuming that she sells the stock after 1 year and pays off her borrowings? How does this return compare with that in part a? Why is there a difference?

6. Crown Chemical Corporation currently pays no dividends and is evaluating the appropriate dividend-payout ratio, if any. The company has an all-equity capital structure, and over the years its capital expenditures have approximately equaled its earnings plus depreciation charges. As a result, any dividend that is paid eventually will have to come from a common stock offering. On the basis of a careful empirical study, Crown has found a net preference in the market for dividends, as opposed to retention, for its type of company. It attributes this net preference to tax-free institutional investors, which are constrained in their investment behavior to dividend-paying stocks and which desire to hold chemical stocks because of portfolio considerations. Crown estimates it could change the market price of its stock by the following formula if it took advantage of this imperfection:

   $$\text{Price change} = .5 \text{ (Dividend-payout ratio)} - .6 \text{ (Dividend-payout ratio)}^2$$

   where the dividend-payout ratio is expressed in decimal form. (For example, a payout ratio of 50 percent is .50.) Any new sale of stock will have an adverse effect on share price, however, owing to flotation costs and underpricing. Crown estimates that this factor, in isolation from the previous factor, will lower share price according to the following formula,

   $$\text{Price change} = -.05 \text{ (Dividend-payout ratio)}$$

   where again the ratio is expressed in decimal form.

   a. The company is considering dividend-payout ratios in increments of .10, going from 0 to 1.00, which represents a 100 percent payout. On the basis of this information, determine the optimal dividend-payout ratio. (*Hint for spreadsheet programming:* Set up the problem with four columns—one for the payout ratio, the second for the first formula, the next for the second formula, and the last for the combined effect. The second column might be determined by 0.5*A6-0.6*A6^2, where A6 refers to specific dividend payout in column-row A6, for example.)

   b. What would happen if the coefficients in the first formula were .6 and .5 instead of .5 and .6?

   c. What if they were .4 and .7, respectively?

   d. What if the coefficient in the second formula were −.08 instead of −.05?

7. The Eureka Mining Company consists of one mine, which has a remaining useful life of 5 years. The owners feel that no new shafts should be sunk for at least this long; indeed, they probably will not continue in this business after five years. Since the initiation of the company, total cash flows have been paid out in dividends. All the firm's stockholders were original investors, have a marginal tax rate of 40 percent (federal and state), and require an after-tax return of 10 percent. The mine will generate the following income during each of the next 5 years:

Net operating income	$25,000	
Less depreciation and depletion	5,000	
Net income before taxes	$20,000	
Less: Taxes	4,400	
Net income	$15,600	

Compute the total value of Eureka to its stockholders if all available funds were paid in dividends at the end of the year they became available. (Assume depreciation and depletion are a return of capital not subject to personal taxation, whereas net income paid in dividends is subject to personal taxation.)

8. Forte Papers Corporation and Great Southern Paper Company are in the same industry, both are publicly held with a large number of stockholders, and they have the following characteristics:

	FORTE	GREAT SOUTHERN
Expected annual cash flow (000)	$ 50,000	$35,000
Standard deviation of cash flows (000)	30,000	25,000
Annual capital expenditures (000)	42,000	40,000
Cash and marketable securities (000)	5,000	7,000
Existing long-term debt (000)	100,000	85,000
Unused short-term line of credit (000)	25,000	10,000
Flotation costs and underpricing on common-stock issues as a percent of proceeds	.05	.08

On the basis of this information, which company is likely to have the higher dividend-payout ratio? Why?

SOLUTIONS TO SELF-CORRECTION PROBLEMS

1. a.

YEAR	INCOME AVAILABLE FOR DIVIDENDS	DIVIDENDS PER SHARE	EXTERNAL FINANCING
1	$1,000	$1.00	0
2	0	0	0
3	500	.50	0
4	800	.80	0
5	0	0	$200
	$2,300		$200

b.

YEAR	(1) NET INCOME	(2) DIVIDENDS	(3) CAPITAL EXPENDITURES	(4) EXTERNAL FINANCING (2) + (3) − (1)
1	$2,000	$1,000	$1,000	0
2	1,500	1,000	1,500	$1,000
3	2,500	1,000	2,000	500
4	2,300	1,000	1,500	200
5	1,800	1,000	2,000	1,200
		$5,000		$2,900

c.

YEAR	(1) NET INCOME	(2) DIVIDENDS	(3) DIVIDENDS PER SHARE	(4) CAPITAL EXPENDITURES	(5) EXTERNAL FINANCING (2) + (4) − (1)
1	$2,000	$1,000	$1.00	$1,000	0
2	1,500	750	.75	1,500	$750
3	2,500	1,250	1.25	2,000	750
4	2,300	1,150	1.15	1,500	350
5	1,800	900	.90	2,000	1,100
		$5,050			$2,950

d. Aggregate dividends are highest under alternative c, which involves a 50 percent dividend payout. However, they are only slightly higher than that which occurs under alternative b. External financing is minimized under alternative a, the residual dividend policy.

2. **a.** Using Eq. (12-1) in the chapter and rearranging, $P_1 = P_0(1 + \rho) - D_1$
With a dividend, $P_1 = \$15(1 + .14) - \$1.35 = \$15.75$
Without a dividend, $P_1 = \$15(1 + .14) - 0 = \$17.10$
The investor would have the same total value (share price plus dividend) either way.

b.

	AMOUNT	TAX RATE	TAX	A.T. AMOUNT
Dividend	$1.35	30%	$.405	$ .945
Capital gain	.75	26%	.195	.555
Total after-tax return				$1.500

c. According to Miller-Scholes, Hernandez should borrow a sufficient sum of money so that his interest expense exactly offsets the expected dividend income of $1.35 per share. The proceeds of the loan are invested in additional stock of the company, so the interest expense must offset not only dividends on the stock already owned but dividends on the new stock as well. The dividend income is neutralized, and all of the return will be a capital gain. To neutralize the added price risk, Hernandez may wish to use an insurance annuity in the manner illustrated in the chapter.

3. The answers assume all things are held constant other than the item in question.
   a. Low payout ratio. Highly taxed owners probably will want to realize their returns through capital gains.

b. Low payout ratio. There will be no residual funds.

c. Medium or high payout ratio. There are likely to be funds left over after funding capital expenditures. Moreover, the liquidity and access to borrowing give the company considerable flexibility.

d. Medium or high payout ratio. Unless the company cuts its dividend, which probably is unlikely in the short run, its payout ratio will rise with the drop in earnings.

e. Low payout ratio. The company will probably wish to retain earnings to build its financial strength in order to offset the high business risk.

SELECTED REFERENCES

ANG, JAMES S., and DAVID R. PETERSON, "Return, Risk and Yield: Evidence from Ex Ante Data," *Journal of Finance*, 40 (June 1985), 537–48.

ASQUITH, PAUL, and DAVID W. MULLINS, JR., "The Impact of Initiating Dividend Payments on Shareholders' Wealth," *Journal of Business*, 56 (January 1983), 77–96.

———, "Signalling with Dividends, Stock Repurchases, and Equity Issues," *Financial Management*, 15 (Autumn 1986), 27–44.

BHATTACHARYA, SUDIPTO, "Imperfect Information, Dividend Policy, and the 'Bird-in-the-Hand' Fallacy," *Bell Journal of Economics*, 10 (Spring 1979), 259–70.

BLACK, FISCHER, "The Dividend Puzzle," *Journal of Portfolio Management*, 2 (Winter 1976), 5–8.

———, and MYRON SCHOLES, "The Effects of Dividend Yield and Dividend Policy on Common Stock Prices and Returns," *Journal of Financial Economics*, 1 (May 1974), 1–22.

BLUME, MARSHALL, "Stock Returns and Dividend Yields: Some More Evidence," *Review of Economics and Statistics*, 62 (November 1980), 567–77.

CAMPBELL, JOHN Y., and ROBERT J. SHILLER, "The Dividend-Price Ratio and Expectations of Future Dividends and Discount Factors," *Review of Financial Studies*, 1 (Fall 1988), 195–228.

CHANG, ROSITA P., and S. GHON RHEE, "The Impact of Personal Taxes on Corporate Dividend Policy and Capital Structure Decisions," *Financial Management*, 19 (Summer 1990), 21–31.

CHEN, NAI-FU, BRUCE GRUNDY, and ROBERT F. STAMBAUGH, "Changing Risk, Changing Risk Premiums, and Dividend Yield Effects," Merton Miller Conference in Honor of His 65th Birthday (August 1988).

ELTON, EDWIN J., and MARTIN J. GRUBER, "Marginal Stockholder Tax Rates and the Clientele Effect," *Review of Economics and Statistics*, 52 (February 1970), 68–74.

GORDON, MYRON J., "Why Corporations Pay Dividends," *Studies in Banking and Finance*, 5 (1988), 77–96.

HEALY, PAUL M., and KRISHNA G. PALEPU, "Earnings Information Conveyed by Dividend Initiations and Omissions," *Journal of Financial Economics*, 21 (September 1988), 149–75.

HIGGINS, ROBERT C., "The Corporate Dividend Saving Decision," *Journal of Financial and Quantitative Analysis*, 7 (March 1972), 1527–41.

JOHN, KOSE, and JOSEPH WILLIAMS, "Dividends, Dilution, and Taxes: A Signalling Equilibrium," *Journal of Finance*, 40 (September 1985), 1053–70.

KALAY, AVNER, "The Ex-Dividend Day Behavior of Stock Prices: A Re-examination of the Clientele Effect," *Journal of Finance*, 37 (September 1982), 1059–70.

KEIM, DONALD B., "Dividend Yields and Stock Returns: Implications of Abnormal January Returns," *Journal of Financial Economics*, 14 (September 1985), 473–89.

LANG, LARRY H. P., and ROBERT H. LITZENBERGER, "Dividend Announcements: Cash Flow Signalling vs. Free Cash Flow Hypothesis," *Journal of Financial Economics*, 24 (September 1989), 181–91.

LINTNER, JOHN, "Distribution of Income of Corporations among Dividends, Retained Earnings, and Taxes," *American Economic Review*, 46 (May 1956), 97–113.

LITZENBERGER, ROBERT H., and KRISHNA RAMISWAMY, "The Effect of Personal Taxes and Dividends on Capital Assest Prices," *Journal of Financial Economics,* 7 (June 1979), 163–95.

———, "Dividends, Short Selling Restrictions, Tax Induced Investor Clienteles and Market Equilibrium," *Journal of Finance,* 35 (May 1980), 469–82.

LITZENBERGER, ROBERT H., and JAMES C. VAN HORNE, "Elimination of the Double Taxation of Dividends and Corporate Financial Policy," *Journal of Finance,* 33 (June 1978), 737–49.

MARSH, TERRY A., and ROBERT C. MERTON, "Dividend Behavior for the Aggregate Stock Market," *Journal of Business,* 60 (January 1987), 1–40.

MILLER, MERTON H., and FRANCO MODIGLIANI, "Dividend Policy, Growth, and the Valuation of Shares," *Journal of Business,* 34 (October 1961), 411–33.

MILLER, MERTON H., and KEVIN ROCK, "Dividend Policy under Asymmetric Information," *Journal of Finance,* 40 (September 1985), 1031–51.

MILLER, MERTON H., and MYRON S. SCHOLES, "Dividends and Taxes," *Journal of Financial Economics,* 6 (December 1978), 333–64.

OFER, AHARON R., and DANIEL R. SIEGEL, "Corporate Financial Policy, Information and Market Expectations: An Empirical Investigation of Dividends," *Journal of Finance,* 42 (September 1987), 889–912.

SHEFRIN, HERSH M., and MEIR STATMAN, "Explaining Investor Preferences for Cash Dividends," *Journal of Financial Economics,* 13 (June 1984), 253–82.

VAN HORNE, JAMES C., and JOHN C. MCDONALD, "Dividend Policy and New Equity Financing," *Journal of Finance,* 26 (May 1971), 507–19.

WATTS, ROSS, "The Information Content of Dividends," *Journal of Business,* 46 (April 1973), 191–211.

13

OTHER ASPECTS OF DIVIDEND POLICY

Although the dividend-payout ratio is a major aspect of the overall dividend policy of a company, it is not the only one. Other aspects may affect valuation. In this chapter, we consider the stability of dividends, stock dividends and stock splits, the repurchase of stock, and the procedural and legal elements of dividend policy.

STABILITY OF DIVIDENDS

In addition to the percentage of dividend payout, stability is attractive to investors. By *stability*, we mean maintaining its position in relation to a trend line, preferably one that is upward sloping. All other things being the same, a stock that pays a stable dividend over time may be priced higher than if it pays out a fixed percentage of earnings. Suppose company A has a long-run dividend payout ratio of 50 percent of earnings. It pays out this percentage every year, despite the fact that its earnings are cyclical. The dividends of company A are shown in Fig. 13-1. Company B, on the other hand, has exactly the same earnings and a long-run dividend-payout ratio of 50 percent, but it maintains a relatively stable dividend over time. It changes the absolute amount of dividend only in keeping with the underlying trend of earnings. The dividends of company B are shown in Fig. 13-2.

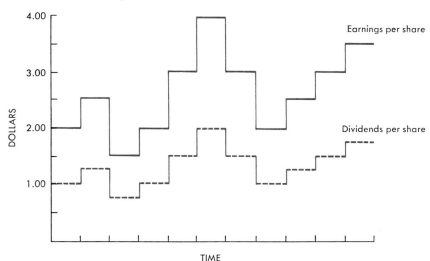

FIGURE 13-1
Hypothetical dividend policy of company A

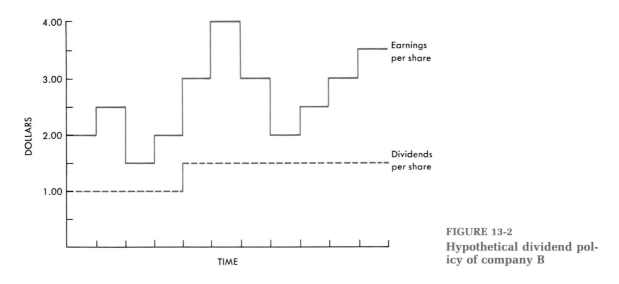

FIGURE 13-2
Hypothetical dividend policy of company B

Over the long run, the total amount of dividends paid by these two firms is the same; however, the market price per share of company B may be higher than that of company A, all other things being the same. Investors may well place a positive utility on dividend stability and pay a premium for the company that offers it. To the extent that investors value dividend stability, the overall dividend policy of company B would be better than that of company A. This policy includes not only the percentage of dividend payout in relation to earnings but also the manner in which the actual dividends are paid. Rather than vary dividends directly with changes in earnings per share, company B raises the dividend only when reasonably confident a higher dividend can be maintained.

VALUATION OF STABILITY

Investors may be willing to pay a premium for stable dividends because of the informational content of dividends, the desire of investors for current income, and certain institutional considerations.

Informational Content. As we said in the preceding chapter, dividends may serve to resolve uncertainty in the minds of investors. When earnings drop and a company does not cut its dividend, the market may have more confidence in the stock than it would have if the dividend were cut. The stable dividend may convey management's view that the future of the company is better than the drop in earnings suggests. Thus, management may be able to influence the expectations of investors through the informational content of dividends. Management will not be able to fool the market permanently. If there is a downward trend in earnings, a stable dividend will not convey forever an impression of a rosy future. Moreover, if a company is in an unstable business with wide swings in earnings, a stable dividend cannot give the illusion of underlying stability.

Current Income Desires. A second factor may favor stable dividends. Investors who desire a specific periodic income will prefer a company with stable dividends to one with unstable dividends, even though both companies may have the same pattern of earnings and long-run dividend payout. Although investors can always sell portions of their stock for income when the dividend is not sufficient to meet their current needs, many investors have an aversion to dipping into principal and to transaction and inconvenience costs. For these reasons, income-conscious investors may place utility on stable dividends.

Institutional Considerations. A stable dividend may be advantageous from the standpoint of permitting certain institutional investors to buy the stock. Various governmental bodies prepare lists of securities in which pension funds, savings banks, trustees, insurance companies, and certain others may invest. In order to qualify, a company often must have an uninterrupted pattern of dividends. A cut in dividends or their omission may result in removal of a company from these lists.

The arguments presented in support of the notion that stable dividends have a positive effect on the market price of the stock are only suggestive. Little empirical evidence sheds light on the question. Although studies of individual stocks often suggest that stable dividends buffer the market price of the stock when earnings turn down, there have been no comprehensive studies of a large sample of stocks dealing with the relationship between dividend stability and valuation. Nevertheless, most companies strive for stability in their dividend payments. This is consistent with a belief that stable dividends have a positive effect on value.

TARGET-PAYOUT RATIOS

A number of companies appear to follow the policy of a target dividend-payout ratio over the long run. Lintner contends that dividends are adjusted to changes in earnings, but only with a lag.[1] When earnings increase to a new level, a company increases dividends only when it feels it can maintain the increase in earnings. Companies are also reluctant to cut the absolute amount of their cash dividend. Both of these factors explain the lag in dividend changes behind changes in earnings. In an economic upturn, the lag relationship becomes visible when retained earnings increase in relation to dividends. In a contraction, retained earnings grow at a slower rate than dividends.

REGULAR AND EXTRA DIVIDENDS

One way for a company to increase its cash distribution in periods of prosperity is to declare an *extra* dividend in addition to the *regular* quarterly or semiannual dividend. By declaring an extra dividend, the company warns investors that the dividend is not an increase in the established dividend rate. The declaration of an extra dividend is particularly suitable for companies with fluctuating earnings. General Motors, for example, sometimes declares extra dividends in good years. The use of the extra dividend enables the company to maintain a stable record of regular dividends but also to distribute to

[1] See John Lintner, "Distribution of Income of Corporations among Dividends, Retained Earnings and Taxes," *American Economic Review*, 46 (May 1956), 97–113.

stockholders some of the rewards of prosperity. Companies that issue extra dividends often are characterized by fluctuating earnings as a result of being in cyclical industries, as well as by a lack of growth opportunities. If a company pays the same extra dividend annually, it defeats its purpose. The extra becomes the expected. When properly labeled, however, an extra or special dividend conveys positive information to the market concerning the firm's present and future performance.[2]

STOCK DIVIDENDS AND STOCK SPLITS

In an economic sense, stock dividends and stock splits are very similar, although typically used for different purposes. Only from an accounting standpoint is there a significant difference.

STOCK DIVIDENDS

A stock dividend simply is the payment of additional stock to stockholders. It represents nothing more than a recapitalization of the company; a stockholder's proportional ownership remains unchanged. Chen Industries had the following capital structure before issuing a stock dividend:

Common stock ($5 par, 400,000 shares)	$ 2,000,000
Additional paid-in capital	1,000,000
Retained earnings	7,000,000
Shareholders' equity	$10,000,000

Chen pays a 5 percent stock dividend, amounting to 20,000 additional shares of stock. The fair market value of the stock is $40 a share. For each 20 shares of stock owned, the stockholder receives an additional share. The balance sheet of the company after the stock dividend is

Common stock ($5 par, 420,000 shares)	$ 2,100,000
Additional paid-in capital	1,700,000
Retained earnings	6,200,000
Shareholders' equity	$10,000,000

With a stock dividend, $800,000 is transferred ($40 × 20,000 shares) from retained earnings to the common stock and paid-in capital accounts. Because the par value stays the same, the increase in number of shares is reflected in a $100,000 increase in the common stock account ($5 par × 20,000 shares). The

[2]James A. Brickley, "Shareholder Wealth, Information Signaling and the Specially Designated Dividend: An Empirical Study," *Journal of Financial Economics,* 12 (August 1983), 187–210, analyzes this phenomenon using the events study methodology and finds support for an information effect. However, a regular dividend increase was found to convey even more positive information.

residual of $700,000 goes into the paid-in capital account. Shareholders' equity of the company remains the same.

Because the number of shares of stock outstanding is increased by 5 percent, earnings per share of the company are reduced proportionately. Total net profit after taxes is $1 million. Before the stock dividend, earnings per share were $2.50 ($1 million/400,000). After the stock dividend, earnings per share are $2.38 ($1 million/420,000). Thus, stockholders have more shares of stock but lower earnings per share. The proportion of total earnings available to common stockholders remains unchanged.

The accounting treatment portrayed holds for what is known as *small-percentage stock dividends*, usually a distribution of 20 percent or less of the number of common shares already outstanding. Because larger stock dividends will materially reduce share price, the accounting authorities usually require that capitalization changes be in terms of the par value of the additional shares issued. (For small-percentage dividends, market value per share is employed.) Suppose in our example that Chen Industries declared a 50 percent stock dividend, amounting to 200,000 additional shares. The capitalization accounts after a *large-percentage stock dividend* of this sort are

Common stock ($5 par, 600,000 shares)	$ 3,000,000
Additional paid-in capital	1,000,000
Retained earnings	6,000,000
Shareholders' equity	$10,000,000

Thus, retained earnings are reduced by only the par value of new shares issued.

STOCK SPLITS

With a stock split, the number of shares is increased through a proportional reduction in the par value of the stock. The capital structure of a lumber company before a 2-to-1 stock split was

Common stock ($5 par, 400,000 shares)	$ 2,000,000
Additional paid-in capital	1,000,000
Retained earnings	7,000,000
Shareholders' equity	$10,000,000

After the split, the capital structure was

Common stock ($2.50 par, 800,000 shares)	$ 2,000,000
Additional paid-in capital	1,000,000
Retained earnings	7,000,000
Shareholders' equity	$10,000,000

With a stock dividend, the par value is not reduced, whereas with a split, it is. As a result, the common stock, paid-in capital, and retained earnings accounts remain unchanged. Shareholders' equity, of course, also stays the same; the only change is in the par value of the stock. Except in accounting treatment, the stock dividend and stock split are very similar. A stock split, however, is usually reserved for occasions when a company wishes to achieve a substantial reduction in the market price per share.

Very seldom will a company maintain the same cash dividends per share before and after a split, but it may increase the effective dividends to stockholders. A company may split its stock 2 for 1 and establish a dividend rate of $1.20 a share, whereas before, the rate was $2.00 a share. A stockholder owning 100 shares before the split would receive $200 in cash dividends per annum. After the split, the stockholder would own 200 shares and would receive $240 in dividends.

VALUE TO INVESTORS
OF STOCK DIVIDENDS AND SPLITS

Theoretically, a stock dividend or stock split is not a thing of value to investors. They receive additional stock certificates, but their proportionate ownership of the company is unchanged. The market price of the stock should decline proportionately, so that the total value of their holdings stays the same. To illustrate with a stock dividend, suppose you held 100 shares of stock worth $40 per share, or $4,000 in total. After a 5 percent stock dividend, share price should drop by $40(1 − 1.00/1.05), or $1.90. The total value of your holdings then would be $38.10 × 105, or $4,000. Under these conditions, the stock dividend does not represent a thing of value to you. You merely have an additional stock certificate evidencing ownership. In theory, the stock dividend or split is purely cosmetic.

To the extent that the investor wishes to sell a few shares of stock for income, the stock dividend may make it easier to do so. Without the stock dividend, of course, stockholders could also sell a few shares of their original holdings for income. In either case, the sale of stock represents the sale of principal and is subject to the capital gains tax. Some investors, however, may not look on the sale of a stock dividend as a sale of principal. To them, the stock dividend represents a windfall gain; they can sell it and still retain their original holdings. The stock dividend may have a favorable psychological effect on these stockholders. In efficient markets, however, we would not expect a favorable impact on share price.

Effect on Cash Dividends. The stock dividend or stock split may be accompanied by an increased cash dividend. For the former, suppose an investor owns 100 shares of a company paying a $1 dividend. The company declares a 10 percent stock dividend and, at the same time, announces that the cash dividend per share will remain unchanged. The investor then will have 110 shares, and total cash dividends will be $110 rather than $100, as before. In this case, a stock dividend increases the total cash dividends. Whether this increase in cash dividend has a positive effect on shareholder wealth will depend on the valuation of dividends, which we discussed in the last chapter. Clearly, the stock dividend in this case represents a decision by the firm to increase modestly the amount of cash dividends. However, it does not need the stock dividend to do so. The firm could merely increase its cash dividend per share from $1.00 to $1.10.

Sometimes a stock dividend is employed to conserve cash. Instead of increasing the cash dividend as earnings rise, a company may desire to retain a greater portion of its earnings and declare a modest stock dividend. The decision then is to lower the dividend-payout ratio, for as earnings rise and total cash dividends remain approximately the same, the payout ratio will decline. Whether shareholder wealth is increased by this action will depend on considerations taken up in the preceding chapter. The decision to retain a higher proportion of earnings, of course, could be accomplished without a stock dividend. However, the stock dividend may tend to please certain investors by virtue of its psychological impact. But the substitution of stock for cash dividends involves a sizable administrative cost. Stock dividends simply are much more costly to administer than are cash dividends, and this out-of-pocket expense works to their disadvantage.

More-Popular Trading Range. A stock split and, to a lesser extent, a stock dividend are used to place the stock in a lower, more-popular trading range. By so doing, more buyers may be attracted. This may affect the mix of stockholders, toward increased individual holdings and decreased institutional holdings. Christopher G. Lamoreux and Percy Poon find that the average number of stockholders increases by some 35 percent in the year of a stock split.[3] Also, trading volume tends to increase after the split. Whether this wider ownership is a thing of value is another matter. Let us look further.

Informational or Signaling Effect. The declaration of a stock dividend or a stock split may convey information about future earnings to investors. As taken up in Chapters 10 and 12 for capital structure and cash dividend changes, there may be asymmetric information between management and investors. With a precise managerial contract, managers will have an incentive to provide favorable information to investors if they believe the stock is truly undervalued. (However, the contract must also have disincentives for false signals.) Instead of a press announcement, a stock dividend or split may connote more convincingly management's belief about the favorable prospects of the company. In this sense, the stock dividend or split is an attention-getting device.

Whether these signals are more convincing is an empirical question. Here there have been a number of event type of studies.[4] Such studies attempt to isolate the abnormal return associated with a particular event—in this case, a stock dividend or split. The abnormal return is simply the residual after

---

[3] Christopher G. Lamoreux and Percy Poon, "The Market Reaction to Stock Splits," *Journal of Finance*, 42 (December 1987), 1347–70.

[4] A classic earlier study is by Eugene F. Fama, Lawrence Fisher, Michael Jensen, and Richard Roll, "The Adjustment of Stock Prices to New Information," *International Economic Review*, 10 (February 1969), 1–21. Subsequent studies include Guy Charest, "Split Information, Stock Returns and Market Efficiency," *Journal of Financial Economics*, 6 (June–September 1978), 265–96; J. Randall Woolridge, "Stock Dividends as Signals," *Journal of Financial Research*, 6 (Spring 1983), 1–12; Mark S. Grinblatt, Ronald W. Masulis, and Sheridan Titman, "The Valuation Effects of Stock Splits and Stock Dividends," *Journal of Financial Economics*, 13 (December 1984), 461–90; Michael J. Brennan and Thomas E. Copeland, "Stock Splits, Stock Prices and Transaction Costs," *Journal of Financial Economics*, 22 (October 1988), 83–101; and Maureen McNichols and Ajay Dravid, "Stock Dividends, Stock Splits, and Signaling," *Journal of Finance*, 45 (July 1990), 857–79.

risk-adjusted market movements (beta), and perhaps other factors, have been taken into account. If stock dividends and splits have a positive signaling effect, a plot of the cumulative residuals might look like that shown in Fig. 13-3. In the several days surrounding the announcement, there is a run-up in the cumulative abnormal return, after which the higher level of security price persists owing to the favorable information effect.

In addition to risk-adjusted market movements, it is important to hold constant changes in cash dividends that may accompany the announcement. The various studies are not uniform in this regard. However, the overwhelming conclusion of them is that there is a statistically significant and positive stock price reaction around the announcement of a stock dividend or a stock split.[5] The evidence is consistent with an information or signaling effect, namely, that the stock is undervalued and should be priced higher. Moreover, Maureen McNichols and Ajay Dravid find that the greater the split factor, the greater the stock price reaction, suggesting that investors draw inferences about value not only from the announcement of a stock split but from the split factor as well.[6] Of course, the company must eventually deliver improved earnings if the stock is to remain higher. The underlying cause for the increase in market price is perceived future earnings, not the stock dividend nor split itself.

REVERSE STOCK SPLITS

Rather than increase the number of shares of stock outstanding, a company may want to reduce the number. It can accomplish this with a *reverse split*. In our stock split example before, had there been a 1-to-4 reverse split instead of the 2-to-1 straight stock split, for each four shares held, the stockholder would receive one share in exchange. The par value per share would become $20, and there would be 100,000 shares outstanding rather than 400,000. Reverse stock splits are employed to increase the market price per

[5] Kenneth M. Eades, Patrick J. Hess, and E. Han Kim, "On Interpreting Security Returns during the Ex-Dividend Period," *Journal of Financial Economics,* 13 (March 1984), 3–34, in testing the ex-day behavior of stock dividends and stock splits find significant excess returns on the ex-day. As the announcement occurs well before the ex-day, the results are most surprising. There is no logical explanation for them.

[6] McNichols and Dravid, "Stock Dividends, Stock Splits, and Signaling."

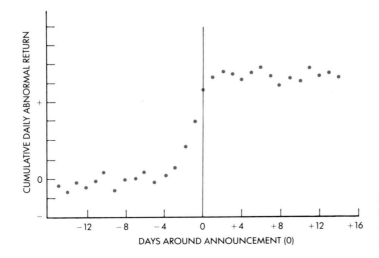

FIGURE 13-3
Cumulative daily abnormal returns around stock dividend or stock split announcement

share when the stock is considered to be selling at too low a price. Many companies have an aversion to seeing their stock fall below $10 per share. If financial difficulty or some other depressant lowers the price into this range, it can be increased with a reverse split.

As with stock dividends and straight stock splits, there is likely to be an information or signaling effect associated with the announcement. Usually the signal is negative, such as would accompany the admission by a company that it is in financial difficulty. However, this need not be the case; the company simply may want to place the stock in a higher trading range where trading costs and servicing expenses are lower. Nonetheless, the empirical evidence is consistent with a statistically significant decline in share price around the announcement date, holding other things constant.[7] The decline is tempered by the company's past earnings performance, but a healthy company should think twice before undertaking a reverse stock split. There are too many bad apples in the barrel not to be tainted by association.

SHARE REPURCHASE

In recent years, the repurchase of stock by corporations has grown dramatically. In the aggregate, share repurchase now comes to roughly one-half of the cash dividends paid. When you look at the total cash distributed to shareholders—cash dividends, share repurchases, and cash tender offers in connection with acquisitions—dividends are no longer the primary mechanism for such distribution.[8] Stock repurchase often is used as part of an overall corporate restructuring, a topic taken up in Chapter 25. In that chapter, we will look at the leveraged recapitalization, which is a means for massive cash distribution to stockholders. In this chapter, our focus is on stock repurchase as a substitute for cash dividends.

METHOD OF REPURCHASE

The two most common methods of repurchase are through a tender offer and through the purchase of stock in the marketplace. With a tender offer, the company makes a formal offer to stockholders to purchase so many shares, typically at a set price. This bid price is above the current market price; stockholders can elect either to sell their stock at the specified price or continue to hold it. Typically, the tender offer period is between 2 and 3 weeks. If stockholders tender more shares than originally sought by the company, the company may elect to purchase all or part of the excess. It is under no obligation to do so. In general, the transaction costs to the firm in making a tender offer are much higher than those incurred in the purchase of stock in the open market.

In open-market purchases, a company buys its stock as any other investor does—through a brokerage house. Usually, the brokerage fee is negotiated. If the repurchase program is gradual, its effect is to drive up the price of the stock. Also, certain Securities and Exchange Commission rules restrict the

---

[7] See J. Randall Woolridge and Donald R. Chambers, "Reverse Splits and Shareholder Wealth," *Financial Management*, 12 (Autumn 1983), 5–15.

[8] See Laurie Simon Bagwell and John B. Shoven, "Cash Distributions to Shareholders," *Journal of Economic Perspectives*, 3 (Summer 1989), 129–40.

manner in which a company bids for its shares. As a result, it takes an extended period of time for a company to accumulate a relatively large block of stock. For these reasons, the tender offer is more suitable when the company seeks a large amount of stock.

Before the company repurchases stock, stockholders must be informed of the company's intentions. In a tender offer, these intentions are announced by the offer itself. Even here, the company must not withhold other information. It would be unethical for a mining company, for example, to withhold information of a substantial ore discovery while making a tender offer to repurchase shares. In open-market purchases especially, it is necessary to disclose a company's repurchase intentions. Otherwise, stockholders may sell their stock not knowing about a repurchase program that will increase earnings per share. Given full information about the amount of repurchase and the objective of the company, the stockholders can sell their stock if they choose. Without proper disclosure, the selling stockholder may be penalized. When the amount of stock repurchased is substantial, a tender offer is particularly suitable, for it gives all stockholders equal treatment.

REPURCHASING AS PART OF A DIVIDEND DECISION

If a firm has excess cash and insufficient profitable investment opportunities to justify the use of these funds, it is in the shareholders' interests to distribute the funds. The distribution can be accomplished either by the repurchase of stock or by paying the funds out in increased dividends. In the absence of personal income taxes and transaction costs, the two alternatives, theoretically, should make no difference to stockholders. With repurchase, fewer shares remain outstanding, and earnings per share and, ultimately, dividends per share rise. As a result, the market price per share should rise as well. In theory, the capital gain arising from repurchase should equal the dividend that otherwise would have been paid.

What repurchase price per share should a company offer to achieve this balance? It depends on the current share price and the proportion of shares a company wishes to repurchase. The idea is to establish a price such that shareholders who do not tender will be no better or worse off than shareholders who tender, and vice versa. The equilibrium share repurchase price, P^*, a company should offer is

$$P^* = \frac{(S \times P_c)}{(S - n)} \tag{13-1}$$

where S = number of shares outstanding prior to the distribution
$\quad P_c$ = current market price per share prior to the distribution
$\quad n$ = number of shares to be repurchased

To illustrate, suppose Apollo Products Inc. has 8 million shares outstanding, whose current market price is $36 per share, and the company wishes to repurchase 1 million shares. The equilibrium share repurchase price offered should be

$$P^* = \frac{(8,000,000 \times \$36)}{(8,000,000 - 1,000,000)} = \$41.14$$

If the offer price were $44, shareholders who tendered their shares would gain at the expense of those who continued to hold the stock. Contrarily, if the offer price were $38, selling stockholders would lose and continuing stockholders would gain. At $41.14, both parties are treated equally.

Recognize that the formula does not take account of the opportunity cost associated with using liquidity to repurchase shares. However, we assume that this liquidity is excess and should be distributed to stockholders. It is merely a question of dividends or share repurchase being the vehicle. With respect to monies realized, stockholders presumably would be indifferent.

Personal Tax Effect.   With a differential tax rate on dividends and capital gains, however, repurchase of stock offers a tax advantage over payment of dividends to the taxable investor. The market price increase resulting from a repurchase of stock is subject to the capital gains tax, whereas dividends are taxed at the ordinary income tax rate. At times in our tax laws, capital gains have been taxed at a more favorable rate; at other times at the same rate. Even here the tax is postponed until the stock is sold, whereas with dividends the tax must be paid on a current basis. With a share repurchase, the stockholder has a timing option. He or she can accept the share repurchase offer or reject it and continue to hold the stock. With a cash dividend, there is no such option.

It is important to recognize that if an investor manufactures a "homemade" dividend by selling off sufficient stock to match the cash dividend that otherwise would have been paid, the proceeds realized are not entirely subject to the capital gains tax. Only the excess of the price realized over original cost is subject to taxation. Capital gains arising from the repurchase are not taxed on the remainder of the investor's holdings until the remaining stock is sold. In essence, the bulk of the capital gains tax is postponed. For tax reasons, then, most taxable investors are better off financially if the firm elects to distribute unused funds via the stock repurchase route rather than via cash dividends. The postponability of the capital gain has present-value advantages over the dividend even if the tax rates on the two types of income are the same.

The repurchase of stock seems particularly appropriate when the firm has a large amount of unused funds to distribute. To pay the funds out through an extra dividend would result in a nonpostponable tax to stockholders. The tax effect could be alleviated somewhat by paying the funds out as extra dividends over a period of time, but this action might result in investors' counting on the extra dividend. The firm must be careful not to undertake a steady program of repurchase in lieu of paying dividends. The Internal Revenue Service will regard such a program as dividend income and not allow stockholders redeeming their shares the capital gains tax advantage.[9] Hence, it is important that the repurchase of stock be somewhat of a "one-shot" nature and not be used as a substitute for regular dividends or even for recurring extra dividends.

---

[9] The tax consequences involved in the repurchase of stock are complex and, in places, ambiguous. In most cases, the monies received by stockholders tendering their shares are subject to the capital gains tax. Under certain circumstances, however, the distribution can be treated as ordinary income to the redeeming stockholder. If the stockholder's percentage of ownership of the company after the tender is greater than .80 of his ownership percentage prior to the tender, the repurchase can be treated as ordinary income by the Internal Revenue Service. This problem can be avoided if the company obtains an advance ruling from the IRS that the repurchase of stock is not equivalent to a dividend.

INVESTMENT OR
FINANCING DECISION?

Some regard the repurchase of stock as an investment decision instead of a dividend decision. Indeed, in a strict sense, it is, even though stock held in the treasury does not provide an expected return as other investments do. No company can exist by investing only in its own stock. The decision to repurchase should involve distribution of unused funds when the firm's investment opportunities are not sufficiently attractive to employ those funds, either now or in the foreseeable future. The repurchase of stock therefore cannot be treated as an investment decision as we define the term.

Repurchase may be regarded as a financing decision, provided its purpose is to alter the capital structure proportions of the firm. By issuing debt and repurchasing stock, a firm can immediately change its debt-to-equity ratio toward a greater proportion of debt. In this case, the repurchase of stock is a financing decision, because the alternative is not to pay out dividends. As we know from Chapter 10, there may be benefits to a greater proportion of debt. For one thing, there is an increased tax subsidy. Also, a repurchase may expropriate debt holders' wealth in favor of stockholders (à la option pricing theory), if they are not protected. These considerations can only be resolved in the overall evaluation of an optimal capital structure. As this was treated in Chapter 10, we do not do so here. However, we must be mindful of the fact that only when there is excess cash can the repurchase be treated as a dividend decision.

POSSIBLE SIGNALING EFFECT

In addition to the factors considered, stock repurchases may have a signaling effect. For example, a positive signal might be sent to the market if management believed the stock were undervalued and they were constrained not to tender shares they owned individually. In this context, the premium in repurchase price over existing market price would reflect management's belief about the degree of undervaluation. The idea is that concrete actions such as repurchase and stock dividends and splits, as well as capital structure changes and cash dividend changes considered in earlier chapters, speak louder than words.

In separate empirical studies, Dann and Vermaelen have found evidence supporting the signaling idea.[10] The methodology employed involved event studies of stock prices around the announcement date, relative to risk-adjusted market movements. In both studies, tender offer repurchase announcements were associated with significant increases in share price, holding other things constant. Virtually all of the effect occurred in the several days surrounding the announcement. Without a signaling effect, it is claimed that stockholders who did not tender would suffer when an excess premium was paid. The fact that share price rose is regarded as evidence of a positive signaling effect. Also, most repurchasing companies were small firms where insiders could not tender shares owned individually; this adds further sup-

---

[10] Larry Y. Dann, "Common Stock Repurchases: An Analysis of Returns to Bondholders and Stockholders," *Journal of Financial Economics*, 9 (June 1981), 113–38; Theo Vermaelen, "Common Stock Repurchases and Market Signalling," *Journal of Economics*, 9 (June 1981), 139–83; and Theo Vermaelen, "Repurchase Tender Offers, Signaling, and Managerial Incentives," *Journal of Financial and Quantitative Analysis*, 19 (June 1984), 163–82.

port to a signaling effect. Finally, the degree of share price improvement was positively related to the size of premium, the fraction of shares repurchased, and the fraction of insider holdings. While the results for tender offers were reasonably conclusive, those for open-market purchases were not. That is not surprising, given our earlier discussion of the nature of open-market purchases.

While dividends and repurchases are similar informationally in that they are paid with cash, they also are somewhat different. The regular cash dividend provides ongoing reinforcement of the underlying ability of the firm to generate cash. It is like a quarterly news release and can be habit forming. In contrast, share repurchase is not a regular event. It may be viewed more as an "extra" used on occasions when management believes the stock is greatly undervalued.[11] Because both dividends and repurchases are done with cash, management has a disincentive to give false signals and implicitly pledges itself to provide cash-flow results consistent with the signal.

PROCEDURAL AND LEGAL ASPECTS

DECLARATION OF DIVIDENDS

When the board of directors of a corporation declares a cash dividend, it specifies a *date of record*. At the close of business that day, a list of stockholders is drawn up from the stock transfer books of the company. Stockholders on the list are entitled to the dividend, whereas stockholders who come on the books after the date of record are not entitled to the dividend. When the board of directors of United Chemical Company met on May 8, it declared a dividend of 25 cents a share payable June 15 to stockholders of record on May 31. Jennifer Doakes owned the stock well before May 31, so she is entitled to the dividend, even though she might sell her stock prior to the dividend actually being paid on June 15.

A problem can develop in the sale of stock in the days immediately before the date of record. The buyer and the seller of the stock have several days to settle, that is, to pay for the stock or to deliver it, in the case of the seller. As a result, the company may not be notified of the stock transfer in sufficient time. For this reason, the brokerage community has a rule whereby new stockholders are entitled to dividends only if they buy the stock more than 4 business days before the date of record. If the stock is bought after that time, the stockholder is not entitled to the dividend. The date itself is known as the *ex-dividend date*. In our example, the date of record was May 31. If this were a Friday, 4 business days before would be May 27, and this would be the ex-dividend date. To receive the dividend, a new stockholder must purchase the stock on May 26 or before. If purchased May 27 or after, the stock is said to be ex-dividend. That is, it is without the 25-cent dividend.

Once a dividend is declared, stockholders become general creditors of the company until the dividend is actually paid; the declared but unpaid dividend is a current liability of the company coming out of retained earnings.

---

[11] See Paul Asquith and David W. Mullins, Jr., "Signalling with Dividends, Stock Repurchases, and Equity Issues," *Financial Management*, 15 (Autumn 1986), 27–44.

LEGAL ASPECTS

Although the legal restrictions we discuss here do not influence most dividend decisions, some companies are affected by them. We have already considered one type of legal restriction, namely, the restriction on dividends imposed in a bond indenture or loan agreement. Other legal restrictions have to do with capital impairment, insolvency, and excess accumulation of cash.

Capital Restriction. Although state laws vary considerably, most states prohibit the payment of dividends if these dividends impair capital. *Capital* is defined in some states as the par value of the common stock. If a firm had 1 million shares outstanding with a $2 par value, total capital would be $2 million. If shareholders' equity of a company were $2.1 million, the company could not pay a cash dividend totaling $200,000 without impairing capital.

Other states define capital to include not only the par value of the common stock but also the paid-in capital. Under such statutes, dividends can be paid only out of retained earnings. The purpose of the capital impairment laws is to protect creditors of a corporation, and they may have some effect when a corporation is relatively new. With established companies that have been profitable in the past and have built up retained earnings, substantial losses will usually have been incurred before the restriction has an effect. By this time, the situation may be sufficiently hopeless that the restriction gives creditors little protection.

Insolvency. Some states prohibit the payment of cash dividends if the company is insolvent. *Insolvency* is defined either in a legal sense, as liabilities exceeding assets, or in a technical sense, as the firm's being unable to pay its creditors as obligations come due. Because the ability of the firm to pay its obligations is dependent on its liquidity rather than on its capital, the technical insolvency restriction gives creditors a good deal of protection. When cash is limited, a company is restricted from favoring stockholders to the detriment of creditors.

Excess Accumulation of Cash. The Internal Revenue Code prohibits the undue retention of earnings. Although *undue retention* is defined vaguely, it usually is thought to be retention significantly in excess of the present and future investment needs of the company. The purpose of the law is to prevent companies from retaining earnings for the sake of avoiding taxes. A company might retain all its earnings and build up a substantial cash and marketable securities position. The entire company then could be sold, and stockholders would be subject to a capital gains tax which was postponed relatively to what would occur if dividends were paid. If the IRS can prove unjustified retention, it can impose penalty tax rates on the accumulation. Whenever a company does build up a substantial liquid position, it has to be sure that it can justify the retention of these funds to the IRS. Otherwise, it may be in order to pay the excess funds out to stockholders as dividends.

SUMMARY

Many people feel that the stability of dividends has a positive effect on the market price of the stock. Stable dividends may resolve uncertainty in the minds of investors, particularly when earnings per share drop. Stable dividends also may have a positive utility to investors interested in current periodic income. Many companies appear to follow the policy of a target dividend-payout ratio, increasing dividends only when they feel that an increase in earnings can be sustained. The use of an extra dividend permits a cyclical company to maintain a stable record of regular dividends while paying additional dividends whenever earnings are unusually high.

A stock dividend pays additional stock to stockholders. Theoretically, it is not a thing of value to the stockholder unless cash dividends per share remain unchanged or are increased. Stock dividends may serve to keep the market price per share in a popular trading range. A more effective device for reducing market price per share is a stock split. With a split, the number of shares is increased by the terms of the split; for example a 3-for-1 split means that the number of shares is tripled. Both stock dividends and stock splits appear to have an informational or signaling effect. When other things are held constant, share price tends to rise around the time of the announcement, consistent with a positive signal. In a reverse stock split, the number of shares outstanding is reduced and the signal to the market usually is negative.

A company's repurchase of its own stock should be treated as a dividend decision when the firm has funds in excess of present and foreseeable future investment needs. It may distribute these funds either by dividends or by the repurchase of stock. In the absence of a tax differential between dividends and capital gains, the monetary value of the two alternatives should be the same if the formula for determining the equilibrium share repurchase price is used. With the tax differential, there is a tax advantage to the repurchase of stock. Because of objections by the Internal Revenue Service, repurchase of stock cannot be used in lieu of regular dividends. Repurchases can be accomplished either with a tender offer or through purchases in the open market. In either case, the repurchase intentions of the company should be made clear to stockholders. Tender offer repurchases of stock appear to have a positive signaling effect, similar to stock dividends and stock splits.

The declaration of dividends involves certain procedures, and their payment is subject to various legal restrictions, which on occasion may influence the dividend policy of the firm.

SELF-CORRECTION PROBLEMS

1. Darcy Dip Doodle Company's earnings per share over the last 10 years were the following:

YEAR	1	2	3	4	5	6	7	8	9	10
EPS ($)	1.70	1.82	1.44	1.88	2.18	2.32	1.84	2.23	2.50	2.73

a. Determine annual dividends per share under the following policies:
   (1) A constant dividend-payout ratio of 40 percent (to the nearest cent).
   (2) A regular dividend of $.80 and an extra dividend to bring the payout ratio to 40 percent if it otherwise would fall below.

(3) A stable dividend that is occasionally raised. The payout ratio may range between 30 percent and 50 percent in any given year, but should average approximately 40 percent.

b. What are the valuation implications of each of these policies?

2. The Kleidon King Company has the following shareholders' equity account:

Common stock ($8 par value)	$ 2,000,000
Additional paid-in capital	1,600,000
Retained earnings	8,400,000
Shareholders' equity	$12,000,000

The current market price of the stock is $60 per share.

a. What will happen to this account and to the number of shares outstanding with a 20 percent "small-percentage" stock dividend?

b. With a 2-for-1 stock split?

c. With a 1-for-2 reverse stock split?

d. In the absence of an informational or signaling effect, at what share price should the common sell after the 20 percent stock dividend? What might happen if there were a signaling effect?

3. Le Pomme de Terre Corporation has enjoyed considerable recent success because Brazil placed a huge order for potatoes. This business is not expected to be repeated, and Le Pomme de Terre has $6 million in excess funds. The company wishes to distribute these funds via the repurchase of stock. Presently, it has 2,400,000 shares outstanding, and the market price per share is $25. It wishes to repurchase 10 percent of its stock, or 240,000 shares.

a. Assuming no signaling effect, at what share price should the company offer to repurchase?

b. In total, how much will the company be distributing through share repurchase?

c. If the company were to pay out the funds through cash dividends instead, what would be the market price per share after the distribution? (Ignore tax considerations.)

4. On July 17, the board of directors of Ipanema Towel and Cloth Company declared its usual 50 cents per share cash dividend payable September 1 to stockholders of record on August 20. The company has 1.7 million shares outstanding.

a. What will happen to cash, the dividend payable account, and to retained earnings on July 17? on September 1?

b. When will the stock trade ex-dividend? What will happen to share price at that time?

PROBLEMS

1. The Axalt Corporation and the Baxalt Corporation have had remarkably similar earnings patterns over the last 5 years. In fact, both firms have had identical earnings per share. Further, both firms are in the same industry, produce the same product, and face the same business and financial risks. In short, these firms are carbon copies of each other in every respect but one: Axalt paid out a constant percentage of its earnings (50 percent) in dividends, while Baxalt paid a constant cash dividend. The financial manager of the Axalt Corporation has been puzzled by the fact that the price of his firm's stock has been generally lower than the

price of Baxalt's stock, even though in some years Axalt's dividend was substantially larger than Baxalt's.

  a. What might account for this condition?

  b. What might be done by both companies to increase the market prices of their stock?

	AXALT			BAXALT		
YEAR	EPS	Div.	Market Price	EPS	Div.	Market Price
1	$1.00	.50	$6	$1.00	.23	4\frac{7}{8}$
2	.50	.25	4	.50	.23	$4\frac{3}{8}$
3	− .25	nil	2	− .25	.23	4
4	.30	.15	3	.30	.23	$4\frac{1}{4}$
5	.50	.25	$3\frac{1}{2}$	.50	.23	$4\frac{1}{2}$

2. The Xavier Industrial Coating Company has hired you as a financial consultant to advise the company with respect to its dividend policy. The coating industry has been very stable for some time, and the firm's stock has not appreciated significantly in market value for several years. The rapidly growing southeastern market provides an excellent opportunity for this old, traditionally midwestern coating manufacturer to undertake a vigorous expansion program. To do so, the company has decided to sell common stock for equity capital in the near future. The company expects its entrance into the southeastern market to be extremely profitable, returning approximately 25 percent on investment each year. Data on earnings, dividends, and common stock prices are given in the following table.

	19x1	19x2	19x3	19x4	ANTICIPATED 19x5
Earn./share	$4.32	$4.17	$4.61	$4.80	$4.75
Cash avail./share	$6.00	$5.90	$6.25	$6.35	$6.25
Dividend/share	$2.90	$2.80	$3.00	$3.20	?
Payout ratio	67%	67%	65%	67%	?
Avg. market price	$60.00	$58.00	$60.00	$67.00	$66.00
P/E ratio	14/1	14/1	13/1	14/1	14/1

What dividend policy recommendations would you make to the company? Specifically, what payout would you recommend for 19x5? Justify your position.

3. The Sherill Corporation capital structure Dec. 30, 19x1

Common stock ($1 par, 1,000,000 shares)	$1,000,000
Additional paid-in capital	300,000
Retained earnings	1,700,000
Shareholders' equity	$3,000,000

The firm earned $300,000 after taxes in 19x1, and paid out 50 percent of these earnings as dividends. The price of the firm's stock on December 30 was $5.

a. If the firm declared a stock dividend of 3 percent on December 31, what would be the reformulated capital structure?

b. Assuming the firm paid no stock dividend, what would be earnings per share for 19x1? dividends per share?

c. Assuming a 3 percent stock dividend, what would happen to EPS and DPS for 19x1?

d. What would be the price of the stock after the 3 percent stock dividend, if there were no signaling or other effects?

4. Zoppo Manufacturers shareholders' equity Dec. 30, 19x1

Common stock ($100 par, 300,000 shares)	$ 30,000,000
Additional paid-in capital	15,000,000
Retained earnings	55,000,000
Shareholders' equity	$100,000,000

On December 31, Zoppo split the stock 2-for-1 and then declared a 10 percent stock dividend. The price of the stock on December 30 was $500. Reformulate the stockholders' capitalization accounts of the firm.

5. Johore Trading Company has 2.4 million shares of common stock outstanding, and the present market price per share is $36. Its equity capitalization is as follows:

Common stock, $2.00 par	$ 4,800,000
Additional paid-in capital	5,900,000
Retained earnings	87,300,000
Shareholders' equity	$98,000,000

a. If the company were to declare a 12 percent stock dividend, what would happen to these accounts? a 5 percent stock dividend?

b. If, instead, the company declared a 3-for-2 stock split, what would happen to the accounts? a 2-for-1 stock split? a 3-for-1 split?

c. What would happen if there were a reverse stock split of 1-for-4? 1-for-6?

6. The Canales Copper Company declared a 25 percent stock dividend on March 10 to stockholders of record on April 1. The market price of the stock is $50 per share. You own 160 shares of the stock.

a. If you sold your stock on March 20, what would be the price per share, all other things the same? (No signaling effect.)

b. After the stock dividend is paid, how many shares of stock will you own?

c. At what price would you expect the stock to sell on April 2, all other things the same? (No signaling effect.)

d. What will be the total value of your holdings before and after the stock dividend, all other things the same?

e. If there were an informational or signaling effect, what would be the effect on share price?

7. In October, Baxter Lorry Company was in a flush cash position and repurchased 100,000 shares of its 1.8 million shares outstanding at a price of $42.50 per share. Immediately prior to the share repurchase announcement, share price was $37.00. The company was surprised that nearly 1 million shares were tendered by stockholders wanting to sell. The company had to repurchase the 100,000 shares on a pro-rata basis according to the number of shares tendered.

a. Why did so many stockholders tender their shares? At what price should the company have made its repurchase offer?

b. Who gained from the offer? Who lost?

8. Singleton Electronics Company repurchased 1 million of 14 million shares outstanding at $98 a share. Immediately before the announcement, market price per share was $91.

   a. Was the offer price by the company the correct repurchase price?

   b. After the repurchase, share price went to $105. What would explain this rise if there were no other information concerning the company or stocks in general?

9. On February 2, the board of directors of International Zinc and Iron Corporation declared a 20 cents per share cash dividend payable March 20 to stockholders of record on March 1.

   a. If you wished to buy the stock before it went ex-dividend, by what date would you need to make your purchase?

   b. If you already own the stock but the company declares bankruptcy on March 10, what happens to your dividend?

SOLUTIONS TO SELF-CORRECTION PROBLEMS

1. a.

YEAR	POLICY 1	POLICY 2	POLICY 3
1	$ .68	$ .80	$ .68
2	.73	.80	.68
3	.58	.80	.68
4	.75	.80	.80
5	.87	.87	.80
6	.93	.93	.80
7	.74	.80	.80
8	.89	.89	1.00
9	1.00	1.00	1.00
10	1.09	1.09	1.00

Other dividend streams are possible under policy 3. This solution is but one.

   b. Policy 1 and, to a much lesser degree, policy 2 result in fluctuating dividends over time, as the company is cyclical. Because of the $.80 minimum regular dividend, policy 2 results in an average payout ratio in excess of 40 percent. Stockholders may come to count on the extra dividend and be disappointed when it is not paid, such as in year 7. To the extent investors value stable dividends and periodic rising dividends over time, and 40 percent is an optimal average payout ratio, dividend policy 3 would be preferred and would likely maximize share price.

2. Present number of common shares = $2,000,000/$8 par value = 250,000.

	a. STOCK DIVIDEND	b. STOCK SPLIT	c. REVERSE SPLIT
Common stock (par)	$ 2,400,000 ($8)	$ 2,000,000 ($4)	$ 2,000,000 ($16)
Additional paid-in capital	4,200,000	1,600,000	1,600,000
Retained earnings	5,400,000	8,400,000	8,400,000
Shareholders' equity	$12,000,000	$12,000,000	$12,000,000
Number of shares	300,000	500,000	125,000

d. The total market value of the firm before the stock dividend is $60 × 250,000 shares = $15 million. With no change in the total value of the firm, market price per share after the stock dividend should be $15 million/300,000 shares = $50 per share. If there is a signaling effect, the total value of the firm might rise and share price be somewhat higher than $50 per share. The magnitude of the effect probably would be no more than several dollars a share, based on empirical findings.

3. a.
$$P^* = \frac{(S \times P_c)}{(S - n)}$$

$$P^* = \frac{(2,400,000 \times \$25)}{(2,400,000 - 240,000)} = \$27.78$$

b. 240,000 × $27.78 = $6,667,200

c. $6,667,200/2,400,000 shares = $2.778 cash dividend

Share price after dividend = $25 − $2.778

= $22.222

4. a.

	CASH (CURRENT ASSET)	DIVIDEND PAYABLE (CURRENT LIABILITY)	RETAINED EARNINGS (NET WORTH)
July 17 declaration date	No change	+$850,000	−$850,000
September 1 payment date	−$850,000	−$850,000	No change

b. The stock will trade ex-dividend 4 business days before August 20. At that time, share price will drop, all other things the same. Owing to a possible favorable capital-gains tax effect for those who buy the stock after it goes ex-dividend, the drop in price may be less than the dividend of 50 cents. (See discussion in the previous chapter for an explanation of this phenomenon.)

SELECTED REFERENCES

ASQUITH, PAUL, and DAVID W. MULLINS, JR., "Signalling with Dividends, Stock Repurchases, and Equity Issues," *Financial Management*, 15 (Autumn 1986), 27–44.

BAGWELL, LAURIE SIMON, and JOHN B. SHOVEN, "Cash Distributions to Shareholders," *Journal of Economic Perspectives*, 3 (Summer 1989), 129–40.

BRENNAN, MICHAEL J., and THOMAS E. COPELAND, "Stock Splits, Stock Prices and Transaction Costs," *Journal of Financial Economics*, 22 (October 1988), 83–101.

BRENNAN, MICHAEL J., and ANJAN V. THAKOR, "Shareholder Preferences and Dividend Policy," *Journal of Finance*, 45 (September 1990), 993–1018.

BRICKLEY, JAMES A., "Shareholder Wealth, Information Signaling and the Specially Designated Dividend: An Empirical Study," *Journal of Financial Economics*, 12 (August 1983) 187–210.

CHAREST, GUY, "Split Information, Stock Returns and Market Efficiency," *Journal of Financial Economics*, 6 (June–September 1978), 265–96.

CONSTANTINIDES, GEORGE M., and BRUCE D. GRUNDY, "Optimal Investment with Stock Repurchase and Financing as Signals," *Review of Financial Studies*, 2, No. 4 (1989), 445–66.

COPELAND, THOMAS E., "Liquidity Changes Following Stock Splits," *Journal of Finance*, 34 (March 1979), 115–42.

DANN, LARRY Y., "Common Stock Repurchases: An Analysis of Returns to Bondholders and Stockholders," *Journal of Financial Economics*, 9 (June 1981), 113–38.

EADES, KENNETH M., PATRICK J. HESS, and E. HAN KIM, "On Interpreting Security Returns during the Ex-Dividend Period," *Journal of Financial Economics*, 13 (March 1984), 3–34.

ELTON, EDWIN J., and MARTIN J. GRUBER, "The Effect of Share Repurchases on the Value of the Firm," *Journal of Finance*, 23 (March 1968), 135–50.

FAMA, EUGENE F., LAWRENCE FISHER, MICHAEL JENSEN, and RICHARD ROLL, "The Adjustment of Stock Prices to New Information," *International Economic Review*, 10 (February 1969), 1–21.

GRINBLATT, MARK S., RONALD W. MASULIS, and SHERIDAN TITMAN, "The Valuation Effects of Stock Splits and Stock Dividends," *Journal of Financial Economics*, 13 (December 1984), 461–90.

KALE, JAYANT R., THOMAS H. NOE, and GERALD D. GAY. "Share Repurchase through Transferable Put Rights: Theory and Case Study," Journal of *Financial Economics*, 25 (November 1989), 141–60.

LAKONISHOK, JOSEF, and BARUCH LEV, "Stock Splits and Stock Dividends: Why, Who, and When," *Journal of Finance*, 42 (September 1987), 913–32.

LAKONISHOK, JOSEF, and THEO VERMAELEN, "Anomalous Price Behavior around Repurchase Tender Offers," *Journal of Finance*, 45 (June 1990), 455–78.

LAMOUREUX, CHRISTOPHER G., and PERCY POON, "The Market Reaction to Stock Splits," *Journal of Finance*, 42 (December 1987), 1347–70.

LINTNER, JOHN, "Distribution of Income of Corporations among Dividends, Retained Earnings and Taxes," *American Economic Review*, 46 (May 1956), 97–113.

MCNICHOLS, MAUREEN, and AJAY DRAVID, "Stock Dividends, Stock Splits, and Signaling," *Journal of Finance*, 45 (July 1990), 857–79.

MASULIS, RONALD, "Stock Repurchases by Tender Offers: An Analysis of the Causes of Common Stock Price Changes," *Journal of Finance*, 35 (May 1980), 305–19.

REILLY, FRANK K., and EUGENE F. DRZYCIMSKI, "Short-Run Profits from Stock Splits," *Financial Management*, 10 (Summer 1981), 64–74.

VERMAELEN, THEO, "Common Stock Repurchases and Market Signalling," *Journal of Financial Economics*, 9 (June 1981) 139–83.

———, "Repurchase Tender Offers, Signaling, and Managerial Incentives," *Journal of Financial and Quantitative Analysis*, 19 (June 1984), 163–82.

WANSLEY, JAMES W., WILLIAM R. LANE, and SALIL SARKAR, "Managements' View on Share Repurchase and Tender Offer Premiums," *Financial Management*, 18 (Autumn 1989), 97–110.

WOOLRIDGE, J. RANDALL, "Stock Dividends as Signals," *Journal of Financial Research*, 6 (Spring 1983), 1–12.

———, and DONALD R. CHAMBERS, "Reverse Splits and Shareholder Wealth," *Financial Management*, 12 (Autumn 1983), 5–15.

PART 4

MANAGEMENT OF LIQUIDITY AND CURRENT ASSETS

Levi Strauss Goes Back to Basics

In the early 1970s, Levi Strauss & Company hired George Daly as chief financial officer. Prior to this time, the company had a strong orientation to sales growth and new products, but little in the way of financial controls. One of the challenges Daly faced was bloated receivable and inventory positions. Profit margins had turned down, and bank loans and payables had escalated in order to finance the buildup in current assets. The average receivable collection period was 57 days, and the average inventory turnover was only 2.6 turns a year. Things were quickly getting out of hand.

One of the first things Daly attacked was the receivable problem. Procedures were instituted to get bills out on time, to monitor payments, and to follow up on tardy collections. Also instituted were changes in credit policies to improve receivable quality and to ensure prompter payment. With respect to inventories, the company selectively pruned slower moving product lines and concentrated on basic jeans. Controls were installed to manage inventories in a tighter, more effective manner.

The combination of these actions produced impressive results. Over a two-year span, the average receivable collection period was reduced to 48 days and the inventory turnover increased to 3.9 turns per year. Profit margins improved, and the company was able to lower its debt ratio with the funds released through better current asset management.

14

WORKING CAPITAL MANAGEMENT AND EFFICIENT MARKET CONSIDERATIONS

In Parts 1 through 3, we thought much about the valuation of the firm under varying assumptions about the perfection of capital markets. We became involved with investment in assets and financing in general, but the implied focus was on fixed assets and long-term financing. By tradition perhaps more than anything else, a split has evolved between consideration of current assets (short-term financing) and fixed assets (long-term financing). *Current assets*, by accounting definition, are normally converted into cash within 1 year. Working capital management is usually described as involving the administration of these assets—namely, cash and marketable securities, receivables, and inventories—and the administration of current liabilities. Administration of *fixed assets* (assets normally not converted into cash within the year) is usually considered to fall within the realm of capital budgeting, whereas administration of long-term financing involves capital structure considerations.

This separation is unfortunate, for it tends to obscure the effect of various decisions on the valuation of the firm as a whole. The typical financial manager spends most of the day managing current assets and liabilities, a repetitive concentration that often results in a myopic approach to such management. Most of the work dealing with working capital management is confined to the left-hand side of the balance sheet, where it is directed to optimizing the levels of cash and marketable securities, receivables, and inventories. For the most part, optimization of these current assets is isolated from the optimization of other current assets and of the overall valuation of the firm.

Conceptually, it does not make sense to divorce the various components of working capital management from the more fundamental decisions of investment and financing. In recent years, some highly sophisticated models for cash, receivables, and inventory management have evolved. In these, the benefits associated with a particular level of current asset are balanced against the risk-adjusted cost of maintaining it. While these models provide efficient decision rules, virtually all of them optimize in a partial equilibrium sense. It is clear that what is needed is an understanding of current asset and liability decisions in light of the overall valuation of the firm.

In this chapter, we shall develop this conceptual understanding. To this end, we categorize the various components of working capital management—liquidity, receivables and inventories, and current liabilities—grouping them according to the way they affect valuation. As the chapter unfolds, we shall see that decisions reached in these areas determine the amount of working capital the firm maintains. We shall also see that working capital emerges as a by-product; it does not represent an active decision in itself. The discussion in this chapter is purposely general, to provide a conceptual overview for judging working capital decisions in relation to the valuation of the firm. This overview will give a better perspective for decisions involving specific current assets and liabilities, which we examine in the remaining chapters of this part and in Part 5.

375

**CHAPTER 14
Working Capital
Management and
Efficient Market
Considerations**

LIQUIDITY AND ITS ROLE

The term *liquid assets* is used to describe money and assets that are readily convertible into money. Different assets may be said to exhibit different degrees of liquidity. Money itself is, by definition, the most liquid of assets; other assets have varying degrees of liquidity, depending on the ease with which they can be turned into cash. For assets other than money, liquidity has two dimensions: (1) the time necessary to convert the asset into money and (2) the degree of certainty associated with the conversion ratio, or price, realized for the asset. Although most assets have a degree of liquidity, we shall focus on the most liquid assets of the firm: cash and marketable securities. Liquidity management, then, involves determining the total amount of these two types of assets the firm will hold.[1] We hold constant the credit policies and procedures of the firm, its inventory management and control, and the administration of its fixed assets, for decisions here affect the overall liquidity of the firm. Thus, a narrow definition of liquidity is taken in order to simplify our discussion of certain principles.

LIQUIDITY WHEN PERFECT CAPITAL MARKETS EXIST

We have seen that under the assumptions of perfect capital markets, a firm could not alter its value by varying its capital structure, its dividend policy, and the diversification of the assets it holds. If we invoke these assumptions again, the degree of liquidity of the firm also would be a matter of indifference to equity holders. Presumably, investors would manage their portfolios of common stocks and other assets, as well as their liabilities, in a way that satisfied their utility for liquidity. As a result, the liquidity of individual firms would not be a factor enhancing shareholder wealth. In essence, the argument is that the firm is unable to do something for investors that they cannot do for themselves. The same argument applies to the irrelevance of capital structure decisions (where investors are able to undertake "homemade" leverage by borrowing on their own), of dividend decisions (where investors are able to manufacture "homemade" dividends by selling a portion of their hold-

[1] The split between the two types of assets is taken up in the subsequent chapter.

ings), and of diversification of asset decisions (where investors are able to diversify on their own).

In this context, excess cash cannot be justified. It is the equity holders' money, and management is only the steward. If the company cannot employ the funds in projects providing expected returns no less than those required by the financial markets, such excess liquidity should be distributed. Put another way, allow the equity holders to use the funds for investment in other endeavors providing appropriate returns.

The assumptions of perfect capital markets imply that if the firm becomes technically insolvent and unable to pay its bills, creditors will be able to step in instantaneously and realize value either by liquidating assets, by running the company themselves, or by effecting a costless reorganization. If the assets are sold, they are assumed to be employed productively without delay or inefficiency in other areas of the economy. When we allow for market imperfections, liquidity may become a desirable characteristic affecting value.

LIQUIDITY MANAGEMENT
WITH IMPERFECTIONS

Chapter 10 pointed out two dimensions of bankruptcy costs. The first is the "shortfall," arising from the liquidation of assets at "distress" prices below their economic values, as well as the productivity lost in going into bankruptcy. The second is the out-of-pocket fees paid to lawyers, trustees in bankruptcy, referees, receivers, liquidators, and so forth. Embodied in the shortfall phenomenon are considerable delays in bankruptcy proceedings, during which the firm and its value can continue to deteriorate.

In effect, bankruptcy costs represent a drain in the system to suppliers of capital. This drain works to the disadvantage of equity holders, who have a residual claim on assets in liquidation. Higher interest rates are another result as creditors seek ways of passing on all or part of the ex ante costs of bankruptcy. This obviously also works to the disadvantage of equity holders. Investors are unable to diversify away the costs of bankruptcy. The firm can reduce the probability of bankruptcy, however, by maintaining liquidity.

Making bankruptcy less probable now and in the future may bestow some benefits upon stockholders as residual owners of the firm. Thus, the firm may be able to do something for stockholders that they cannot do for themselves. To illustrate with a simple example, suppose we have a two-period model. Assume the initial probabilities of insolvency and the bankruptcy costs shown in the upper panel of Table 14-1. If insolvency occurs, creditors will initiate bankruptcy proceedings and liquidate the company. As a result, bankruptcy costs will be incurred. We assume then that all of the costs of bankruptcy are borne by equity holders.[2] The upper panel of the table gives the probability of insolvency in periods 1 and 2, together with the present values of bankruptcy costs, under the assumption that no liquidity is maintained. Note that in period 1 there are two states in which insolvency occurs, each with a different present value of bankruptcy costs. The expected value of

---

[2] This is due to debt holders' charging higher interest rates than would otherwise be the case. In practice, some type of sharing of bankruptcy costs may occur between debt holders and equity holders. For ease of illustration, however, we assume that such costs are borne entirely by equity holders.

TABLE 14-1
Illustration of bankruptcy costs

	PERIOD 1			PERIOD 2	
State	Probability	Present Value of Bankruptcy Costs	State	Probability	Present Value of Bankruptcy Costs
Zero liquidity					
Insolvency	.2	$1,000			
Insolvency	.2	500			
Solvency	.6	0	Insolvency	.1	$500
			Solvency	.9	0
$20,000 liquidity					
Insolvency	.1	$750			
Solvency	.9	0	Insolvency	.1	$1,000
			Insolvency	.2	500
			Solvency	.7	0
$40,000 liquidity					
Insolvency	.1	$750			
Solvency	.9	0	Insolvency	.2	$700
			Solvency	.8	0

present-value bankruptcy costs for the situation of zero liquidity is

$$(.2)(\$1,000) + (.2)(\$500) + (.6)(.1)(\$500) = \$330 \qquad (14\text{-}1)$$

Suppose now that the firm were considering maintaining initial liquidity levels of $20,000 and $40,000 and that these levels changed the probabilities of insolvency and bankruptcy costs to those figures shown in the middle and lower panels, respectively, of Table 14-1. The expected value of present-value bankruptcy costs when the firm maintains an initial liquidity level of $20,000 is

$$(.1)(\$750) + (.9)(.1)(\$1,000) + (.9)(.2)(\$500) = \$225 \qquad (14\text{-}2)$$

while that for a $40,000 initial liquidity level is

$$(.1)(\$750) + (.9)(.2)(\$700) = \$201 \qquad (14\text{-}3)$$

Thus, by increasing liquidity from zero to $20,000, the expected value of present-value bankruptcy costs can be lowered from $330 to $255. By increasing it from $20,000 to $40,000, the expected value is lowered from $255 to $201. In this situation, then, there are positive benefits associated with maintaining liquidity: It lowers the probability of insolvency in period 1 as well as the joint probability of bankruptcy occurring during the two periods.

Another imperfection has to do with contracting costs of managers, workers, suppliers, and customers. If these parties are unable to diversify their claims on the firm properly, they may require additional incentive the riskier the firm.[3] This incentive, whether it be higher compensation, higher prices to

[3] This argument is made by Clifford W. Smith and Rene M. Stulz, "The Determinants of Firms' Hedging Policies," *Journal of Financial and Quantitative Analysis*, 20 (December 1985), 391–405.

suppliers, or lower prices to customers, represents a cost to the firm's equity holders. By increasing liquidity, the risk to these parties can be reduced and the aforementioned costs lowered.

BENEFITS RELATIVE TO COST

Against the benefits associated with maintaining liquidity, one must balance the cost. Liquid assets, like all other assets, have to be financed. Accordingly, the cost of liquidity may be thought of as the differential in interest earned on the investment of funds in liquid assets and the cost of financing. If the firm could both borrow and lend at the same interest rate, there would be no "cost" to maintaining whatever level of liquidity was desired to reduce the probability of technical insolvency. If imperfections in the capital markets result in the borrowing rate exceeding the lending rate, there is a "cost" to maintaining liquidity. Under these conditions, a trade-off exists between the benefits associated with liquidity and the cost of maintaining it. The optimal level of liquidity then could be determined by marginal analysis.

Quantification of this trade-off is complex. Our purpose has been to explore the problem in concept. The important thing to remember is that justification for maintaining cash and marketable securities depends on certain market imperfections rendering financial markets less than perfect. In particular, one needs to concentrate on bankruptcy costs and differences in the borrowing and lending rates of the firm. Even with these imperfections, the firm could avoid or at least reduce the possibility of bankruptcy if it had ready access to external financing. Instead of using a liquidity buffer, it would simply raise funds externally to offset a downside deviation in operating cash flows. In this way the firm would be able to meet its creditor and contractual debt obligations, but it would not need to maintain liquidity in order to do so. If there are flotation costs associated with external financing, this alternative becomes less attractive. In addition to out-of-pocket flotation costs, there may be imperfections that cause delays in the ability of the firm to bring about external financing. Both of these factors would strengthen the case for liquidity to reduce the possibility, and hence the cost, of bankruptcy. More will be said about financing later in the chapter.

Thus, the important thing in establishing a case for a firm maintaining any liquidity is the presence of market imperfections that make liquidity a thing of value. If the various imperfections discussed can be approximated, it is possible to determine in theory, at least, the appropriate level of liquid assets the firm should maintain. We will propose more practical means for looking at the problem in subsequent chapters, but keep in mind the valuation of liquid assets in a market context. In the absence of specific imperfections in financial markets, liquidity management is not a thing of value to shareholders.

RECEIVABLES AND INVENTORIES

Receivables and inventories can and should be evaluated from much the same perspective as fixed assets, which we evaluated in Part 3. Many capital budgeting projects embody receivables and inventories as well as a fixed-asset component. A new distribution system that includes a new warehouse and additional inventories is an example, as is a new product that requires different manufacturing facilities and more receivables and inventories. Receivables and inventories differ from fixed assets in that they are analyzed largely in terms of overall levels; fixed assets are analyzed in terms of specific assets. From the standpoint of the overall valuation of the firm, however, this distinction is unimportant. Capital budgeting projects can be evaluated as a package of assets.

379

CHAPTER 14
Working Capital
Management and
Efficient Market
Considerations

ANALYSIS IN A MARKET CONTEXT

If an overall market valuation approach is employed to analyze risky investments, the package can be judged using a valuation model. You will recall from Chapters 3, 8, and 9 that the appropriate discount rate for a risky investment proposal was the risk-free rate plus a risk premium to capture the unavoidable risk of the project. Unavoidable, or systematic, risk is the risk that cannot be diversified away by holding a broad portfolio of securities. It may be due to one factor, as is the case with the capital asset pricing model (CAPM), or to multiple factors, as is the case with the arbitrage pricing theory (APT). In the latter case, relevant risk variables might include unexpected inflation, unexpected changes in output, and surprise changes in default risk in the capital markets. Whatever model is used, the required return on investment increases with the amount of systematic risk embraced in the project.

Projects that are composed entirely of receivables (e.g., lowering credit standards) or inventories (perhaps stocking more parts) can be evaluated using this approach. The advantage of the approach is that it allows consideration of projects with greatly different risks. A separate required rate of return is determined for each project, and this return is based on the systematic risk of the project in a market context. The lower the risk, the lower the required rate of return.

THE EFFECT OF IMPERFECTIONS

In Chapter 8, we contrasted the evaluation of risky investments when systematic (unavoidable) risk was all that mattered and when firm risk mattered. When market imperfections, such as bankruptcy costs, exist, rational investors become concerned with the total risk of the firm, not just its systematic risk. Total risk, of course, is composed of both systematic and unsystematic risk. We then suggested the use of dual investment hurdle rates—the required return in a systematic-risk context and the required return in a total firm-risk context. The more the real-world conditions involved approximate those of perfect capital markets, the greater the reliance that would be placed on the systematic-risk approach, whereas the greater the imperfections that can be identified, the greater the reliance that would be placed on the total firm-risk approach.

In general, we might expect to find fewer imperfections involved in connection with a receivable investment than we would in connection with an inventory or a fixed-asset investment, and in certain cases fewer imperfections involved in connection with an inventory investment than in connection with a fixed-asset investment. Receivables are a financial asset rather than a real asset. In general, fewer imperfections are evident in financial markets than in product markets. If financial markets were perfect, the firm could not expect to earn an excess return on the investment in receivables. That is, it could not expect to earn a return above the return the financial markets require. Under these circumstances, it would make no difference whether receivables were held as an investment or sold in the market.[4] That is to say, shareholders would be indifferent between the firm having receivables on its books and it selling them for cash once invoices were sent to customers. Only with imperfections in financial markets does the possibility arise for the firm to earn a return above the required return on its investment in receivables.

In contrast to receivables, inventories are real assets, the same as fixed assets. However, there is reason to believe that there may be somewhat fewer imperfections in the product market for inventories than in that for fixed assets. Inventories are portable and have other characteristics that give rise to fewer imperfections. The important thing to be gleaned from this discussion is that if a case can be made for the use of the systematic-risk approach for evaluating fixed assets, an equally strong case can be made for its use with receivables and inventories.

On the basis of this approach, as well as possible allowance for unsystematic risk, decisions can be reached on investment projects that include receivables and inventories. Decisions of this sort over time will determine the level of investment in these two assets. Together with a decision concerning liquidity, which was discussed in the previous section, the current assets of the firm are established. More will be said about this later. We want to turn now to the liability side of the balance sheet and examine the last facet of what has been characterized as working capital management.

LIABILITY STRUCTURE

For purposes of present analysis, we assume that the firm has an established policy with respect to payment for purchases, labor, taxes, and other expenses. As a result, payables and accruals represent passive decision variables; they change in keeping with changes in the level of production or service offered and, in the case of taxes payable, with a change in income before taxes. In a sense, this component of current liabilities represents built-in financing; it tends to rise as the firm expands and fall as the firm contracts. (In Chapter 17, this assumption is relaxed, and we analyze payables and accruals as nonpassive decision variables.)

In contrast, the other component of current liabilities, which we call the active component, would be determined as part of more basic decisions involving determination of the maturity composition and other conditions of the firm's debt. By *other conditions*, we mean such things as whether or not the debt is secured, the type of security, the presence or absence of call feature and/or sinking fund, the coupon rate, and whether or not the security is convertible. Determination of the total amount of debt the firm should maintain was taken up in Chapters 10 and 11, when we examined the capital structure of the firm. Our concern now is with the type of debt that should be used.

VALUE IMPLICATIONS WITH PERFECT AND COMPLETE MARKETS

If perfect and complete financial markets are assumed, not only is the debt versus equity question irrelevant but so are questions about the maturity and other conditions of the debt. Moreover, the company would be indifferent

---

[4] See John J. Pringle and Richard A. Cohn, "Steps toward an Integration of Corporate Financial Planning," in *Management of Working Capital* (New York: West, 1974), pp. 369–75.

between borrowing in the home market or abroad. We previously discussed the requisites of a perfect financial market—an absence of taxes, bankruptcy costs, information costs and delays, transaction costs, and restrictions on market participants. A complete market is somewhat different in concept. It is defined as one where every contingency in the world corresponds to a distinct marketable security. An incomplete financial market exists when the number and types of securities available do not span these contingencies. In a more practical sense, a complete financial market satisfies the desires of potential investors with respect to the kinds of securities offered. Expressed differently, financial instruments with desired features are available in sufficient quantity so as to leave investors satisfied. In an incomplete financial market, issuers of securities would be able to tailor debt offerings to the unfilled desires of investors and thereby reap an interest-cost savings.

Under the assumption of perfect and complete financial markets, all of the firm's financial liabilities would have the same cost on a certainty-equivalent basis. In other words, the risk-adjusted expected returns would be the same. The firm could not hope to profit by issuing debt instruments with different maturities or in domestic or foreign markets. One type of instrument would be as good as the next. Thus, there would be no reward for variety of debt instrument when it comes to the value of the firm to its shareholders.

IMPERFECTIONS AND INCOMPLETENESS

If imperfections exist in financial markets, different financial liabilities may have different certainty-equivalent costs. Imperfections such as taxes, transaction costs, flotation costs, bankruptcy costs, costs of information, and legal constraints on investing by certain institutions may make the maturity and other conditions of a firm's debt relevant considerations when it comes to their impact on value. If flotation costs are roughly the same for all maturities, there would be an incentive for the firm to issue longer-term debt, all other things the same. The reason is that this financing policy would reduce the number of times the firm had to issue debt and incur flotation costs. On the other hand, the presence of bankruptcy costs might cause certain secured debt instruments to be used, whereas they would not be used in the absence of such costs.

If lenders have an unsatisfied demand for a particular type of instrument, it pays the firm to exploit this incomplete market and issue the security. For example, institutional investors, such as pension funds, appeared to have an unfilled appetite for zero coupon bonds in the early 1980s. Many borrowers responded by tailoring their security offerings to the unfilled desires of these lenders. As long as the market remains incomplete, a firm can realize a lower interest cost, all other things the same, by tailoring the type and maturity security it issues to the market. Of course, if enough firms do this, the market becomes complete and no further gains are possible.

We would not expect the impact of market imperfections and incompleteness with respect to maturity and other conditions of debt to be as important as they are in the question of debt versus equity. Nonetheless some effect may cause different financial liabilities to have somewhat different certainty-equivalent costs. With different certainty-equivalent costs, the firm would not be indifferent as to the type of debt instrument it issued. By packaging debt instruments to appeal to certain clienteles of lenders and by taking advantage of imperfections, a company may be able to lower its interest cost. This may

381

CHAPTER 14
Working Capital
Management and
Efficient Market
Considerations

take the form of borrowing in a particular country where favorable opportunities exist owing to market segmentation and other imperfections.[5]

Unfortunately, the differential impact of various financial liabilities has not been written about nearly as much as the debt versus equity question. There has been a reasonable amount of research on the call feature, on the maturity structure of debt, and on the coupon-rate effect.[6] While most of this work supports the notion of efficient markets, at times imperfections and incompleteness seem to exist that might be exploited. However, the effects are subtle and difficult to detect in advance. Little work has been done on the effect of different types of secured positions on the value of debt. With bankruptcy costs, we would expect in theory at least that variations in the type of secured position would have an effect on the debt's value. The same principle would apply to the various protective covenants included in the loan agreement or bond indenture. These covenants give the lender greater flexibility to effect changes should the borrower's financial condition deteriorate.[7]

Clearly, more work needs to be done on the subject. In this book, we allow for the possibility that differences in maturity and other conditions *may* result in differences, although slight, in the certainty-equivalent costs of the various debt instruments available to a company. We assume, therefore, that these factors may be relevant considerations when it comes to structuring the financial liabilities of the firm. To assume otherwise would negate the need to examine the features of various financial instruments. In Part 5, we explore the various real-world conditions associated with short- and intermediate-term debt, in the hope of obtaining a better understanding of their valuation implications.

The important thing to realize is that the amount of current liabilities the firm maintains is the result of more fundamental decisions concerning the maturity composition of its debt. Any debt with a maturity of 1 year or less, by accounting definition, is a current liability. The active component of current liabilities should not be determined in isolation, but rather as a part of an overall determination of the best combination of financial liabilities for the firm. The amount of debt that falls into current liabilities is incidental to such a determination.

IMPLICATIONS FOR WORKING CAPITAL

Our conceptual overview of decisions concerning cash and marketable securities, receivables, inventories, and current liabilities was in keeping with an objective of maximizing the overall value of the firm. Once decisions are

---

[5] See Yong Cheol Kim and Rene M. Stulz, "The Eurobond Market and Corporate Financial Policy: A Test of the Clientele Hypothesis," working paper, Ohio State University (August 1988), who found evidence consistent with such financing opportunities when it came to Eurobond versus American domestic bond issues.

[6] For a review of the empirical work in these areas, see James C. Van Horne, *Financial Market Rates and Flows*, 3d ed. (Englewood Cliffs, NJ: Prentice Hall, 1990).

[7] For a discussion of the various protective covenants, see Chap. 19. See also James C. Van Horne, "Optimal Initiation of Bankruptcy Proceedings by Debt Holders," *Journal of Finance*, 31 (June 1976), 897–910.

reached concerning these areas, the level of working capital, by definition, is also determined. Working capital is not determined in any active decision sense, but falls out as a residual from the decisions just named.

Thus, working capital—current assets less current liabilities—has no economic meaning in the sense of implying some type of normative behavior. According to this line of reasoning, it is largely an accounting artifact. Working capital management, then, is a misnomer; the working capital of the firm is not managed. The term describes a category of management decisions affecting specific types of current assets and current liabilities. In turn, those decisions should be rooted in the overall valuation of the firm.

383

**CHAPTER 14
Working Capital
Management and
Efficient Market
Considerations**

SUMMARY

In this chapter, we took up the valuation of the firm as it pertains in particular to the current assets and liabilities of the firm. In theory, it does not make sense to separate decisions involving specific current assets and liabilities from the overall investment and financing decisions of the firm. Thus, the distinction between current and fixed assets and between current and long-term liabilities is largely an accounting one. In practice, certain characteristics associated with current assets differentiate them somewhat from fixed assets, and these were explored.

Liquidity, receivables and inventories, and current liabilities—the various components of working capital—were categorized along functional lines and analyzed in keeping with the valuation of the firm in a market context. Theoretical justification for maintaining liquidity rests largely on the presence of bankruptcy costs. These costs make liquidity management a thing of value. Receivables and inventories can be evaluated in much the same manner as fixed assets by using a single-factor or multifactor valuation model. The decision processes with respect to current assets were examined under both perfect market assumptions and under imperfections where systematic plus unsystematic risk were important.

The amount of current liabilities the firm maintains falls out as a byproduct of fundamental decisions involving capital structure and the maturity and other conditions of the debt. We touched on the degree of imperfections in the market for financial liabilities and the implications for such imperfections. Also explored was the notion of incomplete markets where the firm tailors its debt instruments to the unfilled desires of investors. Once decisions are reached in the three areas discussed, the level of working capital of the firm emerges as a residual.

In the subsequent chapters of Part 4, we explore the cash and marketable securities, receivables, and inventories of the firm in more detail. The analysis will purposely be partial equilibrium in nature, since most of the analytical work to date has been in this vein, and managerial decisions are framed in this manner. The conceptual overview in this chapter will transcend our discussion and enable us to transform or link decision-making problems to their valuation underpinnings.

SELF-CORRECTION PROBLEMS

1. The Zakuta Fish Company is in a cyclical, risky business. By maintaining liquidity, it lowers the possibility of going into bankruptcy. It is estimated that if bankruptcy were to occur, there would be a $100,000 present-value shortfall in what suppliers of capital would realize from the going concern value of the assets. This "cost" of bankruptcy is attributable to legal expenses and the sale of assets at distress prices. By maintaining the following levels of liquidity, the probabilities of bankruptcy occurring are

LEVEL OF LIQUIDITY	PROBABILITY OF BANKRUPTCY
$ 25,000	.30
50,000	.20
75,000	.15
100,000	.12
125,000	.10
150,000	.08
175,000	.06
200,000	.05
225,000	.04
250,000	.03

Liquidity is increased by borrowing, and it is held in the form of marketable securities. Marketable securities yield less than the interest rate the company must pay on short-term borrowings. The present-value differential amounts to $1,500 for each $25,000 borrowed. If we assume no taxes and no other explicit or implicit costs associated with debt, what is the optimal level of liquidity?

2. The Hollezorin Company must decide among three liability strategies, which differ in maturity structure and type of securities. For each strategy, the annual interest costs, the annual flotation costs, and the annual expected bankruptcy costs (probability weighted) are estimated. On the basis of the information given, which is the best strategy? Why do the various costs change with changes in strategy?

STRATEGY	MATURITY	SECURED OR UNSECURED	ANNUAL INTEREST COSTS	ALL FLOTATION COSTS	BANKRUPTCY COSTS
A	$\frac{1}{2}$ short- $\frac{1}{4}$ medium- $\frac{1}{4}$ long- term debt	All unsecured	$1,400,000	$300,000	$200,000
B	$\frac{1}{3}$ short- $\frac{1}{3}$ medium- $\frac{1}{3}$ long- term debt	Unsecured Secured Unsecured	1,520,000	250,000	150,000
C	$\frac{1}{4}$ short- $\frac{1}{4}$ medium- $\frac{1}{2}$ long- term debt	Unsecured Secured Secured	1,600,000	200,000	75,000

1. The Andersen Corporation has a sales level of $280,000 with a 10 percent net profit margin before interest and taxes. To generate this sales volume, the firm maintains a fixed-asset investment of $100,000. At present, the firm maintains $50,000 in current assets.

   a. Determine the asset turnover (sales/total assets) for the firm. Compute the rate of return on assets.

   b. What would be the rate of return if management assumed a more conservative attitude and increased current assets by $50,000?

   c. What would be the rate of return if management assumed a less conservative attitude and decreased current assets by $25,000?

   d. Appraise the significance of increases and decreases in the level of current assets.

2. The Amos Company has determined that the distribution of expected cash flows (available to meet current obligations of $500,000) for the next 3 months is approximately normal with a mean of $500,000 and a standard deviation of $350,000. The company presently has zero cash, and the expected cash position at the end of the period also would be zero ($500,000 in cash flow minus $500,000 in current obligations). Fortunately, it is able to convert nonliquid assets into liquid assets by selling a portion of its nonliquid assets to a supplier. The sale would be a one-shot occurrence, and no further conversions would be possible. The firm now earns 20 percent on its investment in nonliquid assets; by investing in marketable securities, it could earn only 8 percent.

   In addition, it estimated that lengthening the maturity of the firm's outstanding debt ($6 million) could reduce the outflow of cash in the following manner:

ADDED LENGTH OF MATURITY	REDUCED CASH OUTFLOW
One year	$250,000
Two years	375,000
Three years	450,000
Four years	500,000
Five years	535,000
Six years	560,000
Seven years	580,000

   Lengthening the maturity by 5 years or less would cost the company an additional 1 percent annually on its outstanding debt; lengthening it by 6 or 7 years would result in a $1\frac{1}{2}$ percent annual increase in interest costs on its outstanding debt.

   a. Assuming that the management of the Amos Company is willing to tolerate a 5 percent probability of running out of cash, by how much should it increase its liquid assets?

   b. There are three alternatives that will reduce the probability of running out of cash to 5 percent: (1) increase liquid assets, (2) lengthen maturity of debt, and (3) a combination of 1 and 2. Which alternative is best from the standpoint of management?

3. If the George T. Booker Company increases its inventory investment in glass fibers by $200,000, it can give customers better service. In the past, the sale of the fibers closely paralleled the gross national product. On the basis of this observation, Mr. Booker, the company's president, feels that the underlying risk of the inventory investment is "about that of a typical stock listed on the New York Stock Exchange."

385

At present, the rate on Treasury notes is 8 percent, and in recent years the average return on Standard & Poor's 500-Stock Index has been 14 percent. The Booker Company has an all-equity capital structure and intends to finance all new investment proposals entirely with equity.

a. On the basis of this information, what is the required rate of return on the investment using the CAPM?

b. On what does this required return depend? Is it a realistic acceptance criterion to employ?

SOLUTIONS TO
SELF-CORRECTION PROBLEMS

1.

(1) LEVEL OF LIQUIDITY	(2) PROBABILITY OF BANKRUPTCY	(3) EXPECTED COST OF BANKRUPTCY (2) × $100,000	(4) CHANGE IN (3)
$ 25,000	.30	$30,000	
50,000	.20	20,000	−$10,000
75,000	.15	15,000	−5,000
100,000	.12	12,000	−3,000
125,000	.10	10,000	−2,000
150,000	.08	8,000	−2,000
175,000	.06	6,000	−2,000
200,000	.05	5,000	−1,000
225,000	.04	4,000	−1,000
250,000	.03	3,000	−1,000

As the marginal present-value cost of each $25,000 increment of liquidity is $1,500, the optimal level of liquidity is $175,000. At this level, there is a 6 percent chance that bankruptcy will occur.

2. The total estimated annual costs for the three strategies are

	STRATEGY		
	A	B	C
Total cost	$1,900,000	$1,920,000	$1,875,000

Strategy C, involving the highest portion of long-term debt, is best, despite the higher interest cost. As we see, interest costs increase with the greater use of long-term and medium-term debt. This pattern is consistent with interest rates rising at a decreasing rate with maturity. Flotation costs decrease the longer the average maturity of the debt, which is in keeping with fewer offerings per year. Finally, expected bankruptcy costs decline the longer the average maturity. This occurrence is consistent with less uncertainty associated with long-term debt. Also, expected bankruptcy costs decline as more of the debt is made secured, and lenders can turn directly to assets for payment in cases of adversity as opposed to settlement through the bankruptcy courts.

EMERY, GARY W., "Optimal Liquidity Policy: A Stochastic Process Approach," *Journal of Financial Research*, 5 (Fall 1982), 273–84.

FLANNERY, MARK J., "Asymmetric Information and Risky Debt Maturity Choice," *Journal of Finance*, 41 (March 1986), 19–37.

HAMPTON, JOHN J., and CECILIA L. WAGNER, *Working Capital Management*. New York: John Wiley, 1989.

HAWAWINI, GABRIEL, CLAUDE VIALLET, and ASHOK VORA, "Industry Influence on Corporate Working Capital Decisions," *Sloan Management Review*, 27 (Summer 1986), 15–24.

HO, THOMAS S. Y., and RONALD F. SINGER, "Bond Indenture Provisions and the Risk of Corporate Debt," *Journal of Financial Economics*, 10 (December 1982), 375–406.

KIM, YONG CHEOL, and RENE M. STULZ, "The Eurobond Market and Corporate Financial Policy: A Test of the Clientele Hypothesis," working paper, Ohio State University (August 1988).

MORRIS, JAMES R., "A Model for Corporate Debt Maturity Decisions," *Journal of Financial and Quantitative Analysis*, 11 (September 1976), 339–58.

——, "The Role of Cash Balances in Firm Valuation," *Journal of Financial and Quantitative Analysis*, 18 (December 1983), 533–46.

SARTORIS, WILLIAM L., and NED C. HILL, "A Generalized Cash Flow Approach to Short-Term Financial Decisions," *Journal of Finance*, 38 (May 1983), 349–60.

SMITH, CLIFFORD W., and RENE M. STULZ, "The Determinants of Firms' Hedging Policies," *Journal of Financial and Quantitative Analysis*, 20 (December 1985), 391–405.

VAN HORNE, JAMES C., "A Risk-Return Analysis of a Firm's Working-Capital Position," *Engineering Economist*, 14 (Winter 1969), 71–89.

15

MANAGEMENT OF CASH AND MARKETABLE SECURITIES

If efficiently managed, investment in specific current assets can contribute to the overall objective of the firm. How to do it is the subject of this chapter and the next. First, we delve into the secrets of cash management and the investment of excess funds in marketable securities. Keynes has identified three motives for holding cash: the transactions motive, the precautionary motive, and the speculative motive.[1] The transactions motive is the need for cash to meet payments arising in the ordinary course of business—payments for things such as purchases, labor, taxes, and dividends. The precautionary motive for holding cash has to do with maintaining a cushion or buffer to meet unexpected contingencies. The more predictable the cash flows of the business, the fewer precautionary balances are needed. Ready borrowing power to meet emergency cash drains also reduces the need for this type of balance. It is important to point out that not all of the firm's transactions and precautionary balances need be held in cash; indeed, a portion may be held in marketable securities—near-money assets.

The speculative motive relates to holding cash in order to take advantage of expected changes in security prices. When we expect interest rates to rise and security prices to fall, this motive would suggest that the firm should hold cash until the rise in interest rates ceases. When interest rates are expected to fall, cash may be invested in securities; the firm will benefit by any subsequent fall in interest rates and rise in security prices. For the most part, companies do not hold liquidity for the purpose of taking advantage of expected changes in interest rates. Consequently, we concentrate only on the transactions and precautionary motives of the firm, with these balances held both in cash and in marketable securities.

---

[1] John Maynard Keynes, The General Theory of Employment, Interest, and Money (New York: Harcourt, 1936), pp. 170–74.

388

THE FUNCTION OF CASH MANAGEMENT

389

CHAPTER 15
Management of
Cash and
Marketable
Securities

Cash management involves managing the monies of the firm in order to maximize cash availability and interest income on any idle funds. At one end, the function starts when a customer writes a check to pay the firm on its accounts receivable. The function ends when a supplier, an employee, or the government realizes collected funds from the firm on an account payable or accrual. All activities between these two points fall within the realm of cash management. The firm's efforts to get customers to pay their bills at a certain time fall within accounts receivable management. On the other hand, the firm's decision about when to pay its bills involves accounts payable and accrual management.

The treasurer's office of a company usually manages cash. A cash budget, instrumental in the process, is commonly a monthly forecast of receipts and debts. Since the preparation of cash budgets is discussed in Chapter 28, where we consider financial forecasting, it will not be taken up here. The cash budget tells us the likely availability of cash with respect to both timing and magnitude. In other words, it tells us how much cash we are likely to have, when, and for how long. As Chapter 28 suggests, we must take uncertainty into account, and we can do this by preparing multiple cash budgets under alternative assumptions. Thus, the cash budget serves as a foundation for cash planning and control.

In addition to the cash budget, the firm needs systematic information on cash as well as some kind of control system. Usually the information is computer based, as opposed to manually based. In either case, it is necessary to obtain frequent reports—preferably daily or even more often—on cash balances in each bank account, on the cash disbursed, on the average daily collected balances, and on the marketable security position of the firm, as well as a detailed report of changes in this position. A number of banks provide this information via computer printouts over telephone lines. Also, it is useful to have information on major anticipated cash receipts and cash disbursements. All of this information is essential if a firm is to manage its cash in an efficient manner.

MANAGING COLLECTIONS

The various collection and disbursement methods by which a firm can improve its cash management efficiency constitute two sides of the same coin. They exercise a joint impact on the overall efficiency of cash management. The idea is to collect accounts receivable as soon as possible, but pay accounts payable as late as is consistent with maintaining the firm's credit standing with suppliers. Today, most companies of reasonable size use sophisticated techniques to speed collections and tightly control disbursements. Let us see how they do it.

We consider first the acceleration of collections, which simply means reducing the delay between the time customers pay their bills and the time the checks are collected and become usable funds for the firm. A number of methods are designed to speed up this collection process by doing one or all of the following: (1) speed the mailing time of payments from customers to the firm,

(2) reduce the time during which payments received by the firm remain uncollected funds, and (3) speed the movement of funds to disbursement banks.

The second item, representing float, has two aspects. The first is the time it takes a company to process checks internally. This interval extends from the moment a check is received to the moment it is deposited with a bank for credit to the company's account. The second aspect of float involves the time consumed in clearing the check through the banking system. A check becomes collected funds when it is presented to the drawee bank and actually paid by that bank. In order to streamline the availability of credit, the Federal Reserve System has established a schedule specifying availability for all checks deposited with it for collection. This schedule is based on the time required for a check deposited with a particular Federal Reserve Bank to be collected in a particular geographic area of the country. The maximum period for which credit is deferred is 2 days; most checks involve 1-day deferred availability. This means that even if a check is not actually collected through the Federal Reserve System within 1 or 2 days, it becomes collected funds because the Federal Reserve carries the float.

Float is important to the financial manager because a company usually cannot make withdrawals on a deposit until the checks in that deposit are collected. As the name of the game is usable funds, the financial manager wants to reduce the float as much as possible. In what follows, we examine various ways to speed up the collection process in order to have more usable funds. We first present funds flows based on checks that are written. Later we examine electronic funds transfers. While we are moving in the direction of a "checkless society," due to tradition and preferences checks still are widely used.

TRANSFERRING FUNDS

In the ways discussed as well as in the control of disbursements, moving funds among banks is a factor. There are three principal methods: (1) wire transfers, (2) depository transfer checks, and (3) electronic transfer checks through automatic clearinghouses.

With a wire transfer, funds are immediately transferred from one bank to another. Wire transfers can be through the Federal Reserve Bank's wire transfer service (Fedwire), the Western Union Bank Wire, or the Clearing House Interbank Payments System (CHIPS). With a depository transfer check (DTC) arrangement for the movement of funds, a preprinted depository check is drawn on the local bank, payable to a concentration bank. Funds are not immediately available at the concentration bank, for the check must be collected through the usual channels involving usual delays of 2 or more days. A transfer check costs only 50 cents or so for processing, compared with about $10 for a wire transfer, but it is not nearly as fast. The delay must be analyzed in relation to the difference in cost. For small transfers, a wire transfer may be too costly, compared with a depository transfer check. A variation of the depository transfer check is an electronic check image, which is processed through automatic clearinghouses. The funds become available 1 business day later, and the process is electronic, rather than the physical transportation of the check. As the cost is not particularly large, the electronic DTC has largely replaced the mail-based DTC.

CONCENTRATION BANKING

391

CHAPTER 15
Management of
Cash and
Marketable
Securities

Concentration banking is a means of accelerating the flow of funds of a firm by establishing strategic collection centers. Instead of a single collection center located at the company headquarters, multiple collection centers are established. The purpose is to shorten the period between the time customers mail in their payments and the time when the company has use of the funds. Customers in a particular geographic area are instructed to remit their payments to a collection center in that area. Location of the collection centers usually is based on the geographic areas served and the volume of billings in an area. When payments are received, they are deposited in the collection center's local bank. Surplus funds are then transferred from these local bank accounts to a concentration bank or banks. A bank of concentration is one with which the company has a major account—usually a disbursement account.

An Illustration. This is an actual case of a large company with over 20 collection centers. At the time of the study, each collection center billed customers in its area. In its local bank, it made daily deposits of payments received from customers. On the average, the checks deposited in a bank were collected in $1\frac{1}{4}$ days. In other words, the company had use of the funds $1\frac{1}{4}$ days after deposit. In each of its local banks, the company maintained sufficient collected balances to compensate the bank for the costs of servicing the account. A daily wire transfer arrangement was used to transfer collected balances in excess of compensating balances to one of several concentration banks. The managers of the collection centers initiated the transfer on the basis of a daily report of estimated collected balances from their local banks.

The advantage of a system of decentralized billings and collections over a centralized system is twofold. (Remember that we are comparing a system of multiple collection centers with a single collection center located at company headquarters.)

1. The time required for mailing is reduced. Because the collection center bills customers in its area, these customers usually receive their bills earlier than if bills were mailed from the head office. In turn, when customers pay their bills, the mailing time to the nearest collection center is shorter than the time required for the typical remittance to go to the head office. The company estimated that there was a saving of approximately $1\frac{3}{4}$ days in mailing time from the customer to the company.

2. The time required to collect checks is reduced because remittances deposited in the collection center's local bank usually are drawn on banks in that general area. The company estimated that the average collection period would be 2 days if all remittances were deposited in the company's head office bank, compared with 1 day under the present system. At the margin, then, the company was able to speed up the collection of customer checks by 1 day.

Thus, the company was able to accelerate overall collections by $2\frac{3}{4}$ days; $1\frac{3}{4}$ days were gained by reducing the mailing time and 1 day by reducing the time during which deposited checks remained uncollected. At the time of the study, average daily remittances by customers were $3.1 million. By saving $2\frac{3}{4}$

days in the collection process, approximately $8.5 million in funds were released for investment elsewhere. Profits from the investment of the released funds must be compared with any additional costs of a decentralized system over a centralized one. Also consider any differences between the two systems in total compensating balances. The greater the number of collection centers, the greater the number of local bank accounts that must be maintained.[2]

LOCK-BOX SYSTEM

Another means of accelerating the flow of funds is a lock-box arrangement. With concentration banking, a collection center receives remittances, processes them, and deposits them in a bank. The purpose of a lock-box arrangement is to eliminate the time between the receipt of remittances by the company and their deposit in the bank. A lock-box arrangement usually is on a regional basis, the company choosing regional banks according to its billing patterns. Before determining the regions to be used, a feasibility study is made of the availability of checks that would be deposited under alternative plans vis-à-vis their costs. In this regard, operation research techniques have proved useful in the selection of lock-box sites.[3] If a company divided the country into five sections on the basis of a feasibility study, it might pick New York City for the Northeast, Atlanta for the Southeast, Chicago for the Midwest, Dallas for the Southwest, and San Francisco for the West Coast.

The company rents a local post office box and authorizes its bank in each of these cities to pick up remittances in the box. Customers are billed with instructions to mail their remittances to the lock box. The bank picks up the mail several times a day and deposits the checks in the company's account. The checks are recorded and cleared for collection. The company receives a deposit slip and a list of payments, together with any material in the envelope. This procedure frees the company from handling and depositing the checks.

The main advantage of a lock-box system is that checks are deposited at banks sooner and become collected balances sooner than if they were processed by the company prior to deposit. In other words, the lag between the time checks are received by the company and the time they actually are deposited at the bank is eliminated. The principal disadvantage of a lock-box arrangement is the cost. The bank provides a number of services additional to the usual clearing of checks and requires compensation for them, usually preferring increased deposits. Because the cost is almost directly proportional to the number of checks deposited, lock-box arrangements usually are not profitable if the average remittance is small.

The appropriate rule for deciding whether or not to use a lock-box system—or, for that matter, concentration banking—is simply to compare the added cost of the most efficient system with the marginal income that can be generated from the released funds. If costs are less than income, the system is profitable; if not, the system is not a profitable undertaking. The degree of

---

[2] For a mathematical algorithm for the optimal selection of banks and transfer arrangements, see Bernell K. Stone and Ned C. Hill, "The Design of a Cash Concentration System," *Journal of Financial and Quantitative Analysis*, 16 (September 1981), 301–22.

[3] For an excellent overview of these models and an analysis of the problems involved in their implementation, see Steven F. Maier and James H. Vander Weide, "What Lockbox and Disbursement Models Really Do," *Journal of Finance*, 38 (May 1983), 361–71; and their book, *Managing Corporate Liquidity* (New York: John Wiley, 1985), Chap. 3.

profitability depends primarily on the geographic dispersion of customers, the size of the typical remittance, and the earnings rate on the released funds. Although there is disagreement as to what earnings rate to use, the most appropriate rate for our purpose is the rate on marketable securities. Because a decision on the total amount of liquid assets to maintain was considered in the previous chapter, our present decision affects mainly the proportion of cash to marketable securities, not their sum. Thus, the opportunity cost of tying up funds in cash is the return forgone on marketable securities.

393

CHAPTER 15
Management of
Cash and
Marketable
Securities

OTHER PROCEDURES

Frequently, firms give special attention to handling large remittances so that they may be deposited in a bank as quickly as possible. This special handling may involve personal pickup of checks by the company or by messenger service. When a small number of remittances account for a large proportion of total deposits, it may be worthwhile to initiate controls to accelerate the deposit and collection of large checks. Instead of processing all checks for collection through the Federal Reserve System, some commercial banks offer special services that present high-dollar-volume checks directly to the drawee bank. The benefit is a speedup in collection of these checks, and it is passed on to the bank customer in having usable funds more quickly.

Some companies maintain too many bank accounts, thereby creating unnecessary pockets of idle funds. A company that has an account in every city where it has either a sales office or a production facility might be able to reduce cash balances considerably if it were to eliminate some of these accounts. The banking activities of a sales office can often be handled from a larger account with little loss in service or availability of funds. Even though small accounts may create a degree of goodwill with bankers, they make little sense in the overall cash management of the firm. By closing such unnecessary accounts, a firm may be able to release funds that it then can put to profitable use.

Traditionally, many companies use the postmark date on the envelope to determine whether a payment qualifies for a discount. This requires considerable manual verification. To eliminate such verification as well as speed up collections, some firms are instigating the time of actual receipt as the benchmark for discount qualification. In so doing, the firm may wish to extend the discount period by a day or two in order not to upset customers with the change. Even with such extensions, collections from discount-paying customers usually accelerate on average.

CONTROL OF DISBURSEMENTS

Effective control of disbursements can also result in more availability of cash. Whereas the underlying objective of collections is maximum acceleration, the objective in disbursements is to slow them down as much as possible. The combination of fast collections and slow disbursements will result in maximum availability of funds.

One way of maximizing cash availability is "playing the float." For disbursements, float is the difference between the total dollar amount of checks drawn on a bank account and the balance shown on the bank's books. It is possible, of course, for a company to have a negative balance on its books and a positive bank balance, because checks outstanding have not been collected from the account on which they are drawn. If the size of float can be estimated accurately, bank balances can be reduced and the funds invested to earn a positive return.

MOBILIZING FUNDS AND SLOWING DISBURSEMENTS

A company with multiple banks should be able to shift funds quickly to banks from which disbursements are made, to prevent excessive balances from building up temporarily in a particular bank. The idea is to have adequate cash at the various banks, but not to let excessive balances build up. This requires daily information on collected balances. Excess funds then are transferred to the disbursement banks, either to pay bills or to invest in marketable securities. Many companies have developed sophisticated computer systems to provide the necessary information and to transfer excess funds automatically. Instead of developing one's own system, a firm can hire outside computer services to provide the described functions.

One procedure for tightly controlling disbursements is to centralize payables into a single account, presumably at the company's headquarters. In this way, disbursements can be made at the precise time they are desired. Needless to say, operating procedures for disbursements should be well established. If cash discounts are taken on accounts payable, procedures should aim toward eliminating or minimizing the loss of discounts due to clerical inefficiencies. The timing of payments is important. For maximum use of cash, payments should be made on the due dates, not before.

A means for delaying disbursements is through the use of drafts. Unlike an ordinary check, the draft is not payable on demand. When it is presented to the issuer's bank for collection, the bank must present it to the issuer for acceptance. The funds then are deposited by the issuing firm to cover payment of the draft. The advantage of the draft arrangement is that it delays the time the firm actually has to have funds on deposit to cover the draft. Consequently, it allows the firm to maintain smaller deposits at its banks. A possible disadvantage of a draft system is that certain suppliers may prefer checks. Also, banks do not like to process drafts because they require special attention, often manual. As a result, banks typically impose a higher service charge to process them than they do to process ordinary checks.

When a company has multiple bank accounts throughout the country, the opportunities for "playing the float" expand. Taking advantage of inefficiencies in the check-clearing processes of the Federal Reserve System and of certain commercial banks, as well as inefficiencies in the postal system, a firm may maximize the time the checks it writes remain outstanding. Various models have been proposed to maximize disbursement float through the selection of geographically optimal disbursing banks. The idea is to locate disbursing banks and to draw checks on them in a way that will maximize the time a check will remain outstanding. A check payable to a supplier in Arizona might be drawn on a remote bank in Portland, Maine. The solution depends on the location of, and the amount of billings from, suppliers, on procedural delays in the banking system associated with various supplier location–disbursing bank location combinations, and on the cost of banking services, whether it be compensating balances or fees.

By maximizing disbursement float, the firm can reduce the amount of cash it holds and employ these funds in more profitable ways. One firm's gain, however, is another firm's loss. Maximizing disbursement float means that suppliers will not have collectible funds as early as would otherwise be the case. To the extent that they look with disfavor on such payment habits, supplier relations may be hurt. Some suppliers may simply raise prices to compensate; others may let service slip because the buyer is no longer a favored customer. To the extent supplier relations are adversely impacted by slowing disbursements, this factor must be taken into account.

395

CHAPTER 15
Management of
Cash and
Marketable
Securities

PAYROLL AND DIVIDEND DISBURSEMENTS

Many companies maintain a separate account for payroll disbursements. In order to minimize the balance in this account, one must predict when the payroll checks issued will be presented for payment. If payday falls on a Friday, not all of the checks will be cashed on that day. Consequently, the firm need not have funds on deposit to cover its entire payroll. Even on Monday, some checks will not be presented, owing to delays in their deposit. Based on its experience, the firm should be able to construct a distribution of when, on the average, checks are presented for collection. An example is shown in Fig. 15-1. With this information, the firm can approximate the funds it needs to have on deposit to cover payroll checks. Many firms establish a separate account for dividends, similar to the payroll account. Here, too, the idea is to predict when such checks will be presented for payment, to minimize the cash balance in the account.

ZERO BALANCE ACCOUNT

In order to make transfers automatically into a payroll, dividend, or other special account, some companies employ a zero balance account (ZBA). The ZBA is offered by a number of banks, and it eliminates the need to estimate and fund each disbursement account. Rather, one master disbursing account services all subsidiary accounts. At the end of each day, the bank automatically transfers just enough funds to cover the checks presented for collection. As a result, a zero balance is maintained in each of the special disbursing accounts. While balances must be maintained in the master account, increased efficiency works to reduce the total balances that must be maintained.

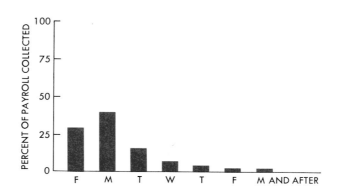

FIGURE 15-1

Percentage of payroll checks collected

ELECTRONIC FUNDS TRANSFER

The procedures for accelerating collections and slowing disbursements discussed in the previous two sections are based on a paper transfer system. However, electronic transfer systems are increasingly being used for both collections and disbursements. The reasons for this evolution are twofold: changes in financial institution regulation and advances in computer-based information systems as well as in electronic communications. Regulatory changes have permitted greater competition among financial institutions and a much broader menu of accounts, instruments, and payments mechanisms.

The second aspect of the changing environment is the increased sophistication in computer applications to cash management and in electronic funds transfers. As individuals, we all are aware of plastic cards with magnetic coding, which can be used to obtain cash, to transfer funds from one account to another, to pay bills, to borrow, and to do other things. These transactions can occur at a financial institution, at an unattended electronic payments machine that is open 24 hours a day, and at certain retail stores. At stores, one is able to pay for a purchase with such a card, as funds are transferred electronically from the customer to the store. The advantage to retailers is obvious; they are ensured that payments for the purchases are good, and they are immediate. Retailers also can reduce the possibility of bad checks by using guarantee systems that a number of banks offer. With such a system, a customer's check is scanned electronically and verified by computer. Because the bank guarantees the checks it verifies, the retailer is not exposed to bad-check losses. The "smart card" has a computer chip embedded in it that allows immediate interface with the retailer. It can be used in a variety of ways, but the important feature is that it is not necessary to go through a central computer. The card contains the relevant information and debits, credits, and other entries can be made directly.

For companies, the electronic transfer of funds is illustrated in Fig. 15-2. The supplier, company Y, sends an invoice to its customer, company X. On the appropriate payment date, company X instructs its bank to pay its supplier via a prearranged procedure. The instructions can be transmitted by central computer, terminal, or some other means. The bank then debits company X's account and either credits directly or wire transfers the credit to company Y's bank, along with communicating electronically the supporting information. The latter bank then credits company Y's account, sending it the supporting information, again electronically. Company Y is then in a position to update its accounts receivable ledgers. In addition to paying bills, electronic funds transfers (EFTs) can be used to deposit payrolls automatically in employee accounts, to pay taxes, and to make dividend and other payments.

Rather than a direct transfer of funds through banks, the transfer can be through an *automatic clearinghouse*. Some of the major networks include *CHIPS*, the Clearing House Interbank System of New York banks involving next-day settlement; *SWIFT*, the Society of Worldwide Interbank Financial Telecommunications consisting of hundreds of banks worldwide, which permits international transfers; and *NACHA*, the National Automated Clearing House Association, which consists of thousands of banks and thrift institutions and is suited to high-volume batch transfers. Continual improvements

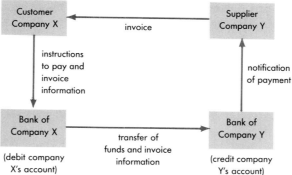

FIGURE 15-2
Example of electronic funds transfer

397

CHAPTER 15
Management of
Cash and
Marketable
Securities

are occurring in these and other networks. Depending on the task involved, one or more of the transfer networks will be most suitable.

With EFT, of course, float is eliminated. Unlike paper transfer, there are no uncollected funds, for one party's account is debited the instant another's is credited. For some corporations, the loss of float in disbursements is too great a cost to pay. To be sure, there are benefits. A tighter control over disbursements is possible, owing to the dates of settlement being known with certainty. Also, supplier relations usually improve. However, these benefits may not offset the perceived cost of float reduction.

Because electronic funds transfer is capital intensive, the cost per transaction is reduced as volume increases. Indeed, this has occurred in recent years, and much of the savings is passed along to users of financial services. The customer benefits from the intense competition among financial institutions and large retailers that provide financial services. For the firm, electronic banking means less time in the collection of receivables, more efficient control of cash, and perhaps a reduction in servicing costs.

Thus, the use of electronic funds transfer can result in greater economization of money balances. In turn, the movement toward these techniques depends in part on the level of interest rates in financial markets. The greater the interest rate, of course, the greater the opportunity cost of holding cash and the more attractive electronic banking techniques become, all other things the same. The use of a new cash management technique, however, typically involves significant start-up costs. As a result, once a new method is in place, there is a tendency to keep it even if interest rates should decline somewhat thereafter.

BALANCING CASH AND MARKETABLE SECURITIES

Given the overall level of transactions and precautionary balances, we wish to consider the appropriate split between cash and marketable securities. Because these securities can be converted into cash on very short notice, they serve the precautionary need of the firm to hold cash. The level of cash, which in turn determines the level of marketable securities, given our assumptions, should be the *greater* of two constraints. The first is any compensating balance requirement of a commercial bank. This requirement is expressed in terms of an average cash balance over some period of time rather than a minimum below which cash cannot fall. The second constraint is self-imposed, and it is determined by the need for cash, the predictability of this need, the interest rate on marketable securities, and the fixed cost of effecting a transfer between marketable securities and cash.

COMPENSATING BALANCES AND FEES

Establishing a minimum level of cash balances depends in part on the compensating balance requirements of banks. These requirements are set on the basis of the profitability of the account. A bank begins by calculating the average collected balance shown on the bank's books over a period of time. The income from the account is determined by multiplying the average collected balance by the bank's earnings rate. Next comes the cost of the account. Most banks have a schedule of costs on a per item basis for such transactions as transfers and processing checks. The account is analyzed for a typical month during which all transactions are multiplied times the per item cost and totaled. If the total cost is less than the total income from the account, the account is profitable; if more, it is unprofitable. The minimum average level of cash balances required is the point at which the account is just profitable. Because banks differ in the earnings rate they use as well as in their costs and method of account analysis, the determination of compensating balances varies. The firm, therefore, may be wise to shop around and find the bank that requires the lowest compensating balances for a given level of activity.

In recent years, there has been a marked trend toward paying cash for services rendered by a bank instead of maintaining compensating balances. The advantage to the firm is that it may be able to earn more on funds used for compensating balances than the fee for the services. The higher the interest rate in the financial markets, the greater the opportunity cost of compensating balances and the greater the advantage of service charges. It is an easy matter to determine if the firm would be better off with service charges as opposed to maintaining compensating balances. Where a service offered can better be paid for by a fee, the firm should be alert to take advantage of the situation and reduce its compensating balances.

MODELS FOR DETERMINING OPTIMAL CASH

In the absence of a binding compensating balance constraint, the optimal levels of cash and marketable securities would be determined by a trade-off between interest income and transaction costs. If the future were known with certainty, it would be an easy matter to determine these optimal levels. Projected cash would be invested as long as the interest earnings exceeded transactions and inconvenience costs, and as long as the delays in conversion between cash and marketable securities did not hinder the firm in paying its bills. If transactions and inconvenience costs were zero and conversion between the two assets were instantaneous, the firm would hold no cash. It simply would sell securities to pay its bills. When transactions and inconvenience costs are positive, however, the firm will want to hold cash when the expected holding period for investment is not long enough to earn sufficient interest to offset them. By the same token, with conversion delays, the firm may need to hold cash. Thus, even if future cash flows were known with certainty, a firm would probably hold some cash.

In the following two sections, we explore two models for determining the appropriate split between cash and marketable securities. The first assumes that the cash flows of the firm are known with certainty while the second assumes they fluctuate randomly. These models portray the extremes of cash-flow certainty, thereby providing useful benchmarks for decision purposes.

399

CHAPTER 15
Management of
Cash and
Marketable
Securities

INVENTORY MODEL

Under conditions of certainty, one simple model for determining the optimal average amount of transaction cash is the economic-order-quantity formula (EOQ) used in inventory management (see the next chapter). It provides a useful conceptual foundation for the cash management problem.[4] In the model, the carrying cost of holding cash—namely, the interest forgone on marketable securities—is balanced against the fixed cost of transferring marketable securities to cash, or vice versa. The model is illustrated by the sawtooth lines in Fig. 15-3.

In the figure, we assume that the firm has a steady demand for cash over some period of time, say, 1 month. The firm obtains cash during this period by selling marketable securities. Suppose it starts out with C dollars in cash, and when this amount is expended, it replenishes it by selling C dollars of marketable securities. Thus, the transfer of funds from securities to cash occurs whenever cash touches zero. If a cushion is desired or if there are lead times to effect a transaction, the threshold for initiating a transfer can be higher. The principle is the same, regardless of whether or not a cushion is used.

The objective is to specify the value of C that minimizes total costs—that is, the sum of the fixed costs associated with transfers and the opportunity

[4] The model was first applied to the problem of cash management by William J. Baumol, "The Transactions Demand for Cash: An Inventory Theoretic Approach," *Quarterly Journal of Economics*, 66 (November 1952), 545–56. It has been further refined and developed by many others.

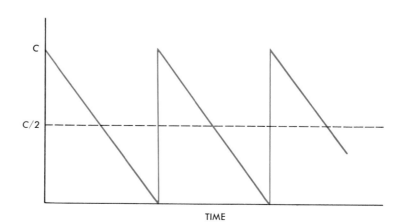

FIGURE 15-3

Inventory model applied to cash management

cost of earnings forgone by holding cash balances. These costs can be expressed as

$$b\left(\frac{T}{C}\right) + i\left(\frac{C}{2}\right) \tag{15-1}$$

where b is the fixed cost of a transaction that is assumed to be independent of the amount transferred, T is the total demand for cash over the period of time involved, and i is the interest rate on marketable securities for the period involved (assumed to be constant). T/C represents the number of transactions during the period, and when it is multiplied times the fixed cost per transaction, we obtain the total fixed cost for the period. $C/2$ represents the average cash balance, and when it is multiplied times the interest rate, we obtain the earnings forgone by virtue of holding cash. The larger the C, the larger the average cash balance, $C/2$, and the smaller the average investment in securities and earnings from these securities. Thus, there is a higher opportunity cost of interest income forgone. The larger the C, however, the fewer the transfers, T/C, that occur and the lower the transfer costs. The object is to balance these two costs so that total costs are minimized.

The optimal level of C is found to be

$$C^* = \sqrt{\frac{2bT}{i}} \tag{15-2}$$

when the derivative of Eq. (15-1) with respect to C is set equal to zero. Thus, cash will be demanded in relation to the square root of the dollar volume of transactions. This phenomenon implies that as the level of cash payments increases, the amount of transaction cash the firm needs to hold increases by a lesser percentage. In other words, economies of scale are possible. The implication is that the firm should try to pool individual bank accounts into as few as possible in order to realize economies in cash management. This does not mean that the firm cannot maintain control over the pooled accounts. Accounting records are kept for each of the accounts and control is maintained; the accounts are pooled only to take advantage of economies of scale available in cash management.

We see also in Eq. (15-2) that C^* varies directly with the fixed cost, b, and inversely with the interest rate on marketable securities, i. The greater the fixed cost of transfers between cash and marketable securities, the fewer the transfers that will take place and the higher the cash balance, all other things the same. The greater the interest rate, the greater the opportunity cost of holding cash and the lower the cash balance, all other things the same. In both cases, the relationship is dampened by the square root sign.

To illustrate the use of the EOQ formula, consider a firm with estimated cash payments of $6 million for a 1-month period, the payments expected to be steady over the period. The fixed cost per transaction is $100, and the interest rate on marketable securities is 12 percent per annum, or 1.0 percent for the 1-month period. Therefore

$$C^* = \sqrt{\frac{2bT}{i}} = \sqrt{\frac{2(100)(6,000,000)}{.01}} = \$346,410$$

Thus, the optimal transaction size is $346,410, and the average cash balance is

$346,410/2 = \$173,205$. This means that the firm should make $\$6,000,000/\$346,410 = 17+$ transactions of marketable securities to cash during the month.

401

CHAPTER 15
Management of
Cash and
Marketable
Securities

It is useful now to consider in more detail the two costs involved. The interest rate is fairly straightforward; it simply represents the rate of interest on securities that would be sold to replenish cash. In most cases, this is the rate on short-term money market instruments, not the average rate of return on all marketable securities. The fixed cost associated with a transaction is more difficult to measure because it consists of both explicit and implied costs. Included are the fixed component of transaction costs, the time it takes the treasurer or other official to place an order with an investment banker, the time consumed in recording the transaction, the secretarial time needed to type the transaction and the purchase order, the time needed to record the transaction on the books, and the time needed to record the safekeeping notification. With a number of transactions, the procedures for placing an order can be streamlined to reduce the average fixed cost per transaction. Nevertheless, these costs do exist and too often are either overlooked or underestimated.

One limitation to the use of the EOQ model is that cash payments are assumed to be steady over the period of time specified. The model is applicable only if this assumption is a reasonable approximation of the situation. When cash payments become lumpy, it may be appropriate to reduce the period for which calculations are made, so that expenditures during the period are relatively steady. The EOQ model can be applied also when receipts are continuous and there are discontinuous large payments. The decision to be made then would be the optimal purchase size of marketable securities.

Another limitation to the use of the model is that cash payments are seldom completely predictable. For modest degrees of uncertainty, one need only add a cushion so that a transfer from marketable securities to cash is triggered at some level of cash above zero. In general, the EOQ model gives the financial manager a benchmark for judging the optimal cash balance. It does not have to be used as a precise rule governing behavior. The model merely suggests what would be the optimal balance under a set of assumptions. The actual balance may be more if the assumptions do not entirely hold.

STOCHASTIC MODELS

In those cases where the uncertainty of cash payments is large, the EOQ model may not be applicable, and other models should be used to determine optimal behavior. If cash balances fluctuate randomly, one can apply control theory to the problem. Assume that the demand for cash is stochastic and unknown in advance. We then can set control limits such that when cash reaches an upper limit, a transfer of cash to marketable securities is consummated, and when it hits a lower limit, a transfer from marketable securities to cash is triggered. As long as the cash balance stays between these limits, no transactions take place.

How the limits are set depends in part on the fixed costs associated with a securities transaction and the opportunity cost of holding cash. As before, we assume these costs are known and that the fixed cost of selling a marketable security is the same as that for buying it. In essence, we want to satisfy the demand for cash at the lowest possible total cost. Although there are a number of applications of control theory to the problem, we discuss a

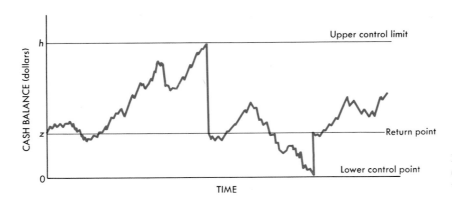

Upper control limit

Return point

Lower control point

FIGURE 15-4
Control-limit model applied
to cash management

relatively simple one. The Miller-Orr model specifies two control limits—
h dollars as an upper bound and zero dollars as a lower bound.[5] The model
is illustrated in Fig. 15-4 under the simplifying assumption that there is no
underlying trend in the cash balance over time.

We see in the figure that when the cash balance touched the upper
bound, $h - z$ dollars of marketable securities are bought, and the new balance
becomes z dollars. When the cash balance touches zero, z dollars of marketable securities are sold, and the new balance again becomes z. As long as
the cash balance fluctuates somewhere between the upper and lower control
limits, no action is taken. The situation is illustrated in the figure. The minimum bound can be set at some amount higher than zero, and h and z would
move up in the figure. We will use zero as the lower bound for purposes of illustration, recognizing that a firm can set the lower bound at some positive
amount. This obviously would be necessary if there were delays in transfer.

The solution for the optimal values of h and z depend not only on the
fixed and opportunity costs but also on the degree of likely fluctuation in cash
balances. The optimal value of z, the return to point for security transactions,
is

$$z = \sqrt[3]{\frac{3b\sigma^2}{4i}}$$
(15-3)

where b = fixed cost associated with a security transaction
σ^2 = variance of daily net cash flows
i = interest rate per day on marketable securities

The optimal value of h is simply 3z. With these control limits set, the model
minimizes the total costs (fixed and opportunity) of cash management. Again,
the critical assumption is that cash flows are random. The average cash
balance cannot be determined exactly in advance, but it is approximately
$(z + h)/3$. As experience unfolds, however, it can easily be calculated.

The equation shows that the wider the variability of cash flows and the
higher the fixed cost of a security transaction, the higher the control limits the
firm sets and the further apart they will be. In contrast, the higher the interest
rate, the lower the control limits, and the closer together they become.

[5] See Merton H. Miller and Daniel Orr, "A Model of the Demand for Money by Firms," *Quarterly
Journal of Economics*, 80 (August 1966), 413–35.

The Miller-Orr model is one of a number of control-limit models designed to deal with the cash management problem under the assumption of stochastic cash flows. As long as cash remains within specified limits, no transactions take place. Thus, we have considered two models for determining the optimal level of cash. The EOQ model assumes cash flows are predictable; the control-limit model assumes they are random. Because of the random cash balance fluctuations assumed, the average cash balance suggested by the control-limit model will be higher than that suggested by the EOQ model.

A PROBABILITY APPROACH

Usually the cash flows of a firm are neither completely predictable nor completely stochastic. Rather, they are predictable within a range. When there is only moderate uncertainty, the EOQ model can be modified to incorporate a precautionary balance to buffer against uncertainty. For many firms, their cash position is reasonably predictable over the near term; therefore, the EOQ model can be employed with some degree of confidence. For these firms, a stochastic model serves primarily as a benchmark for determining cash balances under an extreme assumption of predictability. As we know, the average cash balance will be higher when this model is employed instead of the EOQ model. Thus, when average cash balances of a company are as high as, or higher than, those dictated by a stochastic model, and cash flows are reasonably predictable, we know the cash balance is too high. If, in fact, cash flows are relatively unpredictable, a stochastic model can be used to make automatic transfers between cash and marketable securities.

When cash flows are not reasonably predictable or reasonably unpredictable, a probabilistic approach may be employed. End-of-period cash balances, exclusive of the purchase or sale of marketable securities, can be estimated for various cash-flow outcomes to form a probability distribution. The period used should be short, perhaps a few days or no longer than a week. This probabilistic information, together with information about the fixed cost of a transfer between cash and marketable securities and the return on investment in marketable securities, is all we need to determine the proper initial balance between cash and marketable securities.

For various possible cash-flow outcomes, the expected net earnings associated with different initial levels of marketable securities can be determined. The greater the amount of securities held, of course, the greater the probability that some of those securities will have to be sold in order to meet a cash shortfall. The expected net earnings for a particular level of marketable securities is the gross interest earned on the marketable security position, less the expected fixed cost of selling securities to meet a cash shortfall and less the expected loss of interest income associated with the sale of those securities. When calculations are undertaken for various possible levels of initial marketable security holdings, one obtains the expected net earnings associated with each level.

The optimal level of marketable securities is the level at which expected net earnings are maximized. The mechanics involved in such probabilistic formulations are familiar by now, so we shall not illustrate the probability model approach to cash management. The reader should be able to visualize the approach. Again, probability models may be used when the cash flows of the firm are neither relatively predictable nor relatively unpredictable.

OPTIMAL LEVEL OF CASH

Depending on the situation, one of the models discussed—EOQ, stochastic, or probability—can be used to determine the proper level of cash. Many of the assumptions can be modified, depending on the circumstances. Where these optimization models do not offer improvement over simpler decision rules, they should not be used. Their purpose is to assist in determining the appropriate level of investment in marketable securities. With a known level of total liquid assets, determination of an appropriate level of cash will also be a determination of the level of investment in marketable securities.

Usually, the optimal level of average cash balances will be the greater of two constraints: the compensating balance requirement imposed by a bank, and the average level of cash suggested by an appropriate cash-marketable securities model. In addition to these considerations, the optimal level of cash may be affected by whether a bank allows services to be paid for on a fee basis rather than in compensating balances. If there is a fee schedule, the firm should compare the fee with earnings available on funds that would be tied up in compensating balances. When the earnings are greater, a case can be made for fees. Under this circumstance, the optimal level of cash balances can be determined by an appropriate cash-marketable securities model. To the extent that the firm can use the cash balance so determined as partial or full compensation to the bank for the services rendered, the fees that are paid will be reduced or eliminated altogether.

INVESTMENT IN MARKETABLE SECURITIES

Once the firm has determined an optimal cash balance, the residual of its liquid assets is invested in marketable securities. In the models examined, we assumed a given yield and no risk of fluctuations in market price. These assumptions are realistic for very short-term, high-grade securities used as a buffer to replenish cash. Firms frequently hold securities with lesser characteristics for less immediate needs. In this section, then, we examine the types of marketable securities available to a company as near-money investments, allowing for varying yields and for fluctuations in market price. First, we need to explore the reasons why the yields vary: the differences in default risk, in marketability, in length of time to maturity, in coupon rate, and in taxability.

For accounting purposes, marketable securities and time deposits are shown as "cash equivalents" on the balance sheet if their original maturity is 3 months or less. Other marketable securities are shown as "short-term investments," assuming their maturity is less than 1 year. In what follows, we will not concern ourselves with this accounting distinction.

DEFAULT RISK

When we speak of default risk, we mean the risk that the borrower will not satisfy the contractual obligation to make principal and interest payments. Investors are said to demand a risk premium to invest in other than default-free securities.[6] The greater the possibility that the borrower will default, the greater the financial risk and the premium demanded by the marketplace. Treasury securities are usually regarded as default free, and other securities are judged in relation to them. U.S. government agency issues might be rated next to Treasury securities in creditworthiness. For all practical purposes, these securities are default free. The creditworthiness of other obligations is frequently judged on the basis of security ratings. Moody's Investors Service and Standard & Poor's grade the quality of corporate and municipal securities, for example (see Chapter 22 for a discussion). The greater the default risk of the borrower, the greater the yield of the security should be, all other things held constant. By investing in riskier securities, the firm can achieve higher returns, but it faces the familiar trade-off between expected return and risk.

MARKETABILITY

Marketability of a security relates to the ability of the owner to convert it into cash. There are two dimensions: the price realized and the amount of time required to sell the asset. The two are interrelated in that it is often possible to sell an asset in a short period of time if enough price concession is given. For financial instruments, marketability is judged in relation to the ability to sell a significant volume of securities in a short period of time without significant price concession. The more marketable the security, the greater the ability to execute a large transaction near the quoted price. In general, the lower the marketability of a security, the greater the yield necessary to attract investors. Thus, the yield differential between different securities of the same maturity is caused not only by differences in default risk but also by differences in marketability.

MATURITY

The relationship between yield and maturity can be studied graphically by plotting yield and maturity for securities differing only in the length of time to maturity. In practice, this means holding constant the degree of default risk. An example of the yield-maturity relationship for default-free Treasury securities on two separate dates is shown in Fig. 15-5. Maturity is plotted on the horizontal axis and yield on the vertical; their relationship is described by a yield curve fitted to the observations.

Generally, when interest rates are expected to rise, the yield curve is upward-sloping, whereas it is humped and somewhat downward-sloping when they are expected to fall significantly. However, there is a tendency toward positive-sloped yield curves. Most economists attribute this tendency to the presence of risk for those who invest in long-term securities vis-à-vis short-term securities. In general, the longer the maturity, the greater the risk of fluctuation in the market value of the security. Consequently, investors need to be offered a risk premium to induce them to invest in long-term securities. Only when interest rates are expected to fall significantly are they willing to

405

CHAPTER 15
Management of
Cash and
Marketable
Securities

[6] For an extended discussion of default-risk premiums and of the empirical tests involving such premiums, see James C. Van Horne, *Financial Market Rates and Flows*, 3d ed. (Englewood Cliffs, NJ: Prentice Hall, 1990), Chap. 8.

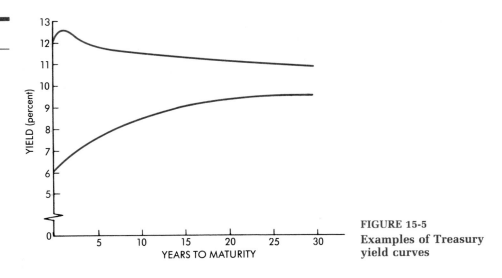

FIGURE 15-5
Examples of Treasury
yield curves

invest in long-term securities yielding less than short- and intermediate-term securities.[7]

COUPON RATE

In addition to maturity, price fluctuations also depend on the level of the coupon. For a given fixed-income security, the lower the coupon rate the greater the price change for a given shift in interest rates. The reason for this is that with lower coupons, more of the total return to the investor is reflected in the principal payment at maturity as opposed to interest payments that are discounted from nearer coupon dates. In effect, investors realize their return sooner with high-coupon bonds than with low-coupon ones. Thus, the volatility of a security depends on the combined effect of maturity and coupon rate. To come to grips with this combined effect, the duration measure explained in Chapter 2 is used.

TAXABILITY

Another factor affecting observed differences in market yields is the differential impact of taxes. The interest income on all but one category of securities is taxable to taxable investors. Interest income from state and local government securities is tax exempt; as a result, they sell in the market at lower yields to maturity than Treasury and corporate securities of the same maturity. For corporations located in states with income taxes, interest income on Treasury securities is exempt from state income taxes. As a result, such instruments may hold an advantage over the debt instruments of corporations or of banks where the interest income is fully taxable at the state level. Under present tax law, capital gains arising from the sale of a security at a profit are taxed at the full corporate tax rate. A final consideration is preferred stock, whose dividends enjoy a special tax advantage to the corporate investor. We will explore this feature shortly.

[7] For a much deeper discussion of this concept, see Van Horne, *Financial Market Rates and Flows*, Chap. 5.

OPTION-TYPE FEATURES

407

CHAPTER 15
Management of
Cash and
Marketable
Securities

A final consideration is whether the security contains any option-type features. The option might be a conversion privilege or a warrant, which links the debt security to equity. That is, it allows the investor to obtain stock in the company upon exercise of the option. The valuation principles are complex, and we devote all of Chapter 23 to them. Rather than a direct option, some debt instruments have embedded in them options of another sort. Examples include the call feature, which enables a company to prepay its debt, and a sinking-fund provision, which enables a company to periodically retire bonds either with cash or by buying bonds at a discount in the secondary market. Both of these embedded options are examined in Chapter 23. Because the marketable securities position of most companies is confined to short-term securities, option-type features usually are not important. Therefore, we defer consideration of them. Bear in mind, however, that if the investor receives an option, such as a conversion feature, the company will be able to borrow at a lower interest cost. If the investor gives the company an option, such as a call option, he or she must be compensated with a higher yield.

We have considered six factors that explain yield differentials on different securities: default risk, marketability, maturity, coupon rate, taxability, and option features. By analyzing securities in terms of these concepts, we can determine what we must give up in order to obtain a higher expected return. In this way, a systematic analysis of marketable securities is possible, so that a portfolio is formed in keeping with the objectives of the firm.

TYPES OF MARKETABLE SECURITIES

In this section, we describe briefly the more prominent marketable securities available for investment. Space prohibits the discussion of longer-term investments, although corporations do invest excess funds in long-term securities that are about to reach maturity. The vast majority of corporations invest in the instruments about to be described, mostly money market instruments, which, by definition, are highly marketable and subject to little default risk. Also, the usual definition restricts maturity of a money market instrument to less than a year.

Treasury Securities. U.S. Treasury obligations constitute the largest segment of the money markets. The principal securities issued are bills, tax anticipation bills, notes, and bonds. The Treasury auctions bills weekly with maturities of 91 days and 182 days. In addition, 9-month and 1-year bills are sold every month., All sales by the Treasury are by auction. Smaller investors can enter a "noncompetitive" bid, which is filled at the average price of successful competitive bids. Treasury bills carry no coupon but are sold on a discount basis. Denominations range from $10,000 to $1 million. These securities are popular with some companies as short-term investments, in part because of the large amount outstanding. The market is very active, and transaction costs are small in the sale of Treasury bills in the secondary market.

The original maturity on Treasury notes is 1 to 10 years, whereas the original maturity on Treasury bonds is over 10 years. With the passage of time, of course, a number of these securities have maturities of less than 1 year and serve the needs of short-term investors. Notes and bonds are coupon issues, and there is an active market for them. Overall, Treasury securities are the safest and most marketable investments. Consequently, they provide the lowest yield for a given maturity of the various instruments we consider. While the interest income on these securities is taxed at the federal level, it is exempt from state income taxes.

Repurchase Agreements. In an effort to tap important sources of financing, government security dealers offer repurchase agreements to corporations. The repurchase agreement, or "repo," is the sale of short-term securities by the dealer to the investor, whereby the dealer agrees to repurchase the securities at a specified future time. The investor receives a given yield while holding the security. The length of the holding period itself is tailored to the needs of the investor. It can be as little as "overnight," meaning a one-day holding period, or it may run several days to a week or more. Thus, repurchase agreements give the investor a great deal of flexibility with respect to maturity. Rates on repurchase agreements are related to the rates on Treasury bills, federal funds, and loans to government security dealers by commercial banks. There is little marketability to the instrument, but the usual maturity is only a few days. Because the instrument involved is a U.S. Treasury security, the default risk depends solely on the financial condition and reliability of the dealer.

Agency Securities. Obligations of various agencies of the federal government are guaranteed by the agency issuing the security, but not by the U.S. government as such. Principal agencies issuing securities include the Federal Housing Administration and the Government National Mortgage Association (Ginnie Mae). In addition, there are a number of government-sponsored, quasi-private agencies. Their securities are not guaranteed by the federal government, nor is there any stated "moral" obligation, but there is an implied backing. It would be hard to imagine the federal government allowing them to fail. Major government-sponsored agencies include the Farm Credit System and the Federal National Mortgage Association (Fannie Mae). Agency issues typically provide a modest yield advantage over Treasury securities of the same maturity, and they have a fairly high degree of marketability. Although interest income on these securities is subject to federal income taxes, issues of the Farm Credit agencies are not subject to state and local income taxes. Maturities range from several days to approximately 15 years. About half of the securities outstanding mature in less than a year.

Bankers' Acceptances. Bankers' acceptances are drafts that are accepted by banks, and they are used in financing foreign and domestic trade. The creditworthiness of bankers' acceptances is judged by the bank accepting the draft, not the drawer. Acceptances generally have maturities of less than 6 months and are of high quality. They are traded in an over-the-counter market dominated by five principal dealers. The rates on bankers' acceptances tend to be slightly higher than rates on Treasury bills of like maturity, and both are sold on a discount basis. Bankers' acceptances can be both on domestic banks and on large foreign banks.

Commercial Paper. Commercial paper consists of short-term unsecured promissory notes issued by finance companies and certain industrial concerns. Commercial paper can be sold either directly or through dealers. Many large sales finance companies have found it profitable, because of the volume, to sell their paper directly to investors, thus bypassing dealers. Among companies selling paper on this basis are the General Electric Credit Corporation, Ford Motor Credit Company, General Motors Acceptance Corporation (GMAC), and Sears, Roebuck Acceptance Corporation. Paper sold through dealers is issued by industrial companies and smaller finance companies. Dealers very carefully screen the creditworthiness of potential issuers. In a sense, dealers stand behind the paper they place with investors.

Rates on commercial paper are somewhat higher than rates on Treasury bills of the same maturity and about the same as the rates available on bankers' acceptances. Paper sold directly generally commands a lower yield than paper sold through dealers. Usually, commercial paper is sold on a discount basis, and maturities generally range from 30 to 270 days. Most paper is held to maturity, for there is essentially no secondary market. Often, direct sellers of commercial paper will repurchase the paper on request. Arrangements may also be made through dealers for repurchase of paper sold through them. Commercial paper is sold only in large denominations, usually $100,000.

Negotiable Certificates of Deposit. A short-term investment, the certificate (CD) is evidence of the deposit of funds at a commercial bank for a specified period of time and at a specified rate of interest. The most common denomination is $100,000, so its appeal is limited to large investors. Money market banks quote rates on CDs; these rates are changed periodically in keeping with changes in other money market rates. Yields on CDs are greater than those on Treasury bills and repos and about the same as those on bankers' acceptances and commercial paper. Original maturities of CDs generally range from 30 to 360 days. A good secondary market has developed for the CDs of the large money market banks. Default risk is that of the bank failing. Like bankers' acceptances, corporations buy domestic as well as CDs of large foreign banks. The latter are known as "Yankee" CDs, and they typically carry a higher expected return.

Eurodollars. Although most Eurodollars are deposited in Europe, the term applies to any dollar deposit in foreign banks or in foreign branches of U.S. banks. There exists a substantial, very active market for the deposit and lending of Eurodollars. This market is a wholesale one in that the amounts involved are at least $100,000. Moreover, the market is free of government regulation, as it is truly international in scope. The rates quoted on deposits vary according to the maturity of the deposit, while the rates on loans depend on maturity and default risk. For a given maturity, the lending rate always exceeds the deposit rate. The bank makes its money on the spread. The benchmark rate in this market is the 6-month London interbank offered rate (LIBOR). This is the rate at which banks make loans to each other. All other borrowers are quoted rates in excess of this rate, such as LIBOR + $\frac{1}{2}$ percent.

As a marketable security, the Eurodollar time deposit is like a negotiable certificate of deposit. Most deposits have a maturity of less than a year, and they can be sold in the market prior to maturity. Call money deposits are available, allowing investors to get their money back on demand, and there

409

CHAPTER 15
Management of
Cash and
Marketable
Securities

are 1-day (overnight) deposits. For the large corporation with ready contact with international money centers, the Eurodollar deposit usually is an important investment.

Short-Term Municipals.   State and local governments are increasingly providing securities tailored to the short-term investor. One is a commercial paper type of instrument, where the interest rate is reset every week. That is, the security is essentially floating rate where the weekly reset ensures that market value will vary scarcely at all. Some corporations invest in longer-term municipal securities, but the maturity usually is kept within one or two years. A problem with longer-term instruments is that marketability is only fair. Shorter-term instruments designed for the corporate treasurer and for municipal money market mutual funds have much better marketability and price stability.

Money Market Preferred Stock.   Beginning in 1982, a special type of preferred stock originated, and it found considerable favor in the marketable security portfolios of corporations. As we shall see in Chapter 22, straight preferred stock is a perpetual security where the dividend can be omitted by the issuer when its financial condition deteriorates. For these reasons, we usually do not think of preferred stock as being suitable for the marketable security portfolio of a corporation. However, the corporate investor gains a considerable tax advantage, in that 70 percent of the preferred stock dividend is exempt from federal taxation. (The full dividend is subject to state income taxes.)

This advantage, together with regulatory changes, prompted the innovation of various floating-rate preferred stock products. One of the largest in use today is money market preferred stock (MMP). With MMP, an auction is held every 49 days. This provides the investor with liquidity and relative price stability as far as interest-rate risk goes. It does not protect the investor against default risk. The new auction rate is set by the forces of supply and demand in keeping with interest rates in the money market. A typical rate might be .75 times the commercial paper rate, with more creditworthy issuers commanding an even greater discount. As long as enough investors bid at each auction, the effective maturity date is 49 days. As a result, there is little variation in the market price of the instrument over time and this represents a substantial advantage. In a failed auction where there are insufficient bidders, there is a default dividend rate for one period that is frequently 110 percent of the commercial paper rate. In addition, the holder has the option to redeem the instrument at its face value. These provisions are attractive to the investor as long as the company is able to meet the conditions. If the company should altogether default, however, the investor loses. There have been only a few instances of failed auctions and default.

Hedging Dividends Received.   Yet another device to take advantage of the 70 percent exemption of intercorporate dividends is the hedged dividend capture. The idea is to invest in stocks, usually preferred, right before a dividend is to be paid and, at the same time, write a call option on the stock. This is known as a covered call in the sense that the investor can deliver stock already owned if the option holder exercises his or her call. This will happen if the stock rises significantly in price, and the corporate investor will realize only the premium paid for the call. If the market price fluctuates, the investor will realize the dividend on favorable tax terms as well as the call premium.

Holding the stock for the mandatory 46 days for tax purposes, the positions in the stock and the option are reversed, and the firm seeks another stock about to pay a dividend. Finally, if the stock should decline significantly in price, the investor's loss is buffered by the call premium paid. Moreover, the positions can be reversed before too much damage occurs.[8]

411

CHAPTER 15
Management of
Cash and
Marketable
Securities

PORTFOLIO MANAGEMENT

The decision to invest excess cash in marketable securities involves not only the amount to invest but also the type of security in which to invest. To some extent, the two decisions are interdependent. Both should be based on an evaluation of expected net cash flows and the uncertainty associated with these cash flows. If future cash-flow patterns are known with reasonable certainty and the yield curve is upward-sloping in the sense of longer-term securities yielding more than shorter-term ones, a company may wish to arrange its portfolio so that securities will mature approximately when the funds will be needed. Such a cash-flow pattern gives the firm a great deal of flexibility in maximizing the average return on the entire portfolio, for it is unlikely that significant amounts of securities will have to be sold unexpectedly.

Suppose the liquidity position of a firm, net of transactions cash and compensating balance requirement needs, were expected to fluctuate in the manner shown by the dotted line in Fig. 15-6. Although the figure shows only 4 months, we assume that the dotted line is not expected to decline below $900,000 over the next 12 months. Based on these projections, an appropriate investment strategy might be that shown by the horizontal bars in the figure. The bottom portion is represented by a 360-day investment in a certificate of deposit, followed by a Federal Home Loan Bank bond with about 10 months to final maturity. Next, the firm has invested in 91-day Treasury bills, and these are expected to be renewed, or rolled over, at maturity. The other investments shown in the figure are designed to match the fluctuating pattern of cash flows shown. Finally, the remaining areas under the dotted line are assumed to be filled as much as possible with repurchase agreements. With repos, maturities of only 1 or a few days can be tailored to the availability of funds for investment. Overall, then, the firm is able to match the maturities of its investments in marketable securities with its expected cash-flow pattern. In this way, it is able to maximize its return on investment insofar as maturity decisions alone will allow.

Again, we have assumed an upward-sloping yield curve. If the yield curve is downward-sloping, the maturity matching strategy outlined above may not be appropriate. The company may wish to invest in securities having maturities shorter than the intended holding period, then to reinvest at maturity. In this way, it can avail itself of the higher initial yield on shorter-term securities, but it does not know what the securities will yield upon reinvestment at maturity. Another key factor is the degree of certainty one has in the cash-flow projections. With a high degree of certainty, the maturity of a marketable security becomes its most important characteristic.[9] If future cash flows are fairly uncertain, the most important characteristics of a security be-

---

[8] For further description and analysis of this technique, see Keith C. Brown and Scott L. Lummer, "Hedged Dividend Capture," *Midland Corporation Finance Journal*, 4 (Fall 1986), 65–72.

[9] This statement assumes that all the securities considered are of reasonably high quality from the standpoint of default risk. Otherwise they would not fall within the usual definition of a marketable security.

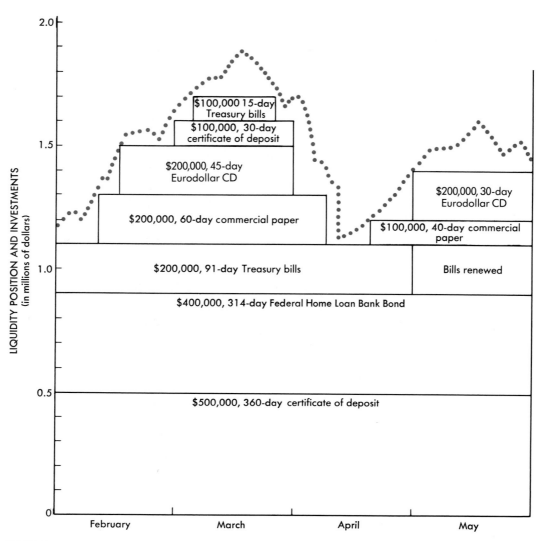

FIGURE 15-6
Investment strategy in relation to projected liquidity position

come its marketability and risk with respect to fluctuations in market value. Treasury bills and short-term repos are perhaps best suited for the emergency liquidity needs of a firm. Higher yields can be achieved by investing in longer-term, less marketable securities with greater risk. Although the firm should always be concerned with risk and marketability, some possibility of loss of principal is tolerable, provided the expected return is high enough. In addition to risk and marketability, transaction costs are a factor with uncertain cash flows. If securities must be sold unexpectedly, transaction costs will be incurred and will result in a lower net return. Thus, the firm faces the familiar trade-off between risk and profitability.

The larger the security portfolio, the more chance there is for specialization and economies of operation. A large enough security portfolio may justify a staff solely responsible for managing the portfolio. Such a staff can undertake research, plan diversification, keep abreast of market conditions, and continually analyze and improve the firm's position. When investment is a specialized function in a firm, the number of different securities considered for investment is likely to be diverse. Moreover, continual effort can be devoted to achieving the highest yield possible in keeping with cash needs of the firm. Trading techniques in such a firm tend to be very sophisticated. For companies with smaller security positions, there may be no economic justification for a staff. Indeed, a single individual may handle investments on a part-time basis. For this type of company, the diversity of securities in the portfolio will probably be limited.

For multinational companies, cash and marketable securities may be kept in multiple currencies. Many companies maintain liquidity in the country where investment takes place and/or where the sourcing of a product occurs. The marketable securities position of such a company is part of a broader management of currency risk exposure. As that topic is addressed in Chapter 26, we do not take it up here.

Although diversification of the short-term marketable security portfolio of a firm might be desirable, there is far less opportunity for such diversification than there is with a portfolio of common stocks.[10] *Diversification* is usually defined as the reduction of the dispersion of possible returns from a portfolio, relative to the expected return from the portfolio. This reduction is achieved by investing in securities not having high degrees of covariance among themselves. Unfortunately, there is a high degree of correlation in the yield movements of money market instruments over time. Consequently, they are ill suited for purposes of diversification. As a result, the objective of most firms is to maximize overall return subject to maintaining sufficient liquidity to meet cash drains. For shorter-term securities, often a two-dimensional analysis of maturity and default risk-marketability is sufficient. With maturity on the horizontal axis and securities in each maturity category listed in descending order of default risk and marketability on the vertical axis, the financial manager obtains a great deal of insight into the risk-return trade-off of the marketable security portfolio.[11]

SUMMARY

A company has three motives for holding liquid assets: the transactions motive, the precautionary motive, and the speculative motive. Our concern is with only the first two of these motives. In the management of cash, we should attempt to accelerate collections and handle disbursements so that maximum cash is available. Collections can be accelerated by means of concentration banking, a lock-box system, and certain other procedures. Disbursements should be handled to give maximum transfer flexibility and the optimum timing of payments, being mindful, however, of supplier relations. Several methods for controlling disbursements were described. Electronic funds transfers are becoming increasingly important, and most corporations use such transfers in one way or another.

Its total level of liquid assets being cash and marketable securities, the company must determine the optimal split between these two assets. The op-

413

CHAPTER 15
Management of
Cash and
Marketable
Securities

---

[10] See Chapter 3 for a review of portfolio analysis and selection.

[11] For a discussion of how risk can be reduced or eliminated through the use of financial futures and debt options markets, both domestic and foreign, see Van Horne, *Financial Market Rates and Flows*, Chaps. 7, 9, and 11.

timal level of cash, which in turn determines the optimal level of marketable securities, is the greater of (1) the compensating balance requirement of a commercial bank or (2) the optimal level determined by an appropriate model. The first constraint is rather straightforward, and its determination was discussed. With respect to the second constraint, the optimal level of cash depends on the predictability of future cash flows, their volatility, the fixed cost of a security transaction, and the carrying cost of holding cash, that is, the interest rate forgone on marketable securities. Several models were examined for determining an optimal level of average cash balances under varying assumptions as to the predictability and pattern of future cash flows.

The company can invest in a number of marketable securities. These securities can be evaluated in relation to their default risk, marketability, maturity, coupon rate, taxability, and option-type features. Depending on the cash-flow pattern of the company and other considerations, a portfolio can be selected in keeping with these characteristics. Specific securities considered included Treasury securities, repurchase agreements, government agency securities, bankers' acceptances, commercial paper, certificates of deposit, Eurodollars, short-term municipals, and money market preferred stock. Because these securities do not offer the diversification that common stocks do, managing the marketable securities portfolio is quite different from managing one composed of common stocks.

SELF-CORRECTION PROBLEMS

1. The Zindler Company currently has a centralized billing system. Payments are made by all customers to the central billing location. It requires, on the average, 4 days for customers' mailed payments to reach the central location. An additional $1\frac{1}{2}$ days are required to process payments before a deposit can be made. The firm has a daily average collection of $500,000. The company has recently investigated the possibility of initiating a lock-box system. It has estimated that with such a system, customers' mailed payments would reach the receipt location $2\frac{1}{2}$ days sooner. Further, the processing time could be reduced by 1 additional day, because each lock-box bank would pick up mailed deposits twice daily.

   a. Determine the reduction in cash balances that can be achieved through the use of a lock-box system.

   b. Determine the opportunity cost of the present system, assuming a 5 percent return on short-term instruments.

   c. If the annual cost of the lock-box system were $75,000, should such a system be initiated?

2. The city of Richmond has two tax dates when it receives cash inflows: February 15 and August 15. On each of these dates, it expects to receive $15 million in tax revenue. Cash expenditures are expected to be steady throughout the subsequent 6 months. Presently, the return on investment in marketable securities is 8 percent per annum, and the cost of transfer from securities to cash is $125 each time a transfer occurs.

   a. What is the optimal transfer size using the EOQ model? What is the average cash balance?

   b. What would be your answers if the return on investment were 12 percent per annum and the transfer cost were $75? Why do they differ from those in part a?

3. Over the next year, El Pedro Steel Company, a California corporation, expects the following returns on continual investment in marketable securities:

415

CHAPTER 15
Management of
Cash and
Marketable
Securities

Treasury bills	8.00%
Commercial paper	8.50
Money market preferred stock	7.00

The company's marginal tax rate for federal income tax purposes is 30 percent (after allowance for the payment of state income taxes), while its marginal, incremental tax rate with respect to California income taxes is 7 percent. On the basis of after-tax returns, which is the most attractive investment? Are there other considerations?

PROBLEMS

1. Speedway Owl Company franchises Gas and Go stations in North Carolina and Virginia. All payments by franchisees for gasoline and oil products are by check, which average in total $420,000 a day. At present, the overall time between a check being mailed by the franchisee to Speedway Owl and the company having available funds at its bank is 6 days.

   a. How much money is tied up in this interval of time?

   b. To reduce this delay, the company is considering daily pickups from the stations. In all, two cars would be needed and two additional people hired. The cost would be $93,000 annually. This procedure would reduce the overall delay by 2 days. Currently, the opportunity cost of funds is 9 percent, that being the interest rate on marketable securities. Should the company inaugurate the pickup plan?

   c. Rather than mail checks to its bank, the company could deliver them by messenger service. This procedure would reduce the overall delay by 1 day and cost $10,300 annually. Should the company undertake this plan?

2. The List Company, which can earn 7 percent on money market instruments, currently has a lock-box arrangement with a New Orleans bank for its southern customers. The bank handles $3 million a day in return for a compensating balance of $2 million.

   a. The List Company has discovered that it could divide the southern region into a southwestern region (with $1 million a day in collections, which could be handled by a Dallas bank for a $1 million compensating balance) and a southeastern region (with $2 million a day in collections, which could be handled by an Atlanta bank for a $2 million compensating balance). In each case, collections would be one-half day quicker than with the New Orleans arrangement. What would be the annual savings (or cost) of dividing the southern region?

   b. In an effort to retain the business, the New Orleans bank has offered to handle the collections strictly on a fee basis (no compensating balance). What would be the maximum fee the New Orleans bank could charge and still retain List's business?

3. The Frazini Food Company has a weekly payroll of $150,000, paid on Friday. On average, its employees cash their checks in the following manner:

DAY CHECK CLEARED ON COMPANY'S ACCOUNT	PERCENT OF CHECKS CASHED
Friday	20
Monday	40
Tuesday	25
Wednesday	10
Thursday	5

As treasurer of the company, how would you arrange your payroll account? Are there any problems involved?

4. Topple Tea Houses, Inc., operates seven restaurants in the state of Pennsylvania. The manager of each restaurant transfers funds daily from the local bank to the company's principal bank in Harrisburg. There are approximately 250 business days during a year in which transfers occur. Several methods of transfer are available. A wire transfer results in immediate availability of funds, but the local banks charge $5 per wire transfer. A transfer through an automatic clearinghouse involves next-day settlement, or a 1-day delay, and costs $3 per transfer. Finally, a depository transfer check arrangement costs $.30 per transfer, and mailing times result in a 3-day delay on average for the transfer to occur. (This experience is the same for each restaurant.) The company presently uses depository transfer checks for all transfers. The restaurants have the following daily average remittances:

			RESTAURANT				
1	2	3	4	5	6	7
$3,000	$4,600	$2,700	$5,200	$4,100	$3,500	$3,800

a. If the opportunity cost of funds is 10 percent, which transfer procedure should be used for each of the restaurants?

b. If the opportunity cost of funds were 5 percent, what would be the optimal strategy?

5. The Schriver Company plans to have $1 million in steady cash outlays for next year. The firm believes that it will face an opportunity interest rate of 10 percent and will incur a cost of $100 each time it borrows (or withdraws). Using the inventory model

a. Determine the transactions demand for cash (the optimal borrowing or withdrawal lot size) for the Schriver Company.

b. What will be the cash cycle for the firm (in days)?

c. What would be the average cash balance for the firm?

6. The Verloom Berloop Tulip Bulb Company has experienced a stochastic demand for its product, with the result that cash balances fluctuate randomly. The standard deviation of daily net cash flows, σ, is $1,000. The company wishes to make the transfer of funds from cash to marketable securities, and vice versa, as automatic as possible. It has heard that this can be done by imposing upper- and lower-bound control limits. The current interest rate on marketable securities is 6 percent. The fixed cost associated with each transfer is $100, and transfers are instantaneous.

a. What are the optimal upper- and lower-bound control limits? (Assume a 360-day year.) Hint: On a calculator, treat the $1,000 as $1 and solve for the cube root by trial and error. Move the decimal point of the final answer two places to the right.

b. What happens at these control limits?

417

CHAPTER 15
Management of
Cash and
Marketable
Securities

7. The O. K. Zarter Company employs a control-limit model for managing its cash position and marketable securities transactions. This is done because of the essential random nature of the cash flows. Using the formula, the company has found the optimal value of z, the return to point, to be $312,000. What approximately are the average transaction balances of the company?

8. Research Project: Examine quotations in the *Wall Street Journal* for each of the following money market instruments:

   a. Treasury bills
   b. Bankers' acceptances
   c. Certificates of deposit
   d. Commercial paper
   e. Government agency issues
   f. Eurodollars

   Evaluate the yield-risk trade-off for each instrument. Consider the appropriateness of each of these securities for the corporation's short-term investment account.

SOLUTIONS TO SELF-CORRECTION PROBLEMS

1. a. Total time savings = $3\frac{1}{2}$ days

   Time savings × Daily average collection = Reduction in cash balances achieved
   $3\frac{1}{2}$ × $500,000 = $1,750,000

   b. 5% × $1,750,000 = $87,500

   c. Since the opportunity cost of the present system ($87,500) exceeds the cost of the lock-box system ($75,000), the system should be initiated.

2. a. $C = \sqrt{\dfrac{2bT}{i}}$

   $C = \sqrt{\dfrac{2(\$125)(\$15 \text{ million})}{.04}} = \$306,186$

   Average cash balance = $\dfrac{C}{2} = \dfrac{\$306,186}{2} = \$153,093$

   Note that the interest rate for 6 months is approximately 4 percent, or one-half the 8 percent annualized rate.

   b. $C = \sqrt{\dfrac{2(\$75)(\$15 \text{ million})}{.06}} = \$193,649$

   Average cash balance = $\dfrac{\$193,649}{2} = \$96,825$

   The amounts are lower because there is a higher opportunity cost to holding cash and the cost of transferring to cash is less. Consequently, more transactions can take place, all other things being the same.

3.

SECURITY	FEDERAL TAX	STATE TAX	COMBINED EFFECT	AFTER-TAX EXPECTED RETURN
Treasury bills	.30	0	.30	(1 − .30)8.00% = 5.60%
Commercial paper	.30	.07	.37	(1 − .37)8.50% = 5.36%
Money market preferred stock	(1 − .70).30 = .09	.07	.16	(1 − .16)7.00% = 5.88%

The money market preferred is the most attractive after taxes, owing to the 70 percent exemption for federal income tax purposes. Commercial paper is less attractive than Treasury bills because of the state income tax from which Treasury bills are exempt. (In states with no income taxes, the after-tax yield on commercial paper would be higher.) Preferred stock may not be the most attractive investment when risk is taken into account.

SELECTED REFERENCES

ALDERSON, MICHAEL J., KEITH C. BROWN, and SCOTT L. LUMMER, "Dutch Auction Rate Preferred Stock," *Financial Management*, 16 (Summer 1987), 68–73.

BATLIN, C. A., and SUSAN HINKO, "Lockbox Management and Value Maximization," *Financial Management*, 10 (Winter 1981), 39–44.

BAUMOL, WILLIAM J., "The Transactions Demand for Cash: An Inventory Theoretic Approach," *Quarterly Journal of Economics*, 65 (November 1952), 545–56.

BROWN, KEITH C., and SCOTT L. LUMMER, "A Reexamination of the Covered Call Option Strategy for Corporate Cash Management," *Financial Management*, 15 (Summer 1986), 13–17.

CONSTANTINIDES, GEORGE, "Stochastic Cash Management with Fixed and Proportional Transaction Costs," *Management Science*, 22 (August 1976), 1320–31.

EMERY, GARY, "Some Empirical Evidence on the Properties of Daily Cash Flow," *Financial Management*, 10 (Spring 1981), 21–28.

GITMAN, LAWRENCE J., D. KEITH FORRESTER, and JOHN R. FORRESTER, JR., "Maximizing Cash Disbursement Float," *Financial Management*, 5 (Summer 1976), 15–24.

KALLBER, JARL G., KENNETH L. PARKINSON, and JOYCE R. OCHS, eds., *Essentials of Cash Management*, 3d ed. Newtown, CT: National Corporate Cash Management Association, 1989.

———, "What Lockbox and Disbursement Models Really Do," *Journal of Finance*, 38 (May 1983), 361–71.

MAIER, STEVEN F., and JAMES H. VANDER WEIDE, "Theory and Application of an Optimizing Procedure for Lockbox Location Analysis," *Management Science*, 27 (August 1981), 855–65.

MILLER, MERTON H., and DANIEL ORR, "A Model of the Demand for Money by Firms," *Quarterly Journal of Economics*, 80 (August 1966), 413–35.

MORRIS, JAMES R., "The Role of Cash Balances in Firm Valuation," *Journal of Financial and Quantitative Analysis*, 18 (December 1983), 533–46.

STONE, BERNELL K., "Design of a Receivable Collection System," *Management Science*, 27 (August 1981), 866–80.

———, "The Design of a Company's Banking System," *Journal of Finance*, 38 (May 1983), 373–85.

———, and NED C. HILL, "Cash Transfer Scheduling for Efficient Cash Concentration," *Financial Management*, 9 (Autumn 1980), 35–43.

———, "The Design of a Cash Concentration System," *Journal of Financial and Quantitative Analysis*, 16 (September 1981), 301–22.

VANDER WEIDE, JAMES, and STEVEN F. MAIER, *Managing Corporate Liquidity*. New York: John Wiley, 1985.

VAN HORNE, JAMES C., *Financial Market Rates and Flows*, 3d ed. Englewood Cliffs, NJ: Prentice Hall, 1990.

ZIVNEY, TERRY L., and MICHAEL J. ALDERSON, "Hedged Dividend Capture with Stock Index Options," *Financial Management*, 15 (Summer 1986), 5–12.

16

MANAGEMENT OF ACCOUNTS RECEIVABLE AND INVENTORIES

For most companies, accounts receivable and inventories are very important investments, often dominating fixed-asset investments. With the concern for return on assets expressed by many companies in recent years, there has come ever-increasing focus on the funds committed to receivables and inventories. Whether these current assets are managed efficiently influences very strongly the amount of funds invested. In this chapter, we explore the key variables involved in efficiently managing receivables and inventories. In both situations, the optimal investment is determined by comparing benefits to be derived from a particular level of investment with the costs of maintaining that level. We consider first the credit and collection policies of the firm as a whole and then discuss procedures for the individual account. The last part of the chapter investigates techniques for efficiently managing inventories. The cash-flow cycle involves inventories being acquired ahead of sales, whereas receivables are generated at the time of sales and become cash only after a further lapse of time.

CREDIT AND COLLECTION POLICIES

Economic conditions and the firm's credit policies are the chief influences on the level of a firm's accounts receivables. Economic conditions, of course, are largely beyond the control of the financial manager. As with other current assets, however, the manager can vary the level of receivables in keeping with the trade-off between profitability and risk. Lowering quality standards may stimulate demand, which, in turn, should lead to higher profits. But there is a cost to carrying the additional receivables, as well as a greater risk of bad-debt losses. It is this trade-off that we wish to examine.

We must emphasize that the credit and collection policies of one firm are not independent of those of other firms. If product and capital markets are reasonably competitive, the credit and collection practices of one company will be influenced by what other firms are doing. If we charge $20 for our product and demand payment within 15 days of shipment, while our competitors sell the identical product for $20 but have 60-day terms, we will have difficulty in selling. In the reverse situation, we will be flooded with orders. Eventually, production will bump capacity, and further production will be very inefficient. Our competitors undoubtedly will respond and change their credit terms. The point is that credit and collection policies are interrelated with the pricing of a product or service and must be viewed as part of the overall competitive process. Our examination of certain policy variables implies that the competitive process is accounted for in the specification of the demand function as well as the opportunity cost associated with taking on additional receivables.

The policy variables we consider include the quality of the trade accounts accepted, the length of the credit period, the cash discount, any special terms—such as seasonal datings—and the collection program of the firm. Together, these elements largely determine the average collection period and the proportion of bad-debt losses. We analyze each element in turn, holding constant certain of the others, as well as any exogenous variables that affect the average collection period and the percentage of bad-debt losses. In addition, we assume that the evaluation of risk is sufficiently standardized so that degrees of risk for different accounts can be compared objectively.

CREDIT STANDARDS

Credit policy can have a significant influence on sales. In theory, the firm should lower its quality standard for accounts accepted as long as the profitability of sales generated exceeds the added costs of the receivables. What are the costs of relaxing credit standards? Some arise from an enlarged credit department, the clerical work of checking additional accounts, and servicing the added volume of receivables. We assume for now that these costs are deducted from the profitability of additional sales to give a net profitability figure for computational purposes. Another cost comes from the increased probability of bad-debt losses. We postpone consideration of this cost to a subsequent section; we assume for now that there are no bad-debt losses.

Finally, there is the opportunity cost of the additional receivables, resulting from increased sales and a slower average collection period. If new customers are attracted by the relaxed credit standards, collecting from these customers is likely to be slower than collecting from existing customers. In addition, a more liberal extension of credit may cause certain existing customers to be less conscientious in paying their bills on time.

To assess the profitability of a more liberal extension of credit, we must know the profitability of additional sales, the added demand for products arising from the relaxed credit standards, the increased slowness of the average collection period, and the required return on investment. Suppose a firm's product sells for $10 a unit, of which $8 represents variable costs before taxes, including credit department costs. The firm is operating at less than full capacity, and an increase in sales can be accommodated without any increase in fixed costs. Therefore, the contribution margin of an additional unit of sales is the selling price less variable costs involved in producing the unit, or $10 − $8 = $2.

At present, annual credit sales are running at a level of $2.4 million, and there is no underlying trend in such sales. The firm may liberalize credit, which will result in an average collection experience of new customers of 2 months.[1] Existing customers are not expected to alter their payment habits and continue to pay in 1 month. The relaxation in credit standards is expected to produce a 25 percent increase in sales, to $3 million annually.[2] This $600,000 increase represents 60,000 additional units if we assume that the price per unit stays the same. Finally, assume that the opportunity cost of carrying additional receivables is 20 percent before taxes.

This information reduces our evaluation to a trade-off between the added profitability on the additional sales and the opportunity cost of the increased investment in receivables. The increased investment arises solely from new, slower-paying customers; we have assumed existing customers continue to pay in 1 month. With the additional sales of $600,000 and receivable turnover of 6 times a year (12 months divided by the average collection period of 2 months), the additional receivables are $600,000/6 = $100,000. For these additional receivables, the firm invests the variable costs tied up in them. For our example, $.80 of every $1.00 in sales represents variable costs. Therefore, the added investment in receivables is .80 × $100,000 = $80,000. With these inputs, we are able to make the calculations shown in Table 16-1. Inasmuch as the profitability on additional sales, $120,000, far exceeds the required return on the additional investment in receivables, $16,000, the firm would be well advised to relax its credit standards. An optimal credit policy would involve extending trade credit more liberally until the marginal profitability on additional sales equals the required return on the additional investment in receivables.

Some Qualifications. Obviously there are many practical problems in effecting a change in credit policy, particularly in estimating the outcomes. In our example, we have worked with only the expected values of additional demand and of the slowing of the average collection period. It is possible and desirable to attach probability distributions to the increased demand and to the increased slowness in receivables and to evaluate a range of possible outcomes. For simplicity of discussion, we shall not incorporate these dimensions into our example.

---

[1] It should be pointed out that if there is either an upward or a downward trend in sales, the average collection period and receivable turnover ratio will not provide an accurate estimate of the new level of receivables outstanding. This problem is investigated at length in Chapter 27, where we explore the use of the average collection period and aging of accounts receivable. For ease of understanding of our example, we assume that there is no trend in sales either before a credit policy decision or after the decision.

[2] In estimating how a change in credit policy affects demand, we should take into account the reaction of competitors to this change. Their reaction will affect demand over the long run.

TABLE 16-1
Profitability versus required return—credit standard change

Profitability of additional sales	= $2 × 60,000 units = $120,000
Additional receivables	= (Additional sales/Receivable turnover) $600,000/6 = $100,000
Investment in additional receivables	= (Variable costs/Sales price)(Additional receivables) (.80)($100,000) = $80,000
Required return on additional investment	= .20 × $80,000 = $16,000

421

CHAPTER 16
Management of
Accounts
Receivable and
Inventories

Another assumption is that we can produce 60,000 additional units at a variable cost of $8 a unit; that is, we do not have to increase our plant. After some point, we are no longer able to meet additional demand with existing plant and would need to add plant. This occurrence would necessitate a change in analysis, for there would be a large block of incremental costs at the point where the existing plant could produce no more units. One implication to all this is that the firm should vary its credit quality standards in keeping with the level of production. As capacity is approached, quality standards might be increased. When production sags and the firm operates at a level below capacity, the lowering of credit quality standards becomes more attractive, all other things the same.

The credit standards of the firm may affect the level of inventories maintained. Easier standards leading to increased sales may require more inventories. If so, the calculations shown in Table 16-1 overstate the profitability of change in credit standards. In order to correct for this overstatement, the additional inventories associated with a new credit policy should be added to the additional receivables, and the opportunity cost should be computed on the basis of the combined increase. Our analysis also implies that the conditions described will be permanent. That is, increased demand as a function of lowering credit quality standards as well as price and cost figures will remain unchanged. If the increase in sales that results from a change in credit policy were a one-shot as opposed to a continuing occurrence, we would need to modify our analysis accordingly.

CREDIT TERMS

Credit Period. Credit terms involve both the length of the credit period and the discount given. The term "2/10, net 30" means that a 2 percent discount is given if the bill is paid before the tenth day after the date of invoice; payment is due by the thirtieth day. The credit period, then, is 30 days. Although the customs of the industry frequently dictate the terms given, the credit period is another means by which a firm may be able to affect product demand, hoping to increase demand by extending the credit period. As before, the trade-off is between the profitability of additional sales and the required return on the additional investment in receivables.

Let us say that the firm in our example increases its credit period from 30 days to 60 days. The average collection period for existing customers goes from 1 month to 2 months. The more liberal credit period results in increased sales of $360,000, and these new customers also pay, on average, in 2 months. The total additional receivables are composed of two parts. The first part represents the receivables associated with the increased sales. In our example, there are $360,000 in additional sales. With a receivable turnover of six times a year, the additional receivables associated with the new sales are $360,000/6 = $60,000. For these additional receivables, the investment by the firm is the variable costs tied up in them. For our example, we have ($8/$10)($60,000) = $48,000.

The second part of the total additional receivables represents the slowing in collections associated with original sales. The old receivables are collected in a slower manner, resulting in a higher receivable level. With $2.4 million in original sales, the firm's level of receivables with a turnover of 12 times a year is $2,400,000/12 = $200,000. The new level with a turnover of 6 times a year is $2,400,000/6 = $400,000. Thus, there are $200,000 in additional receivables associated with the original sales. For this addition, the relevant investment using marginal analysis is the full $200,000. In other words, the use of variable costs pertains only to new sales. The incremental $200,000 in receivables on original sales would have been collected earlier had it not been for the change in credit standards. Therefore, the firm must increase its investment in receivables by $200,000.

Based on these inputs, our calculations are shown in Table 16-2. The appropriate comparison is the profitability of additional sales with the opportunity cost of the additional investment in receivables. Inasmuch as the profitability on additional sales, $72,000, exceeds the required return on the investment in additional receivables, $49,600, the change in credit period from 30 to 60 days is worthwhile. The profitability of the additional sales more than offsets the added investment in receivables, the bulk of which comes from existing customers slowing their payments.

Discount Given. Varying the discount involves an attempt to speed up the payment of receivables. To be sure, the discount also may have an effect on demand and bad-debt losses. We assume that the discount is not regarded as a means of cutting price and thereby affecting demand, and that the discount offered does not affect the amount of bad-debt losses.[3] Holding constant these factors, we must determine whether a speedup in collections would more than offset the cost of an increase in the discount. If it would, the present discount policy should be changed.

Suppose the firm has annual credit sales of $3 million and an average collection period of 2 months, and the sales terms are net 45 days, with no discount given. Consequently, the average receivable balance is $500,000. By instigating terms of 2/10, net 45, the average collection period can be reduced

---

[3] If a price effect does occur, it will depend on the elasticity of demand. The greater the discount, the lower the effective price to customers who take discounts and the greater their demand. The relevant range of discount changes is quite small, however. Unless demand is highly elastic, the effect on demand will be small. For an analysis of the cash discount that embraces the speedup in collections, the effect on sales, and the effect on bad-debt losses, see Ned C. Hill and Kenneth D. Riener, "Determining the Cash Discount in the Firm's Credit Policy," *Financial Management*, 8 (Spring 1979), 68–73.

TABLE 16-2
Profitability versus required return—credit period change

Profitability of additional sales	= $2 × 36,000 units = $72,000
Additional receivables associated with new sales	= (New sales/Receivable turnover) $360,000/6 = $60,000
Additional investment in receivables associated with new sales	= (Variable costs/Sales price)(Additional receivables) (.80)($60,000) = $48,000
Present level of receivables	= (Annual sales/Receivable turnover) $2.4 million/12 = $200,000
New level of receivables associated with original sales	= $2.4 million/6 = $400,000
Additional investment in receivables associated with original sales	= $400,000 − $200,000 = $200,000
Total additional investment in receivables	= $48,000 + $200,000 = $248,000
Carrying cost of additional investment	= .20 × $248,000 = $49,600

to one month, as 60 percent of the customers (in dollar volume) take advantage of the 2 percent discount. The opportunity cost of the discount to the firm is .02 × .6 × $3 million, or $36,000 annually. The turnover of receivables has improved to 12 times a year, so that average receivables are reduced from $500,000 to $250,000.

Thus, the firm realizes $250,000 from accelerated collections. The value of the funds released is their opportunity cost. If we assume a 20 percent rate of return, the opportunity saving is $50,000. In this case, the opportunity saving arising from a speedup in collections is greater than the cost of the discount. The firm should adopt a 2 percent discount. If the speedup in collections had not resulted in sufficient opportunity savings to offset the cost of discount, the discount policy should not be changed. It is possible, of course, that discounts other than 2 percent may result in an even greater difference between the opportunity savings and the cost of the discount.

Seasonal Datings. During periods of slack sales, firms will sometimes sell to customers without requiring payment for some time to come. This seasonal dating can be tailored to the cash flow of the customer and may stimulate demand from customers who cannot pay until later in the season. Again, we should compare the profitability of additional sales with the required return on the additional investment in receivables to determine whether datings are appropriate terms by which to stimulate demand.

Datings also can be used to avoid inventory carrying costs. If sales are seasonal and production is steady throughout the year, there will be buildups in finished goods inventory during certain times of the year. Storage involves warehousing costs that might be avoided by giving datings. If warehousing costs plus the required rate of return on investment in inventory exceed the required rate of return on the additional receivables, datings are worthwhile.

DEFAULT RISK

In the foregoing examples, we assumed no bad-debt losses. Our concern in this section is not only with the slowness of collection but also with the portion of the receivables defaulting. Different credit standard policies will involve both of these factors. Suppose we are considering the present credit standard policy (sales of $2,400,000) together with two new ones, and these policies are expected to produce the following results:

	PRESENT POLICY	POLICY A	POLICY B
Demand (sales)	$2,400,000	$3,000,000	$3,300,000
Default losses on incremental sales (percentage)	2	10	18
Average collection period on incremental sales	1 month	2 months	3 months

We assume that after 6 months an account is turned over to a collection agency and that, on average, 2 percent of the original sales of $2.4 million is never received by the firm, 10 percent is never received on the $600,000 in additional sales under policy A, and 18 percent on the $300,000 in additional sales under policy B is never received. Similarly, the 1-month average collection period pertains to the original sales, 2 months to the $600,000 in additional sales under policy A, and 3 months to the $300,000 in additional sales under policy B. These numbers of months correspond to annual receivable turnovers of 12 times, 6 times, and 4 times, respectively.

The incremental profitability calculations associated with these two new credit standard policies are shown in Table 16-3. We would want to adopt policy A but would not want to go as far as policy B in relaxing our credit standards. The marginal benefit is positive in moving from the present policy to policy A, but negative in going from policy A to policy B. It is possible, of course, that a relaxation of credit standards that fell on one side or the other of policy A would provide an even greater marginal benefit; the optimal policy is the one that provides the greatest marginal benefit.

COLLECTION POLICY

The firm determines its overall collection policy by the combination of collection procedures it undertakes. These procedures include letters, phone calls, personal visits, and legal action. After a point in time, often 90 days past due, many companies turn the account over to a collection agency. Here fees run up to 50 percent of the amount collected. In collections, one of the principal policy variables is the amount expended on collection procedures. Within a range, the greater the relative amount expended, the lower the proportion of bad-debt losses and the shorter the average collection period, all other things the same.

The relationships are not linear. Initial collection expenditures are likely to cause little reduction in bad-debt losses. Additional expenditures begin to have a significant effect up to a point; then they tend to have little effect in further reducing these losses. The hypothesized relationship between expenditures and bad-debt losses is shown in Fig. 16-1. The relationship between the average collection period and the level of collection expenditures is likely to be similar to that shown in the figure.

TABLE 16-3
Profitability versus required return—bad-debt losses and collection period changes

	POLICY A	POLICY B
1. Additional sales	$600,000	$300,000
2. Profitability of additional sales (20%)	120,000	60,000
3. Additional bad-debt losses (additional sales × bad-debt percentage)	60,000	54,000
4. Additional receivables (additional sales/receivables turnover)	100,000	75,000
5. Investment in additional receivables (.8 × additional receivables)	80,000	60,000
6. Required return on additional investment (20 percent)	16,000	12,000
7. Bad-debt losses plus additional required return	76,000	66,000
8. Incremental profitability, line (2) − line (7)	44,000	(6,000)

425

CHAPTER 16
Management of
Accounts
Receivable and
Inventories

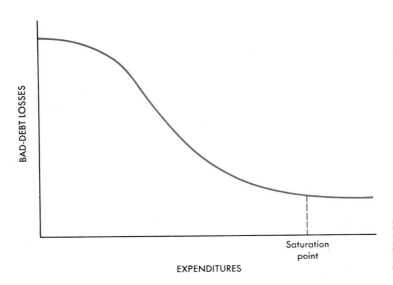

FIGURE 16-1

Relationship between amount of bad-debt losses and collection expenditures

If sales are independent of the collection effort, the appropriate level of collection expenditure again involves a trade-off—this time between the level of expenditure on the one hand and the reduction in the cost of bad-debt losses and reduction in receivables on the other. Suppose we are comparing the present collection program with two new ones, and the programs are expected to produce these results:

	PRESENT PROGRAM	PROGRAM A	PROGRAM B
Annual collection expenditures	$116,000	$148,000	$200,000
Average collection period, all accounts	2 months	$1\frac{1}{2}$ months	1 month
Percentage of default, all accounts	3	2	1

Assume that present sales are $2.4 million and that they are not expected to change with changes in the collection effort. If we go through the same type of reasoning we used for the discount policy where receivables were reduced and for bad-debt losses based on changes in the default percentages for all accounts, we obtain the results in Table 16-4. We see that the opportunity saving resulting from a speedup in collections plus the reduction in bad-debt losses exceeds the additional collection expenditures in going from the present program to program A, but not in going from program A to program B. As a result, the firm should adopt program A but not increase collection expenditures to the extent of program B.

In the example, we have assumed that demand is independent of the collection effort. In most cases, though, sales are likely to be affected adversely if the collection efforts of the firm become too intense and customers become increasingly irritated. If they do, we must take into account the relationship between the collection effort and demand. Reduction in demand can be incorporated into the marginal analysis of collection expenditures in the same manner as was the increase in demand accompanying a relaxation in credit

TABLE 16-4
Evaluation of collection programs

427

CHAPTER 16
Management of
Accounts
Receivable and
Inventories

	PRESENT PROGRAM	PROGRAM A	PROGRAM B
Annual sales	$2,400,000	$2,400,000	$2,400,000
Turnover of receivables	6	8	12
Average receivables	400,000	300,000	200,000
Reduction in receivables from present level		100,000	
Reduction in receivables from program A level			100,000
Return on reduction in receivables (20 percent)		20,000	20,000
Bad-debt losses (percent of annual sales)	72,000	48,000	24,000
Reduction in bad-debt losses from present losses		24,000	
Reduction in bad-debt losses from program A losses			24,000
Opportunity saving on reduced receivables plus reduction in bad-debt losses		44,000	44,000
Additional collection expenditures from present expenditures		32,000	
Additional collection expenditures from program A expenditures			52,000

standards. In addition, if the collection effort has an effect on the percentage of total sales taking a cash discount, this factor must be considered. With increased collection efforts, more customers might take the cash discount.

CREDIT AND COLLECTION POLICIES—SUMMARY

We see that the credit and collection policies of a firm involve several decisions: (1) the quality of account accepted, (2) the credit period, (3) the cash discount given, (4) any special terms such as seasonal datings, and (5) the level of collection expenditures. In each case, the decision should involve a comparison of possible gains from a change in policy and the cost of the change. Optimal credit and collection policies would be those that resulted in the marginal gains equaling the marginal costs.

To maximize profits arising from credit and collection policies, the firm should vary these policies jointly until it achieves an optimal solution. That solution will determine the best combination of credit standards, credit period, cash discount policy, special terms, and level of collection expenditures. Sensitivity analysis might be used to judge the impact of a change in policies on profits. Once functional relationships have been specified for the relationship between a particular policy and marginal sales, average collection period, and bad-debt losses, the policy can be varied from one extreme to the other, holding constant other factors. This variation gives insight into the impact of a change in policy upon profits.

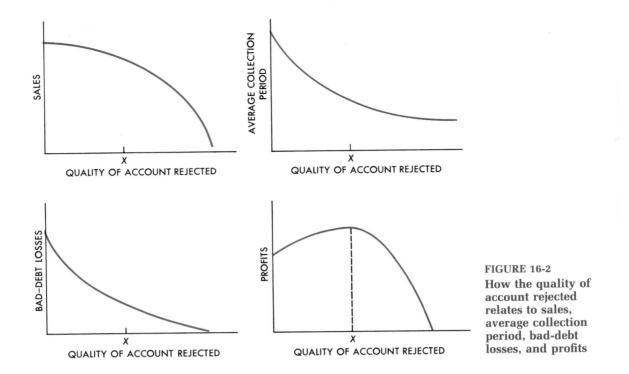

FIGURE 16-2
How the quality of account rejected relates to sales, average collection period, bad-debt losses, and profits

For most policy variables, profits increase at a decreasing rate up to a point and then decrease as the policy is varied from no effort to an extreme effort. Figure 16-2 depicts this relationship with the quality of account rejected. When there are no credit standards, when all applicants are accepted, sales are maximized, but they are offset by large bad-debt losses as well as by the opportunity cost of carrying a very large receivable position. As credit standards are initiated and applicants are rejected, revenue from sales declines, but so do the average collection period and bad-debt losses. Because the latter two decline initially at a faster rate than do sales, profits increase. As credit standards are tightened increasingly, sales revenue declines at an increasing rate. At the same time, the average collection period and bad-debt losses decrease at a decreasing rate. Fewer and fewer bad credit risks are eliminated. Because of the combination of these influences, total profits of the firm increase at a diminishing rate with stricter credit standards up to a point, after which they decline. The optimal policy with respect to credit standards is represented by point x in the figure. In turn, this policy determines the level of accounts receivable held by the firm.[4]

To the extent that decisions on credit standards, the credit period, the discount given, special terms offered, and the level of collection expenditures exercise a joint influence on profits, this interdependency must be recognized in formulating the functional relationships. With assumed relationships specified, the firm can use sensitivity analysis to experiment with different credit and collection policies in order to determine the optimal set of policies. The optimal set establishes the credit terms given, the collection procedures followed, and the cutoff point on quality of account accepted.

[4] For a present-value approach to evaluating credit policy decisions, see Yong H. Kim and Joseph C. Atkins, "Evaluating Investments in Accounts Receivable: A Wealth Maximizing Framework," *Journal of Finance*, 33 (May 1978), 403–12.

When some of the underlying parameters change, sensitivity analysis proves valuable in formulating new credit and collection policies. If the marginal profit per unit of sales declines because of increased competition, the optimal set of policies is likely to change. Lower profits per unit of sale may not justify the present level of receivables carried or the present loss rate. As a result, new credit and collection policies might be in order. Through sensitivity analysis, management could determine the new set of policies that will maximize profit.

The analysis in the last several sections has purposely been rather general, to provide insight into the important concepts of credit and collection policies. Obviously, a policy decision should be based on a far more specific evaluation than that contained in the examples. Estimating the increased demand and increased slowness of collections that might accompany a relaxation of credit standards is extremely difficult. Nevertheless, management must make estimates of these relationships if it is to appraise its existing policies realistically.

429

CHAPTER 16
Management of
Accounts
Receivable and
Inventories

EVALUATING THE CREDIT APPLICANT

Having established the terms of sale to be offered, the firm must evaluate individual credit applicants and consider the possibilities of a bad debt or slow payment. The credit evaluation procedure involves three related steps: obtaining information on the applicant, analyzing this information to determine the applicant's creditworthiness, and making the credit decision. The credit decision, in turn, establishes whether credit should be extended and what the maximum amount of credit should be.

SOURCES OF INFORMATION

A number of sources supply credit information, but for some accounts, especially small ones, the cost of collecting it may outweigh the potential profitability of the account. The firm extending credit may have to be satisfied with a limited amount of information on which to base a decision. In addition to cost, the firm must consider the time it takes to investigate a credit applicant. A shipment to a prospective customer cannot be delayed unnecessarily, pending an elaborate credit investigation. Thus, the amount of information collected needs to be considered in relation to the time and expense required. Depending on these considerations, the credit analyst may use one or more of the following sources of information.

Financial Statement. At the time of the prospective sale, the seller may request a financial statement, one of the most desirable sources of information for credit analysis. Frequently, there is a correlation between a company's refusal to provide a statement and its weak financial position. Audited statements are preferable; when possible, it is helpful to obtain interim statements in addition to year-end figures, particularly for companies having seasonal patterns of sales.

Credit Ratings and Reports. In addition to financial statements, credit ratings are available from various mercantile agencies. Dun & Bradstreet, Inc., is perhaps the best known and most comprehensive of these agencies. It provides credit ratings to subscribers for a vast number of business firms throughout the nation. A key to its individual ratings is shown in Fig. 16-3. As we see, D&B ratings give the credit analyst an indication of the estimated size of net worth and a credit appraisal for companies of a particular size, ranging from "high" to "limited." D&B also indicates when the information available is insufficient to provide a rating for a given business. In addition to its rating service, D&B provides credit reports containing a brief history of a company and its principal officers, the nature of the business, certain financial information, and a trade check of suppliers—the length of their experience with the company and whether payments are discount, prompt, or past due. The quality of the D&B reports varies with the information available externally and the willingness of the company being checked to cooperate with the D&B reporter. The report itself can be accessed via a computer terminal if so desired. The typical D&B contract with a creditor involves a price for a minimum number of reports, with further inquiries bearing an incremental charge.

TRW, Inc., in conjunction with the National Association of Credit Management, has developed a data base on some 8 million businesses. Typically, the information is not as extensive as that of Dun & Bradstreet, but it is of considerable use in credit analysis. TRW information is computer based, so credit reports can be obtained through an automated retrieval system in a matter of minutes.

Bank Checking. Another source of information for the firm is a credit check through a bank. Many banks have large credit departments that undertake credit checks as a service for their customers. By calling or writing a bank in which the credit applicant has an account, a firm's bank is able to obtain information on the average cash balance carried, loan accommodations, expe-

New Key to Ratings.

ESTIMATED FINANCIAL STRENGTH		COMPOSITE CREDIT APPRAISAL			
		HIGH	GOOD	FAIR	LIMITED
5A	Over $50,000,000	1	2	3	4
4A	$10,000,000 to 50,000,000	1	2	3	4
3A	1,000,000 to 10,000,000	1	2	3	4
2A	750,000 to 1,000,000	1	2	3	4
1A	500,000 to 750,000	1	2	3	4
BA	300,000 to 500,000	1	2	3	4
BB	200,000 to 300,000	1	2	3	4
CB	125,000 to 200,000	1	2	3	4
CC	75,000 to 125,000	1	2	3	4
DC	50,000 to 75,000	1	2	3	4
DD	35,000 to 50,000	1	2	3	4
EE	20,000 to 35,000	1	2	3	4
FF	10,000 to 20,000	1	2	3	4
GG	5,000 to 10,000	1	2	3	4
HH	Up to 5,000	1	2	3	4

CLASSIFICATION FOR BOTH
ESTIMATED FINANCIAL STRENGTH AND CREDIT APPRAISAL

FINANCIAL STRENGTH BRACKET	EXPLANATION
1 $125,000 and Over 2 20,000 to 125,000	When only the numeral (1 or 2) appears, it is an indication that the estimated financial strength, while not definitely classified, is presumed to be within the range of the ($) figures in the corresponding bracket and that a condition is believed to exist which warrants credit in keeping with that assumption.

NOT CLASSIFIED OR ABSENCE OF RATING

The absence of a rating, expressed by two hyphens (--), is not to be construed as unfavorable but signifies circumstances difficult to classify within condensed rating symbols. It suggests the advisability of obtaining a report for additional information.

Dun & Bradstreet®

Business Information Systems, Services and Sciences

FIGURE 16-3
Dun & Bradstreet key to ratings

rience, and sometimes financial information. Because banks generally are more willing to share information with other banks than with a direct inquirer, it usually is best for the firm to initiate the credit check through its own bank rather than to inquire directly.

431

CHAPTER 16
Management of
Accounts
Receivable and
Inventories

Trade Checking. Credit information frequently is exchanged among companies selling to the same customer. Through various credit organizations, credit people in a particular area become a closely knit group. A company can ask other suppliers about their experiences with an account. Useful information includes the length of time they have had the account, the maximum credit extended, the amount of the line of credit, and whether payments are prompt or slow.

The Company's Own Experience. A study of the promptness of past payments, including any seasonal patterns, is very useful. Frequently, the credit department will make written assessments of the quality of the management of a company to whom credit may be extended. These assessments are very important, for they pertain to the first of the famous "four C's" of credit: *character, collateral, capital,* and *capacity.* The person who made the sale to a prospective customer frequently can offer useful impressions of the management and operations. Caution is necessary in interpreting this information, because a salesperson has a natural bias toward granting credit and making the sale.

Importance of a Systematic Approach. There is no substitute for consistency in the credit and collection procedures of a company. With a systematic approach, inherent human tendencies to "chase" sales and to "look the other way" when initial collection problems emerge are curbed. In the accompanying "Through the Looking Glass," Charles J. Bodenstab, CEO of Battery & Tire Warehouse Inc. in St. Paul, relates his experiences, both good and bad, with receivable management.

CREDIT ANALYSIS AND DECISION

Having collected credit information, a company must make a credit analysis of the applicant and determine if the company falls above or below the minimum quality standard. If financial statements are provided, the analyst should undertake a ratio analysis, a source and use of funds analysis, and perhaps other analyses, as described in Chapters 27 and 28. As suggested in Chapter 27, empirical studies may determine which financial ratios have the greatest predictive power. The analyst will be particularly interested in the applicant's liquidity and ability to pay bills on time. Such ratios as the quick ratio, receivable and inventory turnovers, the average payable period, debt-to-net-worth ratio, and cash-flow coverage ratio are particularly germane.

In addition to analyzing financial statements, the credit analyst will consider the character and strength of the company and its management, the business risk associated with its operation, and various other matters. Then the analyst attempts to determine the ability of the applicant to service trade credit and the probability of an applicant's not paying on time and of a bad-debt loss. On the basis of this information, together with information about the profit margin of the product or service being sold, a decision is reached on whether or not to extend credit.

Credit Scoring and Expert Systems. *Discriminant analysis,* a statistical technique described in the appendix to this chapter, is being used increasingly. On the basis of a weighted overall score provided by this technique, an

THROUGH THE LOOKING GLASS

THE RECEIVABLE CHALLENGE[5]

When I acquired my business almost six years ago, the accounts receivable were running about 53 days. Within a year, under my brilliant management, that number was up to 60 days. Then we had a write-off of more than $100,000. As you can imagine, that caught my attention.

We had installed some pretty effective systems in other parts of the operation during that first year. The one area we'd neglected, however, was accounts receivable. And there were reasons for that. First of all, it was an area of management in which I had no experience. Second, my optimism and eagerness to grow the company led to my making some less than prudent decisions about extending credit. Finally, let's face it: dealing with receivables is not one of the more enjoyable aspects of running a company. In fact, it's downright distasteful.

After that $100,000 write-off, however, we started a major overhaul of virtually everything we did.

Here's what worked for us:

Look at Personnel.   Often, I've found, the first step toward progress is to put someone different in a key position. That was true in this case. Our credit manager simply wasn't going to be up to the job once we revamped the system. We replaced him with a woman who had started out as our receptionist and had progressed through the organization. Although she didn't have any academic credentials or experience in receivables, she had a certain forcefulness and a personality that seemed just right. And it was. We also put her on an incentive plan—she receives a cash payment of $20 to $100 each month based on the number of days of receivables. And she has been great at doggedly pursuing delinquent accounts and limiting our exposure to losses.

Get Yourself Out.   It finally became clear—even to me—that until I got out of the credit area on a day-to-day basis, we weren't going to make any progress. Owners are optimists. We're customer oriented. And both characteristics are lethal to the credit-approval process.

So we set the rules. I was no longer available for credit approval.

Establish Initial Creditworthiness.   There's an entire body of literature on how to establish the creditworthiness of a prospective customer, so I'm not going to repeat the material except to say: *do it*. Most companies understand that, but they fail to write up the necessary procedures and policies. We were no exception, but we are true believers now.

One technique we initiated helps keep both our sales- and credit people happy. Quite often, in order to lock in a new customer who needed a quick shipment, we'd bypass the initial credit check. While we couldn't continue

[5] Reprinted with permission, *Inc.* magazine (May 1989). Copyright © 1989 by Goldhirsh Group, Inc., 38 Commercial Wharf, Boston, MA 02110.

doing that, we did install an interim "quick credit approval." A salesperson has to supply us with only a bank name and two vendor references, and we will guarantee a response within a half day for the first shipment—with the understanding that the final full credit-approval document will follow.

Check Credit before Shipment. Our basic computer system had some fairly good credit-checking capability at the time an order was entered—in theory, at least. The problem was, we were partly on the system and partly doing the job manually. When we got the system entirely on line, we could implement the credit-checking features. Now, when an order is entered, the computer notes: 1) if there is a credit hold; 2) if a credit limit is being exceeded; and 3) if the customer is 60 days past due. If any of these situations exist, the credit manager has to clear the order.

Monitor Extended Terms. Extending terms is just another form of price cutting. It also extends your receivables and your risk of loss. This was another area where I had to get out of the picture. Our controller has a good protective attitude about letting go of the money, and he now is in charge of approving any extended terms.

Develop Management Reports. While I had to get out of the day-to-day handling of receivables, I did need overall management control. Gross measures, such as percent past due, are fine for estimating general progress, but they are not tools to help get at the heart of various problems. And with more than 3,000 customers, the classic past-due report by customer listing was a mind-boggling mass of data.

Bad judgment: How *not* to handle your receivables

Here's how I managed to wind up with a $100,000 receivables write-off. The technique is infallible, but I wouldn't recommend you try it.

■ Start with an unknown individual who has a minimum of capital and a great story about his prospects in a far corner of the state.

■ Offer extended terms so he can finance the inventory needed to generate the fantastic business he has described.

■ When he is past due on his payments, rationalize that this is temporary, perhaps because of seasonality.

■ Let the account's salesperson verify that the inventory is in fact in place.

■ As you look at the financial statements, be sympathetic that this is a new operation having trouble getting a handle on its operating results.

■ When you start to realize your customer is in trouble, don't take your losses early. Stick with him, and you ought to be able to double the amount you have to write off.

I finally developed a month-end exception reporting system that extracts the critical information that I need to oversee receivables. Briefly, this program isolates two groups of accounts. The first report lists only those customers whose accounts have undergone a statistically significant adverse change. The second report lists the accounts with a history of problems, which need to be monitored.

In both reports, since we display only a small fraction of the accounts, we can print out a six-month history, which aids immensely in tracking them. With these two reports, I have a firm handle on receivables within a half hour after getting the printouts. They're also a useful guide for the credit manager in pinpointing which accounts need following up.

The payoff for all this effort has not been small potatoes. In my company, with $12 million in sales, the result of getting receivables down from 60 to 40 days is roughly $700,000. This may not be the most glamorous end of the business, but figures like that do quicken the pulse.

applicant is judged to be a "good" or a "bad" credit risk. Discriminant analysis has been used with success in consumer credit and other forms of installment lending in which various characteristics of an individual are quantitatively rated and a credit decision is made on the basis of the total score. The plastic credit cards many of us carry often are given out on the basis of a credit scoring system that takes into account such things as age, occupation, duration of employment, home ownership, years of residence, telephone, and annual income. Numerical rating systems also are used by companies extending trade credit. With the overall growth of trade credit, a number of companies are finding it worthwhile to screen out "clear" accept and reject applicants. In other words, routine credit decisions are made on the basis of a numerical score. Marginal applicants, who fall between "clear" accept or reject signals, can then be analyzed in detail by the credit analyst. In this way, a company is able to achieve greater efficiency in its credit investigation process. It uses trained credit analysts to the best advantage.

In a variation of this theme, expert systems using computer software have been designed to analyze financial statements, to undertake credit analyses of credit applicants, and to authorize credits. The idea of an expert system is to mimic the reasoning of experts in analyzing a defined problem and in reaching a decision.[6] By systematically charting the reasoning process of experts, a set of hierarchical rules is designed which embrace the problem area. The task involved is repetitive, but not necessarily structured. By carefully tracking the credit applicant's history, payment record, current status, financial condition, potential for future business, and external (macro) factors, the computer can apply a consistent framework to the task and reach informed decisions. Expert systems allow the leveraging of human talent, often a scarce resource, and can lower costs and increase accuracy.

Sequential Investigation Process. The amount of information collected should be determined in relation to the expected profit from an order and the

[6] For a discussion of a system, see Venkat Srinivasan and Yong H. Kim, "Designing Expert Financial Systems: A Case Study of Corporate Credit Management," *Financial Management*, 17 (Autumn 1988), 32–43.

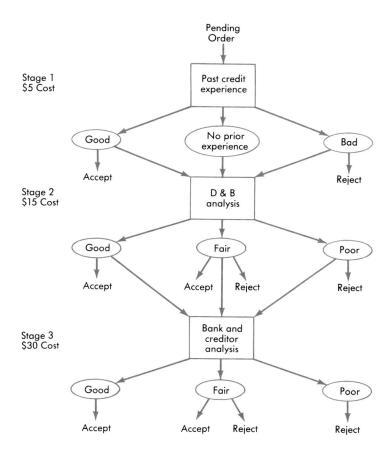

Pending
Order

Stage 1
$5 Cost

Past credit
experience

Good   No prior
experience   Bad

Accept   Reject

Stage 2
$15 Cost

D & B
analysis

Good   Fair   Poor

Accept   Accept   Reject   Reject

Stage 3
$30 Cost

Bank and
creditor
analysis

Good   Fair   Poor

Accept   Accept   Reject   Reject

FIGURE 16-4
Sequential investigation process

cost of investigation. More sophisticated analysis should be undertaken only when there is a chance that a credit decision based on the previous stage of investigation will be changed. If an analysis of a Dun & Bradstreet report resulted in an extremely unfavorable picture of the applicant, an investigation of the applicant's bank and its trade suppliers might have little prospect of changing the reject decision. Therefore, the added cost associated with this stage of investigation would not be worthwhile. With incremental stages of investigation each having a cost, they can be justified only if the information obtained has value in changing a prior decision.[7]

Figure 16-4 is a graphic representation of a sequential approach to credit analysis. The first stage is simply consulting past experience to see if the firm has sold previously to the account and, if it has, whether that experience has been satisfactory. Stage 2 might involve ordering a Dun & Bradstreet report on the applicant and evaluating it. The third, and last, stage could be credit checks of the applicant's bank and creditors. Each stage costs more. The expected profit from accepting an order will depend on the size of the order, as will the opportunity cost associated with its rejection. Rather than perform all stages of investigation, regardless of the size of the order and the firm's past experience, the firm should investigate in stages and go to a new stage only when the expected net benefits of the additional information exceed the cost of acquiring it. When past experience has been favorable, there may be little need for further investigation. In general, the riskier the applicant, the greater

[7] For such an analysis, see Dileep Mehta, "The Formulation of Credit Policy Models," *Management Science*, 15 (October 1968), 30–50.

the desire for more information. By balancing the costs of information with the likely profitability of the order, as well as with information from the next stage of investigation, added sophistication is introduced only when it is beneficial.

The Credit Decision. Once the credit analyst has marshaled the necessary evidence and has analyzed it, a decision must be reached on the disposition of the account. In an initial sale, the first decision to be made is whether or not to ship the goods and extend credit. If repeat sales are likely, the company will probably want to establish procedures so that it does not have to evaluate the extension of credit each time an order is received. One means for streamlining the procedure is to establish a *line of credit* for an account. A line of credit is a maximum limit on the amount the firm will permit to be owing at any one time. In essence, it represents the maximum risk exposure that the firm will allow itself to undergo for an account. In the sequential investigation method illustrated, single orders were evaluated. With a line of credit, multiple orders are assumed. The principle is the same. Likely profits from present and future sales must be balanced against the likely collection period, collection costs, and probability of bad-debt losses over time. Those last three balancing factors depend on the magnitude of the line of credit offered rather than on the size of order. As before, probability concepts can be applied in order to analyze the trade-off between expected benefits and expected costs and to determine an appropriate line of credit for the customer.

The establishment of a credit line streamlines the procedure for shipping goods. One need only determine whether an order brings the amount owed by a customer in excess of the line. If not, the order is shipped; if so, an incremental credit decision must be reached. The line itself must be reevaluated periodically in order to keep abreast of developments in the account. A satisfactory risk exposure today may be more or less than satisfactory a year from today. Despite comprehensive credit procedure, there will always be special cases that must be dealt with individually. Here, too, the firm can streamline the operation by defining responsibilities clearly.

COMPUTER-BASED INFORMATION SYSTEM

Widespread use of computers in credit management provides certain essential up-to-date information for analysis. Information is placed in computer storage, readily accessible to the credit department. At frequent intervals, it can obtain a trial balance that gives a summary of all billings, payments, discounts taken, and amounts still owed. Also, it can obtain an aging of accounts showing the total amounts owed the firm, the portion that is current, the portion that is up to 30 days past due, 30 to 60 days past due, and so forth. In addition to an aging, the average collection period and a collection matrix, which are taken up in Chapter 27, can be computed on a regular basis. By monitoring receivables in this way, the credit manager can detect changes in customer payment behavior. A deteriorating trend can be identified and new credit and collection policies instigated before the erosion becomes serious.

The computer can be programmed to provide complete reports on delinquent accounts, and delinquency letters can be sent out mechanically at regular intervals. Frequent reports on past-due accounts reveal individual problems as they develop. The alerted credit manager is able to stay on top of them and take corrective action. Formerly, the situation might have deteriorated during the information lag. Management also may want to be informed when an account approaches the line of credit established for it, and computers can provide this information easily.

The computer helps the credit manager by providing timely and accurate information on the status of accounts. The payment history of a customer can be drawn from storage and printed out in seconds. It will include the date the account was opened, the amount owed currently, the customer's credit line, any numerical credit ratings, and the promptness of past payments. Special reports can be prepared for categorization or comparisons. If several companies in the same industry are slow in their payments at a particular time of the year, management might want to know the firm's experience with all other companies in that particular industry. Such information enables the credit manager to analyze and deal with the problem more effectively. In another situation, management might wish to compare a customer's incoming orders and payment history. This information also can be provided quickly.

Indeed, the computer can provide a vast array of detailed information—previously impractical to obtain—that may be useful not only to the credit manager but to other management as well. In addition to processing data, the computer can be programmed to make certain routine credit decisions. In particular, small orders from good accounts can be approved by the computer without the order ever going to a credit analyst. All in all, electronic data processing makes a significant contribution to the credit department.

437

CHAPTER 16
Management of
Accounts
Receivable and
Inventories

INVENTORY MANAGEMENT AND CONTROL

Inventories form a link between production and sale of a product. A manufacturing company must maintain a certain amount of inventory during production, the inventory known as work in process. Although other types of inventory—namely, in-transit, raw materials, and finished goods inventory—are not necessary in the strictest sense, they allow the firm to be flexible. Inventory in transit (inventory between various stages of production or storage) permits efficient production scheduling and utilization of resources. Without this type of inventory, each stage of production would have to wait for the preceding stage to complete a unit. Resultant delays and idle time give the firm an incentive to maintain in-transit inventory.

Raw materials inventory gives the firm flexibility in its purchasing. Without it, the firm must exist on a hand-to-mouth basis, buying raw materials in keeping with its production schedule. Conversely, raw materials inventory may be bloated temporarily because the purchasing department has taken advantage of quantity discounts. Finished goods inventory allows the firm flexibility in its production scheduling and in its marketing. Production does not need to be geared directly to sales. Large inventories also allow efficient servicing of customer demands. If a product is temporarily out of stock, present as well as future sales may be lost. Thus, there is an incentive to maintain large stocks of all three types of inventory.

The advantages of increased inventories, then, are several. The firm can effect economies of production and purchasing and can fill orders more quickly. In short, the firm is more flexible. The obvious disadvantages are the total cost of holding the inventory, including storage and handling costs, and the required return on capital tied up in inventory. An additional disadvantage is the danger of obsolescence. Because of the benefits, however, the sales manager and production manager are biased toward relatively large inventories. Moreover, the purchasing manager often can achieve quantity discounts with large orders, and there may be a bias here as well. It falls on the financial manager to dampen the temptation for large inventories. This is done by forcing consideration of the cost of funds necessary to carry inventories as well as perhaps the handling and storage costs. (The latter costs usually will concern the production manager and the purchasing manager as well.)

Like accounts receivable, inventories should be increased as long as the resulting savings exceed the total cost of holding the added inventory. The balance finally reached depends on the estimates of actual savings, the cost of carrying additional inventory, and the efficiency of inventory control. Obviously, this balance requires coordination of the production, marketing, and finance areas of the firm in keeping with an overall objective. Our purpose is to examine various principles of inventory control by which an appropriate balance might be achieved.

ECONOMIC ORDER QUANTITY

The economic order quantity (EOQ) is an important concept in the purchase of raw materials and in the storage of finished goods and in-transit inventories. In our analysis, we wish to determine the optimal order quantity for a particular item of inventory, given its forecasted usage, ordering cost, and carrying cost. Ordering can mean either the purchase of the item or its production. Assume for the moment that the usage of a particular item of inventory is known with certainty. This usage is stationary or steady throughout the period of time being analyzed. In other words, if usage is 2,600 items for a 6-month period, 100 items would be used each week. Although the EOQ model can be modified to take account of increasing and decreasing usage over time, we shall not get into this added degree of complexity.

We assume that ordering costs, O, are constant, regardless of the size of the order. In the purchase of raw materials or other items, these costs represent the clerical costs involved in placing an order as well as certain costs of receiving and checking the goods once they arrive. For finished goods inventories, ordering costs involve scheduling a production run. For in-transit inventories, ordering costs are likely to involve nothing more than record keeping. The total ordering cost for a period is simply the number of orders for that period times the cost per order.

Carrying costs per period, C, represent the cost of inventory storage, handling, and insurance, together with the required rate of return on the investment in inventory. These costs are assumed to be constant per unit of inventory, per unit of time. Thus, the total carrying cost for a period is the average number of units of inventory for the period times the carrying cost per unit. In addition, we assume for now that inventory orders are filled without delay. Because out-of-stock items can be replaced immediately, there is no need to maintain a buffer or safety stock. Though the assumptions made up to now may seem overly restrictive, they are necessary for an initial understanding of the conceptual framework that follows. Subsequently, we shall relax some of them.

If the usage of an inventory item is perfectly steady over a period of time and there is no safety stock, average inventory (in units) can be expressed as

$$\text{Average inventory} = \frac{Q}{2} \qquad (16\text{-}1)$$

439

CHAPTER 16
Management of
Accounts
Receivable and
Inventories

where Q is the quantity (in units) ordered and is assumed to be constant for the period. This problem is illustrated in Fig. 16-5. Although the quantity demanded is a step function, we assume for analytical purposes that it can be approximated by a straight line. We see that zero inventory always indicates that further inventory must be ordered.

The carrying cost of inventory is the carrying cost per unit times the average number of units of inventory, or $CQ/2$. The total number of orders for a period of time is simply the total usage (in units) of an item of inventory for that period, S, divided by Q. Consequently, total ordering costs are represented by the ordering cost per order times the number of orders, or SO/Q. Total inventory costs, then, are the carrying costs plus ordering costs, or

$$T = \frac{CQ}{2} + \frac{SO}{Q} \qquad (16\text{-}2)$$

We see from Eq. (16-2) that the higher the order quantity, Q, the higher the carrying costs but the lower the total ordering costs. The lower the order quantity, the lower the carrying costs but the higher the total ordering costs. We are concerned with the trade-off between the economies of increased order size and the added cost of carrying additional inventory.

To determine the optimal order quantity, Q^*, we differentiate Eq. (16-2) with respect to Q and set the derivative equal to zero, obtaining[8]

$$Q^* = \sqrt{\frac{2SO}{C}} \qquad (16\text{-}3)$$

This equation is known as the economic lot-size formula. To illustrate its use, suppose that usage of an inventory item is 2,000 units during a 100-day period, ordering costs are $100 an order, and the carrying costs are $10 per unit per 100 days. The optimal economic order quantity, then, is

$$Q^* = \sqrt{\frac{2(2,000)(100)}{10}} = 200 \text{ units}$$

With an order quantity of 200 units, the firm would order (2,000/200), or 10 times, during the period under consideration, or every 10 days. We see from Eq. (16-3) that Q^* varies directly with total usage, S, and order cost, O, and inversely with the carrying cost, C. The relationship is dampened by the square root sign in both cases. As usage increases, the optimal order size and

[8] The steps are

$$\frac{dT}{dQ} = \frac{C}{2} - \frac{SO}{Q^2} = 0$$
$$CQ^2 - 2SO = 0$$
$$Q^2 = \frac{2SO}{C}$$
$$Q = \sqrt{\frac{2SO}{C}}$$

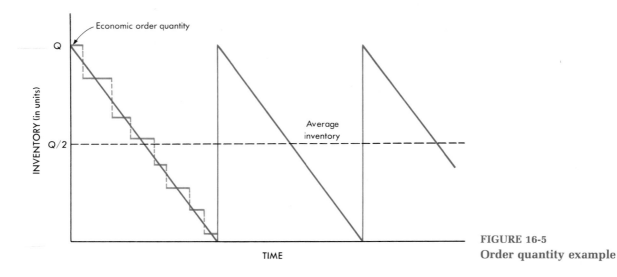

FIGURE 16-5
Order quantity example

the average level of inventory increase by a lesser percentage. In other words, economies of scale are possible.

In our example, we have assumed that inventory can be ordered and received without delay. Usually, there is a time lapse between placement of a purchase order and receipt of the inventory, or in the time it takes to manufacture an item after an order is placed. This lead time must be considered. If it is constant and known with certainty, the optimal order quantity is not affected. In the above example, the firm would still order 200 units at a time and place 10 orders during the specified time period, or every 10 days. If the lead time for delivery were 3 days, the firm simply would place its order 7 days after the delivery of the previous order.

The EOQ function is illustrated in Fig. 16-6. In the figure, we plot ordering costs, carrying costs, and total costs—the sum of the first two costs. We see that whereas carrying costs vary directly with the size of the order, ordering costs vary inversely with the size of the order. The total cost line declines

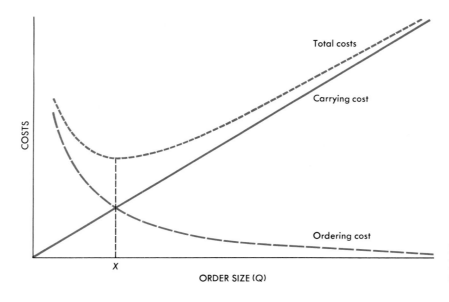

FIGURE 16-6
Economic order quantity relationship

at first as the fixed costs of ordering are spread over more units. The total cost line begins to rise when the decrease in average ordering cost is more than offset by the additional carrying costs. Point x, then, represents the economical order quantity, which minimizes the total cost of inventory. The EOQ formula taken up in this section is a useful tool for inventory control. In purchasing raw materials or other items of inventory, it tells us the amount to order and the best timing of our orders. For finished goods inventory, it enables us to exercise better control over the timing and size of production runs. In general, the EOQ model gives us a rule for deciding when to replenish inventories and the amount to replenish.

441

**CHAPTER 16
Management of
Accounts
Receivable and
Inventories**

UNCERTAINTY AND SAFETY STOCKS

In practice, the demand or usage of inventory generally is not known with certainty; usually it fluctuates during a given period of time. Typically, the demand for finished goods inventory is subject to the greatest uncertainty. In general, the use of raw materials inventory and in-transit inventory, both of which depend on the production scheduling, is more predictable. In addition to demand, the lead time required to receive delivery of inventory once an order is placed usually is subject to some variation. Owing to these fluctuations, it is not feasible usually to allow expected inventory to fall to zero before a new order is anticipated, as the firm could do when usage and lead time were known with certainty. A safety stock is necessary.

ORDER POINT AND SAFETY STOCK

Before discussing safety stocks, we consider at what point inventory will be ordered. Suppose demand for inventory is known with certainty, but that it takes 5 days before an order is received. In our previous illustration of the economic-order-quantity formula, we found that the EOQ for our example firm was 200 units, resulting in an order being placed every 10 days. If usage is steady, the firm now would need to order 5 days before it ran out of stock, or at 100 units of stock on hand. Thus, the order point is 100 units. When the new order is received 5 days later, the firm will just have exhausted its existing stock. This example of an order point is illustrated in Fig. 16-7.

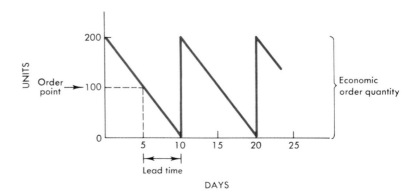

FIGURE 16-7

Order point when lead time is certain

When we allow for uncertainty in demand for inventory as well as in lead time, a safety stock becomes advisable. The concept here is illustrated in Fig. 16-8. In the upper panel of the figure, we show what would happen if the firm had a safety stock of 100 units and if expected demand of 200 units every 10 days and lead time of 5 days were to occur. Note that with a safety stock of 100 units, the order point must be set at 200 units of inventory on hand as opposed to the previous 100 units. In other words, the order point determines the amount of safety stock held.

The bottom panel of the figure shows the actual experience for our hypothetical firm. In the first segment of demand, we see that actual usage is somewhat less than expected. (The slope of the line is less than the expected demand line in the upper panel.) At the order point of 200 units of inventory held, an order is placed for 200 units of additional inventory. Instead of taking the expected 5 days for the inventory to be replenished, we see that it takes only 4 days. The second segment of usage is much greater than expected and, as a result, inventory is rapidly used up. At 200 units of remaining inventory, a 200-unit order again is placed, but here it takes 6 days for the inventory to be received. As a result of both of these factors, heavy inroads are made into the safety stock.

In the third segment of demand, usage is about the same as expected;

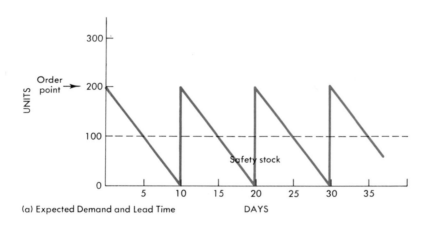

(a) Expected Demand and Lead Time

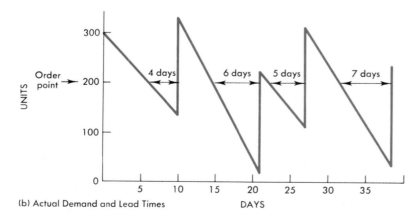

(b) Actual Demand and Lead Times

FIGURE 16-8

Safety stock when demand and lead time are uncertain

that is, the slopes of expected and actual usage lines are about the same. Because inventory was so low at the end of the previous segment of usage, an order is placed almost immediately. The lead time turns out to be 5 days. In the last segment of demand, usage is slightly greater than expected. The lead time necessary to receive the order is 7 days, much longer than expected. The combination of these two factors again causes the firm to go into its safety stock. The example illustrates the importance of safety stock in absorbing random fluctuations in usage and in lead times. Without such stock, the firm would have run out of inventory on two occasions.

443

CHAPTER 16
Management of
Accounts
Receivable and
Inventories

THE AMOUNT OF SAFETY STOCK

The proper amount of safety stock to maintain depends on several things. The greater the uncertainty associated with forecasted demand for inventory, the greater the safety stock the firm will wish to carry, all other things the same. Put another way, the risk of running out of stock is greater, the larger the unforeseen fluctuations in usage. Similarly, the greater the uncertainty of lead time to replenish stock, the greater the risk of running out of stock, and the more safety stock the firm will wish to maintain, all other things being equal. Another factor influencing the safety stock decision is the cost of running out of inventory. The cost of being out of raw materials and in-transit inventories is a delay in production. How much does it cost when production closes down temporarily? Where fixed costs are large, this cost will be quite high, as can be imagined in the case of an aluminum extrusion plant. The cost of running out of finished goods is customer dissatisfaction. Not only will the immediate sale be lost, but future sales will be endangered if customers take their business elsewhere. Although this opportunity cost is difficult to measure, it must be recognized by management and incorporated into the safety stock decision. The greater the costs of running out of stock, of course, the greater the safety stock management will wish to maintain, all other things being the same.

The cost of carrying additional inventory is crucial. If it were not for this cost, a firm could maintain whatever safety stock was necessary to avoid all possibility of running out of inventory. The greater the cost of carrying inventory, the more costly it is to maintain a safety stock, all other things being equal. Determination of the proper amount of safety stock involves balancing the probability and cost of a stockout against the cost of carrying enough safety stock to avoid this possibility. Ultimately, the question reduces to the probability of inventory stockout that management is willing to tolerate.

In recent years, the management of inventory has become very sophisticated. In certain industries, the production process lends itself to "just in time" inventory control. As the name implies, the idea is that inventories are acquired and inserted in production at the exact times they are needed. This requires a very accurate production and inventory information system, highly efficient purchasing, very reliable suppliers, and an efficient inventory-handling system. While raw materials inventory and inventory in transit never can be reduced to zero, the notion with "just in time" is one of extremely tight control so as to minimize inventories. How close a company comes to the ideal depends on the type of production process and the nature of supplier industries, but it is a worthy objective for almost all companies.

The inventory control methods described in this chapter give us a means for determining an optimal level of inventory, as well as how much should be ordered and when. These tools are necessary for managing inventory efficiently and balancing the advantages of additional inventory against the cost of carrying it. Computers have opened new worlds to inventory control, and operations research has many applications to inventory management—all beyond the scope of this book.

Although inventory management is not the direct operating responsibility of the financial manager, the investment of funds in inventory is an important aspect of financial management. Consequently, the financial manager must be familiar with ways to control inventories effectively, so that capital may be allocated efficiently. The greater the opportunity cost of funds invested in inventory, the lower the optimal level of average inventory and the lower the optimal order quantity, all other things held constant. This statement can be verified by increasing the carrying costs, C, in Eq. (16-3). The EOQ model also can be useful to the financial manager in planning for inventory financing.

When demand or usage of inventory is uncertain, the financial manager may try to effect policies that will reduce the average lead time required to receive inventory, once an order is placed. The lower the average lead time, the lower the safety stock needed and the lower the total investment in inventory, all other things held constant. The greater the opportunity cost of funds invested in inventory, the greater the incentive to reduce this lead time. The purchasing department may try to find new vendors that promise quicker delivery, or it may pressure existing vendors to deliver faster. The production department may be able to deliver finished goods faster by producing a smaller run. In either case, there is a trade-off between the added cost involved in reducing the lead time and the opportunity cost of funds tied up in inventory.

The financial manager is concerned also with the risks involved in carrying inventory. The major risk is that the market value of specific inventories will be less than the value at which they were acquired. Certain types of inventory are subject to obsolescence, whether it be in technology or in consumer tastes. A change in technology may make an electronic component worthless. A change in style may cause a retailer to sell dresses at substantially reduced prices. Other inventories, such as agricultural products, are subject to physical deterioration. With deterioration, of course, inventories will have to be sold at lower and lower prices, all other things being the same. In other situations, the principal risk is that of fluctuations in market price. Some items of inventory, such as copper, are subject to rather wide price swings. The financial manager is perhaps in the best place to make an objective analysis of the risks associated with the firm's investment in inventories. These risks must be considered in determining the appropriate level of inventory the firm should carry.

The opportunity cost of funds is the link by which the financial manager ties inventory management to the overall objective of the firm. In this regard, inventory can be treated as an asset to which capital is committed, as in any capital budgeting project. Different items of inventory may involve different risks, and these differences can be incorporated into an analysis of risk similar to that for capital budgeting. As discussed in Chapter 14, the essential difference between a capital asset and inventory is that the former typically involves a discrete investment; the latter represents a continuum of possible investments. Our discussion in this chapter has focused on determining an optimal *level* of investment. We know that the greater the efficiency with which the firm manages its inventory, the lower the required investment and the greater the shareholder wealth, all other things being the same.

445

CHAPTER 16
Management of
Accounts
Receivable and
Inventories

SUMMARY

Credit and collection policies encompass the quality of accounts accepted, the credit period extended, the cash discount given, certain special terms, and the level of collection expenditures. In each case, the credit decision involves a trade-off between the additional profitability and the cost resulting from a change in any of these elements. By liberalizing the quality requirements for accounts, the firm hopes to make more on the additional sales than it spends to carry the additional receivables plus the additional bad-debt losses. To maximize profits arising from credit and collection policies, the firm should vary these policies jointly until an optimal solution is obtained. This variation can be accomplished through simulation, once the functional relationships are specified. The firm's credit and collection policies, together with its credit and collection procedures, determine the magnitude and quality of its receivable position.

In evaluating a credit applicant, the credit analyst obtains financial and other information about the applicant, analyzes this information, and reaches a credit decision. In a sequential analysis process, the firm can decide whether to accept an order, reject it, or obtain additional information. More information is justified only when the expected benefits of the information exceed its cost. In turn, expected benefits arise only if the information allows us to correct a previously wrong decision. If the account is new, the firm must decide whether or not to accept the order. Expert systems, where computer software maps the reasoning process of sophisticated credit analysts, may prove useful in decision making. With repeat orders, a company must decide on the maximum credit to extend. This maximum, known as a line of credit, is based on the creditworthiness of the applicant.

The optimal level of inventories should be judged in relation to the flexibility inventories afford. If we hold constant the efficiency of inventory management, the lower the level of inventories, the less the flexibility of the firm. In evaluating the level of inventories, management must balance the benefits of economies of production, purchasing, and increased product demand against the cost of carrying the additional inventory. Of particular concern to the financial manager is the cost of funds invested in inventory, which is a function of the risk of the specific inventories involved.

In this chapter, we examined several tools of inventory control. One is the economic order quantity (EOQ), whereby we determine the optimal size of order to place, on the basis of the demand or usage of the inventory, the ordering costs, and the carrying costs. Under conditions of uncertainty, the firm usually must provide for a safety stock, owing to fluctuations in demand for inventory and lead times. By varying the point at which orders are placed, one varies the safety stock that is held. The movement toward "just in time" inventory control has reduced the amount of inventory many companies hold.

APPENDIX
Application of Discriminant Analysis to the Selection of Accounts

Discriminant analysis is a statistical tool that can help us decide which prospective accounts to accept or reject on the basis of certain relevant variables. This type of analysis is similar to regression analysis but assumes that the observations come from two or more different universes. In our case, these universes consist of good and bad accounts. Let us start with an evaluation of only two characteristics of trade credit applicants: the quick, or acid-test, ratio and the ratio of net worth to total assets. For purposes of experiment, we extend open-book credit to all new credit applicants for a sample period. We record the quick ratio of each account, its net-worth-to-total-assets ratio, and whether or not after a length of time it defaults in payment. If the account defaults, it is classified as a bad account; if it pays in a reasonable period of time, it is classified as a good account. With this information, we are able to undertake a linear discriminant analysis with two independent variables. We wish to determine the predictive value of these variables for the behavior of the dependent variable, whether the account is good or bad.

We plot quick ratios and net worth/total assets ratios for each account on a scatter diagram, obtaining the results shown in Fig. 16-9. The circles represent bad accounts; the squares represent good accounts. Using the two independent variables, we try to find the linear boundary line that discriminates best between good and bad accounts. We need to find the parameters, or

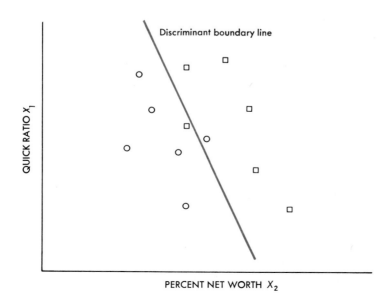

FIGURE 16-9
Discriminant analysis of accounts receivable

weights, of the following discriminant function:

$$f_i = a_1(X_1) + a_2(X_2) \tag{16A-1}$$

447

CHAPTER 16
Management of
Accounts
Receivable and
Inventories

where X_1 is the quick ratio of the firm, X_2 is its net-worth-to-total-assets ratio, and a_1 and a_2 are the parameters or weights we wish to compute. Our purpose is to obtain parameter values such that the average or mean value of f_g in Eq. (16A-1) for good accounts will be significantly larger than the average value of f_b for bad accounts. This notion is illustrated in Fig. 16-10, where the discriminant function value is along the horizontal axis, and the probability of occurrence is along the vertical. In the figure, two universes of credit applicants are shown: good to the right and bad to the left. The average value, f_b, for bad accounts is much lower than the average value, f_g, for good accounts, but the two universes overlap. In general, the smaller the area of overlap, the better the ability of discriminant analysis to predict good and bad accounts. In other words, it is desirable that the averages or means of the two distributions, f_b and f_g, be as far apart as possible.

The coefficients a_1 and a_2 in Eq. (16A-1) can be computed mathematically from the sample data by

$$a_1 = \frac{Szzdx - Sxzdz}{SzzSxx - Sxz^2} \tag{16A-2}$$

$$a_2 = \frac{Sxxdz - Sxzdx}{SzzSxx - Sxz^2} \tag{16A-3}$$

where Sxx and Szz represent the variances of variables X_1 and X_2, respectively, and Sxz is the covariance of variables X_1 and X_2. The difference between the average of X_1's for good accounts and the average of X_1's for bad accounts is represented by dx. Similarly, dz represents the difference between the average of X_2's for good accounts and the average of X_2's for bad accounts. When we solve for a_1 and a_2, we obtain the parameters of the linear discriminant function in Eq. (16A-1). The ratio a_1/a_2 determines the slope of the discriminant boundary line.

We now need to determine the minimum cutoff value of the function. The idea is to refuse credit to those accounts with values of f below the cutoff value and extend credit to those with f values above the cutoff value. In theory

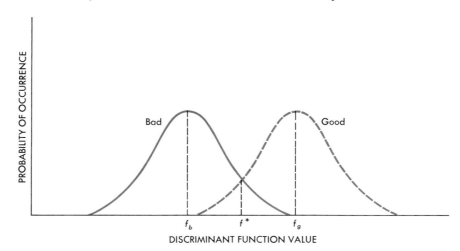

FIGURE 16-10
Universes of good and
bad accounts

we wish to find the discriminant function value denoted by f^* in Fig. 16-10. Using this value for cutoff purposes will minimize the prediction of good accounts when they are bad and the prediction of bad accounts when they are good. To determine the cutoff value in practice, we start by calculating the f_i for each account, given the parameters of Eq. (16A-1). For our example, suppose we obtained the f_i values, arranged in ascending order of magnitude, shown in Table 16-5.

TABLE 16-5
Values of f_i

Account number	7	10	2	3	6	12	11	4	1	8	5	9
Good or bad	B	B	B	B	B	G	B	G	G	G	G	G
f_i	.81	.97	1.36	1.44	1.65	1.77	1.83	1.91	2.12	2.19	2.34	2.48

We see that there is an area of overlap for accounts 6, 12, 11, and 4. We know that the cutoff value must lie between 1.65 and 1.91. For simplicity, we may want to use the midpoint, 1.78, as our cutoff value. Given the cutoff value, we are able to draw the discriminant boundary line in Fig. 16-9 that discriminates best between good and bad accounts. We note that two of the accounts, 11 and 12, are misclassified, given this cutoff value. Account 11 is classified as a good account when, in fact, it was bad; account 12 is classified as a bad account when, in fact, it was good. Rather than assign a strict cutoff value, it may be better to allow for misclassification and designate the area between 1.65 and 1.91 as uncertain, requiring further analysis. In theory, this area would correspond to the area of overlap in Fig. 16-10.

If we have reason to believe that new credit applicants will not differ significantly from the relationships found for the sample accounts, discriminant analysis can be used as a means for selecting and rejecting credit sale customers. If we use a minimum cutoff value, we will reject all sales in which the f_i value for the credit applicant is less than 1.78 and accept all sales in which the f_i value exceeds 1.78. If a range is used, we will accept all sales in which the prospective customer has an f_i value in excess of 1.91 and reject applicants with f_i values below 1.65. For applicants with f_i values lying between these two values, we might want to obtain additional credit information, along with information as to the profitability of the sale, before making a decision.

Although the example we used is simple, it illustrates the potential of discriminant analysis in selecting or rejecting credit applicants. Discriminant analysis can be extended to include a number of other independent variables. In fact, additional independent variables should be added as long as the benefits of greater predictability exceed the costs of collecting and processing the additional information. As before, the idea with more than two independent variables is to determine a set of weights, $a_1, a_2, a_3, \ldots, a_n$, for the various independent variables employed, so that the weighted average, or total score

$$f_i = a_1 X_1 + a_2 X_2 + a_3 X_3 + \cdots + a_n X_n \qquad (16A-4)$$

for the good accounts is as different as possible from that for the bad accounts. Given the optimal set of weights or parameters, one then calculates the total score, f^*, which best discriminates between good and bad accounts.

Assume that we are concerned with four independent variables: the quick ratio, X_1; the net-worth-to-total-assets ratio, X_2; the cash-flow-to-total-debt ratio, X_3; and the net profit margin ratio, X_4. The optimal parameters, or weights, for a_1, a_2, a_3, and a_4 were found to be 2, 5, 13 and 22, respectively. If a new credit applicant had a quick ratio of 1.5, a net worth to total assets ratio of .4, a cash-flow-to-total-debt ratio of .2, and a net profit margin of .05, its total credit score would be

$$f_i = 2(1.5) + 5(.4) + 13(.2) + 22(.05) = 8.7$$

This score is then compared with the optimal discriminant function, or cutoff, value determined on the basis of a sample. If 8.7 exceeds the predetermined cutoff value, the account is accepted. If 8.7 is less than the cutoff value, the account is rejected. Thus, the general approach is the same, whether two independent variables are used or more than two are used.

For discriminant analysis to have predictive value, the credit applicants being analyzed must correspond to the sample applicants on which the discriminant function parameters are based. With the passage of time, the underlying characteristics change. What was once an important financial ratio for predictive purposes may be less important today. In most applications, there is a decay in the validity of the discriminant function over time. As the system decays, there is a tendency to extend credit to more bad customers and to reject more potentially good customers. After a point, the discriminant function system is no longer worthwhile from the standpoint of credit decisions, and the firm would be better off with no system. Therefore, as experience provides new information it is important to assess the validity of the parameters or weights. Where the parameters are no longer realistic, a new sample should be drawn and new parameters generated.

When a linear discriminant function does not fit the data, it is possible to develop nonlinear functions. In particular, the quadratic function has been used with success. Problems other than those discussed exist in the application of discriminant analysis to finance, but space does not permit us to explore them here. Excellent discussions are available, exploring underlying problems in discriminant analysis as they relate to research in finance.[9] In effect, the credit scoring method described is a form of expert system, taken up in the chapter.

In summary, discriminant analysis is a flexible and practical means for evaluating new credit applicants and monitoring existing accounts. Because the information is processed on a high-speed computer, time spent on clerical work and credit analysis can be reduced. Credit analysts can concentrate on only those marginal accounts falling in an uncertain area. Discriminant analysis offers an efficient means by which a company can meet the mounting demands on its credit department.

---

[9] See Robert A. Eisenbeis, "Pitfalls in the Application of Discriminant Analysis in Business, Finance, and Economics," *Journal of Finance*, 32 (June 1977), 875–900; and O. Maurice Joy and John O. Tollefson, "On Financial Applications of Discriminant Analysis," *Journal of Financial and Quantitative Analysis*, 10 (December 1975), 723–40.

449

CHAPTER 16
Management of
Accounts
Receivable and
Inventories

SELF-CORRECTION PROBLEMS

1. Durham-Feltz Corporation presently gives terms of net 30 days. It has $60 million in sales, and its average collection period is 45 days. To stimulate demand, the company may give terms of net 60 days. If it does instigate these terms, sales are expected to increase by 15 percent. After the change, the average collection period is expected to be 75 days, with no difference in payment habits between old and new customers. Variable costs are $.80 for every $1.00 of sales, and the company's required rate of return on investment in receivables is 20 percent. Should the company extend its credit period? (Assume a 360-day year.)

2. Matlock Gauge Company makes wind and current gauges for pleasure boats. The gauges are sold throughout the Southeast to boat dealers, and the average order size is $50. The company sells to all registered dealers without a credit analysis. Terms are net 45 days, and the average collection period is 60 days, which is regarded as satisfactory. Jane Sullivan, vice-president of finance, is now uneasy about the increasing number of bad-debt losses on new orders. With credit ratings from local and regional credit agencies, she feels she would be able to classify new orders into one of three risk categories. Past experience shows the following:

	ORDER CATEGORY		
	Low Risk	Medium Risk	High Risk
Bad-debt loss	1%	4%	24%
Percent of category orders to total orders	30	50	20

The cost of producing and shipping the gauges and of carrying the receivables is 78 percent of sales. The cost of obtaining credit-rating information and of evaluating it is $4 per order. Surprisingly, there does not appear to be any association between the risk category and the collection period; the average for each of the three risk categories is around 60 days. Based on this information, should the company obtain credit information on new orders instead of selling to all new accounts without credit analysis?

3. Vostick Filter Company is a distributor of air filters to retail stores. It buys its filters from several manufacturers. Filters are ordered in lot sizes of 1,000, and each order costs $40 to place. Demand from retail stores is 20,000 filters per month, and carrying cost is $.10 a filter per month.

   a. What is the optimal order quantity with respect to so many lot sizes?

   b. What would be the optimal order quantity if the carrying cost were $.05 a filter per month?

   c. What would be the optimal order quantity if ordering costs were $10?

4. To reduce production start-up costs, Bodden Truck Company may manufacture longer runs of the same truck. Estimated savings from the increase in efficiency are $260,000 per year. However, inventory turnover will decrease from eight times a year to six times a year. Costs of goods sold are $48 million on an annual basis. If the required rate of return on investment in inventories is 15 percent, should the company instigate the new production plan?

450

1. To increase sales from their present annual $24 million, Jefferson Knu Monroe Company, a wholesaler, may try more liberal credit standards. Currently, the firm has an average collection period of 30 days. It believes that with increasingly liberal credit standards, the following will result:

CREDIT POLICY	A	B	C	D
Increase in sales from previous level (in millions)	$2.8	$1.8	$1.2	$.6
Average collection period for incremental sales (days)	45	60	90	144

The prices of its products average $20 per unit, and variable costs average $18 per unit. No bad-debt losses are expected. If the company has a pretax opportunity cost of funds of 30 percent, which credit policy should be pursued? (Assume a 360-day year.)

2. Upon reflection, Jefferson Knu Monroe Company has estimated that the following pattern of bad-debt losses will prevail if it initiates more liberal credit terms:

CREDIT POLICY	A	B	C	D
Bad-debt losses on incremental sales	3%	6%	10%	15%

Given the other assumptions in Problem 1, which credit policy should be pursued?

3. Recalculate Problem 2, assuming the following pattern of bad-debt losses:

CREDIT POLICY	A	B	C	D
Bad-debt losses on incremental sales	1.5%	3.0%	5.0%	7.5%

Which policy now would be best?

4. The Chickee Corporation has a 12 percent opportunity cost of funds and currently sells on terms of net 10, EOM. This means that goods shipped before the end of the month must be paid for by the tenth of the following month. The firm has sales of $10 million a year, which are 80 percent on credit and spread evenly over the year. Currently, the average collection period is 60 days. If Chickee offered terms of 2/10, net 30, 60 percent of its customers would take the discount, and the collection period would be reduced to 40 days. Should Chickee change its terms from net/10, EOM to 2/10, net 30? (Assume a 360-day year.)

5. Porras Pottery Products, Inc., spends $220,000 per annum on its collection department. The company has $12 million in credit sales, its average collection period is $2\frac{1}{2}$ months, and the percentage of bad-debt losses is 4 percent. The company believes that if it were to double its collection personnel, it could bring

down the average collection period to 2 months and bad-debt losses to 3 percent. The added cost is $180,000, bringing total expenditures to $400,000 annually. Is the increased effort worthwhile if the opportunity cost of funds is 20 percent? if it is 10 percent? (Assume a 360-day year.)

6. The Pottsville Manufacturing Corporation is considering extending trade credit to the San Jose Company. Examination of the records of San Jose has produced the following financial statements:

San Jose Company balance sheet (in millions)

	19x1	19x2	19x3
Assets			
Current assets			
Cash	$ 1.5	$ 1.6	$ 1.6
Receivables	1.3	1.8	2.5
Inventories (at lower of cost or market)	1.3	2.6	4.0
Other	.4	.5	.4
Total current assets	$ 4.5	$ 6.5	$ 8.5
Fixed assets:			
Buildings (net)	2.0	1.9	1.8
Machinery and equipment (net)	7.0	6.5	6.0
Total fixed assets	$ 9.0	$ 8.4	$ 7.8
Other assets	1.0	.8	.6
Total assets	$14.5	$15.7	$16.9
Liabilities and shareholders' equity			
Current liabilities:			
Notes payable	$ 2.1	$ 3.1	$ 3.8
Trade payables	.2	.4	.9
Other payables	.2	.2	.2
Total current liabilities	$ 2.5	$ 3.7	$ 4.9
Term loan	4.0	3.0	2.0
Total liabilities	$ 6.5	$ 6.7	$ 6.9
Shareholders' equity			
Common stock	5.0	5.0	5.0
Preferred stock	1.0	1.0	1.0
Retained earnings	2.0	3.0	4.0
Total liabilities and equity	$14.5	$15.7	$16.9

The San Jose Company has a Dun & Bradstreet rating of 4A-2. Inquiries into its banking disclosed balances generally in the low seven figures. Five suppliers to San Jose revealed that the firm takes its discounts from the three offering 2/10, net 30 terms, though it is about 15 days slow in paying the two firms offering terms of net 30.

San Jose Company income statement (in millions)

	19x1	19x2	19x3
Net credit sales	$15.0	$15.8	$16.2
Cost of goods sold	11.3	12.1	13.0
Gross profit	$ 3.7	$ 3.7	$ 3.2
Operating expenses	1.1	1.2	1.2
Net profit before taxes	$ 2.6	$ 2.5	$ 2.0
Taxes	1.3	1.2	1.0
Profit after taxes	$ 1.3	$ 1.3	$ 1.0
Dividends	.3	.3	.0
	$ 1.0	$ 1.0	$ 1.0

Analyze the San Jose Company's application for credit. What positive factors are present? What negative factors are present?

7. The Quigley Company sells and installs ski lifts. It has received an order from Alpine Ski Resort for a $2.3 million system. The production and installation costs of this system amount to 69.6 percent of the total selling price. Because Alpine wishes to go through a full season before paying for the system, it has asked for credit terms of 1 year. Quigley estimates that there is an 80 percent probability that Alpine will pay in full and a 20 percent chance that it will go bankrupt and pay nothing at the end of the year. Alpine's hill will be filled with this installation, so there is no prospect for repeat orders. Quigley's opportunity cost of carrying the receivable at its stated value of $2.3 million is 15 percent per annum.

   a. On the basis of this information, should Quigley accept the order?

   b. If its costs were 74 percent of the selling price, would the order be accepted? If 65 percent?

8. A college bookstore is attempting to determine the optimal order quantity for a popular book on psychology. The store sells 5,000 copies of this book a year at a retail price of $12.50, although the publisher allows the store a 20 percent discount on this price. The store figures that it costs $1 per year to carry a book in inventory and $100 to prepare an order for new books.

   a. Determine the total costs associated with ordering 1, 2, 5, 10, and 20 times a year.

   b. Determine the economic order quantity.

9. The Hedge Corporation manufactures only one product: planks. The single raw material used in making planks is the dint. For each plank manufactured, 12 dints are required. Assume that the company manufactures 150,000 planks per year, that demand for planks is perfectly steady throughout the year, that it costs $200 each time dints are ordered, and that carrying costs are $8 per dint per year.

   a. Determine the economic order quantity of dints.

   b. What are total inventory costs for Hedge (carrying costs plus ordering costs)?

   c. How many times per year would inventory be ordered?

10. Favorite Foods, Inc., buys 50,000 boxes of ice cream cones every 2 months to service steady demand for the product. Order costs are $100 per order, and carrying costs are $.40 per box.

    a. Determine the optimal order quantity.

    b. The vendor now offers Favorite Foods a quantity discount of $.02 per box if it buys cones in order sizes of 10,000 boxes. Should Favorite Foods avail itself of the quantity discount? *Hint:* Determine the increase in carrying cost and decrease in ordering cost relative to your answer in part a. Compare these with the total savings available through the quantity discount.

11. Fouchee Scents, Inc., makes various scents for use in the manufacture of food products. Although the company does maintain a safety stock, it has a policy of "lean" inventories, with the result that customers sometimes must be turned away. In an analysis of the situation, the company has estimated the cost of being out of stock associated with various levels of safety stock:

	LEVEL OF SAFETY STOCK (IN GALLONS)	ANNUAL COST OF STOCKOUTS
Present safety stock level	5,000	$26,000
New safety stock level 1	7,500	14,000
New safety stock level 2	10,000	7,000
New safety stock level 3	12,500	3,000
New safety stock level 4	15,000	1,000
New safety stock level 5	17,500	0

Carrying costs are $.65 per gallon per year. What is the best level of safety stock for the company?

12. Wilstat is contemplating a change in inventory policy. Currently, the firm has an inventory turnover of 24 times a year. Sales have been holding steady at $240,000 per year. Variable costs are 70 percent of the total sales dollar. The company feels that if it were to increase inventories, it could also increase sales by avoiding certain stockouts that now occur. The required rate of return before taxes is 20 percent. The company estimates the following relationship between inventory turnover and sales:

Inventory turnover	24	12	6	4	3
Sales	$240,000	$252,000	$261,000	$266,000	$270,000

Using the marginal analysis procedure developed earlier in the chapter (accounts receivable), determine the optimal inventory policy.

SOLUTIONS TO SELF-CORRECTION PROBLEMS

1. Receivable turnover = 360/75 = 4.8
   Profitability of additional sales = $9 million × .2 = $1,800,000
   Additional receivables associated with the new sales
   $$= \$9 \text{ million}/4.8 = \$1,875,000$$
   Additional investment in receivables associated with the new sales
   $$= \$1,875,000 \times .8 = \$1,500,000$$
   New level of receivables associated with the original sales
   $$= \$60 \text{ million}/4.8 = \$12,500,000$$
   Old level of receivables associated with the original sales
   $$= \$60 \text{ million}/8 = \$7,500,000$$
   Incremental receivable investment, original sales
   $$= \$5,000,000$$
   Total increase in receivable investment
   $$= \$1.5 \text{ million} + \$5 \text{ million} = \$6,500,000$$
   Carrying cost of additional investment = .20 × $6.5 million = $1,300,000
   As the incremental carrying cost is less than the incremental profitability, the company should lengthen its credit period from 30 to 60 days.

2. As the bad-debt loss ratio for the high-risk category exceeds the profit margin of 22 percent, it would be desirable to reject orders from this risk class if such orders could be identified. However, the cost of credit information, as a percentage of the average order, is $4/$50 = 8%, and this cost is applicable to all new orders. As the high-risk category is one-fifth of sales, the comparison would be 5 × 8% = 40% relative to the bad-debt loss of 24%. Therefore, the company should not undertake credit analysis of new orders.

   An example can better illustrate the solution. Suppose new orders were $100,000. The following would then hold:

ORDER CATEGORY

455

CHAPTER 16
Management of
Accounts
Receivable and
Inventories

	Low Risk	Medium Risk	High Risk
Total orders	$30,000	$50,000	$20,000
Bad-debt loss	300	2,000	4,800

Number of orders = $100,000/$50 = 2,000
Credit analysis cost = 2,000 × $4 = $8,000

To save $4,800 in bad-debt losses by identifying the high-risk category of new orders, the company must spend $8,000. Therefore, it should not undertake the credit analysis of new orders. This is a case where the size of order is too small to justify credit analysis. After a new order is accepted, the company will gain experience and can reject subsequent orders if its experience is bad.

3. a.

$$Q^* = \sqrt{\frac{2(20)(40)}{100}} = 4$$

Carrying costs = $.10 × 1,000 = $100
The optimal order size would be 4,000 filters, which represents five orders a month.

b.

$$Q^* = \sqrt{\frac{2(20)(40)}{50}} = 5.66$$

Since the lot size is 1,000 filters, the company would order 6,000 filters each time. The lower the carrying cost, the more important ordering costs become relatively, and the larger the optimal order size.

c.

$$Q^* = \sqrt{\frac{2(20)(10)}{100}} = 2$$

The lower the order cost, the more important carrying costs become relatively and the smaller the optimal order size.

4. Inventories after change = $48 million/6 = $8 million
Present inventories   = $48 million/8 = $6 million

Additional inventories $2 million
Opportunity cost = $2 million × .15 = $300,000

The opportunity cost is greater than the savings. Therefore, the new production plan should not be undertaken.

SELECTED REFERENCES

BRENNAN, MICHAEL, J., VOJISLAV MAKSIMOVIC, and JOSEF ZECHNER, "Vendor Financing," *Journal of Finance*, 43 (December 1988), 1127–41.

EISENBEIS, ROBERT A., "Pitfalls in the Application of Discriminant Analysis in Business, Finance and Economics," *Journal of Finance*, 32 (June 1977), 875–900.

EMERY, GARY W., "A Pure Financial Explanation for Trade Credit," *Journal of Financial and Quantitative Analysis*, 19 (September 1984), 271–86.

GREER, CARL C., "The Optimal Credit Acceptance Policy," *Journal of Financial and Quantitative Analysis,* 2 (December 1967), 399–415.

HALLORAN, JOHN A., and HOWARD P. LANSER, "The Credit Policy Decision in an Inflationary Environment," *Financial Management,* 10 (Winter 1981), 31–38.

HILL, NED C., and KENNETH D. RIENER, "Determining the Cash Discount in the Firm's Credit Policy," *Financial Management,* 8 (Spring 1979), 68–73.

JOY, MAURICE O., and JOHN O. TOLLEFSON, "On the Financial Applications of Discriminant Analysis," *Journal of Financial and Quantitative Analysis,* 10 (December 1975), 723–40.

KIM, YONG H., and JOSEPH C. ATKINS, "Evaluating Investments in Accounts Receivable: A Wealth Maximizing Framework," *Journal of Finance,* 33 (May 1978), 403–12.

KIM, YONG H., and KEE H. CHUNG, "Inventory Management under Uncertainty: A Financial Theory for the Transactions Motive," *Managerial and Decision Economics* (1989).

LONG, MICHAEL S., "Credit Screening System Selection," *Journal of Financial and Quantitative Analysis,* 11 (June 1976), 313–28.

MAGEE, JOHN F., "Guides to Inventory Policy," I–III, *Harvard Business Review,* 34 (January–February 1956), 49–60; (March–April 1956), 103–16; and (May–June 1956), 57–70.

MEHTA, DILEEP, "The Formulation of Credit Policy Models," *Management Science,* 15 (October 1968), 30–50.

OH, JOHN S., "Opportunity Cost in the Evaluation of Investment in Accounts Receivable," *Financial Management,* 5 (Summer 1976), 32–36.

SNYDER, ARTHUR, "Principles of Inventory Management," *Financial Executive,* 32 (April 1964), 13–21.

SRINIVASAN, VENKAT, and YONG H. KIM, "Granting: A Comparative Analysis of Classification Procedures," *Journal of Finance,* 42 (July 1987), 665–81.

STOWE, JOHN D., "An Integer Programming Solution for the Optimal Credit Investigation/Credit Granting Sequence," *Financial Management,* 14 (Summer 1985), 66–76.

WESTON, J. FRED, and PHAM D. TUAN, "Comment on Analysis of Credit Policy Changes," *Financial Management,* 9 (Winter 1980), 59–63.

WHITTRED, GREG, and CLIFFORD SMITH, "Accounts Receivable Management Policy: Theory and Evidence," working paper, University of Rochester (1989).

PART 5

SHORT- AND INTERMEDIATE-TERM FINANCING

Festus McGann Shops for a Loan

In the late 1980s, Festus McGann, president of HiYield Seed Company, approached Nevada National Bank for a seasonal line of credit. HiYield is a processor and distributor of hayseeds, primarily alfalfa, with headquarters in Fallon, Nevada. The loan request was made to finance the accumulation of inventories in the fall until February–April, when heavy seed sales occur. In addition, the company needed to finance an expansion of its processing plant and warehouse. Mr. McGann thought that peak requirements would occur in January, totaling $900,000, and that the company would be out of bank debt by the end of May.

Previously, the company borrowed from another Nevada bank, and its line of credit had been increased over the years to a level of $800,000. However, the other bank expressed dissatisfaction with HiYield Seed Company's mounting financing requirements and its inability to pay off the loan during the prior two years. The banker felt the company was using its seasonal credit line to finance more permanent funds requirements—underlying buildups in receivables, inventories, and fixed assets. While Mr. McGann countered that the company was consistently profitable, having earned $119,000 the previous year, the banker insisted on some term debt or equity being brought into the picture. Mr. McGann hoped for a more understanding treatment from Nevada National Bank.

17

UNSECURED SHORT-TERM FINANCING

THE TYPE OF FINANCING, CONCEPTUALLY

In Chapter 14, we considered the current liabilities of the firm as part of its overall financing decision. The questions of debt versus equity, the maturity composition of the debt, and conditions associated with the debt were considered. (An example of the latter is whether or not the debt is secured and, if so, the type of security.) Decisions on these issues determine the amount of current liabilities of the firm. We suggested that if capital markets were perfect, stockholders would be indifferent to the maturity and type of debt the firm employed. Put another way, the firm would be unable to affect the value of its equity by altering the maturity composition and types of debt contracts employed. Accordingly, there would be no reason to proliferate the types and maturities of debt; one debt strategy would be as good as the next.

If imperfections and/or incompleteness exist in financial markets, stockholders will benefit from the firm's "packaging" its debt instruments in a way that takes advantage of these circumstances. The imperfections that most affect debt financing are flotation costs, bankruptcy costs, costs of information, and restrictions on lenders. Since these imperfections were described earlier in Parts 2 and 3, we touch now on their implications for the problem at hand.

If flotation costs are fixed, either in whole or in part, they create a bias toward less frequent financing, larger offerings of debt each time, and longer maturities. In other words, the presence of fixed costs results in economies of scale in debt offerings. Bankruptcy costs create a bias in favor of lower levels of debt obligations coming due in the near future; that is, longer maturities. To the extent that there are costs of information, they affect the sources of financing the firm is able to tap. If the cost of information is somewhat fixed to either the lender or the borrower, it creates a tendency toward less diversity in debt arrangements. A medium-sized firm may be unable to sell its debt in a public offering simply because the cost of information to ultimate investors is so high that it makes debt issues of less than $10 million infeasible. Instead, the firm will go to a commercial bank or an institutional lender such as an insurance company, where it need negotiate with only one party. If the relationship is continuous over time, the cost of information per financing can be reduced. Thus, economies of scale in information affect the sources of debt financing.

Restrictions, or institutional constraints, on lenders affect the type of loans they can make. These constraints may be caused by things such as legal restrictions or tax differences, or they may simply be self-imposed. Commercial banks tend to make short- to intermediate-term loans, for example, owing to regulations on their investment behavior. Small firms, limited to bank financing because of the cost of information, may be restricted to shorter-term debts. Other examples of imperfections could be cited, but these examples point to the direction of their impact. If financial markets are incomplete with respect to the types of securities offered, the firm may wish to tailor its debt issues to the unfilled desires of investors. By appealing to this excess demand, there will be an interest-cost saving, all other things staying the same.

In this part, we assume that imperfections and/or incompleteness exist in financial markets, even though they may not be substantial. As a result, the way the firm "packages" its debt financing is important. That is, by varying the maturity composition and conditions of its debt, the firm may be able to affect its value, although the impact is likely to be modest. For our purposes in this chapter, the most important aspect of a firm's debt is its maturity.

PERMANENT AND TEMPORARY FINANCING

If the firm adopts a hedging approach to financing, each asset would be offset with a financing instrument of the same approximate maturity. A firm incurs short-term debt to finance short-term or seasonal variations in current assets; it uses long-term debt or equity to finance the permanent component of current assets. The situation is illustrated in Fig. 17-1.

If current assets fluctuate in the manner shown in the figure, only the temporary fluctuations shown at the top of the figure would be financed with temporary debt. To finance short-term requirements with long-term debt would necessitate the payment of interest for the use of funds during times when they were not needed. This occurrence can be illustrated by drawing a

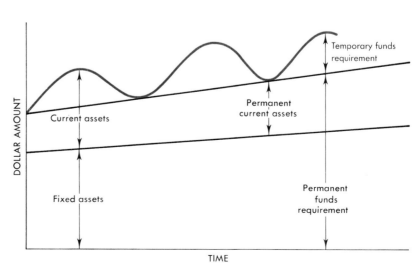

FIGURE 17-1

Funds requirement; hedging financing policy

straight line to represent the total amount of long-term debt and equity across the seasonal humps in Fig. 17-1. It is apparent that financing would be employed in periods of seasonal lull when it was not needed. With a hedging approach to financing, the borrowing and payment schedule for short-term financing would be arranged to correspond to the expected swings in current assets. Fixed assets and the permanent component of current assets would be financed with long-term debt, equity, and the permanent component of current liabilities.

A hedging approach to financing suggests that apart from current installments on long-term debt, a firm would show no current borrowings at the seasonal troughs in Fig. 17-1. Short-term borrowings would be paid off with surplus cash. As the firm moved into a period of seasonal funds needs, it would borrow on a short-term basis, again paying off the borrowings as surplus cash was generated. In this way, financing would be employed only when it was needed. In a growth situation, permanent financing would be increased in keeping with underlying increases in permanent funds requirements.

MATURITY OF DEBT

Although an exact synchronization of the schedule of expected future net cash flows and the payment schedule of debt is appropriate under conditions of certainty, it usually is not appropriate under uncertainty. Net cash flows will deviate from expected flows in keeping with the business risk of the firm. As a result, the schedule of debt maturities is important in assessing the risk-profitability trade-off. We assume that the firm will not arrange its debt obligations so that the composite maturity schedule calls for payments of principal and interest before expected net cash flows are available. The question is, What margin of safety should be built into the maturity schedule in order to allow for adverse fluctuations in cash flows? This depends on the trade-off between risk and profitability.

The Risks Involved. In general, the shorter the maturity schedule of a firm's debt obligations, the greater the risk that it will be unable to meet principal and interest payments. On the other hand, the longer the maturity schedule, the less risky the financing of the firm, all other things the same.

Suppose a company borrows on a short-term basis in order to build a new plant. The short-term cash flows from the plant are not sufficient in the short run to pay off the loan. As a result, the company bears the risk that the lender may not renew the loan at maturity. This risk could be reduced by financing the plant on a long-term basis, the expected cash flows being sufficient to retire the debt in an orderly manner. Thus, committing funds to a long-term asset and borrowing short carries the risk that the firm may not be able to renew its borrowings. If the company should fall on hard times, creditors may regard renewal as too risky and may demand immediate payment. This, in turn, will cause the firm to either retrench or go into bankruptcy.

In addition to this sort of risk, there is also the uncertainty associated with interest costs. When the firm finances with long-term debt, it knows precisely what its interest costs will be over the time period it needs the funds. If it finances with short-term debt, it is uncertain of interest costs on refinancing. In a sense, then, the uncertainty of interest costs represents risk to the borrower. We know that short-term interest rates fluctuate more than long-term interest rates. A firm forced to refinance its short-term debt in a period of rising interest rates may pay an overall interest cost on short-term debt that is higher than it would have been on long-term debt. Therefore, the absence of knowledge of future short-term interest costs represents a risk to the company.

A mitigating factor is the possible covariance of short-term interest costs with operating income. With covariance, when operating income is high it will be offset by higher interest costs, thereby dampening the rise in net income. When operating income is low, net income will benefit from the lower interest costs at that time.[1] Net income therefore would be somewhat lower in periods of economic prosperity and somewhat higher in periods of economic contraction than it would be if constant interest had been paid on long-term debt. It is only if the financing is short-term and rolled over at maturity that interest costs vary over time and there is the possibility for covariance with the firm's operating income. Marriott Corporation is said to have found that hotel operating income was correlated with the level of interest rates. As a result, a case was made for financing in part on a short-term basis.

Taking all the foregoing factors into account, we can say that for most companies the longer the maturity schedule of a firm's debt in relation to its expected net cash flows, the less the risk. The major risk in this regard is the possible inability to refinance short-term debt at its maturity. There is also the uncertainty associated with interest costs on the rollover of short-term borrowings, which can either dampen or accentuate fluctuations in the firm's operating income.

The Trade-off with Costs.   Differences in risk between short-and long-term financing must be balanced against differences in interest costs. The longer the maturity schedule of a firm's debt, the more costly the financing is likely to be. For one thing, the expected cost of long-term financing usually is more than that of short-term financing. In periods of high interest rates, the rate on short-term corporate borrowings may exceed that on long-term borrowings; but over an extended period of time, the firm typically pays more for long-term borrowings. Expressed differently, the long-run expected cost of short-term borrowings, represented by the present short-term interest rate and expected future short-term rates when the debt is rolled over, will be lower than the expected cost of long-term debt. In addition to the higher expected costs of long-term borrowings, the firm may pay interest on debt over periods of time when the funds are not needed. Thus, there usually is an inducement to finance funds requirements on a short-term basis.

Consequently, we have the familiar trade-off between risk and profitability. The margin of safety, or lag between expected net cash flows and payments on debt, will depend on the risk preferences of management. In turn, its decision on the maturity composition of the firm's debt will determine the portion of current assets financed by current liabilities and the portion financed on a long-term basis.

To allow for a margin of safety, management might decide on the proportions of short-term and long-term financing shown in Fig. 17-2. Here we see that the firm finances a portion of its expected seasonal funds requirement on a long-term basis. If the expected net cash flows do occur, it will pay interest on debt during seasonal troughs when the funds are not needed. During these troughs, moreover, it will be financing with the higher expected cost long-term debt. If there is a shortfall in net cash flows, the firm will have in place a

---

[1] This proposition is advanced by James R. Morris, "On Corporate Debt Maturity Strategies," *Journal of Finance*, 31 (March 1976), 29–37.

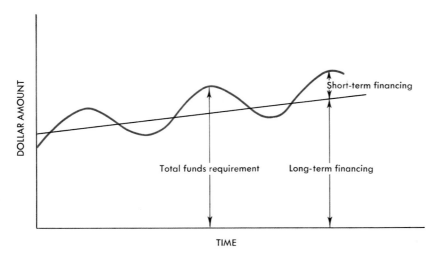

FIGURE 17-2
Funds requirement; margin of safety

cushion of long-term financing with which it hopes to cover its permanent funds requirements. If the shortfall is great enough, it will need to resort to short-term financing or other measures. These examples are sufficient to show that the firm can reduce the risk of cash insolvency by increasing the maturity schedule of its debt.

With this general framework in mind, we are now able to examine in detail specific methods of short-term financing. The major sources are trade credit, accruals, commercial paper, and short-term loans. The first three as well as unsecured short-term loans are considered in this chapter; secured short-term loans are taken up in the next. We wish to see how these sources of short-term financing may be used for seasonal and temporary fluctuations in funds requirements, as well as the more permanent needs of the firm.

TRADE CREDIT FINANCING

Trade credit is a form of short-term financing common to almost all businesses. In fact, it is the largest source of short-term funds for business firms collectively. In an advanced economy, most buyers are not required to pay for goods on delivery but are allowed a short deferment period before payment is due. During this period, the seller of the goods extends credit to the buyer. Because suppliers generally are more liberal in the extension of credit than are financial institutions, small companies in particular rely on trade credit.

Of the three types of trade credit—open account, notes payable, and trade acceptances—by far the most common type is the open-account arrangement. The seller ships goods to the buyer and sends an invoice that specifies the goods shipped, the price, the total amount due, and the terms of the sale. Open-account credit derives its name from the fact that the buyer does not sign a formal debt instrument evidencing the amount owed the seller. The seller extends credit based on a credit investigation of the buyer (see Chapter 16).

In some situations, promissory notes are employed instead of open-account credit. The buyer signs a note that evidences a debt to the seller. The note itself calls for the payment of the obligation at some specified future date. This arrangement is employed when the seller wants the buyer to recognize the debt formally. For example, a seller might request a promissory note from a buyer if the buyer's open account became past due. A trade acceptance is another arrangement by which the indebtedness of the buyer is recognized formally. Under this arrangement, the seller draws a draft on the buyer, ordering the buyer to pay the draft at some date in the future. The seller will not release the goods until the buyer accepts the time draft.[2]

TERMS OF SALE

Because the use of promissory notes and trade acceptances is limited, the subsequent discussion will be confined to open-account trade credit. The terms of sale make a great deal of difference in this type of credit. These terms, specified in the invoice, may be placed in several broad categories according to the net period within which payment is expected and according to the terms of the cash discount.

COD and CBD—No Extension of Credit. COD terms mean *cash on delivery* of the goods. The only risk the seller undertakes in this type of arrangement is that the buyer may refuse the shipment. Under such circumstances, the seller will be stuck with the shipping costs. Occasionally, a seller might ask for cash before delivery (CBD) to avoid all risk. Under either COD or CBD terms, the seller does not extend credit. CBD terms must be distinguished from progress payments, which are common in certain industries. With progress payments, the buyer pays the manufacturer at various stages of production prior to actual delivery of the finished product. Because large sums of money are tied up in work in progress, aircraft manufacturers request progress payments from airlines in advance of the actual delivery of aircraft.

Net Period—No Cash Discount. When credit is extended, the seller specifies the period of time allowed for payment. The terms, net 30, indicate that the invoice or bill must be paid within 30 days. It the seller bills on a monthly basis, it might require such terms as net/15 EOM, which means that all goods shipped before the end of the month must be paid for by the fifteenth of the following month.

Net Period with Cash Discount. In addition to extending credit, the seller may offer a cash discount if the bill is paid during the early part of the net period. The terms 2/10, net 30 indicate that the seller offers a 2 percent discount if the bill is paid within 10 days; otherwise, the buyer must pay the full amount within 30 days. Usually, a cash discount is offered as an incentive to the buyer to pay early. In Chapter 16, we discussed the optimal cash discount the seller might offer. A cash discount differs from a trade discount and from a quantity discount. A trade discount is greater for one class of customers (e.g., wholesalers) than for others (e.g., retailers). A quantity discount is offered on large shipments.

Datings. In a seasonal business, sellers frequently use datings to encourage customers to place their orders before a heavy selling period. A manufacturer of lawn mowers may give seasonal datings specifying that any shipment to a dealer in the winter or spring does not have to be paid for until

---

[2] If the instrument is a sight draft, the buyer is ordered to pay the draft upon presentation. Under this arrangement, trade credit is not extended.

summer. Earlier orders benefit the seller, who can gauge the demand more realistically and schedule production more efficiently. Also, the seller does not have to store finished goods inventory. The buyer has the advantage of not having to pay for the goods until the height of the selling period. Under this arrangement, credit is extended for a longer than normal period of time.

TRADE CREDIT AS A MEANS OF FINANCING

We have seen that trade credit is a source of funds, because the buyer does not have to pay for goods until after they are delivered. If the firm automatically pays its bills a certain number of days after the date of invoice, trade credit becomes a built-in source of financing that varies with the production cycle. As the firm increases its production and corresponding purchases, accounts payable increase and provide part of the funds needed to finance the increase in production. As production decreases, accounts payable tend to decrease. Under these circumstances, trade credit is not a discretionary source of financing. It is entirely dependent on the purchasing plans of the firm, which, in turn, are dependent on its production cycle. In examining trade credit as a discretionary form of financing, we want to consider situations in which (1) a firm does not take a cash discount but pays on the last day of the net period and (2) a firm pays its bills beyond the net period.

PAYMENT ON THE FINAL DUE DATE

In this section, we assume that the firm forgoes a cash discount but does pay its bill on the final due date of the net period. If no cash discount is offered, there is no cost for the use of credit during the net period. By the same token, if a firm takes the discount, there is no cost for the use of trade credit during the discount period. If a cash discount is offered but not taken, there is a definite opportunity cost. If the terms of sale are 2/10, net 30, the firm has the use of funds for an additional 20 days if it does not take the cash discount but pays on the final day of the net period. For a $100 invoice, it would have the use of $98 for 20 days. The approximate annual interest cost is

$$\frac{2}{98} \times \frac{365}{20} = 37.2\%$$

Thus, we see that trade credit can be a very expensive form of short-term financing when a cash discount is offered.

The cost of trade credit declines as the net period becomes longer in relation to the discount period. Had the terms in the above example been 2/10, net 60, the annual interest cost would have been

$$\frac{2}{98} \times \frac{365}{50} = 14.9\%$$

The relationship between the annual interest cost of trade credit and the number of days between the end of the discount period and the end of the net period is shown in Fig. 17-3. In the figure, we assume 2/10 discount terms. We see that the cost of trade credit decreases at a decreasing rate as the net period

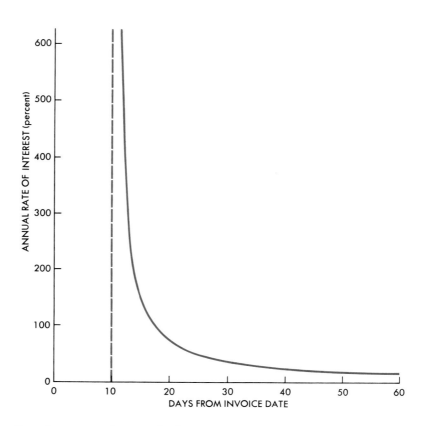

FIGURE 17-3
Annual rate of interest on
accounts payable with terms
of 2/10

increases. The point is that if a firm does not take a cash discount, its cost of
trade credit declines with the length of time it is able to postpone payment.

STRETCHING ACCOUNTS PAYABLE

In the preceding section, we assumed that payment was made at the end
of the due period; however, a firm may postpone payment beyond this period.
We shall call this postponement "stretching" accounts payable or "leaning on
the trade." The cost of stretching accounts payable is twofold: the cost of the
cash discount forgone and the possible deterioration in credit rating. In Chapter 16, we discussed the rating system of credit agencies such as Dun & Bradstreet. If a firm stretches its payables excessively, so that trade payables are
significantly delinquent, its credit rating will suffer. Suppliers will view the
firm with apprehension and may insist on rather strict terms of sale if, indeed,
they sell at all. In assessing a company, banks and other lenders do not favorably regard excessive slowness in the trade. Although it is difficult to measure, there is certainly an opportunity cost to a deterioration in a firm's credit
reputation.

Notwithstanding the possibility of a deteriorating credit rating, it may be
possible to postpone certain payables beyond the net period without severe
consequences. Suppliers are in business to sell goods, and trade credit may
increase sales. A supplier may be willing to go along with stretching payables,
particularly if the risk of bad-debt loss is negligible. If the funds requirement
of the firm is seasonal, suppliers may not view the stretching of payables in an
unfavorable light during periods of peak requirements, provided that the firm
is current in the trade during the rest of the year. There may be an indirect

465

charge for this extension of credit, in the form of higher prices, a possibility that the firm should carefully consider in evaluating the cost of stretching accounts payable.

Periodic and reasonable stretching of payables is not necessarily bad per se. It should be evaluated objectively in relation to its cost and in relation to alternative sources of short-term credit. When a firm does stretch its payables, effort should be made to keep suppliers fully informed of its situation. Many suppliers will allow a firm to stretch payables if the firm is honest with the supplier and consistent in its payments. Sometimes a firm with seasonal funds requirements is able to obtain a dating from a supplier. When a firm obtains a dating, it does not stretch its payables; as long as it pays the bill by the final date, no deterioration in its credit rating is likely. Here, as before, the company must be mindful of the likelihood that the supplier will charge a higher price to recoup its cost of carrying the receivable.

ADVANTAGES OF TRADE CREDIT

The firm must balance the advantages of trade credit against the cost of forgoing a cash discount, the opportunity cost associated with possible deterioration in credit reputation if it stretches its payables, and the possible increase in selling price the seller imposes on the buyer. There are several advantages of trade credit as a form of short-term financing. Probably the major advantage is its ready availability. The accounts payable of most firms represent a continuous form of credit. There is no need to arrange financing formally; it is already there. If the firm is now taking cash discounts, additional credit is readily available by not paying existing accounts payable until the end of the net period. There is no need to negotiate with the supplier; the decision is entirely up to the firm. In stretching accounts payable, the firm will find it necessary, after a certain degree of postponement, to negotiate with the supplier.

In most other types of short-term financing, it is necessary to negotiate formally with the lender over the terms of the loan. The lender may impose restrictions on the firm and seek a secured position. Restrictions are possible with trade credit, but they are not nearly as likely. With other sources of short-term financing, there may be a lead time between the time the need for funds is recognized and the time the firm is able to borrow them. Trade credit is a more flexible means of financing. The firm does not have to sign a note, pledge collateral, or adhere to a strict payment schedule on the note. A supplier views an occasional delinquent payment with a far less critical eye than does a banker or other lender.

The advantages of using trade credit must be weighed against the cost. As we have seen, the cost may be very high when all factors are considered. Many firms utilize other sources of short-term financing in order to be able to take advantage of cash discounts. The savings in cost over other forms of short-term financing, however, must offset the flexibility and convenience of trade credit. For certain firms there are no alternative sources of short-term credit.

WHO BEARS THE COST?

We must recognize that trade credit involves a cost for the use of funds over time. In the previous sections, it was implied that there is no explicit cost to trade credit if the buyer pays the invoice during the discount period or during the net period, if no cash discount is given. Although this supposition is valid from the standpoint of marginal analysis, it overlooks the fact that somebody must bear the cost of trade credit, for the use of funds over time is not free. The burden may fall on the supplier, the buyer, or both parties. The supplier may be able to pass the cost on to the buyer in the form of higher prices.

The supplier of a product for which demand is elastic may be reluctant to increase prices and may end up absorbing most of the cost of trade credit. Under other circumstances, the supplier is able to pass the cost on to the buyer. The buyer should determine who is bearing the cost of trade credit. A buyer who is bearing the cost may shop around for a better deal. The buyer should recognize that the cost of trade credit changes over time. In periods of rising interest rates and tight money, suppliers may raise the price of their products to take account of the rising cost of carrying receivables. This rise in price should not be confused with other rises caused by changing supply and demand conditions in the product markets.

ACCRUAL ACCOUNTS AS SPONTANEOUS FINANCING

Perhaps even more than accounts payable, accrual accounts represent a spontaneous source of financing. The most common accrual accounts are for wages and taxes. For both accounts, the expense is incurred or accrued but not paid. Usually a date is specified indicating when the accrual must be paid. Income taxes are paid quarterly; property taxes are paid semiannually. Wages are typically paid weekly, every other week, bimonthly, or monthly. Like accounts payable, accruals tend to expand with the scope of the operation. As sales increase, labor costs usually increase; and with them, accrued wages increase. As profits increase, accrued taxes increase.

In a sense, accruals represent costless financing. Services are rendered for wages, but employees are not paid and do not expect to be paid until the end or after the end of the pay period. The lapse is established by the company, although union and competing employers in the labor market influence its length. Similarly, taxes are not expected to be paid until their due date. Thus, accruals represent an interest-free source of financing.

Unfortunately for the company, they do not represent discretionary financing. For taxes, the government is the creditor, and it likes to be paid on time. A company in extreme financial difficulty can postpone tax payment for a short while, but there is a penalty charge. It may also postpone payment of wages at the expense of employees and morale. Employees may respond with absenteeism or reduced efficiency or may seek employment elsewhere. A company must be extremely careful in postponing wages. It must fully inform employees and set a firm date for payment. Such a measure is one of last resort; nevertheless, many a company on the brink of cash-flow disaster finds itself having to postpone wages as well as all other payments.

ACCRUED WAGES AND PAY PERIOD CHANGES

Accrued wages are partially discretionary in that a company can change the frequency of wage payments and thereby affect the amount of financing. If the interval of time between the last working day of a pay period and payday stays the same, the less frequent the paydays the more the financing. Suppose a company had a weekly payroll of $400,000 with an average amount accrued of $200,000. If the company were to increase its pay period from 1 to 2 weeks, the payroll at the end of the period would be $800,000. The average amount of accrued wages would now be $400,000 ($800,000 divided by 2). Therefore, the company increases its interest-free financing by $200,000.

The longer the pay period, the greater the amount of accrued wage financing. Obviously, it would be desirable from the standpoint of a company to have as long a pay period as possible, but competition for labor from other employers and union pressures limit the feasible range of options. Moreover, an increase in the pay period is usually "one-shot" in that it is not possible to repeat with a subsequent increase. In summary, then, accruals are a discretionary source of financing only within a very narrow range.

MONEY MARKET CREDIT

Large, well-established companies sometimes borrow on a short-term basis through commercial paper and other money market instruments. Commercial paper represents an unsecured, short-term, negotiable promissory note sold in the money market. Because these notes are unsecured and are a money market instrument, only the more creditworthy companies are able to use commercial paper as a source of short-term financing.

COMMERCIAL PAPER MARKET

The commercial paper market is composed of two parts: the dealer market and the direct-placement market.[3] Industrial firms, utilities, and medium-sized finance companies sell commercial paper through dealers. The dealer organization is composed of a half-dozen major dealers who purchase commercial paper from the issuer and, in turn, sell it to investors. The typical commission a dealer earns is $\frac{1}{8}$ percent, and maturities on dealer-placed paper generally range from 30 to 90 days. The market is a highly organized and sophisticated one; paper is generally sold in denominations of $100,000. Although the dealer market has been characterized in the past by a significant number of issuers who borrow on a seasonal basis, the trend definitely is toward financing on a revolving or more permanent basis.

A number of large sales finance companies, such as General Motors Acceptance Corporation, bypass the dealer organization in favor of selling their paper directly to investors. These issuers tailor both the maturity and the amount of the note to the needs of investors, mostly large corporations with excess cash. Maturities on directly placed paper can range from as little as a few days up to 9 months. Unlike many industrial issuers, finance companies use the commercial paper market as a permanent source of funds. Both dealer-placed and directly placed paper are rated as to its quality by one or more of the independent rating agencies—Moody's, Standard & Poor's, and Fitch's. The top ratings are P-1, A-1, and F-1 for the three agencies, respectively. Only 1 and 2 grades of paper find favor in the market.

---

[3] For a discussion of commercial paper from the standpoint of a short-term investor, see Chapter 15.

The principal advantage of commercial paper as a source of short-term financing is that it is generally cheaper than a short-term business loan from a commercial bank. Depending on the interest rate cycle, the rate on commercial paper is from 1 to 6 percent lower than the prime rate of bank loans to the highest-quality borrower, with the differential dependent on the phase of the interest rate cycle. Commercial paper dealers require borrowers to maintain lines of credit at banks in order to backstop the use of commercial paper. This assures them that commercial paper borrowings can be paid off. In the aggregate, however, the growth of the commercial paper and other money markets has been at the expense of bank borrowings. The market share of total corporate financing enjoyed by banks has declined over time.

Instead of issuing "stand-alone" paper, some corporations issue what is known as "bank-supported" commercial paper. Here a bank provides a letter of credit guaranteeing the investor that the company's obligation will be paid. The quality of the investment then depends on the creditworthiness of the bank, and the paper is rated as such by the rating agencies. For making available the letter of credit arrangement, the bank charges a commitment fee on the maximum credit it will provide. Usually the commitment fee is $\frac{1}{8}$ or $\frac{1}{4}$ percent. In addition, the bank frequently charges a usage fee on the amount of funds actually borrowed in the commercial paper market, again usually $\frac{1}{8}$ or $\frac{1}{4}$ percent. For example, suppose the Second National Bank of Palo Alto issued a letter of credit of $50 million in support of commercial paper borrowings by Insell Corporation. The commitment fee is $\frac{1}{4}$ percent, and the usage fee is $\frac{1}{8}$ percent. If commercial paper borrowings averaged $20 million, the annual cost of the letter of credit arrangement would be $\frac{1}{4}\% \times \$50$ million = $125,000 plus $\frac{1}{8}\% \times \$20$ million = $25,000, or $150,000 in total. For companies not well known, such as those privately held, as well as for companies that would be rated somewhat less than prime quality if they were to try to issue "stand-alone" paper, a "bank-supported" arrangement makes sense. It affords access to the commercial paper market at times when the total cost is less than that for direct borrowings at the bank.

BANKERS' ACCEPTANCES

For a company engaged in foreign trade or the domestic storage and shipment of certain marketable goods, bankers' acceptances can be a major source of financing. When an American company wishes to import $100,000 worth of electronic components from a company in Japan, the two companies may agree that a 90-day time draft will be used in settlement of the trade. The American company arranges a letter of credit with its bank, whereby the bank agrees to honor drafts drawn on the company as presented through a Japanese bank. The Japanese company ships the goods and at the same time draws a draft ordering the American company to pay in 90 days. It then takes the draft to its Japanese bank. By prearrangement, the draft is sent to the American bank and is accepted by the bank. At the time it becomes a bankers' acceptance. In essence, the bank accepts responsibility for payment, thereby substituting its creditworthiness for that of the drawee, the American company.

If the bank is large and well known, and most banks accepting drafts are, the instrument becomes highly marketable upon acceptance. As a result, the drawer, the Japanese company, does not have to hold the draft until the final due date; it can sell the draft in the market for less than its face value. The discount involved represents the interest payment to the investor. At the end of

90 days, the investor presents the acceptance to the accepting bank for payment and receives $100,000. At this time, the American company is obligated to have funds on deposit to cover the draft. In the manner described, the American company finances its import for a 90-day period. Presumably, the Japanese exporter would have charged a lower price if payment were to be made upon shipment. In this sense, the American company is the borrower.

The presence of an active and viable bankers' acceptance market makes possible the financing of foreign trade at interest rates approximating those on commercial paper. Although the principles by which the acceptance is created are the same for foreign and domestic trade, a smaller portion of the total bankers' acceptances outstanding is domestic. In addition to trade, domestic acceptance financing is used in connection with the storage of such things as grain. The bank involved advances funds on the basis of a draft from the company. By accepting the draft, it then can be sold in the bankers' acceptance market. The borrower's interest rate is the rate the investor receives plus fees to the bank and dealer, which frequently aggregate $\frac{7}{8}$ percent. In recent years, bankers' acceptances have multiplied as more companies recognize the usefulness of this form of financing.

SHORT-TERM LOANS

For expository purposes, it is convenient to separate business loans into two categories: unsecured loans and secured loans. Almost without exception, finance companies do not offer unsecured loans, simply because a borrower who deserves unsecured credit can borrow at a lower cost from a commercial bank. Consequently, our discussion of unsecured loans will involve only commercial banks. Secured loans will be examined in the next chapter.

Short-term, unsecured bank loans typically are regarded as "self-liquidating" in that the assets purchased with the proceeds generate sufficient cash flows to pay off the loan eventually. At one time, banks confined their lending mostly to this type of loan, but they now provide a wide variety of business loans tailored to the specific needs of the borrower. Still, the short-term, self-liquidating loan is a popular source of business financing, particularly in financing seasonal buildups in accounts receivable and inventories. Unsecured short-term loans may be extended under a line of credit, under a revolving credit agreement, or on a transaction basis. The debt itself is evidenced formally by a promissory note signed by the borrower, showing the time and amount of payment and the interest to be paid.

LINE OF CREDIT

A line of credit is an arrangement between a bank and its customer, specifying the maximum amount of unsecured credit the bank will permit the firm to owe at any one time. Usually, credit lines are established for a 1-year period and are subject to 1-year renewals. Frequently, lines of credit are set for renewal after the bank receives the audited annual report and has had a chance to review the progress of the borrower. If the borrower's year-end statement date is December 31, a bank may set its line to expire some time in March. At that time, the bank and the company meet to discuss the credit needs of the firm for the coming year in light of its past year's performance. The amount of the line is based on the bank's assessment of the creditworthiness and credit needs of the borrower. Depending on changes in these conditions, a line of credit may be adjusted at the renewal date or before, if conditions necessitate a change.

The cash budget (see Chapter 28) gives the best insight into the borrower's short-term credit needs. If maximum or peak borrowing needs over the forthcoming year are estimated at $800,000, a company might seek a line of credit of $1 million to give it a margin of safety. Whether the bank will go along with the request, of course, will depend on its evaluation of the creditworthiness of the firm. If the bank agrees, the firm then may borrow on a short-term basis—usually 90 days—up to the full $1 million line. Because certain banks regard borrowing under lines of credit as seasonal or temporary financing, they may require that the borrower be out of bank debt at some time during the year. Frequently, the borrower will be required to clean up (pay off) bank debt for a period of time during the year. The cleanup period required usually is 1 or 2 months. The cleanup itself is evidence to the bank that the loan is truly seasonal in nature. If the interval during which a profitable firm were out of bank debt decreased from 4 months two years ago to 2 months last year and to no cleanup this year, the trend would suggest the use of bank credit to finance permanent funds requirements.

Despite its many advantages to the borrower, a line of credit does not constitute a legal commitment on the part of the bank to extend credit. The borrower is usually informed of the line by means of a letter indicating that the bank is willing to extend credit up to a certain amount. An example of such a letter is shown in Fig. 17-4. This letter is not a legal obligation of the bank to extend credit. If the creditworthiness of the borrower should deterio-

Second National Bank
Palo Alto, California

March 23, 1992

Mr. Joseph A. Ralberg
Vice President & Treasurer
Barker Manufacturing Corporation
Palo Alto, California 94302

Dear Mr. Ralberg:

Based upon our analysis of your year-end audited statements, we are pleased to renew your $1 million unsecured line of credit for the forthcoming year. Borrowings under this line wiil be at a rate of one-half percent (½%) over the prime rate.

This line is subject to only the understanding that your company will maintain its financial position and that it will be out of bank debt for at least 45 days during the fiscal year.

Yours very truly,

John D. Myers
Vice President

FIGURE 17-4
Sample letter extending line of credit

rate over the year, the bank may not want to extend credit and would not be required to do so. Under most circumstances, however, a bank feels morally bound to honor a line of credit.

REVOLVING CREDIT AGREEMENT

A revolving credit agreement is a legal commitment by a bank to extend credit up to a maximum amount. While the commitment is in force, the bank must extend credit whenever the borrower wishes to borrow, provided total borrowings do not exceed the maximum amount specified. If the revolving credit is for $5 million, and $3 million is already owing, the borrower can borrow an additional $2 million at any time. For the privilege of having this formal commitment, the borrower usually is required to pay a commitment fee on the unused portion of the revolving credit. If the revolving credit is for $5 million, and borrowing for the year averages $2 million, the borrower will be required to pay a commitment fee on the $3 million unused portion. If the fee is $\frac{1}{2}$ percent, the cost of this privilege will be $15,000 for the year. Revolving credit agreements frequently extend beyond 1 year. Because lending arrangements of more than a year must be regarded as intermediate rather than short-term credit, we shall examine revolving credits more extensively in Chapter 18. The purpose of introducing them at this time is to illustrate the formal nature of the arrangement in contrast to the informality of a line of credit.

TRANSACTION LOANS

Borrowing under a line of credit or under a revolving credit arrangement is not appropriate when the firm needs short-term funds for only one purpose. A contractor may borrow from a bank in order to complete a job. When the contractor receives payment for the job, the loan is paid. For this type of loan, a bank evaluates each request by the borrower as a separate transaction. In these evaluations, the cash-flow ability of the borrower to pay the loan is usually of paramount importance.

EXPERT SYSTEMS

In recent years, expert systems have been developed for use by banks in making business loans. As taken up in the previous chapter, computer software mimics the reasoning process of experienced lending officers. By so doing, credit analysis and decision making can be streamlined and made more consistent for routine types of loans. For complex lending situations, however, the individual lending officer must be involved. The idea with an expert system is to leverage the talent of seasoned lending officers.[4] Such systems are likely to see increased use, but again only in well-defined domains of lending.

---

[4] For a survey of uses, see Clyde W. Holsapple, Kar Yan Tam, and Andrew B. Whinston, "Adapting Expert System Technology to Financial Management," *Financial Management,* 17 (Autumn 1988), 12–22. For specific systems of loan evaluation, see Michael J. Shaw and James A. Gentry, "Using an Expert System with Inductive Learning to Evaluate Business Loans," *Financial Management,* 17 (Autumn 1988), 45–57; and Peter Duchessi, Harry Shawsky, and John P. Seagle, "A Knowledge-Engineered System for Commercial Loan Decisions," *Financial Management,* 17 (Autumn 1988), 57–65.

INTEREST RATES

Unlike interest rates on impersonal money market instruments such as Treasury bills, bankers' acceptances, and commercial paper, most business loans are determined through personal negotiation between the borrower and lender. In some measure, banks try to vary the interest rate charged according to the creditworthiness of the borrower; the lower the creditworthiness, the higher the interest rate. Interest rates charged also vary in keeping with money market conditions. One measure that changes with underlying market conditions is the *prime rate*. The prime rate is the rate charged on business loans to financially sound companies. The rate itself is usually set by large money market banks and is relatively uniform throughout the country.

Differentials from Prime.   Despite the term *prime rate* implying the price a bank charges its most creditworthy customers, this has not been the recent practice. With banks becoming more competitive for corporate customers and facing extreme competition from the commercial paper market, the well-established, financially sound company often is able to borrow at a rate of interest below prime. The rate charged is based on the bank's marginal cost of funds, as typically reflected by the rate paid on money market certificates of deposit. An interest rate margin is added to the cost of funds, and the sum becomes the rate charged the customer. This rate is changed daily in keeping with changes in money market rates. Generally, the rate paid by the customer is $\frac{1}{4}$ to 1 percent below the prime rate. The differential depends on competitive conditions and on the relative bargaining power of the borrower.

Other borrowers will pay either the prime rate or a rate above prime, the bank's pricing of the loan being relative to the prime rate. A bank might extend a line of credit to a company at a rate of $\frac{1}{2}$ percent above prime. If the prime rate is 10 percent, the borrower is charged an interest rate of 10.5 percent. If the prime rate changes to 9 percent, the borrower will pay 9.5 percent. Interest rate differentials among the various customers of a bank supposedly should reflect only differences in creditworthiness.

Other factors, however, influence the differential. Among them are the balances maintained and other business the borrower has with a bank (such as trust business). A good customer who has maintained very attractive balances in the past may be able to obtain a more favorable interest rate than will a firm of equal creditworthiness that has carried rather meager balances. Also, the cost of servicing a loan is a factor determining the differential in rate from prime. Certain collateral loans are costly to administer, and this cost must be passed on to the borrower either in the interest rate charged or in a special fee.

Thus, the interest rate charged on a short-term loan will depend on the prevailing cost of funds to banks, the existing prime rate, the creditworthiness of the borrower, present and prospective relationships of the borrower with the bank, and sometimes other conditions. Because of the fixed costs involved in credit investigation and in the processing of a loan, we would expect the interest rate on small loans to be higher than the rate on large loans.

Methods of Computing Interest Rates.   There are three ways in which interest on a loan may be paid: on a collect basis, a discount basis, and an add-on basis. When paid on a collect basis, the interest is paid at the maturity of the note; when paid on a discount basis, interest is deducted from the initial loan. On a $10,000 loan at 12 percent interest for 1 year, the effective rate of interest on a collect note is

$$\frac{\$1,200}{\$10,000} = 12.00\%$$

On a discount basis, the effective rate of interest is not 12 percent but

$$\frac{\$1,200}{\$8,800} = 13.64\%$$

When we pay on a discount basis, we have the use of only $8,800 for the year but must pay back $10,000 at the end of that time. Thus, the effective rate of interest is higher on a discount note than on a collect note. We should point out that most bank business loans are on a collect note basis.

On installment loans, banks and other lenders usually charge interest on an add-on basis. This means that interest is added to the funds disbursed in order to determine the face value of the note. Suppose in our example that an installment loan were involved with 12 equal monthly installments and that the interest rate were 12 percent. The borrower would receive $10,000, and the face value of the note would be $11,200. Thus, $1,200 in interest is paid. However, the borrower has use of the full $10,000 for only 1 month and at the end of that month must pay one-twelfth of $11,200, or $933.33. Installments in that amount are due at the end of each of the subsequent 11 months until the note is paid. For the full year, then, the borrower has use of only about one-half of the $10,000. Instead of a 12 percent rate, the effective rate is nearly double that, about 22 percent with monthly compounding. Thus, add-on interest is paid on the initial amount of the loan and not on the declining balance, as is customary with other types of loans.

COMPENSATING BALANCES

In addition to charging interest on loans, commercial banks often require the borrower to maintain demand-deposit balances at the bank in direct proportion to either the amount of funds borrowed or the amount of the commitment. These minimum balances are known as compensating balances. The amount required in the compensating balance varies according to competitive conditions in the market for loans and specific negotiations between the borrower and lender. Suppose a bank were able to obtain from a customer compensating balances equal to 10 percent of a line of credit. If the line is $2 million, the borrower would be required to maintain average balances of at least $200,000 during the year. Another arrangement might be for the bank to require average balances of 5 percent of the line and 5 percent more on the amount owing when the line is in use. If a firm's line were $2 million and its borrowings averaged $600,000, it would be required to maintain $130,000 in compensating balances.

The effect of a compensating balance requirement is to raise the effective cost of borrowing if the borrower is required to maintain balances above the amount the firm would maintain ordinarily. To the extent that a compensating balance requirement does not require the borrower to maintain balances above those that it would maintain ordinarily, such a requirement does not raise the effective cost of borrowing. However, if balances above the ordinary must be maintained, the effective cost of borrowing is raised. If we borrow $1 million at 12 percent and are required to maintain $100,000 more in demand-deposit balances than we would ordinarily, we would then have use of only $900,000 of the $1 million loan. The effective annual interest cost is $120,000/$900,000 = 13.33 percent, rather than 12 percent.

The notion of compensating balances for loans is weakening. Banks are profit as opposed to deposit oriented and, accordingly, they "fine-tune" their profitability analyses of customer relationships. With the rapid and significant fluctuations in the cost of funds to banks in recent years, as well as the accelerated competition among financial institutions, banks make a number of loans without compensating balance requirements. The interest rate charged is in line with the bank's incremental cost of obtaining funds. The movement toward sophisticated profitability analysis has driven banks to direct compensation for loans through interest rates and fees as opposed to indirect compensation through deposit balances.

SUMMARY

If imperfections and/or incompleteness exist in financial markets, the financial manager should be concerned with the type of debt that is issued. By "packaging" debt instruments to take advantage of imperfections and incompleteness, the firm can maximize shareholder wealth. A debt instrument has a number of features, but one of the most meaningful is its maturity. In general, short-term debt is less costly than long-term debt, but it is also more risky. Thus, a decision as to the maturity composition of the firm's debt involves a trade-off between profitability and risk. A number of types of short-term financing are available.

Trade credit can be a significant source of short-term financing. It is a discretionary source only if a firm does not have a strict policy regarding its promptness in paying bills. When a cash discount is offered but not taken, the cost of trade credit is the cash discount forgone. The longer the period between the end of the discount period and the time the bill is paid, the less this opportunity cost. "Stretching" accounts payable involves postponement of payment beyond the due period. The opportunity cost of stretching payables is the possible deterioration in the firm's credit rating. The firm must balance the cost of trade credit against its advantages and the costs of other short-term credit. A major advantage of trade credit is the flexibility it gives the firm.

Like accounts payable, accruals represent a spontaneous source of financing, albeit offering the firm even less discretion than it has with trade credit financing. The principal accrual items are wages and taxes, and both are expected to be paid on established dates. In the interim, interest-free financing is available to the company, and for an ongoing company, this financing is continuous. A company can increase the amount of its accrued wages by lessening the frequency of paydays within a narrow range.

Commercial paper is used only by well-established, high-quality companies. The evidence of debt is an unsecured, short-term promissory note that is sold in the money market. Commercial paper is sold either through dealers or directly to investors. Rather than "stand-alone" paper, a firm may issue "bank-supported" paper where a bank guarantees the creditworthiness of the paper.

The principal advantage of commercial paper is that its yield typically is less than the rate of interest a company would have to pay on a bank loan. Bankers' acceptance financing is another type of money market credit. Usually associated with a foreign trade transaction, the acceptance is highly marketable and can be a very desirable source of short-term funds.

Short-term loans can be divided into two types: unsecured and secured. Unsecured credit is usually confined to bank loans under a line of credit, under a revolving credit agreement, or on a transaction basis. Interest rates on business loans are a function of a bank's cost of funds, the existing prime rate, the creditworthiness of the borrower, and the profitability of the relationship to the bank. If the borrower is required to maintain compensating balances above those that it would maintain ordinarily, the effective cost of borrowing is increased.

SELF-CORRECTION PROBLEMS

1. The Dud Company purchases raw materials on terms of 2/10, net 30. A review of the company's records by the owner, Mr. Dud, revealed that payments are usually made 15 days after purchases are received. When asked why the firm did not take advantage of its discounts, the bookkeeper, Mr. Grind, replied that it cost only 2 percent for these funds, whereas a bank loan would cost the firm 12 percent.
   a. What mistake is Grind making?
   b. What is the real cost of not taking advantage of the discount?
   c. If the firm could not borrow from the bank and was forced to resort to the use of trade credit funds, what suggestion might be made to Grind that would reduce the annual interest cost?

2. The Halow Harp and Chime Company is negotiating a new labor contract. Among other things, the union is demanding that the company pay its workers weekly instead of twice a month. The payroll currently is $260,000 per payday, and accrued wages average $130,000. What is the annual cost of the union's demand if the company's opportunity cost of funds is 9 percent?

3. Burleigh Mills Company has a $5 million revolving credit agreement with First State Bank of Arkansas. Being a favored customer the rate is set at 1 percent over the bank's cost of funds, where the cost is the rate on negotiable certificates of deposit (CDs). In addition, there is a $\frac{1}{2}$ percent commitment fee on the unused portion of the revolving credit. If the CD rate is expected to average 9 percent for the coming year and if the company expects to utilize on average 60 percent of the total commitment, what is the expected annual dollar cost of this credit arrangement? What is the percentage cost when both the interest rate and the commitment fee paid are considered? What happens to the percentage cost if on average only 20 percent of the total commitment is utilized?

PROBLEMS

1. Mendez Metal Specialties, Inc., has a seasonal pattern to its business. It borrows under a line of credit from Central Bank at 1 percent over prime. Its total asset requirements now (at year end) and estimated requirements for the coming year are

	NOW	1ST QUARTER	2ND QUARTER	3RD QUARTER	4TH QUARTER
Amount	$4,500,000	$4,800,000	$5,500,000	$5,900,000	$5,000,000

477

CHAPTER 17
Unsecured
Short-Term
Financing

Assume that these requirements are level throughout the quarter. Presently, the company has $4,500,000 in equity capital plus long-term debt plus the permanent component of current liabilities, and this amount will remain constant throughout the year.

The prime rate presently is 11 percent, and the company expects no change in this rate for the next year. Mendez Metal Specialties is also considering issuing intermediate-term debt at an interest rate of $13\frac{1}{2}$ percent. In this regard, three alternative amounts are under consideration: zero, $500,000, and $1 million. All additional funds requirements will be borrowed under the company's bank line of credit.

a. Determine the total dollar borrowing costs for short- and intermediate-term debt under each of the three alternatives for the coming year. (Assume there are no changes in current liabilities other than borrowings.) Which is lowest?

b. Are there other considerations in addition to expected cost?

2. Determine the annual percentage interest cost for each of the following terms of sale, assuming the firm does not take the cash discount but pays on the final day of the net period (assume a 365-day year):

a. 1/20, net 30 ($500 invoice)

b. 2/30, net 60 ($1,000 invoice)

c. 2/5, net 10 ($100 invoice)

d. 3/10, net 30 ($250 invoice)

3. Does the dollar size of the invoice affect the percentage annual interest cost of not taking discounts? Illustrate with an example.

4. Recompute Problem 2, assuming a 10-day stretching of the payment date. What is the major advantage of stretching? What are the disadvantages?

5. On January 1, Faville Car Company, a large car dealer, gave its employees a 10 percent pay increase in view of the substantial profits the preceding year. Before the increase, the weekly payroll was $50,000. What is the effect of the change on accruals?

6. The Fox Company is able to sell $1 million of commercial paper every 3 months at a rate of 10 percent and a placement cost of $3,000 per issue. The dealers require Fox to maintain bank lines of credit demanding $100,000 in bank balances, which otherwise would not be held. Fox has a 40 percent tax rate. What do the funds from commercial paper cost Fox after taxes?

7. Commercial paper has no stipulated interest rate. It is sold on a discount basis, and the amount of the discount determines the interest cost to the issuer. On the basis of the following information, determine the percentage interest cost on an annual basis for each of the following issues.

ISSUE	FACE VALUE	PRICE	TIME TO MATURITY
(a)	$25,000	$24,500	60 days
(b)	100,000	96,500	180
(c)	50,000	48,800	90
(d)	75,000	71,300	270
(e)	100,000	99,100	30

8. The Sphinx Supply Company needs to increase its working capital by $10 million. It has decided that there are essentially three alternatives of financing available:

   a. Forgo cash discounts, granted on a basis of 3/10, net 30.

   b. Borrow from the bank at 15 percent. This alternative would necessitate maintaining a 12 percent compensating balance.

   c. Issue commercial paper at 12 percent. The cost of placing the issue would be $100,000 each 6 months.

   Assuming that the firm would prefer the flexibility of bank financing, provided the additional cost of this flexibility is no more than 2 percent, which alternative should Sphinx select?

9. Bork Corporation wishes to borrow $100,000 for 1 year. It must choose one of the following alternatives:

   a. An 8 percent loan on a discount basis with 20 percent compensating balances required

   b. A 9 percent loan on a discount basis with 10 percent compensating balances required

   c. A $10\frac{1}{2}$ percent loan on a collect basis with no compensating balance requirement

   Which alternative should Bork Corporation choose if it is concerned with the effective interest rate?

SOLUTIONS TO SELF-CORRECTION PROBLEMS

1. a. Grind is confusing the percentage cost of using funds for 5 days with the cost of using funds for a year. These costs are clearly not comparable. One must be converted to the time scale of the other.

   b.
   $$\frac{2}{98} \times \frac{365}{5} = 149.0\%$$

   c. Assuming that the firm has made the decision not to take the cash discount, it makes no sense to pay before the due date. In this case, payment 30 days after purchases are received rather than 15 would reduce the annual interest cost to 37.2 percent.

2. New average amount of accrued wages $= (\$130,000)\left(\frac{1}{52}\right)\left(\frac{24}{1}\right)$

   $$= \$60,000$$

   Note: Fifty-two is the number of paydays in a year if wages are paid weekly; 24 is the number if wages are paid twice a month.

   Decrease in average accrued wages $= \$130,000 - \$60,000$
   $$= \$70,000$$

   Cost $= \$70,000 \times .09 = \$6,300$

3. Cost $= (\$3,000,000).10 + (\$2,000,000).005 = \$310,000$
   Percentage cost $= \$310,000/\$3,000,000 = 10.33\%$
   Dollar cost with 20% utilization $= (\$1,000,000).10 + (\$4,000,000).005$
   $$= \$120,000$$
   Percentage cost with 20% utilization $= \$120,000/\$1,000,000$
   $$= 12\%$$
   The percentage cost goes up as less of the total revolving credit agreement is utilized, owing to the commitment fee of $\frac{1}{2}$ percent on the unused portion.

SELECTED REFERENCES

BRENNAN, MICHAEL J., VOJISLAV MAKSIMOVIC, and JOHN M. PINKERTON, "Vendor Financing," *Journal of Finance*, 43 (December 1988), 1127–42.

DUCHESSI, PETER, HARRY SHAWSKY, and JOHN P. SEAGLE, "A Knowledge-Engineered System for Commercial Loan Decisions," *Financial Management*, 17 (Autumn 1988), 57–65.

FISCHER, GERALD C., "The Myth and the Reality of the Prime Rate," *Journal of Commercial Bank Lending*, 64 (July 1982), 16–26.

HARRINGTON, DIANA R., and BRENT D. WILSON, *Corporate Financial Analysis*, 3d ed. Homewood, IL: BPI/Irwin, 1989, Chap. 2.

JAMES, CHRISTOPHER, "Some Evidence on the Uniqueness of Bank Loans," *Journal of Financial Economics*, 19 (December 1987), 217–36.

MORRIS, JAMES R., "On Corporate Debt Maturity Strategies," *Journal of Finance*, 31 (March 1976), 29–37.

RAMASWAMY, KRISHNA, and SURESH M. SUNDARESAN, "The Valuation of Floating-Rate Instruments: Theory and Evidence," *Journal of Financial Economics*, 17 (December 1986), 251–72.

SHAW, MICHAEL J., and JAMES A. GENTRY, "Using an Expert System with Inductive Learning to Evaluate Business Loans," *Financial Management*, 17 (Autumn 1988), 45–56.

STONE, BERNELL K., "The Design of a Company's Banking System," *Journal of Finance*, 38 (May 1983), 373–85.

THAKOR, ANJAN V., "Toward a Theory of Bank Loan Commitments," *Journal of Banking and Finance*, 6 (March 1982), 55–84.

479

18

SECURED LOANS AND TERM FINANCING

In this chapter, we extend our examination of short-term loans to consider secured types of lending arrangements. The principal characteristic of short-term loans is that they are self-liquidating over a period of time of less than a year. Frequently, these types of loans are employed to finance seasonal and temporary funds requirements. Intermediate-term financing, on the other hand, is employed to finance more permanent funds requirements, such as underlying buildups in receivables and inventories, as well as to provide flexibility in a period of uncertainty. In the second part of the chapter, we examine various types of intermediate-term loans. In the following chapter, we consider lease financing, another means of intermediate-term financing.

SECURED LENDING ARRANGEMENTS

Many firms cannot obtain credit on an unsecured basis, either because they are new and unproven or because bankers do not highly regard the firms' ability to service debt. In order to make a loan, lenders require security that will reduce their risk of loss. With security, lenders have two sources of loan payment: the cash-flow ability of the firm to service the debt and, if that source fails for some reason, the collateral value of the security. Most lenders will not make a loan unless the firm has sufficient expected cash flows to make proper servicing of debt probable. To reduce their risk further, lenders require security.

SOME THEORETICAL NOTIONS

We know that secured lending arrangements are more costly to administer than unsecured loans and that the incremental cost is passed on to the borrower in the form of fees and higher interest costs than would otherwise be the case. The question that might be asked is, Why is it in either party's interest to create the additional cost? The answer is that the market for loans is a competitive one. If unsecured credit is available somewhere at less total cost, one can be sure that a borrower will go there to get it. Beyond a point in risk, however, all lenders in the market will want some type of safeguard in addition to the general credit standing of the company. This safeguard can come in the form of security or a set of protective covenants that afford the lender the ability to take corrective steps prior to maturity if the borrower's financial condition should deteriorate. We discuss protective covenants later in the chapter; our focus now is on secured loans. In both cases, we must be aware that the conditions imposed on a borrower are determined in competitive financial markets. A lender cannot demand security and expect to get it unless the borrower has no other alternatives![1] The use of security is negotiated in keeping with conditions in the overall market for loans.

With secured loans, a company's cash flows are segregated with respect to payments to creditors. This may reduce conflict between creditors and reduce monitoring, enforcement, and foreclosure costs, which, in turn, can work to the advantage of a company and its stockholders.[2] Rene M. Stulz and Herb Johnson portray the use of secured debt as an option to segregate the cash flows emanating from a new investment project from those arising from old projects.[3] As a result, the underinvestment problem described in Chapter 9 can be reduced. In turn, this benefits stockholders, at the expense of existing debt holders. The idea, then, is that a company plays one set of debt holders off against another, thereby extracting gain in the option pricing model context illustrated earlier in the book.

COLLATERAL VALUE

The excess of the market value of the security pledged over the amount of the loan determines the lender's margin of safety. If the borrower is unable to meet an obligation, the lender can sell the security to satisfy the claim. If the security is sold for an amount exceeding the amount of the loan and interest owed, the difference is remitted to the borrower. If the security is sold for less, the lender becomes a general, or unsecured, creditor for the amount of the difference. Because secured lenders do not wish to become general creditors, they usually seek security with a market value sufficiently above the amount of the loan to minimize the likelihood of their not being able to sell the security in full satisfaction of the loan. The degree of security protection a lender seeks varies with the creditworthiness of the borrower, the security the borrower has available, and the financial institution making the loan.

The value of the collateral to the lender varies according to several factors. Perhaps the most important is marketability. If the collateral can be sold quickly in an active market without depressing the price, the lender is likely to be willing to lend an amount that represents a fairly high percentage of the collateral's stated value. On the other hand, if the collateral is a special-purpose machine designed specifically for a company and it has no viable secondary market, the lender may choose to lend nothing at all. The life of the collateral also matters. If the collateral has a cash-flow life that closely paral-

---

[1] See James H. Scott, Jr., "Bankruptcy, Secured Debt, and Optimal Capital Structure," *Journal of Finance*, 32 (March 1977), 1–19, for an extension of this notion. In addition, Scott posits that a firm can increase its value to its shareholders by issuing secured debt. The reason advanced is that with a secured lending arrangement, the present value of expected payments to unsecured creditors is reduced. Essentially, equity holders sell the right to be first in order of priority in the event of bankruptcy. As this right is valuable, equity holders are said to obtain value for it in some form of side payment from the secured lender.

[2] Clifford W. Smith, Jr., and Jerold B. Warner, "On Financial Contracting: An Analysis of Bond Covenants," *Journal of Financial Economics*, 7 (June 1979), 117–61.

[3] Rene M. Stulz and Herb Johnson, "An Analysis of Secured Debt," *Journal of Financial Economics*, 14 (December 1985), 501–21.

lels the life of the loan, it will be more valuable to the lender than collateral that is much longer-term in nature. As the collateral is liquidated into cash, the proceeds may be used to pay down the loan. Still another factor is the basic riskiness associated with the collateral. The greater the fluctuation in its market value or the more uncertain the lender is concerning market value, the less desirable the collateral from the standpoint of the lender. Thus, marketability, life, and riskiness determine the attractiveness of various types of collateral to a lender and, hence, the amount of financing available to a company. Before taking up specific short-term secured lending arrangements, we take a brief look at how lenders protect themselves under the Uniform Commercial Code, which is in force in all states.

Article 9 of the code deals with security interests of lenders, the specific aspect with which we are concerned. A lender who requires collateral of a borrower obtains a *security interest* in the collateral. The collateral may be accounts receivable, inventory, equipment, or other assets of the borrower. The security interest in the collateral is created by a *security agreement,* also known as a *security device.* This agreement is signed by the borrower and the lender and contains a description of the collateral. To "perfect" a security interest in the collateral, the lender must file a copy of the security agreement or a financing statement with a public office of the state in which the collateral is located. Frequently, this office is that of the secretary of state. The filing gives public notice to other parties that the lender has a security interest in the collateral described. Before accepting collateral as security for a loan, a lender will search the public notices to see if the collateral has been pledged previously in connection with another loan. Only the lender with a valid security interest in the collateral has a prior claim on the assets and can sell the collateral in settlement of the loan.

ASSIGNMENT OF ACCOUNTS RECEIVABLE

Accounts receivable are one of the most liquid assets of the firm; consequently, they make desirable security for a loan. From the standpoint of the lender, the major difficulties with this type of security are the cost of processing the collateral and the risk of fraud. To illustrate the nature of the arrangement, we trace through a typical assignment of accounts receivable loan. A company may seek a receivable loan from either a commercial bank or a finance company. Because a bank usually charges a lower interest rate than a finance company does, the firm will generally try first to borrow from a bank.

Quality and Size of Receivables. In evaluating the loan request, the lender will analyze the quality of the firm's receivables to determine how much to lend against them. The higher the quality of the accounts the firm maintains, the higher the percentage the lender is willing to advance against the face value of the receivables pledged. A lender does not have to accept all the borrower's accounts receivable; usually, accounts that have low credit ratings or that are unrated will be rejected. Also, government and foreign accounts usually are ineligible unless special arrangements are made. Depending on the quality of the receivables accepted, a lender typically advances between 50 percent and 80 percent of their face value.

The lender is concerned not only with the quality of receivables but also with their size. The lender must keep records on each account receivable that is pledged; the smaller the average size of the accounts, the more it costs per dollar of loan to process them. Consequently, a firm that sells low-priced items on open account will generally be unable to obtain a receivable loan, regardless of the quality of the accounts. The cost of processing the loan is simply too high. Sometimes a general assignment, known also as a "floating" or "blanket" assignment, will be used to circumvent the problem of cost. With a general assignment, the lender does not keep track of the individual accounts but records only the total amounts in the accounts assigned and the payments received. Because preventing fraud is difficult with a "general" assignment, the percentage advance against the face value of receivables may be lower.

Procedure. Suppose a lender has decided to extend credit to a firm on the basis of a 75 percent advance against the face value of accounts receivable assigned. The firm then sends in a schedule of accounts showing the name of the account, the date of billings, and the amounts owed. The lender will sometimes require evidence of shipment, such as an invoice. Having received the schedule of accounts, the lender has the borrower sign a promissory note and a security agreement. The firm then receives 75 percent of the face value of the receivables shown on the schedule of accounts.

A receivable loan can be on either a nonnotification or a notification basis. Under the former arrangement, customers of the firm are not notified that their accounts have been pledged to the lender. When the firm receives payment on an account, it forwards this payment, together with other payments, to the lender. The lender checks the payments against its record of accounts outstanding and reduces the amount the borrower owes by 75 percent of the total payments. The other 25 percent is credited to the borrower's account. With a nonnotification arrangement, the lender must take precautions to make sure the borrower does not withhold a payment check. With a notification arrangement, the account is notified of the assignment, and remittances are made directly to the lender. Under this arrangement, the borrower cannot withhold payments. Most firms naturally prefer to borrow on a nonnotification basis; however, the lender reserves the right to place the arrangement on a notification basis.

An accounts receivable loan is a more or less continuous financing arrangement. As the firm generates new receivables that are acceptable to the lender, they are assigned, adding to the security base against which the firm is able to borrow. New receivables replace the old, and the security base and the amount of loan fluctuate accordingly. A receivable loan is a very flexible means of secured financing. As receivables build up, the firm is able to borrow additional funds to finance this buildup. Thus, it has access to "built-in" financing. Many banks do not require compensating balances for receivable loans. Compensation comes in the form of a higher rate—usually 2 to 4 percent above the prime rate. Also, a service fee of 1 to 3 percent typically is charged to cover bookkeeping and other administrative costs of the lender. Finally, a "cleanup" of the loan is not required, because it is regarded as a more or less permanent source of financing.

FACTORING RECEIVABLES

In the assignment of accounts receivable, the firm retains title to the receivables. When a firm *factors* its receivables, it actually sells them to a factor. The sale may be either with or without recourse, depending on the type of arrangement negotiated. The factor maintains a credit department and makes credit checks on accounts. Based on its credit investigation, the factor may refuse to buy certain accounts that it deems too risky. By factoring, a firm frequently relieves itself of the expense of maintaining a credit department and making collections. Any account that the factor is unwilling to buy is an unacceptable credit risk unless, of course, the firm wants to assume this risk on its own and ship the goods. Factoring arrangements are governed by a contract between the factor and the client. The contract frequently is for 1 year with an automatic provision for renewal and can be canceled only with prior notice of 30 to 60 days. Although it is customary in a factoring arrangement to notify customers that their accounts have been sold and that payments on the account should be sent directly to the factor, in some instances notification is not made. Customers continue to remit payments to the firm, which, in turn, endorses them to the factor. These endorsements are frequently camouflaged to prevent customers from learning that their accounts have been sold.

Factoring Costs. For bearing risk and servicing the receivables, the factor receives a commission, typically somewhat over 1 percent of the face value of the receivables. The commission varies according to the size of the individual accounts, the volume of receivables sold, and the quality of the accounts. Since receivables sold to the factor will not be collected from the various accounts for a period of time, the firm may wish to receive payment for the sale of its receivables before they are actually collected. On that advance, it must pay interest. Advancing payment is a lending function of the factor in addition to risk bearing and servicing the receivables. For this additional function, the factor requires compensation.

If the receivables total $10,000 and the factoring fee is 2 percent, the factor will credit the firm's account with $9,800. If the firm wants to draw on this account before the receivables are collected, it will have to pay an interest charge—say, $1\frac{1}{2}$ percent a month—for the use of the funds. If it wishes a cash advance and the receivables are collected, on the average, in 1 month, the interest cost will be approximately .015 × $9,800, or $147.[4] Thus, the total cost of factoring is composed of a factoring fee plus an interest charge if the firm draws on its account before the receivables are collected. If the firm does not draw on its account until the receivables are collected, there is no interest charge. In a third alternative, the firm may leave its funds with the factor beyond the time when the receivables are collected and receive interest on the account from the factor.

Flexibility. The typical factoring arrangement is continuous. As new receivables are acquired, they are sold to the factor, and the firm's account is credited. The firm then draws on this account as it needs funds. Sometimes the factor will allow the firm to overdraw its account during periods of peak needs and thereby borrow on an unsecured basis. Under other arrangements, the factor may withhold a reserve from the firm's account as a protection against losses. The principal sources of factoring are commercial banks, factoring subsidiaries of bank holding companies, and certain old-line factors. While factoring appears to be expensive, one must remember that the factor relieves the company of credit checks, of the cost of processing receivables, and of collection expenses. As the factor has the advantage of economies of

---

[4] The actual cash advance would be $9,800 less the interest cost, or $9,653.

scale, it often can do the job at a lower cost. Also, the factor has access to more extensive credit information than does the individual company. This may make for better credit decisions. For the small company in particular, these advantages may well outweigh the cost.

INVENTORY LOANS

Inventories also represent a reasonably liquid asset and are therefore suitable as security for loans. As with a receivable loan, the lender determines a percentage advance against the market value of the collateral. This percentage varies according to the quality of the inventory. Certain inventories, such as grains, are very marketable and when properly stored resist physical deterioration. The margin of safety required by the lender on a loan of this sort is fairly small, and the advance may be as high as 90 percent. On the other hand, the market for a highly specialized piece of equipment may be so narrow that a lender is unwilling to make any advance against its reported market value. Thus, not every kind of inventory can be pledged as security for a loan. The best collateral is inventory that is relatively standard and for which a ready market exists apart from the marketing organization of the borrower.

Lenders determine the percentage that they are willing to advance by considering marketability, perishability, market price stability, and the difficulty and expense of selling the inventory to satisfy the loan. The cost of selling some inventory may be very high. Lenders do not want to be in the business of liquidating collateral, but they do want to assure themselves that collateral has adequate value in case borrowers default in the payment of principal or interest. As is true with most secured loans, the actual decision to make the loan will depend on the cash-flow ability of the borrower to service debt. There are a number of different ways a lender can obtain a secured interest in inventories, and we consider each in turn. In the first methods (floating lien, chattel mortgage, and trust receipt), the inventory remains in the possession of the borrower. In the last two methods (terminal warehouse and field warehouse receipts), the inventory is in the possession of a third party.

Floating Lien. Under the Uniform Commercial Code, the borrower may pledge inventories "in general" without specifying the kind of inventory involved. Under this arrangement, the lender obtains a floating lien on all inventory of the borrower. This lien by its very nature is loose, and the lender may find it difficult to police. Frequently, a floating lien is requested only as additional protection and does not play a major role in determining whether or not the loan will be made. Even if the collateral is valuable, the lender usually is willing to make only a moderate advance because of the difficulty in exercising tight control over the collateral. The floating lien can be made to cover both receivables and inventories, as well as the collection of receivables. This modification gives the lender a lien on major portion of a firm's current assets. In addition, the lien can be made to encompass almost any length of time, so that it includes future as well as present inventory as security.

Chattel Mortgage. With a chattel mortgage, inventories are identified specifically by serial number or by some other means. While the borrower holds title to the goods, the lender has a lien on inventory. This inventory cannot be sold unless the lender consents. Because of the rigorous identification requirements, chattel mortgages are ill suited for inventory with rapid turnover or inventory that is not easily identified because of size or other reasons. Chattel mortgages are well suited for certain capital assets, such as machine tools.

Trust Receipt Loans. Under a trust receipt financing arrangement, the borrower holds in trust for the lender the inventory and the proceeds from its sale. This type of lending arrangement, known also as floor planning, has been used extensively by automobile dealers, equipment dealers, and consumer durable goods dealers. An automobile manufacturer will ship cars to a dealer who, in turn, may finance the payment for these cars through a finance company. The finance company pays the manufacturer for the cars shipped. The dealer signs a trust receipt security agreement, which specifies what can be done with the inventory. The car dealer is allowed to sell the cars but must turn the proceeds of the sale over to the lender, in payment of the loan. Inventory in trust, unlike inventory under a floating lien, is specifically identified by serial number or by other means. In our example, the finance company periodically audits the cars the dealer has on hand. The serial numbers of these cars are checked against those shown in the security agreement. The purpose of the audit is to see if the dealer has sold cars without remitting the proceeds of the sale to the finance company.

As the dealer buys new cars from the automobile manufacturer, a new trust receipt security agreement is signed, taking account of the new inventory. The dealer then borrows against this new collateral, holding it in trust. Although there is tighter control over collateral with a trust receipt agreement than with a floating lien, there is still the risk of inventory being sold without the proceeds being turned over to the lender. Consequently, the lender must exercise judgment in deciding to lend under this arrangement. A dishonest dealer can devise numerous ways to fool the lender.

Many durable goods manufacturers finance the inventories of their distributors or dealers. Their purpose is to encourage dealers or distributors to carry reasonable stocks of goods. It is reasoned that the greater the stock, the more likely the dealer or distributor is to make a sale. Because the manufacturer is interested in selling its product, financing terms are often more attractive than they are with an "outside" lender.

Terminal Warehouse Receipt Loans. A borrower secures a terminal warehouse receipt loan by storing inventory with a public, or terminal, warehousing company. The warehouse company issues a warehouse receipt, which evidences title to specified goods that are located in the warehouse. An example of a warehouse receipt is shown in Fig. 18-1. The warehouse receipt gives the lender a security interest in the goods, against which a loan can be made to the borrower. Under such an arrangement, the warehouse can release the collateral to the borrower only when authorized to do so by the lender. Consequently, the lender is able to maintain strict control over the collateral and will release collateral only when the borrower pays a portion of the loan. For protection, the lender usually requires the borrower to take out an insurance policy with a loss-payable clause in favor of the lender.

Warehouse receipts may be either nonnegotiable or negotiable. A nonnegotiable warehouse receipt is issued in favor of a specific party—in this case, the lender—who is given title to the goods and has sole authority to release them. A negotiable warehouse receipt can be transferred by endorse-

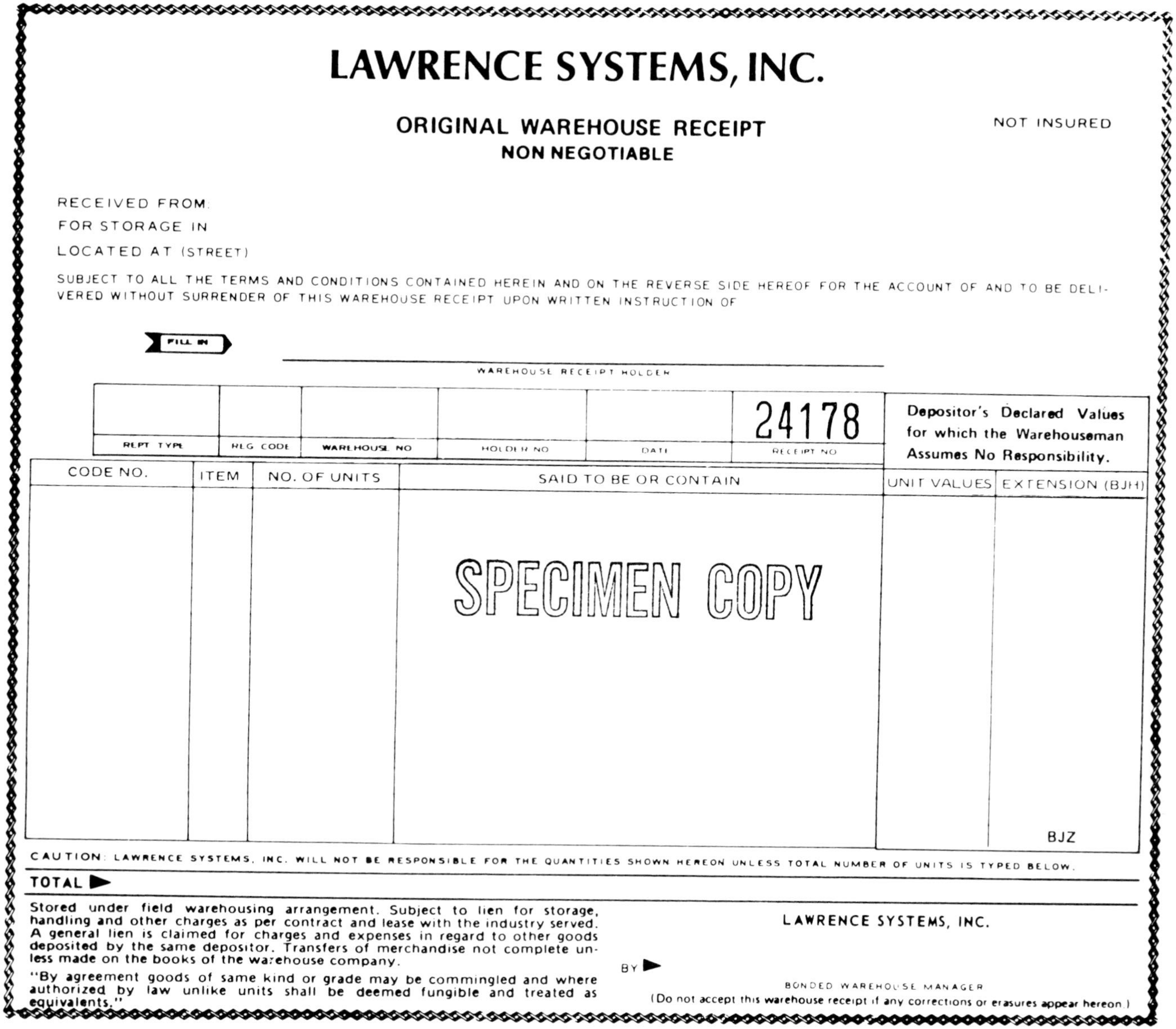

LAWRENCE SYSTEMS, INC.

ORIGINAL WAREHOUSE RECEIPT
NON NEGOTIABLE

NOT INSURED

RECEIVED FROM
FOR STORAGE IN
LOCATED AT (STREET)

SUBJECT TO ALL THE TERMS AND CONDITIONS CONTAINED HEREIN AND ON THE REVERSE SIDE HEREOF FOR THE ACCOUNT OF AND TO BE DELIVERED WITHOUT SURRENDER OF THIS WAREHOUSE RECEIPT UPON WRITTEN INSTRUCTION OF

FILL IN

WAREHOUSE RECEIPT HOLDER

REPT TYPE	REG CODE	WAREHOUSE NO	HOLDER NO	DATE	RECEIPT NO
					24178

Depositor's Declared Values for which the Warehouseman Assumes No Responsibility.

CODE NO.	ITEM	NO. OF UNITS	SAID TO BE OR CONTAIN	UNIT VALUES	EXTENSION (BJH)
			SPECIMEN COPY		BJZ

CAUTION: LAWRENCE SYSTEMS, INC. WILL NOT BE RESPONSIBLE FOR THE QUANTITIES SHOWN HEREON UNLESS TOTAL NUMBER OF UNITS IS TYPED BELOW.

TOTAL ▶

Stored under field warehousing arrangement. Subject to lien for storage, handling and other charges as per contract and lease with the industry served. A general lien is claimed for charges and expenses in regard to other goods deposited by the same depositor. Transfers of merchandise not complete unless made on the books of the warehouse company.

"By agreement goods of same kind or grade may be commingled and where authorized by law unlike units shall be deemed fungible and treated as equivalents."

LAWRENCE SYSTEMS, INC.

BY ▶

BONDED WAREHOUSE MANAGER

(Do not accept this warehouse receipt if any corrections or erasures appear hereon.)

FIGURE 18-1
Example of warehouse receipt *Source: Lawrence Systems, Inc. Reprinted by permission.*

ment. Before goods can be released, the negotiable receipt must be presented to the warehouse operator. A negotiable receipt is useful when title to the goods is transferred from one party to another while the goods are in storage. With a nonnegotiable receipt, the release of goods can be authorized only in writing. Most lending arrangements are based on nonnegotiable receipts.

Field Warehouse Receipt Loans. In a terminal warehouse receipt loan, the goods are located in a public warehouse. Another arrangement, known as field warehousing, permits loans to be made against inventory that is located on the borrower's premises. Under this arrangement, a field warehousing company sets off a designated storage area on the borrower's premises for the inventory pledged as collateral. The field warehousing company has sole access to this area and is supposed to maintain strict control over it. (The goods that serve as collateral are segregated from the borrower's other inventory.) The field warehousing company issues a warehouse receipt as described in the preceding section, and the lender extends a loan based on the collateral value of the inventory. The field warehouse arrangement is a useful means of financing when it is not desirable, either because of the expense or because of the inconvenience, to place the inventory in a public warehouse. Field warehouse receipt lending is particularly appropriate when a borrower must make frequent use of inventory. Because of the need to pay the field warehousing company's expenses, the cost of this method of financing can be relatively high.

The warehouse receipt, as evidence of collateral, is only as good as the issuing warehousing company. When administered properly, a warehouse receipt loan affords the lender a high degree of control over the collateral; however, sufficient examples of fraud show that the warehouse receipt does not always evidence actual value. The warehouse operator must exercise strict control. A grain elevator that is alleged to be full may, in fact, be empty. Upon close examination, we may find that barrels reported to contain grain oil actually contain water.[5]

INTERMEDIATE-TERM DEBT

Typically, intermediate-term financing is self-liquidating and in that way resembles short-term financing. However, it also can satisfy more permanent funds requirements and, in addition, it can serve as an interim substitute for long-term financing. If a firm wishes to float long-term debt or issue common stock, but conditions are unfavorable in the market, the firm may seek intermediate-term debt to bridge the gap until long-term financing can be undertaken on favorable terms. Thus, intermediate-term debt may give a firm flexibility in the timing of long-term financing. It also can provide flexibility when the firm is uncertain about the size and nature of its future funds requirements. As uncertainty is resolved, intermediate-term financing can be replaced by a more appropriate means of financing. The most important use of intermediate-term financing, however, is to provide credit when the expected cash flows of the firm are such that the debt can be retired steadily over a period of several years. Even though it is sometimes linked to a particular asset,

---

[5] For a lively discussion of various frauds against secured lenders, see Monroe R. Lazere, "Swinging Swindles and Creepy Frauds," *Journal of Commercial Bank Lending*, 60 (September 1977), 44–52.

such as a piece of equipment, intermediate-term financing must be considered in relation to the firm's total funds requirements.

In this section, we examine various forms of intermediate-term debt. The maturity range for this type of debt generally is felt to be 1 to 5 years. We begin by considering bank term loans.

BANK TERM LOANS

An ordinary term loan is a business loan with an original, or final, maturity of more than 1 year, repayable according to a specified schedule. For the most part, these loans are repayable in periodic installments—quarterly, semiannually, or yearly. The payment schedule of the loan usually is geared to the borrower's cash-flow ability to service the debt. Typically, this schedule calls for equal periodic installments, but it may specify irregular amounts or repayment in a lump sum at final maturity. Sometimes the loan is amortized in equal periodic installments except for the final payment, known as a "balloon" payment, which is larger than any of the others. Most bank term loans are written with original maturities in the 3- to 5-year range.

Generally, the interest rate on a term loan is higher than the rate on a short-term loan to the same borrower. If a firm could borrow at the prime rate on a short-term basis, it might pay .25 percent to .50 percent more on a term loan. The interest rate on a term loan can be set in one of two ways: (1) a fixed rate that is effective over the life of the loan, or (2) a variable rate may be set, to be adjusted in keeping with changes in the prime rate. Sometimes a ceiling or a floor rate is established, limiting the range within which the rate may fluctuate.

In addition to interest costs, the borrower usually is required to pay the legal expenses that the bank incurs in drawing up the loan agreement. Also, a commitment fee may be charged for the time during the commitment period when the loan is not taken down. For an ordinary term loan, these additional costs usually are rather small in relation to the total interest cost of the loan. A typical fee on the unused portion of a commitment is .50 percent. This means that if the commitment were $1 million, and the company took down all of the loan 3 months after the commitment, it would owe the bank $1 million $\times$ .005 $\times$ 3/12 = $1,250.

The principal advantage of an ordinary bank term loan is flexibility. The borrower deals directly with the lender, and the loan can be tailored to the borrower's needs through direct negotiation. The bank usually has had previous experience with the borrower, so it is familiar with the company's situation. Should the firm's requirements change, the terms and conditions of the loan may be revised. In many instances, bank term loans are made to small businesses that do not have access to the capital markets and cannot readily float a public issue. The ability to sell a public issue varies over time in keeping with the tone of the capital markets, whereas access to term loan financing is more dependable. Even large companies that are able to go the public market may find it quicker and more convenient to seek a bank term loan than to float a public issue.

REVOLVING CREDITS

As we said in Chapter 17, a revolving credit is a formal commitment by a bank to lend up to a certain amount of money to a company over a specified period of time. The actual notes evidencing debt are short term, usually 90 days, but the company may renew them or borrow additionally, up to the specified maximum, throughout the duration of the commitment. Many revolving credit commitments are for 3 years, although it is possible for a firm to obtain a shorter commitment. As with an ordinary term loan, the interest rate is usually .25 to .50 percent higher than the rate at which the firm could borrow on a short-term basis under a line of credit. When a bank makes a revolving credit commitment, it is legally bound under the loan agreement to have funds available whenever the company wants to borrow. The borrower usually must pay for this availability in the form of a commitment fee, perhaps .50 percent per annum, on the difference between the amount borrowed and the specified maximum.

Because most revolving credit agreements are for more than 1 year, they are regarded as intermediate-term financing. This borrowing arrangement is particularly useful at times when the firm is uncertain about its funds requirements. A revolving credit agreement has the features of both a short-term borrowing arrangement and a term loan, for the firm can borrow a fixed amount for the duration of the commitment. Thus, the borrower has flexible access to funds over a period of uncertainty and can make more definite credit arrangements when the uncertainty is resolved. Revolving credit agreements can be set up so that at the maturity of the commitment, borrowings then owing can be converted into a term loan at the option of the borrower. Someday your company may introduce a new product and face a period of uncertainty over the next several years. To provide maximum financial flexibility, you might arrange a 3-year revolving credit that is convertible into a 5-year term loan at the expiration of the revolving credit commitment. At the end of 3 years, the company should know its funds requirements better. If these requirments are permanent, or nearly so, the firm might wish to exercise its option and take down the term loan.

INSURANCE COMPANY TERM LOANS

Insurance companies and certain other institutional lenders also extend term loans to companies. The important differences are in the maturity of the loan extended and in the interest rate charged. In general, life insurance companies are interested in term loans with final maturities in excess of 10 years. Because these companies do not have the benefit of compensating balances or other business from the borrower, and because their loans usually have a longer maturity than bank term loans, typically the rate of interest is higher. To the insurance company, the term loan represents an investment and must yield a return commensurate with the costs involved in making the loan, the risk, the maturity, and prevailing yields on alternative investments. Because an insurance company is interested in keeping its funds employed without interruption, it normally has a prepayment penalty, whereas ordinarily the bank does not. One of the simpler prepayment formulas calls for a premium of .25 percent for each year remaining to maturity. Insurance company term loans generally are not competitive with bank term loans. Indeed, they are complementary, for they serve different maturity ranges.

EQUIPMENT FINANCING

Equipment represents another asset of the firm that may be pledged to secure a loan. If the firm either has equipment that is marketable or is purchasing such equipment, it is usually able to obtain some sort of secured financing. Because such loans usually are for more than a year, we classify them as intermediate-term financing. As with other secured loans, the lender evaluates the marketability of the collateral and will advance a percentage of the market value, depending on the quality of the equipment. Frequently, the repayment schedule for the loan is set in keeping with the economic life of the equipment. In setting the repayment schedule, the lender wants to be sure that the market value of the equipment always exceeds the balance of the loan.

The excess of the expected market value of the equipment over the amount of the loan is the margin of safety, which will vary according to the specific situation. The rolling stock of a trucking company is movable collateral and reasonably marketable. As a result, the advance may be as high as 80 percent. Less marketable equipment, such as that with a limited use, will not command as high an advance. A certain type of lathe may have a thin market, and a lender might not be willing to advance more than 50 percent of its reported market value. Some equipment is so specialized that it has no value as collateral.

Sources of Equipment Financing. Commercial banks, finance companies, and the sellers of equipment are among the sources of equipment financing. Because the interest charged by a finance company on an equipment loan is usually higher than that charged by a commercial bank, a firm will turn to a finance company only if it is unable to obtain the loan from a bank. The seller of the equipment may finance the purchase either by holding the secured note itself or by selling the note to its captive finance subsidiary. The interest charge will depend on the extent to which the seller uses financing as a sales tool. The seller who uses financing extensively may charge only a moderate interest rate but make up for part of the cost of carrying the notes by charging higher prices for the equipment. The borrower must consider this possibility in judging the true cost of financing. Equipment loans may be secured either by a chattel mortgage or by a conditional sales contract arrangement.

Chattel Mortgage. A chattel mortgage is a lien on property other than real estate. The borrower signs a security agreement that gives the lender a lien on the equipment specified in the agreement. In order to perfect the lien, the lender files a copy of the security agreement or a financing statement with a public office of the state in which the equipment is located. Given a valid lien, the lender can sell the equipment if the borrower defaults in the payment of principal or interest on the loan.

Conditional Sales Contract. With a conditional sales contract arrangement, the seller of the equipment retains title to it until the purchaser has satisfied all the terms of the contract. The buyer signs a conditional sales contract security agreement to make periodic installment payments to the seller over a specified period of time. These payments usually are monthly or quarterly. Until the terms of the contract are satisfied completely, the seller retains title to the equipment. Thus, the seller receives a down payment and a promissory note for the balance of the purchase price upon the sale of the equipment. The note is secured by the contract, which gives the seller the authority to repossess the equipment if the buyer does not meet all the terms of the contract.

The seller may either hold the contract or sell it, simply by endorsing it, to a commercial bank or finance company. The bank or finance company then becomes the lender and assumes the security interest in the equipment. If the buyer should default under the terms of the contract, the bank or finance company could repossess the equipment and sell it in satisfaction of its loan. Often the vendor will sell the contract to a bank or finance company with recourse. Under this arrangement, the lender has the additional protection of recourse to the seller in case the buyer defaults.

PROTECTIVE COVENANTS AND LOAN AGREEMENTS

When a lender makes a term loan or revolving credit commitment, it provides the borrower with available funds for an extended period of time. Much can happen to the financial condition of the borrower during that period. To safeguard itself, the lender requires the borrower to maintain its financial condition and, in particular, its current position at a level at least as favorable as when the commitment was made. The provisions for protection contained in a loan agreement are known as protective covenants.

The loan agreement itself simply gives the lender legal authority to step in should the borrower default under any of the provisions. Otherwise, the lender would be locked into a commitment and would have to wait until maturity before being able to effect corrective measures. The borrower who suffers losses or other adverse developments will default under a well-written loan agreement; the lender then will be able to act. The action usually takes the form of working with the company to straighten out its problems. Seldom will a lender demand immediate payment, despite the legal right to do so in cases of default. More typically, the condition under which the borrower defaults is waived or the loan agreement is amended. The point is that the lender has the authority to act, even though negotiation with the borrower may be instituted to resolve the problem.

The formulation of the different restrictive provisions should be tailored to the specific loan situation. The lender fashions these provisions for the overall protection of the loan. No one provision is able by itself to provide the necessary safeguards; but together with the other provisions, it is designed to ensure overall liquidity and ability to pay a loan. The important protective covenants of a loan agreement may be classified as follows: (1) general provisions used in most loan agreements, which are variable to fit the situation; (2) routine provisions used in most agreements, which usually are not variable; and (3) specific provisions that are used according to the situation. Although we focus on a bank loan agreement, the protective covenants used and the philosophy underlying their use are the same for a bond indenture, which is described in Chapter 21.

GENERAL PROVISIONS

The *working capital requirement* is probably the most commonly used and most comprehensive provision in a loan agreement. Its purpose is to preserve the company's current position and ability to pay the loan. Frequently, a straight dollar amount, such as $6 million, is set as the minimum working capital the company must maintain during the duration of the commitment.

When the lender feels that it is desirable for a specific company to build working capital, it may increase the minimum working capital requirement throughout the duration of the loan. The establishment of a working capital minimum normally is based on the amounts of present working capital and projected working capital, allowing for seasonal fluctuations. The requirement should not restrict the company unduly in the ordinary generation of profit. Should the borrower incur sharp losses or spend too much for fixed assets, purchase of stock, dividends, redemption of long-term debt, and so forth, it would probably breach the working capital requirement.

The *cash dividend and repurchase of stock restriction* is another major restriction in this category. Its purpose is to limit cash going outside the business, thus preserving the liquidity of the company. Most often, cash dividends and repurchase of stock are limited to a percentage of net profits on a cumulative basis after a certain base date, frequently the last fiscal year end prior to the date of the term loan agreement. A less flexible method restricts dividends and repurchase of stock to an absolute dollar amount each year. In most cases, the prospective borrower must be willing to undergo a cash dividend and repurchase of stock restriction. If tied to earnings, this restriction still will allow adequate dividends as long as the company is able to generate satisfactory profits.

The *capital expenditures limitation* is third in the category of general provisions. Capital expenditures may be limited to a fixed dollar amount yearly or, probably more commonly, either to depreciation or to a percentage thereof. The capital expenditures limitation is another tool the lender uses to ensure the maintenance of the borrower's current position. By limiting capital expenditures directly, the bank can be surer that it will not have to look to liquidation of fixed assets for payment of its loan. Again, the provision should not be so restrictive that it prevents adequate maintenance and improvement of facilities.

A *limitation on other indebtedness* is the last general provision. This limitation may take a number of forms, depending on the circumstances. Frequently, a loan agreement will prohibit a company from incurring any other long-term debt. This provision protects the lender, inasmuch as it prevents future lenders from obtaining a prior claim on the borrower's assets. Usually a company is permitted to borrow within reasonable limits for seasonal and other short-term purposes arising in the ordinary course of business.

ROUTINE PROVISIONS

The second category of restrictions includes routine, usually invariable provisions found in most loan agreements. Ordinarily, the loan agreement requires the borrower to furnish the bank with financial statements and to maintain adequate insurance. Additionally, the borrower normally must not sell a significant portion of its assets and must pay, when due, all taxes and other liabilities, except those it contests in good faith. A provision forbidding the pledging or mortgaging of any of the borrower's assets is almost always included in a loan agreement; this important provision is known as a *negative pledge clause.*[6]

---

[6] For a critical analysis of the effectiveness of a negative pledge clause, see Morey W. McDaniel, "Are Negative Pledge Clauses in Public Debt Issues Obsolete?" *Business Lawyer,* 38 (May 1983), 867–81.

Usually, the company is required not to discount or sell its receivables. Moreover, the borrower generally is prohibited from entering into any leasing arrangement of property, except up to a certain dollar amount of annual rental. The purpose of this provision is to prevent the borrower from taking on a substantial lease liability, which might endanger its ability to pay the loan. A lease restriction also prevents the firm from leasing property instead of purchasing it and thereby getting around the limitations on capital expenditures and debt. Usually, too, there is a restriction on other contingent liabilities.

In addition to these restrictions, there typically is a restriction on the acquisition of other companies. This restriction often is a straight prohibition of such mergers unless specifically approved by the lender. It is possible to have other kinds of restrictions on mergers, but a flat prohibition is most prevalent. The provisions in this "routine" category appear as a matter of course in most loan agreements. Although somewhat mechanical, they are necessary because they close many loopholes and provide a tight, comprehensive loan agreement.

SPECIAL PROVISIONS

In specific loan agreements, the bank uses special provisions to achieve a desired total protection of its loan. A loan agreement may contain a definite understanding regarding the use of the loan proceeds, so that there will be no diversion of funds to purposes other than those contemplated when the loan was negotiated. A provision for limiting loans and advances often is found in a bank term loan agreement. Closely allied to this restriction is a limitation on investments, which is used to safeguard liquidity by preventing certain non-liquid investments.

If one or more executives are essential to a firm's effective operation, a bank may insist that the company carry life insurance on them. Proceeds of the insurance may be payable to the company or directly to the bank, to be applied to the loan. An agreement may also contain a management clause under which certain key individuals must remain actively employed in the company during the time the loan is owing. Aggregate executive salaries and bonuses are sometimes limited in the loan agreement to prevent excessive compensation of executives, which might reduce profits. This provision closes another loophole; it prevents large stockholders who are officers of the company from increasing their own salaries in lieu of paying higher dividends, which are limited under the agreement.

NEGOTIATING RESTRICTIONS
AND THE OPTION PRICING THEORY

The provisions just described represent the most frequently used protective covenants in a loan agreement. From the standpoint of the lender, the aggregate impact of these provisions should be to safeguard the financial position of the borrower and its ability to pay the loan. Under a well-written agreement, a borrower cannot get into serious financial difficulty without defaulting under an agreement, thereby giving the lender legal authority to take action. Although the lender is instrumental in establishing restrictions, the restrictiveness of protective covenants is subject to negotiation between borrower and lender. The final result will depend on the relative bargaining power of each of the parties involved.[7]

From our discussion in Chapters 5 and 10 concerning the application of the option pricing theory, it is easy to visualize the debt holder–equity holder relationship as being essentially an option arrangement. Looking at the relationship in this manner affords a better understanding of a lender's desire for protective covenants. A firm may have a single debt issue outstanding which is denoted by the obligation of the company to pay D at time T.[8] If total value of the company at time T, which we denote by V, exceeds D, debt holders will be paid the face value of the obligation. If V is less than D, the firm is assumed to default. Therefore, the value of the debt obligation at time T is min (D, V). This merely states that debt holders receive the lesser of the contractual amount of the debt obligation or the value of the firm if this obligation cannot be entirely paid at time T. In other words, in default, the ownership of the firm passes to the debt holders; they realize a value on their claim which is less than the contractual amount.

On the other hand, the value of the common stock at time T is max $(V - D, 0)$. Equity holders are the residual owners of the company and are entitled to any value of the firm that remains after the debt has been paid, $V - D$. In the event the debt cannot be paid in its entirety because V is less than D, they receive nothing. In this sense, the equity holders have an option on the total value of the firm at time T. If V exceeds D, they exercise this option, so to speak, by paying off the loan and they receive the total value of the firm at time T less the debt claim. (The face value of the debt can be thought of as the exercise price of the option.) If V is less than D, the option is worth zero. Now we know from Chapter 5 that with an option, the greater the variance of the distribution of possible values of the firm at time T, the greater the value of the option, all other things the same. Put another way, it is the variance of the value of the associated asset—in this case, the firm—that gives an option value. The same principles that apply to options on stock apply here.

In the context of our example, it behooves the equity holders to increase the risk of the firm in order to increase the variance of its total value. By undertaking more risky ventures, the value of the equity holders' option increases. While greater risk works to the advantage of equity holders, it is at the expense of the option writer, the debt holders. In fact, the increase in value of the equity holders' option means a corresponding decrease in the value of debt. Expressed differently, there is a transfer of wealth from debt holders to equity holders. The same thing occurs when the capital structure is changed by issuing new debt and repurchasing stock. As illustrated in Chapter 10, the probability of default increases and, as a result, the value of existing debt de-

---

[7] For a linear-programming approach to analyzing the opportunity costs of protective covenants, see James C. Van Horne, "A Linear-Programming Approach to Evaluating Restrictions under a Bond Indenture or Loan Agreement," *Journal of Financial and Quantitative Analysis*, 1 (June 1966), 68–83. In the article, the dual variable values are taken as measures of the opportunity costs of protective covenants. Through sensitivity analysis, one can evaluate the effect on the optimal solution of given changes in the protective covenant restrictions.

[8] This example is based on James C. Van Horne, "Optimal Initiation of Bankruptcy Proceedings by Debt Holders," *Journal of Finance*, 31 (June 1976), 897–910. See also Fischer Black and John C. Cox, "Valuing Corporate Securities: Some Effects of Bond Indenture Provisions," *Journal of Finance*, 31 (May 1976), 351–67; Fischer Black and Myron Scholes, "The Pricing of Options and Corporate Liabilities," *Journal of Political Economy*, 81 (May–June 1973), 649–51; and Clifford W. Smith Jr., and Jerold B. Warner, "On Financial Contracting: An Analysis of Bond Covenants," *Journal of Financial Economics*, 7 (June 1979), 117–61.

clines. In essence, the stockholders expropriate some of the wealth of the old debt holders. (New debt holders are not affected because they lend money on the basis of the new, more risky capital structure.)

If a lender recognizes the possibility that the equity holders may substantially alter the riskiness of the firm or issue new debt after a loan is made, it will probably want to institute some safeguards against these occurrences before making the loan. This can be done by imposing protective convenants of the sort described earlier. If the firm should breach any of these restrictions, default occurs, and the lender can then declare the loan immediately payable. Protective covenants obviously give the lender the additional ability to force bankruptcy. With bankruptcy, ownership of the firm effectively passes to the debt holders, and they can seize upon the value of the firm at that time. Therefore, lenders are in a position to preclude equity holders from increasing the risk of the company or issuing new debt at their expense. They have only to write protective covenants that will trigger default.

When protective covenants are initially formulated, the key question from the standpoint of the lender is their potential benefits. One way to judge the benefits is in terms of the present value of the debt with, and without, a particular covenant. If the present value of the existing debt is no higher with the addition of a particular protective covenant than it is without it, the covenant does not really benefit the lender.[9] Decisions by the firm that affect the overall riskiness of its assets can be restrained but not altogether precluded by such protective covenants as the working capital provision, capital expenditures restrictions, and a restriction on the sale of assets. Limitation on the issuance of additional debt is the only way that existing lenders can preclude new lenders from coming in with the same claim on assets or with a superior one.

Conceptually, then, the purpose of these restrictions should be to protect against a transfer of value from the debt holders to the equity holders. As stated before, the benefit to the debt holders of protective covenants is the ability to initiate bankruptcy proceedings earlier than would otherwise be the case. In this way, they can limit the increase in risk allowed before default is triggered, thereby limiting the potential transfer of value to the equity holders. Still we have to remember that protective covenants are negotiated between the borrower and the lender. What the lender might want, the borrower might not want to give up.

As discussed in Chapter 10, there are monitoring costs associated with the writing of protective covenants and with their enforcement.[10] These costs ultimately are borne by the equity holders, so it is in their interests to see that monitoring activities are administered efficiently. The greater the safeguards to the lender, the greater its protection and the lower the interest rate, all other things the same; however, the incremental protection afforded the lender increases at a decreasing rate. On the other hand, monitoring costs increase, probably at an increasing rate, as more safeguards are added. It is therefore necessary to strike a balance that embraces this trade-off. The final position will be a compromise between the borrower and the lender, one that

[9] For an approach to determining the incremental present value of the debt associated with a protective covenant using a multiperiod state-preference mode, see Van Horne, "Optimal Initiation of Bankruptcy Proceedings by Debt Holders," pp. 908–9.

[10] See Michael C. Jensen and William H. Meckling, "Theory of the Firm: Managerial Behavior, Agency Cost and Ownership Structure," *Journal of Financial Economics*, 3 (October 1976), 305–60, for a discussion of these as well as other agency costs.

is influenced by relative conditions in the financial markets and by the costs of monitoring (see Chapter 10).

SUMMARY

Many firms unable to obtain unsecured credit are required to pledge security. In giving a secured loan, the lender looks first to the cash-flow ability of the company to service debt and, if this source of loan repayment should fail, to the collateral value of the security. To provide a margin of safety, a lender usually will advance somewhat less than the market value of the collateral. The percentage advance varies according to the quality of the collateral pledged and the control the lender has over this collateral. Accounts receivable and inventory are the principal assets used to secure short-term business loans. Receivables may either be assigned to secure a loan or sold to a factor. Inventory loans can be under a floating lien, under a trust receipt, or under terminal warehouse or field warehouse receipt arrangements.

Intermediate-term financing generally is thought to include maturities of 1 to 5 years. There are a number of sources of intermediate-term financing. Commercial banks, insurance companies, and other institutional investors make term loans to business firms. Banks also provide financing under a revolving credit arrangement, which represents a formal commitment on the part of the bank to lend up to a certain amount of money over a specified period of time. On a secured basis, firms can obtain intermediate-term financing by pledging equipment that they own or are purchasing. Banks, finance companies, and sellers of the equipment are active in providing this type of secured financing.

Lenders who offer unsecured credit usually impose restrictions on the borrower. These restrictions are called protective covenants and are contained in a loan agreement. If the borrower defaults under any of the provisions of the loan agreement, the lender may initiate immediate corrective measures. The use of protective covenants can be viewed in the option pricing model framework of debt holders versus equity holders. This framework was illustrated, as was the influence of monitoring costs.

SELF-CORRECTION PROBLEMS

1. The Barnes Corporation has just acquired a large account. As a result, it needs an additional $75,000 in working capital immediately. It has been determined that there are three feasible sources of funds:

    a. Trade credit: the company buys about $50,000 of materials per month on terms of 3/30, net 90. Discounts are taken.

    b. Bank loan: the firm's bank will lend $100,000 at 13 percent. A 10 percent compensating balance will be required.

    c. A factor will buy the company's receivables ($100,000 per month), which have a collection period of 60 days. The factor will advance up to 75 percent of the face value of the receivables at 12 percent on an annual basis. The factor will also charge a 2 percent fee on all receivables purchased. It has been estimated that the factor's services will save the company a credit department expense and bad-debt expenses of $1,500 per month.

On the basis of annual percentage cost, which alternative should Barnes select?

2. The Kedzie Cordage Company needs to finance a seasonal bulge in inventories of $400,000. The funds are needed for 6 months. The company is considering the following possibilities:

a. Warehouse receipt loan from a finance company. Terms are 12 percent annualized with an 80 percent advance against the value of the inventory. The warehousing costs are $7,000 for the 6-month period. The residual financing requirement, which is $400,000 less the amount advanced, will need to be financed by forgoing cash discounts on its payables. Standard terms are 2/10, net 30; however, the company feels it can postpone payment until the fortieth day without adverse effect.

b. A floating lien arrangement from the supplier of the inventory at an effective interest rate of 20 percent. The supplier will advance the full value of the inventory.

c. A field warehouse loan from another finance company at an interest rate of 10 percent annualized. The advance is 70 percent, and field warehousing costs amount to $10,000 for the 6-month period. The residual financing requirement will need to be financed by forgoing cash discounts on payables as in the first alternative.

Which is the least costly method of financing the inventory needs of the firm?

3. Sir Toby Ales is expanding its chain of retail liquor stores. This program will require a capital expenditure of $3 million, which must be financed. The company has settled on a 3-year revolving credit of $3 million, which may be converted into a 3-year term loan at the expiration of the revolving credit commitment. The commitment fee for both credit arrangements is .50 percent of the unused portions. The bank has quoted Sir Toby Ales an interest rate of 1 percent over prime for the revolving credit and $1\frac{1}{2}$ percent over prime for the term loan, if that option is taken. The company expects to borrow $1.4 million at the outset and another $1.6 million at the very end of the first year. At the expiration of the revolving credit, the company expects to take down the full term loan. At the end of the fourth, fifth, and sixth years, it expects to make principal payments of $1 million.

a. For each of the next 6 years, what is the expected commitment fee in dollars?

b. What is the expected dollar interest cost above the prime rate?

PROBLEMS

1. Fritz-Polakoff Finance Company makes a variety of secured loans. Both the percentage of advance and the interest rate charged vary with the marketability, life, and riskiness of the collateral. It has established the following advances and interest rate charges for certain types of equipment:

ITEM	ADVANCE AGAINST APPRAISAL VALUE	INTEREST RATE
1. Forklift truck	75%	18%
2. Back hoe truck	80	18
3. Drill press	50	20
4. Bottle filler	40	22
5. Turret lathe	60	20

L. Bradford Company has used equipment of this sort with appraised values of $13,000, $19,000, $6,000, $38,000, and $24,000, respectively. How much can it borrow and what will be the total annual interest cost in dollars? in percentage? (Assume that the company owns only one item of each.)

more long-term debt; its total liabilities cannot be more than .6 of its total assets; and capital expenditures in any year are limited to depreciation plus $3 million. The company's balance sheet at December 31, before the term loan, is

Current assets	$ 7 million	Current liabilities	$ 3 million
Net fixed assets	10	Long-term debt (due in 5 years)	5
		Net worth	9
	$17 million		$17 million

The proceeds of the term loan will be used to increase Sharpe's investment in inventories and receivables in response to introducing a new "closer-to-the-face" razor blade. The company anticipates a subsequent need to grow at a rate of 24 percent a year, equally divided between current assets and net fixed assets. Profits after taxes of $1.5 million are expected this year, and these profits are further expected to grow by $250,000 per year over the subsequent 3 years. The company pays no dividends and does not intend to pay any over the next 4 years. Depreciation in the past year was $2.5 million, and this is predicted to grow over the next 4 years at the same rate as the increase in net fixed assets. Under the loan agreement, will the company be able to achieve its growth objectives?

6. Max-Fli Toy Company currently has a total value of $10 million. The face value of the debt outstanding is $7 million, and it is represented by discount bonds that all mature in 4 years. The standard deviation of the continuously compounded rate of return on the total value of the firm is .30. The short-term risk-free rate is currently 6 percent.

   a. Using the Black-Scholes option model, Eq. (5-2) in Chapter 5, determine the value of the equity and the value of the debt.

   b. If the company goes into a new, riskier toy line that increases the standard deviation to .50, what will be the effect on the value of the debt?

   c. How can the debt holders protect themselves?

7. *Research project:* Examine several bond indentures or loan agreements (if available). What major restrictions are imposed? Do you note any differences between restrictions outlined in bond indentures and those in loan agreements? Why might these differences exist? Do you find any correlation between the maturity length of the instrument and the number (and degree) of the restrictions? What might account for your findings?

SOLUTIONS TO SELF-CORRECTION PROBLEMS

1. a. Cost of trade credit: If discounts are not taken, up to $97,000 can be raised after the second month. The cost would be

$$\frac{3}{97} \times \frac{365}{60} = 18.81\%$$

   b. Cost of bank loan: Assuming the compensating balance would not otherwise be maintained, the cost would be

$$\frac{13}{90} = 14.44\%$$

   c. Cost of factoring: The factor fee for the year would be

$$2\% \times \$1,200,000 = \$24,000$$

The savings effected, however, would be $18,000, giving a net factoring cost of $6,000. Borrowing $75,000 on the receivables would thus cost

$$\frac{(12\%)(\$75,000) + \$6,000}{\$75,000} = \frac{\$9,000 + \$6,000}{\$75,000} = 20.00\%$$

Bank borrowing would be the cheapest source of funds.

2. a. Twelve percent of 80 percent of $400,000 for 6 months   = $19,200
    Warehousing cost   = 7,000
    Cash discount forgone to extend payables
      from 10 days to 40 days

$$\left(\frac{2}{98} \times \frac{365}{30}\right)(\$80,000)(\tfrac{1}{2}\text{ year}) = .2483 \times 80,000 \times .5 \qquad = \underline{9,932}$$

Total cost   = $36,132

   b. $400,000 × 20% × $\frac{1}{2}$ year   = $40,000

   c. Ten percent of 70 percent of $400,000 for 6 months   = $14,000
    Field warehousing cost   = 10,000
    Cash discount forgone to extend payables
      from 10 days to 40 days

$$\left(\frac{2}{98} \times \frac{365}{30}\right)(\$120,000)(\tfrac{1}{2}\text{ year}) = .2483 \times 120,000 \times .5 \qquad = \underline{14,898}$$

Total cost   = $38,898
The warehouse receipt loan results in the lowest cost.

3 a. and b.

	YEAR					
	Revolving Credit			Term Loan		
	1	2	3	4	5	6
Amount borrowed during year (in thousands)	$1,400	$3,000	$3,000	$3,000	$2,000	$1,000
Unused portion (in thousands)	1,600	0	0	0	1,000	2,000
Commitment fee (.005)	8,000	0	0	0	5,000	10,000
Interest cost above prime (1% first 3 years and $1\frac{1}{2}$% the last 3)	14,000	30,000	30,000	45,000	30,000	15,000

SELECTED REFERENCES

ARNOLD, JASPER H., III, "How to Negotiate a Term Loan," *Harvard Business Review*, 60 (March–April 1982), 131–38.

BLACK, FISCHER, and JOHN C. COX, "Valuing Corporate Securities: Some Effects of Bond Indenture Provisions," *Journal of Finance*, 31 (May 1976), 351–67.

DIAMOND, DOUGLAS W., "Reputation Acquisition in Debt Markets," *Journal of Political Economy*, 97, No. 4 (1989), 828–62.

GILL, RICHARD C., "Term Loan Agreements," *Journal of Commercial Bank Lending*, 62 (February 1980), 22–27.

HAWKINS, GREGORY D., "An Analysis of Revolving Credit Agreements," *Journal of Financial Economics*, 10 (March 1982), 59–81.

HO, THOMAS S. Y., and RONALD F. SINGER, "Bond Indenture Provisions and the Risk of Corporate Debt," *Journal of Financial Economics*, 10 (December 1982), 375–406.

JENSEN, MICHAEL C., and WILLIAM H. MECKLING, "Theory of the Firm: Managerial Behavior, Agency Costs and Ownership Structure," *Journal of Financial Economics*, 3 (October 1976), 305–60.

LAZERE, MONROE R., "Swinging Swindles and Creepy Frauds," *Journal of Commercial Bank Lending*, 60 (September 1977), 44–52.

LUMMAR, SCOTT L., and JOHN J. MCCONNELL, "Further Evidence on the Bank Lending Process and the Capital Market Response to Bank Loan Agreements," *Journal of Financial Economics*, 25 (November 1989), 99–122.

SCOTT, JAMES H., JR., "Bankruptcy, Secured Debt, and Optimal Capital Structure," *Journal of Finance*, 32 (March 1977), 1–19.

SMITH, CLIFFORD W., JR., and JEROLD B. WARNER, "On Financial Contracting: An Analysis of Bond Covenants," *Journal of Financial Economics*, 7 (June 1980), 117–61.

STULZ, RENE M., and HERB JOHNSON, "An Analysis of Secured Debt," *Journal of Financial Economics*, 14 (December 1985), 501–21.

VAN HORNE, JAMES C., "A Linear-Programming Approach to Evaluating Restrictions under a Bond Indenture or Loan Agreement," *Journal of Financial and Quantitative Analysis*, 1 (June 1966), 68–83.

———, "Optimal Initiation of Bankruptcy Proceedings by Debt Holders," *Journal of Finance*, 31 (June 1976), 897–910.

19

LEASE
FINANCING

A lease is a contract whereby the owner of an asset (the lessor) grants to another party (the lessee) the exclusive right to use the asset, usually for an agreed period of time, in return for the payment of rent.[1] Most of us are familiar with leases of houses, apartments, offices, or telephones. Recent decades have seen an enormous growth in the leasing of business assets such as cars and trucks, computers, other equipment, and manufacturing plants. In fact, leasing accounts for over 30 percent of external equipment financing. An obvious advantage to the lessee is the use of an asset without having to buy it. For this advantage, the lessee incurs several obligations. First and foremost is the obligation to make periodic lease payments, usually monthly or quarterly and in advance. Also, the lease contract specifies who is to maintain the asset. Under a *maintenance lease,* the lessor pays for maintenance, repairs, taxes, and insurance. Under a *net lease,* the lessee pays these costs.

The lease may be *cancellable* or *noncancellable.* When cancellable, there sometimes is a penalty. An *operating lease* for office space, for example, is relatively short-term in length and is cancellable with proper notice. The term of this type of lease is shorter than the asset's economic life. In other words, the lessor does not recover its investment during the first lease period. It is only in releasing the space over and over, either to the same party or to others, that the lessor recovers its cost.[2] Other examples of operating leases include the leasing of copying machines, certain computer hardware, word processors, and automobiles. In contrast, a *financial lease* is longer term in nature and is noncancellable. The lessee is obligated to make lease payments until the lease's expiration, which corresponds to the useful life of the asset. These payments not only amortize the cost of the asset but provide the lessor an interest return. Our focus in this chapter is on financial as opposed to operating leases.

Finally, the lease contract typically specifies some kind of option to the lessee at expiration. It may involve renewal, where the lessee has the right to renew the lease for another lease period, either at the same rent or at a different, usually lower, rent. The option might be to purchase the asset at expiration. For tax reasons, the purchase price must not be significantly lower than fair market value. If the lessee does not exercise its option, the lessor takes possession of the asset and is entitled to any *residual value* associated with it.

[1] The development of most of this chapter assumes that the reader has studied Parts 2 and 3.

[2] For an analysis of cancellable operating leases as financial leases with a put option, see Thomas E. Copeland and J. Fred Weston, "A Note on the Evaluation of Cancellable Operating Leases," *Financial Management,* 11 (Summer 1982), 60–67.

Because of the contractual nature of a financial lease obligation, it must be regarded as a form of financing. It is used in place of other methods of financing to acquire the use of an asset. An alternative method of financing might be to purchase the asset and finance its acquisition with debt. Both the lease payment and the payment of principal and interest on debt are fixed obligations that must be met. Inability to meet these obligations will result in financial embarrassment. Thus, lease financing and debt financing are very similar from the standpoint of analyzing the ability of the firm to service fixed obligations.

FORMS OF LEASE FINANCING

Virtually all lease financing arrangements fall into one of three main types of lease financing: a sale and leaseback arrangement, the direct acquisition of an asset under a lease, and leveraged leasing. Before analyzing lease financing or its basic valuation implications, let us look at the three categories.

SALE AND LEASEBACK

Under a sale and leaseback arrangement, a firm sells an asset to another party, and this party leases it back to the firm. Usually, the asset is sold at approximately its market value. The firm receives the sales price in cash and the economic use of the asset during the basic lease period. In turn, it contracts to make periodic lease payments and gives up title to the asset. As a result, the lessor realizes any residual value the asset might have at the end of the lease period, whereas before, this value would have been realized by the firm. The firm may realize an income tax advantage if the asset involves a building on owned land. Whereas land is not depreciable if owned outright, lease payments are tax deductible, so the firm indirectly is able to amortize the value of the land. Lessors engaged in sale and leaseback arrangement include insurance companies, other institutional investors, finance companies, and independent leasing companies.

DIRECT LEASING

Under direct leasing, a company acquires the use of an asset it did not own previously. A firm may lease an asset from the manufacturer: IBM leases computers: Xerox leases copiers. Indeed capital goods are available today on a lease-financed basis. A wide variety of direct leasing arrangements meet various needs of firms. The major types of lessors are manufacturers, finance companies, banks, independent leasing companies, special-purpose leasing companies, and partnerships. For leasing arrangements involving all but manufacturers, the vendor sells the asset to the lessor, who in turn, leases it to the lessee. In certain cases, a lessor may achieve economies of scale in the purchase of capital assets and may pass them on to the lessee in the form of lower lease payments.

LEVERAGED LEASING

A special form of leasing sometimes is used in financing assets requiring large capital outlays. It is known as *leveraged leasing*. In contrast to the two parties involved in the forms of leasing previously described, there are three parties involved in leveraged leasing: (1) the lessee, (2) the lessor, or equity participant, and (3) the lender. We examine each in turn.

From the standpoint of the lessee, there is no difference between a leveraged lease and any other of type of lease. The lessee contracts to make periodic payments over the basic lease period and, in return, is entitled to the use of the asset over that period of time. The role of the lessor, however, is changed. The lessor acquires the asset in keeping with the terms of the lease arrangement and finances the acquisition in part by an equity investment of, say, 20 percent (hence the name *equity participant*). The remaining 80 percent is provided by a long-term lender or lenders. The loan is usually secured by a mortgage on the asset, as well as by the assignment of the lease and lease payments.[3] The lessor is the borrower.

As owner of the asset, the lessor is entitled to deduct all depreciation charges associated with the asset. The cash-flow pattern for the lessor typically involves (1) a cash outflow at the time the asset is acquired, which represents its equity participation; (2) a period of cash inflows represented by lease payments and tax benefits, less payments on the debt (principal and interest); and (3) a period of net cash outflows during which, because of declining tax benefits, the sum of lease payments and tax benefits falls below the debt payments due. If there is any residual value at the end of the lease period, this of course represents a cash inflow to the lessor. From the standpoint of the lessor, the reversal of signs of the cash flows from negative to positive to negative gives rise to the possibility of multiple internal rates of return.[4] (This problem is addressed in the Appendix to Chapter 6.) For this reason, it is best for the lessor to use a net-present-value approach when evaluating the situation.

Although the leveraged lease may at first seem more complicated than either the sale and leaseback arrangement or direct leasing, it reduces to certain basic concepts that, from the standpoint of the lessee, can be analyzed in the same manner as for any lease. We therefore shall not treat it separately in the rest of this chapter.

ACCOUNTING AND TAX TREATMENTS OF LEASES

Where once leases were not disclosed and were attractive to some as "off balance sheet" financing, this no longer is the case. Financial Accounting Standards Board Statement No. 13 requires capitalization on the balance sheet of certain types of leases. In essence, this statement says that if the lessee acquires essentially all of the economic benefits and risks of the leased property, then the value of the asset along with the corresponding lease liability must be shown on the balance sheet.

---

[3] Sometimes, in addition, the lessee guarantees the debt.

[4] For a discussion of this problem as well as presentations of possible approaches, see Robert C. Wiar, "Economic Implications of Multiple Rates of Return in the Leveraged Lease Context," *Journal of Finance*, 28 (December 1973), 1275–86: Richard A. Grimlund and Robert Capettini, "A Note on the Evaluation of Leveraged Leases and Other Investments," *Financial Management*, 11 (Summer 1982), 68–72; and Bruce D. Smith, "Accelerated Debt Repayment in Leverage Leases," *Financial Management*, 11 (Summer 1982), 73–80.

CAPITAL AND OPERATING LEASES

Leases that conform in principle to this definition are called *capital leases*. More specifically, a lease is regarded as a capital lease if it meets any one of the following conditions:[5]

1. The lease transfers title to the asset to the lessee by the end of the lease period.
2. The lease contains an option to purchase the asset at a bargain price.
3. The lease period is equal to, or greater than, 75 percent of the estimated economic life of the asset.
4. At the beginning of the lease, the present value of the minimum lease payments equals or exceeds 90 percent of the fair value of the leased property to the lessor.

If any of these conditions is met, the lessee is said to have acquired most of the economic benefits and risks associated with the leased property; therefore, a capital lease is involved. If a lease does not meet any of these conditions, it is classified as an *operating lease*. Essentially, operating leases give the lessee the right to use the leased property over a period of time, but they do not give the lessee all the benefits and risks associated with the asset.

Recording the Value of a Capital Lease. With a capital lease, the lessee must report the value of the leased property on the asset side of the balance sheet. The amount reflected is the present value of the minimum lease payments over the lease period. If executory costs, such as insurance, maintenance, and taxes, are a part of the total lease payment, these are deducted and only the remainder is used for purposes of calculating the present value. As required by the accounting rules, the discount rate employed is the lower of (1) the lessee's incremental borrowing rate or (2) the lessor's implicit interest rate if, in fact, that rate can be determined.

The present value of the lease payments should be recorded as an asset on the lessee's balance sheet. (If the fair value of the leased property is lower than the present value of the minimum lease payments, then the fair value would be shown.) The associated lease obligation would be shown on the liability side of the balance sheet, with the present value of payments due within 1 year being reflected as current liabilities and the present value of payments due after 1 year being shown as noncurrent liabilities. The leased property may be combined with similar information on assets that are owned, but there must be a disclosure in a footnote with respect to the value of the leased property and its amortization. A hypothetical balance sheet might look like the following:

ASSETS		LIABILITIES	
Gross fixed assets*	$3,000,000	Current:	
Less: Accumulated		Obligations under	
depreciation and		capital leases	$90,000
amortization	1,000,000	Noncurrent:	
Net fixed assets	$2,000,000	Obligations under	
		capital leases	$270,000

* Gross fixed assets include leased property of $500,000. Accumulated depreciation and amortization includes $140,000 in amortization associated with such property.

[5] *Statement of Financial Accounting Standards No. 13, Accounting for Leases* (Stamford, CT: Financial Accounting Standards Board, November 1976).

Here we see in the footnote that the capitalized value of leases of the company is $500,000 less $140,000 in amortization, or $360,000 in total. The liability is split with $90,000 current and $270,000 due beyond 1 year. In addition to this information, more details are required in footnotes. Relevant information here includes the gross amounts of leased property by major property categories (these can be combined with categories of owned assets), the total future minimum lease payments, a schedule by years of future lease payments required over the next 5 years, the total minimum sublease rentals to be received, the existence and terms of purchase or renewal options and escalation clauses, rentals that are contingent on some factor other than the passage of time, and any restrictions imposed in the lease agreement.

Disclosure of Operating Leases. For operating leases, as for capital leases, some of the same disclosure is required, but it can be in footnotes. For noncancellable leases having remaining terms in excess of 1 year, the lessee must disclose total future minimum lease payments, a schedule by year for the next 5 years, the total sublease rentals to be received, the basis for contingent rental payments, the existence and terms of purchase and renewal options and escalation clauses, and any lease agreement restrictions. The last two categories are included in a general description of the leasing arrangement.

AMORTIZING THE CAPITAL LEASE AND REDUCING THE OBLIGATION

A capital lease must be amortized and the liability reduced over the lease period. The method of amortization can be the lessee's usual depreciation method for assets that are owned. It should be pointed out that the period of amortization is always the lease term, even if the economic life of the asset is longer. If the latter occurs, the asset would have an expected residual value, which would go to the lessor. FASB No. 13 also requires that the capital lease obligation be reduced over the lease period by the "interest" method. Under this method, each lease payment is separated into two components: the payment of principal and the payment of interest. The obligation is reduced by the amount of the principal payment.

Reporting Earnings. For income-reporting purposes, FASB No. 13 requires that both the amortization of the leased property and the annual interest embodied in the lease payment be treated as an expense. This expense then is deducted in the same way that any expense is, to obtain net income. This treatment differs from that for the operating lease, for which only the lease payment itself is deductible as an expense. It also differs from the way all leases were treated prior to FASB No. 13, when only the lease payment was deductible. As you can appreciate, the accounting for leases can become quite complicated.[6]

TAX TREATMENT

Recognize that the treatment of capital leases for tax purposes differs from that for income statement purposes. For tax purposes, most companies

---

[6] The reader interested in the refinements should refer to an intermediate or advanced financial accounting textbook.

report the lease payment as an expense. In other words, for tax purposes, a company does not deduct the amortization of the asset and the interest as the expense of a capital lease. It deducts the annual lease payment.

The Internal Revenue Service wants to be sure that the lease contract truly represents a lease and not an installment purchase of the asset. To assure itself that a true lease in fact is involved, it may check on whether there is a meaningful residual value at the end of the lease term. Usually this is construed to mean that the term of the lease cannot exceed 90 percent of the useful life of the asset. In addition to this criterion, the lessee must not be given an option to purchase the asset or to re-lease it at a nominal price at the end of the lease period. Any option must be based on fair market value at the lease's expiration, such as would occur with an outside offer. The lease payments must be reasonable in that they provide the lessor not only a return of principal but a reasonable interest return as well. In addition, the lease term must be less than 30 years, or it will be construed as a purchase of asset.

In essence, the IRS wants to assure itself that the lease contract is not, in effect, a purchase of the asset, for which payments are much more rapid than would be allowed with depreciation. As lease payments are deductible for tax purposes, such a contract would allow the lessor to effectively "depreciate" the asset more quickly than allowed under a straight purchase. If the lease contract meets the conditions described, the full lease payment is deductible for tax purposes.

TO LEASE OR TO BORROW

Whether lease financing or borrowing is favored will depend on the patterns of cash outflows for each financing method and on the opportunity cost of funds. Several different methods may be used to compare the two alternatives. Our hypothetical examples will show the more frequently used methods.

At the outset, understand that not all lease contracts are paid according to the contractual specifications at the time the lease was negotiated. Some are paid in advance, some default, and others are renegotiated in minor ways. For still others, there are differences between actual residual value and that which was expected at the time the contract was negotiated. In a study of financial leases, Ronald C. Lease, John J. McConnell, and James S. Schallheim found that 31 percent of their sample prepaid and 19 percent of the contracts ended in default.[7] On average, realized returns were 2.6 percent less than contractual returns, reflecting the fact that a significant proportion defaulted. For non-defaulted leases, actual returns were greater than contractual returns, which the authors attribute to unanticipated inflation favorably affecting residual values. As our focus is on the cost of funds to the lessee as opposed to the likely return to the lessor, we use the contractual stream of payments in our analysis.

INVESTMENT FOLLOWED
BY FINANCING DECISION

A decision to acquire an asset is an investment decision. Using the discounted cash-flow methods and the required rate of return discussed in Part 2,

---

[7] Ronald C. Lease, John J. McConnell, and James S. Schallheim, "Realized Returns and the Default and Prepayment Experience of Financial Leasing Contracts," *Financial Management*, 19 (Summer 1990), 11–20.

the firm will decide whether or not to accept the project. Expressed differently, the investment worthiness of the project should be evaluated separately from the specific method of financing to be employed.

Once a decision is reached to acquire an asset, the firm must decide how it is to be financed. In this regard, we assume that it has determined an appropriate capital structure and that this structure calls for financing the project with either debt or a capital lease. The relevant comparison, then, is the cost of debt financing versus that of lease financing. The firm will wish to use the least costly alternative.

In the rest of this part, we present two ways in which to analyze the lease versus borrow decision—the present value method and the internal rate of return method. To illustrate them, we will use a common example.

EXAMPLE FOR ANALYSES

Suppose Kennedy Electronics, Inc., has decided to acquire a piece of equipment costing $148,000 to be used in the fabrication of microprocessors. If it were to lease finance the equipment, the manufacturer will provide such financing over 7 years. The terms of the lease call for the annual payment of $27,500. Lease payments are made in advance, that is, at the end of the year prior to each of the 7 years. The lessee is responsible for maintenance of the equipment, insurance, and taxes.

Embodied in the lease payments is an implied interest return to the lessor. If we ignore possible residual value, this before-tax return can be found by solving the following equation for R:

$$\$148,000 = \sum_{t=0}^{6} \frac{\$27,500}{(1 + R)^t} \qquad (19\text{-}1)$$

Because lease payments are made in advance, we solve for the internal rate of return that equates the cost of the asset with one lease payment at time 0 plus the present value of six lease payments at the end of each of the next 6 years. When we solve for R, we find it to be 9.79 percent. If instead of this return, the lessor wished a return of 11 percent, it would need to obtain annual lease payments of x in the following equation:

$$\$148,000 = \sum_{t=0}^{6} \frac{x}{(1.11)^t} \qquad (19\text{-}2)$$

$$\$148,000 = x + 4.2305x$$

$$x = \frac{\$148,000}{5.2305}$$

$$x = \$28,296$$

In the equation, 4.2305 is the present-value discount factor for an even stream of cash flows for 6 years, discounted at 11 percent (see Table B at the back of the book). Therefore, the annual lease payment would be $28,296.

If the asset is purchased, Kennedy Electronics would finance it with a 7-year term loan at 12 percent. The company is in a 40 percent tax bracket. The asset falls in the 5-year property class for accelerated cost recovery (depreciation) purposes. Accordingly, the schedule discussed in Chapter 6 is used:

Year	1	2	3	4	5	6
Depreciation	20.00%	32.00%	19.20%	11.52%	11.52%	5.76%

The cost of the asset is then depreciated at these rates, so that first-year depreciation is $.20 \times \$148,000 + \$29,600$, and so forth. At the end of the 7 years, the equipment is expected to have a scrap value of $15,000. If purchased, Kennedy Electronics would be entitled to this residual value, as it would be the owner of the asset.

PRESENT-VALUE ANALYSIS OF ALTERNATIVES

The first method of analysis we consider is a comparison of the present values of cash outflows for each of the alternatives. According to this method, whichever alternative has the lowest present value is the most desirable. Remember that the company will make annual lease payments of $27,500 if the asset is leased. Because these payments are an expense, they are deductible for tax purposes, but only in the year for which the payment applies. The $27,500 payment at the end of year 0 represents a prepaid expense and is not deductible for tax purposes until year 1. Similarly, the other six payments are not deductible until the following year.

As leasing is analogous to borrowing, an appropriate discount rate for discounting the after-tax cash flows might be the after-tax cost of borrowing. For our example, the after-tax cost of borrowing = $12\%(1 - .40) = 7.2\%$. The use of this rate assumes that the firm's future taxable income will be sufficient to utilize fully the tax shield associated with lease payments. It also assumes that the tax rate will not change. These assumptions are not unreasonable approximations of reality for many firms, but we must point out that there is disagreement over the appropriate discount rate to employ.[8]

Given the foregoing assumptions, we are able to derive a schedule of cash outflows after taxes and compute their present value. These computations are shown in Table 19-1. The present value of the total cash outflows under the leasing alternative is $98,904. This figure, then, must be compared with the present value of cash outflows under the borrowing alternative.

[8] See Richard S. Bower, "Issues in Lease Financing," *Financial Management*, 2 (Winter 1973), 31; and Myron J. Gordon, "A General Solution to the Buy or Lease Decision: A Pedagogical Note," *Journal of Finance*, 29 (March 1974), 245–46.

TABLE 19-1
Schedule of cash outflows: leasing alternative

END OF YEAR	(1) LEASE PAYMENT	(2) TAX SHIELD (1)(.4)	(3) CASH OUTFLOW AFTER TAXES (1) − (2)	(4) PRESENT VALUE OF CASH OUTFLOWS (7.2%)
0	$27,500	—	$27,500	$27,500
1–6	27,500	$11,000	16,500	78,165
7		11,000	(11,000)	(6,761)
				$98,904

Analysis of Debt.   If the asset is purchased, Kennedy Electronics is assumed to finance it entirely with a 12 percent unsecured term loan, its payment schedule of the same configuration as the lease payment schedule. In other words, loan payments are assumed to be payable at the beginning, not the end, of each year. This assumption places the loan on an equivalent basis with the lease and allows us to compare apples with apples, as most lease arrangements call for payment in advance.[9] A loan of $148,000 is taken out at time 0 and is payable over 7 years with annual payments of $28,955 at the beginning of each year.[10] The proportion of interest in each payment depends on the unpaid principal amount owing during the year. The principal amount owing during year 1 is $148,000 minus the payment at the very start of the year of $28,955, which is equal to $119,045. The annual interest for the first year is $119,045 × 12% = $14,285.[11] As subsequent payments are made, the interest component decreases. Table 19-2 shows these components over time.

To compute the cash outflows after taxes for the debt alternative, we must determine the tax effect. This requires knowing the amounts of annual interest and annual depreciation. Using the cost recovery schedule for the 5-year property class listed earlier, we show the annual depreciation charges in the third column of Table 19-3. Because both depreciation and interest are deductible expenses for tax purposes, they provide a tax shield equal to their sum times the tax rate of 40 percent. This is shown in column 4 of the table. When this shield is deducted from the debt payment, we obtain the cash outflow after taxes at the end of each year, column 5. At the end of the seventh year, the asset is expected to have a residual value of $15,000. This amount is subject to the corporate tax rate of 40 percent for the company, which leaves an expected after-tax cash inflow of $9,000. Finally, we compute the present value of all of these cash flows at a 7.2 percent discount rate and find that they total $93,484.

This present value of cash outflow is less than that for the lease alternative, $98,904. Therefore, the analysis suggests that the company use debt as opposed to lease financing in acquiring use of the asset. This conclusion

---

[9] If the loan payments were payable at the end of the year and lease payments were payable at the beginning, the earlier payments under the lease alternative would, in theory at least, release capacity for raising funds by other means of financing earlier than under the debt alternative. See Richard S. Bower, Frank C. Herringer, and J. Peter Williamson, "Lease Evaluations," *Accounting Review*, 41 (April 1966), 257–65.

[10] This amount is computed in the same manner as in Eq. (19-2), using 12 percent instead of 11 percent.

[11] For ease of illustration, we round to the nearest dollar throughout. This results in the final debt payment in Table 19-2 being slightly less than would otherwise be the case.

TABLE 19-2
Schedule of debt payments

END OF YEAR	LOAN PAYMENT	PRINCIPAL AMOUNT OWING AT END OF YEAR	ANNUAL INTEREST
0	$28,955	$119,045	$ 0
1	28,955	104,375	14,285
2	28,955	87,945	12,525
3	28,955	69,544	10,553
4	28,955	48,934	8,345
5	28,955	25,851	5,872
6	28,953	0	3,102

TABLE 19-3
Schedule of cash outflows: debt alternative

END OF YEAR	(1) LOAN PAYMENT	(2) INTEREST	(3) DEPRECIATION	(4) TAX SHIELD [(2) + (3)].4	(5) CASH OUTFLOWS AFTER TAXES (1) − (4)	(6) PRESENT VALUE OF CASH OUTFLOWS (7.2%)
0	$28,955	$ 0	$ 0	0	$28,955	$28,955
1	28,955	14,285	29,600	17,554	11,401	10,635
2	28,955	12,525	47,360	23,954	5,001	4,352
3	28,955	10,553	28,416	15,588	13,367	10,851
4	28,955	8,345	17,050	10,158	18,797	14,233
5	28,955	5,872	17,050	9,169	19,786	13,976
6	28,953	3,102	8,524	4,650	24,303	16,013
7	(15,000)			(6,000)	(9,000)	(5,532)
						$93,484

arises despite the fact that the implied interest rate embodied in the lease payments, 9.79 percent, is less than the explicit cost of debt financing, 12 percent. However, if the asset is bought, the company is able to avail itself of accelerated cost recovery depreciation, and this helps the situation from a present-value standpoint. Moreover, the residual value at the end of the project is a favorable factor, whereas this value goes to the lessor with lease financing.

Another factor that favors the debt alternative is the deductibility of interest payments for tax purposes. Because the amount of interest embodied in a "mortgage-type" debt payment is higher at first and declines with successive payments, the tax benefits associated with these payments follow the same pattern over time. From a present-value standpoint, this pattern benefits the firm relative to the pattern of lease payments, which typically are constant over time. These positive factors to purchase and debt financing more than offset the implied interest rate advantage to lease financing. The lease payment terms simply are not attractive enough to give up the tax and other benefits associated with ownership.

RESIDUAL VALUE UNCERTAINTY

A final consideration is the fact that the residual value is seldom known with certainty. The economic value of an asset at the end of a period of time is usually subject to considerable uncertainty, whether it be sold or continues to be employed in the firm. One way to treat the problem is with a probability distribution of residual values. Another way is to analyze the asset in terms of the value of services that are expected over its remaining life where these values are subject to a stochastic process. Such an approach is beyond the scope of this book; but we must bring residual value into our analysis if, in fact, a significant residual value is expected to occur.

INTERNAL-RATE-OF-RETURN ANALYSIS

Instead of computing the present value of cash outflows for the two financing alternatives, we could compute the internal rates of return. This approach avoids the problem of having to choose a rate of discount. In general, managers feel more comfortable in comparing percentages than they do in comparing present values.

To begin with consideration of the lease, the after-tax cost of leasing can be determined by solving the following equation for r:

$$A_0 - \sum_{t=0}^{n-1} \frac{L_t}{(1+r)^t} + \sum_{t=1}^{n} \frac{T(L_{t-1} - P_t)}{(1+r)^t} - \frac{RV(1-T)}{(1+r)^n} = 0 \qquad (19\text{-}3)$$

where A_0 = cost of the asset to be leased
n = number of periods to the end of the lease
L_t = lease payment at the end of period t
T = corporate tax rate
P_t = depreciation in period t
RV = amount of expected residual value at the end of the lease

In this construct, the cost of leasing is the rate of discount that equates the cost of the asset with the present value of lease payments, net of their tax shields, together with the present value of expected residual value after taxes. In other words, the cost of leasing includes not only the lease payments but the depreciation tax deductions and residual value that are forgone by virtue of leasing the asset as opposed to purchasing it. The last two represent opportunity costs if the asset is leased. If there is no expected residual value, the RV term drops out of Eq. (19-3).

Using our previous example and drawing on Tables 19-1 and 19-3, the information necessary to solve for the after-tax cost of leasing is shown in Table 19-4. The cash-flow stream appears in the last column. When we solve for the rate of discount that equates the negative cash flows with the positive ones in column 6, we find it to be 8.79 percent. This figure then serves as the after-tax cost of lease financing, and it should be compared with the after-tax cost of debt financing to determine which method results in the lower cost of financing. The after-tax cost of debt financing is merely the before-tax cost times 1 minus the tax rate. With the before-tax interest cost of 12 percent and a tax rate of .4 for our example problem, the after-tax cost of debt financing is $12.00(1 - .4) = 7.2$ percent. According to this method of analysis, then, borrowing is the preferred alternative because its effective yield is less than that for the leasing alternative.

TABLE 19-4
Schedule of cash flows—IRR analysis of lease

END OF YEAR	(1) COST OF ASSET	(2) L_t LEASE PAYMENT	(3) P_t DEPRECIATION	(4) TAX SHIELD $T(L_{t-1} - P_t)$	(5) RESIDUAL VALUE AFTER TAXES	(6) CASH FLOW (1) − (2) + (4) − (5)
0	$148,000	$27,500	—	—	—	$120,500
1	—	27,500	$29,600	$ (840)	—	(28,340)
2	—	27,500	47,360	(7,944)	—	(35,444)
3	—	27,500	28,416	(366)	—	(27,866)
4	—	27,500	17,050	4,180	—	(23,320)
5	—	27,500	17,050	4,180	—	(23,320)
6	—	27,500	8,524	7,590	—	(19,910)
7	—	—	—	11,000	$9,000	2,000

In summary, the internal-rate-of-return method of analysis permits a simple comparison of the after-tax costs of the lease and borrowing alternatives. Whichever alternative has the lowest rate would be selected according to this method. Again, this assumes that decisions have already been reached with respect to acquiring the asset and to financing it with a fixed-income type of instrument—either debt or a lease. Either method of financing is understood to have the same effect on the capacity of the firm to raise additional funds.

UNCERTAIN BORROWING COSTS

Rather than a fixed-rate term loan, sometimes the debt alternative is floating rate in nature, where the rate is geared to the prime rate. While the lease payments in the lease versus borrow analysis are known and contractual, debt payments are not, owing to fluctuations in the prime rate. When confronted with a situation of this sort, most analysts employ either the present short-term borrowing rate or some average of expected future short-term borrowing rates. In such situations, sensitivity analysis may be helpful. If our evaluation using the present borrowing rate shows debt financing to be the preferred alternative, we may wish to know how much the interest rate would need to rise before lease financing were favored. Also, a time dimension may be introduced to determine not only how much but how fast the rate must rise before we are indifferent between lease and debt financing. If such a rise is improbable, this will strengthen the case for debt financing. If it is probable, the case is weakened. Similarly, if lease financing dominates on the basis of present borrowing costs, an interesting question is how far and how quickly must interest rates decline before debt financing dominates. Again probability assessments are in order.

By employing sensitivity analysis in this manner, one can come to grips with situations where the cost of borrowing is uncertain in lease versus borrow analyses. This approach is applicable to both the present-value and the internal-rate-of-return methods for analyzing the lease versus borrow decision. In the final section of this chapter, we explore the circumstances under which lease financing can be a thing of value. Before we do that, let us consider a special lease situation.

ANALYSIS OF AN ASSET THAT CAN ONLY BE LEASED

Occasionally, the firm must evaluate an asset that it can acquire only by leasing. For example, ocean freighters may use certain dock facilities only through a long-term lease. The purchase alternative is not available. In situations of this sort, the firm does not choose between leasing or borrowing; the only decision is whether or not to lease. As a result, the investment and financing decisions are inextricably intertwined.

Although no method of analysis is entirely satisfactory, perhaps the best approach is to determine the merit of the project as an investment. The first step is to compute the cash-equivalent price of the lease alternative, beginning by establishing an interest rate that is consistent with other current leasing arrangements. The cash-equivalent price is the present value of all required lease payments, discounted by this rate. The next step is to compute the present value of expected future cash benefits associated with the project, discounted at the required rate of return. Obviously these benefits should be estimated only for the duration of the lease period. If the present value of the expected future cash benefits exceeds the cash-equivalent price, the project is worthwhile, and the firm should enter into the lease.[12] If the present value of the cash benefits is less than the cash-equivalent price, the project should be rejected.

If the project is accepted, obviously it can be financed only by leasing. Our method of analysis implies that lease financing does not alter the firm's cost of capital. In other words, the firm must be able to balance this method of financing with others so that it maintains a desired capital structure. If for some reason this balancing is not possible, perhaps because the project is large, then the effect of financing the project on the firm's cost of capital must be taken into account.

THE ECONOMICS OF LEASING

Now that we have an understanding of leasing and how it might be analyzed in relation to debt financing, we focus on the factors that give rise to leasing's being a thing of value in the capital markets. These factors are the differences in effective taxes paid by lessors and lessees and the differences in the protection afforded the lender and the lessor in bankruptcy. In the end, we will demonstrate why a firm should concentrate its evaluation on these factors to determine whether lease financing is appropriate for its situation.

LEASE FINANCING IN PERFECT CAPITAL MARKETS

It is useful to begin by assuming that capital markets are perfect and complete. Discussed in Part 2 and other parts of the book, this implies that there are no transaction costs, information is costless and readily available to all, securities are infinitely divisible, there are no bankruptcy costs, and there are no taxes. Complete financial markets imply that the desires of borrowers are satisfied with respect to the kinds of financial instruments available in the marketplace. Under these assumptions and the implied perfect competition among financial markets that results, it can be shown that the debt and lease obligations of a firm will be valued by secured lenders and lessors in the same manner.[13] The costs of debt and lease financing will therefore be the same, and the firm would be indifferent between the two as methods of financing.

When we relax the assumptions of perfect and complete capital markets, debt and lease instruments may not be valued in the same manner. As a result, their costs to the firm may differ. The introduction of transaction costs,

---

[12] We assume that the acceptance of the project does not change the business-risk complexion of the firm (see Part 2). Under no circumstances should the lease payments be deducted from the expected cash benefits and the project judged on the basis of whether or not the present value of the residuals is positive.

[13] In James C. Van Horne, "The Cost of Leasing with Capital Market Imperfections," *Engineering Economist*, 23 (Fall 1977), 1–12, this is demonstrated, using a state-preference model. Because the model is complicated, it is not presented here; however, the conclusion logically follows from all of our earlier discussion of the impact of the perfect market assumption on the valuation of financial instruments.

information costs, and less than infinite divisibility of securities results in impediments to arbitraging between financial instruments. These imperfections do not have a systematic effect in the sense that they favor leasing or favor debt financing all of the time. Rather, arbitrage between the markets is impeded; consequently, it may be possible for the firm to take "advantage" of the situation by issuing one type of instrument or the other. Since the advantage is likely to be small and extremely difficult to predict in practice, we do not concentrate on these imperfections. In contrast, the presence of bankruptcy costs and taxes affects things in a systematic manner, and the direction of their effect is predictable. It is to these factors that we now turn.

BANKRUPTCY COSTS TO THE LENDER OR LESSOR

If a lessee or borrower liquidates, the lessor's position is superior to that of a supplier of capital.[14] The lessor owns the asset and can retrieve it when the lessee defaults. The lender finds it more difficult and costly to gain possession when the borrower defaults, even though the loan was secured with the asset. As we know from our analysis of capital structure decisions and liquidity decisions earlier in the book, there are costs associated with the initiation of bankruptcy proceedings. In addition to out-of-pocket costs, there are delays to the secured lender in taking over the asset involved; these delays have an obvious opportunity cost. Neither the out-of-pocket costs nor the delays affect the lessor nearly to the extent that they encumber the secured lender.

The riskier the firm that seeks financing, the greater the incentive for the supplier of capital to make the arrangement a lease rather than a loan. Many suppliers of capital are either lenders or lessors but not both; some, such as bank holding companies, are both. The author is familiar with situations in which loans have been converted to leases when the risk of default has increased significantly. The purpose, of course, is to improve one's position should liquidation become necessary. In the total scheme of things, there is less "external drain" due to bankruptcy costs with lease financing than there is with debt financing. To the extent that any of the ex ante costs of bankruptcy avoided by leasing instead of borrowing are passed on to the lessee in the form of lower lease payments than would otherwise be the case, the firm might have an incentive to lease as opposed to borrow.[15]

Although the superior position of the lessor in bankruptcy relative to that of the lender is one reason for the development of the leasing industry, it is not the dominant one. But it is important and should not be overlooked, as it often distinguishes a lease from a loan in the eyes of a supplier of capital. Its significance varies over time. As the default risk of companies in general increases, as it might in a recession, this factor looms larger, the incentive for lease financing increases, and we would expect to see a greater amount of it.

THE EFFECT OF DIFFERING TAXES

The dominant economic reason for the existence of leasing is that companies, financial institutions, and individuals derive different tax benefits

---

[14] See Appendix A at the back of the book for a discussion of bankruptcy proceedings.

[15] This advantage may be offset by the fact that leasing sometimes introduces an additional intermediary with a resulting increment in administrative costs.

from owning assets. The greater the divergence in these benefits, the greater the attraction of lease financing overall, all other things staying the same. We know from our previous discussion that the tax benefit associated with owning an asset is the tax shield afforded by the deduction of depreciation over the depreciable life of the asset.

If the effective tax benefits associated with owning an asset were the same for all economic units in the economy and if capital markets were perfect in every other way, debt and lease obligations would be valued in the same manner. As a result, their costs would be the same. If the lessor did not lower lease payments to give the lessee all the tax benefits of ownership, the prospective lessee could simply purchase the asset and finance it with debt. In this way, it could avail itself of all the tax benefits. Therefore, it is not the existence of taxes per se that gives rise to leasing being a thing of value, but it is a situation in which different companies, financial institutions, and individuals have different abilities to realize the tax benefits.

Such differences are due to

1. *Different tax rates among economic units in the economy.* Examples: differences in personal and corporate income tax rates and differences in tax rates among various individuals and corporations.

2. *Different levels of past and current taxable income among economic units.* Example: a company that carries forward a tax loss and pays little or no taxes.

3. *Different effects related to the alternative minimum tax.* The presence of the alternative minimum tax (AMT) causes divergences in the ability of different corporations and individuals to use fully accelerated depreciation and the deduction of interest as an expense. Example: A company with redundant tax deductions will have an incentive to lease finance because the lease payment is not classified as a preference item when computing the AMT. Companies not so affected will have an incentive to act as lessors.

A firm that pays little or no taxes may lease an asset from another party that pays higher taxes. The lessee gets part of the tax benefits of ownership because its lease payments are lower than they would otherwise be. In turn, the lessor is able to use the full tax credit, which might not otherwise be available to it. As a result, both parties gain.[16]

MARKET EQUILIBRATION PROCESS

How much realization of the tax benefits the lessee is able to achieve depends on the supply and demand conditions in the market for lease financing. A lessor is unlikely to give up all the tax benefits, because realization of such benefits by the company seeking financing depends on its favorable tax situation. By the same token, competition among lessors will ensure that part of the benefits will be transferred to the lessee in the form of lower lease payments than would otherwise be the case. The exact sharing of the tax benefits is negotiable, but it will depend on equilibrium conditions in the capital markets.

[16] In studying sale and leaseback announcements, Myron B. Slovin, Marie E. Sushka, and John A. Poloncheck, "Corporate Sale-and-Leasebacks and Shareholder Wealth," *Journal of Finance*, 45 (March 1990), 289–99, find a positive stock market reaction for the lessee. They interpret this as being consistent with a reduction in expected taxes.

Our discussion shows that a company should concentrate its analysis on the tax considerations when approaching the question of whether to lease or borrow. For the consistently profitable company, lease financing may make little sense. Whenever a third-party lessor is involved, an added financial intermediary is introduced. This additional intermediation adds administrative costs ultimately borne by the lessee. For the marginally profitable firm or for the firm that has had a temporary setback and expects to pay little in the way of taxes in the near future, lease financing may prove very beneficial.

The economic benefits passed off to the lessee are reflected in the amount of periodic lease payments relative to the cost of the asset involved, or simply in the implied interest cost of the lease. By concentrating on this cost and the economic benefits associated with leasing relative to those for borrowing, the firm is able to determine whether lease financing is promising. It also is able to shop around better among lessors and to negotiate the lease. In this way, the decision will be grounded in sound economic reasoning, as opposed to the sales pitch used by many a leasing company to sell its financial service.

In the United States, a sophisticated market has developed in the leasing of large, expensive assets such as airplanes, ships, railroad cars, computers, and machinery. As would be expected, the lessees of such assets are primarily companies that have relatively low profitability and are unable to take full advantage of the tax benefits. The airlines' leasing of jets is an illustration of this arrangement. The profitability of many airlines has been relatively low or negative, and therefore they are unable to take full advantage of the tax benefits available. Lease financing enables them to realize a significant portion of these benefits.

In addition to bankruptcy costs and differences in tax situations, there may be other reasons for the existence of lease financing. For one thing, the lessor may enjoy economies of scale in the purchase of assets that are not available to the lessee. The lessor simply may be a large purchaser of certain types of assets. Also, the lessor may have a different estimate of the life of the asset, its salvage value, or of the discount rate than the lessee. Moreover, the lessor may face different borrowing costs than the lessee, lower, it is hoped, if leasing is to be stimulated. Finally, the lessor may be able to provide expertise to its customers in equipment selection and maintenance. While all of these factors may give rise to leasing, we would not expect them to be nearly as important as the tax reason.

SUMMARY

In lease financing, the lessee agrees to pay the lessor, periodically, for economic use of the lessor's asset. Because of this contractual obligation, leasing is regarded as a method of financing similar to borrowing. Leasing can involve the direct acquisition of an asset under a lease, a sale and leaseback arrangement whereby the firm sells an asset it owns and leases it back from the buyer, or a leveraged lease.

The accounting treatment of leases depends on the type. Leases that convey most of the economic benefits and risks associated with ownership are known as capital leases. Noncancellable leases not meeting this criterion are called operating leases. For a capital lease, the capitalized value of the leased property must be shown on the balance sheet as an asset, with the obligation shown as a liability. Moreover, the reported lease expense is the amortization of the lease property plus the implied interest rate embodied in the lease payments, not the amount of the lease payment. For the operating lease, the reported lease expense is the latter. For tax purposes, the lease payment usually is what is deductible as an expense.

Cash-flow methods may be used for evaluating lease financing in relation to debt financing. Unless an asset can be used only by leasing it, the decision to lease or borrow can be made on the basis of which alternative has the lowest present value of cash outflows or the lowest after-tax internal rate of return. Because the latter does not require specifying a discount rate, it is preferred by some. In both cases, a key factor is the interest rate on debt funds relative to the implied discount rate embodied in the lease payments. Unless the latter is relatively low, owing to the lessor enjoying the tax and residual value benefits associated with ownership, debt financing will dominate. The decision to employ lease or debt financing occurs only after a firm decides to invest in the project.

The foundation for the growth in leasing is (1) differences in the protection afforded the lessor and the lender in the event of bankruptcy and (2) differences in the ability of companies, financial institutions, and individuals to take advantage of the tax benefits associated with owning an asset. The impact of both of these factors varies over time with changes in perceived default risk; in bankruptcy costs; in federal, state, and local tax rates; and in the overall profitability of companies. As a result, the use of lease financing in the economy can change over time.

Of the two factors, the second has by far the greater influence. Firms that pay low taxes may be able to reap significant economic benefit from lease as opposed to debt financing. By leasing an asset from a lessor that pays substantial taxes, a firm is able to realize part of the tax benefits associated with accelerated depreciation. These tax benefits allow the lessor to lower the lease payments. At the expense of the federal government, both parties can gain by the lease arrangement.

SELF-CORRECTION PROBLEMS

1. Assuming that annual lease payments are in advance and that there is no residual value, solve for the unknown in each of the following situations:

    a. Purchase price of $46,000, implicit interest rate of 11 percent, a 6-year lease period; solve for the annual lease payment.

    b. Purchase price of $210,000, a 5-year lease period, annual lease payments of $47,030; solve for the implied interest rate.

    c. Implied interest rate of 8 percent, a 7-year lease period, annual lease payments of $16,000; solve for the purchase price.

    d. Purchase price of $165,000, implied interest rate of 10 percent, annual lease payments of $24,412; solve for the lease period.

2. Cordillera Pisco Company wishes to acquire a $100,000 press, which has a useful life of 8 years. At the end of this time, its scrap value will be $8,000. The asset falls into the 5-year property class for cost recovery (depreciation) purposes. The company can use either lease or debt financing. Lease payments of $16,000 at the beginning of each of the 8 years would be required. If debt financed, the interest rate would be 14 percent and debt payments would be due at the beginning of

each of the 8 years. (Interest would be amortized as a mortgage type of debt instrument.) The company is in a 40 percent tax bracket. Which method of financing has the lower present value of cash outflows?

3. The Xenia-Youngstown Zipper Company (XYZ) has decided to invest in a computer-controlled measuring device costing $120,000. The device has an economic life of 7 years, after which no salvage value is expected. The company must determine whether it is better to finance the acquisition through debt or leasing. XYZ expects profits before taxes of $10,000 next year, $20,000 the following year, $30,000 the third year, and $40,000 each year thereafter (before depreciation on the device). It has a high degree of confidence in these estimates. The tax rate is 15 percent on the first $50,000 in profits, 25 percent on the next $25,000, and 34 percent on any profits above $75,000. The company has had break-even operations during the previous 3 years.

   If the machine is financed with debt, the Atticks National Bank of Youngstown is willing to extend a loan for the full purchase price at an 11 percent rate of interest payable in equal annual amounts over 7 years. The bank also has a leasing division and has indicated that it is willing to lease finance the acquisition for XYZ over the 7-year period. The bank is and has been quite profitable, and it is in a 34 percent tax bracket. Describe in words whether lease or debt financing is likely to be more favorable for XYZ. Why? Is the bank likely to want to accommodate the company more on a lease basis or on a debt basis?

PROBLEMS

1. Given the following information, compute the annual lease payment that a lessor will require. (Lease payments are in advance.)

   a. Purchase price of $260,000, interest rate of 13 percent, 5-year lease period, and no residual value

   b. Purchase price of $138,000, interest rate of 6 percent, 9-year lease period, and a near certain residual value of $20,000

   c. Purchase price of $773,000, interest rate of 9 percent, 10-year lease period, and no residual value

2. Lucky Locker Corporation has just leased a metal bending machine that calls for annual lease payments of $30,000 payable in advance. The lease period is 6 years, and the lease is classified as a capital asset for accounting purposes. The company's incremental borrowing rate is 11 percent, whereas the lessor's implicit interest rate is 12 percent. Amortization of the lease in the first year amounts to $16,332. On the basis of this information, compute

   a. The accounting lease liability that will be shown on the balance sheet immediately after the first lease payment.

   b. The annual lease expense (amortization plus interest) in the first year as it will appear on the accounting income statement. (The interest expense is based on the accounting value determined in part a.)

   c. The annual lease expense for tax purposes.

3. Fez Fabulous Fabrics wishes to acquire a $100,000 multifacet cutting machine. The machine has a useful life of 8 years, after which there is no expected salvage value. If it were to lease finance the machine over 8 years, annual lease payments of $16,000 would be required, payable in advance. The company also could borrow at a 12 percent rate. The asset falls in the 5-year property class for cost recovery (depreciation) purposes and the company has a 35 percent tax rate. What is the present value of cash outflows for each of these alternatives, using the after-tax cost of debt as the discount rate? Which alternative is preferred?

4. In Problem 3, suppose now the machine were expected to have a scrap value of $14,000 at the end of year 8. Using the internal rate of return method of analysis, determine the best alternative. Does it differ from your answer to Problem 3?

5. Valequez Ranches, Inc., wishes to acquire a mechanized feed spreader that costs $80,000. The ranch company intends to operate the equipment for 5 years, at which time it will need to be replaced. However, it is expected to have a salvage value of $10,000 at the end of the fifth year. The asset will be depreciated on a straight-line basis ($16,000 per year) over the 5 years, and Valequez Ranches is in a 30 percent tax bracket. Two means for financing the feed spreader are available. A lease arrangement calls for lease payments of $19,000 annually, payable in advance. A debt alternative carries an interest cost of 10 percent. Debt payments will be at the start of each of the 5 years using mortgage type of debt amortization.

  a. Using the present-value method, determine the best alternative.

  b. Using the internal rate of return alternative, which is the best alternative? Does your answer differ from that to part a?

6. Pacific-Baja Shipping Company may need dock facilities in Valdez, Alaska. It would use the facilities for 4 years in connection with supplying heavy-duty equipment and other cargo to the area. The Port of Valdez Authority leases the facilities at an annual cost of $200,000 payable at the beginning of each year. Although the port authority has not stated the implied interest rate embodied in the lease payments, officials of Pacific-Baja believe a 9 percent rate would be appropriate. Over the 4 years, the company expects the project to show net cash flows of $180,000 in the first year, $250,000 in the second, $320,000 in the third, and $240,000 in the last year. (For simplicity assume these cash flows are realized at the end of each of the years.) The project is subject to risk, and it has been determined that the required after-tax rate of return is 18 percent.

  Should the company undertake the project and lease the dock facilities or should it reject the project?

SOLUTIONS TO SELF-CORRECTION PROBLEMS

1. a. Using Eq. (19-2) as the formula throughout

$$\$46,000 = \sum_{t=0}^{5} \frac{x}{(1.11)^t}$$

$$\$46,000 = x + 3.6959x$$

$$x = \frac{\$46,000}{4.6959} = \$9,795.78$$

  b. $\$210,000 = \sum_{t=0}^{4} \frac{\$47,030}{(1 + x)^t}$

$210,000/$47,030 = 4.4652

Subtracting 1 from this gives 3.4652. Looking in Appendix Table B across the year 4 row, we find that 3.4652 is very near the 3.4651 shown for 6 percent. Therefore, the implied interest rate is approximately 6 percent.

  c. $x = \sum_{t=0}^{6} \frac{\$16,000}{(1.08)^t}$

x = $16,000(1 + 4.6229)

x = $89,966.40

  d. $\$165,000 = \sum_{t=0}^{x} \frac{\$24,412}{(1.10)^t}$

$165,000/$24,412 = 6.759

Subtracting 1 from this gives 5.759. Looking in Appendix Table B down the 10 percent column, we find that 5.759 corresponds to year 9. Therefore, the lease period is 9 + 1, or 10 years.

2. Lease cash outflows:

END OF YEAR	(1) LEASE PAYMENT	(2) TAX SHIELD (1)(.40)	(3) CASH OUTFLOWS AFTER TAXES (1) − (2)	(4) PRESENT VALUE OF CASH OUTFLOWS (8.4%)
0	$16,000	—	$16,000	$16,000
1–7	$16,000	$6,400	9,600	49,305
8	—	$6,400	(6,400)	(3,357)
			PV of cash outflows =	$61,948

The discount rate is the before-tax cost of borrowing, 14 percent, times one minus the tax rate.

Debt cash outflows:

$$\text{Annual debt payment: } \$100,000 = \sum_{t=0}^{7} \frac{x}{(1.14)^t}$$

$$\$100,000 = x + 4.2883x$$

$$x = \frac{\$100,000}{5.2883} = \$18,910$$

END OF YEAR	(1) DEBT PAYMENT	(2) PRINCIPAL AMOUNT OWING AT END OF YEAR	(3) ANNUAL INTEREST
0	$18,910	$81,090	$ 0
1	18,910	73,533	11,353
2	18,910	64,917	10,295
3	18,910	55,096	9,088
4	18,910	43,899	7,713
5	18,910	31,135	6,146
6	18,910	16,584	4,359
7	18,906	0	2,322

The last payment is slightly lower due to rounding throughout.

END OF YEAR	(1) DEBT PAYMENT	(2) INTEREST	(3) DEPRECIATION	(4) TAX SHIELD (2 + 3).40	(5) A.T. CASH FLOW (1) − (4)	(6) PV OF CASH FLOWS (8.4%)
0	$18,910	$ 0	$ 0	$ 0	$18,910	$18,910
1	18,910	11,353	20,000	12,541	6,369	5,875
2	18,910	10,295	32,000	16,918	1,992	1,695
3	18,910	9,088	19,200	11,315	7,595	5,962
4	18,910	7,713	11,520	7,693	11,217	8,124
5	18,910	6,146	11,520	7,066	11,844	7,913
6	18,910	4,359	5,760	4,048	14,862	9,160
7	18,906	2,322	—	929	17,977	10,222
8	(8,000)	Residual value		(3,200)	(4,800)	(2,518)
				Present value of cash outflows =		$65,344

As the lease alternative has the lower present value of cash outflows, it is preferred.

3. The company is in a low tax bracket and has relatively low profits. If the asset is purchased, XYZ will be unable to utilize fully accelerated depreciation tax benefits in the early years. Finally, the applicable tax rate on XYZ's expected profits is 15 percent, very low.

In contrast, the applicable tax rate for the bank is 34 percent. Moreover, it will be able to utilize fully the accelerated depreciation charges at the times they occur. As a result, ownership of the asset is more valuable to the bank than it is to XYZ. If the bank is willing to lend money at 11 percent, it should be willing to lease finance at a lower implicit rate. Therefore, lease financing is likely to be the more favorable alternative to XYZ. Assuming that the bank does not have to pass on all the tax benefits to XYZ in the form of lower lease payments than otherwise would be the case, it should have a preference for leasing as opposed to lending. The problem serves to illustrate that with divergent tax rates and levels of profits, both parties can gain through lease as opposed to debt financing. The source of this incremental value, of course, is the government through its tax policies.

SELECTED REFERENCES

ANG, JAMES, and PAMELA P. PETERSON, "The Leasing Puzzle," *Journal of Finance,* 39 (September 1984), 1055–66.

BOWER, RICHARD S., "Issues in Lease Financing," *Financial Management,* 2 (Winter 1973), 25–34.

————, FRANK C. HERRINGER, and J. PETER WILLIAMSON, "Lease Evaluation," *Accounting Review,* 41 (April 1966), 257–65.

BOWER, RICHARD S., and GEORGE S. OLDFIELD, JR., "Of Lessees, Lessors, and Discount Rates and Whether Pigs Have Wings," *Journal of Business Research,* 9 (March 1981), 29–38.

COPELAND, THOMAS E., and J. FRED WESTON, "A Note on the Evaluation of Cancellable Operating Leases," *Financial Management,* 11 (Summer 1982), 60–67.

FRANKS, JULIAN R., and STEWART D. HODGES, "Lease Valuation When Taxable Earnings Are a Scarce Resource," *Journal of Finance,* 42 (September 1987), 987–1006.

GORDON, MYRON J., "A General Solution to the Buy or Lease Decision: A Pedagogical Note," *Journal of Finance,* 29 (March 1974), 245–50.

HULL, JOHN C., "The Bargaining Positions of the Parties to a Lease Agreement," *Financial Management,* 11 (Autumn 1982), 71–79.

KIM, E. HAN, WILBUR G. LEWELLEN, and JOHN J. MCCONNELL, "Sale and Leaseback Agreements and Enterprise Valuation," *Journal of Financial and Quantitative Analysis,* 13 (December 1978), 871–84.

LEASE, RONALD C., JOHN J. MCCONNELL, and JAMES S. SCHALLHEIM, "Realized Returns and the Default and Prepayment Experience of Financial Leasing Contracts," *Financial Management,* 19 (Summer 1990), 11–20.

LEWELLEN, WILBUR G., and DOUGLAS R. EMERY, "On the Matter of Parity among Financial Obligations," *Journal of Finance,* 36 (March 1981), 97–111.

LEWELLEN, WILBUR G., MICHAEL S. LONG, and JOHN J. MCCONNELL, "Asset Leasing in Competitive Capital Markets," *Journal of Finance,* 31 (June 1976), 787–98.

MCCONNELL, JOHN J., and JAMES S. SCHALLHEIM, "Valuation of Asset Leasing Contracts," *Journal of Financial Economics,* 12 (August 1983), 237–61.

MILLER, MERTON H., and CHARLES W. UPTON, "Leasing, Buying, and the Cost of Capital Services," *Journal of Finance,* 31 (June 1976), 787–98.

MYERS, STEWART C., DAVID A. DILL, and ALBERTO J. BAUTISTA, "Valuation of Financial Lease Contracts," *Journal of Finance,* 31 (June 1976), 799–820.

SCHALLHEIM, JAMES S., RAMON E. JOHNSON, RONALD C. LEASE, and JOHN J. MCCONNELL, "The Determinants of Yields on Financial Leasing Contracts," *Journal of Financial Economics,* 19 (September 1987), 45–68.

SLOVIN, MYRON B., MARIE E. SUSHKA, and JOHN A. POLONCHEK, "Corporate Sale-and-Leasebacks and Shareholder Wealth," *Journal of Finance*, 45 (March 1990), 289–99.

VAN HORNE, JAMES C., "The Cost of Leasing with Capital Market Imperfections," *Engineering Economist*, 23 (Fall 1977), 1–12.

WEINGARTNER, H. MARTIN, "Leasing, Asset Lives and Uncertainty: Guides to Decision Making," *Financial Management*, 16 (Summer 1987), 5–12.

PART 6

LONG-TERM FINANCING

Long-Term Financing at Dow

"We had to use financial leverage to obtain our growth objectives," said Enrique Falla,[*] chief financial officer of Dow Chemical Company. He was describing the era in which Dow was small relative to such giants as DuPont, Monsanto, and Union Carbide. As the company expanded, it spent large sums on research and development, on capital investments, and on acquisitions. By any measure, Dow has been successful and is now a giant itself in the chemical and related industries.

In financing its needs, Dow has been very innovative. It was one of the first companies to employ interest-rate swaps, and it pioneered the use of convertible debentures. Dow was *the* first to finance with "shogun" bonds, that is, bonds of U.S. corporations issued in Japan. In acquisitions, Dow literally invented the use of contingent value rights. "What we've done is to effectively use financial tools and techniques to support the company and its business objectives and to enhance shareholder value," remarks Falla. This approach to raising funds in imaginative ways plays a vital role in the overall management of Dow. It is an example of the finance function contributing in an important way to a company's value objectives.

[*] "Dow's Enrique Falla: Financial Innovator," *Institutional Investor*, 24 (June 1990), 124.

20

CHANGING FINANCIAL MARKETS

When considering the price equilibration process by which financial instruments are valued, our focus so far has been micro. We assumed that the firm was a price taker in its dealings with suppliers of capital. (An exception was the last part of Chapter 19 where we investigated the economics of leasing.) In this chapter, we introduce some broader notions, which might fall under the label of macrofinance. One can hardly open the financial section of a newspaper today without reading about rapidly changing financial markets. Like it or not, the financial services industry is in a period of rapid change. Deregulation, globalization, volatile interest rates and currency exchange rates, and heightened competition are some of the reasons. Today the financial manager of any medium to large corporation must search for "best price" across a wide spectrum of possibilities, both domestic and global. In what follows, we investigate the purpose of financial markets and the ever-changing environment in which capital is raised. This is important not only for its own sake but also because many of the remaining chapters draw on these concepts.

THE PURPOSE OF FINANCIAL MARKETS

Financial assets exist in an economy because the savings of various individuals, corporations, and governments during a period of time differ from their investment in real assets. By real assets, we mean things such as houses, buildings, equipment, inventories, and durable goods. If savings equaled investment in real assets for all economic units in an economy over all periods of time, there would be no external financing, no financial assets, and no money and capital markets. Each economic unit would be self-sufficient; current expenditures and investment in real assets would be paid for out of current income. A financial asset is created only when the investment of an economic unit in real assets exceeds its savings, and it finances this excess by borrowing or issuing equity securities. Of course, another economic unit must be willing to lend. This interaction of borrowers with lenders determines interest rates. In the economy as a whole, savings-surplus economic units (those whose savings exceed their investment in real assets) provide funds to savings deficit units (those whose investment in real assets exceeds their savings). This exchange of funds is evidenced by pieces of paper representing a financial asset to the holder and a financial liability to the issuer.

EFFICIENCY OF FINANCIAL MARKETS AND INTERMEDIATION

The purpose of financial markets in an economy is to allocate savings efficiently to ultimate users. If those economic units that saved were the same as those that engaged in capital formation, an economy could prosper without financial markets. In modern economies, however, the economic units most responsible for capital formation—nonfinancial corporations—use more than their total savings for investing in real assets. Households, on the other hand, have total savings in excess of total investment. The more diverse the patterns of desired savings and investment among economic units, the greater the need for efficient financial markets to channel savings to ultimate users. The ultimate investor in real assets and the ultimate saver should be brought together at the least possible cost and inconvenience.

Efficient financial markets are absolutely essential to ensure adequate capital formation and economic growth in an economy. With financial intermediaries in an economy, the flow of savings from savers to users of funds can be indirect. Financial intermediaries include institutions such as commercial banks, life insurance companies, and pension and profit-sharing funds. These intermediaries come between ultimate borrowers and lenders by transforming direct claims into indirect ones. They purchase primary securities and, in turn, issue their own securities. The primary security that a bank might purchase is a mortgage, a commercial loan or a consumer loan; the indirect claim issued is a demand deposit, a savings account or a certificate of deposit. A life insurance company, on the other hand, purchases corporate bonds, among other things, and issues life insurance policies.

Financial intermediaries transform funds in such a way as to make them more attractive. On one hand, the indirect security issued to ultimate lenders is more attractive than is a direct, or primary, security. In particular, these indirect claims are well suited to the small saver. On the other hand, the ultimate borrower is able to sell its primary securities to a financial intermediary on more attractive terms than it could if the securities were sold directly to ultimate lenders. Financial intermediaries provide a variety of services and economies that make the transformation of claims attractive.

1. *Transaction costs.* Because financial intermediaries are continually in the business of purchasing primary securities and selling indirect securities, economies of scale not available to the borrower or to the individual saver are possible. As a result, transactions costs and costs associated with locating potential borrowers and savers are lowered.

2. *Information production.* The financial intermediary is able to develop information on the ultimate borrower in a more efficient manner than the saver. Moreover, the intermediary may be able to reduce the moral hazard problem of unreliable information. Another possible advantage is that intermediaries can protect the confidentiality of information.

3. *Divisibility and flexibility.* A financial intermediary is able to pool the savings of many individual savers to purchase primary securities of vary-

ing sizes. In particular, the intermediary is able to tap small pockets of savings for ultimate investment in real assets. The offering of indirect securities of varying denomination makes financial intermediaries more attractive to the saver. Moreover, borrowers have more flexibility in dealing with a financial intermediary than with a large number of lenders and are able to obtain terms better suited to their needs.

4. *Diversification and risk.* By purchasing a number of different primary securities, the financial intermediary is able to spread risk. If these securities are less than perfectly correlated with each other, the intermediary is able to reduce the risk associated with fluctuations in value of principal. The benefits of reduced risk are passed on to the indirect security holders. As a result, the indirect security provides a higher degree of liquidity to the saver than does a like commitment to a single primary security. To the extent individuals are unable, because of size or other reasons, to achieve adequate diversification on their own, the financial intermediation process is beneficial.

5. *Maturity.* A financial intermediary is able to transform a primary security of a certain maturity into indirect securities of different maturities. As a result, the maturities on the primary and the indirect securities may be more attractive to the ultimate borrower and lender than they would be if the loan were direct.

6. *Expertise and convenience.* The financial intermediary is an expert in making purchases of primary securities and in so doing eliminates the inconvenience to the saver of making direct purchases. For example, not many individuals are familiar with the intricacies of making a mortgage loan; they have neither the time nor the inclination to learn. For the most part, they are happy to let savings and loan associations, commercial banks, savings banks, and life insurance companies engage in this type of lending and to purchase the indirect securities of these intermediaries. The financial intermediary is also an expert in dealing with ultimate savers—an expertise lacking in most borrowers.

Financial intermediaries tailor the denomination and type of indirect securities they issue to the desires of savers. Their purpose, of course, is to make a profit by purchasing primary securities yielding more than the return they must pay on the indirect securities issued and on operations. In so doing, they must channel funds from the ultimate lender to the ultimate borrower at a lower cost or with more convenience or both than is possible through a direct purchase of primary securities by the ultimate lender. Otherwise, they have no reason to exist.

DISINTERMEDIATION AND SECURITIZATION

We usually think of financial intermediation making the markets more efficient by lowering the cost and/or inconvenience to consumers of financial services. However, this is not always the case. Sometimes the intermediation process becomes cumbersome and expensive. When this occurs, there is a reversion toward direct loans and security issues. This reversal process is known as *disintermediation.* In other words, when financial intermediation no longer makes the financial markets more efficient, disintermediation occurs. One manifestation of this phenomenon is securitization.

Securitization involves taking an illiquid asset, such as a residential mortgage, packaging it into a pool of like assets, and then issuing securities

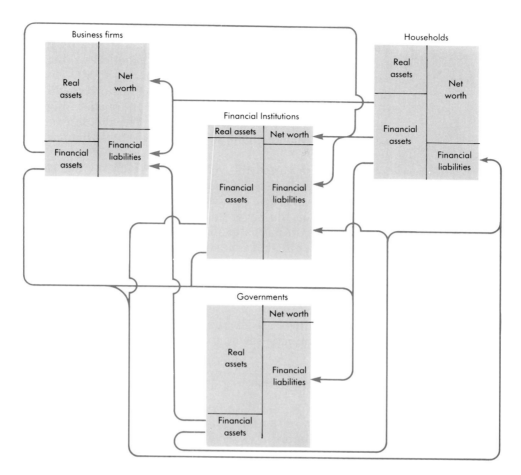

FIGURE 20-1
Relationship
of claims

backed by the asset pool. The investor has a direct claim on a portion of the mortgage pool. That is to say, interest and principal payments on the mortgages are passed directly along to the investor. Other securities involve bonds backed by the pool of assets. While securitization of assets was originally confined to residential mortgages, in the mid- to late 1980s it spread to auto loans, to credit card receivables, to commercial mortgages, and to lease contracts. In addition, attempts have been made to securitize trade credit and commercial loans. The reason for its spread is that the total transaction costs of credit often are less with securitization than they are when a depository institution intermediates between borrowers and savers. The forces of competition work to lower costs.

The securitization movement has implications for the financial manager in financing the corporation, so the movement requires careful monitoring. It is the wave of the future, not only in the United States but in Asia and Europe. When a company's assets include consumer receivables and loans, securitization may be a logical, cost effective means of financing.

FINANCIAL FLOWS IN THE ECONOMY

There are four main sectors in an economy: households, nonfinancial business firms, governments, and financial institutions. These four sectors form a matrix of claims against one another. This matrix is illustrated in Fig. 20-1, which shows hypothetical balance sheets for each sector. Financial assets of each sector include money as well as primary securities. Households, of course, are the ultimate owners of all business enterprises, whether they are nonfinancial corporations or private financial institutions. The figure illustrates the distinct role of financial intermediaries. Their assets are predominantly financial assets; they hold a relatively small amount of real assets. On the right-hand side of the balance sheet, financial liabilities are predominant. Financial institutions, then, are engaged in transforming direct claims into indirect claims that have a wider appeal. The relationships of financial to real assets and of financial liabilities to net worth distinguish them from other economic units.

The more varied the vehicles by which savings can flow from ultimate savers to ultimate users of funds, the more efficient the financial markets of an economy usually are. The more developed the financial markets, the greater the choices of the saver in putting savings to work and the greater the financing opportunities available to the borrower. The utility of both is increased. With efficient financial markets, then, there can be sharp differences between the pattern of savings and the pattern of investment for economic units in the economy. The result is a higher level of capital formation, growth, and want satisfaction. Individual economic units are not confined either to holding their savings in money balances or to investing them in real assets. Their alternatives are many; each contributes to the efficient channeling of funds from ultimate savers to users.

ALLOCATION OF FUNDS

The allocation of funds in an economy occurs primarily on the basis of price, expressed in terms of expected return. Economic units in need of funds must outbid others for their use. Although the allocation process is affected by capital rationing, government restrictions, and institutional constraints, expected returns are the primary mechanism whereby supply and demand are brought into balance for a particular financial instrument across financial markets. If risk is held constant, economic units willing to pay the highest expected return are the ones entitled to the use of funds. If rationality prevails, the economic units bidding the highest prices will have the most promising investment opportunities. As a result, savings will tend to be allocated to the most efficient uses.

It is important to recognize that the equilibration process by which savings are allocated in an economy occurs not only on the basis of expected return but on the basis of risk as well. Different financial instruments have different degrees of risk. In order for them to compete for funds, these instruments must provide different expected returns, or yields. If all financial instruments had exactly the same risk characteristics, they would provide the same expected return in market equilibrium.

From our discussion of marketable securities in Chapter 15, we know that the relative risk and, hence, expected return of different financial instruments are a function of a number of things:

1. Differences in default risk
2. Differences in maturity
3. Differences in the level of coupon rate
4. Differences in taxation of interest, dividend, and capital gains returns
5. Differences in option-type features, such as conversion rights, other equity links, call features, and sinking funds

As the effects of these factors on expected returns were explained in that chapter, and some will be expanded upon in Chapters 22 and 23, we do not dwell on them here.

Finally, the expected return on a financial instrument depends on the real rate of interest in the economy and on expected inflation. It generally is agreed that the nominal rate of interest that we observe on a fixed-income security embodies in it a premium for expected inflation. However, there is disagreement about the stability and consistency of this effect over time.

NOMINAL AND
REAL RATES OF RETURN

As we know from earlier chapters, the expected return to a supplier of capital is the rate of discount that equates the present value of the stream of expected cash inflows with the purchase price. For a fixed-income security, inflows consist of interest and principal payments together with the sales price if the security is sold before maturity. For an equity security, inflows consist of dividends and the sales price of the security if it is sold.[1] The expected return from holding a security is expressed in *nominal terms;* that is, the cash inflows received are in current dollars at the time of receipt. They have not been adjusted for inflation.

With inflation, these dollars will be worth less in purchasing power than were the dollars put out at the time the security was bought. As a result, the *real rate of return* on the security will be less than the nominal return. Suppose the expected nominal return on a security to be held 5 years is 10 percent, and expectations are realized. If the rate of inflation over the period turns out to be 5 percent per annum, the real rate of return is less than the nominal return. In this case, the real return is approximately 5 percent. The real return, then, is simply the return realized when dollars received in the future are placed on the same purchasing-power basis as the dollars put out to buy the security.

THE FISHER EFFECT

Many years ago, Irving Fisher expressed the nominal rate of interest on a bond as the sum of the real rate and the rate of price change expected to occur over the life of the instrument.[2] More formally, the nominal rate, r, is

$$1 + r = (1 + R)(1 + \alpha)$$
$$r = R + \alpha + R\alpha \tag{20-1}$$

where R is the real rate and α is the rate of inflation per annum expected to prevail over the life of the instrument. Where inflation is only moderate, the cross-product term, $R\alpha$, is small and usually ignored in the formulation. As a result, we would have

$$r = R + \alpha \tag{20-2}$$

[1] See Chapter 2 for the mathematics of finance as it pertains to stocks and bonds.
[2] "Appreciation and Interest," *Publications of the American Economic Association,* 11 (August 1896), 1–100.

Traditionally, this formulation is known as the *Fisher effect*. It states merely that the nominal rate of interest embodies in it an inflation premium sufficient to compensate lenders for the expected loss of purchasing power associated with the receipt of future dollars. Put another way, lenders require a nominal rate of interest high enough for them to earn an expected real rate of interest. In turn, the real rate required is a function of productive returns on real assets in our society plus a risk premium commensurate with risk of the borrower. The Fisher effect implies that if expected inflation rises by 1 percent, the nominal interest rate will rise by 1 percent as well. In other words, the effect is one to one. If r and α are the nominal rate and the expected inflation rate now, and r' and α' are those that prevail after a change in expected inflation, the Fisher effect suggests that

$$r' - r = \alpha' - \alpha \qquad (20\text{-}3)$$

According to this expression, the nominal rate of interest fully adjusts to changes in expected inflation; that is, the relationship of changes in nominal interest rates to changes in expected inflation is one to one. Financial markets would equilibrate in terms of their expected real rates of return, according to this notion. Put another way, investors would be indifferent between investing in a real asset or a financial asset, holding risk constant, for both would provide the same expected return after adjusting for inflation.

CHANGES IN NOMINAL RATES VERSUS EXPECTED INFLATION CHANGES

The question of whether the relationship between changes in nominal interest rates and changes in expected inflation is one to one is subject to much controversy, both theoretically and empirically. On a theoretical level, there are reasons why the nominal interest rate may not conform exactly to changes in inflation. Arguments exist to justify the relationship being less than one to one, as well as more. Robert Mundell, followed by James Tobin, presents a theory where changes in the expected rate of inflation raise or lower the nominal rate of interest by less than the expected inflation rate change.[3] In the case of an increase in expected inflation, this change is said to be reflected in both an increase in the nominal rate of interest and a decrease in the real rate.

The crux of Mundell's contention that the real rate of interest declines under such circumstances is that inflation reduces real money balances. In other words, money assets depreciate in real terms. As a result, real wealth declines, and this stimulates increased savings. In turn, this brings downward pressure on the real rate of interest. Finally, the decline in the real rate of interest stimulates investment and an acceleration in growth, according to this theory. In the case of a decrease in expected inflation or increased deflation, the opposite occurs. Here the real rate rises and, as a result, the nominal rate falls by less than the change in inflation. Because the change in real rate is opposite to that of the change in expected inflation, the response of the nominal rate of interest to the expected inflation change is less than one to one.

The principal argument for the response being more than one to one has

---

[3] Robert Mundell, "Inflation and Real Interest," *Journal of Political Economy*, 71 (June 1963), 280–83; and James Tobin, "Money and Economic Growth," *Econometrica*, 33 (October 1965), 671–84.

to do with taxes. This argument has been advanced by Michael R. Darby and by Martin Feldstein.[4] With taxes, it is shown that a rise in expected inflation results in nominal rates rising by a greater percentage. The after-tax real return to a lender whose loan is specified in nominal dollars is

$$R^* = r - rt - \alpha \qquad (20\text{-}4)$$

where r = the nominal rate of interest
$\quad t$ = the marginal tax rate
$\quad \alpha$ = the expected rate of inflation

all of which are expressed in terms of the length of the loan.
    Rearranging Eq. (20-4), the nominal rate of interest is

$$r = \frac{(R^* + \alpha)}{(1 - t)} \qquad (20\text{-}5)$$

Suppose now that expected inflation increases from α to α' but that the marginal tax rate remains unchanged, as does the after-tax real return that is required. From Eq. (20-5), it is seen that the nominal rate must rise by

$$\Delta r = \frac{\alpha' - \alpha}{(1 - t)} \qquad (20\text{-}6)$$

If the tax rate were positive, the nominal rate would increase by more than the increase in anticipated inflation. This is needed simply to pay the additional taxes. The higher the tax rate, the greater the nominal rate increase that is required.
    To illustrate, suppose the expected rate of inflation is presently 5 percent and it rises to 7 percent. If the lenders' effective tax rate is 40 percent, the nominal interest rate must rise by

$$\Delta r = \frac{7\% - 5\%}{(1 - .4)} = 3\tfrac{1}{3}\%$$

for lenders to be as well off in real terms on new loans as they were before the change in expected inflation. The implication is that lenders require compensation not only for inflation but for the additional tax burden as well.

EMPIRICAL EVIDENCE

Theoretically, we see—depending on the strength of the argument—that inflation may affect nominal interest rates in different ways. The Fisher effect postulates a one-to-one change in the nominal rate of interest to a change in expected inflation. Other arguments suggest that it is less than one to one (Mundell-Tobin) or more than one to one (Darby-Feldstein). The actual effect is an empirical question, and one to which a great deal of inquiry has been di-

[4] Michael R. Darby, "The Financial and Tax Effects of Monetary Policy on Interest Rates," *Economic Inquiry*, 13 (June 1975), 266–76; and Martin Feldstein, "Inflation, Income Taxes and the Rate of Inflation: A Theoretical Analysis," *American Economic Review*, 66 (December 1976), 809–20.

rected. Rather than going through the evidence article by article, we will summarize it. A detailed analysis is available elsewhere.[5]

Prior to the 1960s, there was little evidence of a relationship between inflation and nominal rates of interest. From the mid-1960s to 1980, however, there was a reasonably strong and positive relationship. That is, when there was an unexpected change in inflation, interest rates responded in the same direction, a behavior consistent with an inflation premium being embraced in the nominal rate of interest. In the 1980s, the rate of inflation declined and so did interest rates, but not by as much. The result, at least through the mid-1980s, was a sizable increase in real rates of interest. Only in the late 1980s and early 1990s did inflation and nominal interest rates come into reasonable balance. Real interest rates declined, not to the low levels of the 1970s but to levels that could at least be explained by underlying savings and investment patterns.

With respect to the Fisher effect, many earlier empirical studies, based on data for the 1960s and 1970s, suggested a less than one-to-one relationship between changes in nominal rates of interest and changes in inflation. Later studies, however, suggested either a one-to-one or greater than one-to-one relationship, the latter being consistent with a tax effect. The relationship between inflation and interest rates does not lend itself to simple explanations, nor does it appear to be consistent over time. There are a host of factors affecting interest rates, one of which is inflation. Our ability to explain, let alone predict, nominal rates of interest in terms of inflation leaves much to be desired.

NOMINAL CONTRACTING EFFECTS

With an unanticipated change in inflation, contracts specified in nominal terms are affected. Debtor-creditor claims are one example where there are redistribution consequences when unexpected inflation occurs. Another example is the tax contract between corporations and the government, where tax shields on capital assets are historically based. A third example is the increased tax burden arising from inflation-induced accounting profits on inventories. We consider these as well as other issues in this section.

Debtor-Creditor Claims. Whenever an unanticipated change in inflation occurs, an existing loan is not repaid in keeping with the real return expected at the time the loan was made. If there is an unanticipated increase in inflation, the borrower tends to gain. This gain occurs in an opportunity sense in that the loan is repaid with "cheaper" money than originally anticipated. To illustrate, suppose the nominal rate of interest on a 10-year loan is 10 percent, of which 5 percent is the expected real rate and 5 percent represents a premium for expected inflation. However, suppose that over the 10 years, inflation of 8 percent per annum actually occurs. As a result, the borrower's real interest cost is 2 percent instead of 5 percent. The lender loses, of course, because the real return is less than anticipated at the time the loan contract was made. With an unanticipated decrease in inflation, the borrower loses, in that the loan has to be repaid in more "expensive" dollars than originally anticipated, whereas the lender gains.

---

[5] See James C. Van Horne, *Financial Market Rates and Flows*, 3d ed. (Englewood Cliffs, NJ: Prentice Hall, 1990), Chap. 4.

Unanticipated increases in inflation result in a transfer of real wealth from net creditors to net debtors, whereas the opposite occurs with unanticipated decreases. A *net creditor* is defined as an economic unit whose financial assets exceed its financial liabilities, whereas the opposite holds for the *net debtor*. Whether a given economic unit gains or loses with respect to inflation depends on whether there is an unanticipated increase or decrease in inflation and whether the economic unit is a net debtor or a net creditor. In the aggregate, nonfinancial corporations have been consistent net debtors. However, individual companies can be net debtors or net creditors, and this can vary over time.

Price-Cost Sensitivity. Wages, cost of materials, and prices of a firm's products may be responsive to an unanticipated change in inflation. Their sensitivity or insensitivity can make a noticeable change in a firm's value. Because supply and demand functions for different products and for different resource inputs change in different degrees with unanticipated inflation, the effect on value is different for different firms. When prices, wages, and other costs vary proportionally with unanticipated changes in inflation, the firm's value should rise so that it leaves the real return on capital roughly unchanged. For many firms, prices change more or less quickly than wages and other costs when there is an unanticipated change in inflation. If they rise more rapidly, firm value should increase, all other things the same; if they rise more slowly, firm value should fall.[6] Thus, the lag or lead of costs to prices will strongly influence future operating earnings and firm value.

Depreciation and Inventories. Other nominal contracting effects may be reflected in depreciation and inventories. Depreciation charges, based on the historical costs of assets acquired in the past, do not change with inflation. If inflation results in larger operating cash flows, an increasing portion of these cash flows is subject to taxation. Because the corporation is able to deduct only historical cost depreciation and not replacement cost depreciation, its real rate of return is lower, creating a depressing influence on share value, all other things the same.

Under certain circumstances, the same phenomenon applies to inventories. Inventories can be deducted as a corporate expense only when sold or put into a product that is sold. Moreover, they are deductible only at original cost, not at replacement cost. If a company uses the first-in, first-out method of inventory accounting (FIFO), recorded inventory costs will be lower than replacement costs in an inflationary world. The reason is that the inventory first in was acquired in the past at a lower cost than presently prevails. When this cost is used in the cost of goods sold, accounting profits are overstated, and this overstatement results in higher taxes than would be paid if replacement costs were used. In other words, the real return on capital is lower, owing to the increased tax bite on operating cash flows. The problem can be reduced substantially if the company uses the last-in, first-out (LIFO) method of inventory accounting. With this method, the inventory last in is used in the cost of goods sold, and the cost figure here approximates the replacement cost of the inventory sold. In general, the more capital intensive the firm, the greater the

[6] For further analysis of this point and its precise effect on firm value, see James C. Van Horne and William F. Glassmire, Jr., "The Impact of Unanticipated Changes in Inflation on the Value of Common Stocks," *Journal of Finance*, 27 (December 1972), 1081–92.

influence of depreciation and inventory (FIFO) considerations, and the greater the difference between accounting and real profits in an inflationary environment.

Another nominal contracting issue has to do with a firm's pension plan and its explicit as well as implicit obligation to existing and future employees. As this aspect is very involved, we do not describe it. The effect of nominal contracts is particularly important when it comes to the valuation of a corporation. Unanticipated changes in inflation should be reflected in common stock prices. Individual stocks may be affected differently, depending on the nature of the nominal contracting. However, another explanation has been offered.

Money Illusion by Corporate Stockholders?   With increasing inflation and rising interest rates, Franco Modigliani and Richard A. Cohn argue that stockholders of a corporation suffer a money illusion, which results in a valuation of the stock lower than its true value.[7] Because corporations are able to deduct all of the higher interest expense, even though part of it is a return of capital, accounting profits are said to seriously underestimate the "true" profits of the corporation. By increasing its nominal debt to offset an increase in inflation, a company is able to hold constant its debt in real terms. Modigliani and Cohn suggest that the increase in nominal debt generates sufficient funds not only to pay interest but also to maintain real dividends and reinvestment. To the extent stockholders are fooled by accounting earnings, as opposed to real dividends, stock prices will suffer. The Modigliani-Cohn proposition has stirred considerable controversy, both theoretically and empirically. One troubling aspect of their proposition, however, is that the money illusion applies only to one set of security holders—namely, stockholders—and not to the other set, lenders. Often economic units are both lenders and investors in stock. If both suffer money illusion or if neither lenders nor investors in stock suffer it, the proposition does not hold.

FINANCIAL INNOVATIONS AND THE CHANGING FINANCIAL ENVIRONMENT

The last 15 years have been characterized by tremendous financial innovation, first in the United States and then in Europe and the developed countries of the Far East. The listing of developments is awesome; it includes zero-coupon bonds, money market preferred stock, the securitization of assets previously described, options and futures markets, interest-rate swaps, interest-cap loans, multicurrency loans and hedges, point-of-sale terminal transactions, and many more. These innovations encompass new or improved products as well as processes. Recognize that financial innovations do not just happen. There are reasons for their occurrence, both conceptual and environmental.

---

[7] Franco Modigliani and Richard A. Cohn, "Inflation, Rational Valuation and the Market," *Financial Analysts Journal*, 35 (March–April 1979), 24–44.

MAKING MARKETS MORE EFFICIENT
AND/OR COMPLETE

537

CHAPTER 20
Changing
Financial Markets

The principal force behind any financial innovation is the profit motive. In an economic sense, a new financial product or process will be profitable only if it makes the market more *efficient* and/or *complete*. Recall from earlier in the chapter that the purpose of financial markets is to channel savings in our society to the most efficient uses. However, the intermediation process is not costless. Costs are represented by the spread between what the ultimate saver receives for funds and what the ultimate borrower pays, holding risk constant, transaction fees, and the inconvenience to one or both parties. A financial innovation may make the market more efficient in the sense of reducing the spread, as defined above, or of lowering transaction and inconvenience costs. If this occurs, the overall cost of intermediation is reduced by definition.

Market completeness is different in concept. As explained in Chapter 14, a complete market exists when every contingency in the world corresponds to a distinct marketable security.[8] Incomplete markets exist when the number and types of securities available do not span these contingencies. More practically speaking, with an incomplete market, there is an unfilled desire for a particular type of security on the part of an investor clientele. If the market is incomplete, it pays the firm or financial institution to exploit the opportunity by tailoring security offerings to the unsatisfied desires of investors. By so doing, a lower financing cost will be achieved. As long as the market remains incomplete, a firm or financial institution should continue to tailor the securities it issues to the market.

CAUSES OF FINANCIAL INNOVATIONS

In steady state, of course, we would not expect to be able to make the market more efficient and/or complete. Presumably all opportunities for profitable exploitation would be exhausted, and no further gains would be possible. As a result, there would be no financial innovations. Indeed, an unchanging world would be marked by a lack of new financial products and/or processes. The environment simply must change for there to be exploitable opportunities with respect to inefficiencies and/or incompleteness. There are a number of causes for change, and we consider them in turn. Underlying each is a shift in savings flows or composition and/or a change in risk or utility with respect to risk.

What are some of the catalysts for change? They are (1) tax law changes, (2) technological advances, (3) changing inflation, interest-rate and currency levels, as well as their volatilities, (4) changes in the level of economic activity, and (5) regulatory change. With a change in one or more of these factors, the equilibrium is upset. Profit opportunities arise, and new financial products and processes are introduced to exploit the opportunity.

When tax laws change, the equilibrium structure of risk versus after-tax return is altered. As a result, new financial products often emerge as do revi-

---

[8] See J. Hirshleifer, *Investment, Interest and Capital* (Englewood Cliffs, NJ: Prentice Hall, 1970), pp. 264–75.

sions in existing products. New technology in computer-based information and funds transfers prompts changes in the delivery of financial services. To remain competitive, efficiency is crucial, and financial institutions that do not adapt to new technology are quickly left behind. To survive, an institution must be cost effective in processing transactions.

Rapidly changing inflation and fluctuating nominal and real rates of interest provoke the introduction of new financial instruments. Volatile foreign exchange rates have a similar effect. Increased interest-rate and/or currency volatility cause a number of market participants to want to shift risk to others. As a result, hedging and other devices come into being. Closely related to volatility of inflation and interest rates is the level of economic activity. In periods of economic prosperity, the focus tends to be on growth, and the thrust of new product development is on achieving this objective. In a sharp recession, the focus shifts to risk-reducing devices.

Last but not least is the change in environment caused by changes in regulations. In the United States, dramatic deregulation of the financial services industry has occurred, beginning in the late 1970s. Banking, insurance, securities firms, mortgages, payments mechanisms, and many other aspects of financial services were deregulated. Geographic and product differentiation, once the hallmarks of the financial services industry, are now very difficult to sustain. Barriers to entry were largely dismantled, competition heightened, and a lower average pricing of services followed. In this atmosphere, financial innovation flourished. Deregulation of financial markets followed in Britain, France, Germany, Japan, the Netherlands, and Switzerland, as well as in other countries.

IMPLICATIONS FOR THE FINANCIAL MANAGER

Whatever the nature of the catalyst, financial innovations occur in response to profit opportunities. In competitive markets, the profitability of a financial innovation to its original promoter will decline over time. The profitability associated with an innovation does not go unnoticed. Others enter the marketplace with a like product or process. As this occurs, the profit margins of promoters erode and consumers of financial services increasingly benefit from the financial innovation. While the promoter takes most of the benefits initially, this does not last long. Increasingly, these benefits are realized by the consumer in lower costs, in greater choice, and in less inconvenience. This occurs only if the financial markets are truly competitive.[9]

The financial manager must be alert to the changing environment. Investment as well as financing opportunities emerge which can increase a company's profitability. In particular, as a financial innovation becomes seasoned and promoter profit margins erode, the financial manager may wish to seize upon the opportunity. This requires a careful tracking of innovations to see which have a lasting economic foundation, which have become cost effective, and which make sense for the firm. There are literally hundreds of financial innovations every year, and many do not survive. You must have an effective

[9] In James C. Van Horne, "Of Financial Innovations and Excesses," *Journal of Finance*, 40 (July 1985), 621–31, I investigate ideas posed as financial innovations by their promoters but which are lacking in economic substance.

tracking system, or you will become lost in a bewildering display of new financial products and processes.

While this chapter introduces the topic of financial innovation, we do not stop here. Indeed, we merely set the stage for many of the remaining chapters of the book. Later we learn about specific financial innovations. The fact that the environment in which capital is raised is rapidly changing requires the financial manager to remain ever vigilant. Not only do financial innovations change the cost, features, and access to certain types of financing, but they affect cash and marketable security management as well. The ability to shift risk through financial markets has expanded enormously as a result of financial innovation—options, futures, currency, and swap markets. For the most part, financial deregulation has helped the corporation, particularly the large corporation.

SUMMARY

Financial assets exist in an economy because an economic unit's investment in real assets frequently differs from its savings. An excess of investment over savings is financed by issuing a financial liability; a surplus of savings over investment in real assets is held in the form of financial assets. The purpose of financial markets is the efficient allocation of savings to ultimate users of funds. A number of factors make financial markets efficient. Among the important is the presence of financial intermediaries. A financial intermediary transforms the direct claims of an ultimate borrower into an indirect claim, which is sold to ultimate lenders. At times, intermediation is no longer effective and is reversed either by securitization or by other means.

The allocation of funds in an economy occurs primarily on the basis of expected return and risk. We reviewed the reasons for differing risks and returns on financial market instruments. Among these was the effect of inflation. With inflation, the real return on a security is less than its nominal return, and the difference is known as an inflation premium. The Fisher effect suggests that the nominal return on a bond is the sum of the real rate of interest plus the rate of inflation expected over the life of the instrument. Certain empirical evidence was reviewed, and we found that the relationship between inflation and nominal rates is not consistent over time. Nominal contracting pertains to such things as debtor-creditor claims, price and wage lags to inflation, inflation-induced inventory profits, depreciation tax shields, and pension plans. As a result of these contracts, wealth transfers may occur when there is an unanticipated change in inflation. As a result, the company's stock price may be affected.

Financial innovation, where new products and processes are introduced, occurs because of the profit motive. By making financial markets more efficient and/or complete, financial innovations reward the initiator while at the same time they benefit other market participants through reduced costs and inconvenience together with a greater variety of financial instruments. There are a number of causes of financial innovation: volatile inflation rates and interest rates, regulatory changes, tax changes, technological advances, and the business cycle. The financial services industry has undergone deregulation and the adjustment process is ongoing. As a result, the financial manager must keep abreast of the ever-changing environment in which capital is raised. The ideas developed in this chapter will be drawn upon in subsequent chapters.

SELF-CORRECTION PROBLEMS

1. Wallopalooza Financial, Inc., believes that it can intermediate successfully in the mortgage market. Presently, borrowers pay 12 percent on adjustable rate mortgages. The deposit rate necessary to attract funds to lend is 8 percent, also adjustable with market conditions. Wallopalooza's administrative expenses, including information costs, are $2 million per annum on a base business of $100 million in loans.

    a. What interest rates on mortgage loans and on deposits would you recommend to obtain business?

    b. If $100 million in loans and an equal amount of deposits are attracted, what would be Wallopalooza's annual before-tax profit on the new business? (Assume that interest rates do not change.)

    c. In a market equilibration process, what would likely happen?

2. First Financial Corporation has made a 1-year loan to Xcor at an interest rate of 11 percent. For the year, it expects inflation of 4 percent. First Financial Corporation's tax rate is 30 percent.

    a. What after-tax real return does First Financial expect to earn?

    b. Suppose Xcor wishes to renew the loan at the end of the year, but expected inflation has increased to 7 percent. What interest rate would First Financial need to charge to be as well off as before with respect to expected after-tax real return?

    c. Suppose in part b the expected inflation rate were 2 percent. What interest rate would be appropriate to be as well off?

3. Abra Axle Company has a heavy inventory position, which is on a FIFO basis. It finances this inventory with floating rate loans. As it is in an extremely competitive business, it cannot quickly pass along cost increases to its customers in the form of higher prices. Its fixed assets are old, and it has no long-term debt. On the other hand, Elexir Extracts Company uses the LIFO method of inventory accounting. Its fixed assets are short-lived, and the company must continually replace older ones. The company has no short-term debt but does have fixed-rate long-term debt. It is the price leader in its industry and enjoys a relatively inelastic demand for its product.

    a. If there is an unanticipated increase in inflation, what is likely to happen to the share values of these two companies? Why?

    b. If there is an unanticipated decrease, what is likely to happen?

PROBLEMS

1. For 19xx, suppose the following changes in the balance sheets of business firms, households, and governments in the aggregate occur (in billions):

	BUSINESS FIRMS	HOUSEHOLDS	GOVERNMENTS
Net worth (savings)	$220	$380	−$50
Real assets	275	280	
Money	5	10	2
Other financial assets	75	215	70
Financial liabilities	135	125	122

    a. Which sectors are savings-deficit sectors? savings-surplus sectors? Why?

    b. From which sector do the savings-deficit sectors finance their deficits? How is it done?

2. Loquat Foods Company is able to borrow at an interest rate of 12 percent for 1 year. For the year, inflation of 7 percent is expected by market participants.

    a. What approximate real rate of return does the lender expect? What is the inflation premium embodied in the nominal interest rate?

    b. If inflation proves to be 4 percent for the year, does the lender suffer? Does the borrower suffer? Why?

    c. If inflation proves to be 10 percent, who gains and who loses?

3. The 3 percent British consols are an obligation of the British government issued in the Napoleonic wars. They are perpetual and obligate the British government to pay 30 pounds per 1,000 pounds face value bond forever.

    a. If the present yield on the instrument is 15 percent, what is the market price per bond?

    b. Suppose there is an unanticipated increase in inflation of 5 percent and the Fisher effect held exactly. What would be the new market price?

    c. If there is an unanticipated decrease in inflation of 5 percent, what is the new market price?

4. Companies X and Y have the following balance sheets at the latest year end (in thousands):

	COMPANY X	COMPANY Y
Cash	$ 1,000	$ 500
Receivables	7,000	2,000
Inventories	2,000	4,000
Net fixed assets	2,000	5,500
Total	$12,000	$12,000
Current liabilities	2,000	3,000
Long-term debt	1,000	5,000
Shareholders' equity	9,000	4,000
Total	$12,000	$12,000

    a. Are the companies net monetary creditors or debtors?

    b. If the rate of inflation should increase unexpectedly from 8 percent presently to 10 percent, who gains and who loses?

    c. If inflation goes from 8 percent to 6 percent, what happens?

5. Suppose the interest rate on high-grade corporate bonds were $12\frac{1}{2}$ percent and the present rate of inflation were 5 percent. If these percentages were to continue, what would be the effect on capital expenditures?

6. Lexalt Systems, Inc., has observed that computer-aided access to corporate bond price quotations and other information could be improved. Beare, Kelly and Zlotney, an investment banking firm, is particularly interested in an application proposed by Lexalt, as it wishes to introduce a new financial product—options on convertible bonds. To develop the necessary secondary market, information availability to market participants is critical. Beare, Kelly and Zlotney believe that the computer application and new financial product must be treated as a package, and the two parties have agreed to a joint venture. In words, what are the requisites for this innovation to succeed?

SOLUTIONS TO SELF-CORRECTION PROBLEMS

1. **a.** At $2 million in expenses per $100 million in loans, administrative costs come to 2 percent. As a result, the deposit rate must be no more than 10 percent, and the mortgage rate no less than 10 percent. Suppose Wallopalooza wished to increase the deposit rate and lower the mortgage rate by equal amounts while earning a before-tax return spread of 1 percent. It would then offer a deposit rate of $8\frac{1}{2}$ percent and a mortgage rate of $11\frac{1}{2}$ percent. Of course, other answers are possible depending on your profit assumptions.

    b. One percent of $100 million in loans equals $1 million.

    c. The intermediation spread is reduced from 4 percent to 3 percent by the entry of Wallopalooza. As both the depositor and the borrower gain, Wallopalooza will attract a lot of new business. In competitive markets, other financial institutions will respond to this price-cutting by offering the same or perhaps even lower mortgage rates and the same or higher deposit rates. As a result, Wallopalooza's gains will be checked, particularly if other institutions engage in a price war. However, consumers of financial services are well served with lower borrowing rates and higher deposit rates.

2. **a.** After-tax real return $= r - rt - \alpha = 11\% - (11\%)(.30) - 4\% = 3.70\%$

    b. $\Delta r = \dfrac{\alpha' - \alpha}{(1 - t)} = \dfrac{7\% - 4\%}{(1 - .3)} = 4.29\%$

    New interest rate $= 11\% + 4.29\% = 15.29\%$

    After-tax real return $= 15.29\% - (15.29\%)(.30) - 7\%$
    $= 3.70\%$

    c. $\Delta r = \dfrac{2\% - 4\%}{(1 - .3)} = -2.86\%$

    New interest rate $= 11\% - 2.86\% = 8.14\%$

    After-tax real return $= 8.14\% - (8.14\%)(.30) - 2\%$
    $= 3.70\%$

3. **a.** Abra Axle Company's share price is likely to decline. Costs are likely to increase faster than prices in response to the higher inflation. The FIFO method of inventory accounting will result in higher taxes on real income. Depreciation much below replacement depreciation will also have an adverse tax effect in real terms. As it has no long-term debt and floating rate short-term debt, it will not enjoy the benefits of existing debt values declining.

    Elexir Extracts Company's shares are likely to increase in value. It is able to pass along inflation-induced cost increases in higher prices. It may be able to raise prices even more than costs. Its LIFO method of inventory accounting and rapid replacement of fixed assets will largely shield the company from adverse tax effects. Its long-term debt will decline in value, thereby benefiting stockholders.

    b. For just the opposite reasons, Abra Axle Company's shares are likely to increase in value, while Elexir Extracts Company's shares are likely to decline in value.

SELECTED REFERENCES

CAMPBELL, TIM S., *Money and Capital Markets*. Glenview, IL: Scott, Foresman, 1988.

DARBY, MICHAEL R., "The Financial Effects of Monetary Policy on Interest Rates," *Economic Inquiry*, 13 (June 1975), 266–76.

FAMA, EUGENE F., "Short-Term Interest Rates as Predictors of Inflation," *American Economic Review*, 65 (June 1975), 269–82.

———, and MICHAEL R. GIBBONS, "Inflation, Real Returns and Capital Investment," *Journal of Monetary Economics*, 9 (May 1982), 297–323.

FELDSTEIN, MARTIN, "Inflation, Income Taxes and the Rate of Inflation: A Theoretical Analysis," *American Economic Review*, 66 (December 1976), 809–20.

FISHER, IRVING, *Appreciation and Interest*. New York: Macmillan, 1896.

———, *The Theory of Interest*. New York: Macmillan, 1930.

HENDERSHOTT, PATRIC H., and JAMES C. VAN HORNE, "Expected Inflation Implied by Capital Market Rates," *Journal of Finance*, 28 (May 1973), 301–14.

HIGGINS, ROBERT C., "Sustainable Growth under Inflation," *Financial Management*, 10 (Autumn 1981), 36–40.

LIVINGSTON, MILES, *Money & Capital Markets*. Englewood Cliffs, NJ: Prentice Hall, 1990.

MUNDELL, ROBERT, "Inflation and Real Interest," *Journal of Political Economy*, 71 (June 1963), 280–83.

ROSE, PETER S., *Money and Capital Markets*, 3d ed. Homewood, IL: BPI/Irwin, 1989.

VAN HORNE, JAMES C., "Of Financial Innovation and Excesses," *Journal of Finance*, 40 (July 1985), 621–31.

———, *Financial Market Rates and Flows*, 3d ed. Englewood Cliffs, NJ: Prentice Hall, 1990.

21

ISSUING SECURITIES

When we discussed external and internal long-term financing, back in Part 3, we analyzed the theoretical aspects. We broadly categorized the methods as equity and nonequity portions of the capital structure of the firm. Now we are going to be more specific about the methods of external long-term financing. We shall see how a firm employs the various methods, their features, certain valuation concepts, information effects, and their integration into the theory previously discussed. We shall meet the people whose title is *investment banker*.

PUBLIC OFFERING OF SECURITIES

The efficient functioning of financial markets requires a number of financial institutions.[1] One of these institutions, the investment banking firm, acts as middleman in the distribution of new securities to the public. Its principal function is to buy the securities from the company and then resell them to investors. For this service, investment bankers receive the difference, or spread, between the price they pay for the security and the price at which the securities are resold to the public. Because most companies make only occasional trips to the capital market, they are not specialists in the distribution of securities. On the other hand, investment banking firms have the expertise, the contacts, and the sales organization necessary to do an efficient job of marketing securities to investors. Because they are continually in the business of buying securities from companies and selling them to investors, investment bankers usually can perform this service at a lower cost than can the individual firm.

There are two means by which companies offer securities to the public: a traditional underwriting and a shelf registration. In recent years, the latter has come to dominate, at least with respect to larger corporations. Let us explore the two methods for offering bonds and stocks to investors.

---

[1] For a theoretical discussion of the efficiency of financial markets and savings flows, see James C. Van Horne, *Financial Markets Rates and Flows*, 3d ed. (Englewood Cliffs, NJ: Prentice Hall, 1990), Chaps. 1 and 2.

When an investment banking institution buys a security issue, it underwrites the sale of the issue by giving the company a check for the purchase price. At that time, the company is relieved of the risk of not being able to sell the issue at the established price. If the issue does not sell well, either because of an adverse turn in the market or because it is overpriced, the underwriter, not the company, takes the loss. Thus, the investment banker insures, or underwrites, the risk of adverse market price fluctuations during the period of distribution.

Typically, the investment banking institution with whom a company discusses the offering does not handle the underwriting alone. To spread risk and obtain better distribution, it invites other investment bankers to participate in the offering. The originating house usually is the manager and has the largest participation. Other investment bankers are invited into the syndicate, and their participations are determined primarily on the basis of their ability to sell securities. A traditional underwriting can be either on a *competitive bid* basis or on a *negotiated* basis. With a competitive bid, the issuing company specifies the date that sealed bids will be received, and competing syndicates submit bids at the specified time and place. The syndicate with the highest bid wins the security issue. With a negotiated offering, the company issuing the securities selects an investment banking firm and works directly with that firm in determining the essential features of the issue. Together, they discuss and negotiate a price for the security and the timing of the issue. Depending on the size of the issue, the investment banker may invite other firms to join it in sharing the risk and selling the issue. In either case, for the risk-bearing function investment bankers are compensated by an underwriting profit.

Compensation to Investment Bankers. To illustrate the compensation of investment bankers, we turn to an example. Figure 21-1 shows the essential features of a bond issue. The issue involves a syndicate of eight underwriters, with Hendershott, Kane and Kaufman being the manager that put it together. Its participation was the largest, being $22.5 million. Other participations ranged from $15 million down to $2 million. We see in the figure that the syndicate bought the bonds from the company for $74,156,250, or $988.75 per bond. In turn, it priced the bonds to the public at $997.50 a bond, or $74,812,500 in total. The spread of $8.75 per bond, or $656,205 in total, represents the gross commission to the syndicate for underwriting the issue, for selling it, and for covering the various expenses incurred.

Of the total spread of $8.75 per bond, $3.75, or 43 percent of it, is the gross underwriting profit. A portion of this gross goes to the originating house as manager of the offering. In our example, the manager receives a fee of $100,000, which represents approximately 15 percent of the total spread. After the bonds are sold, total underwriting profits less expenses and manager's fee are distributed to members of the syndicate on the basis of their percentage participation. It should be noted that the amount of underwriting profit to a member of a syndicate after expenses and the manager's fee is not large. In our example, it probably is less than $2 a bond.

With a respect to underwriter risk, each member of the syndicate is liable for its percentage participation in the unsold securities of the syndicate,

$75,000,000

Northern California Public Utility Company

$11\frac{1}{2}$% FIRST MORTGAGE BONDS DUE 2022

Interest payable September 1 and March 1. The bonds are redeemable on 30 days' notice at the option of the company at 111.5% to and including March 1, 1993, at decreasing prices thereafter to and including March 1, 2017, and thereafter at 100%. Due March 1, 2022.

Application will be made to list the bonds on the New York Stock Exchange.

THESE SECURITIES HAVE NOT BEEN APPROVED OR DISAPPROVED BY THE SECURITIES AND EXCHANGE COMMISSION NOR HAS THE COMMISSION PASSED UPON THE ACCURACY OR ADEQUACY OF THIS PROSPECTUS. ANY REPRESENTATION TO THE CONTRARY IS A CRIMINAL OFFENSE.

	Price to Public (1)	*Underwriting Discounts and Commissions (2)*	*Proceeds to Company (1) (3)*
Per unit	99.750%	.875%	98.875%
Total	$74,812,500	$656,250	$74,156,250

(1) Plus accrued interest from March 1, 1992 to date of delivery and payment.
(2) The company has agreed to indemnify the several purchasers against certain civil liabilities.
(3) Before deducting expenses payable by the company estimated at $200,000.

The new bonds are offered by the several purchasers named herein subject to prior sale, when, as and if issued and accepted by the purchasers and subject to their right to reject any orders for the purchase of the new bonds, in whole or in part. It is expected that the new bonds will be ready for delivery on or about March 12, 1992 in New York City.

HENDERSHOTT, KANE AND KAUFMAN

ELTON AND GRUBER — *LITZENBERGER, MCDONALD, PARKER AND PORTERFIELD*

BRENNAN, KRAUS AND SCHWARTZ — *UPSTAIRS AND DOWNING*

CARLETON, PINCHES, REILLY, AND YAWITZ

BLACK, MERTON AND SCHOLES — *MODIGLIANI, MILLER, KIM, ROLL AND SHARPE*

The date of this prospectus is March 5, 1992.

FIGURE 21-1
A cover of a prospectus

regardless of the number of securities the individual member sells. If a member of a syndicate has a 20 percent participation in an offering involving 40,000 bonds, and 10,000 remain unsold at the termination of the syndicate, the member would be responsible for 2,000 bonds. Its liability would be the same whether it had sold 20,000 bonds or none.

The principal reward for an investment banker participating in a syndicate comes from selling the securities to investors. As we discussed earlier, investment bankers are invited into syndicates, and their participation is determined primarily on the basis of their ability to distribute securities. For this function, an investment banker is rewarded by a selling concession of so many dollars a bond. In the Northern California Public Utility offering, the selling concession was $5 per bond, or 57 percent of the total spread of $8.75. The ultimate seller can be either a member of the underwriting syndicate or a qualified outside security dealer. To earn the full concession, however, the seller must be a member of the syndicate. An outside security dealer must purchase bonds from a member and will obtain only a dealer concession, which is less than the full selling concession. In our example, the outside dealer concession was $2.50 per bond out of a total selling concession of $5.

Best Efforts Offering.   Instead of underwriting a security issue, investment bankers may sell the issue on a *best efforts* basis. Under this arrangement, the investment bankers agree only to sell as many securities as they can at an established price. They have no responsibility for securities that are unsold. In other words, they bear no risk. Investment bankers frequently are unwilling to underwrite a security issue of smaller, nontechnological companies. For these companies, the only feasible means by which to place securities may be through a best efforts offering.[2]

Making a Market.   On occasion, the underwriter will make a market for a security after it is issued. In the first public offering of common stock, making a market is important to investors. In making a market, the underwriter maintains a position in the stock, quotes bid and asked prices, and stands ready to buy and sell it at those prices. These quotations are based on underlying supply and demand conditions. With a secondary market, the stock has greater liquidity to investors; this appeal enhances the success of the original offering.

SHELF REGISTRATIONS

The distinguishing feature of the traditional underwriting is that the registration process with the Securities and Exchange Commission (SEC) takes at least several weeks to complete. (The process itself is described at the end of this section.) Often 2 or more months elapse between the time a company decides to finance and the time the security offering actually takes place. As a result of this time lapse, as well as the fixed costs associated with a registration, there is an incentive for having a large as opposed to a small security offering.

Large corporations, whose securities are listed on an exchange, are able to shortcut the registration process by filing only a brief statement under Rule 415. This rule, which was initiated in 1982, permits what is known as a *shelf registration*. Here a company files an amendment to its detailed SEC filing every time it wishes to sell new securities. Mostly, this amendment contains details about the specific security being offered. Information about the company and risks inherent in its operations is found in the regular required SEC re-

[2] For a theoretical analysis of a best efforts offering relative to an underwritten one from the standpoint of the firm seeking the "best" contract with an investment banker, see Gershon Mandelker and Artur Raviv, "Investment Banking: An Economic Analysis of Optimal Underwriting Contracts," *Journal of Finance*, 32 (June 1977), 638–94. See also David P. Baron and Bengt Holmstrom, "The Investment Banking Contract for New Issues under Asymmetric Information," *Journal of Finance*, 35 (September 1980), 1115–38.

port, which provides the authority under which the individual shelf registrations occur. By using a shelf registration, a company is able to go to market with a new issue in a matter of days as opposed to weeks or months. As a result, it has the flexibility to time issues to market conditions, and the issues themselves need not be large.

Flotation Costs and Other Repercussions. In effect, a corporation places securities it expects to use in financing over the next 2 years on the "shelf," and from time to time it auctions off some of them. Therein lies the second major distinction between a shelf registration and a traditional underwriting. Obviously, the company will select the low-cost bidder. In this regard, large corporations are able to play investment bankers off against each other, and the resulting competition is felt in reduced spreads. For example, a typical spread on a traditional underwriting of corporate bonds is $7.50 or $8.75 per bond; the spread on a shelf registration might be $2.00 or $3.00 a bond. Flotation costs for a large common stock issue, again using a traditionl underwriting, might run 3 to 4 percent of the gross proceeds.[3] With a shelf registration, an SEC study indicated that these costs would run about 2 to 3 percent. In addition, the fixed costs of public debt issues (legal and administrative) are lower with a shelf registration because there is but one registration. Therefore, it is not surprising that large corporations have turned to shelf registrations.

For the somewhat smaller corporation, which must resort to a traditional underwriting, the widespread use of shelf registrations may work to its disadvantage. While there are far fewer traditional underwritings than before, the spreads for these underwritings do not appear to have widened. Mostly investment banks have absorbed the lower profitability associated with shelf registrations in reduced overall underwriting profitability. However, the amount of free advice available to a company is less than before. When overall underwriting profits were large, investment banks competed with all kinds of free advisory services, concerning such things as conditions and timing in the capital markets and financial strategy. As the lucrative underwriting business suffered, investment banks cut back on the free services they offered. Overall, then, shelf registrations have had a profound effect on the way in which securities, particularly debt instruments, are distributed, on the number of traditional underwritings, and on the function of investment banks.

GOVERNMENT REGULATIONS

Both the federal and state governments regulate the sale of new securities to the public, but federal authority is far more encompassing in its influence.

---

[3] For smaller issues, flotation costs, as a percentage of the gross proceeds of the issue, are higher. For empirical tests showing lower interest costs for shelf registrations versus traditional underwritings, see David S. Kidwell, M. Wayne Marr, and G. Rodney Thompson, "SEC Ruling 415: The Ultimate Competitive Bid," *Journal of Financial and Quantitative Analysis*, 19 (June 1984), 183–95; Robert J. Rogowski and Eric H. Sorensen, "Deregulation in Investment Banking: Shelf Registrations, Structure, and Performance," *Financial Management*, 14 (Winter 1985), 5–15; and F. Douglas Foster, "Syndicate Size, Spreads, and Market Power during the Introduction of Shelf Registration," *Journal of Finance*, 44 (March 1989), 195–204. Others suggest that the observed differences in flotation costs may be due to differences in issuing corporation as opposed to the registration method. Arguments for such an issuer self selection bias are contained in Robert Hansen, "Evaluating the Costs of a New Equity Issue," *Midland Corporate Finance Journal*, 4 (Spring 1986), 42–55; and David S. Allen, Robert E. Lamy, and G. Rodney Thompson, "The Shelf Registration of Debt and Self Selection Bias," *Journal of Finance*, 45 (March 1990), 275–87.

Federal Regulation.   With the collapse of the stock market in 1929 and the subsequent depression, there came a cry to protect investors from misinformation and fraud. Congress undertook extensive investigations and proposed federal regulation of the securities industry. The Securities Act of 1933 dealt with the sale of new securities and required the full disclosure of information to investors. The Securities Exchange Act of 1934 dealt with the regulation of securities already outstanding. Moreover, it created the Securities and Exchange Commission to enforce the two acts.

Most corporations selling securities to the public must register the issue with the SEC. Certain types of corporations, such as railroads, are exempt because they are regulated by other authorities. In addition, a corporation selling $1.5 million or less in new securities is required to file only a limited amount of information with the SEC under Regulation A. Also, if the issue is entirely sold to citizens of a single state, it does not necessarily fall under the SEC. Most corporations, however, must file a detailed registration statement, which contains information such as the nature and history of the company, the use of the proceeds of the security issue, financial statements, the management and directors and their security holdings, competitive conditions and risks, legal opinions, and a description of the security being issued. Along with the registration statement, the corporation must file a copy of the prospectus (see Fig. 21-1), which is a summary of the essential information in the registration statement. The prospectus must be available to prospective investors and others who request it.

The SEC reviews the registration statement and the prospectus to see that all the required information is presented and that it is not misleading. If the SEC is satisfied with the information, it approves the registration, and the company then is able to issue a final prospectus and sell the securities. If not, the SEC issues a *stop order*, which prevents the sale of the securities. Most deficiencies can be corrected by the company, and approval will usually be given eventually, except in cases of fraud or misrepresentation. For serious violations of the 1933 Securities Act, the SEC is empowered to go to court and seek an injunction. It should be pointed out that the SEC is not concerned with the investment value of the securities being issued, only with the presentation of complete and accurate information on all material facts regarding the security. Investors must make their own decisions based on that information. The security being issued may well be a highly speculative one subject to considerable risk. As long as the information is correct, the SEC will not prevent its sale.

The minimum period required between the time a registration statement is filed and the time it becomes effective is 20 days. The usual time lapse, however, is around 40 days. As we discussed earlier, large corporations are able to use shelf registrations. Once a detailed report is filed covering a block of securities, the company is able to sell off the shelf by filing a simple amendment. The lapse in time in this case is very short—perhaps a day.

The SEC regulates the sale of securities in the secondary markets in addition to the sale of new issues. In this regard, it regulates the activities of the security exchanges, the over-the-counter market, investment bankers and brokers, the National Association of Security Dealers, and investment companies. It requires monthly reports on inside stock transactions by officers, directors, and large stockholders. Whenever an investor or group obtains 5 percent or more of the stock, it must file a form 13D, which alerts all to the accumulation and to subsequent changes in ownership. In its regulatory capacity, the SEC seeks to prevent manipulative practices by investment dealers and by officers and directors of the company, abuses by insiders (officers and directors) in transactions involving the company's stock, fraud by any party, and other abuses affecting the investing public.

State Regulation. Individual states have security commissions that regulate the issuance of new securities in their states. Like the SEC, these commissions seek to prevent the fraudulent sale of securities. The laws providing for state regulation of securities are known as blue-sky laws because they attempt to prevent the false promotion and sale of securities representing nothing more than blue sky. State regulations are particularly important when a security issue is sold entirely to people within the state and is not subject to SEC scrutiny. In addition, it can be important when the amount of the issue is less than $1.5 million and subject to only limited SEC scrutiny. Unfortunately, the laws of the individual states vary greatly in their effectiveness. Some states are strict, and others are fairly permissive, with the result that misrepresentative promotion can thrive.

SELLING COMMON STOCK
THROUGH A RIGHTS ISSUE

Instead of selling a security issue to new investors, some firms offer the securities first to existing shareholders on a privileged subscription basis. Sometimes the corporate charter requires that a new issue of common stock or an issue of securities convertible into common be offered first to existing shareholders because of their preemptive right.

PREEMPTIVE RIGHT

Under a preemptive right, existing common stockholders have the right to preserve their proportionate ownership in the corporation. If the corporation issues additional common stock, they must be given the right to subscribe to the new stock so that they maintain their pro rata interest in the company. You may own 100 shares of a corporation that decides to make a new common stock offering for the purpose of increasing outstanding shares by 10 percent. If you have a preemptive right, you must be given the option to buy 10 additional shares so that you can preserve your proportionate ownership in the company. Various states have different laws regarding preemptive rights, but most of them provide that a stockholder has a preemptive right unless the corporate charter otherwise denies it.

OFFERING THROUGH RIGHTS

When a company sells securities by privileged subscription, it mails to its stockholders one right for each share of stock held. With a common stock offering, the rights give stockholders the option to purchase additional shares according to the terms of the offering. The terms specify the number of rights required to subscribe for an additional share of stock, the subscription price per share, and the expiration date of the offering. The holder of rights has three choices: (1) exercise them and subscribe for additional shares, (2) sell them, because they are transferable, or (3) do nothing and let them expire. The last usually occurs only if the value of a right is negligible or if the stockholder owns but a few shares of stock. Generally, the subscription period is about 3 weeks. A stockholder who wishes to buy a share of additional stock but does not have the necessary number of rights may purchase additional rights. If you now own 85 shares of stock in a company, and the number of rights required to purchase 1 additional share is 10, your 85 rights would allow you to purchase only 8 full shares of stock. If you would like to buy the ninth share, you may do so by purchasing an additional 5 rights.

In a rights offering, the board of directors establishes a date of record. Investors who buy the stock prior to that date receive the right to subscribe to the new issue. The stock is said to sell with *rights-on* through the date of record. After the date of record, the stock is said to sell *ex-rights*; that is, the stock is traded without the rights attached. An investor who buys the stock after this date does not receive the right to subscribe to additional stock.

VALUE OF RIGHTS

The market value of a right is a function of the present market price of the stock, the subscription price, and the number of rights required to purchase an additional share of stock. The theoretical market value of one right after the offering is announced but while the stock is still selling rights-on is

$$R_0 = \frac{P_0 - S}{N + 1} \qquad (21\text{-}1)$$

where R_0 = market value of one right when stock is selling rights-on
P_0 = market value of a share of stock selling rights-on
S = subscription price per share
N = number of rights required to purchase one share of stock

If the market price of a stock is $100 a share, the subscription price is $90 a share, and it takes four rights to buy an additional share of stock, the theoretical value of a right when the stock is selling rights-on would be

$$R_0 = \frac{100 - 90}{4 + 1} = \$2 \qquad (21\text{-}2)$$

We note that the market value of the stock with rights-on contains the value of one right.

When the stock goes ex-rights, the market price theoretically declines, for investors no longer receive the right to subscribe to additional shares. The theoretical value of one share of stock when it goes ex-rights is

$$P_x = \frac{(P_0 \times N) + S}{N + 1} \qquad (21\text{-}3)$$

where P_x is the market price of the stock when it goes ex-rights. For our example

$$P_x = \frac{(100 \times 4) + 90}{4 + 1} = \$98 \qquad (21\text{-}4)$$

From this example we see that, theoretically, the right does not represent a thing of value to the stockholder, whose stock is worth $100 before the date of record; after the date of record, it is worth $98 a share. The decline in market price is offset exactly by the value of the right. Thus, theoretically, the stockholder does not benefit from a rights offering; the right represents merely a return of capital. Another way to look at a rights offering is to equate it with a stock dividend to existing stockholders coupled with a new stock issue to which these stockholders have the first right to subscribe. The fall in stock price caused by the right offering $P_0 - P_x$ is the same as the fall in price caused by a stock dividend. In neither case does the stockholder receive a thing of value.

The theoretical value of a right when the stock sells ex-rights is

$$R_x = \frac{P_x - S}{N} \tag{21-5}$$

where R_x is the market value of one right when the stock is selling ex-rights. If, in our example, the market price of the stock is $98 when it goes ex-rights

$$R_x = \frac{98 - 90}{4} = \$2 \tag{21-6}$$

or the same value as before.

We should be aware that the actual value of a right may differ somewhat from its theoretical value on account of transaction costs, speculation, and the irregular exercise and sale of rights over the subscription period. However, arbitrage limits the deviation of actual value from theoretical value. If the price of a right is significantly higher than its theoretical value, stockholders will sell their rights and purchase the stock in the market. Such action will exert downward pressure on the market price of the right and upward pressure on its theoretical value. The latter occurs because of the upward pressure on the market price of the stock. If the price of the right is significantly lower than its theoretical value, arbitragers will buy the rights, exercise their option to buy stock, and then sell the stock in the market. This occurrence will exert upward pressure on the market price of the right and downward pressure on its theoretical value. These arbitrage actions will continue as long as they are profitable.

THE SUCCESS OF THE OFFERING

One of the most important aspects of a successful rights offering is the subscription price. If the market price of the stock should fall below the subscription price, stockholders obviously will not subscribe to the stock, for they can buy it in the market at a lower price. Consequently, a company will set the subscription price at a value lower than the current market price, to reduce the risk of the market price's falling below it. We know that the stock should fall in price when it goes ex-rights. Its new theoretical value is determined by Eq. (21-3), and we see that it strongly depends upon N, the number of rights required to purchase one share of stock. The greater the N, the less the theoretical price decline when the stock goes ex-rights. Thus, the risk that the market price will fall below the subscription price is inversely related to

N.[4] To illustrate, suppose the following were true:

	COMPANY A	COMPANY B
Market value per share rights-on, P_0	$60.00	$60.00
Subscription price, S	$46.00	$46.00
Number of rights needed to purchase one share, N	1	10
Theoretical value of one share ex-rights, P_x	$53.00	$58.73

We see that company A will have a greater decline in value per share when its stock goes ex-rights than will company B. All other things staying the same, there is a greater probability, or risk, that company A's stock will fall below the subscription price of $46 than there is that company B's stock will fall below it.

Amount of Discount. Apart from the number of rights required to purchase one share, the risk that the market price of a stock will fall below the subscription price is a function of the volatility of the company's stock, the tone of the market, expectations of earnings, and other factors. To avoid all risk, a company could set the subscription price so far below the market price that there is virtually no possibility that the market price will fall below it. The greater the discount from the current market price, the greater the value of the right, and the greater the probability of a successful sale of stock, all other things the same. As long as stockholders do not allow their rights to expire, theoretically they neither gain nor lose by the offering. In other words, the subscription price is irrelevant if stockholders exercise their rights and subscribe for more shares or if they sell them. Therefore, it might seem feasible to set the subscription price at a substantial discount to assure a successful sale.

The greater the discount, however, the more shares will have to be issued to raise a given amount of money, and the greater the dilution in earnings per share. This dilution may be of practical concern, for the investment community analyzes closely the growth trend in earnings per share. Significant underpricing of the new issue will dampen the growth trend in earnings per share. Although theoretically the stockholders are equally well off regardless of the subscription price set, in practice the market value of their stock holdings may suffer if investors in any way are fooled by the dilution in reported earnings per share. Obviously this would be an imperfection in the market, but imperfections on occasion can make a difference.[5]

If the firm wishes to maintain the same dividend per share, underpricing, which results in more shares being issued, will increase the total amount of dividends the company will need to pay and lower its coverage ratio. The

[4] See Haim Levy and Marshall Sarnat, "Risk, Dividend Policy, and the Optimal Pricing of a Rights Offering," *Journal of Money, Credit and Banking*, 3 (November 1971), 840–49.

[5] For a study that partly supports the imperfection notion as it has to do with rights offerings versus public underwritings, see Cleveland S. Patterson and Nancy D. Ursel, "Public Utility Equity Financing Practices: A Test of Market Efficiency," in *Regulating Utilities in an Era of Deregulation*, ed. Michael A. Crew (London: Macmillan, 1987).

disadvantages of underpricing must be balanced against the risk of the market price's falling below the subscription price. The primary consideration in setting the subscription price is to reduce the probability of this occurrence to a tolerable level. If, then, the subscription price appears to result in excessive dilution and this dilution seems to matter, the company should consider a public issue wherein the amount of underpricing is less. For most rights offerings, the subscription price discount from the current market price ranges between 10 and 20 percent.

Other Factors. The size of the capital outlay in relation to a stockholder's existing ownership of the stock is an influence on the success of a rights offering. Stockholders are likely to be more willing to subscribe to an issue amounting to a 10 percent addition to the stock they now hold than to an issue amounting to a 50 percent addition. The mix of existing stockholders may also be a factor. If a substantial number of stockholders hold only a few shares, the success of the offering may be less than if most stockholders held units of 100 shares. The balance between institutional and individual investors may also bear on the success of the rights offering. The current trend and tone of the stock market are influential. If the trend is upward and the market is relatively stable in this upward movement, the probability of a successful sale is quite high. The more uncertain the stock market, the greater the underpricing that may be necessary in order to sell the issue. There are times when the market is so unstable that an offering will have to be postponed.

STANDBY ARRANGEMENT AND OVERSUBSCRIPTIONS

A company can ensure the complete success of a rights offering by having an investment banker or a group of investment bankers "stand by" to underwrite the unsold portion of the issue. In fact, most companies use a standby arrangement in a rights offering. For this standby commitment, the underwriter charges a fee that varies with the risk involved in the offering. Often the fee consists of two parts: a flat fee and an additional fee for each unsold share of stock that the underwriter has to buy. From the standpoint of the company issuing the stock, the greater the risk of an unsuccessful sale, the more desirable a standby arrangement, although it also is more costly.[6] In essence, the underwriter sells a put option to the firm and its shareholders. If the stock price declines below the subscription price, the stock will be put to the underwriter at the subscription price. That is bad for the underwriter, but it all is in the nature of writing options. If the stock price remains above the subscription price, rights will be exercised and the underwriter will pocket the standby fee. Because of the risk, standby fees are significant and increase with the volatility of the stock. Therefore, the firm must pay for its put option. In view of the high costs relative to experience, it is surprising that so many companies have their rights offerings underwritten.

Another, and less used, means of increasing the probability that the entire issue will be sold is through oversubscriptions. This device gives stock-

---

[6] For an analysis of an underwriter's risk in a standby agreement, see Levy and Sarnat, "Risk, Dividend Policy, and the Optimal Pricing of a Rights Offering," pp. 842–45. For an analysis of its use from the standpoint of the company, see Simon M. Keane, "Significance of the Issue Price in Rights Issues," *Journal of Business Finance*, 4 (1972), 40–45.

holders not only the right to subscribe for their proportional share of the total offering but also the right to oversubscribe for any unsold shares. Oversubscriptions are then awarded on a pro rata basis relative to the number of unsold shares. Stockholders may subscribe to 460,000 shares of a 500,000-share rights offering. Perhaps some of them would like to purchase more shares, and their oversubscriptions total 100,000 shares. As a result, each stockholder oversubscribing is awarded four-tenths of a share for each share oversubscribed. This results in the entire issue being sold. Although the use of the oversubscription increases the chances that the issue will be entirely sold, it does not assure this occurrence, as does the standby agreement. It is possible that the combination of subscriptions and oversubscriptions will fall short of the amount of stock the company desires to sell.

Underwriters sometimes obtain the option to purchase additional stock at the offering price. Known as a *green shoe provision*, after an actual company, the option usually lasts several weeks after the offering. As with any option, the green shoe provision benefits the holder and works to the disadvantage of the issuer—the company, in this case. If the shares rise in price immediately after the offering, the underwriter can exercise the option and purchase the shares, then sell them at a gain.

RIGHTS ISSUE VERSUS PUBLIC OFFERING

By offering stock first to existing stockholders, the company taps investors who are familiar with the operations of the company. The principal sales tool is the discount from the current market price, whereas with a public issue, the major selling tool is the investment banking organization. When the issue is not underwritten with a standby arrangement, the flotation costs of a rights offering are lower than the costs of an offering to the general public. Therefore, there is less drain in the system from the standpoint of existing stockholders.[7] Moreover, many stockholders feel that they should be given the first opportunity to buy new common shares. When this preemptive right is taken away from them by amendment to the corporate charter, share price typically declines upon announcement of the event.[8]

Offsetting these advantages in the minds of some is that a rights offering will have to be sold at a lower price than will an issue to the general public. If a company goes to the equity market with reasonable frequency, this means that there will be somewhat more dilution with rights offerings than there will be with public issues. Even though this consideration is not relevant theoretically, many companies wish to minimize dilution. To the extent that there are information, legal, and institutional imperfections that influence this choice, existing shareholder wealth may be enhanced by a decision to go the public

---

[7] Clifford W. Smith, Jr., "Alternative Methods for Raising Capital," *Journal of Financial Economics*, 5 (November 1977), 273–307, analyzes empirically flotation costs for underwritings, rights offerings with standby arrangements, and pure rights offerings. He found that the total average cost as a percentage of proceeds was slightly higher for the underwriting, 6.17 percent, than it was for the rights offering with a standby arrangement, 6.05 percent, and both were significantly higher than the cost for a pure rights offering, 2.45 percent. The differences were most dramatic for issues of $100 million or more, in which the total cost as a percent of proceeds was but .13 percent for the pure rights offering compared with approximately 4 percent for both the underwriting and the rights offering with a standby arrangement.

[8] For an empirical study that confirms this notion, see Sanjai Bhagat, "The Effect of Pre-emptive Right Amendments on Shareholder Wealth," *Journal of Financial Economics*, 12 (November 1983), 289–310. This study uses the standard abnormal return, event study technique.

issue route. Examples of imperfections include financial reporting that masks the "true" trend in earnings per share, restraints on a company issuing stock at below its book value, and possible institutional incentives for a company to sell stock at as high a price per share as possible. Also, a public offering will tend to result in a wider distribution of shares, which may be desirable to the company.

Although these factors may have an effect on shareholder wealth, we would expect their effect to be slight. The issue remains as to why so many companies incur the costs associated with underwriting when they could sell securities through a rights issue without a standby agreement at less cost. Hansen and Pinkerton contend that companies that issue securities through a rights offering have a different stockholder mix than those that use a public offering.[9] The more concentrated the ownership of a company, the lower the merchandising expense of a rights offering. These expenses include printing, mailing, stock transfer, and payment of fees to a subscription agent to promote the sale. The more concentrated the stock ownership, the lower these costs. In testing ownership patterns for a sample of stock offerings, the authors claim to find a higher concentration of ownership for companies that use rights offerings. They suggest the choice of offering is a function of the flotation cost structure of the company.

In a separate paper, Hansen analyzes why companies prefer underwritten public offerings to underwritten rights offerings (those with a standby agreement).[10] This is perplexing because direct flotation costs are higher. However, underwritten rights offerings are associated with a price decline of more than 4 percent just prior to the sale, in contrast to public offerings where there is little price concession. Hansen argues that the price dip is a transaction cost for placing new securities. Inasmuch as total transactions costs (flotation and price concession) are higher for an underwritten rights offering, he suggests it is not surprising that companies prefer public offerings.

In summary, the introduction of imperfections in the capital markets may explain the wide use of public offerings versus rights offerings. Still, the greater direct flotation cost must be weighted in reaching a financing decision, particularly if the price concession is viewed not as a transaction cost but simply as a proportional renumbering of shares within the family of stockholders.

INITIAL FINANCING

When a company is formed, it obviously must be financed. Often the seed money comes from the founders and their families and friends. For some companies, this is sufficient to get things launched, and, with retained earnings, no more equity is needed. In other situations, equity infusions are necessary. In this section, we look at venture capital and initial public offerings.

VENTURE CAPITAL

Venture capital represents funds invested in a new enterprise. Debt funds sometimes are provided, but for the most part, common stock is involved. Almost always this stock is not registered for a period of years.

[9] Robert S. Hansen and John M. Pinkerton, "Direct Equity Financing: A Resolution of a Paradox," *Journal of Finance*, 37 (June 1982), 651–65.

[10] Robert S. Hansen, "The Demise of the Rights Issue," *Review of Financial Studies*, 1 (Fall 1988), 289–309.

Known as *letter stock*, it cannot be sold until the issue is registered; therefore, investors have no liquidity for a period of time. Their hope is that the company will thrive and that after 5 years or so it will be large and profitable enough to sell its stock in the public market. In turn, venture capitalists hope to sell their stock for many times what they paid for it. This is one scenario. Others, unfortunately, are possible. The risks associated with a new venture are many, and the frequency of failure can be high. With failure, the investor loses everything. The probability distribution of possible returns for most venture capital portfolio investments is skewed to the right. That is, there is a significant chance that investors will lose all their investment, but there also is some probability that their investment will increase in value fiftyfold. The overall portfolio return to the venture capitalist is very sensitive to those few investments that do very well, perhaps 1 or 2 in 10.

New venture proposals in the high-technology area are more attractive to venture capitalists than are new ventures in a mundane industry. The reason is simple. In high technology, there is the perceived possibility of substantial growth and ultimate capital gains. Thus, there are a number of venture capital firms in the greater Boston and San Francisco areas, owing to the hotbed of electronic activities in these areas. In addition, there are a number of venture capitalists in New York, Chicago, and some other cities. Whereas high-tech situations once were the only type of venture funded, this no longer is the case. Some low-tech and service companies lend themselves to venture capital financing. The keys are the quality of management and the potential market niche for the product or service.

The sources of venture capital are several. Wealthy individuals, the traditional source, are still important but no longer dominant. Individuals make venture capital investments directly or indirectly. In a direct investment, the individual or partnership of individuals screens applicants, investigates the investment, and reaches a decision. With an indirect approach, the first step is undertaken by a venture capitalist who presents situations and a certain amount of analysis to the investor. More common today, the venture capitalist will form a partnership and seek capital in advance from investors. The venture capitalist then will develop venture situations in which to invest. As general partner, the venture capitalist receives 20 to 25 percent of the ultimate profits of the partnership, known as carried interest, together with an annual management fee, say, 2 percent.

In addition to individuals, investors include institutions such as pension funds, trusts, life insurance companies, and universities. The intent is to invest a certain portion of the overall portfolio, usually less than 10 percent, in new ventures.

The enterprise seeking financing must convince any of the various sources that sizable returns will offset the substantial risks involved. That may be hard to do, so venture capital is not available to all new companies, but it gives some of them their start. There are several stages to venture-capital financing—start-up and, typically, several rounds of follow-up financing for expansion purposes. Such financing may carry the company for five years.

INITIAL PUBLIC OFFERINGS

If the private firm is successful, usually the owners will want to take the company public with a sale of stock to outsiders. Often this is prompted by venture capitalists, who wish to realize a cash return on their investment. In other situations, the founders simply want to establish a value, and liquidity, for their stock. Whatever the motivation, a decision is reached to become a public corporation. There are exceptions; some large, successful companies choose to remain private. Bechtel Corporation is one of the largest construction and engineering companies in the world, but it is private.

While there are advantages to being a public company, there are disadvantages. The public company must conform to SEC requirements in having a board of directors, disclosing sensitive information, having to employ certain accounting conventions, and incurring expenses as a public company not incurred by a private one. In addition, there is an investor fixation on quarterly earnings. At times this is a hindrance to management in trying to make long-term decisions. More will be said about this in Chapter 25, when we examine public companies that go private. Suppose for now, however, that a private company has decided to go public.

Most initial public offerings (IPOs) are through an underwriter. Having no previous public market, there is no stock price benchmark. Consequently, there is more uncertainty than there is when a public company sells additional stock. Empirical studies suggest that on average IPOs are sold at a significant discount (over 15 percent) from the prices that prevail in the aftermarket.[11] Several explanations have been offered. There may be an asymmetry in information between the company and the investment banker and among investors who are informed in varying degree. Beatty and Ritter posit a reputational effect for the investment banker that causes him or her to seek an optimal underpricing.[12] If the issue is underpriced too much, the investment banker will lose potential future issuers; if too little, potential investors. The authors test this proposition empirically and find that underwriters with the most deviation from an estimated normal underpricing lose market share.

Another reason for the discount, Ritter argues, is that there are both informed and uninformed investors in an IPO.[13] The informed investors will invest only in successful offerings where share price subsequently rises. Yet some IPOs are unsuccessful and the investor loses money. If the "average" uninformed investor is to be drawn into the market, the average return to them must be positive. But it will not be if informed investors invest only in the good deals and uninformed investors must pick up all the bad. (A winner's curse: Though they win the bid, they are cursed with the outcome.) To lure uninformed investors into the IPO market, Ritter suggests the need for a substantial discount.

For the corporation, the implication is that the initial public stock offering will need to be significantly underpriced from what is believed to be its true value. This is the price of admission to the public market. If reputational effects prevail, investment bankers should be motivated to seek a fair underpricing. Due to asymmetric information, however, significant underpricing probably will be necessary. Subsequent public offerings will not need to be underpriced as much, as a benchmark price will exist and there will be less uncertainty.

[11] For a synthesis of these studies, see Clifford W. Smith, Jr., "Investement Banking and the Capital Acquisition Process," *Journal of Financial Economics*, 15 (January–February 1986), 19–22.

[12] Randolph P. Beatty and Jay R. Ritter, "Investment Banking, Reputation, and the Underpricing of Initial Public Offerings," *Journal of Financial Economics*, 15 (January–February 1986), 213–32.

[13] Jay R. Ritter, "The Costs of Going Public," *Journal of Financial Economics*, 19 (December 1987), 269–82.

When a public company announces a security issue, there may be an information effect that causes a stock market reaction. Holding constant market movements, scholars have found negative stock price reactions (or abnormal returns) to a common stock or convertible security issue.[14] Straight debt and preferred stock announcements do not tend to show a statistically significant effect. A typical reaction for stock issue announcements is shown in Fig. 21-2, where days around the event are on the horizontal axis and the cumulative average abnormal return, after isolating overall market movement effects, is along the vertical axis. As seen, a stock price reduction occurs around the announcement date and it tends to average about 3 percent.

EXPECTATIONS OF FUTURE CASH FLOWS

Several explanations have been offered for this phenomenon. For one thing, the security issue announcement may be telling us something about future cash flows. When a company announces a security issue, the implication is that these funds will go to one or more purposes: investment in assets, reduction of debt, stock repurchase or increased dividends, or to make up for lower than expected operating cash flows. To the extent an unexpected security sale is associated with the last, the event will be bad news and the stock

[14] For an excellent synthesis of the empirical evidence, see Smith, "Investment Banking and the Capital Acquisition Process," pp. 3–29. See also Paul Asquith and David W. Mullins, Jr., "Signalling with Dividends, Stock Repurchases, and Equity Issues," *Financial Management*, 15 (Autumn 1986), 27–44; and Michael J. Barclay and Robert H. Litzenberger, "Announcement Effects of New Equity Issues and the Use of Intraday Price Data," *Journal of Financial Economics*, 21 (May 1988), 71–99.

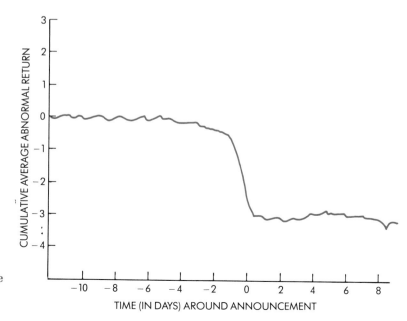

FIGURE 21-2

Relative stock returns around the announcement of a new equity issue

price accordingly may suffer. The cash-flow argument for an information effect is associated with Miller and Rock.[15]

When Smith summarized a number of empirical studies on new security sales, stock repurchases, dividend changes, and changes in capital expenditures, the evidence was consistent with a cash-flow information effect.[16] Repurchase of stock, dividend increases, and investment plan increases were accompanied by positive abnormal stock returns in the 2 days immediately prior to the announcement, whereas stock sales, dividend decreases, and investment plan decreases were accompanied by negative abnormal returns. The more anticipated or predictable the announcement, the less the stock price change. As a debt issue is more predictable than an equity issue and utility issues are more predictable than industrial issues, the price effect was found to be less.

ASYMMETRIC INFORMATION

A second effect has to do with asymmetric information between investors and management. In this argument, associated with Myers and Majluf, potential investors in securities have less information than management, and management tends to issue securities when the market's assessment of their value is higher than its assessment.[17] This would be particularly true with common stock, where investors have only a residual claim to income and assets. Because cash flows are affected when a new security is offered, an asymmetric information effect is difficult to sort out using new issue data.

With an exchange offering of one security for another, however, cash flows are not affected. When empirical studies on exchange offers are categorized into those that increase leverage and those that decrease leverage, the results are striking.[18] Leveraging-increasing transactions are accompanied by positive abnormal stock returns in the 2 days prior to announcement, while leverage-reducing transactions are accompanied by negative returns. The effect is greatest for debt for common exchanges (positive return) and common for debt exchanges (negative return), followed by preferred for common (positive return) and preferred for debt (negative return). Thus, the evidence is consistent with an asymmetric information effect. In other words, managers are more likely to issue debt or preferred when they believe the common stock is underpriced in the market and to issue common when it is believed to be overpriced.

In summary, the issuance of new securities as well as exchange offerings appears to bring with it information effects that impact stock prices. The financial manager must be mindful of these potential effects before a decision is reached.

---

[15] Merton H. Miller and Kevin Rock, "Dividend Policy under Asymmetric Information," *Journal of Finance*, 40 (September 1985), 1031–51.

[16] Smith, "Investment Banking and the Capital Acquisition Process," pp. 7–9.

[17] See Stewart C. Myers and Nicholas S. Majluf, "Corporate Financing and Investment Decisions When Firms Have Information That Investors Do Not Have," *Journal of Financial Economics*, 13 (June 1984), 187–221.

[18] Again, the source of this categorization is Smith, "Investment Banking and the Capital Acquisition Process," pp. 10–12. Included in exchange offers are pairwise combinations of debt, convertibles, preferred stock, and common stock.

In contrast to a public sale of stock where share price falls by 3 percent on average, the announcement of a private sale is associated with an increase. Wruck found the average increase to be 4.5 percent.[19] In a private sale, a company sells stock to a single investor or to a small group of investors. With a private sale, ownership concentration tends to increase. In contrast to the previous information effects, the effect here has to do with control of the company. Wruck found that when the level of ownership concentration after the sale was less than 5 percent or more than 25 percent, the announcement effect was positive. In the mid range, the effect on share price was negative, owing perhaps to incumbents becoming more entrenched. Much more will be said about corporate control in Chapter 24; it will suffice for now to distinguish between public and private sales of stock.

SUMMARY

When companies finance their long-term needs externally, they may obtain funds from the capital markets. If the financing involves a public offering, the company often will use the services of an investment banking firm. The investment banker's principal functions are risk bearing, or underwriting, and selling the securities. For these functions, the investment banking firm is compensated by the spread between the price it pays for the securities and the price at which it resells the securities to investors. The offering itself can be either a traditional underwriting or, in the case of a large corporation, a shelf registration. With a shelf registration, a company sells securities "off the shelf" without the delays associated with a lengthy registration process. Instead, only an amendment is filed with the Securities and Exchange Commission. Not only is the shelf registration faster, but the cost of the issue is a good deal less.

A company may give its existing stockholders the first opportunity to purchase a new security issue on a privileged subscription basis. This type of issue is known as a rights offering, because existing stockholders receive one right for each share of stock they hold. A right represents an option to buy the new security at the subscription price, and it takes a specified number of rights to purchase the security. Depending on the relationship between the current market price of the stock and the subscription price, a right usually will have a market value. Security offerings to the general public and offerings on a privileged subscription basis must comply with federal and state regulations. The enforcement agency for the federal government is the Securities and Exchange Commission, whose authority encompasses both the sale of new securities and the trading of existing securities in the secondary market.

In its early stages, a company needs financing. One source is the venture captialist who specializes in financing new enterprises, particularly if they involve high technology. If the company is successful, it often will "go public"

---

[19]Karen Hopper Wruck, "Equity Ownership Concentration and Firm Value," *Journal of Financial Economics*, 23 (June 1989), 3–28.

with an initial public offering of common stock. Because there is no benchmark stock price, much uncertainty exists and the new issue usually must be sold at a sizable discount from the price that will prevail in the after-market.

The announcement of a debt or stock issue may be accompanied by a stock market reaction. For one thing, the announcement may connote information about future cash flows of the company. Or the reaction may be due to asymmetric information between investors and management. The latter presumes management will finance with stock when it believes the stock is overvalued and with debt when it is believed to be undervalued. Empirical evidence is consistent with both of these notions, so the financial manager must recognize the likelihood of an information effect when issuing securities.

SELF-CORRECTION PROBLEMS

1. The Homex Company wishes to raise $5 million in additional equity capital through a traditional underwriting. After considering the potential difficulty of selling the shares, the investment banker decides that the selling concession should be between 3 percent and 4 percent of the value of the issue. When the risks of underwriting are evaluated, it is decided that the selling concession should constitute between 50 percent and 60 percent of the gross spread. If the manager's fee (which constitutes part of the underwriting profit) is taken to be 15 percent of the gross spread, answer the following questions:

    a. Assuming that the selling concession is set at 4 percent of gross proceeds and 50 percent of the gross spread, what would be the dollar value of the manager's fee, net underwriting profit, selling concession, and gross spread on the Homex underwriting?

    b. Rework part a, assuming that the selling concession was set at 3 percent of gross proceeds and 60 percent of the gross spread.

    c. Assuming that the managing underwriter underwrote 25 percent and sold 20 percent of the issue, what would be the manager's total compensation under part a? under part b?

2. The stock of the Dunbar Company is selling for $150 per share. The company issues rights to subscribe for one additional share of stock at $125 a share, for each nine held. Compute the theoretical value of

    a. A right when the stock is selling rights-on

    b. One share of stock when it goes ex-rights

    c. A right when the stock sells ex-rights and the actual market price goes to $143 per share

PROBLEMS

1. Caldacci Copper Company, a risky company, needs to raise $75 million in long-term debt funds. The company is negotiating the offering through First Columbia Corporation. First Columbia believes it can bring together a syndicate of investment bankers to underwrite and sell the issue. The bonds will be given a coupon rate, so that they may be priced to the public at their face value of $1,000. The selling concession will be $6 per bond; in addition, administrative expenses of $115,000 will be incurred. Typically, First Columbia requires a manager's fee of 15 percent of the total spread. To sell this issue, it feels that the underwriting

commission, net of expenses, and manager's fee must be 25 percent of the total spread.

   a. What will be the total spread? the total spread per bond?

   b. What will be the net proceeds of the issue to Caldacci Copper?

   c. What is the selling concession as a percentage of the total spread?

   d. What are the total costs of issuing the securities as a percentage of the net proceeds to the company?

2. Black Telecommunications Company needs to raise $1.8 billion (face value) of debt funds over the next 2 years. If it were to use traditional underwritings, the company would expect to have six underwritings over the 2-year span. The underwriter spread would likely be $7.50 per bond, and out-of-pocket expenses paid by the company would total $350,000 per underwriting. With shelf registrations, the average size of offering would probably be $75 million. Here the estimated spread is $3.00 per bond, and out-of-pocket expenses of $40,000 per issue are expected.

   a. Ignoring interest costs, what are the total absolute costs of flotation over the 2 years for the traditional underwriting method of offering securities?

   b. For the shelf registration method?

   c. Which is lower?

3. Two different companies are considering rights offerings. The current market price per share is $48 in both cases. To allow for fluctuations in market price, company X wants to set a subscription price of $42. Company Y feels a subscription price of $41.50 is in order. The number of rights necessary to purchase an additional share is 14 for company X and 4 for company Y.

   a. Which company has the larger stock issue relatively? Is it the larger stock issue in absolute terms?

   b. In which case is there less risk that the market price will fall below the subscription price?

4. The stock of the National Corporation is selling for $50 per share. The company then issues rights to subscribe to one new share at $40 for each five rights held.

   a. What is the theoretical value of a right when the stock is selling rights-on?

   b. What is the theoretical value of one share of stock when it goes ex-rights?

   c. What is the theoretical value of a right when the stock sells ex-rights at $50?

   d. Joe Speculator has $1,000 at the time National stock goes ex-rights at $50 per share. He feels that the price of the stock will rise to $60 by the time the rights expire. Compute his return on his $1,000 if he (1) buys National stock at $50, or (2) buys the rights at the price computed in part c, assuming his price expectations are valid.

5. Instead of a rights offering, National Corporation (see Problem 4) could undertake a public offering of $45 per share with a 6 percent gross spread. National currently has 1 million shares outstanding and earns $4 million a year. All earnings are paid in dividends. In either case, National would sell enough shares to raise $8 million, which would be invested at an after-tax return of 10 percent.

   a. Compute the earnings per share, dividends per share, and market price of the stock (assuming a 12.5 P/E ratio) for (1) the rights offering and (2) the public offering alternatives.

   b. Mr. Brown owns one share of National stock. On a rights offering, he will sell the right (assume for $2), thereby reducing his investment to $48. On a public offering, he would not buy any more shares. Compute Brown's earnings and dividend return on his investment and his price gain or loss on his investment under each of the two financing alternatives facing National.

6. Zeus Electronics Company is a new enterprise formed to exploit a technological innovation. It is to be capitalized with $6 million in equity, of which venture capitalists are being asked to provide $5.6 million. For this cash investment, venture capitalists will receive 70 percent of the common stock, with the management/founders keeping 30 percent. At the end of 6 years, management believes that the equity portion of the company is likely to be worth $50 million. At that time, it envisions an initial public offering where venture capitalists and the management/founders can sell all their stock if they so choose.

For initial public offerings, a discount of 20 percent is believed to be required from the "true" worth of the company. While $50 million is the most likely "true" value of the company's stock 6 years hence, there is a 30 percent probability the company will fail and be worth nothing to stockholders and a 20 percent probability that its true worth (equity portion) will be worth $80 million.

If the most likely value prevails, what will be the compound annual return on investment to a venture capitalist who decides to sell stock at the end of 6 years? What is the compound expected annual return based on all possibilities?

7. Doubletree Foods, Inc., is considering either a new stock issue or a new debt issue to raise capital. What are the likely information effect and stock market reaction that accompany the announcement of a stock issue? of a debt issue? Why?

SOLUTIONS TO SELF-CORRECTION PROBLEMS

1. a. SC $\quad$ = 4% of GP = 50% of GS
   GS $\quad$ = 8% × $5,000,000 = $400,000
   SC $\quad$ = $200,000
   MF $\quad$ = $60,000
   Net UP = $140,000

   b. SC $\quad$ = 3% of GP = 60% of GS
   GS $\quad$ = 5% × $5,000,000 = $250,000
   SC $\quad$ = $150,000
   MF $\quad$ = $37,500
   Net UP = $62,500

   c. Case A: $60,000 + .25($140,000) + .20($200,000) = $135,000
   Case B: $37,500 + .25($62,500) + .20($150,000) = $83,125

2. a.
$$R_0 = \frac{P_0 - S}{N + 1}$$

$$R_0 = \frac{\$150 - \$125}{9 + 1} = \frac{\$25}{10} = \$2.50$$

   b.
$$P_x = \frac{(P_0 \times N) + S}{N + 1} = \frac{(\$150 \times 9) + \$125}{9 + 1}$$

$$= \frac{\$1,350 + \$125}{10} = \frac{\$1,475}{10} = \$147.50$$

   c.
$$R_x = \frac{P_x - S}{N} = \frac{\$143 - 125}{9} = \frac{\$18}{9} = \$2$$

SELECTED REFERENCES

ALLEN, DAVID S., ROBERT E. LAMY, and G. RODNEY THOMPSON, "The Shelf Registration and Self Selection Bias," *Journal of Finance*, 45 (March 1990), 275–87.

ALLEN, FRANKLIN, and GERALD R. FAULHABER, "Signaling by Underpricing in the IPO Market," *Journal of Financial Economics*, 23 (August 1989), 303–24.

ASQUITH, PAUL, and DAVID MULLINS, JR., "Equity Issues and Offering Dilution," *Journal of Financial Economics*, 15 (January–February 1986), 61–90.

———, "Signalling with Dividends, Stock Repurchases, and Equity Issues," *Financial Management*, 15 (Autumn 1986), 27–44.

BARCLAY, MICHAEL J., and ROBERT H. LITZENBERGER, "Announcement Effects of New Equity Issues and the Use of Intraday Price Data," *Journal of Financial Economics*, 21 (May 1988), 71–99.

BEATTY, RANDOLPH P., and JAY R. RITTER, "Investment Banking, Reputation and the Underpricing of Initial Public Offerings," *Journal of Financial Economics*, 15 (January–February 1986), 213–32.

BHAGAT, SANJAI, "The Effect of Pre-emptive Right Amendments on Shareholder Wealth," *Journal of Financial Economics*, 12 (November 1983), 289–310.

BLACKWELL, DAVID W., and DAVID S. KIDWELL, "An Investigation of Cost Differences between Public Sales and Private Sales of Debt," *Journal of Financial Economics*, 22 (December 1988), 253–78.

CARTER, RICHARD, and STEVEN MANASTER, "Initial Public Offerings and Underwriter Reputation," *Journal of Finance*, 45 (September 1990), 1045–68.

ECKBO, B. ESPEN, "Valuation Effects of Corporate Debt Offerings," *Journal of Financial Economics*, 15 (January–February 1986), 119–52.

FUNG, W.K.H., and ANDREW RUDD, "Pricing New Corporate Bond Issues: An Analysis of Issue Cost and Seasoning Effects," *Journal of Finance*, 41 (July 1986), 633–42.

GLADSTONE, DAVID, *Venture Capital Handbook*. Englewood Cliffs, NJ: Prentice Hall, 1988.

HANSEN, ROBERT S., "The Demise of the Rights Issue," *Review of Financial Studies*, 1 (Fall 1988), 289–309.

———, BEVERLY R. FULLER, and VAHAN JANJIGIAN, "The Over-Allotment Option and Equity Financing Flotation Costs," *Financial Management*, 16 (Summer 1987), 24–32.

HANSEN, ROBERT S., and JOHN M. PINKERTON, "Direct Equity Financing: A Resolution of a Paradox," *Journal of Finance*, 37 (June 1982), 651–65.

HEINKEL, ROBERT, and EDUARDO S. SCHWARTZ, "Rights versus Underwritten Offerings: An Asymmetric Information Approach," *Journal of Finance*, 41 (March 1986), 1–18.

HESS, ALAN C., and PETER A. FROST, "Tests for Price Effects of New Issues of Seasoned Securities," *Journal of Finance*, 37 (March 1982), 11–26.

HUNTSMAN, BLAINE, and JAMES P. HOBAN, JR., "Investment in New Enterprise: Some Empirical Observations on Risk, Return, and Market Structure," *Financial Management*, 9 (Summer 1980), 44–51.

JOHNSON, JAMES M., and ROBERT E. MILLER, "Investment Banker Prestige and the Underpricing of Initial Public Offerings," *Financial Management*, 17 (Summer 1988), 19–29.

LEVY, HEIM, and MARSHALL SARNAT, "Risk, Dividend Policy, and the Optimal Pricing of a Rights Offering," *Journal of Money, Credit, and Banking*, 3 (November 1971), 840–49.

MASULIS, RONALD W., and ASHOK N. KORWAR, "Seasoned Equity Offerings: An Empirical Investigation," *Journal of Financial Economics*, 15 (January–February 1986), 91–118.

MIKKELSON, WAYNE H., and M. MEGAN PARTCH, "Valuation Effects of Security Offerings and the Issuance Process," *Journal of Financial Economics*, 15 (January–February 1986), 31–60.

MYERS, STEWART C., and NICHOLAS S. MAJLUF, "Corporate Financing and Investment Decisions When Firms Have Information That Investors Do Not Have," *Journal of Financial Economics*, 13 (June 1984), 187–221.

PARKER, GEORGE G. C., and DAVID COOPERMAN, "Competitive Bidding in the Underwriting of Public Utilities Securities," *Journal of Financial and Quantitative Analysis*, 5 (December 1978), 885–902.

PARSONS, JOHN E., and ARTUR RAVIV, "Underpricing of Seasoned Issues," *Journal of Financial Economics*, 14 (September 1985), 377–98.

RITTER, JAY R., "The Costs of Going Public," *Journal of Financial Economics*, 19 (December 1987), 269–82.

SMITH, CLIFFORD W., JR., "Alternative Methods for Raising Capital," *Journal of Financial Economics*, 5 (November 1977), 273–307.

———, "Investment Banking and the Capital Acquisition Process," *Journal of Financial Economics*, 15 (January–February 1986), 3–29.

TINIC, SEHA M., "Anatomy of Initial Public Offerings of Common Stock," *Journal of Finance*, 43 (September 1988), 789–822.

VAN HORNE, JAMES C., *Financial Market Rates and Flows*, 3d ed. Englewood Cliffs, NJ: Prentice Hall, 1990.

WRUCK, KAREN HOPPER, "Equity Ownership Concentration and Firm Value: Evidence from Private Equity Financings," *Journal of Financial Economics*, 23 (June 1989), 3–28.

22

FIXED-INCOME FINANCING AND PENSION LIABILITY

When we analyzed the theoretical aspects of fixed-income securities in conjunction with the use of equity capital (Chapters 10 and 11), we were thinking in terms of fixed-income securities in general rather than in terms of specific types of instruments. In this chapter, we work with the wide spectrum of long-term debt instruments available to the firm, consider certain conceptual and valuation issues associated with long-term debt, and evaluate the use of preferred stock financing. From the standpoint of common stockholders, preferred stock represents a form of leverage and must be evaluated in much the same way as debt.

FEATURES OF DEBT

The holders of a company's long-term debt, of course, are creditors. Generally they cannot exercise control over the company and do not have a voice in management. If the company violates any of the provisions of the debt contract, then these holders may be able to exert some influence on the direction of the company. Holders of long-term debt do not participate in the residual earnings of the company; instead, their return is fixed. Their debt instrument has a specific maturity, whereas a share of common or preferred stock does not. In liquidation, the claim of debt holders is before that of preferred and common stockholders. Depending on the nature of the debt instrument, however, there may be differences in the priority of claim among the various creditors of a company.

SOME DEFINITIONS

The fixed return of a long-term debt instrument is denoted by the *coupon* rate. A $10\frac{1}{2}$ percent debenture indicates that the issuer will pay bondholders $52.50 semiannually for every $1,000 face value bond they hold. The yield to maturity on a bond is determined by solving for the rate of discount that equates the present value of principal and interest payments with the current market price of the bond. (See Chapter 2 for the mathematics of bond interest.) The yield on a bond is the same as the internal rate of return for an investment project.

A company issuing bonds to the public designates a qualified *trustee* to represent the interests of the bondholders. The obligations of a trustee are specified in the Trust Indenture Act of 1939, administered by the Securities and Exchange Commission. The trustee's responsibilies are to authenticate the bond issue's legality at the time of issuance, to watch over the financial condition and behavior of the borrower to make sure all contractual obligations are carried out, and to initiate appropriate actions if the borrower does not meet any of these obligations. The trustee is compensated directly by the corporation, a compensation that adds to the cost of borrowing.

The legal agreement between the corporation issuing the bonds and the trustee, who represents the bondholders, is defined in the *indenture*. The indenture contains the terms of the bond issue as well as the restrictions placed on the company. These restrictions, known as *protective covenants*, are very similar to those contained in a term loan agreement. Because we analyzed protective covenants in detail in Chapter 18, it is not necessary to describe these restrictions here. The terms contained in the indenture are established jointly by the borrower and the trustee. (If the issue is a negotiated underwriting, the underwriter also will be involved.) If the corporation defaults under any of the provisions of the indenture, the trustee, on behalf of the bondholders, can take action to correct the situation. If not satisfied the trustee then can call for the immediate payment of all outstanding bonds.

BOND RATINGS

The creditworthiness of a publicly traded debt instrument often is judged by investors in terms of the credit rating assigned to it by investment agencies. The principal rating agencies are Moody's Investors Service and Standard & Poor's. The issuer of a new corporate bond contracts with the agency to evaluate and rate the bond as well as to update the rating throughout the bond's life. For this service, the issuer pays a fee. In addition, the rating agency charges subscribers to its rating publications.

Based on their evaluations of a bond or preferred stock issue, the agencies give their opinion in the form of letter grades, which are published for use by investors. In their ratings, the agencies attempt to rank issues according to the probability of default. The highest-grade issues, whose risk of default is felt to be negligible, are rated triple A, followed by double A, single A, B double a, and so forth through C and D, which are the lowest grades of the two agencies, respectively. The first four grades mentioned are considered to represent investment-quality issues, whereas other rated bonds are considered speculative. For each rating category, a modifier of 1, 2, or 3 is applied. For example, Aa-1 means that a security is in the higher end of the Aa rating category. Baa-3 indicates that a security is in the lower end of the Baa category. The ratings by the two agencies are widely respected as measures of default risk. In fact, many investors do not separately analyze the default risk of a company.

JUNK BONDS

During the 1980s, there developed an active market for non-investment-grade bonds. These are bonds with a grade of Ba or less, and they are called "junk" or "high-yield" bonds. The market was promulgated by the investment banking firm of Drexel Burnham Lambert, which dominated this market until its demise in 1990. A number of companies used the market to raise billions and billions of dollars of funds, displacing what was previously bank and private-placement financing. In addition, junk bonds were used in acquisitions and leveraged buyouts (topics taken up in Chapters 24 and 25).

Principal investors in junk bonds include pension funds, high-yield bond mutual funds, and some individuals who invest directly. A secondary market of sorts exists, but in any kind of "flight to quality" in the bond markets, such liquidity dries up. In the late 1980s, bonds issued in connection with highly levered transactions (i.e., leveraged buyouts) began to experience difficulty and many defaulted. Investors lost confidence and there was a sharp drop in new issues. While junk bonds are a viable means of financing for some companies, it must be recognized that there are windows of opportunity. In an unstable market, few investors are to be found.

SINKING FUNDS

The retirement of bonds may be accomplished in a number of ways: by payment at final maturity, by conversion if the bonds are convertible, by calling the bonds if there is a call feature, or by periodic repayment. Periodic repayment of the debt is possible if the bond issue is a sinking-fund issue. Conversion is taken up in the next chapter, and calling is examined later in this chapter.

The majority of corporate bond issues carry a provision for a sinking fund, which requires the corporation to make periodic sinking-fund payments to a trustee, in order to retire a specified face amount of bonds each period. Many sinking funds begin not at the time of issuance, but after a period of 5 or 10 years. The sinking-fund retirement of a bond issue can take two forms: (1) The corporation can make a cash payment to the trustee, who in turn calls the bonds for redemption at the sinking-fund call price. (This usually is lower than the regular call price of a bond, often being the face value of the instrument.) The bonds themselves are called on a lottery basis by their serial numbers, which are published in the *Wall Street Journal* and other papers. (2) The corporation can purchase bonds in the open market and pay the trustee by delivering to it a given number of bonds.

The corporation should purchase the bonds in the open market as long as the market price is less than the sinking-fund call price; when the market price exceeds the call price, it should make cash payments to the trustee. In this context, the sinking fund represents a delivery option to the corporation. It can satisfy the provision by paying cash to the trustee or by repurchasing bonds in the market. Expressed differently, it has an option to retire debt at the sinking-fund call price or at the market price, whichever is lower. If interest rates increase and/or credit quality deteriorates, the bond's price will decline in relation to the sinking-fund call price. As a result, the delivery option can have significant value. As with any option, it works to the advantage of the holder, in this case the corporation, and to the disadvantage of bondholders. The greater the volatility of interest rates and/or volatility of firm value, the more valuable the option to the corporation.

However, the sinking-fund provision may benefit the bondholder. By delivering bonds whose cost is lower than the call price, the company conserves cash, which may lower the probability of default. Because of the orderly retirement of sinking-fund debt, known as the amortization effect, some feel that it has less default risk than non-sinking-fund debt. In addition, steady repurchase activity adds liquidity to the market, which may be benefical to investors.

The two factors discussed work in opposite directions. The delivery option works to the disadvantage of bondholders, but amortization and other things that reduce risk and/or increase liquidity work to their advantage. The limited empirical evidence available supports both effects, but the amortization effect somewhat more so.

Some corporations, in purchasing bonds for sinking-fund payment, find that *accumulators* have got there first. Accumulators are institutional or other investors that buy bonds in advance of the corporation going into the market to acquire them for sinking funds. If supply is sufficiently restricted, the corporation will be able to purchase bonds only by bidding up the price. In this way, the accumulator hopes to sell the bonds at an inflated price, knowing the corporation must purchase them in order to satisfy the sinking-fund requirement. For example, an accumulator might buy bonds at a price of $810 per pond to yield 11.2 percent and sell them to the corporation for $875, which corresponds to a yield of 10.3 percent. While the price is significantly above the previous going market price, imperfections allow the accumulator to partially corner the market, thereby forcing the corporation to pay the inflated price.[1] Although perfectly legal, accumulators are not looked upon with great favor by financial managers. Only when the bonds sell at a discount from the sinking-fund call price, of course, does accumulation occur. Otherwise, the corporation will make a cash payment to the trustee, who will purchase bonds at the sinking-fund call price.

FLOATING RATE NOTES

Instead of a fixed interest rate over the life of the debt instrument, the interest rate can float with some short-term rate, such as the Treasury bill or commercial paper rate. With the high and volatile interest rate environment of the early 1980s, many corporations were reluctant to commit to long-term debt. Floating rate notes (FRNs) were looked to as a way to reduce some of the risk of volatile interest rates. A typical FRN might have a 5-year maturity with the interest rate adjusted every 3 months in keeping with changes in the Treasury bill rate. An initial interest rate is set for the first 3 months, but after that the instrument might provide an interest rate $\frac{1}{2}$ percent above the 3-month Treasury bill rate.

Often a minimum or floor rate is specified, and there may be some special features, such as options, a declining spread, or even a fixed-rate provision after a specified change in rates. The FRN is a financial innovation that

[1] For an analysis of the accumulation problem in a game theory context, see Kenneth B. Dunn and Chester S. Spatt, "A Strategic Analysis of Sinking Bond Funds," *Journal of Financial Economics,* 13 (September 1984), 399–423. See also Andrew J. Kalotay, "On the Management of Sinking Funds," *Financial Management,* 10 (Summer 1981), 34–40, for an evaluation of the problem.

came about in response to volatile interest rates. During such times, its use is widespread.

TYPES OF DEBT FINANCING

DEBENTURES

The term *debenture* usually applies to the unsecured bonds of a corporation. Investors look to the earning power of the corporation as their security. Because these general credit bonds are not secured by specific property, in the event of liquidation the holder becomes a general creditor. Although the bonds are unsecured, debenture holders are protected by the restrictions imposed in the indenture, particularly the negative pledge clause, which precludes the corporation from pledging its assets to other creditors. This provision safeguards the investor in that the borrower's assets will not be impaired in the future. Because debenture holders must look to the general credit of the borrower to meet principal and interest payments, only well-established and creditworthy companies are able to issue debentures.

SUBORDINATED DEBENTURES

Subordinated debentures represent debt that ranks behind debt senior to these debentures with respect to the claim on assets. In the event of liquidation, subordinated debenture holders usually only receive settlement if all senior creditors are paid the full amount owed them. These holders still would rank ahead of preferred stockholders in the event of liquidation. The existence of subordinated debentures may work to the advantage of senior holders, because senior holders are able to assume the claims of the subordinated debenture holders. To illustrate: A corporation is liquidated for $600,000. It had $400,000 in straight debentures outstanding, $400,000 in subordinated debentures outstanding, and $400,000 in obligations owed to general creditors. One might suppose that the straight debenture holders and the general creditors would have an equal and prior claim in liquidation, that each would receive $300,000. The fact is, the straight debenture holders are entitled to the subordinated debenture holders' claims, giving them $800,000 in total claims. As a result, they are entitled to two-thirds of the liquidating value, or $400,000, whereas general creditors are entitled to only one-third, or $200,000.

Because of the nature of the claim, a straight subordinated debenture issue has to provide a yield significantly higher than a regular debenture issue in order to be attractive to investors. Frequently, subordinated debentures are convertible into common stock and therefore may sell at a yield that actually is less than what the company would have to pay on an ordinary debenture. From the standpoint of a creditor, the equity base of the firm is the same whether the issue remains as subordinated debentures or is converted into common stock.

MORTGAGE BONDS

A mortgage bond issue is secured by a lien on specific assets of the corporation—usually fixed assets. The specific property securing the bonds is described in detail in the mortgage, which is the legal document giving the bondholder a lien on the property. As with other secured lending arrangements, the market value of the collateral should exceed the amount of the bond issue by a reasonable margin of safety. If the corporation defaults in any of the provisions of the bond indenture, the trustee, on behalf of the bondholders, has the power to foreclose. In a foreclosure, the trustee takes over the property and sells it, using the proceeds to pay the bonds. If the proceeds are less than the amount of the issue outstanding, the bondholders become general creditors for the residual amount. A company may have more than one bond issue secured by the same property. If a bond issue is secured by a *second mortgage* and the first mortgagee forecloses, the first-mortgage bondholders must be paid the full amount owed them before there can be any distribution to the second-mortgage bondholders.

A mortgage may be either *closed-end* or *open-end*. When a mortgage is closed, additional bonds cannot be issued under that lien. To raise additional funds through mortgage bonds, the company must mortgage additional properties. The result is frequently a hodgepodge of mortgage bond issues outstanding. Under an open-end mortgage, the company can issue additional bonds under an existing lien. This arrangement allows the company to issue various series of bonds at different times under the same lien. In this respect, it gives the company considerable flexibility in its financing. To protect the position of the bondholders of earlier series, certain restrictions usually are imposed that limit the amount of additional debt. These restrictions include a maximum percentage on the amounts of bonds in relation to the value of the property securing these bonds and a minimum earning power of the company in relation to the bonds outstanding. Public utilities and railroads have used open-end mortgages rather extensively.

INCOME BONDS

A company is obligated to pay interest on an income bond only when it is earned. There may be a cumulative feature in the issue where unpaid interest in a particular year accumulates. If the company does generate earnings, it will have to pay the cumulative interest to the extent that earnings permit. However, the cumulative obligation usually is limited to no more than 3 years. As should be evident, this type of security offers the investor a rather weak promise of a fixed return. Nevertheless, the income bond is still senior to preferred and common stock, as well as to any subordinated debt. Unlike preferred stock dividends, the interest payment is deductible for tax purposes. Because income bonds are not popular with investors, they have been used principally in reorganizations.[2]

EQUIPMENT TRUST CERTIFICATES

Although equipment trust financing is a form of lease financing, the certificates themselves represent an intermediate- to long-term fixed-income investment. This method of financing is used by railroads to finance the acquisition of rolling stock. Under this method, the railroad arranges with a trustee to purchase equipment from a manufacturer. The railroad signs a contract with the manufacturer for the construction of specific equipment. When the equipment is delivered, equipment trust certificates are sold to investors.

[2] For an extensive analysis of income bonds, see John J. McConnell and Gary G. Schlarbaum, "Returns, Risks, and Pricing of Income Bonds," *Journal of Business*, 54 (January 1981), 33–57.

The proceeds of this sale, together with the down payment by the railroad, are used to pay the manufacturer. Title to the equipment is held by the trustee, who in turn leases the equipment to the railroad. Lease payments are used by the trustee to pay a fixed return on the certificates outstanding—actually a dividend—and to retire a specified portion of the certificates at regular intervals. Upon the final lease payment by the railroad, the last of the certificates is retired, and title to the equipment passes to the railroad.

The duration of the lease varies according to the equipment involved, but 15 years is common. Because rolling stock is essential to the operation of a railroad and it has a ready market value, equipment trust certificates enjoy a very high standing as fixed-income investments. As a result, railroads are able to acquire cars and locomotives on favorable financing terms. Airlines, too, use a form of equipment trust certificate to finance jet aircraft. Usually, airlines' certificates are sold to institutional investors; some issues are sold to the public.

CONVERTIBLE BONDS

A convertible bond is one that may be changed, at the option of the holder, into a certain number of shares of common stock of the corporation. The number of shares into which the bond is convertible is specified in the bond, and these shares remain unissued until actual conversion. We consider convertible securities in depth in Chapter 23.

PROJECT FINANCING

The term *project financing* describes a variety of financing arrangements for large, individual investment projects. Often a separate legal entity is formed to own the project. Suppliers of capital then look at the earnings stream of the project for repayment of their loan or for the return on their equity investment. Often, the projects involve energy: not only large explorations of gas, oil, and coal but also tankers, port facilities, refineries, and pipelines. Other projects include aluminum plants, fertilizer plants, and power plants. These projects require huge amounts of capital, often beyond the reach of a single company. Many times a consortium of companies is formed to spread risk and to finance the project. Part of the capital comes from equity participations by the companies, and the rest comes from lenders or lessors.

If the loan or lease is on a nonrecourse basis, the lender or lessor pays exclusive attention to the size of the equity participation and to the economic feasibility of the project. In other words, the lender or lessor can look only to the project for payout, so the larger the equity cushion and the greater the confidence that can be placed in the projections, the better the project. In another type of arrangement, each sponsor may guarantee its share of the project's obligations. Under these circumstances, the lender or lessor places emphasis on the creditworthiness of the sponsors as well as on the economic feasibility of the project.

For the sponsors of the project there are several types of sharing rules. In a "take-or-pay" arrangement, each sponsor agrees to purchase a specific percentage of the output of the project and to pay that percentage of the operating costs of the project plus debt-servicing charges. This obligation exists whether or not output actually occurs. When pipelines are involved, the type of sharing rule is frequently a "throughput" arrangement. Here each sponsor is required to ship through the facility a certain amount, or percentage, of product. If the total shipped is insufficient to cover the expenses of running the facility, sponsors are assessed additional amounts to cover the shortfall. The amount of assessment is proportional to their participation. The maturity of the loan or lease corresponds to the likely ability of the project to generate cash over time. Although the financing need not be long term, in most cases it extends over a period of 8 or more years. In this type of arrangement, the lender or lessor has limited recourse to the project's sponsors in the sense of being assured of minimum cash flows.

CALL PROVISION AND REFUNDING

Most corporate bond issues provide for a call feature, which gives the corporation the option to buy back the bonds at a stated price before their maturity. Not all bond issues are callable; in times of low interest rates in particular, some corporations issue noncallable or "noncall-life" bonds as they are known. When a bond is callable, the call price usually is above the par value of the bond and decreases over time. A bond with 20 years to maturity might be callable at $110 ($1,100 per $1,000 face value bond) the next 2 years, $109 the following 2 years, and so on until the final 2 years, when it is callable at $101. Frequently, the call price in the first year is established at 1 year's interest above the face value of the bond. If the coupon rate is 14 percent, the initial call price may be $114 ($1,140 per $1,000 face value).

There are two types of call provision, according to when they can be exercised. The security may be immediately callable, which simply means that the instrument may be bought back by the issuer at the call price at any time. Rather than being immediately callable, the call provision may be deferred for a period of time. The most widely used deferred call periods are 5 years for public utility bonds and 10 years for industrial bonds. During this deferment period, the investor is protected from a call by the issuer. In recent years, virtually all issues of corporate bonds have involved a deferred call as opposed to an immediate call feature.

The call provision gives the company flexibility in its financing. If interest rates should decline significantly, it can call the bonds and refinance the issue at a lower interest cost. Thus, the company does not have to wait until the final maturity to refinance. In addition, the provision may be advantageous to the company if it finds any of the protective convenants in the bond indenture to be unduly restrictive. By calling the bonds before maturity, the company can eliminate these restrictions. Of course, if the issue is refinanced with bonds, similar restrictions may be imposed.

The deferment period protects the investor from early call. However, this protection is not always what it seems. Many issues reserve the right to redeem a bond issue at any time under a set of conditions different from those that govern the call. In most bond indentures, call deferment is restricted to situations where a refunding takes place. By *refunding*, we mean refinancing the bond issue with a new bond issue at a lower interest cost.

However, many bond issues can be redeemed provided the source of the redemption is not a refunding. It may be the issuer has excess liquidity, or it could sell assets. It might issue common stock or be acquired in a merger. As long as the funds used to redeem the bond issue do not come from a new one, the investor has no deferred call protection. As though this were not bad enough, the redemption price often is the face value of the bond as opposed to the higher call price. The line of demarcation between a call and a redemption is blurred. For example, if a company redeems a bond issue out of cash and later issues bonds to restore its liquidity, is it a redemption or a call? Sometimes legal redress is sought, but seldom does the investor win. Investors had best read the fine print before investing to see the conditions under which redemption is possible. Many are surprised.

VALUE OF CALL PRIVILEGE

Although the call privilege is beneficial to the issuing corporation, it works to the detriment of investors. If interest rates fall and the bond issue is called, they can invest in other bonds only at a sacrifice in yield to maturity. Consequently, the call privilege usually does not come free to the borrower. Its cost, or value, is measured at the time of issuance by the difference in yield on the callable bond and the yield that would be necessary if the security were noncallable. This value is determined by supply and demand forces in the market for callable securities. In equilibrium, the value of the call feature will be just sufficient to bring the demand for callable securities by investors into balance with the supply of callable securities by borrowers. In the equilibrating process, both borrowers and investors are influenced by expectations of the future course of interest rates.

When interest rates are high and expected to fall, the call feature is likely to have significant value. Investors are unwilling to invest in callable bonds unless such bonds yield more than bonds that are noncallable, all other things the same. In other words, they must be compensated for assuming the risk that the bonds might be called. On the other hand, borrowers are willing to pay a premium in yield for the call privilege in the belief that yields will fall and that it will be advantageous to refund the bonds. In equilibrium, both the marginal borrower and the marginal investor will be indifferent to whether the bond issue is callable or noncallable.[3]

When interest rates are low and expected to rise, the call privilege may have a negligible value in that the company might pay the same yield if there were no call privilege. For the privilege to have value, interest-rate expectations must make it seem possible that the issue will be called. If interest rates are very low and not expected to fall further, there is little probability that the bonds will be called. The key factor is that the borrower has to be able to refund the issue at a profit and that cannot be done unless interest rates drop significantly, for the issuer must pay the call price—which is usually at a premium above par value—as well as the flotation costs involved in refinancing. If there is no probability that the borrower can refund the issue at a profit, the call privilege is unlikely to have a value.

The announcement of a call may convey information to investors about the future of the company. If the call changes the capital structure of the company, for example, investors may react to the leverage change apart from whether or not the bond issue is refunded at a lower interest cost. As we dis-

---

[3] See Gordon Pye, "The Value of the Call Option on a Bond," *Journal of Political Economy,* 74 (April 1966), 200–203.

cussed in the previous chapter, the leverage change may convey information about an unanticipated change in the earnings prospects of the company—positive for increases in leverage and negative for decreases.[4]

Valuation in an Option Pricing Context. The call feature, of course, is an option given by investors to the corporation. Consequently, much of the thinking that went into our discussion of the option pricing theory in Chapter 5 applies here. Rather than the variance of a common stock's value determining the value of the option, in this case it is the variance of future interest rates. The greater the expected volatility of future interest rates, the greater the value of the call option. This principle stems from the fact that it is the variance of the value of the associated asset that determines the value of the option.

This concept is illustrated in Figure 22-1. In the figure, we assume that the call option pertains only to a given future date. In other words, the option can be exercised at only one time, this being the option date. The value of the bond appears on the vertical axis, and the interest rate in the market on the horizontal axis. For a noncallable bond, value decreases at a decreasing rate as the interest rate increases. For a callable bond, value is constrained on the upside by the call price. This occurs for lower levels of interest rates—to the left of X on the horizontal axis. In this range, the difference between the value of a noncallable bond and the value of a callable bond represents the value of the option on the option date. If interest rates are such that the bond's value as a noncallable bond is less than the call price, the company obviously will not call the issue. As a result, the value of the callable bond is the same as that of a noncallable bond for interest rates higher than X on the horizontal axis. The key to valuation of the option is the likelihood that interest rates will be less than X on the horizontal axis on the option date. This, in turn, depends on the variance of the distribution of possible interest rates. The greater the variance, the greater the expected value of call option to the company.

[4] Mild support for this notion is found in Joseph D. Vu, "An Empirical Investigation of Calls of Non-Convertible Bonds," *Journal of Financial Economics*, 14 (June 1986), 235–65. For a theoretical inquiry into why the issuance of callable bonds may serve as a signaling device to convey "good news" to investors, see Edward Henry Robbins and John D. Schatzberg, "Callable Bonds: A Risk-Reducing Signalling Mechanism," *Journal of Finance*, 41 (September 1986), 935–49.

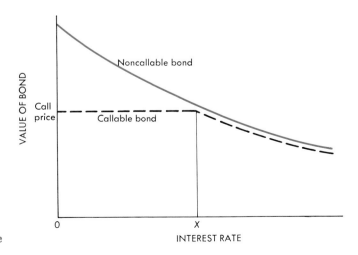

FIGURE 22-1
Valuation of callable
bond on the option date

The equilibration mechanism for valuation is

$$\text{Callable bond} = \text{Noncallable bond} - \text{Call option} \qquad (22\text{-}1)$$

where the noncallable bond is identical to the callable bond in all respects except the call feature. The greater the value of the call feature, the lower the value of the callable bond relative to that of the noncallable one. The level and volatility of interest rates are key factors in giving value to the call feature. A sharp drop in interest rates will cause the option to have more value. In turn, such a drop is related to volatility.

Once the call option has been valued, Eq. (22-1) may be used to determine if the callable bond and the noncallable bond are mispriced. This type of analysis identifies arbitrage opportunities. For example, if it were determined that the standard deviation of bond returns necessary to bring about the equality was 26 percent, and you believed 15 percent was more realistic, you would conclude the two bonds were mispriced. More specifically, the noncallable bond in Eq. (22-1) is priced too high in relation to the callable one. This is merely to say that if the "true" standard deviation is 15 percent, then the call option is less valuable than the difference in prices of the two bonds would suggest. To arbitrage, you would buy the callable bond and sell short the noncallable bond.

In summary, we see that the principles of the option pricing theory apply to the valuation of the call feature. The greater the variance or uncertainty of future interest rates, the greater the value of the option to the corporation and, in efficient financial markets, the greater its cost to the company. We turn now to the question of refinancing an existing bond issue, given a call feature on the bond.

REFUNDING A BOND ISSUE

In this section, we analyze the profitability of a company refunding a bond issue before its maturity. By *refunding*, we mean calling the issue and replacing it with a new issue of bonds. In this regard, we focus our attention on only one reason for refunding—profitability—which, in turn, is due to interest rates having declined since the bonds were issued. On occasion, other reasons prompt companies to refund outstanding bonds. Sometimes a company will refund a bond issue simply to eliminate overly restrictive protective covenants in the bond indenture. This assumes, of course, that the protective covenants in the new bond indenture will be less onerous.

Analysis in a Capital Budgeting Framework.   The refunding decision can be regarded as a form of capital budgeting: There is an initial cash outlay followed by future interest savings. These savings are represented by the difference between the annual cash outflow required under the old bonds and the net cash outflow required on the new, or refunding, bonds. Calculating the initial cash outlay is more complex. Consequently, it is best to show an example of this method of evaluation.[5]

---

[5] This example draws upon Oswald D. Bowlin, "The Refunding Decision: Another Special Case in Capital Budgeting," *Journal of Finance*, 21 (March 1966), 55–68.

A company currently has a $20 million, 12 percent debenture issue outstanding, and the issue still has 20 years to final maturity. Because interest rates are significantly lower than at the time of the original offering, the company can now sell a $20 million issue of 20-year bonds at a coupon rate of 10 percent that will net it $19,600,000 after the underwriting spread.

For federal income tax purposes, the unamortized issuing expense of the old bonds, the call premium, and the unamortized discount of the old bonds, if they were sold at a discount, are deductible as expenses in the year of the refunding. The old bonds were sold originally at a slight discount from par value, and the unamortized portion now is $200,000. Moreover, the legal fees and other issuing expenses involved with the old bonds have an unamortized balance of $100,000. The call price on the old bonds is $109, issuing expenses on the new bonds are $150,000, the income tax rate is 40 percent, and there is a 30-day period of overlap. The period of overlap is the lag between the time the new bonds are sold and the time the old bonds are called. This lag occurs because most companies wish to have the proceeds from the new issue on hand before they call the old issue. Otherwise, there is a certain amount of risk associated with calling the old issue and being at the mercy of the bond market in raising new funds. During the period of overlap, the company pays interest on both bond issues.

With this rather involved background information in mind, we can calculate the initial cash outflow and the future cash benefits. The net cash outflow at the time of the refunding is as follows:

Cost of calling old bonds (call price $109)		$21,800,000
Net proceeds of new bond issue		19,600,000
Difference		$ 2,200,000
Expenses		
Issuing expense of new bonds	$ 150,000	
Interest expense on old bonds during overlap period	200,000	350,000
Gross cash outlay		$ 2,550,000
Less tax savings		
Interest expense on old bonds during overlap period	200,000	
Call premium	1,800,000	
Unamortized discount on old bonds	200,000	
Unamortized issuing expense on old bonds	100,000	
Total	$2,300,000	
Tax savings (40% of amount above)		920,000
Net cash outflow		$ 1,630,000

For ease of presentation, we ignore any interest that might be earned by investing the refunding bond proceeds in marketable securities during the 30-day period of overlap. The annual net cash benefits may be determined by calculating the difference between the net cash outflow required on the old bonds and the net cash outflow required on the new or refunding bonds. We assume for simplicity that interest is paid but once a year, at year end. The annual net cash outflow on the old bonds is

Interest expense 12%		$2,400,000
Less: Tax savings		
Interest expense	$2,400,000	
Amortization of bond discount ($200,000/20)	10,000	
Amortization of issuing costs ($100,000/20)	5,000	
Total	$2,415,000	
Tax savings (40% of amount above)		966,000
Annual net cash outflow, old bonds		$1,434,000

The annual net cash outflow on the new bonds is

Interest expense 10%		$2,000,000
Less: Tax savings		
Interest expense	$2,000,000	
Amortization of bond discount ($400,000/20)	20,000	
Amortization of issuing costs ($150,000/20)	7,500	
Total	$2,027,500	
Tax savings (40% of amount above)		811,000
Annual net cash outflow, new bonds		$1,189,000
Difference between annual net cash outflows ($1,434,000 − $1,189,000)		$ 245,000

Discounting. Thus, for an initial net cash outflow of $1,630,000, the company can achieve annual net cash benefits of $245,000 over the next 20 years. Because the net cash benefits occur in the future, they must be discounted back to present value. But what discount rate should be used? Certain authors advocate the use of the cost of capital. However, a refunding operation differs from other investment proposals. Once the new bonds are sold, the net cash benefits are known with certainty. From the standpoint of the corporation, the refunding operation is essentially a riskless investment project. The only risks associated with the cash flows are that of the firm defaulting in the payment of principal or interest. Because a premium for default risk is embodied in the market rate of interest, most agree that the appropriate discount rate is the cost of debt. It is assumed, then, that the net cash outflow is financed by issuing additional bonds in the refunding.

There is disagreement as to whether the before-tax or the after-tax cost should be used. Gordon argues that the before-tax cost of debt is the appropriate discount rate, even though the cash flows are after taxes.[6] The logic of his position is that the opportunity cost of the funds employed in the refunding is that which investors in the company require. Since an investor can earn the before-tax rate by buying the refunding bonds directly, Gordon argues that this rate is the appropriate opportunity cost. Ofer and Taggart show that this is true only if the net refunding outlay is financed with equity.[7] If additional

[6] Myron J. Gordon, "A General Solution to the Buy or Lease Decision: A Pedagogical Note," *Journal of Finance*, 29 (March 1974), 245–50.

[7] Aharon R. Ofer and Robert A. Taggart, Jr., "Bond Refunding: A Clarifying Analysis," *Journal of Finance*, 32 (March 1977), 21–30. Ofer and Taggart also analyze the favorable effect of a refunding on the firm's debt capacity. They propose a means for analyzing the tax savings that result from the increase in debt capacity. See also Wilbur G. Lewellen and Douglas R. Emery, "On the Matter of Parity among Financial Obligations," *Journal of Finance*, 36 (March 1981), 97–111; and Gene Laber, "Implications of Discount Rates and Financing Assumptions for Bond Refunding Decisions," *Financial Management*, 8 (Spring 1979), 7–12.

bonds are issued to finance the refunding outlay, stockholders will realize additional tax savings through the corporation, and the relevant discount rate becomes the after-tax cost of the refunding bonds.

The after-tax cost of the refunding bonds in our example is 10 percent $(1 - .4) = 6$ percent. If this percent is used as the discount rate, under the assumption that the initial outlay of $1,630,000 is financed with the sale of additional bonds, the net present value of the refunding operation is found to be $1,180,131. As this amount is positive, the refunding operation would be worthwhile.[8] If the before-tax cost of the new bonds of 10 percent is used as the discount rate, the net present value is found to be $455,823. Again the refunding operation would be worthwhile, though less obviously.

Several points should be raised with respect to the calculations in our example. First, most firms refund an existing issue with a new bond issue of a longer maturity. In our example, we assumed that the new bond issue has the same maturity as that of the old bond issue. The analysis needs to be modified somewhat when the maturity dates are different. The usual procedure is to consider only the net cash benefits up to the maturity of the old bonds. A second assumption in our example was that neither issue involved sinking-fund bonds or serial bonds. If either issue calls for periodic reduction of the debt, we must adjust our procedure for determining future net cash benefits. Finally, the annual cash outflows associated with the refunding bonds usually are less than those associated with the refunded bonds. As a result, effectively there is a decrease in the leverage of the firm. While this effect is likely to be small, leverage is not held constant. To remedy these problems, one may wish to use something different.

AN ALTERNATIVE APPROACH

Another way to look at the bond refunding decision is to replicate the cash outflows of the old bond issue and then determine the net inflow to be realized from the sale of the new bonds in the current market. If the new bonds can be sold so that the net inflow exceeds the outflow associated with calling the old bonds at their call price, bond refunding is favorable; if the inflow is less, it is unfavorable. If refunding is favorable, the firm will end up issuing new bonds with a higher present value than the call price of the old bonds. Since the stream of future net cash outflows is the same, the refunding action will transfer present value from creditors to equity holders.[9] Expressed differently, the firm's leverage, as depicted by the stream of debt-servicing outflows, remains the same, but the firm exchanges one bond issue for another. In so doing, it receives cash for the difference between the sales price of the new bond and the call price of the old. Equity holders obviously are better off.

A company currently has a $5 million, 10 percent debenture issue outstanding that has 25 years to maturity with a call price of $108. Interest on the

---

[8] We recall from Chapter 6 that the net present value is the present value of net cash benefits less the initial cash outflow.

[9] This approach is used by Gordon Pye, "The Value of the Call Option on a Bond," *Journal of Political Economy*, 74 (April 1966), 200–205; and by Jess B. Yawitz and James A. Anderson, "The Effect of Bond Refunding on Shareholder Wealth," *Journal of Finance*, 32 (December 1977), 1738–46. For an analysis of this approach as well as a reconciliation with the previous one, see Kenneth D. Riener, "Financial Structure Effects of Bond Refunding," *Financial Management*, 9 (Summer 1980), 18–23.

bonds is paid annually. To replicate the coupon and principal payment stream, the company must issue a bond with a coupon rate of 10 percent and a maturity of 25 years. Currently, the issue can be sold to the public at a yield to maturity of 8 percent. The present value of a 10 percent, $5 million issue yielding 8 percent to maturity in 25 years is determined by

$$X = \frac{\$500,000}{(1.08)} + \frac{\$500,000}{(1.08)^2} + \cdots + \frac{\$500,000}{(1.08)^{25}} +$$

$$\frac{\$5,000,000}{(1.08)^{25}} + \$6,067,478 \qquad (22\text{-}2)$$

The underwriting spread is 1 percent, so that the net proceeds of the new issue to the company are $6,067,478 (1 − .01) = $6,006,795. The tax rate is 40 percent, and there is an overlap period of 1 month.[10] Thus, the net cash inflow at the time of the refunding is

Net proceeds of new bond issue		$6,006,795
Cost of calling old bonds (call price $108)		5,400,000
Difference		$ 606,795
Expenses		
Interest expense on old bonds during overlap period		41,667
Gross cash inflow		$ 565,128
Plus tax savings		
Interest expense on old bonds during overlap period	$ 41,667	
Call premium	400,000	
Total	$441,667	
Tax savings (40% of amount above)		176,667
Net cash inflow		$ 741,795

Therefore, with the contractual stream of cash outflows to service debt over the next 25 years the same as before, the company can realize present cash of $741,795. The refunding obviously is worthwhile.

We see, then, that there are different ways the bond refunding decision might be approached. The latter method is appropriate only if the firm intends to replicate the debt-service stream of payments. Generally, companies will issue new bonds at coupon rates approximating current yields in the market. As a result, the cash-outflow stream will not be precisely replicated, even if more bonds are issued. For this reason, the alternative method presented here may not be practical in most situations. Still, it serves as a conceptual way to deal with a refunding decision and under most circumstances gives accurate answers even if the input data are not precise.

TIMING OF REFUNDING

We must recognize that just because a refunding operation is found to be worthwhile, it should not necessarily be undertaken right away. If interest rates are declining, and this decline is expected to continue, management may prefer to delay the refunding. At a later date, the refunding bonds can be sold

[10] For simplicity, we assume that there is no unamortized discount or unamortized issuing expenses on the old bonds and no issuing expenses on the new bonds.

at an even lower rate of interest, making the refunding operation even more worthwhile. The decision concerning timing must be based on expectations of future interest rates. In determining whether or not to postpone refunding, the financial manager should also consider the dispersion and shape of the probability distribution of possible future interest rates.

PRIVATE PLACEMENTS

Rather than sell securities to the public, a corporation can sell the entire issue to a single institutional investor or a small group of such investors. This type of sale is known as a private or direct placement, for the company negotiates directly with the investor over the terms of the offering, eliminating the function of the underwriter. In what follows, we focus on the private placement of debt issues. Equity placements involving venture capitalists were discussed in the previous chapter.

FEATURES

One of the more frequently mentioned advantages of a private placement is the speed of the commitment. A public issue must be registered with the SEC, documents prepared and printed, and extensive negotiations undertaken. All of this requires a certain lead time. In addition, the public issue always involves risks with respect to timing. With a private placement, the terms can be tailored to the needs of the borrower, and the financing can be consummated quickly. However, the large corporation also can quickly tap the public market through a *shelf registration,* which was described in the last chapter.

Because the private placement of debt is negotiated, the exact timing in the market is not a critical problem. The fact that there is but a single investor or small group of investors is attractive if it becomes necessary to change any of the terms of the issue. It is much easier to deal with a single investor than with a large group of public security holders. A possible disadvantage in this regard is that a single investor may monitor the company's operations in much greater detail than will a trustee for the purchasers of a public issue.

Another advantage of a privately placed debt issue is that the actual borrowing does not necessarily have to take place all at once. The company can enter into an arrangement whereby it can borrow up to a fixed amount over a period of time. For this nonrevolving credit arrangement, the borrower usually will pay a commitment fee. This type of arrangement gives the company flexibility, allowing it to borrow only when it needs the funds. Because the private placement does not have to be registered with the SEC, the company avoids making available to the public the detailed information required by the SEC. However, the shelf registration process has lessened this advantage for the large company. It can issue bonds in the public market quickly and with little "red tape."

RECENT DEVELOPMENTS

In recent years, private placements have rekindled in importance. With public bonds, it is possible for the issuing corporation to be restructured, with much higher debt. The bonds previously outstanding become less creditworthy and drop in price. This event risk is not precluded by the bond indenture. With a private placement, such event risk can be avoided with tightly written protective covenants (see Chapter 18). Should the corporation be restructured, the bonds become immediately payable at their face value.

Another advantage to the institutional investors is that the SEC now permits them to sell securities generated in the private-placement market to other institutions. Thus, U.S. as well as non-U.S. companies can issue bonds and stocks in the market without having to go through public-market registration procedures. Qualified buyers (large institutions) can trade the securities to other qualified buyers. As a result, the market becomes broader and more liquid.

For the issuer, these developments make private-placement financing less costly than before. While public issues of bonds tend to bear a lower interest rate than do private placements, the differential has narrowed as a result of these recent developments.

PREFERRED STOCK

Preferred stock is a hybrid form of financing, combining features of debt and common stock. In the event of liquidation, a preferred stockholder's claim on assets comes after that of creditors but before that of common stockholders. Usually, this claim is restricted to the par value of the stock. If the par value of a share of preferred stock is $100, the investor will be entitled to a maximum of $100 in settlement of the principal amount. Although preferred stock carries a stipulated dividend, the actual payment of a dividend is a discretionary rather than a fixed obligation of the company. The omission of a dividend will not result in a default of the obligation or insolvency of the company. The board of directors has full power to omit a preferred stock dividend if it so chooses.

The maximum return to preferred stockholders usually is limited to the specified dividend, and these stockholders ordinarily do not share in the residual earnings of the company. Thus, if you own 100 shares of $10\frac{1}{2}$ percent preferred stock, $50 par value, the maximum return you can expect in any one year is $525, and this return is at the discretion of the board of directors. The corporation cannot deduct this dividend on its tax return; this fact is the principal shortcoming of preferred stock as a means of financing.

CUMULATIVE FEATURE

Almost all preferred stocks have a cumulative feature, providing for unpaid dividends in any one year to be carried forward. Before the company can pay a dividend on its common stock, it must pay the dividends *in arrears* on its preferred stock. A board of directors may omit the preferred stock dividend on a company's 8 percent cumulative preferred stock for 3 consecutive years. If the stock has a $100 par value, the company would be $24 per share in arrears on its preferred stock. Before it can pay a dividend to its common stockholders, it must pay preferred stockholders $24 for each share of preferred stock held. It should be emphasized that just because preferred stock dividends are in arrears, there is no guarantee that they will ever be paid. If the corporation has no intention of paying a common stock dividend, there is no need to clear up the arrearage on the preferred. The preferred stock dividend typically is omitted for lack of earnings, but the corporation does not have to pay a dividend if earnings are restored.

If the preferred stock dividends are in arrears, and the company wishes to pay a common stock dividend, it may choose not to clear up the arrearage but to make an exchange offering to preferred stockholders. Say that the dividend arrearages on an issue of $100 par value preferred stock are $56 and that the market price of the stock is $61 a share. The company might offer preferred stockholders common stock in the company, valued at $110, for each share of preferred stock held. Although theoretically the preferred stockholder is asked to give up $156 ($100 par value plus $56 dividend arrearages), the exchange offering promises $110 relative to a current preferred stock market value of only $61 per share. In order to eliminate the preferred stock, the company must obtain the approval of a required percentage of the stock outstanding, often two-thirds. Consequently, it probably will make its exchange offering contingent upon obtaining the required acceptance.

If a preferred stock is noncumulative, dividends not paid in one year do not carry forward. As a result, a company can pay a common stock dividend without regard to any dividends it did not pay in the past on its preferred stock. From the standpoint of an investor, a noncumulative preferred stock is little more than an income bond. In fact, there is somewhat less uncertainty with income bonds, for the conditions under which interest will be paid are specified clearly, and bondholders have a prior claim on assets. Because of the obvious disadvantage to investors, noncumulative preferred stock issues are rare.

PARTICIPATING FEATURE

A participating feature allows preferred stockholders to participate in the residual earnings of the corporation according to some specified formula. The preferred stockholder might be entitled to share equally with common stockholders in any common stock dividend beyond a certain amount. Suppose a 6 percent preferred stock ($100 par value) were participating, so that the holders were entitled to share equally in any common stock dividends in excess of $6 a share. If the common stock dividend is $7, the preferred stockholder will receive $1 in extra dividends for each share of stock owned. The formula for participation can vary greatly. The essential feature is that preferred stockholders have a prior claim on income and an opportunity for additional return if the dividends to common stockholders exceed a certain amount. Unfortunately for the investor, practically all preferred stock issues are nonparticipating, with the maximum return limited to the specified dividend rate.

VOTING POWER

Because of their prior claim on assets and income, preferred stockholders normally are not given a voice in management unless the company is unable to pay preferred stock dividends during a specified period of time. Arrearages on four quarterly dividend payments might constitute such a default, and under such circumstances, preferred stockholders as a class would be entitled to elect a specific number of directors. Usually, the number of directors is rather small in relation to the total, and by the time the preferred stockholders obtain a voice in management, the company probably is in considerable financial difficulty. Consequently, the voting power that preferred stockholders are granted may be virtually meaningless.

Depending on the agreement between the preferred stockholders and the company, they may obtain voting power under other conditions as well. The company may default under restrictions in the agreement that are similar to those found in a loan agreement or a bond indenture. One of the more frequently imposed restrictions is that dividends on common stock are prohibited if the company does not satisfy certain financial ratios. We note, however, that default under any of the provisions of the agreement between the corporation and its preferred stockholders does not result in the obligation's becoming immediately payable, as does default under a loan agreement or bond indenture. The preferred stockholders merely are given a voice in management and assurance that common stock dividends will not be paid during the period of default. Thus, preferred stockholders do not have nearly the same legal power in default as do debt holders.

RETIREMENT OF PREFERRED STOCK

The fact that preferred stock, like common stock, has no maturity does not mean that most preferred stock issues will remain outstanding forever, because provision for retirement of the stock invariably is made.

Call Feature.   Almost all preferred stock issues have a stated call price, which is above the original issuance price and may decrease over time. Like the call feature on bonds, the call feature on preferred stock affords the company flexibility. Because the market price of a straight preferred stock tends to fluctuate in keeping wih interest rate cycles, the value of the preferred stock call feature is determined by the same considerations as is the call feature for bonds, which we discussed earlier. Unlike preferred stock, long-term debt has a final maturity that assures the eventual retirement of the issue. Without a call feature on preferred stock, the corporation would be able to retire the issue only by the often more expensive and less efficient methods of purchasing the stock in the open market, inviting *tenders* of stock from preferred stockholders at a price above the market price or offering the preferred stockholders another security in its place.

Sinking Fund.   Many preferred stock issues provide for a sinking fund, which partially assures an orderly retirement of the stock. Like bond issues, a preferred stock sinking fund is advantageous to investors because the retirement process exerts upward pressure on the market price of the remaining shares. However, the issuing corporation often has the option to make payment in cash or with preferred shares it purchases in the market.

Convertibility.   Certain preferred stock issues are convertible into common stock at the option of the holder. Upon conversion, of course, the preferred stock is retired. Because virtually all convertible securities have a call feature, the company can force conversion by calling the preferred stock if the market price of the preferred is significantly above the call price. Convertible preferred stock is used frequently in the acquisition of other companies. In part, its use stems from the fact that the transaction is not taxable for the company that is acquired or its stockholders at the time of acquisition. It becomes a taxable transaction only when the preferred stock is sold. We shall examine convertible securities in much more detail in the next chapter.

FINANCING WITH PREFERRED STOCK

Nonconvertible preferred stock is not used extensively as a means of long-term financing: only public utilities employ it with any degree of regularity. The reason is that the preferred stock dividend is not deductible as an expense for tax purposes. The public utility, however, is able to pass along this tax disadvantage to its customers through higher rates approved by state regulators.[11] For the corporate investor, preferred stock may be more attractive than debt instruments because 70 percent of the dividends received by the corporation is not subject to taxation.

This attraction has given rise to floating-rate preferred stock. In one variation, money market preferred stock (MMP), the rate is set by auction every 49 days. Put another way, the rate is established by the forces of supply and demand in keeping with money market rates in general. A typical rate might be .75 times the commercial paper rate, with more creditworthy issuers commanding an even greater discount. As long as enough investors bid at each auction, the effective maturity date is 49 days. As a result, there is little variation in the market price of the investment over time. The tax arbitrage, which benefits both investor and issuer, is at the expense of the federal government. For the issuer, the relevant cost comparison is with the after-tax cost of other methods of short-term financing.

Apart from such short-term financing considerations, one advantage of a regular (long-term) preferred stock arrangement is that the dividend is not a legal obligation of the corporation issuing the securities. If earnings turn bad and the financial condition of the company deteriorates, the dividend can be omitted. With debt financing, interest must be paid, regardless of whether earnings are good or bad. To be sure, companies that are accustomed to paying dividends on their common stock certainly regard the preferred dividend as a fixed obligation. Nevertheless, under dire circumstances, a company that omits its common stock dividend can also omit its preferred dividend.

Another advantage of a straight preferred stock issue is that it has no final maturity; in essence, it is a perpetual loan. From the standpoint of creditors, preferred stock adds to the equity base of the company and thereby strengthens its financial condition. The additional equity base enhances the ability of the company to borrow in the future. Although the explicit after-tax cost of preferred stock is higher than that of bonds, the implied benefits discussed earlier may offset this cost. In addition, the implicit cost of preferred stock financing, from the standpoint of investors penalizing the equity-capitalization rate of the common stock, may be somewhat less than that of debt financing. To the extent that investors are apprehensive over legal bankruptcy, they would regard debt as a riskier form of leverage. Unlike credi-

---

[11] S. C. Linn and J. Michael Pinegar, "The Effect of Issuing Preferred Stock on Common and Preferred Stockholder Wealth," *Journal of Financial Economics*, 22 (October 1988), 155–84, find that common stock prices of utilities showed a small but positive reaction when a preferred stock issue was announced.

tors, preferred stockholders cannot force a company into legal bankruptcy.[12] Therefore, the potential costs of bankruptcy are not a factor as they are with debt financing.

PENSION FUND LIABILITY

Although it does not appear on the balance sheet, many companies have a contractual obligation to make present and future pension payments. Under the Employee Retirement Income Security Act of 1974 (ERISA), this liability is every bit as binding a claim as a federal tax lien and is senior to all other claims. In other words, it is awfully important and goes to the head of the line of creditors if the firm were to be liquidated. In the aggregate, corporate pension fund liabilities have grown enormously during the last two decades, representing a huge source of investment funds. For some companies, this liability exceeds tangible assets. As a financial manager, you will be involved in any pension fund your company might have, so a basic understanding is essential.

TYPES OF PENSION PLANS

Corporate pension plans may be one of two types. A *defined benefit plan* either pays a retired employee so many dollars per month or it pays the individual a percentage of his or her average final salaries. To illustrate the former, after 25 years a participant might be entitled to $18 times the number of years of service, or $450 per month. This is known as a *flat benefit formula*. With respect to the latter method, a person might be paid 2 percent of his or her average salary during the last 5 years of employment multiplied by the number of years of service. If these years were 20 and average monthly salary were $3,000, the monthly pension would be $1,200. This is known as a *unit benefit formula*. Under ERISA, a person who leaves a company prior to regular retirement age will qualify for pension benefits, provided that he or she has been with the firm a sufficient time. This provision is known as *vesting*. A plan must be 100 percent vested after a certain period of employment, the maximum length of time a company may take before fully vesting an employee being 10 years.

The second type of plan is a *defined contribution plan*. Here a company agrees to make a specified monthly or annual payment to the pension plan. All contributions to the plan are a tax-deductible expense by the corporation.[13] (Usually, these payments may be augmented by the employee making individual contributions on a voluntary basis.) The contributions are invested,

---

[12] Gordon Donaldson, "In Defense of Preferred Stock," *Harvard Business Review*, 40 (July–August 1962), 123–36, defends rigorously the use of preferred stock as a means of financing under certain circumstances. He argues that when a company has utilized its debt capacity, it may be able to finance further with preferred stock because the preferred stock capacity of a company is distinct from its debt capacity.

[13] In separate papers, Fischer Black, "The Tax Consequences of Long Run Pension Policy," *Financial Analysts Journal*, 36 (July–August 1980), 21–28, and Irwin Tepper, "Taxation and Corporate Pension Policy," *Journal of Finance*, 36 (March 1981), 1–13, argue that because of the tax feature corporations should maximize their contributions to pension funds. Moreover, these funds should be invested entirely in bonds in order to maximize the tax arbitrage opportunity.

and at retirement the employee is entitled to the cumulative total of contributions plus investment earnings on those contributions. Only when the employee retires and actually receives payment are taxes paid on the benefits. In the accumulation/investment phase, no taxes are paid. Actual future benefits paid to an employee are not known with certainty; they depend on what can be earned by investing the contributions. As most corporate employees are covered by defined benefit plans, we concentrate on the former type of plan.

FUNDED AND UNFUNDED LIABILITIES

The pension liability of a company with a defined benefit plan is composed of two parts. There is the liability to currently retired employees. The present value of this obligation depends on their average life expectancy as well as the discount rate used. The second obligation is to employees not yet retired. This obligation is further subdivided into (1) the benefits earned by employees by virtue of past employment and (2) likely benefits to be earned based on future service. The latter is a forecast, and obviously subject to error. The total pension liability of a company must be valued, usually by an actuary. The idea is to determine the amount of funds necessary for a company to be able to make good on its pension obligations. The *present value of liabilities* is calculated by discounting to present value likely future benefits to be paid, where these benefits are based on past service as well as on expected future service.

The magnitude of present-value liability obviously is sensitive to the discount rate employed—the higher the rate, the lower the liability. However, the rate must correspond to a realistic return on investment in stocks, bonds, and other assets. Usually, actuaries are conservative in the rate they use. This may make sense, inasmuch as they typically ignore the effect of inflation on future salaries and wages. By changing actuarial assumptions, companies sometimes are able to reduce pension fund liabilities in relation to assets. However, the change is an accounting one and usually does not affect the obligation in an economic sense. Moreover, auditors and government agencies restrict the degree to which "creative" actuarial changes can occur.

Once the liabilities are valued, the assets must be valued. This valuation process also consists of two parts. The first involves past corporate contributions. These contributions are paid to a trust or insurance company and are invested in a diversified portfolio of assets. The market value of this portfolio then is its value, although some actuaries value the portfolio using historical costs. The second part involves the present value of expected future contributions by the company for future service by employees. Again this is an estimate, and this total also is sensitive to the discount rate. The present value of assets is the sum of the two parts.

It is desirable, of course, for the present value of the assets to equal the present value of the pension liabilities. This seldom is the case. When the former is less than the latter, there is said to be an unfunded liability, which is simply

Unfunded liability = PV of pension liabilities − PV of pension assets

If a company has an unfunded liability, it must be reported on the balance sheet as a liability.[14] (FASB 87) If there is a surplus, nothing appears. For some companies, the unfunded liability is large and is a matter of concern to creditors. Why? Because it represents a claim that ultimately must be paid. If the underfunded plan is terminated, the company is responsible for the deficit up to 30 percent of its net worth. Credit- and bond-rating agencies are mindful of this obligation and analyze it closely before assigning a rating.

We must recognize that the unfunded liability of a company is not a precise figure. It is an actuary's estimate and is subject to a number of assumptions. However, suppliers of capital should watch closely a company's unfunded liability and dig into the assumptions. For many a company, it simply is too large a potential liability to be ignored, despite problems of estimation. In fact, for some companies the unfunded pension liability dwarfs all other liabilities.

OTHER ASPECTS

If a company should go into bankruptcy and there not be enough funds on hand to meet its pension obligations, the Pension Benefit Guarantee Corporation makes good on most of the total obligation. This government agency is funded by premiums paid to it by companies with pension plans. Because the premium is invariant with respect to default risk, there is option pricing gamesmanship to it. From the standpoint of the stockholders of a company, the bias is for the pension fund to invest in risky assets. If the investments go well, they gain in enhanced share value; if badly, the PBGC is left holding the bag.[15]

Another variant is that when interest rates decline and actuarial assumptions result in a plan being overfunded, many companies voluntarily terminate their plans and start new ones. The "excess overfunding" in the old plan then reverts to the company, boosting earnings and net worth. Whether wealth is expropriated in favor of the company's equity holders depends on the circumstances, but some sizable increases in share price have been found around the time of the reversion.[16] Obviously, the PBGC would like to reduce the "games" played against it, but its legislated tools to do so are limited.

Throughout our discussion, we have dealt with pensions for nonunion employees. Unions have their own pension plans, and the labor contracts they negotiate with corporations include contributions to the union pension fund. Union employees look to this fund and not to the company's for their retirement income.

With respect to accounting for pension expenses, FASB 87 is explicit. There are four components: (1) the interest cost, which is the interest rate times the pension liability; (2) the service cost for additional benefits that employees earn during the year; (3) amortization of any accumulated deficit in

---

[14] As accountants are wont to do, smoothing is possible for companies that have a sudden change putting them in an unfunded liability position. First, they can spread the effect over several years. Second, they can record an intangible asset (for more productive employees!) which is amortized over several years.

[15] The first to articulate this argument was William F. Sharpe, "Corporate Pension Funding Policy," *Journal of Financial Economics*, 4 (June 1976), 183–94.

[16] See Michael J. Alderson and K. C. Chen, "Excess Asset Reversions and Shareholder Wealth," *Journal of Finance*, 41 (March 1986), 225–41, who test and find significant share price improvement. They claim this is consistent with a separation hypothesis of the pension fund and the corporation, where unanticipated reversion results in a windfall gain to stockholders.

the pension fund (unfunded liability); and (4) the expected investment return. The pension expense recorded is the sum of the first three components, offset by number 4. This expense usually differs from the cash actually contributed to the plan for the year.

An important responsibility of the financial manager is to oversee the management of the pension fund's investments. This involves determining asset allocations, choosing investment managers, and monitoring their investment performance. These responsibilities are in addition to analyzing actuarial assumptions, determining the proper funding of a plan, and overseeing the record keeping. These topics as well as those discussed could occupy an entire book. We have just skimmed the surface, but in so doing we hope we have conveyed the importance of pension plans and of the unfunded liability to suppliers of capital. The interested reader is referred to more detailed discussions and analyses.[17]

SUMMARY

The principal features of debt include the fixed or floating rate return, the final maturity, the priority of claim on assets, the credit quality (going from the highest investment grade to junk bonds), the call privilege, and the presence or absence of a sinking-fund provision.

In financing with long-term debt, the company must bargain with investors over the terms of the debt instrument. If the company wishes to include terms that are not beneficial to investors, it must be prepared to pay a higher yield in order to sell the instrument. If debentures are subordinated, investors will demand a higher yield than if the issue involves straight debentures. Another interesting aspect of the bargaining process relates to the call privilege. If interest rate expectations in the market lead investors to think that the issue may be called, the company will have to pay a higher yield for the privilege of being able to call it. As with any option, the value of it depends on variability; for the call option, the variance of future interest rates is paramount. When there is a call feature on a bond, one method for analyzing the refunding of the issue before maturity treats the refunding operation as a riskless capital budgeting project. An alternative method replicates the cash payment stream on the old bonds and focuses attention on the net cash provided by the refunding.

Rather than offer securities to the general public, a company may place them privately with an institutional investor. With a private placement, the company negotiates directly with the investor; there is no underwriting and no registration of the issue with the SEC. The private placement has the virtue of flexibility and affords the medium-sized and even the small company the opportunity to sell its securities.

Preferred stock is a hybrid form of security having characteristics both of debt and common stock. The payment of dividends is not a legal but a discretionary obligation, although many companies regard the obligation as fixed. Preferred stockholders' claims on assets and income come after those of credi-

---

[17] Dan M. McGill and Donald S. Grubbs, Jr., *Fundamentals of Private Pensions*, 6th ed. (Homewood, IL: Pension Research Council, Richard D. Irwin, 1989).

tors but before those of common stockholders. The return on their investment is almost always limited to the specified dividend. Because preferred stock has no final maturity, almost all issues have call features that give the corporation financial flexibility. Retirement of the preferred stock can be accomplished also by a sinking fund, convertibility, or an exchange offering. Because of the 70 percent exemption of dividends to the corporate investor, preferred stock typically has a lower yield than corporate bonds. Particularly popular for marketable security portfolios is money market preferred stock.

The financial manager necessarily is involved in the company's pension plan. Most corporate plans involve defined benefits, and the present value of the pension liability must be compared with the present value of assets earmarked to meet that obligation. If the former exceeds the latter, the company has an unfunded liability. The magnitude of this liability as well as the assumptions inherent in its calculation should be watched closely by suppliers of capital, for pensions are a prior claim in the event of liquidation.

From time to time, a financial manager will wish to hedge the company's fixed-rate financing or investments. There are several devices for doing so, and these are taken up in the Appendix.

APPENDIX
Hedging Fixed-Income Instruments

At times it is desirable to shift risk to others. Unfortunately, this does not come free. There is a cost, in the form of either a spread or a premium paid. The idea is to hedge out unpredictable changes in value. One means for doing so is with stock options, the topic of Chapter 5. The focus here is on how we might hedge fixed-income instruments. In this regard, we examine interest-rate futures, debt options, and interest-rate swaps.[18]

FUTURES MARKETS

By way of definition, a *futures contract* is a standardized agreement that calls for delivery of a commodity at some specified future date. In the case of financial futures, the commodity is a security. Once a contract is traded, the clearinghouse of the exchange interposes itself between the buyer and seller. Its creditworthiness is substituted for that of the other party, and each exchange has a number of rules governing transactions. As in commodities, very few financial futures contracts involve actual delivery at maturity. Rather, buyers and sellers of a contract independently take offsetting positions to close out the contract. The seller cancels a contract by buying another contract; the buyer, by selling another contract.

[18] For a more extensive treatment of these topics, see James C. Van Horne, *Financial Market Rates and Flows,* 3d ed. (Englewood Cliffs, NJ: Prentice Hall, 1990).

MONEY MARKET INSTRUMENTS

Futures markets are available for Eurodollars, Treasury bills, Treasury notes, Treasury bonds, and municipal bonds. Each market is different, but contracts are available anywhere out to 1 to 3 years in the future. To illustrate a transaction, consider first the market for Eurodollars. Each contract is for $1 million face value of Eurodollar deposits, with delivery months of March, June, September, and December (second Wednesday of the month). At present, 10 delivery months are traded, going out nearly 3 years. In the case of Eurodollars, there is no physical settlement on the delivery day. Rather, it is a cash settlement procedure against the LIBOR rate. In contrast, the Treasury bill futures market calls for the actual delivery of a 90- to 92-day bill. Cash settlements involve fewer complications concerning delivery, but the derivation of an index, such as obtaining and averaging Eurodollar quotations, also has its problems.

LONGER-TERM INSTRUMENTS

The features of a longer-term contract, such as Treasury bond futures, are somewhat different from those for Eurodollars and Treasury bills. The trading unit for a single contract is $100,000, in contrast to $1 million. Delivery months are March, June, September, and December, and contracts go out about $2\frac{3}{4}$ years. Price quotations are given as a percentage of the face value ($100) of an 8 percent coupon with 20 years to maturity. A quotation of $91\frac{4}{32}$ means $91\frac{1}{8}$ percent of $100, or $91.125.

For delivery, any Treasury bond with at least 15 years to the earliest call date or to maturity may be used. This contrasts with Treasury bills, where a specific maturity bill is stated in the contract. Because most bonds have a coupon rate other than 8 percent, the invoice is the settlement price multiplied by a *conversion factor*. Recall that the futures contract settlement price is based on a coupon rate of 8 percent. Therefore, the conversion factor is greater than 1.00 for coupon rates greater than 8 percent, 1.00 for an 8 percent coupon bond, and less than 1.00 for coupon rates less than 8 percent. The greater the deviation in coupon rate from 8 percent, the greater the deviation in conversion factor from 1.00. Conversion factors are established for each delivery date and are used in all transactions.

HEDGING A POSITION

Hedging represents taking a future contract position opposite to a position taken in the spot market. The purpose is to reduce risk exposure by protecting oneself from unexpected price changes. In contrast, a *speculator* takes positions in futures markets in the pursuit of profits and assumes price risk in this endeavor.

A *long hedge* involves buying (going long in) a futures contract. It is generally employed to lock in an interest rate that is believed to be high. Suppose an investor will have $1 million to invest in Treasury bonds 2 months hence—on November 1, for example. The investor believes interest rates have peaked at present and wishes to lock in the current high rates (on September 1), even though the funds will not be available for investment for 2 months.

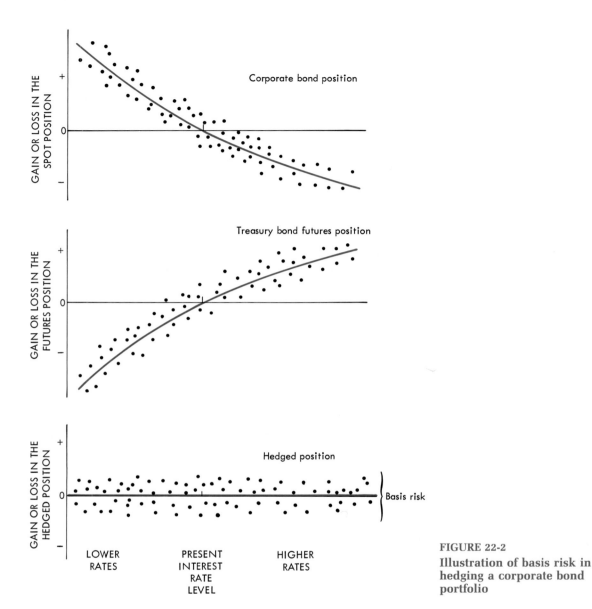

FIGURE 22-2
Illustration of basis risk in hedging a corporate bond portfolio

A *short hedge* involves the opposite sort of transactions from a long hedge. Here the idea is to sell a futures contract now because of a belief that interest rates will rise. The sale of the futures contract is used as a substitute for the sale of an actual security held. Another example of a short hedge is a corporation that needs to borrow in the future and sells a futures contract now to protect itself against an expected rise in interest rates. Suppose on February 1, a corporation knows it will need to borrow $1 million in the long-term market 3 months hence. The company feels interest rates will rise and wishes to hedge against this possibility.

Unfortunately, there is no futures market for long-term corporate bonds. Therefore, the company must look to a related market and settles on the Treasury bond futures market. While interest rates in these two markets do not move entirely in concert, there is a close relationship, so a *cross hedge* across markets makes sense.

Hedging is not perfect in eliminating the risk of a position. In hedging, market participants are concerned with fluctuations in the *basis*, which portrays the risk to the hedger. The basis is simply the price of a security in the spot market minus its future price (adjusted by the appropriate conversion factor). To illustrate basis risk as well as hedging in general, suppose you hold a portfolio of corporate bonds and wish to hedge it. If interest rates rise, the value of your portfolio declines, and vice versa. This is illustrated in the top panel of Fig. 22-2. The mathematical relationship between value and interest-rate changes is given by the curvilinear line. Because the corporate bond market is subject to imperfections, there may be deviations about the line, as depicted by the scatter of dots.

To hedge a portfolio, one would want to write Treasury bond futures contracts. As there is not a viable corporate bond futures market, one must resort to a cross hedge. By writing futures contracts, one offsets the long position in the spot market with a short position in the futures market. As interest rates rise, the value of the futures contract will increase and vice versa. The relationship is illustrated by the middle panel of Fig. 22-2. Here, too, there is a random component, as depicted by the scatter of dots.

On average, the long and the short positions are offsetting. As shown in the bottom panel of Fig. 22-2, the overall position (spot and futures) is insensitive to changes in interest rates. However, there is risk left over, again depicted by the dispersion of dots about the line. This basis risk arises because of somewhat divergent movements in the spot and futures markets.

DEBT OPTIONS

We turn now to options on debt instruments. Exchange markets for such options began in 1982 with options on individual Treasury securities and options on interest-rate futures contracts. The former have withered, but there is an over-the-counter market for such options. In contrast, options on futures have grown dramatically, and there now are futures options on Eurodollars, Treasury bills, Treasury notes, Treasury bonds, and on the municipal bond futures index. As was the case for futures markets, volume is heaviest for options on Eurodollar futures and on Treasury bond futures.

FUTURES VERSUS OPTIONS

With a futures contract, an investor's gain or loss depends on interest-rate movements. If one wished to hedge a long position in a fixed-income security, he or she would take a short position in a futures contract, that is, a hedger would write a contract. By such action a hedger largely neutralizes risk. Such a hedge is illustrated in the top panel of Fig. 22-3.

With an option, the potential loss is limited to the premium paid. This contrasts with a futures position where the loss is not so bounded. If an individual wished to hedge a long position in a fixed-income security, he or she would buy a put option. The situation is illustrated in the bottom panel of Fig. 22-3. As taken up in Chapter 5, debt options are suited for hedging "one-

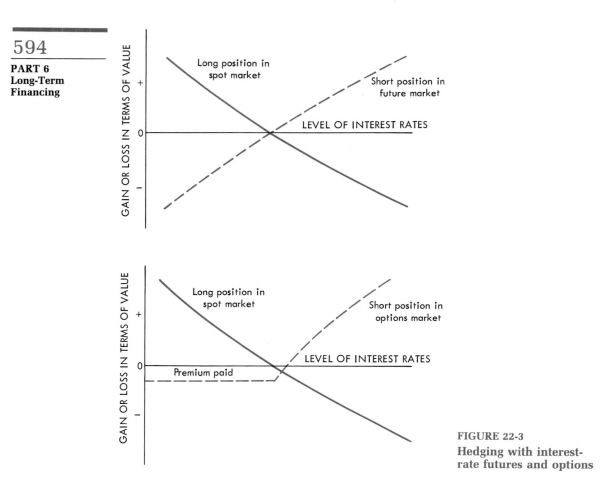

FIGURE 22-3
Hedging with interest-rate futures and options

sided" risk. They also can be used to place bets on the direction and/or volatility of interest rates.

INTEREST-RATE SWAPS

When a company can borrow to advantage with one type of financing but really prefers another, it sometimes will engage in a swap. A *swap,* as the name implies, represents an exchange of obligations. There are two principal types: *currency swaps* and *interest-rate swaps.* With the former, two parties exchange interest obligations on debt dominated in different currencies. At maturity the principal amounts are exchanged, usually at a rate of exchange agreed upon in advance. With an interest-rate swap, interest-payment obligations are exchanged between two parties, but they are denominated in the same currency. Our focus in this chapter is on interest-rate swaps; in Chapter 26 we consider currency swaps.

SOME DEFINITIONS AND ILLUSTRATION

The most common swap is the *floating-/fixed-rate* exchange. For example, a corporation that has borrowed on a fixed-rate, term basis may swap with a counterparty to make floating-rate interest payments. The counterparty, which has borrowed directly on a floating-rate basis, agrees to make fixed-rate interest payments in the swap. There is no transfer of principal; only the interest obligation is exchanged. This exchange is done at periodic intervals, and usually on a net settlement basis. That is, the party that owes more interest than it receives in the swap pays the difference. Often the arrangement is blind in that the counterparties do not know each other. An intermediary—a commercial or investment bank—makes the arrangements.

Typically, floating-rate payments are tied to the London interbank offer rate (LIBOR), though this does not need to be the case. LIBOR is the rate for top-quality Eurodollar borrowings by banks. For standardized swaps, a secondary market of sorts developed in the mid- to late 1980s. This market allows contracts to be reversed or terminated, providing a degree of liquidity.

To illustrate a basic floating-/fixed-rate swap, consider the example in Fig. 22-4. Company A has an AAA credit rating and is able to borrow directly in the market at a rate of 10 percent for a 10-year loan and at LIBOR + 0.20 percent for a floating-rate loan. Company B has a BBB credit rating and can borrow directly at interest rates of 11.20 percent term and LIBOR + 0.75 percent floating. In our example, company A borrows directly at a fixed rate of 10 percent and swaps to pay floating rate at LIBOR. It is called the *floating-rate payer*. In contrast, company B borrows directly in the floating-rate market at LIBOR + 0.75 percent, and agrees to pay a fixed rate of 10.20 percent in the swap. It is called the *fixed-rate payer*. Finally, the intermediary is interposed between the two parties. It passes the floating-rate payments through directly but retains 0.10 percent of the fixed-rate payments as its margin.

At the bottom of the figure is a recap which portrays the "alleged" savings. For company A, its all-in cost of floating-rate financing is the LIBOR rate it pays in the swap minus (10.10 percent − 10.00 percent), which represents the excess of what it receives in the swap over its fixed-rate cost of borrowing directly. As a result, it realizes an opportunity savings of 0.30 percent relative to the LIBOR + 0.20 percent it would pay to borrow directly on a floating-rate basis. Company B's all-in cost of fixed-rate financing is 10.95 percent. This is

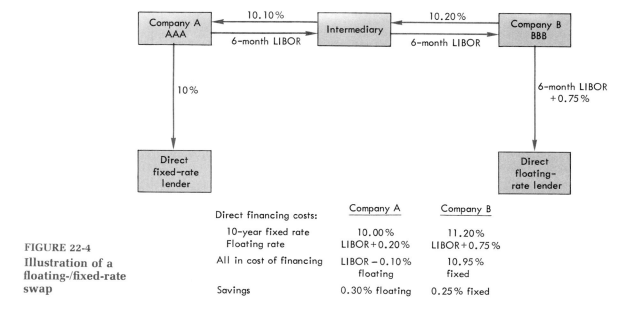

FIGURE 22-4

Illustration of a
floating-/fixed-rate
swap

Direct financing costs:	Company A	Company B
10-year fixed rate	10.00%	11.20%
Floating rate	LIBOR+0.20%	LIBOR+0.75%
All in cost of financing	LIBOR−0.10% floating	10.95% fixed
Savings	0.30% floating	0.25% fixed

comprised of the 10.20 percent rate it pays in the swap plus (LIBOR + 0.75 percent − LIBOR), which represents the excess of its floating-rate cost of direct borrowing over what it receives in the swap. It realizes an opportunity savings of 0.25 percent, relative to the 11.20 percent it would pay to borrow directly on a fixed-rate basis. Thus, both parties as well as the intermediary seem to gain in this floating-/fixed-rate swap. From whence do these gains come?

VALUATION ISSUES

One argument is comparative advantage in financing, which rests on market segmentation occurring.[19] It is argued that institutional restrictions (regulatory, tax, and tradition) limit the ability of a party to borrow in the way or in the currency desired. Closely allied is an argument that asymmetric information causes the opportunity. Different lenders are said to have access to different information about borrowers. As disclosure requirements are different in Europe than in the United States, for example, a potential corporate borrower may be able to borrow to better advantage in the home market where lenders have an information edge.

As a result of imperfections and disparate information, borrowers are said to have comparative advantage. It may be that United Fruit can borrow more effectively on a term basis in the United States than it can on a floating-rate basis either in the United States or in Europe, while Foreaux Company can place floating-rate debt more effectively in France than it can place term debt either in Europe or in the United States. If United Fruit really wants to borrow on a floating-rate basis and Foreaux really wants to borrow on a term basis, it makes sense for each to borrow where they have comparative advantage. By swapping interest obligations, both parties can realize cost savings similar to those shown in Fig. 22-4, so the argument goes.

The key is whether the arbitrage opportunity persists. One would think that as more and more swaps occur, the rate differences would be reduced and eventually eliminated. In other words, any initial opportunity would be arbitraged out as the swap market seasoned. So while institutional rigidities may persist, arbitrage would eliminate savings possible from comparative advantage. Moreover, informational asymmetry would be reduced as more swaps occur, and credit rating services endeavor to fill information gaps. Thus, the comparative advantage argument is suspect.

Typically, the counterparties in a swap are not of equal credit risk. Default risk does not apply to principal; each party is responsible for whatever principal obligation it has incurred in direct borrowings. However, there is default risk with respect to the differential in interest payments. In the early 1980s, default risk was borne by the two counterparties in most swaps. However, intermediaries increasingly interposed themselves between the parties in such a way as to assume the default risk.

If a fixed-rate counterparty should default, the exposed intermediary will need to assume its position. If interest rates have declined from the time of the contract, there is a shortfall between the payment required and what could be obtained in the current swap market. The exposed intermediary must make

[19] Leading proponents of this explanation for the existence of the swap market are James Bicksler and Andrew H. Chen, "An Economic Analysis of Interest Rate Swaps," *Journal of Finance*, 41 (July 1986), 645–55.

up the difference. It can bring in another counterparty to pay fixed rate, but it will be at a lower rate and the intermediary is obligated to pay the difference. Most default risk is on the fixed-rate side, and then only if interest rates decline. If interest rates rise, the intermediary will have no difficulty replacing the defaulted counterparty. In fact, it will gain from any excess in interest rate over the fixed-rate contracted for in the swap. Thus, default risk is one-sided. It depends on (1) the fixed-rate payer defaulting and (2) interest rates declining. If the floating-rate payer defaults, a new counterparty can be brought in with little loss other than transaction costs and the loss of an interest payment difference or two.

In general, the weaker counterparty in a swap is the one that swaps to pay fixed rate. That is, it borrows directly on a floating-rate basis and swaps to pay fixed rate. It would borrow to advantage on a direct basis if it could do so. The scenario under which both default tends to occur for lower grade credits *and* interest rates tend to decline is a steep recession.

Yet another reason for the differences observed in Fig. 22-4 is that there are call feature differences. The 10-year loan rate on direct U.S. borrowings has embraced in it a premium for call risk. In contrast, swaps typically do not have a call option.[20] For this reason alone, the fixed rate in a swap should be lower than the fixed rate on a direct bond issue in the United States. This is simply the yield differential between a callable and a non-callable bond, discussed earlier.

Apart from these considerations, the swap market provides a hedging vehicle not otherwise available. The interest-rate futures and debt options markets extend out only 2 or 3 years. The swap market serves to complete the market for hedges in longer maturity areas, and it can prove quite useful to the financial manager.

SELF-CORRECTION PROBLEMS

1. The Lemand Corporation has $8 million of 10 percent mortgage bonds outstanding under an open-end indenture. The indenture allows additional bonds to be issued as long as all the following conditions are met:

   a. Pretax interest coverage [(income before taxes + bond interest)/bond interest] remains greater than 4.

   b. Net depreciated value of mortgaged assets remains twice the amount of mortgage debt.

   c. Debt-to-equity ratio remains below .5.

   The Lemand Corporation has net income after taxes of $2 million and a 50 percent tax rate, $40 million in equity, and $30 million in depreciated assets, covered by the mortgage. Assuming that 50 percent of the proceeds of a new issue would be added to the base of mortgaged assets and that the company has no sinking-fund payments until next year, how much more 10 percent debt could be sold under each of the three conditions? Which protective covenant is binding?

2. Northern California Public Service Company is considering refunding its preferred stock. The dividend rate on this stock is $6 and it has a par value of $50 a share. The call price is $52 a share, and 500,000 shares are outstanding. George Arroya, vice-president, finance, feels the company can issue new preferred stock in the current market at an interest rate of 11 percent. With this rate, the new is-

[20] See Clifford W. Smith, Jr., Charles W. Smithson, and Lee MacDonald Wakeman, "The Market for Interest Rate Swaps," research paper, University of Rochester (1987).

sue could be sold at par; the total par value of the issue would be $25 million. Flotation costs of $780,000 are tax deductible, but the call premium is not tax deductible; the company's marginal tax rate is 30 percent. A 90-day period of overlap is expected between the time the new preferred stock is issued and the time the old preferred stock is retired. Should the company refund its preferred stock using a capital budgeting analysis of refunding?

3. Alvarez Apparel, Inc., could sell preferred stock with a dividend cost of 12 percent. If it were to sell bonds in the current market, the interest rate cost would be 14 percent. The company is in a 40 percent tax bracket.

   a. What is the after-tax cost of each of these methods of financing?

   b. Setlec Corporation holds a limited number of preferred stocks in its marketable security portfolio. It is in a 36 percent tax bracket. If it were to invest in the preferred stock of Alvarez Apparel, what would be its after-tax return? What would be its after-tax return if it were to invest in the bonds?

PROBLEMS

1. Bragon Manufacturing Company has in its capital structure $20 million of $13\frac{1}{2}$ percent sinking-fund debentures. The sinking-fund call price is $1,000 per bond, and sinking-fund payments of $1 million in face amount of bonds are required annually. Presently, the yield to maturity on the debentures in the market is 12.21 percent. To satisfy the sinking-fund payment, should the company deliver cash to the trustee or bonds? What if the yield to maturity were 14.60 percent?

2. The Hirsch Corporation is in bankruptcy. Mortgaged assets have been sold for $5 million, and other assets have yielded $10 million. Hirsch has $10 million in mortgage bonds, $5 million in subordinated (to the mortgage bonds) debentures, $15 million owed to general creditors, and $10 million par value of common stock. How would distribution of the $15 million in liquidating value be made?

3. Crakow Machine Company wishes to borrow $10 million for 10 years. It can issue either a noncallable bond at 11.40 percent interest or a bond callable at the end of 5 years for 12 percent. For simplicity, we assume that the bond will be called only at the end of year 5. The interest rate that is likely to prevail 5 years hence for a 5-year straight bond can be described by the following probability distribution:

Interest rate	9%	10%	11%	12%	13%
Probability	.1	.2	.4	.2	.1

Issuing and other costs involved in selling a bond issue 5 years hence will total $200,000. The call price is assumed to be par.

a. What is the total absolute amount of interest payments for the noncallable issue over the 10 years? (Do not discount.) What is the expected value of total interest payments and other costs if the company issues callable bonds? (Assume that the company calls the bonds and issues new ones only if there is a savings in interest costs after issuing expenses.) On the basis of total costs, should the company issue noncallable or callable bonds?

b. What would be the outcome if the probability distribution of interest rates 5 years hence were the following?

Interest rate	7%	9%	11%	13%	15%
Probability	.2	.2	.2	.2	.2

Assume that all other conditions stay the same.

4. Five years ago, Zapada International issued $50 million of 10 percent, 25-year debentures at a price of $990 per bond to the public. The call price was originally $1,100 per bond the first year after issuance, and this price declined by $10 each subsequent year. Zapada now is calling the bonds in order to refund them at a lower interest rate.

   a. Ignoring taxes, what is the bondholder's return on investment for the 5 years? (Assume that interest is paid once a year and that the investor owns one bond.)

   b. If the bondholder can now invest $1,000 in a 20-year bond of equivalent risk that provides 8 percent interest, what is his overall cash-flow return over the 25-year holding period? How does this compare with the return on the Zapada bonds had they not been called? (Assume again that interest is paid once a year.)

5. The U.S. Zither Corporation has $50 million of 14 percent debentures outstanding, which are due in 25 years. USZ could refund these bonds in the current market with new 25-year bonds, sold to the public at par ($1,000 per bond) with a 12 percent coupon rate. The spread to the underwriter is 1 percent, leaving $990 per bond in proceeds to the company. The old bonds have an unamortized discount of $1 million, unamortized legal fees and other expenses of $100,000, and a call price of $1,140 per bond ($114 on $100 face value convention). The tax rate is 40 percent. There is a 1-month overlap during which both issues are outstanding, and issuing expenses are $200,000. Compute the present value of the refunding, using the after-tax rate on the new bonds as the discount rate. Is the refunding worthwhile?

6. Velcor Electrical Products Company presently has $10 million in 15 percent bonds outstanding with 10 years to final maturity. The call price is $1,120 per bond ($112 on $100 face value convention), and the company presently could sell a 10-year bond in the market at a yield of 13 percent to the public. Interest would be paid annually, the underwriter spread would be 2 percent of gross proceeds received from the public, and a 2-month overlap period would occur. The company is in the 35 percent tax bracket, and there is no unamortized discount or issuing costs on the old bonds. Using a replication-of-cash-outflows approach (alternative approach), is the refunding worthwhile?

7. The Riting Railroad needs to raise $9.5 million for capital improvements. One possibility is a new preferred stock issue: 8 percent, $100 par value stock that would yield 9 percent to investors. Flotation costs for an issue this size amount to 5 percent of the total amount of preferred stock sold; these costs are deducted from gross proceeds in determining the net proceeds to the company. (Ignore any tax considerations.)

   a. At what price per share will the preferred stock be offered to investors? (Assume that the issue will never be called.)

   b. How many shares must be issued to raise $9.5 million for Riting Railroad?

8. Lost Horizon Silver Mining Company has 200,000 shares of $7 cumulative preferred stock outstanding, $100 par value. The preferred stock has a participating feature. If dividends on the common stock exceed $1 per share, preferred stockholders receive additional dividends per share equal to one-half of the excess. In other words, if the common stock dividend were $2, preferred stockholders would receive an additional dividend of $.50. The company has 1 million shares of common outstanding. What would dividends per share be on the preferred stock and on the common stock if earnings available for dividends in three successive years were (a) $1,000,000, $600,000, and $3,000,000; (b) $2,000,000, $2,400,000, and $4,600,000; and (c) $1,000,000, $2,500,000, and $5,700,000. (Assume that all the available earnings are paid in dividends, but nothing more is paid.)

9. Solie Sod and Seed Company (SSS) has a defined benefit pension plan for its salaried employees. The balance sheet of the plan has the following format:

Value of existing pension fund assets	PV of expected benefits to retired employees
PV of expected future contributions	PV of expected benefits for future service
Total assets	Total pension fund liabilities

Presently the fund has an unfunded liability. Determine in general the effect of each of the following on the appropriate balance sheet item and on the unfunded liability:

a. Sal Zambrano joins the firm and is expected to be entitled to a pension of $25,000 a year starting in 20 years.

b. In a good earnings year, SSS buys $400,000 in bonds and contributes them to the plan over and above its regular contribution.

c. In view of inflation, SSS raises the monthly pension of existing retirees by $10 per month.

d. As interest rates have risen, the discount rate used for determining present values is raised by 1 percent.

SOLUTIONS TO SELF-CORRECTION PROBLEMS

1. (dollars in millions) Let x = the number of millions of dollars of new debt that can be issued.

a.
$$\frac{\$4.8}{\$.8 + .10x} = 4$$
$$4(\$.8) + 4(.10x) = \$4.8$$
$$.40x = \$1.6$$
$$x = \$4$$

b.
$$\frac{\$30 + .5x}{\$8 + x} = 2$$
$$2(\$8) + 2(x) = \$30 + .5x$$
$$1.5x = \$14$$
$$x = \$9.333$$

c.
$$\frac{\$10 + x}{\$40} = .5$$
$$.5(\$40) = \$10 + x$$
$$x = \$10$$

Condition a is binding and it limits the amount of new debt to $4 million.

2. Net cash outflow:

Cost of calling old preferred ($52)	$26,000,000
Net proceeds of new issue: $25 million – flotation costs of $780,000	24,220,000
Difference	$ 1,780,000
Preferred stock dividends on old preferred during overlap	750,000
Gross cash outlay	$ 2,530,000
Less: Tax savings on flotation costs $780,000 (.3)	234,000
Net cash outflow	$ 2,296,000
Annual net cash outflow on old preferred: Preferred stock dividend	$ 3,000,000
Annual net cash outflow on new preferred: Preferred stock dividend	$ 2,750,000

Difference = \$3,000,000 − \$2,750,000 = \$250,000
Discounted at a rate of 11 percent for a perpetuity:

$$PV = \frac{\$250,000}{.11} = \$2,272,727$$

The preferred stock issue should not be refunded. The net benefit is negative (\$2,272,727 − \$2,296,000).

3. a. After-tax cost:
Preferred stock = 12%
Bonds = 14%(1 − .40) = 8.40%

b. The dividend income to a corporate investor is 70 percent exempt from taxation. With a corporate tax rate of 36 percent, we have for the preferred stock:

After-tax return = 12%[1 − .3(.36)] = 10.70%

For the bonds, the after-tax return = 14%(1 − .36) = 8.96%

SELECTED REFERENCES

ALDERSON, MICHAEL J., and K. C. CHEN, "Excess Asset Reversions and Shareholder Wealth," *Journal of Finance*, 41 (March 1986), 225–41.

ANG, JAMES S. "The Two Faces of Bond Refunding," *Journal of Finance*, 20 (June 1975), 869–74.

BLACK, FISCHER, "The Tax Consequences of Long Run Pension Policy," *Financial Analysts Journal*, 36 (July–August 1980), 21–28.

BODIE, ZVI, and ROBERT A. TAGGART, JR., "Future Investment Opportunities and the Value of the Call Provisions on a Bond," *Journal of Finance*, 33 (September 1978), 1187–1200.

BOWLIN, OSWALD D., "The Refunding Decision: Another Special Case in Capital Budgeting," *Journal of Finance*, 21 (March 1966), 55–68.

BRENNAN, MICHAEL J., and EDUARDO S. SCHWARTZ, "Savings Bonds, Retractable Bonds and Callable Bonds," *Journal of Financial Economics*, 5 (1977), 67–88.

DONALDSON, GORDON, "In Defense of Preferred Stock," *Harvard Business Review*, 40 (July–August 1962), 123–36.

DUNN, KENNETH B., and CHESTER S. SPATT, "A Strategic Analysis of Sinking Fund Bonds," *Journal of Financial Economics*, 13 (September 1984), 399–424.

DYL, EDWARD A., and MICHAEL D. JOEHNK, "Sinking Funds and the Cost of Corporate Debt," *Journal of Finance*, 34 (September 1979), 887–94.

EMERY, DOUGLAS R., and WILBUR G. LEWELLEN, "Refunding Noncallable Debt," *Journal of Financial and Quantitative Analysis*, 19 (March 1984), 73–82.

FINNERTY, JOHN D., "Preferred Stock Refunding Analysis: Synthesis and Extension," *Financial Management*, 13 (Autumn 1984), 22–28.

FOOLADI, IRAJ, and GORDON S. ROBERTS, "On Preferred Stock," *Journal of Financial Research*, 9 (Winter 1986), 319–24.

HO, THOMAS, and RONALD F. SINGER, "Bond Indenture Provisions and the Risk of Corporate Debt," *Journal of Financial Economics*, 10 (December 1982), 375–406.

———, "The Value of Sinking Fund Provisions on Corporate Debt," *Journal of Business*, 57 (1984), 315–36.

HOUSTON, ARTHUR L., JR., and CAROL OLSON HOUSTON, "Financing with Preferred Stock," *Financial Management*, 19 (Autumn 1990), 42–54.

KALOTAY, A. J., "On the Management of Sinking Funds," *Financial Management*, 10 (Summer 1981), 34–40.

———, "On the Structure and Valuation of Debt Refunding," *Financial Management*, 11 (Spring 1982), 41–42.

LEWELLEN, WILBUR G., and DOUGLAS R. EMERY, "On the Matter of Parity among Financial Obligations," *Journal of Finance*, 36 (March 1981), 97–111.

LINN, S. C., and J. MICHAEL PINEGAR, "The Effect of Issuing Preferred Stock on Common and Preferred Stockholder Wealth," *Journal of Financial Economics*, 22 (October 1988), 155–84.

MCCONNELL, JOHN J., and GARY G. SCHLARBAUM, "Returns, Risks, and Pricing of Income Bonds, 1956–76," *Journal of Business*, 54 (January 1981), 33–57.

MCDANIEL, MOREY W., "Bondholders and Corporate Governance," *Business Lawyer*, 41 (February 1986), 413–60.

MCGILL, DAN M., and DONALD S. GRUBBS, JR., *Fundamentals of Private Pensions*, 6th ed. Homewood, IL: Pension Research Council, Richard D. Irwin, 1989.

MARSHALL, WILLIAM J., and JESS B. YAWITZ, "Optimal Terms of the Call Provision on a Corporate Bond," *Journal of Financial Research*, 3 (Fall 1980), 203–11.

OFER, AHARON R., and ROBERT A. TAGGART, JR., "Bonding Refunding: A Clarifying Analysis," *Journal of Finance*, 32 (March 1977), 21–30.

ROBBINS, EDWARD HENRY, and JOHN D. SCHATZBERG, "Callable Bonds: A Risk-Reducing Signalling Mechanism," *Journal of Finance*, 41 (September 1986), 935–49.

SMITH, CLIFFORD W., JR., CHARLES W. SMITHSON, and LEE MACDONALD WAKEMAN, "The Market for Interest Rate Swaps," research paper, University of Rochester (1987).

SMITH, CLIFFORD W., JR., and JEROLD B. WARNER, "On Financial Contracting: An Analysis of Bond Covenants," *Journal of Financial Economics*, 7 (June 1979), 117–61.

SORENSEN, ERIC H., and CLARK A. HAWKINS, "On the Pricing of Preferred Stock," *Journal of Financial and Quantitative Analysis*, 16 (November 1981), 515–28.

TEPPER, IRWIN, "Taxation and Corporate Pension Policy," *Journal of Finance*, 36 (March 1981), 1–14.

VAN HORNE, JAMES C., "Implied Fixed Costs in Long-Term Debt Issues," *Journal of Financial and Quantitative Analysis*, 8 (December 1973), 821–34.

———, "Called Bonds: How Does the Investor Fare?" *Journal of Portfolio Management*, 6 (Summer 1980), 58–61.

———, *Financial Market Rates and Flows*, 3d ed. Englewood Cliffs, NJ: Prentice Hall, 1990.

VU, JOSEPH D., "An Empirical Investigation of Calls of Non-Convertible Bonds," *Journal of Financial Economics*, 14 (June 1986), 235–65.

23

OPTION FINANCING: WARRANTS, CONVERTIBLES, AND EXCHANGEABLES

Warrants, convertible securities, and exchangeable securities, the subjects of this chapter, are forms of options. We know from Chapter 5 that an option is merely an instrument that gives its owner the right to buy or sell the common stock of a company within a specific period of time. The price paid for the stock, or the price at which it is sold, is known as the *exercise price*, and it is stated in the contract. We might have a "call" option to buy one share of stock of ABC Corporation at $10 through December 31 of the current year.[1] Thus, the option has an exercise price of $10 and an expiration date of December 31. The option itself may be traded in a market. If it is, its value will be closely related to the value of the associated stock—the two securities are close substitutes with respect to market price movements.

We also know from Chapter 5 that the value of the option should bear a relationship to certain other variables. It is useful to review them briefly. Obviously, the higher the current price of the stock or the lower the exercise price of the option, the greater the value of the option. Increased volatility of the common stock works to the advantage of the option holder. This is because the downside risk of the option is bounded at zero. Therefore, an increase in variance expands the upside potential of the option while the downside risk continues to be bounded at zero. The result is an increase in the option's value. Also we saw in Chapter 5 that the longer the length of time to the expiration of the option, the more valuable it becomes, all other things staying the same. Moreover, the higher the short-term, risk-free interest rate, the greater the value of the option, holding all else constant. Finally, the higher the dividend on the common stock, the lower the value of the option. This is due to the fact that option holders are not entitled to dividends, nor is their option readjusted to reflect the payment of dividends to the common stockholders. All the factors discussed govern the value of an option in the marketplace.

---

[1] In contrast, a "put" option entitles the holder to sell stock at a specified exercise price through the expiration date. In the remainder of our discussion, we will be concerned only with call options.

We discovered in Chapter 5 that the relationship between the value of the stock and the value of the option is affected by the ability of market participants to hold a fully hedged, risk-free position. This can be accomplished by buying stock and writing options or buying options and shorting stock. By holding such a combination, movements upward or downward in the price of the stock are offset by opposite movements in the value of the option position. With efficient financial markets, a risk-free hedged position should return only the risk-free rate. To the extent that returns in excess of the risk-free rate can be earned, individuals will have an incentive to take such positions. The impact of their buying and selling of stocks and options to establish hedged positions will affect relative prices in a way that drives out any excess returns that might be earned. Black and Scholes have provided a precise formula for determining the equilibrium value of an option under these conditions,[2] and this model was illustrated in Chapter 5. In equilibrium, then, excess returns should not be possible, and stocks and options should be priced in the market in such a way that one is not overvalued or undervalued relative to the other.

With this general discussion of options in mind, we now examine three types of options employed by business firms in their financing—the warrant, the convertible security, and the exchangeable security. As we shall see, the warrant is like a pure call option, although the number of shares of stock a warrant will purchase can be more than or less than one. Virtually all of our discussion on option valuation in Chapter 5 is directly applicable here, so we mainly explore the use of warrants as a financing vehicle. Convertible securities are somewhat different in that they represent a hybrid security—part bond or preferred stock and part common stock. As a result, their valuation is somewhat different from that of a straight option and we will need to spend more time on them. Exchangeable bonds are convertible, but into the common stock of another corporation as opposed to the stock of the issuer.

THE USE OF WARRANTS

A *warrant* is an option to purchase a specified number of shares of common stock at a stated price. When holders exercise options, they surrender the warrants. Warrants are often employed as "sweeteners" to a public issue of bonds or debt that is privately placed. The investor obtains not only the fixed return associated with debt but also an option to purchase common stock at a stated price. If the market price of stock should rise, this option can be valuable. As a result, the corporation should be able to obtain a lower interest rate than it would otherwise. For companies that are marginal credit risks, the use of warrants may make the difference between being able and not being able to raise funds through a debt issue. In addition to being a "sweetener" to debt financing, warrants are used in the founding of a company as compensation to underwriters and venture capitalists.

FEATURES

The warrant itself contains the provisions of the option. It states the number of shares the holder can buy for each warrant. Frequently, a warrant will provide the option to purchase 1 share of common stock for each warrant

---

[2] Fischer Black and Myron Scholes, "The Pricing of Options and Corporate Liabilities," *Journal of Political Economy*, 81 (May–June 1973), 637–54.

held, but it might be 2 shares, 3 shares, or 2.54 shares. Another important provision is the price at which the warrant is exercisable, such as $12 a share. This means that in order to buy one share, the warrant holder must put up $12. This exercise price may be either fixed or "stepped up" over time. For example, the exercise price might increase from $12 to $13 after 3 years and to $14 after another 3 years.

605

CHAPTER 23
Option Financing:
Warrants,
Convertibles, and
Exchangeables

The warrant must specify the date the option expires, unless it is perpetual, having no expiration date. Because a warrant is only an option to purchase stock, warrant holders are not entitled to any cash dividends paid on the common stock, nor do they have voting power. If the common stock is split or a stock dividend is declared, the option price of the warrant usually is adjusted to take this change into account.

For accounting reporting purposes, a company with warrants outstanding is required to report earnings per share in such a way that those who read the financial statement can visualize the potential dilution. More specifically, it must report earnings on two bases: *primary earnings per share* and *fully diluted earnings per share,* which recognizes the negative EPS effect of all potentially dilutive securities.

EXERCISE OF WARRANTS

When warrants are exercised, the common stock of the company is increased. Moreover, the debt that was issued in conjunction with the warrants remains outstanding, assuming the warrants are detachable. At the time of the issue of the warrants, the exercise price usually is set in excess of the market price of the common stock. The premium often is 15 percent or so above the stock's value. If the share price is $40 and the holder can purchase one share of common stock for each warrant held, this translates into an exercise price of $46.

To see how new capital can be infused with the exercise of warrants, let us take a company we shall call Western Rig. It has just raised $25 million in debt funds with warrants attached. The debentures carry an 11 percent coupon rate, and with each debenture ($1,000 face value) investors receive one warrant entitling each to purchase four shares of common stock at $30 a share. The capitalization of the company before financing, after financing, and after complete exercise of the warrants is as follows (in millions):

	BEFORE FINANCING	AFTER FINANCING	AFTER EXERCISE
Debentures		$25	$25
Common stock ($10 par value)	$10	10	11
Additional paid-in capital			2
Retained earnings	40	40	40
Shareholders' equity	$50	$50	$53
Total capitalization	$50	$75	$78

The retained earnings of the company remain unchanged, and the debenture issue has neither matured nor been called. Exercising their options, the warrant holders purchase 100,000 shares of stock at $30 a share, or $3 million in total. Consequently, the total capitalization of the company is increased by that amount.

A company cannot force the exercise of the warrant option as it can force the exercise of the conversion option by calling a convertible security. Consequently, it is unable to control when, if ever, the warrant will be exercised and there will be an infusion of new equity capital into the corporation. Only the expiration date sets a limit on how long the warrants can remain outstanding and unexercised.

VALUATION OF WARRANTS

The theoretical value of a warrant can be determined by

$$NP_s - E \qquad (23\text{-}1)$$

where N = the number of shares that can be purchased with one warrant
P_s = the market price of one share of stock
E = the exercise dollar amount associated with the purchase of N shares

Note that this formula is exactly the same as that discussed in Chapter 5 for the valuation of an option where $N = 1$. Most warrants sell at prices in excess of their theoretical values. The reasons for this occurrence were discussed in Chapter 5, and they relate to the volatility of the common stock, to the length of time to the expiration of the warrant, and to the time value of money. The typical relationship between the market value of a warrant and the value of the associated common stock is shown in Fig. 23-1. The theoretical value of the warrant is represented by the solid line in the figure, and the actual market value of the warrant by the dashed line. When the market value of the associated stock is less than the exercise price, the theoretical value of the warrant is zero and it is said to be trading "out of the money." When the value of the associated common stock is greater than the exercise price, the theoretical value of the warrant is positive, as depicted by the solid diagonal line. Under these circumstances, the warrant is said to be trading "in the money."

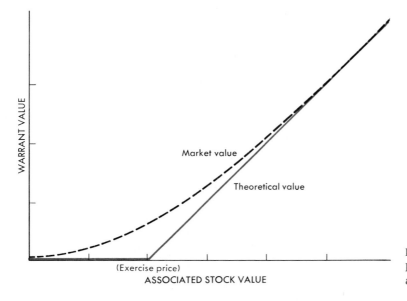

FIGURE 23-1

Relationship between theoretical and market values of a warrant

The shorter the length of time to the expiration of the option, the more convex the market-value line. With only a few days to expiration, the market-value line will approach the theoretical value line. It should be noted that the typical warrant has a longer time to expiration than does the option. The same relationship holds as the dividend on the common stock increases. Because the investor in the warrant does not participate in dividends paid on the common, the greater the dividend, the less attractive the warrant in relation to its associated stock. As a result, the greater the dividend, the more the actual value line would approach the theoretical value line. All of these factors are familiar from our discussion of option valuation in Chapter 5.

THE EFFECT OF DILUTION

Option valuation and warrant valuation differ in one fundamental respect. With the exercise of an option, there is no change in the number of shares of stock of the company or in its net worth. Essentially, we have a side bet between two parties. With the exercise of a warrant, however, the number of shares increases, and there is a cash infusion into the firm. To illustrate, suppose Sigma Corporation has two equal owners, Gamma Jones and Delta Smith.[3] The company owns 1 ounce of gold worth $400, so each share of stock is worth $200. Jones decides to sell an option to a third party, Alpha Brown, which enables Brown to buy Jones's share of stock for $240. If the market price of gold were to go above $480 per ounce, Brown could exercise her option at a profit. Note that if this is done, the number of total shares remains at two; Jones merely sells her stock to Brown.

Instead of an option, suppose the company issues a warrant to Brown to buy one share of stock at $240 per share. Let us assume further that the price of gold goes to $510 per ounce and that the warrant is exercised. As a result, an additional share of stock is issued and the company receives a cash infusion of $240. The value of the company now is $510 in gold plus $240 in cash, or $750 total. Therefore, the value per share is $750/3 = $250. Thus, Brown pays out $240 to obtain a one-third interest in a larger company—larger by virtue of the exercise price paid into it. The gain to Brown is $10. Another way to look at the situation is that part of the exercise price paid in actually belongs to Brown. Effectively, she gives up only two-thirds of it, or $160. For this, she obtains a one-third interest in the gold of the company before the exercise. At $510 per ounce, this is worth $170. Therefore, Brown gains $10, the same as calculated before.

If the Black-Scholes option pricing formula is used to value a warrant, certain adjustments are necessary if the number of new shares issued is relatively large. The exercise price used in the formula should be the money actually given up, or $160 in our example, not $240. The stock price employed should be the value of the equity before exercise divided by the number of shares in existence after the exercise of all warrants. Therefore, this value is

607

CHAPTER 23
Option Financing:
Warrants,
Convertibles, and
Exchangeables

[3] This example is based on Paul Pfleiderer, Teaching Note, Stanford Graduate School of Business, Stanford, CA. See also Black and Scholes, "The Pricing of Options and Corporate Liabilities," pp. 648–49. We assume the other conditions associated with the Black-Scholes model hold, including the absence of dividends. For further analysis of the warrant and optimal exercise strategy, see David C. Emanuel, "Warrant Valuation and Exercise Strategy," *Journal of Financial Economics*, 12 (August 1983), 211–35. For an empirical valuation of warrants, see Beni Lauterbach and Paul Schultz, "Pricing Warrants: An Empirical Study of Black-Scholes Model and its Alternatives," *Journal of Finance*, 45 (September 1990), 1181–1209.

$170 in our example. Finally, the variance rate used is the variance rate of return of the company's overall equity—stocks and warrants—not just its common stock. While in general the same factors that affect the valuation of an option affect the valuation of a warrant, certain adjustments are necessary if the option pricing model is used.

CONVERTIBLE SECURITIES

A *convertible security* is a bond or a share of preferred stock that can be converted at the option of the holder into common stock of the same corporation. Once converted into common stock, the stock cannot be exchanged again for bonds or preferred stock. The ratio of exchange between the convertible security and the common stock can be stated in terms of either a *conversion price* or a *conversion ratio*. McKesson Corporation's $9\frac{3}{4}$ percent convertible subordinated debentures ($1,000 face value) have a conversion price of $43.75, meaning that each debenture is convertible into 22.86 shares of common stock. We simply divide the face value of the security by the conversion price to obtain the conversion ratio, $1,000/$43.75 = 22.86 shares. The conversion privilege can be stated in terms of either the conversion price or the conversion ratio.

The conversion terms are not necessarily constant over time. Some convertible issues provide for increases or "step-ups" in the conversion price at periodic intervals. A $1,000 face value bond might have a conversion price of $40 a share for the first 5 years, $48 a share for the second 5 years, $56 for the third 5, and so on. In this way, the bond converts into fewer shares of common stock as time goes by. Usually, the conversion price is adjusted for any stock splits or stock dividends that occur after the securities are sold. If the common stock were split 2 for 1, the conversion price would be halved. This provision protects the convertible bondholders and is known as an antidilution clause.

CONVERSION VALUE AND PREMIUM

The *conversion value* of a convertible security is the conversion ratio of the security times the market price per share of the common stock. If McKesson stock were selling for $50, the conversion value of one convertible subordinated debenture would be 22.86 × $50, or $1,143.

The convertible security provides the investor with a fixed return from a bond or with a specified dividend from preferred stock. In addition, the investor receives an option to convert the security into common stock and thereby participates in the possibility of capital gains associated with being a residual owner of the corporation. Because of this option, the company is able to sell the convertible security at a lower yield than it would have to pay on a straight bond or preferred stock issue.

At the time of issuance, the convertible security will be priced higher than its conversion value. The differential is known as the *conversion premium*. The McKesson convertible subordinated debentures were sold to the public for $1,000 a bond. The market price of the common stock at the time of issuance of the convertibles was approximately $38\frac{1}{2}$ per share. Therefore, the conversion value of each bond was 22.86 × $38\frac{1}{2}$ = $880, and the differential of $120 between this value and the issuing price represented the conversion premium. Frequently, this premium is expressed as a percentage; in our example, the conversion premium is $120/$880 = 13.6%. For most issues of convertibles, the conversion premium ranges from 10 to 20 percent. For a growth company, the conversion premium can be in the upper part of this range, or perhaps even higher in the case of super growth. For companies with more moderate growth, the conversion premium may be closer to 10 percent. The range itself is established mainly by market tradition, in keeping with the idea that the issuer should be in a position to force conversion within a reasonable period of time. (Forcing conversion will be illustrated shortly.)

Almost without exception, convertible securities provide for a *call price*. As was true with the straight bond or preferred stock, the call feature enables the corporation to call the security for redemption. Few convertible securities, however, are ever redeemed. Instead, the purpose of the call is to force conversion when the conversion value of the security is above its call price.

OTHER FEATURES

Almost all convertible bond issues are subordinated to other creditors. That fact permits the lender to treat convertible subordinated debt or convertible preferred stock as a part of the equity base when evaluating the financial condition of the issuer. In the event of liquidation, it makes no difference to the lender if the issue is actually converted; in either case, the lender has a prior claim. The dilution effect with convertibles can be seen in a company that issues $20 million in 9 percent convertible debentures. The conversion price is $20 a share. The total number of additional shares upon conversion would be $20 million/$20 = 1 million shares. The company has 3 million common shares outstanding and no other debt. It expects earnings before interest and taxes 2 years from now to be $10 million, and the income-tax rate is 40 percent. Earnings per share before and after conversion would be

	CONVERTIBLE DEBENTURES OUTSTANDING	DEBENTURES CONVERTED
Earnings before interest and taxes	$10,000,000	$10,000,000
Interest 9% debentures	1,800,000	—
Profit before taxes	$ 8,200,000	$10,000,000
Taxes	3,280,000	4,000,000
Profit after taxes	$ 4,920,000	$ 6,000,000
Shares outstanding	3,000,000	4,000,000
Earnings per share	$1.64	$1.50

We see that upon future conversion, there is dilution in earnings per share in this example. We note also that upon conversion, the company no longer has to pay interest on the debentures; this factor has a favorable influence on earnings per share. As with warrants, it is necessary for companies to report earnings per share on a primary and on a fully diluted basis.

609

CHAPTER 23
Option Financing:
Warrants,
Convertibles, and
Exchangeables

Convertible securities, in many cases, are employed as deferred common stock financing. Technically, these securities represent debt or preferred stock, but in essence they are delayed common stock. Companies that issue convertibles expect them to be converted in the future. By selling a convertible security instead of common stock, they create less dilution in earnings per share, both now and in the future. The reason is that the conversion price on a convertible security is higher than the issuing price on a new issue of common stock.

The current market price of the common stock of the mythical ABC Corporation is $40 per share. If the company raises capital with an issue of common stock, it will have to underprice the issue in order to sell it in the market. Suppose the issue's net proceeds to the company are $36 per share. If the company wishes to raise $18 million, the issue will involve 500,000 shares of additional stock. On the other hand, if ABC Corporation sells a convertible issue, it is able to set the conversion price above the current market price per share. If the conversion premium is 15 percent, the conversion price would be $46 per share. Assuming an $18 million issue of convertibles, the number of shares of additional stock after conversion would be

$$\frac{\$18 \text{ million}}{\$46} = 391,305$$

We see that potential dilution with a convertible issue is less than that with a common issue because fewer shares are being added.

Another advantage to the company in using convertible securities is that the interest rate or preferred dividend rate is lower than the rate the company would have to pay on a straight bond or a straight preferred stock issue. The conversion feature makes the issue more attractive to investors. The greater the value of the conversion feature to investors, the lower the yield the company will need to pay in order to sell the issue. The lower interest payments early on may be particularly useful to a company in a growth phase, for it allows it to keep more cash for growth. Moreover, companies with relatively low credit ratings but good prospects of growth may find it difficult to sell a straight issue of bonds or preferred stock. The market may respond favorably to a convertible issue of these companies, not because of its quality as a bond or as preferred stock but because of its quality as common stock.

FORCING OR STIMULATING CONVERSION

Companies usually issue convertible securities with the expectation that these securities will be converted within a certain length of time. Investors can exercise their options voluntarily at any time and exchange the convertible security for common stock; however, they may prefer to hold the security, for its price will increase as the price of the common stock increases. During this time, also, they receive regular interest payments or preferred stock dividends. For the convertible security in which the common stock pays no dividend, it is to the convertible security holder's advantage never to convert voluntarily. In other words, the investor should delay conversion as long as possible. (When a company pays a common stock dividend, it may be in the interest of the convertible security holder to convert voluntarily.) On the other hand, it is in the company's interest, in behalf of existing stockholders, to force conversion as soon as the conversion value exceeds the call price, thereby taking the option away from the holder. In so doing, it also eliminates the cost of paying interest on the convertible debenture or dividends on the convertible preferred stock.[4]

611

CHAPTER 23
Option Financing:
Warrants,
Convertibles, and
Exchangeables

In order to force conversion, companies issuing convertible securities usually must call the issue. To do so, the market price of the security must be higher than the call price, so that investors will convert rather than accept the lower call price. Many companies regard a 15 percent premium of conversion value over call price as a sufficient cushion for possible declines in market price and for enticing investors to convert their securities. The conversion price of a convertible debenture ($1,000 face value) might be $50 and the call price $1,080. For the conversion value of the bond to equal the call price, the market price of the stock must be $1,080/20, or $54 a share. If the bonds are called when the market price is $54, many investors might choose to accept the call price rather than convert.[5] The company then would have to redeem many of the bonds for cash, in part defeating the purpose of the original financing. In order to ensure almost complete conversion, it might wait to call the debentures until the conversion value of the bond is 15 percent above the call price, a value that corresponds to a common stock market price of $62.10. Many companies require a much greater cushion. They simply do not force conversion when academics think they should—when the security's conversion value first exceeds the call price. The wide divergence between theory and practice is difficult to explain.[6]

Upon announcement that a convertible bond issue is to be called, the market price of the company's common stock typically declines by a small but significant amount. This decline may be due to several reasons, though all are somewhat dubious. It is clear that the company will have lower interest expenses after conversion than before. As a result, it loses a tax shield, which, we know from Chapter 10, may have value to the common stockholders. However, this argument supposes that investors are surprised by the call and that they do not expect the company to replace the called debt. Another reason for the decline in share price might be the dilution in earnings per share, which results from an increased number of shares. However, the potential dilution surely is recognized in the marketplace before the convertible bond is called,

---

[4] See Jonathan E. Ingersoll, Jr., "A Contingent-Claims Valuation of Convertible Securities," *Journal of Financial Economics*, 4 (January 1977), 297–301; and M. J. Brennan and E. S. Schwartz, "Convertible Bonds: Valuation and Optimal Strategies for Call and Conversion," *Journal of Finance*, 32 (December 1977), 1699–1715.

[5] Under the usual conditions associated with the option pricing model and with the Modigliani-Miller irrelevance of capital structure position, Ingersoll, "A Contingent-Claims Valuation of Convertible Securities," demonstrates for the company that pays no common stock dividend that the optimal time to force conversion is when the conversion value just equals the call price. The author recognizes that this is at odds with the practice of most companies, which wait until the conversion value is substantially in excess of the call price before calling the issue. He cites as a possible explanation market imperfections. See also Brennan and Schwartz, "Convertible Bonds," for further discussion of the optimal time to convert and to call.

[6] In a study of convertible preferred stocks, Kenneth B. Dunn and Kenneth M. Eades, "Voluntary Conversion of Convertible Securities and the Optimal Call Strategy," *Journal of Financial Economics*, 23 (August 1989), 273–301, find that a substantial number of investors do not convert voluntarily when the common dividend income they would realize as common stockholders exceeds the convertible preferred's dividend plus its premium of conversion value over call price. Under these circumstances, a company could rationally delay forcing conversion, and the authors offer this as a reason for the phenomenon observed above.

although the timing of the call may be somewhat uncertain. Finally, there may be a wealth transfer from stockholders to senior security holders if the calling of the convertible bond issue is unexpected. The senior claims simply become more creditworthy with the elimination of a debt issue.

Mikkelson tests these notions and finds convertible bond calls to result in a decline in share price at the announcement date, but convertible preferred stock calls not to result in a decline.[7] He finds a significant relationship between the stock behavior for bond calls and the decrease in interest tax deduction. Moreover, he suggests that there may be an information effect at play and that the calling of a convertible bond conveys unfavorable information about the company's earnings prospects. Aharon R. Ofer and Ashok Natarajan follow up this study with further support for convertible calls conveying bad news.[8] More specifically, the authors find that the convertible call is associated with subsequent declines in profit performance by the company.

Other means are available to a company for "stimulating," as opposed to "forcing," conversion. By establishing an acceleration or "step-up" in the conversion price at steady intervals in the future, there is persistent pressure on bondholders to convert, assuming the conversion value of the security is relatively high. If the conversion price is scheduled to increase from $50 to $56 at the end of next month, convertible bondholders have an incentive to convert prior to that time, all other things the same. If the holders wait, they receive fewer shares of stock. Be aware that the "step-up" provision must be established at the time the convertible issue is sold. It cannot be used for purposes of stimulating conversion at a particular moment in time.

Another means for stimulating conversion is to increase the dividend on the common stock, thereby making the common more attractive.[9] If the dividend income available on the associated common exceeds interest income on the convertible security, there is particular incentive to convert. Although the two stimulants just discussed enhance conversion, invariably a portion of the convertible bondholders will not convert, owing to the downside protection of the bond, the superior legal claim on assets, and other reasons. Consequently, calling the issue may be the only means for ensuring that the issue will be substantially converted.

DEBT PLUS OPTION CHARACTERISTIC

The simplistic view that a convertible bond is the best of all possible things because it offers a lower interest cost than straight debt and less dilution than equity financing overlooks the option nature of the contract. The convertible bond may be viewed as straight debt plus a warrant to purchase common stock. If the following conditions hold—the conversion ratio and the relative number of warrants are the same; the warrants are not detachable from the debt; the straight debt's maturity, the expiration date of the warrant,

[7] Wayne H. Mikkelson, "Convertible Calls and Security Returns," *Journal of Financial Economics,* 9 (September 1981), 237–64; and Mikkelson, "Capital Structure Change and Decreases in Stockholders' Wealth: A Cross-Sectional Study of Convertible Security Calls," working paper, National Bureau of Economic Research, Washington, D.C. (1983).

[8] Aharon R. Ofer and Ashok Natarajan, "Convertible Call Policies," *Journal of Financial Economics,* 19 (September 1987), 91–108.

[9] For an analysis of voluntary conversion by the security holder in the presence of a conversion price "step-up" or dividends being paid on the common stock, see Ingersoll, "Contingent-Claims Valuation of Convertible Securities," pp. 314–19.

and the maturity of the convertible are all the same; and the coupon rates and redemption features are the same—then it can be demonstrated that[10]

613

CHAPTER 23
Option Financing:
Warrants,
Convertibles, and
Exchangeables

$$\text{Debt} + \text{Warrants} = \text{Convertible bond} \qquad (23\text{-}2)$$

The greater the uncertainty, or risk, of the firm's cash flows, the less the value of the debt, all other things the same. Expressed differently, the greater the risk, the higher the interest rate the company is required to pay on its borrowings and the lower the value of any fixed rate debt that is outstanding. On the other hand, the greater the uncertainty or volatility of cash flows, the greater the value of the warrant component. This follows from our earlier discussion.

Thus, risk cuts both ways. As firm risk increases, a company incurs higher interest costs on straight debt. However, with convertible debt the option component becomes more valuable. As a result, the interest rate may not increase with more firm risk and actually could decrease. This offset means the convertible security is less affected by the issuing company's risk than are other types of securities.[11] Put another way, differences in coupon rates and conversion premiums for the convertible debentures of companies having different risk complexions are not likely to be nearly as large as they would be for other types of securities. This suggests that when a company's future is highly uncertain, the convertible security should be the financing method of choice.

Agency Costs. Thus, the convertible security serves an important role for the company faced with operating uncertainty. Similarly, it may serve a useful role when there are agency problems. Here straight debt holders are concerned about expropriation of wealth in favor of equity holders. The convertible bond bridges this problem by giving lenders a potential equity stake. Finally, when the economy overall enters a period of great uncertainty, we might expect more utilization of convertible security issues. In summary, the greater the risk faced by the firm and/or the greater the agency problems, the more difficult it is to sell straight debt and the more valuable the conversion feature becomes. In the appendix to this chapter, we explore the option characteristic of a convertible issue in detail. But now we look at convertible security valuation in more traditional ways.

VALUE OF CONVERTIBLE SECURITIES

As we know, the value of a convertible security to an investor is twofold: its value as a bond or preferred stock and its potential value as common stock. (Because the principles of valuation of a convertible bond and a convertible preferred stock are nearly the same, our subsequent discussion will refer to convertible bonds.) Investors obtain a hedge when they purchase convertible

---

[10] See E. Philip Jones and Scott P. Mason, "Equity-Linked Debt," *Midland Corporate Finance Journal*, 3 (Winter 1986), 47–58; and John D. Finnerty, "The Case for Issuing Synthetic Convertible Bonds," *Midland Corporate Finance Journal*, 4 (Fall 1986), 72–82.

[11] See Michael J. Brennan and Eduardo S. Schwartz, "The Case for Convertibles," *Journal of Applied Corporate Finance*, 1 (Summer 1988), 55–64.

bonds. If the market price of the stock rises, the value of the convertible is determined largely by its conversion value. If the market for the stock turns down, the investor still holds a bond whose value provides a floor below which the price of the convertible is unlikely to fall.

BOND VALUE

The bond value of a convertible security is the price at which a straight bond of the same company would sell in the open market. For semiannual compounding, it can be determined by solving the following equation for B:

$$B = \sum_{t=1}^{2n} \frac{I}{\left(1 + \dfrac{r}{2}\right)^t} + \frac{F}{\left(1 + \dfrac{r}{2}\right)^{2n}} \tag{23-3}$$

where B = straight bond value of the convertible
I = semiannual interest payments determined by the coupon rate
F = face value of the bond
n = years to final maturity
r = market yield to maturity on a straight bond of the same company

In the equation, we assume semiannual interest payments, which are typical with corporate bonds, so the total number of interest payments is two times the years to maturity, n, and the semiannual interest rate on a straight bond is r divided by 2.

Amos White Company has outstanding a 9 percent convertible debenture with a final maturity 20 years hence. If the company is to sell a straight 20-year debenture in the current market, the yield will have to be 12 percent to be attractive to investors. For a 20-year bond with a 9 percent coupon to yield 12 percent to maturity, the bond has to sell at a discount. Using Eq. (23-3) and rounding, we have the following equation;

$$B = \sum_{t=1}^{40} \frac{\$45}{(1.06)^t} + \frac{\$1,000}{(1.06)^{40}} = \$774$$

Although it is possible to solve this equation using present-value tables, we need only consult a bond table to determine the market price. (An example of a bond table is shown in Chapter 2, where we take up the mathematics of bond interest.) Thus the bond-value floor of Amos White Company's convertible bonds is $774. This floor suggests that if the price of the common stock were to fall sharply, the price of the convertible would fall only to $774. At that price, the security would sell as a straight bond in keeping with prevailing bond yields for that grade of security.

The bond-value floor of a convertible is not constant over time. It varies with (1) interest rate movements in the capital markets and (2) changes in the financial risk of the company involved. If interest rates in general rise, the bond value of a convertible will decline. If the yield to maturity on a straight bond in our example increases from 12 to 14 percent, the bond value of the convertible will drop from $774 to $667. Moreover, the company's credit rating can either improve or deteriorate over time. If it improves, and the company is able to sell a straight bond at a lower yield to maturity, the bond value of the convertible security will increase, all other things held constant. If the company's credit standing deteriorates, and the yield on a straight bond increases, the bond-value floor will decline. Unfortunately for investors, when the market price of the stock falls because of poor earnings and/or increased risk, its credit standing may suffer. As a result, the straight bond value of the convertible may decline along with the decline in its conversion value, giving investors less downside protection than they might have expected originally.[12]

615

CHAPTER 23
Option Financing:
Warrants,
Convertibles, and
Exchangeables

PREMIUMS

Convertible securities frequently sell at premiums over both their bond value and their conversion value. Recall that the conversion value of a convertible is simply the current market price per share of the company's common stock times the number of shares into which the security is convertible. The fact that the convertible bond provides the investor with a degree of downside protection, given the qualifications just mentioned, often results in its selling at a market price somewhat higher than its conversion value. The difference is known as the *premium-over-conversion value*.

Moreover, a convertible bond typically will sell at a *premium-over-bond* value, primarily because of the conversion feature. Unless the market price of the stock is very low relative to the conversion price, the conversion feature usually will have value, in that investors may eventually find it profitable to convert the securities. To the extent that the conversion feature does have value, the convertible will sell at a premium over its straight bond value. The higher the market price of the common relative to the conversion price, the greater this premium.

RELATION BETWEEN PREMIUMS

The trade-off between the two premiums depicts the value of the option to investors and is illustrated in Fig. 23-2. The market price of the common is on the horizontal axis; the value of the convertible security is on the vertical. It should be pointed out that the two axes are on different scales. The diagonal line, which starts at the origin, represents the conversion value of the bond. It is linear, as the conversion ratio is invariant with respect to the market price of the stock. The bond-value line, however, is related to the market price of the common. If a company is doing badly financially, the prices of both its common stock and its bonds are likely to be low. At the extreme, if the total value of the company were zero, both the bonds and the stock would have a value of zero. As the company becomes sounder financially and the common stock increases in price, bond value increases but at a decreasing rate. After a point, the bond-value line becomes flat, and further increases in common stock price are unrelated to it. At this point, the bond-value floor is determined by what other high-grade bonds sell for in the market. The upper curved line represents the market price of the convertible security. The distance between this line and the bond-value line is the premium over bond

---

[12] Mathematically, the straight bond value of a convertible security will rise over time, all other things held constant, if the face value of the convertible is above the straight bond value at the time of issuance. At final maturity, the straight bond value will equal the face value of the convertible, assuming the company is not in default. See Chapter 2.

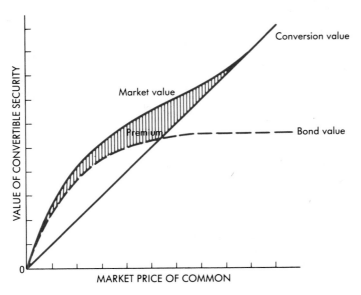

Conversion value

Market value

Premium

Bond value

VALUE OF CONVERTIBLE SECURITY

MARKET PRICE OF COMMON

0

FIGURE 23-2
Relationship between bond-value and
conversion-value premiums

value, while the distance between the market-value line and the conversion-value line represents the premium-over-conversion value.

We see that at relatively high common stock price levels, the value of the convertible as a bond is insignificant. Consequently, its premium-over-bond value is high, whereas its premium-over-conversion value is negligible. The security sells mainly for its stock equivalent. Investors are unwilling to pay a significant premium-over-conversion value for the following reasons. First, the greater the premium of market price of the convertible over its bond value, the less valuable the bond-value protection is to the investor. Second, when the conversion value is high, the convertible may be called; if it is, the investor will want to convert rather than redeem the bond for the call price. Upon conversion, of course, the bond is worth only its conversion value.

On the other hand, when the market value of the convertible is close to its straight bond value, the conversion feature has little value. At this level, the convertible security is valued primarily as a straight bond. Under these circumstances, the market price of the convertible is likely to exceed its conversion value by a significant premium.

The principal reason for premiums in the market price over both conversion value and bond value is the unusual attribute of a convertible as both a bond and an option on common stock. It offers the holder partial protection on the downside together with participation in upward movements in stock price. Thus, the distribution of possible outcomes is skewed to the right, and this characteristic finds favor with investors. Both the bond-value and the stock-value components of the convertible security can be valued using the option pricing notions discussed earlier. In the appendix to this chapter, we investigate such valuation in more detail.

OTHER REASONS FOR PREMIUMS

Although we have concentrated on the main reasons for premiums, other factors appear to have at least a modest influence. Some of the influence stems from the presence of certain impediments to the perfect market assumptions invoked earlier in our discussion of options. For one thing, lower transaction costs on convertible bonds relative to those on common stocks enhance the attractiveness of these bonds. By purchasing convertible bonds and converting them into common stock, investors incur lower transaction costs than they would by purchasing the stock outright. This attraction should exert upward pressure on the premiums-over-conversion value and over-bond value. Yet another influence that may raise premiums is that certain institutional investors, such as life insurance companies, are restricted with respect to investing in common stock. By investing in convertible bonds, they gain the benefits of a common stock investment without actually investing in common stock.

The duration of the convertible option also should affect the premiums. In general, the longer the duration, the more valuable the option. Unlike other options, the duration until expiration is uncertain, owing to the fact that the company can force conversion if the price of the common stock is high enough. The longest duration is the maturity of the security, but the actual duration typically is much shorter. Another factor is the dividend on the common. The greater the dividend, the greater the attraction of the common vis-à-vis the convertible security and the lower the premiums, all other things the same. All of these influences affect the premiums at which convertible securities sell. Although they tend to carry less weight than the influences discussed in the previous section, they need to be considered nonetheless in determining the value of a convertible security.

EXCHANGEABLE BONDS

An exchangeable bond is like a convertible bond, but the common stock involved is that of another corporation. National Distillers and Chemical Corporation issued $49 million in 6 percent subordinated debentures exchangeable into stock of Cetus Corporation, a biotechnology firm. While still not a widespread means of financing, exchangeables are increasing in importance.

FEATURES

Like the conversion price and conversion ratio for a convertible security, the *exchange price* and *exchange ratio* must be set at the time of issuance. The National Distillers debentures have an exchange price of $49, which translates into 20.41 shares of Cetus for each $1,000 face value debenture. At the time of issuance, Cetus was selling for $37.50 per share. Therefore, the *exchange premium* was 30.7 percent, which is very high as conversion premiums go. This reflected the nature of Cetus—good potential but little revenue and much uncertainty. The more variable the outcome, of course, the higher the option value. As with convertible bonds, there typically is a call feature with an exchangeable bond, and most issues are subordinated.

USE IN FINANCING

Exchangeable bond issues usually occur only when the issuer owns common stock in the company in which the bonds can be exchanged. National Distillers, for example, owned 4 percent of the outstanding stock of Cetus Corporation. Exchange requests presumably will be satisfied from this

617

CHAPTER 23
Option Financing:
Warrants,
Convertibles, and
Exchangeables

holding, as opposed to acquiring stock in the open market. Therefore, the decision to go with an exchangeable bond issue may bring with it the reduction in or elimination of stock ownership in another company. A conscious decision of this sort is embraced in the financing.

Like the convertible, interest costs are lower because of the option value of the instrument. So far most companies issuing exchangeables have been large and would not have experienced difficulty financing with a straight debt issue. The attraction is a lower interest cost together with the possibility of disposing of a common stock investment at a premium above the present price. Finally, some exchangeable issues of U.S. companies have been placed with investors outside the United States.

VALUATION OF AN EXCHANGEABLE

The valuation of an exchangeable security is identical in most respects to that of a convertible security. Exchangeable debt can be viewed as

$$\text{Debt} + \text{Call option} = \text{Exchangeable debt} \qquad (23\text{-}4)$$

where the call option is on the stock of the company in which the debt is exchangeable. Therefore, the investor must analyze and track the bond of one company and the stock of another.

One advantage of the exchangeable bond is diversification; the bond-value floor and the stock value are not directly linked. Poor earnings and financial performance in one company will not lead to a simultaneous decline in bond-value floor and in the stock value. If the companies are in unrelated industries, the investor achieves diversification. With market imperfections, this may lead to a higher valuation for the exchangeable than for the convertible, all other things the same.

Because option values are driven by the volatility of the associated asset, differences in volatility may affect the choice between an exchangeable and a convertible bond issue. If the stock of the company in exchange is more volatile than that of the issuer, the option value will be greater with an exchangeable bond issue than it will with a convertible bond issue, all other things the same.

A relative disadvantage has to do with taxation. The difference between the market value of the stock at the time of exchange and the cost of the bond is treated as a capital gain for tax purposes. In the case of a convertible, this gain goes unrecognized until the stock is sold. The net effect of these factors is unclear. In summary, exchangeable securities are a variant of convertible securities that may increase in use what with the rapid innovation now occurring in corporate financing.

SUMMARY

Warrants, convertible securities, and exchangeable securities are options under which the holder can obtain common stock. The conversion or exchange feature enables the investor to transfer a debt instrument or preferred stock into common stock, whereas a warrant attached to a bond enables the holder to purchase a specified number of shares at a specified price. With a warrant, the exercise of the option does not result in the elimination of the bonds.

Normally, warrants are employed as a "sweetener" for a public or private issue of debt. They are like a call option, but the beginning time to expiration tends to be longer. Also, there is a dilution effect on value, which is not the case with call options. When the market price of the stock is near the exercise price, the market value of the warrant tends to be high relative to its theoretical value. The greater the volatility of the associated stock, the more valuable the warrant. Other factors also influence the price of this type of option.

The convertible security can be viewed as a straight debt or preferred stock issue plus an option to buy common stock. For the corporation, convertibles often represent delayed common stock financing. For a given amount of financing, there will be less dilution with a convertible issue than with a common stock issue, assuming it eventually converts. As a hybrid security, the convertible security has a bond-value floor and a conversion, or stock, value. As a result, the distribution of possible returns is skewed to the right and there is a trade-off between the two factors.

The premiums at which a convertible security sells above its conversion value and above its bond value are due to the security's partial downside protection as a bond and its upside potential as stock (the same in principle as with any option), the volatility of the common stock, the dividend on the common, the duration of the convertible option, and certain institutional imperfections that affect investors. Convertibles are particularly suited as a financing vehicle when there is much uncertainty concerning the company. If things go well, the company will be in a position to force conversion by calling the issue.

An exchangeable bond may be exchanged for common stock in another corporation. It is like the convertible security in its valuation underpinnings with a few exceptions. This method of financing is applicable to companies that have stock holdings in another company.

619

CHAPTER 23
Option Financing:
Warrants,
Convertibles, and
Exchangeables

APPENDIX
Valuing Convertible Bonds in the Face of Firm Volatility, Default Risk, and Fluctuating Interest Rates

Because a convertible bond is both a debt instrument and a stock option, its precise valuation is complex. In this chapter as well as in certain preceding chapters, we discussed the valuation of stock options and debt in an option pricing model framework. We have not put the various components together as they relate to convertible bonds, and that is the purpose of this appendix. Briefly reviewing, a convertible bond is an option to obtain stock in a corporation. As with any option, the greater the volatility of the stock and the underlying volatility of firm value, the greater the value of the option to the convertible security holder.

In Chapters 10 and 18, we saw that debt holders could be viewed as option writers and the equity holders could be viewed as holding a call option on the firm's total value. At the maturity of the debt, the equity holders have the option of buying back the firm from the debt holders at a specified price, which is the face value of the debt instrument. In this context, the greater the volatility of the value of the total firm, the greater the value of the option to the equity holders. On the other hand, the greater the volatility, the greater the default risk in the sense that the firm will be worth less than the debt's face value. If default occurs, equity holders will not exercise their option, bankruptcy by definition will occur, and debt holders will suffer a loss. In Chapter 22, we explored the valuation of the call option on straight debt. Here we found that the greater the volatility of future interest rates, the greater the value of the call option to the equity holders and the greater the value loss to the debt holders. If such interest rate volatility is anticipated at the time of the loan, lenders will demand a higher interest rate to compensate them for the call risk.

All three factors influence the valuation of convertible bonds, and it is useful to explore the interrelationships. What will emerge is not a precise model, if indeed one were possible, but a general overview of the valuation underpinnings. To begin, let us assume that financial markets are perfect, that a firm has no debt other than convertible bonds, and that bondholders and the firm follow optimal strategies. Under these circumstances, optimal strategies consist of (1) bondholders converting their bonds into stock if the value of the convertible is less than its conversion value; (2) bondholders forcing the firm into bankruptcy and seizing its value if the value of the firm falls below the debt's face value, assuming that the ability to do so is written into the contract; and (3) the firm calling the bonds when their value equals the call price.[13]

Given these actions, the boundaries for the valuation of convertible bonds are shown in Fig. 23-3. If the value of bonds should exceed the call price, they will be called so their value is bounded on the upside by the call price. On the downside, bondholders will force bankruptcy, should the value of the firm fall below the total value of the bonds outstanding.[14] Moreover,

---

[13] See footnote 5 in this chapter.

[14] This assumes that at the time of the loan, the firm's value exceeds the face value of the bonds.

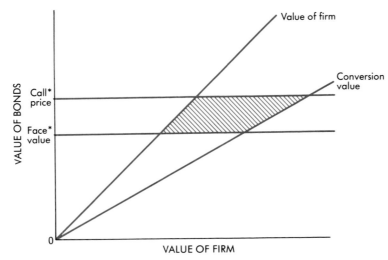

VALUE OF FIRM

*Represents the total value of all bonds at the call price and at face value.

FIGURE 23-3

Boundaries of convertible bond valuation

bondholders will convert if the value of their bonds falls below the conversion value, so we have another lower boundary. Finally, the total value of the bonds cannot exceed the total value of the firm. As a result of these constraints, the value of the bonds must fall within the shaded area in the figure.

Within these boundaries, certain relationships are likely to hold. For one, we would expect an inverse relationship between the risk of default and the value of the firm. That is, increases in firm value would be associated with decreases in default risk up to a point. As a result, we might expect the relationship shown in the upper panel of Fig. 23-4. Here we see that the value of the bonds increases at a decreasing rate until the curve eventually turns up, in keeping with the change in conversion value. This phenomenon was discussed in the chapter, and we know that it embraces both default risk and firm value volatility.

For a given firm value, companies can have different business-risk strategies, which result in different default risks. Therefore, the relationship be-

621

CHAPTER 23
Option Financing:
Warrants,
Convertibles, and
Exchangeables

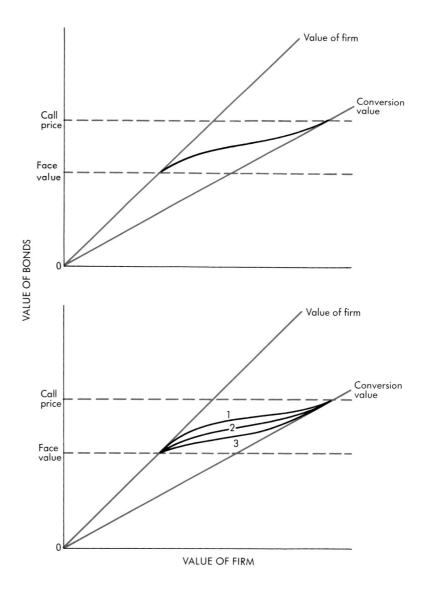

FIGURE 23-4

Convertible bond valuation with default risk

tween bond value and firm value will differ, depending on the risk strategy chosen by the firm. In the bottom panel of Fig. 23-4, risk strategy 1 is safer than strategies 2 and 3, in the sense of less volatility of firm value. Accordingly, the risk of default is less for any level of firm value, and the value of the convertible bonds is higher.

Having considered default risk, we turn now to interest rate risk. For given levels of firm value and default risk, the greater the interest rate, the lower the value of the outstanding convertible bonds. The relationship is depicted by upper panel of Fig. 23-5. For a hypothetical interest rate of 6 percent, the bond-value line is higher than it is for interest rates of 10 percent and 14 percent, respectively. This follows, of course, from the valuation of any fixed-income security. Apart from the expected level of interest rates, the greater the volatility of future interest rates, the greater the value of the call option to the company and the lower the value of the convertible security to the holder. This situation is depicted in the lower panel of Fig. 23-5. Bear in mind that if the bond is called, the holder has the option to convert it into common stock; therefore, the impact of the call is far less than it is in the case of straight debt. Finally, we should point out that in determining whether a

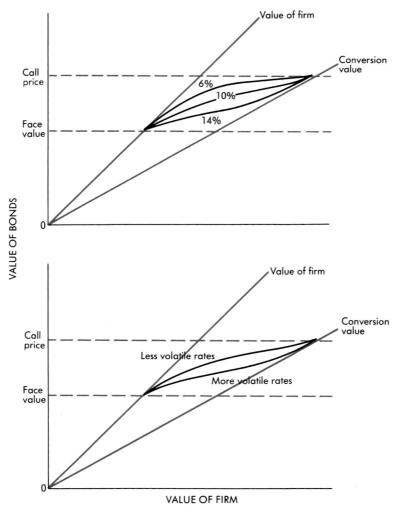

FIGURE 23-5
Convertible bond valuation and interest rates

convertible security is called, stock price volatility usually dominates interest-rate volatility.

623

CHAPTER 23
Option Financing:
Warrants,
Convertibles, and
Exchangeables

We have described the more important "two-way" relationships affecting the valuation of convertible bonds, but there are others that complicate the picture. For one thing, there is likely to be an association among the level of interest rates, default risk, and the value of the firm. High interest rates often are associated with periods of high and uncertain inflation. Consequently, the value of the firm will be less, all other things staying the same, than it is in times of low inflation, moderate uncertainty, and low interest rates. Similarly, periods of high inflation, great uncertainty, and high interest rates may be characterized by greater default risk. Thus, the volatility of firm value and of interest rates are not independent, and this makes the valuation of the hybrid convertible security very complicated indeed.

Our purpose in this appendix is not to present a model but to point out the direction of bond-value changes that are likely to accompany parameter changes.[15] This discussion gives us a richer understanding of the valuation of convertible securities, a topic that will see increasing research in the vein taken up in this appendix.

SELF-CORRECTION PROBLEMS

1. Camelot Pizza has outstanding warrants, where each warrant entitles the holder to purchase two shares of stock at $24 per share. The market price per share of stock and market price per warrant were the following over the last year:

	OBSERVATION					
	1	2	3	4	5	6
Stock price	$20	$18	$27	$32	$24	$38
Warrant price	5	3	12	20	8	29

Determine the theoretical value per warrant for each of these observations. Plot the market value per warrant in relation to its theoretical value. At what price per common share is the warrant premium over theoretical value the greatest? Why?

2. The Charrier Boat Company has current earnings of $3 a share with 500,000 shares outstanding. The company plans to issue 40,000 shares of 7 percent, $50 par value convertible preferred stock at par. The preferred stock is convertible into two shares of common for each preferred share held. The common stock has a current market price of $21 per share.

    a. What is the preferred stock's conversion value?

    b. What is its conversion premium?

    c. Assuming that total earnings stay the same, what will be the effect of the issue on primary earnings per share before conversion? on a fully diluted basis?

    d. If profits after taxes increase by $1 million, what will be primary earnings per share before conversion? on a fully diluted basis?

[15] For one approach to modeling the relationships, see Michael J. Brennan and Eduardo S. Schwartz, "Analyzing Convertible Bonds," *Journal of Financial and Quantitative Analysis*, 15 (November 1980), 907–29.

3. Sadfield Manufacturing Company plans to issue $10 million in 10 percent convertible subordinated debentures. Currently, the stock price is $36 per share, and the company believes it could obtain a conversion premium (issuing price in excess of conversion value) of approximately 12 percent. The call price of the debenture in the first 10 years is $1,060 per bond, after which it drops to $1,030 in the next 10 years and to $1,000 in the last 10 years. To allow for fluctuations in the market price of the stock, the company does not want to call the debentures until their conversion value is at least 15 percent in excess of the call price. Earnings per share are expected to grow at an 8 percent compound annual rate in the foreseeable future, and the company envisions no change in its price/earnings ratio.

a. Determine the expected length of time that must elapse before the company is in a position to force conversion.

b. Is the issuance of a convertible security a good idea for the company?

PROBLEMS

1. Using Eq. (23-1), compute the theoretical value of each of the following warrants:

	N	P_s	E
(a)	5	$100	$400
(b)	10	10	60
(c)	2.3	4	10
(d)	3.54	$27\frac{1}{8}$	35.40

2. Max Murphy, Inc., has warrants outstanding that allow the holder to purchase three shares of stock for a total of $60 for each warrant. Currently, the market price per share of Max Murphy common is $18. Investors hold the following probabilistic beliefs about the stock 6 months hence:

Market price per share	$16	$18	$20	$22	$24
Probability	.15	.20	.30	.20	.15

a. What is the present theoretical value of the warrant?

b. What is the expected value of stock price 6 months hence?

c. What is the expected value of theoretical value of the warrant 6 months hence?

d. Would you expect the present market price of the warrant to equal its theoretical value? If not, why not?

3. The Beruth Company is contemplating raising $10 million by means of a debt issue. It has the following alternatives:

a. A 20-year, 8 percent convertible debenture issue with a $50 conversion price and $1,000 face value

b. A 20-year, 10 percent straight bond issue

Each $1,000 bond has a detachable warrant to purchase four shares for $50 a share. The company has a 50 percent tax rate, and its stock is currently selling at

$40 a share. Its earnings before interest and taxes are a constant 20 percent of its total capitalization, which currently appears as follows:

625

CHAPTER 23
Option Financing:
Warrants,
Convertibles, and
Exchangeables

Common stock (par $5)	$ 5,000,000
Additional paid-in capital	10,000,000
Retained earnings	15,000,000
Total	$30,000,000

(1) Show the capitalizations resulting from each alternative, both before and after conversion or exercise (a total of four capitalizations).

(2) Compute primary earnings per share currently and under each of the four capitalizations determined in part 1.

(3) If the price of Beruth stock went to $75, determine the theoretical value of each warrant issued under alternative b.

4. The common stock of the Draybar Corporation earns $2.50 per share, has a dividend payout of two-thirds, and sells at a P/E ratio of 16. Draybar wishes to offer $10 million of 9 percent, 20-year convertible debentures with an initial conversion premium of 20 percent and a call price of 105. Draybar currently has 1 million common shares outstanding and has a 50 percent tax rate.

a. What is the conversion price?

b. What is the conversion ratio per $1,000 debenture?

c. What is the initial conversion value of each debenture?

d. How many new shares of common must be issued if all debentures are converted?

e. If Draybar can increase operating earnings by $1 million per year with the proceeds of the debenture issue, compute the new earnings per share and earnings retained before and after conversion.

5. Assume that the Draybar Corporation (in Problem 4) could sell $10 million in straight debt at 12 percent as an alternative to the convertible issue. Compute the earnings per share and earnings retained after issuance of the straight debt under the assumption of a $1 million increase in operating earnings and compare your answers with those obtained in Problem 4, part e.

6. What are the straight bond values of the following convertible bonds?

a. An 8 percent coupon convertible bond with 20 years to maturity where a straight bond of this maturity would yield 13 percent

b. A 10 percent coupon convertible bond with 15 years to maturity where the straight bond would yield 12 percent

7. Curran Consolidated Industries has outstanding a $7\frac{3}{4}$ percent, 20-year convertible debenture issue. Each $1,000 debenture is convertible into 25 shares of common stock. The company also has a straight debt issue outstanding of the same approximate maturity, so it is an easy matter to determine the straight bond value of the convertible issue. The market price of Curran stock is volatile. Over the last year, the following was observed:

	OBSERVATION				
	1	2	3	4	5
Market price per share	$ 40	$ 45	$ 32	$ 23	$ 18
Straight bond value	690	700	650	600	550
Market price of convertible debenture	1,065	1,140	890	740	640

a. Compute the premium-over-conversion value (in dollars) and the premium-over-straight-bond value for each of the observations.

b. Compare the two premiums either visually or by graph. What do the relationships tell you with respect to the valuation of the convertible debenture?

8. The following year, Curran Consolidated Industries falls on further hard times. Its stock price drops to $10 per share and the market price of the convertible debentures to $440 per debenture. The straight bond value goes to $410. Determine the premium-over-conversion value and the premium-over-bond value. What can you say about the bond-value floor?

9. Singapore Enterprises is considering an exchangeable bond issue, where each bond can be exchanged for $16\frac{2}{3}$ shares of Malaysian Palm Oil Company. The latter company's stock is presently selling for $50 a share. At what premium-over-exchange value will the bonds be sold if they are sold for $1,000 a bond? Are there advantages to this type of financing versus a convertible issue?

10. Fujiwara Electronics Company has a warrant outstanding that enables the holder to acquire two shares of stock for $32 a share for each warrant held. The present market price of the stock is $39 a share, and the expected standard deviation of its continuously compounded return is .20. The warrant has 3 years until expiration. The current rate on short-term Treasury bills is 5 percent.

a. If one values the warrant as a "European" option and uses the Black-Scholes option pricing model, Eq. (5-2) in Chapter 5, what is the value of the warrant? Assume that the added shares of stock upon exercise of the warrants are small relative to the number of shares outstanding and that no adjustments to the Black-Scholes formula are necessary.

b. What would happen to the value of the warrant if the standard deviation were .40? Why does this occur?

SOLUTIONS TO
SELF-CORRECTION PROBLEMS

1. Market price of warrant and theoretical value at various common stock prices (in ascending order):

Common price	$18	$20	$24	$27	$32	$38
Warrant price	3	5	8	12	20	29
Theoretical value	0	0	0	6	16	28

When plotted, the relationship is of the same pattern as that shown in Fig. 23-1. The maximum premium over theoretical value occurs when share price is $24 and the warrant has a theoretical value of zero. Here the greatest leverage occurs, and since volatility is what gives an option value, the premium over theoretical value tends to be greatest at this point.

2. a. Conversion ratio × market price per share = 2 × $21 = $42

   b. ($50/$42) − 1 = 19.05%

   c. Primary earnings per share effect:

627

CHAPTER 23
Option Financing:
Warrants,
Convertibles, and
Exchangeables

Total after-tax earnings = $3 × 500,000 shares =	$1,500,000
Preferred stock dividend	140,000
Earnings available to common stockholders	$1,360,000
Number of shares	500,000
Earnings per share	$2.72
Total after-tax earnings	$1,500,000
Number of shares (500,000 + 80,000)	580,000
Earnings per share	$2.59

d. Primary earnings per share effect with profit increase:

Total after-tax earnings	$2,500,000
Preferred stock dividend	140,000
Earnings available to common stockholders	$2,360,000
Number of shares	500,000
Earnings per share	$4.72
Total after-tax earnings	$2,500,000
Number of shares (500,000 + 80,000)	580,000
Earnings per share	$4.31

3. **a.** Conversion price = $36 × 1.12 = $40.32

Call price per share the first 10 years = $40.32 × 1.06 = $42.74

Price to which the common must rise before the company will be in a position to force conversion = $42.74 × 1.15 = $49.15

Increase from present price = $49.15/$36 = 1.365

At an 8 percent compound growth rate, earnings per share will grow to 1.36 in 4 years. (This is simply $(1.08)^4$.) If the price/earnings ratio stays the same, it will take approximately 4 years before the company will be in a position to force conversion.

b. This period is somewhat longer than the 2 to 3 years that market participants have come to expect for the convertible security. Still, it is not far out of line and the company may wish to go ahead. However, if uncertainty as to earnings per share increases with the length of time in the future, there may be considerable risk of an overhanging issue. This may cause the company to reconsider.

SELECTED REFERENCES

ALEXANDER, GORDON J., and ROGER D. STOVER, "The Effect of Forced Conversion on Common Stock Prices," *Financial Management*, 9 (Spring 1980), 39–45.

BLACK, FISCHER, and MYRON SCHOLES, "The Valuation of Option Contracts and a Test of Market Efficiency," *Journal of Finance*, 27 (May 1972), 339–417.

———, "The Pricing of Options and Corporate Liabilities," *Journal of Political Economy*, 81 (May–June 1973), 637–54.

BRENNAN, M. J., and E. S. SCHWARTZ, "Convertible Bonds: Valuation and Optimal Strategies for Call and Conversion," *Journal of Finance*, 32 (December 1977), 1699–1715.

——, "Analyzing Convertible Bonds," *Journal of Financial and Quantitative Analysis,* 15 (November 1980), 907–29.

——, "The Case for Convertibles," *Journal of Applied Corporate Finance,* 1 (Summer 1988), 55–64.

CONSTANTINIDES, GEORGE M., "Warrant Exercise and Bond Conversion in Competitive Markets," *Journal of Financial Economics,* 13 (September 1984), 371–98.

DANN, LARRY Y., and WAYNE H. MIKKELSON, "Convertible Debt Issuance, Capital Structure Change and Financing-Related Information: Some New Information," *Journal of Financial Economics,* 13 (June 1984), 157–86.

DUNN, KENNETH B., and KENNETH M. EADES, "Voluntary Conversion of Convertible Securities and the Optimal Call Strategy," *Journal of Financial Economics,* 23 (August 1989), 273–301.

EMANUEL, DAVID C., "Warrant Valuation and Exercise Strategy," *Journal of Financial Economics,* 12 (August 1983), 211–35.

FERRI, MICHAEL G., JOSEPH W. KREMER, and H. DENNIS OBERHELMAN, "An Analysis of Corporate Warrants," *Advances in Futures and Options Research,* 1 (1986), 201–26.

FINNERTY, JOHN D., "The Case for Issuing Synthetic Convertible Bonds," *Midland Corporate Finance Journal,* 4 (Fall 1986), 73–82.

GALAI, DAN, and MIER I. SCHNELLER, "Pricing of Warrants and the Value of the Firm," *Journal of Finance,* 33 (December 1978), 1333–42.

GREEN, RICHARD C., "Investment Incentives, Debt, and Warrants," *Journal of Financial Economics,* 13 (March 1984), 115–36.

HARRIS, MILTON, and ARTUR RAVIV, "A Sequential Signalling Model of Convertible Debt Call Policy," *Journal of Finance,* 40 (December 1985), 1263–81.

INGERSOLL, JONATHAN E., JR., "A Contingent-Claims Valuation of Convertible Securities," *Journal of Financial Economics,* 4 (January 1977), 289–321.

——, "An Examination of Corporate Call Policies on Convertible Securities," *Journal of Finance,* 32 (May 1977), 463–78.

JONES, E. PHILIP, and SCOTT P. MASON, "Equity-Linked Debt," *Midland Corporate Finance Journal,* 3 (Winter 1986), 47–58.

LAUTERBACH, BENI, and PAUL SCHULTZ, "Pricing Warrants: An Empirical Study of Black-Scholes Model and Its Alternatives," *Journal of Finance,* 45 (September 1990), 1181–1209.

LONG, MICHAEL S., and STEPHAN E. SEFCIK, "Participation Financing: A Comparison of the Characteristics of Convertible Debt and Straight Bonds Issued in Conjunction with Warrants," *Financial Management,* 19 (Autumn 1990), 23–34.

MARR, M. WAYNE, and G. RODNEY THOMPSON, "The Pricing of New Convertible Bond Issues," *Financial Management,* 13 (Summer 1984), 31–37.

MIKKELSON, WAYNE H., "Convertible Calls and Security Returns," *Journal of Financial Economics,* 9 (September 1981), 237–64.

OFER, AHARON R., and ASHOK NATARAJAN, "Convertible Call Policies: An Empirical Analysis of an Information-Signaling Hypothesis," *Journal of Financial Economics,* 19 (September 1987), 91–108.

RUBINSTEIN, MARK, and JOHN C. COX, *Options Markets.* Englewood Cliffs, NJ: Prentice Hall, 1985.

VAN HORNE, JAMES C., "Warrant Valuation in Relation to Volatility and Opportunity Costs," *Industrial Management Review,* 10 (Spring 1969), 19–32.

PART 7

EXPANSION
AND RESTRUCTURING

Sweet Georgia-Pacific Grows Sweeter

In 1990, Georgia-Pacific Corporation acquired Great Northern Nekoosa Corporation[*] for $3.8 billion in a hostile bid. The acquisition was interesting not only as to the usual particulars but as to the tone it set for the 1990s. First of all, it was a strategic acquisition, allowing GP to gain valuable manufacturing capacity through buying another company as opposed to building. Great Northern had new, efficient plants in Georgia, Mississippi, and Arkansas. Had Georgia-Pacific built the same primary mill capacity, it would have cost over $6 billion. Estimates of the efficiency gains resulting from the merger range from $40 to $80 million annually. The merger, one of the first of the 1990s, was the vanguard of many more strategic mergers to come. These are in contrast to financial mergers, which were the rage during the 1980s.

Community relations played an important role in the acquisition. Great Northern was an exemplary corporate citizen. In Maine in particular, local constituencies could be counted on to oppose the bid by Georgia-Pacific. The thrust of GP's message was that it too was a good corporate citizen, and that unlike timberland acquisitions by others, GP was not acquiring Great Northern as a breakup situation. The fact that GP was able to easily and quickly arrange financing allayed the latter fear. GP convinced people that it was a long-term employer interested in communities. The payoff was that Maine legislators remained neutral in the corporate control contest. Georgia-Pacific captured its prize, and this large strategic merger set the stage for more to come in the 1990s.

[*] "How GP Won the Battle of the Paper Giants," Institutional Investor, 24 (May 1990), 159.

24

MERGERS AND THE MARKET FOR CORPORATE CONTROL

The market for corporate control can alter dramatically the setting in which business firms compete. In an idealized world, this market is a positive thing for stockholders and for the economy as a whole. Assets, people, and products may be transferred to more productive uses. By loosening management control over these resources, higher-value employment is possible. With rapidly changing technology and product markets, what was once a viable corporate strategy may no longer be so. Yet existing management may be wedded to the old strategy and reluctant to change. Moreover, a top-heavy bureaucracy may have little incentive to run a company efficiently, enjoying high compensation and perquisites while paying insufficient attention to cost-effectiveness and competitive advantage.

Realistically, the contested takeover is the only means for replacing ineffective management and better utilizing corporate resources. Moreover, the ever-present threat of a takeover may stimulate existing management to perform better. In other words, competition among management teams to control corporate resources may motivate better management throughout the economy.

However, the takeover movement is not without its critics. There is the "short-termism" argument. It is alleged that management sacrifices long-term goals for short-term preservation. Put another way, it is argued that management is consumed with the potential takeover and possible defenses, and that this works to the detriment of the long-run viability of the enterprise. Research and development, capital expenditures, advertising, and personnel development are cut in a myopic way. In addition to this argument, there are out-of-pocket costs associated with a takeover—payments to lawyers, investment banks, newspapers for pages and pages of ads, proxy solicitors, and others who are able to mine the rich lode called merger mania. In such a frenzy, it is posited by some that irrational prices are paid for corporate control—premiums above present stock values that cannot be justified by the likely economies to be realized.

Thus, the market for corporate control has both supporters and detractors. In this chapter, we sort out the issues as to their valuation underpinnings. We will look at mergers, tender offers, resistance to takeovers, and the empirical evidence on valuation. This will be followed in the next chapter by other aspects of corporate restructuring. Recall that in Chapters 7 and 9 we treated the acquisition of another company as a capital budgeting decision. The acquisition requires an initial outlay, which is expected to be followed by free cash flows. These are cash flows in excess of necessary investments in working capital and in fixed assets. In those earlier chapters, we developed a conceptual framework for analyzing and evaluating the likely effect of an acquisition on the value of the firm in both firm-risk and market-risk contexts.

The value of the combined company was found to be the sum of the values of the parts plus any synergy that might be involved.

$$Vab = Va + Vb + \text{Synergy} \qquad (24\text{-}1)$$

where Vab = value of company post merger
Va = value of company A pre merger
Vb = value of company B pre merger
Synergy = economies realized in the merger through increased revenues and/or cost reductions

The maximum price that company A should pay for company B is $Vab - Va$. Apart from the arithmetic of valuation, the effect of any change in risk (usually a reduction) on the required rate of return also was addressed. With these foundations in place, we deal with more applied aspects of acquisitions and the market for corporate control. Now some definitions.

FEATURES OF A MERGER

A merger is a combination of two corporations in which only one survives. The merged corporation goes out of existence, leaving its assets and liabilities to the acquiring corporation. A merger must be distinguished from a *consolidation*, which involves the combination of two or more corporations whereby an entirely new corporation is formed. The old companies cease to exist, and shares of their common stock are exchanged for shares in the new company. When two companies of about the same size combine, they usually consolidate. When two companies differ significantly in size, they usually merge. Though it is necessary to understand the distinction, the terms *merger* and *consolidation* tend to be used interchangeably to describe the combination of two companies. A term also used is *takeover*, which can mean a friendly merger of two companies or an unfriendly acquisition by tender offer. However, the term usually is associated with the latter.

PURCHASE OF ASSETS
OR PURCHASE OF STOCK

A company may be acquired either by the purchase of its assets or its common stock. The acquirer evaluates many facets of a target company, as the rather exhaustive checklist in Fig. 24-1 shows. The buying company may purchase all or a portion of the assets of another company and pay for them in cash or with its own stock. Frequently, the buyer acquires only the assets of

General Information
- [ ] Exact corporate name
- [ ] Address
- [ ] Date and state of incorporation
- [ ] States in which the company is qualified to do business
- [ ] Location of minute books, by-laws, and certificate of incorporation
- [ ] History
- [ ] Description of products
- [ ] Fiscal year
- [ ] Capitalization
- [ ] Rights of each class of stock and other securities
- [ ] Stockholders' agreements and terms thereof
- [ ] Names of stockholders and holdings
- [ ] Bank depositaries and average bank balances
- [ ] Bank references
- [ ] Credit rating
- [ ] Location of company records
- [ ] Accountants: Name, address, and reputation
- [ ] Attorneys: Name and address

Personnel
- [ ] Directors and their affiliations
- [ ] Officers: For each — position, duties, age, health, salary, service, experience, personal plans for the future, other interests (including time devoted thereto), and stockholdings
- [ ] Organization chart
- [ ] Employee contracts: Terms, expiration date(s)
- [ ] Number of employees in production, sales, administration, etc.
- [ ] Union contracts: Terms, expiration dates
- [ ] Strike record, labor morale, handling of labor relations
- [ ] Labor market
- [ ] Pension, profit sharing, insurance, stock bonus, deferred compensation, and severance plans
- [ ] Comparison with industry as to number of employees, hours per week, and wage rates for the past five years and for the past twelve months

Operations
- [ ] Description, including significant changes in the past few years
  1. Capacity and per cent of utilization
  2. Production controls (scheduling and inventories)
  3. Shipping and receiving controls
  4. Accounting controls
- [ ] Principal suppliers and terms
- [ ] Distribution methods and terms (also, brokers or agents and compensation arrangements)
- [ ] Branch offices and their operations
- [ ] Subsidiaries, their operations and inter-company dealings
- [ ] Government contracts and subcontracts
- [ ] Seasonal factors
- [ ] Public and stockholder relations

Sales
- [ ] Description of market
- [ ] Number of customers and names of principal customers
- [ ] Gross and net sales for the past five years and for the past twelve months
  1. Penetration of market by product
  2. Possibilities of increase through existing lines and by diversification
- [ ] Sales comparison with the industry for the past five years and for the past twelve months
- [ ] Sales backlog, accounts receivable activity, customer continuity
- [ ] Sales correspondence
- [ ] Sales policies and method of compensation of sales personnel
- [ ] Pricing policies and fluctuations in the past five years
- [ ] Principal competitors
- [ ] Relative size in the industry
- [ ] Comparative advantages and disadvantages
- [ ] Anything significant in lines produced in the past few years
- [ ] Any nonrelated activities
- [ ] Missing product lines
- [ ] Advertising and other sales promotion programs: Cost and effectiveness in the past five years
- [ ] Research program: Cost, history, scope, potential, results, work by outsiders
- [ ] New developments
- [ ] Industry trends
- [ ] Current and future prospects

Earnings and Dividends
- [ ] Earnings record and budget for the past five years and the last twelve months, break-even point, gross profit margins and reasons for variations, nonrecurring income and expenses, changes in overabsorbed and underabsorbed burden
- [ ] Earnings comparison with the industry for the past five years
- [ ] Dividend and earnings record for the past five years in total and per share
- [ ] Potential economies
- [ ] Current and future prospects
- [ ] Analysis of selling and general and administrative expenses
- [ ] Contribution of company's effort to profit

Plant Facilities
- [ ] Location
- [ ] Shipping facilities
- [ ] Real estate taxes
- [ ] Land
  1. Acreage
  2. Cost
  3. Assessed value
  4. Fair market value

FIGURE 24-1

Acquisition evaluation checklist SOURCE: *PMM & Co./Management Focus/May–June 1980.*
Copyright Peat, Marwick, Mitchell & Co. Reprinted by permission.

- ☐ Buildings
  1. Description, including pictures, if available
  2. Age and condition
  3. Area
  4. Depreciation: Reserves, methods, rates, policies
  5. Assessed value
  6. Fair market value (recent appraisals)
  7. Fire insurance
- ☐ Title to realty and title policy
- ☐ Machinery and equipment
  1. Description
  2. Age, condition, efficiency, insurance coverage
  3. Depreciation: Reserves, methods, rates, policies
  4. Total acquisitions during the past five years
  5. Analysis of most recent additions
- ☐ Future plant, machinery, and equipment requirements
- ☐ Capitalization versus repair policies
- ☐ Capital expenditures and repairs for the past five years
- ☐ Percentage relationship of production costs and comparison with the industry
- ☐ Efficiency of operations
- ☐ Subcontracting done by others
- ☐ Certificates of necessity
- ☐ Facility contracts or leases
- ☐ Surplus or idle buildings or equipment

Assets

- ☐ Relationship of cash to current liabilities
- ☐ Age and number of accounts receivable (latest accounts receivable aging)
- ☐ Provision for bad debts
- ☐ Inventories for the past five years
  1. Relationship of inventories to current assets
  2. Location
  3. Finished goods by product
  4. Work in process by product
  5. Raw materials by product
  6. Pricing methods
  7. Accounting procedures and practices
  8. Provision for obsolete or slow-moving stock (latest inventory aging)
- ☐ Analysis of notes receivable
- ☐ Analysis of investments
- ☐ Subsidiaries
  1. Treatment on parent company's balance sheet
  2. Analysis (per check list) of significant items
- ☐ Analysis of other assets
- ☐ Patents held

Liabilities

- ☐ Renegotiable business
- ☐ Renegotiation status
- ☐ Current federal and state tax status and tax payments for the past three years
- ☐ Commitments for new buildings, machinery, inventories
- ☐ Long-term loans outstanding and terms
- ☐ Debentures outstanding and terms
- ☐ Dividend and interest arrearages
- ☐ Leases: Locations, areas, terms
- ☐ Insurance coverage, fidelity bonds, and amounts
- ☐ Pensions, etc.
- ☐ Contingent liabilities: Warranties; patent, etc., infringements; loss contracts; compensation for services
- ☐ Litigation record and present status

Financial Data

- ☐ Annual statements and audit reports for the past five years
- ☐ Tax returns for the past five years
- ☐ Surplus statements
- ☐ Disposition of funds statements
- ☐ Reports to Securities and Exchange Commission
- ☐ Explanation of how consolidations, if any, were effected and separate statement for each company involved
- ☐ Chart of accounts
- ☐ Book, net quick, liquidating, and market values for the past five years
- ☐ Working capital for the past five years and normal requirements based on trade practices, credit terms to customers, consignments, finished inventory, and raw inventory
- ☐ Net working capital ratios for the past five years
- ☐ Net quick position for the past five years
- ☐ Annual depreciation compared with capital additions for the past five years
- ☐ Inventory turnover for the past five years
- ☐ Cash, inventory, and working capital requirements for the past two years
- ☐ Interest charges for the past five years
- ☐ Exchange, if any, on which the company's stock is traded
- ☐ Recent stock sales and prices paid

Comparison with Comparable Companies

The following ratios for the subject company should be compared with those of comparable companies for the past five years and, if data are available, by quarters for the current year:

- ☐ Price to earnings
- ☐ Price to book value
- ☐ Sales to accounts receivable
- ☐ Sales to inventories
- ☐ Sales to fixed assets
- ☐ Earnings to book value

Terms of Acquisition

- ☐ Reasons for sale
- ☐ Price to be paid
- ☐ Terms of payment
- ☐ Financing
- ☐ Brokerage fees
- ☐ Tax considerations

Projected Financial Data

- ☐ Pro forma balance sheet
- ☐ Earnings forecast

the other company and does not assume its liabilities. If all the assets are purchased, the selling company is but a corporate shell. After the sale, its assets are composed entirely of cash or the stock of the buying company. The selling company can hold the cash or stock, or distribute it to its stockholders as a liquidating dividend, after which the company is dissolved. Thus, when its assets are purchased, the selling company can continue to exist if it holds the cash or stock arising from the sale. If it has cash, it may invest in other assets, such as a division of another company. Obviously, if only a portion of its assets are sold, the selling company will continue as a corporate entity.

When an acquiring company purchases the stock of another company, the latter is combined into the acquiring company. The company that is acquired ceases to exist, and the surviving company assumes all its assets and liabilities. As with a purchase of assets, the means of payment to the stockholders of the company being acquired can be either cash or stock. A purchase of assets is easier to effect than a purchase of stock, for all that is needed on the part of the buying company is approval by the board of directors. The selling company, however, needs the approval of its stockholders.

TAXABLE OR TAX-FREE TRANSACTION

If the acquisition is made with cash or with a debt instrument, the transaction is taxable to the selling company or to its stockholders at that time. This means that they must recognize any capital gain or loss on the sale of the assets or the sale of the stock at the time of the sale. If payment is made with voting preferred or common stock, the transaction is not taxable at the time of the sale. The capital gain or loss is recognized only when the stock is sold. In addition to the requirement of voting stock, in order for a combination to be tax free it must have a business purpose. In other words, it cannot be entirely for tax reasons. Moreover, in a purchase of assets the acquisition must involve substantially all the assets of the selling company, and no less than 80 percent of those assets must be paid for with voting stock. In a purchase of stock, the buying company must own at least 80 percent of the selling company's stock immediately after the transaction.

In most cases, a tax-free transaction is preferred by the selling company and its stockholders. A tax-free combination allows the selling company—in a purchase of assets—or its stockholders—in a purchase of stock—to postpone taking the gain and paying taxes on it until it is desirable to do so. To qualify as a tax-free transaction, not only must preferred or common stock be used but there must be a continuity of the surviving enterprise, the combination must not be solely for tax purposes, and the selling company stockholders must receive a significant and continuing equity stake in the acquiring company. While technical, the Internal Revenue Service wishes to discourage tax avoidance schemes that have no economic justification.

The form of the transaction, cash or stock, may have financial signaling implications to investors in the acquiring company. Following up our discussion in Chapter 21, a cash bid, which implicitly is financed with debt, may be interpreted as "good news" by investors, whereas a stock-financed bid may be interpreted as "bad news." Empirical evidence suggests that acquiring company stockholders realize lower returns (negative) upon the announcement of an equity-financed merger than they do when a cash merger is announced.[1]

---

[1] Paul Asquith, Robert F. Bruner, and David W. Mullins, Jr., "Merger Returns and the Form of Financing," research paper, Harvard University (October 1986).

ACCOUNTING TREATMENT

From an accounting standpoint, a combination of two companies is treated as either a *purchase* or a *pooling of interests*. In a purchase, the buyer treats the acquired company as an investment. If the buyer pays a premium above the book value of the assets, this premium must be reflected on the buyer's balance sheet. The purchase method requires tangible assets to be reported at fair market value. As a result, it may be possible to write up the acquired company's tangible assets. If such occurs, there will be higher depreciation charges.

If the premium paid exceeds the writeup, however, the difference must be reflected as goodwill on the buyer's balance sheet. Moreover, goodwill must be written off against future income, the logic being that it will be reflected in such income. An estimate must be made of the life of goodwill, as of any asset, and goodwill is amortized over this period, which cannot exceed 40 years. Thus, earnings are reduced by the amount of the charge. Note that goodwill charges are not deductible for tax purposes. Therefore, the acquiring firm generally views as a disadvantage the reduction of reported future earnings associated with this accounting treatment.

In a pooling of interests, the balance sheets of the two companies are combined, with assets and liabilities simply being added together. As a result, asset writeups and/or goodwill are not reflected in the combination, and there are no charges against future income. Because reported earnings will be higher with the pooling of interests accounting treatment than they will be with the purchase treatment, many acquiring companies prefer it.

The choice of accounting treatment does not rest entirely with the acquiring company, but rather is governed by the circumstances of the merger and the rules of the accounting profession. Only under the following rather restricted conditions can a merger be treated as a pooling of interests.

1. Each of the combined companies must be autonomous for at least 2 years prior to the pooling and independent of the others in the sense that no more than 10 percent of the stock is owned.

2. The combination must be consummated in a single transaction or in accordance with a specific plan within 1 year after the plan is initiated. In this regard, no contingent payments are permitted.

3. The acquiring corporation can issue only common stock, with rights identical to those of the majority of outstanding voting stock, in exchange for *substantially* all of the voting common stock of another company. Here, "substantially" means 90 percent or more.

4. The surviving corporation must not later retire or reacquire common stock issued in connection with the combination, must not enter into an arrangement for the benefit of former stockholders, and must not dispose of a significant portion of the assets of the combining companies for at least 2 years.

The most limiting condition is number 3, which states that common must be exchanged for common. The next most limiting is the prohibition of contingent payments. The result of these conditions is a significant constraint on the number of poolings of interests.

ABC Company acquired XYZ Company in an exchange of stock valued at $2 million. XYZ Company had debt of $1 million and shareholders' equity of $1.2 million prior to the merger, the net book value of its assets being $2.2 million. On the other hand, ABC Company, the acquirer, had shareholders' equity of $10 million, debt of $5 million, and assets having a net book value of $15 million prior to the merger. With the purchase method, the total assets of the acquired company are written up by $800,000, which is the price paid in excess of book value. Part of this figure, $300,000, can be treated as a writeup of tangible assets to their fair market value. The remainder, $500,000, must be reflected as goodwill. Under the pooling of interests accounting treatment, the assets shown for the surviving company are simply the sum of the book values of assets shown for the two companies prior to the merger.

| | BEFORE MERGER | | AFTER MERGER | |
	ABC Company	XYZ Company	Purchase	Pooling
Net tangible assets	$15,000	$2,200	$17,500	$17,200
Goodwill	0	0	500	0
Total assets	$15,000	$2,200	$18,000	$17,200
Debt	$ 5,000	$1,000	$ 6,000	$ 6,000
Shareholders' equity	10,000	1,200	12,000	11,200
Total liabilities and equity	$15,000	$2,200	$18,000	$17,200

Corporate executives with a focus on accounting income do not like the purchase method. Goodwill must be amortized as an expense, while any writeup in asset value means higher depreciation charges. Neither provides a tax advantage.[2] Therefore, reported income is lower. Note that cash flows are not affected by the choice of accounting method, so there is no effect on the economic value of the merger. While many executives prefer pooling, the previously mentioned restrictions constrain their choice.

STRATEGIC ACQUISITIONS INVOLVING STOCK

A *strategic acquisition* occurs when one company acquires another as part of its overall strategy. Perhaps cost advantages result, or it may be that the target company provides revenue enhancement through product extension or market dominance. The key is that there is a strategic reason for blending two companies together. In contrast, a *financial acquisition* is where a financial promoter, such as Kohlberg, Kravis and Roberts (KKR), is the acquirer. The motivation is to sell off assets, cut costs, and operate whatever remains more efficiently than before, in the hope of producing value above what was paid. The acquisition is not strategic, for the company acquired is operated as an independent entity.

A financial acquisition invariably involves cash, and payment to the selling stockholders is financed largely with debt. Known as a leveraged buyout (LBO), this type of acquisition is taken up in the next chapter. Our focus here is on strategic acquisitions. As we know, an acquisition can be either for cash or for stock. Cash acquisitions are examined later in the chapter. With a stock acquisition, a ratio of exchange occurs, denoting the relative value weightings

---

[2] Goodwill amortization is not an expense for tax purposes. If assets are written up in value for tax purposes, the higher depreciation charges can be deducted. However, the entire writeup must be treated as taxable income at the time of writeup, a present-value disadvantage to say the least.

of the two companies. In this section, we consider ratios of exchange for earnings and for market prices.

EARNINGS

In evaluating a possible acquisition, the acquiring firm usually considers the effect the merger will have on the earnings per share of the surviving corporation. Company A is considering the acquisition, by stock, of company B. The financial data on the acquisition at the time it is being considered follow:

	COMPANY A	COMPANY B
Present earnings	$20,000,000	$5,000,000
Shares	5,000,000	2,000,000
Earnings per share	$4.00	$2.50
Price of stock	$64.00	$30.00
Price/earnings ratio	16X	12X

Company B has agreed to an offer of $35 a share to be paid in company A stock. The exchange ratio, then, is $35/$64, or about .547 share of company A's stock for each share of company B's stock. In total, 1,093,750 shares of company A will need to be issued in order to acquire company B. Assuming that the earnings of the component companies stay the same after the acquisition, earnings per share of the surviving company would be

	SURVIVING COMPANY A
Earnings	$25,000,000
Shares	6,093,750
Earnings per share	$4.10

Thus, there is an immediate improvement in earnings per share for company A as a result of the merger. Company B's former stockholders experience a reduction in earnings per share, however. For each share of B's stock they had held, they now hold .547 share of A. Thus, the earnings per share on each share of company B's stock they had held is (.547)(4.10), or $2.24, compared with $2.50 before.

Suppose now that the price agreed upon for company B's stock is $45 a share. The ratio of exchange, then, would be $45/$64, or about .703 share of A for each share of B. In total, 1,406,250 shares would have to be issued, and earnings per share after the merger would be

	SURVIVING COMPANY A
Earnings	$25,000,000
Shares	6,406,250
Earnings per share	$3.90

In this case, there is initial dilution in company A's earnings per share on account of the acquisition of company B.[3] Dilution in earnings per share will occur any time the price/earnings ratio paid for a company exceeds the price/earnings ratio of the company doing the acquiring. In our example, the price/earnings ratio in the first case was $35.00/$2.50, or 14, and in the second case, it was $45.00/$2.50, or 18. Because the price/earnings ratio of company A was 16, there was an increase in earnings per share in the first case and a decrease in the second.

Thus, initial increases and decreases in earnings per share are both possible. The *amount* of increase or decrease is a function of (1) the differential in price/earnings ratios and (2) the relative size of the two firms as measured by total earnings.[4] The higher the price/earnings ratio of the acquiring company in relation to that of the company being acquired, and the larger the earnings of the acquired company in relation to those of the acquiring company, the greater the increase in earnings per share of the acquiring company. These relationships are illustrated in Fig. 24-2 for three different earnings relationships. The a subscript for total earnings, T_a, and for price/earnings ratio, P_a/E_a, denotes the acquiring company, while the b subscript for T_b and P_b/E_b denotes the company being acquired.

Future Earnings. If the decision to acquire another company were based solely on the initial impact on earnings per share, an initial dilution in earnings per share would stop any company from acquiring another. This type of analysis, however, does not take into account the possibility of a future growth in earnings owing to the merger. This growth may be due to the expected growth in earnings of the acquired company as an independent entity and to any synergistic effects that result from the fusion of the two companies. If the earnings of company B are expected to grow at a faster rate than those of company A or if there is expected synergy, a high ratio of exchange for the stock may be justified, despite the fact that there is initial dilution in earnings

[3] Company B's former stockholders obtain an improvement in earnings per share. Earnings per share on each share of stock they had held are $2.74.

[4] See Walter J. Mead, "Instantaneous Merger Profit as a Conglomerate Merger Motive," *Western Economics Journal*, 7 (December 1969), 295–306.

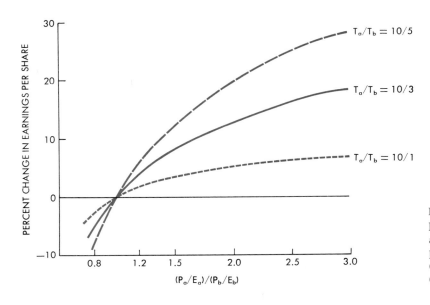

FIGURE 24-2

Earnings per share change as a function of the price/earnings ratio differential and relative earnings

per share for stockholders of company A. The superior growth in earnings of the acquired company may eventually result in higher earnings per share for these stockholders relative to earnings without the merger.

It is useful to graph likely future earnings per share with and without the acquisition. Figure 24-3 shows this for a hypothetical merger. The graph tells us how long it will take for the dilution in earnings per share to be eliminated, and for an accretion to take place. In this example, it is $1\frac{1}{2}$ years; earnings per share drop \$.30 initially, but this relative dilution is eliminated by the middle of the second year. The greater the duration of dilution, the less desirable the acquisition is said to be from the standpoint of the acquiring company. Some companies set a ceiling on the number of years dilution will be tolerated, and this ceiling serves as a constraint in establishing the exchange ratio to be paid in the acquisition. When an acquisition is being considered, graphs should be prepared under differing assumptions as to the exchange ratio. They also should be made under differing earnings assumptions for the combination; preparing multiple graphs gives management greater information on which to base negotiations.

MARKET VALUE

The major emphasis in the bargaining process is on the ratio of exchange of market prices per share. Judging the intrinsic value of a company, investors focus on the market price of its stock. That price reflects the earnings potential of the company, dividends, business risk, capital structure, asset values, and other factors that bear upon valuation. The ratio of exchange of market prices is simply

$$\frac{\text{Market price per share of acquiring company} \times \text{Number of shares offered}}{\text{Market price per share of acquired company}}$$

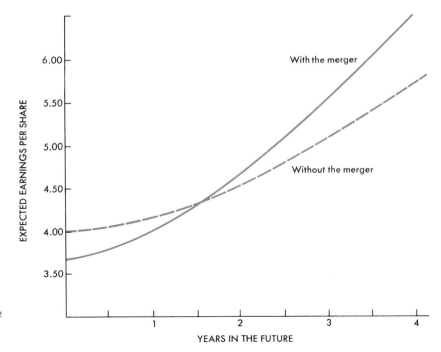

FIGURE 24-3
Expected earnings per share with and without the merger

If the market price of Acquiring Company is $60 per share and that of Bought Company is $30, and Acquiring offers a half share of its stock for each share of Bought Company, the ratio of exchange would be

$$\frac{\$60 \times .5}{\$30} = 1.00$$

In other words, the stocks of the two companies would be exchanged on a one-to-one market price basis. If the market price of the surviving company is relatively stable at $60 a share, stockholders of both companies are about as well off as before with respect to market value. The company being acquired finds little enticement to accept a one-to-one market-value ratio of exchange, however. The acquiring company must offer a price in excess of the current market price per share of the company it wishes to acquire. Instead of a half share of stock, Acquiring might have to offer .667 share, or $40 a share in current market value.

Bootstrapping Earnings per Share.   In the absence of synergism, improved management, or of the underpricing of Bought Company's stock in an inefficient market, we would not expect it to be in the interest of Acquiring's stockholders to offer a price in excess of Bought Company's current market price. Acquiring stockholders could be better off if their company's price/earnings ratio is higher than Bought Company's and if somehow the surviving company is able to keep that same higher price/earnings ratio after the merger. Perhaps Bought Company has a price/earnings ratio of 10. Acquiring Company, on the other hand, has a price/earnings ratio of 18. Assume the following financial information:

	COMPANY A	COMPANY B
Present earnings	$20,000,000	$6,000,000
Shares	6,000,000	2,000,000
Earnings per share	$3.33	$3.00
Market price per share	$60.00	$30.00
Price/earnings ratio	18X	10X

With an offer of .667 share of Acquiring Company for each share of Bought Company, or $40 a share in value, the market price exchange ratio of Bought Company is

$$\frac{\$60 \times .667}{\$30} = 1.33$$

Stockholders of Bought Company are being offered a stock with a market value of $40 for each share of stock they own. Obviously, they benefit from the acquisition with respect to market price, because their stock was formerly worth $30 a share. Stockholders of Acquiring Company also stand to benefit, *if the price/earnings ratio of the surviving company stays at 18.* The market price per share of the surviving company after the acquisition, all other things held constant, would be

SURVIVING COMPANY

641

CHAPTER 24
Mergers and the
Market for
Corporate Control

Total earnings	$26,000,000
Number of shares	7,333,333
Earnings per share	$3.55
Price/earnings ratio	18X
Market price per share	$63.90

The reason for this apparent bit of magic whereby the stockholders of both companies benefit is the difference in price/earnings ratios.

Under the conditions described, companies with high price/earnings ratios would be able to acquire companies with lower price/earnings ratios and obtain an immediate increase in earnings per share, despite the fact that they pay a premium with respect to the market-value exchange ratio. The key factor is what happens to the price/earnings ratio after the merger. If it stays the same, the market price of the stock will increase. As a result, an acquiring company would be able to show a steady growth in earnings per share if it acquired a sufficient number of companies over time in this manner. This increase is not the result of economies or underlying growth but is due to the "bootstrap" increase in earnings per share through acquisitions. If the marketplace values this illusory growth, a company presumably could increase shareholder wealth through acquisitions alone. In reasonably efficient capital markets, however, it is unlikely that the market will hold constant the price/earnings ratio of a company that cannot demonstrate growth potential in ways other than acquiring companies with lower price/earnings ratios.

Thus, the acquiring company must allow for the price/earnings ratio changing with an acquisition. If the market is relatively free from imperfections and if synergism and/or improved management is not anticipated, we would expect the price/earnings ratio of the surviving firm to approach a weighted average of the two previous price/earnings ratios. Under these circumstances, the acquisition of companies with lower price/earnings ratios would not enhance shareholder wealth. In fact, if the market price exchange ratio were more than one, as occurs with a premium being paid, there would be a transfer of wealth from the stockholders of the acquiring company to those of the acquired firm. If synergism were expected, shareholder wealth could be increased through the acquisition. All of this is in keeping with our earlier discussion of the issue in Chapter 9. Let us turn now to the fundamental valuation underpinnings of a merger.

SOURCES OR REARRANGEMENTS OF VALUE

The purpose of a merger or takeover is to create value. There are a handful of reasons why we might expect value to be created or rearranged, and we consider them in turn. Some were discussed in Chapter 9, so this treatment is an extension of those ideas together with some new ones.

SALES ENHANCEMENT AND OPERATING ECONOMIES

An important reason for some acquisitions is the enhancement of sales. By gaining market share, ever-increasing sales may be possible through market dominance. There may be other marketing and strategic benefits. Perhaps the acquisition will bring technological advances to the product table. Or it may be that it will fill a gap in the product line, thereby enhancing sales throughout. To be a thing of value, such sales enhancement must be cost effective.

Operating economies can often be achieved through a combination of companies. Duplicate facilities can be eliminated, and marketing, accounting, purchasing, and other operations can be consolidated. The sales force may be reduced to avoid duplication of effort in a particular territory. In a railroad merger, the principal objective is to realize economies of operation through elimination of duplicate facilities and runs. When industrial companies merge, a firm with a product that complements an existing product line may fill out that line and increase the total demand for products of the acquiring company. The realization of such economies is known as *synergism*; the fused company is of greater value than the sum of the parts, that is, $2 + 2 = 5$.

In addition to operating economies, economies of scale may be possible with a merger of two companies. Economies of scale occur when average cost declines with increases in volume. Usually we think of economies of scale in production and overlook their possibilities in marketing, purchasing, distribution, accounting, and even finance. The idea is to concentrate a greater volume of activity into a given facility, into a given number of people, into a given distribution system, and so forth. In other words, increases in volume permit a more efficient utilization of resources. Like anything else, it has limits. Beyond a point, increases in volume may cause more problems than they remedy, and a company may actually become less efficient. Economists speak of an "envelope curve" with economies of scale possible up to some optimal point, after which diseconomies occur.

Economies can perhaps best be realized with a *horizontal* merger, combining two companies in the same line of business. The economies achieved by this means result primarily from eliminating duplicate facilities and offering a broader product line in the hope of increasing total demand. A *vertical merger*, whereby a company expands either forward toward the ultimate consumer or backward toward the source of raw material, may also bring about economies. This type of merger gives a company more control over its distribution and purchasing. There are few operating economies in a *conglomerate merger*, combining two companies in unrelated lines of business.

IMPROVED MANAGEMENT

Some companies are inefficiently managed, with the result that profitability is lower than it might be. This topic was discussed at the outset of the chapter when we considered the market for corporate control. To the extent the acquirer can provide better management, an acquisition may make sense for this reason alone. While a company can change management itself, the practical realities of entrenchment may be such that an external acquisition is required for anything to happen. This motivation would suggest that poor-earning, low-return companies are ripe acquisition candidates, and there appears to be some evidence in support of this contention. The idea is that the external financial markets discipline management.

Many people maintain that the possibilities of sales enhancement, operating economies, and improved management are the only important justifications for a combination where the objective is to maximize shareholder wealth. Their reasons are essentially those discussed in Chapter 9, namely, that investors are able to achieve on their own the other benefits associated with mergers. In particular, conglomerate mergers are viewed as lacking economic justification unless the acquiring company can manage more productively the assets and people of the companies being acquired.

INFORMATION EFFECT

Value also could occur if new information is conveyed as a result of the merger negotiations or takeover attempt. This notion implies asymmetric information between management (or the acquirer) and the general market for the stock. To the extent a stock is believed to be undervalued, a positive signal may occur via the merger announcement, which causes share price to rise. The idea is that the merger/takeover event provides information on underlying profitability that otherwise cannot be convincingly conveyed. This argument has been examined elsewhere in the book and, in a nutshell, it is that specific actions speak louder than words.

Whether a company is truly undervalued is always questionable. Invariably management believes it is, and in certain cases it has information that is not properly reflected in market price. However, the market for acquisitions is an active one with extensive information networks being maintained by investment banks and merger brokers. Moreover, there is considerable competition among potential buyers, so the argument for sizable numbers of undervalued bargains existing is dubious. However, there may be situations where it is cheaper to buy assets through an acquisition than it is to acquire them directly. The market value of some companies is considerably below the replacement value of the assets. If another company wishes to invest in those assets, say, a plant, and faces a decision to build or acquire through acquisition, it will choose the latter if the price paid is less than the cost of building from scratch.

TAX REASONS

A motivation in some mergers is tax. In the case of a tax-loss carryforward, a company with cumulative tax losses may have little prospect of earning enough in the future to utilize fully its tax-loss carryforward.[5] By merging with a profitable company, it may be possible for the surviving company to utilize the carryforward more effectively. However, there are restrictions that limit its utilization to a percentage of the fair market value of the acquired company. Still, there can be an economic gain—at the expense of the government—that cannot be realized by either company separately.

---

[5] A loss is carried back 3 years and forward 15 years to offset taxable income in those years. It first must be applied to the earliest preceding year and then to the next 2 years in order. If the loss is not entirely offset by earnings in the 3 prior years, the residual is carried forward sequentially to reduce future profits and taxes in each of the next 15 years.

There are other tax motivations, but they tend to be of minor importance. In general, the Tax Reform Act of 1986 sharply reduced tax-motivated mergers. Almost across the board, previous tax motivations were blunted—from the use of the installment sales method to postpone capital gains to the writeup of asset value, which permitted higher depreciation charges and lower taxes.[6] While certain technical tax advantages remain, they are small.

DIVERSIFICATION

Diversification is the motive in some mergers. By acquiring a firm in a different line of business, a company may be able to reduce cyclical instability in earnings. To the extent that investors in a company's stock are averse to risk and are concerned only with the total risk of the firm, a reduction in earnings instability would have a favorable impact on share price.

This argument assumes that investors evaluate risk solely in relation to the *total* risk of the firm. We know from Chapters 3 and 9, however, that investors are able to diversify risk on their own. If they evaluate risk in an overall market context, they will diversify at least as effectively on their own as the firm is able to do for them. Particularly when the stock of the company being acquired is publicly traded, there is no reason to believe that investors are not able to diversify their portfolios efficiently. Because the firm is unable to do something for them that they cannot do for themselves, diversification as a reason for merging usually is not a thing of value.[7] Consequently, it would not lead to an increase in share price.

WEALTH TRANSFERS

However, there may be wealth transfers from equity holders to debt holders, via diversification, when a merger occurs. To the extent the combination lowers the relative variability of cash flows, debt holders benefit in having a more creditworthy claim. As a result, the market value of their claim should increase, all other things the same. Unless equity holders protect themselves, they will lose value to debt holders in the option pricing model context illustrated in Chapters 9 and 10. In effect it is a zero-sum game, and one party gains only at the expense of the other. Equity holders can protect themselves by increasing the amount of debt or instigating "me-first" rules. (See Chapter 10.)

HUBRIS HYPOTHESIS

Richard Roll argues that takeovers are motivated by bidders who get caught up in believing they can do no wrong and that their foresight is perfect.[8] *Hubris* refers to an animal-like spirit of arrogant pride and self-

[6] See Myron S. Scholes and Mark A. Wolfson, "The Effects of Changes in Tax Laws on Corporate Reorganization Activity," working paper, National Bureau of Economic Research (September 1989). For an analysis of wealth effects pre-1986 TRA, see Carla Hayn, "Tax Attributes as Determinants of Shareholder Gains in Corporate Acquisitions," *Journal of Financial Economics*, 23 (June 1989), 121–53.

[7] In Chapter 9, we discussed certain conditions under which diversification through merging may have a positive effect—though minor, compared to any synergistic effect—on the total value of the firm.

[8] Richard Roll, "The Hubris Hypothesis of Corporate Takeovers," *Journal of Business*, 59 (April 1986), 197–216.

confidence. Such individuals are said not to have the rational behavior necessary to refrain from bidding. They get caught up in the "heat of the hunt" where the prey must be had regardless of cost. As a result, bidders pay too much for their targets. The hubris hypothesis suggests that the excess premium paid for the target company benefits those stockholders, but that stockholders of the acquiring company suffer a diminution in wealth.

MANAGEMENT'S PERSONAL AGENDA

Rather than hubris, it may be that the acquiring company overpays because management pursues personal as opposed to corporate wealth-maximizing goals. Sometimes management chases growth. Being larger may bring prestige, in whose glow management basks. The goal may be diversification, because with unrelated businesses and risk spread out, management jobs may be more secure. In testing these notions, Randall Morck, Andrei Shleifer, and Robert W. Vishny find that stock price returns are lower when a company diversifies, when it buys a rapidly growing company, and when management performance has been poor before the acquisition.[9]

From the standpoint of the selling company, personal reasons also may come into play. In a tightly held company, the individuals who have controlling interest may want their company acquired by another company that has an established market for its stock. For estate tax purposes, it may be desirable for these individuals to hold shares of stock that are readily marketable and for which market-price quotations are available. The owners of a tightly held company may have too much of their wealth tied up in the company. By merging with a publicly held company, they obtain a marked improvement in their liquidity, enabling them to sell some of their stock and diversify their investments. Unlike the previous reasons we have investigated, this reason relates to specific stockholders as opposed to investors at large.

Now that we have explored various reasons for a merger/takeover, we need to consider corporate voting by which control is determined.

CORPORATE VOTING
AND CONTROL

Inasmuch as the common stockholders of a company are its owners, they are entitled to elect a board of directors. The board, in turn, selects the management, and management actually controls the operations of the company. In a proprietorship, partnership, or small corporation, the owners usually directly control the operations of the business; in a large corporation, the owners have but an indirect and often very faint voice in the affairs of the company. Because common stockholders frequently are widely dispersed geographically and therefore disorganized, management may be able to exercise effective control of a corporation if it controls only a moderate percentage of the stock outstanding.

---

[9]Randall Morck, Andrei Shleifer, and Robert W. Vishny, "Do Managerial Objectives Drive Bad Acquisitions?" *Journal of Finance*, 45 (March 1990), 31–48.

IS CONTROL VALUABLE?

Some contend that control is valuable because management can enjoy private benefits. These include high salaries, extensive perquisites like cars, club memberships, and corporate planes, or simply the peace of mind that comes with entrenchment. Where there are private control benefits, they work to the disadvantage of public stockholders, at least theoretically. For these stockholders, the one vote–one share rule is usually optimal.[10] The idea then is that control has value apart from the ordinary trading of shares. If this is true, it would not be surprising for large premiums to be paid to wrest control from incumbent management. With these concepts in mind, let us see how voting works.

VOTING PROCEDURES

Depending on the corporate charter, the board of directors is elected either under a *majority voting system* or under a *cumulative voting system*. Under the majority system, stockholders have one vote for each share of stock they own, and they must vote for each director position that is open. A stockholder who owns 100 shares will be able to cast 100 votes for each director's position open. Because each person seeking a position on the board must win a majority of the total votes cast for that position, the system precludes minority interests from electing directors. If management can obtain proxies for over 50 percent of the shares voted, it can select the entire board.

Under a cumulative voting system, a stockholder is able to accumulate votes and cast them for less than the total number of directors being elected. The total number of votes is the number of shares the stockholder owns times the number of directors being elected. If you are a stockholder who owns 100 shares, and 12 directors are to be elected, you may cast 1,200 votes for any number of directors you choose, the maximum being 1,200 votes for one director.

A cumulative voting system, in contrast to the majority system, permits minority interests to elect a certain number of directors. The minimum number of shares necessary to elect a specific number of directors is determined by

$$\frac{\text{Total shares outstanding times specific number of directors sought}}{\text{Total number of directors to be elected plus one}} + 1$$

(24-2)

If there are 3 million shares outstanding, the total number of directors to be elected is 14, and if a minority group wishes to elect two directors, it will need at least the following numbers of shares:

$$\frac{3,000,000 \times 2}{14 + 1} + 1 = 400,001$$

Cumulative voting gives minority interests a better opportunity to be represented on the board of directors of a corporation. Because the system is

[10] Sanford J. Grossman and Oliver D. Hart, "One Share–One Vote and the Market for Corporate Control," *Journal of Financial Economics*, 20 (January/March 1988), 175–202; Milton Harris and Artur Raviv, "Corporate Governance," *Journal of Financial Economics*, 20 (January/March 1988), 203–35; and Milton Harris and Artur Raviv, "The Design of Securities," *Journal of Financial Economics*, 24 (October 1989), 203–35.

more democratic, a number of states require that companies in the state elect directors in this way. Even with cumulative voting, however, management can reduce the number of directors and sometimes preclude minority interests from obtaining a seat on the board of directors. Suppose the minority group just described actually owns 400,001 shares. With 14 directors to be elected, the group can elect 2 directors. If the board is reduced to 6 members, the minority group can elect no directors, because the minimum number of shares needed to elect a signal director is

$$\frac{3,000,000 \times 1}{6 + 1} + 1 = 428,572$$

Another method of thwarting a minority interest from obtaining representation is to stagger the terms of the directors so that only a portion is elected each year. If a firm has 12 directors and the term is 4 years only, only 3 are elected each year. As a result, a minority group needs considerably more shares voted in its favor to elect a director than it would need if all 12 directors came up for election each year.

PROXIES

Voting may be either in person at the stockholders' annual meeting or by proxy. As most stockholders do not attend the meeting, the latter is the mechanism by which most votes are garnered. A *proxy* is a form a stockholder signs giving his or her right to vote to another person or persons. The SEC regulates the solicitation of proxies and also requires companies to disseminate information to its stockholders through proxy mailings. Prior to the annual meeting, management solicits proxies from stockholders to vote for the recommended slate of directors and for any other proposals requiring stockholder approval. If stockholders are satisfied with the company, they generally sign the proxy in favor of management, giving written authorization to management to vote their shares. If some stockholders do not vote their shares, the number of shares voted at the meeting and the number needed to constitute a majority are lower. Because of the proxy system and the fact that management is able to mail information to stockholders at the company's expense, management has a distinct advantage in the voting process.

But the fortress is not invulnerable. Outsiders can seize control of a company through a proxy contest. Obviously, they would not attempt a takeover if management controlled a large percentage of shares outstanding. When an outside group undertakes a proxy raid, it is required to register its proxy statement with the Securities and Exchange Commission to prevent the presentation of misleading or false information. In a proxy contest, the odds favor existing management to win. It has both the organization and the use of the company's resources to carry on the proxy fight. Insurgents are likely to be successful only when the earnings performance of the company has been bad and management obviously ineffective.

Still, the undertaking of a proxy contest often is associated with higher share price performance than otherwise would be the case.[11] The challenge it-

---

[11] For empirical studies of the phenomena that support this notion, see Peter Dodd and Jerold B. Warner, "On Corporate Governance: A Study of Proxy Contests," *Journal of Financial Economics*, 11 (April 1983), 401–38; and Harry DeAngelo and Linda DeAngelo, "Proxy Contests and the Governance of Publicly Held Corporations," *Journal of Financial Economics*, 23 (June 1989), 29–59.

self may be sufficient to change expectations about management in the future behaving more in keeping with maximizing shareholder wealth. With the advantages to management, together with certain institutional imperfections, the proxy contest is an inefficient means for a corporate control challenge.[12] Whereas the proxy contest was a dominant means for gaining corporate control in the 1950s and 1960s, it gave way to the tender offer in the 1970s and 1980s, a topic we explore shortly. In the early 1990s, however, the proxy challenge reemerged with some rather highly publicized contests. One reason was the abatement of highly levered transactions.

DUAL-CLASS COMMON STOCK

To retain control for management, founders, or some other group, a company may have more than one class of common stock. For example, its common stock might be classified according to voting power and to the claim on income. Class A common may have inferior voting privilege but may be entitled to a prior claim to dividends, while the class B common has superior voting rights but a lower claim to dividends. Usually, the promoters of a corporation and its management will hold the class B common stock, whereas the class A common is sold to the public.

Suppose the class A and class B common stockholders of a company are entitled to one vote per share, but the class A stock is issued at an initial price of $20 a share. If $2 million is raised in the original offering through the issuance of 80,000 shares of class A common for $1.6 million and 200,000 shares of class B common for $400,000, the class B stockholders will have over twice as many votes as the class A holders have, despite the fact that their original investment is only one-quarter as large. Thus, the class B holders have effective control of the company. Indeed, this is the purpose of classified stock. Rather than requiring a cash investment, sometimes the class B common is given to the founders/promoters of a corporation for their human capital.

Perhaps the most famous example of a company with classified common stock is the Ford Motor Company. The class B stock is owned by members of the Ford family, while the class A stock is held by the general public. Regardless of the number of class A shares issued, the class B common constitutes 40 percent of the total voting power of the company. Thus, members of the Ford family retain substantial voting power in the company, despite the fact that they hold far fewer shares than does the general public.

A number of scholars have examined the valuation of dual-class stock.[13] The superior voting-right stock tends to trade at a premium above the class of

[12] See John Pound, "Proxy Contests and the Efficiency of Shareholder Oversight," *Journal of Financial Economics*, 18 (January/March 1988), 237–65.

[13] Harry DeAngelo and Linda DeAngelo, "Management Ownership of Voting Rights: A Study of Public Corporations with Dual Classes of Common Stock," *Journal of Financial Economics*, 14 (March 1985), 33–70; Ronald C. Lease, John J. McConnell, and Wayne H. Mikkelson, "The Market Value of Control in Publicly-Traded Corporations," *Journal of Financial Economics*, 11 (April 1983), 439–71; Megan Partch, "The Creation of a Class of Limited Voting Common Stock and Shareholders' Wealth," *Journal of Financial Economics*, 18 (June 1987), 313–39; Ronald J. Gilson, "Evaluating Dual Class Common Stock: The Relevance of Substitutes," *Virginia Law Review*, 73 (August 1987), 807–44; Gregg A. Jarrell and Annette B. Poulsen, "Dual-Class Recapitalizations as Antitakeover Mechanisms," *Journal of Financial Economics*, 20 (January/March 1988), 129–52; and Marcia Millon Cornett and Michael R. Vetsuypens, "Voting Rights and Shareholder Wealth: The Issuance of Limited Voting Common Stock," *Managerial and Decision Economics*, 10 (September 1989), 175–88.

common having inferior voting power. While one would think that announcement of a new superior voting-right stock would result in a negative stock price reaction, the empirical evidence is mixed in this regard.

TENDER OFFERS
AND COMPANY RESISTANCE

Rather than a proxy contest, the threatening party can make a *tender offer* directly to stockholders of the company it wishes to acquire. A tender offer is an offer to purchase shares of stock of another company at a fixed price per share from stockholders who "tender" their shares. The tender price is usually set significantly above the present market price, as an incentive. Use of the tender offer allows the acquiring company to bypass the management of the company it wishes to acquire and, therefore, serves as a threat in any negotiations with that management.

The tender offer can be used also when there are no negotiations but when one company simply wants to acquire another. It no longer is possible to surprise another company, because the Securities and Exchange Commission requires rather extensive disclosures. In both cash and stock tenders, the primary selling tool is the premium that is offered over the existing market price of the stock. In addition, brokers are often given attractive commissions for shares tendered through them. The tender offer itself is usually communicated through financial newspapers. Direct mailings are made to the stockholders of the company being bid for if the bidder is able to obtain a list of stockholders. Although a company is legally obligated to provide such a list, it usually is able to delay delivery long enough to frustrate the bidder.

Instead of one tender offer, some bidders make a two-tier offer. The first tier of stock usually represents control and, for example, might be 45 percent of the stock outstanding if the bidder already owned 5 percent. The first-tier offer is more attractive in terms of price and/or the form of payment than is the second-tier offer for the remaining stock. The differential is designed to increase the probability of successfully gaining control, by providing an incentive to tender early. The two-tier offer avoids the "free-rider" problem associated with a single tender offer where individual stockholders have an incentive to hold out in the hope of realizing a higher counteroffer by someone else.[14]

The company being bid for may use a number of defensive tactics. Management may try to persuade stockholders that the offer is not in their best interests. Usually, the argument is that the bid is too low in relation to the true, long-run value of the firm. Hearing that, stockholders may look at an attractive premium and find the long run too long. Some companies raise the cash dividend or declare a stock split in hopes of gaining stockholder support. Legal actions are often undertaken, more to delay and frustrate the bidder than with the expectation of winning. When the two firms are competitors, an antitrust suit may prove a powerful deterrent to the bidder. As a last resort, management of the company being bid for may seek a merger with a "friendly" company, known as a "white knight."

[14] For a detailed analysis of the two-tier offer and its implications for acquisitions, see Sanford Grossman and Oliver Hart, "Takeover Bids, the Free-Rider Problem, and the Theory of the Corporation," *Bell Journal of Economics*, 11 (Spring 1980), 42–64.

650

PART 7
Expansion and
Restructuring

ANTITAKEOVER AMENDMENTS
AND OTHER DEVICES

In addition to the defensive tactics already described, some companies use more formal methods that are put into place prior to an actual takeover attempt. Known as antitakeover or "shark-repellent" devices, they are designed to make a takeover more difficult. Before describing them, it is useful to consider their motivation. The managerial entrenchment hypothesis suggests that the barriers erected are to protect management jobs and that such actions work to the detriment of stockholders. On the other hand, the stockholders interest hypothesis implies that corporate control contests are dysfunctional and take management time away from profit-making activities. Therefore, antitakeover devices ensure more attention being paid to these activities and are in the interest of stockholders. Moreover, the barriers erected are said to cause individual stockholders not to accept a low offer price but to join other stockholders in a cartel response to any offer. Therefore, antitakeover devices would enhance shareholder wealth, according to this hypothesis.[15]

A handful of devices exist to make it more difficult for another party to take you over. As we know, some companies *stagger the terms of their board of directors* so that fewer stand for election each year, and, accordingly, more votes are needed to elect a director. Sometimes it is desirable to *change the state of incorporation.* Charter rules differ state by state, and many companies like to incorporate in a state with few limitations, such as Delaware. By so doing, it is easier for the corporation to install antitakeover amendments as well as to defend itself legally if a takeover battle ensues. Some companies put into place a *super-majority merger approval provision.* Instead of an ordinary majority being needed for approval of a merger, a higher percentage is required, often two-thirds. The percentage may be even higher; 80 percent is used in a number of instances. The ability to install this provision depends on the state of incorporation.

Another device is a *fair merger price provision.* Here the bidder must pay noncontrolling stockholders a price at least equal to a "fair price," which is established in advance. Usually this minimum price is linked to earnings per share through a price/earnings ratio, but it may simply be a stated market price. Often the fair price provision is coupled with a *supermajority provision.* If the stated minimum price is not satisfied, the combination can only be approved if a supermajority of stockholders are in favor. It also is frequently accompanied with a *freeze-out provision,* which allows the transaction to proceed, at a "fair price," only after a delay of between two and five years.

To discourage potential acquirers, some companies instigate a distribution of rights to stockholders, allowing them to purchase a new series of securities, often convertible preferred stock. However, the security offering is triggered only if an outside party acquires some percentage, frequently 20 percent, of the company's stock. The idea is to have available a security offering that is unpalatable to the acquirer. This can be with respect to voting rights, with respect to a low exercise price paid for the security (a bargain), or with

[15] See Harry DeAngelo and Edward M. Rice, "Antitakeover Charter Amendments and Stockholder Wealth," *Journal of Financial Economics,* 11 (April 1983), 329–60; Scott C. Linn and John J. McConnell, "An Empirical Investigation of the Impact of Antitakeover Amendments on Common Stock Prices," *Journal of Financial Economics,* 11 (April 1983), 361–99; Michael C. Jensen, "The Takeover Controversy: Analysis and Evidence," *Midland Corporate Finance Journal,* 4 (Summer 1986); and Gregg A. Jarrell and Annette B. Poulsen, "Shark Repellents and Stock Prices," *Journal of Financial Economics,* 19 (September 1987), 127–68, for a discussion of these hypotheses, various antitakeover devices, and empirical evidence concerning them.

respect to precluding a control transaction unless a substantial premium, often several hundred percent, is paid. Known as a *poison pill*, the provision is meant to force the potential acquirer into negotiating directly with the board of directors. The board reserves the ability to redeem the rights at any time for a token amount. Thus, the poison pill puts power in the hands of the board to dissuade a takeover, which may or may not be in the interest of stockholders overall.

A *lock-up provision* is used in conjunction with other provisions. This provision requires supermajority stockholder approval to modify the corporate charter and any previously passed antitakeover provisions. In addition to these charter amendments, many companies enter into *management contracts* with their top management. Typically, high compensation is triggered if the company is taken over. Known as a "golden parachute," these contracts effectively increase the price the acquiring company must pay in an unfriendly takeover. Their nuisance value may serve as a deterrent, but golden parachutes are so common that most acquiring companies have grown used to coping with them.

Despite these devices, outside groups do acquire blocks of stock in a corporation preparatory to either a takeover attempt or the sale of their stock to someone else who poses such a threat. Indication of unusual accumulation of stock comes from watching trading volume and stock transfers. If a group acquires more than 5 percent of a company, it is required to file a *13-D form* with the Securities and Exchange Commission. This form describes the people involved with the group, its holdings, and its intention. The standard response to the last is "we bought it only as an investment," so little information is really conveyed. Each time the group acquires an additional 1 percent of the stock, it must file an amendment to the 13-D form. Therefore, a company can accurately track the amount of stock accumulated.

Sometimes the company will negotiate a *standstill agreement* with the outside party. Such an agreement is a voluntary contract where, for a period of several years, the substantial stockholder group agrees not to increase its stock holdings. Often this limitation is expressed as a maximum percentage of stock the group may own. The agreement also specifies that the group will not participate in a control contest against management and that it gives the right of first refusal to the company if it should decide to sell its stock. For this agreement, the group often negotiates a premium if the stock is sold to the company. The standstill agreement, together with the other provisions discussed, serves to reduce competition for corporate control. For the most part, legal obstacles have not proven particularly effective in thwarting takeovers, so we must not make too much of them. Whether they are in the interests of stockholders is taken up in the next section, where we review the empirical evidence.

As a last resort, some companies make a *premium buy-back* offer to the threatening party. As the name implies, the repurchase of stock is at a premium over its market price and usually is in excess of what the accumulator paid. Moreover, the offer is not extended to other stockholders. Known as *greenmail*, the idea is to get the threatening party off management's back by making it attractive for the party to leave. Of course the premium paid to one party may work to the disadvantage of stockholders left "holding the bag."

Takeover Defenses and the Courts.   Whether defensive devices work for the besieged company depends in some measure on the courts. When confronted with a hostile takeover or the potential for such, a board of directors must be guided by the legal environment in which it finds itself. Doctrines of behavior involve rules of *business judgment, intrinsic fairness,* and *proportionality.* The first is that the board acts in the interests of shareholders and exercises good business judgment when it comes to a bid or to the instigation of antitakeover devices. Taken to the extreme, it says management and the board can "just say no," a defense associated with Martin Lipton, the famous attorney.[16] The second notion is that the board acts in a way that is fair to all parties, in particular to its shareholders.

The rule of proportionality is that a company's response to a takeover threat must be proportional, with respect to value, to the threat itself. For the most part, this rule has revolved around the poison pill. If an acquirer makes an offer conditional on an existing pill being removed, the company under attack must eliminate its pill or the response will be construed as not being proportional.

The principal state in which companies are incorporated is Delaware. In the 1980s and in 1990, the Delaware Supreme Court and Chancery Court made some landmark rulings: *Moran v. Household; Unocal v. Mesa Petroleum; Interco;* and *Paramount v. Time Warner.* The first case affirmed the use of the poison pill under the business-judgment rule. The *Unocal* decision established the rule of proportionality, which was a blow to the poison pill because it had to be redeemed when under attack. The *Interco* decision upheld the proportionality rule. Finally, the *Time Warner* decision cast doubt on proportionality. It did not overturn the rule but made it ambiguous. Perhaps future cases will resolve the uncertainty, but recently the tilt has been toward management entrenchment.

While Delaware law is the most important, as nearly half of the NYSE companies are incorporated there, companies do incorporate elsewhere. For them, other laws and rulings regulate corporate takeovers. In the 1980s, a number of state courts seemed to shift toward less protection of incumbent management. However, Indiana, Minnesota, and Pennsylvania promulgated laws making hostile takeovers difficult and limiting the personal liability of officers and directors. The purpose seemed to be to preserve employment in the state as well as the independence of local companies. Thus, the legal environment differs according to the state of incorporation.[17]

EMPIRICAL EVIDENCE ON MERGERS AND TAKEOVERS

In recent years, there have been a number of empirical studies on takeovers, and these studies provide a wealth of information. However, differences in samples, sample periods, and research methods render some of the valuation implications ambiguous. Nonetheless, with the ever-increasing number of

---

[16] Martin Lipton, "Corporate Governance: The Role of the Board of Directors in Takeover Bids and Defenses," *Journal of Applied Corporate Finance,* 2 (Summer 1989), 14–22.

[17] For a discussion of these issues, see Ronald J. Gilson and Reinier Kraakman, "Delaware's Intermediate Standard for Defensive Tactics: Is there Substance to Proportionality Review," *Business Lawyer,* 44 (May 1989), 247–74; Michael D. Ryngaert, "Firm Valuation, Takeover Defenses, and the Delaware Supreme Court," *Financial Management,* 18 (Autumn 1989), 20–28; Jeffrey Netter and Annette Poulsen, "State Corporation Laws and Shareholders: The Recent Experience," *Financial Management,* 18 (Autumn 1989), 29–40; and Jonathan M. Karpoff and Paul H. Malatesta, "The Wealth Effects of Second-Generation State Takeover Legislation," *Journal of Financial Economics,* 25 (December 1989), 263–90.

studies, certain patterns emerge that make generalizations possible. In this section, we review the overall evidence for valuation implications; no attempt is made to analyze the many individual empirical studies.[18] The implications can be categorized into those for target, or acquired, company stockholders and those for buying, or acquiring, company stockholders and debt holders.

TARGET COMPANY SHAREHOLDER RETURNS

For the successful, or completed, takeover, all studies show the target company stockholders realizing appreciable increments in wealth relative to the market value of their holdings prior to any takeover activity. This wealth increment is due to the premium paid by the acquiring company, the size of which has run around 30 percent on average during the last few decades. However, premiums as high as 100 percent have occurred. Moreover, there has been an upward shift in premiums over time. That is, premiums in the 1980s were nearly double what they were in the 1960s, tending to average in the 50 to 60 percent range. In part, this upward shift was due to the leveraged buyout movement, a phenomenon described in the next chapter. As this movement has abated, the 1990s saw a reduction in the average premium paid. The market price of the target company's stock tends to rise once information about a potential takeover becomes available or rumors of such develop. Typically the stock price improvement begins prior to the takeover announcement, perhaps 1 month in advance. The pattern usually observed for the target or selling company is shown in Fig. 24-4. However, it makes a difference whether the takeover is by tender offer or by merger agreement. Share price improvement usually is much greater with a tender offer than with a merger. For example, whereas share price may be 50 percent higher than the preoffer price with a tender offer, it might be only 30 percent higher with a merger. This difference is attributable to the competition and multiple bids often associated with a tender offer as opposed to merger negotiation with only one party.

For the unsuccessful takeover, the results are even more affected by whether a tender offer or a merger agreement is involved. With an unsuccess-

---

[18] Studies on which this section draws include Paul Asquith and E. Han Kim, "The Impact of Merger Bids on the Participating Firms' Security Holders," *Journal of Finance,* 37 (December 1982), 1209–28; Peter Dodd, "Merger Proposals, Management Discretion and Stockholder Wealth," *Journal of Financial Economics,* 8 (June 1980), 105–38; Michael Bradley, "Interfirm Tender Offers and the Market for Corporate Control," *Journal of Business,* 53 (September 1980), 345–76; Paul Asquith, "Merger Bids, Uncertainty, and Stockholder Returns," *Journal of Financial Economics,* 11 (April 1983), 51–84; Paul H. Malatesta, "The Wealth Effect of Merger Activity and the Objective Functions of Merging Firms," *Journal of Financial Economics,* 11 (April 1983), 155–82; Michael Bradley, Anand Desai, and E. Han Kim, "The Rationale behind Interfirm Tender Offers: Information or Synergy," *Journal of Financial Economics,* 11 (April 1983), 183–206; Michael C. Jensen, "The Takeover Controversy: Analysis and Evidence," *Midland Corporate Finance Journal,* 4 (Summer 1986), 6–32; Wayne H. Mikkelson and Richard S. Ruback, "An Empirical Analysis of the Interfirm Equity Investment Process," *Journal of Financial Economics,* 14 (December 1985), 523–54; Debra K. Dennis and John J. McConnell, "Corporate Mergers and Security Returns," *Journal of Financial Economics,* 16 (June 1986), 143–88; Julian R. Franks and Robert S. Harris, "Shareholder Wealth Effects of Corporate Takeovers: The UK Experience," *Journal of Financial Economics,* 23 (August 1989), 225–50; Bernard S. Black and Joseph A. Gundfest, "Shareholder Gains from Takeovers and Restructurings," *Journal of Applied Corporate Finance,* 1 (Spring 1988), 5–15; Kevin S. Nathan and Terrence B. O'Keefe, "The Rise in Takeover Premiums: An Exploratory Study," *Journal of Financial Economics,* 23 (June 1989), 101–20; and Greg A. Jarrell and Annette B. Poulsen, "The Returns to Acquiring Firms in Tender Offers: Evidence from Three Decades," *Financial Management,* 18 (Autumn 1989), 12–19.

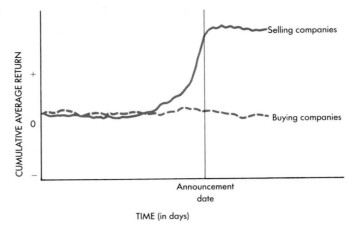

FIGURE 24-4
Relative stock returns around a successful takeover

ful tender offer, the target company's share price typically remains high after the failure announcement. The reason is the prospect of future tender offers that will enhance share price. If no subsequent acquisition attempts occur, share price usually slips and may even fall back as far as the preoffer level. If subsequent bids occur, however, share price of the target company may show further improvement. For the unsuccessful takeover, share price tends to fall quickly to its preoffer level, after the failure becomes evident. In summary, target company stockholders realize substantial gains in a successful takeover, more for a tender offer than for a merger. For the unsuccessful takeover, share price falls back toward the preoffer level unless there is a subsequent bid.

ACQUIRING COMPANY STOCKHOLDER RETURNS

For the buying, or acquiring, company, the evidence is less clear. In all cases of a successful takeover, a premium obviously is paid, and its justification must be expected synergy and/or more efficient management of the resources of the target company. The question is whether likely synergy and/or improved management will result in a wealth increment sufficient to offset the premium. Answers to this question from empirical studies are mixed. Some studies suggest stockholders of acquiring firms obtain a small improvement in share price while others find no effect at all. The situation of no effect is illustrated in Fig. 24-4. Still others find that stockholders of acquiring companies earn negative returns, holding constant other factors. The small negative returns observed were found in the 1980s, but not in earlier decades. They could be due to sampling biases.

Another explanation, of course, is that acquiring companies simply pay too much. This would agree with the hubris hypothesis, which predicts a decrease in value of the acquiring firm. In other words, potential synergy and management improvement are not enough to offset the premium paid. In certain bidding wars, the frenzy is such that rational decision making seems to disappear. In some contests, the quest of the prize is so important that the premium is bid up beyond what synergy and/or improved management will justify. This is fueled in part by investment bankers who earn ever more handsome fees the greater the price paid. One of the problems in testing is the fact that the typical acquiring firm is many times larger than the typical target firm. The return to the acquiring firm's stockholders, either positive or negative, may be hidden in statistical noise. Still, the fact that some studies show negative post-takeover returns should give acquiring companies pause for concern.

In summary, the evidence on returns to stockholders of acquiring companies is mixed. It is difficult to make an overall case for takeovers being a thing of value to the stockholders of the acquiring company. Clearly, some acquisitions are worthwhile, because of synergy and managerial improvement, and some are bad. The key for the financial manager is to be careful because, on average, a case cannot be made for corporations overall making consistently good acquisitions. For the acquired and the acquiring companies collectively, there is an increment in wealth associated with takeovers. This is primarily the result of the premium paid to the selling company's stockholders. As long as it is not offset by a significant decline in share price of the acquiring company, wealth overall is increased.

When the bidder does not acquire the target but instead its stock position is bought out, the outcome is different. If the investment is repurchased by the target company (greenmail) or the shares are sold to a third party, stockholders of the acquiring company tend to be rewarded with positive abnormal returns.[19]

OTHER SECURITY HOLDER RETURNS

There have been only a limited number of studies dealing with what happens to debt instrument returns around the time of a merger.[20] The results suggest that nonconvertible debt holders neither gain nor lose in a merger. For both acquiring and acquired companies, the abnormal returns at the time of the merger announcement do not differ significantly from zero. Therefore, the wealth transfer hypothesis, which suggests bondholders gain with a merger because of diversification leading to a reduction in default risk, is not supported. A merger not involving substantial changes in leverage must be distinguished from a highly levered transaction, such as a leveraged buyout. Whether existing bondholders suffer in such a transaction is a topic for the next chapter.

TAKEOVERS AND PRODUCTIVITY

Most empirical evidence on takeovers has involved event studies of target and acquiring company security returns around the time of the announcement. The effect on overall societal wealth is seldom examined. Andrei Shleifer and Lawrence H. Summers argue that what passes as value creation for stockholders may be value redistribution from other stakeholders—lower wages or layoffs for employees, lower prices or renegotiated contracts for suppliers, lower tax revenues for the government, and adverse community

---

[19] Mikkelson and Ruback, "An Empirical Analysis of the Interfirm Equity Investment Process."

[20] Asquith and Kim, "The Impact of Merger Bids on the Participating Firms' Security Holders"; E. Han Kim and John J. McConnell, "Corporate Merger and the Co-insurance of Corporate Debt," *Journal of Finance*, 32 (May 1977), 349–65; and Dennis and McConnell, "Corporate Mergers and Security Returns."

effects.[21] They argue that takeovers abrogate implicit contracts with stakeholders. However, others argue that this is not so, and that there is a net creation of wealth due to productivity gains.

Shedding light on the matter, Frank R. Lichtenberg and Donald Siegel examine the productivity of some 19,000 relatively large manufacturing plants, 21 percent of which changed ownership.[22] They found that the beforehand productivity of plants that changed ownership was 3.2 percent lower than that of plants that did not. After the change in ownership, the productivity gap shrank progressively. By 7 years after the control change, the gap had fallen to −1.2 percent. This appeared not to be at the expense of workers, as labor input increased on average after the change in control. However, administrative personnel experienced sharp declines in employment following the ownership change. The authors conclude that takeovers and other ownership changes are associated with higher productivity and are in the interest of society.

EFFECT OF ANTITAKEOVER DEVICES

There have been various tests of antitakeover devices, usually in conjunction with the two hypotheses discussed earlier. The managerial entrenchment hypothesis works to the detriment of present stockholders. The stockholders interest hypothesis holds that antitakeover devices benefit stockholders in ensuring management's attention to the profit-generating affairs of the company as well as giving individual stockholders a greater incentive to hold out for a high price, thereby benefiting all stockholders. The empirical evidence, which uses event study analysis, shows that for some of the devices there is a negative share price effect accompanying the announcement.[23] The effectiveness of shark repellents, of course, depends importantly on the legal environment, previously discussed.

It appears that the use of standstill agreements has a negative effect on stockholder returns, holding other things constant.[24] In addition, stock repurchase by the company from a large block owner (greenmail) appears to hurt nonparticipating stockholders around the time of the announcement.[25] However, where control subsequently changes hands, stockholders in the corpora-

[21] Andrei Shleifer and Lawrence H. Summers, "Breach of Trust in Hostile Takeovers," *Corporate Takeovers: Causes and Consequences*, Alan J. Auerbach, ed. (Chicago: University of Chicago Press, 1988). They undertook case studies of Carl Icahn and TWA and of Youngstown Sheet & Tube, which they claim support their redistribution hypothesis.

[22] Frank R. Lichtenberg and Donald Siegel, "The Effect of Control Changes on the Productivity of U.S. Manufacturing Plants," *Journal of Applied Corporate Finance*, 2 (Summer 1989), 60–67. A similar conclusion is reached by Paul M. Healy, Krishna G. Palepu, and Richard S. Ruback, "Does Corporate Performance Improve after Mergers?" working paper, National Bureau of Economic Research (May 1990).

[23] The evidence is not one sided, as a number of studies show inconclusive results. See DeAngelo and Rice, "Antitakeover Charter Amendments and Stockholders Returns"; Linn and McConnell, "An Empirical Investigation of the Impact of Antitakeover Amendments on Common Stock Prices"; and Jarrell and Poulsen, "Shark Repellents and Stock Prices."

[24] See Dann and DeAngelo, "Standstill Agreements, Privately Negotiated Stock Repurchases, and the Market for Corporate Control"; and Wayne H. Mikkelson and Richard S. Ruback, "Target Repurchases and Common Stock Returns," research paper, Massachusetts Institute of Technology (June 1986).

[25] Michael Bradley and L. Macdonald Wakeman, "The Wealth Effects of Targeted Share Repurchases," *Journal of Financial Economics*, 11 (April 1983), 301–28; and Mikkelson and Ruback, op. cit.

tion that yields to greenmail enjoy positive abnormal returns. A lot depends on previous information embedded in the stock price. In essence, the block stockholder is treated differently from others, and there is a wealth transfer away from nonparticipating stockholders. Such repurchases are for the purpose of eliminating the threat of a takeover. Both of these results are consistent, of course, with the managerial entrenchment hypothesis.

Finally, the use of a poison pill appears to have a negative, though modest, effect on share price around the time of the announcement.[26] Companies that adopt poison pill defenses have been found to be less profitable than other firms in the industry. These results are consistent with a managerial entrenchment hypothesis.

SUMMARY

The market for corporate control is one where various management teams compete to gain control of corporate resources, hoping to put them to more productive uses. One company may acquire another through the purchase of its assets or its stock, and payment can be cash or stock. Whether a combination is taxable or tax free is highly consequential to the selling company and its stockholders and, sometimes, to the buying company. Accounting considerations come into play in that the merger must be treated either as a purchase or as a pooling of interests. In a purchase, any goodwill arising from the merger must be amortized against future earnings.

Whenever two companies exchange stock, certain financial relationships come into prominence. Some companies focus on the impact on earnings per share. When the price/earnings ratio of the company being acquired is lower than the price/earnings ratio of the acquiring company, there is an initial improvement in earnings per share of the latter company; a dilution occurs when the price/earnings ratio is higher. Instead of looking only at the effect on initial earnings per share, it is desirable to look at the effect on expected future earnings per share as well. In efficient financial markets and in the absence of synergism, we would expect the price/earnings ratio of the surviving company to be a weighted average of the price/earnings ratios of the two pre-merger companies.

The foundations for value creation through a merger are several. Sales enhancement, operating economies, economies of scale, and more effective management may give rise to synergy. Moreover, there may be an information effect, leading to the correction of an undervalued situation. Tax effects can lead to value creation, while diversification tends to benefit debt holders in having a more creditworthy claim. If this is the case, there may be a wealth transfer from equity holders to debt holders when a merger occurs. The hubris hypothesis is that acquirers become irrational in bidding wars and pay too much. Finally, personal motives of the owners of a company being sold or of the management of the acquiring company may be a reason for a merger.

Corporate voting determines who will be successful in a merger skir-

[26] Paul H. Malatesta and Ralph A. Walking, "Poison Pill Securities," *Journal of Financial Economics*, 20 (January/March 1988), 347–76; and Michael Ryngaert, "The Effect of Poison Pill Securities on Shareholder Wealth," *Journal of Financial Economics*, 20 (January/March 1988), 377–417.

mish. Common stockholders elect the board of directors by proxy. These directors can be elected under a majority voting system or a cumulative voting one, the latter allowing minority interests to gain board membership. The use of different classes of common stock permits promoters and management of a corporation to retain voting control. Proxy contests are one means by which outsiders can seize corporate control. More prevalent is the tender offer to purchase shares directly from the stockholders of that company. A number of antitakeover devices exist, and they were explored, as were defenses against the takeover and the legal environment in which they hold.

Certain empirical evidence indicates substantial excess returns to the stockholders of the selling company if the merger or tender offer is successful. If it fails, share price falls back to the preoffer level unless, in the case of a tender offer, there is a subsequent bid. For the acquiring company stockholders, the evidence is mixed. It is hard to make a case for positive excess returns to buying company stockholders, and some recent studies show negative excess returns. Although there has been little direct study of productivity gains accompanying an acquisition, limited evidence suggests there may be some. Using event-time analysis, modest negative share price effects have been found around the announcement of some antitakeover amendments.

SELF-CORRECTION PROBLEMS

1. Yablonski Cordage Company is considering the acquisition of Yawitz Wire and Mesh Corporation with stock. Relevant financial information is as follows:

	YABLONSKI	YAWITZ
Present earnings (in thousands)	$4,000	$1,000
Common shares (in thousands)	2,000	800
Earnings per share	$2.00	$1.25
Price/earnings ratio	12X	8X

Yablonski plans to offer a premium of 20 percent over the market price of Yawitz stock.

a. What is the ratio of exchange of stock? How many new shares will be issued?

b. What are earnings per share for the surviving company immediately following the merger?

c. If the price/earnings ratio stays at 12 times, what is the market price per share of the surviving company? What would happen if it went to 11 times?

2. Karoo Company has merged into Sandoz Pharmacies, Inc., where $1\frac{1}{2}$ shares of Sandoz were exchanged for each share of Karoo. The balance sheets of the two companies before the merger were as follows (in millions):

	KAROO	SANDOZ
Current assets	$ 5	$20
Fixed assets	7	30
Goodwill	0	2
Total assets	$12	$52
Current liabilities	3	9
Long-term debt	2	15
Shareholders' equity	7	28
Total	$12	$52
Number of shares (in millions)	.2	1.4
Market value per share	$35	$28

The fair market value of Karoo's fixed assets is $400,000 higher than their book value. Construct the balance sheets for the company after the merger using the purchase and pooling of interests methods of accounting.

3. Aggressive Incorporated wishes to make a tender offer for the Passive Company. Passive has 100,000 shares of common stock outstanding and earns $5.50 per share. If it were combined with Aggressive, total economies of $1.5 million could be realized. Presently the market price per share of Passive is $55. Aggressive makes a two-tier tender offer: (1) $65 per share for the first 50,001 shares tendered and (2) $50 per share for the remaining shares.

a. If successful, what will Aggressive end up paying for Passive? How much incrementally will stockholders of Passive receive for the economies?

b. Acting independently, what will each stockholder do to maximize his or her wealth? What might they do if they could respond collectively as a cartel?

c. How can a company increase the probability of individual stockholders resisting too low a tender offer?

d. What might happen if Aggressive offered $65 in the first tier and only $40 in the second tier?

PROBLEMS

1. The following data are pertinent for companies A and B:

	COMPANY A	COMPANY B
Present earnings (in millions)	$20	$ 4
Shares (in millions)	10	1
Price/earnings ratio	18X	10X

a. If the two companies were to merge and the exchange ratio were one share of company A for each share of company B, what would be the initial impact on earnings per share of the two companies? What is the market-value exchange ratio? Is a merger likely to take place?

b. If the exchange ratio were two shares of company A for each share of company B, what would happen with respect to part a?

c. If the exchange ratio were 1.5 shares of company A for each share of company B, what would happen?

d. What exchange ratio would you suggest?

2.

	NET INCOME	NUMBER OF SHARES	MARKET PRICE PER SHARE	TAX RATE
Nimbus Company	$5,000,000	1,000,000	$100	50%
Noor Company	1,000,000	500,000	20	50

The Nimbus Company wishes to acquire the Noor Company. If the merger were effected through an exchange of stock, Nimbus would be willing to pay a 25 percent premium for the Noor shares. If done for cash, the terms would have to be as favorable to the Noor shareholders. To obtain the cash, Nimbus would have to sell its own stock in the market.

a. Compute the combined earnings per share for an exchange of stock.

b. If we assume that all Noor shareholders have held their stock for more than 1 year, have a 20 percent marginal capital gains tax rate, and paid an average of $14 for their shares, what cash price would have to be offered to be as attractive as the terms in part a? (Assume that Noor shareholders equate value per share in cash after capital gains taxes with value per share in Nimbus stock.)

3. Assume the exchange of Nimbus shares for Noor shares as outlined in Problem 2.

a. What is the ratio of exchange?

b. Compare the earnings per Noor share before and after the merger. Compare the earnings per Nimbus share. On this basis alone, which group fared better? Why?

c. Why do you imagine that old Nimbus commanded a higher P/E than Noor? What should be the change in P/E ratio resulting from the merger?

d. If the Nimbus Company were in a high-technology growth industry and Noor made cement, would you revise your answers?

e. In determining the appropriate P/E ratio for Nimbus, should the increase in earnings resulting from this merger be added as a growth factor?

f. In light of the foregoing discussion, do you feel that the Noor shareholders would have approved the merger if Noor stock paid a $1 dividend and Nimbus paid $3? Why?

4. Biggo Stores, Inc. (BSI), has acquired the Nail It, Glue It, and Screw It Hardware Company (NGS) for $4 million in stock and the assumption of $2 million in NGS liabilities. The balance sheets of the two companies before the merger were

	BSI	NGS
Tangible and total assets	$10.0 million	$5.0 million
Liabilities	4.0	2.0
Shareholders' equity	6.0	3.0

Determine the balance sheet of the combined company after the merger under the purchase and pooling of interests methods of accounting.

5. Copper Tube Company currently has annual earnings of $10 million, with 4 million shares of common stock outstanding and a market price per share of $30. In

the absence of any mergers, Copper Tube's annual earnings are expected to grow at a compound rate of 5 percent per annum. Brass Fitting Company, which Copper Tube is seeking to acquire, has present annual earnings of $2 million, 1 million shares of common outstanding, and a market price per share of $36. Its annual earnings are expected to grow at a compound annual rate of 10 percent per annum. Copper Tube will offer 1.2 shares of its stock for each share of Brass Fitting Company. No synergistic effects are expected from the merger.

   a. What is the immediate effect on the surviving company's earnings per share?

   b. Would you want to acquire Brass Fitting Company? If it is not attractive now, when will it be attractive from the standpoint of earnings per share?

6. D. Sent, a disgruntled stockholder of the Zebec Corporation, desires representation on the board. The Zebec Corporation, which has ten directors, has 1 million shares outstanding.

   a. How many shares would Sent have to control to be assured of one directorship under a majority voting system?

   b. Recompute part a, assuming a cumulative voting system.

   c. Recompute parts a and b, assuming the number of directors was reduced to five.

7. Joe Miller has formed a company that can earn a 12 percent return after taxes, although no investment has yet been made. Joe plans to take $1 million in $1 par value stock for his promotion efforts. All financing for the firm will be in stock, and all earnings will be paid in dividends.

   a. Joe desires to keep 50 percent control of the company after he has acquired new financing. He can do this by taking his stock in the form of $1 par value, class B, with two votes per share, while selling $1 par value class A stock. The investors, however, would require a dividend formula that would give them a 10 percent dividend return. How many class A shares would be issued? What dividend formula would meet the investors' requirements? What dividend payment would be left for Joe's class B shares?

   b. If Joe were willing to accept one share—one vote, he could have just one class of common stock and sell the same amount of class A stock as in part a. The investors would require only an 8 percent rate of return. What would be the dividend distribution in this case? Comparing this answer with that obtained in part a, what is Joe paying to retain control?

   c. Rework part b under the assumption that the investors require a 9 percent dividend return. What happens to Joe?

8. Friday Harbor Lime Company presently sells for $24 per share. Management, together with their families, control 40 percent of the 1 million shares outstanding. Roche Cement Company wishes to acquire Friday Harbor Lime because of likely synergies. The estimated present value of these synergies is $8 million. Moreover, Roche Cement Company feels that management of Friday Harbor Lime is overpaid and "overperked." It feels that with better management motivation, lower salaries, and fewer perks for controlling management, including the disposition of two yachts, approximately $400,000 per year in expenses can be saved. This would add $3 million in value to the acquisition.

   a. What is the maximum price per share that Roche Cement Company can afford to pay for Friday Harbor Lime Company?

   b. At what price per share will the management of Friday Harbor Lime be indifferent to giving up the present value of their private control benefits?

   c. What price per share would you offer?

9. Collect data on situations in which one company made a tender offer for the shares of another, and management hurriedly conducted negotiations with a third company. Compare the terms of the two offers, especially the price of the offer. Did the offer endorsed by management always bear the highest price? Should this not be the case under the theory? Examine the other terms of the offers, including employment contracts, options, bonuses, and retirement provisions. Correlate management's endorsement with

   a. Offers having the highest price, and then

b.   Offers having the most favorable employment terms

Which correlation is higher? Why? Finally, determine which offer was accepted by the stockholders. Correlate this with (1) those having the highest price and (2) those endorsed by management. Which correlation is higher? Why?

SOLUTIONS TO SELF-CORRECTION PROBLEMS

1.   a.

	YABLONSKI	YAWITZ
Earnings per share	$2.00	$1.25
Price/earnings ratio	12X	8X
Market price per share	$24	$10

Offer to Yawitz shareholders in Yablonski stock (including the premium) = $10 × 1.20 = $12 per share

Exchange ratio = $12/$24 = .5, or one-half share of Yablonski stock for every share of Yawitz stock

Number of new shares issued = 800,000 shares × .5 = 400,000 shares

b.

Surviving company earnings (in thousands)	$5,000
Common shares (in thousands)	2,400
Earnings per share	$2.0833

There is an increase in earnings per share by virtue of acquiring a company with a lower price/earnings ratio.

c.   Market price per share $2.0833 × 12 = $25.00
     Market price per share $2.0833 × 11 = $22.92

In the first instance, share price rises, from $24, due to the increase in earnings per share. In the second case, share price falls owing to the decline in the price/earnings ratio. In efficient markets, we might expect some decline in price/earnings ratio if there was not likely to be synergy and/or improved management.

2.   With an exchange ratio of $1\frac{1}{2}$, Sandoz would issue 300,000 new shares of stock with a market value of $28 × 300,000 = $8.4 million for the stock of Karoo. This exceeds the net worth of Karoo by $1.4 million. With the purchase method, Karoo's fixed assets will be written up by $400,000 and goodwill of Sandoz by $1 million. This does not happen, of course, with a pooling of interests. The balance sheets after the merger under the two methods of accounting are (in millions)

	PURCHASE	POOLING OF INTERESTS
Current assets	$25.0	$25.0
Fixed assets	37.4	37.0
Goodwill	3.0	2.0
Total	$65.4	$64.0
Current liabilities	$12.0	$12.0
Long-term debt	17.0	17.0
Shareholders' equity	36.4	35.0
Total	$65.4	$64.0

3. a.

$$
\begin{aligned}
50{,}001 \text{ shares} \times \$65 &= \$3{,}250{,}065 \\
49{,}999 \text{ shares} \times \$50 &= \underline{\ \ 2{,}499{,}950} \\
\text{Total purchase price} &= \$5{,}750{,}015 \\
\text{Total value of stock before} = 100{,}000 \text{ shares} \times \$55 &= \underline{\ \ 5{,}500{,}000} \\
\text{Increment to Passive stockholders} &= \$\ \ \ \ 250{,}015
\end{aligned}
$$

The total value of the economies to be realized is $1,500,000. Therefore, Passive stockholders receive only a modest portion of the total value of the economies; in contrast, Aggressive stockholders obtain a large share.

b. With a two-tier offer, there is a great incentive for individual stockholders to tender early, thereby ensuring success for the acquiring firm. Collectively, Passive stockholders would be better off holding out for a larger fraction of the total value of the economies. They can do this only if they act as a cartel in their response to the offer.

c. By instigating antitakeover amendments and devices, some incentives may be created for individual stockholders to hold out for a higher offer. However, in practice, it is impossible to achieve a complete cartel response.

d.

$$
\begin{aligned}
50{,}000 \text{ shares} \times \$65 &= \$3{,}250{,}065 \\
49{,}999 \text{ shares} \times \$40 &= \underline{\ \ 1{,}999{,}960} \\
\text{Total purchase price} &= \$5{,}250{,}025
\end{aligned}
$$

This value is lower than the previous total market value of $5,500,000. Clearly, stockholders would fare poorly if in the rush to tender shares the offer were successful. However, other potential acquirers would have an incentive to offer more than Aggressive, even with no economies to be realized. Competition among potential acquirers should ensure counterbids, so that Aggressive would be forced to bid no less than $5,500,000 in total, the present market value.

SELECTED REFERENCES

Asquith, Paul, "Merger Bids, Uncertainty, and Stockholder Returns," *Journal of Financial Economics*, 11 (April 1983), 51–84.

———, Robert F. Bruner, and David W. Mullins, Jr., "The Gains to Bidding Firms from Merger," *Journal of Financial Economics*, 11 (April 1983), 121–40.

Asquith, Paul, and E. Han Kim, "The Impact of Merger Bids on the Participating Firms' Security Holders," *Journal of Finance*, 37 (December 1982), 1209–28.

Baron, David P., "Tender Offers and Management Resistance," *Journal of Finance*, 38 (March 1983), 331–43.

Black, Bernard S., and Joseph A. Grundfest, "Shareholder Gains from Takeovers and Restructurings," *Journal of Applied Corporate Finance*, 1 (Spring 1988), 5–15.

BRADLEY, MICHAEL, ANAND DESAI, and E. HAN KIM, "The Rationale behind Interfirm Tender Offers: Information on Synergy," *Journal of Financial Economics*, 11 (April 1983), 183–206.

CARLETON, WILLARD T., DAVID K. GUILKEY, ROBERT S. HARRIS, and JOHN F. STEWART, "An Empirical Analysis of the Role of the Medium of Exchange in Mergers," *Journal of Finance*, 38 (June 1983), 813–26.

DANN, LARRY Y., and HARRY DEANGELO, "Standstill Agreements, Privately Negotiated Stock Repurchases, and the Market for Corporate Control," *Journal of Financial Economics*, 11 (April 1983), 275–300.

DEANGELO, HARRY, and LINDA DEANGELO, "Managerial Ownership of Voting Rights: A Study of Public Corporations with Dual Classes of Common Stock," *Journal of Financial Economics*, 14 (March 1985), 33–70.

DEANGELO, HARRY, and EDWARD M. RICE, "Antitakeover Charter Amendments and Stockholder Wealth," *Journal of Financial Economics*, 11 (April 1983), 329–60.

DENNIS, DEBRA K., and JOHN J. MCCONNELL, "Corporate Mergers and Security Returns," *Journal of Financial Economics*, 16 (June 1986), 143–88.

DODD, PETER, and JEROLD B. WARNER, "On Corporate Governance: A Study of Proxy Contests," *Journal of Financial Economics*, 11 (April 1983) 401–38.

ELGERS, PIETER T., and JOHN J. CLARK, "Merger Types and Shareholder Returns: Additional Evidence," *Financial Management*, 9 (Summer 1980), 66–72.

HARRIS, MILTON, and ARTUR RAVIV, "Corporate Governance," *Journal of Financial Economics*, 20 (January/March 1988), 203–35.

———, "The Design of Securities," *Journal of Financial Economics*, 24 (October 1989), 255–88.

HIGGINS, ROBERT C., and LAWRENCE D. SCHALL, "Corporate Bankruptcy and Conglomerate Merger," *Journal of Finance*, 30 (March 1975), 93–114.

JARRELL, GREGG, A., and ANNETTE B. POULSEN, "Shark Repellents and Stock Prices," *Journal of Financial Economics*, 19 (September 1987), 127–68.

———, "The Returns to Acquiring Firms in Tender Offers: Evidence from Three Decades," *Financial Management*, 18 (Autumn 1989), 12–19.

JENSEN, MICHAEL C., "The Takeover Controversy: Analysis and Evidence," *Midland Corporate Finance Journal*, 4 (Summer 1986), 6–32.

———, and RICHARD S. RUBACK, "The Market for Corporate Control: The Scientific Evidence," *Journal of Financial Economics*, 11 (April 1983), 5–50.

KIM, E. HAN, and JOHN J. MCCONNELL, "Corporate Merger and the Co-insurance of Corporate Debt," *Journal of Finance*, 32 (May 1977), 349–65.

LARSON, KERMIT D., and NICHOLAS J. GONEDES, "Business Combinations: An Exchange-Ratio Determination Model," *Accounting Review*, 44 (October 1969), 720–28.

LEASE, RONALD C., JOHN J. MCCONNELL, and WAYNE H. MIKKELSON, "The Market Value of Control in Publicly-traded Corporations," *Journal of Financial Economics*, 11 (April 1983), 439–71.

LEVY, HAIM, "Economic Evaluation of Voting Power of Common Stock," *Journal of Finance*, 38 (March 1983), 79–94.

LEWELLEN, WILBUR G., "A Pure Financial Rationale for the Conglomerate Merger," *Journal of Finance*, 26 (May 1971), 521–37.

LINN, SCOTT C., and JOHN J. MCCONNELL, "An Empirical Investigation of the Impact of Antitakeover Amendments on Common Stock Prices," *Journal of Financial Economics* 11 (April 1983), 361–99.

MCCONNELL, JOHN J., "Equity Ownership and Corporate Value," working paper, Purdue University (January 1990).

MALATESTA, PAUL H., "The Wealth Effect of Merger Activity and the Objective Functions of Merging Firms," *Journal of Financial Economics*, 11 (April 1983), 155–82.

———, and RALPH A. WALKING, "Poison Pill Securities," *Journal of Financial Economics*, 20 (January/March 1988), 347–76.

MORCK, RANDALL, ANDREI SHLEIFER, and ROBERT W. VISHNY, "Management Ownership and Market Valuation: An Empirical Analysis," *Journal of Financial Economics*, 20 (January/March 1988), 293–316.

NATHAN, KEVIN S., and TERRENCE B. O'KEEFE, "The Rise in Takeover Premiums: An Exploratory Study," *Journal of Financial Economics*, 23 (June 1989), 101–20.

PARTCH, M. MEGAN, "The Creation of a Class of Limited Voting Common Stock and Shareholder Wealth," *Journal of Financial Economics*, 18 (June 1987), 313–39.

POUND, JOHN, "Proxy Contests and the Efficiency of Shareholder Oversight," *Journal of Financial Economics*, 18 (January/March 1988), 237–65.

ROLL, RICHARD, "The Hubris Hypothesis of Corporate Takeovers," *Journal of Business*, 59 (April 1986), 197–216.

SCHOLES, MYRON S., and MARK A. WOLFSON, "The Effects of Changes in Tax Laws on Corporate Reorganization Activity," working paper, National Bureau of Economic Research (September 1989).

———, "Employee Stock Ownership Plans and Corporate Restructuring: Myths and Realities," *Financial Management*, 19 (Spring 1990), 12–28.

SHLEIFER, ANDREI, and LAWRENCE H. SUMMERS, "Breach of Trust in Hostile Takeovers," *Corporate Takeovers: Causes and Consequences*, Alan J. Auerbach, ed. Chicago: University of Chicago Press, 1988.

SHLEIFER, ANDREI, and ROBERT W. VISHNY, "Management Entrenchment: The Case of Manager-Specific Investments," *Journal of Financial Economics*, 25 (November 1989), 123–39.

SMALTER, DONALD J., and RODERIC C. LANCEY, "P/E Analysis in Acquisition Strategy," *Harvard Business Review*, 44 (November–December 1966), 85–95.

STULZ, RENE M., RALPH A. WALKING, and MOON H. SONG, "The Distribution of Target Ownership and the Division of Gains in Successful Takeovers," *Journal of Finance*, 45 (July 1990), 817–34.

WANSLEY, JAMES W., RODNEY L. ROENFELDT, and PHILIP L. COOLEY, "Abnormal Returns from Merger Profiles," *Journal of Financial and Quantitative Analysis*, 18 (June 1983), 149–62.

25

CORPORATE RESTRUCTURING

Corporate restructuring is a broad umbrella that covers many things. One thing is the merger or takeover, which we considered in the last chapter. From the standpoint of the buyer, this represents expansion, where from the perspective of the seller it represents a change in ownership that may or may not be voluntary. In addition to mergers, takeovers, and contests for corporate control, there are other types of corporate restructuring. In this chapter, we consider such things as sell-offs, spin-offs, equity carve-outs, going private, leveraged buyouts, and leveraged recapitalizations. The name *corporate restructuring* can be construed as almost any change in capital structure, in operations, or in ownership that is outside the ordinary course of business. In Table 25-1, various kinds of restructuring are listed, together with the chapters in which the topic is discussed. As shown, we already have considered

TABLE 25-1
Aspects of corporate restructuring

EXPANSION

Mergers and acquisitions (Chapters 9 and 24)
Takeovers and tender offers (Chapter 24)

DIVESTITURE AND REARRANGEMENTS

Abandoning capital assets (Chapter 7)
Liquidation and bankruptcy (Appendix to Chapter 11 and Appendix at back of book)
Sell-off of part of the enterprise (Chapter 25)
Spin-offs (Chapter 25)
Equity carveouts (Chapter 25)

OWNERSHIP RESTRUCTURING

Selling the company (Chapters 24 and 25)
Market for corporate control (Chapter 24)
Stock repurchase (Chapters 13 and 21)
Other exchange offers (Chapter 21)
Going private (Chapter 25)
Leveraged buyouts, LBOs (Chapter 25)
Leveraged recapitalizations (Chapter 25)

some of these topics in earlier chapters. Our focus now is on topics not previously discussed.

Before we begin, we must emphasize that stock repurchase often is part of an overall corporate restructuring plan. That is, excess funds that arise from accumulation, asset sales, or simply from increasing the amount of debt in capital structure are used to repurchase the company's stock. As this topic was addressed in Chapters 13 and 21, we do not take it up here. However, bear in mind that a comprehensive restructuring plan often includes stock repurchase.

DIVESTITURE IN GENERAL

As reflected in the table, there are different ways a corporation can divest itself of part or all of the enterprise. Before we get into specifics, let us reflect on the reasons for divestiture. Divestiture can be involuntary or voluntary. An involuntary divestiture usually is the result of an antitrust ruling by the government. When another company is acquired, for example, the Federal Trade Commission and/or the Justice Department sometimes will stipulate that a certain activity must be divested. Otherwise undue concentration will occur. A voluntary divestiture, on the other hand, is a willful decision by management to divest. It presumably is based on one or more reasons. What are the possible reasons? Some are efficiency gains, information effects and undervaluation, wealth transfers, and tax reasons. Whatever the reason, it is clear that the number of divestitures increased dramatically in the 1980s and so far in the 1990s. We consider each of the reasons in turn; most are familiar from the previous chapter.

EFFICIENCY GAINS

Simply put, a particular operation may be more valuable to someone else than it is to the company. With synergy in a merger, the whole is said to be greater than the sum of the parts: $2 + 2 = 5$. With a divestiture, reverse synergy may occur, such that $4 - 2 = 3$. That is, the operation may be more valuable to someone else in generating cash flows and positive net present value. As a result, that someone is willing to pay a higher price for the operation than its present value to you. In some situations, the operation may be a chronic loser, and the owner is unwilling to commit the necessary resources to make it profitable. This was the case with Borg Warner Corporation when it decided to divest itself of York International, a maker of heating and air-conditioning equipment. As in the case of abandoning a capital investment project, which we considered in Chapter 7, an operation should be sold when it no longer earns its economic keep relative to its external market value.

An allied reason for divestiture is a strategic change by the company. Periodically, most companies review their long-range plans in an effort to answer the eternal question, What businesses should we be in? Strategic considerations include internal capabilities (capital, plant, and people), the external product markets, and competitors. The market, as well as the competitive advantage of a company within a market, changes over time, sometimes very quickly. New markets emerge, as do new capabilities within the firm. What was a good fit before may no longer be a good fit. As a result, a decision may be reached to divest a particular operation. In the case of an acquisition of another company, not all of the parts may fit the strategic plan of the acquiring company. As a result, a decision may be reached to divest one or more of the parts. Strategic realignment is the most cited reason chief executive officers give for divestiture.

INFORMATION EFFECT

A second reason for divestiture may involve the information it conveys to investors. If there is asymmetric information in that management has information not known by investors, the announcement of a divestiture may have signaling implications. If the announcement is interpreted as a change in investment strategy or in operating efficiency, for example, there may be a positive effect on share price. On the other hand, if the announcement is interpreted as the sale of the most marketable subsidiary to deal with adversities elsewhere in the company, the signal will be negative. Whether a good or bad signal is conveyed depends on the circumstances.

To the extent management believes a business unit is undervalued as a part of the company's total stock value and that asymmetry in information is the culprit, the divestiture announcement may have a positive share price impact. However, information effects are tricky when it comes to perceived undervaluation. There may be effective ways to convey the subsidiary's value other than by selling it. Then again the subsidiary's worth may be properly assessed by the market, and management simply has a fixation on undervaluation.

WEALTH TRANSFERS

If a company divests a portion of the enterprise and distributes the proceeds to stockholders, there will be a wealth transfer from debt holders to stockholders. The transaction reduces the probability that the debt will be paid, and it will have a lesser value, all other things the same. If the value of the debt declines by virtue of more default risk, the value of the equity will increase, assuming the total value of the firm remains unchanged. Here equity value is composed of the value of the shares as well as the distribution to stockholders. In essence, the stockholders have "stolen away" a portion of the enterprise, thereby reducing its remaining collateral value.[1] As a result, there is a wealth transfer from debt holders to stockholders.

A variation of this theme is that of Myers, who reasons that companies with risky debt sometimes reject positive net-present-value projects.[2] The reason is that existing debt holders capture too many of the benefits through the improved creditworthiness of the company. There results a wealth transfer from equity holders to debt holders. The same behavior may occur in farming, where the heavily levered farmer is unwilling to take out crop insurance because most of the payoff goes to lenders. In the case of the corporation, suppose a subsidiary with attractive investment opportunities is divested. In this way, equity holders may be able to capture most of the positive value from investments, whereas before these investments might largely benefit debt hold-

[1] See Dan Galai and Ronald W. Masulis, "The Option Pricing Model and the Risk Factor of Stocks," *Journal of Financial Economics*, 3 (January–March 1976), 53–81.

[2] Stewart C. Myers, "Determinants of Corporate Borrowing," *Journal of Financial Economics*, 5 (November 1977), 147–76.

ers. At the margin, then, there is a wealth transfer from debt holders to equity holders.

TAX REASONS

As in mergers, sometimes tax considerations enter into a decision to divest. If a company loses money and is unable to use a tax loss carryforward, divestiture in whole or in part may be the only way to realize value from this tax benefit. In the past, assets acquired in a merger were marked up to market value in order to obtain a stepped-up basis for depreciation. However, the 1986 Tax Reform Act eliminated this advantage by treating the writeup as taxable income in the year taken.

Where corporate restructuring involves increased leverage, there is a tax shield advantage owing to interest payments being tax deductible. With a buyout, a possible tax advantage arises in the use of an employee stock ownership plan (ESOP). In the past, principal as well as interest payments on a loan were tax deductible by the ESOP. Moreover, the interest received on the loan by a financial institution was partially tax exempt. These things made the ESOP method of buyout tax advantaged.

With these four motivations in mind, let us turn to the specific divestiture techniques that are listed in Table 25-1.

VOLUNTARY LIQUIDATION OR SELL-OFFS

A *sell-off* can consist of the entire company or of some business unit, such as a subsidiary, a division, or a product line.

LIQUIDATING THE OVERALL FIRM

The decision to sell a firm in its entirety should be rooted in value creation for the stockholders. Assuming the situation does not involve financial failure, which we address in Appendix A at the back of the book, the idea is that the assets may have a higher value in liquidation than the present value of the expected cash-flow stream emanating from them. By liquidating, the seller is able to sell the assets to multiple parties, which may result in a higher value being realized than if they had to be sold as a whole, as occurs in a merger. With a complete liquidation, the debt of the company must be paid off at its face value. If the market value of the debt was previously below this, debt holders realize a wealth gain, which ultimately is at the expense of equity holders.

PARTIAL SELL-OFFS

In the case of a sell-off, only part of the company is sold. When a business unit is sold, payment generally is in the form of cash or securities. The decision should result in some positive net present value to the selling company. The key is whether the value received is more than the present value of the stream of expected future cash flows if the operation were to be continued.

This excess value may be due to one or more of the reasons taken up in the previous section.

EMPIRICAL STUDIES OF LIQUIDATIONS/SELL-OFFS

There have been a handful of empirical studies of voluntary liquidations/sell-offs. Event-study methodology is employed. In this case, the event is the announcement of the sell-off. The idea is to study daily security return behavior before and after the event. To hold constant influences other than the event, the capital asset pricing model is used to predict the daily return for the security, given the return that day for the overall market index. (This methodology was described in Chapter 24 and in earlier chapters, so we do not dwell on it here.) The predicted return then is subtracted from the actual return, and the residual is known as the abnormal return. The daily residuals then are averaged for all companies in the sample and summed over various time intervals to obtain cumulative average residuals or abnormal returns.

For liquidation of the entire company, the results indicate a large abnormal return or gain to stockholders of the liquidating company, in the range of 12 to 20 percent.[3] Companies choosing to liquidate appear to be worth more this way than as going concerns. In addition, one study (Kim-Schatzberg) found that the average beta dropped significantly upon the liquidation announcement. Once liquidation is announced, the value of the firm becomes more certain and its underlying risk decreases.

The results of partial sell-off studies indicate a slight positive (2 to 3 percent), but statistically significant, abnormal return to the seller's stock around the announcement date.[4] Thus, there appears to be positive value associated with the sell-off, as investors on average react positively to the information. In the studies, it was found that sell-offs frequently follow a period of poor performance for the seller's stock. Moreover, stockholders in the buying company also seem to experience a positive abnormal return around the time of the announcement, particularly if the business purchased is similar to that of the acquirer.[5] This evidence is consistent with there being economic gains to the sell-off. That is, the business unit is more valuable to the buyer than it is to the seller. Because of expected operating or other competitive advantages inherent in the buyer managing the business, the sell-off is viewed by investors as a positive net present value transaction. This is not to say that all sell-offs

---

[3] E. Han Kim and John D. Schatzberg, "Voluntary Corporate Liquidations," *Journal of Financial Economics*, 19 (December 1987), 311–28; Terrance R. Skantz and Roberto Marchesini, "The Effect of Voluntary Corporate Liquidation on Shareholder Wealth," *Journal of Financial Research*, 10 (Spring 1986), 65–76; and Gailen L. Hite, James E. Owers, and Ronald C. Rogers, "The Market for Interfirm Asset Sales," *Journal of Financial Economics*, 18 (June 1987), 229–52.

[4] See Gordon J. Alexander, P. George Benson, and Joan M. Kampmeyer, "Investigating the Valuation Effects of Announcements of Voluntary Selloffs," *Journal of Finance*, 39 (June 1984), 503–17; Prem C. Jain, "The Effect of Voluntary Sell-off Announcements on Shareholder Wealth," *Journal of Finance*, 40 (March 1985), 209–24; James D. Rosenfeld, "Additional Evidence on the Relation between Divestiture Announcements and Shareholder Wealth," *Journal of Finance*, 39 (December 1984), 1437–48; April Klein, "The Timing and Substance of Divestiture Announcements," *Journal of Finance*, 41 (July 1986), 685–96; Hite, Owers, and Rogers, "The Market for Interfirm Asset Sales"; Bernard S. Black and Joseph A. Grundfest, "Shareholder Gains from Takeovers and Restructurings between 1981 and 1986," *Journal of Applied Corporate Finance*, 1 (Spring 1988), 11–14.

[5] Neil W. Sicherman and Richard H. Pettway, "Acquisition of Divested Assets and Shareholders Wealth," *Journal of Finance*, 42 (December 1987), 1261–73.

will be so viewed, only that the evidence is consistent with such transactions on average being associated with excess stock returns for both the seller and the buyer.

CORPORATE SPIN-OFFS

Similar to a sell-off, a *spin-off* involves a decision to divest a business unit such as a stand-alone subsidiary or division. In a spin-off, the business unit is not sold for cash or securities. Rather, common stock in the unit is distributed to the stockholders of the company on a pro rata basis, after which the operation becomes a completely separate company with its own traded stock. There is no tax to the stockholder at the time of the spin-off; taxation occurs only when the stock is sold.

REASONS FOR SPIN-OFFS

The motivations for a spin-off are similar in some ways to those for a sell-off. In the case of a spin-off, however, another company will not operate it. Therefore, there is no opportunity for synergy in the usual sense of the term. It is possible that as an independent company with different management incentives, the operation will be better run. In this sense, an economic gain may be achieved from the transaction. However, costs are involved. New shares must be issued and there are the ongoing costs of servicing stockholders, together with new agency costs involving auditors and other monitoring devices. Thus, there is duplication of costs in having two public companies as opposed to one. The net case for economic gain is not clear.

Other reasons would appear to have more substance. The previously cited argument of a wealth transfer from debt holders to equity holders might be applicable. Moreover, the agency theory argument that with a spin-off positive net present value projects now will be accepted where previously they were rejected may also hold. Still another factor from our earlier discussion is any information concerning improved operating performance that is associated with the spin-off. It may be that there is a divergence of opinion between current owners of the company and nonowners. To the extent some nonowners think that the value of the business unit to be spun off is higher than do the current owners, the spin-off may increase value. The greater the divergence, the greater the excess return associated with the spin-off.[6]

With a spin-off, in contrast to a sell-off, the new publicly traded company may make the financial markets more complete. The opportunity set of securities available to investors is expanded, allowing more ability to invest in "pure plays." As a result, the spin-off may have scarcity value in the stock market and be accorded a premium price. This value is not reflected in the stock of the company of which the business unit is a part.

Also with a spin-off, it may be possible to obtain flexibility in contracting. With a separate operation, one sometimes can rearrange labor contracts, get out from under tax regulations, or skirt regulatory constraints that no

---

[6] See Edward M. Miller, "Risk, Uncertainty, and Divergence of Opinion," *Journal of Finance*, 32 (September 1977), 151–68. Empirical support for the Miller hypothesis is found in Ronald J. Kudla and Thomas H. McInish, "Divergence of Opinion and Corporate Spin-Offs," *Quarterly Review of Economics and Business*, 28 (Summer 1988), 20–29.

longer are directly applicable. Another type of contract involves management. With a spin-off, there is a separation of the business units management from that of the parent. As a result, it may be possible to restructure incentives in order to gain improved managerial productivity. Finally, the spin-off may permit greater flexibility in debt contracts when it comes to protective covenants imposed.[7] All of these things may influence the decision to spin off a business unit, and the valuation of the transaction.

EMPIRICAL EVIDENCE ON SPIN-OFFS

Valuation studies of corporate spin-offs involve the same event-study methodology described for sell-offs. The idea is to analyze share price behavior around the date of the announcement, holding constant other factors influencing market valuation. The studies undertaken suggest moderate, positive abnormal stock returns (5 percent or more) around the announcement date.[8] On average, the cumulative abnormal return associated with the spin-off was larger than that associated with the sell-off discussed in the last section. When, in some of the studies, the samples were partitioned, the evidence was consistent with contractual flexibility. In addition, the expectation of improved management efficiency was supported in one study. However, the evidence was not consistent with a wealth transfer from debt holders to equity holders. On balance, there appears to be a significant and positive information effect to the spin-off announcement.

EQUITY CARVEOUTS

An *equity carveout* is similar in some ways to the two previous forms of divestiture. However, common stock in the business unit is sold to the public. The initial public offering of the subsidiary's stock usually involves only some of it. Typically, the parent continues to have an equity stake in the subsidiary and does not relinquish control. Under these circumstances, a minority interest is sold and the carveout represents a form of equity financing. The difference between it and the parent selling stock under its own name is that the claim is on the subsidiary's cash flows and assets. For the first time, the value of the subsidiary becomes observable in the marketplace. Examples of equity carveouts include McKesson Corporation's public offering of 17 percent of the shares of Armor All Products, a maker of vinyl and leather treatments, and General Motors' offering of GM "E" shares in its EDS subsidiary.

One motivation for the equity carveout is that with a separate stock price and public trading, managers may have more incentive to perform well. For one thing, the size of the operation is such that their efforts will not go unno-

---

[7] For an analysis of these various reasons, see Katherine Schipper and Abbie Smith, "Effects of Recontracting on Shareholder Wealth," *Journal of Financial Economics*, 12 (December 1983), 437–67.

[8] See ibid.; Gailen L. Hite and James E. Owers, "Security Price Reactions around Corporate Spin-off Announcements," *Journal of Financial Economics*, 12 (December 1983), 409–36; James D. Rosenfeld, "Additional Evidence on the Relation between Divestiture Announcements and Shareholder Wealth," *Journal of Finance*, 39 (December 1984), 1437–48; James A. Miles and James D. Rosenfeld, "The Effect of Voluntary Spin-off Announcements on Shareholder Wealth," *Journal of Finance*, 38 (December 1983), 1597–1606; and Thomas E. Copeland, Eduardo F. Lemgruber, and David Mayers, "Corporate Spinoffs: Multiple Announcement and Ex-Date Abnormal Performance," research paper, University of California, Los Angeles (June 1986).

ticed, as they sometimes do in a large, multibusiness company. With separate stock options, it may be possible to attract and retain better managers and to motivate them. Also, information about the subsidiary is more readily available. In turn, this may reduce asymmetric information between managers and investors and cause the subsidiary's worth to be more accurately assessed by the marketplace. By being able to finance separately from the parent, there may be a greater inclination to accept positive net-present-value projects as opposed to forgoing some of them because the relative benefits to debt holders are too high.

Some suggest that the equity carveout is a favorable means for financing growth. When the subsidiary is in leading edge technology but not particularly profitable, the equity carveout may be a more effective vehicle for financing than is financing through the parent. With a separate subsidiary, the market may become more complete because investors are able to obtain a "pure play" investment in the technology.

There has been little empirical testing of equity carveouts. The one thorough study is by Schipper and Smith, and they used the event-study methodology previously described.[9] The authors found a moderate, positive (1.8 percent) abnormal return around the announcement date. On average, then, there is a positive information effect associated with the equity carveout announcement. The reasons could be any one or combination of those discussed. In the sample survey, the authors find that in over 90 percent of the cases the equity carveout is accompanied by a change in incentive compensation.

In all three cases—the sell-off, the spin-off, and the equity carveout—scholars have observed a positive share price effect. The results contrast with those for the straight sale of new equity by a company. For the reasons taken up in Chapters 10 and 21, negative abnormal returns are associated with the announcement of a stock offering by a company. For the three methods of divestiture discussed, the results are positive, which indicates a different informational effect to the event.

GOING PRIVATE

A number of well-known companies have "gone private," including RJR Nabisco, Safeway Stores, and Levi Strauss & Company. Going private simply means transforming a company whose stock is publicly held into a private one. The privately held stock is owned by a small group of investors, with incumbent management usually having a large equity stake. In this ownership reorganization, a variety of vehicles are used to buy out the public stockholders. Probably the most common involves cashing them out and merging the company into a shell corporation owned solely by the private investor/management group. Rather than a merger, the transaction may be treated as an asset sale to the private group. There are other ways, but the result is the same: The company ceases to exist as a publicly held entity and the stockholders receive a valuable consideration for their shares. While most transactions involve cash, sometimes noncash compensation, such as notes, is employed.

The stockholders must agree to a company going private, and the incentive to them is the premium in price paid. Even when the majority vote in fa-

[9]Katherine Schipper and Abbie Smith, "A Comparison of Equity Carve-outs and Seasoned Equity Offerings," *Journal of Financial Economics*, 15 (January–February 1986), 153–86.

vor, other stockholders can sue, claiming the price is not high enough. Class action suits prompted by hungry lawyers also are common.

MOTIVATIONS FOR GOING PRIVATE

A number of factors may prompt management to take a company private.[10] There are costs to being a publicly held company. The stock must be registered, stockholders must be serviced, there are administrative expenses in paying dividends and sending out materials, and there are legal and administrative expenses in filing reports with the Securities and Exchange Commission and other regulators. In addition, there are annual meetings and meetings with security analysts leading to embarrassing questions that most chief executive officers would rather do without. All of these things can be avoided by being a private company.

With a publicly held company, some feel there is a fixation on quarterly accounting earnings as opposed to long-run economic earnings. To the extent decisions are directed more toward building economic value, going private may improve resource allocation decisions and thereby enhance value.

Another motivation is to realign and improve management incentives. With increased equity ownership by management, there may be an incentive to work more efficiently and longer. The money saved and the profits generated through more effective management largely benefit the company's management as opposed to a wide group of stockholders. As a result, they may be more willing to make the tough decisions, to cut costs, to reduce management "perks," and simply to work harder. The rewards are linked more closely to their decisions. The greater the performance and profitability, the greater the reward. In a publicly held company, the compensation level is not so directly linked, particularly for decisions that produce high profitablity. When compensation is extremely high, there are always questions from security analysts, stockholders, and the press.

While there are a number of reasons for going private, there are some off-setting arguments. For one thing there are transaction costs to investment bankers, lawyers, and others that can be quite substantial. A private company gives little liquidity to its owners with respect to their stock ownership. A large portion of their wealth may be tied up in the company. Management, for example, may create value for the company but be unable to realize this value unless the company goes public in the future. If the company later goes public, transaction costs are repeated—wonderful for investment bankers and lawyers but a sizable cost nonetheless.

LEVERAGED BUYOUTS

Going private can be a straight transaction, where the investor group simply buys out the public stockholders, or it can be a leveraged buyout, where there are third- and sometimes fourth-party investors. As the name implies, a leveraged buyout represents an ownership transfer consummated primarily with debt. Sometimes called asset-based financing, the debt is secured by the assets

[10] The major paper dealing with going private is by Harry DeAngelo, Linda DeAngelo, and Edward M. Rice, "Going Private: Minority Freezeouts and Stockholder Wealth," *Journal of Law and Economics*, 27 (June 1984), 367–401, where most of these motivations are discussed.

of the enterprise involved. While some leveraged buyouts involve the acquisition of an entire company, many involve the purchase of a division of a company or some other subunit. Frequently, the sale is to the management of the division being sold, the company having decided that the division no longer fits its strategic objectives. Another distinctive feature is that leveraged buyouts are cash purchases, as opposed to stock purchases. Finally, the business unit involved invariably becomes a privately held as opposed to a publicly held company.

Desirable LBO candidates have certain common characteristics. Frequently, the company has a several-year window of opportunity where major expenditures can be deferred. Often it is a company that has gone through a heavy capital expenditures program, and whose plant is modern. Companies with high R&D requirements, like drug companies, are not good LBO candidates. For the first several years, cash flows must be dedicated to debt service. Capital expenditures, R&D, advertising, and personnel development take a back seat. If the company has subsidiary assets that can be sold without adversely impacting the core business, this may be attractive. Such asset sales provide cash for debt service in the early years.

Stable, predictable operating cash flows are prized. In this regard, consumer-branded products dominate "commodity-type" businesses. Proven historical performance with an established market position means a lot. Turnaround situations tend to be spurned. The less cyclical the company or business unit, the better. A service company, where people are the franchise value, is seldom a good LBO candidate. If the people should leave, little of value remains. As a rule, the assets must be physical assets and/or brand names. Management, however, is important. The experience and quality of senior management are critical to success. While the above characteristics are not all inclusive, they give a flavor of the ingredients that make for desirable, and undesirable, LBO candidates.

AN ILLUSTRATION

To illustrate a typical leveraged buyout, suppose Alsim Corporation wishes to divest itself of its dairy products division. The assets of the division consist of plants, equipment, truck fleets, inventories, and receivables. These assets have a book value of $120 million. While their replacement value is $170 million, if the division were to be liquidated the assets would fetch only $95 million. Alsim has decided to sell the division if it can obtain $110 million in cash, and it has enlisted an investment banker to assist it in the sale. After surveying the market for such a sale, the investment banker concludes that the best prospect is to sell the division to existing management. The four top divisional officers are interested and eager to pursue the opportunity. However, they are able to come up with only $2 million in personal capital among them. More obviously is needed.

The investment banker agrees to try to arrange a leveraged buyout. Financial projections and cash budgets are prepared for the division, to determine how much debt can be serviced. On the basis of these forecasts as well as the curtailment of certain capital expenditures, research and development expenses, and advertising expenses, it is felt that the likely cash throw-off is sufficient to service approximately $100 million in debt. The reduction in expenditures is regarded as temporary for the company to service debt during the next several years. The investment banker has drawn on a limited partnership to make an additional equity investment of $13 million, bringing total equity to $15 million. For this cash contribution, the partnership is to receive 60 percent of the initial common stock, with management receiving the remainder.

ARRANGING DEBT FINANCING

With this equity capital commitment, the investment banker proceeds to arrange debt financing. In a leveraged buyout, two forms of debt typically are employed: senior debt and junior subordinated debt. For the senior debt, a large New York bank, through its asset-based lending subsidiary, has agreed to provide $70 million toward the cost plus an additional $8 million revolving credit for seasonal needs. The rate on both arrangements is 2 percent over the prime rate, and the loans are secured by liens on all the assets—real estate, buildings, equipment, rolling stock, inventories, and receivables. The term of the $70 million loan is 6 years, and it is payable in equal monthly installments of principal with interest for the month being added on. All major banking will be with the bank, and company receipts will be deposited into a special account at the bank for purposes of servicing the debt. In addition to the collateral, the usual protective covenants are imposed in a loan agreement.

Junior subordinated debt in the amount of $25 million has been arranged with the merger-funding subsidiary of a large finance company. This debt sometimes is referred to as "mezzanine-layer" financing, as it falls between senior debt and the equity. The loan is for 7 years with an interest rate of 13 percent being fixed throughout. Only monthly interest payments are required during the 7 years, the full principal amount being due at the end. As the senior lender will have liens on all assests, the debt is unsecured and subordinated to the senior debt as well as to trade creditors. For this subordinated financing, the lender receives warrants exercisable for 40 percent of the stock. These warrants may be exercised any time throughout the 7 years at a price of $1 per share, quite nominal. If exercised, management's stock will go from 40 percent of the total outstanding to 24 percent, and the limited partnership from 60 percent to 36 percent. To recapitulate, the financing is as follows:

Senior debt	$70 million
Junior subordinated debt	25
Equity	15
	$110 million

In addition, the company will have access to an $8 million revolving credit for seasonal needs.

The mezzanine layer of financing fills the gap between what senior lenders are willing to provide and what equity holders/management are able to commit. Because of the highly levered nature of the transaction, mezzanine debt invariably is rated speculative grade, Ba or lower (junk bonds). Expected returns, including the exercise of stock warrants or other equity participation, are in the 20 to 30 percent per annum range. The security itself is illiquid, so the bulk of the return comes at the end when the company goes public, is sold, or is further restructured. If the LBO is unsuccessful, of course, mezzanine lenders may lose everything. Such lenders like to see total EBIT (earnings before interest and taxes) coverage of all interest payments in the neighborhood of 1.25 to 1. For more speculative deals, coverage may be closer to 1 to 1.

EMPIRICAL EVIDENCE ON LBOs

There have been a handful of studies on the valuation implications of LBOs and of management buyouts (MBOs).[11] In a buyout, one implication is whether public stockholders realize fair value for their holdings. Depending on the study, the average premium to pre-buyout shareholders has been found to be between 25 percent and 42 percent. Thus, stockholders typically receive a sizable premium for their stock when a company goes private. This is consistent with the economic gains being shared between pre-buyout stockholders and post-buyout owners.

Operating performance and cash flows have been found to improve after the buyout, as has the productivity of capital. This gives credence to efficiency gains being one source of value. Often this is attributable to improved management incentives. Another source is tax benefits. Before the 1986 Tax Reform Act, a sizable portion of the premium paid to stockholders could be explained by tax benefits. This source of value is not nearly as important today, owing to changes in the tax laws. Wealth transfers from pre-buyout bondholders to post-buyout equity holders also are a factor. We know that when leveraged buyouts occur, bond ratings are downgraded, sometimes several notches. However, wealth transfers have been found to be small. Typically, the pre-buyout company has only a moderate amount of debt outstanding, and some of this is protected by covenants from the expropriation of value. The notion of wealth transfers from workers via lost jobs has not been supported, though administrative personnel tend to be cut. The evidence also is consistent with buyouts reducing agency problems between management and stockholders. These arise because management sometimes squanders free cash flow on wasteful expenditures when it should be directing such cash flow to stockholders.

OBSERVATIONS ON LBOs

We see that leveraged buyouts permit going private with little equity. The assets of the acquired company or division are used to secure a large amount of debt. The equity holders, of course, are residual owners. If things go according to plan and the debt is serviced according to schedule, after 5 years they will own a healthy company with moderate debt. Of course, their position will be diluted as the junior subordinated lender exercises its war-

---

[11] Among them are Harry DeAngelo, Linda DeAngelo, and Edward M. Rice, "Going Private: Minority Freezeouts and Stockholder Wealth," *Journal of Law and Economics*, 27 (June 1984), 367–401; Laurentius Marias, Katherine Schipper, and Abbie Smith, "Wealth Effects of Going Private for Senior Securities," *Journal of Financial Economics*, 23 (June 1989), 155–91; Gailen L. Hite and Michael R. Vetsuypens, "Management Buyouts of Divisions and Shareholder Wealth," *Journal of Finance*, 44 (June 1989), 953–80; Kenneth Lehn and Annette Poulsen, "Free Cash Flow and Stockholder Gains in Going Private Transactions," *Journal of Finance*, 44 (July 1989), 771–87; Steven Kaplan, "Management Buyouts: Evidence on Taxes as a Source of Value," *Journal of Finance*, 44 (July 1989), 611–32; and Steven Kaplan, "The Effects of Management Buyouts on Operating Performance and Value," *Journal of Financial Economics*, 24 (October 1989), 217–54.

rants to purchase stock. In any leveraged buyout, the first several years are key. The company initially operates with a very thin equity base. If somehow it can make its payments, the interest burden declines over time as operating profits, it is hoped, improve.

There are two kinds of risk. The first is business risk. Operations may not go according to plan, and the cash-flow wherewithal to service debt may be lower than forecasted. The other risk involves changing interest rates. As the senior debt typically is floating rate and changes with the prime rate, a sharp rise in interest rates may very well carry the business under. By their very nature, leveraged buyouts have a modest safety cushion built into the calculations for the first several years. Even with good management of operations, a sizable increase in interest costs will eliminate this cushion and cause the firm to default. To mitigate the effect of adverse interest-rate movements, some firms hedge through interest-rate options.

Thus, the equity holders are playing a high-risk game, and the principle of leverage being a two-edged sword becomes abundantly clear. The reader can visualize their position in the option pricing model framework used earlier in the book. Another potential problem with the need to service debt is the focus on short-run profitability. This may work to the detriment of the long-run viability of the enterprise. If capital expenditures, research and development, and advertising are cut not only to but through the bone, the company may not be competitive once the debt is paid off. Once lost, the company may not be able to regain its competitive position despite reasonable expenditures later on. A rule of thumb is that the total value placed on an LBO (debt and equity) should be no more than six to eight times pretax operating cash flow. If higher than this, and if leverage is a large component of the total value, the probability of default is accentuated beyond what most would regard as reasonable.

During the 1980s, there was considerable hype to the LBO movement. One incentive was high fees to promoters and investment bankers. As long as lenders could be found and the economy was benign, there seemed to be no end to the types of deals that could be done. The reward-to-risk ratio to lenders was relatively low, which meant that financial promoters and equity holders could borrow on relatively favorable terms. This changed in the late 1980s. A number of highly levered transactions ran into trouble—Campeau, Southland, Resorts International, and many others.

The junk bond market deteriorated, and yields increased sharply to reflect default risk and illiquidity concerns. When Drexel Burnham Lambert, an investment bank specializing in junk bonds, failed in 1990, liquidity suffered greatly. When this was coupled with increased regulatory scrutiny of depository institutions, highly levered transactions of this sort abated sharply in the early 1990s. Participants gained respect for the risks involved, and mezzanine financing and senior financing were difficult to arrange. Although LBOs may well come back in the American capital markets, a greater rationality will certainly prevail than in the mid-1980s—a rationality and self-discipline by lenders/investors that should have been there all along.

LEVERAGED RECAPITALIZATIONS

The leveraged buyout (LBO) must be distinguished from a leveraged recapitalization, or leveraged cash out (LCO) as it is also known. With an LBO, public stockholders are bought out and the company, or business unit of a company, becomes private. With a leveraged recap, a publicly traded company raises cash through increased leverage, usually massive leverage. The cash then is distributed to stockholders, often by means of a huge dividend. In contrast to an LBO, stockholders continue to hold shares in the company. The firm remains a public corporation with a traded stock.

These shares are known as "stub" shares. Obviously, they are worth a lot less per share, owing to the huge cash payout. (While a cash payout is most common, stockholders could receive debt securities or even preferred stock.) In the transaction, management and other insiders do not participate in the payout but take additional shares instead. As a result, their proportional ownership of the corporation increases sharply.[12] For example, rather than receive one share of new stock plus a large cash dividend for each old share, management might receive five shares, but no cash dividend. Thus, management obtains a large equity stake in the company, but unlike an LBO, this stake is represented by publicly traded stock. The leveraged recap does not lend itself to a business unit, as does an LBO. It must involve the company as a whole.

While the number of leveraged recaps is limited, the ones that have occurred have been large. They include Colt Industries, FMC, Owens-Corning, USG Corporations, and Harcourt Brace Jovanovich. Often leveraged recaps occur in response to a hostile takeover threat or to management's perception that the company is vulnerable even though it is not actually under attack. A leveraged recap can occur without putting the company up for sale, or "into play," as is required with an LBO. The disadvantage, relative to an LBO, is that as a public company, shareholder-servicing costs and security regulations and disclosures remain.

VALUATION IMPLICATIONS

How do the outside, or public, stockholders fare? While the leveraged recap usually is a defensive tactic and antitakeover devices generally work to the disadvantage of stockholders, this is different. For one thing, leverage and a greater equity stake may give management more incentive to manage efficiently and to reduce wasteful expenditures. There also is the tax shield that accompanies the use of debt. Event studies, which analyze share price reaction around the time of announcement of a leveraged recap, have found excess returns somewhat in excess of 30 percent.[13] This is in the same general area as LBOs and returns to acquired company stockholders in a takeover. Thus, leveraged recaps are not adverse to stockholders, as are other antitakeover devices.

SUMMARY

Corporate restructuring involves many types of transactions, only a handful of which were taken up in this chapter. Transactions fall into the broad categories of expansion, divestiture, and ownership restructuring, with the focus

---

[12] See Robert T. Kleiman, "The Shareholder Gains from Leveraged Cash-Outs: Some Preliminary Evidence," *Journal of Applied Corporate Finance*, 1 (Spring 1988), 46–53, for various forms of leveraged recaps.

[13] Ibid.; and Black and Grundfest, "Shareholder Gains from Takeovers and Restructurings," 14–15.

of this chapter on the last two. Voluntary divestitures have several motives: (1) expected efficiency gains, sometimes through strategic realignment; (2) information effects to correct asymmetric information between investors and management; (3) wealth transfers from debt holders to equity holders; and (4) tax reasons.

Voluntary liquidations, sell-offs, spin-offs, and equity carveouts have similar characteristics and some that are different. A voluntary liquidation involves the sale of the overall company. A sell-off usually involves the sale of a business unit for cash or securities. In contrast, a spin-off involves distribution of common stock in the business unit to stockholders of the company spinning off the unit. In both the sell-off and the spin-off, the company divests itself of all ownership and control. In an equity carveout, common stock in a business unit is sold to the public, but the company usually keeps majority ownership and control. The various motives for these divestitures were taken up, as was the empirical evidence on valuation. In all three situations, there typically is a positive return to stockholders around the announcement date, after isolating the effect of market movements.

When a company goes private, it is transformed from public ownership to private ownership by a small group of investors, including management. There are a number of motivations for going private, and some reasons for expecting economic gain. The empirical evidence suggests sizable premiums being paid to the public stockholders, similar to those for mergers. One means for going private is the leveraged buyout. Here a large amount of debt is used to finance a cash purchase of a division of a company or a company as a whole. Both senior debt secured by assets and junior subordinated debt are employed. The latter is known as mezzanine financing and usually comes with warrants or some other type of equity link. Given the small equity base, LBOs are risky. It does not take a very large adverse change in operations or in interest rates for default to occur, as attested to by the sizable number of defaults in recent years.

A leveraged recapitalization is similar to an LBO in that massive leverage is employed. However, the cash raised through debt is used to pay a large dividend to stockholders. They continue to hold stock, known as stub shares, and the company remains a public corporation. In the transaction, management does not receive cash. It takes stock instead, thereby sizably increasing its proportional ownership of the company.

SELF-CORRECTION PROBLEMS

1. What are the similarities and differences between sell-offs, spin-offs, and equity carveouts? Is one method better than the others? Why would a company want to divest itself of a business unit?

2. Rumpole Bailey Company recently has become subject to a hostile takeover attempt. Management is considering either a leveraged buyout or a leveraged recapitalization. With the LBO, it would initially own 30 percent of the stock, but this would be diluted if mezzanine lenders were to exercise their warrants. These warrants, upon exercise, give holders 30 percent of the total shares. Management presently owns 400,000 shares of the 10 million shares outstanding. With a leveraged recap, it would receive 6 shares of "stub" stock for each old share owned, but no dividend, while public stockholders would receive 1 new share for each old share owned plus a large cash dividend.

a. In the case of the LBO, after exercise of the warrants what will be management's proportion of ownership of the company?

b. If a leveraged recap were to occur, what would be management's proportion of ownership?

c. Are there other factors to consider? What are they?

3. Tokay Enterprises is considering going private through a leveraged buyout by management. Management presently owns 21 percent of the 5 million shares outstanding. Market price per share is $20, and it is felt that a 40 percent premium over the present price will be necessary to entice public stockholders to tender their shares in a cash offer. Management intends to keep their shares and to obtain senior debt equal to 80 percent of the funds necessary to consummate the buyout. The remaining 20 percent will come from junior subordinated debentures.

Terms on the senior debt are 2 percent above the prime rate, with principal reductions of 20 percent of the initial loan at the end of each of the next 5 years. The junior subordinated debentures bear a 13 percent interest rate and must be retired at the end of 6 years with a single balloon payment. The debentures have warrants attached that enable the holders to purchase 30 percent of the stock at the end of year 6. Management estimates that earnings before interest and taxes will be $25 million per year. Because of tax loss carryforwards, the company expects to pay no taxes over the next 5 years. The company will make capital expenditures in amounts equal to its depreciation.

a. If the prime rate is expected to average 10 percent over the next 5 years, is the leveraged buyout feasible?

b. What if it averaged only 8 percent?

c. What minimal EBIT is necessary to service the debt?

PROBLEMS

1. R. Leonard Company has three divisions, and the total market value (debt and equity) of the firm is $71 million. Its debt-to-total-market-value ratio is .40, and bond indentures provide the usual protective covenants. However, they do not preclude the sale of a division. Leonard has decided to divest itself of its Eltron division for a consideration of $20 million. In addition to this payment to Leonard, the buyer will assume $5 million of existing debt of the division. The full $20 million will be distributed to Leonard Company stockholders. In words, are the remaining debt holders of Leonard Company better or worse off? Why? In theory, are the equity holders better or worse off?

2. Lorzo-Perez International has a subsidiary, the DelRay Sorter Company. The company believes the subsidiary on average will generate $1 million per year in annual net cash flows, after necessary capital expenditures. These annual net cash flows are projected into the far future (assume infinity). The required rate of return for the subsidiary is 12 percent. If the company were to invest an additional $10 million now, it is believed that annual net cash flows could be increased from $1 million to $2 million. Exson Corporation has expressed an interest in DelRay, because it is in the sorter business and believes it can achieve some economies. Accordingly, it has made a cash offer of $10 million for the subsidiary.

Should Lorzo-Perez (a) continue the business as is? (b) invest the additional $10 million? (c) sell the subsidiary to Exson? (Assume the subsidiary is entirely equity financed.)

3. Biglow Carpet Company is considering divesting itself of its linoleum division. It is considering either a sell-off, a spin-off, or an equity carveout, where the carveout would be for 48 percent of the value of the division. Event studies for similar situations suggest the following abnormal returns around the announcement date: sell-offs, 1 percent; spin-offs, 3 percent; equity carveouts, 1 percent. Which

method would you advise the company to use? Are there considerations other than these data that would influence your decision?

4. Hogs Breath Inns, a chain of restaurants, is considering going private. The president, Clint Westwood, believes that with the elimination of stockholder servicing costs and other costs associated with public ownership, the company could save $800,000 per annum before taxes. In addition, the company believes management incentives and hence performance will be higher as a private company. As a result, annual profits are expected to be 10 percent greater than present after-tax profits of $9 million. The effective tax rate is 30 percent, the price/earnings ratio of the stock is 12, and there are 10 million shares outstanding. What is the present market price per share? What is the maximum dollar premium above this price that the company could pay in order to take the company private?

5. Bulaweyo Industries wishes to sell its valve division for $10 million. Management of the division wishes to buy it and has arranged a leveraged buyout. The management will put $1 million in cash. A senior lender will advance $7 million secured by all the assets of the company. The rate on the loan is 2 percent above the prime rate, which is presently 12 percent. The loan is payable in equal annual principal installments over 5 years, with interest for the year payable at the end of each year. A junior subordinated loan of $2 million also has been arranged, and this loan is due at the end of 6 years. The interest rate is fixed at 15 percent, and interest payments only are due at the end of each of the first 5 years. Interest and principal are due at the end of the sixth year. In addition, the lender has received warrants exercisable for 50 percent of the stock.

The valve division expects earnings before interest and taxes of $3.4 million in each of the first 3 years and $3.7 million in each of the next 3 years. The tax rate is $33\frac{1}{3}$ percent, and the company expects capital expenditures and investments in receivables and inventories to equal depreciation charges in each year. All debt servicing must come from profits. (Assume also that the warrants are not exercised and that there is no cash infusion as a result.)

a. If the prime rate stays at 12 percent on average throughout the 6 years, will the enterprise be able to service the debt properly?

b. If the prime rate were to rise to 20 percent in the second year and average that for years 2 through 6, would the situation change?

6. USB Corporation is considering a leveraged recapitalization. Currently, its balance sheet consists of the following:

Total assets	$941 million
Total debt	295 million
Shareholders' equity	646 million

There are 20 million shares outstanding, of which management owns 1 million. The leveraged recap involves $703 million in new debt, paying public stockholders a cash dividend of $37 per share, and giving them 1 new share of stub stock for each old share of stock owned. Management will receive no cash dividend but will get 9 new shares of stock for each old share held.

a. What will the balance sheet look like after the leveraged recap? What will give the shares value?

b. What proportional ownership will management have after the transaction compared with what it had before?

c. Determine the after-recap value per share implicit in cash-dividend and exchange-offer differentials between management and public stockholders. Assume there is no control value and that management and stockholders are indifferent between having cash dividends or value in the shares they own.

7. Research Project. Obtain legal documentation to stockholders for some spin-offs, equity carveouts, and going-private transactions. Compare and contrast these types of corporate restructuring. What kinds of companies engage in them? Did the stockholders benefit from the restructuring as far as you are able to tell from the share price behavior around the announcement date?

SOLUTIONS TO
SELF-CORRECTION PROBLEMS

1. In sell-offs and spin-offs, the company divests itself entirely of the business unit. In an equity carveout, only a portion of the equity ownership of the unit is divested, through a sale of stock to the public. Usually this portion is a minority interest, and the company continues to manage the business unit. With a sell-off and equity carveout, the company receives a consideration for the business unit, usually cash. With a spin-off, it receives no such consideration. Rather, stock in the business unit is distributed to stockholders. The most appropriate method depends on the circumstances and what the company wishes to accomplish by the transaction.

   As taken up in the chapter, the motives to divest a business unit are several. There may be an economic gain in the business unit being more valuable to someone else than it is to the company. If there is asymmetric information between management and investors, it may be possible to achieve a favorable information effect, and valuation, by divesting. A wealth transfer from old debt holders to stockholders will sometimes occur if lenders have a lesser claim after the transaction. Finally, there may be tax advantages to the divestiture.

2. a. $30\% \times (1 - .30) = 21\%$

   b.
Management shares after recap	2.4 million
Public stockholder shares after recap	9.6 million
Total shares after the recap	12.0 million

   Proportion of ownership by management = 2.4/12.0 = 20%

   Management obtains a slightly lesser ownership position with the leveraged recap than with the LBO.

   c. With the leveraged recap, the company remains a public corporation and management can trade its shares. With an LBO, it owns stock in a private company and such stock is illiquid. There are certain costs for the public corporation and, perhaps, an undue focus on quarterly earnings, which would not be the case with the private-company LBO. The leveraged recap can be consummated without putting the company up for sale and obligating the board of directors to accept the highest offer. However, with the leveraged recap, 80 percent of the stock will stay in public hands, so the company still could be subject to hostile takeover attempts. However, the high degree of leverage may serve as a deterrent.

3. a. Shares owned by outsiders = 5 million $\times$ .79 = 3,950,000

   Price to be offered = $20 $\times$ 1.40 = $28 per share
   Total buyout amount = 3,950,000 shares $\times$ $28 = $110,600,000

   Senior debt = $110,600,000 $\times$ .80 = $88,480,000
   Annual principal payment = $88,480,00/5 = $17,696,000
   Junior debt = $110,600,000 $\times$ .20 = $22,120,000

   Annual EBIT to service debt:
Senior debt interest	$88,480,000 $\times$ .12 =	$10,617,600
Senior debt principal		17,696,000
Junior debt interest	$22,120,000 $\times$ .13 =	2,875,600
Total EBIT necessary		$31,189,200

   During the first 5 years, EBIT of $25 million will not be sufficient to service the debt.

   b. $88,480,000 $\times$ .10 = $8,848,000, which together with the two other amounts above, comes to $29,419,600. Still, expected EBIT will not be sufficient to service the debt.

   c. $31,189,200

SELECTED REFERENCES

ALEXANDER, GORDON J., P. GEORGE BENSON, and JOAN M. KAMPMEYER, "Investigating the Valuation Effects of Announcements of Voluntary Selloffs," *Journal of Finance,* 39 (June 1984), 503–17.

BAKER, GEORGE P., and KAREN H. WRUCK, "Organizational Changes and Value Creation in Leveraged Buyouts: The Case of O. M. Scott & Sons Company," *Journal of Financial Economics,* 25 (December 1989), 163–90.

DEANGELO, HARRY, LINDA DEANGELO, and EDWARD M. RICE, "Going Private: Minority Freezeouts and Stockholder Wealth," *Journal of Law and Economics,* 27 (June 1984), 367–401.

HITE, GAILEN L., and JAMES E. OWERS, "Security Price Reactions around Corporate Spin-off Announcements," *Journal of Financial Economics,* 12 (December 1983), 409–36.

———, and RONALD C. ROGERS, "The Market for Interfirm Asset Sales," *Journal of Financial Economics,* 18 (June 1987), 229–52.

HITE, GAILEN L., and MICHAEL R. VETSUYPENS, "Management Buyouts of Divisions and Shareholder Wealth," *Journal of Finance,* 44 (June 1989), 953–80.

JAIN, PREM C., "The Effect of Voluntary Sell-off Announcements on Shareholder Wealth," *Journal of Finance,* 40 (March 1985), 209–24.

KAPLAN, STEVEN, "Management Buyouts: Evidence on Taxes as a Source of Value," *Journal of Finance,* 44 (July 1989), 611–32.

———, "The Effects of Management Buyouts on Operating Performance and Value," *Journal of Financial Economics,* 24 (October 1989), 217–54.

KIM, E. HAN, and JOHN D. SCHATZBERG, "Voluntary Corporate Liquidations," *Journal of Financial Economics,* 19 (December 1987), 311–28.

KLEIMAN, ROBERT T., "The Shareholder Gains from Leveraged Cash-Outs: Some Preliminary Evidence," *Journal of Applied Corporate Finance,* 1 (Spring 1988), 46–53.

KLEIN, APRIL, "The Timing and Substance of Divestiture Announcements," *Journal of Finance,* 41 (July 1986), 685–96.

KUDLA, RONALD J., and THOMAS H. MCINISH, "Divergence of Opinion and Corporate Spin-Offs," *Quarterly Review of Economics and Business,* 28 (Summer 1988), 20–29.

MCDANIEL, MOREY W., "Bondholder and Corporate Governance," *Business Lawyer,* 41 (February 1986), 413–60.

MARIAS, LAURENTIUS, KATHERINE SCHIPPER, and ABBIE SMITH, "Wealth Effects of Going Private for Senior Securities," *Journal of Financial Economics,* 23 (June 1989), 155–91.

MILES, JAMES A., and JAMES D. ROSENFELD, "The Effect of Voluntary Spin-off Announcements on Shareholder Wealth," *Journal of Finance,* 38 (December 1983), 1597–1606.

MYERS, STEWART C., "Determinants of Corporate Borrowing," *Journal of Financial Economics,* 5 (November 1977), 147–76.

ROSENFELD, JAMES D., "Additional Evidence on the Relation between Divestiture Announcements and Shareholder Wealth," *Journal of Finance,* 39 (December 1984), 1437–48.

SCHIPPER, KATHERINE, and ABBIE SMITH, "Effects of Recontracting on Shareholder Wealth," *Journal of Financial Economics,* 12 (December 1983), 437–67.

———, "A Comparison of Equity Carve-outs and Seasoned Equity Offerings," *Journal of Financial Economics,* 15 (January–February 1986), 153–86.

SICHERMAN, NEIL W., and RICHARD H. PETTWAY, "Acquisition of Divested Assets and Shareholders' Wealth," *Journal of Finance,* 42 (December 1987), 1261–73.

SKANTZ, TERRANCE R., and ROBERTO MARCHESINI, "The Effect of Voluntary Corporate Liquidation on Shareholder Wealth," *Journal of Financial Research,* 10 (Winter 1987), 65–76.

WESTON, J. FRED, "Divestitures: Mistakes or Learning," *Journal of Applied Corporate Finance,* 2 (Summer 1989), 68–76.

26

INTERNATIONAL FINANCIAL MANAGEMENT

In the 1980s and 1990s, there has been an explosion in international investments, through mutual funds and other intermediaries by the individual and through direct investments by the institution. On the other side, capital raising is increasingly occurring across national boundaries. The financial manager must search for "best price" in a global marketplace, sometimes with currency and other hedges. To accommodate the underlying demands of investors and capital raisers, financial institutions and instruments have changed dramatically. Financial deregulation, first in the United States and then in Europe and Asia, has prompted increased integration of world financial markets. As a result of the rapidly changing scene, the financial manager today must be global in his or her perspective. While the concepts developed earlier in this book are applicable here, the environment in which decisions are made is different. In this chapter, we develop an understanding of this environment and describe how a company goes about protecting itself.

SOME BACKGROUND

The motivation to invest capital in a foreign operation, of course, is to provide a return in excess of that required. There may be gaps in foreign markets where excess returns can be earned. Domestically, competitive pressures may be such that only a normal rate of return can be earned. Although expansion into foreign markets is the reason for most investment abroad, there are other reasons. Some firms invest in order to produce more efficiently. Another country may offer lower labor and other costs, and a company will choose to locate production facilities there in the quest for lower operating costs. The electronics industry has moved toward foreign production facilities for this saving. Finally, some companies invest abroad to secure necessary raw materials. Oil companies and mining companies in particular invest abroad for this reason. All of these pursuits—markets, production facilities, and raw materials—are in keeping with an objective of securing a higher rate of return than is possible through domestic operations alone.

INTERNATIONAL CAPITAL BUDGETING

The relevant cash inflows for a foreign investment are those that can be repatriated to the parent. If the expected return on investment is based on nonremittable cash flows that build up in a foreign subsidiary, the investment is unlikely to be attractive. If cash flows can be freely repatriated, however, capital budgeting is straightforward. The U.S. firm would

1. Estimate expected cash flows in the foreign currency
2. Compute their U.S. dollar equivalents at the expected exchange rate (foreign currency per dollar)
3. Determine the net present value of the project using the U.S. required rate of return, adjusted upward or downward for any risk premium effect associated with the foreign investment

Suppose Jacklin Jersey Company is considering an investment in Malaysia costing 1.5 million ringgits. The product has a short life, 4 years, and the required rate of return on repatriated U.S. dollars is 18 percent. The ringgit, now 2.70 to the dollar, is expected to depreciate over time. That is, a dollar is expected to be worth more ringgits in the future than it is worth now. Table 26-1 illustrates the three steps used to calculate dollar cash flows and their net present value, which we see to be approximately $49,000.

Although the calculations are straightforward, obviously much goes into the assumptions concerning projected cash flows, projected exchange rates, and the required rate of return. Learning about these things is the purpose of this chapter.

RISK FACTORS

With respect to required returns, international diversification is a consideration. Recall from our discussion of portfolio risk in Chapter 3 that the key element is the correlation among projects in the asset portfolio. By combining projects with low degrees of correlation with each other, a firm is able to reduce risk in relation to expected return. Since domestic investment projects tend to be correlated with each other, most being highly dependent on the state of the economy, foreign investments have an advantage. The economic cycles of different countries do not tend to be completely synchro-

TABLE 26-1
Expected cash flows for Jacklin Jersey Company's Malaysian project (000 omitted)

	YEAR				
	0	1	2	3	4
Expected cash flow (in ringgits)	−1,500	500	800	700	600
Exchange rate (R/$)	2.70	2.76	2.84	2.92	3.00
Expected cash flow (in dollars)	−556	181	282	240	200

Net present value at 18 percent = $49.

nized, so it is possible to reduce risk relative to expected return by investing across countries. The idea is simply that returns on investment projects tend to be less correlated among countries than they are in any one particular country.

Whether foreign diversification by a company benefits its stockholders depends on whether capital markets between countries are segmented. If they are not, there is little reason to believe that foreign diversification by a company will increase its value. This notion is the same as that for diversification of assets involving domestic projects, which was discussed earlier. If capital markets are perfect, investors can effectively replicate any asset diversification by the firm. Therefore, such diversification adds nothing at the margin to shareholder wealth. If currency restrictions, investment barriers, legal restrictions, lack of information, and other capital market imperfections of this sort exist, capital markets between countries may be segmented. Under these circumstances, foreign diversification may enhance shareholder wealth.

Thus, whether stocks are better regarded as being traded in domestic markets, where the market models (CAPM or APT) would hold, or in an international market is the question. The former implies a segmented capital market, whereas the latter suggests an integrated one with the relevant market portfolio being worldwide. The situation is illustrated in Fig. 26-1. With a domestic portfolio of stocks, one is able to reduce total risk through diversification in the manner shown by the top line. This illustration corresponds to Fig. 3-9, which dealt with the relationship among total, systematic, and unsystematic risk. With an integrated market for securities, the investor is able to reduce risk more quickly and further by diversifying across international stocks as opposed to only domestic ones. The evidence suggests that world security markets are at least partially integrated. To the extent there is some segmentation, however, the corporation may be able to do something for its stockholders that they cannot do for themselves, namely, reduce risk through direct foreign investments.

Some of the things that make direct foreign investments different from domestic investments are taxation and political risk. Before we get into currency exposure of a company, we consider these topics.

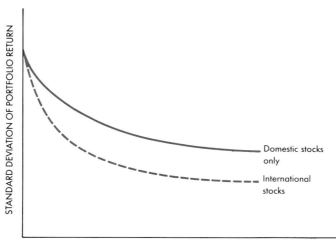

FIGURE 26-1

Domestic versus international stock diversification

TAXATION

Owing to different tax laws and different treatments of foreign investment, the taxation of a multinational firm is complex. Our purpose is to discuss some of the salient aspects of the problem, and we begin with the way in which the U.S. government taxes a company with foreign operations. Then we can move on to taxation by foreign countries.

Taxation by U.S. Government. If a U.S. corporation carries on business abroad through a branch or division, the income from that operation is reported on the company's U.S. tax form and is taxed in the same way as domestic income. If business is carried on through a foreign subsidiary, the income normally is not taxed in the United States until it is distributed to the parent in the form of dividends. The advantage here, of course, is that the tax is deferred until the parent receives a cash return. In the meantime, earnings are reinvested in the subsidiary to finance expansion. Unlike dividends from a domestic corporation (70 percent exempt), dividends received by a U.S. corporation from a foreign subsidiary are fully taxable.

Taxation by Foreign Governments. Every country taxes income of foreign companies doing business in that country. The type of tax imposed varies. Some of these countries differentiate between income distributed to stockholders and undistributed income, with a lower tax on distributed income. Less-developed countries frequently have lower taxes and provide certain other tax incentives to encourage foreign investment. One method of taxation that has been prominent in Europe is the value-added tax, in essence a sales tax on each stage of production, which is taxed on the value added. It works this way: An aluminum fabricator buys aluminum sheets for $1,000, cuts, shapes, and otherwise works them into doors, which are sold for $1,800. The value added is $800, and the fabricator is taxed on this amount. If the fabricator sold its doors to a wholesaler who, in turn, sold them to retailers for $2,000, the value added would be $200 and taxed accordingly.

The taxation policies of foreign governments are not only varied but also highly complex. The definition of what constitutes taxable income is different for different countries, and the tax rate varies among countries. Certain nations, such as Luxembourg, Panama, and the Bahamas, have low tax rates on corporate profits in order to encourage foreign investment, whereas the tax rates in most advanced industrial countries are high. The picture is complicated further by the numerous tax treaties that the United States has with other nations. Although the U.S. government restricts use of a low-tax country as a tax haven, enough latitude remains so that companies still devise complicated legal structures in order to take advantage of such havens.

To avoid double taxation, the United States gives a federal income tax credit for foreign taxes paid by a U.S. corporation. If a foreign country has a tax rate of less than that of the U.S. corporation, it will pay combined taxes at the full U.S. tax rate. Part of the taxes are paid to the foreign government, the other part to the U.S. government. Suppose a foreign branch of a U.S. corporation operates in a country where the income tax rate is 27 percent. The branch earns $2 million and pays $540,000 in foreign income taxes. The $2 million earnings are subject to a 34 percent tax rate in the United States, or $680,000 in taxes. The company receives a tax credit of $540,000; thus, it pays only $140,000 in U.S. taxes on earnings of its foreign branch. If the foreign tax rate were 50 percent, the company would pay $1 million in foreign taxes on those earnings, nothing in U.S. taxes. Here, total taxes paid are obviously higher.

Moreover, the size of foreign tax credit may be constrained. The United States taxes companies on their worldwide income and permits a foreign tax credit only to the extent that the foreign source income would have been taxed in the United States. Suppose 30 percent of a multinational company's total income is attributable to foreign sources. If its precredit U.S. tax liability is $10 million, only $3 million in foreign tax credits may be used to offset the U.S. tax liability. If the company pays more in foreign taxes, it will be subject to double taxation on that portion. Relative sourcing of assets, income, or value becomes important also in allocating certain corporate expenses, in particular, interest expenses.

It is clear that tax planning for an international operation is complex and highly technical. From time to time, various special tax incentives come into existence to help export industries, the Foreign Sales Corporation (FSC) being a current example. Other tax provisions, both U.S. and foreign, are constantly changing. The advice of tax experts and legal counsel, both foreign and domestic, should be sought at the time the foreign operation is organized.

POLITICAL RISK

A multinational company faces political risks ranging from mild interference to complete confiscation of all assets. Interference includes laws that specify a minimum percentage of nationals who must be employed in various positions, required investment in environmental and social projects, and restrictions on the convertibility of currencies. The ultimate political risk is expropriation, such as that which occurred in Chile in 1971, when the country took over the copper companies. Between mild interference and outright expropriation, there are discriminatory practices such as higher taxes, higher utility charges, and the requirement to pay higher wages than a national company. In essence, they place the foreign operation of the U.S. company at a competitive disadvantage.

Because political risk has a serious influence on the overall risk of an investment project, it must be assessed realistically. Essentially, the job is one of forecasting political instability. How stable is the government involved? What are the prevailing political winds? What is likely to be a new government's view of foreign investment? How efficient is the government in processing requests? How much inflation and economic stability are there? How strong and equitable are the courts? Answers to these questions should give considerable insight into the political risk involved in an investment. Some companies have categorized countries according to their political risk. If a country is classified in the undesirable category, probably no investment will be permitted, no matter how high its expected return.

Once a company decides to invest, it should take steps to protect itself. By cooperating with the host country in hiring nationals, making the "right" types of investment, and in other ways being desirable, political risk can be reduced. A joint venture with a company in the host country can improve the public image of the operation. Indeed, in some countries a joint venture may be the only way to do business, because direct ownership, particularly of manufacturing, is prohibited. The risk of expropriation also can be reduced by making the subsidiary dependent on the parent for technology, markets, and/or supplies. A foreign government is reluctant to expropriate when the enterprise is not self-sustaining. Although every effort should be made to protect an investment once it is made, often when sharp political changes occur nothing can be done. The time to look hardest at political risk is before the investment is made.

TYPES OF EXPOSURE

The company with foreign operations is at risk in various ways. Apart from political danger, risk fundamentally emanates from changes in exchange rates. In this regard, the *spot rate* represents the number of units of one currency that can be exchanged for another. Put differently, it is the price of one currency relative to another. The currencies of the major countries are traded in active markets, where rates are determined by the forces of supply and demand. Quotations can be in terms of the domestic currency or in terms of the foreign currency. If the U.S. dollar is the domestic currency and the British pound the foreign, a quotation might be .625 pounds per dollar or 1.60 dollars per pound. The result is the same, for one is the reciprocal of the other.

We must distinguish a spot exchange rate from a *forward exchange rate*. Forward transactions involve an agreement today for settlement in the future. It might be the delivery of 1,000 pounds 90 days hence, where the settlement rate is 1.59 dollars per pound. The forward exchange rate usually differs from the spot exchange rate for reasons we will explain shortly.

With these definitions in mind, there are three types of exposure with which we are concerned:

1. Translation exposure
2. Transactions exposure
3. Economic exposure

The first, translation exposure, is the change in accounting income and balance sheet statements caused by changes in exchange rates. This will be illustrated in the next section. Transactions exposure has to do with settling a particular transaction, like a receivable, at one exchange rate when the obligation was originally recorded at another. Finally, economic exposure involves changes in expected future cash flows, and hence economic value, caused by a change in exchange rates. For example, if we budget 1.3 million deutschemarks to build an extension to our German plant and the exchange rate now is DM1.70 per dollar, this corresponds to DM1.3 million/1.70 = $764,706. When we go to pay for materials and labor, the DM might strengthen, say to 1.60. The plant now has a dollar cost of DM1.3 million/1.60 = $812,500. The difference, $47,794, represents an economic loss.

Having briefly defined these three exposures, we investigate them in detail. This will be followed by how exposure can be managed.

TRANSLATION EXPOSURE

As we know, translation exposure relates to the accounting treatment of changes in exchange rates. Statement No. 52 of the Financial Accounting Standards Board deals with the translation of foreign currency changes on the balance sheet and income statement. Under these accounting rules, a U.S. company must determine a functional currency for each of its foreign subsidiaries. If the subsidiary is a stand-alone operation that is integrated within a particular country, the functional currency may be the local currency; otherwise, it is the dollar.[1] Where high inflation occurs (over 100 percent per annum), the functional currency must be the dollar regardless of the conditions given.

The functional currency used is important because it determines the translation process. If the local currency is used, all assets and liabilities are translated at the *current rate of exchange*. Moreover, translation gains or losses are not reflected in the income statement, but rather are recognized in owners' equity as a translation adjustment. The fact that such adjustments do not affect accounting income is appealing to many companies. If the functional currency is the dollar, however, this is not the case. Gains or losses are reflected in the income statement of the parent company using what is known as the *temporal method*. In general, the use of the dollar as the functional currency results in greater fluctuations in accounting income, but in smaller fluctuations in balance sheet items than does the use of the local currency. Let us examine the differences.

DIFFERENCES IN METHODS

With the dollar as the functional currency, balance sheet and income statement items are categorized as to historical exchange rates or as to current exchange rates. Cash, receivables, liabilities, sales, expenses, and taxes are translated using current exchange rates, whereas inventories, plant and equipment, equity, cost of goods sold, and depreciation are translated at the historical exchange rates existing at the time of the transactions. This differs from the situation where the local currency is used as the functional currency; here all items are translated at current exchange rates.

To illustrate, a company we shall call Richmond Precision Instruments has a subsidiary in the Kingdom of Spamany where the currency is the liso. At the first of the year, the exchange rate is 8 lisos to the dollar, and that rate has prevailed for many years. During 19x2, however, the liso declines steadily in value to 10 lisos to the dollar at year end. The average exchange rate during the year is 9 lisos to the dollar. Table 26-2 shows the balance sheet and income statement for the foreign subsidiary at the beginning and at the end of the year and the effect of the method of translation.

Taking the balance sheet first, the 12/31/x1 date serves as a base, and the dollar statement in column 3 is simply the liso amounts shown in column 1 divided by the exchange rate of 8 lisos to the dollar. For the two separate dollar statements at 12/31/x2, shown in the last two columns, we see that cash, receivables, current liabilities, and long-term debt are the same for both methods of accounting. These amounts are determined on a current exchange rate basis by dividing the amounts shown in column 2 by the exchange rate at year end of 10 lisos to the dollar. For the local functional currency statement, column 4, inventories and fixed assets are determined in the same manner, that is, by use of the current exchange rate. For the dollar functional currency

---

[1] Various criteria are used to determine if the foreign subsidiary is self-contained, including whether sales, labor, other costs, and debt are primarily dominated in the local currency. Also, the nature and magnitude of intercompany transactions are important. Under certain circumstances, it is possible for a foreign currency other than the local one to be used.

TABLE 26-2
Foreign subsidiary
Richmond Precision Instruments

	IN LISOS		IN DOLLARS		
				Local Functional Currency	Dollar Functional Currency
	12/31/x1	12/31/x2	12/31/x1	12/31/x2	12/31/x2
Balance Sheet (in thousands)					
Cash	L 600	L 1,000	$ 75	$ 100	$ 100
Receivables	2,000	2,600	250	260	260
Inventories (FIFO)	4,000	4,500	500	450	500
Current assets	6,600	8,100	825	810	860
Net fixed assets	5,000	4,400	625	440	550
Total	L11,600	L12,500	$1,450	$1,250	$1,410
Current liabilities	L 3,000	L 3,300	$ 375	$ 330	$ 330
Long-term debt	2,000	1,600	250	160	160
Common stock	600	600	75	75	75
Retained earnings	6,000	7,000	750	861	845
Accumulated translation adjustment				−176	
Total	L11,600	L12,500	$1,450	$1,250	$1,410
Income Statement (in thousands with rounding)					
Sales		L10,000		$1,111	$1,111
Cost of goods sold		4,000		444	500
Depreciation		600		67	75
Expenses		3,500		389	389
Taxes		900		100	100
Operating income		L 1,000		$ 111	$ 47
Translation gain					48
Net income		L 1,000		$ 111	$ 95
Translation adjustment				−$176	

statement, inventories and fixed assets are valued using historical exchange rates. Because cost of goods sold equals beginning inventory, the ending inventory is purchased throughout the year. Assuming steady purchases, we divide the ending liso amount by the average exchange rate (9 : 1) to obtain $500,000. Using historical exchange rates again, net fixed assets are determined by dividing the liso amount at year end by the earlier 8 lisos to the dollar exchange rate. The common stock account is carried at the base amount under both methods.

Finally, the change in retained earnings is a residual. (We defer until the discussion of the income statement the accumulated translation adjustment item.) Because of the upward adjustment in inventories and fixed assets, total assets are higher with the dollar functional currency (temporal method) than they are with the local functional currency (current method). The opposite would occur in our example if the liso increased in value relative to the dollar. We see that there is substantially more change in total assets when a local functional currency is used than when a dollar functional currency is employed.

The opposite occurs for the income statement. In our example, sales are adjusted by the average exchange rate that prevailed during the year (9 : 1) for both accounting methods. For column 4, local functional currency, all cost and expense items are adjusted by this exchange rate. For the last column, dollar functional currency, cost of goods sold, and depreciation are translated at historical exchange rates (8 : 1), whereas the other items are translated at the current average rate (9 : 1). We see that operating income and net income are larger when the local functional currency is used than when the functional currency is the dollar. For the latter method, the translation gain is factored in, so that net income agrees with the change in retained earnings from 12/31/x1 to 12/31/x2. We see that this change is $845 − $750 = $95. In contrast, when the functional currency is local, the translation adjustment occurs after the income figure of $111. The adjustment is that amount, −$176, that, together with net income, brings the liability and net worth part of the balance sheet into balance. This amount then is added to the sum of past translation adjustments to obtain the new accumulated translation adjustment figure that appears on the balance sheet. As we assume past adjustments total zero, this item becomes −$176.

Thus, the translation adjustments for the two methods are in opposite directions. Should the liso increase in value relative to the dollar, the effect would be the reverse of that illustrated; operating income would be higher if the functional currency were the dollar.

IMPLICATIONS

Because translation gains or losses are not reflected directly on the income statement, reported operating income tends to fluctuate less when the functional currency is local than when it is the dollar. However, the variability of balance sheet items is increased, owing to the translation of all items by the current exchange rate. Because many corporate executives are concerned with accounting income, FASB No. 52 is popular, as long as a subsidiary qualifies for a local functional currency. However, this accounting method also has its drawbacks. For one thing, it distorts the balance sheet and the historical cost numbers. Moreover, it may cause return on asset calculations and other measures of return to be meaningless. It is simply inconsistent with the nature of other accounting rules, which are based on historical costs. Most financial ratios are affected by the functional currency employed, so the financial analyst must be careful when foreign subsidiaries account for a sizable portion of a company's operations.[2] The method also has been criticized for not allowing proper assessment of the parent's likely future cash flows. In summary, there is no universally satisfactory way to treat foreign currency translations, and the accounting profession continues to struggle with the issue.

TRANSACTIONS EXPOSURE

Transactions exposure involves the gain or loss that occurs when settling a specific foreign transaction. The transaction might be the purchase or sale of a product, the lending or borrowing of funds, or some other transaction involv-

---

[2] See Thomas I. Selling and George H. Sorter, "FASB Statement No. 52 and Its Implications for Financial Statement Analysis," *Financial Analysts Journal*, 39 (May–June 1983), 64–69.

ing the acquisition of assets or the assumption of liabilities denominated in a foreign currency. While any transaction will do, the term "transactions exposure" usually is employed in connection with foreign trade, that is, specific imports or exports on open account credit.

Suppose a deutschemark receivable of DM680 is booked when the exchange rate is 1.70 DM to the dollar. Payment is not due for two months. In the interim, the DM weakens and exchange rate goes to 1.74. As a result, there is a transactions loss. Before, DM680/1.70 = $400. When payment is received, DM680/1.74 = $390.80. Thus, we have a transactions loss of $9.20. If the DM were to strengthen, say to 1.66, there would be a transactions gain. We would have DM680/1.66 = $409.64. With this example in mind, it is easy to produce examples of other types of transactions losses and gains.

ECONOMIC EXPOSURE

Perhaps the most important of the three exposures—translation, transactions, and economic—is the last. Economic exposure is the change in value of a company that accompanies an *unanticipated* change in exchange rates. Note that we distinguish anticipated from unanticipated. Anticipated changes in exchange rates already are reflected in the market value of the firm. If we do business with Brazil, the anticipation is that the cruzeiro will weaken relative to the dollar. The fact that it weakens should not impact market value. If it weakens more than or less than expected, however, this will affect value. Economic exposure is not as precise as translation or transactions exposures. It depends on what happens to expected future cash flows, so subjectivity necessarily is involved.

DEGREES OF EXPOSURE

Not all assets and liabilities are equally exposed. For example, inventories may be less exposed than monetary assets, such as cash, marketable securities, and accounts receivable. Christine R. Hekman has derived a framework for categorizing assets and liabilities as to their degree of exposure.[3] To illustrate her approach, suppose we had a Singapore subsidiary, Tan Lee Feu Limited, that had the balance sheet shown in the first column of Table 26-3. The Singaporean dollar assets and liabilities are converted to their U.S. dollar equivalents. In the second column, market values appear. The last asset requires explanation. For book-value purposes, it is net property, plant, and equipment (cost less cumulative depreciation). For the market-value column, it is the total value of the subsidiary less the market value of the other assets. As such, it is a residual.

The next task in the Hekman framework is to assign an exposure coefficient to each asset and liability. A coefficient of 1.0 means the market value of the balance sheet item is entirely exposed. When exchange rates change, (Singaporean dollar in relation to the U.S. dollar), the full brunt of the change is felt. If the Singaporean dollar rises by 10 percent and the item involved is receivables, the U.S. dollar market value declines by 10 percent, and vice versa.

[3] Christine R. Hekman, "Measuring Foreign Exchange Exposure: A Practical Theory and Its Application," *Financial Analysts Journal,* 39 (September–October 1983), 59–65; and Hekman, "Don't Blame Currency Values for Strategic Errors," *Midland Corporate Finance Journal,* 4 (Fall 1986), 45–55.

TABLE 26-3
Balance sheet of the Tan Lee Feu subsidiary (in millions)

695

CHAPTER 26
International
Financial
Management

	BOOK VALUE	MARKET VALUE	EXPOSURE COEFFICIENT	EXPOSURE
Cash	$1.5	$1.5	1.0	$1.5
Marketable securities	5.6	5.6	1.0	5.6
Receivables	16.3	16.3	1.0	16.3
Inventories	21.8	24.2	0.6	14.5
Value of market position and operating capacity	34.1	71.9	0.3	21.6
Total assets	$79.3	$119.5		$59.5
Accounts payable	$14.9	$14.9	1.0	$14.9
Accruals	8.7	8.7	1.0	8.7
Debt	17.0	15.8	1.0	15.8
Total liabilities	$40.6	$39.4		$39.4
Shareholders' equity	38.7	80.1		
Total	$79.3	$119.5		
Net aggregate market-value exposure				+$20.1

A coefficient of 0.0 means the market value of the balance sheet item is unexposed. When the Singaporean dollar rises by 10 percent in value, there is no change in the market value of the balance sheet item as expressed in U.S. dollars. An example here is a commodity whose price is set in world markets completely apart from Singapore and the United States. For coefficients between these two extremes, the item is partially exposed.

In Table 26-3, monetary assets—cash, marketable securities, and accounts receivable—and all monetary liabilities have an exposure coefficient of 1.0. They are totally exposed. Real assets, however, are only partially exposed. Because the Singaporean plant produces fabricated products sold in Southeast Asia, the inventory exposure coefficient is 0.6. If the inventory were heavily commodity oriented, the coefficient would be lower, maybe 0.2. The inventory coefficient depends on sourcing, competitive position, technology, and things of this sort.

Finally, the exposure coefficient for market position/operating capacity is due to some of these same factors. For the Tan Lee Feu subsidiary, it is estimated to be 0.3. Thus, the value of the future operations is only moderately exposed to changes in the Sing. $/U.S. $ exchange rate. Just because an operation is located in Singapore does not mean that it is highly sensitive to the value of the Singapore dollar. To be sure, the labor component of costs will be sensitive, but raw materials are likely to come from other markets. If the finished product is sold in non-Singaporean markets, there may be little sensitivity here as well. The key is whether prices can be adjusted to provide a U.S. dollar margin. If the goods are priced in world markets, which are U.S. dollar sensitive, the market position/operating capacity value of the subsidiary will be relatively insensitive to the Sing. $/U.S. $ exchange rate.

AGGREGATE ECONOMIC EXPOSURE

When the market-value column is multiplied by the exposure coefficient column, we obtain the exposed market value for the various balance sheet items. Liability exposure, of course, offsets asset exposure. Thus, we subtract total liability exposure from total asset exposure to obtain net aggregate market-value exposure. In our case, net aggregate market-value exposure is seen at the bottom of the table to be $20.1 million. This compares with the market value of shareholders' equity of $80.1 million.

It is useful to put things on a relative basis with the following:

$$\text{Aggregate exposure coefficient} = \frac{\text{Net aggregate market-value exposure}}{\text{Market value of equity}} \qquad (26\text{-}1)$$

For our example, the aggregate exposure coefficient for the Tan Lee Feu subsidiary is

$$\text{Aggregate exposure coefficient} = \$20.1/\$80.1 = 25.1\%$$

This means that its exposure is asset sensitive. If the Singaporean dollar should rise by 10 percent, the subsidiary's U.S. dollar value will decline by $10\% \times .251 = 2.51$ percent, and vice versa. If the aggregate exposure coefficient were negative, the subsidiary would be liability sensitive and a rise in value of the Singaporean dollar would result in a rise in U.S. dollar value of the subsidiary. For most situations, there will be net asset sensitivity. Typically, the more global the markets served, the less the overall exposure.

We see that the Hekman framework can be used to assess the economic exposure of a company. This perspective is essential before we can address what to do. Simply put, we must know what exposure we face before we can go about managing it.

MANAGEMENT OF EXPOSURE

There are a number of ways by which exchange-rate exposure can be managed. Natural hedges, cash management, adjusting intercompany accounts, financing hedges, and currency hedges, through forward contracts, futures contracts, exchange-rate options, and currency swaps, all serve this purpose.

NATURAL HEDGES

The relationship between revenues (prices) and costs often provides a natural hedge, giving the firm ongoing protection from exchange-rate fluctuations. The key is the extent to which cash flows adjust naturally to currency changes. It is not the country in which a subsidiary is located that matters, but whether its revenue and cost functions are sensitive to global or to domestic market conditions. At the extremes there are four situations.[4]

---

[4] For further categorization and explanation, see Hekman, "Don't Blame Currency Values for Strategic Errors."

SCENARIO	GLOBALLY DETERMINED	DOMESTICALLY DETERMINED
1. Pricing	x	
Cost	x	
2. Pricing		x
Cost		x
3. Pricing	x	
Cost		x
4. Pricing		x
Cost	x	

In the first category, we might have a copper fabricator in Taiwan. Its principal cost is copper, the raw material, whose price is determined in global markets and quoted in dollars. Moreover, the fabricated product produced is sold in markets dominated by global pricing. Therefore, the subsidiary has little exposure to exchange-rate fluctuations. In other words, there is a natural hedge. The second category might correspond to a cleaning service company in Belgium. The dominant cost component is labor, and both it and the pricing of the service are determined domestically. As domestic inflation hits costs, the subsidiary is able to pass along the increase in its pricing to customers. Margins, expressed in U.S. dollars, are relatively insensitive to the combination of domestic inflation and exchange-rate changes. This situation also constitutes a natural hedge.

The third situation might involve a British-based international consulting firm. Pricing is largely determined in global markets, whereas costs, again mostly labor, are determined in the domestic market. If, due to inflation, the British pound should decrease in value relative to the dollar, costs will rise relative to prices, and margins will suffer. Here the subsidiary is exposed. Finally, the last category might correspond to a Japanese importer of foreign foods. Costs are determined globally, whereas prices are determined domestically. Here too, the subsidiary would be subject to much exposure.

These simple notions, together with the Hekman framework presented earlier, illustrate the nature of natural hedging. A company's strategic positioning largely determines its natural exposure. However, such exposure can be modified. For one thing, a company can internationally diversify its operations when it is overexposed in one currency. It also can source differently in the production of a product. Apple Computer was exposed in its revenues to pounds sterling. By locating a manufacturing plant in Ireland, a sterling-linked currency, it reduced its net exposure. Any strategic decision that affects markets served, pricing, operations, or sourcing can be thought of as a form of natural hedging. In the remainder of this section, we consider various financial hedges.

CASH MANAGEMENT AND INTERCOMPANY ACCOUNTS

If a company knew a currency were going to fall in value, it would want to do a number of things. First, it should reduce its cash to a minimum by purchasing inventories or other real assets. Moreover, the company should try to avoid extended trade credit. As quick a turnover as possible of receivables into cash is desirable. In contrast, it should try to obtain extended terms on its accounts payable. It may also want to borrow in the local currency to replace advances made by the U.S. parent. The last step will depend on relative interest rates. If the currency were going to appreciate in value, opposite steps should be undertaken. Without knowledge of the future direction of currency value movements, aggressive policies in either direction are inappropriate. Under most circumstances, we are unable to predict the future, so the best policy may be one of balancing monetary assets against monetary liabilities in order to neutralize the effect of exchange-rate fluctuations.

A company with multiple foreign operations can protect itself against foreign exchange risks by adjusting transfer of funds commitments between countries. You may hold a high position in such a company at a time when you think the German mark will soon be revalued upward, but the French franc will hold steady. Your company has foreign subsidiaries in both countries. The French subsidiary purchases approximately $100,000 of goods each month from the German subsidiary. Normal billing calls for payment 3 months after delivery of the goods. Instead of this arrangement, you instruct the French subsidiary to pay for the goods on delivery, in view of the likely revaluation upward of the German mark.

In addition to these arrangements, the multinational company also can adjust intercompany dividends and royalty payments. Sometimes the currency in which a sale is billed is varied in keeping with anticipated foreign exchange movements. Transfer pricing of components or of finished goods, which are exchanged between the parent and various foreign affiliates, can be varied. (However, the tax authorities in most countries look very closely at transfer prices to ensure that taxes are not being avoided.) In all of these cases as well as others, intercompany payments are arranged so that they fit into the company's overall management of its currency exposure.

INTERNATIONAL FINANCING

If a company is exposed in one currency, it can borrow in that country to offset the exposure. In the context of the framework presented earlier, asset sensitive exposure would be balanced with borrowings. Monetary assets and monetary liabilities both have an exposure coefficient of 1.0, so they serve as offsets. A wide variety of sources of external financing are available to the foreign affiliate. These range from commercial bank loans within the host country to loans from international lending agencies. In this section, we consider the chief sources of external financing.

COMMERCIAL BANK LOANS AND TRADE BILLS

One of the major sources of financing abroad, commercial banks perform essentially the same financing function as domestic banks—a topic discussed in Chapter 18. One subtle difference is that banking practices in Europe allow longer-term loans than are available in the United States. Another is that loans tend to be on an overdraft basis. That is, a company writes a check that overdraws its account and is charged interest on the overdraft. Many of these banks are known as merchant banks, which simply means that they offer a full menu of financial services to business firms. Corresponding to the growth in multinational companies, international banking operations of U.S. banks have accommodated. All the principal cities of the free world have branches or offices of a U.S. bank.

In addition to commercial bank loans, discounting trade bills is a common method of short-term financing. Although this method of financing is not used extensively in the United States, it is widely used in Europe to finance both domestic and international trade. More will be said about the instruments involved later in the chapter.

EURODOLLAR FINANCING

A *Eurodollar* is defined as a dollar deposit held in a bank outside the United States. Since the late 1950s, an active market has developed for these deposits. Foreign banks and foreign branches of U.S. banks, mostly in Europe, bid actively for Eurodollar deposits, paying interest rates that fluctuate in keeping with supply and demand. The deposits are in large denominations, frequently $100,000 or more, and the banks use them to make dollar loans to quality borrowers. The loans are made at a rate in excess of the deposit rate; the differential varies according to the relative risk of the borrower. Essentially, borrowing and lending Eurodollars is a wholesale operation, with far fewer costs than are usually associated with banking. The market itself is unregulated, so supply and demand forces have free rein. The Eurodollar deposit rate usually is slightly above the rate paid by American banks on large, domestic certificates of deposit of the same maturity.

The Eurodollar market is a major source of short-term financing for the working capital requirements of the multinational company. Many American firms arrange for lines of credit and revolving credits from Eurodollar banks. For the revolving credit arrangement, the firm pays a commitment fee, the same as it does for a domestic revolving credit. In addition, there often is a front-end fee that is expressed as a percentage of the total loan. This one-time load charge might be 1 to 3 percent. The interest rate on loans is based on the Eurodollar deposit rate and bears only an indirect relationship to the prime rate. Typically, rates on loans are quoted in terms of the London interbank offered rate, commonly called LIBOR. The greater the risk, the greater the spread above LIBOR. A prime borrower will pay about one-half percent over LIBOR for an intermediate-term loan. One should realize that LIBOR is more volatile than the U.S. prime rate, owing to the sensitive nature of supply and demand for Eurodollar deposits. Consequently, it is more difficult to project the cost of a Eurodollar loan than that of a domestic loan. Nevertheless, no compensating balances are required, thus enhancing the attractiveness of this kind of financing.

We should point out that the Eurodollar market is part of a larger Eurocurrency market where deposit and lending rates are quoted on the stronger currencies of the world. The principles involved in these markets are the same as for the Eurodollar market, so we do not repeat them. The development of Eurocurrency markets has greatly facilitated international borrowing and financial intermediation. In addition to the Eurocurrency markets, the Asiadollar market has developed rapidly during the last decade, what with the large trade surpluses of Japan and other Far Eastern countries.

INTERNATIONAL BOND FINANCING

The Eurocurrency market must be distinguished from the *Eurobond market*. The latter market is a more traditional one, with underwriters placing securities. While a bond issue is dominated in a single currency, it is placed in multiple countries. Once issued, it is traded over the counter in multiple countries and by a number of security dealers. A Eurobond is different from a *foreign bond*, where a bond is issued by a foreign government or corporation in a local market. Such a bond is sold in a single country and falls under the security regulations of that country. "Yankee bonds" are issued by non-Americans in the U.S. market; "samurai bonds" are issued by non-Japanese in the Japanese market.

With Eurobonds, foreign bonds, and domestic bonds of different countries, there are numerous differences in terminology, in the way interest is computed, and in features. We do not address these differences, as that would require a separate book. The total amount of bonds outstanding worldwide is over $10 trillion, a staggering sum, even larger than equities. The leading currencies of denomination are the U.S. dollar, the yen, the deutschemark, the pound sterling, the lira, and the French franc. In recent years, the *European Currency Unit* (ECU) has become important. The ECU is a composite of a number of European currencies. This weighted currency basket provides a degree of exchange rate stability not found in any one currency. The ECU exchange rate is the average exchange rate of the currencies involved.

Many debt issues in the international arena are floating-rate notes (FRNs). These instruments have a variety of features, often involving multiple currencies. Some instruments are indexed to price levels or to commodity prices. Others are linked to an interest rate, such as LIBOR. The reset interval may be annual, semiannual, quarterly, or even more frequent. Still other instruments have option features.

CURRENCY-OPTION
AND MULTIPLE-CURRENCY BONDS

Certain bonds provide the holder with the right to choose the currency in which payment is received, usually prior to each coupon or principal payment. Typically this option is confined to two currencies, though it can be more. For example, a 6 percent bond might be issued in deutschemarks with semiannual coupons of DM30 per bond. The bond might have the option to receive payment in either DMs or in pounds sterling. The exchange rate is fixed at the time of issue.

If the £/DM exchange rate were 3.0, the bondholder could choose to receive a coupon payment of 30 deutschemarks or 10 pounds sterling, and a final principal payment of either DM1,000 or 333.33 pounds. The bondholder obviously will choose the payment that is most advantageous at the time. If the DM should appreciate relative to the pound, holders will elect payment in DMs; if it should depreciate, they will choose pounds. (This assumes the exchange rate at the time of issue is roughly the same as the spot exchange rate.) As with any option, it benefits the holder in being able to choose the stronger currency.

Another option feature is a *conversion option*, which permits an instrument dominated in one currency to be converted into an instrument dominated in another. A Japanese company might issue a U.S. dollar bond, which is convertible into shares of stock quoted in yen. The exchange rate of yen into dollars is fixed at the time of issuance (via the combined conversion/exchange ratio). Thus, two options are involved: (1) a conversion option of the bond into so many shares of common stock (see Chapter 23), and (2) a currency option. If the yen rises in value relative to the U.S. dollar, the investor benefits in being able to exchange a dollar asset, the bond, into a yen asset, common stock.

Bond issues sometimes are floated in multiple currencies. Known as a "currency cocktail," the market value of the bond is less volatile than that of a bond dominated in a single currency. With a *dual currency bond*, interest and principal payments are made in different currencies. For example, a Swiss bond might call for interest payments in Swiss francs and principal payments in U.S. dollars. In this case, the value of the bond is found by (1) discounting the interest payments to present value using a Swiss interest rate, and (2) discounting the principal payment at maturity to present value using a dollar interest rate. We see, then, that a variety of currency features are possible.

CURRENCY MARKET HEDGES

Yet another means to hedge currency exposure is through one of several currency markets—forward contracts, futures contracts, currency options, and currency swaps. Let us see how these markets work to protect us.

FORWARD EXCHANGE MARKET

In the forward exchange market, one buys a forward contract for the exchange of one currency for another at a specific future date and at a specific exchange ratio. A forward contract provides assurance of being able to convert into a desired currency at a price set in advance.

The Xicon Electronics Company is hedging through the forward market. It sold equipment to a French customer through its Paris branch for 1 million francs with terms of 90 days. Upon payment, Xicon intends to convert the francs into dollars. The spot and 90-day forward rates of French francs in terms of dollars were the following:

Spot rate	$.168
90-day forward	.166

The spot rate is simply the current market-determined exchange rate for French francs. In our example, 1 franc is worth 16.8 cents, and $1 will buy $1.00/.168 = 5.95$ francs. A foreign currency sells at a *forward discount* if its forward price is less than its spot price. In our example, the French franc sells at a discount. If the forward price exceeds the spot price, it is said to sell at a *forward premium*. For example, the deutschemark sells at a forward premium. In other words, deutschemarks buy more dollars for future delivery than they do for present delivery.

If Xicon wishes to avoid foreign exchange risk, it should sell 1 million francs forward 90 days. When it delivers the francs 90 days hence, it will receive $166,000 (1 million francs times the 90-day forward price of $.166). If the spot rate stays at $.168, of course, Xicon would be better off not having sold francs forward. It could sell 1 million francs in the spot market for $168,000. In this sense, Xicon pays $.002 per franc, or $2,000 in total, to insure its ability to convert French francs to dollars. On an annualized basis, the cost of this protection is

$$\left(\frac{.002}{.168}\right)\left(\frac{365}{90}\right) = 4.83\%$$

For stable pairs of currencies, the discount or premium of the forward rate over the spot rate varies from zero to 10 percent on an annualized basis. For somewhat less stable currencies, the discount or premium will be higher. For an unstable currency, the discount may go as high as 25 percent. Much beyond this point of instability, the forward market for the currency ceases to exist. In summary, the forward exchange market allows a company to insure against devaluation or market-determined declines in value.

Quotations on selected foreign exchanges at a moment in time are shown in Table 26-4. The spot rates reported in the first column indicate the conversion rate into dollars. What is quoted in the financial press is the interbank or wholesale rate. Retail transactions provide fewer units of the foreign currency per U.S. dollar. At the top of the table, the Australian dollar is seen to be worth $.798, or $1/.798 = A$1.253. Forward rates for 30, 90, and 180 days are shown for the British pound, the Canadian dollar, the French franc, the German deutschemark, and the Japanese yen.

Through the use of the forward market, the effect of exchange-rate fluctuations on cash flows can be blunted. The forward market is particularly suited for hedging transactions exposure. For this protection, there is a cost, determined by the relationship between the forward rate and the subsequent future spot rate. The greater the possibility of currency value changes and the greater the risk aversion of the firm, the greater the case that can be made for the use of the forward market. If others feel the same way, unfortunately, the cost of this insurance will rise.

CURRENCY FUTURES

Closely related to the use of a forward contract is a futures contract. Currency futures markets exist for the major currencies of the world—the Australian dollar, the Canadian dollar, the British pound, the French franc, the Swiss franc, the Japanese yen, and the German deutschemark. A futures contract is a standardized agreement that calls for delivery of a currency at some specified future date, either the third Wednesday of March, or June, or September, or December. Contracts are traded on an exchange, and the clearinghouse of the exchange interposes itself between the buyer and the seller. This means that all transactions are with the clearinghouse, not direct between the two parties. Very few contracts involve actual delivery at expiration. Rather, buyers and sellers of a contract independently take offsetting positions to close out a contract. The seller cancels a contract by buying another contract; the buyer, by selling another contract.

Each day, the futures contract is *marked-to-market* in the sense that it is valued at the closing price. Price movements affect the buyer and seller in op-

TABLE 26-4
Foreign exchange rates, July 6, 1990

	U.S. DOLLARS REQUIRED TO BUY ONE UNIT	UNITS REQUIRED TO BUY ONE U.S. DOLLAR
Australia (dollar)	$.798	1.253
Austria (schilling)	.086	11.64
Brazil (cruzeiro)	.016	65.83
Britain (pound)	1.785	.560
30-day forward	1.775	.563
90-day forward	1.756	.569
180-day forward	1.730	.578
Canada (dollar)	.861	1.162
30-day forward	.857	1.167
90-day forward	.850	1.177
180-day forward	.840	1.190
France (franc)	.180	5.550
30-day forward	.180	5.558
90-day forward	.179	5.574
180-day forward	.179	5.599
Germany (deutschemark)	.605	1.653
30-day forward	.605	1.653
90-day forward	.605	1.653
180-day forward	.604	1.655
Hong Kong (dollar)	.129	7.778
Italy (lira)	.0008	1,213.50
Japan (yen)	.0066	151.60
30-day forward	.0066	151.49
90-day forward	.0066	151.35
180-day forward	.0066	151.12
Malaysia (ringgit)	.369	2.706
Mexico (peso)	.0003	2,859.01
Netherlands (guilder)	.537	1.863
Saudi Arabia (rial)	.267	3.748
Singapore (dollar)	.546	1.830
Spain (peseta)	.010	101.40
Sweden (krona)	.167	5.998
Switzerland (franc)	.715	1.399
Taiwan (dollar)	.037	26.75
Thailand (baht)	.039	25.64

posite ways. Every day there is a winner and a loser, depending on the direction of price movement. The loser must come up with more margin (a small deposit), while the winner can draw off excess margin. Futures contracts are different from forward contracts in this regard; the latter need to be settled only at expiration. Another difference is that only a set number of maturities are available. Finally, futures contracts come only in multiples of standard-size contracts—for example, multiples of 125,000 deutschemarks or 12.5 million yen. Forward contracts can be for almost any size.

The two instruments, however, are used for the same hedging purpose. Suppose Poipu Manufacturing Company will collect a 250,000 Swiss franc receivable 90 days hence. If we now are in the middle of March, it could sell June futures contracts that call for the delivery of Swiss francs for dollars. In this way, the company locks in a certain conversion ratio today. This is the same principle as with a forward contract; the future conversion ratio of one currency for another is set in advance.[5] The futures markets are liquid, and this affords the company flexibility in reversing a position if a condition should change.

CURRENCY OPTIONS

Forward and futures contracts provide a "two-sided" hedge against currency movements. That is, if the currency involved moves in one direction, the forward or futures position offsets it. *Currency options*, in contrast, enable the hedging of "one-sided" risk. Only adverse currency movements are hedged, either with a call option to buy the foreign currency or with a put option to sell it. The holder has the right, but not the obligation, to buy or sell the currency over the life of the contract. If not exercised, of course, the option expires. For this protection, one pays a premium.

There are both options on spot market currencies and options on currency futures contracts. Because currency options are traded on a number of exchanges throughout the world, one is able to trade with relative ease. The use of currency options and their valuation are largely the same as described in Chapter 5 for stock options, so we do not repeat that discussion. The value of the option, and hence the premium paid, depend importantly on exchange-rate volatility.

CURRENCY SWAPS

Yet another device for shifting risk is the currency swap. In a currency swap, two parties exchange debt obligations dominated in different currencies. Each party agrees to pay the other's interest obligation. At maturity, principal amounts are exchanged, usually at a rate of exchange agreed upon in advance. The currency swap market traces its roots to the 1960s, when *parallel loans* were arranged between two borrowers of different nationalities. Suppose a U.S. parent company wishes to lend $1 million to its German subsidiary for 3 years. At the same time, a German company wishes to lend money to its U.S. subsidiary. If the amounts and maturities are the same, an intermediary might bring the two companies together in a parallel loan arrangement. Instead of lending to its German subsidiary, the U.S. company extends a $1 million 3-year loan to the U.S. subsidiary of the German company. Likewise, the German company makes a deutschemark loan to the German subsidiary of the U.S. company. The parallel loan was the antecedent to the currency swap.

The currency swap, as we know it today, is a product of the 1970s. In a *straight currency swap*, two parties agree to pay each other's debt obligations. An illustration is shown in Fig. 26-2, involving a British company and a U.S. company. The annual interest obligations are 12 percent in British pounds and 11 percent in U.S. dollars. Maturity is 3 years, the exchange rate fixed in the swap is 1.80 dollars to the pound, and the amount of debt involved in the swap is 1 million pounds. On an annual basis, the U.S. company pays the British company £120,000 in interest, (£1 million × .12), while the British company pays the U.S. company $198,000, (£1 million × 1.80 × .11). At the

---

[5] See James C. Van Horne, *Financial Market rates and Flows*, 3d ed. (Englewood Cliffs, NJ: Prentice Hall, 1990), Chaps. 7 and 11, for a detailed discussion of futures markets.

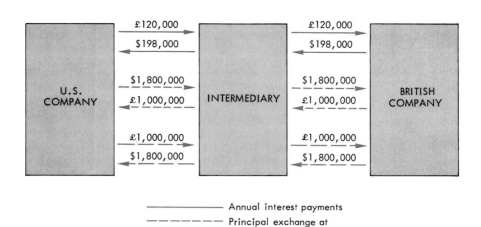

FIGURE 26-2

Illustration of a
currency swap (fixed
rate-to-fixed rate)

——————————— Annual interest payments

— — — — — — Principal exchange at
beginning of year 1

— — — — Principal exchange at
end of year 3

end of 3 years, the principal amounts of $1.8 million and £1 million are ex-changed back.

The exchanges themselves are notational in that only cash flow differ-ences are paid. If the exchange rate in the first year stays at 1.80 pounds to the dollar, on paper the British company owes the U.S. company the equivalent of £110,000 ($198,000/1.80) in annual interest. The U.S. company owes the British company £120,000 in interest, but it pays only the difference of £10,000. In the second year, suppose the pound appreciates to 2.00 dollars to the pound. In this situation, the British company owes the U.S. company the equivalent of £99,000 ($198,000/2.00) in interest. The differential the U.S. company now pays is £21,000 (£120,000 − £99,000). If at the end of 3 years the exchange rate were again 2.00 dollars to the pound, the interest differen-tial owed by the U.S. company would be £21,000. With respect to principal, the British company owes the U.S. company the equivalent of £900,000 ($1.8 million/2.00). As the U.S. company owes £1 million in principal, the principal differential payment it must make is £100,000.

As with an interest-rate swap, there is not an actual exchange of princi-pal. If one party defaults, there is no loss of principal per se. There is, how-ever, the opportunity cost associated with currency movements after the swap's initiation. These movements affect both interest and principal pay-ments, as we have seen. In this respect, currency swaps are more risky than interest-rate swaps, where the exposure is only to interest. The example just cited is a fixed rate-to-fixed rate exchange of borrowings.

Currency/Interest-Rate Swaps.   Currency swaps can be, and often are, combined with interest-rate swaps. In Chapter 22, we examined the mechan-ics and valuation of interest-rate swaps. With a combined swap, there is a ex-change of fixed-rate for floating-rate payments where the two payments are in different currencies. For example, a Japanese company might swap a 3-year, fixed-rate German deutschemark liability for a 3-year French franc liability where the floating rate is tied to LIBOR. From the standpoint of the Japanese company, there is a combination deutschemark/French franc currency swap, together with a fixed/floating interest-rate swap. A number of extensions are possible: more than two currencies, options, and other features. As can be imagined, things get complicated rather quickly.

SHOULD EXPOSURE BE MANAGED?

In the foregoing, we have looked at ways to manage a company's exposure to exchange-rate fluctuations. If international product and financial markets were perfect and complete, it would not be optimal for a company to engage in any of the defensive tactics just considered. The transaction costs of such moves would be a net drain to suppliers of capital. Instantaneous price adjustments to change would occur in both markets, and suppliers of capital would not be concerned with the variability of cash flows and earnings of an individual firm. It is only when we admit to imperfections and incompleteness in such markets that a case can be made for the various hedging strategies discussed.[6]

When it comes to international investments, certain scholars argue that one should always hedge currency exposure. The idea is that one can achieve substantial reductions in risk with no significant loss of expected return.[7] The average expected return on a currency hedge is zero, and transactions costs are minimal. While this argument has been modified theoretically by Fischer Black, who shows that some unhedged currency risk should be borne,[8] it is rather compelling in its risk-reduction implications.

Only if the financial markets of the world are unrestricted and fully integrated would such risk reduction not be a thing of value. The disadvantage to hedging, of course, is transactions costs. Although these costs are minimal for a single transaction, they mount up with multiple transactions and the rebalancing of a hedged position. In addition, there are accounting costs associated with recording transactions on the firm's books. Neither of these costs is large, but they are sufficient to make currency hedging a losing proposition *unless* risk reduction is a thing of value to the company's stockholders. In turn, this depends on imperfections and/or incompleteness in world financial markets.

While large companies may engage in self-insurance, based on the notion that changes in exchange rates average out over time with enough commercial transactions, costs of bankruptcy and agency costs make extensive exposure, particularly for the smaller firm, unwise. For reasons of imperfections and incompleteness in international product and financial markets, then, most companies manage their currency-risk exposure. Certainly, a degree of self-insurance occurs, but few companies are willing to risk everything on future exchange rates. Not only is currency exposure management consistent with managerial survival, but it can be defended on the basis of maximizing shareholder wealth. The real issue is not so much whether a company manages currency-risk exposure or not, but the degree of management. It may well overemphasize such management in an attempt to ensure managerial survival when shareholders would be better off with a degree of self-insurance.

---

[6] For an excellent review of the arguments for and against exchange-risk management, see Gunter Dufey and S. L. Srinivasulu, "The Case for Corporate Management of Foreign Exchange Risk," *Financial Management*, 12 (Winter 1983), 54–62.

[7] This argument is associated with Andre F. Perold and Evan C. Schulman, "The Free Lunch in Currency Hedging: Implications for Investment Policy and Performance Standards," *Financial Analysts Journal*, 44 (May–June 1988), 45–50.

[8] Fischer Black, "Equilibrium Exchange Rate Hedging," *Journal of Finance*, 45 (July 1990), 899–908.

Fluctuations in exchange rates are continual and often defy explanation, at least in the short run. In the longer run, however, there are linkages between domestic and foreign inflation, and between interest rates and foreign exchange rates. These relationships provide an underlying theory of international product and financial market equilibrium. We first present the theory, which assumes free trade and an absence of imperfections, and then touch on the empirical evidence.

THE LAW OF ONE PRICE

Simply put, the *law of one price* says that a commodity will sell for the same price regardless of where it is purchased. More formally, for a single good

$$P^{FC} = P^{\$} \times S^{(FC/\$)} \tag{26-2}$$

where P^{FC} is the price of the good in a foreign currency, $P^{\$}$ is the price of the good in the United States, and $S^{(FC/\$)}$ is the spot exchange rate of the foreign currency per dollar.

If it is cheaper to buy wheat from Argentina than it is from a U.S. producer, after transportation costs and after adjusting the Argentine price for the exchange rate, a rational U.S. buyer will purchase Argentine wheat. This action, together with commodity arbitrage, will cause the Argentine wheat price to rise relative to the U.S. price and, perhaps, for the austral exchange rate to strengthen. The combination of rising Argentine wheat prices and a changing austral value raises the dollar price of Argentine wheat to the U.S. buyer. Theory would have it that these transactions would continue until the dollar cost of wheat was the same. At that point, the purchaser would be indifferent between U.S. and Argentine wheat. For that matter, an Argentine buyer of wheat also would be indifferent. For this to hold, of course, transportation and transactions costs must be zero, and there must be no impediments to trade.

PURCHASING POWER PARITY

The law of one price is really a way to express *purchasing power parity* (PPP). Invoking the law of one price, PPP says that the rate of exchange between currencies of two countries is directly related to the differential rate of inflation between them. Any change in the differential rate of inflation is offset by an opposite movement in the spot exchange rate. From Eq. (26-2), PPP implies

$$1 + P^{\wedge FC} = [1 + P^{\wedge \$}] \times [1 + S^{\wedge(FC/\$)}] \tag{26-3}$$

where the $\wedge$ represents the rate of change in the price level or in the exchange rate. Rearranging,

$$\frac{1 + P^{\wedge FC}}{1 + P^{\wedge \$}} = 1 + S^{\wedge(FC/\$)} \tag{26-4}$$

If the annual rate of inflation is 5 percent in the United States and 3 percent in Belgium, the implication is

$$1.03/1.05 = .9810$$

or that the Belgium franc must appreciate in value relative to the dollar by approximately 1.90 percent on an annualized basis. If instead the rate of inflation in Belgium were 10 percent, we would have

$$1.10/1.05 = 1.0476$$

which means the Belgium franc should decline in value, relative to the dollar, by approximately 4.76 percent.

As an approximation to Eq. (26-4), many people use

$$P^{\wedge FC} - P^{\wedge \$} = S^{\wedge (FC/\$)} \tag{26-5}$$

where the exchange-rate change is directly related to the inflation differential. For our examples, the changes in the Belgium franc per dollar would be +2 percent and −5 percent. In the context of this formula, purchasing power parity is illustrated in Figure 26-3. Eq. (26-5) can be used in an expectational sense. For example, suppose we expect inflation in Belgium to exceed that in the United States by 3 percent and the spot exchange rate now is 35 Belgium francs to the dollar. At the end of one year, the exchange rate should be BF35(1 − .03) = BF33.95. Again remember that this is but an approximation. For greater accuracy, we whould use Eq. (26-4).

How closely a country's exchange rate corresponds to purchasing power parity depends on the price elasticity of exports and imports. To the extent exports are traded in world competitive markets, there usually is close conformity to PPP. Commodities and fabricated products like steel and clothing are

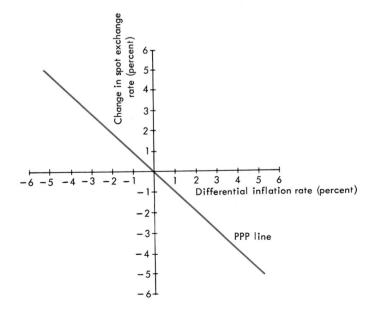

FIGURE 26-3

Approximation of purchasing power parity (PPP) between two countries

highly price sensitive. In general, products in mature industries conform more closely to PPP than products in newer industries with emerging technology. To the extent a country's inflation is dominated by services, there tends to be less conformity to PPP. We know also that PPP does not work well when a country intervenes in the exchange-rate market, either propping up its currency or keeping it artificially low. Before we look at the empirical evidence on PPP, we present the third link to our conceptual framework.

INTEREST-RATE PARITY

The last link concerns the interest-rate differential between two countries. *Interest-rate parity* suggests that if interest rates are higher in one country than they are in another, the former's currency will sell at a discount in the forward market. Expressed differently, interest-rate differentials and forward-spot exchange-rate differentials are offsetting. How does it work? The starting point is the relationship between nominal interest rates and inflation. Recall from Chapter 21 that the *Fisher effect* implies that the nominal rate of interest is comprised of the real rate plus the rate of inflation expected to prevail over the life of the instrument. Thus

$$r = R + P^\wedge \qquad (26\text{-}6)$$

where r is the nominal rate, R is the inflation-adjusted real rate of interest, and $P^\wedge$ is rate of inflation per annum expected over the life of the instrument.[9]

In an international context, sometimes called the *international Fisher effect,* the equation suggests that differences in interest rates between two countries serve as a proxy for differences in expected inflation. For example, if the nominal interest rate were 8 percent in the United States but 15 percent in Australia, the expected differential in inflation would be 7 percent. That is, inflation in Australia is expected to be 7 percent higher than in the United States. Does this hold exactly? While there is disagreement as to the precise relationship between nominal interest rates and inflation, most people feel that expected inflation for a country has a powerful effect on interest rates in that country. The more open the capital markets, the closer the conformity to an international Fisher effect.

Remember from purchasing power parity that exchange rates were directly tied to the inflation differential between two countries. Through the common link of inflation differentials, it figures that exchange-rate differentials should be related to interest-rate differentials. The mechanism by which this manifests itself is the difference between the spot rate of exchange and the forward exchange rate.

To illustrate interest-rate parity, consider the relationship between the U.S. dollar (\$) and the British pound (£) both now and 90 days in the future; the theorem suggests that

$$\frac{F(£/\$)}{S(£/\$)} = \frac{1 + r_£}{1 + r_\$}$$

---

[9] Mathematically, the correct expression is $r = R + P^\wedge + RP^\wedge$. Unless the inflation rate is large, most ignore the cross product term.

where $F(£/\$)$ = current 90-day forward exchange rate in pounds per dollar
$S(£/\$)$ = current spot exchange rate in pounds per dollar
$r_£$ = nominal British interbank Euromarket interest rate, expressed in terms of the 90-day return
$r_\$$ = nominal U.S. interbank Euromarket interest rate, expressed in terms of the 90-day return

If the nominal interest rate in Britain were 10 percent and the nominal U.S. rate 8 percent, these annualized rates translate into 90-day rates of 2.5 percent and 2 percent, respectively. If the current spot rate were .60 pounds per dollar, we would have

$$\frac{F(£/\$)}{.60} = \frac{1.025}{1.02}$$

Solving for the implied forward rate

$$1.02F(£/\$) = .615$$

$$F(£/\$) = .603$$

Thus, the implied forward rate is .603 British pounds per U.S. dollar. The British pound forward rate is at a discount from the spot rate of .60 pounds to the dollar. That is, a pound is worth less in terms of dollars in the forward market, $1/.603 = \$1.658$, than it is in the spot market, $1/.60 = \$1.667$. The discount is $(.603 - .60)/.60 = .005$. With interest-rate parity, the discount must equal the relative difference in interest rates and, indeed, this is the case, for $(1.025 - 1.02)/1.02 = .005$. If the interest rate in Britain were less than that in the United States, the implied forward rate in our example would be less than the spot rate. In this case, the British pound forward rate would be at a premium above the spot rate. For example, if the U.S. interest rate (annualized) were 10 percent and the British rate 8 percent, the implied 90-day forward rate for British pounds would be

$$\frac{F(£/\$)}{.60} = \frac{1.02}{1.025}$$

Solving for $F(£/\$)$, we have

$$1.025F(£/\$) = .612$$

$$F(£/\$) = .597$$

Therefore, the forward rate is at a premium in the sense that it is worth more in terms of dollars in the forward market than it is in the spot market.

COVERED INTEREST ARBITRAGE

If interest rate parity did not occur, presumably arbitragers would be alert to the opportunity for profit. In our first example, had the British pound 90-day forward rate been .610 instead of .603, an arbitrager, recognizing this deviation, would borrow in Britain at 10 percent interest for 90 days. If the amount involved were £100,000, the amount due at the end of 90 days would be £100,000(1.025) = £102,500. Upon receipt of the pound loan, the arbitrager should convert the £100,000 into dollars in the spot market. At an exchange rate of .65, this comes to $166,667. This amount then should be invested at 8 percent interest for 90 days. At the end of 90 days, the arbitrager will have $166,667(1.02) = $170,000. To cover the loan's repayment in pounds, the arbitrager should buy British pounds 90 days forward. He or she will need £102,500 to repay the loan. At a 90-day forward rate of .61 British pounds per U.S. dollar, it will require £102,500/.61 = $168,033.

In this series of transactions, which is known as *covered interest arbitrage*, the profit is equal to the receipt of funds from investment less the repayment of the loan. For our example

$$\text{Arbitrage profit} = \$170,000 - \$168,033 = \$1,967$$

Arbitrage actions of this sort increase the demand for British pounds in the forward market and increase the supply of dollars. Moreover, borrowing in Britain will tend to increase interest rates there, while lending in the United States will lower American rates. The combination of these forces will work to reduce the interest rate differential as well as reduce the discount for the British pound forward exchange rate. Arbitrage actions will continue until interest-rate parity is established and there is zero profit potential on covered interest arbitrage.

INTEREST-RATE PARITY APPROXIMATION

On an annualized basis, interest-rate parity can be expressed as

$$\frac{F^{(FC/\$)} - S^{(FC/\$)}}{S^{(FC/\$)}} = r_{FC} - r_\$ \tag{26-7}$$

where the forward rate and the two interest rates are for one-year contracts/instruments. Using our earlier example for British pounds, where the current spot exchange rate is .60 and U.K. and U.S. interest rates are 10 percent and 8 percent, respectively, the implied discount in the one-year forward market is 2 percent of the spot rate. This means that the forward rate is greater than the spot rate by 2 percent; more pounds per dollar in the future implies a weaker pound over time. The absolute, as opposed to the percentage, discount using Eq. (26-7) is

$$F^{(£/\$)} - S^{(£/\$)} = (.10 - .08).60 = .012$$

Thus, the implied forward rate of pounds per dollar one year hence is .60 + .012 = .612.

This simple formula tells us that interest-rate differentials are a proxy for forward exchange rate/spot exchange rate differentials, and vice versa. Equation (26-7) is expressed graphically in Figure 26-4. The upper right-hand quadrant represents a foreign currency discount because the forward exchange rate of the foreign currency per dollar exceeds the spot rate. That is to say, the foreign currency is expected to depreciate in terms of dollars. In contrast, the lower left-hand quadrant represents a foreign currency premium, for the forward exchange rate is less than the spot rate.

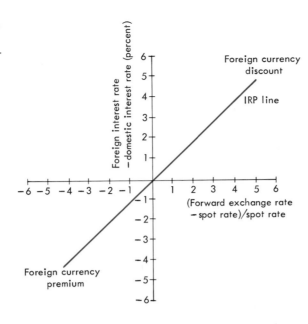

FIGURE 26-4

Approximation of interest-rate parity between two countries (IRP)

EMPIRICAL EVIDENCE IN GENERAL

The theories presented provide a useful framework for understanding the way things should work for international equilibrium to be achieved. Do they work this way? Not in the short run. For purchasing-power parity to hold, there cannot be significant imperfections. We know there are frictions, trade barriers, government intervention in the exchange market, and other things of this sort. In addition, different people have different consumption patterns and different baskets of goods and services they prefer. Thus, there is not a common inflation measure for all peoples of the world, so there are measurement problems in establishing what is inflation. For these reasons, it often takes several years for an imbalance, or deviation from PPP, to be corrected.[10] Still, PPP seems to hold in the long run, and it helps us to understand the likely direction of change. The problem is that the long run can prove to be very long.

For the interest-rate parity theorem, results are similar; in general, it does not hold in the short run. For certain European currencies, however, where imperfections are less prevalent, interest-rate parity shows some explanatory power even in the short run. In the longer run (more than one year), support for interest-rate parity is convincing.

FINANCING INTERNATIONAL TRADE

Foreign trade differs from domestic trade with respect to the instruments and documents employed. Most domestic sales are on open-account credit; the customer is billed and has so many days to pay. In international trade, sellers are seldom able to obtain as accurate or as thorough credit information on po-

---

[10] For a review of the evidence on this and other theories, see Bruno Solnik, *International Investments* (Reading, MA: Addison-Wesley, 1988), Chap. 1. See also Niso Abuaf and Philippe Jorion, "Purchasing Power Parity in the Long Run," *Journal of Finance*, 45 (March 1990), 157–74.

tential buyers as they are in domestic sales. Communication is more cumbersome, and transportation of the goods is slower and less certain. Moreover, the channels for legal settlement in cases of default are more complicated and more costly to pursue. For these reasons, procedures for international trade differ from those for domestic trade. There are three key documents: an order to pay, or draft; a bill of lading, which involves the physical movement of the goods; and a letter of credit, which gurantees the creditworthiness of the buyer. We examine each in turn.

THE TRADE DRAFT

The international draft, sometimes called a bill of exchange, is simply a written statement by the exporter ordering the importer to pay a specific amount of money at a specific time. Although the word "order" may seem harsh, it is the customary way of doing business internationally. The draft may be either a *sight* draft or a *time* draft. A sight draft is payable on presentation to the party to whom the draft is addressed. This party is known as the *drawee.* If the drawee, or importer, does not pay the amount specified upon presentation of the draft, he or she defaults, and redressment is achieved through the letter of credit arrangement to be discussed later. A time draft is payable so many days after presentation to the drawee.[11] A 90-day time draft indicates that the draft is payable 90 days after sight. An example of a time draft is shown in Fig. 26-5.

Several features should be noted about the draft. First, it is an unconditional order in writing signed by the drawer, the exporter. It specifies an exact amount of money that the drawee, the importer, must pay. Finally, it specifies an exact interval after sight at which time this amount must be paid. Upon presentation of the time draft to the drawee, it is accepted. The *acceptance* can be by either the drawee or a bank. If the drawee accepts the draft, he or she acknowledges in writing on the back of the draft the obligation to pay the amount specified 90 days hence. The draft then is known as a trade acceptance. If a bank accepts the draft, it is known as a bankers' acceptance. The

---

[11] The draft itself can be either "clean" or "documentary." A clean draft is one to which documents of title are not attached. They are attached to a documentary draft and are delivered to the importer at the time the draft is presented. Clean drafts are usually used when there is no trade as such and the drawer is simply collecting a bill. Most drafts are documentary.

```
    $10,000.00                              January 5, 1992

    ------ Ninety ------ Days after sight
                         Pay to the order of OURSELVES

    Ten thousand and no/100 --------------------- Dollars

To
    Dorts Imports

    Hamburg, Germany              J. Kelly Company Exporters

                                  Palo Alto, California, U.S.A.

                                  By  Joseph Kelly
```

FIGURE 26-5

A time draft

bank accepts responsibility for payment and thereby substitutes its creditworthiness for that of the drawee.

If the bank is large and well known—and most banks accepting drafts are—the instrument becomes highly marketable upon acceptance. As a result, the drawer, or exporter, does not have to hold the draft until the due date; he or she can sell it in the market. In fact, an active market exists for bankers' acceptances of well-known banks. A 90-day draft for $10,000 may be accepted by a well-known bank. Say that 90-day interest rates in the bankers' acceptance market are 8 percent. The drawer then could sell the draft to an investor for $9,800, or $10,000 − [$10,000 × .08(90/360)]. At the end of 90 days, the investor would present the acceptance to the accepting bank for payment and would receive $10,000. Thus, the existence of a strong secondary market for bankers' acceptances has facilitated international trade by providing liquidity to the exporter.

BILLS OF LADING

A bill of lading is a shipping document used in the transportation of goods from the exporter to the importer. It has several functions. First, it serves as a receipt from the transportation company to the exporter, showing that specified goods have been received. Second, it serves as a contract between the transportation company and the exporter to ship the goods and deliver them to a specific party at a specific point of destination. Finally, the bill of lading can serve as a document of title. It gives the holder title to the goods. The importer cannot take title until receipt of the bill of lading from the transportation company or its agent. This bill will not be released until the importer satisfies all the conditions of the draft.[12]

The bill of lading accompanies the draft, and the procedures by which the two are handled are well established. Banks and other institutions able to handle these documents efficiently exist in virtually every country. Moreover, the procedures by which goods are transferred internationally are well grounded in international law. These procedures allow an exporter in one country to sell goods to an unknown importer in another and not release possession of the goods until paid, if there is a sight draft, or until the obligation is acknowledged, if there is a time draft.

LETTERS OF CREDIT

A commercial letter of credit is issued by a bank on behalf of the importer. In the document, the bank agrees to honor a draft drawn on the importer, provided the bill of lading and other details are in order. In essence, the bank substitutes its credit for that of the importer. Obviously, the local bank will not issue a letter of credit unless it feels the importer is creditworthy and will pay the draft. The letter of credit arrangement almost eliminates the exporter's risk in selling goods to an unknown importer in another country.

Illustration of a Confirmed Letter. The arrangement is strengthened further if a bank in the exporter's country *confirms* the letter of credit. A New York exporter wishes to ship goods to a Brazilian importer located in Rio de Janeiro. The importer's bank in Rio regards the importer as a sound credit risk

---

[12] The bill of lading can be negotiable if specified at the time it is made out. It also can be used as collateral for a loan.

and is willing to issue a letter of credit guaranteeing payment for the goods when they are received. Thus, the Rio bank substitutes its credit for that of the importer. The contract is now between the Rio bank and the beneficiary of the letter of credit, the New York exporter. The exporter may wish to work through her bank, because she has little knowledge of the Rio bank. She asks her New York bank to confirm the Rio bank's letter of credit. If the New York bank is satisfied with the creditworthiness of the Rio bank, it will agree to do so. When it does, it obligates itself to honor drafts drawn in keeping with the letter of credit arrangement.

Thus, when the exporter ships the goods, she draws a draft in accordance with the terms of the letter of credit arrangement. She presents the draft to her New York bank and the bank pays her the amount designated, assuming all the conditions of shipment are met. As a result of this arrangement, the exporter has her money, with no worries about payment. The New York bank then forwards the draft and other documents to the Rio bank. Upon affirming that the goods have been shipped in a proper manner, the Rio bank honors the draft and pays the New York bank. In turn, it goes to the Brazilian importer and collects from him once the goods have arrived in Rio and are delivered.

Facilitation of Trade. From the description, it is easy to see why the letter of credit facilitates international trade. Rather than extending credit directly to an importer, the exporter relies on one or more banks, and their creditworthiness is substituted for that of the importer. The letter itself can be either *irrevocable* or *revocable*, but drafts drawn under an irrevocable letter must be honored by the issuing bank. This obligation can be neither cancelled nor modified without the consent of all parties. On the other hand, a revocable letter of credit can be cancelled or amended by the issuing bank. A revocable letter specifies an arrangement for payment but is no guarantee that the draft will be paid. Most letters of credit are irrevocable, and the process described assumes an irrevocable letter.

The three documents described—the draft, the bill of lading, and the letter of credit—are required in most international transactions. Established procedures exist for doing business on this basis. Together, they afford the exporter protection in selling goods to unknown importers in other countries. They also give the importer assurance that the goods will be shipped and delivered in a proper manner. The financial manager should be acquainted with the mechanics of these transactions if the firm is engaged in exporting or importing.

SUMMARY

The financial manager is increasingly becoming involved in global product and financial markets. The globalization movement means that investment and financing decisions must be made in an international arena. Capital budgeting, for example, embraces estimates of future rates of exchange between two currencies. Owing to market segmentation, foreign projects sometimes afford risk-reduction properties that are not available in domestic projects. If capital markets are partially segmented, diversification of stocks internationally may reduce portfolio risk further than can be accomplished through domestic stock diversification.

Expansion abroad is undertaken to go into new markets, acquire less costly production facilities, and secure raw materials. A number of factors make foreign investment different from domestic investment. Taxation is different, and there are risks present in political conditions.

A company faces three types of risk in its foreign operations: translation exposure, transactions exposure, and economic exposure. *Translation exposure* is the change in accounting income and balance sheet statements caused by changes in exchange rates. FASB No. 52 governs the accounting treatment of a foreign subsidiary. *Transactions exposure* relates to settling a particular transaction, like open account credit, at one exchange rate when the obligation was booked at another. *Economic exposure* has to do with the impact of changing exchange rates on expected future cash flows and, hence, on the economic value of the firm. A framework was presented for measuring the degree of economic exposure, which aggregated the individual exposure coefficients for all balance sheet items.

Management of exchange-rate exposure embraces a number of things. Natural hedges involve offsets between revenues and costs with respect to different sensitivities to exchange-rate changes. Natural hedges depend on the degree to which prices and costs are globally determined or domestically determined. A company can protect itself also by balancing monetary assets and liabilities, and by adjusting intercompany accounts. It can hedge by financing in different currencies. The major sources of international financing are commercial banks, discounted trade drafts, Eurodollar and Asiadollar loans, and international bonds. The last includes Eurobonds, foreign bonds, floating rate notes linked to LIBOR, currency-option bonds, and multiple-currency bonds.

Finally, there are currency hedges, which include forward contracts, futures contracts, currency options, and currency swaps. For the first, one buys a forward contract for the exchange of one currency for another at a specific future date and at an exchange ratio set in advance. For this protection, there is a cost that is determined by the difference in the forward and spot exchange rates. Currency futures contracts are like forward contracts in function, but there are differences in settlement and other features. Currency options afford protection against adverse currency movements, for which one pays a premium for the right, but not the obligation, to exercise the option. They are suited for hedging "one-sided" risk. Finally, currency swaps are an important longer-term risk-shifting device. Here, two parties exchange debt obligations in different currencies. Often currency swaps are combined with interest-rate swaps, involving fixed-rate-for-floating-rate exchanges.

Certain underlying theories provide a better understanding of the relationship between inflation, interest rates, and exchange rates. Purchasing-power parity is the idea that a basket of goods should sell at the same price internationlly, after factoring into account exchange rates. Relative inflation has an important influence on exchange rates and on relative interest rates. Interest-rate parity suggests that the difference between forward and spot currency exchange rates can be explained by differences in nominal interest rates between two countries. Empirical evidence is consistent with these theories in the long run but not in the short run.

Three principal documents are involved in international trade. The *draft* is an order by the exporter to the importer to pay a specified amount of money either upon presentation of the draft or a certain number of days after presentation. A *bill of lading* is a shipping document that can serve as a receipt, as a shipping contract, and as title to the goods involved. A *letter of credit* is an agreement by a bank to honor a draft drawn on the importer. It greatly reduces the risk to the exporter and may be confirmed by another bank. These three documents greatly facilitate international trade.

SELF-CORRECTION PROBLEMS

1. The following exchange rates prevail in the foreign currency market:

	U.S. DOLLARS REQUIRED TO BUY ONE UNIT
Spamany (liso)	.100
Britland (ounce)	1.500
Chilaquay (peso)	.015
Trance (franc)	.130
Shopan (ben)	.005

Determine the number of
a. Spamany lisos that can be acquired for $1,000
b. Number of dollars that 30 Britland ounces will buy
c. Chilaquay pesos that $900 will acquire
d. Number of dollars that 100 Trench francs will purchase
e. Shopan ben that $50 will acquire

2. Fog Industries, Inc., has a subsidiary in Lolland where the currency is the guild-note. The exchange rate at the beginning of the year is 3 guildnotes to the dollar; at the end of the year, it is 2.5 guildnotes, as the guildnote strengthens in value. The subsidiary's balance sheets at the two points in time and the income statement for the year are as follows (in thousands):

	IN GUILDNOTES	
	12/31/x1	12/31/x2
Balance Sheet		
Cash	300	400
Receivables	1,800	2,200
Inventories (FIFO)	1,500	2,000
Net fixed assets	2,100	1,800
Total	5,700	6,400
Current liabilities	2,000	1,900
Common stock	600	600
Retained earnings	3,100	3,900
Total	5,700	6,400
Income Statement		
Sales		10,400
Cost of goods sold		6,000
Depreciation		300
Expenses		2,400
Taxes		900
Operating Income		800

The historical exchange rate for the fixed assets is 3 guildnotes to the dollar. The historical cost exchange rate for inventories and cost of goods sold, using the dollar as the functional currency, is 2.70. Using the guildnote, it is 2.60 for cost of goods sold purposes. The average exchange rate for the year is 2.75 guildnotes to the dollar, and sales, depreciation, expenses, and taxes paid are steady throughout the year. Also assume no previous translation adjustments. On the basis of this information, determine to the nearest thousand dollars the balance sheet and income statement for 12/31/X2, assuming that the functional currency is the guildnote. Assuming that it is the dollar, what are the differences?

3. Zike Athletic Shoe company sells to a wholesaler in Germany. The purchase price of a shipment is 50,000 deutschemarks with terms of 90 days. Upon payment, Zike will convert the DM to dollars. The present spot rate for DM per dollar is 1.71, whereas the 90-day forward rate is 1.70.

   a. If Zike were to hedge its foreign exchange risk, what would it do? What are the transactions necessary?

   b. Is the deutschemark at a premium or at a discount?

   c. What is the implied differential in interest rates between the two countries? (Use interest-rate parity assumptions.)

PROBLEMS

1. The following spot rates are observed in the foreign currency market:

CURRENCY	FOREIGN CURRENCY PER U.S. DOLLAR
Britain pound	.62
Netherlands guilder	1.90
Sweden krona	6.40
Switzerland franc	1.50
Italy lira	1,300.00
Japan yen	140.00

On the basis of this information, compute to the nearest second decimal the number of

   a. British pounds that can be acquired for $100
   b. Dollars that 50 Dutch guilders will buy
   c. Swedish krona that can be acquired for $40
   d. Dollars that 200 Swiss francs can buy
   e. Italian lira that can be acquired for $10
   f. Dollars that 1,000 Japanese yen will buy

2. The U.S. Imports Company purchased 100,000 marks' worth of machines from a firm in Dortmund, Germany. The value of the dollar in terms of the mark has been decreasing. The firm in Dortmund offers 2/10, net 90 terms. The spot rate for the mark is $.55; the 90-day forward rate is $.56.

   a. Compute the dollar cost of paying the account within the 10 days.

   b. Compute the dollar cost of buying a forward contract to liquidate the account in 90 days.

   c. The differential between part a and part b is the result of the time value of money (the discount for prepayment) and protection from currency value fluctuation. Determine the magnitude of each of these components.

3. Loco Boost Vehicles, Inc., is considering a new plant in the Netherlands. The plant will cost 26 million guilders. Incremental cash flows are expected to be 3 million guilders per year for the first three years, 4 million guilders the next three, 5 million guilders in years 7 through 9, and 6 million guilders in years 10 through 19, after which the project will terminate with no residual value. The present exchange rate is 1.90 guilders per dollar. The required rate of return on repatriated dollars is 16 percent.

a. If the exchange rate stays at 1.90, what is the project's net present value?

b. If the guilder appreciates to 1.84 for years 1–3, to 1.78 for years 4–6, to 1.72 for years 7–9, and to 1.65 for years 10–19, what happens to the net present value?

4. Fleur du Lac, a French company, has shipped goods to an American importer under a letter of credit arrangement, which calls for payment at the end of 90 days. The invoice is for $124,000. Presently the exchange rate is 5.70 French francs to the dollar. If the French franc were to strengthen by 5 percent by the end of 90 days, what would be the transactions gain or loss in French francs? If it were to weaken by 5 percent, what would happen? (*Note:* Make all calculations in francs per dollar.)

5. Itoh Selangor Berhad is the Malaysian subsidiary of USD Corporation. Presently the subsidiary has the following balance sheet items expressed in U.S. dollar equivalents using book values (in millions):

Monetary assets	$24
Inventories	16
Value of operating capacity	30
Total assets	$70
Monetary liabilities	$40
Shareholders' equity	30
Total	$70

The market values of monetary assets and liabilities are the same as book values, whereas inventories are 1.25 times book value and the value of operating capacity is 1.667 times book value. Suppose the exposure coefficients for these two assets are 0.5 and 0.2, respectively, for the Malaysian ringgit/U.S. dollar exchange rate. Using the Hekman framework, what is the net aggregate market value exposure for the subsidiary and its aggregate exposure coefficient (on equity)?

6. Wheat sells for $4.00 a bushel in the United States. The price in Canada is Can.$4.56. The exchange rate is 1.2 Canadian dollars to 1 U.S. dollar. Does purchasing power parity exist? If not, what changes would need to occur for it to exist?

7. Presently, the dollar is worth 140 Japanese yen in the spot market. The interest rate in Japan on 90-day government securities is 4 percent; it is 8 percent in the United States. If the interest-rate parity theorem holds, what is the implied 90-day forward exchange rate in yen per dollar? What would be implied if the U.S. interest rate were 6 percent?

8. Cordova Leather Company is in a 38 percent U.S. tax bracket. It has sales branches in Algeria and in Spain, each of which generates earnings of $200,000 before taxes. If the effective income tax rate is 52 percent in Algeria and 35 percent in Spain, what total U.S. and foreign taxes will Cordova pay on the above earnings?

9. McDonnoughs Hamburger Company wishes to lend $500,000 to its Japanese subsidiary. At the same time, Yasufuku Heavy Industries is interested in making a medium-term loan of approximately the same amount to its U.S. subsidiary. The two parties are brought together by an investment bank for the purpose of making parallel loans. McDonnoughs will lend $500,000 to the U.S. subsidiary of Yasufuku for 4 years at 13 percent. Principal and interest are payable only at the

end of the fourth year, with interest compounding annually. Yasufuku will lend the Japanese subsidiary of McDonnoughs 70 million yen for 4 years at 10 percent. Again the principal and interest (annual compounding) are payable at the end. The current exchange rate is 140 yen to the dollar. However, the dollar is expected to decline by 5 yen to the dollar per year over the next 4 years.

a. If these expectations prove to be correct, what will be the dollar equivalent of principal and interest payments to Yasufuku at the end of 4 years?

b. What total dollars will McDonnoughs receive at the end of 4 years from the payment of principal and interest on its loan by the U.S. subsidiary of Yasufuku?

c. Which party is better off with the parallel loan arrangement? What would happen if the yen did not change in value?

10. The government of Zwill presently encourages investment in the country. Comstock International Mining Corporation, a U.S. company, is planning to open a new copper mine in Zwill. The front-end investment is expected to be $25 million, after which cash flows are expected to be more than sufficient to cover further capital needs. Preliminary exploration findings suggest that the project is likely to be very profitable, providing an expected internal rate of return of 34 percent, based on business considerations alone.

The government of Zwill, like that of many countries, is unstable. The management of Comstock, trying to assess this instability and its consequences, forecasts a 10 percent probability that the government will be overthrown and a new government will expropriate the property, with no compensation. The full $25 million would be lost, and the internal rate of return would be −100 percent. There also is a 15 percent probability that the government will be overthrown but that the new government will make partial payment for the properties; this would result in an internal rate of return of −40 percent. Finally, there is a 15 percent probability that the present government will stay in power, but that it will change its policy on repatriation of profits. More specifically, it will allow the corporation to repatriate its original investment, $25 million, but all other cash flows generated by the project would have to be reinvested in the host country forever. These probabilities still leave a 60 percent chance that a 34 percent internal rate of return will be achieved.

Given these political risks, approximate the likely return to Comstock. Should the mining venture be undertaken?

SOLUTIONS TO SELF-CORRECTION PROBLEMS

1. a. $1,000/.100 = 10,000$ lisos
   b. $30 \times \$1.500 = \$45$
   c. $\$900/.015 = 60,000$ pesos
   d. $100 \times \$.13 = \$13$
   e. $\$50/.005 = 10,000$ ben

2.

	IN DOLLARS 12/31/x2	
	Functional Currency Guildnote	Functional Currency Dollar
Balance Sheet		
Cash	$ 160	$ 160
Receivables	880	880
Inventories	800	741
Net fixed assets	720	600
Total	$2,560	$2,381

Current liabilities	$ 760	$ 760
Common stock	200	200
Retained earnings		
($1,033 at 12/31/x1)	1,198	1,421
Accumulated translation adjustment	402	
Total	$2,560	$2,381

Income Statement

Sales	$3,782	$3,782
Cost of goods sold	2,308	2,222
Depreciation	109	100
Expenses	873	873
Taxes	327	327
Operating income	$ 165	$ 260
Translation gain		128
Net income	$ 165	$ 388
Translation adjustment	$ 402	

When the guildnote is used as the functional currency, all balance sheet items except common stock and retained earnings are translated at the current exchange rate, 2.50. All income statement items are translated at the average exchange rate for the year, 2.75, except cost of goods sold, which is translated at 2.60. Net income is a residual, after deducting costs and expenses from sales. Retained earnings are net income, $165, plus retained earnings at the beginning of the year, $1,033, to give $1,198. The translation adjustment is that amount necessary to bring about an equality in the two totals on the balance sheet. It is $402. For the dollar as the functional currency, inventories and cost of goods sold are translated at the historical exchange rate of 2.70, and fixed assets and depreciation at the historical exchange rate of 3.00. Other items are translated in the same manner as with the other method. Retained earnings are a balancing factor to bring equality between the balance sheet totals. Operating income is a residual. The translation gain is that amount necessary to make net income equal to the change in retained earnings: $1,421 − $1,033 = $388 − $260 = $128. Depending on the accounting method, income is more variable with the dollar as the functional currency, whereas balance sheet totals are more variable with the guildnote as the functional currency.

3. a. It would hedge by selling marks forward 90 days. Upon delivery of 50,000 marks in 90 days, it would receive DM50,000/1.70 = $29,412. If it were to receive payment today, Zike would get DM50,000/1.71 = $29,240.

b. The DM is at a premium because the 90-day forward rate of DM per dollar is less than the current spot rate. The DM is expected to strengthen (fewer DM to buy a dollar).

c. $[(1.70 − 1.71)/1.71] \times [365/90] = r_{DM} − r_{\$} = −.0237$
The differential in interest rates is −2.37 percent, which means if interest-rate parity holds, interest rates in the U.S. should be 2.37 percent higher than in Germany.

SELECTED REFERENCES

ABUAF, NISO, and PHILIPPE JORION, "Purchasing Power Parity in the Long Run," *Journal of Finance*, 45 (March 1990), 157–74.

ADLER, MICHAEL, and BERNARD DUMAS, "International Portfolio Choice and Corporation Finance: A Synthesis," *Journal of Finance*, 38 (June 1983), 925–84.

———, "Exposure to Currency Risk: Definition and Measurement," *Financial Management*, 13 (Summer 1984), 41–50.

BALDWIN, CARLISS Y., "Competing for Capital in a Global Environment," *Midland Corporate Finance Journal*, 5 (Spring 1987), 43–64.

BLACK, FISCHER, "Equilibrium Exchange Rate Hedging," *Journal of Finance*, 45 (July 1990), 899–908.

DUFEY, GUNTER, and S. L. SRINIVASULU, "The Case for Corporate Management of Foreign Exchange Risk," *Financial Management*, 12 (Winter 1983), 54–62.

EITEMAN, DAVID K., and ARTHUR I. STONEHILL, *Multinational Business Finance*, 5th ed. Reading, MA: Addison-Wesley, 1989.

ERRUNZA, VIHANG R., and LEMMA W. SENBET, "The Effects of International Operations on the Market Value of the Firm: Theory and Evidence," *Journal of Finance*, 36 (May 1981), 401–18.

FLOOD, EUGENE, JR., and DONALD R. LESSARD, "On the Measurement of Operating Exposure to Exchange Rates," *Financial Management*, 15 (Spring 1986), 25–36.

HEKMAN, CHRISTINE R., "Measuring Foreign Exchange Exposure: A Practical Theory and Its Application," *Financial Analysts Journal*, 39 (September–October 1983), 59–65.

———, "Don't Blame Currency Values for Strategic Errors," *Midland Corporate Finance Journal*, 4 (Fall 1986), 45–55.

KIM, YONG CHEOL, and RENE M. STULZ, "The Eurobond Market and Corporate Financial Policy: A Test of the Clientele Hypothesis," *Journal of Financial Economics*, 22 (December 1988), 189–206.

KORAJCZYK, ROBERT A., and CLAUDE J. VIALLET, "An Empirical Investigation of International Asset Pricing," *Review of Financial Studies*, 2, No. 4 (1989), 553–86.

LESSARD, DONALD, "International Portfolio Diversification: A Multivariate Analysis for a Group of Latin American Countries," *Journal of Finance*, 28 (June 1973), 619–34.

LEVY, HAIM, and MARSHALL SARNAT, "International Diversification of Investment Portfolios," *American Economic Review*, 60 (September 1970), 668–75.

PEROLD, ANDRE F., and EVAN C. SCHULMAN, "The Free Lunch in Currency Hedging: Implications for Investment Policy and Performance Standards," *Financial Analysts Journal*, 44 (May–June 1988), 45–50.

SHAPIRO, ALAN C., "International Capital Budgeting," *Midland Corporate Finance Journal*, 1 (Spring 1983), 26–45.

———, *Multinational Financial Management*, 2d ed. Boston: Allyn & Bacon, 1986.

SOLNIK, BRUNO, "The International Pricing of Risk: An Empirical Investigation of the World Capital Market Structure," *Journal of Finance*, 29 (May 1974), 365–78.

———, "The Relation between Stock Prices and Inflationary Expectations: The International Evidence," *Journal of Finance*, 38 (March 1983), 25–48.

———, *International Investments*. Reading, MA: Addison-Wesley, 1988.

STULZ, RENE M., "A Model of International Asset Pricing," *Journal of Financial Economics*, 10 (December 1981), 923–34.

———, "The Pricing of Currency Options: A Review," working paper, Ohio State University (April 1990).

VAN HORNE, JAMES C., *Financial Market Rates and Flows*, 3d ed. Englewood Cliffs, NJ: Prentice Hall, 1990, Chap. 11.

PART 8

TOOLS OF FINANCIAL ANALYSIS AND CONTROL

Financial Planning at Hewlett-Packard

In 1957, David Packard set forth various corporate objectives that have guided the company ever since. Among them were (1) to operate the business to obtain a before-tax profit of about 20 percent of sales and (2) to let growth be determined by profits and the ability to produce innovative products that satisfy customer needs. The latter effectively constrained the company to financing growth internally (without debt).

In the 1960s, Hewlett-Packard committed these objectives to a formal financial planning model. The key ratios in the model are (1) asset-to-sales, (2) new equity-to-assets (primarily through an employee stock purchase plan), (3) profit margin, (4) percent of profits retained, (5) equity-to-assets, and (6) sales growth rate. The last can be solved for, given targets for the other ratios. What evolved was a framework for determining the sustainable growth rate in sales, given likely operating efficiency and financing objectives.

Each year, the various components of the corporation are brought together in the overall plan. As George Newman, treasurer, explains: "The model serves as a discipline on all aspects of the business. It forces us to be internally consistent within our objective of self-financing." The model permits sensitivity analysis in answering "What if?" questions, a theme that has carried over into Hewlett-Packard's advertisements. The key ingredients in supporting growth, both in the company overall and in the subunits, are easily identified. The planning model instills a realism and consistency across business units as to what is possible financially in supporting the growth objectives.

27

FINANCIAL RATIO ANALYSIS

INTRODUCTION TO FINANCIAL ANALYSIS

To make rational decisions in keeping with the objectives of the firm, the financial manager must have certain analytical tools. The more useful tools of financial analysis are the subjects of this chapter and the next. The company itself and outside suppliers of capital—creditors and investors—all undertake financial analysis. The firm's purpose is not only internal control but also better understanding of what capital suppliers seek in financial condition and performance from it. The type of analysis varies according to the specific interests of the party involved. Trade creditors are interested primarily in the liquidity of a firm. Their claims are short term, and the ability of a firm to pay these claims is best judged by means of a thorough analysis of its liquidity. The claims of bondholders, on the other hand, are long term. Accordingly, they are more interested in the cash-flow ability of the firm to service debt over the long run. The bondholder may evaluate this ability by analyzing the capital structure of the firm, the major sources and uses of funds, its profitability over time, and projections of future profitability.

Investors in a company's common stock are concerned principally with present and expected future earnings and the stability of these earnings about a trend, as well as their covariance with the earnings of other companies. As a result, investors might concentrate their analysis on the profitability of the firm. They would be concerned with its financial condition insofar as it affects the ability of the company to pay dividends and to avoid bankruptcy. In order to bargain more effectively for outside funds, the management of a firm should be interested in all aspects of financial analysis that outside suppliers of capital use in evaluating the firm. Management also employs financial analysis for purposes of internal control. In particular, it is concerned with profitability on investment in the various assets of the company and in the efficiency of asset management. In addition to suppliers of capital and the firm itself, various government regulators may use financial analysis. In particular, regulatory agencies are concerned with the rate of return a company earns on its assets as well as with the proportion of nonequity funds employed in the business. Thus, the type of financial analysis undertaken varies according to the specific interests of the analyst. Financial statement analysis is part of a larger information processing system on which informed decisions can be based.

In analyzing financial statements, many of you will want to use a computer spreadsheet program. For repetitive analyses, such a program permits changes in assumptions and simulations to be done with ease. In fact, financial statements are an ideal application for these powerful programs, and their use by financial statement analysts and companies is quite common. In the supplement, *Financial Management Computer Applications*, programs are provided for analyzing the financial condition and performance of a company.

USE OF FINANCIAL RATIOS

To evaluate the financial condition and performance of a firm, the financial analyst needs certain yardsticks. The yardstick frequently used is a ratio, or index, relating two pieces of financial data to each other. Analysis and interpretation of various ratios should give experienced, skilled analysts a better understanding of the financial condition and performance of the firm than they would obtain from analysis of the financial data alone.

Trend Analysis.   The analysis of financial ratios involves two types of comparison. First, the analyst can compare a present ratio with past and expected future ratios for the same company. The current ratio (the ratio of current assets to current liabilities) for the present year end could be compared with the current ratio for the preceding year end. When financial ratios are arrayed on a spreadsheet over a period of years, the analyst can study the composition of change and determine whether there has been an improvement or a deterioration in the financial condition and performance over time. Financial ratios also can be computed for projected, or pro forma, statements and compared with present and past ratios. In the comparisons over time, it is best to compare not only financial ratios but also the raw figures.

Comparison with Others.   The second method of comparison involves comparing the ratios of one firm with those of similar firms or with industry averages at the same point in time. Such a comparison gives insight into the relative financial condition and performance of the firm. Financial ratios for various industries are published by Robert Morris Associates, by Dun & Bradstreet, by Prentice Hall (*Almanac of Business and Industrial Financial Ratios*), by the Federal Trade Commission–Securities and Exchange Commission, and by various credit agencies and trade associations.[1]

The analyst should avoid using rules of thumb indiscriminately for all industries. For example, the criterion that all companies should have at least a 2-to-1 current ratio is inappropriate. The analysis must be in relation to the type of business in which the firm is engaged and to the firm itself. The true test of liquidity is whether a company has the ability to pay its bills on time.

---

[1] Robert Morris Associates, an association of bank credit and loan officers, publishes industry averages based upon financial statements supplied to banks by borrowers. Sixteen ratios are computed annually for over 150 lines of business. In addition, each line of business is divided into four size categories. Dun & Bradstreet calculates annually 14 important ratios for over 100 lines of business. The *Almanac of Business and Industrial Financial Ratios* (Englewood Cliffs, NJ: Prentice Hall, 1989) shows industry averages for 22 financial ratios. Approximately 170 businesses and industries are listed, covering the complete spectrum. The data for this publication come from U.S. corporate tax filings with the Internal Revenue Service. *The Quarterly Financial Report of Manufacturing Corporations* is published jointly by the Federal Trade Commission and the Securities and Exchange Commission. This publication contains balance sheet and income statement information by industry groupings and by asset-size categories.

Many sound companies, including electric utilities, have this ability despite current ratios substantially below 2 to 1. It depends on the nature of the business. Only by comparing the financial ratios of one firm with those of similar firms can one make a realistic judgment.

Similarly, analysis of the deviation from the norm should be based on some knowledge of the distribution of ratios for the companies involved. If the company being studied has a current ratio of 1.4 and the industry norm is 1.8, one would like to know the proportion of companies whose ratios are below 1.4. If it is only 2 percent, we are likely to be much more concerned than if it is 25 percent. Therefore, we need information on the dispersion of the distribution in order to judge the significance of the deviation of a financial ratio for a particular company from the industry norm.

Comparisons with the industry must be approached with caution. It may be that the financial condition and performance of the entire industry is less than satisfactory, and a company's being above average may not be sufficient. The company may have a number of problems on an absolute basis and should not take refuge in a favorable comparison with the industry. In addition, the analyst should realize that the various companies within an industry grouping may not be homogeneous. Companies with multiple product lines often defy precise industry categorization. They may be placed in the most "appropriate" industry grouping, but comparison with other companies in that industry may not be consistent. Also, companies in an industry may differ substantially in size. In these circumstances, it may be best to subdivide the industry to compare companies of similar size. All of these things signal caution when comparing financial ratios of one company with those of other companies in the industry.

Because reported financial data and the ratios computed from these data are numerical, there is a tendency to regard them as precise portrayals of a firm's true financial status. For some firms, the accounting data may closely approximate economic reality. For others, it is necessary to go beyond the reported figures in order to analyze properly their financial condition and performance. Accounting data such as depreciation, reserve for bad debts, and other reserves are estimates at best and may not reflect economic depreciation, bad debts, and other losses. To the extent possible, accounting data from different companies should be standardized. Compare apples with apples and oranges with oranges; even with standardized figures, however, the analyst should use caution in interpreting the comparisons.

TYPES OF RATIOS

For our purposes, financial ratios can be grouped into four types: liquidity, debt, profitability, and coverage ratios. No one ratio gives us sufficient information by which to judge the financial condition and performance of the firm. Only when we analyze a group of ratios are we able to make reasonable judgments. We must be sure to take into account any seasonal character of a business. Underlying trends may be assessed only through a comparison of raw figures and ratios at the same time of year. We would not compare a December 31 balance sheet with a May 31 balance sheet, but we would compare December 31 with December 31.

Although the number of financial ratios that might be computed increases geometrically with the amount of financial data, we concentrate only on the more important ratios in this chapter. Actually, the ratios needed to assess the financial condition and performance of a company are relatively few in number. Computing unneeded ratios adds both complexity and confusion to the problem. To illustrate the ratios discussed in this chapter, we use the balance sheet and income statements of the Aldine Manufacturing Company shown in Tables 27-1 and 27-2. In the balance sheet, cash equivalents represent marketable securities and time deposits with an original maturity of three

TABLE 27-1
Aldine Manufacturing Company balance sheet (in thousands of dollars)

ASSETS	MARCH 31, 1992	MARCH 31, 1991
Cash and cash equivalents	$ 177,689	$ 175,042
Accounts receivable	678,279	740,705
Inventories	1,328,963	1,234,725
Prepaid expenses	20,756	17,197
Other current assets	35,203	29,165
Current assets	$2,240,890	$2,196,834
Property, plant, and equipment	1,596,886	1,538,495
Less: Accumulated depreciation	856,829	791,205
	$ 740,057	$ 747,290
Investment, long term	65,376	—
Other assets	205,157	205,624
	$3,251,480	$3,149,748

LIABILITIES AND SHAREHOLDERS' EQUITY	MARCH 31, 1992	MARCH 31, 1991
Bank loans and notes payable	$ 448,508	$ 356,511
Accounts payable	148,427	136,793
Accrued taxes	36,203	127,455
Other accrued liabilities	190,938	164,285
Current liabilities	$ 824,076	$ 785,044
Long-term debt	630,783	626,460
Shareholders' equity		
Common stock	420,828	420,824
Additional paid-in capital	361,158	361,059
Retained earnings	1,014,635	956,361
Total shareholders' equity	$1,796,621	$1,738,244
	$3,251,480	$3,149,748

TABLE 27-2
Aldine Manufacturing Company statement of earnings (in thousands of dollars)

	YEAR ENDED MARCH 31, 1992	YEAR ENDED MARCH 31, 1991
Net sales	$3,992,758	$3,721,241
Cost of goods sold	2,680,298	2,499,965
Selling, general, and administrative expenses	801,395	726,959
Depreciation	111,509	113,989
Interest expense	85,274	69,764
Earnings before taxes	$ 314,282	$ 310,564
Provision for taxes	113,040	112,356
Earnings after taxes	$ 201,242	$ 198,208
Cash dividends	142,968	130,455
Retained earnings	$ 58,274	$ 67,753

months or less. A third accounting statement required in the presentation of audited financial results, a statement of cash flows, is taken up in the next chapter.

LIQUIDITY RATIOS

Liquidity ratios are used to judge a firm's ability to meet short-term obligations. From them, much insight can be obtained into the present cash solvency of the firm and its ability to remain solvent in the event of adversities. Essentially, we wish to compare short-term obligations with the short-term resources available to meet these obligations.

CURRENT RATIO

One of the most general and most frequently used of these ratios is the *current ratio:*

$$\frac{\text{Current assets}}{\text{Current liabilities}} \qquad (27\text{-}1)$$

For Aldine, the ratio for the 1992 year end is

$$\frac{\$2,240,890}{\$824,076} = 2.72$$

The higher the ratio, supposedly, the greater the ability of the firm to pay its bills. The ratio must be regarded as a crude measure of liquidity, however, because it does not take into account the liquidity of the individual components of the current assets. A firm having current assets composed principally of cash and current receivables is generally regarded as more liquid than a firm whose current assets consist primarily of inventories.[2] Consequently, we must turn to "finer" tools of analysis if we are to evaluate critically the liquidity of the firm.

ACID-TEST RATIO

A somewhat more accurate guide to liquidity is the *quick,* or *acid-test, ratio:*

$$\frac{\text{Current assets less inventories}}{\text{Current liabilities}} \qquad (27\text{-}2)$$

---

[2] We have defined *liquidity* as the ability to realize value in money, the most liquid of assets. Liquidity has two dimensions: (1) the time required to convert the asset into money and (2) the certainty of the price realized. To the extent that the price realized on receivables is as predictable as that realized on inventories, receivables would be a more liquid asset than inventories, owing to the shorter time required to convert the asset into money. If the price realized on receivables is more certain than is that on inventories, receivables would be regarded as being even more liquid.

For Aldine, this ratio is

$$\frac{\$2,240,890 - \$1,328,963}{\$824,076} = 1.11$$

This ratio is the same as the current ratio, except that it excludes inventories—presumably the least liquid portion of current assets—from the numerator. The ratio concentrates on cash, marketable securities, and receivables in relation to current obligations and thus provides a more penetrating measure of liquidity than does the current ratio.

LIQUIDITY OF RECEIVABLES

When there are suspected imbalances or problems in various components of the current assets, the financial analyst will want to examine these components separately in assessing liquidity. Receivables, for example, may be far from current. To regard all receivables as liquid, when in fact a sizable portion may be past due, overstates the liquidity of the firm being analyzed. Receivables are liquid assets only insofar as they can be collected in a reasonable amount of time. For our analysis of receivables, we have two basic ratios, the first of which is the *average collection period:*

$$\frac{\text{Receivables} \times \text{Days in year}}{\text{Annual credit sales}} \qquad (27\text{-}3)$$

If we assume for Aldine that all sales are credit sales, this ratio is

$$\frac{\$678,279 \times 365}{\$3,992,758} = 62 \text{ days}$$

The average collection period tells us the average number of days receivables are outstanding, that is, the average time it takes to convert them into cash.

The second ratio is the *receivable turnover ratio:*

$$\frac{\text{Annual credit sales}}{\text{Receivables}} \qquad (27\text{-}4)$$

For Aldine, this ratio is

$$\frac{\$3,992,758}{\$678,279} = 5.89$$

These two ratios are reciprocals of each other. The number of days in the year, 365, divided by the average collection period, 62 days, gives the receivable turnover ratio, 5.89. The number of days in the year divided by the turnover ratio gives the average collection period. Thus, either of these two ratios can be employed.

When credit sales figures for a period are not available, we must resort to the total sales figures. The receivable figure used in the calculation ordinarily represents year-end receivables. When sales are seasonal or have grown considerably over the year, using the year-end receivable balance may not be appropriate. With seasonality, an average of the monthly closing balances may be the most appropriate figure to use. With growth, the receivable balance at the end of the year will be deceptively high in relation to sales. The result is that the collection period calculated is a biased and high estimate of the time it will take for the receivable balance at year end to be collected. In this case, an average of receivables at the beginning and at the end of the year might be appropriate if the growth in sales were steady throughout the year. The idea is to relate the relevant receivable position to the credit sales over the year so that apples are compared with apples.

The average collection period ratio or the receivable turnover ratio indicates the slowness of receivables. Either ratio must be analyzed in relation to the billing terms given on the sales. If the average collection period is 45 days and the terms are 2/10, net 30,[3] the comparison would indicate that a sizable proportion of the receivables is past due beyond the final due date of 30 days. On the other hand, if the terms are 2/10, net 60, the typical receivable is being collected before the final due date. A comparison of the average collection period and terms given by a specific company with those of other companies in the industry gives us additional insight into the investment in receivables. Too low an average collection period may suggest an excessively restrictive credit policy. The receivables on the books may be of prime quality, yet sales may be curtailed unduly—and profits less than they might be—because of this policy. In this situation, credit standards for an acceptable account should be relaxed somewhat. On the other hand, too high an average collection period may indicate too liberal a credit policy. As a result, a large number of receivables may be past due—some uncollectible. Here, too, profits may be less than those possible, because of bad-debt losses and the need to finance a large investment in receivables. In this case, credit standards should be raised.

Aging of Accounts. Another means by which we can obtain insight into the liquidity of receivables is through an *aging of accounts*. With this method, we categorize the receivables at a moment in time according to the proportions billed in previous months. We might have the following hypothetical aging of accounts receivable at December 31:

Proportion of receivables billed

DECEMBER	NOVEMBER	OCTOBER	SEPTEMBER	AUGUST AND BEFORE	TOTAL
67%	19%	7%	2%	5%	100%

If the billing terms are 2/10, net 30, this aging tells us that 67 percent of the receivables at December 31 are current, 19 percent are up to 1 month past due, 7 percent are 1 to 2 months past due, and so on. Depending on the conclusions drawn from our analysis of the aging, we may want to examine more closely the credit and collection policies of the company. In the example, we might be prompted to investigate the individual receivables that were billed in August and before, in order to determine if any should be charged off. The receivables shown on the books are only as good as the likelihood that they will be collected. An aging of accounts receivables gives us considerably more

[3] The notation means that the supplier gives a 2 percent discount if the receivable invoice is paid within 10 days and that payment is due within 30 days if the discount is not taken.

information than the calculation of the average collection period, because it pinpoints the trouble spots more specifically.

Receivable Collection Matrix. Both the average collection period and the aging of accounts receivable are affected by the patterns of sales. With rising sales, the average collection period and the aging will be more current than if sales are level, all other things the same. The reason is that a greater portion of sales is billed currently. On the other hand, when sales are declining over time, the average collection period and the aging will be less current than if sales are level. Here the reason is that a smaller portion of sales is billed currently. Although the average collection period and the aging measures will not be significantly affected if there is only a modest and steady trend in sales, they will be affected if there is a rapid change in the pattern of sales or if there is a fluctuating pattern of sales behavior over time. For these situations, the average collection period and the aging schedule are not realistic portrayals of the liquidity of receivables. Adjustments in analysis should be made. For seasonal sales patterns, it is useful to compare the average collection period and aging at one point with the average collection period and aging at the same point in another year. We might compare the average collection period and an aging at the end of May with those at the end of May in another year.

The meaningful thing is to try to separate changes in the payment behavior of customers from changes in the pattern of sales. One way to do so is with a conversion matrix of receivables into cash.[4] Such a matrix is illustrated in Table 27-3. As we see, the matrix tells us the amount of credit sales in a given month and the months when the receivables so generated are collected. At the right of each collection amount, the percentage that amount represents in rela-

TABLE 27-3
Conversion matrix of credit sales to cash

MONTH	CREDIT SALES	MONTHLY COLLECTIONS (IN THOUSANDS OF DOLLARS)					
		January	February	March	April	May	June
Oct.	$6,000	600(10%)					
Nov.	4,000	900(23%)	300(8%)	125(3%)			
Dec.	3,000	1,400(47%)	700(23%)	400(13%)			
Jan.	5,000	700(14%)	2,500(50%)	1,200(24%)	600(12%)		
Feb.	6,000		900(15%)	3,200(53%)	1,500(25%)	400(7%)	
Mar.	7,000			1,200(17%)	3,300(47%)	1,900(27%)	600(9%)
Apr.	8,000				1,100(14%)	4,100(51%)	1,900(24%)
May	7,000					1,300(19%)	3,300(47%)
June	5,000						700(14%)
Total collections		3,600	4,400	6,125	6,500	7,700	6,500

Note: The percentages are in relation to credit sales shown in the second column.

[4] Similar approaches have been proposed by W. G. Lewellen and R. W. Johnson, "Better Way to Monitor Accounts Receivable," *Harvard Business Review*, 50 (May–June 1972), 101–9; W. G. Lewellen and R. O. Edmister, "A General Model for Accounts Receivable Analysis and Control," *Journal of Financial and Quantitative Analysis*, 8 (March 1973), 195–206; and Bernell K. Stone, "The Payments-Pattern Approach to the Forecasting and Control of Accounts Receivable," *Financial Management*, 5 (Autumn 1976), 65–82. In all three articles, there is a detailed analysis of the problem as it relates in particular to the average collection period and the aging of accounts receivable.

tion to total credit sales is shown. At the bottom of the table, total collections are shown for each month. The advantage of this type of calculation is that it permits the financial analyst to concentrate on the payment pattern of customers month by month as opposed to the combined payment and sales patterns. By tracing the collections in a month to the date of sales, we can determine if the firm's collection experience is improving or deteriorating. If sales change significantly over time, this isolation of payments behavior from sales behavior is critical. The principal limitation to the use of a conversion matrix is that such information is available only from the company and cannot be derived from financial statements. The same limitation applies to an aging of accounts receivable. In fact, the same information necessary to prepare an aging schedule can be used to derive a conversion matrix.

DURATION OF PAYABLES

From a creditor's point of view, it is desirable to obtain an *aging of accounts payable* or a *conversion matrix for payables*. These measures, combined with the less exact turnover of payables (annual purchases divided by payables), allow us to analyze payables in much the same manner as we analyze receivables. Also, we can compute the average age of a firm's accounts payable. The *average payable period* is

$$\frac{\text{Accounts payable} \times 365}{\text{Purchases}} \tag{27-5}$$

where accounts payable is the average balance outstanding for the year and the denominator is external purchases during the year.

When information on purchases is not available, one can occasionally use the cost of goods sold in the denominator. A department store chain, for example, typically does no manufacturing. As a result, the cost of goods sold consists primarily of purchases. However, in situations where there is sizable value added, such as with a manufacturer, the use of the cost of goods sold is inappropriate. One must have the amount of purchases if the ratio is to be used. Another caveat has to do with growth. As with receivables, the use of a year-end payable balance will result in a biased and high estimate of the time it will take a company to make payment on its payables if there is strong underlying growth. In this situation, it may be better to use an average of payables at the beginning of the year and at the end.

The average payable period is valuable in evaluating the probability that a credit applicant will pay on time. If the average age of payables is 48 days, and the terms in the industry are net 30, we know that a portion of the applicant's payables are not being paid on time. A credit check of other suppliers will give insight into the severity of the problem.

LIQUIDITY OF INVENTORIES

We may compute the *inventory turnover ratio* as an indicator of the liquidity of inventory:

$$\frac{\text{Cost of goods sold}}{\text{Average inventory}} \tag{27-6}$$

For Aldine, the ratio is

$$\frac{\$2,680,298}{\$1,281,844} = 2.09$$

The figure for cost of goods sold used in the numerator is for the period being studied—usually 1 year; the average inventory figure used in the denominator typically is an average of beginning and ending inventories for the period. As was true with receivables, however, it may be necessary to compute a more sophisticated average when there is a strong seasonal element. The inventory turnover ratio tells us the rapidity with which the inventory is turned over into receivables through sales. This ratio, like other ratios, must be judged in relation to past and expected future ratios of the firm and in relation to ratios of similar firms, the industry average, or both.

Generally, the higher the inventory turnover, the more efficient the inventory management of a firm. Sometimes a relatively high inventory turnover ratio may be the result of too low a level of inventory and frequent stockouts. It might also be the result of too many small orders for inventory replacement. Either of these situations may be more costly to the firm than carrying a larger investment in inventory and having a lower turnover ratio. Again, caution is necessary in interpreting the ratio. When the inventory turnover ratio is relatively low, it indicates slow-moving inventory or obsolescence of some of the stock. Obsolescence may necessitate substantial write-downs, which, in turn, would negate the treatment of inventory as a liquid asset. Because the turnover ratio is a somewhat crude measure, we would want to investigate any perceived inefficiency in inventory management. In this regard, it is helpful to compute the turnover of the major categories of inventory to see if there are imbalances, which may indicate excessive investment in specific components of the inventory. Once we have a hint of a problem, we must investigate it more specifically to determine its cause.

DEBT RATIOS

Extending our analysis to the long-term liquidity of the firm (that is, its ability to meet long-term obligations), we may use several debt ratios. The *debt-to-net-worth ratio* is computed by simply dividing the total debt of the firm (including current liabilities) by its shareholders' equity:

$$\frac{\text{Total debt}}{\text{Shareholders' equity}} \qquad (27\text{-}7)$$

For Aldine, the ratio is

$$\frac{\$1,454,859}{\$1,796,621} = .81$$

When intangible assets are significant, they frequently are deducted from net worth to obtain the tangible net worth of the firm.

The ratio of debt to equity varies according to the nature of the business and the volatility of cash flows. An electric utility, with very stable cash flows, usually will have a higher debt ratio than will a machine tool company, whose cash flows are far less stable. A comparison of the debt ratio for a given company with those of similar firms gives us a general indication of the creditworthiness and financial risk of the firm. The reason that it is a general indication is that the assets and cash flows of the firm provide the wherewithal for payment of debt. To the extent that the asset totals are either overstated or understated with respect to their economic and liquidating values, the measure is faulty. Much more was said about the analysis of financial risk in Chapters 10 and 11.

In addition to the ratio of total debt to equity, we may wish to compute the following ratio, which deals with only the long-term capitalization of the firm:

$$\frac{\text{Long-term debt}}{\text{Total capitalization}} \qquad (27\text{-}8)$$

where total capitalization represents all long-term debt and shareholders' equity. For Aldine, the ratio is

$$\frac{\$630,783}{\$2,427,404} = .26$$

This measure tells us the relative importance of long-term debt in the capital structure. The ratios computed here have been based on book-value figures; it is sometimes useful to calculate these ratios using market values. In summary, debt ratios tell us the relative proportions of capital contribution by creditors and by owners.

CASH FLOW TO DEBT AND CAPITALIZATION

A measure of the ability of a company to service its debt is the relationship of annual cash flow to the amount of debt outstanding. The cash flow of a company often is defined as the cash generated from the operation of the company. This is defined as *earnings before interest, taxes, and depreciation (EBITD)*. *The cash-flow-to-total-liabilities ratio* is simply

$$\frac{\text{Cash flow (EBITD)}}{\text{Total liabilities}} \qquad (27\text{-}9)$$

For Aldine, the ratio is

$$\frac{\$511,065}{\$1,454,859} = .35$$

The cash flow is composed of earnings before taxes, $314,282, plus interest, $85,274, and depreciation, $111,509. This ratio is useful in assessing the creditworthiness of a company seeking debt funds.

Another ratio is the *cash-flow-to-long-term-debt ratio:*

$$\frac{\text{Cash flow (EBITD)}}{\text{Long-term debt}} \qquad (27\text{-}10)$$

Here we have the following for Aldine:

$$\frac{\$511,065}{\$630,783} = .81$$

This ratio tends to be used in the evaluation of the bonds of a company. The two cash-flow ratios just described have proven useful in predicting the deteriorating financial health of a company.

This is particularly helpful in corporate restructuring, where heavily levered transactions occur. Another ratio sometimes used in this regard is total interest-bearing debt plus equity in relation to operating cash flows.

$$\frac{\text{Total borrowings + Equity}}{\text{Cash flow (EBITD)}} \qquad (27\text{-}11)$$

For Aldine, this ratio is

$$\frac{\$2,875,912}{\$511,065} = 5.63$$

where bank loans, notes payable, and long-term debt represent total borrowings. The higher this ratio, the greater the value that is being placed on the securities. Lenders in highly levered transactions become concerned when the ratio exceeds 8, as the possibility of default has been found to be significant at this point.

COVERAGE RATIOS

Coverage ratios are designed to relate the financial charges of a firm to its ability to service them. Bond-rating services such as Moody's Investors Service and Standard & Poor's make extensive use of these ratios.

INTEREST COVERAGE RATIO

One of the most traditional of the coverage ratios is the *interest coverage ratio,* simply the ratio of earnings before interest and taxes for a particular reporting period to the amount of interest charges for the period. We must differentiate which interest charges should be used in the denominator. The *overall coverage method* stresses a company's meeting all fixed interest, regardless of the seniority of the claim. We have the following financial data for a hypothetical company:

Average earnings before interest and taxes	$2,000,000
Interest on senior 12% bonds	−400,000
	$1,600,000
Interest on junior 14% bonds	160,000

The overall interest coverage would be $2,000,000/$560,000, or 3.57. This method implies that the creditworthiness of the senior bonds is only as good as the firm's ability to cover all interest charges.

Of the various coverage ratios, the most objectionable is the *prior deductions method*. Using this method, we deduct interest on the senior bonds from average earnings and then divide the residual by the interest on the junior bonds. We find that the coverage on the junior bonds in our example is 10 times ($1,600,000/$160,000). Thus, the junior bonds give the illusion of being more secure than the senior obligations. Clearly, this method is inappropriate. The *cumulative deduction method*, perhaps, is the most widely used method of computing interest coverage. Under this method, coverage for the senior bonds would be 5 times. Coverage for the junior bonds is determined by adding the interest charges on both bonds and relating the total to average earnings. Thus, the coverage for the junior bonds would be $2,000,000/$560,000 = 3.57 times.

CASH-FLOW COVERAGE RATIO

One of the principal shortcomings of an interest coverage ratio is that a firm's ability to service debt is related both to interest and to principal payments. Moreover, these payments are not met out of earnings per se, but out of cash. Hence, a more appropriate coverage ratio relates the cash flow of the firm to the sum of interest and principal payments. The *cash-flow coverage ratio* may be expressed as

$$\frac{\text{EBIT} + \text{Depreciation}[1/(1 - t)]}{\text{Interest} + \text{Principal payments}[1/(1 - t)]} \qquad (27\text{-}12)$$

where EBIT is earnings before interest and taxes, and t is the income tax rate.[5] Because principal payments are made after taxes, it is necessary to gross up this figure by $[1/(1 - t)]$ so that it corresponds to interest payments, which are made before taxes. If the tax rate were $33\frac{1}{3}$ percent and annual principal payments $100,000, before-tax earnings of $150,000 would be needed to cover these payments. Similarly, the depreciation charges in the numerator need to be grossed up to put them on a basis equivalent to the principal payments. If there is tax rate uncertainty owing to fluctuating earnings, both of these adjustments would be less.

A broader type of analysis would evaluate the ability of the firm to cover all charges of a fixed nature in relation to its cash flow. In addition to interest and principal payments on debt obligations, we would include preferred stock dividends, lease payments, and possibly even certain essential capital expenditures. As we saw in Chapter 11, an analysis of this type is a far more

---

[5] I am grateful to Professor Robert J. Angell for suggesting this equation.

realistic gauge than is a simple interest coverage ratio in determining whether a firm has the ability to meet its long-term obligations.

In assessing the financial risk of a firm, then, the financial analyst should first compute the debt ratios as a rough measure of financial risk. Depending on the payment schedule of the debt and the average interest rate, debt ratios may or may not give an accurate picture of the ability of the firm to meet its financial obligations. Therefore, it is necessary to analyze additionally the cash-flow ability of the firm to service debt. This is done by relating cash flow not only to the amount of debt outstanding but also to the amount of financial charges. In this way, the financial analyst is able to get an accurate idea of the financial risk of the firm. Neither debt ratios nor coverage ratios are sufficient by themselves.

PROFITABILITY RATIOS

Profitability ratios are of two types: those showing profitability in relation to sales, and those showing profitability in relation to investment. Together these ratios indicate the firm's efficiency of operation.

PROFITABILITY IN RELATION TO SALES

The first ratio we consider is the gross *profit margin*:

$$\frac{\text{Sales less cost of goods sold}}{\text{Sales}} \qquad (27\text{-}13)$$

For Aldine, the gross profit margin is

$$\frac{\$1,312,460}{\$3,992,758} = 32.9\%$$

This ratio tells us the profit of the firm relative to sales after we deduct the cost of producing the goods sold. It indicates the efficiency of operations as well as how products are priced. A more specific ratio of profitability is the *net profit margin*:

$$\frac{\text{Net profits after taxes}}{\text{Sales}} \qquad (27\text{-}14)$$

For Aldine, this ratio is

$$\frac{\$201,242}{\$3,992,758} = 5.04\%$$

The net profit margin tells us the relative efficiency of the firm after taking into account all expenses and income taxes, but not extraordinary charges.

By considering both ratios jointly, we are able to gain considerable insight into the operations of the firm. If the gross profit margin is essentially unchanged over a period of several years, but the net profit margin has declined over the same period, we know that the cause is either higher expenses relative to sales or a higher tax rate. Therefore, we would analyze these factors more specifically to determine the cause of the problem. On the other hand, if the gross profit margin falls, we know that the cost of producing the goods relative to sales has increased. This occurrence, in turn, may be due to problems in pricing or costs.

There are any number of combinations of changes possible in the gross and net profit margins. Indications of the sort illustrated here tell us where we should investigate further. In our analysis, it is useful to examine over time each of the individual expense items as a percentage of sales. By so doing, we can pick out specific areas of deterioration or improvement.

PROFITABILITY IN RELATION TO INVESTMENT

The second group of profitability ratios relates profits to investments. One of these measures is the *rate of return on equity,* or the *ROE:*

$$\frac{\text{Net profits after taxes} - \text{Preferred stock dividend}}{\text{Shareholders' equity}}$$

For Aldine, the rate of return is

$$\frac{\$201,242}{\$1,796,621} = 11.20\%$$

This ratio tells us the earning power on shareholders' book investment and is frequently used in comparing two or more firms in an industry. The figure for shareholders' equity used in the ratio may be expressed in terms of market value instead of book value. When we use market value, we obtain the earnings/price ratio of the stock.

A more general ratio used in the analysis of profitability is the *return on assets,* or the *ROA:*

$$\frac{\text{Net profits after taxes}}{\text{Total assets}} \qquad (27\text{-}15)$$

For Aldine, the ratio is

$$\frac{\$201,242}{\$3,251,480} = 6.19\%$$

This ratio is somewhat inappropriate, inasmuch as profits are taken after interest is paid to creditors. Because these creditors provide means by which part of the total assets are supported, there is a fallacy of omission. When financial charges are significant, it is preferable, for comparative purposes, to compute a net operating profit rate of return instead of a return on assets ratio. The *net operating profit rate of return* may be expressed as

$$\frac{\text{Earnings before interest and taxes}}{\text{Total assets}} \qquad (27\text{-}16)$$

Using this ratio, we are able to abstract from differing financial charges (interest and preferred stock dividends). Thus, the relationship studied is independent of the way the firm is financed.

TURNOVER AND EARNING POWER

Frequently, the financial analyst relates total assets to sales to obtain the *asset turnover ratio*:

$$\frac{\text{Sales}}{\text{Total assets}} \qquad (27\text{-}17)$$

Aldine's turnover for the 1992 fiscal year was

$$\frac{\$3,992,758}{\$3,251,480} = 1.23$$

This ratio tells us the relative efficiency with which the firm utilizes its resources in order to generate output. It varies according to the type of company being studied. A food chain has a considerably higher turnover, for example, than does an electric utility. The turnover ratio is a function of the efficiency with which the various asset components are managed: receivables as depicted by the average collection period, inventories as portrayed by the inventory turnover ratio, and fixed assets as indicated by the throughput of product through the plant or the sales to net fixed asset ratio.

When we multiply the asset turnover of the firm by the net profit margin, we obtain the return on assets ratio, or *earning power* on total assets:

$$\text{Earning power} = \frac{\text{Sales}}{\text{Total assets}} \times \frac{\text{Net profits after taxes}}{\text{Sales}}$$
$$= \frac{\text{Net profits after taxes}}{\text{Total assets}} \qquad (27\text{-}18)$$

For Aldine, we have

$$\frac{\$3,992,758}{\$3,251,480} \times \frac{\$201,242}{\$3,992,758} = 6.19\%$$

Neither the net profit margin nor the turnover ratio by itself provides an adequate measure of operating efficiency. The net profit margin ignores the utilization of assets, whereas the turnover ratio ignores profitability on sales. The return on assets ratio, or earning power, resolves these shortcomings. An improvement in the earning power of the firm will result if there is an increase in turnover on existing assets, an increase in the net profit margin, or both. Two companies with different asset turnovers and net profit margins may have the same earning power. Firm A, with an asset turnover of 4 to 1 and a net profit margin of 3 percent, has the same earning power—12 percent—as firm B, with an asset turnover of $1\frac{1}{2}$ to 1 and a net profit margin of 8 percent.

Another way to look at the return on equity (ROE) is

$$\text{ROE} = \text{Earning power} \times (1 + \text{Debt/Equity}) \qquad (27\text{-}19)$$

In this equation, earning power is grossed up by the equity multiplier associated with the use of debt. For Aldine,

$$ROE = 6.19\% \times 1.81 = 11.20\%$$

or the same as we determined earlier when we computed it directly.

With all the profitability ratios, comparing one company with similar companies is extremely valuable. Only by comparison are we able to judge whether the profitability of a particular company is good or bad, and why. Absolute figures provide some insight, but relative performance is most revealing.

PREDICTIVE POWER OF FINANCIAL RATIOS

In the previous sections, we presented the principal ratios used in financial analysis. Reliance on certain ratios depends on the analyst's perception of their predictive power relative to the problem at hand—a perception based on either subjective beliefs or empirical analysis. In predicting the future value of a stock, an investor might feel that the return on investment ratio and various profit margin ratios would be the greatest help. Most estimates of the predictive power of financial ratios are based on the analyst's past experience with them. By their very nature, then, these estimates tend to be subjective and to differ from one analyst to the next.

A number of empirical studies have tested the predictive power of financial ratios.[6] In many of these studies, financial ratios are used to predict business failure. Others have tested the power of financial ratios to predict corporate bond ratings. With these ratios as the dependent variable, regression analysis and discriminant analysis have been employed, using various financial ratios for a sample of companies. The best ratios for predictive purposes are debt-to-equity, cash-flow-to-debt, net operating profit margin, debt coverage and its stability, return on investment, size, and earnings stability. On the basis of these studies, it appears that a handful of ratios can be used to predict the long-term credit standing of a firm.

PREDICTING FINANCIAL DISTRESS

For our purposes, financial distress is the event of particular interest. (For a discussion of failure and bankruptcy laws, see Appendix A at the back of the book.)

William H. Beaver was the first to use statistical techniques to predict corporate failure. A broad definition of failure was employed, namely, the inability to meet financial obligations of any type. Beaver collected a large sample of firms that failed.[7] Another firm was compared with each of these com-

[6] For an excellent overall discussion of this type of research, see George Foster, *Financial Statement Analysis*, 2d ed. (Englewood Cliffs, NJ: Prentice Hall, 1986). See also Edward I. Altman, *Corporate Financial Distress* (New York: John Wiley, 1983), for a review.
[7] William H. Beaver, "Financial Ratios as Predictors of Failure," *Empirical Research in Accounting: Selected Studies*, supplement to *Journal of Accounting Research*, 41 (1966), 71–111.

panies—a firm that did not fail, that was in the same industry, and that was of approximately the same size as the firm that failed. The data collected for the nonfailed companies were for the same years as those for the failed firms. These samples were used to test the predictive ability of 30 financial ratios. The mean values of the ratios for the two samples were compared over the 5-year period prior to failure. The mean ratio for the failed firms was found to be significantly lower and to deteriorate markedly as failure approached. Although not all of the ratios predicted failure equally well, many showed excellent predictive power.

In a similar type of study, Edward I. Altman employed multiple discriminant analysis to predict bankruptcy, using various financial ratios.[8] This statistical technique is described in the Appendix to Chapter 16. Altman worked with a sample of corporations that filed for bankruptcy. Like Beaver, he collected a paired sample of nonbankrupt firms on a stratified random basis. Starting with 22 financial ratios, he selected the 5 that did the best combined job of predicting bankruptcy. These ratios were used to discriminate between bankrupt and nonbankrupt firms, using data from 1 to 5 years prior to bankruptcy. As expected, the predictive accuracy of the multiple discriminant model declined with the increase in years prior to bankruptcy; however, the model was able to forecast failure quite well up to 2 years before bankruptcy.

The Z score model itself was the following:

$$Z = 1.2X_1 + 1.4X_2 + 3.3X_3 + .6X_4 + 1.0X_5 \qquad (27\text{-}20)$$

where X_1 = working capital to total assets
X_2 = cumulative retained earnings to total assets
X_3 = earnings before interest and taxes to total assets
X_4 = market value of equity to book value of total liabilities
X_5 = sales to total assets

The Z ratio is the overall index of the multiple discriminant function. (See the Appendix to Chapter 16 for further explanation.) Altman found that companies with Z scores below 1.81 (including negative amounts) always went bankrupt, whereas Z scores above 2.99 represented healthy firms. Firms with Z scores in between were sometimes misclassified, so this represents an area of gray. On the basis of these cutoffs, Altman suggests that one can predict whether or not a company is likely to go bankrupt in the near future.

ZETA MODEL

Because of a changing underlying environment for bankruptcy as well as the desire for other improvements in the Z score model, the Zeta model was developed by Altman and others.[9] The authors extended the Z score model to include, among other things, the capitalization of leases, and they updated its application. A sample of 53 bankrupt firms and a matched sample of 58 non-bankrupt firms were employed. Manufacturing and, for the first time in any

---

[8] Edward I. Altman, "Financial Ratios, Discriminant Analysis and the Prediction of Corporate Bankruptcy," *Journal of Finance*, 23 (September 1968), 589–609. For additional discussion of this and other models, see Edward I. Altman, *Corporate Financial Distress* (New York: John Wiley, 1983).

[9] Edward I. Altman, Robert G. Haldeman, and P. Narayanan, "Zeta Analysis: A New Model to Identify Bankruptcy Risk of Corporations," *Journal of Banking and Finance*, 1 (June 1977), 29–54. For additional discussion of it, see Altman, *Financial Distress*, Chap. 4.

study, retailing companies were included. On the basis of discriminatory ability, 27 original variables were reduced to 7: the return on assets ratio, the stability of earnings, the interest coverage ratio, the retained earnings to total assets ratio, the current ratio, the common equity to total capital ratio, and the size of total assets. Using a linear discriminant model, the authors were successful in predicting bankruptcy up to 5 years prior to failure. Successful classification ranged from 96 percent 1 year before failure to 70 percent 5 years before failure, a better performance than the Z score model. Both quadratic and linear models were tested, with the linear function winning out.

Unfortunately for those of us interested in the process, the Zeta model was developed with a private party, called ZETA Services, Inc., so that the coefficients are not published. While the model is used in practice, one must be a subscriber to the service to obtain its output. This output consists of Zeta scores for each of the past 10 years on some 2,400 firms, together with certain other financial data. In testing the model on 64 firms that filed for bankruptcy, Altman found that 95 percent of the bankruptcies could have been predicted on the basis of financial statement information 1 year before and 63 percent on the basis of information 5 years before.

OTHER STUDIES

In addition to the studies described, there has been other empirical work on distress prediction. Space does not permit a thorough review, but we will mention one study. Abdul Aziz and Gerald H. Lawson use a cash-flow-based model (CFB) to predict corporate bankruptcy.[10] The various components of cash flow—operating, investing, financing, and liquidity changes—are employed. Testing the predictive accuracy of the model for 1 to 5 years prior to bankruptcy, the authors find 92 percent accuracy for 1 year prior to the event, declining to 72 percent 5 years before. In comparing their results with those for Altman's Z model and the Zeta model, the CBF model is found to be slightly more accurate than the former and slightly less accurate than the latter. However, the comparisons are mixed with little in the way of statistically significant differences; all three models do a good job.

Additional studies have used regression analysis, discriminant analysis, conditional probability models, and LOGIT techniques to predict financial failure on the basis of financial ratios. Some of these studies are listed in the references at the end of the chapter. It appears that the signs of potential failure are evident before actual failure occurs. For the creditor, the lag allows time to take corrective actions.

SOME FINAL OBSERVATIONS

As a result of the empirical testing of financial ratios, we have a better understanding of which ratios are important in predicting certain types of events. Rather than analyze a host of ratios indiscriminately, the financial analyst can home in on those ratios that are really important with respect to the problem at hand. These are the ratios that have underlying predictive ability. In addition to telling us which ratios are important, empirical testing can

[10] Abdul Aziz and Gerald H. Lawson, "Cash Flow Reporting and Financial Distress Models: Testing of Hypotheses," *Financial Management*, 18 (Spring 1989), 55–63.

show us how these ratios can best be combined so that the analysis is most meaningful in prediction of a future event. As a result of this work, financial ratio analysis has become more scientific and objective than before.

One indication of this is expert systems. As described in Chapter 16, computer software mimics the reasoning process of experienced financial analysts.[11] When the company being analyzed is relatively straightforward in its financial statements, the software routine will analyze the statements and draw conclusions about the company's financial condition and performance. The idea with an expert system is to leverage the talent of experienced financial analysts.

COMMON SIZE AND INDEX ANALYSES

It is often useful to express balance sheet and income statement items as percentages. The percentages can be related to totals, such as total assets or total sales, or to some base year. Called *common size analysis* and *index analysis*, respectively, the evaluation of trends in financial statement percentages over time affords the analyst insight into the underlying improvement or deterioration in financial condition and performance. While a good portion of this insight is revealed in the analysis of financial ratios, a broader understanding of the trends is possible when the analysis is extended to include the foregoing considerations. To illustrate these two types of analyses, we shall use the balance sheet and income statements of Riker Electronics Company for the 19x1 through 19x4 fiscal years. These statements are shown in Tables 27-4 and 27-5.

STATEMENT ITEMS AS PERCENTAGES OF TOTALS

In common size analysis, we express the various components of a balance sheet as percentages of the total assets of the company. In addition, this can be done for the income statement, but here items are related to sales. The gross and net profit margins, taken up earlier, are examples of this type of expression; and it can be extended to all the items on the income statement. The expression of individual financial items as percentages of totals usually permits insights not possible from a review of the raw figures themselves.

To illustrate, common size balance sheet and income statements are shown in Tables 27-6 and 27-7 for Riker Electronics Company for the fiscal years 19x1 through 19x4. In the first of the two tables, we see that over the 4 years the percentage of current assets increased and that this was particularly true of cash. In addition, we see that accounts receivable showed a relative increase from 19x3 to 19x4. On the liability and shareholders' equity side of the balance sheet, the debt of the company declined on a relative basis from 19x1 to 19x3. With the large absolute increase in assets that occurred in 19x4, however, the debt ratio increased from 19x3 to 19x4. This is particularly apparent in accounts payable, which increased substantially in both absolute and relative terms.

[11] For a survey of uses, see Clyde W. Holsapple, Kar Yan Tam, and Andrew B. Whinston, "Adapting Expert System Technology to Financial Management," *Financial Management*, 17 (Autumn 1988), 12–22.

TABLE 27-4
Riker Electronics Corporation balance sheet (in thousands)

	19x1	19x2	19x3	19x4
Assets				
Cash	$ 2,507	$ 4,749	$ 11,310	$ 19,648
Accounts receivable	70,360	72,934	85,147	118,415
Inventory	77,380	86,100	91,378	118,563
Other current assets	6,316	5,637	6,082	5,891
Current assets	$156,563	$169,420	$193,917	$262,517
Fixed assets, net	$ 79,187	$ 91,868	$ 94,652	$115,461
Other long-term assets	4,695	5,017	5,899	5,491
Total assets	$240,445	$266,305	$294,468	$383,469
Liabilities and Shareholders' Equity				
Accounts payable	$ 35,661	$ 31,857	$ 37,460	$ 62,725
Notes payable	20,501	25,623	14,680	17,298
Other current liabilities	11,054	7,330	8,132	15,741
Current liabilities	$ 67,216	$ 64,810	$ 60,272	$ 95,764
Long-term debt	888	979	1,276	1,917
Total liabilities	$ 68,104	$ 65,789	$ 61,548	$ 97,681
Preferred stock	0	0	0	2,088
Common stock	$ 12,650	$ 25,649	$ 26,038	$ 26,450
Additional paid-in capital	36,134	33,297	45,883	63,049
Retained earnings	123,557	141,570	160,999	194,201
Shareholders' equity	$172,341	$200,516	$232,920	$285,788
Total liabilities and equity	$240,445	$266,305	$294,468	$383,469

TABLE 27-5
Riker Electronics Corporation income statement (in thousands)

	19x1	19x2	19x3	19x4
Sales	$323,780	$347,322	$375,088	$479,077
Cost of goods sold	148,127	161,478	184,507	223,690
Gross profit	$175,653	$185,844	$190,581	$255,387
Selling expenses	79,399	98,628	103,975	125,645
General and administrative expenses	43,573	45,667	45,275	61,719
Total expenses	$122,972	$144,295	$149,250	$187,364
Earnings before interest and taxes	$52,681	$41,549	$41,331	$68,023
Other income	1,757	4,204	2,963	3,017
Earnings before taxes	$54,438	$45,753	$44,294	$71,040
Taxes	28,853	22,650	20,413	32,579
Earnings after taxes	$ 25,585	$ 23,103	$ 23,881	$ 38,461

TABLE 27-6

Riker Electronics Corporation common size balance sheet

	19x1	19x2	19x3	19x4
Assets				
Cash	1.0	1.8	3.8	5.1
Accounts receivable	29.3	27.4	28.9	30.9
Inventory	32.2	32.3	31.0	30.9
Other current assets	2.6	2.1	2.1	1.5
Current assets	65.1	63.6	65.9	68.5
Fixed assets, net	32.9	34.5	32.1	30.1
Other long-term assets	2.0	1.9	2.0	1.4
Total assets	100.0	100.0	100.0	100.0
Liabilities and Shareholders' Equity				
Accounts payable	14.8	12.0	12.7	16.4
Notes payable	8.5	9.6	5.0	4.5
Other current liabilities	4.6	2.8	2.8	4.1
Current liabilities	28.0	24.3	20.5	25.0
Long-term debt	.4	.4	.4	.5
Total liabilities	28.3	24.7	20.9	25.5
Preferred stock	.0	.0	.0	.5
Common stock	5.3	9.6	8.8	6.9
Additional paid-in capital	15.0	12.5	15.6	16.4
Retained earnings	51.4	53.2	54.7	50.6
Shareholders' equity	71.7	75.3	79.1	74.5
Total liabilities and equity	100.0	100.0	100.0	100.0

TABLE 27-7

Riker Electronics Corporation common size income statement

	19x1	19x2	19x3	19x4
Sales	100.0	100.0	100.0	100.0
Cost of goods sold	45.7	46.5	49.2	46.7
Gross profit	54.3	53.5	50.8	53.3
Selling expenses	24.5	28.4	27.7	26.2
General and administrative expenses	13.5	13.1	12.1	12.9
Total expenses	38.0	41.5	39.8	39.1
Earnings before interest and taxes	16.3	12.0	11.0	14.2
Other income	.5	1.2	.8	.6
Earnings before taxes	16.8	13.2	11.8	14.8
Taxes	8.9	6.5	5.4	6.8
Earnings after taxes	7.9	6.7	6.4	8.0

The common size income statement in Table 27-7 shows the gross profit margin fluctuating from year to year. When this is combined with selling, general, and administrative expenses, which also fluctuate over time, the end result is a net profit picture that varies from year to year. Although 19x4 shows a sharp improvement over 19x3 and 19x2, it still is not as good as 19x1 on a before-tax relative basis.

STATEMENT ITEMS AS INDEXES RELATIVE TO A BASE YEAR

The common size balance sheet and income statement can be supplemented by the expression of items as trends from a base year. For Riker Electronics Corporation, the base year is 19x1, and all financial statement items are 100.0 for that year. Items for the three subsequent years are expressed as an index relative to that year. If a statement item were $22,500 compared with $15,000 in the base year, the index would be 150. Tables 27-8 and 27-9 are an indexed balance sheet and an income statement. In the first of these two tables, the buildup in cash from the base year is particularly apparent, and this agrees with our previous assessment. Note also the large increase in accounts receivable and inventories from 19x3 to 19x4. The latter was not apparent in the common size analysis. To a lesser extent, there was a sizable increase in fixed assets. On the liability side of the balance sheet, we note the large increase in accounts payable as well as in other current liabilities that occurred from 19x3 to 19x4. This, coupled with retained earnings and the sale of com-

TABLE 27-8
Riker Electronics Corporation indexed balance sheet

	19x1	19x2	19x3	19x4
Assets				
Cash	100.0	189.4	451.1	783.7
Accounts receivable	100.0	103.7	121.0	168.3
Inventory	100.0	111.3	118.1	153.2
Other current assets	100.0	89.2	96.3	93.3
Current assets	100.0	108.2	123.9	167.7
Fixed assets, net	100.0	116.0	119.5	145.8
Other long-term assets	100.0	106.9	125.6	117.0
Total assets	100.0	110.8	122.5	159.5
Liabilities and Shareholders' Equity				
Accounts payable	100.0	89.3	105.0	175.9
Notes payable	100.0	125.0	71.6	84.4
Other current liabilities	100.0	66.3	73.6	142.4
Current liabilities	100.0	96.4	89.7	142.5
Long-term debt	100.0	110.2	143.7	215.9
Total liabilities	100.0	96.6	90.4	143.4
Preferred stock	0.0	0.0	0.0	100.0
Common stock	100.0	202.8	205.8	209.1
Additional paid-in capital	100.0	92.1	127.0	174.5
Retained earnings	100.0	114.6	130.3	157.2
Shareholders' equity	100.0	116.3	135.2	164.3
Total liabilities and equity	100.0	110.8	122.5	159.5

TABLE 27-9
Riker Electronics Corporation indexed income statement

747

CHAPTER 27
Financial Ratio
Analysis

	19x1	19x2	19x3	19x4
Sales	100.0	107.3	115.8	148.0
Cost of goods sold	100.0	109.0	124.6	151.0
Gross profit	100.0	105.8	108.5	145.4
Selling expenses	100.0	124.2	131.0	158.2
General and administrative expenses	100.0	104.8	103.9	141.6
Total expenses	100.0	117.3	121.4	152.4
Earnings before interest and taxes	100.0	78.9	78.5	129.1
Other income	100.0	239.3	168.6	171.7
Earnings before taxes	100.0	84.0	81.4	130.5
Taxes	100.0	78.5	70.7	112.9
Earnings after taxes	100.0	90.3	93.3	150.3

mon stock, financed the large increase in assets that occurred between these two points in time.

The indexed income statement in Table 27-9 gives much the same picture as the common size income statement, namely, fluctuating behavior. The sharp improvement in 19x4 profitability is more easily distinguished, and the indexed statement gives us information on the magnitude of absolute change in profits and expenses. With the common size statement, we have no information about how total assets or total sales change over time.

In summary, the standardization of balance sheet and income statement items as percentages of totals and as indexes to a base year often gives us insights additional to those obtained from analysis of financial ratios. Common size and index analyses are much easier when a computer spreadsheet program is employed. The division calculations by rows or by columns can be done quickly and accurately with such a program.

SUMMARY

Financial ratios can be derived from the balance sheet and the income statement. They are categorized into four types: liquidity, debt, profitability, and coverage. Each type has a special use for the financial analyst. Outside creditors, investors, and government regulators extensively employ the ratios discussed in this chapter. These ratios are also helpful for managerial control and for a better understanding of what outside suppliers of capital expect in financial condition and performance. The usefulness of the ratios depends on the ingenuity and experience of the financial analyst who employs them. By themselves, financial ratios are fairly meaningless; they must be analyzed on a comparative basis.

A comparison of ratios of the same firm over time uncovers leading clues in evaluating changes and trends in the firm's financial condition and profitability. The comparison may be historical and predictive. It may include

748

**PART 8
Tools of Financial
Analysis and
Control**

an analysis of the future based on projected financial statements. Ratios may also be judged in comparison with those of similar firms in the same line of business and, when appropriate, with an industry average. Caution is necessary in such comparisons, because the distributions of financial ratios for companies in an industry vary a good deal. The financial analyst must heed other caveats and be aware of various sources of industry financial ratio information.

From empirical testing in recent years, it appears that financial ratios can be used successfully to predict certain events, bankruptcy in particular. With this testing, financial ratio analysis has become more scientific and objective than ever before, and we can look to further progress in this regard. One example is the development of computer-software expert systems to analyze financial statements and draw implications.

Additional insight often is obtained when balance sheet and income statement items are expressed as percentages. The percentages can be in relation to total assets or total sales for some base year. Called common size analysis and index analysis, respectively, the idea is to study trends in financial statement items over time. In this regard, a rich understanding of the underlying funds movement of the firm as well as of its profitability is possible with these two types of analyses.

APPENDIX
Inflation and Financial Analysis

In financial ratio analysis, inflationary forces may mask the results. Part of the financial performance of a company may result from management decisions, but part may be attributable to external factors over which management has little control. In particular, inflation may give rise to holding period gains that are not attributable to management decisions. The problem with holding period gains is that they vary with inflation and this clouds the analysis of the overall results. To the extent that financial analysts wish to differentiate performance based on conventional accounting data from economic profitability, they will need to adjust the accounting numbers.

THE PROBLEM ILLUSTRATED

Foster Tool Company, a wholesaler of tools, began business on December 31, 19X1, and had the following balance sheet at that time:

ASSETS		LIABILITIES AND SHAREHOLDERS' EQUITY	
Cash	$ 40,000	Common stock	$240,000
Inventory	100,000		
Net fixed assets	100,000		
	$240,000		$240,000

The fixed assets are depreciable over 10 years, and for ease of illustration we assume straight-line depreciation. Inventory is reported on a first-in, first-out (FIFO) basis.[12] Sales occurred entirely at the end of the first year of operation, and inflation for that year was 20 percent. For ease of understanding, we assume that inflation occurred at the beginning of 19x2 and that we live in a world of no taxes.

Operations for the first year are reported on an historical cost basis and are as follows:

INCOME		
Sales		$170,000
Cost of goods sold		
Beginning inventory	$100,000	
Purchases	120,000	
Ending inventory	(120,000)	100,000
Depreciation ($100,000/10)		10,000
Selling and administrative expenses		30,000
Net profit		$ 30,000

Note that the company's ending inventory is higher than its beginning inventory by the percentage increase in prices, namely, 20 percent. The balance sheet of the company at December 31, 19x2, would be

ASSETS		LIABILITIES AND SHAREHOLDERS' EQUITY	
Cash	$ 60,000		
Inventory	120,000	Common stock	$240,000
Net fixed assets	90,000	Retained earnings	30,000
	$270,000		$270,000

If we compute two of the more widely used profitability ratios, we find them to be

Net profit margin ($30,000/$170,000) = 17.65%

Return on assets ($30,000/$240,000) = 12.50%

In both cases, the underlying economic profitability of the company is overstated. For one thing, with the FIFO method, inventories that are sold are assumed to have been purchased at the prices prevailing when the oldest items in the inventory were purchased. With inflation, these prices will be considerably below their replacement costs. In the case of Foster Tool Company, the inventories sold are valued at $100,000 for accounting purposes, whereas their replacement cost at the time they were sold was $120,000. The costing of

---

[12] This example draws on Lawrence Revsine, *Accounting in an Inflationary Environment* (New York: Laventhol and Horwath, 1977).

inventories in this manner tends to understate economic costs and to over-state economic profits. A remedy is to use the last-in, first-out (LIFO) method. With this method, the inventory most recently purchased is employed in the cost of goods sold. As a result, the value attached to the inventory approxi-mates the replacement cost.

In addition to inventory valuation on a FIFO basis overstating economic profits, depreciation charges in our example are based on the original cost of the fixed assets, less accumulated depreciation. Again with inflation, the origi-nal cost is less than the current replacement cost of these assets. If these assets increase in value by 20 percent, their replacement value is $120,000, and eco-nomic depreciation would be $12,000 instead of the $10,000 used for account-ing depreciation purposes.

Restating the income statement of Foster Tool Company on a replace-ment cost basis, we have for 19X2

INCOME

Sales	$170,000
Cost of goods sold (replacement cost)	120,000
Depreciation ($120,000/10)	12,000
Selling and administrative expenses	30,000
Net profit	$ 8,000

The profitability ratios are as follows when economic profits as opposed to profits on an historical cost basis are used:

Net profit margin ($8,000/$170,000) = 4.70%

Return on assets ($8,000/$240,000) = 3.33%

We see, then, that the economic performance results are substantially lower than those originally supposed when accounting data were used.

IMPLICATIONS

The example illustrates the problems involved when the analyst tries to compare the financial ratios of a company over time in the face of differing rates of inflation. Historical cost accounting data are distorted from year to year as a result of inflation. Financial ratios, particularly those dealing with profitability, likewise are distorted. Some of the operating results are due to inflation, which is beyond management's control. What may appear to be a significant change in profitability may, upon closer examination, be due to the vagaries of inflation.

In addition to a company's financial ratios being distorted over time, in-tercompany comparisons may be distorted. When historical costs are used, the company with older fixed assets will often show a higher return on invest-ment in an inflationary environment than will a company whose fixed assets were acquired more recently. Not only will the depreciation charges for the former company be less, which, in turn, will result in greater reported profits, but total assets will be lower. This combination of higher profits and lower in-vestment will result in a higher return on investment, all other things being the same. The difference in return performance, however, may be due entirely to assets being purchased at different times, not to the relative efficiency of management. The danger is that the company with older fixed assets may be much less efficient in an economic sense, but that its return on investment, as based on conventional accounting data, is as good as, if not better than, that of a more efficient producer.

For both types of comparisons—intercompany and financial ratios of the same company over time—inflation can lead the financial analyst to derive faulty economic assessments. In periods of rapidly changing inflation, particular caution is necessary. Under these circumstances, it is desirable to recompute financial ratios using replacement cost accounting data. This can be done in the manner illustrated. By doing so, the financial analyst is able to differentiate between performance attributable to inflation and performance more directly under management's control.

SELF-CORRECTION PROBLEMS

1. High-Low Plumbing Company sells plumbing fixtures on terms of 2/10, net 30. Its financial statements over the last 3 years follow:

	19x1	19x2	19x3
Cash	$ 30,000	$ 20,000	$ 5,000
Accounts receivable	200,000	260,000	290,000
Inventory	400,000	480,000	600,000
Net fixed assets	800,000	800,000	800,000
	$1,430,000	$1,560,000	$1,695,000
Accounts payable	230,000	300,000	380,000
Accruals	200,000	210,000	225,000
Bank loan, short term	100,000	100,000	140,000
Long-term debt	300,000	300,000	300,000
Common stock	100,000	100,000	100,000
Retained earnings	500,000	550,000	550,000
	$1,430,000	$1,560,000	$1,695,000
Sales	$4,000,000	$4,300,000	$3,800,000
Cost of goods sold	3,200,000	3,600,000	3,300,000
Net profit	300,000	200,000	100,000

Using the ratios taken up in the chapter, analyze the company's financial condition and performance over the last 3 years. Are there any problems?

2. Using the following information, complete this balance sheet.

Long-term debt to net worth	5 to 1
Total asset turnover	2.5×
Average collection period*	18 days
Inventory turnover	9×
Gross profit margin	10%
Acid-test ratio	1 to 1

*Assume a 360-day year and all sales on credit.

Cash	$_____	Notes and payables	$100,000
Accounts receivable	_____	Long-term debt	
Inventory	_____	Common stock	$100,000
Plant and equipment	_____	Retained earnings	100,000
Total assets	$_____	Total liabilities and equity	$_____

3. Stella Stores, Inc., has sales of $6 million, an asset turnover ratio of 6 for the year, and net profits of $120,000.

  a. What is the company's return on assets or earning power?

  b. The company will install new point-of-sales cash registers throughout its stores. This equipment is expected to increase efficiency in inventory control, reduce clerical errors, and improve record keeping throughout the system. The new equipment will increase the investment in assets by 20 percent and is expected to increase the net profit margin from 2 percent now to 3 percent. No change in sales is expected. What is the effect of the new equipment on the return on assets ratio or earning power?

4. Kedzie Kord Company had the following balance sheets and income statements over the last 3 years (in thousands):

	19x1	19x2	19x3
Cash	$ 561	$ 387	$ 202
Receivables	1,963	2,870	4,051
Inventories	2,031	2,613	3,287
Current assets	$ 4,555	$ 5,870	$ 7,540
Net fixed assets	2,581	4,430	4,364
Total assets	$ 7,136	$10,300	$11,904
Payables	$ 1,862	$ 2,944	$ 3,613
Accruals	301	516	587
Bank loan	250	900	1,050
Current liabilities	$ 2,413	$ 4,360	$ 5,250
Long-term debt	500	1,000	950
Shareholders' equity	4,223	4,940	5,704
Total liabilities and equity	$ 7,136	$10,300	$11,904
Sales	$11,863	$14,952	$16,349
Cost of goods sold	8,537	11,124	12,016
Selling, general, and administrative expenses	2,349	2,659	2,993
Profit before taxes	$ 977	$ 1,169	$ 1,340
Taxes	390	452	576
Profit after taxes	$ 587	$ 717	$ 764

Using common size and index analyses, evaluate trends in the company's financial condition and performance.

PROBLEMS

1. Cordillera Carson Company has the following balance sheet and income statement for 19X2 (in thousands):

Balance Sheet

Cash	$ 400	Accounts payable	$ 320
Accounts receivable	1,300	Accruals	260
Inventories ($1,800 for 19x1)	2,100	Short-term loans	1,100
Current assets	$3,800	Current liabilities	$1,680
Net fixed assets	3,320	Long-term debt	2,000
Total assets	$7,120	Shareholders' equity	3,440
		Total liabilities and equity	$7,120

Income Statement

Net sales (all credit)	$12,680
Cost of goods sold*	8,930
Gross profit	$ 3,750
Selling, general, and admin. expenses	2,230
Interest expense	460
Profit before taxes	$ 1,060
Taxes	390
Profit after taxes	$ 670

*Includes depreciation of $480.

On the basis of this information, compute (a) the current ratio, (b) the acid-test ratio, (c) the average collection period, (d) the inventory turnover ratio, (e) the debt-to-net-worth ratio, (f) the long-term-debt-to-total-capitalization ratio, (g) the gross profit margin, (h) the net profit margin, (i) the rate of return on common stock equity, and (j) the ratio of cash flow to long-term debt.

2. Parker Phial Company has current assets of $1 million and current liabilities of $600,000.

    a. What is the company's current ratio?

    b. What would be its current ratio if each of the following occurred, holding all other things constant?

    (1) A machine costing $100,000 is paid for with cash.

    (2) Inventories of $120,000 are purchased and financed with trade credit.

    (3) Accounts payable of $50,000 are paid off with cash.

    (4) Accounts receivable of $75,000 are collected.

    (5) Long-term debt of $200,000 is raised for investment in inventories ($100,000) and to pay down short-term borrowings ($100,000).

3. A company has total annual sales (all credit) of $400,000 and a gross profit margin of 20 percent. Its current assets are $80,000; current liabilities, $60,000; inventories, $30,000; and cash, $10,000.

    a. How much average inventory should be carried if management wants the inventory turnover to be 4? (Assume a 360-day year for calculations.)

    b. How rapidly (in how many days) must accounts receivable be collected if management wants to have only an average of $50,000 invested in receivables? (Assume a 360-day year.)

4. The data for various companies in the same industry and of about the same size follow:

COMPANY	A	B	C	D	E	F
Sales (in millions)	$10	$20	$8	$5	$12	$17
Total assets (in millions)	8	10	6	2.5	4	8
Net income (in millions)	0.7	2.0	0.8	0.5	1.5	1.0

Determine the asset turnover, net profit margin, and earning power for each of the companies.

5. The long-term debt section of the balance sheet of the Diters Corporation appears as follows:

$9\frac{1}{4}\%$ mortgage bonds	$2,500,000
$12\frac{3}{8}\%$ second-mortgage bonds	1,500,000
$10\frac{1}{4}\%$ debentures	1,000,000
$14\frac{1}{2}\%$ subordinated debentures	1,000,000
	$6,000,000

a. If the average earnings before interest and taxes of the Diters Corporation are $1.5 million, what is the overall interest coverage?

b. Using the cumulative deduction method, determine the coverage for each issue.

6. **U.S. Republic Corporation balance sheet,**
December 31, 19X3

ASSETS		LIABILITIES AND STOCKHOLDERS' EQUITY	
Cash	$ 500,000	Notes payable	$ 2,000,000
Accounts receivable	2,500,000	Accounts payable	1,000,000
Inventory*	3,500,000	Accrued wages and taxes	1,000,000
Fixed assets, net	7,500,000		
Excess over book value		Long-term debt	6,000,000
of assets acquired		Preferred stock	2,000,000
(intangible assets)	1,000,000		
		Common stock	1,000,000
		Retained earnings	2,000,000
		Total liabilities	
Total assets	$15,000,000	and equity	$15,000,000

*Inventory at December 31, 19X2 = $1,500,000.

U.S. Republic Corporation statement of income and retained earnings, year ended December 31, 19X3

Net sales		
Credit	$ 8,000,000	
Cash	2,000,000	
Total	$10,000,000	
Costs and expenses		
Cost of goods sold	$6,000,000	
Selling, general, and administrative expenses	1,100,000	
Depreciation	700,000	
Interest on long-term debt	600,000	8,400,000
Net income before taxes		$ 1,600,000
Taxes on income		600,000
Net income after taxes		$ 1,000,000
Less: Dividends on preferred stock		120,000
Net income available to common		880,000
Add: Retained earnings 1/1/x3		1,300,000
Subtotal		$ 2,180,000
Less: Dividends paid on common		180,000
Retained earnings at 12/31/x3		$ 2,000,000

a. Fill in the 19X3 column in the data presented.

U.S. Republic Corporation

RATIO	19x1	19x2	19x3	INDUSTRY 19x3
1. Current ratio	250%	200%		225%
2. Acid-test ratio	100%	90%		110%
3. Receivables turnover	5.0×	4.5×		6.0×
4. Inventory turnover	4.0×	3.0×		4.0×
5. Long-term debt to capitalization	35%	40%		33%
6. Gross profit margin	39%	41%		40%
7. Net profit margin	17%	15%		15%
8. Rate of return on equity	15%	20%		20%
9. Return on tangible assets	15%	12%		10%
10. Tangible asset turnover	.9×	.8×		1.0×
11. Overall interest coverage	11×	9×		10×
12. Cash flow to long-term debt	.66	.59		.60

b. Evaluate the position of the company from the table. Cite specific ratio levels and trends as evidence.

c. Indicate which ratios would be of most interest to you and what your decision would be in each of the following situations:

(1) U.S. Republic wants to buy $500,000 worth of raw materials from you, with payment to be due in 90 days.

(2) U.S. Republic wants you, a large insurance company, to pay off its note at the bank and assume it on a 10-year maturity basis at the current coupon of 14 percent.

(3) There are 100,000 shares outstanding, and the stock is selling for $80 a share. The company offers you an opportunity to buy 50,000 additional shares at this price.

7. The following information is available on the Vanier Corporation. Assuming sales and production are steady throughout the year and a 360-day year, complete the balance sheet and income statement for Vanier Corporation.

Balance Sheet   December 31, 19x6 (in thousands of dollars)

Cash and marketable securities	$500	Accounts payable	$ 400
Accounts receivable	?	Bank loan	?
Inventories	?	Accruals	200
Current assets	?	Current liabilities	?
		Long-term debt	?
Net fixed assets	?	Common stock and retained earnings	3,750
Total assets	?	Total liabilities and equity	?

Income Statement for 19x6 (in thousands of dollars)

Credit sales	$8,000
Cost of goods sold	?
Gross profit	?
Selling and administrative expenses	?
Interest expense	400
Profit before taxes	?
Taxes, @ 44%	?
Profit after taxes	?

Other Information

Current ratio	3 to 1
Depreciation	$500
(Net profit & depreciation) to long-term debt	.40
Net profit margin	7%
Total liabilities to net worth	1 to 1
Average collection period	45 days
Inventory turnover ratio	3 to 1

8. Tic Tac Homes has had the following balance sheet statements during the past 4 years (in thousands):

	19x1	19x2	19x3	19x4
Cash	$ 214	$ 93	$ 42	$ 38
Receivables	1,213	1,569	1,846	2,562
Inventories	2,102	2,893	3,678	4,261
Net fixed assets	2,219	2,346	2,388	2,692
Total assets	$5,748	$6,901	$7,954	$9,553
Accounts payable	$1,131	$1,578	$1,848	$2,968
Notes payable	500	650	750	750
Accruals	656	861	1,289	1,743
Long-term debt	500	800	800	800
Common stock	200	200	200	200
Retained earnings	2,761	2,812	3,067	3,092
Total liabilities and shareholders' equity	$5,748	$6,901	$7,954	$9,553

Using index analysis, what are the major problems in the company's financial condition?

9. Two companies have the following financial characteristics (in thousands):

	ZOOM COMPANY	ZING COMPANY
Working capital	$10,500	−$ 1,600
Total assets	50,000	21,000
Total liabilities	22,000	13,000
Equity value (market)	38,000	5,100
Retained earnings	19,000	3,000
Sales	86,000	23,000
Earnings before interest and taxes	12,000	1,300

Using Altman's model for predicting bankruptcy presented in this chapter, determine the Z score index for each company. On the basis of these indexes, is either company likely to go into bankruptcy? Why?

Appendix Problem

1. Using historical costs, Patell Patterns, Inc., had the following income statement for the year, which was one in which 15 percent inflation occurred (in thousands of dollars):

Sales		$5,000
Cost of goods sold		
Beginning inventory	$ 800	
Purchases	3,200	
Ending inventory	(920)	3,200
Depreciation		500
Selling and administrative expenses		800
Profit before taxes		620
Taxes @ 40%		248
Profit after taxes		$ 372

At the beginning of the year, the fixed assets of the company amounted to $6 million on an historical cost basis, and they were depreciated on a straight-line basis with an average depreciable life of 12 years. The FIFO method is used for inventories.

a. Determine the income statement on a replacement cost basis.

b. What is the difference between the two methods?

SOLUTIONS TO
SELF-CORRECTION PROBLEMS

1.

	19x1	19x2	19x3
Current ratio	1.19	1.25	1.20
Acid-test ratio	.43	.46	.40
Average collection period	18	22	27
Inventory turnover	NA	8.2	6.1
Total debt to net worth	1.38	1.40	1.61
Long-term debt to total capitalization	.33	.32	.32
Gross profit margin	.200	.163	.132
Net profit margin	.075	.047	.026
Asset turnover	2.80	2.76	2.24
Return on assets	.21	.13	.06

NA—not available.

The company's profitability has declined steadily over the period. As only $50,000 is added to retained earnings, the company must be paying substantial dividends. Receivables are growing slower, although the average collection period is still very reasonable relative to the terms given. Inventory turnover is slowing as well, indicating a relative buildup in inventories. The increase in receivables and inventories, coupled with the fact that net worth has increased very little, has resulted in the total debt-to-worth ratio increasing to what would have to be regarded on an absolute basis as a quite high level.

The current and acid-test ratios have fluctuated, but the current ratio is not particularly inspiring. The lack of deterioration in these ratios is clouded by the relative buildup in both receivables and inventories, evidencing a deterioration in the liquidity of these two assets. Both the gross profit and net profit margins have declined substantially. The relationship between the two suggests that the company has reduced relative expenses in 19x3 in particular. The buildup in inventories and receivables has resulted in a decline in the asset turnover ratio, and this, coupled with the decline in profitability, has resulted in a sharp decrease in the return on assets ratio.

2. $\dfrac{\text{Long-term debt}}{\text{Net worth}} = .5 = \dfrac{\text{Long-term debt}}{200,000}$ Long-term debt = $100,000

Total liabilities and net worth = $400,000

Total assets = $400,000

$\dfrac{\text{Sales}}{\text{Total assets}} = 2.5 = \dfrac{\text{Sales}}{400,000}$ Sales = $1,000,000

Cost of goods sold = (.9)($1,000,000) = $900,000

$\dfrac{\text{Cost of goods sold}}{\text{Inventory}} = \dfrac{900,000}{\text{Inventory}} = 9$ Inventory = $100,000

$\dfrac{\text{Receivables} \times 360}{1,000,000} = 18 \text{ days}$ Receivables = $50,000

$\dfrac{\text{Cash} + 50,000}{100,000} = 1$ Cash = $50,000

Plant and equipment = $200,000

Balance sheet

Cash	$ 50,000	Notes and payables	$100,000
Accounts		Long-term debt	100,000
receivable	50,000	Common stock	100,000
Inventory	100,000	Retained earnings	100,000
Plant and equipment	200,000		
Total	$400,000	Total	$400,000

3. a. Total assets = Sales/turnover = $6 million/6 = $1 million

Earning power = Net profits/total assets
$$= \$120{,}000/\$1 \text{ million} = 12\%$$

b. Total assets = $1 million × 1.2 = $1.2 million

Earning power = Turnover × Net profit margin
$$= \frac{\$6 \text{ million}}{\$1.2 \text{ million}} \times 3\% = 15\%$$

4. The common size analysis shows that receivables are growing faster than total assets and current assets, while cash declined dramatically as a percentage of both. Net fixed assets surged in 19X2, but then fell back as a percentage of the total to almost the 19X1 percentage. The absolute amounts suggest that the company spent less than its depreciation on fixed assets in 19X3. With respect to financing, shareholders' equity has not kept up, so the company has had to use somewhat more debt percentagewise. It appears to be leaning more on the trade as payables increased percentagewise. Bank loans and long-term debt also increased sharply in 19X2, no doubt to finance the bulge in net fixed assets. The bank loan remained about the same in 19X3 as a percentage of total liabilities and equity, while long-term debt declined as a percentage. Profit after taxes slipped slightly as a percentage of sales over the 3 years. In 19X2, this decline was a result of the cost of goods sold, as expenses and taxes declined as a percentage of sales. In 19X3, cost of goods sold declined as a percentage of sales, but this was more than offset by increases in expenses and taxes as percentages of sales.

	19X1	19X2	19X3
	Common Size Analysis		
Cash	7.9%	3.8%	1.7%
Receivables	27.5	27.8	34.0
Inventories	28.4	25.4	27.6
Current assets	63.8%	57.0%	63.3%
Net fixed assets	36.2	43.0	36.7
Total assets	100.0%	100.0%	100.0%
Payables	26.1%	28.6%	30.4%
Accruals	4.2	5.0	4.9
Bank loan	3.5	8.7	8.8
Current liabilities	33.8%	42.3%	44.1%
Long-term debt	7.0	9.7	8.0
Shareholders' equity	59.2	48.0	47.9
Total liabilities and equity	100.0%	100.0%	100.0%
Sales	100.0%	100.0%	100.0%
Cost of goods sold	72.0	74.4	73.5
Selling, general, and administrative expenses	19.8	17.8	18.3
Profit before taxes	8.2%	7.8%	8.2%
Taxes	3.3	3.0	3.5
Profit after taxes	4.9%	4.8%	4.7%

	19x1	19x2	19x3
		Index Analysis	
Cash	100.0	69.0	36.0
Receivables	100.0	146.2	206.4
Inventories	100.0	128.7	161.8
Current assets	100.0	128.9	165.5
Net fixed assets	100.0	171.6	169.1
Total assets	100.0	144.3	166.8
Payables	100.0	158.1	194.0
Accruals	100.0	171.4	195.0
Bank loan	100.0	360.0	420.0
Current liabilities	100.0	180.7	217.6
Long-term debt	100.0	200.0	190.0
Shareholders' equity	100.0	117.0	135.1
Total liabilities and equity	100.0	144.3	166.8
Sales	100.0	126.0	137.8
Cost of goods sold	100.0	130.3	140.8
Selling, general, and administrative expenses	100.0	113.2	127.4
Profit before taxes	100.0	119.7	137.2
Taxes	100.0	115.9	147.7
Profit after taxes	100.0	122.2	130.2

Index analysis shows much the same picture. Cash declined faster than total assets and current assets, and receivables increased faster than these two benchmarks. Inventories fluctuated, but were about the same percentagewise to total assets in 19X3 as they were in 19X1. Net fixed assets increased more sharply than total assets in 19X2 and then fell back into line in 19X3. The sharp increase in bank loans in 19X2 and 19X3 and the sharp increase in long-term debt in 19X2 are evident. Equity increased less than total assets, so debt increased more percentagewise. With respect to profitability, net profits increased less than sales, for the reasons indicated earlier.

SELECTED REFERENCES

Almanac of Business and Industrial Ratios. Englewood Cliffs, NJ: Prentice Hall, 1989.

ALTMAN, EDWARD I., "Financial Ratios, Discriminant Analysis and the Prediction of Corporate Bankruptcy," *Journal of Finance*, 23 (September 1968), 589–609.

———, ROBERT G. HALDEMAN, and P. NARAYANAN, "Zeta Analysis: A New Model to Identify Bankruptcy Risk of Corporations," *Journal of Banking and Finance*, 1 (June 1977), 29–54.

AZIZ, ABDUL, and GERALD H. LAWSON, "Cash Flow Reporting and Financial Distress Models: Testing of Hypotheses," *Financial Management*, 18 (Spring 1989), 55–63.

BACKER, MORTON, and MARTIN L. GOSMAN, "The Use of Financial Ratios in Credit Downgrade Decisions," *Financial Management*, 9 (Spring 1980), 53–56.

BEAVER, WILLIAM H., "Financial Ratios as Predictors of Failure," *Empirical Research in Accounting: Selected Studies in Journal of Accounting Research* (1966), 71–111.

———, *Financial Reporting: An Accounting Revolution.* Englewood Cliffs, NJ: Prentice Hall, 1981.

CHEN, KUNG H., and THOMAS A. SHIMERDA, "An Empirical Analysis of Useful Financial Ratios," *Financial Management*, 10 (Spring 1981), 51–60.

DAMBOLENA, ISMAEL G., and SARKIS J. KHOURY, "Ratio Stability and Corporate Failure," *Journal of Finance*, 35 (September 1980), 1017–26.

DEAKIN, EDWARD B., "Distributions of Financial Accounting Ratios: Some Empirical Evidence," *Accounting Review*, 51 (January 1976), 90–96.

FOSTER, GEORGE, *Financial Statement Analysis*, 2d ed. Englewood Cliffs, NJ: Prentice Hall, 1986.

FRYDMAN, HALINA, EDWARD I. ALTMAN, and DUEN-LI KAO, "Introducing Recursive Partitioning for Financial Classification: The Case of Financial Distress," *Journal of Finance*, 40 (March 1985), 269–91.

GOMBOLA, MICHAEL J., and J. EDWARD KETZ, "Financial Ratio Patterns in Retail and Manufacturing Organizations," *Financial Management*, 12 (Summer 1983), 45–56.

HARRINGTON, DIANA R., and BRENT D. WILSON, *Corporate Financial Analysis*, 3d ed. Homewood, IL: BPI/Irwin, 1989.

HELFERT, ERICH A., *Techniques of Financial Analysis*, 7th ed. Homewood, IL: Richard D. Irwin, 1991, Chap. 3.

HIGGINS, ROBERT C., *Analysis for Financial Management*. 2d ed. Homewood, IL: Richard D. Irwin, 1989.

HOLSAPPLE, CLYDE W., KAR YAN TAM, and ANDREW B. WHINSTON, "Adapting Expert System Technology to Financial Management," *Financial Management*, 17 (Autumn 1988), 12–22.

LEWELLEN, W. G., and R. O. EDMISTER, "A General Model for Accounts Receivable Analysis and Control," *Journal of Financial and Quantitative Analysis*, 8 (March 1973), 195–206.

OHLSON, JAMES, "Financial Ratios and Probabilistic Prediction of Bankruptcy," *Journal of Accounting Research*, 18 (Spring 1980), 109–31.

QUEEN, MAGGIE, and RICHARD ROLL, "Mortality Tables for Firms: Predicting Survival with Market Indicators," working paper, UCLA Graduate School of Management (February 1987).

REVSINE, LAWRENCE, *Accounting in an Inflationary Environment*. New York: Laventhol and Horwath, 1977.

STONE, BERNELL K., "The Payments-Pattern Approach to the Forecasting of Accounts Receivable," *Financial Management*, 5 (Autumn 1976), 65–82.

28

FINANCIAL PLANNING

Financial planning involves analyzing the financial flows of a company; forecasting the consequences of various investment, financing, and dividend decisions, and weighing the effects of various alternatives. The idea is to determine where the firm has been, where it is now, and where it is going—not only the most likely course of events, but deviations from the most likely outcome. If things become unfavorable, the company should have a backup plan, so that it is not caught flat-footed, without financial alternatives.

These steps lead to a financial plan or strategy embracing investment, financing and dividend decisions of the company, for the firm's financial results are the product of these decisions. In financial planning, the *integrated* effect of these decisions must be considered, because seldom does the sum of the parts equal the whole. Since one tries to take account of possible surprises, risk necessarily is involved. Indeed, the focus of this book is on risk and return, for they determine the valuation of the firm in the marketplace. The advantage of financial planning is that it forces management to take account of possible deviations from the company's anticipated path. Usually a firm will establish goals for itself; helping it achieve these goals is one of the main responsibilities of the chief financial officer and his or her planning staff.

The planning horizon depends on the company. Most firms have a horizon of at least 1 year. Many will produce detailed plans for 1 year and more general financial plans for 3 to 5 years. Some companies will plan ahead 10 or even more years. Public utilities and energy companies, having very long lead times for capital projects, make much longer financial plans than do most companies.

METHODS OF ANALYSIS

This chapter looks through the tool kit for financial planning and the analysis of past financial progress. One of the valuable aids we find is a funds-flow statement, with which a financial manager or a creditor may evaluate how a firm uses funds and may determine how these uses are financed. In addition to studying past flows, the analyst can evaluate future flows by means of a funds statement based on forecasts. Such a statement provides an efficient method for the financial manager to assess the growth of the firm and its resulting financial needs as well as to determine the best way in which to finance those needs. In particular, funds statements are very useful in planning intermediate- and long-term financing.

In the analysis of future funds flows, we have the cash budget and pro forma statements. The cash budget is indispensable to the financial manager in determining the short-term cash needs of the firm and, accordingly, in planning its short-term financing. When cash budgeting is extended to include a range of possible outcomes, the financial manager can evaluate the business risk and liquidity of the firm and plan a realistic margin of safety. This margin of safety might come from adjusting the firm's liquidity cushion, rearranging the maturity structure of its debt, arranging a line of credit with a bank, or a combination of the three. Cash budgets prepared for a range of possible outcomes are valuable also in appraising the ability of the firm to adjust to unexpected changes in cash flows. The preparation of pro forma balance sheets and income statements enables the financial manager to analyze the effect of various policy decisions on the future financial condition and performance of the firm.

The final method of analysis involves sustainable growth modeling. Here we determine whether the sales growth objectives of the company are consistent with its operating efficiency and with its financial ratios. This powerful tool of analysis allows us to simulate the likely effects of changes in target ratios when we move from a steady state environment. The integration of marketing, operational, and financial objectives permits better management of growth.

As we discussed in the previous chapter, a computer-based spreadsheet program is particularly applicable. Cash budgeting, the preparation of pro forma statements, and even sustainable growth modeling are made easier. In the supplement, *Financial Management Computer Applications*, such programs are provided. They make possible wide-ranging analyses not possible if things have to be redone by hand each time there is a change in assumptions.

SOURCE AND USE OF FUNDS

The flow of funds in a firm may be visualized as a continuous process. For every use of funds, there must be an offsetting source. In a broad sense, the assets of a firm represent the net uses of funds; its liabilities and net worth represent net sources. A funds-flow cycle for a typical manufacturing company is illustrated in Fig. 28-1. For the going concern, there is really no starting or stopping point. A finished product is a variety of inputs—namely, raw material, fixed assets, and labor—ultimately paid for in cash. The product then is sold either for cash or on credit. A credit sale involves a receivable, which, when collected, becomes cash. If the selling price of the product exceeds all costs (including depreciation on assets) for a period of time, there is a profit for the period; if not, there is a loss. The reservoir of cash, the focal point in the figure, fluctuates over time with the production schedule, sales, collection of receivables, capital expenditures, and financing. On the other hand, reservoirs of raw materials, work in process, finished goods inventory, accounts receivable, and trade payables fluctuate with sales, the production schedule, and policies on managing receivables, inventories, and trade payables.

The funds statement is a method by which we study the net funds flow between two points in time. These points conform to beginning and ending

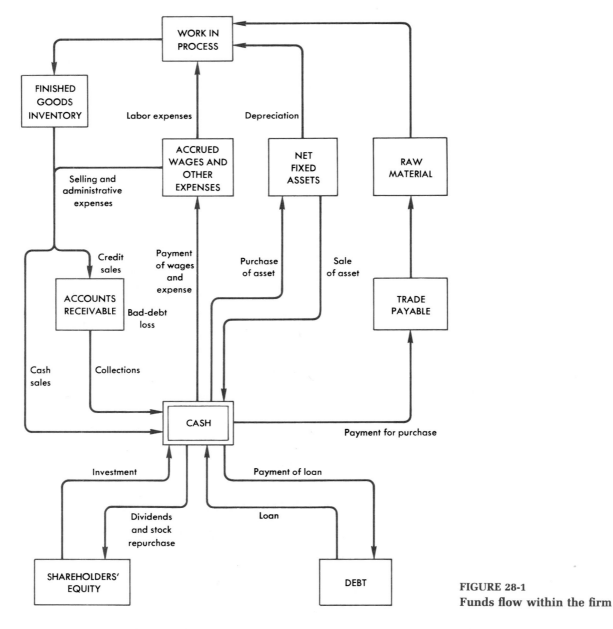

FIGURE 28-1
Funds flow within the firm

financial statement dates for whatever period of examination is relevant—a quarter, a year, or 5 years. We must emphasize that the funds statement portrays net rather than gross changes between two comparable financial statements at different dates. For example, gross changes might be thought to include all changes that occur between the two statement dates, rather than the sum of these changes—the net change as defined. Although an analysis of the gross funds flow of a firm over time would be much more revealing than an analysis of net funds flow, we are usually constrained by the financial information available, namely, balance sheets and income statements that span particular periods of time. Funds may be defined in several different ways, depending on the purpose of the analysis. Although they are often defined as cash, many analysts treat funds as working capital, a somewhat broader definition. Other definitions are possible, although the two described are the most common by far. Depending on the analyst's objective, the definition can be broadened or narrowed. Because a funds-flow analysis on a cash basis serves as a building block for analyses using broader definitions of funds, we begin by defining funds as cash.

In what follows, we present two similar but somewhat different approaches to analyzing funds flows on a cash basis. The first is a traditional way used by many financial analysts. The second is an accounting statement of cash flows required in the presentation of audited financial results. This statement supplements the balance sheet and income statement.

FUNDS STATEMENT ON A CASH BASIS

Basically, one prepares a funds statement on a cash basis by (1) classifying net balance sheet changes that occur between two points in time: changes that increase cash and changes that decrease cash; (2) classifying, from the income statement and the surplus statement, the factors that increase cash and the factors that decrease cash; and (3) consolidating this information in a source and use of funds statement form. In the first of these steps, we simply place one balance sheet beside the other and compute the changes in the various accounts.

Sources of funds that increase cash are

1. A net decrease in any asset other than cash or fixed assets
2. A gross decrease in fixed assets
3. A net increase in any liability
4. Proceeds from the sale of preferred or common stock
5. Funds provided by operations

Funds provided by operations usually are not expressed directly on the income statement. To determine them, one must add back depreciation to net income after taxes. For Aldine Manufacturing Company, our example in the preceding chapter, we have (in thousands):

Net income after taxes	$201,242
Add noncash expenses: depreciation	111,509
Funds provided by operations	$312,751

Thus, the net income of Aldine understates funds provided by operations by $111,509. Depreciation is not a source of funds, for funds are generated only from operations. If operating losses before depreciation are sustained, funds are not provided regardless of the magnitude of depreciation charges.

Uses of funds include

1. A net increase in any asset other than cash or fixed assets
2. A gross increase in fixed assets
3. A net decrease in any liability
4. A retirement or purchase of stock
5. Cash dividends

To avoid double counting, we compute gross changes in fixed assets by adding depreciation for the period to net fixed assets at the ending financial statement date and subtract from this amount net fixed assets at the beginning financial statement date. The residual represents the gross change in fixed assets for the period. If the residual is positive, as is usually the case, it represents a use of funds; if negative, it represents a source.

Once all sources and uses are computed, they may be arranged in statement form, so that we can analyze them better. Table 28-1 shows a source and use of funds statement for the Aldine Manufacturing Company for the fiscal year ended March 31, 1992. The balance sheet and income statement for this corporation, on which the funds statement is based, are shown in Tables 27-1 and 27-2 of Chapter 27. When we subtract the total uses of funds in Table 28-1 from the total sources, the difference should equal the actual change in cash between the two statement dates. If it does not, then the analyst must search for the cause of the discrepancy. Frequently, discrepancies will be due to surplus adjustments, and the analyst should be alert to this possibility.

TABLE 28-1
**Aldine Manufacturing Company sources and uses of funds March 31, 1991,
to March 31, 1992 (in thousands)**

SOURCES		USES	
Funds provided by operations			
Net profit	$201,242	Dividends	$142,968
Depreciation	111,509	Additions to fixed assets	104,276
		Increase, inventories	94,238
Decrease, accounts receivable	62,426	Increase, prepaid expenses	3,559
Decrease, other assets	467		
Increase, bank loans	91,997	Increase, tax prepayments	6,038
Increase, accounts payable	11,634	Increase, investments	65,376
Increase, other accruals	26,653	Decrease, accrued taxes	91,252
Increase, long-term debt	4,323		
Increase, common stock and			
paid-in capital	103	Increase, cash position	2,647
	$510,354		$510,354

In Table 28-1, we see that the principal uses of funds for the 1992 fiscal year were additions to fixed assets, increases in inventories and in investments, and a sizable decrease in taxes payable. These uses were financed primarily by funds provided by operations in excess of dividends; a decrease in accounts receivable; and by increases in bank loans, payables, and accruals. As sources exceeded slightly the uses of funds, cash and cash equivalents (marketable securities and time deposits with original maturities of less than 3 months) rose by $2,647. In a sources and uses of funds analysis, it is useful to place cash dividends opposite net profits and additions to fixed assets opposite depreciation. Doing this allows the analyst to evaluate easily both the amount of dividend payout and the increase in fixed assets.

A statement of cash flows (using the "indirect" method employed by most firms) is shown in Table 28-2. Again this statement is derived from balance sheet and income statement information in Tables 27-1 and 27-2 of the previous chapter. Notice that changes that increase cash, all other things the same, are shown as positive numbers, while changes that decrease cash are shown as negative numbers, and that they all appear in a single column. This contrasts with the presentation in Table 28-1, where positive changes are shown in the sources column and negative changes in the uses column.

Moreover, changes in Table 28-2 are categorized into operating activities, investing activities, and financing activities. For many analysts, this categorization is helpful; no such categorization occurs in the previous Table 28-1. A third difference is that the accounting statement of cash flows records not only gross investment in property, plant, and equipment (fixed assets) but also

TABLE 28-2
Aldine Manufacturing Company statement of cash flows March 31, 1991 to March 31, 1992 (in thousands)

	YEAR ENDED March 31, 1992
Cash flows from operating activities:	
Net earnings	$201,242
Adjustments to reconcile net earnings to cash provided by operating activities:	
Depreciation	111,509
Changes in assets and liabilities:	
Accounts receivable	62,426
Inventories	(94,238)
Prepaid expenses	(3,559)
Other current assets	(6,038)
Accounts payable	11,634
Accrued taxes	(91,252)
Other accrued liabilities	26,653
	$218,377
Cash flows from investing activities:	
Investment in property, plant, & equipment	(113,730)
Disposition of property, plant, & equipment	9,454
Purchase of long-term investments	(65,376)
Other	467
	($169,185)
Cash flows from financing activities:	
Increase (decrease) short-term borrowings	91,997
Increase (decrease) long-term debt	4,323
Issuance of common stock	103
Dividends	(142,968)
	($46,545)
Increase (decrease) in cash & cash equivalents	2,647
Cash and cash equivalents at beginning of year	175,042
Cash and cash equivalents at end of year	$177,689

dispositions. The two are combined in Table 28-1. While not shown in Table 28-2, because there were none, repurchase of stock is a separate item in the accounting statement of cash flows. In the approach shown in Table 28-1, only the net change in stock is shown.

Having explained the differences there are a number of similarities, as the reader can appreciate when comparing the two statements. The final reconciliation, the change in cash position, +$2,647, is the same. Which approach, or both, the analyst uses is a matter of taste. The accounting statement of cash flows appears in audited statements and does not have to be derived. This obviously is an advantage. The same generalizations are possible with either format. The important thing is to be able to quickly identify the major uses of funds and how those uses were financed.

FUNDS AS WORKING CAPITAL

Financial analysts sometimes prepare a source and use of working capital statement. This statement is very similar to the source and use of funds statement on a cash basis, but it takes into account working capital instead of cash. A statement of the source and use of working capital for Aldine Manufacturing Company for the year ended March 31, 1992 is shown in Table 28-3.

We see that the only difference between this statement and a funds statement on a cash basis is the omission of changes in the various components of current assets and current liabilities. This statement is analyzed much as is the source and use of funds statement. Bankers frequently use a source and use of working capital statement, for they often require a borrower to maintain some sort of minimum working capital. Other lenders and management use it for internal control.

TABLE 28-3
Aldine Manufacturing Company sources and uses of working capital
March 31, 1991, to March 31, 1992 (in thousands)

SOURCES		USES	
Funds provided by operations			
Net profit	$201,242	Dividends	$142,968
Depreciation	111,509	Additions to fixed assets	104,276
Decrease, other assets	467		
Increase, long-term debt	4,323	Increase, investments	65,376
Increase, common stock and			
paid-in capital	103	Increase, working capital	5,024
	$317,644		$317,644

IMPLICATIONS

The analysis of cash and working capital funds statements gives us a rich insight into the financial operations of a firm—an insight that will be especially valuable to you as a financial manager analyzing past and future expansion plans of the firm and the impact of these plans on liquidity. You can detect imbalances in the uses of funds and undertake appropriate actions. An analysis spanning the past several years might reveal a growth in inventories out of proportion with the growth of other assets and with sales. Upon analysis, you might find that the problem was due to inefficiencies in inventory management. Thus, a funds statement alerts you to problems that you can analyze in detail and take proper actions to correct. When a company has a number of divisions, individual funds statements may prove useful. These statements enable top management to appraise the performance of divisions in relation to the funds committed to them.

Another use of funds statements is in the evaluation of the firm's financing. An analysis of the major sources of funds in the past reveals what portion of the firm's growth was financed internally and what portion externally. In evaluating the firm's financing, you will wish to evaluate the ratio of dividends to earnings relative to the firm's total need for funds. Funds statements are useful also in judging whether the firm has expanded at too fast a rate and whether financing is strained. You can determine if trade credit has increased out of proportion to increases in current assets and sales. If trade credit has increased at a significantly faster rate, you would wish to evaluate the consequences of increased slowness in trade payments on the credit standing of the firm and its ability to finance in the future. It is also revealing to analyze the mix of short- and long-term financing in relation to the funds needs of the firm. If these needs are primarily for fixed assets and permanent increases in working capital, you might be disturbed if a significant portion of total financing came from short-term sources.

An analysis of a funds statement for the future will be extremely valuable to you as a financial manager planning the intermediate- and long-term financing of your firm. It reveals the firm's total prospective need for funds, the expected timing of these needs, and their nature, that is, whether the increased investment is primarily for inventories, fixed assets, and so forth. Given this information, along with the expected changes in trade payables and the various accruals, you can arrange your firm's financing more effectively. In addition, you can determine the expected closing cash position of the firm simply by adjusting the beginning cash balance for the change in cash reflected on the projected source and use statement. In essence, the projected change in cash is a residual.

CASH BUDGETING

A cash budget is arrived at through a projection of future cash receipts and cash disbursements of the firm over various intervals of time. It reveals the timing and amount of expected cash inflows and outflows over the period studied. With this information, the financial manager is better able to determine the future cash needs of the firm, plan for the financing of these needs, and exercise control over the cash and liquidity of the firm.

Cash budgets may be made for almost any period of time. For near-term forecasts, monthly periods probably are most frequently used because they take into account seasonal variations in cash flows. When cash flows are extremely volatile but predictable, budgets at more frequent intervals may be necessary for determining peak cash requirements. By the same token, when cash flows are relatively stable, budgeting at quarterly or even longer intervals may be justified. Generally, the further into the future the period for which one is trying to predict cash flows, the more uncertain the forecast. The expense of preparing monthly cash budgets usually is warranted only for predictions concerning the near future.

The cash budget is only as useful as the accuracy of the forecasts that are relied on in its preparation. The greater the possible dispersion of actual results from those estimated, the more the allowance that must be made for unexpected swings in cash flow. A firm whose cash flows are subject to much uncertainty should provide for a cash cushion or ready borrowing power or both to tide it over in periods of adverse cash developments.

PREPARATION OF THE CASH BUDGET: RECEIPTS

The key to the accuracy of most cash budgets is the forecast of sales. This forecast can be based on an internal analysis, an external one, or both. With an internal approach, sales representatives are asked to project sales for the forthcoming period. The product sales managers screen these estimates and consolidate them into sales estimates for product lines. The estimates for the various product lines then are combined into an overall sales estimate for the firm. The basic problem with an internal approach is that it can be myopic. Significant trends in the economy and in the industry are often overlooked.

For this reason, many companies use an external analysis as well. With an external approach, economic analysts make forecasts of the economy and of industry sales for several years to come. They may use regression analysis to estimate the association between industry sales and the economy in general. After these basic predictions of business conditions and industry sales, the next step is to estimate market share by individual products, prices that are likely to prevail, and the expected reception of new products. Usually, these estimates are made in conjunction with marketing managers, but the ultimate responsibility should lie with the economic forecasting department. From this information, an external forecast of sales can be prepared.

When the internal forecast of sales differs from the external one, as it is likely to do, a compromise must be reached. Past experience will show which of the two forecasts is more accurate. In general, the external forecast should serve as the foundation for the final sales forecast, often modified by the internal forecast. For example, the firm might expect several large orders from customers, and these orders might not show up in the external forecast. A final sales forecast based on both internal and external analyses is usually more accurate than either an internal or an external forecast by itself. The final sales forecast should be based on prospective demand, not modified initially by internal constraints such as physical capacity. The decision to remove these constraints will depend on the forecast. The value of accurate sales forecasts cannot be overestimated, for most of the other forecasts, in some measure, are based on expected sales.

The sales forecast out of the way, the next job is to determine the cash receipts from these sales. For cash sales, cash is received at the time of the sale; for credit sales, receipts do not come until later. How much later will depend on the billing terms given, the type of customer, and the credit and collection policies of the firm. The Continental Sheetmetal Company offers terms of net 30, meaning that payment is due within 30 days after the invoice date. In the company's experience, 90 percent of receivables are collected, on the average, 1 month from the date of the sale, and 10 percent are collected 2 months from the date of the sale, with no bad-debt losses. Moreover, on the average, 10 percent of total sales are cash sales.

If the sales forecast are those shown in the first line of Table 28-4, we can compute a schedule of the expected sales receipts based on the foregoing assumptions. This schedule appears in Table 28-4. For January, we see that total sales are estimated to be $250,000, of which $25,000 are cash sales. Of the $225,000 in credit sales, 90 percent, or $202,500, are expected to be collected in February, and 10 percent, or $22,500, are expected to be collected in March. Similarly, sales in other months are estimated according to the same percentages. The firm should be ready to change its assumptions with respect to collections when there is an underlying shift in the payment habits of its customers. If there is a slowdown in the economy, certain customers are likely to become slower in their trade payments. The firm must take account of this change if its cash budget is to be realistic.

TABLE 28-4
Schedule of sales receipts (in thousands)

	NOV.	DEC.	JAN.	FEB.	MAR.	APR.	MAY	JUNE
Total sales	$300.0	$350.0	$250.0	$200.0	$250.0	$300.0	$350.0	$380.0
Credit sales	270.0	315.0	225.0	180.0	225.0	270.0	315.0	342.0
Collections, 1 month		243.0	283.5	202.5	162.0	202.5	243.0	283.5
Collections, 2 months			27.0	31.5	22.5	18.0	22.5	27.0
Total collections			$310.5	$234.0	$184.5	$220.5	$265.5	$310.5
Cash sales			25.0	20.0	25.0	30.0	35.0	38.0
Total sales receipts			$335.5	$254.0	$209.5	$250.5	$300.5	$348.5

From this example, it is easy to see the effect of a variation in sales on the magnitude and timing of cash receipts, all other things being held constant. For most firms, there is a degree of correlation between sales and collection experience. In times of recession and sales decline, the average collection period is likely to lengthen; bad-debt losses are likely to increase. Thus, the collection experience of a firm may reinforce a decline in sales and magnify the downward impact on total sales receipts.

Cash receipts may arise from the sale of assets as well as from sales of the product. If Continental intends to sell $40,000 in fixed assets in February, total cash receipts that month would be $294,000. For the most part, the sale of assets is planned in advance and is easily predicted for purposes of cash budgeting. In addition, cash receipts may arise from interest and dividend income.

RECEIVABLE COLLECTION PERIOD

Digressing for the moment, consider now how other collection forecasts might be set up for cash budgeting purposes. In our example, we assumed 90 percent of credit sales in 1 month was collected 1 month later and that 10 percent was collected 2 months later. If credit sales are steady throughout the month and each month has 30 days, this corresponds to an average collection period of 33 days (the weighted average of 30 and 60 days). If the average collection period were 30 days, all credit sales would be collected 1 month later. That is, the $315,000 in December credit sales would be collected in January, and so forth. If the average collection period were 60 days, of course, collections would be lagged 2 months, so that the $315,000 in December would be collected in February.

If the average collection period were 45 days, however, one-half of December credit sales, or $157,500, would be collected in January and the other half in February. The assumption is that credit sales billed in the first half of December will be collected in the last half of January, and sales billed in the last half of December will be collected in the first half of February. Other months will reflect this lag structure as well. If the average collection period were 40 days, implied is that two-thirds of December sales, or $210,000, will be collected in January and that one-third, or $105,000, will be collected in February. The weighted average of $(2/3 \times 30 \text{ days}) + (1/3 \times 60 \text{ days})$ equals 40 days.

By similar reasoning, an average collection period of 50 days means that one-third of December credit sales, or $105,000, will be collected in January and two-thirds, or $210,000, will be collected in February. Similarly, the 30-day month can be divided into fifths, sixths, tenths, fifteenths, and thirtieths to come to grips with other average collection periods. The situation for tenths was illustrated in our example. Finally, if the average collection period were 37 days, the implication is that 23/30 of December credit sales, or $241,500, will be collected in January, while 7/30, or $73,500, will be collected in February. These are enough examples to illustrate the effect of a change in average collection period assumptions on collections. With a computer-based spreadsheet program, it is an easy matter to set up lagged collections for credit sales. Now, back to our example.

FORECASTING DISBURSEMENTS

Next comes a forecast of cash disbursements. Given the sales forecast, management may choose either to gear production closely to sales or to produce at a relatively constant rate over time. When production is geared to sales, inventory carrying costs generally are lower, but total production costs are higher than they are when work continues steadily. If sales fluctuate, finished goods inventories build up during certain periods and require storage. Because storage is uneven throughout the year, inventory carrying costs are generally higher than they would be if production were geared to sales. On the other hand, steady production typically is more efficient. Which alternative is better will depend on the cost of carrying inventory when production is geared to sales compared with the savings available if production is steady. The final production schedule embodies decisions with respect to inventory management, a topic taken up in Chapter 16.

Once a production schedule has been established, estimates can be made of the needs in materials, labor, and additional fixed assets. As with receivables, there is a lag between the time a purchase is made and the time of actual cash payment. If suppliers give average billing terms of net 30 and the firm's policy is to pay its bills at the end of this period, there is approximately a 1-month lag between a purchase and the payment. If the production program of Continental Sheetmetal calls for the manufacture of goods in the month preceding forecasted sales, we might have a schedule like that in Table 28-5. As we see, there is a 1-month lag between the time of purchase and the payment for the purchase. As with the collection of receivables, payment for purchases can be lagged for other average payable periods. The setup is the

TABLE 28-5

Schedule of disbursements for purchases and expenses (in thousands)

	DEC.	JAN.	FEB.	MAR.	APR.	MAY	JUNE
Purchases	$100	$ 80	$100	$120	$140	$150	$150
Cash payment							
for purchases		100	80	100	120	140	150
Wages		80	80	90	90	95	100
Other expenses		50	50	50	50	50	50
Total cash expenses		$230	$210	$240	$260	$285	$300

same as illustrated for collections, and the lagged structure is facilitated using a computer-based spreadsheet program.

Wages are assumed to increase with the amount of production. Generally, wages are more stable over time than are purchases. When production dips slightly, workers usually are not laid off. When production picks up, labor becomes more efficient with relatively little increase in total wages. Only after a certain point is overtime work required or new workers have to be hired to meet the increased production schedule. Included in other expenses are general, administrative, and selling expenses; property taxes; interest expenses; power, light, and heat expenses; maintenance expenses; and indirect labor and material expenses. These expenses tend to be reasonably predictable over the short run.

In addition to cash expenses, we must take into account capital expenditures, dividends, federal income taxes, and any other cash outflows. Because capital expenditures are planned in advance, they usually are predictable for the short-term cash budget. As the forecast becomes more distant, however, prediction of these expenditures becomes less certain. Dividend payments for most companies are stable and are paid on specific dates. Estimation of federal income taxes must be based on projected profits for the period under review. Other cash outlays might consist of the repurchase of stock or payment of long-term debt. These outlays are combined with total cash expenses to obtain the schedule of total cash disbursements shown in Table 28-6.

NET CASH FLOW AND CASH BALANCE

Once we are satisfied that we have taken into account all foreseeable cash inflows and outflows, we combine the cash receipts and cash disbursements schedules to obtain the net cash inflow or outflow for each month. The

TABLE 28-6

Schedule of cash disbursements (in thousands)

	JAN.	FEB.	MAR.	APR.	MAY	JUNE
Total cash expenses	$230	$210	$240	$260	$285	$300
Capital expenditures		150	50			
Dividend payments			20			20
Income taxes	30			30		
Total cash disbursements	$260	$360	$310	$290	$285	$320

TABLE 28-7
Net cash flow and cash balance (in thousands)

	JAN.	FEB.	MAR.	APR.	MAY	JUNE
Total cash receipts	$335.5	$294.0*	$ 209.5	$250.5	$300.5	$348.5
Total cash disbursements	260.0	360.0	310.0	290.0	285.0	320.0
Net cash flow	$ 75.5	$(66.0)	$(100.5)	$(39.5)	$ 15.5	$ 28.5
Beginning cash without financing	100.0	175.5	109.5	9.0	(30.5)	(15.0)
Ending cash without financing	175.5	109.5	9.0	(30.5)	(15.0)	13.5

*Includes sales receipts of $254,000 and cash sales of assets of $40,000.

net cash flow may then be added to beginning cash in January, which is assumed to be $100,000, and the projected cash position computed month by month for the period under review. This final schedule is shown in Table 28-7.

The cash budget shown indicates that the firm is expected to have a cash deficit in April and May. Its deficit is caused by a decline in collections through March, capital expenditures totaling $200,000 in February and March, and a cash dividend of $20,000 in March. With the increase in collections in May and June, the cash balance without financing rises to $13,500 in June. The cash budget indicates that peak cash requirements occur in April. If the firm has a policy of maintaining a minimum cash balance of $75,000 and of borrowing from its bank to maintain this minimum, it will need to borrow an additional $66,000 in March. Additional borrowings will peak at $105,500 in April, after which they will decline to $61,500 in June, if all goes according to prediction.

Alternative means of meeting the cash deficit are available. The firm may be able to delay its capital expenditures or its payments for purchases. Indeed, one of the principal purposes of a cash budget is to determine the timing and magnitude of prospective financing needs, so that the most appropriate method of financing can be arranged. A decision to obtain long-term financing should be based on long-range funds requirements and on considerations apart from a cash forecast. In addition to helping the financial manager plan for short-term financing, the cash budget is valuable in managing the firm's cash position. On the basis of a cash budget, the manager can plan to invest excess funds in marketable securities. The result is an efficient transfer of funds from cash to marketable securities and back.

DEVIATIONS FROM EXPECTED CASH FLOWS

Often, there is a tendency to place considerable faith in the cash budget simply because it is expressed in numbers. We stress again that a cash budget represents merely an *estimate* of future cash flows. Depending on the care devoted to preparing the budget and the volatility of cash flows resulting from the nature of the business, actual cash flows will deviate more or less widely from those that were expected. In the face of uncertainty, we must provide information about the range of possible outcomes. Analyzing cash flows under only one set of assumptions, as is the case with conventional cash budgeting, results in a faulty perspective of the future.

To take into account deviations from expected cash flows, it is desirable to work out additional cash budgets. We might want to base one cash forecast on the assumption of a maximum probable decline in business and another on the assumption of the maximum probable increase in business. By bringing possible events into the open for discussion, management is better able to plan for contingencies. Not only will such discussion sharpen its perspective on the probability of occurrence of a particular event, but it will give management a better understanding of the magnitude of its impact on the firm's cash flows.[1]

Given the preparation of a cash budget based on expected cash flows, it is often a simple matter to trace through a change in one or a series of figures in order to take into account a large number of possibilities. In determining the spectrum of possible outcomes, simulation techniques can be useful. A spreadsheet program may be used to calculate cash budgets under varying assumptions. With such a program, the analyst can type in a change, such as an increase in the average collection period, and the computer will recompute and display a new cash budget in seconds. A cash budget format for such simulations is found in the supplement, *Financial Management Computer Applications.*

The expected cash position plus the probability distribution of possible outcomes gives us a considerable amount of information. We can see the additional funds required or the funds released under various possible outcomes. This information enables us to determine more accurately the minimum cash balance, maturity structure of debt, and borrowing power necessary to give the firm a margin of safety. It enables the financial manager to anticipate sharp changes in the firm's cash position.

We also can analyze the ability of the firm to adjust to deviations from the expected outcomes. If sales should fall off, how flexible are our expenses? What can be cut? By how much? How quickly? How much effort should be devoted to the collection of receivables? If there is an unexpected increase in business, what additional purchases will be required, and when? Can labor be expanded? Can the present plant handle the additional demand? How much in funds will be needed to finance the buildup? Answers to these questions provide valuable insight into the efficiency and flexibility of the firm under a variety of conditions.[2] An analysis of this sort helps to answer the important question of the costs of various deviations from expected outcomes. Again, simulation is a useful method for evaluating these costs.

The final product might be a series of distributions of end-of-the-month cash without financing. Figure 28-2 shows relative frequency distributions for the months of January through June. Bar graphs are used, as these are usually the product of a simulation. The most likely values of ending cash are depicted by the highest bar; these conform with the values shown in Table 28-7. We note that while several of the distributions are reasonably symmetrical, others are skewed. In particular, the distributions for March and April are skewed to the left. As a result, the need for cash during these months might be considerably greater than that depicted in Table 28-7. It is clear that the type

---

[1] See Gordon Donaldson, "Strategy for Financial Emergencies," *Harvard Business Review,* 47 (November–December 1969), 69.

[2] Donaldson, "Strategy for Financial Emergencies," pp. 71–79, develops a framework for evaluating the resources available to meet adverse financial contingencies.

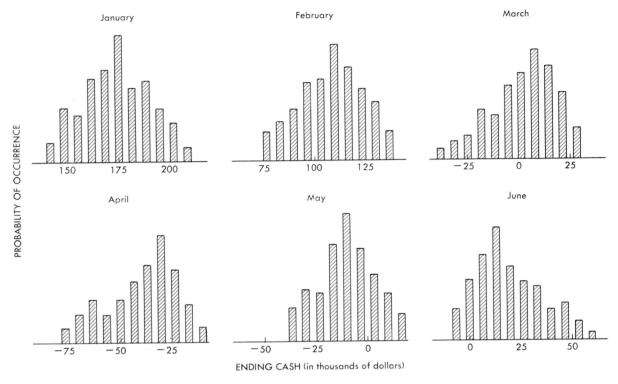

FIGURE 28-2
Distributions of ending cash

of information portrayed in Fig. 28-2 better enables management to plan for contingencies than does information giving only single-point estimates of monthly cash flows.

From the standpoint of internal planning, it is far better to allow for a range of possible outcomes than to rely solely on the expected outcome. This allowance is particularly necessary for firms whose business is relatively unstable. If the firm bases its plans on only expected cash flows, it is likely to be caught flat-footed if there is a significant deviation from the expected outcome, and it will have difficulty making an adjustment. An unforeseen deficit in cash may be difficult to finance on short notice. Therefore, it is essential for the firm to be honest with itself and attempt to minimize the costs associated with deviations from expected outcomes. It may do this by taking the steps necessary to ensure accuracy and by preparing additional cash budgets to take into account the range of possible outcomes.

PRO FORMA STATEMENTS

In addition to projecting the cash flow of a firm over time, it often is useful to prepare a projected, or pro forma, balance sheet and income statement for selected future dates. A cash budget gives us information about only the prospective future cash positions of the firm, whereas pro forma statements embody forecasts of all assets and liabilities as well as of income statement items. Much of the information that goes into the preparation of the cash budget, however, can be used to derive a pro forma statement. As before, the key to accuracy is the sales forecasts.

PRO FORMA INCOME STATEMENT

The pro forma income statement is a projection of income for a period of time in the future. As was true of our cash budget, the sales forecast is the key to scheduling production and estimating production costs. The analyst may wish to evaluate each component of the cost of goods sold. A detailed analysis of purchases, production wages, and overhead costs is likely to produce the most accurate forecasts. Often, however, costs of goods sold are estimated on the basis of past ratios of costs of goods sold to sales.

Selling, general, and administrative expenses are estimated next. Because these expenses usually are budgeted in advance, estimates of them are fairly accurate. Typically, these expenses are not overly sensitive to changes in sales in the very short run, particularly to reductions in sales. Next, we estimate other income and expenses as well as interest expenses to obtain net income before taxes. Income taxes are then computed—based on the applicable tax rate—and deducted, to arrive at estimated net income after taxes. All of these estimates are then combined into an income statement.

To illustrate for Continental Sheetmetal Company, suppose projected sales for January through June in Table 28-4 are $1,730,000, as reflected in our cash budget in Table 28-4. In the cash budget, the cost of goods sold is not depicted directly. However, we know that purchases fall into this category. For financial statement purposes, the purchases associated with January through June sales are those for December through May, because production occurs in the month preceding forecasted sales. Purchases are shown in Table 28-5, and they total $690,000 for December through May. Wages also are a cost of goods sold, and here, too, the relevant period for financial statement purposes is December through May. For this period, wages totaling $505,000 are expected to be paid. (See Table 28-5.) We stated earlier that depreciation of $110,000 was expected for the January–June period. Other expenses (selling, general, and administrative) are expected to be $50,000 a month and are also shown in Table 28-5. For the 6-month period they total $300,000. Finally, let us assume a federal plus state income tax rate of 48 percent. Given this information, we can derive a pro forma income statement for the January–June period (in thousands):

Sales		$1,730
Cost of goods sold		
Purchases	$690	
Wages	505	
Depreciation	110	$1,305
Gross profit		425
Selling, general, and administrative		
expenses		300
Profit before taxes		125
Taxes		60
Profit after taxes		$ 65

The pro forma income statement need not be based on a cash budget. Instead, one can make direct estimates of all the items. By first estimating a sales level, one can multiply historical ratios of cost of goods sold and various expense items by the level in order to derive the statement. Where historical ratios no longer are appropriate, new estimates should be employed.

PRO FORMA BALANCE SHEET

Let us prepare a pro forma statement for Continental Sheetmetal for June 30. The company has the following balance sheet at December 31:

ASSETS (IN THOUSANDS)		LIABILITIES (IN THOUSANDS)	
Cash	$ 100	Bank borrowings	$ 50
Receivables	342	Accounts payable	200
Inventory	350	Accrued wages and expenses	250
Current assets	$ 792	Accrued income taxes	70
		Current liabilities	$ 570
Net fixed assets	800	Shareholders' equity	1,022
Total assets	$1,592	Total liabilities and equity	$1,592

Receivables at June 30 can be estimated by adding to the receivable balance at December 31 the total projected credit sales from January through June, less total projected credit collections for the period. On the basis of the information in the cash budget, receivables at June 30 would be $342,000 + $31,500, or $373,500.

If a cash budget is not available, the receivable balance may be estimated on the basis of a turnover ratio. This ratio, which depicts the relationship between credit sales and receivables, should be based on past experience. To obtain the estimated level of receivables, projected sales simply are divided by the turnover ratio. If the sales forecast and turnover ratio are realistic, the method will produce a reasonable approximation of the receivable balance. The estimated investment in inventories at June 30 may be based on the production schedule, which, in turn, is based on the sales forecast. This schedule should show expected purchases, the expected use of inventory in production, and the expected level of finished goods. On the basis of this information, together with the beginning inventory level, a pro forma estimate of inventory can be made.

Rather than use the production schedule, estimates of future inventory can be based on a turnover ratio of cost of goods sold to inventory. This ratio is applied in the same manner as for receivables, except that we solve for the ending inventory position that emanates from the average. We have

$$\frac{\text{Cost of goods sold}}{(\text{Beginning} + \text{Ending inventory})/2} = \text{Turnover ratio} \qquad (28\text{-}1)$$

Given an assumed turnover ratio and assumed cost of goods sold figure, and knowing the beginning inventory, we rearrange the equation to solve for the unknown:

$$\text{Ending inventory} = \frac{2(\text{CofGS})}{\text{Turnover ratio}} - \text{Beginning inventory}$$

If the estimated inventory turnover ratio in our example were 3.39 and the estimated cost of goods sold were $1,305,000, we would have (with rounding)

$$\text{Ending inventory} = \frac{2(1,305,000)}{3.39} - 350,000 = \$420,000$$

Thus, $420,000 would be our estimate of inventory on June 30, a figure that represents a moderate increase over the inventory level of December 31, in keeping with the buildup in sales.

Future net fixed assets are estimated by adding planned expenditures to existing net fixed assets and subtracting from this sum depreciation for the period, plus any sale of fixed assets at book value. From the cash budget, we note that capital expenditures are estimated at $200,000 over the period and that $40,000 in fixed assets will be sold at what we assume to be their depreciated book values. If depreciation for the period is expected to be $110,000, the expected net addition to fixed assets would be $50,000, ($200,000 − $40,000 − $110,000), and projected net fixed assets at June 30 would be $850,000. Because capital expenditures are planned in advance, fixed assets generally are fairly easy to forecast.

Turning now to the liabilities, we estimate accounts payable by adding total projected purchases for January through June, less total projected cash payments for purchases for the period, to the December 31 balance. Our estimate of accounts payable, therefore, is $200,000 + $50,000, or $250,000. The calculation of accrued wages and expenses is based on the production schedule and the historical relationship between these accruals and production. We assume the estimate of accrued wages and expenses to be $240,000. Accrued income taxes are estimated by adding to the current balance taxes on forecasted income for the 6-month period, less the actual payment of taxes. If income taxes for the period are forecast at $60,000, and the firm is scheduled to make $60,000 in actual payments, estimated accrued income taxes at June 30 would be $70,000.

Shareholders' equity at June 30 would be that at December 31 plus profits after taxes for the period, less the amount of cash dividends paid. If profits after taxes are estimated at $65,000 in the pro forma income statement, shareholders' equity at June 30 would be $1,022,000 plus $65,000 minus dividends of $40,000, or $1,047,000. Two items remain: cash and bank loans. We see from the cash budget that estimated cash at June 30 would be $13,500 without additional financing. If the firm has the policy of maintaining a minimum cash balance of $75,000, and borrowing from its bank to maintain this balance, cash at June 30 would be $75,000, and bank borrowings would increase by $61,500 to $111,500. In general, cash and notes payable serve as balancing factors in the preparation of pro forma balance sheets, whereby assets and liabilities plus shareholders' equity are brought into balance.

Once we have estimated all the components of the pro forma balance sheet, they are combined into a balance sheet format. The pro forma balance sheet at June 30 is

ASSETS (IN THOUSANDS)		LIABILITIES (IN THOUSANDS)	
Cash	$ 75.0	Bank borrowings	$ 111.5
Receivables	373.5	Accounts payable	250.0
Inventories	420.0	Accrued wages and expenses	240.0
Current assets	$ 868.5	Accrued income taxes	70.0
		Current liabilities	$ 671.5
Net fixed assets	850.0	Shareholders' equity	1,047.0
Total assets	$1,718.5	Total liabilities and equity	$1,718.5

USE OF RATIOS AND IMPLICATIONS

780

PART 8
Tools of Financial
Analysis and
Control

As before, the cash budget method is but one way to prepare a pro forma statement. One can also make direct estimates of all the items on the balance sheet by projecting financial ratios into the future and then making estimates on the basis of these ratios. Receivables, inventories, accounts payable, and accrued wages and expenses frequently are based on historical relationships to sales and production when a cash budget is not available. For example, if the average collection period is 45 days, turnover would be eight times a year. If receivables were $500,000 but the firm were predicting a $2 million increase in sales for the coming year, it would take approximately $2 million/8 = $250,000 in additional receivables to support the added sales. Thus, the level of receivables 1 year hence might be forecast at $750,000.

Pro forma statements allow us to study the composition of expected future balance sheets and income statements. Financial ratios may be computed for analysis of the statements; these ratios and the raw figures may be compared with those for present and past balance sheets. Using this information, the financial manager can analyze the direction of change in the financial condition and performance of the firm over the past, the present, and the future. If the firm is accustomed to making accurate estimates, the preparation of a cash budget, pro forma statements, or both literally forces it to plan ahead and to coordinate policy in the various areas of operation. Continual revision of these forecasts keeps the firm alert to changing conditions in its environment and in its internal operations. Again, it is useful to prepare more than one set of pro forma statements to take into account the range of possible outcomes.

SUSTAINABLE GROWTH MODELING

The management of growth requires careful balancing of the sales objectives of the firm with its operating efficiency and financial resources. Many a company overreaches itself financially at the altar of growth; the bankruptcy courts are filled with such cases. The trick is to determine what sales growth rate is consistent with the realities of the company and of the financial marketplace. In this regard, sustainable growth modeling is a powerful planning tool and has found enthusiastic use in companies like Hewlett-Packard. In the way of definition, the *sustainable growth rate (SGR)* is the maximum annual percentage increase in sales that can be achieved based on target operating, debt, and dividend-payout ratios. If actual growth exceeds the SGR, something must give, and frequently it is the debt ratio. By modeling the process of growth, we are able to make intelligent trade-offs.

A STEADY STATE MODEL

To illustrate the calculation of a sustainable growth rate, we begin with a steady state model where the future is exactly like the past with respect to balance sheet and performance ratios. Assumed also is that the firm engages in no external equity financing; the equity account builds only through earnings retention. Both of these assumptions will later be relaxed when we consider sustainable growth modeling under changing assumptions.

Variables Employed.   In a steady state environment, the variables necessary to determine the sustainable growth rate are

A/S = the total assets-to-sales ratio
NP/S = the net profit margin (net profits divided by sales)
b = the retention rate of earnings ($1 - b$ is the dividend-payout ratio)
$D/Eq.$ = the debt-to-equity ratio
S_0 = the most recent annual sales (beginning sales)
ΔS = the absolute change in sales from the most recent annual sales

The first four variables are target variables. The total assets-to-sales ratio is a measure of operating efficiency, the reciprocal of the traditional asset turnover ratio. The lower the ratio, the more efficient the utilization of assets. In turn, this ratio is a composite of (1) receivable management, as depicted by the average collection period; (2) inventory management, as indicated by the inventory turnover ratio; (3) fixed-asset management, as reflected by the throughput of product through the plant; and (4) liquidity management, as suggested by the proportion of and return on liquid assets. For purposes of illustration, we assume liquid assets are kept at moderate levels.[3]

The net profit margin is a relative measure of operating efficiency, after taking account of all expenses and income taxes. While both the assets-to-sales ratio and the net profit margin are affected by the external product markets, they largely capture internal management efficiency. The earnings retention rate and the debt ratio should be determined in keeping with dividend and capital structure theory and practice. They are influenced importantly by the external financial markets. Our purpose is not to touch on how they are established, as that is done elsewhere in this book, but to incorporate them in the planning model presented.

Sustainable Growth Rate.   With these variables, we can derive the sustainable growth rate (SGR). The idea is that an increase in assets (a use of funds) must equal the increase in liabilities and shareholders' equity (a source of funds). The increase in assets can be expressed as $\Delta S(A/S)$, the change in sales times the total assets-to-sales ratio. The increase in shareholders' equity (through retained earnings) is $b(NP/S)(S_0 + \Delta S)$, or the retention rate times the net profit margin times total sales. Finally, the increase in total debt is simply the net worth increase multiplied by the target debt-to-equity ratio, or $[b(NP/S)(S_0 + \Delta S)]D/Eq.$ Putting these things together, we have[4]

$$\underset{\substack{\text{Asset}\\\text{increase}}}{\Delta S\left(\frac{A}{S}\right)} = \underset{\substack{\text{Retained}\\\text{earning}\\\text{increase}}}{b\left(\frac{NP}{S}\right)(S_0 + \Delta S)} + \underset{\substack{\text{Increase in}\\\text{debt}}}{\left[b\left(\frac{NP}{S}\right)(S_0 + \Delta S)\right]\frac{D}{Eq.}} \qquad (28\text{-}2)$$

---

[3] If this is not the case, it may be better to use the operating-assets-to-sales ratio.
[4] This is the same formulation as in Robert C. Higgins, *Analysis for Financial Management* (Homewood, IL: Richard D. Irwin, 1984), Chap. 5. See his book for application and further illustration.

By rearrangement, this equation can be expressed as[5]

$$\frac{\Delta S}{S} \text{ or } SGR = \frac{b\left(\dfrac{NP}{S}\right)\left(1 + \dfrac{D}{Eq.}\right)}{\left(\dfrac{A}{S}\right) - \left[b\left(\dfrac{NP}{S}\right)\left(1 + \dfrac{D}{Eq.}\right)\right]} \tag{28-3}$$

This is the maximum rate of growth in sales that is consistent with the target ratios. Whether or not this growth rate can be achieved, of course, depends on the external product markets and on the firm's marketing efforts. A particular growth rate may be feasible financially, but the product demand simply may not be there. Implicit in the formulations presented is that depreciation charges are sufficient to maintain the value of operating assets.[6] A final caveat has to do with interest on new borrowings. The implicit assumption is that all interest expenses are incorporated in the target net profit margin. While it would be possible to specify interest costs separately, it complicates the modeling considerably with simultaneous equations. As sustainable growth modeling is a broad-gauged planning tool, we will skirt this dimension.

An Illustration. Suppose a company were characterized by the data shown in Table 28-8. If this were the case, the sustainable growth rate would be

$$SGR = \frac{.70(.04)(1.8)}{.60 - [.70(.04)(1.80)]} = 9.17\%$$

Thus, 9.17 percent is the sales growth rate consistent with the steady state variables shown in Table 28-8. It can be demonstrated that initial equity increases by 9.17 percent to $109.17 and that debt grows by 9.17 percent to $87.34, as everything increases in stable equilibrium. If the actual growth rate is other than 9.17 percent, however, one or more of the variables must change. In other words, operating efficiency, leverage, or earnings retention must change or there must be the sale or repurchase of stock.

---

[5] Equation (28-2) can be expressed as

$$\Delta S\left(\frac{A}{S}\right) = b\left(\frac{NP}{S}\right)(S_0 + \Delta S)\left(1 + \frac{D}{Eq.}\right)$$

$$\Delta S\left(\frac{A}{S}\right) = b\left(\frac{NP}{S}\right)\left(1 + \frac{D}{Eq.}\right)S_0 + b\left(\frac{NP}{S}\right)\left(1 + \frac{D}{Eq.}\right)\Delta S$$

$$\Delta S\left(\frac{A}{S}\right) - b\left(\frac{NP}{S}\right)\left(1 + \frac{D}{Eq.}\right)\Delta S = b\left(\frac{NP}{S}\right)\left(1 + \frac{D}{Eq.}\right)S_0$$

$$\Delta S\left[\left(\frac{A}{S}\right) - b\left(\frac{NP}{S}\right)\left(1 + \frac{D}{Eq.}\right)\right] = b\left(\frac{NP}{S}\right)\left(1 + \frac{D}{Eq.}\right)S_0$$

$$\frac{\Delta S}{S_0} = \frac{b\left(\dfrac{NP}{S}\right)\left(1 + \dfrac{D}{Eq.}\right)}{\left(\dfrac{A}{S}\right) - \left[b\left(\dfrac{NP}{S}\right)\left(1 + \dfrac{D}{Eq.}\right)\right]}$$

[6] For an analysis of the effect of different inflation assumptions on the SGR via depreciation, see Robert C. Higgins, "How Much Growth Can a Firm Afford?" *Financial Management*, 6 (Fall 1977), 7–16.

TABLE 28-8
Initial inputs and variables used to illustrate sustainable growth rates

SYMBOL	INITIAL INPUT AND/OR VARIABLE	
$Eq._0$	Beginning equity capital (in millions)	$100
$Debt_0$	Beginning debt (in millions)	$ 80
$Sales_0$	Sales the previous year (in millions)	$300
b	Target earnings retention rate	.70
NP/S	Target net profit margin	.04
$D/Eq.$	Target debt-to-equity ratio	.80
A/S	Target assets-to-sales ratio	.60

MODELING UNDER CHANGING ASSUMPTIONS

To see what happens when we move from steady state, and variables change from year to year, we must model sustainable growth in a different way. In effect, the growth in equity base and the growth in sales are unbalanced over time. More specifically, we must bring in beginning sales, S_0, and beginning equity capital, $Eq._0$, as foundations on which to build. Additionally, we express dividend policy in terms of the absolute amount of dividends a company wishes to pay. Finally, we allow for the sale of common stock in a given year, though this can be specified as zero.

With these variables, the sustainable growth rate in sales for the next year, SGR in decimal form, becomes

$$SGR = \left[\frac{(Eq._0 + \text{New Eq.} - \text{Div.})\left(1 + \frac{D}{Eq.}\right)\left(\frac{S}{A}\right)}{1 - \left[\left(\frac{NP}{S}\right)\left(1 + \frac{D}{Eq.}\right)\left(\frac{S}{A}\right)\right]} \right] \left[\frac{1}{S_0}\right] - 1 \qquad (28\text{-}4)$$

where New Eq. is the amount of new equity capital raised, Div. is the absolute amount of annual dividend, and S/A is the sales-to-total-assets ratio. The latter is simply the reciprocal of the assets-to-sales ratio that we used before. Intuitively, the numerator in the first bracket in Eq. (28-4) represents the sales that could occur on the basis of existing capital plus any change occasioned by common stock sales or dividends. The equity base is expanded by the debt employed and then multiplied by the sales-to-asset ratio. The denominator in the first bracket is one minus the target earning power of the company, $(NP/S)(S/A)$, magnified by the proportion of debt employed. When the numerator is divided by the denominator, we obtain the new level of sales that can be achieved. In the last bracket, we divide this new level by beginning sales to determine the change in sales that is sustainable for the next year.

To illustrate, suppose the target dividend were $3.93 million, no new equity issuance was planned, and the other variables in Table 28-8 held. The sustainable growth rate, using Eq. (28-4), is

$$SGR = \left[\frac{(100 - 3.93)(1.80)(1.6667)}{1 - [(.04)(1.80)(1.6667)]} \right] \left[\frac{1}{300}\right] - 1 = 9.17\%$$

This is exactly the same as computed with the steady state model, Eq. (28-3), because a dividend of $3.93 million corresponds to an earnings retention rate of .70. Note also that an assets-to-sales ratio of .60 is the same as a sales-to-assets ratio of 1.6667.

Suppose now that the target assets-to-sales ratio is .55 (a sales-to-assets ratio of 1.8182) instead of .60. Moreover, the target net profit margin also is better, .05 instead of .04. Finally, the target debt-to-equity ratio is moved from .80 to 1.00. Assuming a dividend of $4 million, the sustainable growth rate becomes

$$SGR = \left[\frac{(100 - 4)(2.00)(1.8182)}{1 - [(.05)(2.00)(1.8182)]}\right]\left[\frac{1}{300}\right] - 1 = 42.22\%$$

This substantial increase in SGR is due to improved operating efficiency, which generates more retained earnings, and a higher debt ratio. It is important to recognize that the sales growth rate possible is for 1 year only. Even if operating efficiency continues on an improved basis, the debt ratio would have to increase continually in order to generate an SGR of 42.22 percent. The change in debt ratio affects all assets, not just the growth component.

To illustrate, suppose the debt-to-equity ratio were to remain at 1.00 and the other ratios also stayed the same. At the end of the year, we would be building from higher equity and sales bases:

$$S_1 = \$300(1.4222) = \$426.66$$

$$E_1 = \$300(1.4222).05 - \$4 + 100 = \$117.333$$

The sustainable growth rate for year 2 becomes

$$SGR_2 = \left[\frac{(117.333 - 4)(2.00)(1.8182)}{1 - [(.05)(2.00)(1.8182)]}\right]\left[\frac{1}{426.66}\right] - 1 = 18.06\%$$

Thus, the model produces the sustainable growth rate year by year in a changing environment. Just because a high SGR is possible one year does not mean that this growth rate is sustainable in the future. In fact, it will not be sustainable unless further variable changes in the same direction occur. In this sense, it represents a one-shot occurrence.

Let us return to our earlier example that produced a 9.17 percent SGR under the assumptions of

$$NP/S = .04 \qquad S/A = 1.6667 \qquad D/Eq. = .80 \qquad Div. = \$3.93$$

If the company were to raise $10 million in new equity capital, we would have

$$SGR = \left[\frac{(100 + 10 - 3.93)(1.80)(1.6667)}{1 - [(.04)(1.80)(1.6667)]}\right]\left[\frac{1}{300}\right] - 1 = 20.54\%$$

This SGR is higher than earlier because of the new equity infusion, which, again, may be a one-shot occurrence. In summary, sustainable growth modeling year by year is considerably different from steady state modeling.

SOLVING FOR OTHER VARIABLES

With any five of the six variables, together with beginning equity and beginning sales, it is possible to solve for the sixth. For example, suppose we wished to determine the *assets-to-sales ratio* consistent with a growth in sales of 25 percent next year and the following other target variables:

$$NP/S = .05 \qquad D/Eq. = .50 \qquad Div. = \$4 \qquad New\ Eq. = \$10$$

The relevant formula is

$$\frac{S}{A} = \frac{(1 + SGR)\,S_0}{\left[1 + \dfrac{D}{E}\right]\left[Eq._0 + New\ Eq. - Div. + \left(\dfrac{NP}{S}\right)(1 + SGR)S_0\right]} \tag{28-5}$$

and solving for our example, we have

$$\frac{S}{A} = \frac{(1.25)300}{[1.50][100 + 10 - 4 + (.05)(1.25)300]} = 2.00$$

$$\frac{A}{S} = 1/2.00 = .50$$

This suggests that the company will need to have an assets-to-sales ratio of .50 if it is to grow at a 25 percent rate next year. This assumes a 5 percent net profit margin and the sale of $10 million in new equity capital.

If a sales growth rate of 25 percent is again desired but a sales-to-assets ratio of 1.70 is all that is likely (assets-to-sales ratio of .5882), we might be interested in the *debt-to-equity ratio* consistent with this and the other variables. The relevant formula is

$$\frac{D}{Eq.} = \frac{(1 + SGR)S_0}{\left[Eq._0 + New\ Eq. - Div. + \left(\dfrac{NP}{S}\right)(1 + SGR)S_0\right]\left[\dfrac{S}{A}\right]} - 1 \tag{28-6}$$

For our example

$$\frac{D}{Eq.} = \frac{(1.25)300}{[(100 + 10 - 4 + (.05)(1.25)300][1.70]} - 1 = .7682$$

If the sales-to-assets ratio were 1.70 instead of 2.00, an increase in debt ratio from .50 to .7682 would be necessary to sustain a growth in sales of 25 percent next year. Thus, the sales-to-assets ratio and the debt-to-equity ratio have a powerful effect on the results.

Finally, suppose the company wished to grow at 20 percent in sales, raise no new equity capital, and had other target variables of

$$S/A = 1.90 \qquad D/Eq. = .60 \qquad Div. = \$4$$

TABLE 28-9
Simulations using sustainable growth modeling

VARIABLE	1	2	3	4	5	6	7	8	9	10	11	12	13
A/S	.60	.60	.55	.50	.65	.70	.50	.4292	.5263	.60	.5882	.60	.60
NP/S	.04	.04	.05	.05	.035	.03	.05	.04	.0623	.0538	.05	.04	.04
D/E	.80	.80	1.00	.50	.80	.80	.50	.50	.60	1.00	.7682	1.0272	1.1659
Div.	4.00	4.00	4.00	4.00	4.00	4.00	4.00	4.00	4.00	4.00	4.00	4.00	4.00
New Eq.	0	10.00	0	0	5.00	0	10.00	0	0	0	10.00	0	0
SGR	.0909	.2046	.4222	.1294	.0325	−.1083	.25	.30	.20	.30	.25	.25	.35

Beginning sales = $300.
Beginning equity = $100.

786

It now wishes to determine the net profit margin it would need to achieve in order to make this happen. The formula is

$$\frac{NP}{S} = 1 \bigg/ \left(1 + \frac{D}{Eq.}\right)\left(\frac{S}{A}\right) - (Eq._0 + \text{New Eq.} - \text{Div.})/(1 + SGR)S_0 \qquad (28\text{-}7)$$

which for our example becomes

$$\frac{NP}{S} = 1/(1.60)(1.90) - (100 - 4)/(1.20)300 = .0623$$

To achieve a 20 percent growth in sales in the face of no new equity financing, the net profit margin needs to be 6.23 percent.

By simulation, then, one is able to gain insight into the sensitivity of certain variables in the overall growth picture. With an algorithm for solving for the variables, these simulations can be made with ease. In Table 28-9, we present certain simulations where the missing variables for which we solve are shown in the boxes. Sustainable growth algorithms can be found in the supplement, *Financial Management Computer Applications.*

IMPLICATIONS

To grow in a stable, balanced way, the equity base must grow proportionally with sales. When this is not the case, one or more of the financial ratios must change in order for the divergence in the two growth rates to be accommodated. By putting things into a sustainable growth model, we are able to check the consistency of various growth plans. Often in corporate planning the company wants a number of good things: high sales growth, manufacturing flexibility, moderate use of debt, and high dividends. However, these things may be inconsistent with one another.

Sustainable growth modeling enables one to check for such inconsistency. By simulation, we can better understand the sensitivity of certain factors to the growth objectives of the firm and vice versa. In this way, more informed and wiser marketing, finance, and manufacturing decisions can be reached. Sustainable growth modeling provides an integrative tool for helping the decision-making process. With the current emphasis in corporations on return on assets and on asset management, such modeling can play an integral part.

SUMMARY

Continuing our examination of the analytical tools of the financial manager, we looked at source and use of funds statements, the cash budget, pro forma statements, and sustainable growth modeling. The funds statement on a cash basis (either a traditional sources and uses statement or an accounting statement of cash flows) or a funds statement of working capital gives the financial analyst considerable insight into the uses of funds and how these uses are financed over a specific period of time. Funds-flow analysis is valuable in analyzing the commitment of funds to assets and in planning the firm's interme-diate- and long-term financing. The flow of funds studied, however, repre-sents net rather than gross transactions between two points in time.

A cash budget is a forecast of the future cash receipts and cash disburse-ments of a firm. This forecast is particularly useful to the financial manager in determining the probable cash balances of the firm over the near future and in planning for the financing of prospective cash needs. In addition to analyzing expected cash flows, the financial manager should take into account possible deviations from the expected outcome. An analysis of the range of possible outcomes enables management to better assess the efficiency and flexibility of the firm and to determine the appropriate margin of safety.

We considered the preparation of pro forma balance sheets and income statements. These statements give financial managers insight into the prospec-tive future financial condition and performance of the firm, giving them yet another tool for financial planning and control.

Finally, we took up sustainable growth modeling and learned that it is a powerful tool for checking the consistency between sales growth goals, oper-ating efficiency, and financial objectives. Two variations of the model exist: steady state, where the equity base and sales grow in concert; and unbalanced growth, where the ratios and growth change from year to year. With the latter, the sustainable growth rate is determined year by year. Given a desired growth in sales, through simulation, one is able to determine the operating and financial variables necessary to achieve it.

SELF-CORRECTION PROBLEMS

1. Serap-Jones, Inc., had the following financial statements for 19X1 and 19X2.
   a. Prepare a source and use of funds statement on a cash basis.
   b. Prepare an accounting statement of cash flows.
   c. Evaluate your findings.

	19X1	19X2
Assets		
Cash and cash equivalents	$ 140,000	$ 31,000
Accounts receivable	346,000	528,000
Inventories	432,000	683,000
Current assets	$ 918,000	$1,242,000
Net fixed assets	1,113,000	1,398,000
Total	$2,031,000	$2,640,000

Liabilities and equity		
Accounts payable	$ 413,000	$ 627,000
Accruals	226,000	314,000
Bank borrowings	100,000	235,000
Current liabilities	$ 739,000	$1,176,000
Common stock	100,000	100,000
Retained earnings	1,192,000	1,364,000
Total	$2,031,000	$2,640,000

Note: Depreciation was $189,000 for 19X2 and no dividends were paid.

2. Consider the balance sheet of Rodriguez Malting Company at December 31 (in thousands). The company has received a large order and anticipates the need to go to its bank to increase its borrowings. As a result, it has to forecast its cash requirements for January, February, and March. Typically, the company collects 20 percent of its sales in the month of sale, 70 percent in the subsequent month, and 10 percent in the second month after the sale. All sales are credit sales.

Cash	$ 50	Accounts payable	$ 360
Accounts receivable	530	Bank loan	400
Inventories	545	Accruals	212
Current assets	$1,125	Current liabilities	$ 972
Net fixed assets	1,836	Long-term debt	450
		Common stock	100
		Retained earnings	1,439
Total assets	$2,961	Total liabilities and equity	$2,961

Purchases of raw materials to produce malt are made in the month prior to the sale and amount to 60 percent of sales in the subsequent month. Payments for these purchases occur in the month after the purchase. Labor costs, including overtime, are expected to be $150,000 in January, $200,000 in February, and $160,000 in March. Selling, administrative, taxes, and other cash expenses are expected to be $100,000 per month for January through March. Actual sales in November and December and projected sales for January through April are as follows (in thousands):

November	$500	January	$ 600	March	$650
December	600	February	1,000	April	750

On the basis of this information:

a. Prepare a cash budget for the months of January, February, and March.

b. Determine the amount of additional bank borrowings necessary to maintain a cash balance of $50,000 at all times.

c. Prepare a pro forma balance sheet for March 31.

3. Zippo Industries has equity capital of $12 million, total debt of $8 million, and sales last year of $30 million.

a. It has a target assets-to-sales ratio of .6667, a target net profit margin of .04, a target debt-to-equity ratio of .6667, and a target earnings retention rate of .75. In steady state, what is its sustainable growth rate?

b. Suppose, now, the company has established for next year a target assets-to-sales ratio of .62, a target net profit margin of .05, and a target debt-to-equity ratio of .80. It wishes to pay an annual dividend of $0.3 million and raise $1 million in equity capital next year. What is its sustainable growth rate for next year? Why does it differ from that in part a?

PROBLEMS

1. Galow Fish Canning Company reports the following changes from the preceding year end. Categorize these changes as either a source of funds or a use of funds.

ITEM	CHANGE
Cash	−$100
Accounts receivable	700
Inventory	−300
Gross fixed assets	900
Depreciation	1,000
Accounts payable	300
Accruals	−100
Long-term debt	−200
Net profit	600
Dividends	400

2. Kohn Corporation comparative balance sheets at December 31 (in millions):

ASSETS	19x1	19x2	LIABILITIES AND EQUITY	19x1	19x2
Cash	$ 5	$ 3	Notes payable	$20	$ 0
Accounts receivable	15	22	Accounts payable	5	8
Inventories	12	15	Accrued wages	2	2
Fixed assets, net	50	55	Accrued taxes	3	5
Other assets	8	5	Long-term debt	0	15
			Common stock	20	26
			Retained earnings	40	44
Total assets	$90	$100	Total liabilities and equity	$90	$100

Kohn Corporation statement of income and retained earnings year ended December 31, 19X2:

				$48,000,000
Net sales				
Expenses				
Cost of goods sold		$25,000,000		
Selling, general, and				
administrative expenses		5,000,000		
Depreciation		5,000,000		
Interest		2,000,000		37,000,000
Net income before taxes				$11,000,000
Less: Taxes				4,000,000
Net income				$ 7,000,000
Add: Retained earnings at 12/31/x1				40,000,000
Subtotal				$47,000,000
Less: Dividends				3,000,000
Retained earnings at 12/31/x2				$44,000,000

a. Prepare a source and use of funds statement on a cash basis for 19X2 for the Kohn Corporation.

b. Prepare an accounting statement of cash flows.

c. Prepare a source and use of working capital statement for 19X2.

3. Financial statements for the Sennet Corporation follow:

Sennet Corporation balance sheet at December 31 (in millions)

	19X1	19X2		19X1	19X2
Cash	$ 4	$ 5	Accounts payable	$ 8	$10
Accounts receivable	7	10	Notes payable	5	5
Inventory	12	15	Accrued wages	2	3
Current assets	$23	$30	Accrued taxes	3	2
Net plant	40	40	Current liabilities	$18	$20
			Long-term debt	20	20
			Common stock	10	10
			Retained earnings	15	20
			Total liabilities		
Total assets	$63	$70	and equity	$63	$70

Sennet Corporation income statement 19X2 (in millions)

Sales		$95
Cost of goods sold	$50	
Selling, general, and administrative expenses	15	
Depreciation	3	
Interest	2	70
Net income before taxes		$25
Taxes		10
Net income		$15

a. Prepare a source and use of funds statement for Sennet.

b. Prepare a source and use of working capital statement.

4. Prepare a cash budget for the Ace Manufacturing Company indicating receipts and disbursements for May, June, and July. The firm wishes to maintain, at all times, a minimum cash balance of $20,000. Determine whether or not borrowing will be necessary during the period, and if it is, when and for how much. As of April 30, the firm had a balance of $20,000 in cash.

	ACTUAL SALES		FORECASTED SALES	
January	$50,000	May	$ 70,000
February	50,000	June	80,000
March	60,000	July	100,000
April	60,000	August	100,000

Accounts receivable: 50 percent of total sales are for cash. The remaining 50 percent will be collected equally during the following 2 months (the firm incurs a negligible bad-debt loss).

Cost of goods manufactured: 70 percent of sales; 90 percent of this cost is paid during the first month after incurrence, the remaining 10 percent is paid the following month.

Sales and administrative expenses: $10,000 per month plus 10 percent of sales. All of these expenses are paid during the month of incurrence.

Interest payments: Semiannual interest of $18,000 is paid during July. An annual $50,000 sinking-fund payment is also made at that time.

Dividends: A $10,000 dividend payment will be declared and made in July.

Capital expenditures: $40,000 will be invested in plant and equipment in June.

Taxes: Income tax payments of $1,000 will be made in July.

5. Downeast Nautical Company expects sales of $2.4 million next year and expects sales of the same amount the following year. Sales are spread evenly throughout the year. On the basis of the following information, prepare a pro forma balance sheet and income statement for year end:

Cash	= Minimum of 4 percent of annual sales.
Accounts receivable	= 60-day average collection period based on annual sales.
Inventories	= Turnover of 8 times a year.
Net fixed assets	= $500,000 now. Capital expenditures are equal to depreciation.
Accounts payable	= One month's purchases.
Accruals	= 3 percent of sales.
Bank borrowings	= $50,000 now. Can borrow up to $250,000.
Long-term debt	= $300,000 now; $75,000 payable at year end.
Common stock	= $100,000. No additions planned.
Retained earnings	= $500,000 now.
Net profit margin	= 8 percent of sales.
Dividends	= None.
Cost of goods sold	= 60 percent of sales.
Purchases	= 50 percent of costs of goods sold.
Income taxes	= 50 percent of before-tax profits.

6. Given the information that follows, prepare a cash budget for the Central City Department Store for the first 6 months of 19X2 under the following assumptions:

a. All prices and costs remain constant.

b. Sales are 75 percent for credit and 25 percent for cash.

c. In terms of credit sales, 60 percent are collected in the month after the sale, 30 percent in the second month, and 10 percent in the third. Bad-debt losses are insignificant.

d. Sales, actual and estimated, are

October 19x1	$300,000	March 19x2	$200,000
November 19x1	350,000	April 19x2	300,000
December 19x1	400,000	May 19x2	250,000
January 19x2	150,000	June 19x2	200,000
February 19x2	200,000	July 19x2	300,000

e. Payments for purchases of merchandise are 80 percent of the following month's anticipated sales.

f. Wages and salaries are

January	$30,000	March	$50,000	May	$40,000
February	40,000	April	50,000	June	35,000

g. Rent is $2,000 a month.

h. Interest of $7,500 is due at the end of each calendar quarter.

i. A tax prepayment on 19x2 income of $50,000 is due in April.

j. A capital investment of $30,000 is planned in June.

k. The company has a cash balance of $100,000 at December 31, 19x1, which is the minimum desired level for cash. Funds can be borrowed in multiples of $5,000 on a monthly basis. (Ignore interest on such borrowings.)

7. Use the cash budget worked out in Problem 6 and with the following additional information prepare a pro forma income statement for the first half of 19x2 for the Central City Department Store.

a. Inventory at December 31, 19x1, was $200,000.

b. Depreciation is taken on a straight-line basis on $250,000 of assets with an average remaining life of 10 years and no salvage value. It is recorded as an operating expense apart from cost of goods sold.

c. The tax rate is 40 percent.

8. Liz Clairsorn Industries has $40 million in shareholders' equity and sales of $150 million last year.

a. Its target ratios are: assets-to-sales, .40; net profit margin, .07; debt-to-equity, .50; and earnings retention, .60. If these ratios correspond to steady state, what is its sustainable growth rate?

b. If instead of these ratios, what would be the sustainable growth rate next year if the company moved from steady state and had the following targets? Assets-to-sales ratio, .42; net profit margin, .06; debt-to-equity, .45; dividend of $5 million; and no new equity financing.

9. Hildebrand Hydronics Corporation wishes to achieve a 35 percent increase in sales next year. Sales last year were $30 million, and the company has equity capital of $12 million. It intends to raise $.5 million in new equity by sale of stock to officers. No dividend is planned. Tentatively, the company has set the following target ratios: assets-to-sales, .67; net profit margin, .08; and debt-to-equity, .60. The company has determined that these ratios are not sufficient to produce a growth in sales of 35 percent.

a. Holding the other two target ratios constant, what assets-to-sales ratio would be necessary to attain the 35 percent sales increase?

b. Holding the other two ratios constant, what net profit margin would be necessary?

c. Holding the other two ratios constant, what debt-to-equity ratio would be necessary?

SOLUTIONS TO
SELF-CORRECTION PROBLEMS

1. a. Source and use of funds statement for Serap-Jones, Inc. (in thousands):

SOURCES		USES	
Funds provided by operations			
Net profit	$172		
Depreciation	189	Addition to fixed assets	$474
	$361		
		Increase, accounts receivable	182
Increase, accounts payable	214		
Increase, accruals	88	Increase, inventories	251
Increase, bank borrowings	135		
Decrease, cash	109		
	$907		$907

b. Statement of cash flows for Serap-Jones, Inc. (in thousands):

Cash flows from operating activities:	
Net earnings	$172
Adjustments to reconcile net earnings to cash provided by operating activities:	
Depreciation	189
Changes in assets and liabilities:	
Accounts receivable	(182)
Inventories	(251)
Accounts payable	214
Accruals	88
	$230
Cash flows from investing activities:	
Investment in fixed assets	($474)
Cash flows from financing activities:	
Increase (decrease) short-term borrowings	$135
Increase (decrease) in cash & cash equivalents	($109)
Cash & cash equivalents at beginning of year	140
Cash & cash equivalents at end of year	$31

c. The company has had substantial capital expenditures and increases in accounts receivable and inventories. To finance this growth, which is greatly in excess of the growth in equity base, the company has leaned on the trade, has increased its accruals, and has increased its bank borrowings significantly. This not being enough, there was a substantial draw down of the cash position. The financing is short term in nature, but it is being used mostly for long-term buildups in assets.

2. a. Cash budget (in thousands):

	NOV.	DEC.	JAN.	FEB.	MAR.	APR.
Sales	$500	$600	$600	$1,000	$650	$750
Collections, current month sales			120	200	130	
Collections, previous month sales			420	420	700	
Collections, previous 2 months' sales			50	60	60	
Total cash receipts			$590	$680	$890	
Purchases		$360	$600	$390	$450	
Payment for purchases			360	600	390	
Labor costs			150	200	160	
Other expenses			100	100	100	
Total cash disbursements			$610	$900	$650	
Receipts less disbursements			($20)	($220)	$240	

b.

	JAN.	FEB.	MAR.
Additional borrowings	$ 20	$220	($240)
Cumulative borrowings	420	640	400

The amount of financing peaks in February owing to the need to pay for purchases made the previous month and higher labor costs. In March, substantial collections are made on the prior month's billings, causing a large net cash inflow sufficient to pay off the additional borrowings.

c. Pro forma balance sheet, March 31 (in thousands):

Cash	$ 50	Accounts payable	$ 450
Accounts receivable	620	Bank loan	400
Inventories	635	Accruals	212
Current assets	$1,305	Current liabilities	$1,062
Net fixed assets	1,836	Long-term debt	450
		Common stock	100
		Retained earnings	1,529
Total assets	$3,141	Total liabilities and equity	$3,141

Accounts receivable = Sales in March × .8 + Sales in February × .1

Inventories = $545 + Total purchases January through March − Total sales
January through March × .6

Accounts payable = Purchases in March

Retained earnings = $1,439 + Sales − Payment for purchases − Labor
costs and − Other expenses, all for January through March

3. a. $\text{SGR} = \dfrac{.75(.04)(1.6667)}{.6667 - [.75(.04)(1.6667)]} = 8.11\%$

b. $\text{SGR} = \left[\dfrac{(12 + 1 - 0.3)(1.80)(1.6129)}{1 - [(.05)(1.80)(1.6129)]} \right]\left[\dfrac{1}{30} \right] - 1 = 43.77\%$

The company has moved from steady state with higher target operating efficiency, a higher debt ratio, and the sale of common stock. All of these things permit a high rate of growth in sales next year. Unless further changes in these directions occur, the SGR will decline.

SELECTED REFERENCES

HELFERT, ERICH A., *Techniques of Financial Analysis*, 7th ed. Homewood, IL: Richard D. Irwin, 1991, Chaps. 1, 2, and 4.

HIGGINS, ROBERT C., "Sustainable Growth under Inflation," *Financial Management*, 10 (Autumn 1981), 36–40.

———, *Analysis for Financial Management*. Homewood, IL: Richard D. Irwin, 1984.

HILL, NED C., "Planning and Control Techniques," in *Handbook of Corporate Finance*, ed. Edward I. Altman. New York: John Wiley, 1986, Chap. 1.

PARKER, GEORGE G. C., "Financial Forecasting," in *Handbook of Corporate Finance*, ed. Edward I. Altman. New York: John Wiley, 1986, Chap. 2.

VANDER WEIDE, JAMES, and STEVEN F. MAIER, *Managing Corporate Liquidity*. New York: John Wiley, 1984.

VAN HORNE, JAMES C., "Sustainable Growth Modeling," *Journal of Corporate Finance*, 1 (Winter 1988), 19–25.

APPENDIX A: REMEDIES FOR A FAILING COMPANY

The remedies for a failing company vary in harshness according to the degree of financial difficulty. If the outlook is sufficiently hopeless, liquidation may be the only feasible alternative. Some failing companies, however, can be rehabilitated to the gain of creditors, stockholders, and society. The purpose of this appendix is to review the remedies available, beginning with those that are voluntary and then move on to examine legal actions.

VOLUNTARY SETTLEMENTS

An *extension* involves creditors postponing the maturity of their obligations. By not forcing legal proceedings, creditors avoid considerable legal expense and the possible shrinkage of value in liquidation. As all creditors must agree to extend their obligations, the major creditors usually form a committee whose function is to negotiate with the company and to formulate a plan mutually satisfactory to all concerned.

A *composition* involves a pro rata settlement of creditors' claims in cash or in cash and promissory notes. All creditors must agree to accept this partial settlement in discharge of their entire claim. As with an extension, dissenting creditors must be either brought into the fold or paid in full.

Voluntary liquidation represents an orderly private liquidation of a company apart from the bankruptcy courts. Not only is it likely to be more efficient, but creditors are likely to receive a higher settlement, as many of the costs of bankruptcy are avoided. However, the company and all creditors must go along. As a result, voluntary liquidations usually are restricted to companies with a limited number of creditors.

LEGAL PROCEEDINGS

Legal procedures undertaken in connection with a failing company fall under bankruptcy law as carried out through bankruptcy courts. Bankruptcy law is composed of many facets, but we are concerned with only two, which pertain to business failure. Chapter 7 of the bankruptcy law deals with liquidation; Chapter 11 deals with the rehabilitation of an enterprise through its reorganization.

In both cases, proceedings begin with the debtor or creditors filing a petition in the bankruptcy court. When the debtor initiates the petition, it is called a voluntary proceeding; if the initiative is taken by creditors, it is said to be involuntary. In voluntary proceedings, merely filing the petition gives the debtor immediate protection from creditors. A stay restrains creditors from collecting their claims or taking actions until the court decides on the merit of the petition. The court can either accept the petition and order relief or dismiss it.

For an involuntary bankruptcy, three or more unsecured creditors with claims totaling $5,000 or more are required. Here the petition must give evidence that the debtor has not paid debts on a timely basis or has assigned possession of most of its property to someone else. The bankruptcy court then must decide whether the involuntary petition has merit. If the decision is negative, the petition is dismissed. Moreover, petitioning creditors sometimes are required to pay the debtor's court costs. (This is designed to protect debtors from nuisance petitions being filed.) If the petition is accepted, the court issues an order of relief pending a more permanent solution. The idea behind this stay of creditor action is to give the debtor breathing space to propose a solution to the problem. In what follows, we observe the solutions of liquidation and the reorganization of an enterprise.

LIQUIDATION

If there is no hope for the successful operation of a company, liquidation is the only feasible alternative. Upon petition of bankruptcy, the debtor obtains temporary relief from creditors until a decision is reached by the bankruptcy court. After issuing the order of relief, the court frequently appoints an interim trustee to take over the operation of the company and to call a meeting of creditors. The interim trustee is a "disinterested" private citizen who is appointed from an approved list and who serves until at least the first meeting of creditors. At the meeting, claims are proven, and the creditors then may elect a new trustee to replace the interim trustee. Otherwise, the interim trustee serves as the regular trustee, continuing to function in that capacity until the case is completed. The trustee has responsibility for liquidating the property of the company and distributing liquidating dividends to creditors.

In distributing the proceeds of a liquidation to creditors with unsecured claims, the priority of claims must be observed. The order of distribution is as follows:

1. Administrative expenses associated with liquidating the property, including the trustee's fee and attorney fees.
2. Creditor claims that arise in the ordinary course of the debtor's business from the time the case starts to the time a trustee is appointed.
3. Wages employees earned within 90 days of the bankruptcy petition. These are limited to $2,000 per employee.
4. Claims for contributions to employee benefit plans for services rendered within 120 days of the bankruptcy petition. These claims are limited to $2,000 per employee times the number of employees.
5. Claims of customers who make money deposits for goods or services not provided by the debtor.

6. Income tax claims for 3 tax years prior to the petition, property taxes for 1 year prior to the petition, and all taxes withheld from employees' paychecks.
7. Unsecured claims either filed on time or tardily filed if the creditor did not know of the bankruptcy.
8. Unsecured claims filed late by creditors who had knowledge of the bankruptcy.
9. Fines and punitive damages.
10. Interest that accrues to claims after the date of the petition.

Claims in each of these classes must be paid in full before any payment can be made to claims in the next class. If anything is left over after all of these claims are paid in full, liquidating dividends can then be paid to subordinated debt holders, to preferred stockholders, and, finally, to common stockholders. It is unlikely, however, that common stockholders will receive any distribution from a liquidation. Special provision is made in the Bankruptcy Act for damage claims by lessors to the debtor. In general, lessors are limited to the greater of 1 year of payments or 15 percent of the total remaining payments, but not to exceed 3 years. Upon the payment of all liquidating dividends, the debtor is discharged and relieved of any further claims.

REORGANIZATION

It may be in the best interests of all concerned to reorganize a company rather than liquidate it. Conceptually, a firm should be reorganized if its economic worth as an operating entity is greater than its liquidation value. It should be liquidated if the converse is true, that is, if it is worth more dead than alive. Reorganization is an effort to keep a company alive by changing its capital structure. The rehabilitation involves the reduction of fixed charges by substituting equity and limited-income securities for fixed-income securities.

Reorganizations occur under Chapter 11 of the bankruptcy law and are initiated in the same general manner as liquidation in bankruptcy. Either the debtor or the creditors file a petition, and the case begins. The idea in a reorganization is to keep the business going. In most cases, the debtor will continue to run the business, although a trustee can assume operating responsibility of the company. One of the great needs in rehabilitation is interim credit. To provide inducements, Chapter 11 gives postpetition creditors priority over prepetition creditors. If this inducement is not sufficient, the bankruptcy court is empowered to authorize new creditors to obtain a lien on the debtor's property.

If a trustee is not appointed, the debtor has the sole right to draw up a reorganization plan and to file it within 120 days. Otherwise, the trustee has the responsibility for seeing that a plan is filed. It may be drawn up by the trustee, the debtor, the creditors' committee, or individual creditors, and more than one plan can be filed. All reorganization plans must be submitted to creditors and stockholders for approval. The role of the court is to review the information in the plan, to make sure disclosure is full.

In a reorganization, the plan should be *fair, equitable,* and *feasible.* This means that all parties must be treated fairly and equitably and that the plan must be workable with respect to the earning power and financial structure of the reorganized company as well as the ability of the company to obtain trade credit and, perhaps, short-term bank loans. Each class of claimholders must vote on a plan. More than one-half in number and two-thirds in amount of total claims in each class must vote in favor of the plan if it is to be accepted. If the reorganization plan is rejected by creditors, the case goes to what is known as a "cram down." Here the court imposes a plan on all claimholders, being bound by the principle that it is fair and equitable. Upon confirmation of a plan by the bankruptcy court, the debtor then must perform according to the terms of the plan. Moreover, all creditors and stockholders, including dissenters, are bound by the plan.

REORGANIZATION PLAN

The difficult aspect of a reorganization is the recasting of the company's capital structure to reduce the amount of fixed charges. In formulating a reorganization plan, there are three steps. First, the total valuation of the reorganized company must be determined. This step, perhaps, is the most difficult and the most important. The technique favored by trustees is a capitalization of prospective earnings. If future annual earnings of the reorganized company are expected to be $2 million, and the overall capitalization rate of similar companies averages 10 percent, a total valuation of $20 million would be set for the company. The valuation figure is subject to considerable variation, owing to the difficulty of estimating prospective earnings and determining an appropriate capitalization rate. Thus, the valuation figure represents nothing more than a best estimate of potential value. Although the capitalization of prospective earnings is the generally accepted approach of valuing a company in reorganization, the valuation may be adjusted upward if the assets have substantial liquidating value.

Once a valuation figure has been determined, the next step is to formulate a new capital structure for the company, to reduce fixed charges, so that there will be an adequate coverage margin. To reduce these charges, the total debt of the firm is scaled down by being partly shifted to income bonds, preferred stock, and common stock. In addition to being scaled down, the terms of the debt may be changed. The maturity of the debt can be extended to reduce the amount of annual sinking-fund obligation. If it appears that the reorganized company will need new financing in the future, the trustee may feel that a more conservative ratio of debt to equity is in order to provide for future financial flexibility.

Once a new capital structure is established, the last step involves the valuation of the old securities and their exchange for new securities. In general, all senior claims on assets must be settled in full before a junior claim can be settled. In the exchange process, bondholders must receive the par value of their bonds in another security before there can be any distribution to preferred stockholders. The total valuation figure arrived at in step 1 sets an upper limit on the amount of securities that can be issued. The existing capital structure of a company undergoing reorganization may be as follows:

Debentures	$ 9 million
Subordinated debentures	3 million
Preferred stock	6 million
Common stock equity (at book value)	10 million
	$28 million

If the total valuation of the reorganized company is to be $20 million, the trustee might establish the following capital structure in step 2:

Debentures	$ 3 million
Income bonds	6 million
Preferred stock	3 million
Common stock	8 million
	$20 million

Having established the "appropriate" capital structure for the reorganized company, the trustee then must allocate the new securities. In this regard, the trustee may propose that the debenture holders exchange their $9 million in debentures for $3 million in new debentures and $6 million in income bonds, that the subordinated debenture holders exchange their $3 million in securities for preferred stock, and that preferred stockholders exchange their securities for $6 million of common stock in the reorganized company. The common stockholders would then be entitled to $2 million in stock in the reorganized company, or 25 percent of the total common stock of the reorganized company.

Thus, each claim is settled in full before a junior claim is settled. The example represents a relatively mild reorganization. In a harsh reorganization, debt instruments may be exchanged entirely for common stock in the reorganized company, and the old common stock may be eliminated completely. Had the total valuation figure in the example been $12 million, the trustee might have proposed a new capital structure consisting of $3 million in preferred stock and $9 million in common stock. Only the straight and subordinated debenture holders would receive a settlement in this case. The preferred and the common stockholders of the old company would receive nothing.

These examples show that the common stockholders of a company undergoing reorganization suffer under an absolute priority rule, whereby claims must be settled in the order of their legal priority. From their standpoint, they would much prefer to see claims settled on a *relative priority basis*. Under this rule, new securites are allocated on the basis of the relative market prices of the securities. The common stockholders could never obtain senior securities in a reorganization, but they would be entitled to some common stock if their present stock had value. Because the company is not actually being liquidated, common stockholders argue that a rule of relative priority is really the fairest. The Supreme Court decided otherwise when it upheld the absolute priority rule (*Case* v. *Los Angeles Lumber Products Company*, 1939).

By and large, the principle of absolute priority is used in reorganization cases, although the Bankruptcy Reform Act of 1978 did provide a degree of flexibility, shifting in the direction of relative priority. The practical reality is that during Chapter 11 reorganization proceedings, often protracted, management frequently controls the company. Under these circumstances, creditors sometimes will give something to the stockholders in order to move the process along and to reduce bankruptcy costs overall.

Appendix Problems

1. Merry Land, an amusement park in Atlanta, has experienced increased difficulty in paying its bills. Although the park has been marginally profitable over the years, the current outlook is not encouraging, as profits during the last 2 years have been negative. The park is located on reasonably valuable real estate and has an overall liquidating value of $5 million. After much discussion with creditors, management has agreed to a voluntary liquidation. A trustee, who is appointed by the various parties to liquidate the properties, will charge $200,000 for his services. The Merry Land Company owes $300,000 in back property taxes. It has a $2 million mortgage on certain amusement park equipment that can be sold for only $1 million. Creditor claims are as follows:

PARTY	BOOK VALUE CLAIM
General creditors	$1,750,000
Mortgage bonds	2,000,000
Long-term subordinated debt	1,000,000
Common stock	5,000,000

What amount is each party likely to receive in liquidation?

2. The Greenwood Corporation is in Chapter 11. The trustee has estimated that the company can earn $1.5 million before interest and taxes (40 percent) in the future. In the new capitalization, he feels that debentures should bear a coupon of 10 percent and have coverage of 5 times, income bonds (12 percent) should have overall coverage of 2 times, preferred stock (10 percent) should have after-tax coverage of 3 times, and common stock should be issued on a price/earnings ratio basis of 12 times. Determine the capital structure that conforms to the trustee's criteria.

3. Facile Fastener Company had the following liabilities and equity position when it filed for bankruptcy under Chapter 11 (in thousands):

Accounts payable	$500
Accrued wages	200
Bank loan, 12% rate (secured by receivables)	600
Current liabilities	$1,300
13% First-mortgage bonds	500
15% Subordinated debentures	1,700
Total debt	$3,500
Common stock and paid-in capital	500
Retained earnings	420
Total liabilities and equity	$4,420

After straightening out some operating problems, the company is expected to be able to earn $800,000 annually before interest and taxes. Based on other going-concern values, it is felt that the company as a whole is worth 5 times its EBIT. Court costs associated with the reorganization will total $200,000, and the expected tax rate is 40 percent for the reorganized company. As trustee, suppose you have the following instruments to use for the long-term capitalization of the company: 13 percent first-mortgage bonds, 15 percent capital notes, 13 percent preferred stock, and common stock.

With the new capitalization, the capital notes should have an overall coverage ratio, after bank loan interest, of 4 times, and preferred stock should have a coverage ratio after interest and taxes of 2 times. Moreover, it is felt that common stock equity should equal at least 30 percent of the total assets of the company.

a. What is the total valuation of the company after reorganization?

b. If the maximum amounts of debt and preferred stock are employed, what will be the new capital structure and current liabilities of the company?

c. How should these securities be allocated, assuming a rule of absolute priority?

APPENDIX B:
PRESENT-VALUE TABLES
AND NORMAL
PROBABILITY
DISTRIBUTION TABLE

TABLE A
Present value of one dollar due at the end of *n* years

N	1%	2%	3%	4%	5%	6%	7%	8%	9%	10%	N
01	.99010	.98039	.97007	.96154	.95238	.94340	.93458	.92593	.91743	.90909	01
02	.98030	.96117	.94260	.92456	.90703	.89000	.87344	.85734	.84168	.82645	02
03	.97059	.94232	.91514	.88900	.86384	.83962	.81630	.79383	.77218	.75131	03
04	.96098	.92385	.88849	.85480	.82270	.79209	.76290	.73503	.70843	.68301	04
05	.95147	.90573	.86261	.82193	.78353	.74726	.71299	.68058	.64993	.62092	05
06	.94204	.88797	.83748	.79031	.74622	.70496	.66634	.60317	.59627	.56447	06
07	.93272	.87056	.81309	.75992	.71068	.66506	.62275	.58349	.54703	.51316	07
08	.92348	.85349	.78941	.73069	.67684	.62741	.58201	.54027	.50187	.46651	08
09	.91434	.83675	.76642	.70259	.64461	.59190	.54393	.50025	.46043	.42410	09
10	.90529	.82035	.74409	.67556	.61391	.55839	.50835	.46319	.42241	.38554	10
11	.89632	.80426	.72242	.64958	.58468	.52679	.47509	.42888	.38753	.35049	11
12	.88745	.78849	.70138	.62460	.55684	.49697	.44401	.39711	.35553	.31863	12
13	.87866	.77303	.68095	.60057	.53032	.46884	.41496	.36770	.32618	.28966	13
14	.86996	.75787	.66112	.57747	.50507	.44230	.38782	.34046	.29925	.26333	14
15	.86135	.74301	.64186	.55526	.48102	.41726	.36245	.31524	.27454	.23939	15
16	.85282	.72845	.62317	.53391	.45811	.39365	.33873	.29189	.25187	.21763	16
17	.84438	.71416	.60502	.51337	.43630	.37136	.31657	.27027	.23107	.19784	17
18	.83602	.70016	.58739	.49363	.41552	.35034	.29586	.25025	.21199	.17986	18
19	.82774	.68643	.57029	.47464	.39573	.33051	.27651	.23171	.19449	.16351	19
20	.81954	.67297	.55367	.45639	.37689	.31180	.25842	.21455	.17843	.14864	20
21	.81143	.65978	.53755	.43883	.35894	.29415	.24151	.19866	.16370	.13513	21
22	.80340	.64684	.52189	.42195	.34185	.27750	.22571	.18394	.15018	.12285	22
23	.79544	.63416	.50669	.40573	.32557	.26180	.21095	.17031	.13778	.11168	23
24	.78757	.62172	.49193	.39012	.31007	.24698	.19715	.15770	.12640	.10153	24
25	.77977	.60953	.47760	.37512	.29530	.23300	.18425	.14602	.11597	.09230	25

TABLE A (*cont.*)
Present value of one dollar due at the end of *n* years

N	11%	12%	13%	14%	15%	16%	17%	18%	19%	20%	N
01	.90090	.89286	.88496	.87719	.86957	.86207	.85470	.84746	.84034	.83333	01
02	.81162	.79719	.78315	.76947	.75614	.74316	.73051	.71818	.70616	.69444	02
03	.73119	.71178	.69305	.67497	.65752	.64066	.62437	.60863	.59342	.57870	03
04	.65873	.63552	.61332	.59208	.57175	.55229	.53365	.51579	.49867	.48225	04
05	.59345	.56743	.54276	.51937	.49718	.47611	.45611	.43711	.41905	.40188	05
06	.53464	.50663	.48032	.45559	.43233	.41044	.38984	.37043	.35214	.33490	06
07	.48166	.45235	.42506	.39964	.37594	.35383	.33320	.31392	.29592	.27908	07
08	.43393	.40388	.37616	.35056	.32690	.30503	.28478	.26604	.24867	.23257	08
09	.39092	.36061	.33288	.30751	.28426	.26295	.24340	.22546	.20897	.19381	09
10	.35218	.32197	.29459	.26974	.24718	.22668	.20804	.19106	.17560	.16151	10
11	.31728	.28748	.26070	.23662	.21494	.19542	.17781	.16192	.14756	.13459	11
12	.28584	.25667	.23071	.20756	.18691	.16846	.15197	.13722	.12400	.11216	12
13	.25751	.22917	.20416	.18207	.16253	.14523	.12989	.11629	.10420	.09346	13
14	.23199	.20462	.18068	.15971	.14133	.12520	.11102	.09855	.08757	.07789	14
15	.20900	.18270	.15989	.14010	.12289	.10793	.09489	.08352	.07359	.06491	15
16	.18829	.16312	.14150	.12289	.10686	.09304	.08110	.07078	.06184	.05409	16
17	.16963	.14564	.12522	.10780	.09293	.08021	.06932	.05998	.05196	.04507	17
18	.15282	.13004	.11081	.09456	.08080	.06914	.05925	.05083	.04367	.03756	18
19	.13768	.11611	.09806	.08295	.07026	.05961	.05064	.04308	.03669	.03130	19
20	.12403	.10367	.08678	.07276	.06110	.05139	.04328	.03651	.03084	.02608	20
21	.11174	.09256	.07680	.06383	.05313	.04430	.03699	.03094	.02591	.02174	21
22	.10067	.08264	.06796	.05599	.04620	.03819	.03162	.02622	.02178	.01811	22
23	.09069	.07379	.06014	.04911	.04017	.03292	.02702	.02222	.01830	.01509	23
24	.08170	.06588	.05322	.04308	.03493	.02838	.02310	.01883	.01538	.01258	24
25	.07361	.05882	.04710	.03779	.03038	.02447	.01974	.01596	.01292	.01048	25

TABLE A (*cont.*)
Present value of one dollar due at the end of *n* years

N	21%	22%	23%	24%	25%	26%	27%	28%	29%	30%	N
01	.82645	.81967	.81301	.80645	.80000	.79365	.78740	.78125	.77519	.76923	01
02	.68301	.67186	.66098	.65036	.64000	.62988	.62000	.61035	.60093	.59172	02
03	.56447	.55071	.53738	.52449	.51200	.49991	.48819	.47684	.46583	.45517	03
04	.46651	.45140	.43690	.42297	.40906	.39675	.38440	.37253	.36111	.35013	04
05	.38554	.37000	.35520	.34411	.32768	.31488	.30268	.29104	.27993	.26933	05
06	.31863	.30328	.28878	.27509	.26214	.24991	.23833	.22737	.21700	.20718	06
07	.26333	.24859	.23478	.22184	.20972	.19834	.18766	.17764	.16822	.15937	07
08	.21763	.20376	.19088	.17891	.16777	.15741	.14776	.13878	.13040	.12259	08
09	.17986	.16702	.15519	.14428	.13422	.12493	.11635	.10842	.10109	.09430	09
10	.14864	.13690	.12617	.11635	.10737	.09915	.09161	.08470	.07836	.07254	10
11	.12285	.11221	.10258	.09383	.08590	.07869	.07214	.06617	.06075	.05580	11
12	.10153	.09198	.08339	.07567	.06872	.06245	.05680	.05170	.04709	.04292	12
13	.08391	.07539	.06780	.06103	.05498	.04957	.04472	.04039	.03650	.03302	13
14	.06934	.06180	.05512	.04921	.04398	.03934	.03522	.03155	.02830	.02540	14
15	.05731	.05065	.04481	.03969	.03518	.03122	.02773	.02465	.02194	.01954	15
16	.04736	.04152	.03643	.03201	.02815	.02478	.02183	.01926	.01700	.01503	16
17	.03914	.03403	.02962	.02581	.02252	.01967	.01719	.01505	.01318	.01156	17
18	.03235	.02789	.02408	.02082	.01801	.01561	.01354	.01175	.01022	.00889	18
19	.02673	.02286	.01958	.01679	.01441	.01239	.01066	.00918	.00792	.00684	19
20	.02209	.01874	.01592	.01354	.01153	.00983	.00839	.00717	.00614	.00526	20
21	.01826	.01536	.01294	.01092	.00922	.00780	.00661	.00561	.00476	.00405	21
22	.01509	.01259	.01052	.00880	.00738	.00619	.00520	.00438	.00369	.00311	22
23	.01247	.01032	.00855	.00710	.00590	.00491	.00410	.00342	.00286	.00239	23
24	.01031	.00846	.00695	.00573	.00472	.00390	.00323	.00267	.00222	.00184	24
25	.00852	.00693	.00565	.00462	.00378	.00310	.00254	.00209	.00172	.00142	25

TABLE A (cont.)
Present value of one dollar due at the end of _n_ years

N	31%	32%	33%	34%	35%	36%	37%	38%	39%	40%	N
01	.76336	.75758	.75188	.74627	.74074	.73529	.72993	.72464	.71942	.71429	01
02	.58272	.57392	.56532	.55692	.54870	.45066	.53279	.52510	.51757	.51020	02
03	.44482	.43479	.42505	.41561	.40644	.39745	.38890	.38051	.37235	.36443	03
04	.33956	.32939	.31959	.31016	.30107	.29231	.28387	.27573	.26788	.26031	04
05	.25920	.24953	.24029	.23146	.22301	.21493	.20720	.19980	.19272	.18593	05
06	.19787	.18904	.18067	.17273	.16520	.15804	.15124	.14479	.13865	.13281	06
07	.15104	.14321	.13584	.12890	.12237	.11621	.11040	.10492	.09975	.09486	07
08	.11530	.10849	.10214	.09620	.09064	.08545	.08058	.07603	.07176	.06776	08
09	.08802	.08219	.07680	.07179	.06714	.06283	.05882	.05509	.05163	.04840	09
10	.06719	.06227	.05774	.05357	.04973	.04620	.04293	.03992	.03714	.03457	10
11	.05129	.04717	.04341	.03998	.03684	.03397	.03134	.02893	.02672	.02469	11
12	.03915	.03574	.03264	.02984	.02729	.02498	.02887	.02096	.01922	.01764	12
13	.02989	.02707	.02454	.02227	.02021	.01837	.01670	.01519	.01383	.01260	13
14	.02281	.02051	.01845	.01662	.01497	.01350	.01219	.01101	.00995	.00900	14
15	.01742	.01554	.01387	.01240	.01109	.00993	.00890	.00789	.00716	.00643	15
16	.01329	.01177	.01043	.00925	.00822	.00730	.00649	.00578	.00515	.00459	16
17	.01015	.00892	.00784	.00691	.00609	.00537	.00474	.00419	.00370	.00328	17
18	.00775	.00676	.00590	.00515	.00451	.00395	.00346	.00304	.00267	.00234	18
19	.00591	.00512	.00443	.00385	.00334	.00290	.00253	.00220	.00192	.00167	19
20	.00451	.00388	.00333	.00287	.00247	.00213	.00184	.00159	.00138	.00120	20
21	.00345	.00294	.00251	.00214	.00183	.00157	.00135	.00115	.00099	.00085	21
22	.00263	.00223	.00188	.00160	.00136	.00115	.00098	.00084	.00071	.00061	22
23	.00201	.00169	.00142	.00119	.00101	.00085	.00072	.00061	.00051	.00044	23
24	.00153	.00128	.00107	.00089	.00074	.00062	.00052	.00044	.00037	.00031	24
25	.00117	.00097	.00080	.00066	.00055	.00046	.00038	.00032	.00027	.00022	25

TABLE B
Present value of one dollar per year, *n* years at *r*%

YEAR	1%	2%	3%	4%	5%	6%	7%	8%	9%	10%	YEAR
1	.9901	.9804	.9709	.9615	.9524	.9434	.9346	.9259	.9174	.9091	1
2	1.9704	1.9416	1.9135	1.8861	1.8594	1.8334	1.8080	1.7833	1.7591	1.7355	2
3	2.9410	2.8839	2.8286	2.7751	2.7232	2.6730	2.6243	2.5771	2.5313	2.4868	3
4	3.9020	3.8077	3.7171	3.6299	3.5459	3.4651	3.3872	3.3121	3.2397	3.1699	4
5	4.8535	4.7134	4.5797	4.4518	4.3295	4.2123	4.1002	3.9927	3.8896	3.7908	5
6	5.7955	5.6014	5.4172	5.2421	5.0757	4.9173	4.7665	4.6229	4.4859	4.3553	6
7	6.7282	6.4720	6.2302	6.0020	5.7863	5.5824	5.3893	5.2064	5.0329	4.8684	7
8	7.6517	7.3254	7.0196	6.7327	6.4632	6.2098	5.9713	5.7466	5.5348	5.3349	8
9	8.5661	8.1622	7.7861	7.4353	7.1078	6.8017	6.5152	6.2469	5.9852	5.7590	9
10	9.4714	8.9825	8.5302	8.1109	7.7217	7.3601	7.0236	6.7101	6.4176	6.1446	10
11	10.3677	9.7868	9.2526	8.7604	8.3064	7.8868	7.4987	7.1389	6.8052	6.4951	11
12	11.2552	10.5753	9.9539	9.3850	8.8632	8.3838	7.9427	7.5361	7.1607	6.8137	12
13	12.1338	11.3483	10.6349	9.9856	9.3935	8.8527	8.3576	7.9038	7.4869	7.1034	13
14	13.0038	12.1062	11.2960	10.5631	9.8986	9.2950	8.7454	8.2442	7.7861	7.3667	14
15	13.8651	12.8492	11.9379	11.1183	10.3796	9.7122	9.1079	8.5595	8.0607	7.6061	15
16	14.7180	13.5777	12.5610	11.6522	10.8377	10.1059	9.4466	8.8514	8.3125	7.8237	16
17	15.5624	14.2918	13.1660	12.1656	11.2740	10.4772	9.7632	9.1216	8.5436	8.0215	17
18	16.3984	14.9920	13.7534	12.6592	11.6895	10.8276	10.0591	9.3719	8.7556	8.2014	18
19	17.2261	15.6784	14.3237	13.1339	12.0853	11.1581	10.3356	9.6036	8.9501	8.3649	19
20	18.0457	16.3514	14.8774	13.5903	12.4622	11.4699	10.5940	9.8181	9.1285	8.5136	20
21	18.8571	17.0111	15.4149	14.0291	12.8211	11.7640	10.8355	10.0168	9.2922	8.6487	21
22	19.6605	17.6580	15.9368	14.4511	13.1630	12.0416	11.0612	10.2007	9.4424	8.7715	22
23	20.4559	18.2921	16.4435	14.8568	13.4885	12.3033	11.2722	10.3710	9.5802	8.8832	23
24	21.2435	18.9139	16.9355	15.2469	13.7986	12.5503	11.4693	10.5287	9.7066	8.9847	24
25	22.0233	19.5234	17.4131	15.6220	14.0939	12.7833	11.6536	10.6748	8.8226	9.0770	25

TABLE B (*cont.*)
Present value of one dollar per year, *n* years at *r*%

YEAR	11%	12%	13%	14%	15%	16%	17%	18%	19%	20%	YEAR
1	.9009	.8929	.8850	.8772	.8696	.8621	.8547	.8475	.8403	.8333	1
2	1.7125	1.6901	1.6681	1.6467	1.6257	1.6052	1.5852	1.5656	1.5465	1.5278	2
3	2.4437	2.4018	2.3612	2.3216	2.2832	2.2459	2.2096	2.1743	2.1399	2.1065	3
4	3.1024	3.0373	2.9745	2.9137	2.8550	2.7982	2.7432	2.6901	2.6386	2.5887	4
5	3.6959	3.6048	3.5172	3.4331	3.3522	3.2743	3.1993	3.1272	3.0576	2.9906	5
6	4.2305	4.1114	3.9976	3.8887	3.7845	3.6847	3.5892	3.4976	3.4098	3.3255	6
7	4.7122	4.5638	4.4226	4.2883	4.1604	4.0386	3.9224	3.8115	3.7057	3.6046	7
8	5.1461	4.9676	4.7988	4.6389	4.4873	4.3436	4.2072	4.0776	3.9544	3.8372	8
9	5.5370	5.3282	5.1317	4.9464	4.7716	4.6065	4.4506	4.3030	4.1633	4.0310	9
10	5.8892	5.6502	5.4262	5.2161	5.0188	4.8332	4.6586	4.4941	4.3389	4.1925	10
11	6.2065	5.9377	5.6869	5.4527	5.2337	5.0286	4.8364	4.6560	4.4865	4.3271	11
12	6.4924	6.1944	5.9176	5.6603	5.4206	5.1971	4.9884	4.7932	4.6105	4.4392	12
13	6.7499	6.4235	6.1218	5.8424	5.5831	5.3423	5.1183	4.9095	4.7147	4.5327	13
14	6.9819	6.6282	6.3025	6.0021	5.7245	5.4675	5.2293	5.0081	4.8023	4.6106	14
15	7.1909	6.8109	6.4624	6.1422	5.8474	5.5755	5.3242	5.0916	4.8759	4.6755	15
16	7.3792	6.9740	6.6039	6.2651	5.9542	5.6685	5.4053	5.1624	4.9377	4.7296	16
17	7.5488	7.1196	6.7291	6.3729	6.0472	5.7487	5.4746	5.2223	4.9897	4.7746	17
18	7.7016	7.2497	6.8399	6.4674	6.1280	5.8178	5.5339	5.2732	5.0333	4.8122	18
19	7.8393	7.3658	6.9380	6.5504	6.1982	5.8775	5.5845	5.3162	5.0700	4.8435	19
20	7.9633	7.4694	7.0248	6.6231	6.2593	5.9288	5.6278	5.3527	5.1009	4.8696	20
21	8.0751	7.5620	7.1016	6.6870	6.3125	5.9731	5.6648	5.3837	5.1268	4.8913	21
22	8.1757	7.6446	7.1695	6.7429	6.3587	6.0113	5.6964	5.4099	5.1486	4.9094	22
23	8.2664	7.7184	7.2297	6.7921	6.3988	6.0442	5.7234	5.4321	5.1668	4.9245	23
24	8.3481	7.7843	7.2829	6.8351	6.4338	6.0726	5.7465	5.4509	5.1822	4.9371	24
25	8.4217	7.8431	7.3300	6.8729	6.4641	6.0971	5.7662	5.4669	5.1951	4.9476	25

TABLE B (cont.)
Present value of one dollar per year, n years at $r\%$

YEAR	21%	22%	23%	24%	25%	26%	27%	28%	29%	30%	YEAR
1	.8264	.8197	.8130	.8065	.8000	.7937	.7874	.7813	.7752	.7692	1
2	1.5095	1.4915	1.4740	1.4568	1.4400	1.4235	1.4074	1.3916	1.3761	1.3609	2
3	2.0739	2.0422	2.0114	1.9813	1.9520	1.9234	1.8956	1.8684	1.8420	1.8161	3
4	2.5404	2.4936	2.4483	2.4043	2.3616	2.3202	2.2800	2.2410	2.2031	2.1662	4
5	2.9260	2.8636	2.8035	2.7454	2.6893	2.6351	2.5827	2.5320	2.4830	2.4356	5
6	3.2446	3.1669	3.0923	3.0205	2.9514	2.8850	2.8210	2.7594	2.7000	2.6427	6
7	3.5079	3.4155	3.3270	3.2423	3.1611	3.0833	3.0087	2.9370	2.8682	2.8021	7
8	3.7256	3.6193	3.5179	3.4212	3.3289	3.2407	3.1564	3.0758	2.9986	2.9247	8
9	3.9054	3.7863	3.6731	3.5655	3.4631	3.3657	3.2728	3.1842	3.0997	3.0190	9
10	4.0541	3.9232	3.7993	3.6819	3.5705	3.4648	3.3644	3.2689	3.1781	3.0915	10
11	4.1769	4.0354	3.9018	3.7757	3.6564	3.5435	3.4365	3.3351	3.2388	3.1473	11
12	4.2785	4.1274	3.9852	3.8514	3.7251	3.6060	3.4933	3.3868	3.2859	3.1903	12
13	4.3624	4.2028	4.0530	3.9124	3.7801	3.6555	3.5381	3.4272	3.3224	3.2233	13
14	4.4317	4.2646	4.1082	3.9616	3.8241	3.6949	3.5733	3.4587	3.3507	3.2487	14
15	4.4890	4.3152	4.1530	4.0013	3.8593	3.7261	3.6010	3.4834	3.3726	3.2682	15
16	4.5364	4.3567	4.1894	4.0333	3.8874	3.7509	3.6228	3.5026	3.3896	3.2832	16
17	4.5755	4.3908	4.2190	4.0591	3.9099	3.7705	3.6400	3.5177	3.4028	3.2948	17
18	4.6079	4.4187	4.2431	4.0799	3.9279	3.7861	3.6536	3.5294	3.4130	3.3037	18
19	4.6346	4.4415	4.2627	4.0967	3.9424	3.7985	3.6642	3.5386	3.4210	3.3105	19
20	4.6567	4.4603	4.2786	4.1103	3.9539	3.8083	3.6726	3.5458	3.4271	3.3158	20
21	4.6750	4.4756	4.2916	4.1212	3.9631	3.8161	3.6792	3.5514	3.4319	3.3198	21
22	4.6900	4.4882	4.3021	4.1300	3.9705	3.8223	3.6844	3.5558	3.4356	3.3230	22
23	4.7025	4.4985	4.3106	4.1371	3.9764	3.8273	3.6885	3.5592	3.4384	3.3254	23
24	4.7128	4.5070	4.3176	4.1428	3.9811	3.8312	3.6918	3.5619	3.4406	3.3272	24
25	4.7213	4.5139	4.3232	4.1474	3.9849	3.8342	3.6943	3.5640	3.4423	3.3286	25

TABLE B (*cont.*)
Present value of one dollar per year, *n* years at *r*%

YEAR	31%	32%	33%	34%	35%	36%	37%	38%	39%	40%	YEAR
1	.7634	.7576	.7519	.7463	.7407	.7353	.7299	.7246	.7194	.7143	1
2	1.3461	1.3315	1.3172	1.3032	1.2894	1.2760	1.2627	1.2497	1.2370	1.2245	2
3	1.7909	1.7663	1.7423	1.7188	1.6959	1.6735	1.6516	1.6302	1.6093	1.5889	3
4	2.1305	2.0957	2.0618	2.0290	1.9969	1.9658	1.9355	1.9060	1.8772	1.8492	4
5	2.3897	2.3452	2.3021	2.2604	2.2200	2.1807	2.1427	2.1058	2.0699	2.0352	5
6	2.5875	2.5342	2.4828	2.4331	2.3852	2.3388	2.2939	2.2506	2.2086	2.1680	6
7	2.7386	2.6775	2.6187	2.5620	2.5075	2.4550	2.4043	2.3555	2.3083	2.2628	7
8	2.8539	2.7860	2.7208	2.6582	2.5982	2.5404	2.4849	2.4315	2.3801	2.3306	8
9	2.9419	2.8681	2.7976	2.7300	2.6653	2.6033	5.5437	2.4866	2.4317	2.3790	9
10	3.0091	2.9304	2.8553	2.7836	2.7150	2.6495	2.5867	2.5265	2.4689	2.4136	10
11	3.0604	2.9776	2.8987	2.8236	2.7519	2.6634	2.6180	2.5555	2.4956	2.4383	11
12	3.0995	3.0133	2.9314	2.8534	2.7792	2.7084	2.6409	2.5764	2.5148	2.4559	12
13	3.1294	3.0404	2.9559	2.8757	2.7994	2.7268	2.6576	2.5916	2.5286	2.4685	13
14	3.1522	3.0609	2.9744	2.8923	2.8144	2.7403	2.6698	2.6026	2.5386	2.4775	14
15	3.1696	3.0764	2.9883	2.9047	2.8255	2.7502	2.6787	2.6106	2.5457	2.4839	15
16	3.1829	3.0882	2.9987	2.9104	2.8337	2.7575	2.6852	2.6164	2.5509	2.4885	16
17	3.1931	3.9071	3.0065	2.9209	2.8398	2.7629	2.6899	2.6206	2.5546	2.4918	17
18	3.2008	3.1039	3.0124	2.9260	2.8443	2.7668	2.6934	2.6236	2.5573	2.4941	18
19	3.2067	3.1090	3.0169	2.9299	2.8476	2.7697	2.6959	2.6258	2.5592	2.4958	19
20	3.2112	3.1129	3.0202	2.9327	2.8501	2.7718	2.6977	2.6274	2.5606	2.4970	20
21	3.2147	3.1158	3.0227	2.9349	2.8519	2.7734	2.6991	2.6285	2.5616	2.4979	21
22	3.2173	3.1180	3.0246	2.9365	2.8533	2.7746	2.7000	2.6294	2.5623	2.4985	22
23	3.2193	3.1197	3.0260	2.9377	2.8543	2.7754	2.7008	2.6300	2.5628	2.4989	23
24	3.2209	3.1210	3.0271	2.9386	2.8550	2.7760	2.7013	2.6304	2.5632	2.4992	24
25	3.2220	3.1220	3.0279	2.9392	2.8556	2.7765	2.7017	2.6307	2.5634	2.4994	25

TABLE C
Normal probability distribution table*

NUMBER OF STANDARD DEVIATIONS FROM MEAN (X)	AREA TO THE LEFT OR RIGHT (ONE TAIL)	NUMBER OF STANDARD DEVIATIONS FROM MEAN (X)	AREA TO THE LEFT OR RIGHT (ONE TAIL)
.00	.5000	1.55	.0606
.05	.4801	1.60	.0548
.10	.4602	1.65	.0495
.15	.4404	1.70	.0446
.20	.4207	1.75	.0401
.25	.4013	1.80	.0359
.30	.3821	1.85	.0322
.35	.3632	1.90	.0287
.40	.3446	1.95	.0256
.45	.3264	2.00	.0228
.50	.3085	2.05	.0202
.55	.2912	2.10	.0179
.60	.2743	2.15	.0158
.65	.2578	2.20	.0139
.70	.2420	2.25	.0122
.75	.2264	2.30	.0107
.80	.2119	2.35	.0094
.85	.1977	2.40	.0082
.90	.1841	2.45	.0071
.95	.1711	2.50	.0062
1.00	.1577	2.55	.0054
1.05	.1469	2.60	.0047
1.10	.1357	2.65	.0040
1.15	.1251	2.70	.0035
1.20	.1151	2.75	.0030
1.25	.1056	2.80	.0026
1.30	.0968	2.85	.0022
1.35	.0885	2.90	.0019
1.40	.0808	2.95	.0016
1.45	.0735	3.00	.0013
1.50	.0668		

* Area of normal distribution that is X standard deviations to the left or right of the mean.

INDEX

815